FREE ONLINE COURSES – AVAILABLE IN WEBCT, BLACKBOARD, AND COURSECOMPASS!

Are you teaching an online course now? Or would you like to teach a Web-enhanced course? Here's how Prentice Hall can help you to optimize your class!

- **Online Quizzes** automatically feed results into the Gradebook.
- **Bulletin Boards** let you and your students post critical messages.
- An **Online Syllabus** keeps students aware of deadlines and updates.

- **Discussion Groups** enable you to hold synchronous or asynchronous meetings with classes, speakers, or groups of students.
- **Link** your students (via the syllabus) to key Internet sites.

- **Custom-created content** supports each chapter and includes:
  - On Location video segments feature real business practices
  - "Coaching" video segments help students understand key topics
  - PowerPoints with audio provide "mini" lectures
  - "Helpful Hints" summarize key concepts

MASTERING ACCOUNTING CD-ROM SERIES

Package Mastering Accounting with Harrison and Horngren (or any other Prentice Hall accounting text) for a small, additional price.

- Mastering Accounting, part of the Mastering Business program, is an **interactive, multimedia CD-ROM** that uses video and interactive exercises to help students link the THEORY they learn in class with **realistic business situations.**
- The episodes and interactive exercises on the CD-ROM are based on CanGo, a fictional e-commerce startup that sells a variety of entertainment products and services online.
- The **dramatic situations** show students how all **the functional areas of business work together** to ensure the growth of the company – as well as how to apply business theories to CanGo's daily operations.
- All of the content – including videos and exercises – was **created and reviewed by university professors** and experts in interactive instructional design.

Financial Accounting

Charles T. Horngren Series in Accounting

AUDITING: AN INTEGRATED APPROACH, 9/E
Arens/Loebbecke

FINANCIAL STATEMENT ANALYSIS, 2/ED
Foster

GOVERNMENTAL AND NONPROFIT ACCOUNTING: THEORY AND PRACTICE, 7/ED
Freeman/Shoulders

FINANCIAL ACCOUNTING, 5/ED
Harrison/Horngren

COST ACCOUNTING: A MANAGERIAL EMPHASIS, 11/ED
Horngren/Datar/Foster

ACCOUNTING, 5/ED
Horngren/Harrison/Bamber

CASES IN FINANCIAL REPORTING, 3/ED
Hirst/McAnally

INTRODUCTION TO FINANCIAL ACCOUNTING, 8/ED
Horngren/Sundem/Elliott

INTRODUCTION TO MANAGEMENT ACCOUNTING, 12/ED
Horngren/Sundem/Stratton

BUDGETING, 6/E
Welsch/Hilton/Gordon

Financial Accounting

FIFTH EDITION

Walter T. Harrison Jr.
Baylor University

Charles T. Horngren
Stanford University

Upper Saddle River, New Jersey 07458

Library of Congress Cataloging-in-Publication Data

Harrison, Walter T.
Financial accounting / Walter T. Harrison, Jr., Charles T.
Horngren. — 4th ed.
752 pp.
Includes indexes.
ISBN 0-13-008213-9
1. Accounting. I. Horngren, Charles T., 1926– II. Title
HF5635.H333 2000
657—dc21 00-029798

Executive Editors: Debbie Hoffman; Mac Mendelsohn
Editor-in-Chief: P.J. Boardman
Assistant Editor: Sam Goffinet
Senior Editorial Assistant: Jane Avery
Developmental Editor: Jeannine Ciliotta
Director of Development: Steve Deitmer
Media Project Manager: Nancy Welcher
Marketing Manager: Beth Toland
Managing Editor (Production): Cynthia Regan
Senior Production Editor: Anne Graydon
Permissions Coordinator: Suzanne Grappi
Associate Director, Manufacturing: Vincent Scelta
Production Manager: Arnold Vila
Design Manager: Maria Lange
Designer: Steve Frim
Interior Design: Jill Little
Photo Researcher: Diane Austin
Photo Permissions Coordinator: Michelina Viscusi
Cover Design: Steve Frim
Cover Image: Courtesy of Fossil, Inc.
Illustrator (Interior): Progressive Publishing Alternatives
Manager, Print Production: Christy Mahon
Composition: Progressive Information Technologies
Full-Service Project Management: Progressive Publishing Alternatives
Printer/Binder: R.R. Donnelley/Willard

Credits and acknowledgements borrowed from other sources and reproduced, with permission [6, Fossil, Inc.; 54, Michael Newman/PhotoEdit; 110, ARS Technical Images; 178, James Nielsen/Getty Images, Inc.–Liaison; 222, Reuters NewMedia Inc./CORBIS; 262, Deborah Davis/PhotoEdit; 316, Alan Schein/CORBIS; 364, Michael Newman/PhotoEdit; 416, Chuck Nacke/Woodfin Camp & Associates; 464, AFP Photo/Raveendran/CORBIS; 506, PhotoEdit; 544, These materials have been reproduced with the permission of eBay Inc. Copyright © eBay Inc. All rights reserved; 604, Bristol-Meyers Squibb Company; 661, Fossil, Inc.; 675, pier 1 Imports.]

Pearson Education LTD
Pearson Education Australia PTY, Limited
Pearson Education Singapore, Pte. Ltd
Pearson Education North Asia Ltd
Pearson Education, Canada, Ltd
Pearson Educación de Mexico, S.A. de C.V.
Pearson Education—Japan
Pearson Education Malaysia, Pte. Ltd

10 9 8 7 6 5 4 3 2 1 ISBN 0-13-008213-9

For our wives,

Nancy and Joan

Brief Contents

Contents

SUCCESS STARTS WITH:

Welcome to accounting!

In your personal life and in your professional career, **you will use accounting information each day to make basic business decisions**. Think about it... Did you write a check today? Did you pay bills? Do you have a part-time or full-time position while taking this course? Did you make a purchase on eBay?

As a consumer, you may skip using credit cards to avoid high interest balances. Or, you may buy over the Internet to save time and avoid paying sales tax. If you decide to open a retail store, you may need to weigh how much inventory you should carry of classic lines versus the latest styles.

Our goal in preparing the Fifth Edition is to provide you with the best tools and resources to understand how accounting will affect your personal and professional life.

Walter T. Harrison, Jr.

Charles T. Horngren

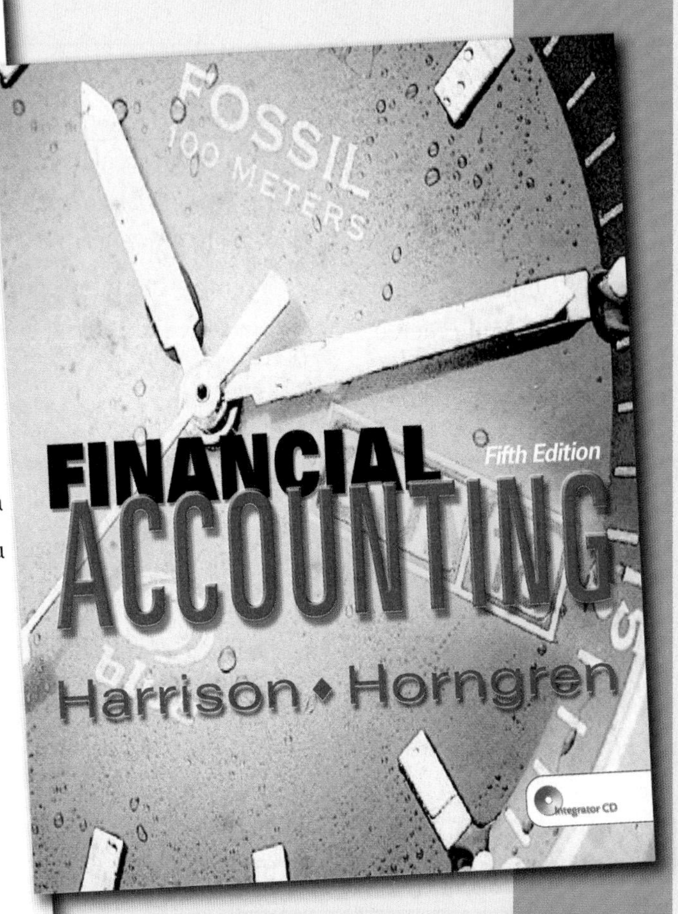

How do we do this?

- We **emphasize decisions** and how to use accounting information to make those decisions.
- We use examples of **real businesses** you know such as eBay to show you accounting issues at those companies.
- We start with **basic procedures and concepts** and then place them in a business context.
- We provide **tools for active learning and review material** to help you perform better in the classroom and on tests.
- We introduce you to **the "Integrator"** – an innovative CD-ROM that enables you to explore all concepts covered in each chapter and then to test your understanding!
- We provide you (and your professor) with **the most complete supplements package available.**

SUCCESS IS WITHIN YOUR GRASP.

Let's get started by helping you succeed in this first accounting course!

STEP ONE: Focus on the

Financial Accounting, fifth edition, continues its clear, concise presentation of accounting concepts and procedures. Students know the accounting cycle by the end of Chapter 3. *Financial Accounting* sets a new standard by merging merchandising and inventory concepts in a single-chapter (Chapter 6, "Merchandise Inventory, Cost of Goods Sold, and Gross Profit") that enables students to review all of this material in a unified treatment.

By being grounded in the basics, students are effectively prepared to understand and prepare all four financial statements. And, see the new coverage in Chapter 1 on Understanding the Relationship Between the Financial Statements.

Highlights of the Fifth Edition

As always, we have responded to student, adopter, and reviewer feedback in preparing the Fifth Edition. Some of the highlights include:

Chapter 1–The Financial Statements

- ***New*** feature company, *Fossil, Inc.*, is integrated throughout the chapter
- ***New*** material on the Ethics of Biased Information: *Enron, WorldCom, Qwest*
- ***New*** discussion of B2B and Electronic Accounting
- Statement of Cash Flows features the Indirect Method
- Moved "Accounting's Role in Business" to Prologue—to show students why accounting is a dynamic and powerful field in which to work

Chapter 2–Processing Information

- Updated chapter-opening vignette on *Pepsi Co.*
- ***New*** exercises, Ethical Issue, and Decision Case

Chapter 3–Accrual Accounting

- ***New*** chapter-opening vignette on *Vodafone Plc* and *Deutsche Telekom*
- ***New*** comparison of Accrual versus Cash-basis accounting
- Comparison of *Vodafone* and *Best Buy* income statements
- Two new Decision Cases

Chapter 4–Internal Control and Cash

- ***New*** chapter-opening vignette on *Enron*
- ***New*** discussion of Computer Fraud
- Streamlined Internal Control exhibits
- ***New*** section on Compensating Balances

Chapter 5–Short-Term Investments and Receivables

- Updated chapter-opening vignette on *Oracle Corporation*
- Streamlined coverage of Accounting for Uncollectibles

Basic Concepts & Procedures

Chapter 6–Inventory

- ***New*** chapter-opening vignette on *General Motors*
- Added graphs to distinguish FIFO from LIFO

Chapter 7–Plant Assets

- ***New*** chapter-opening vignette on *FedEx*
- ***New*** section on Ethical Considerations
- Updated accounting for *Goodwill*

Chapter 8–Current and Long-Term Liabilities

- ***New*** chapter-opening vignette compares *Home Depot* and *H. J. Heinz*
- ***New*** material on the Times-Interest-Earned Ratio

Chapter 9–Stockholders' Equity

- Updated and revised chapter-opening vignette on *IHOP*
- Streamlined Accounting for Treasury Stock
- Shortened Accounting for Stock Dividends

Chapter 10–Long-Term Investments and International Operations

- ***New*** chapter-opening vignette on *General Electric*
- Updated coverage of Accounting for International Operations

Chapter 11–The Income Statement and the Statement of Stockholders' Equity

- ***New*** chapter-opening vignette on *Lockheed Martin*
- Scaled down the detail of Discontinued Operations and Earnings Per Share Calculations
- ***New*** section on the Pitfalls of Pro Forma Earnings
- ***New*** section on Using the P/E Ratio

Chapter 12–The Statement of Cash Flows

- ***New*** chapter-opening vignette on *eBay*
- Now the Indirect Method for operating cash flows precedes coverage of the Direct Method
- Simplified computations for Cash-Flow amounts

Chapter 13–Financial Statement Analysis

- ***New*** *Bristol-Myers Squibb* chapter-opening vignette
- Streamlined discussions of Horizontal and Vertical Analyses
- Comparison of *Bristol-Myers Squibb* and *Procter & Gamble*
- ***New*** discussion of Using the Statement of Cash Flows in Financial Statement Analysis
- ***New*** section on Red Flags in Financial Statement Analysis

STEP TWO: Decision-Making

New! Decision-Making Tools

- ***NEW!*** chapter-opening vignettes now feature a "decision to be made."
- ***NEW!*** *Pier 1* and *Fossil* Annual Report financials are available in end-of-book appendixes. Both reports are referenced in the end-of-chapter cases. Using both reports for the financial statement cases enables you to compare financial statements.
- ***NEW!*** Within each chapter, numerous decision-making topics are highlighted to show students how accountants make decisions that affect the rest of the business.

Fossil

Pier 1

The **Decision Guidelines** appear in every chapter and are designed to show **when**, **why**, and **how** managers use accounting information to make business decisions. Students are presented with realistic scenarios and specific guidelines for solving dilemmas presented in these scenarios.

Decision Guidelines

Any entrepreneur must determine whether the venture is profitable. To do this, he or she needs to know its results of operations and financial position. If Michael Dell, for example, wanted to know whether the business he had begun from his dorm room at The University of Texas was making money, the Decision Guidelines that follow would help him. They identify some of the questions he needs to ask, and tell him how to get the answers. The guidelines also show how Dell, you, or anyone else would start a business.

HOW TO MEASURE RESULTS OF OPERATIONS AND FINANCIAL POSITION

Decision	Guidelines
Has a transaction occurred?	If the event affects the entity's financial position and can be reliably recorded—Yes. If either condition is absent—No.
Where to record the transaction?	In the *journal*, the chronological record of transactions
How to record an increase or decrease in the following accounts?	Rules of *debit* and *credit*:

	Increase	Decrease
Asset	Debit	Credit
Liability	Credit	Debit
Stock	Credit	
	Credit	

Skills & Real-World Examples

Excel

Excel Application Problem

Goal: Create an Excel spreadsheet to help evaluate various options for an ethical dilemma.

Scenario: Consider the dilemma of Max Shauk, in problem P4-7A. In addition to the facts in the problem, Shauk's board is considering additional options. First, they've been told that there is a comparable site in the same general area with an appraised value of $2.9 million. It has, however, recently been found to be home to a delicate species of woodland fungus that scientists believe holds promise in the treatment of diabetes. Second, the board is considering remodeling and expanding the existing location square footage by 25%. The board has received a bid of $2.2 million on the remodel and new construction from

2. Which option does your spreadsheet suggest the board choose?
3. For each option, which issue did you weight the most (in other words, which issue was most important to consider)?
4. If you were Shauk, which option would you recommend the board choose, and why?

Step-by-step:

1. Open a new Excel worksheet.
2. Create a bold-faced heading for your spreadsheet that contains the following:
   a. Chapter 4 Decision Guidelines
   b. Ethical Dilemma
   c. Today's Date

... create the following column headings:

EXCEL is the single most important piece of business software that you should be familiar with. Harrison/Horngren incorporates Excel into every chapter and shows students how Excel is used to make major business decisions.

- Application Problems appear with the Decision Guidelines in each chapter and provide you with a **step-by-step** guide to **creating Excel templates** to solve accounting dilemmas.
- Selected end-of-chapter problems appear on **templates created for immediate use** on the Student ***Integrator*** CD-ROM
- Package *Getting Started with Excel with Tom's Wear* free (upon faculty request) with new texts.

Real-World Vignettes & *On Location!* Videos

What do a professional football team and a billion-dollar software company have in common? The answer in more than you might think. When New York Jets linemen must decide which opposing player to block, the answer depends on the formation the opposing team is using. In the information age, the Jets use software, not playbooks with *X* and *O* diagrams, to map out plays. With help from the Oracle Corporation, an interactive multimedia show turns football formations into live animation.

Using Developer/2000 and multimedia software, Carl Banks, director of player development, has a state-of-the-art teaching model. Says Banks, "By the time [the players] hit the practice field, [they] lose the ability to visualize *X*'s and *O*'s as actual plays. Oracle has helped create [a] learning environment that increases [players'] retention by as much as 250%."

Oracle is the world's second largest software company. With annual revenues exceeding $10 billion, the company offers products and services to clients around the world. As Oracle's balance sheet shows, Trade receivables (another name for Accounts receivable) are a significant asset.

Receivables present a challenge: How much of a company's receivables will it be able to collect in cash? This chapter shows how to answer this and other questions about receivables. It also covers short-term investments, Oracle's second most liquid asset, which is listed immediately after cash on the balance sheet.

The **Chapter-Opening Stories** thrust you into the real world of accounting—where business decisions affect the future of actual organizations. These vignettes—including such companies as General Electric, FedEx, New York Jets, and eBay—provide the real business context for chapter concepts. These motivational stories are linked to our custom-crafted *On Location!* videos.

This set of custom-crafted videos (each 5-10 minutes in length) is provided free to faculty upon adoption and is also available on the Student and Instructor ***Integrator*** (see Step Four for details) CD-ROMs.

STEP THREE: Learn

New! Sitemap

Sitemap

Accrual Accounting Versus Cash Basis Accounting ■
Updating the Accounts: The Adjustment Process ■
Preparing Financial Statements ■
Formats for Financial Statements ■
Decision Making: Using Accounting Ratios ■

Whether the business is Vodafone in England, Gap, Inc. in San Francisco, or Air & Sea Travel across town, the profit motive drives the business. As you study this chapter, consider how net income affects the behavior of managers and investors.

How does a business know whether it is profitable? By analyzing its financial statements. Vodafone's income statement, like th British companies, is reported in pounds sterling (denoted symbol £). The statements of many foreign companies, suc Vodafone, give fewer details than those of companies in th States. But even without many details, the Vodafone staten "net loss!"

Like to know what's ahead? Each chapter's text begins with a Sitemap–a listing of the major topics that tells you the skills you will learn in that chapter.

New! Running Glossary & Concept Links

The *amount* of revenue to record is the cash value of the ... the customer. Suppose that in order to obtain a new client, Air & Sea Travel arranges a trip for the price of $500. Ordinarily, Air & Sea would charge $600 for this service. How much revenue should it record? The answer is $500—the cash value of the transaction. The cash to be received, $500, pinpoints the amount of revenue earned.

← An expense, defined in Chapter 1, page 12, is a decrease in retained earnings that occurs from using assets and creating liabilities in the course of operating a business.

The Matching Principle

The **matching principle** is the basis for recording expenses →. *Expenses* are the costs of assets used up, and liabilities created, in the earning of revenue. Expenses have no future benefit to the company. The matching principle includes two steps:

1. Identify all the expenses incurred during the accounting period.
2. Measure the expenses ... the revenues earned.

To *match* expenses agains... compute net income or ne...

Matching principle The basis for recording expenses. Directs accountants to identify all expenses incurred during the period, to measure the expenses, and to match them against the revenues earned during that same period.

Is terminology important to your success? Absolutely! *New!* All key terms are now highlighted in boldface within the text and given a **full definition** in the side margin.

Concept Links are designed to **help you recall previous concepts and see how these are linked** to new material. Whenever possible, the margin links include a page number for reference.

Stop & Think Boxes

STOP & THINK

At the beginning of the month, supplies were $5,000. During the month, $7,800 of supplies were purchased. At month's end, $3,600 of supplies were still on hand. What are the adjusting entry and the ending balance in the Supplies account?

Answer:

Supplies Expense ($5,000 + $7,800 − $3,600) ....
Supplies ....

Ending balance of supplies = $3,600 (the supplies still on ha...

Several *Stop & Think* exercise boxes appear within the text in every chapter. These exercises encourage you to **practice immediately what you have just learned.** If you can correctly solve the problem, great! Keep on reading! If you need some assistance, you can go back and review what you have just read rather than waiting until the end of the chapter. This feature helps you see where you may need extra help, and reinforces points you have already mastered!

& Review

Mid-Chapter and End-of-Chapter Summary Problems

End-of-Chapter Summary Problem

Refer to the mid-chapter summary problem that begins on page 133.

Required

1. Make State Service Company's closing entries at December 31, 20X5. Explain what the closing entries accomplish and why they are necessary.
2. Post the closing entries to Retained Earnings and compare Retained Earnings' ending balance with the amount reported on the balance sheet on page 000. The two amounts should be the same.
3. Prepare State Service Company's classified balance sheet to identify the company's current assets and current liabilities. (State has no long-term liabilities.) Then compute the company's current ratio and debt ratio at December 31, 20X5.
4. The top management of State Service Company has asked you for a $500,000 loan to expand the business. State proposes to pay off the loan over a 10-year period. Recompute State's debt ratio assuming you make the loan. Use the company financial statements plus the ratio values to decide whether to grant the loan at an interest rate of 8%, 10%, or 12%. State Service Company's cash flow is strong. Give the reasoning underlying your decision.

Answers

Requirem...

This **unique** Harrison/Horngren feature enables you to pause and assess your understanding of chapter concepts at two locations within each chapter–midway and again at the end of the chapter. Solutions appear with the problems for immediate feedback.

Assignment Material with Unique "Check Points"

Assess Your Progress

Check Points

Linking accrual accounting and cash flows **(Obj. 1)**

CP3-1 Pier 1 Imports, Inc. made sales of $1,411 million during 20X1. O... 1 collected cash for all but $3 million. The company's cost of goods so... and all other expenses for the year totaled $499 million. Also during 20... million for its inventory and $356 million for everything else. Begi... million. Suppose Pier 1's top management is interviewing you for a job a... questions:

a. How much was Pier 1's net income for 20X1?
b. How much was Pier ... balance at the end of 20X1?

Ease into your homework! These unique, single-concept exercises frequently use real-world companies and are designed to serve as warm-ups.

✔ Check Point 3-1

✔ Check Point 3-2

The income statement reports the revenue earned, and the balance sheet reports the wireless service that Vodafone still owes its customers. T... ing amounts. The statement of cash flows reports cash re... are needed to report what happened to Vodafone during 2...

Accrual accounting is based on a conceptual framew... and principles. We turn now to the time-period concept, ... the matching principle.

The Time-Period Concept

Read the exercise, above. If you can solve it, great. If not, look for the exercise icon and number within the margin of the text. You will find information that will help you reach the solution.

STEP FOUR: The

The Student *Integrator* CD-ROM contains a vast array of tools designed to assist you in learning accounting concepts and testing your understanding of these concepts prior to taking examinations.

Integrator CD

Click & Learn

Simply insert the *Integrator* Student CD-ROM into your PC and click on the chapter you are reading. You can browse, search (by chapter, key word, and file type), and view resources. You can also export resources to your own computer and customize your study materials.

Here's what you can do:

1. Review the PowerPoints **often used in class.**
2. Watch short video clips: ***On Location!* clips show real companies using accounting information. *Tutorial* clips teach financial accounting topics.**
3. Install General Ledger software or use Excel Spreadsheet templates **to complete homework assignments.**
4. Install PH ReEnforcer software **to test your understanding of basic principles and practices.**
5. Use the Excel Tutorial **and the** eWorking Papers **as a learning tool or a refresher.**
6. Use Getting Started with Peachtree or QuickBooks **data files.**

ATTENTION FACULTY

We didn't forget you!

There's a special version of the ***Integrator*** just for YOU! It contains the entire ancillary package on CD-ROM... perfect for customizing supplements, accessing the package in the classroom, or transporting the package from class to home to office. You can export resources to your own computer for editing or inclusion in online courses or other projects. We've included the entire test bank in the correct format for quick uploading into WebCT, Blackboard, or Course Compass. Just ask your Prentice Hall Representative for details.

"Integrator" CD-ROM

Active Learning Resources for Each Chapter

Journalizing adjusting entries
(Obj. 3)

general ledger

E3-9 Suppose **The Home Depot, Inc.** faced the following situations. Journalize the adjusting entry needed at December 31 for each situation. Consider each fact separately.

a. Equipment was purchased at the beginning of last year at a cost of $50,000. The equipment's useful life is 4 years. Record the depreciation for this year and then determine the equipment's book value.

b. On September 1, when we prepaid $1,200 for a 1-year insuran...
Prepaid Insurance and credited Cash.

c. The business will ... expense of $9,000 early in the ...

You want to play an active role in learning accounting, right? On the opening page of each chapter and several times within each chapter, you will see the ***Integrator*** icon in the side margin. This is a cue that there are resources available to help you to understand the material.

Internal Contro... & Managing Cash

Learning Objectives

1. **Set** up an effective system of internal control
2. **Use** a bank reconciliation as a control device
3. **Apply** internal controls to cash receipts and cash payments
4. **Use** a budget to manage cash
5. **Weigh** ethical judgments in business

Integrator CD

Need additional help? Go to the **Integrator CD** *and search these key words: bank reconciliation, cash budget, cash disbursements, cash payments, ethics, internal control*

The Best

Technology Resources

- INNOVATION!
  Instructor & Student *Integrator* CD-ROMs
  The *Integrator* is a powerful teaching and learning tool. It serves as a roadmap through the chapters to first identify key concepts and then guides you to material that can help you further develop your skills.

  The Instructor ***Integrator*** CD-ROM contains all print (Instructor's Manual, Solutions Manual, Test Bank) and technology (e.g., software, spreadsheets, videos, data files) supplements on a single CD-ROM. Enjoy the freedom to transport the entire package from office, to home, to classroom. The Instructor CD-ROM enables you to customize any of the ancillaries, print only the chapters or materials you wish, or access any item from the package within the classroom! The *Integrator* also contains a special option for faculty who wish to build their own online courses! Faculty can pick and choose from the various supplements (organized by chapter and topic), and export them to their hard drive in HTML. From hard drive to online course is an easy step!

  The Student ***Integrator*** CD-ROM is free (upon your request with new text purchase only; it can also be sold stand-alone) and contains the Excel spreadsheets, tutorial and general ledger software, powerpoints, and other valuable tools for students.

- INNOVATION!
  Getting Started Series
  Upon faculty request, you may package your choice of these approximately 70-page manuals on the latest professional accounting software packages with Harrison/Horngren **at no charge.** Each manual introduces students to the concepts of **Excel, Peachtree, QuickBooks,** or **Simply Accounting.**

- INNOVATION!
  SPECIAL OFFERS–Professional Accounting Software Packages
  Package your choice of the latest software releases of Peachtree or Simply Accounting at $10.00 net with new text purchase.

- PH ReEnforcer and General Ledger Software
  The tutorial software enables students to test their understanding of chapter concepts via a variety of problem types. The General Ledger software enables students to complete homework assignments using a general ledger software package. Students may also enter and solve their own problems. Available on the Student *Integrator* CD-ROM, Instructor *Integrator* CD-ROM, and downloadable from Companion Website.

- INNOVATION!
  Standard Online Courses in WebCT, CourseCompass, and BlackBoard
  Teach a complete online course or a Web-enhanced course. Add your own course materials, take advantage of online testing and Gradebook opportunities, and utilize the bulletin board and discussion board functions. Free upon request. This is an excellent time to build your own course using our ***Integrator*** CD-ROM with your choice of platform.

Teaching & Learning Resources

- **PH Professor: A Classroom Presentation on PowerPoint**
  PowerPoint presentations are available for each chapter of the text. Instructors have the flexibility to add slides and/or modify the existing slides to meet the course needs. Free upon adoption. Available on the Instructor Course Organizer CD and on the text Web site. Use the ***Integrator*** to create your own slideshow!

- **Companion Website at www.prenhall.com/Harrison**
  Prentice Hall's Learning on the Internet Partnership offers the most expansive Internet-based support available. Our Web sites provides a wealth of resources for students and faculty–resources including: Student Study Hall, Online Tutorial Assistance, Study Guide with Quizzes, Internet Exercises, and much more.

Instructor Supplements

- **INNOVATION!**
  Instructor *Integrator* CD-ROM
  The *Integrator* is a powerful teaching and learning tool. It first serves as a roadmap through the chapters to identify key concepts and then guides students through to the CD-ROM where they can further develop their skills.

  The **Instructor *Integrator* CD** contains all print and technology (e.g., spreadsheets, videos) supplements on a single CD-ROM. Enjoy the freedom to transport the entire package from office, to home, to classroom. This enables you to customize any of the ancillaries, print only the chapters or materials you wish to use, or access any item from the package within the classroom!

- **Instructor's Manual**
  Each chapter of this comprehensive resource consists of a list of the student learning objectives, a narrative overview of main topics, an outline with teaching tips interspersed, a 10-problem multiple-choice quiz cross-referenced to the outline and arranged for easy copying (answers are at end of the outline and solutions for all quizzes are on separate pages at the end of the manual), suggested readings, examples of ways to integrate the supplements, and transparency masters.

- **Test Item File**
  The printed Test Item File consists of over 1,800 questions, including true/false questions, conceptual and quantitative multiple-choice questions, critical thinking problems, and exercises. Each question will identify the difficulty level and the corresponding learning objective. **Prentice Hall Test Generator** can create exams and evaluate and track student results. It also provides online testing capabilities. Test items are drawn from the Test Item File.

- **Solutions Manual**
  In addition to fully worked-out and accuracy-checked solutions for every question, exercise, and problem in the text, this manual provides suggestions for alternative chapter sequences, a categorization of assignment material, and check figures.

- **Solutions Transparencies**
  Every page of the Solutions Manual has been reproduced in acetate form for use on the overhead projector.

- ***On Location* Videos**
  These brief videos take students "on location" to real companies where real accounting situations are discussed and explained.

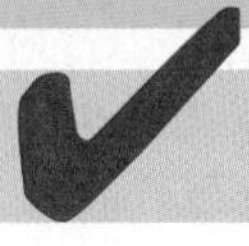

Student Supplements

- INNOVATION!
  Student *Integrator* CD-ROM
  The **Student *Integrator* CD-ROM** is free (upon faculty request with new text purchase only; it can also be purchased separately) and contains the Excel spreadsheets, PH ReEnforcer (tutorial) and General Ledger software packages, PowerPoints, Getting Started data files, and other valuable tools for students.

- Student Study Guide
  This chapter-by-chapter learning aid systematically and effectively helps students study financial accounting and get the maximum benefit from their study time. Each chapter provides a Chapter Overview and a Chapter Review, a Featured Exercise that covers in a single exercise all of the most important material included in the chapter, and Review Questions and Exercises with Solutions that best test the student's understanding of the material.

- Working Papers and eWorking Papers
  Working Papers and eWorking Papers are available.

- Mastering Accounting CD-ROM
  Package Mastering Accounting with Harrison/Horngren (or any other Prentice Hall text) for only $5.00 net.

  Mastering Accounting, part of the Mastering Business program, is an **interactive, multimedia CD-ROM** that uses video and interactive exercises to help students **link the THEORY** they learn in class with **realistic business situations.** The episodes and interactive exercises on the CD are based on CanGo, a fictional e-commerce startup that sells a variety of entertainment products and services online. The **dramatic situations** show students how all the **functional areas of business work together** to ensure the growth of the company—as well as how to apply business theories to CanGo's daily operations. All of the content—including videos and exercises—was **created and reviewed by university professors** and experts in interactive instructional design.

Financial Accounting

Prologue: Accounting's Role in Business

Every organization has a mission. Hospitals provide health care. Law firms advise clients. Auto dealers sell cars. All these organizations use *accounting* because no one can physically observe all the aspects of a business. Accounting helps managers view the organization as a whole without drowning in the details. Let's see how people use accounting to make decisions.

Suppose you own a software consulting firm. How will you decide on office rent, employee salaries, and computer software? You will be limited by your cash balance, which you can access from accounting records. After the business becomes a success how will you decide whether to expand?

Good contacts and intelligence are important, but they are not enough for wise decision making. You must "run the numbers" to determine how much you will earn from the business. Your banker will be more impressed with a detailed plan than with a few vague ideas. Accounting will help you develop a business plan.

Good managers plan for the future. They develop a *budget*, which is a formal plan stated in monetary terms. For example, a product manager for Best Buy will have an annual sales budget. If she makes more than the budgeted level of sales, she will receive a bonus. You need to know how a budget works because a budget will be used to evaluate your own performance.

Accounting helps banks decide to whom they will lend money. Bankers can study customers' financial statements to predict their ability to repay the loan. And they monitor borrowers' progress by examining their financial reports.

Accounting provides information that helps investors pick stocks. An investor may not be able to check every detail of a company before buying its stock. But he can examine the company's financial reports and figure out whether the company is profitable and well managed. Why are investors willing to spend their money this way? Because accounting statements and other reports provide data that people trust.

Let's examine the two main paths that an accounting career can take.

Private Accounting

Private accountants work for a single business, such as Dillard's Department Stores, McDonald's restaurant chain, or Eastman Kodak Company. Charitable organizations, educational institutions, and government agencies also employ accountants. You'll find private accountants in Wall Street brokerage firms, agencies for the homeless, and rock bands. Accountants services include:

- *Budgeting* sets goals and develops plans for achieving those goals. The most successful companies in the United States have pioneered budgeting—Procter & Gamble and General Electric, for example.
- *Information systems design* identifies the organization's information needs. Systems designers develop information systems to meet those needs.
- *Cost accounting* analyzes costs to help control expenses.
- *Internal auditing* is performed by a business's own accountants. Most organizations have internal auditors who work to improve operating efficiency.

A company's chief accounting officer usually has the title of controller, treasurer, or chief financial officer (CFO). This person operates as a vice president. Accountants who have met certain professional requirements in the area of management accounting are designated as *certified management accountants (CMAs)*.

The CFO and other accounting professionals have become increasingly important as businesses compete in global markets. At FedEx Corporation, some financial managers visited Intel to learn how to improve efficiency.

People in accounting careers need more than a financial and accounting background. They must be good communicators, analysts, and problem solvers. They work in teams composed of members from production, distribution, sales, and marketing, so they need good people skills too.

Public Accounting

Public accountants serve the general public and collect professional fees, as do doctors and lawyers. Public accountants are only a small fraction (about 10%) of all accountants. Accountants who have met certain professional requirements in accounting, auditing, and law are designated as *certified public accountants (CPAs)*.

Like private accountants, public accountants provide valuable services:

- *Assurance services* include auditing. In conducting an audit, CPAs from outside a business examine its financial statements. The CPAs give a professional opinion stating whether the firm's financial statements agree with generally accepted accounting principles (GAAP). Stockholders and creditors need assurance that the financial picture of a potential investment is complete and accurate.
- *Tax accounting* has two aims: complying with the tax laws and minimizing the company's tax bill. Because federal income tax rates run as high as 38.6% for individuals and 35% for corporations, reducing a tax bill is important. Accountants plan business transactions to minimize taxes, and they advise clients on investments.
- *Consulting* describes the wide scope of advice CPAs provide to help managers run a business. CPAs look deep into a business's operations. With the insights they gain, they make suggestions for improvements in the business's structure.
- *Financial planning* helps individuals map out their investments to save for retirement and children's college expenses.

Most professional employees of accounting firms are CPAs. Accounting firms vary greatly in size. Some are small businesses and others are large partnerships. There are four large, international accounting firms:

PricewaterhouseCoopers	Deloitte & Touche
Ernst & Young	KPMG

All of these firms are organized as partnerships, and they each have approximately 2,000 partners worldwide. These firms serve the largest corporations in the world (such as General Motors, Sony, and British Petroleum) and many other clients as well. Other CPA firms operate nationally and regionally in the United States. Some of these firms include

Grant Thornton	Crowe Chizek
BDO Seidman	Moss Adams
RSM McGladrey	Plante & Moran

Each of these firms has 150 to 300 partners and usually specializes in some area (a particular industry, a geographical region, or a type of business).

Public accountants spend most of their time at their clients' locations: across town, around the country, and around the world. Public accountants may even find themselves in some unlikely places. Consider the following examples:

- Josh Young's first consulting engagement found him on the site of the Northridge earthquake outside Los Angeles. One of his clients was a supermarket chain with 150 damaged stores. Young needed to visit the actual site at 4:00 A.M.—as the tremors continued—to determine how much damage had occurred to help prepare the insurance claims.
- Mike Nugent, a supervising senior at KPMG, took on a consulting job, at which his business attire included boots, overalls, and a hairnet. To conduct an audit for a chicken producer recently acquired by a Japanese company, Nugent drove to Heartland, Indiana, where he found himself surrounded by 2,000 screaming chickens.
- Jennifer Tufer is a Deloitte & Touche senior manager on assignment in Moscow. As she sifts through faxes from various Deloitte & Touche offices around the world, she finds a request from a U.S. manufacturer interested in expanding into Russia. "The company wanted to know how they would be taxed," Ms. Tufer says.

Accounting Today

Accountants are as diverse as their job assignments. They are male or female, outgoing or conservative, but they are all analytical. They may have backgrounds in art history or computer programming. And they come from every ethnic and cultural background.

Many accountants enjoy flexible work arrangements. "I'm probably one of the first people who stayed in public accounting because of quality-of-life advantages," says Eileen Garvey, an audit partner at Ernst & Young in New York. Garvey works a 3-day-a-week schedule. The mother of two, she became a partner as a part-timer. Flexibility works for men, too. Carl Moellenkamp, a manager with a firm in Chicago, took a summer leave to pursue his other career as a chef.

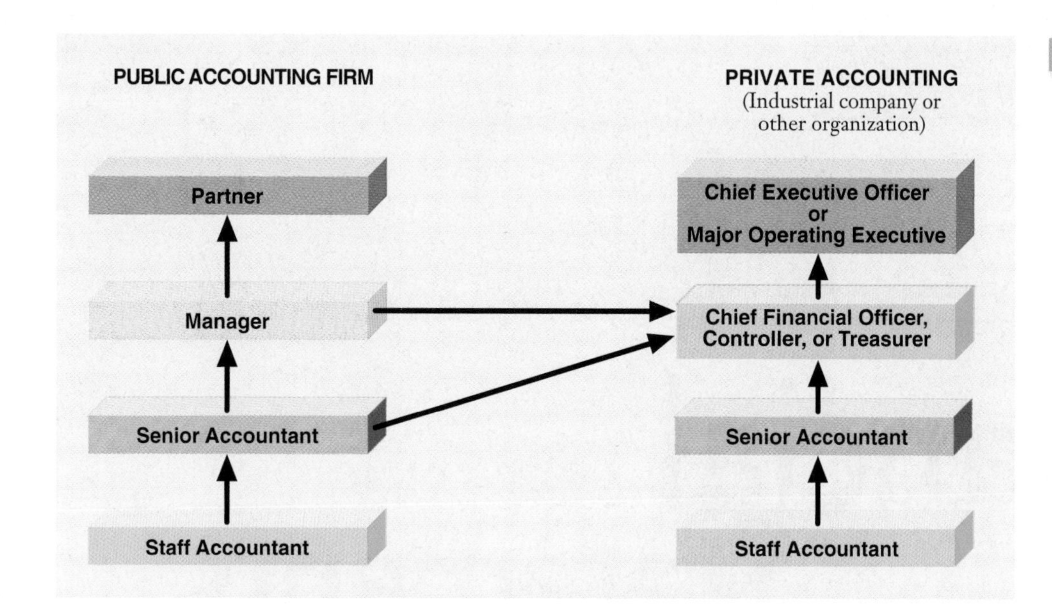

Exhibit 1

Accounting Positions within Organizations

Using computers, phones, and fax machines, accountants now work from home. Janet Caswell, a Michigan accountant with her own business, has a staff but no office. Her computer server and equipment are located in a rented storage space, and her telephone is an 800 number. Ms. Caswell follows her employees electronically. Hers is a "virtual office."

What can you expect if you enter accounting? Exhibit 1 shows the positions within public accounting firms and other organizations. An accounting background opens doors in many lines of business because accounting deals with all facets of an organization. This is why accounting provides such an excellent basis for gaining business experience. After all, accounting is the language of business.

1

The Financial Statements

Learning Objectives

1. **Use** accounting vocabulary for decision making
2. **Analyze** a business using accounting concepts and principles
3. **Use** the accounting equation to describe an organization
4. **Evaluate** a company's operating performance, financial position, and cash flows
5. **Explain** the relationships among the financial statements

Integrator CD

Need additional help? Go to the **Integrator CD** *and search these key words:* accounting concepts, accounting equation, asset, balance sheet, expense, financial statements, income statement, liability, owners' equity, revenue, statement of cash flows

Fossil, Inc.

Consolidated Statement of Income (Adapted)

Amounts in millions	Years Ended December 31, 2001	2000
1 Net sales revenue	$546	$504
2 Cost of goods sold	274	248
3 Gross profit	272	256
4 Operating expenses:		
5 Selling and distribution expense	150	126
6 General and administrative expense	45	36
7 Total operating expenses	195	162
8 Operating income	77	94
9 Other income (expense):		
10 Write-off of investment	(5)	—
11 Other income (expense), net	1	1
12 Income before income tax	73	95
13 Income tax expense	29	39
14 Net income	$ 44	$ 56

What company comes to mind when you think of innovative wristwatches, sunglasses, and leather goods—fashion, nostalgia, a look forward and a look back in time? If you guessed Fossil, you're right. This company burst onto the fashion scene in 1984 with its trademark watch brand. Some companies farm out product design to one entity and rely on others for distribution. Not Fossil—it controls everything from design to distribution. And Fossil products are sold in over 90 countries around the world.

But 2001 was a disappointing year: Fossil's sales were up, yet profits were down. Why the decline in profits? Was it because Fossil shifted to making watches for upscale brands like Armani, DKNY, and Diesel? Are people unwilling to pay a premium price for a Fossil watch with a DKNY dial?

Sitemap

This course will help you develop the skills to address real business questions like these. You will learn how companies represent themselves to the public. You will also master some of the analytical techniques managers, investors, and lenders use to make decisions every day. We start with business decisions, by both managers and investors.

Business Decisions

Fossil's managers make lots of decisions in the course of leading the company. Which watches are selling the fastest? Are the company's leather goods bringing in profits? Should Fossil expand into China and the Pacific Rim? Accounting helps managers make these decisions.

Fossil managers must determine how much to invest in watches, sunglasses, and leather products. Should they automate the warehouse and use robotic equipment to handle merchandise? If so, they will purchase equipment that moves goods rapidly and at the lowest cost. Accounting measures the cost of the equipment.

Fossil managers must also decide how to finance operations. What works best—selling stock to the owners or borrowing from outsiders? Sometimes borrowing has the advantage. In other cases, it is better to issue stock. Accounting measures the cost of financing.

Take a look at Fossil, Inc.'s income statement on page 7. Focus on net income (line 14). Net income represents Fossil's profit, the excess of revenues over expenses. You can see that Fossil earned a $44 million profit in 2001. That's good because it means that Fossil had $44 million more revenue than expenses for the year.

Fossil's income statement also conveys some bad news. Net income for 2001 was less than net income for 2000. The managers of companies prefer net income to grow from year to year. So Fossil managers had to get the company back on track in 2002. Why do managers strive to earn ever larger amounts of net income each year? Increasing profits usually indicates that the company is growing, and investors buy the stocks of growing companies.

Now suppose you have $9,000 to invest. You can deposit the money in a bank and earn interest. This investment is safe because U.S. bank deposits are insured, but your money won't grow very fast. You can also invest in Fossil stock. Your $9,000 will buy 400 shares of Fossil stock because its price was recently quoted at $22.49 per share ($400 \times \$22.49 = \$8,996$).

What information would you need before deciding to invest in Fossil? You want Fossil to have a track record of profitable operations—earning a profit (net earnings or net income) year after year. Fossil also needs a steady stream of cash coming in. How would you determine whether the company meets these criteria? Accounting provides this information through Fossil's financial statements.

✔ Check Point 1-1

Accounting: The Language of Business

financial statements

Objective

1 **Use** accounting vocabulary for decision making

Accounting is the information system that measures business activities, processes data into reports, and communicates results to decision makers. Accounting is "the language of business." The better you understand the language, the better you can manage your own finances. Personal planning, education expenses, auto loans, and income taxes all depend on accounting information.

A key product of accounting is the set of **financial statements** that report information about a business entity. The financial statements are standard documents that tell us how well a business is performing and where it stands in financial terms. In this chapter we focus on Fossil, Inc. After completing this chapter, you will be familiar with the financial statements that companies use to represent themselves to the public. **This book's major goal is to help you use financial statements for decision making.**

Don't mistake bookkeeping for accounting. Bookkeeping is the procedural part of accounting, just as arithmetic is a part of mathematics. Exhibit 1-1 illustrates accounting's role in business. The process starts and ends with people making decisions.

Accounting
The information system that measures business activities, processes that information into reports and financial statements, and communicates the results to decision-makers.

Financial statements
Business documents that report financial information about a business entity to decision-makers.

✔ Check Point 1-2

Exhibit 1-1 **The Flow of Accounting Information**

1. People make decisions

2. Business transactions occur.

3. Businesses prepare reports to show the results of their operations.

DECISION: An Information System or a Valuation System?

Accounting can be viewed as a system for providing information, or it can be treated as a system for assigning value to things. The information perspective focuses on the data that accounting provides for decision making. Valuation assigns values to assets (resources), liabilities (debts), and other items used by an organization. Two examples will clarify the distinction between the two.

> *Information system.* Suppose General Motors (GM) is negotiating to purchase BMW, the German automaker. How much should GM pay to acquire BMW? GM's decision will depend largely upon BMW's profits, and the accounting system will help GM make this decision. Accounting is therefore an information system.

> *Valuation system.* Again, suppose GM is negotiating to purchase BMW. Suppose the price for BMW depends on the value of the company's assets. BMW's accounting records will *not* show the current value of BMW's assets. Why not? Because accounting is not designed to show the current values of a company's assets and liabilities. GM will hire an appraiser to tell the current values.

Who Uses Accounting Information?

Decision makers need information. A banker must decide who gets a loan. An investor selects which stock to buy. A manager decides whether to sell goods in foreign countries. The more important the decision, the greater the need for accounting information. Let's see how some other decision makers use accounting information.

INDIVIDUALS. People use accounting to manage their bank accounts and to decide whether to rent an apartment or buy a house. Accounting helps them decide which automobile they can afford and how to pay for it.

BUSINESSES. Business managers use accounting information to set goals, evaluate progress, and to take corrective action. Decisions based on accounting information may include where to locate a Fossil store, how many watches and sunglasses to keep on hand, and how much cash to borrow.

INVESTORS AND CREDITORS. Investors and creditors provide the money to finance a business. To decide whether to invest in Fossil or any other company people predict the level of income to expect on their investment. This requires accounting data. Before making a loan to Fossil, banks evaluate Fossil's ability to make payments on time.

GOVERNMENT REGULATORY AGENCIES. Most organizations face government regulation. For example, the Securities and Exchange Commission (SEC), a federal agency, requires businesses to report to the investing public. Fossil, eBay, GM, and other companies publish annual reports. The company's income statement on page 7 was taken from Fossil, Inc.'s annual report for the year ended December 31, 2001.

TAXING AUTHORITIES. Governmental units levy taxes on individuals and businesses. Fossil pays property tax on its assets and income tax on profits. Fossil also collects sales tax from customers and forwards the money to the government. Individuals pay income tax on their earnings. Most taxes are based on accounting data.

NONPROFIT ORGANIZATIONS. Nonprofit organizations—churches, hospitals, and charities such as the Red Cross—use accounting information the same way profit-oriented businesses do. They must deal with payrolls, rent payments, and the like—information that accounting provides.

Financial Accounting and Management Accounting

The users of accounting information may be categorized as *external users* or *internal users*. This distinction allows us to classify accounting into financial accounting and management accounting.

Financial accounting
The branch of accounting that provides information to people outside the firm.

Financial accounting provides information to managers and to people outside the firm, such as investors on Wall Street and creditors who lend money. Government agencies and the general public also depend on accounting information. To meet these needs, financial information must meet certain standards of relevance and reliability.

Management accounting
The branch of accounting that generates information for the internal decision-makers of a business, such as top executives.

Management accounting generates confidential information for internal decision makers, such as the executives and other managers of Fossil, Inc. Management information is tailored to the needs of managers and thus does not have to meet external standards of reliability.

Ethics in Accounting and Business

Ethical considerations pervade accounting. Companies need money to operate. To attract investors and obtain loans, they must provide information to the public. Without information, people won't invest their money. To keep the economy going strong, the federal government therefore strives to keep investments flowing. The United States has laws that require companies to report relevant, reliable information to investors and creditors.

The top managers of a company such as Fossil know this. They also know a lot more about the company than anyone else. As they report on Fossil's operations, there is a natural temptation for them to slant the information to make the company look good—even if times are hard. The legal requirement for relevant, reliable information, coupled with managers' having inside information, creates an ethical challenge for executives. Most managers meet this challenge by providing full and fair information to the public. Capital flows to the most successful companies, the economy moves along, and living standards improve. That is the goal of economic policy makers.

Occasionally, a company will report biased information. It may misstate its financial statements—overstate profits or understate debts. In 2002, several well-known companies were charged with reporting misleading information. Enron Corporation, at the time one of the largest companies in the United States, admitted understating its liabilities (debts). Xerox, WorldCom, and Qwest were accused of overstating profits. If true, these companies' data were unreliable and their information thus failed the basic test of good ethics. The result? People invested in the wrong companies, lost money, and filed lawsuits to recover their losses. Reporting relevant, reliable information to the public is the ethical course of action. It also provides the most benefit to individuals and to the economy.

STANDARDS OF PROFESSIONAL CONDUCT FOR ACCOUNTANTS. What are the criteria for ethical judgments in accounting? The *American Institute of Certified Public Accountants (AICPA)*, other professional organizations, and large companies have codes of conduct that require high levels of ethical conduct. The AICPA is the country's largest organization of professional accountants, similar to the American Medical Association for physicians and the American Bar Association for attorneys.

The Code of Professional Conduct of the AICPA provides guidance in performing professional duties. The preamble to the Code states: "[A] certified public accountant assumes an obligation of self-discipline above and beyond the requirements of laws and regulations . . . [and] an unswerving commitment to honorable behavior, even at the sacrifice of personal advantage." The result of ethical behavior by accountants is information that people can rely on for decision making.

✔ Check Point 1-3

The events of 2002 drove home the need for good ethics among accountants as never before. The accounting firm of Arthur Andersen was the auditor of Enron, WorldCom, and Qwest, and, as mentioned previously, these companies' financial reports proved to be unreliable. The damage to Arthur Andersen's reputation was so great that the firm lost all of its large public clients and was denied the right to practice accounting in a number of states.

DECISION: How to Organize a Business

A business takes one of three forms of organization, and the accounting can depend on which form the organization takes. Therefore, you need to understand the differences

Exhibit 1-2

The Three Forms of Business Organization

	Proprietorship	*Partnership*	*Corporation*
Owner(s)	Proprietor—one owner	Partners—two or more owners	Stockholders—generally many owners
Life of entity	Limited by owner's choice or death	Limited by owners' choices or death	Indefinite
Personal liability of owner(s) for business debts	Proprietor is personally liable	Partners are personally liable	Stockholders are not personally liable
Accounting status	Accounting entity is separate from proprietor	Accounting entity is separate from partners	Accounting entity is separate from stockholders

among the three types: proprietorships, partnerships, and corporations. Exhibit 1-2 compares the three types.

Proprietorship A business with a single owner.

PROPRIETORSHIPS. A **proprietorship** has a single owner, called the proprietor, who is generally also the manager. Lands' End, the catalog merchant, may have started out as a proprietorship, with its founder as the owner. Proprietorships tend to be small retail stores or individual professional businesses—physicians, attorneys, and accountants. From a legal perspective the business *is* the proprietor and the proprietor is personally liable for business debts. But from the accounting viewpoint, each proprietorship is distinct from its proprietor. Thus, the accounting records of the proprietorship do not include the proprietor's personal financial records.

Partnership An association of two or more persons who co-own a business for profit.

PARTNERSHIPS. A **partnership** joins two or more persons as co-owners. Each owner is a partner. Many retail establishments and some professional organizations of physicians, attorneys, and accountants are partnerships. Most partnerships are small or medium-sized, but some are gigantic, with 2,000 or more partners. Accounting treats the partnership as a separate organization, distinct from the personal affairs of each partner. But the law views a partnership as the partners: Each partner is personally liable for all the partnership's debts. For this reason, partnerships are quite risky. In a recent example, the accounting firm of Arthur Andersen was found guilty of obstructing justice. A few Andersen partners virtually killed the entire firm.

Corporation A business owned by stockholders. A corporation is a legal entity, an "artificial person" in the eyes of the law.

Stockholder A person who owns stock in a corporation. Also called a *shareholder*.

Shareholder Another name for *stockholder*.

Stock Shares into which the owners' equity of a corporation is divided.

CORPORATIONS. A **corporation** is a business owned by **stockholders**, or **shareholders.** These people own **stock,** which represents shares of ownership, in a corporation. Corporations dominate business activity in the United States even though proprietorships and partnerships are more numerous. Corporations transact much more business and are larger in terms of total assets, income, and number of employees. Most well-known companies, such as Fossil, General Motors, and American Airlines, are corporations. Their full names include *Corporation* or *Incorporated* (abbreviated *Corp.* and *Inc.*) to indicate that they are corporations—for example, Fossil, Inc. and General Motors Corporation. Some bear the name "Company," such as Ford Motor Company. A proprietorship and a partnership can also bear the name "Company."

A corporation is a business entity formed under state law. From a legal perspective, a corporation is distinct from its owners. The corporation is like an artificial person and possesses many of the rights that a person has. For example, a corporation may buy, own, and sell property. It may enter into contracts, sue, and be sued. Unlike proprietors and partners, the stockholders who own a corporation have no personal obligation for its debts. Proprietors and partners *are* personally liable for the debts of their businesses. The most that a stockholder can lose on an investment in stock is the cost of the investment.

A corporation's ownership is divided into shares of stock. One becomes a stockholder by purchasing the corporation's stock. Fossil, for example, has issued over 30 million shares of stock. An investor with no personal relationship to Fossil can become a co-owner by buying 1, 30, 100, 5,000, or any number of shares of its stock through NASDAQ, a national stock exchange similar to the New York Stock Exchange.

Ultimate control of a corporation rests with the stockholders. They get one vote for each share of stock they own. Stockholders elect the members of the **board of directors,** which sets policy for the corporation and appoints officers. The board elects a chairperson, who is the most powerful person in the corporation and often carries the title chief executive officer (CEO). The board also designates the president, who is the chief operating officer (COO) in charge of day-to-day operations. Most corporations also have vice presidents in charge of sales, manufacturing, accounting and finance, and other key areas.

Board of directors
Group elected by the stockholders to set policy for a corporation and to appoint its officers.

How to Do Accounting: Principles and Concepts

accounting concepts

Accountants follow professional guidelines. The rules that govern accounting are called **GAAP,** which stands for **generally accepted accounting principles.**

In the United States, the *Financial Accounting Standards Board (FASB)* determines how accounting is practiced. The FASB works with the SEC and AICPA. Exhibit 1-3 diagrams the relationships among these organizations and the rules that govern them. To read the diagram, start at the top and move to your right, following the arrows.

Generally accepted accounting principles (GAAP)
Accounting guidelines, formulated by the Financial Accounting Standards Board, that govern how accountants measure, process, and communicate financial information.

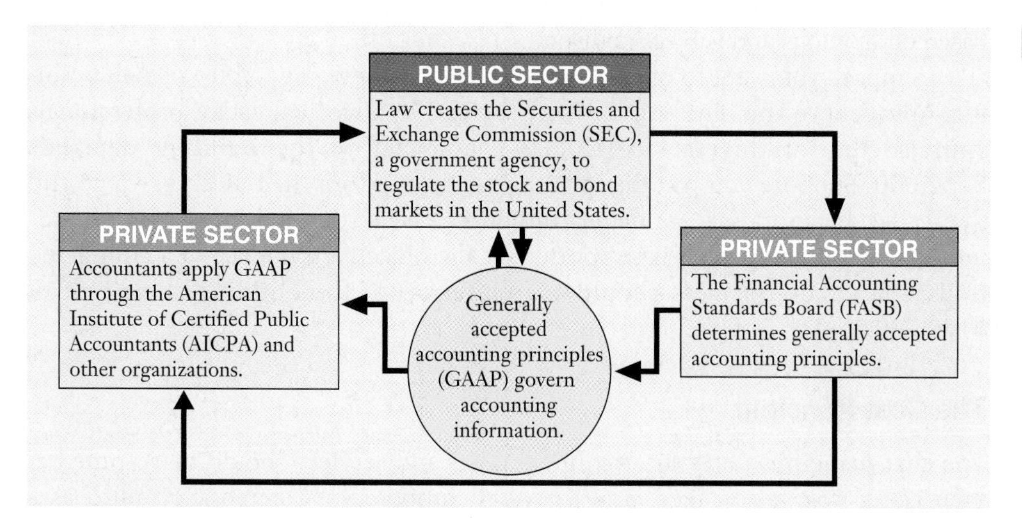

Exhibit 1-3

Key Accounting Organizations

GAAP rests on a conceptual framework produced by the FASB: To be useful, information must be relevant, reliable, and comparable. This course will expose you to the generally accepted methods of accounting; we will discuss these as they become relevant in each chapter. We also summarize them in Appendix E. First, however, you need to understand several basic concepts that provide the foundation for accounting practice.

Objective

2 **Analyze** a business using accounting concepts and principles

The Entity Concept

Entity
An organization or a section of an organization that, for accounting purposes, stands apart from other organizations and individuals as a separate economic unit.

The most basic concept in accounting is that of the **entity.** An accounting entity is an organization that stands apart as a separate economic unit. From an accounting perspective, sharp boundaries are drawn around each entity so as not to confuse its affairs with those of others.

Consider Tom Kartsotis, Chairman of the Board of Fossil, Inc. Mr. Kartsotis owns a home and several automobiles, among other family possessions. He may owe money on some personal loans. All these assets and liabilities belong to Tom Kartsotis and have nothing to do with Fossil, Inc. Likewise, Fossil's cash, computers, and store equipment belong to the company and do not belong to Kartsotis. Why? Because the entity concept draws a sharp boundary around each entity; in this case Fossil is one entity and Tom Kartsotis is a separate entity.

Now consider Toyota, which has several divisions. Toyota management evaluates each division as a separate entity. If Lexus sales are dropping, Toyota can identify the reason. But if sales figures from all divisions of the company are combined, then management cannot tell how many Lexuses the company is selling. To correct the problem, managers need data for each division of the company. The transactions of different entities should not be accounted for together. Each entity should be evaluated separately.

✔ Check Point 1-4

The Reliability Principle

Reliability principle
The accounting principle that ensures that accounting records and statements are based on the most reliable data available. Also called the *objectivity principle.*

To ensure that they are relevant and reliable, accounting records and statements are based on the most objective data available. This guideline is the **reliability principle,** also called the **objectivity principle.** Reliable data (1) are verifiable and (2) can be confirmed by an independent observer. Ideally, accounting records are based on information supported by objective evidence. For example, a $40 purchase of a Fossil wristwatch is supported by a paid invoice. This invoice is objective evidence of the cost of the watch. Without the reliability principle, accounting records would be based on opinions and subject to dispute.

Suppose you want to open a stereo shop and are trying to buy a small building. You believe the building is worth $155,000. Two real estate professionals appraise the building at $147,000. The owner of the building demands $160,000. Suppose you pay that price. Your belief about the building's value and the real-estate appraisals are merely opinions. The accounting value of the building is $160,000 because it is supported by the objective evidence of a completed transaction. The business should therefore record the building at its cost of $160,000.

The Cost Principle

Cost principle
Principle that states that acquired assets and services should be recorded at their actual cost.

The **cost principle** states that acquired assets and services should be recorded at their actual cost (also called *historical cost*). Suppose your stereo shop purchases stereo equipment from a supplier who is going out of business. Assume that you get a good deal on this purchase and pay only $2,000 for merchandise that would have cost you $3,000 elsewhere. The cost principle requires you to record this merchandise at its actual cost of $2,000, not the $3,000 that you believe it is worth.

The cost principle also holds that accounting records should maintain the historical cost of an asset for as long as the business holds the asset. Why? Because cost is a reliable measure. Suppose your store holds the stereo equipment for 6 months. Stereo prices increase and the equipment can be sold for $3,500. Should its accounting value—the figure *on the books*—be the actual cost of $2,000 or the current market value of $3,500? According to the cost principle, the equipment remains on the books at cost of $2,000.

The Going-Concern Concept

Another reason for measuring assets at historical cost is the **going-concern concept,** which assumes that the entity will remain in operation for the foreseeable future. Under the going-concern concept, accountants assume that the business will remain in operation long enough to use existing assets—land, buildings, supplies—for their intended purpose.

Going-concern concept
Holds that the entity will remain in operation for the forseeable future.

Consider the alternative to the going-concern concept: going out of business. A store holding a going-out-of-business sale is trying to sell all its assets. In that case, the relevant measure of the assets is their current market value. But going out of business is the exception rather than the rule, and for this reason accounting lists a going concern's assets at their historical cost.

The Stable-Monetary-Unit Concept

In the United States, we record transactions in dollars, the medium of exchange. British accountants record transactions in pounds sterling, and Japanese accountants in yen. Europeans who belong to the European Union price goods and services in euros.

Unlike the value of a liter or a mile, the value of a dollar or of a Mexican peso changes over time. A rise in the general price level is called *inflation*. During inflation, a dollar will purchase less milk, less toothpaste, and less of other goods. When prices are stable—when there is little inflation—a dollar's purchasing power is also stable.

Accountants assume that the dollar's purchasing power is relatively stable. The **stable-monetary-unit concept** is the basis for ignoring inflation in accounting records. It allows accountants to add and subtract dollar amounts as though each dollar has the same purchasing power as any other dollar at any other time.

Stable-monetary-unit concept
The basis for ignoring the effect of inflation in the accounting records, based on the assumption that the dollar's purchasing power is relatively stable.

You are considering the purchase of land for future expansion. The seller is asking $50,000 for land that cost him $35,000. An appraisal shows a value of $47,000. You first offer $44,000, the seller makes a counteroffer of $48,000, and you agree on $46,000. What dollar value is reported for the land on your financial statements?

Answer:
Report the land at $46,000, which is its historical cost.

The Accounting Equation

accounting equation, asset, liability, owners' equity, revenue, expense

As we saw for Fossil, Inc., the financial statements tell us how a business is performing and where it stands. They are the final product of financial accounting. But how do we arrive at the financial statements?

Objective

3 **Use** the accounting equation to describe an organization

Accounting equation
The most basic tool of accounting: Assets = Liabilities + Owners' Equity.

Asset
An economic resource that is expected to be of benefit in the future.

Liability
An economic obligation (a debt) payable to an individual or an organization outside the business.

Owners' equity
The claim of the owners of a business to the assets of the business. Also called *capital* for proprietorships and partnerships and *stockholders' equity* for corporations. Sometimes called *net assets.*

Assets and Liabilities

The financial statements are based on the basic tool of accounting, the **accounting equation.** This equation presents the resources of the business and the claims to those resources.

- **Assets** are the economic resources of a business that are expected to produce a benefit in the future. Cash, office supplies, merchandise, furniture, land, and buildings are examples of assets.

Claims on assets come from two sources:

- **Liabilities** are "outsider claims." They are economic obligations—debts—payable to outsiders, called *creditors.* For example, a creditor who has loaned money to a business has a claim—a legal right—to a part of the company's assets until the business repays the debt.
- **Owners' equity** (also called **capital**) represents the "insider claims" of a business. Equity means ownership, so stockholders' equity is the owners' interest in the assets of a corporation.

The accounting equation shows the relationship among assets, liabilities, and owners' equity. Assets appear on the left side of the equation. The legal and economic claims against the assets—the liabilities and owners' equity—appear on the right side. As Exhibit 1-4 shows, the two sides must be equal:

Economic Resources = Claims to Economic Resources
Assets = Liabilities + Owners' Equity

Exhibit 1-4

The Accounting Equation

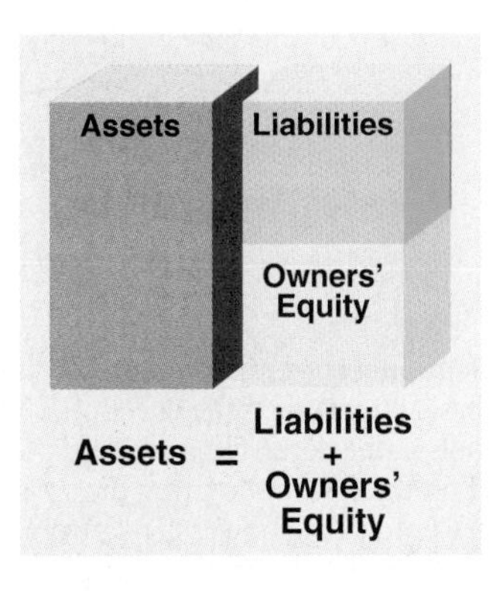

Consider the assets and the liabilities of Fossil, Inc. What are some of Fossil's assets? The first asset listed for all businesses is **cash,** the liquid (cash) asset that is the medium of exchange. Another important Fossil asset is **merchandise inventory** (often called Inventories)—the watches, sunglasses, and other goods—that Fossil sells. Fossil also has assets in the form of property, plant, and equipment. These are the long-lived assets that Fossil uses to manufacture and sell its merchandise—buildings, machinery, computers, and so on. Land, buildings, and equipment are called **plant assets,** or *property, plant, and equipment* (often abbreviated as *PPE*).

Fossil's liabilities include a number of payables, such as accounts payable and notes payable. The word *payable* always signifies a liability. An **account payable** is a liability for goods or services purchased on credit and supported only by the credit standing of the purchaser. A **note payable** is a written promise to pay on a certain date. **Long-term debt** is a liability that falls due beyond 1 year from the date of the financial statements.

Capital
Another name for the *owners' equity* of a business.

Cash
Money and any medium of exchange that a bank accepts at face value.

Merchandise inventory
The merchandise that a company sells to customers.

Plant asset
Long-lived assets, such as land, buildings, and equipment, used in the operation of the business. Also called *fixed assets.*

Account payable
A liability backed by the general reputation and credit standing of the debtor.

Owners' Equity

The owners' equity of any business is the assets of the business minus its liabilities. This applies equally to private individuals and the largest corporations such as Fossil, Microsoft, or GM. We often write the accounting equation to show that the owners' claim to assets is a residual—what is left over after a subtraction process:

Assets − Liabilities = Owners' Equity

The owners' equity of a corporation—called **stockholders' equity,** or simply **equity**—is divided into two main categories, paid-in capital and retained earnings. For a corporation, the accounting equation can be written as

Assets = Liabilities + Stockholders' Equity

Assets = Liabilities + Paid-in Capital + Retained Earnings

Paid-in capital is the amount invested in the corporation by its owners. The basic component of paid-in capital is **common stock**, which the corporation issues to stockholders as evidence of ownership.

Retained earnings is the amount earned by income-producing activities and kept for use in the business. Two types of transactions that affect retained earnings are revenues and expenses.

- **Revenues** are increases in retained earnings from delivering goods or services to customers. For example, Fossil's receipt of cash from the sale of a leather wallet brings in revenue and increases Fossil's retained earnings.
- **Expenses** are decreases in retained earnings that result from operations. For example, the wages that Fossil pays its salespeople constitute an expense and decrease retained earnings. Expenses are the cost of doing business and are thus the opposite of revenues. Expenses include office rent, salaries, and utility payments. Expenses also include depreciation of computers and buildings.

Businesses strive for profitability. When total revenues exceed total expenses, the result of operations is called **net income, net earnings**, or **net profit.** When expenses exceed revenues, the result is a **net loss.** Net income or net loss is the "bottom line" on an income statement. Fossil's bottom line reports net income of $44 million on page 7 (line 14).

A successful business may pay dividends. **Dividends** are distributions to stockholders of assets (usually cash) generated by net income. Remember: **Dividends are not expenses. Dividends never affect net income.** Exhibit 1-5 shows the relationships among

- Retained earnings
- Revenues − expenses = net income (or net loss)
- Dividends

✔ Check Point 1-5

Note payable
A liability evidenced by a written promise to make a future payment.

Long-term debt
A liability that falls due beyond one year from the date of the financial statements.

✔ Check Point 1-6

✔ Check Point 1-7

Stockholders' equity
The stockholders' ownership interest in the assets of a corporation.

Paid-in capital
The amount of stockholders' equity that stockholders have contributed to the corporation. Also called *contributed capital.*

Common stock
The most basic form of capital stock. Common stockholders own a corporation.

Retained earnings
The amount of stockholders' equity that the corporation has earned through profitable operation of the business and has not given back to stockholders.

Revenue
Increase in retained earnings from delivering goods or services to customers or clients.

Expense
Decrease in retained earnings that results from operations; the cost of doing business; opposite of revenues.

Exhibit 1-5 Components of Retained Earnings

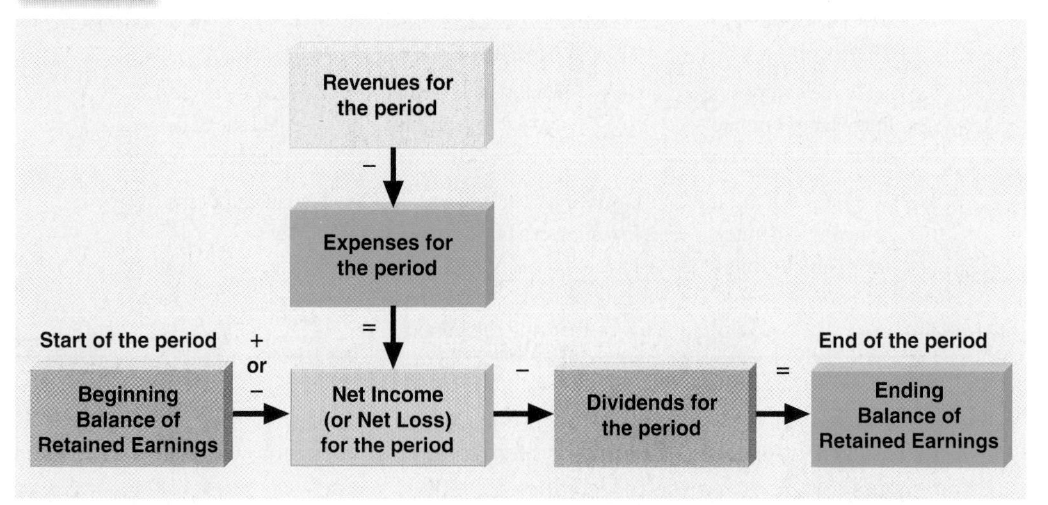

Net income
Excess of total revenues over total expenses. Also called *net earnings* or *net profit.*

Net loss
Excess of total expenses over total revenues.

The owners' equity of proprietorships and of partnerships is different. These types of businesses make no distinction between paid-in capital and retained earnings. Instead, the equity of each owner is accounted for under the single heading of Capital—for example, Randall Walker, Capital, if the company were a proprietorship. The partnership of Pratt and Muesli has a separate record for the capital of each partner: Pratt, Capital, and Muesli, Capital.

1. If the assets of a business are $174,300 and the liabilities are $82,000, how much is the owners' equity?
2. If the owners' equity in a business is $22,000 and the liabilities are $36,000, how much are the assets?
3. A company reported monthly revenues of $77,600 and expenses of $81,300. What is the result of operations for the month?

Answers:
1. $92,300 ($174,300 − $82,000)
2. $58,000 ($22,000 + $36,000)
3. Net loss of $3,700 ($77,600 − $81,300); expenses minus revenues

Dividends
Distributions (usually cash) by a corporation to its stockholders.

The Financial Statements

balance sheet, income statement, statement of cash flows

The financial statements are a picture of the company in financial terms. Each financial statement relates to a specific date or covers a particular period. What would managers and investors want to know about Fossil, Inc., at the end of a period? Exhibit 1-6 summarizes four basic questions decision makers may ask. The answer to each question is given by one of the financial statements.

Exhibit 1-6

Information Reported on the Financial Statements

Question	Answer	Financial Statement
1. How well did the company perform (or operate) during the period?	Revenues − Expenses Net income (or Net loss)	Income statement (also called the Statement of operations)
2. Why did the company's retained earnings change during the period?	Beginning retained earnings + Net income (or − Net loss) − Dividends Ending retained earnings	Statement of retained earnings
3. What is the company's financial position at the end of the period?	Assets = Liabilities + Owners' Equity	Balance sheet (also called the Statement of financial position)
4. How much cash did the company generate and spend during the period?	Operating cash flows ± Investing cash flows ± Financing cash flows Increase (or decrease) in cash during the period	Statement of cash flows

To learn how to use financial statements, let's work our way through Fossil's statements for the year ended December 31, 2001.

We begin with the income statement in Exhibit 1-7. Its final amount, net income (line 14), feeds into the statement of retained earnings (Exhibit 1-8, line 2), which also appears on the balance sheet (Exhibit 1-9, line 28). As you can see, there is a natural progression from the income statement, to the statement of retained earnings, to the balance sheet, and finally to the statement of cash flows (Exhibit 1-10).

Objective

4 **Evaluate** a company's operating performance, financial position, and cash flows

Exhibit 1-7

Income Statement (Statement of Income and Comprehensive Income, Adapted)

Fossil, Inc.

Consolidated Statement of Income (Adapted)

Amounts in millions	*Years Ended December 31,* 2001	2000
1 Net sales revenue	$546	$504
2 Cost of goods sold	274	248
3 Gross profit	272	256
4 Operating expenses:		
5 Selling and distribution expense	150	126
6 General and administrative expense	45	36
7 Total operating expenses	195	162
8 Operating income	77	94
9 Other revenue (expense):		
10 Write-off of investment	(5)	—
11 Other income (expense), net	1	1
12 Income before income tax	73	95
13 Income tax expense	29	39
14 Net income	$ 44	$ 56

The Income Statement: Measuring Operating Performance

The **income statement, statement of operations,** or **statement of earnings** reports the company's revenues, expenses, and net income or net loss for the period. At the top of Exhibit 1-7 (same as the income statement in the chapter opener) is the company's name, Fossil, Inc. Fossil, the parent company, owns other companies that are its subsidiaries. To include all the resources that Fossil controls, the amounts reported on the statements include figures for both Fossil and its subsidiaries. Most companies' financial statements show consolidated totals and thus include the word *consolidated* in the title.

Income statement
A financial statement listing an entity's revenues, expenses, and net income or net loss for a specific period. Also called the *statement of operations.*

The date of Fossil's income statement is "Years ended December 31, 2001 and 2000." Fossil uses the calendar period as its accounting year, as do around 60% of large companies. Some use a fiscal year, which ends on a date other than December 31. For example, Pier 1 Imports, Wal-Mart, and most other retailers end their accounting year on or around January 31. FedEx's year end falls on May 31. Companies adopt an accounting year that ends on the low point of their operations.

Fossil's income statement in Exhibit 1-7 reports operating results for 2 years, 2001 and 2000. The income statement includes more than 1 year of data to show trends for sales expenses, and net income. To avoid cluttering the statement with zeros, we show Fossil's figures in millions of dollars. During 2001, Fossil increased net sales from $504 million to $546 million (see line 1). But net income dropped from $56 million to $44 million (line 14). This might mean that Fossil was able to sell more watches and sunglasses in 2001 but failed to control expenses. That is one explanation for the decline in profit.

The income statement reports two main categories:

- Revenues and gains
- Expenses and losses

Revenues and expenses measure net income as follows:

Net Income = Total Revenues and Gains − Total Expenses and Losses

In accounting, the word "net" means the result after a subtraction. *Net* income is the income left over after subtracting expenses and losses from revenues and gains.

REVENUES. Revenues and expenses do not always carry the terms *revenue* and *expense* in their titles. For example, net sales revenue is often abbreviated as *net sales*. During 2001, Fossil had net sales of $546 million (line 1). The term *net* sales means total sales minus sales returns received from customers.

EXPENSES. *Cost of goods sold* (also called *cost of sales,* line 2) represents the cost to Fossil of the goods it sold to customers. For example, suppose it costs Fossil $25 to make a wristwatch. Assume Fossil sells the watch for $60. Sales revenue is $60, and cost of goods sold is $25. Cost of goods sold is the major expense of merchandising entities such as Fossil, Wal-Mart, and Safeway (the grocery chain).

✔ Check Point 1-8

✔ Check Point 1-9

Fossil follows the common practice of dividing operating expense (line 4) into two categories:

- *Selling and distribution expense (line 5).* This category includes all expenses directly related to selling merchandise. Advertising, promotion, compensation of sales persons, and depreciation of store fixtures and equipment are selling expenses. The cost of transporting merchandise to stores is a distribution expense.
- *General and administrative (G & A) expense (line 6).* These expenses include all operating costs not directly related to selling products. Examples include the salaries paid to company executives, home-office expenses, and depreciation of computers and other equipment not used to sell and distribute merchandise. For Fossil and for most other companies, G & A expenses are less than selling expenses.

Fossil's income statement includes other items, as follows:

- *Other revenue (expense) (line 9).* These revenues and expenses arise from activities outside the company's central, ongoing operations. During 2001, Fossil wrote off an investment and suffered a $5 million loss (line 10; a loss has the same effect as an expense). This loss is an "other" expense because Fossil's investments in other companies fall outside the merchandising of wristwatches and sunglasses. The parentheses around $5 million tell us that this is like an expense and not a revenue. A gain on an investment would also be reported as *other revenue*. Line 11 reports other income (expense), which may be the interest revenue that Fossil earned on its bank deposits. This amount has no parentheses, so it is like a revenue. Interest expense would be reported in parentheses.

- *Income tax expense (line 13)*. Corporations pay income tax just as individuals do. During 2001, Fossil's income tax expense totaled $29 million, roughly 40% of the $73 million income before tax.

COMPREHENSIVE INCOME. The FASB also requires companies to report another income amount called comprehensive income. **Comprehensive income** includes net income from the income statement plus several additional items that we will cover in later chapters. These additional items do not affect net income and do not need to be reported on the income statement. At this point, it remains to be seen how useful comprehensive income will be for decision making. Now let's move on to the statement of retained earnings and Exhibit 1-8.

Comprehensive income
A company's change in total stockholders' equity from all sources other than from the owners of the business.

Exhibit 1-8

Statement of Retained Earnings (Adapted)

Fossil, Inc.

Consolidated Statement of Retained Earnings (Adapted)

	Amounts in millions	*Years Ended December 31,* *2001*	*2000*
	Retained earnings:		
1	Balance, beginning of year	$208	$152
2	Net income	44	56
3	Less: Cash dividends declared	(0)	(0)
4	Balance, end of year	$252	$208

Statement of Retained Earnings

Fossil's *retained earnings* represent exactly what the term implies: that portion of net income the company has retained. Net income from the income statement also appears on the **statement of retained earnings** (line 2 in Exhibit 1-8). Net income increases retained earnings and thus links the income statement to retained earnings.

Statement of retained earnings
Summary of the changes in the retained earnings of a corporation during a specific period.

After Fossil earns net income, the board of directors must decide whether to use some cash to pay a dividend to the stockholders. Thus far, Fossil has declared no dividends (line 3). But if they existed, dividends would decrease retained earnings (the parentheses indicate a subtraction). Fossil ended 2000 with retained earnings of $208 million. This ending balance carries over and becomes the beginning balance of 2001. Fossil added more net income in 2001, again declared no dividends, and ended that year with a still larger balance of retained earnings (line 4).

✔ Check Point 1-10

The Balance Sheet: Measuring Financial Position

Fossil's comparative balance sheet appears in Exhibit 1-9. The balance sheet is dated December 31, 2001, the end of the company's accounting year. The balance sheet gives a snapshot of the company's financial position at a moment in time. This is in contrast to the dates of the other three statements. The income statement, the statement of retained earnings, and the statement of cash flows (discussed in the next section) are dated "Year Ended December 31, 2001," because they report on events that occurred throughout the year.

Exhibit 1-9

Balance Sheet (Adapted)

Fossil, Inc.

Consolidated Balance Sheet (Adapted)

Amounts in millions		*December 31,* 2001		*2000*
1 **Assets**				
2 Current assets:				
3 Cash and cash equivalents		$ 68		$ 80
4 Short-term investments		5		11
5 Accounts receivable		74		63
6 Inventories		104		81
7 Prepaid expenses		19		18
8 Total current assets		270		253
9 Investments		1		6
10 Property, plant, and equipment, at cost	$123		$ 66	
11 Less: accumulated depreciation	(33)		(24)	
12 Property, plant, and equipment, net		90		42
13 Intangible and other assets		20		7
14 Total assets		$381		$308
15 **Liabilities**				
16 Current liabilities:				
17 Notes payable, short-term		$ 16		$ 5
18 Accounts payable		21		19
19 Advertising payable		15		14
20 Compensation (salary) payable		8		6
21 Other accrued expenses payable		28		19
22 Income taxes payable		18		20
23 Total current liabilities		106		83
24 Long-term liabilities		11		4
25 Total liabilities		117		87
26 **Stockholders' equity**				
27 Common stock		16		15
28 Retained earnings		252		208
29 Other equity		(4)		(2)
30 Total stockholders' equity		264		221
31 Total liabilities and stockholders' equity		$381		$308

A company's **balance sheet,** also called the **statement of financial position,** reports three main categories: assets, liabilities, and owners' equity (which Fossil, Inc. calls *stockholders' equity*).

Balance sheet
List of an entity's assets, liabilities, and owners' equity as of a specific date. Also called the *statement of financial position.*

ASSETS. Assets are subdivided into two categories: current assets and long-term assets. **Current assets** are those assets the company expects to convert to cash, sell, or consume during the next 12 months or within the business's normal operating cycle if longer than a year. Current assets for Fossil, Inc. consist of Cash, Short-term investments, Accounts receivable, Merchandise inventory, and Prepaid expenses (lines 3 to 7). Fossil's current assets at December 31, 2001, total $270 million (line 8).

Current asset
An asset that is expected to be converted to cash, sold, or consumed during the next 12 months, or within the business' normal operating cycle if longer than a year.

Fossil has $68 million in cash. Cash is the liquid asset that is the medium of exchange. Short-term investments include stocks and bonds that the company intends to sell within the next year. Accounts receivable are amounts the company expects to collect from customers. Cash, short-term investments, and accounts receivable are the most liquid assets, in that order.

Merchandise inventory (line 6) is the company's largest current asset, totaling over $100 billion. *Inventory* is a common abbreviation for *Merchandise inventory*; the two names are used interchangeably. Prepaid expenses represent prepayments for advertisements and for rent, insurance, and supplies that have not yet been used up. Prepaid expenses are assets because Fossil will benefit from these expenditures in the future. **An asset always represents a future benefit.**

The main categories of *long-term assets* are Investments (line 9), Property, plant, and equipment (lines 10 to 12), and Intangibles and other assets (line 13). Investments (line 9), with no other words attached, are *long-term* in nature. They may include stocks and bonds. They are long-term because Fossil does not expect to sell them for cash within the next year.

Property, plant, and equipment (PPE) includes Fossil's land, buildings, computers, store fixtures, and equipment. Fossil reports PPE on three lines. Line 10 shows the company's cost of PPE, which is $123 million through December 31, 2001. Cost means the acquisition price to Fossil. It does not mean that Fossil could sell its PPE for $123 million. After all, the company may have acquired the assets several years ago.

Line 11 lists the accumulated depreciation that Fossil has recorded on its PPE. (*Depreciation* is the process of allocating an asset's cost to expense; we discuss depreciation in later chapters. It is useful to think of depreciation as the using up of property, plant, and equipment.) Accumulated depreciation refers to the cumulative amount of depreciation that Fossil has recorded on PPE from acquisition through the end of the year. It can be viewed as the used-up portion of the asset. Observe that Fossil subtracts accumulated depreciation from the cost of PPE to determine the net carrying amount of PPE ($90 million on line 12). The net amount of PPE ($90 million) is the portion of the asset that has not yet been depreciated (used up).

Fossil reports Intangible and other assets on line 13. Intangibles are long-term assets with no physical form, such as company trademarks and noncompete agreements that Fossil purchases to protect its products. "Other assets" is a catchall category for items that are difficult to classify. Overall, Fossil reports total assets of $381 million at December 31, 2001 (line 14).

Examine Fossil's balance sheet in Exhibit 1-9. Look at total assets on line 14. What is your opinion of the change in total assets during 2001? Is it good news, bad news, or no news? Why? To what other item should you relate the change in total assets? Identify that item, its change during $2001, and state why it too is important.

Answer:
It is *good news* that total assets grew from $308 million to $381 million. This means that Fossil has $73 million more resources (assets) to use for operations.

We should relate the change in total assets ($73 million = $381 − $308) to the change in total liabilities ($30 million = $117 − $87). It's not enough to examine only the change in assets. The change in liabilities is also important because Fossil may be racking up huge debts to build its assets. As it turns out, Fossil's increase in assets ($73 million) far exceeds the increase in liabilities ($30 million). That is *good news* for Fossil because it shows that the company is building assets without excessive debt.

Current liability
A debt due to be paid within one year or within the entity's operating cycle if the cycle is longer than a year.

LIABILITIES. Liabilities are also divided into current and long-term categories. **Current liabilities** (lines 16 to 23) are debts payable within 1 year or within the entity's normal operating cycle if longer than a year. Chief among the current liabilities for Fossil, Inc. are Notes payable, short-term; Accounts payable; Advertising and compensation payable; Other accrued expenses payable; and Income taxes payable. *Long-term liabilities* are payable after 1 year.

Notes payable, short term (line 17) are promissory notes that Fossil has promised to pay back within 1 year or less. Accounts payable (line 18) represents amounts owed for goods and services that Fossil has purchased but not yet paid for. Advertising payable (line 19) is the amount Fossil owes to advertising agencies, magazines, and other outlets that carry company ads. Compensation payable (line 20) includes salaries owed to employees plus all the payroll taxes payable to the government.

The company's largest current liability is Other accrued expenses payable, $28 million (line 21). Included among Other accrued expenses payable are interest payable on borrowed money, property taxes, utility payables, and other expenses that Fossil has incurred but not yet paid. Income taxes payable (line 22) are amounts owed to the government for income taxes. At December 31, 2001, Fossil's current liabilities total $106 million. Fossil has very little in long-term debt—only $11 million at December 31, 2001 (line 24). These liabilities may be notes payable that are due after 1 year. At the end of 2001, total liabilities are $117 million (line 24). This is low in comparison to total assets (line 14), and that is a sign of a strong financial position.

OWNERS' EQUITY. The accounting equation states that

Assets − Liabilities = Owners' Equity

The assets (resources) and the liabilities (debts) of Fossil are fairly easy to understand. Owners' equity is harder to pin down. Owners' equity is simple to calculate, but what does it *mean*?

Fossil, Inc. calls its owners' equity *stockholders' equity* (line 26), and this title is descriptive. Remember that a company's owners' equity represents the shareholders' ownership of business assets. Owners' equity for Fossil consists of common stock, represented by millions of shares issued to stockholders for approximately $16 million through December 31, 2001 (line 27).

The largest part of the owners' equity is Retained earnings of $252 million (line 28). The large amount of Retained earnings explains why liabilities are so low: Profitable operations have financed most of the company's operations, and Fossil has not needed to borrow heavily. Trace the $252 million ending balance of retained earnings from the statement of retained earnings in Exhibit 1-8 (line 4) to the balance sheet (line 28). Retained earnings links the statement of retained earnings to the balance sheet.

Fossil's equity holds another item. Other equity is a collection of miscellaneous items. For now you can focus on the two main components of stockholders' equity: common stock and retained earnings.

At December 31, 2001, Fossil has Total stockholders' equity of $264 million (line 30). We can now prove that Fossil's, total assets equal the company's total liabilities and equity (amounts in $ millions):

Total assets (line 14)		$381	← Must equal
= Total liabilities:			
Current (line 23)	$106		
Long-term (line 24)	11		
Total liabilities		$117	
+ Total stockholders' equity (line 30)		264	
Total liabilities and stockholders' equity (line 31)		$381	← Must equal

The statement of cash flows is the last required financial statement.

✔ Check Point 1-11

The Statement of Cash Flows: Measuring Cash Receipts and Payments

Organizations engage in three basic types of activities:

1. **Operating activities** 2. **Investing activities** 3. **Financing activities**

The **statement of cash flows** reports cash flows under these three categories. Think about the cash flows (cash receipts and cash payments) in each category:

- ***Companies operate by buying, and then selling, goods and services to customers.*** Operating activities result in net income or net loss, and they either increase or decrease cash. The income statement tells whether the company is profitable. The statement of cash flow reports whether operations provided cash or used cash. Cash flow from operating activities is the most important piece of information on the cash-flow statement. It should always be positive; negative cash flow from operations can send an organization into bankruptcy.
- ***Companies invest in long-term assets for use in operations.*** Fossil pays cash to acquire other companies and also to buy buildings and equipment. When these assets wear out, the company sells them for cash. Both purchases and sales of long-term assets are investing cash flows. Investing cash flows are next most important after operations because what a company invests in determines where its cash comes from.
- ***Companies need money for financing.*** Financing includes both issuing stock and borrowing. Fossil has issued stock to its shareholders and has borrowed money from banks. These are cash receipts. The company pays off loans. Other companies such as Procter & Gamble, Gap, Inc., and Nike pay dividends to stockholders. These payments are financing cash flows.

Operating activities
Activity that creates revenue or expense in the entity's major line of business; a section of the statement of cash flows. Operating activities affect the income statement.

Investing activities
Activities that increase or decrease the long-term assets available to the business; a section of the statement of cash flows.

Financing activities
Activities that obtain from investors and creditors the cash needed to launch and sustain the business; a section of the statement of cash flows.

Statement of cash flows
Reports cash receipts and cash disbursements classified according to the entity's major activities: operating, investing, and financing.

OVERVIEW. Companies organize the statement of cash flows into operating, investing, and financing activities. Each category results either in an increase or a decrease in cash. In Exhibit 1-10, Fossil's operating activities provided cash of $49 million in 2001 (line 4). This increase in cash signals strong cash flow from operations. Investing activities used cash of $68 million in 2001 (line 10). Financing activities brought in $7 million (line 16). On a statement of cash flows, cash receipts appear as positive amounts with no signs. Cash payments are negative amounts and are, therefore, enclosed by parentheses.

Exhibit 1-10

Statement of Cash Flows (Adapted)

Fossil, Inc.

Consolidated Statement of Cash Flows (Adapted)

Amounts in millions	*December 31, 2001*	*2000*
1 **Operating activities:**		
2 Net income	$ 44	$ 56
3 Adjustments to reconcile net income to net cash provided by operating activities	5	(16)
4 Net cash provided by operating activities	49	40
5 **Investing activities:**		
6 Business acquisitions	(16)	(2)
7 Additions to property, plant, and equipment	(56)	(20)
8 Sale of investments	6	—
9 Other investing activities	(2)	(2)
10 Net cash used for investing activities	(68)	(24)
11 **Financing activities:**		
12 Issuance of common stock	3	1
13 Purchase and retirement of common stock	(4)	(28)
14 Issuance of notes payable (borrowing)	9	—
15 Other financing activities	(1)	—
16 Net cash provided by financing activities	7	(27)
17 Net increase in cash and cash equivalents	(12)	(11)
18 Cash and cash equivalents, beginning of year	80	91
19 Cash and cash equivalents, end of year	$ 68	$ 80

Overall, Fossil's cash decreased by $12 million during 2001 (line 17); Fossil ended the year with cash of $68 million (line 19). Trace the ending cash balance of $68 million to the balance sheet in Exhibit 1-9. The cash balance links the statement of cash flows to the balance sheet.

Let's now examine the three major sections of the statement of cash flows more closely.

CASH FLOWS FROM OPERATING ACTIVITIES. The vast majority of companies report cash flows from operating activities, starting with net income. They then make some standard adjustments to reconcile from net income to net cash provided by operating activities. Fossil follows this practice in Exhibit 1-10 (lines 2 to 4).

CASH FLOWS FROM INVESTING ACTIVITIES. During 2001, Fossil spent $16 million to acquire Avia Watch Company, Pulse Time, Ltd., and other companies (line 6). Fossil also paid $56 million for property, plant, and equipment (line 7). The company sold investments for $6 million during the year. Overall, Fossil used $68 million for investing activities (line 10). Negative cash flow for investing activities is generally healthy because it indicates that a company is buying new assets and growing.

CASH FLOWS FROM FINANCING ACTIVITIES. Borrowing (line 14) was modest during 2001. Fossil received $3 million from the issuance of stock (line 12) and paid $4 million to buy back its own stock (line 13). Most large companies also pay cash dividends to their stockholders. Fossil does *not* pay cash dividends.

NET INCREASE (DECREASE) IN CASH. The overall result of the statement of cash flows is the net increase (or decrease) in cash during the year. As we have seen, Fossil's cash decreased by $12 million during 2001 (line 17). Lines 18 and 19 of the cash flow statement show both the beginning cash balance and the ending cash balance for the year. Fossil began 2001 with $80 million and ended with $68 million. Trace both amounts to the balance sheet in Exhibit 1-9 (line 3).

The purpose of the statement of cash flows is to show *why* cash changed during the year. Should Fossil be alarmed that cash decreased by $12 million during 2001? Probably not, for three reasons:

✔ Check Point 1-12

1. The cash balance is still a healthy $68 million.
2. Operating activities provided the bulk of Fossil's cash during 2001.
3. Fossil earned net income on the income statement. (However, top managers of Fossil should determine why net income dropped from 2000.)

These are but a few of the evaluations you will learn to make throughout this course. Now let's review the relationships among the financial statements.

Relationships Among the Financial Statements

financial statements

Exhibit 1-11 summarizes the relationships among the financial statements of ABC Company. Study the exhibit carefully because these relationships apply to all organizations. Specifically, note the following:

Objective

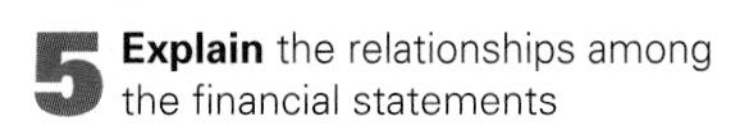

1. The income statement for the year ended December 31, 2003
   a. Reports all revenues and all expenses during the period. Revenues and expenses are reported *only* on the income statement.
   b. Reports net income if total revenues exceed total expenses. If expenses exceed revenues, there is a net loss.
2. The statement of retained earnings for the year ended December 31, 2003
   a. Opens with the beginning retained earnings balance.
   b. Adds net income (or subtracts net loss). Net income comes directly from the income statement (arrow ① in Exhibit 1-11).
   c. Subtracts dividends.
   d. Ends with the retained earnings balance at the end of the period.

Exhibit 1-11

Relationships Among the Financial Statements (These statements are summarized, with all amounts assumed for the illustration)

ABC Company
Income Statement
Year Ended December 31, 2003

Revenues	$700,000
Expenses	670,000
Net income	$ 30,000

①

ABC Company
Statement of Retained Earnings
Year Ended December 31, 2003

Beginning retained earnings	$180,000
Net income	30,000
Cash dividends	(10,000)
Ending retained earnings	$200,000

②

ABC Company
Balance Sheet
December 31, 2003

Assets	
Cash	$ 25,000
All other assets	275,000
Total assets	$300,000
Liabilities	
Total liabilities	$120,000
Stockholders' Equity	
Common stock	40,000
Retained earnings	200,000
Other equity	(60,000)
Total liabilities and stockholders' equity	$300,000

③

ABC Company
Statement of Cash Flows
Year Ended December 31, 2003

Net cash provided by operating activities	$ 90,000
Net cash used for investing activities	(110,000)
Net cash provided by financing activities	40,000
Net increase in cash	20,000
Beginning cash balance	5,000
Ending cash balance	$ 25,000

3. The balance sheet at December 31, 2003, at the end of the accounting year
   a. Reports all assets, liabilities, and stockholders' equity at the end of the period. Only the balance sheet reports assets and liabilities.
   b. Reports that assets equal the sum of liabilities plus stockholders' equity. This balancing feature gives the balance sheet its name; it follows the accounting equation.
   c. Reports ending retained earnings, which comes from the statement of retained earnings (arrow ② in Exhibit 1-11).
4. The statement of cash flows for the year ended December 31, 2003
   a. Reports cash flows from operating activities, investing activities, and financing activities. Each category results in net cash provided (an increase) or net cash used (a decrease).
   b. Reports that cash increased or decreased during the period and ends with the cash balance on December 31, 2003. Ending cash is reported on the balance sheet (arrow ③ in Exhibit 1-11).

✔ Check Point 1-13

DECISION: Which Company to Invest In? Electronic Analysis of Financial Statements

How do investors decide which company's stock to buy? How do bankers decide which customer will get a loan? How do managers decide whether they are beating competitors? They analyze financial statements.

A well-worn path up the career ladder begins as an "analyst." Many college graduates begin their careers analyzing financial statements—electronically. They use software such as Standard & Poor's (S&P) Research Insight. With this program, you can access companies included in the S&P Index. Companies' financial statements are available online, along with other data that aid decisions.

S&P Research Insight includes ratios that shed light on a company's performance. Ratios compare related financial-statement items for decision making. For example, can General Electric (GE) Company pay its bills? To address this question, we compare GE's current assets to its current liabilities. This is called the current ratio, and we will show you how to use this ratio and many others throughout the book.

There are other financial databases. The SEC Edgar file includes the financial statements of all public corporations in the United States. Edgar is easy to use because it is keyword activated. Simply enter the company name, and its recent SEC documents appear. The 10-K Report holds the financial statements. You can then drop GE's data into an Excel spreadsheet and compute whatever ratios you need for the decision at hand.

Business-to-Business (B2B) Accounting

Many companies use (business-to-business) B2B information systems. B2B refers to online transmission of data from one company to another. For example, suppose Frito-Lay needs 10 tons of potatoes for potato chips. The information system automatically orders potatoes when supplies run low. In a B2B system, Frito-Lay is linked electronically to its supplier of potatoes. B2B takes the guesswork out of deciding when to order goods and how much to order. It also speeds the ordering process to help Frito-Lay get fresh products to stores. And in the process, it makes accounting for these purchases simpler, automatic, and more accurate.

Decision Guidelines

The Decision Guidelines illustrate how managers, investors, and lenders use financial statements. Decision Guidelines appear throughout the book to show how accounting information aids decision making.

Suppose you are considering an investment in Fossil stock. How do you proceed? Where do you get the information you need? What do you look for?

How Managers, Investors, and Lenders Analyze Financial Statements:

IN EVALUATING A COMPANY, WHAT DO THESE DECISION MAKERS LOOK FOR?

Question/Decision	What to Look for
1. Can the company sell its products?	**1.** Sales revenue on the income statement. Are sales growing or falling?
2. What are the main income measures to watch for trends?	**2. a.** Gross profit (sales – cost of goods sold) **b.** Operating income (gross profit – operating expenses) **c.** Net income (bottom line of the income statement) All three income measures should be increasing over time.
3. What percentage of sales revenue ends up as profit?	**3.** Divide net income by sales revenue. Examine the trend of the net income percentage from year to year.
4. Can the company collect its receivables?	**4.** From the balance sheet, compare the percentage increase in accounts receivable to the percentage increase in sales. If receivables are growing much faster than sales, collections may be too slow, and a cash shortage may result.
5. Can the company pay its **a.** Current liabilities? **b.** Current and long-term liabilities?	**5.** From the balance sheet, compare **a.** Current assets to current liabilities. Current assets should be somewhat greater than current liabilities. **b.** Total assets to total liabilities. Total assets must be quite a bit greater than total liabilities.
6. Where is the company's cash coming from? How is cash being used?	**6.** On the cash-flow statement, operating activities should provide the bulk of the company's cash during most years. Otherwise the business will fail. Examine investing cash flows to see if the company is purchasing long-term assets—property, plant, and equipment and intangibles (this signals growth). Examine financing cash flows for heavy borrowing (a bad sign) or issuance of stock (less risky).

Excel Application Problem

Goal: Create a simple spreadsheet that a stockholder or creditor could use to quickly analyze the financial performance of a company.

Scenario: After receiving a Fossil watch for graduation, you are thinking about investing some of your savings in the company's stock. Before doing so, however, you want to perform a quick check of the company's financial performance. Use the Fossil Annual Report to gather your data (also found online at **www.fossil.com**; Investor Relations).

When you have completed your spreadsheet, answer the following questions (You may wish to reference the annual report's Financial Highlights, Consolidated Statements of Income, Consolidated Balance Sheets, Consolidated Statements of Cash Flows, and Management's Analysis for explanations):

1. Since net income affects both stock prices and dividends, what changes have occurred in Fossil's net income over the past five years? Why might Fossil's management not include a net income trend chart like yours in the annual report?
2. Cash flows indicate how a company generates and uses cash. For the past few years, what has happened with Fossil's cash from operating activities? Why?

3. Bankers and creditors look for assets to exceed liabilities. When a company's current liabilities are subtracted from its current assets, a measure of the company's working capital can be determined. For Fossil, what has been the company's working capital trend? Why?

Step-by-step:

1. Open a new Excel spreadsheet.
2. In column 1, create a bold-faced heading as follows:
   a. Chapter 1 Decision Guidelines
   b. Fossil Financial Performance
   c. Today's Date
3. Two rows down, enter the following labels (one in each row):
   a. Income Statement Data (bold)
   b. Net Income (in 000's)
   c. Percentage Change
   d. (skip this row)
   e. Statement of Cash flows Data (bold)
   f. Net Cash from Operating Activities (in 000's)
   g. Percentage Change
   h. (skip this row)
   i. Balance Sheet Data (bold)
   j. Current Assets (in 000's)
   k. Current Liabilities (in 000's)
   l. Working Capital
4. Two rows below your heading, starting in the second column, set up five column headings, beginning with FY 1997 and ending with FY 2001 (or the last five fiscal years, if different from these).
5. Using the Fossil annual report, enter the net income data for the past five years, and use formulas to calculate the percentage change from year to year.
6. Enter the net cash from operating activities for at least three years, and use formulas to calculate the percentage change from year to year.
7. Enter the current assets and current liabilities data for at least two years. To calculate working capital, subtract current liabilities from current assets.
8. Use the Chart Wizard to create a column chart showing how net income has changed (in percent). Title the chart "Net Income Trend" and use the "percentage change" data for the chart data range. Position the chart appropriately on your spreadsheet.
9. Format all cells appropriately (width, dollars, percent, decimal places).
10. Save your worksheet and print a copy for your files.

End-of-Chapter Summary Problem

Air & Sea Travel, Inc., a travel agency, began operations on April 1, 20X3. During April, the business provided travel services for clients. It is now April 30, and investors wonder how well Air & Sea Travel performed during its first month. They also want to know the business's financial position at the end of April and its cash flows during the month.

They have assembled the following data, listed in alphabetical order. They have requested your help in preparing the Air & Sea Travel financial statements at the end of April 20X3.

Accounts payable	$ 100	Land	$18,000
Accounts receivable	2,000	Office supplies	500
Adjustments to reconcile net income to net cash provided by operating activities	(2,400)	Payments of cash:	
Cash balance at beginning of April	0	Acquisition of land	40,000
Cash balance at end of April	33,300	Dividends	2,100
Cash receipts:		Rent expense	1,100
Issuance (sale) of stock to owners	50,000	Retained earnings at beginning of April	0
Sale of land	22,000	Retained earnings at end of April	?
Common stock	50,000	Salary expense	1,200
Dividends	2,100	Service revenue	8,500
		Utilities expense	400

Required

1. Prepare the income statement, the statement of retained earnings, and the statement of cash flows for the month ended April 30, 20X3, and the balance sheet at April 30, 20X3. Draw arrows linking the pertinent items in the statements.
2. Answer the investors' underlying questions.
   a. How well did Air & Sea Travel perform during its first month of operations?
   b. Where does Air & Sea Travel stand financially at the end of the first month?
3. If you were a banker, would you be willing to lend money to Air & Sea Travel, Inc.?

Answers

Requirement 1

Financial Statements of Air & Sea Travel, Inc.

Air & Sea Travel, Inc.
Income Statement
Month Ended April 30, 20X3

Revenue:		
Service revenue		$8,500
Expenses:		
Salary expense	$1,200	
Rent expense	1,100	
Utilities expense	400	
Total expenses		2,700
Net income		$5,800

①

Air & Sea Travel, Inc.
Statement of Retained Earnings
Month Ended April 30, 20X3

Retained earnings, March 31, 20X3	$ 0
Add: Net income for the month	5,800
	5,800
Less: Dividends	(2,100)
Retained earnings, April 30, 20X3	$3,700

②

Air & Sea Travel, Inc.
Balance Sheet
April 30, 20X3

Assets		Liabilities	
Cash	$33,300	Accounts payable	$ 100
Accounts receivable	2,000		
Office supplies	500	**Stockholders' Equity**	
Land	18,000	Common stock	50,000
		Retained earnings	3,700
		Total stockholders' equity	53,700
		Total liabilities and	
Total assets	$53,800	stockholders' equity	$53,800

③

Air & Sea Travel, Inc.

Statement of Cash Flows
Month Ended April 30, 20X3

Cash flows from operating activities:		
Net income		$ 5,800
Adjustments to reconcile net income to net cash provided by operating activities		(2,400)
Net cash provided by operating activities		3,400
Cash flows from investing activities:		
Acquisition of land	$(40,000)	
Sale of land	22,000	
Net cash used for investing activities		(18,000)
Cash flows from financing activities:		
Issuance (sale) of stock	$ 50,000	
Payment of dividends	(2,100)	
Net cash provided by financing activities		47,900
Net increase in cash		$33,300
Cash balance, April 1, 20X3		0
Cash balance, April 30, 20X3		$33,300

Requirements 2 and 3

2. a. The company performed rather well in April. Net income was $5,800—very good in relation to service revenue of $8,500. The company was able to pay cash dividends of $2,100.
   b. The business ended April with cash of $33,300. Total assets of $53,800 far exceed total liabilities of $100. Stockholders' equity of $53,700 provides a good cushion for borrowing. The business's financial position at April 30, 20X3, is strong.
3. The company has plenty of cash, and assets far exceed liabilities. Operating activities generated positive cash flow in the first month of operations. Lenders like to see these features before making a loan. Most bankers would be willing to lend to Air & Sea Travel at this time.

Review The Financial Statements

Lessons Learned

1. **Use accounting vocabulary for decision making.** *Accounting* is an information system for measuring, processing, and communicating financial information. As the "language of business," accounting helps a wide range of decision makers. Accountants are expected to perform their jobs in an ethical manner consistent with generally accepted accounting principles (GAAP).

   The three forms of business organization are the proprietorship, the partnership, and the corporation.
2. **Analyze a business using accounting concepts and principles.** Accountants use the *entity concept* not only to keep the business's records separate from the personal records of the people who run it but to separate corporate divisions from one another. Other important concepts that guide accountants are the *reliability principle,* the *cost principle,* the *going-concern concept,* and the *stable-monetary-unit concept.*
3. **Use the accounting equation to describe an organization.** In its most common form, the accounting equation is

   Assets = Liabilities + Owners' Equity

   Assets are the economic resources of a business that are expected to be of benefit in the future. *Liabilities* are economic debts payable to people or organizations outside the firm. *Owners' equity* refers to the claims held by the owners of a proprietorship or partnership. In a corporation, owners' equity is usually called *stockholders' equity* and is subdivided into two categories: *paid-in capital* and *retained earnings.*
4. **Evaluate a company's operating performance, financial position, and cash flow.** The *financial statements* communi-

cate information about a business entity to decision makers. The *income statement* reports the company's revenues, expenses, and net income or net loss for a period. The *statement of retained earnings* summarizes the changes in a corporation's retained earnings during the period. The *balance sheet* is a snapshot of a business on a particular day; it reports on three main categories of items—assets, liabilities, and owners' equity. The *statement of cash flows* reports cash receipts and payments over a period, classified according to operating, investing, and financing activities.

5. **Explain the relationships among the financial statements.** The bottom line of the income statement, net income, feeds into the statement of retained earnings. The final value of retained earnings then appears on the balance sheet. The final cash balance on the statement of cash flows also appears on the balance sheet.

Accounting Vocabulary

Accounting, like many other subjects, has a special vocabulary. It is important that you understand the following terms. They are defined in the chapter and also in the glossary at the end of the book.

account payable (p. 16)
accounting (p. 9)
accounting equation (p. 16)
assets (p. 16)
balance sheet (p. 23)
board of directors (p. 13)
capital (p. 16)
cash (p. 16)
common stock (p. 17)
comprehensive income (p. 21)
corporation (p. 12)
cost principle (p. 14)
current assets (p. 23)
current liabilities (p. 24)
dividends (p. 18)
entity (p. 14)
expenses (p. 17)
financial accounting (p. 10)
financial statements (p. 9)
financing activities (p. 25)
generally accepted accounting principles (GAAP) (p. 13)
going-concern concept (p. 15)
income statement (p. 19)
investing activities (p. 25)
liabilities (p. 16)
long-term debt (p. 17)
management accounting (p. 10)
merchandise inventory (p. 16)
net earnings (p. 18)
net income (p. 18)
net loss (p. 18)
net profit (p. 18)
note payable (p. 17)
objectivity principle (p. 14)
operating activities (p. 25)
owners' equity (p. 16)
paid-in capital (p. 17)
partnership (p. 12)
plant assets (p. 16)
proprietorship (p. 12)
reliability principle (p. 14)
retained earnings (p. 17)
revenues (p. 17)
shareholders (p. 12)
stable-monetary-unit concept (p. 15)
statement of cash flows (p. 25)
statement of earnings (p. 19)
statement of financial position (p. 23)
statement of operations (p. 19)
statement of retained earnings (p. 21)
stock (p. 12)
stockholders (p. 12)
stockholders' equity (p. 17)

Questions

1. Identify five users of accounting information and explain how they use it.
2. What organization formulates generally accepted accounting principles? Is this organization a government agency?
3. What are the owner(s) of a proprietorship, a partnership, and a corporation called?
4. Why do ethical standards exist in accounting?
5. Why is the entity concept so important to accounting?
6. Give four examples of accounting entities.
7. Briefly describe the reliability principle.
8. What role does the cost principle play in accounting?
9. If assets = liabilities + owners' equity, then how can liabilities be determined?
10. Explain the difference between an account receivable and an account payable.
11. In what two ways can a business use its net income?
12. Give a more descriptive title for the balance sheet.
13. What feature of the balance sheet gives this statement its name?
14. Give another title for the income statement.
15. Which financial statement is like a snapshot of the entity at a specific time? Which statement provides a moving picture of operations?
16. What piece of information flows from the income statement to the statement of retained earnings? What information flows from the statement of retained earnings to the balance sheet?
17. List the cash-flow activities in the order they are likely to occur for a new business. Then rank the cash-flow activities in the order of their importance to a business.

Assess Your Progress

Check Points

CP1-1 Suppose you manage a **Fossil, Inc.**, store. Identify three decisions you must make. How will accounting aid your decisions? Answer in your own words.

Now suppose you are considering the purchase of Fossil stock as an investment. Study Fossil's income statement at the beginning of the chapter and identify certain items that will help you decide whether to make this investment.

Making management and investor decisions
(Obj. 1)

CP1-2 Briefly discuss the difference between accounting and bookkeeping. How does bookkeeping fit into accounting?

Distinguishing accounting from bookkeeping
(Obj. 1)

CP1-3 Accountants follow ethical guidelines in the conduct of their work. What are these standards of professional conduct designed to produce? Why is this goal important? Assume that there are no ethical guidelines for accountants and that managers could report to the public whatever they wish about their companies. What would be a likely result?

Making ethical judgments
(Obj. 1)

CP1-4 Return to the discussion of Tom Kartsotis, Chairman of the Board of **Fossil, Inc.**, on page 14. Suppose Mr. Kartsotis has just founded Fossil, and assume that he treats his home and other personel assets as part of Fossil, Inc. Answer these questions about the evaluation of Fossil, Inc.

1. What can Kartsotis be misled into believing?
2. Which accounting concept governs this situation?
3. How can the proper application of this accounting concept give Kartsotis a realistic view of Fossil, Inc.? Explain in detail.

Applying accounting concepts
(Obj. 2)

CP1-5 Review the accounting equation on page 16.

1. Show how to determine the amount of **eBay's** owners' equity. How would your answer change if you were analyzing your own household? A neighborhood restaurant?
2. If you know assets and owners' equity, how can you measure liabilities? Give the equation.
3. Can you compute assets with the knowledge of owners' equity and liabilities? If so, show how. If not, explain why it is impossible.

Using the accounting equation
(Obj. 3)

CP1-6 Accounting definitions are precise, and you must understand the vocabulary to properly use accounting. Sharpen your understanding of key terms by answering the following questions:

1. How do the *assets* and *owners' equity* of **Nike, Inc.** differ? Which one (assets or owners' equity) must be at least as large as the other? Which one can be smaller than the other?
2. How are Nike's *liabilities* and *owners' equity* similar? Different?

Defining key accounting terms
(Obj. 1)

CP1-7 Consider **Oracle**, the world's second largest software company. Classify the following items as an Asset (A), a Liability (L), or an Owners' Equity (E) for Oracle:

a. Accounts payable
b. Common stock
c. Receivables
d. Retained earnings
e. Land
f. Prepaid expenses
g. Cash
h. Long-term debt
i. Merchandise inventory
j. Notes payable
k. Accrued expenses payable
l. Equipment

Classifying assets, liabilities, and owners' equity
(Obj. 1)

CP1-8 Use **Fossil's** income statement in Exhibit 1-7 (page 19) to answer the following questions about the company's operations during the year ended December 31, 2001:

Using the income statement
(Obj. 4)

1. Identify the two basic categories of items on Fossil's income statement.
2. What do we call the bottom line of the income statement?
3. Fossil's total assets are $381 million, as reported on the company's balance sheet (page 22). How are total assets used to measure net income? Explain your answer.

Preparing an income statement
(Obj. 4)

CP1-9 Return to **Fossil's** income statement in Exhibit 1-7 (page 19). Compute the percentage of cost of goods sold to sales for 2001 and 2000. Is the trend in this percentage favorable or unfavorable for Fossil? Give the reason for your answer.

Preparing a statement of retained earnings
(Obj. 4)

CP1-10 **Kraft Foods, Inc.** began 2001 with retained earnings of $992 million. Revenues during the year were $33,875 million and expenses totaled $31,993 million. Kraft declared dividends of $483 million. What was the company's ending balance of retained earnings? To answer this question, prepare Kraft's statement of retained earnings for the year ended December 31, 2001, complete with its appropriate heading.

Preparing a balance sheet
(Obj. 4)

CP1-11 At December 31, 2004, $40,000 Nye Printing Company has cash of $13,000, receivables of $2,000, and inventory of $40,000. The company's land, buildings, and equipment total $110,000, and other assets amount to $10,000. Nye owes accounts payable of $8,000, short-term notes payable of $12,000, and also has long-term debt of $80,000.

Common stock is $15,000. The general manager of Nye is unsure about the amount of retained earnings.

Prepare Nye's balance sheet at December 31, 2004, complete with its appropriate heading.

Preparing a statement of cash flows
(Obj. 4)

CP1-12 Doubletree Builders, Inc. ended 2005 with cash of $16,000. During 2006, Doubletree earned net income of $80,000 and had adjustments to reconcile net income to net cash provided by operations totaling $20,000 (this is a negative amount).

Doubletree paid $300,000 for equipment during 2006 and had to borrow half of this amount. During the year, the company paid dividends of $10,000 and sold old equipment for $90,000.

Prepare Doubletree's statement of cash flows for the year ended December 31, 2006, complete with its appropriate heading. Follow the format of the summary problem on pages 31–33.

Identifying items with the appropriate financial statement
(Obj. 5)

CP1-13 Suppose you are analyzing the financial statements of **McDonald's Corporation.** Identify each item with its appropriate financial statement, using the following abbreviations: Income statement (IS), Statement of retained earnings (SRE), Balance sheet (BS), and Statement of cash flows (SCF). Three items appear on two financial statements, and one item shows up on three statements.

1. Dividends ____
2. Salary expense ____
3. Inventory ____
4. Sales revenue ____
5. Retained earnings ____
6. Operating cash flows ____
7. Net income (or net loss) ____
8. Cash ____
9. Cash flows from financing activities ____
10. Accounts payable ____
11. Common stock ____
12. Interest revenue ____
13. Long-term debt ____
14. Increase or decrease in cash ____

Exercises

Organizing a business
(Obj. 1)

E1-1 FasTech Company develops Web sites for other companies. FasTech needs funds, and Mel O'Conner, the president, has asked you to consider investing in the business. Answer the following questions about the different ways that O'Conner might organize the business. Explain each of your answers.

a. What form of business organization will give O'Conner the most freedom to manage the business as he wishes?
b. What form of organization will give creditors the maximum protection in the event that FasTech fails and cannot pay its liabilities?

c. What form of organization will enable the owners of FasTech to limit their risk of loss to the amount they have invested in the business?
d. Under what form of organization will FasTech be likely to have the longest life?
e. What form of organization will probably enable FasTech to raise the most money from owners' equity over the life of the business?

If you were O'Conner and could organize the business as you wish, what form of organization would you choose for FasTech Company? Explain your reasoning.

Explaining the income statement and the balance sheet
(Obj. 1)

E1-2 Lia Saxenian wants to open a Mediterranean restaurant in Atlanta. In need of cash, she asks Georgia Bank & Trust for a loan. The bank requires financial statements to show likely results of operations for the year and the expected financial position at year end. With little knowledge of accounting, Saxenian doesn't know how to proceed. Explain to her the information provided by the statement of operations (the income statement) and the statement of financial position (the balance sheet). Indicate why a lender would require this information.

Applying accounting concepts and principles
(Obj. 2)

E1-3

a. **Dell Computer** has several divisions. Managers of each division are evaluated on their division's profit performance. Which concept or principle helps Dell Computer design an accounting system to identify the most profitable division managers?
b. Suppose Dell Computer decides to get out of the magnetic imaging business and offers its magnetic imaging division for sale. Which accounting concept or principle helps Dell account for its magnetic imaging division differently from its main operations?
c. Dell Computer must pay for the materials, labor, and overhead that go into its computers. After assembly, a computer is much more valuable than the sum of the inputs. Which accounting concept or principle tells how to account for the materials, labor and overhead?
d. Dell Computer began in Michael Dell's dorm room at The University of Texas at Austin. Suppose Dell kept a single check book to account for both his personal affairs and Dell Computer transactions. Would he be able to determine the success or failure of the business? Which accounting concept or principle is applicable to Dell's situation?
e. Dell Computer owns real estate around Austin, Texas. Suppose the company purchased land for $3 million in 2002, and its value has risen. The business is offering the land for sale. One appraiser says the land is worth $10 million; another values the land at $15 million. Should Dell record a gain on the value of the land, or wait to record the gain after selling the land? Which accounting concept or principle controls this situation?

Accounting equation
(Obj. 3)

E1-4 Compute the missing amount in the accounting equation for each company (amounts in billions):

	Assets	Liabilities	Owners' Equity
3M	$?	$ 8.0	$ 6.5
Intel	48	?	37
Bank One	269	250	?

How can Bank One operate with such a high ratio of liabilities to assets? What makes Bank One different from 3M Company and Intel?

Accounting equation
(Obj. 3, 4)

E1-5 **Pier 1 Imports** has current assets of $605 million; property, plant, and equipment of $210 million; and other assets totaling $48 million. Current liabilities are $208 million and long-term liabilities add up to $69 million.

Required

1. Use these data to write Pier 1's accounting equation.
2. How much in resources does Pier 1 have to work with?

3. How much does Pier 1 owe creditors?
4. How much of the company's assets do the Pier 1 stockholders actually own?
5. Does Pier 1 appear able to pay its current liabilities? Its total liabilities? How can you tell?

Accounting equation
(Obj. 3)

E1-6 **The Coca-Cola Company's** comparative balance sheet at December 31, 2001, and 2000, reports (in billions):

	Dec. 31, 2001	Dec. 31, 2000
Total assets	$22	$21
Total liabilities	11	12

Required

Three situations about Coca-Cola's issuance of stock and payment of dividends during the year ended December 31, 2001, follow. For each situation, compute the amount of Coca-Cola's net income or net loss during the year ended December 31, 2001.

1. Coke issued $1 billion of stock and paid no dividends.
2. Coke issued no stock but paid dividends of $2 billion.
3. Coke issued $5 billion of stock and paid dividends of $1 billion.

Which situation indicates the strongest operating results for Coca-Cola? Which situation indicates the weakest operating results? Give your reason for each answer.

Accounting equation
(Obj. 3, 4)

E1-7 Answer these questions about two actual companies.

1. **Gap, Inc.** began the year with total liabilities of $4.1 billion and total stockholders' equity of $2.9 billion. During the year, total assets increased by 8.5%. How much are total assets at the end of the year?
2. **Johnson & Johnson** famous for Band-Aids and other health-care products, began the year with total assets of $34.2 billion and total liabilities of $13.8 billion. Net income for the year was $5.7 billion, and dividends and other decreases in stockholders' equity totaled $1.9 billion. How much is stockholders' equity at the end of the year?

Identifying financial statement information
(Obj. 4)

E1-8 Assume top managers at **PepsiCo** are expanding bottling operations in Japan. They must decide where to locate the plant, how much to spend on the building, and how to finance construction. The level of net income they can expect to earn is important. Identify the financial statement where these decision makers can find the following information about PepsiCo, Inc. (In some cases, more than one statement will report the needed data.)

a. Cash spent to acquire the building
b. Selling, general, and administrative expenses
c. Adjustments to reconcile net income to net cash provided by operations
d. Ending cash balance
e. Liabilities that must be paid next year
f. Net income
g. Total assets
h. Long-term debt
i. Revenue
j. Common stock
k. Income tax payable
l. Dividends
m. Income tax expense
n. Ending balance of retained earnings
o. Cost of goods sold

Business organization, balance sheet
(Obj. 2, 5)

E1-9 Amounts of the assets and liabilities of **The Home Depot, Inc.**, as of January 31, 2002, are adapted as follows. Also included are revenue and expense figures for the year ended on that date (amounts in millions):

Sales revenue	$53,553	Property and equipment, net	$15,375
Accounts receivable	920	Merchandise inventory	6,725
Accounts payable	3,436	Other liabilities	4,876
Common stock	5,309	Other expenses (summarized)	2,940
Cost of goods sold	37,406	Cash	2,477
Selling and store operating expense	10,163	Retained earnings, beginning	10,151
Other assets	897	Retained earnings, ending	?

spreadsheet

Required

Prepare the balance sheet of The Home Depot, Inc., at January 31, 2002.

E1-10 This exercise should be worked only in connection with Exercise 1-9. Refer to the data of The Home Depot, Inc., in Exercise 1-9.

Income statement
(Obj. 2, 5)

spreadsheet

Required

1. Prepare the income statement of The Home Depot, Inc., for the year ended January 31, 2002.
2. What amount of dividends did Home Depot pay during the year ended January 31, 2002?

E1-11 Assume that **Sprint Corporation**, the telecommunications company, began the year 20X4 with $185 million in cash. During 20X4, Sprint earned net income of $395 million. Adjustments to reconcile net income to net cash provided by operations totaled $2,334 million, a positive amount. Investing activities used cash of $3,141 million, and financing activities provided cash of $422 million. Sprint ended 20X4 with total assets of $15,195 million and total liabilities of $10,553 million.

Statement of cash flows
(Obj. 2, 4, 5)

Required

Prepare Sprint Corporation's statement of cash flows for the year ended December 31, 20X4. Identify the data items given that do not appear on the statement of cash flows. Also identify the financial statement that reports the unused items.

E1-12 Instiprint, Inc. ended the month of July 20X6, with these data:

Preparing an income statement and a statement of retained earnings
(Obj. 5)

Cash balance at beginning of July	$ 0	Payments of cash:	
Cash balance at end of July	6,500	Acquisition of equipment	$30,000
Cash receipts:		Dividends	1,000
Issuance (sale) of stock to owners	35,000	Retained earnings at beginning of July	0
Rent expense	700	Retained earnings at end of July	?
Common stock	35,000	Utilities expense	200
Equipment	30,000	Adjustments to reconcile net income to cash provided by operations	1,000
Office supplies	1,200		
Accounts payable	2,200		
Service revenue	2,400		

Required

Prepare the income statement and the statement of retained earnings of Instiprint, Inc., for the month ended July 31, 20X6.

E1-13 Refer to the data in the preceding exercise. Prepare the balance sheet of Instiprint, Inc., at July 31, 20X6.

Preparing a balance sheet
(Obj. 5)

E1-14 Refer to the data in Exercise 1-12. Prepare the statement of cash flows of Instiprint, Inc., for the month ended July 31, 20X6. Draw arrows linking the pertinent items in the statements you prepared for Exercises 1-12 through 1-14.

Preparing a statement of cash flows
(Obj. 5)

Advising a business
(Obj. 4, 5)

E1-15 This exercise should be used in conjunction with Exercises 1-12 through 1-14.

The owners of Instiprint, Inc., now seek your advice as to whether they should cease operations or continue the business. Write a report giving them your opinion of operating results, dividends, financial position, and cash flows during their first month of operations. Cite specifics from the financial statements to support your opinion. Conclude your report with advice on whether to stay in business or cease operations.

Applying accounting concepts to explain business activity
(Obj. 2, 5)

E1-16 Apply your understanding of the relationships among the financial statements to answer these questions.

a. Give two reasons why a business can have a steady stream of net income over a 5-year period and still experience a cash shortage.
b. If you could pick a single source of cash for your business, what would it be? Why?
c. How can a business lose money several years in a row and still have plenty of cash?
d. How can a business earn large profits but have a small balance of retained earnings?
e. Suppose your business has $100,000 of current liabilities that must be paid within the next 3 months. Your current assets total only $70,000, and your sales and collections from customers are slow. Identify two ways to finance the extra $30,000 that you will need to pay your current liabilities when they come due.

Problems

(Group A)

Analyzing a loan request
(Obj. 1, 5)

P1-1A As an analyst for Edward Jones Company, it is your job to write recommendations to the firm's loan committee. Kaiser Corporation, a pharmaceutical company, has submitted these summary data to support the company's request for a $4.5 million loan.

	All amounts in millions		
Statement of Cash Flow Data	2007	2006	2005
Net cash flow from operations	$ 70	$ 90	$110
Net cash flow from investing	(40)	(100)	60
Net cash flow from financing	(80)	(40)	(190)
Increase (decrease) in cash	$ (50)	$(50)	$ (20)
Income Statement Data			
Total revenues	$890	$830	$820
Total expenses	640	570	540
Net income	$250	$260	$280
Statement of Retained Earnings Data			
Dividends	$290	$280	$270
Balance Sheet Data			
Total assets	$730	$700	$660
Total liabilities	$390	$320	$260
Total stockholders' equity	340	380	400
Total liabilities and stockholders' equity	$730	$700	$660

Required

Analyze these financial statement data to determine whether the firm should lend $4.5 million to Kaiser. Write a one-paragraph recommendation to the loan committee.

Applying accounting concepts and principles to the income statement
(Obj. 2, 4, 5)

P1-2A Assume that the **Chrysler Division of DaimlerChrysler Corporation**, the automaker, experienced the following transactions during the year ended December 31, 20X5:

a. Suppose Chrysler sold automobiles and other manufactured products for the discounted price of $69.4 billion. Under normal conditions Chrysler would have sold these products for $73 billion. Other revenues totaled $5.8 billion.

b. It cost Chrysler $59.0 billion to manufacture the products it sold. If Chrysler had purchased the products instead of manufacturing them, the cost would have been $61.6 billion.

c. Selling and administrative expenses were $3.9 billion. All other expenses, excluding income taxes, totaled $4.5 billion for the year. Income tax expense was 35% of income before tax. Round to the nearest 1/10 billion (for example, $3.2 billion).

d. Chrysler has several operating subdivisions: Dodge, Chrysler, Jeep, and Eagle. Each subdivision is accounted for separately to indicate how well each is performing. However, Chrysler combines the statements of all subdivisions to show results for the Chrysler Division as a whole.

e. Inflation affects the amounts that Chrysler must pay for steel and other components of the company's manufactured goods. If Chrysler's financial statements were to show the effects of inflation, the company's reported net income would drop by $0.4 billion.

f. If Chrysler were to go out of business, the sale of its assets would bring in over $90 billion in cash.

Required

1. Prepare the Chrysler Division's income statement for the year ended December 31, 20X5.
2. For items a through f, identify the accounting concept or principle that provides guidance in accounting for the item described. State how you have applied the concept or principle in preparing Chrysler's income statement.

Using the accounting equation **(Obj. 3)**

P1-3A Compute the missing amount (?) for each company (adapted and in billions).

	Best Buy	*Pier 1*	*Wal-Mart*
Beginning			
Assets	$ 3.0	$0.7	$ 78
Liabilities	1.9	0.2	47
Ending			
Assets	$ 4.8	$0.9	$?
Liabilities	3.0	0.3	48
Owners' Equity			
Issuances of stock	$?	$ 0	$ 0
Dividends	0	0	3
Income Statement			
Revenues	$15.3	$1.5	$218
Expenses	14.9	?	211

At the end of the year, which company has the

- Lowest percentage of liabilities to assets?
- Highest percentage of net income to revenues?

On these two measures, which company looks strongest? Why?

Balance sheet **(Obj. 2, 5)**

P1-4A Greg Ogden, the manager of **Shipp Belting, Inc.**, which manufactures conveyor belts, prepared the company's balance sheet while the accountant was ill. The balance sheet contains some errors. In particular, Ogden knew that the balance sheet should balance, so he plugged in the stockholders' equity amount needed to achieve this balance. The stockholders' equity amount is *not* correct. All other amounts are accurate.

Shipp Belting, Inc.

Balance Sheet
Month Ended October 31, 20X4

Assets		Liabilities	
Cash	$ 15,400	Notes receivable	$ 14,000
Equipment	36,700	Interest expense	2,000
Accounts payable	3,000	Office supplies	800
Utilities expense	2,100	Accounts receivable	2,600
Advertising expense	300	Note payable	50,000
Land	80,500		
Salary expense	3,300	**Stockholders' Equity**	
		Stockholders' equity	71,900
Total assets	$141,300	Total liabilities	$141,300

Required

1. Prepare the correct balance sheet and date it properly. Compute total assets, total liabilities, and stockholders' equity.
2. Is Shipp Belting actually in better (or worse) financial position than the erroneous balance sheet reports? Give the reason for your answer.
3. Identify the accounts listed on the incorrect balance sheet that are not reported on the balance sheet. State why you excluded them from the correct balance sheet you prepared for Requirement 1. On which financial statement should these accounts appear?

Balance sheet, entity concept
(Obj. 2, 5)

P1-5A Mike Cassell is a realtor. He buys and sells properties on his own, and he also earns commission as an agent for buyers and sellers. He organized his business as a corporation on March 10, 2008. The business received $75,000 cash from Cassell and issued common stock. Consider the following facts as of March 31, 2008:

a. Cassell has $9,000 in his personal bank account and $16,000 in the business bank account.
b. Office supplies on hand at the real estate office total $1,000.
c. Cassell's business spent $35,000 for a **Century 21** franchise, which entitles him to represent himself as an agent. Century 21 is a national affiliation of independent real estate agents. This franchise is a business asset.
d. Cassell's business owes $33,000 on a note payable for some undeveloped land acquired for a total price of $100,000.
e. Cassell owes $65,000 on a personal mortgage on his personal residence, which he acquired in 2002 for a total price of $190,000.
f. Cassell owes $300 on a personal charge account with **Sears**.
g. Cassell acquired business furniture for $12,000 on March 26. Of this amount, Cassell's business owes $6,000 on open account at March 31.

Required

1. Prepare the balance sheet of the real estate business of Mike Cassell Realtor, Inc., at March 31, 2008.
2. Does it appear that Cassell's realty business can pay its debts? How can you tell?
3. Identify the personal items given in the preceding facts that would not be reported on the balance sheet of the business.

P1-6A The assets and liabilities of Kellogg Services, Inc., as of December 31, 20X7 and revenues and expenses for the year ended on that date are listed here.

Income statement, statement of retained earnings, balance sheet
(Obj. 5)

spreadsheet

Equipment	$31,000	Land	$ 8,000
Interest expense	4,000	Note payable	31,000
Interest payable	1,000	Property tax expense	2,000
Accounts payable	12,000	Rent expense	14,000
Accounts receivable	10,000	Salary expense	34,000
Building	26,000	Service revenue	115,000
Cash	4,000	Supplies	2,000
Common stock	10,000	Utilities expense	3,000

Beginning retained earnings was $11,000, and dividends totaled $42,000 for the year.

Required

1. Prepare the income statement of Kellogg Services, Inc. for the year ended December 31, 20X7.
2. Prepare the company's statement of retained earnings for the year.
3. Prepare the company's balance sheet at December 31, 20X7.
4. Analyze Kellogg Services by answering these questions:
   a. Was Kellogg profitable during 20X7? By how much?
   b. Did retained earnings increase or decrease? By how much?
   c. Which is greater, total liabilities or total equity? Who owns more of Kellogg's assets, creditors or the Kellogg stockholders?

P1-7A The following data are adapted from the financial statements of **The Home Depot, Inc.**, at the end of a recent year (in millions):

Preparing a statement of cash flows
(Obj. 4)

Purchases of property, plant, and equipment	$ 3,393	Other investing cash payments	$ 263
Long-term debt	1,250	Accounts receivable	920
Net income	3,044	Borrowing	532
Adjustments to reconcile net income to cash provided by operations	2,919	Payment of dividends	396
Revenues	53,553	Common stock	5,529
Cash, beginning of year	167	Issuance of common stock	445
end of year	2,477	Sales of property, plant, and equipment	176
Cost of goods sold	37,406	Retained earnings	12,799
		Payment of long-term debt	754

Required

1. Prepare Home Depot's statement of cash flows for the year ended January 31, 20X3. Follow the format of the summary problem on pages 31 to 33.

2. What was Home Depot's largest source of cash. Is this a sign of financial strength or weakness?

Analyzing a company's financial statements
(Obj. 4, 5)

P1-8A McConnell Corporation manufactures recreational aircraft. Adapted versions of the company's financial statements are given for two recent years.

	20X5	20X4
	(In Thousands)	
Statement of Operations		
Revenues	$ k	$15,487
Cost of goods sold	11,026	a
Other expenses	1,230	1,169
Earnings before income taxes	920	1,496
Income taxes (35% in 20X5)	l	100
Net earnings	$ m	$ b
Statement of Retained Earnings		
Beginning balance	$ n	$ 2,702
Net earnings	o	c
Dividends	(65)	(55)
Ending balance	$ p	$ d
Balance Sheet		
Assets:		
Cash	$ q	$ e
Property, plant, and equipment	1,597	1,750
Other assets	r	10,190
Total assets	$ s	$13,026
Liabilities:		
Current liabilities	$ t	$ 5,403
Notes payable and long-term debt	2,569	3,138
Other liabilities	69	72
Total liabilities	$ 8,344	$ f
Shareholders' Equity:		
Common stock	$ 117	$ 118
Retained earnings	u	g
Other shareholders' equity	179	252
Total shareholders' equity	v	4,413
Total liabilities and shareholders' equity	$ w	$ h
Statement of Cash Flows		
Net cash provided by operating activities	$ x	$ 475
Net cash provided by investing activities	58	574
Net cash used for financing activities	(709)	(1,045)
Increase (decrease) in cash	335	i
Cash at beginning of year	y	1,082
Cash at end of year	$ z	$ j

Required

1. Determine the missing amounts denoted by the letters.
2. Use McConnell's financial statements to answer these questions about the company. Explain each of your answers.

a. Did operations improve or deteriorate during 20X5?

b. What is the company doing with most of its income—retaining it for use in the business or using it for dividends?

c. How much in total resources does the company have to work with as it moves into the year 20X6?

d. At the end of 20X4, how much did the company owe outsiders? At the end of 20X5, how much did the company owe? Is this trend good or bad in comparison to the trend in assets?

e. What is the company's major source of cash? Is cash increasing or decreasing? What is your opinion of the company's ability to generate cash?

(Group B)

Analyzing a loan request
(Obj. 1, 5)

P1-1B Assume **Prudential Financial Services** is considering an investment in Genome Science Corporation. It is your job to write recommendations to the firm's investment committee. Genome Science has submitted these summary data to support its request for Prudential to purchase $100,000 of the company's stock.

	2005	2004	2003
Statement of Cash Flow Data			
Net cash flow from operations	$190,000	$170,000	$170,000
Net cash flow from investing	(180,000)	(180,000)	(50,000
Net cash flow from financing	30,000	20,000	(110,000)
Increase (decrease) in cash	$ 40,000	$ 10,000	$ 10,000
Income Statement Data			
Total revenues	$950,000	$820,000	$720,000
Total expenses	640,000	570,000	540,000
Net income	$310,000	$250,000	$180,000
Statement of Retained Earnings Data			
Dividends	$160,000	$140,000	$120,000
Balance Sheet Data			
Total assets	$990,000	$720,000	$590,000
Total liabilities	$440,000	$320,000	$300,000
Total stockholders' equity	550,000	400,000	290,000
Total liabilities and stockholders' equity	$990,000	$720,000	$590,000

Required

Analyze these financial statement data to decide whether the firm should purchase Genome stock. Write a one-paragraph recommendation to the investment committee.

Applying accounting concepts and principles to the income statement
(Obj. 2, 4, 5)

P1-2B Assume that **General Electric (GE)** experienced the following transactions during the year ended December 31, 20X5:

a. GE sold products for $53 billion. Company management believes that the value of these products is approximately $80 billion. Other revenues totaled $73 billion.

b. It cost GE $36 billion to manufacture the products it sold. If GE had purchased the products instead of manufacturing them, GE's cost would have been $42 billion.

c. All other expenses, excluding income taxes, totaled $70 billion for the year. Income tax expense was 30% of income before tax.
d. GE has several operating divisions including aircraft engines, appliances, and NBC, the television network. Each division is accounted for separately to show how well each division is performing. However, GE's financial statements combine the statements of all the divisions to report on the company as a whole.
e. Inflation affects GE's cost to manufacture goods. If GE's financial statements were to show the effects of inflation, assume the company's reported net income would drop by $0.7 billion.
f. If GE were to go out of business, the sale of its assets may bring in over $500 billion in cash.

Required

1. Prepare GE Company's income statement for the year ended December 31, 20X5.
2. For items a through f, identify the accounting concept or principle that tells how to account for the item described. State how you have applied the concept or principle in preparing GE's income statement.

Using the accounting equation
(Obj. 3)

P1-3B Compute the missing amount (?) for each company (adapted and in billions).

	FedEx Corporation	Coca-Cola Company	Ford Corporation
Beginning			
Assets	$12	$17	$279
Liabilities	7	10	228
Ending			
Assets	$13	$19	$?
Liabilities	7	11	204
Owners' Equity			
Issuance of stock	$?	$ 0	$ 1
Dividends	1	3	9
Income Statement			
Revenues	$20	$19	$119
Expenses	19	?	97

At the end of the year, which company has the

- Lowest percentage of liabilities to assets?
- Highest percentage of net income to revenues?

On these two measures, which company looks strongest? Why?

Balance sheet
(Obj. 2, 5)

P1-4B The manager of ICON, Inc. prepared the balance sheet of the company while the accountant was ill. The balance sheet contains numerous errors. In particular, the manager knew that the balance sheet should balance, so he plugged in the stockholders' equity amount needed to achieve this balance. The stockholders' equity amount, however, is *not* correct. All other amounts are accurate.

ICON, Inc.
Balance Sheet
Month Ended July 31, 20X7

Assets		Liabilities	
Cash	$15,000	Accounts receivable	$12,000
Office furniture	10,000	Service revenue	50,000
Note payable	16,000	Property tax expense	800
Rent expense	4,000	Accounts payable	9,000
Office supplies	1,000		
Land	44,000	**Stockholders' Equity**	
Advertising expense	2,500	Stockholders' equity	20,700
Total assets	$92,500	Total liabilities	$92,500

Required

1. Prepare the correct balance sheet and date it properly. Compute total assets, total liabilities, and stockholders' equity.
2. Is ICON, Inc. actually in better (or worse) financial position than the erroneous balance sheet reports? Give the reason for your answer.
3. Identify the preceding accounts that are *not* reported on the balance sheet. State why you excluded them from the correct balance sheet you prepared for Requirement 1. Which financial statement should these accounts appear on?

Balance sheet, entity concept **(Obj. 2, 5)**

P1-5B Marjorie Caballero is a realtor. She buys and sells properties on her own, and she also earns commission as an agent for buyers and sellers. Caballero organized her business as a corporation on November 24, 2004. The business received $50,000 from Caballero and issued common stock. Consider these facts as of November 30, 2004:

a. Caballero has $10,000 in her personal bank account and $6,000 in the business bank account.
b. Caballero owes $1,800 on a personal charge account with **Nordstrom** department store.
c. Caballero acquired business furniture for $17,000 on November 25. Of this amount, her business owes $6,000 on open account at November 30.
d. Office supplies on hand at the real estate office total $1,000.
e. Caballero's business owes $40,000 on a note payable for some undeveloped land acquired for a total price of $120,000.
f. Caballero's business spent $20,000 for a **Century 21** real estate franchise, which entitles her to represent herself as a Century 21 agent. Century 21 is a national affiliation of independent real estate agents. This franchise is a business asset.
g. Caballero owes $100,000 on a personal mortgage on her personal residence, which she acquired in 2001 for a total price of $160,000.

Required

1. Prepare the balance sheet of the real estate business of Marjorie Caballero, Realtor, Inc., at November 30, 2004.
2. Does it appear that Caballero's realty business can pay its debts? How can you tell?
3. Identify the personal items given in the preceding facts that would not be reported on the balance sheet of the business.

Income statement, statement of retained earnings, balance sheet **(Obj. 5)**

P1-6B The assets and liabilities of Hercules, Inc., as of December 31, 20X3, and revenues and expenses for the year ended on that date follow.

spreadsheet

Land	$ 98,000	Accounts payable	$ 19,000
Note payable	85,000	Accounts receivable	12,000
Property tax expense	4,000	Advertising expense	13,000
Rent expense	23,000	Building	150,000
Cash	10,000	Salary expense	63,000
Common stock	100,000	Salary payable	1,000
Furniture	20,000	Service revenue	220,000
Interest expense	9,000	Supplies	3,000

Beginning retained earnings were $50,000, and dividends totaled $70,000 for the year.

Required

1. Prepare the income statement of Hercules, Inc., for the year ended December 31, 20X3.
2. Prepare Hercules' statement of retained earnings for the year.
3. Prepare Hercules' balance sheet at December 31, 20X3.
4. Analyze Hercules, Inc., by answering these questions:
   a. Was Hercules profitable during 20X3? By how much?
   b. Did retained earnings increase or decrease? By how much?
   c. Which is greater, total liabilities or total equity? Who owns more of Hercules' assets, creditors or the Hercules stockholders?

Preparing a statement of cash flows
(Obj. 4)

P1-7B The *data below* are adapted from the financial statements of **Nike, Inc.**, at the end of a recent year (in millions).

Required

Revenues	$9,187	Sales of property, plant, and equipment	$ 24
Cash, beginning of year	262	Adjustments to reconcile net income to cash provided by operations	(473)
end of year	445	Cost of goods sold	5,503
Purchases of property, plant, and equipment	510	Other investing cash receipts	33
Long-term debt	296	Accounts receivable	1,754
Net income	796	Borrowing	388
Payment of dividends	101		
Common stock	2,858		
Issuance of common stock	26		
Retained earnings	2,974		

1. Prepare Nike, Inc.'s statement of cash flows for the year ended May 31, 20X4. Follow the format of the summary problem on pages 31 to 33. Not all the items given appear on the statement of cash flows.
2. Which activities provided the bulk of Nike's cash? Is this a sign of financial strength or weakness?

Analyzing a company's financial statements
(Obj. 4, 5)

P1-8B StrideRite, Inc. operates discount shoe stores. Condensed versions of the company's financial statements, with certain items omitted, follow for two recent years.

	20X6	20X5
Statement of Income	*(Thousands)*	
Revenues	$ k	$88,412
Cost of goods sold	74,564	a
Other expenses	15,839	13,564
Income before income taxes	4,346	9,262

(continued)

Income taxes (36.95% in 20X6)	l	1,581
Net income	$ m	$ b
Statement of Retained Earnings		
Beginning balance	$ n	$ 9,987
Net income	o	c
Dividends	(559)	(455)
Ending balance	$ p	$ d
Balance Sheet		
Assets:		
Cash	$ q	$ e
Property, plant, and equipment	23,894	20,874
Other assets	r	16,900
Total assets	$ s	$37,819
Liabilities:		
Current liabilities	$ t	$ 9,973
Long-term debt and other liabilities	11,331	10,120
Total liabilities	22,785	f
Shareholders' Equity:		
Common stock	$ 229	$ 230
Retained earnings	u	g
Other shareholders' equity	133	283
Total shareholders' equity	v	17,726
Total liabilities and shareholders' equity	$ w	$ h
Statement of Cash Flows		
Net cash provided by operating activities	$ x	$ 2,906
Net cash used for investing activities	(3,332)	(3,792)
Net cash provided by financing activities	987	911
Increase (decrease) in cash	38	i
Cash at beginning of year	y	20
Cash at end of year	$ z	$ j

Required

1. Determine the missing amounts denoted by the letters.
2. Use StrideRite's financial statements to answer these questions about the company. Explain each of your answers.
   a. Did operations improve or deteriorate during 20X6?
   b. What is the company doing with most of its income—retaining it for use in the business or using it for dividends?
   c. How much in total resources does the company have to work with as it moves into 20X7? How much in total resources did the company have at the end of 20X5?
   d. At the end of 20X5, how much did the company owe outsiders? At the end of 20X6, how much did the company owe?
   e. What is the company's major source of cash? What is your opinion of the company's ability to generate cash? How is the company using most of its cash? Is the company growing or shrinking?

Apply Your Knowledge

Decision Cases

Analyzing a company as an investment **(Obj. 2, 4, 5)**

Case 1. After a year out of college, you now have $5,000 to invest. You visit the Web sites of eBay, AOL Time Warner, and Yahoo!, but their stocks seem overpriced. A friend has started a dot.com, and she asks you to invest in her company. You obtain Dot.com, Inc.'s, financial statements, which are summarized at the end of the first year as follows:

Dot.com, Inc.
Income Statement
Year Ended Dec. 31, 20X4

Revenues	$80,000
Expenses	60,000
Net income	$20,000

Dot.com, Inc.
Balance Sheet
Dec. 31, 20X4

Cash	$ 3,000	Liabilities	$30,000
Other assets	67,000	Equity	40,000
		Total liabilities	
Total assets	$70,000	and equity	$70,000

Visits with your friend turn up the following facts:

a. Software costs of $25,000 were recorded as assets. These costs should have been expensed. Dot.com paid cash for these expenses and recorded the cash payment correctly.
b. Revenues and receivables of $10,000 were overlooked and omitted.
c. The company owes an additional $5,000 for TV ads that aired in December.

Required

1. What is Dot.com's most pressing need?
2. Prepare corrected financial statements.
3. Use your corrected statements to evaluate Dot.com's results of operations and financial position.
4. Will you invest in Dot.com? Give your reason.

Using financial statements to evaluate a loan request
(Obj. 1, 2)

Case 2. Two businesses, MLK, Inc. and JFK Corporation, have sought business loans from you. To decide whether to make the loans, you have requested their balance sheets.

JFK Corporation
Balance Sheet
August 31, 2005

Assets		Liabilities	
Cash	$ 11,000	Accounts payable	$ 3,000
Accounts receivable	4,000	Notes payable	388,000
Supplies	1,000	Total liabilities	391,000
Furniture	36,000		
Land	79,000	**Owners' Equity**	
Equipment	300,000	Owners' equity	40,000
		Total liabilities and	
Total assets	$431,000	owners' equity	$431,000

MLK, Inc.
Balance Sheet
August 31, 2005

Assets		Liabilities	
Cash	$ 9,000	Accounts payable	$ 12,000
Accounts receivable	14,000	Note payable	18,000
Merchandise inventory	85,000	Total liabilities	30,000

(continued)

Supplies	500		
Furniture and fixtures	9,000		
Building	82,000	**Stockholders' Equity**	
Land	14,000	Stockholders' equity	183,500
		Total liabilities and	
Total assets	$213,500	stockholders' equity	$213,500

Required

1. Solely on the basis of these balance sheets, to which entity would you be more comfortable lending money? Explain fully, citing specific items and amounts from the respective balance sheets.
2. In addition to the balance sheet data, what other information would you require? Be specific.

Using accounting information **(Obj. 1, 2, 3, 4, 5)**

Case 3. A friend learns that you are taking an accounting course. Knowing that you do not plan a career in accounting, the friend asks you why you are "wasting your time." Explain to the friend how you and your friends will use accounting information in

a. Your personal life.
b. The business of your friend, who plans to be a farmer.
c. The business life of another friend, who plans a career in sales.

Ethical Issue

During 2002, **Enron Corporation** admitted hiding large liabilities from its balance sheet. **WorldCom** confessed to recording expenses as assets. Both companies needed to improve their appearance as reported in their financial statements.

Required

1. What is the fundamental ethical issue in these situations?
2. Use the accounting equation to show how Enron abused good accounting. Use a separate accounting equation to demonstrate WorldCom's error.
3. What can happen when companies report financial data that are untrue?

Financial Statement Case

Identifying items from a company's financial statements **(Obj. 4)**

This and similar cases in succeeding chapters are based on the financial statements of **Fossil, Inc.** As you work with Fossil throughout this course, you will develop the ability to use actual financial statements.

Required

Refer to the Fossil, Inc., financial statements in Appendix A at the end of the book.

1. Use the Fossil income statement for the current year to answer these questions: Suppose you own stock in Fossil. If you could pick one item on the company's income statement to increase year after year, what would it be? Why is this item so important? Did this item increase or decrease during 2001? Is this good news or bad news for the company?
2. What was Fossil's largest expense each year? In your own words, explain the meaning of this item. Give specific examples of items that make up this expense. Why is this expense less than sales revenue?
3. Use the balance sheet of Fossil in Exhibit 1-9 (page 22) to answer these questions: At the end of 2001, how much in total resources did Fossil have to work with? How much did the company owe (treat minority interest as an amount that Fossil owes)? How much of its assets did the company's stockholders actually own? Use these amounts to write Fossil's accounting equation at January 5, 2002. Round to the nearest $1 million.
4. Use Fossil's statement of cash flows in Appendix A at the back of the book to answer these questions: Where does Fossil get most of its cash? How does the company spend its cash?

How much cash did Fossil have at the beginning of the most recent year? How much cash did it have at the end of the year?

Analytical Case

Evaluating a leading company
(Obj. 3, 4)

This and similar cases in succeeding chapters are based on the financial statements of **Pier 1 Imports, Inc.** As you work with Pier 1 throughout this course, you will develop the ability to analyze financial statements.

Required

Refer to the Pier 1 Imports financial statements in Appendix B at the end of the book.

1. Write Pier 1's accounting equation at the end of 2002 (express all items in millions). Does Pier 1's financial condition look strong or weak? How can you tell?
2. Examine accounts payable on the balance sheet. What caused accounts payable to increase so much during 2002?
3. Which part of shareholders' equity increased the most during 2002? What caused this item to increase?
4. Cash rose dramatically in 2002. Which statement reports cash as part of Pier 1's financial position? Which statement tells *why* cash increased (or decreased) during the year? What caused Pier 1's cash to increase during 2002?
5. What was the result of Pier 1's operations during 2002? Identify both the name and the dollar amount of the result of operations for 2002, and indicate whether it increased or decreased during the year. Does an increase signal good news or bad news for the company and its stockholders?

Group Projects

Project 1. As instructed by your professor, obtain the annual report of a well-known company.

Required

1. Take the role of a loan committee of Charter Bank, a large banking company headquartered in Charlotte, North Carolina. Assume the company has requested a loan from Charter Bank. Analyze the company's financial statements and any other information you need to reach a decision regarding the largest amount of money you would be willing to lend. Go as deeply into the analysis and the related decision as you can. Specify the following:
   a. The length of the loan period—that is, over what period will you allow the company to pay you back?
   b. The interest rate you will charge on the loan. Will you charge the prevailing interest rate, a lower rate, or a higher rate? Why?
   c. Any restrictions you will impose on the borrower as a condition for making the loan.

   Note: The long-term debt note to the financial statements gives details of the company's existing liabilities.
2. Write your group decision in a report addressed to the bank's board of directors. Limit your report to two double-spaced word-processed pages.
3. If your professor directs, present your decision and your analysis to the class. Limit your presentation to 10 to 15 minutes.

Project 2. You are the owner of a company that is about to "go public"—that is, issue its stock to outside investors. You wish to make your company look as attractive as possible to raise $1 million of cash to expand the business. At the same time, you want to give potential investors a realistic picture of your company.

Required

1. Design a booklet to portray your company in a way that will enable outsiders to reach an informed decision as to whether to buy some of your stock. The booklet should include the following:

   a. Name and location of your company.
   b. Nature of the company's business (be as detailed as possible).
   c. How you plan to spend the money you raise.
   d. The company's comparative income statement, statement of retained earnings, balance sheet, and statement of cash flows for 2 years: the current year and the preceding year. Make the data as realistic as possible with the intent of receiving $1 million.
2. Word-process your booklet, not to exceed five pages.
3. If directed by your professor, make a copy for each member of your class. Distribute copies to the class and present your case with the intent of interesting your classmates in investing in the company. Limit your presentation to 10 to 15 minutes.

2

Processing Accounting Information

Learning Objectives

1. **Analyze** business transactions
2. **Understand** how accounting works
3. **Record** business transactions
4. **Use** a trial balance
5. **Analyze** transactions for quick decisions

Need additional help? Go to the **Integrator CD** *and search these key words:*
account, journal, ledger, t-account, transaction, trial balance

Integrator CD

PepsiCo, Inc.

Statement of Income (Adapted)
Fiscal Years Ended December 29, 2001 and December 25, 2000

	Millions	
	2001	2000
Net Sales	$26,935	$25,479
Expenses		
Cost of sales	10,754	10,226
Selling, general and administrative expenses	11,608	11,104
Other operating expense	552	331
Operating Profit	4,021	3,818
Interest expense	(219)	(272)
Interest and other income	227	215
Income Before Income Taxes	4,029	3,761
Provision for Income Taxes (Income tax expense)	1,367	1,218
Net Income	$ 2,662	$ 2,543

Have you ever looked at a supermarket shelf and wondered how a Frito-Lay route manager knows what and when to order, and how to keep shelves stocked with fresh chips? How does the manager do this and not waste material? Part of the answer comes from a sophisticated information system: Frito-Lay route managers use handheld computers to control how many products are left on the shelves each day. When relayed to company headquarters, the information tells Frito-Lay what and where products are selling, along with the quantities. Then managers can make wise investments in the corn, potatoes, and new technology that contribute to a healthy bottom line.

The results? Frito-Lay, the most profitable of PepsiCo's three business units, dominates the prepared snack foods industry worldwide. The bottom line of the PepsiCo income statement shows huge profits. Let's see how the cost of potatoes becomes part of the financial statements that tell PepsiCo executives how their company is doing.

Sitemap

Chapter 1 gives you a good grounding in the financial statements. Chapters 2 and 3 cover the accounting process that produces these statements. Chapter 2 discusses the processing of accounting information, beginning with the accounting equation from Chapter 1. The second half of the chapter then illustrates the way accounting systems actually work. Chapter 3 covers the end-of-period process that results in the financial statements.

account

The Account

Chapter 1 shows that the accounting equation is the basic tool of accounting. It measures the assets of the business and the claims to those assets.

Account
The detailed record of the changes that have occurred in a particular asset, liability, or stockholders' equity during a period. The basic summary device of accounting.

The main summary device of accounting is the **account.** This is the record of all changes in a particular asset, liability, or stockholders' (or owners') equity. Accounts are of three broad types, according to the accounting equation:

$$\text{Assets} = \text{Liabilities} + \text{Stockholders' (or Owners') Equity}$$

Assets

Assets are economic resources that benefit a business and will continue to be useful. Most firms use the following asset accounts:

Cash
Money and any medium of exchange that a bank accepts at face value.

CASH. **Cash** means money and any medium of exchange including bank account balances, paper currency, coins, certificates of deposit, and checks. Most business failures result from a shortage of cash.

ACCOUNTS RECEIVABLE. A business may sell its goods or services and receive a promise for future payment. Such sales are made on credit (on account). The Accounts Receivable account contains these amounts.

INVENTORY. PepsiCo's most important asset is its inventory—the drinks and snack foods the company sells to customers. Other titles for this account include *Merchandise* and *Merchandise Inventory*.

NOTES RECEIVABLE. A business may sell its goods or services for a note receivable called a *promissory note*. The company will collect cash from a customer, who must pay a fixed amount of money by a certain date.

Prepaid expense
A category of miscellaneous assets that typically expire or get used up in the near future. Examples include prepaid rent, prepaid insurance, and supplies. Also called a *deferral*.

PREPAID EXPENSES. A business may pay certain expenses in advance. A **prepaid expense** is an asset because the payment provides a *future* benefit for the business. Prepaid Rent, Prepaid Insurance, and Office Supplies are prepaid expenses.

LAND. The Land account is a record of the cost of land a business uses in its operations.

BUILDINGS. The cost of the business buildings—office building, manufacturing plant, and the like—appears in the Buildings account.

Equipment, Furniture, and Fixtures. A business has a separate asset account for each type of equipment, for example, Office Equipment, Manufacturing Equipment, and Store Equipment. The Furniture and Fixtures account shows the cost of these assets, which are similar to equipment.

Liabilities

Recall that a *liability* is a debt. A receivable is always an asset; a payable is always a liability. The most common types of liabilities include these:

Notes Payable. The Notes Payable account is the opposite of the Notes Receivable account. Notes Payable includes the amounts that the business must *pay* because it signed promissory notes that require a future payment.

Accounts Payable. The Accounts Payable account is the direct opposite of Accounts Receivable. The promise to pay a debt arising from a credit purchase of inventory appears in the Accounts Payable account. This purchase is said to be made "on account" or "on credit."

Accrued Liabilities. An **accrued liability** is a liability for an expense that has not yet been paid. Interest Payable and Salary Payable are accrued liability accounts for most companies. Income Taxes Payable is also an accrued liability.

Accrued liability
A liability incurred but not yet paid by the company. Another name for *accrued expense.*

Stockholders' (Owners') Equity

The owners' claims to the assets of a corporation are called *stockholders' equity, shareholders' equity*, or simply *owners' equity*. In a proprietorship, there is a single capital account. For a partnership, owner equity is held in separate accounts for each owner's capital balance. A corporation uses Common Stock, Retained Earnings, and Dividends accounts.

Common Stock. The Common Stock account shows the owners' investment in the corporation. A corporation receives cash and issues common stock to the investor. A stock certificate lists the stockholder's name as proof of ownership.

Retained Earnings. A for-profit business must earn income to survive. The Retained Earnings account shows the cumulative net income earned by the corporation over its lifetime, minus cumulative net losses and dividends.

Dividends. The owners of a corporation demand a return on their investment. They want cash dividends. After profitable operations, the board of directors may (or may not) declare and pay a cash dividend. Dividends are optional and decided by the board of directors. The corporation may keep a separate account titled *Dividends*, which indicates a decrease in Retained Earnings.

Revenues. The increase in stockholders' equity from delivering goods or services to customers is called *revenue*. The company uses as many revenue accounts as needed. PepsiCo uses a Sales Revenue account for revenue earned by selling drinks and chips to customers. A lawyer provides legal services for clients and uses a Service Revenue account. If a business loans money to an outsider, it needs an Interest Revenue account. If the business rents a building to a tenant, it needs a Rent Revenue account.

EXPENSES. The cost of operating a business is called *expense*. Expenses *decrease* stockholders' equity, the opposite of revenues. A business needs a separate account for each type of expense, such as Cost of Sales, Salary Expense, Rent Expense, Advertising Expense, and Utilities Expense. Businesses strive to minimize expenses and thereby maximize net income.

Name two things that (1) increase PepsiCo's stockholders' equity; (2) decrease PepsiCo's stockholders' equity.

Answer:

(1) Sale of stock and net income (revenue greater than expenses). (2) Declaration and payment of dividends and net loss (expenses greater than revenue).

DECISION: Why Does the Type of Accounting System Matter?

Transaction
An event that both affects the financial position of a business entity and can be reliably recorded.

There are two basic ways to do accounting—the accrual basis and the cash basis. In accrual accounting we record all the events that have a financial impact on a business and that can be measured reliably. We call these events business **transactions.** In cash basis accounting we record only those events that affect cash, and we ignore all others.

Suppose America Online (AOL) Time Warner sells advertising space to two customers, Dell Computer and Kinko's Copy Centers. AOL collects cash from Dell and takes an account receivable from Kinko's. How should AOL record these transactions under the cash basis and under the accrual basis?

Cash Basis	*Accrual Basis*
Record only receipt of cash from Dell	Record both sales
Ignore the sale on account to Kinko's	**a.** Cash sale to Dell
because AOL received no cash	**b.** Sale on account to Kinko's

Which accounting system captures more information? Why is this important to the person running the business? The accrual basis is superior because it records both sales and collections and, therefore, gives an accurate picture of the firm's assets. With the cash basis, you would not know you actually have more assets than the cash collected from Dell. Banks require accrual-basis financial statements before they make loans, and outside investors want to see profits and losses measured by the accrual basis. This is why generally accepted accounting principles (GAAP) require firms to use the accrual basis.

Now let's see how to use accrual accounting.

Accounting for Business Transactions

transaction

In accounting terms, a **transaction** is any event that both affects the financial position of the business entity and can be reliably recorded. Many events may affect a company, including elections, economic booms and recessions, purchases and sales of merchandise inventory, and payment of rent. But accountants record only those events with effects that can be measured reliably as transactions.

Objective

1 Analyze business transactions

Which of the preceding events would an accountant record? Record the purchases and sales, and the payment of rent. The dollar effects of elections and economic trends cannot be measured reliably, even though they might affect the business.

To illustrate accounting for business transactions, let's return to Gary and Monica Lyon. We met the Lyons in Chapter 1, when they opened a travel agency in April 20X3 and incorporated it as Air & Sea Travel, Inc. We consider 11 events and analyze each in terms of its effect on the accounting equation of Air & Sea Travel.

TRANSACTION 1. The Lyons invest $50,000 to begin the business, and Air & Sea Travel issues common stock to Gary and Monica Lyon. The effect of this transaction on the accounting equation of the business entity Air & Sea Travel, Inc. is a receipt of $50,000 cash and issuance of common stock:

	ASSETS	=	LIABILITIES	+	STOCKHOLDERS' EQUITY	TYPE OF STOCKHOLDERS' EQUITY TRANSACTION
	Cash				Common Stock	
(1)	+ 50,000				+ 50,000	Issued stock

For every transaction, the net amount on the left side of the equation must equal the net amount on the right side. The first transaction increases both the assets (in this case, Cash) and the owners' equity (Common Stock). The transaction involves no liabilities because it creates no obligation for Air & Sea Travel to pay an outside party. To the right of the transaction we write "Issued stock" to record the reason for the $50,000 increase in stockholders' equity.

Every transaction affects the financial statements, and we can prepare the statements after one, two, or any number of transactions. For example, Air & Sea Travel, Inc. could report the company's balance sheet after its first transaction, shown below.

This balance sheet shows that Air & Sea Travel holds cash of $50,000 and that the company owes no liabilities. Thus, the stockholders own all the assets of the business. Their equity (ownership) is denoted simply as *Common stock* on the balance sheet. A bank would look favorably on the Air & Sea Travel balance sheet because the business has $50,000 cash and no debt—a strong financial position. This would make a loan decision easy for a banker.

Air & Sea Travel, Inc.
Balance Sheet
April 1, 20X3

Assets		***Liabilities***	
Cash	$50,000	None	
		Stockholders' Equity	
		Common stock	$50,000
		Total stockholders' equity	50,000
		Total liabilities and	
Total assets	$50,000	stockholders' equity	$50,000

As a practical matter, most entities report their financial statements at the end of the accounting period—not after each transaction. But an accounting system can produce statements whenever managers and owners need to know where the business stands.

TRANSACTION 2. Air & Sea Travel purchases land for an office location and pays cash of $40,000. The effect of this transaction on the accounting equation is:

	ASSETS				LIABILITIES	+	STOCKHOLDERS' EQUITY	TYPE OF STOCKHOLDERS' EQUITY TRANSACTION
	Cash	+	Land	=			Common Stock	
(1)	50,000						50,000	Issued stock
(2)	−40,000	+	40,000					
Bal.	10,000		40,000				50,000	
	50,000						50,000	

The purchase increases one asset (Land) and decreases another asset (Cash) by the same amount. After the transaction is completed, Air & Sea Travel has cash of $10,000, land of $40,000, no liabilities, and stockholders' equity of $50,000. Note that the sums of the balances (which we abbreviate Bal.) on both sides of the equation are equal. This equality must always exist.

✔ Check Point 2-1

TRANSACTION 3. The business buys stationery and other office supplies, agreeing to pay $500 within 30 days. This transaction increases both the assets and the liabilities of the business. Its effect on the accounting equation is as follows:

	ASSETS						LIABILITIES	+	STOCKHOLDERS' EQUITY
	Cash	+	Office Supplies	+	Land	=	Accounts Payable	+	Common Stock
Bal.	10,000				40,000				50,000
(3)			+500				+500		
Bal.	10,000		500		40,000		500		50,000
	50,500						50,500		

The new asset is Office Supplies, and the liability is an Account Payable. Because Air & Sea Travel must pay $500 in the future but signs no formal promissory note, the liability is an account payable, not a note payable.

TRANSACTION 4. Air & Sea Travel earns service revenue by providing travel services. Assume the business earns $5,500 and collects this amount in cash. The effect on the accounting equation is an increase in the asset Cash and an increase in Retained Earnings, as follows:

	ASSETS						LIABILITIES	+	STOCKHOLDERS' EQUITY			TYPE OF STOCKHOLDERS' EQUITY TRANSACTION
	Cash	+	Office Supplies	+	Land	=	Accounts Payable	+	Common Stock	+	Retained Earnings	
Bal.	10,000		500		40,000		500		50,000			
(4)	+ 5,500										+5,500	Service revenue
Bal.	15,500		500		40,000		500		50,000		5,500	
	56,000						56,000					

TRANSACTION 5. Air & Sea Travel performs services for customers who do not pay immediately. Air & Sea gets the customers' promise to pay $3,000 within 1 month. This promise is an account receivable of Air & Sea Travel. (In accounting, we say that Air & Sea performed this service *on account*.) Performing a service for a customer earns revenue for the business regardless of whether it receives cash now or collects later. Air & Sea Travel records an increase in the asset Accounts Receivable and an increase in Retained Earnings as follows:

	ASSETS					LIABILITIES +	STOCKHOLDERS' EQUITY		TYPE OF STOCKHOLDERS' EQUITY TRANSACTION
	Cash	+ Accounts Receivable	+ Office Supplies	+ Land		Accounts Payable	+ Common Stock	+ Retained Earnings	
Bal.	15,500		500	40,000	=	500	50,000	5,500	
(5)		+3,000						+3,000	Service revenue
Bal.	15,500	3,000	500	40,000		500	50,000	8,500	
	59,000					59,000			

TRANSACTION 6. During the month, Air & Sea Travel pays $2,700 for the following cash expenses: office rent, $1,100; employee salary, $1,200; and utilities, $400. The effect on the accounting equation is:

✔ Check Point 2-2

	ASSETS					LIABILITIES +	STOCKHOLDERS' EQUITY		TYPE OF STOCKHOLDERS' EQUITY TRANSACTION
	Cash	+ Accounts Receivable	+ Office Supplies	+ Land		Accounts Payable	+ Common Stock	+ Retained Earnings	
Bal.	15,500	3,000	500	40,000		500	50,000	8,500	
(6)	−1,100				=			−1,100	Rent expense
	−1,200							−1,200	Salary expense
	− 400							− 400	Utilities expense
Bal.	12,800	3,000	500	40,000		500	50,000	5,800	
	56,300					56,300			

The expenses decrease the asset Cash and the owners' equity account, Retained Earnings.

TRANSACTION 7. Air & Sea Travel pays $400 to the store from which it purchased office supplies in Transaction 3. (In accounting, we say that Air & Sea Travel pays $400 *on account*.) The effect on the accounting equation is a decrease in the asset Cash and a decrease in the liability Accounts Payable as follows:

	ASSETS					LIABILITIES	+ STOCKHOLDERS' EQUITY	
	Cash	+ Accounts Receivable	+ Office Supplies	+ Land		Accounts Payable	+ Common Stock	+ Retained Earnings
Bal.	12,800	3,000	500	40,000	=	500	50,000	5,800
(7)	− 400					− 400		
Bal.	12,400	3,000	500	40,000		100	50,000	5,800
	55,900					55,900		

The payment of cash on account has no effect on Office Supplies because the payment does not increase or decrease the supplies. The payment is not an expense. Instead, the business is paying off a liability.

TRANSACTION 8. The Lyons paid $30,000 to remodel their home. This event is a personal transaction and therefore is not recorded by the business. We focus solely on the business entity, and this event does not affect it. The transaction illustrates the application of the entity concept from Chapter 1.

TRANSACTION 9. In Transaction 5, Air & Sea Travel performed service for customers on account. The business now collects $1,000 from a customer. (We say that Air & Sea Travel *collects the cash on account.*) Air & Sea will record an increase in Cash and a decrease in Accounts Receivable. It should not record service revenue now because Air & Sea already recorded the revenue in Transaction 5, when it performed the service. Performing the service, not collecting the cash, earns the revenue. The effect of collecting cash on account is:

	ASSETS					LIABILITIES	+ STOCKHOLDERS' EQUITY	
	Cash	+ Accounts Receivable	+ Office Supplies	+ Land		Accounts Payable	+ Common Stock	+ Retained Earnings
Bal.	12,400	3,000	500	40,000	=	100	50,000	5,800
(9)	+ 1,000	− 1,000						
Bal.	13,400	2,000	500	40,000		100	50,000	5,800
	55,900					55,900		

Total assets are unchanged from the preceding transaction's total. Why? Because Air & Sea Travel merely received one asset and gave up another.

TRANSACTION 10. Air & Sea Travel sells land for $22,000, which is the same amount it paid for the land. Air & Sea receives $22,000 cash, and the effect on the accounting equation is:

	ASSETS				=	LIABILITIES +	STOCKHOLDERS' EQUITY	
	Cash	+ Accounts Receivable	+ Office Supplies	+ Land		Accounts Payable	+ Common Stock	+ Retained Earnings
Bal.	13,400	2,000	500	40,000		100	50,000	5,800
(9)	+22,000			−22,000				
Bal.	35,400	2,000	500	18,000		100	50,000	5,800
	55,900					55,900		

Note that the company did not sell all its land; it still owns $18,000 worth of land.

TRANSACTION 11. Air & Sea Travel declares a dividend and pays Gary and Monica Lyon $2,100 cash. The effect on the accounting equation is:

	ASSETS				=	LIABILITIES +	STOCKHOLDERS' EQUITY		TYPE OF STOCKHOLDERS' EQUITY TRANSACTION
	Cash	+ Accounts Receivable	+ Office Supplies	+ Land		Accounts Payable	+ Common Stock	+ Retained Earnings	
Bal.	35,400	2,000	500	18,000		100	50,000	5,800	
(11)	− 2,100							−2,100	Dividends
Bal.	33,300	2,000	500	18,000		100	50,000	3,700	
	53,800					53,800			

The dividend decreases both the asset Cash and the retained earnings of the business. *But dividends are not an expense.*

Transactions and Financial Statements

Exhibit 2-1 summarizes the 11 preceding transactions. Panel A gives the details of the transactions, and Panel B is the analysis. As you study the exhibit, note that every transaction maintains the following equality:

Assets = Liabilities + Stockholders' Equity

Exhibit 2-1 provides the data for Air & Sea Travel's financial statements:

- *Income statement* data appear as revenues and expenses under Retained Earnings. The revenues increase retained earnings; the expenses decrease retained earnings.
- The *balance sheet* data are composed of the ending balances of the assets, liabilities, and stockholders' equities shown at the bottom of the exhibit. The accounting equation shows that total assets ($53,800) equal total liabilities plus stockholders' equity ($53,800).
- The *statement of retained earnings*, which shows net income (or net loss) and dividends, can also be prepared.
- Data for the *statement of cash flows* are aligned under the Cash account. Cash receipts increase cash, and cash payments are decreases.

Exhibit 2-1 **Analysis of Air & Sea Travel, Inc., Transactions**

PANEL A—Details of Transactions

(1) Received $50,000 cash and issued stock to the owners
(2) Paid 40,000 cash for land
(3) Bought $500 of office supplies on account
(4) Received $5,500 cash from customers for service revenue earned
(5) Performed services for customers on account, $3,000
(6) Paid cash expenses: rent, $1,100; employee salary, $1,200; utilities, $400
(7) Paid $400 on the account payable created in Transaction 3
(8) Owners paid personal funds to remodel home, *not* a transaction of the business
(9) Received $1,000 on account
(10) Sold land for cash at its cost of $22,000
(11) Declared and paid a dividend of $2,100 to the stockholders

PANEL B—Analysis of Transactions

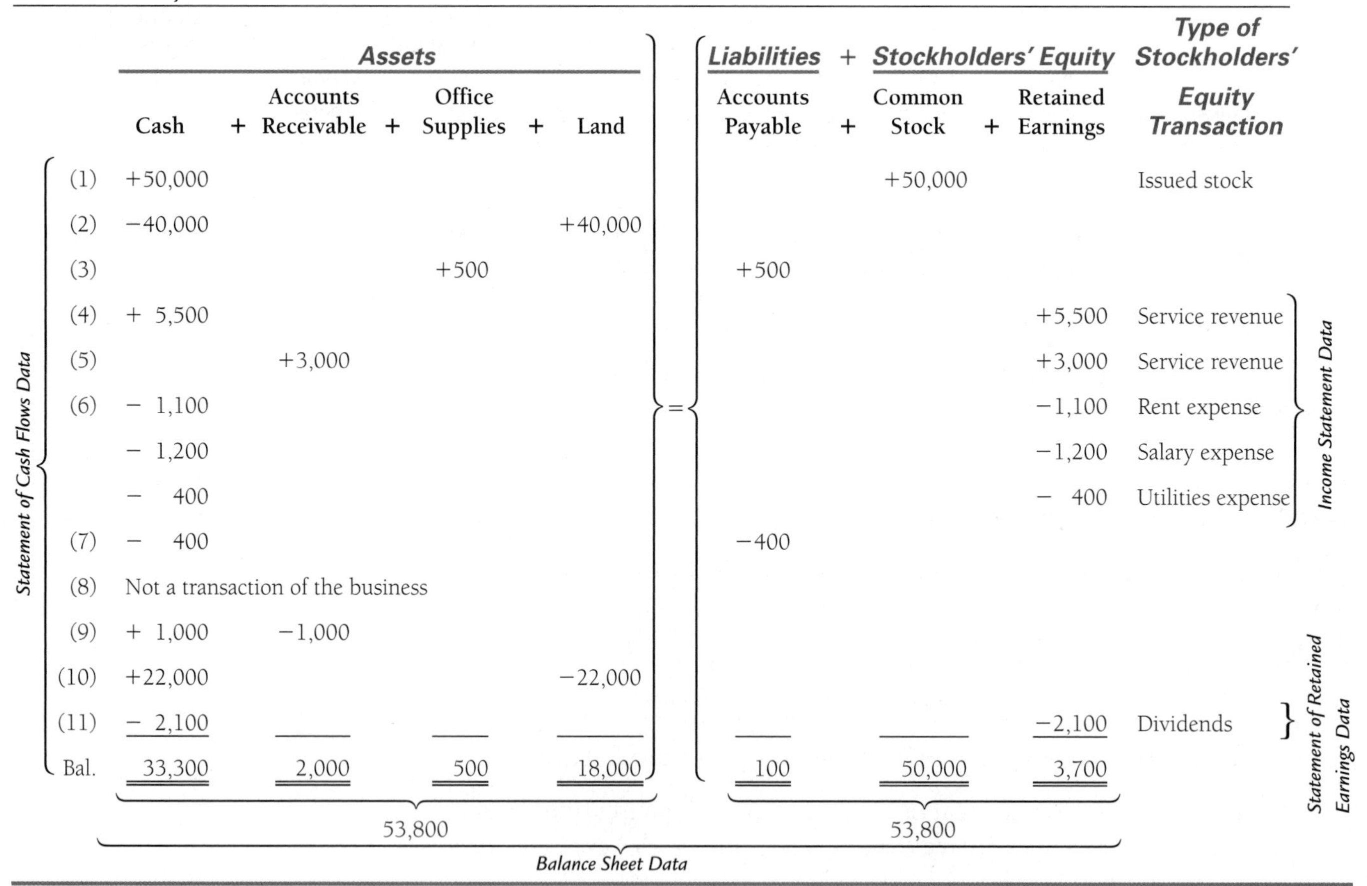

	Assets				=	Liabilities +	Stockholders' Equity		Type of Stockholders' Equity Transaction
	Cash	+ Accounts Receivable	+ Office Supplies	+ Land		Accounts Payable	+ Common Stock	+ Retained Earnings	
(1)	+50,000						+50,000		Issued stock
(2)	−40,000			+40,000					
(3)			+500			+500			
(4)	+ 5,500							+5,500	Service revenue
(5)		+3,000						+3,000	Service revenue
(6)	− 1,100							−1,100	Rent expense
	− 1,200							−1,200	Salary expense
	− 400							− 400	Utilities expense
(7)	− 400					−400			
(8)	Not a transaction of the business								
(9)	+ 1,000	−1,000							
(10)	+22,000			−22,000					
(11)	− 2,100							−2,100	Dividends
Bal.	33,300	2,000	500	18,000		100	50,000	3,700	
	53,800					53,800			

Exhibit 2-2 shows the Air & Sea Travel financial statements at the end of April, the company's first month of operations. You can recognize the statements from the solution to the summary problem at the end of Chapter 1. We repeat the statements here. Follow the flow of data to observe the following:

1. The income statement reports revenues, expenses, and either a net income or a net loss for the period. During April, Air & Sea earned net income of $5,800. Compare the Air & Sea Travel income statement with that of PepsiCo at the

Exhibit 2-2

Financial Statements of Air & Sea Travel, Inc.

Air & Sea Travel, Inc.
Income Statement
Month Ended April 30, 20X3

Revenue		
Service revenue ($5,500 + $3,000)		$8,500
Expenses		
Salary expense	$1,200	
Rent expense	1,100	
Utilities expense	400	
Total expenses		2,700
Net income		$5,800

①

Air & Sea Travel, Inc.
Statement of Retained Earnings
Month Ended April 30, 20X3

Retained earnings, April 1, 20X3	$ 0
Add: Net income for the month	5,800
	5,800
Less: Dividends	(2,100)
Retained earnings, April 30, 20X3	$3,700

②

Air & Sea Travel, Inc.
Balance Sheet
April 30, 20X3

Assets		***Liabilities***	
Cash	$33,300	Accounts payable	$ 100
Accounts receivable	2,000		
Office supplies	500	***Stockholders' Equity***	
Land	18,000	Common stock	50,000
		Retained earnings	3,700
		Total stockholders' equity	53,700
		Total liabilities and	
Total assets	$53,800	stockholders' equity	$53,800

beginning of the chapter. The income statement includes only two types of accounts: revenues and expenses.

2. The statement of retained earnings starts with the beginning balance of retained earnings, which for a new business is zero. Add net income for the period (arrow ①), subtract dividends, and obtain the ending balance of retained earnings ($3,700).

3. The balance sheet lists the assets, liabilities, and stockholders' equity of the business at the end of the period. Included in stockholders' equity is retained earnings, which comes from the statement of retained earnings (arrow ②).

The analysis in Exhibit 2-1 can be used, but it is cumbersome for even small organizations. Consider PepsiCo, Inc., with its hundreds of accounts and thousands of transactions. The spreadsheet to account for the PepsiCo transactions would be much too large. For this reason, accountants use a different accounting system called *double-entry accounting* to create the financial statements. In the second half of this chapter we discuss double-entry accounting as it is used in business. First, let us put into practice what you have learned thus far.

Mid-Chapter Summary Problem

Suzanne Abbey opens a research service near a college campus. She names the corporation Abbey Researchers, Inc. During the first month of operations, July 20X3, the business engages in the following transactions:

a. Abbey Researchers, Inc. issues its common stock to Suzanne Abbey, who invests $25,000 to open the business.
b. The company purchases on account office supplies costing $350.
c. Abbey Researchers pays cash of $20,000 to acquire a lot next to the campus. The company intends to use the land as a building site for a business office.
d. Abbey Researchers performs research for clients and receives cash of $1,900.
e. Abbey Researchers pays $100 on the account payable it created in Transaction b.
f. Abbey pays $2,000 of personal funds for a vacation.
g. Abbey Researchers pays cash expenses for office rent ($400) and utilities ($100).
h. The business sells a small parcel of the land for its cost of $5,000.
i. The business declares and pays a cash dividend of $1,200.

Required

1. Analyze the preceding transactions in terms of their effects on the accounting equation of Abbey Researchers, Inc. Use Exhibit 2-1 as a guide.
2. Prepare the income statement, statement of retained earnings, and balance sheet of the business after recording the transactions. Draw arrows linking the statements.

Answers

Requirements 1 and 2

PANEL A—Details of Transactions

(a) Received $25,000 cash and issued common stock
(b) Purchased $350 of office supplies on account
(c) Paid $20,000 to acquire land as a building site
(d) Earned service revenue and received cash of $1,900
(e) Paid $100 on account
(f) Paid for a personal vacation, not a transaction of the business
(g) Paid cash expenses for rent ($400) and utilities ($100)
(h) Sold land for $5,000, its cost
(i) Declared and paid cash dividends of $1,200

PANEL B—Analysis of Transactions

	Assets				Liabilities +	Stockholders' Equity		Type of Stockholders' Equity Transaction
	Cash	+ Office Supplies +	Land		Accounts Payable +	Common Stock +	Retained Earnings	
(a)	+25,000					+25,000		Issued stock
(b)		+350			+350			
(c)	−20,000		+20,000					
(d)	+ 1,900						+1,900	Service revenue
(e)	− 100			=	−100			
(f)	Not a transaction of the business							
(g)	− 400						− 400	Rent expense
	− 100						− 100	Utilities expense
(h)	+ 5,000		− 5,000					
(i)	− 1,200						−1,200	Dividends
Bal.	10,100	350	15,000		250	25,000	200	
	25,450				25,450			

Abbey Researchers, Inc.

Income Statement
Month Ended July 31, 20X3

Revenue		
Service revenue		$1,900
Expenses		
Rent expense	$400	
Utilities expense	100	
Total expenses		500
Net income		$1,400

Abbey Researchers, Inc.

Statement of Retained Earnings
Month Ended July 31, 20X3

Retained earnings, July 1, 20X3	$ 0
Add: Net income for the month	1,400
	1,400
Less: Dividends	(1,200)
Retained earnings, July 31, 20X3	$ 200

continued

Abbey Researchers, Inc.
Balance Sheet
July 31, 20X3

Assets		Liabilities	
Cash	$10,100	Accounts payable	$ 250
Office supplies	350		
Land	15,000	**Stockholders' Equity**	
		Common stock	25,000
		Retained earnings	200
		Total stockholders' equity	25,200
Total assets	$25,450	Total liabilities and stockholders' equity	$25,450

Double-Entry Accounting

t-account

Objective

2 **Understand** how accounting works

Double-entry system
An accounting system that uses debits and credits to record the dual effects of each business transaction.

All business transactions include two parts. You give something and you receive something. Accounting is, therefore, based on a **double-entry system,** which records the giving and receiving—the *dual effects* on the entity. *Each transaction affects at least two accounts.* For example, Air & Sea Travel's receipt of $50,000 cash and issuance of stock increased both the Cash and the Common Stock of the business. It would be incomplete to record only the increase in Cash or only the increase in Common Stock.

Consider a cash purchase of supplies. What are the dual effects of this transaction? The purchase (1) decreases cash and (2) increases supplies. Other examples:

- A *purchase of supplies on credit* (1) increases supplies and (2) increases accounts payable.
- A *cash payment on account* (1) decreases cash and (2) decreases accounts payable.

All transactions have at least two effects on the entity.

The T-Account

To record transactions, accountants often use *T-accounts*. The term gets its name from the capital letter *T*. The vertical line in the letter divides the account into its two sides: left and right. The account title rests on the horizontal line at the top of the T. For example, the Cash account of a business can appear as follows:

Cash	
(Left side)	**(Right side)**
Debit	***Credit***

Debit
The left side of an account.

Credit
The right side of an account.

The left side of the account is called the **debit** side, and the right side is called the **credit** side. Often, students are confused by the words *debit* and *credit*. To become comfortable using them, remember that

Debit = Left side Credit = Right side

Every business transaction involves both a debit and a credit.[1]

Increases and Decreases in the Accounts

The type of account determines how we record an increase or a decrease. For any given account, all increases are recorded on one side and all decreases on the other side. *The rules of debit and credit are as follows* (Exhibit 2-3):

- Increases in assets are recorded on the left (debit) side of the account. Decreases in assets are recorded on the right (credit) side.
- Conversely, increases in liabilities and stockholders' equity are recorded by credits. Decreases in liabilities and stockholders' equity are recorded by debits.

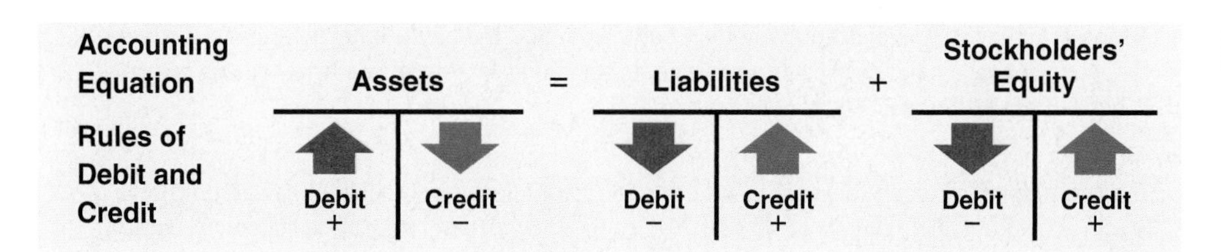

Exhibit 2-3

Accounting Equation and the Rules of Debit and Credit

In everyday conversation, we may praise someone by saying, "She deserves credit for her good work." As you study accounting, forget this general usage. Remember that in accounting

- *Debit means left side.*
- *Credit means right side.*

In a computerized accounting system, the program interprets debits and credits as increases or decreases. Whether a debit is an increase or a decrease depends on the type of account. For example, the program reads a debit to Cash as an increase because Cash is an asset. It reads a debit to Accounts Payable as a decrease because a payable is a liability.

This pattern of recording debits and credits is based on the accounting equation:

ASSETS = LIABILITIES + STOCKHOLDERS' EQUITY

Debits (Assets) — **Credits** (Liabilities + Stockholders' Equity)

Assets (debit-balance accounts) are on the opposite side of the equation from the credit-balance accounts—liabilities and stockholders' equity. Therefore, increases and decreases in assets are recorded in the opposite manner from liabilities and stockholders' equity. Also liabilities and stockholders' equity are treated similarly because both are credit-balance accounts. Exhibit 2-3 shows the relationship between the accounting equation and the rules of debit and credit.

[1]The words *debit* and *credit* have Latin origins (*debitum* and *creditum*). Pacioli, the Italian monk who wrote about accounting in the 15th century, used these terms.

To illustrate the ideas diagrammed in Exhibit 2-3, let's review the first transaction. Air & Sea Travel received $50,000 and issued stock. Which accounts are affected? How will the accounts appear after the transaction? The Cash account and the Common Stock account will hold these amounts:

Assets = ***Liabilities*** + ***Stockholders' Equity***

Cash	
Debit for Increase, 50,000	

Common Stock	
	Credit for Increase, 50,000

The amount remaining in an account is called its *balance*. This first transaction gives Cash a $50,000 debit balance and Common Stock a $50,000 credit balance.

Suppose Air & Sea Travel is applying for a bank loan, and the bank requires a financial statement. Can you prepare a balance sheet and an income statement for Air & Sea Travel at this point? What would the financial statements report?

Answer:
You can prepare a balance sheet that would report Cash, an asset, of $50,000 and Common Stock, a stockholders' equity, of $50,000. You cannot yet prepare an income statement because the business has experienced no revenues or expenses.

The second transaction in our Air & Sea Travel illustration is a $40,000 cash purchase of land. This transaction affects two assets: Cash and Land. It decreases Cash with a credit and increases Land with a debit, as shown in the following T-accounts:

Assets = ***Liabilities*** + ***Stockholders' Equity***

Cash	
Bal. 50,000	**Credit for Decrease, 40,000**
Bal. 10,000	

Land	
Debit for Increase, 40,000	
Bal. 40,000	

Common Stock	
	Bal. 50,000

After this transaction, Cash has a $10,000 debit balance ($50,000 debit balance minus the $40,000 credit amount), Land has a debit balance of $40,000, and Common Stock has a $50,000 credit balance, as shown in Exhibit 2-4.

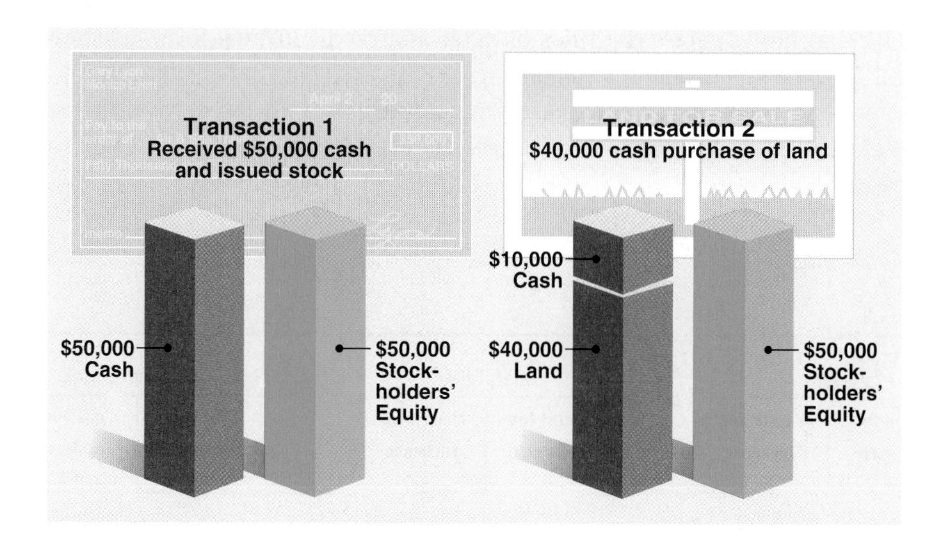

Exhibit 2-4

The Accounting Equation and the First Two Transactions of Air & Sea Travel, Inc.

Additional Stockholders' Equity Accounts: Revenues and Expenses

Stockholders' equity also includes the two types of income statement accounts, Revenues and Expenses:

- *Revenues* are increases in stockholders' equity that result from delivering goods or services to customers.
- *Expenses* are decreases in stockholders' equity due to the cost of operating the business.

Therefore, the accounting equation may be expanded as shown in Exhibit 2-5.

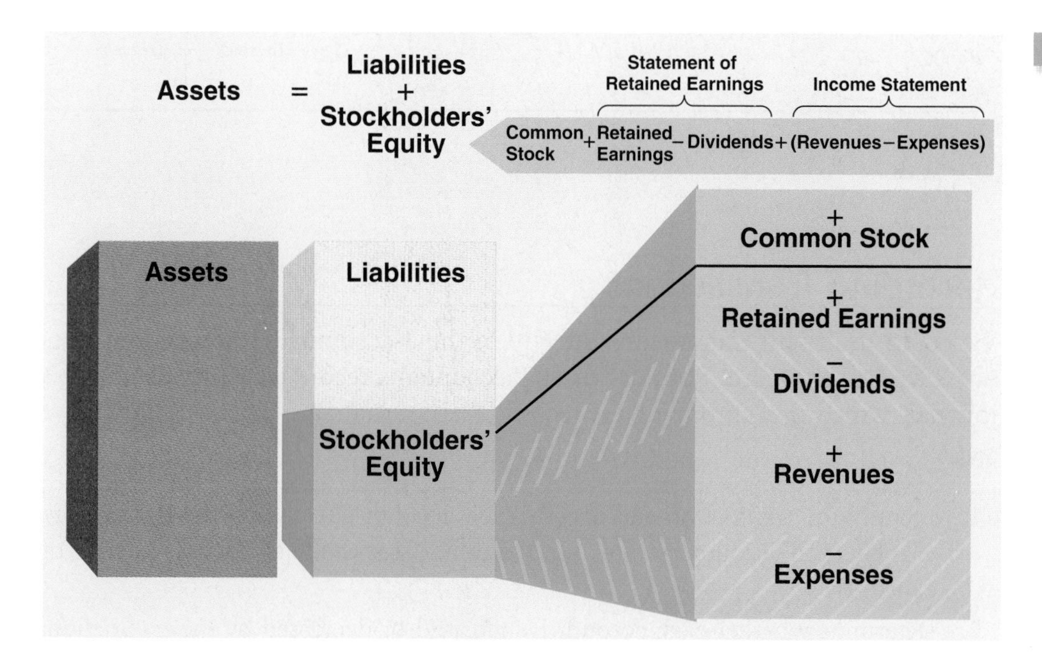

Exhibit 2-5

Expansion of the Accounting Equation

Revenues and expenses appear in parentheses because their net effect—revenues minus expenses—equals net income, which increases stockholders' equity. If expenses exceed revenues, there is a net loss, which decreases stockholders' equity.

We can now express the rules of debit and credit in final form, as shown in Exhibit 2-6. *You should not proceed until you have learned these rules*. For example, you must remember that a debit increases an asset account and a credit decreases an asset. Liabilities are the opposite. A credit increases a liability account and a debit decreases a liability.

Exhibit 2-6

Expanded Rules of Debit and Credit

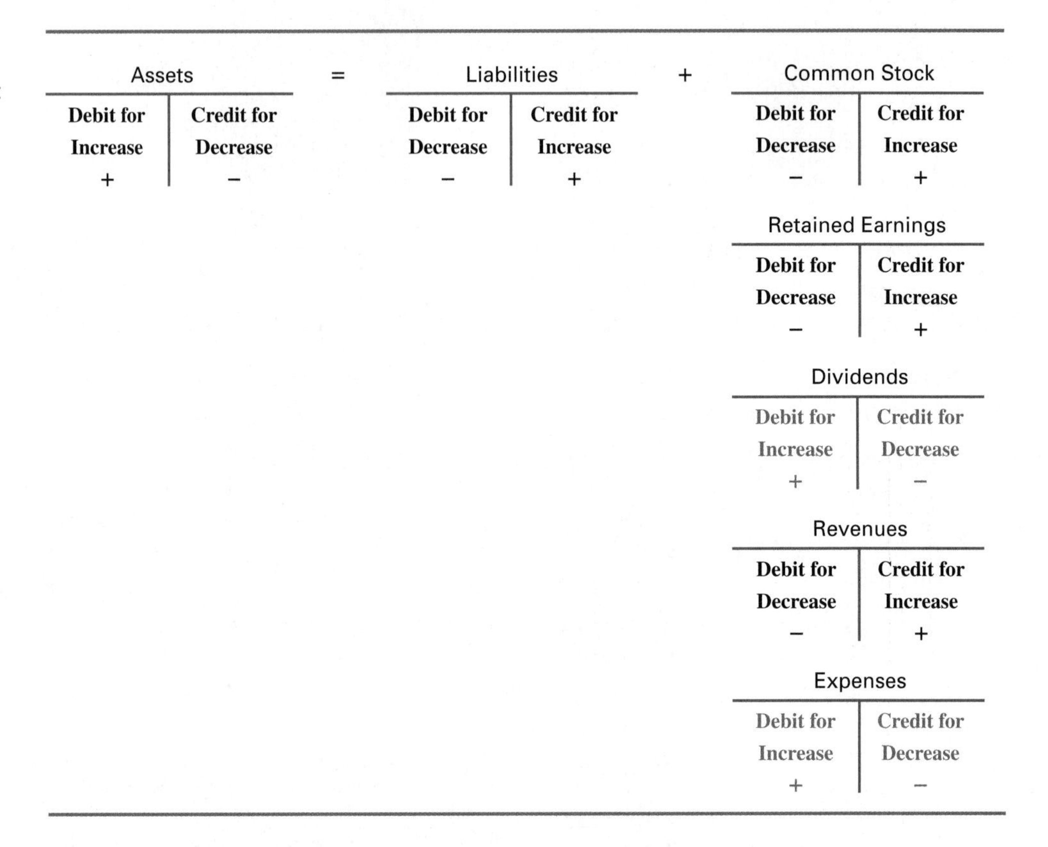

Recording Transactions

journal, ledger

Objective 3 **Record** business transactions

Journal The chronological accounting record of an entity's transactions.

We could record all transactions directly in the T-accounts. However, that does not leave a clear record. For this reason, accountants record transactions first in a **journal**, which is a chronological record. The journalizing process follows five steps:

1. Identify the transaction and specify each account affected by the transaction. Classify each account by type (asset, liability, stockholders' equity, revenue, or expense).
2. Determine whether each account is increased or decreased by the transaction. Use the rules of debit and credit to determine whether to debit or credit the account to record its increase or decrease.
3. Enter the transaction in the journal, including a brief explanation for the entry. The debit side is entered first and the credit side next.

"Enter the transaction in the journal," means to record the transaction in the journal. This step is also called "making the journal entry" or "journalizing the transaction." Let's apply the steps to journalize the first transaction of Air & Sea Travel, Inc.—receiving cash of $50,000 and issuing common stock.

STEP 1 The transaction is a cash receipt for the issuance of stock. Cash and Common Stock are the accounts affected by the transaction. Cash is an asset and Common Stock is stockholders' equity.

STEP 2 Both accounts, Cash and Common Stock, increase by $50,000. Debit Cash to record an increase in this asset account. Credit Common Stock to record an increase in this stockholders' equity account.

STEP 3 Journalize the transaction:

Date	Accounts and Explanation	Debit	Credit
Apr. 2[a]	Cash[b]	50,000[d]	
	Common Stock[c]		50,000[e]
	Issued common stock[f]		

A complete journal entry includes the following elements:

a. Date of the transaction
b. Title of the account debited (placed flush left)
c. Title of the account credited (indented slightly)
d. Dollar amount of the debit (left)
e. Dollar amount of the credit (right)
f. Short explanation of the transaction (not indented)
Note that dollar signs are omitted in the money columns.

When analyzing a transaction, first pinpoint its effects (if any) on cash. Did cash increase or decrease? Typically, it is easiest to identify a transaction's effect on cash. Then identify the effects on other accounts.

In the discussions that follow, we temporarily ignore the date of each transaction to focus on the accounts and their dollar amounts.

Copying Information (Posting) from Journal to Ledger

The journal is a chronological record of all company transactions listed by date of the transaction, but the journal does not indicate how much cash the business has to use. The **ledger** is a grouping of all the accounts; it shows their balances. For example, the balance of the Cash account indicates how much cash the business has. The balance of Accounts Receivable shows the amount due from customers. The balance of Accounts Payable tells how much the business owes suppliers on open account, and so on.

Ledger
The book of a company's accounts and their balances.

In the phrase "keeping the books," *books* refers to the accounts in the ledger. In most accounting systems, the ledger is computerized. Exhibit 2-7 shows how the asset, liability, and stockholders' equity accounts are grouped in the ledger.

Exhibit 2-7

The Ledger (Asset, Liability, and Stockholders' Equity Accounts)

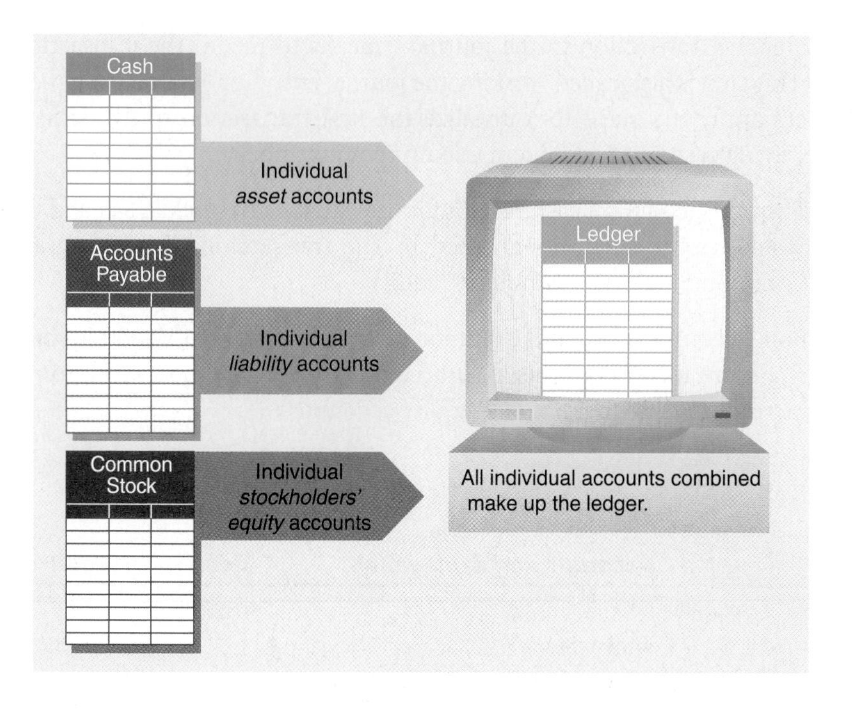

Posting Copying amounts from the journal to the ledger.

Entering a transaction in the journal does not get the data into the ledger accounts. Data must be copied to the ledger—a process called **posting.** Debits in the journal are posted as debits in the accounts, and likewise for credits. Exhibit 2-8 shows how Air & Sea Travel's stock issuance transaction is posted to the accounts.

Exhibit 2-8

Journal Entry and Posting to the Accounts

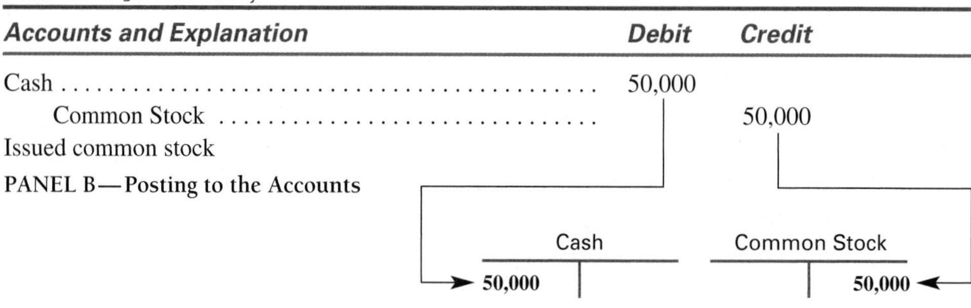

PANEL A—Journal Entry

Accounts and Explanation	*Debit*	*Credit*
Cash	50,000	
Common Stock		50,000
Issued common stock		

PANEL B—Posting to the Accounts

The Flow of Accounting Data: From Theory to Practice

Exhibit 2-9 summarizes the flow of accounting data from the business transaction to the ledger. Let's continue the example of Air & Sea Travel, Inc., and account for the same 11 transactions we illustrated earlier in terms of their effects on the accounting equation, the journal, and the accounts.

Each journal entry posted to the accounts is keyed by date or by transaction number. In this way, any transaction can be traced from the journal to the accounts and, if need be, back to the journal. This linking allows you to locate any information you may need.

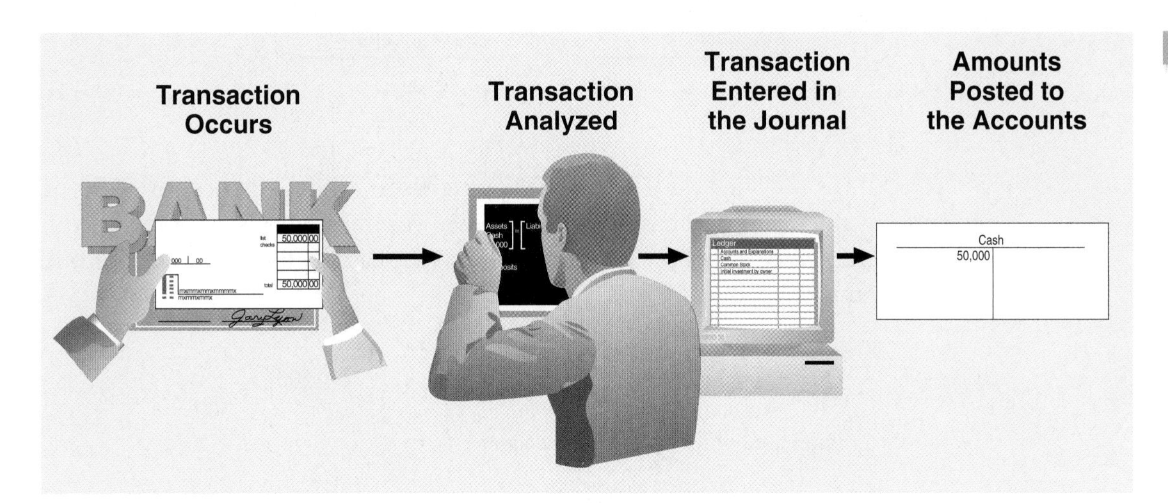

Exhibit 2-9

Flow of Accounting Data

TRANSACTION 1 ANALYSIS. Air & Sea Travel, Inc., received $50,000 cash from the Lyons and in turn issued common stock to them. Air & Sea Travel increased its asset cash; to record this increase, debit Cash. The issuance of stock increased the stockholders' equity of the corporation; to record this increase, credit Common Stock.

Journal entry

	Debit	Credit
Cash	50,000	
Common Stock		50,000
Issued common stock.		

Accounting equation

ASSETS	=	LIABILITIES	+	STOCKHOLDERS' EQUITY
50,000	=	0	+	50,000

The accounts

Cash	
(1) **50,000**	

Common Stock	
	(1) **50,000**

TRANSACTION 2 ANALYSIS. The business paid $40,000 cash for land as a future office location. The purchase decreased cash; therefore, credit Cash. The purchase increased the asset land; to record this increase, debit Land.

Journal entry

	Debit	Credit
Land	40,000	
Cash		40,000
Paid cash for land.		

Accounting equation

ASSETS	=	LIABILITIES	+	STOCKHOLDERS' EQUITY
+40,000	=	0	+	0
−40,000				

The accounts

Cash		Land	
(1) 50,000	(2) 40,000	(2) 40,000	

Transaction 3 Analysis. The business purchased office supplies for $500 on account payable. The purchase increased office supplies, an asset; to record this increase, debit Office Supplies. The purchase also increased a liability; to record this, credit Accounts Payable.

Journal entry

	Debit	Credit
Office Supplies	500	
Accounts Payable		500
Purchased office supplies on account.		

Accounting equation

ASSETS	=	LIABILITIES	+	STOCKHOLDERS' EQUITY
+500	=	+500	+	0

The accounts

Office Supplies		Accounts Payable	
(3) 500			(3) 500

Transaction 4 Analysis. The business performed travel service for clients and received cash of $5,500. The transaction increased the business's cash, so debit Cash. Service revenue was increased. To record an increase in revenue, credit Service Revenue.

Journal entry

	Debit	Credit
Cash	5,500	
Service Revenue		5,500
Performed services for cash.		

Accounting equation

ASSETS	=	LIABILITIES	+	STOCKHOLDERS' EQUITY	+	REVENUES
+5,500	=	0	+		+	5,500

The accounts

Cash		Service Revenue	
(1) 50,000	(2) 40,000		(4) 5,500
(4) 5,500			

Transaction 5 Analysis. The business performed services for clients who did not pay immediately and billed the clients for $3,000 on account. The transaction increased the asset accounts receivable; therefore, debit Accounts Receivable. Service revenue was also increased, so credit Service Revenue.

Journal entry

	Debit	Credit
Accounts Receivable	3,000	
Service Revenue		3,000
Performed services on account.		

Accounting equation

ASSETS	=	LIABILITIES	+	STOCKHOLDERS' EQUITY	+	REVENUES
+3,000	=	0	+		+	3,000

The accounts

Accounts Receivable	
(5) 3,000	

Service Revenue	
	(4) 5,500
	(5) 3,000

TRANSACTION 6 ANALYSIS. The business paid $2,700 for the following expenses: office rent, $1,100; employee salary, $1,200; and utilities, $400. The asset cash is decreased; therefore, credit Cash for the sum of the expense amounts. The following expenses are increased: Rent Expense, Salary Expense, and Utilities Expense. Debit each of these expense accounts.

Journal entry

	Debit	Credit
Rent Expense	1,100	
Salary Expense	1,200	
Utilities Expense	400	
Cash		2,700
Paid expenses.		

Accounting equation

ASSETS	=	LIABILITIES	+	STOCKHOLDERS' EQUITY	−	EXPENSES
−2,700	=	0	+		−	2,700

✔ Check Point 2-3
✔ Check Point 2-4
✔ Check Point 2-5

The accounts

Cash	
(1) 50,000	(2) 40,000
(4) 5,500	(6) 2,700

Rent Expense	
(6) 1,100	

Salary Expense	
(6) 1,200	

Utilities Expense	
(6) 400	

TRANSACTION 7 ANALYSIS. The business paid $400 on the account payable created in Transaction 3. The payment decreased the asset cash; therefore, credit Cash. The payment also decreased a liability; to record this decrease, debit Accounts Payable.

Journal entry

	Debit	Credit
Accounts Payable	400	
Cash		400
Paid cash on account.		

Accounting equation

ASSETS	=	LIABILITIES	+	STOCKHOLDERS' EQUITY
−400	=	−400	+	0

✔ Check Point 2-6

The accounts

Cash	
(1) 50,000	(2) 40,000
(4) 5,500	(6) 2,700
	(7) 400

Accounts Payable	
(7) 400	(3) 500

TRANSACTION 8 ANALYSIS. The Lyons remodeled their personal residence. This is not a transaction of the travel agency, so the business makes no journal entry.

TRANSACTION 9 ANALYSIS. The business collected $1,000 cash on account from the clients in Transaction 5. The receipt of cash increased this asset; debit Cash. The asset accounts receivable decreased; therefore, credit Accounts Receivable.

Journal entry

	Debit	Credit
Cash	1,000	
Accounts Receivable		1,000
Collected cash on account.		

✔ Check Point 2-7

Accounting equation

ASSETS	=	LIABILITIES	+	STOCKHOLDERS' EQUITY
+1,000	=	0	+	0
−1,000				

The accounts

Cash			
(1)	50,000	(2)	40,000
(4)	5,500	(6)	2,700
(9)	1,000	(7)	400

Accounts Receivable			
(5)	3,000	(9)	1,000

TRANSACTION 10 ANALYSIS. The business sold land for its cost of $22,000, receiving cash. The asset cash increased; debit Cash. The asset land decreased; credit Land.

Journal entry

	Debit	Credit
Cash	22,000	
Land		22,000
Sold land.		

Accounting equation

ASSETS	=	LIABILITIES	+	STOCKHOLDERS' EQUITY
+22,000	=	0	+	0
−22,000				

The accounts

Cash			
(1)	50,000	(2)	40,000
(4)	5,500	(6)	2,700
(9)	1,000	(7)	400
(10)	22,000		

Land			
(2)	40,000	(10)	22,000

TRANSACTION 11 ANALYSIS. Air & Sea Travel, Inc., paid the Lyons cash dividends of $2,100. The dividends decreased the entity's cash; therefore, credit Cash. The transaction also decreased stockholders' equity and must be recorded by a debit to a stockholders' equity account. Decreases in a corporation's stockholders' equity that result from distributions to owners are debited to a separate stockholders' equity account titled Dividends. Therefore, debit Dividends.

Journal entry

	Debit	Credit
Dividends	2,100	
Cash		2,100
Declared and paid dividends.		

Accounting equation

ASSETS	=	LIABILITIES	+	STOCKHOLDERS' EQUITY	–	DIVIDENDS
−2,100	=	0	+		–	2,100

The accounts

Cash

	Debit		Credit
(1)	50,000	(2)	40,000
(4)	5,500	(6)	2,700
(9)	1,000	(7)	400
(10)	22,000	(11)	2,100

Dividends

	Debit		Credit
(11)	2,100		

Accounts after Posting

Exhibit 2-10 shows how the accounts look when the preceding transactions have been posted. The exhibit groups the accounts under assets, liabilities, and equity.

Each account has a balance, denoted as Bal., which is the difference between the account's total debits and its total credits. For example, the balance in the Accounts Payable account is the difference between the credit ($500) and the debit ($400). Thus, the Accounts Payable balance is $100. The Cash account has a debit balance of $33,300.

We set an account balance apart from the transaction amounts by a horizontal rule that runs all the way across the account. If the sum of an account's debits is greater than the sum of its credits, that account has a debit balance, as the Cash account does here. If the sum of its credits is greater, that account has a credit balance, as for Accounts Payable.

Exhibit 2-10 Air & Sea Travel's Ledger Accounts after Posting

ASSETS = LIABILITIES + STOCKHOLDERS' EQUITY

ASSETS

Cash

	Debit		Credit
(1)	50,000	(2)	40,000
(4)	5,500	(6)	2,700
(9)	1,000	(7)	400
(10)	22,000	(11)	2,100
Bal.	33,300		

Accounts Receivable

	Debit		Credit
(5)	3,000	(9)	1,000
Bal.	2,000		

Office Supplies

	Debit		Credit
(3)	500		
Bal.	500		

Land

	Debit		Credit
(2)	40,000	(10)	22,000
Bal.	18,000		

LIABILITIES

Accounts Payable

	Debit		Credit
(7)	400	(3)	500
		Bal.	100

STOCKHOLDERS' EQUITY

Common Stock

	Debit		Credit
		(1)	50,000
		Bal.	50,000

Dividends

	Debit		Credit
(11)	2,100		
Bal.	2,100		

REVENUE

Service Revenue

	Debit		Credit
		(4)	5,500
		(5)	3,000
		Bal.	8,500

EXPENSES

Rent Expense

	Debit		Credit
(6)	1,100		
Bal.	1,100		

Salary Expense

	Debit		Credit
(6)	1,200		
Bal.	1,200		

Utilities Expense

	Debit		Credit
(6)	400		
Bal.	400		

The Trial Balance

trial balance

A **trial balance** lists all accounts with their balances—assets first, followed by liabilities and then stockholders' equity. It summarizes all the account balances for the

Objective

4 Use a trial balance

Trial balance
A list of all the ledger accounts with their balances.

financial statements and shows whether total debits equal total credits. A trial balance may be taken at any time, but the most common time is at the end of the period. Exhibit 2-11 is the trial balance of Air & Sea Travel, Inc. after its first 11 transactions have been journalized and posted.

Exhibit 2-11 **Trial Balance**

✔ Check Point 2-8

✔ Check Point 2-9

Air & Sea Travel, Inc.
Trial Balance
April 30, 20X3

	Balance	
Account Title	Debit	Credit
Cash	$33,300	
Accounts receivable	2,000	
Office supplies	500	
Land	18,000	
Accounts payable		$ 100
Common stock		50,000
Dividends	2,100	
Service revenue		8,500
Rent expense	1,100	
Salary expense	1,200	
Utilities expense	400	
Total	$58,600	$58,600

DECISION: Air & Sea Travel Needs a Loan

Suppose you are Monica Lyon, one of the owners. Your accountant is out of town, and the only accounting record available to you is the trial balance. Your banker requests some information. Use the trial balance in Exhibit 2-11 to answer the following questions:

1. How much are Air & Sea Travel's total assets? [*Answer*: $53,800 = $33,300 + $2,000 + $500 + $18,000.]
2. Does the business already have any loans payable to other banks? [*Answer*: No.]
3. How much does the business owe in total? [*Answer*: $100 for accounts payable.]
4. What was the business's net income or net loss for the month of April? [*Answer*: Net income was $5,800 [Revenues of $8,500 − Expenses of $2,700 ($1,100 + $1,200 + $400)].]

Correcting Accounting Errors

Accounting errors can occur even in computerized systems. Input data may be wrong, or they may be entered twice or not at all. A debit may be entered as a credit, and vice versa. You can detect the reason or reasons behind many out-of-balance conditions by computing the difference between total debits and total credits. Then perform one or more of the following actions:

1. Search the records for a missing account. Trace each account back and forth from the journal to the ledger. A $200 transaction may have been recorded incorrectly in the journal or posted incorrectly to the ledger. Search the journal for a $200 transaction.
2. Divide the out-of-balance amount by 2. A debit treated as a credit, or vice versa, doubles the amount of error. Suppose Air & Sea Travel added $300 to Cash instead of subtracting $300. The out-of-balance amount is $600, and dividing by 2 identifies $300 as the amount of the transaction. Search the journal for the $300 transaction and trace to the account affected.
3. Divide the out-of-balance amount by 9. If the result is evenly divisible by 9, the error may be a *slide* (writing $61 as $610) or a *transposition* (treating $61 as $16). Suppose Air & Sea Travel listed the $100 Accounts Payable balance as $1,000. The accounts would be out of balance by $900 ($1,000 − $100 = $900). Dividing $900 by 9 yields $100, the correct amount of the accounts payable. Trace this amount through the journal and then to the Accounts Payable account.

✔ Check Point 2-10

Chart of Accounts

As you know, the ledger contains the business accounts grouped under these headings:

1. **Balance sheet accounts: Assets, Liabilities, and Stockholders' Equity**
2. **Income statement accounts: Revenues and Expenses**

To keep track, organizations have a **chart of accounts,** which lists all accounts and account numbers. Account numbers usually have two or more digits. Assets are often numbered beginning with 1, liabilities with 2, stockholders' equity with 3, revenues with 4, and expenses with 5. The second, third, and higher digits in an account number indicate the position of the individual account within the category. For example, Cash may be account number 101, which is the first asset account. Accounts Payable may be number 201, the first liability account. All accounts are numbered by this system.

Chart of accounts
List of all a company's accounts and their account numbers.

Organizations with many accounts use lengthy account numbers. For example, the chart of accounts of Johnson & Johnson, famous for Band-Aids and other health products, may use five-digit account numbers. The chart of accounts for Air & Sea Travel, Inc. appears in Exhibit 2-12. Notice the gap between the account

Exhibit 2-12

Chart of Accounts—Air & Sea Travel, Inc.

Balance Sheet Accounts

Assets	Liabilities	Stockholders' Equity
101 Cash	201 Accounts Payable	301 Common Stock
111 Accounts Receivable	231 Notes Payable	311 Dividends
141 Office Supplies		312 Retained Earnings
151 Office Furniture		
191 Land		

Income Statement Accounts (Part of Stockholders' Equity)

Revenues	Expenses
401 Service Revenue	501 Rent Expense
	502 Salary Expense
	503 Utilities Expense

numbers 111 and 141. The Lyons realize that at some later date the business may need to add another category of receivables, for example, Notes Receivable, which may be numbered 121.

The appendix to this book gives two expanded charts of accounts that you can find helpful as you work through this course. The first chart lists the typical accounts that a *service* corporation, such as Air & Sea Travel, would have after a period of growth. The second chart is for a *merchandising* corporation, one that sells a product instead of a service.

The Normal Balance of an Account

An account's *normal balance* falls on the side of the account—debit or credit—where increases are recorded (the side that is positive). The normal balance of assets is on the debit side. Assets are called *debit-balance accounts*. Conversely, liabilities and stockholders' equity usually have a credit balance, so their normal balances are on the credit side. They are called *credit-balance accounts*. Exhibit 2-13 illustrates the normal balances of all the assets, liabilities, and stockholders' equities, including revenues and expenses.

Exhibit 2-13

Normal Balances of the Accounts

Assets	Debit	
Liabilities		Credit
Stockholders' Equity—overall		Credit
Common stock		Credit
Retained earnings		Credit
Dividends	Debit	
Revenues		Credit
Expenses	Debit	

✔ Check Point 2-11

As explained earlier, stockholders' equity usually contains several accounts. In total, these accounts show a normal credit balance for the stockholders' equity of the business. But there are exceptions. Dividends and expenses are equity accounts that carry debit balances because they represent decreases in stockholders' equity.

Account Formats

So far we have illustrated accounts in a two-column T-account format, with the debit column on the left and the credit column on the right. Another format has four *amount* columns, as illustrated for the Cash account in Exhibit 2-14. The first pair of amount columns are for the debit and credit amounts. The second pair of amount

Exhibit 2-14

Account in Four-Column Format

Account: Cash **Account No. 101**

				Balance	
Date	Item	Debit	Credit	Debit	Credit
20X3					
Apr. 2		50,000		50,000	
3			40,000	10,000	

columns are for the account balance. This four-column format keeps a running balance in the two right columns.

Quick Decision Making

Objective

5 **Analyze** transactions for quick decisions

Business people must often make decisions without the benefit of a complete accounting system. For example, the managers of PepsiCo may consider buying equipment that costs $100,000. PepsiCo will borrow the money. To see how the borrowing and purchase of the equipment affects the PepsiCo financial position, the manager can analyze the effects of the transactions by going directly to T-accounts, as follows (transaction amounts in color):

Transaction		Cash		Note Payable / Equipment		Note Payable	
Transaction A Borrow $100,000	T-accounts:	(a) 100,000			(a) 100,000		
Transaction B Purchase equipment	T-accounts:	(a) 100,000	(b) 100,000	(b) 100,000			(a) 100,000

(In Transaction A the accounts are Cash and Note Payable; in Transaction B they are Cash, Equipment, and Note Payable.)

This informal analysis shows immediately that PepsiCo will add $100,000 of equipment and a $100,000 note payable to its financial position. By assuming PepsiCo began with zero balances, the equipment and note payable transactions would result in the following balance sheet (date assumed for illustration only):

PepsiCo, Inc
Balance Sheet
September 12, 20X3

Assets		***Liabilities***	
Cash	$ 0	Note payable	$100,000
Equipment	100,000	Total liabilities	100,000
		Stockholders' Equity	**0**
Total assets	$100,000	Total liabilities and stockholders' equity	$100,000

✔ Check Point 2-12

Companies do not actually keep records in this shortcut fashion, but a decision maker who needs information immediately can do this to analyze how the transactions will affect the company.

This chapter covers a lot of material on the processing of accounting information. The Decision Guidelines feature "How to Measure Results of Operations and Financial Position," should help you focus on the essential elements covered in the chapter. The guidelines start with the most fundamental consideration in accounting: Has a transaction occurred? As you work through the guidelines, do not lose sight of your goal. The final guideline zeros in on the financial statements, which are the focal points of the accounting process.

The statements are where the fun begins—the place people go for information to make decisions. As we proceed through this book, we emphasize the use of the information for decision making. The more accounting you learn, the better equipped you are to make decisions in your organization.

Decision Guidelines

Any entrepreneur must determine whether the venture is profitable. To do this, he or she needs to know its results of operations and financial position. If Michael Dell, for example, wanted to know whether the business he had begun from his dorm room at The University of Texas was making money, the Decision Guidelines that follow would help him. They identify some of the questions he needs to ask, and tell him how to get the answers. The guidelines also show how Dell, you, or anyone else would start a business.

HOW TO MEASURE RESULTS OF OPERATIONS AND FINANCIAL POSITION

Decision	Guidelines
Has a transaction occurred?	If the event affects the entity's financial position and can be reliably recorded—Yes. If either condition is absent—No.
Where to record the transaction?	In the *journal*, the chronological record of transactions
How to record an increase or decrease in the following accounts?	Rules of *debit* and *credit*:

	Increase	Decrease
Asset	Debit	Credit
Liability	Credit	Debit
Stockholders' equity	Credit	Debit
Revenue	Credit	Debit
Expense	Debit	Credit

Decision	Guidelines
Where to store all the information for each account?	In the *ledger*, the book of accounts
Where to list all the accounts and their balances?	In the *trial* balance
Where to report the:	
Results of operations?	In the *income* statement (revenues − expenses = net income or net loss)
Financial position?	In the *balance sheet* (assets = liabilities + stockholders' equity)

End-of-Chapter Summary Problem

The trial balance of Calderon Computer Service Center, Inc., on March 1, 20X3, lists the entity's assets, liabilities, and stockholders' equity on that date.

	Balance	
Account Title	*Debit*	*Credit*
Cash	$26,000	
Accounts receivable	4,500	
Accounts payable		$ 2,000
Common stock		10,000
Retained earnings		18,500
Total	$30,500	$30,500

During March, the business completed the following transactions:

a. Borrowed $45,000 from the bank, with Calderon signing a note payable in the name of the business.
b. Paid cash of $40,000 to a real estate company to acquire land.
c. Performed service for a customer and received cash of $5,000.
d. Purchased supplies on credit, $300.
e. Performed customer service and earned revenue on account, $2,600.
f. Paid $1,200 on account.
g. Paid the following cash expenses: salaries, $3,000; rent, $1,500; and interest, $400.
h. Received $3,100 on account.
i. Received a $200 utility bill that will be paid next week.
j. Declared and paid dividend of $1,800.

Required

1. Open the following accounts, with the balances indicated, in the ledger of Calderon Computer Service Center, Inc. Use the T-account format.
   - Assets—Cash, $26,000; Accounts Receivable, $4,500; Supplies, no balance; Land, no balance
   - Liabilities—Accounts Payable, $2,000; Note Payable, no balance
   - Stockholders' Equity—Common Stock, $10,000; Retained Earnings, $18,500; Dividends, no balance
   - Revenues—Service Revenue, no balance
   - Expenses—(none have balances) Salary Expense, Rent Expense, Interest Expense, Utilities Expense
2. Journalize the preceding transactions. Key journal entries by transaction letter.
3. Post to the ledger and show the balance in each account after all the transactions have been posted.
4. Prepare the trial balance of Calderon Computer Service Center, Inc., at March 31, 20X3.
5. To determine the net income or net loss of the entity during the month of March, prepare the income statement for the month ended March 31, 20X3. List expenses in order from the largest to the smallest.
6. Suppose the organizers of Calderon Computer Service Center ask you to invest $5,000 in the company stock. Cite specifics from the income statement and the trial balance to support your decision.

Answers

Requirement 1

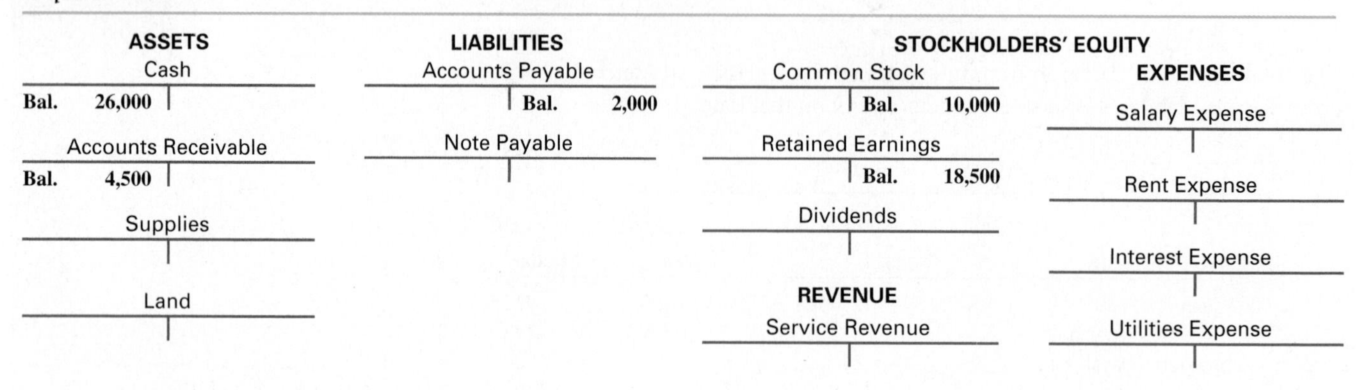

Requirement 2

Accounts and Explanation	Debit	Credit
a. Cash	45,000	
Note Payable		45,000
Borrowed cash on note payable.		
b. Land	40,000	
Cash		40,000
Purchased land for cash.		
c. Cash	5,000	
Service Revenue		5,000
Performed service and received cash.		
d. Supplies	300	
Accounts Payable		300
Purchased supplies on account.		
e. Accounts Receivable	2,600	
Service Revenue		2,600
Performed service on account.		
f. Accounts Payable	1,200	
Cash		1,200
Paid on account.		

Accounts and Explanation	Debit	Credit
g. Salary Expense	3,000	
Rent Expense	1,500	
Interest Expense	400	
Cash		4,900
Paid cash expenses.		
h. Cash	3,100	
Accounts Receivable		3,100
Received on account.		
i. Utilities Expense	200	
Accounts Payable		200
Received utility bill.		
j. Dividends	1,800	
Cash		1,800
Declared and paid dividends.		

Requirement 3

ASSETS

Cash

Bal.	26,000	(b)	40,000
(a)	45,000	(f)	1,200
(c)	5,000	(g)	4,900
(h)	3,100	(j)	1,800
Bal.	31,200		

Accounts Receivable

Bal.	4,500	(h)	3,100
(e)	2,600		
Bal.	4,000		

Supplies

(d)	300		
Bal.	300		

Land

(b)	40,000		
Bal.	40,000		

LIABILITIES

Accounts Payable

(f)	1,200	Bal.	2,000
		(d)	300
		(i)	200
		Bal.	1,300

Note Payable

		(a)	45,000
		Bal.	45,000

STOCKHOLDERS' EQUITY

Common Stock

		Bal.	10,000

Retained Earnings

		Bal.	18,500

Dividends

(j)	1,800		
Bal.	1,800		

REVENUE

Service Revenue

		(c)	5,000
		(e)	2,600
		Bal.	7,600

EXPENSES

Salary Expense

(g)	3,000		
Bal.	3,000		

Rent Expense

(g)	1,500		
Bal.	1,500		

Interest Expense

(g)	400		
Bal.	400		

Utilities Expense

(i)	200		
Bal.	200		

Requirement 4

Calderon Computer Service Center, Inc.

Trial Balance
March 31, 20X3

	Balance	
Account Title	*Debit*	*Credit*
Cash	$31,200	
Accounts receivable	4,000	
Supplies	300	
Land	40,000	
Accounts payable		$ 1,300
Note payable		45,000
Common stock		10,000
Retained earnings		18,500
Dividends	1,800	
Service revenue		7,600
Salary expense	3,000	
Rent expense	1,500	
Interest expense	400	
Utilities expense	200	
Total	$82,400	$82,400

Requirement 5

Calderon Computer Service Center, Inc.

Income Statement
Month Ended March 31, 20X3

Revenue		
Service revenue		$7,600
Expenses		
Salary expense	$3,000	
Rent expense	1,500	
Interest expense	400	
Utilities expense	200	
Total expenses		5,100
Net income		$2,500

Requirement 6

A $5,000 investment in Calderon appears to be warranted because

a. The company earned net income of $2,500, so the business appears profitable.

b. Total assets of $75,500 ($31,200 + $4,000 + $300 + $40,000) far exceed total liabilities of $46,300 ($45,000 + $1,300), which suggests that Calderon can pay its debts and remain in business.

c. Calderon is paying a dividend, so an investment in the stock may yield a quick return in the form of dividends.

Review Processing Accounting Information

Lessons Learned

1. **Analyze business transactions.** A *transaction* is any event that affects the financial position of the business entity and can be reliably recorded. Analyzing business transactions involves determining each transaction's effects on the accounting equation: assets = liabilities + stockholders' equity. The summary of all the transactions over a period forms the basis for the financial statements of a business.
2. **Understand how accounting works.** *Double-entry accounting* is a system that uses debits and credits to record the effects of each business transaction. Every transaction involves both a debit and a credit, and the total amount debited must equal the total amount credited. *Debits* are simply the left side of an account; *credits* are the right side of an account. Assets and expenses are increased by debits and decreased by credits. Liabilities, stockholders' equity, and revenues are increased by credits and decreased by debits.
3. **Record business transactions.** Accountants first record business transactions in a *journal*, a chronological record of the entity's transactions. Each journal entry includes a date, the titles of the accounts debited and credited, the dollar amounts debited and credited, and a short explanation of the transaction. This information is then *posted* (copied) to the *ledger*, a grouping of all the individual accounts and their balances. The balance of each account in the ledger may be taken after all posting is done.
4. **Use a trial balance.** A *trial balance* is a list of all accounts with their balances—assets first, followed by liabilities, stockholders' equity, revenues, and expenses. It shows whether total debits equal total credits. If total debits do not equal total credits, an accounting error has occurred somewhere in journalizing or posting.
5. **Analyze transactions for quick decisions.** Managers must often make decisions without complete accounting results. With some basic accounting knowledge, you can analyze certain situations by going directly to the ledger: compressing transaction analysis, journalizing, and posting into one step.

Accounting Vocabulary

account (p. 56)
accrued liability (p. 57)
cash (p. 56)
chart of accounts (p. 81)
credit (p. 69)
debit (p. 69)
double-entry system (p. 68)
journal (p. 72)
ledger (p. 73)
posting (p. 74)
prepaid expense (p. 56)
transaction (p. 58)
trial balance (p. 80)

Questions

1. Name the basic summary device of accounting. Name its two sides.
2. Is the following statement true or false? "Debit means decrease and credit means increase." Explain your answer.
3. What are the three basic types of accounts? Name two additional types of accounts. To which one of the three basic types are these two additional types of accounts most closely related?
4. What role do transactions play in accounting?
5. Briefly describe the flow of accounting information from the business transaction to the ledger.
6. Label each of the following transactions as increasing stockholders' equity (+), decreasing stockholders' equity (−), or having no effect on stockholders' equity (0). Write the appropriate symbol in the space provided.
   ___ a. Issuance of stock
   ___ b. Revenue transaction
   ___ c. Purchase of supplies on credit
   ___ d. Expense transaction
   ___ e. Cash payment on account
   ___ f. Dividends
   ___ g. Borrowing money on a note payable
   ___ h. Sale of service on account
7. Rearrange the following accounts in their logical sequence in the ledger:

Notes Payable	Cash
Accounts Receivable	Common Stock
Sales Revenue	Salary Expense

8. What is the meaning of the following statement? "Accounts Payable has a credit balance of $1,700."
9. Jack Brown Campus Cleaners launders the shirts of customer Bobby Baylor, who has a charge account at the cleaners. When Bobby picks up his clothes and is short of cash, he asks Jack Brown if he can pay later in the month. Bobby receives his monthly statement from the cleaners, writes a check on Dear Old Dad's bank account, and mails the check to Jack Brown. Identify the two business transactions described here. Which transaction increases Jack Brown's stockholders' equity? Which transaction increases cash?
10. Why do accountants prepare a trial balance?
11. To what does the normal balance of an account refer?
12. Indicate the normal balance of the five types of accounts.

Account Type	Normal Balance
Assets	________
Liabilities	________
Stockholders' equity	________
Revenues	________
Expenses	________

13. The accountant for Bower Construction Company mistakenly recorded a $500 purchase of supplies on account as a $5,000 purchase. He debited Supplies and credited Accounts Payable for $5,000. Does this error cause the trial balance to be out of balance? Explain your answer.
14. What is the effect on total assets of collecting cash on account from customers?
15. What is the advantage of analyzing transactions without the use of a journal? Describe how this "journalless" analysis works.

Assess Your Progress

Check Points

Explaining an asset versus an expense **(Obj. 1)**

CP2-1 Erica Nelson opened a software consulting firm that immediately paid $20,000 for equipment. Was Nelson's payment an expense of the business? If not, what did Nelson acquire?

Analyzing the effects of transactions
(Obj. 1)

CP2-2 Review transactions 4, 5, and 6 of Air & Sea Travel on pages 60 and 61. Suppose Air & Sea Travel is applying for a business loan, and the bank requires the following financial information (after transaction 6 is completed):

a. How much in total assets does the business have?
b. How much cash does the business have?
c. How much cash does the business hope to collect from clients?
d. Thus far, how much net income has the business earned?
e. How much does Air & Sea Travel owe?

Answer these questions.

Analyzing transactions
(Obj. 1)

CP2-3 Mario Portofino, M.D., opened a medical practice in Columbus, Ohio. The business completed the following transactions:

May	1	Portofino invested $22,000 cash to start his medical practice. The business issued stock to Portofino.
	1	Purchased medical supplies on account totaling $9,000.
	2	Paid monthly office rent of $4,000.
	3	Recorded $3,000 revenue for service rendered to patients, received cash of $2,000, and sent bills to patients for the remainder.

After these transactions, how much cash and how much in accounts receivable does the business have to work with? Use T-accounts to show your answer.

Analyzing transactions
(Obj. 1)

CP2-4 Refer to Check Point 2-3. Which of the transactions of Mario Portofino, M.D., increased the total assets of the business? Which transaction decreased total assets? For each transaction, identify the asset that was increased or decreased.

Recording transactions
(Obj. 2, 3)

CP2-5 After operating for several months, attorney Steven Eisenbarth completed the following transactions during the latter part of April:

April	15	Borrowed $20,000 from the bank, signing a note payable.
	22	Performed service for clients on account totaling $4,000.
	28	Received $1,000 cash on account from clients.
	29	Received a utility bill of $200, which will be paid during May.
	30	Paid monthly salary of $3,000 to assistant.
	30	Paid interest expense of $300 on the bank loan.

Journalize the transactions of Steven Eisenbarth, Attorney. Include an explanation with each journal entry.

Journalizing transactions; posting
(Obj. 2, 3)

CP2-6 Architect Lane Stanton purchased supplies on account for $1,500. Two weeks later, Stanton paid $500 on account.

1. Journalize the two transactions on the books of Lane Stanton, Architect. Include an explanation for each transaction.
2. Open a T-account for Accounts Payable and post to Accounts Payable. Compute the balance and denote it as Bal.
3. How much does Stanton's business owe after both transactions? In which account does this amount appear?

CP2-7 Childhood Development Center (The Center) performed legal service for a client who could not pay immediately. The Center expected to collect the $800 the following month. A month later, The Center received $500 cash from the client.

Journalizing transactions; posting **(Obj. 2, 3)**

1. Record the two transactions on the books of Childhood Development Center. Include an explanation for each transaction.
2. Open these T-accounts: Cash, Accounts Receivable, Service Revenue. Post to all three accounts. Compute each account balance and denote as Bal.
3. Answer these questions based on your analysis:
   a. How much did The Center earn? Which account shows this amount?
   b. How much in total assets did The Center acquire as a result of the two transactions? Show the amount of each asset.

CP2-8 Assume that Old Navy, a division of Gap, Inc., reported the following summarized data at December 31, 20X3. Accounts appear in no particular order; dollar amounts are in millions.

Preparing and using a trial balance **(Obj. 4)**

Revenues	$30	Other liabilities	$ 5
Other assets	10	Cash	3
Accounts payable	1	Expenses	26
Stockholders' equity	3		

Prepare the trial balance of Old Navy at December 31, 20X3. List the accounts in their proper order, as on page 80. How much was Old Navy's net income or net loss?

CP2-9 Refer to Air & Sea Travel's trial balance on page 80. Compute these amounts for the business:

Using a trial balance **(Obj. 4)**

1. Total assets
2. Total liabilities
3. Total stockholders' equity
4. Net income or net loss during April

CP2-10 Refer to Air & Sea Travel's trial balance on page 80. The purpose of this check point is to help you learn how to correct three common errors in accounting:

Using a trial balance **(Obj. 4)**

ERROR 1. Slide. Assume the trial balance lists Accounts receivable as $20,000 instead of $2,000. Recompute column totals, take the difference, and divide by 9. You get back to the original amount of Accounts receivable, $2,000.

ERROR 2. Transposition: Assume the trial balance lists Land as $81,000 instead of $18,000. Recompute column totals, take the difference, and divide by 9. The result is an integer (no decimals), which suggests that the error is either a transposition or a slide.

ERROR 3. Mislabelling an item: Assume that Air & Sea Travel accidentally listed Accounts receivable as a credit balance instead of a debit. Recompute the trial balance totals for debits and credits. Then take the difference between total debits and total credits. Finally, divide the difference by 2, and you get back to the original amount of Accounts receivable.

CP2-11 Accounting has its own vocabulary and basic relationships. Match the accounting terms at left with the corresponding definition or meaning at right.

Using key accounting terms **(Obj. 2)**

______	1. Ledger	A. Using up assets in the course of operating a business
______	2. Posting	B. Always a liability
______	3. Normal balance	C. Revenues − expenses
______	4. Payable	D. Grouping of accounts

______	5. Journal	E. Assets − liabilities
______	6. Receivable	F. Record of transactions
______	7. Owners' equity	G. Always an asset
______	8. Debit	H. Left side of an account
______	9. Expense	I. Side of an account where increases are recorded
______	10. Net income	J. Copying data from the journal to the ledger

Analyzing transactions without a journal
(Obj. 5)

CP2-12 First National Bank began by issuing common stock for cash of $500,000. The bank immediately purchased equipment on account for $200,000.

1. Set up the following T-accounts of First National Bank: Cash, Equipment, Accounts Payable, Common Stock.
2. Record the first two transactions of First National Bank directly in the T-accounts without using a journal.
3. Compute the balance in each account and show that total debits equal total credits.

Exercises

Reporting on business activities
(Obj. 1)

E2-1 Assume **Discount Tire Company** has opened a store in Baton Rouge, Louisiana. Starting with cash and stockholders' equity (common stock) of $40,000, Keith Farris, the store manager, borrowed $320,000 by signing a note payable in the name of the store. Prior to opening the store, Farris purchased land for $70,000 and a building for $120,000. He also paid $100,000 for equipment and $40,000 for supplies to use in the business.

Suppose the home office of Discount Tire Company requires a weekly report from store managers. Write Farris's memo to the home office to report on his borrowing and purchases. Include the store's balance sheet as the final part of your memo.

Business transactions and the accounting equation
(Obj. 1)

E2-2 The EuroShop, which specializes in imported clothing, completed a series of transactions. For each of the following items, give an example of a business transaction that has the described effect on the accounting equation of the EuroShop:

a. Increase an asset and increase a liability.
b. Increase one asset and decrease another asset.
c. Decrease an asset and decrease owners' equity.
d. Decrease an asset and decrease a liability.
e. Increase an asset and increase owners' equity.

Transaction analysis
(Obj. 1)

E2-3 The following events were experienced by either **Tetco Oil Company**, a corporation, or Renée Firestone, the major stockholder. State whether each event (1) increased, (2) decreased, or (3) had no effect on the total assets of the business. Identify any specific asset affected.

a. Borrowed $50,000 from the bank.
b. Made cash purchase of land for a building site, $85,000.
c. Received $20,000 cash and issued stock to a stockholder.
d. Paid $60,000 cash on accounts payable.
e. Purchased machinery and equipment for a manufacturing plant, and signed a $100,000 promissory note in payment.
f. Performed service for a customer on account totaling $15,000.
g. The business paid Firestone a cash dividend of $4,000.
h. Received $90,000 cash from customers on accounts receivable.
i. Firestone used personal funds to purchase a swimming pool for her home.
j. Sold land and received cash of $11,000 (the land was carried on the company's books at $11,000.)

Transaction analysis; accounting equation
(Obj. 1)

E2-4 Deborah Austin opens a medical practice specializing in gynecology. During the first month of operation (October), her business, titled Deborah Austin, Professional Corporation (P.C.), experienced the following events:

October	6	Austin invested $35,000 in the business, which in turn issued its common stock to her.
	9	The business paid cash for land costing $15,000. Austin plans to build an office building on the land.
	12	The business purchased medical supplies for $2,000 on account.
	15	Deborah Austin, P.C., officially opened for business.
	15–31	During the rest of the month, Austin treated patients and earned service revenue of $8,000, receiving cash for half the revenue earned.
	15–31	The business paid cash expenses: employee salaries, $1,400; office rent, $1,000; utilities, $300.
	31	The business sold supplies to another physician for cost of $500.
	31	The business borrowed $10,000, signing a note payable to the bank.
	31	The business paid $1,500 on account.

Required

1. Analyze the effects of these events on the accounting equation of the medical practice of Deborah Austin, P.C. Use a format similar to that of Exhibit 2-1, Panel B, with headings for Cash, Accounts Receivable, Medical Supplies, Land, Accounts Payable, Note Payable, Common Stock, and Retained Earnings.
2. After completing the analysis, answer these questions about the business.
   a. How much are total assets?
   b. How much does the business expect to collect from patients?
   c. How much does the business owe in total?
   d. How much net income or net loss did the business experience during its first month of operations?

Journalizing transactions
(Obj. 2, 3)

E2-5 Refer to Exercise 2-4. Record the transactions in the journal of Deborah Austin, P.C. List the transactions by date and give an explanation for each transaction.

Integrator CD
general ledger

Analyzing transactions
(Obj. 1)

E2-6 Pegasus Satellite Communications, Inc., provides satellite TV and Internet services to rural areas of the United States. Assume Pegasus began business in 20X3 by issuing common stock for $100 million and completed the following transactions. The company paid $70 million to purchase satellite and other communication equipment. During the remainder of the year, Pegasus bought supplies and other equipment on account for $60 million. Before year end the company paid $55 million on account. Cash ran low, so Pegasus borrowed $30 million on a note payable. Revenues for the year totaled $20 million, and expenses were $22 million. All revenues were collected in cash, and $21 million of the expenses were paid during the year. Pegasus has a liability for the remaining expenses.

The top managers of the company are evaluating Pegasus at December 31, 20X3, and they wish to know where the company stands financially. They ask you the following questions:

1. What is the company's cash balance?
2. How much does the company owe?
3. What was the net income or net loss for the year?

Journalizing transactions
(Obj. 2, 3)

E2-7 American Learning Systems, Inc. engaged in the following transactions during August 20X6, its first month of operations:

spreadsheet

Aug.	1	Received $18,000 and issued common stock.
	2	Purchased $800 of office supplies on account.
	4	Paid $14,000 cash for land to use as a building site.
	6	Performed service for customers and received cash of $2,000.
	9	Paid $100 on accounts payable.
	17	Performed service for **IBM** on account totaling $1,200.
	23	Received $1,200 cash from IBM on account.
	30	Paid the following expenses: salary, $1,000; rent, $500.

Required

1. Record the preceding transactions in the journal of American Learning Systems, Inc. Key transactions by date and include an explanation for each entry, as illustrated in the chapter.
2. After these transactions, how much cash does American have to work with?
   a. How much does American expect to collect from customers on account?
   b. How much are total liabilities?
   c. Did American have a profit or a loss and how much?

Posting to the ledger and preparing and using a trial balance
(Obj. 3, 4)

E2-8 Refer to Exercise 2-7.

Required

1. After journalizing the transactions of Exercise 2-7, post the entries to the ledger, using a T-account format. Key transactions by date. Date the ending balance of each account August 31.
2. Prepare the trial balance of American Learning Systems, Inc., at August 31, 20X6.
3. How much are total assets, total liabilities, and total stockholders' equity on August 31?

Journalizing transactions
(Obj. 2, 3)

E2-9 The first seven transactions of Martinez Marble Company have been posted to the company's accounts as follows:

Cash

(1)	20,000	(3)	8,000
(2)	7,000	(6)	6,000
(5)	100	(7)	300

Supplies

(4)	600	(5)	100

Equipment

(6)	6,000		

Land

(3)	31,000		

Accounts Payable

(7)	300	(4)	600

Note Payable

		(2)	7,000
		(3)	23,000

Common Stock

		(1)	20,000

Required

Prepare the journal entries that served as the sources for the seven transactions. Include an explanation for each entry. As Martinez moves into the next period, how much cash does the business have? How much does Martinez owe?

Preparing and using a trial balance
(Obj. 4)

E2-10 The accounts of Sunbeam Appliance Service follow with their normal balances at May 31, 20X6. The accounts are listed in no particular order.

spreadsheet

Account	Balance	Account	Balance
Common stock	$48,800	Building	$75,250
Accounts payable	4,300	Dividends	6,000
Service revenue	22,000	Utilities expense	1,400
Land	29,000	Accounts receivable	15,500
Note payable	13,000	Delivery expense	300
Cash	9,000	Retained earnings	?
Salary expense	8,650		

Required

1. Prepare the company's trial balance at May 31, 20X6, listing accounts in proper sequence, as illustrated in the chapter. For example, Supplies comes before Building and Land. List the expense with the largest balance first, the expense with the next largest balance second, and so on.
2. Prepare the financial statement for the month ended May 31, 20X6, that will tell the Sunbeam top managers the results of operations for the month.

E2-11 The trial balance of AAmco Auto Paint, at February 28, 20X3, does not balance:

Correcting errors in a trial balance **(Obj. 4)**

Cash	$ 4,200	
Accounts receivable	13,000	
Inventory	17,400	
Supplies	600	
Land	46,000	
Accounts payable		$ 3,000
Common stock		47,900
Sales revenue		35,700
Salary expense	1,700	
Rent expense	800	
Utilities expense	300	
Total	$84,000	$86,600

The accounting records hold the following errors:

a. Understated Common Stock by $400.
b. Omitted Cost of Goods Sold, an expense of $3,900, from the trial balance.
c. Recorded a $400 cash revenue transaction by debiting Accounts Receivable, with the credit part of the entry correct.
d. Posted a $1,000 credit to Accounts Payable as $100.
e. Did not record utilities expense or the related account payable in the amount of $200.

Required

Prepare the correct trial balance at February 28, complete with a heading. Journal entries are not required.

E2-12 Set up the following T-accounts: Cash, Accounts Receivable, Office Supplies, Office Furniture, Accounts Payable, Common Stock, Dividends, Service Revenue, Salary Expense, and Rent Expense.

Recording transactions without a journal **(Obj. 5)**

general ledger

Record the following transactions directly in the T-accounts without using a journal. Use the letters to identify the transactions.

a. Linda English opened a law firm by investing $8,000 cash and office furniture valued at $12,400. Organized as a professional corporation, the business issued common stock to English.

b. Paid monthly rent of $1,500.
c. Purchased office supplies on account, $800.
d. Paid employees' salaries of $1,800.
e. Paid $400 of the account payable created in Transaction c.
f. Performed legal service on account, $1,700.
g. Declared and paid dividends of $2,000.

Preparing and using a trial balance
(Obj. 4)

E2-13 Refer to Exercise 2-12.

1. After recording the transactions in Exercise 2-12, prepare the trial balance of Linda English, Attorney, at July 31, 20X8.
2. How well did the business perform during its first month? Give the basis for your answer.

Serial Exercise

Exercise 2-14 begins an accounting cycle that is completed in Chapter 3.

Recording transactions and preparing a trial balance
(Obj. 2, 3, 4)

general ledger

E2-14 Sandy Lloyd, Certified Public Accountant, Professional Corporation (P.C.), completed these transactions during the first part of December:

Dec.	2	Received $7,000 cash from Lloyd, and issued common stock to her.
	2	Paid monthly office rent, $500.
	3	Paid cash for a Dell computer, $3,000, with the computer expected to remain in service for 5 years.
	4	Purchased office furniture on account, $3,600, with the furniture projected to last for 5 years.
	5	Purchased supplies on account, $300.
	9	Performed tax service for a client and received cash for the full amount of $800.
	12	Paid utility expenses, $200.
	18	Performed consulting service for a client on account, $1,700.

Required

1. Set up T-accounts for Cash, Accounts Receivable, Supplies, Equipment, Furniture, Accounts Payable, Common Stock, Dividends, Service Revenue, Rent Expense, Utilities Expense, and Salary Expense.
2. Journalize the transactions. Explanations are not required.
3. Post to the T-accounts. Key all items by date and denote an account balance on December 18 as Bal.
4. Prepare a trial balance at December 18. In the Serial Exercise of Chapter 3, we add transactions for the remainder of December and will require a trial balance at December 31.

Challenge Exercises

Computing financial statement amounts
(Obj. 5)

E2-15 The owner of Biznet Internet Service is an engineer with little understanding of accounting. He needs to compute the following summary information from the accounting records:

a. Net income for the month of March
b. Total cash paid during March
c. Cash collections from customers during March
d. Cash paid on a note payable during March

The quickest way to compute these amounts is to analyze the following accounts:

Account	Balance Feb. 28	Balance Mar. 31	Additional Information for the Month of March
1. Retained Earnings	$ 6,200	$10,500	Dividends, $15,800
2. Cash	4,600	5,400	Cash receipts, $81,200
3. Accounts Receivable	24,300	26,700	Sales on account, $60,500
4. Note Payable	13,900	21,400	New borrowing, $16,300

The net income for March can be computed as follows:

RETAINED EARNINGS

March dividends	**15,800**	**Feb. 28 Bal.**	**6,200**
		March net income	x **= $20,100**
		March 31	**Bal. 10,500**

Use a similar approach to compute the other three items.

E2-16 The trial balance of Road Runner, Inc., at December 31, 20X5, does not balance.

Analyzing transactions; using a trial balance
(Obj. 1, 4)

Cash	$ 4,200	Common stock	$25,000
Accounts receivable	2,200	Retained earnings	7,300
Supplies	800	Service revenue	9,100
Land	39,000	Salary expense	3,400
Accounts payable	5,800	Advertising expense	900
Note payable	5,000		

Required

1. How much out of balance is the trial balance? Determine the out-of-balance amount. The error lies in the Accounts Receivable account. Add the out-of-balance amount to, or subtract it from, Accounts Receivable to determine the correct balance of Accounts Receivable.
2. Road Runner also failed to record the following transactions during December:
   a. Purchased additional land for $80,000 by signing a note payable.
   b. Earned service revenue on account, $7,000.
   c. Paid salary expense of $400.
   d. Purchased a television advertisement for $2,000. This account will be paid during January.

   Add these amounts to, or subtract them from, the appropriate accounts to properly include the effects of these transactions. Then prepare the corrected trial balance of Road Runner, Inc.
3. After correcting the accounts, advise the top management of Road Runner, Inc. on (a) the amount of the company's total assets and (b) whether the business was profitable during December.

E2-17 This question concerns the items and the amounts that two entities, City of Denver (Denver), and Hillcrest Health Maintenance Organization, Inc. (Hillcrest) should report in their financial statements. During June, Hillcrest provided City of Denver with medical exams for Denver employees and sent a bill for $10,000. On July 7 Denver sent a check to Hillcrest for $8,000. Denver began June with a cash balance of $15,000; Hillcrest began with cash of $0.

Analyzing transactions
(Obj. 1)

Required

For this situation, show everything that both Denver and Hillcrest will report on their June and July income statements and on their balance sheets at June 30 and July 31. Use the following format for your answer:

Denver		
Income statement	June	July
Balance sheet	June 30	July 31
Hillcrest		
Income statement	June	July
Balance sheet	June 30	July 31

After showing what each company should report, briefly explain how the Denver and the Hillcrest data relate to each other. Be specific.

Problems

(Group A)

Analyzing a trial balance
(Obj. 1)

P2-1A The owners of Mach-1, Inc., a credit-counseling service, are selling the business. They offer the following trial balance to prospective buyers:

Mach-1, Inc.
Trial Balance
December 31, 20X6

Cash	$ 16,000	
Accounts receivable	11,000	
Prepaid expenses	4,000	
Equipment	171,000	
Building	100,000	
Accounts payable		$ 31,000
Note payable		120,000
Common stock		103,000
Retained earnings		40,000
Dividends	21,000	
Service revenue		86,000
Rent expense	14,000	
Advertising expense	3,000	
Wage expense	33,000	
Supplies expense	7,000	
	$380,000	$380,000

Clay Cornelius, your best friend, is considering buying Mach-1, Inc. He seeks your advice in interpreting this information. Specifically, he asks whether this trial balance is the same as a balance sheet and an income statement. He also wonders whether Mach-1, Inc. is a sound company. After all, the accounts are in balance.

Required

Write a short note to answer Cornelius's questions. To aid his decision, state how he can use the information on the trial balance to compute the Mach-1 net income or net loss for the current period. State the amount of net income or net loss in your note.

Analyzing transactions with the accounting equation and preparing the financial statements
(Obj. 1)

P2-2A Dudley Haas operates and is the major stockholder of an interior design studio called Haas Interiors, Inc. The following amounts summarize the financial position of the business on August 31, 20X8:

	ASSETS				=	LIABILITIES	+	STOCKHOLDERS' EQUITY	
		Accounts				Accounts		Common	Retained
	Cash +	Receivable +	Supplies +	Land	=	Payable	+	Stock +	Earnings
Bal.	1,250	1,500		12,000		8,000		4,000	2,750

During September 20X8, the business completed these transactions:

a. Haas inherited $9,000 and deposited the cash in the business bank account. The business issued common stock to Haas.
b. Performed services for a client and received cash of $6,700.
c. Paid $5,000 on accounts payable.
d. Purchased supplies on account, $1,000.
e. Collected cash from a customer on account, $500.
f. Received cash of $1,000 and issued common stock to Haas.
g. Consulted on the interior design of a major office building and billed the client for services rendered, $2,400.
h. Recorded the following business expenses for the month: (1) paid office rent—$900; (2) paid advertising—$300.
i. Declared and paid a cash dividend of $1,800.

Required

1. Analyze the effects of the preceding transactions on the accounting equation of Haas Interiors, Inc. Adapt the format of Exhibit 2-1, Panel B.
2. Prepare the income statement of Haas Interiors, Inc., for the month ended September 30, 20X8. List expenses in decreasing order by amount.
3. Prepare the entity's statement of retained earnings for the month ended September 30, 20X8.
4. Prepare the balance sheet of Haas Interiors, Inc., at September 30, 20X8.

Recording transactions, posting
(Obj. 2, 3)

Integrator CD

general ledger

P2-3A This problem should be used only in conjunction with Problem 2-2A. Refer to Problem 2-2A.

Required

1. Journalize the transactions of Haas Interiors, Inc. Explanations are not required.
2. Set up the following T-accounts: Cash, Accounts Receivable, Supplies, Land, Accounts Payable, Common Stock, Retained Earnings, Dividends, Service Revenue, Rent Expense, and Advertising Expense. Insert in each account its balance as given (example: Cash $1,250). Post the transactions to the accounts.
3. Compute the balance in each account. For each asset account, each liability account, and for Common Stock, compare its balance to the ending balance you obtained in Problem 2-2A. Are the amounts the same or different? (In Chapter 3, we complete the accounting process. There you will learn how the Retained Earnings, Dividends, Revenue, and Expense accounts work together in the processing of accounting information.)

Analyzing transactions with the accounting equation
(Obj. 1, 2)

P2-4A Don Gerbing practiced law with a large firm, a partnership, for 5 years after graduating from law school. Recently, he resigned his position to open his own law office, which he operates as a professional corporation. The name of the new entity is Don Gerbing, Attorney, Professional Corporation (P.C.). Gerbing experienced the following events during the organizing phase of his new business and its first month of operations. Some of the events were personal and did not affect his law practice. Others were business transactions and should be accounted for by the business.

Feb. 4	Gerbing received $65,000 cash from his former partners in the law firm from which he resigned.
5	Gerbing deposited $22,000 cash in a new business bank account titled Don Gerbing, Attorney, P.C. The business issued common stock to Gerbing.
6	The business paid $300 cash for letterhead stationery for the new law office.
7	The business purchased office furniture. The company paid cash of $10,000 and agreed to pay the account payable for the remainder, $7,000, within 6 months.
10	Gerbing sold IBM stock, which he had owned for several years, receiving $75,000 cash from his stockbroker.
11	Gerbing deposited the $75,000 cash from sale of the IBM stock in his personal bank account.
12	A representative of a large company telephoned Gerbing and told him of the company's intention to transfer its legal business to Gerbing.
18	Gerbing finished court hearings on behalf of a client and submitted his bill for legal services, $4,000. Gerbing expected to collect from this client within 2 weeks.
21	The business paid half its account payable for the furniture purchased on February 7.
25	The business paid office rent of $1,000.
28	The business declared and paid a cash dividend of $2,000.

Required

1. Classify each of the preceding events as one of the following:
   a. A business transaction to be recorded by the business of Don Gerbing, Attorney, P.C.
   b. A business-related event but not a transaction to be recorded by the business of Don Gerbing, Attorney, P.C.
   c. A personal transaction not to be recorded by the business of Don Gerbing, Attorney, P.C.

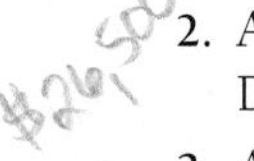

2. Analyze the effects of the preceding events on the accounting equation of the business of Don Gerbing, Attorney, P.C. Use a format similar to that in Exhibit 2-1, Panel B.
3. At the end of the first month of operations, Gerbing has a number of questions about the financial standing of the business. Explain to him
   a. How the business can have more cash than retained earnings.
   b. How much in total resources the business has, how much it owes, and what Gerbing's ownership interest is in the assets of the business.
4. Record the transactions of the business in its journal. Include an explanation for each entry.

Analyzing and recording transactions
(Obj. 2, 3)

general ledger

P2-5A Patricia Libby practices medicine under the business title Patricia Libby, M.D., Professional Corporation (P.C.). During May, Libby's medical practice completed the following transactions:

May 1	Libby deposited $9,000 cash in the business bank account. The business issued common stock to her.
5	Paid monthly rent on medical equipment, $700.
9	Paid $1,000 cash and signed a $25,000 note payable to purchase land for an office site.
10	Purchased supplies on account, $1,200.
19	Paid $1,000 on account.

May 22	Borrowed $20,000 from the bank for business use. Libby signed a note payable to the bank in the name of the business.
31	Revenues earned during the month included $6,000 cash and $5,000 on account.
31	Paid employees' salaries ($2,400), office rent ($1,500), and utilities ($400).
31	Declared and paid a cash dividend of $4,000.

Libby's business uses the following accounts: Cash, Accounts Receivable, Supplies, Land, Accounts Payable, Notes Payable, Common Stock, Dividends, Service Revenue, Salary Expense, Rent Expense, and Utilities Expense.

Required

1. Journalize each transaction of Patricia Libby, M.D., P.C. Explanations are not required.
2. After these transactions, how much cash does the business have? How much in total does it owe?

Journalizing transactions, posting, and preparing and using a trial balance
(Obj. 2, 3, 4)

general ledger

P2-6A Pat O'Dell opened a law office on January 2 of the current year. During the first month of operations, the business completed the following transactions:

Jan. 2	O'Dell deposited $33,000 cash in the business bank account Pat O'Dell, Attorney, Professional Corporation (P.C.). The corporation issued common stock to O'Dell.
3	Purchased supplies, $500, and furniture, $2,600, on account.
4	Performed legal service for a client and received cash, $1,500.
7	Paid cash to acquire land for an office site, $22,000.
11	Defended a client in court and billed the client $800.
16	Paid for the furniture purchased January 3 on account.
17	Paid the telephone bill, $110.
18	Received partial payment from client on account, $400.
22	Paid the water and electricity bills, $130.
29	Received $1,800 cash for helping a client sell real estate.
31	Paid secretary's salary, $1,300.
31	Declared and paid dividends of $2,200.

Required

Set up the following T-accounts: Cash, Accounts Receivable, Supplies, Furniture, Land, Accounts Payable, Common Stock, Dividends, Service Revenue, Salary Expense, and Utilities Expense.

1. Record each transaction in the journal, using the account titles given. Key each transaction by date. Explanations are not required.
2. Post the transactions to the T-accounts, using transaction dates as posting references. Label the ending balance of each account Bal., as shown in the chapter.
3. Prepare the trial balance of Pat O'Dell, Attorney, P.C., at January 31 of the current year.
4. O'Dell asks you how much in total resources the business has to work with, how much it owes, and whether January was profitable (and by how much).

Recording transactions directly in T-accounts; preparing and using a trial balance
(Obj. 3, 4)

P2-7A Betty Doss obtained a corporate charter from the state of Michigan and started CableVision, Inc. During the first month of operations (January 20X7), the business completed the following selected transactions:

general ledger

a. Doss began the business with an investment of $10,000 cash and a building valued at $50,000. The corporation issued common stock to Doss.
b. Borrowed $20,000 from the bank; signed a note payable.
c. Paid $22,000 for transmitting equipment.
d. Purchased office supplies on account, $400.
e. Paid employees' salaries, $1,300.
f. Received $500 for cable TV service performed for customers.
g. Sold cable service to customers on account, $1,800.
h. Paid $100 of the account payable created in Transaction d.
i. Received a $600 bill for utility expense that will be paid in the near future.
j. Received cash on account, $1,100.
k. Paid the following cash expenses: (1) rent on land, $1,000; (2) advertising, $800.
l. Declared and paid dividends of $2,600.

Required

1. Set up the following T-accounts: Cash, Accounts Receivable, Office Supplies, Transmitting Equipment, Building, Accounts Payable, Note Payable, Common Stock, Dividends, Service Revenue, Salary Expense, Rent Expense, Advertising Expense, and Utilities Expense.
2. Record the foregoing transactions directly in the T-accounts without using a journal. Use the letters to identify the transactions.
3. Prepare the trial balance of CableVision, Inc., at January 31, 20X7.
4. Doss is afraid total liabilities of the business exceed total assets. She also fears that the business suffered a net loss during January. Compute the amounts needed to answer her questions.

(Group B)

Analyzing a trial balance
(Obj. 1)

P2-1B The owners of Salon Adeva, Inc. a small chain of hair-design salons, are selling the business. They offer the following trial balance to prospective buyers.

Your best friend is considering buying Salon Adeva. She seeks your advice in interpreting this information. Specifically, she asks whether this trial balance is the same as a balance sheet and an income statement. She also wonders whether Salon Adeva is a sound company. After all, the accounts are in balance.

Salon Adeva, Inc.
Trial Balance
December 31, 20X5

Account	Debit	Credit
Cash	$ 12,000	
Accounts receivable	47,000	
Prepaid expenses	4,000	
Equipment	231,000	
Accounts payable		$105,000
Note payable		92,000
Common stock		30,000
Retained earnings		50,000
Dividends	18,000	
Service revenue		134,000
Salary expense	63,000	
Rent expense	26,000	
Supplies expense	7,000	
Advertising expense	3,000	
	$411,000	$411,000

Required

Write a memo to answer your friend's questions. To aid her decision, state how she can use the information on the trial balance to compute the Salon Adeva net income or net loss for the current period. State the amount of net income or net loss in your note.

P2-2B Lisa Lane operates and is the major stockholder of an interior design studio called Lane Designers, Inc. The following amounts summarize the financial position of the business on April 30, 20X5:

Analyzing transactions with the accounting equation and preparing the financial statements
(Obj. 1)

	ASSETS							=	LIABILITIES	+	STOCKHOLDERS' EQUITY		
			Accounts						Accounts		Common		Retained
	Cash	+	Receivable	+	Supplies	+	Land	=	Payable	+	Stock	+	Earnings
Bal.	1,720		2,240				24,100		5,400		10,000		12,660

During May 20X5, the business completed these transactions:

a. Lane received $42,000 as a gift and deposited the cash in the business bank account. The business issued common stock to Lane.
b. Paid $1,400 on accounts payable.
c. Performed services for a client and received cash of $4,100.
d. Collected cash from a customer on account, $750.
e. Purchased supplies on account, $720.
f. Consulted on the interior design of a major office building and billed the client for services rendered, $5,000.
g. Received cash of $1,700 and issued common stock to Lane.
h. Recorded the following expenses for the month: (1) paid office rent—$1,200; (2) paid advertising—$660.
i. Declared and paid a cash dividend of $2,400.

Required

1. Analyze the effects of the preceding transactions on the accounting equation of Lane Designers, Inc. Adapt the format of Exhibit 2-1, Panel B.
2. Prepare the income statement of Lane Designers, Inc., for the month ended May 31, 20X5. List expenses in decreasing order by amount.
3. Prepare the statement of retained earnings of Lane Designers, Inc., for the month ended May 31, 20X5.
4. Prepare the balance sheet of Lane Designers, Inc., at May 31, 20X5.

P2-3B This problem should be used only in conjunction with Problem 2-2B. Refer to Problem 2-2B.

Recording transactions, posting
(Obj. 2,3)

general ledger

Required

1. Journalize the transactions of Lane Designers, Inc. Explanations are not required.
2. Set up the following T-accounts: Cash, Accounts Receivable, Supplies, Land, Accounts Payable, Common Stock, Retained Earnings, Dividends, Service Revenue, Rent Expense, and Advertising Expense. Insert in each account its balance as given (example: Cash $1,720). Post to the accounts.
3. Compute the balance in each account. For each asset account, each liability account, and for Common Stock, compare its balance to the ending balance you obtained in Problem 2-2B. Are the amounts the same or different? (In Chapter 3, we complete the accounting process. There you will learn how the Retained Earnings, Dividends, Revenue, and Expense accounts work together in the processing of accounting information.)

Analyzing transactions with the accounting equation
(Obj. 1, 2)

general ledger

P2-4B Charles Ming practiced law with a large firm, a partnership, for 10 years after graduating from law school. Recently, he resigned his position to open his own law office, which he operates as a professional corporation. The name of the new entity is Charles Ming, Attorney and Counselor, Professional Corporation (P.C.). Ming experienced the following events during the organizing phase of his new business and its first month of operations. Some of the events were personal and did not affect the law practice. Others were business transactions and should be accounted for by the business.

July 1	Ming sold 1,000 shares of **Eastman Kodak** stock, which he had owned for several years, and received $88,000 cash from his stockbroker.
2	Ming deposited in his personal bank account the $88,000 cash from sale of the Eastman Kodak stock.
3	Ming received $150,000 cash from his former partners in the law firm from which he resigned.
5	Ming deposited $30,000 cash in a new business bank account titled Charles Ming, Attorney and Counselor, P.C. The business issued common stock to Ming.
6	A representative of a large company telephoned Ming and told him of the company's intention to transfer its legal business to the new entity of Charles Ming, Attorney and Counselor, P.C.
7	The business paid $550 cash for letterhead stationery for the law office.
9	The business purchased office furniture. Ming paid cash of $10,000 and agreed to pay the account payable for the remainder, $9,500, within 3 months.
23	Ming finished court hearings on behalf of a client and submitted his bill for legal services, $3,000. He expected to collect from this client within 1 month.
29	The business paid $5,000 of its account payable on the furniture purchased on July 9.
30	The business paid office rent of $1,900.
31	The business declared and paid a cash dividend of $500.

Required

1. Classify each of the preceding events as one of the following:
   a. A business transaction to be recorded by the business of Charles Ming, Attorney and Counselor, P.C.
   b. A business-related event but not a transaction to be recorded by the business of Charles Ming, Attorney and Counselor, P.C.
   c. A personal transaction not to be recorded by the business of Charles Ming, Attorney and Counselor, P.C.
2. Analyze the effects of the preceding events on the accounting equation of the business of Charles Ming, Attorney and Counselor, P.C. Use a format similar to Exhibit 2-1, Panel B.
3. At the end of the first month of operations, Ming has a number of questions about the financial standing of the business. Explain the following to him:
   a. How the business can have more cash than retained earnings.
   b. How much in total resources the business has, how much it owes, and what Ming's ownership interest is in the assets of the business.
4. Record the transactions of the business in its journal. Include an explanation for each entry.

Analyzing and recording transactions
(Obj. 2, 3)

P2-5B Schwartz, Inc. owns movie theaters in the shopping malls of a major metropolitan area. The business completed the following transactions:

Integrator CD
general ledger

Feb.	1	Received cash of $30,000 and issued common stock to the investor.
	2	Paid $20,000 cash and signed a $30,000 note payable to purchase land for a theater site.
	5	Borrowed $100,000 from the bank to finance part of the construction of the new theater and signed a note payable to the bank.
	7	Received $15,000 cash from ticket sales and deposited that amount in the bank (labeling the revenue as Sales Revenue).
	10	Purchased theater supplies on account, $1,700.
	15	Paid employees' salaries, $2,800, and rent on a theater building, $1,800.
	15	Paid property tax expense, $1,200.
	16	Paid $800 on account.
	17	Declared and paid a cash dividend of $3,000.

Schwartz, Inc. uses the following accounts: Cash, Supplies, Land, Accounts Payable, Notes Payable, Common Stock, Dividends, Sales Revenue, Salary Expense, Rent Expense, and Property Tax Expense.

Required

1. Journalize each transaction. Explanations are not required.
2. After these transactions, how much cash does the business have? How much does it owe in total?

P2-6B Tomás Lopez opened a law office on September 3 of the current year. During the first month of operations, the business completed the following transactions:

Journalizing transactions, posting, and preparing and using a trial balance **(Obj. 2, 3, 4)**

general ledger

Sept.	3	Transferred $25,000 cash from the Lopez personal bank account to a business account titled Tomás Lopez, Attorney, Professional Corporation (P.C.). The corporation issued common stock to Lopez.
	4	Purchased supplies, $200, and furniture, $1,800, on account.
	6	Performed legal services for a client and received $1,000 cash.
	7	Paid $15,000 cash to acquire land for an office site.
	10	Defended a client in court, billed the client, and received his promise to pay the $600 within 1 week.
	14	Paid for the furniture purchased September 4 on account.
	16	Paid the telephone bill, $120.
	17	Received partial payment from client on account, $500.
	24	Paid the water and electricity bills, $110.
	28	Received $1,500 cash for helping a client sell real estate.
	30	Paid secretary's salary, $1,200.
	30	Declared and paid dividends of $2,400.

Required

Set up the following T-accounts: Cash, Accounts Receivable, Supplies, Furniture, Land, Accounts Payable, Common Stock, Dividends, Service Revenue, Salary Expense, and Utilities Expense.

1. Record each transaction in the journal, using the account titles given. Key each transaction by date. Explanations are not required.
2. Post the transactions to the T-accounts, using transaction dates as posting references. Label the ending balance of each account Bal., as shown in the chapter.
3. Prepare the trial balance of Tomás Lopez, Attorney, P.C., at September 30 of the current year.
4. Lopez asks you how much in total resources the business has to work with, how much it owes, and whether September was profitable (and by how much).

Recording transactions directly in T-accounts; preparing and using a trial balance
(Obj. 3, 4)

general ledger

P2-7B Britt Hendrix obtained a corporate charter from the state of Connecticut and started a computer graphics firm. During the first month of operations (June 20X3), the business completed the following selected transactions:

a. Began the business with an investment of $11,000 cash and a building valued at $60,000. The corporation issued common stock to Hendrix.
b. Borrowed $90,000 from the bank; signed a note payable.
c. Purchased office supplies on account for $1,300.
d. Paid $88,000 for computer equipment.
e. Paid employees' salaries totaling $2,200.
f. Performed computer graphic service on account for a client, $2,100.
g. Paid $800 of the account payable created in Transaction c.
h. Received a $600 bill for advertising expense that will be paid in the near future.
i. Performed service for clients and received $1,100 in cash.
j. Received $1,200 cash on account.
k. Paid the following cash expenses: (1) rent on land, $700; (2) utilities, $400.
l. Declared and paid dividends of $500.

Required

1. Set up the following T-accounts: Cash, Accounts Receivable, Office Supplies, Computer Equipment, Building, Accounts Payable, Note Payable, Common Stock, Dividends, Service Revenue, Salary Expense, Advertising Expense, Rent Expense, and Utilities Expense.
2. Record each transaction directly in the T-accounts without using a journal. Use the letters to identify the transactions.
3. Prepare the trial balance of Hendrix Computer Graphics Service, Inc., at June 30, 20X3.
4. Hendrix is afraid the business's total liabilities exceed its total assets. He also fears that the business suffered a net loss during June. Compute the amounts needed to answer his questions.

Decision Cases

Recording transactions directly in T-accounts, preparing a trial balance, and measuring net income or loss
(Obj. 4, 5)

Case 1. You have been requested by a friend named Dirk Khoury to give advice on the effects that certain business transactions will have on the entity he has started. Time is short, so you will not be able to do all the detailed procedures of journalizing and posting. Instead, you must analyze the transactions without the use of a journal. Khoury will continue the business only if it can be expected to earn monthly net income of $5,000. The following transactions have occurred this month:

a. Khoury deposited $10,000 cash in a business bank account, and the corporation issued common stock to Khoury.
b. Borrowed $4,000 cash from the bank and signed a note payable due within 1 year.
c. Paid $300 cash for supplies.
d. Purchased advertising in the local newspaper for cash, $800.
e. Purchased office furniture on account, $4,400.
f. Paid the following cash expenses for 1 month: secretary's salary, $1,750; office rent, $600.
g. Earned revenue on account, $7,650.
h. Earned revenue and received $2,500 cash.
i. Collected cash from customers on account, $1,200.
j. Paid on account, $1,000.
k. Declared and paid dividends of $900.

Required

1. Set up the following T-accounts: Cash, Accounts Receivable, Supplies, Furniture, Accounts Payable, Notes Payable, Common Stock, Dividends, Service Revenue, Salary Expense, Advertising Expense, and Rent Expense.
2. Record the transactions directly in the accounts without using a journal. Key each transaction by letter.
3. Prepare a trial balance at the current date. List expenses with the largest amount first, the next largest amount second, and so on. The business name will be Khoury Furniture Finishing, Inc.
4. Compute the amount of net income or net loss for this first month of operations. Why or why not would you recommend that Khoury continue in business?

Correcting financial statements; deciding whether to expand a business **(Obj. 2)**

Case 2. Ming Fu opened a Chinese restaurant in Toledo, Ohio. Business has been good, and Ming Fu is considering doubling the size of the restaurant. A cousin, Lei Ma, has been doing the accounting for the restaurant, and Lei Ma has produced the following financial statements at December 31, 20X5, end of the first year of operations:

Ming Fu's Fine Foods, Inc.
Income Statement
Year Ended December 31, 20X5

Sales revenue	$50,000
Common stock	38,000
Total revenue	88,000
Accounts payable	8,000
Advertising expense	5,000
Rent expense	6,000
Total expenses	19,000
Net income	$69,000

Ming Fu's Fine Foods, Inc.
Balance Sheet
December 31, 20X5

Assets	
Cash	$14,000
Cost of goods sold (expense)	19,000
Food inventory	5,000
Furniture	47,000
Total assets	$85,000
Liabilities	
None	
Owners' Equity	$85,000

In these financial statements all *amounts* are correct, except for Owners' Equity. Lei Ma heard that total assets should equal total liabilities plus owners' equity, so he plugged the amount of owners' equity at $85,000 to make the balance sheet come out even.

Required

Ming Fu has asked whether she should double the size of the restaurant. Her banker tells her to expand if (a) net income for the year reached $50,000 and (b) total assets are at least $75,000. It appears that the business has reached these milestones, but Ming Fu has a nagging doubt about Lei Ma's understanding of accounting. She needs your help in making this decision. Prepare a corrected income statement and balance sheet. (Remember that Retained Earnings, which Lei Ma omitted, should equal net income for the first year; there were no dividends). After preparing the statements, give Ming Fu your recommendation.

Ethical Issues

Issue 1. Blaine McCormick is the president and principal stockholder of McCormick's Restaurant, Inc. During 20X4, the company earned total revenue of $800,000 and incurred expenses of $450,000. The resulting net income is $350,000, which is quite good. To expand, the business is applying for a $250,000 bank loan, and the bank requires the company to have owners' equity of at least as much as the loan. The present balance sheet of McCormick's

Restaurant, Inc. reports total assets of $300,000 and liabilities of $200,000. To get the loan, McCormick is considering two options for beefing up the owners' equity of the business:

OPTION 1. Issue common stock for cash. A friend has been wanting to invest in the company. This may be the right time to extend the offer.

OPTION 2. Transfer land to the business, and issue common stock to McCormick. Then, after obtaining the loan, he can transfer the land back to himself and zero out the common stock.

Journalize the transactions required by each option. Which plan is ethical? Which is unethical and why?

Issue 2. Human Habitat, a charitable organization in Taos, New Mexico, has a standing agreement with Taos State Bank. The agreement allows Habitat to overdraw its cash balance at the bank when donations are running low. In the past, Habitat managed funds wisely and rarely used this privilege. Douglas Byrd has been named president of Habitat. To expand operations, he is acquiring office equipment and spending a lot for fund-raising. During Byrd's presidency, Habitat has maintained a negative bank balance of about $3,000.

Required

What is the ethical issue in this situation? Do you approve or disapprove of Byrd's management of Habitat's and Taos State Bank's funds? Why?

Financial Statement Case

Recording transactions and computing net income
(Obj. 3, 4)

Refer to **Fossil, Inc.**'s financial statements in Appendix A at the end of the book. Assume that Fossil completed the following selected transactions during 2001.

a. Made sales on account, $546 million.
b. Incurred cost of goods sold (an expense) of $274 million. Credit the Inventories account.
c. Paid operating and other expenses of $199 million.
d. Paid income tax expense, $29 million.
e. Collected accounts receivable, $535 million.
f. Paid cash for other assets, $319 million.

Required

1. Set up T-accounts for: Cash (debit balance of $80 million); Accounts Receivable (debit balance of $63 million); Inventories (debit balance of $378 million); Other Assets ($0 balance); Net Sales ($0 balance); Cost of Goods Sold ($0 balance); Operating and Other Expenses ($0 balance); Income Tax Expense ($0 balance).
2. Journalize Fossil's transactions a–f. Explanations are not required.
3. Post to the T-accounts, and compute the balance for each account. Key postings by transaction letters a–f.
4. For each of the following accounts, compare your computed balance to Fossil's actual balance as shown on Fossil's fiscal year 2001 income statement or balance sheet (dated January 5, 2002). All your amounts should agree to the actual figures, rounded to the nearest million dollars. There may be a slight rounding error.
   a. Cash
   b. Accounts Receivable
   c. Inventories
   d. Net Sales
   e. Cost of Goods Sold
   f. Income Tax Expense (listed as Provision for Income Taxes on the income statement)
5. Use the relevant accounts from requirement 4 to prepare a summary income statement for Fossil, Inc., for fiscal year 2001. Compare the net income you computed to Fossil's actual net income. The two net income amounts should be equal.

Analytical Case

Analyzing a leading company's financial statements
(Obj. 2, 6)

Refer to the **Pier 1 Imports** financial statements in Appendix B at the end of the book. Suppose you are an investor considering buying Pier 1 stock. The following questions are important:

1. Explain whether Pier 1 made more sales, or collected more cash from customers, during 2002. Combine Pier 1's two receivable accounts, and then analyze total receivables to answer this question.
2. A major concern of lenders, such as banks, is the amount of "long-term debt" a company owes. How much long-term debt does Pier 1 owe at the end of 2002? Consider both the current portion and the long-term portions of the long-term debt. Assume Pier 1 paid off no long-term debt during 2002. How much new long-term debt did the company take on during 2002?
3. Investors are vitally interested in a company's sales and profits, and its trends of sales and profits over time. Consider Pier 1's net sales and net income during the period from 2000 to 2002. Compute the percentage increases in net sales and also in net income from 2000 to 2002. Which item grew faster during this period, net sales or net income? (For convenience, show dollar amounts in millions.) Which would you prefer to grow faster, net sales or net income? Give the reason for your answer.

Group Projects

Project 1. Contact a local business and arrange with the owner to learn what accounts the business uses.

Required

1. Obtain a copy of the business's chart of accounts.
2. Prepare the company's financial statements for the most recent month, quarter, or year. You may use either made-up account balances or balances supplied by the owner.

   If the business has a large number of accounts within a category, combine related accounts and report a single amount on the financial statements. For example, the company may have several cash accounts. Combine all cash amounts and report a single Cash amount on the balance sheet.

   You will probably encounter numerous accounts that you have not yet learned. Deal with these as best you can. The charts of accounts given in the appendix at the end of the book can be helpful.

Project 2. You are promoting a rock concert in your area. Your purpose is to earn a profit, so you need to establish the formal structure of a business entity. Assume you organize as a corporation.

Required

1. Make a detailed list of 10 factors you must consider as you establish the business.
2. Describe 10 of the items your business must arrange to promote and stage the rock concert.
3. Identify the transactions that your business can undertake to organize, promote, and stage the concert. Journalize the transactions, and post to the relevant T-accounts. Set up the accounts you need for your business ledger. Refer to the appendix at the end of book if needed.
4. Prepare the income statement, statement of retained earnings, and balance sheet immediately after the rock concert, that is, before you have had time to pay all the business's bills and to collect all receivables.
5. Assume that you will continue to promote rock concerts if the venture is successful. If it is unsuccessful, you will terminate the business within 3 months after the concert. Discuss how to evaluate the success of your venture and how to decide whether to continue in business.

3

Accrual Accounting & The Financial Statements

Learning Objectives

1. **Relate** accrual accounting and cash flows
2. **Apply** the revenue and matching principles
3. **Update** the financial statements by adjusting the accounts
4. **Prepare** the financial statements
5. **Close** the books
6. **Use** the current ratio and the debt ratio to evaluate a business

Integrator CD

Need additional help? Go to the **Integrator CD** *and search these key words:* accrual basis, cash basis, current assets, current liabilities, current ratio, debt ratio, depreciation, matching principle, prepaid expenses, revenue principle, unearned revenue.

Vodafone Group Plc

Statement of Profit and Loss (Adapted)
Year Ended March 31, 2001

	Millions
Total revenues	£15,004
Operating expenses	21,443
Operating profit (loss)	(6,439)
Other revenue (expense)	(3,324)
Net income (net loss)	£ (9,763)

The dot-com bubble grew larger and larger in Austin, Boston, and Silicon Valley. Lots of entrepreneurs with great ideas founded dot-com companies and became millionaires overnight. Reality hit when the companies failed to earn a profit: Someone forgot to tell the young entrepreneurs that revenues must exceed expenses for a company to stay afloat.

The same thing happened in Europe, and it ended up costing investors billions. Europeans bet large sums on the third-generation, or "3G," wireless market. Giant companies like Vodafone (England) and Deutsche Telekom (Germany) spent $103 billion on radio spectrum in 16 European countries, plus $200 billion for equipment. "It's too early to say how we'll price 3G or what the popular services will be," says an official at Vodafone. According to the president of Qwest, an American company, "[The Europeans] overpriced the air." Like the dot-coms, few wireless phone companies had a clear view of how their fantasies would become profitable.

Vodafone's income statement bears this out. For the year ended March 31, 2001, Vodafone lost £9,763, or around $14 billion in U.S. dollars. (£ is the symbol for a British pound sterling, the monetary unit in Great Britain.) Let's see what accounting information might have warned Vodafone managers of the coming crunch.

Source: Adapted from Quentin Hardy, "Third (DeGeneration)," *Forbes* (April 16, 2001), p. 72; and Vodafone Group Plc Annual Report for the year ended March 31, 2001, p. 39.

Sitemap

Whether the business is Vodafone in England, Gap, Inc. in San Francisco, or Air & Sea Travel across town, the profit motive drives the business. As you study this chapter, consider how net income affects the behavior of managers and investors.

How does a business know whether it is profitable? By analyzing its financial statements. Vodafone's income statement, like that of other British companies, is reported in pounds sterling (denoted by the symbol £). The statements of many foreign companies, such as Vodafone, give fewer details than those of companies in the United States. But even without many details, the Vodafone statement screams, "net loss!"

This chapter completes the accounting cycle, which begins with recording transactions (see Chapter 2) and ends with the financial statements.

Businesses start with cash. They purchase inventory and essential services, earn revenue, and collect cash. This is called the business cycle. Exhibit 3-1 diagrams the business cycle.

Exhibit 3-1

The Business Cycle

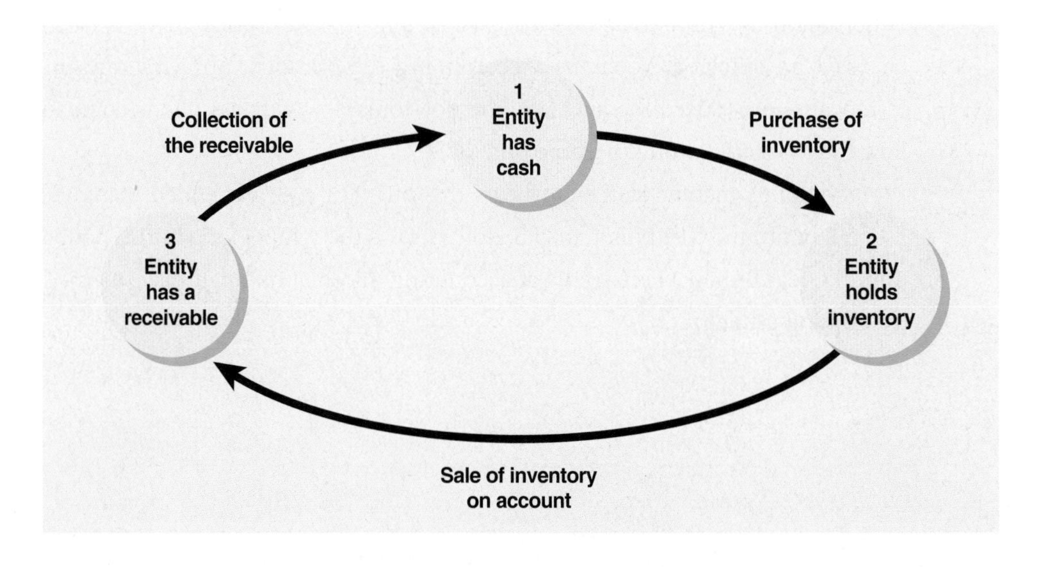

The cycle for service entities such as Vodafone or Air & Sea Travel is similar, except they do not hold inventory. The **accounting cycle** reports on the following facts about the entity:

Accounting cycle The process by which accountants produce an entity's financial statements for a specific period.

- Results of operations (income statement)
- Financial position (balance sheet)
- Cash flows (statement of cash flows)

Accrual Accounting Versus Cash Basis Accounting

accrual basis, cash basis, matching principle, revenue principle

People like investors and lenders use accounting data to evaluate companies. Investors are always on the lookout for corporations whose stock price will increase and that pay high dividends. Banks want to lend to borrowers who will pay their loans on time. Accounting provides a framework for organizing the necessary financial information. Accounting can be based on the accrual basis or the cash basis.

In **accrual accounting**, an accountant recognizes the impact of a business transaction as it occurs. When the business performs a service, makes a sale, or incurs an expense, the accountant records the transaction even if it receives or pays no cash. In **cash-basis accounting,** the accountant records a transaction only when it receives or pays cash. Cash receipts are treated as revenues and cash payments are handled as expenses.

Accrual accounting
Accounting that recognizes (records) the impact of a business event as it occurs, regardless of whether the transaction affected cash.

Cash-basis accounting
Accounting that records only transactions in which cash is received or paid.

Generally accepted accounting principles (GAAP) require that businesses use accrual accounting. This means that the business records revenues as they are *earned* and expenses as they are *incurred*—not necessarily when cash changes hands.

DECISION: Which System Is Better—Accrual or Cash-Basis Accounting?

To answer this question, suppose you are Gary Lyon, the co-owner of Air & Sea Travel. At the end of April, your clients owe the business $2,500. Is this receivable a real asset, or should you forget it? Also at April 30, Air & Sea Travel owes $13,100 on accounts payable. Must you pay these liabilities, or can you safely ignore them? Is the depreciation of Air & Sea Travel's office furniture merely an illusion, or is the wear-and-tear real?

Accrual accounting records all types of transactions, including receivables, payables, and depreciation. The cash basis of accounting ignores these important items. Before deciding to expand the business, you must keep your liabilities in mind. If you ignore your payables, you may spend too much on expansion and find yourself unable to pay bills. Managers also need to know the amount of depreciation on equipment in order to decide when to replace worn-out assets. For these and other reasons, we do accounting by the accrual basis. It provides more complete information than the cash basis.

Accrual Accounting and Cash Flows

Objective

1 **Relate** accrual accounting and cash flows

Accrual accounting is more complex—and more complete—than cash-basis accounting. Accrual accounting records *cash* transactions, including

- Collecting from customers
- Receiving cash from interest earned
- Paying salaries, rent, and other expenses
- Borrowing money
- Paying off loans
- Issuing stock

Accrual accounting also records *noncash* transactions such as

- Purchases of inventory on account
- Sales on account
- Accrual of expenses incurred but not yet paid
- Depreciation expense
- Usage of prepaid rent, insurance, and supplies

This chapter shows how accrual accounting completes the process leading up to the financial statements. Before launching into the detailed accounting procedures, let's illustrate how accrual accounting gives a complete picture of a company's operations. Vodafone provides an interesting illustration.

Suppose that on September 30, 2005, Vodafone receives £24 (24 pounds sterling, the British monetary unit) for a 1-year connection to wireless phone service. By December 31, Vodafone has earned the service revenue for 3 months (October, November, and December). At year end Vodafone reports the results shown in Exhibit 3-2.

Exhibit 3-2

Accrual Accounting and Cash Flows for Vodafone

	December 31, 2005
Income statement reports for the year:	
Service revenue (when earned; £24 × 3/12)	£6
Balance sheet reports at year end:	
Liabilities	
Unearned service revenue (company still owes £24 × 9/12)	£18
Statement of cash flows reports for the year:	
Cash receipts and cash payments	

✔ Check Point 3-1

✔ Check Point 3-2

The income statement reports the revenue earned, and the balance sheet reports the wireless service that Vodafone still owes its customers. These are accrual-accounting amounts. The statement of cash flows reports cash receipts. All three statements are needed to report what happened to Vodafone during 2005.

Accrual accounting is based on a conceptual framework of accounting concepts and principles. We turn now to the time-period concept, the revenue principle, and the matching principle.

The Time-Period Concept

The only way for a business to know for certain how well it performed is to close its doors, sell the assets, pay the liabilities, and return any leftover cash to the owners. This process, called *liquidation*, means going out of business. On-going businesses cannot measure income this way. Instead, they need regular progress reports. Accountants, therefore, prepare financial statements for specific periods. The **time-period concept** ensures that accounting information is reported at regular intervals.

Time-period concept Ensures that accounting information is reported at regular intervals.

The basic accounting period is 1 year, and virtually all businesses prepare annual financial statements. Around 60% of large companies use the calendar year from January 1 through December 31. Vodafone, on the other hand, uses a fiscal year as its annual reporting period. A *fiscal year* ends on a date other than December 31. Vodafone's accounting year runs from April 1 through March 31 of the following year. This is why Vodafone's income statement is dated "Year Ended March 31, 2001."

Most retailers, including JC Penney Company use a fiscal year that ends on January 31 because the low point in their business activity falls during January, after Christmas sales. JC Penney does more than 30% of its yearly sales during November and December but only 5% in January.

Managers and investors cannot wait until the end of the year to gauge a company's progress. Companies prepare financial statements for interim periods of less than a year, such as a quarter (3 months) or a semiannual period (6 months). Because managers want financial information even more often, monthly statements are common. Most of the discussions in this text are based on an annual accounting period.

The Revenue Principle

Objective

2 **Apply** the revenue and matching principles

The **revenue principle** governs two things:

1. *When* to record revenue (make a journal entry)
2. The *amount* of revenue to record →

← *Revenue, defined in Chapter 1, page 17, is the increase in retained earnings from delivering goods and services to customers in the course of operating a business.*

When should you record revenue? When it has been earned—and not before. In most cases, revenue is earned when the business has delivered a good or service to a customer. The business has done everything required to earn the revenue by transferring the good or service to the customer.

Revenue principle The basis for recording revenues; tells accountants when to record revenue and the amount of revenue to record.

Exhibit 3-3 shows two situations that provide guidance on when to record revenue. Situation 1 illustrates when *not* to record revenue: No transaction has occurred, so Air & Sea Travel makes no journal entry. Situation 2 illustrates when revenue should be recorded, after a business transaction has occurred. Air & Sea Travel records either Cash or Accounts Receivable, depending on the agreement with the client. In either case, the travel agency records Service Revenue when it is earned. The earning of revenue, not the collection of cash, is the critical event for recording revenue.

Exhibit 3-3 **When to Record Revenue**

The *amount* of revenue to record is the cash value of the service transferred to the customer. Suppose that in order to obtain a new client, Air & Sea Travel arranges a trip for the price of $500. Ordinarily, Air & Sea would charge $600 for this service. How much revenue should it record? The answer is $500—the cash value of the transaction. The cash to be received, $500, pinpoints the amount of revenue earned.

← *An expense, defined in Chapter 1, page 17, is a decrease in retained earnings that occurs from using assets and creating liabilities in the course of operating a business.*

The Matching Principle

The **matching principle** is the basis for recording expenses →. *Expenses* are the costs of assets used up, and liabilities created, in the earning of revenue. Expenses have no future benefit to the company. The matching principle includes two steps:

Matching principle The basis for recording expenses. Directs accountants to identify all expenses incurred during the period, to measure the expenses, and to match them against the revenues earned during that same period.

1. Identify all the expenses incurred during the accounting period.
2. Measure the expenses, and match expenses against the revenues earned.

To *match* expenses against revenues means to subtract expenses from revenues to compute net income or net loss. Exhibit 3-4 illustrates the matching principle.

Exhibit 3-2

The Matching Principle

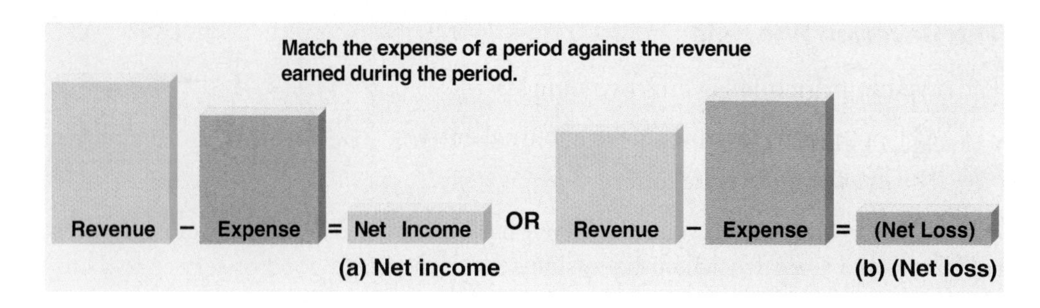

✔ Check Point 3-3

Some expenses are paid in cash. Other expenses arise from using up an asset such as supplies. Still other expenses occur when a company creates a liability. For example, Vodafone's salary expense occurs when employees work for the company. Vodafone may pay the salary expense immediately, or it may record a liability for the expense. In either case, Vodafone has salary expense. The critical event for recording an expense is the occurrence of the expense, not the payment of cash.

1. A client pays Air & Sea $900 on March 15 for service to be performed April 1 to June 30. Has Air & Sea earned revenue on March 15? When will Air & Sea earn the revenue?
2. Air & Sea Travel pays $4,500 on July 31 for office rent for the next 3 months. Has the company incurred an expense on July 31?

Answers:

1. No. Air & Sea has received the cash but will not perform the service until later. Air & Sea earns the revenue when it performs the service.
2. No. Air & Sea has paid cash for rent in advance. This prepaid rent is an asset because Air & Sea has the use of an office in the future.

Ethical Issues in Accrual Accounting

Accrual accounting provides some ethical challenges that cash accounting avoids. For example, suppose that in 2006. Shop Online (SOL) prepays a $3 million advertising campaign to be conducted by Saatchi & Saatchi, a leading advertising agency. The advertisements are scheduled to run during December, January, and February. SOL is buying an asset, a prepaid expense. Suppose SOL pays for the advertisements on December 1 and the ads start running immediately. SOL should record one-third of the expense ($1 million) during the year ended December 31, 2006, and two-thirds ($2 million) during 2007.

Suppose 2006 is a great year for SOL—net income is better than expected. SOL's top managers believe that 2007 will not be as profitable. In this case, the company has a strong incentive to expense the full $3 million during 2006 in order to report all the expense in the 2006 income statement. This unethical action would keep $2 million of advertising expense off the 2007 income statement and make 2007's net income look better.

In cash-basis accounting, this particular ethical challenge could not arise. Under the cash basis, SOL would record the full $3 million as expense in December 2006 because the cash payment occurred during that month. But the cash basis is unacceptable because it distorts reported figures for assets, expenses, and net income.

Another ethical challenge in accrual accounting arises because it is easy to overlook an expense at the end of the period. Suppose it is now December 31, 2007, and the year has not turned out very well for *Herald-Tribune* newspapers. If top managers are unethical, the company can "manufacture" net income by failing to record some expenses. Suppose the company owes $4 million in interest expense that it will pay in January 2008. At December 31, 2007, company accountants can "overlook" the $4 million interest expense and add several million dollars to net income.

This ethical challenge cannot arise under the cash basis. The company records only the cash payment. At December 31, 2007, there is no expense to accrue as a liability. Again, this is the weakness of the cash basis: It fails to report some expenses and liabilities. This is why GAAP require the accrual basis, despite the ethical temptations it poses.

DECISION: Earnings Management and Cookie Jar Reserves

In a competitive market, it is important for a company to meet or beat Wall Street forecasts. Companies that report higher-than-expected profits are rewarded with high stock prices. And companies that fail to meet their earnings forecasts are punished severely. Therefore, managers try not to surprise the market with bad news. How can a company keep earnings trending upward and stay within GAAP? The best way is to deliver superior products to customers. If that fails, some companies try to "manage their earnings," a practice frowned on by the Securities and Exchange Commission (SEC).

During the 1990s, the world economy grew at a record pace. Profits rose, and stock prices soared. Some companies abused the adjusting process by creating "cookie-jar reserves." An example of a cookie-jar reserve is a liability created when a company records an expense that is not directly linked to a specific accounting period—the expense may fall in one period or another. Companies may record such a *discretionary* expense when profits are high because they can afford to take the hit to income. When profits are low, the company reduces the liability (the reserve) rather than recording an expense in the lean year. The result is a "smoothing" of net income over the course of several years, with net income still trending upward. Analysts push the company's stock, and everyone is happy. Now let's return to accounting as it is supposed to be practiced.

Updating the Accounts: The Adjustment Process

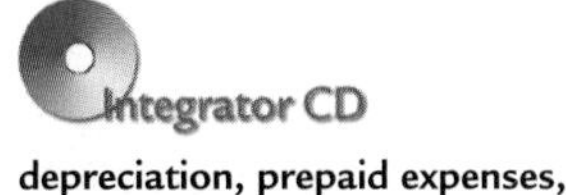

depreciation, prepaid expenses, unearned revenues

Objective

3 **Update** the financial statements by adjusting the accounts

At the end of the period, the business reports its financial statements. This process begins with the trial balance from Chapter 2. Exhibit 3-5 is the trial balance of Air & Sea Travel, Inc., at April 30, 20X3. We refer to this trial balance as *unadjusted* because the accounts are not yet ready for the financial statements. In most cases we drop the label "unadjusted" and refer simply to the "Trial Balance."

Which Accounts Need to Be Updated (Adjusted)?

At the end of the month, Gary and Monica Lyon need to know how well Air & Sea Travel performed during April. To provide this information, the business presents its financial statements, which report the balances of the accounts on that date. All accounts must show up-to-date amounts, and that means some accounts must be adjusted at year end. The end-of-period accounting process starts with the trial balance from Chapter 2. Exhibit 3-5 gives the trial balance of Air & Sea Travel, Inc., at April 30, 20X3.

Exhibit 3-5

Unadjusted Trial Balance

Air & Sea Travel, Inc.
Unadjusted Trial Balance
April 30, 20X3

Cash	$24,800	
Accounts receivable	2,250	
Supplies	700	
Prepaid rent	3,000	
Furniture	16,500	
Accounts payable		$13,100
Unearned service revenue		450
Common stock		20,000
Retained earnings		11,250
Dividends	3,200	
Service revenue		7,000
Salary expense	950	
Utilities expense	400	
Total	$51,800	$51,800

Scan the trial balance in Exhibit 3-5. Can you identify the accounts with balances that are already up-to-date on April 30? Those accounts are ready to be reported on the April 30 balance sheet. Start with Cash. Cash, Furniture, Accounts Payable, Common Stock, and Dividends are up-to-date and need no further adjustment. Why? Because the everyday buy and sell transactions of the period provide all the relevant data for these accounts.

Accounts Receivable, Supplies, Prepaid Rent, and the other accounts are another story. These accounts are not yet up-to-date on April 30. Why? Because certain transactions have not yet been recorded. Take Supplies. All during April, Air & Sea Travel used stationery, printed catalogs, and other supplies to serve clients. But Air & Sea Travel did not make a journal entry every time someone printed a travel itinerary for a client. That would waste time and money. Instead, Air & Sea Travel waits until the end of the period and then accounts for the supplies used up during the month.

The cost of supplies used up is an expense and must be recorded by making an adjusting entry at the end of April. The adjustment updates both the Supplies account (an asset) and the Supplies Expense account. Once adjusted, these accounts are ready to be reported in the April financial statements. We must adjust all other accounts whose balances are not yet up-to-date at the end of the period.

Categories of Adjusting Entries

Accounting adjustments fall into three basic categories: *deferrals, depreciation,* and *accruals.*

Deferral
A category of miscellaneous assets that typically expire or get used up in the near future. Examples include prepaid rent, prepaid insurance, and supplies. Also called a *prepaid expense.*

DEFERRALS. A **deferral** is an adjustment for which the business paid or received cash in advance. Vodafone purchases supplies for use in its operations. During the period, some supplies (assets) are used up and thus become expenses. At the end of the period, an adjustment is needed to decrease the Supplies account for the supplies used up. This is Supplies Expense. Prepaid rent, prepaid insurance, and all other prepaid expenses require deferral adjustments.

There are also deferral adjustments for liabilities. Companies such as Vodafone collect cash in advance of earning the revenue. Vodafone collects cash up front and then provides wireless phone service. When Vodafone receives cash up front, the company has a liability to provide a service for the client. This liability is called Unearned Service Revenue. Then, over the course of the contract period, Vodafone earns Service Revenue by providing the phone service. This earning process requires an adjustment at the end of each accounting period. The adjustment decreases the liability account and increases the revenue account for the amount of revenue earned during the period. Publishers such as Time, Inc. and your local newspaper sell subscriptions and collect cash in advance. Their accounting parallels that of Vodafone.

DEPRECIATION. **Depreciation** is the allocation of the cost of a plant asset to expense over the asset's useful life. Depreciation is the most common long-term deferral. The business buys long-term plant assets, such as buildings, equipment, and furniture. As the company uses the assets it records depreciation for their wear-and-tear and obsolescence. The accounting adjustment records Depreciation Expense, which decreases the book value of the asset over its life. The process is identical to a deferral-type adjustment; the only difference is the type of asset involved.

Depreciation
Expense associated with spreading (allocating) the cost of a plant asset over its useful life.

ACCRUALS. An **accrual** is the opposite of a deferral. For an accrued expense, the business records an expense before paying cash. For an accrued revenue, it records the revenue before receiving the cash. Selling on account creates an accrued revenue.

Accrual
An expense or a revenue that occurs before the business pays or receives cash. An accrual is the opposite of a deferral.

Salary Expense is an example of an accrual adjustment for an expense. As employees work for Vodafone, the company's salary expense accrues with the passage of time. Suppose that at year end, Vodafone owes employees salaries of £1,000 and will pay them on January 2 of the next year. At December 31, Vodafone must record Salary Expense and Salary Payable for the £1,000. Other examples of expense accruals include interest expense and income tax expense.

For an accrued revenue, Vodafone earns service revenue that it will collect in cash next year. At December 31, Vodafone must accrue the service revenue. The adjustment is made to Accounts Receivable and Service Revenue. An accrual of interest revenue requires an adjustment of Interest Receivable and Interest Revenue.

Let's see how the adjusting process actually works. We begin with prepaid expenses. Recall that prepaid expenses are assets, not expenses.

Prepaid Expenses

A **prepaid expense** is an expense paid in advance. The prepayment will be used up in the near future. Therefore, prepaid expenses are assets, because they provide a future benefit for the owner. Let's do the adjustment for prepaid rent and supplies.

PREPAID RENT. Rent is paid in advance. This prepayment creates an asset for the renter, who can then use the rented item in the future. Suppose Air & Sea Travel prepays 3 months' office rent on April 1, 20X3. The lease specifies a monthly rental of $1,000, so the entry for the prepayment of 3 months' rent debits Prepaid Rent as follows:

Apr. 1	Prepaid Rent ($1,000 × 3)	3,000	
	Cash.		3,000
	Paid 3 months' rent in advance.		

The accounting equation shows that one asset increases and another decreases. Total assets are unchanged.

ASSETS	=	LIABILITIES	+	STOCKHOLDERS' EQUITY
3,000	=	0	+	0
−3,000				

After posting, the Prepaid Rent account appears as follows:

Prepaid Rent		
Apr. 1	**3,000**	

Throughout April, the Prepaid Rent account maintains this beginning balance, as shown in Exhibit 3-5 (p. 118). At April 30, Prepaid Rent must be adjusted. Rent expense is 1 month of the prepayment ($3,000 × 1/3 = $1,000). The adjustment transfers $1,000 from Prepaid Rent to Rent Expense as follows:

Apr. 30*	Rent Expense ($3,000 × 1/3)	1,000	*Adjusting entry a*
	Prepaid Rent		1,000
	To record rent expense.		

The accounting equation shows that both assets and stockholders' equity decrease.

ASSETS	=	LIABILITIES	+	STOCKHOLDERS' EQUITY	−	EXPENSES
−1,000	=	0			−	1,000

After posting, Prepaid Rent and Rent Expense appear as follows:

Prepaid Rent			
Apr. 1	**3,000**	**Apr. 30**	**1,000** →
Bal.	**2,000**		

Rent Expense		
Apr. 30	**1,000**	
Bal.	**1,000**	

This expense illustrates the matching principle, that is, recording an expense for the purpose of measuring net income.

SUPPLIES. Supplies are another type of prepaid expense. On April 2, Air & Sea Travel paid cash of $700 for office supplies:

Apr. 2	Supplies	700	
	Cash		700
	Paid cash for supplies.		

ASSETS	=	LIABILITIES	+	STOCKHOLDERS' EQUITY
700	=	0	+	0
−700				

The April 30 trial balance lists Supplies with a $700 debit balance (Exhibit 3-5).

*See Exhibit 3-10, page 129, for a summary of adjustments a–g.

The cost of the supplies Air & Sea Travel used during April is *supplies expense* for the month. To measure supplies expense during April, the business counts the supplies on hand at the end of the month. The count shows that supplies costing $400 remain. Subtracting the $400 of supplies on hand at the end of April from the supplies available ($700) measures supplies expense for the month ($300):

ASSET AVAILABLE DURING THE PERIOD	–	ASSET ON HAND AT THE END OF THE PERIOD	=	ASSET USED (EXPENSE) DURING THE PERIOD
$700	–	$400	=	$300

The April 30 adjusting entry debits the expense and credits the asset, as follows:

Apr. 30	Supplies Expense ($700 – $400)	300		Adjusting entry b
	Supplies.		300	
	To record supplies expense.			

ASSETS	=	LIABILITIES	+	STOCKHOLDERS' EQUITY	–	EXPENSES
–300	=	0			–	300

After posting, the Supplies and Supplies Expense accounts appear as follows:

Supplies

Apr. 2	700	Apr. 30	300
Bal.	400		

→

Supplies Expense

Apr. 30	300		
Bal.	300		

The Supplies account then enters the month of May with a $400 balance, and the adjustment process is repeated month after month.

✔ Check Point 3-4

At the beginning of the month, supplies were $5,000. During the month, $7,800 of supplies were purchased. At month's end, $3,600 of supplies were still on hand. What are the adjusting entry and the ending balance in the Supplies account?

Answer:

Supplies Expense ($5,000 + $7,800 – $3,600)	9,200	
Supplies		9,200

Ending balance of supplies = $3,600 (the supplies still on hand)

Depreciation of Plant Assets

Plant assets are long-lived tangible assets, such as land, buildings, furniture, machinery, and equipment. All plant assets but land decline in usefulness as they age, and this decline is an *expense*. Accountants spread the cost of each plant asset, except land, over its useful life. This process of allocating cost to expense is called *depreciation*. Depreciation is an expense as much as the salary that a business pays its employees.

Plant assets
Long-lived assets, such as land, buildings, and equipment, used in the operation of the business. Also called *fixed assets*.

To illustrate depreciation, consider Air & Sea Travel. Suppose that on April 3 the business purchased furniture on account for $16,500:

Apr. 3	Furniture	16,500	
	Accounts Payable		16,500
	Purchased office furniture on account.		

ASSETS	=	LIABILITIES	+	STOCKHOLDERS' EQUITY
16,500	=	16,500	+	0

After posting, the Furniture account appears as follows:

Furniture	
Apr. 3 **16,500**	

Air & Sea Travel records an asset when it purchases furniture. Then, a portion of the asset's cost is transferred to Depreciation Expense each period the asset is used. Accounting matches the asset's expense against revenue—this is the matching principle. In computerized systems, the depreciation entry is programmed for each month of the asset's life.

Air & Sea Travel's office furniture will remain useful for 5 years and than be virtually worthless. One way to compute the amount of depreciation for each year is to divide the cost of the asset ($16,500 in our example) by its expected useful life (5 years). This procedure—called the *straight-line method*—gives annual depreciation of $3,300. The depreciation amount is an *estimate*. (Chapter 7 covers plant assets and depreciation in more detail.)

$16,500/5 years = $3,300 per year

Depreciation for April is $275.

$3,300/12 months = $275 per month

THE ACCUMULATED DEPRECIATION ACCOUNT. Depreciation expense for April is recorded as follows:

Apr. 30	Depreciation Expense—Furniture	275		*Adjusting entry c*
	Accumulated Depreciation—Furniture. . . .		275	
	To record depreciation on furniture.			

Note that assets decrease by the amount of the expense:

ASSETS	=	LIABILITIES	+	STOCKHOLDERS' EQUITY	−	EXPENSES
−275	=	0			−	275

The Accumulated Depreciation account (not Furniture) is credited to preserve the original cost of the furniture in the Furniture account. Managers can then refer to the Furniture account if they need to know how much the asset cost.

Accumulated Depreciation The cumulative sum of all depreciation expense from the date of acquiring a plant asset.

The **Accumulated Depreciation** account shows the sum of all depreciation expense from the date of acquiring the asset. Therefore, the balance in the Accumulated Depreciation account increases over the asset's life.

Contra account An account that always has a companion account and whose normal balance is opposite that of the companion account.

Accumulated Depreciation is a *contra asset* account—an asset account with a normal credit balance. A **contra account** has two distinguishing characteristics:

1. It always has a companion account.
2. Its normal balance is opposite that of the companion account.

In this case, Accumulated Depreciation is the contra (companion) account to the asset account Furniture, so Accumulated Depreciation appears directly after

Furniture on the balance sheet. A business carries an accumulated depreciation account for each depreciable asset, for example, Accumulated Depreciation—Building and Accumulated Depreciation—Machinery.

After posting, the plant asset accounts of Air & Sea Travel are as follows:

Furniture			
Apr. 3	16,500		
Bal.	16,500		

Accumulated Depreciation—Furniture			
		Apr. 30	275
		Bal.	275

Depreciation Expense—Furniture			
Apr. 30	275		
Bal.	275		

Book Value. The net amount of a plant asset (cost minus accumulated depreciation) is called that asset's **book value** or *carrying amount*. Exhibit 3-6 shows how Air & Sea Travel would report the book value of its furniture and building at April 30.

Book value (of a plant asset) The asset's cost minus accumulated depreciation.

✔ Check Point 3-5

Exhibit 3-6

Plant Assets on the Balance Sheet of Air & Sea Travel (April 30)

Air & Sea Travel
Plant Assets at April 30

Furniture	$16,500	
Less Accumulated Depreciation	(275)	$16,225
Building	$48,000	
Less Accumulated Depreciation	(200)	47,800
Book value of plant assets		$64,025

At April 30, the book value of furniture is $16,225; the book value of the building is $47,800.

1. What is the book value of Air & Sea Travel's furniture at the end of May?
2. Is book value what the furniture could be sold for?

Answers:

1. $16,500 − $275 − $275 = $15,950.
2. Not necessarily. Book value represents the part of the asset's cost that has not yet been depreciated. Book value is not necessarily related to the amount that an asset can be sold for.

Exhibit 3-7 shows how Johnson & Johnson—maker of Band-Aids, Tylenol, and other health-care products—can show Property, Plant, and Equipment in its annual report. Lines 1 to 4 list specific assets and their cost. Line 5 shows the cost of all Johnson & Johnson plant assets. Line 6 gives the sum of the accumulated depreciation, and line 7 shows the assets' book value of $4,115 million.

Accrued Expenses

Businesses incur expenses before they pay cash. Consider an employee's salary. The employer's expense and payable grow as the employee works, so the liability is said to accrue. Another example is interest expense on a note payable. Interest accrues as the

Exhibit 3-7

Johnson & Johnson's Reporting of Property, Plant, and Equipment (Adapted, in Millions)

1 Land and land improvements	$ 262
2 Buildings and building equipment	2,226
3 Machinery and equipment	3,143
4 Construction in progress	672
5 Plant assets, at cost	6,303
6 Less Accumulated depreciation	(2,188)
7 Plant assets, net	$ 4,115

Accrued expense An expense incurred but not yet paid in cash.

clock ticks. The term **accrued expense** refers to a liability that arises from an expense that has not yet been paid.

It wastes time to record expenses daily or weekly. Consequently, the accountant waits until the end of the period. Then an adjusting entry brings each expense (and related liability) up-to-date just before the financial statements are prepared. Let's look at salary expense.

Most companies pay their employees at set times. Suppose Air & Sea Travel pays its employee a monthly salary of $1,900, half on the 15th and half on the last day of the month. The following calendar for April has the paydays circled:

April

Sun.	Mon.	Tue.	Wed.	Thur.	Fri.	Sat.
					1	2
3	4	5	6	7	8	9
10	11	12	13	14	(15)	16
17	18	19	20	21	22	23
24	25	26	27	28	29	(30)

Assume that if a payday falls on the weekend, Air & Sea Travel pays the employee on the following Monday. During April, the agency paid its employee's first half-month salary of $950 and made the following entry:

Apr. 15	Salary Expense	950	
	Cash		950
	To pay salary.		

ASSETS	=	LIABILITIES	+	STOCKHOLDERS' EQUITY	–	EXPENSES
−950	=	0			–	950

After posting, the Salary Expense account is

Salary Expense		
Apr. 15	**950**	

The trial balance at April 30 (Exhibit 3-5, p. 118) includes Salary Expense, with its debit balance of $950. Because April 30, the second payday of the month, falls on a Saturday, the second half-month amount of $950 will be paid on Monday, May 2. At April 30, therefore, Air & Sea adjusts for additional *salary expense* and *salary payable* of $950 as follows:

Apr. 30	Salary Expense	950	*Adjusting entry d*
	Salary Payable.		950
	To accrue salary expense.		

The accounting equation shows that an accrued expense increases liabilities and decreases stockholders' equity:

ASSETS	=	LIABILITIES	+	STOCKHOLDERS' EQUITY	−	EXPENSES
0	=	950			−	950

After posting, the Salary Payable and Salary Expense accounts appear as follows:

Salary Payable

	Apr. 30	950
	Bal.	**950**

Salary Expense

Apr. 15	950	
Apr. 30	950	
Bal.	**1,900**	

The accounts at April 30 now contain the full month's salary information. Salary Expense has a full month's salary, and Salary Payable shows the amount owed at April 30. All accrued expenses are recorded this way—debit the expense account and credit the liability account.

✔ Check Point 3-6

✔ Check Point 3-7

Computerized systems contain a payroll module. The adjustment for accrued salaries is automatically journalized and posted at the end of each accounting period.

What is the adjusting entry at April 30 for the following situation? Weekly salaries for a 5-day work week total $3,500, payable on Friday; April 30 falls on a Tuesday.

Answer: $3,500 × 2/5 = $1,400. The adjusting entry is

Salary Expense	1,400	
Salary Payable		1,400
To accrue salary expense.		

Accrued Revenues

Businesses often earn revenue before they receive the cash—collection occurs later. A revenue that has been earned but not yet received in cash is called an **accrued revenue.**

Accrued revenue
A revenue that has been earned but not yet received in cash.

Bank One employees must travel in their work. Assume that Bank One hires Air & Sea Travel on April 15 to arrange travel services on a monthly basis. Suppose Bank One will pay the travel agency $500 monthly, with the first payment on May 15. During April, Air & Sea will earn half a month's fee, $250, for work done April 15 through April 30. On April 30, Air & Sea Travel makes the following adjusting entry:

Apr. 30	Accounts Receivable ($500 × 1/2).	250	*Adjusting entry e*
	Service Revenue		250
	To accrue service revenue.		

Revenue increases both total assets and stockholders' equity:

ASSETS	=	LIABILITIES	+	STOCKHOLDERS' EQUITY	+	REVENUES
250	=	0			+	250

Recall that Accounts Receivable has an unadjusted balance of $2,250, and Service Revenue's unadjusted balance is $7,000 (Exhibit 3-5, p. 118). This April 30 adjusting entry has the following effects:

Accounts Receivable

	Debit	Credit
	2,250	
Apr. 30	250	
Bal.	2,500	

Service Revenue

Debit		Credit
		7,000
	Apr. 30	250
	Bal.	7,250

✔ Check Point 3-8

All accrued revenues are accounted for similarly—debit a receivable and credit a revenue.

Suppose Air & Sea Travel holds a note receivable from a client. At the end of April, $125 of interest revenue has been earned. Prepare the adjusting entry at April 30.

Answer:

Interest Receivable	125	
Interest Revenue		125
To accrue interest revenue.		

Unearned Revenues

Unearned revenue
A liability created when a business collects cash from customers in advance of doing work for them. The obligation is to provide a product or a service in the future.

Some businesses collect cash from customers before earning the revenue. This creates a liability called **unearned revenue**, which is an obligation arising from receiving cash before providing a service. Only when the job is completed can the business earn the revenue. Suppose Plantation Foods, a major producer of turkey food products, engages Air & Sea, agreeing to pay the travel agency $450 monthly, beginning immediately. If Air & Sea Travel collects the first amount on April 20, Air & Sea records this transaction as follows:

Apr. 20	Cash	450	
	Unearned Service Revenue.		450
	Received cash for revenue in advance.		

ASSETS	=	LIABILITIES	+	STOCKHOLDERS' EQUITY
450	=	450	+	0

After posting, the liability account appears as follows:

Unearned Service Revenue

Debit		Credit
	Apr. 20	450

Unearned Service Revenue is a liability because Air & Sea is obligated to perform services for the client. The April 30 unadjusted trial balance (Exhibit 3-5, p. 118) lists Unearned Service Revenue with a $450 credit balance. During the last 10 days of the month—April 21 through April 30—the travel agency will *earn* one-third

(10 days divided by April's total of 30 days) of the $450, or $150. Therefore, the accountant makes the following adjustment on April 30:

Apr. 30	Unearned Service Revenue ($450 × 1/3)......	150	
	Service Revenue		150
	To record unearned service revenue that has been earned.		

Adjusting entry f

ASSETS	=	LIABILITIES	+	STOCKHOLDERS' EQUITY	+	REVENUES
0	=	−150			+	150

This adjusting entry shifts $150 of the total amount received ($450) from liability to revenue. After posting, Unearned Service Revenue is reduced to $300, and Service Revenue is increased by $150, as follows:

Unearned Service Revenue

Apr. 30	**150**	**Apr. 20**	**450**
		Bal.	**300**

Service Revenue

			7,000
		Apr. 30	**250**
		Apr. 30	**150**
		Bal.	**7,400**

All revenues collected in advance are accounted for this way.

✔ Check Point 3-9

An unearned revenue is a liability, not a revenue. An unearned revenue to one company can be a prepaid expense to the company that made the payment. For example, Plantation Foods' prepayment to Air & Sea Travel is a prepaid expense of Plantation. Air & Sea Travel has a liability for the unearned revenue.

Exhibit 3-8 diagrams the distinctive timing of prepaid and accrual adjustments. Study prepaid expenses all the way across. Then study unearned revenues, and so on.

Exhibit 3-8

Prepaid and Accrual Adjustments

PREPAIDS—The Cash Transaction Occurs First

	First				***Later***		
Prepaid expenses	Pay cash and record an asset:			→	Record an expense and decrease the asset:		
	Prepaid Expense	XXX			Expense	XXX	
	Cash		XXX		Prepaid Expense ...		XXX
Unearned revenues	Receive cash and record unearned revenue:			→	Record a revenue and decrease unearned revenue:		
	Cash	XXX			Unearned Revenue	XXX	
	Unearned Revenue		XXX		Revenue		XXX

ACCRUALS—The Cash Transaction Occurs Later

	First				***Later***		
Accrued expenses	Record (accrue) an expense and the related payable:			→	Pay cash and decrease the payable:		
	Expense............	XXX			Payable	XXX	
	Payable		XXX		Cash		XXX
Accrued revenues	Record (accrue) a revenue and the related receivable:			→	Receive cash and decrease the receivable:		
	Receivable	XXX			Cash	XXX	
	Revenue		XXX		Receivable		XXX

The authors thank Darrel Davis and Alfonso Oddo for suggesting this exhibit.

Summary of the Adjusting Process

A key purpose of the adjusting process is to measure business income. Therefore, each adjusting entry affects at least one income statement account—a revenue or an expense. Another purpose of the adjusting process is to update the balance sheet. Therefore, the other side of each adjustment affects an asset or a liability. Adjusting entries do not affect Cash. The adjusting process is reserved for the non-cash transactions required by accrual accounting. Exhibit 3-9 summarizes the adjusting entries.

Exhibit 3-9

Summary of Adjusting Entries

	Type of Account	
Category of Adjusting Entry	***Debit***	***Credit***
Prepaid expense	Expense	Asset
Depreciation	Expense	Contra asset
Accrued expense	Expense	Liability
Accrued revenue	Asset	Revenue
Unearned revenue	Liability	Revenue

Adapted from material provided by Beverly Terry.

Exhibit 3-10 on page 129 summarizes the adjustments of Air & Sea Travel, Inc., at April 30—the adjusting entries we've examined over the past few pages. Panel A repeats the data for each adjustment, Panel B gives the adjusting entries, and Panel C shows the accounts after posting the adjusting entries ←. The adjustments are keyed by letter.

→ Recall from Chapter 2, page 74, that posting is the process of transferring amounts from the journal to the ledger.

Exhibit 3-10 includes an additional adjusting entry that we have not yet discussed—the accrual of income tax expense. Like individual taxpayers, corporations are subject to income tax. They typically accrue income tax expense and the related income tax payable as the final adjusting entry of the period. Air & Sea Travel, Inc. accrues income tax expense with adjusting entry g, as follows:

Apr. 30	Income Tax Expense	540	
	Income Tax Payable		540
	To accrue income tax expense.		

Adjusting entry g

The Adjusted Trial Balance

This chapter began with the unadjusted trial balance (see Exhibit 3-5, p. 118). After the adjustments are journalized and posted, the accounts appear as shown in Exhibit 3-10, Panel C. A useful step in preparing the financial statements is to list the accounts, along with their adjusted balances, on an **adjusted trial balance.** This document lists all the accounts and their final balances in a single place. Exhibit 3-11 shows the adjusted trial balance of Air & Sea Travel.

Adjusted trial balance
A list of all the ledger accounts with their adjusted balances.

Note how clearly the adjusted trial balance presents the data. The Account Title and the Trial Balance data come from the trial balance. The two Adjustments columns summarize the adjusting entries. The Adjusted Trial Balance columns give the final account balances. Each amount on the *adjusted* trial balance of Exhibit 3-11 is the *unadjusted* balance plus or minus the adjustments. For example, Accounts Receivable starts with a balance of $2,250. Add the $250 debit adjustment to get Accounts Receivable's ending balance of $2,500. Spreadsheets are designed for this type of analysis.

Exhibit 3-10

The Adjusting Process of Air & Sea Travel, Inc.

PANEL A—Information for Adjustments at April 30, 20X3

(a) Prepaid rent expired, $1,000.
(b) Supplies on hand, $400.
(c) Depreciation on furniture, $275.
(d) Accrued salary expense, $950.
(e) Accrued service revenue, $250.
(f) Amount of unearned service revenue that has been earned, $150.
(g) Accrued income tax expense, $540.

PANEL B—Adjusting Entries

		Debit	Credit
(a)	Rent Expense	1,000	
	Prepaid Rent		1,000
	To record rent expense.		
(b)	Supplies Expense	300	
	Supplies		300
	To record supplies used.		
(c)	Depreciation Expense—Furniture	275	
	Accumulated Depreciation—Furniture		275
	To record depreciation on furniture.		
(d)	Salary Expense	950	
	Salary Payable		950
	To accrue salary expense.		
(e)	Accounts Receivable	250	
	Service Revenue		250
	To accrue service revenue.		
(f)	Unearned Service Revenue	150	
	Service Revenue		150
	To record unearned revenue that has been earned.		
(g)	Income Tax Expense	540	
	Income Tax Payable		540
	To accrue income tax expense.		

PANEL C—Ledger Accounts

Assets

Cash

Debit	Credit
Bal. 24,800	

Accounts Receivable

Debit	Credit
2,250	
(e) 250	
Bal. 2,500	

Supplies

Debit	Credit
700	(b) 300
Bal. 400	

Prepaid Rent

Debit	Credit
3,000	(a) 1,000
Bal. 2,000	

Furniture

Debit	Credit
Bal. 16,500	

Accumulated Depreciation—Furniture

Debit	Credit
	(c) 275
	Bal. 275

Liabilities

Accounts Payable

Debit	Credit
	Bal. 13,100

Salary Payable

Debit	Credit
	(d) 950
	Bal. 950

Unearned Service Revenue

Debit	Credit
(f) 150	450
	Bal. 300

Income Tax Payable

Debit	Credit
	(g) 540
	Bal. 540

Stockholders' Equity

Common Stock

Debit	Credit
	Bal. 20,000

Retained Earnings

Debit	Credit
	Bal. 11,250

Dividends

Debit	Credit
Bal. 3,200	

Revenue

Service Revenue

Debit	Credit
	7,000
	(e) 250
	(f) 150
	Bal. 7,400

Expenses

Rent Expense

Debit	Credit
(a) 1,000	
Bal. 1,000	

Salary Expense

Debit	Credit
950	
(d) 950	
Bal. 1,900	

Supplies Expense

Debit	Credit
(b) 300	
Bal. 300	

Depreciation Expense—Furniture

Debit	Credit
(c) 275	
Bal. 275	

Utilities Expense

Debit	Credit
Bal. 400	

Income Tax Expense

Debit	Credit
(g) 540	
Bal. 540	

Exhibit 3-11

Adjusted Trial Balance

Air & Sea Travel, Inc.

Preparation of Adjusted Trial Balance
April 30, 20X3

Trial Balance	Adjustments		Adjusted Trial Balance			
Account Title	***Debit***	***Credit***	***Debit***	***Credit***	***Debit***	***Credit***
Cash	24,800				24,800	
Accounts receivable	2,250		(e) 250		2,500	
Supplies	700			(b) 300	400	
Prepaid rent	3,000			(a) 1,000	2,000	
Furniture	16,500				16,500	
Accumulated depreciation—furniture				(c) 275		275
Accounts payable		13,100				13,100
Salary payable				(d) 950		950
Unearned service revenue		450	(f) 150			300
Income tax payable				(g) 540		540
Common stock		20,000				20,000
Retained earnings		11,250				11,250
Dividends	3,200				3,200	
Service revenue		7,000		(e) 250		7,400
				(f) 150		
Rent expense			(a) 1,000		1,000	
Salary expense	950		(d) 950		1,900	
Supplies expense			(b) 300		300	
Depreciation expense			(c) 275		275	
Utilities expense	400				400	
Income tax expense			(g) 540		540	
	51,800	51,800	3,465	3,465	53,815	53,815

✔ Check Point 3-10

✔ Check Point 3-11

Preparing the Financial Statements

Objective

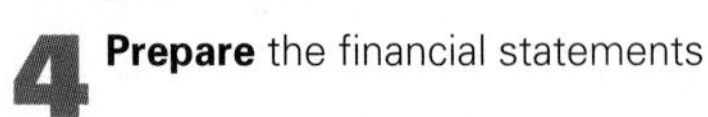

4 Prepare the financial statements

The April financial statements of Air & Sea Travel can be prepared from the adjusted trial balance. Exhibit 3-12 shows how the accounts are distributed from the adjusted trial balance to the financial statements. The income statement (Exhibit 3-13) comes from the revenue and expense accounts. The statement of retained earnings (Exhibit 3-14) shows the changes in retained earnings. The balance sheet (Exhibit 3-15) reports assets, liabilities, and stockholders' equity.

The arrows in Exhibits 3-13, 3-14, and 3-15 show the flow of data from one statement to the next. Let's examine the statements ←. Why is the income statement prepared first and the balance sheet last?

→ The relationships among the financial statements were introduced in Chapter 1, page 27.

1. The income statement reports net income or net loss, revenues minus expenses. Because revenues and expenses affect stockholders' equity, net income is then transferred to retained earnings. The first arrow tracks net income.

Account Title	Adjusted Trial Balance Debit	Credit	
Cash	24,800		Balance Sheet (Exhibit 3-15)
Accounts receivable	2,500		
Supplies	400		
Prepaid rent	2,000		
Furniture	16,500		
Accumulated depreciation—furniture		275	
Accounts payable		13,100	
Salary payable		950	
Unearned service revenue		300	
Income tax payable		540	
Common stock		20,000	
Retained earnings		11,250	Statement of Retained Earnings (Exhibit 3-14)
Dividends	3,200		
Service revenue		7,400	Income Statement (Exhibit 3-13)
Rent expense	1,000		
Salary expense	1,900		
Supplies expense	300		
Depreciation expense	275		
Utilities expense	400		
Income tax expense	540		
	53,815	53,815	

Exhibit 3-12

The Financial Statements of Air & Sea Travel, Inc. can be taken from the Adjusted Trial Balance

✔ Check Point 3-12

Exhibit 3-13

Income Statement

Air & Sea Travel, Inc.

Income Statement
Month Ended April 30, 20X3

Revenue:		
Service revenue		$7,400
Expenses:		
Salary expense	$1,900	
Rent expense	1,000	
Utilities expense	400	
Supplies expense	300	
Depreciation expense	275	3,875
Income before tax		3,525
Income tax expense		540
Net income		$2,985

①

Exhibit 3-14

Statement of Retained Earnings

Air & Sea Travel, Inc.

Statement of Retained Earnings
Month Ended April 30, 20X3

Retained earnings, April 1, 20X3	$11,250
Add: Net income	2,985
	14,235
Less: Dividends	(3,200)
Retained earnings, April 30, 20X3	$11,035

Exhibit 3-15

Balance Sheet

Air & Sea Travel. INC.

Balance Sheet
April 30, 20X3

②

Assets			***Liabilities***	
Cash		$24,800	Accounts payable	$13,100
Accounts receivable		2,500	Salary payable	950
Supplies		400	Unearned service revenue	300
Prepaid rent		2,000	Income tax payable	540
Furniture	$16,500		Total liabilities	14,890
Less Accumulated depreciation	(275)	16,225	***Stockholders' Equity***	
			Common stock	20,000
			Retained earnings	11,035
			Total stockholders' equity	31,035
Total assets		$45,925	Total liabilities and stockholders' equity	$45,925

2. Retained Earnings is a balance sheet account, so its ending balance appears on the balance sheet. Retained Earnings is the final balancing element of the balance sheet. To solidify your understanding, trace the $11,035 retained earnings figure from Exhibit 3-14 to Exhibit 3-15. Arrow ② tracks retained earnings.

Mid-Chapter Summary Problem

The trial balance of State Service Company shown below pertains to December 31, 20X5, which is the end of its year-long accounting period. Data needed for the adjusting entries include the following:

a. Supplies on hand at year end, $2,000.
b. Depreciation on furniture and fixtures, $20,000.
c. Depreciation on building, $10,000.
d. Salaries owed but not yet paid, $5,000.
e. Accrued service revenue, $12,000.
f. Of the $45,000 balance of unearned service revenue, $32,000 was earned during the year.
g. Accrued income tax expense, $35,000.

Required

1. Open the ledger accounts with their unadjusted balances. Show dollar amounts in thousands, as shown for Accounts Receivable:

Accounts Receivable	
370	

2. Journalize the State Service Company adjusting entries at December 31, 20X5. Key entries by letter, as in Exhibit 3-10.
3. Post the adjusting entries.
4. Enter the trial balance on a work sheet, enter the adjusting entries, and prepare an adjusted trial balance, as shown in Exhibit 3-11.
5. Prepare the income statement, the statement of retained earnings, and the balance sheet. (At this stage, it is not necessary to classify assets or liabilities as current or long term.) Draw arrows linking these three financial statements.

State Service Company
Trial Balance
December 31, 20X5

Cash	$ 198,000	
Accounts receivable	370,000	
Supplies	6,000	
Furniture and fixtures	100,000	
Accumulated depreciation—furniture and fixtures		$ 40,000
Building	250,000	
Accumulated depreciation—building		130,000
Accounts payable		380,000
Salary payable		
Unearned service revenue		45,000
Income tax payable		
Common stock		100,000
Retained earnings		193,000
Dividends	65,000	
Service revenue		286,000
Salary expense	172,000	
Supplies expense		
Depreciation expense—furniture and fixtures		
Depreciation expense—building		
Income tax expense		
Miscellaneous expense	13,000	
Total	$1,174,000	$1,174,000

Answers

Requirements 1 and 3

ASSETS

Cash

	Debit		Credit
Bal.	198		

Accounts Receivable

	Debit		Credit
	370		
(e)	12		
Bal.	382		

Supplies

	Debit		Credit
	6	(a)	4
Bal.	2		

Furniture and Fixtures

	Debit		Credit
Bal.	100		

Accumulated Depreciation—Furniture and Fixtures

	Debit		Credit
			40
		(b)	20
		Bal.	60

Building

	Debit		Credit
Bal.	250		

Accumulated Depreciation—Building

	Debit		Credit
			130
		(c)	10
		Bal.	140

LIABILITIES

Accounts Payable

	Debit		Credit
		Bal.	380

Salary Payable

	Debit		Credit
		(d)	5
		Bal.	5

Unearned Service Revenue

	Debit		Credit
(f)	32		45
		Bal.	13

Income Tax Payable

	Debit		Credit
		(g)	35
		Bal.	35

STOCKHOLDERS' EQUITY

Common Stock

	Debit		Credit
		Bal.	100

Retained Earnings

	Debit		Credit
		Bal.	193

Dividends

	Debit		Credit
Bal.	65		

REVENUE

Service Revenue

	Debit		Credit
			286
		(e)	12
		(f)	32
		Bal.	330

EXPENSES

Salary Expense

	Debit		Credit
	172		
(d)	5		
Bal.	177		

Supplies Expense

	Debit		Credit
(a)	4		
Bal.	4		

Depreciation Expense—Furniture and Fixtures

	Debit		Credit
(b)	20		
Bal.	20		

Depreciation Expense—Building

	Debit		Credit
(c)	10		
Bal.	10		

Income Tax Expense

	Debit		Credit
(g)	35		
Bal.	35		

Miscellaneous Expense

	Debit		Credit
Bal.	13		

Requirement 2

	20X5			
(a)	Dec. 31	Supplies Expense ($6,000 – $2,000)	4,000	
		Supplies		4,000
		To record supplies used.		
(b)	31	Depreciation Expense—Furniture and Fixtures	20,000	
		Accumulated Depreciation—Furniture and Fixtures		20,000
		To record depreciation expense on furniture and fixtures.		
(c)	31	Depreciation Expense—Building	10,000	
		Accumulated Depreciation—Building		10,000
		To record depreciation expense on building.		
(d)	31	Salary Expense	5,000	
		Salary Payable		5,000
		To accrue salary expense.		

(e)	31	Accounts Receivable	12,000	
		Service Revenue		12,000
		To accrue service revenue.		
(f)	31	Unearned Service Revenue	32,000	
		Service Revenue		32,000
		To record unearned service revenue that has been earned.		
(g)	31	Income Tax Expense	35,000	
		Income Tax Payable		35,000
		To accrue income tax expense.		

Requirement 4

State Service Company

Preparation of Adjusted Trial Balance
December 31, 20X5

(Amounts in Thousands)

	Trial Balance		Adjustments		Adjusted Trial Balance	
	Debit	**Credit**	**Debit**	**Credit**	**Debit**	**Credit**
Cash	198				198	
Accounts receivable	370		(e) 12		382	
Supplies	6			(a) 4	2	
Furniture and fixtures	100				100	
Accumulated depreciation—furniture and fixtures		40		(b) 20		60
Building	250				250	
Accumulated depreciation—building		130		(c) 10		140
Accounts payable		380				380
Salary payable				(d) 5		5
Unearned service revenue		45	(f) 32			13
Income tax payable				(g) 35		35
Common stock		100				100
Retained earnings		193				193
Dividends	65				65	
Service revenue		286		(e) 12 (f) 32		330
Salary expense	172		(d) 5		177	
Supplies expense			(a) 4		4	
Depreciation expense—furniture and fixtures			(b) 20		20	
Depreciation expense—building			(c) 10		10	
Income tax expense			(g) 35		35	
Miscellaneous expense	13				13	
	1,174	1,174	118	118	1,256	1,256

Requirement 5

State Service Company
Income Statement
Year Ended December 31, 20X5

	(Amounts in Thousands)	
Revenue:		
Service revenue		$330
Expenses:		
Salary expense	$177	
Depreciation expense—furniture and fixtures	20	
Depreciation expense—building	10	
Supplies expense	4	
Miscellaneous expense	13	224
Income before tax		106
Income tax expense		35
Net income		$ 71

State Service Company
Statement of Retained Earnings
Year Ended December 31, 20X5

	(Amounts in Thousands)
Retained earnings, January 1, 20X5	$193
Add: Net income	71
	264
Less: Dividends	(65)
Retained earnings, December 31, 20X5	$199

State Service Company
Balance Sheet
December 31, 20X5

(Amounts in Thousands)

Assets			Liabilities	
Cash		$198	Accounts payable	$380
Accounts receivable		382	Salary payable	5
Supplies		2	Unearned service revenue	13
Furniture and fixtures	$100		Income tax payable	35
Less accumulated depreciation	(60)	40	Total liabilities	433
			Stockholders' Equity	
Building	$250		Common stock	100
Less accumulated depreciation	(140)	110	Retained earnings	199
			Total stockholders' equity	299
Total assets		$732	Total liabilities and stockholders' equity	$732

DECISION: Which Accounts Need to Be Closed?

It is now April 30, the end of the month. Gary and Monica Lyon have Air & Sea Travel's income statement and balance sheet. The income statement lets them know the business profit for April, and the balance sheet reports its financial position. Presumably, the Lyons will continue operating the travel agency into May, June, and beyond. But wait—the revenue and the expense accounts still hold amounts for April. At the end of each accounting period, it is necessary to close the books.

Objective

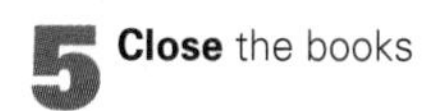

5 Close the books

Closing the books means to prepare the accounts for the next period's transactions. The **closing entries** set the balances of the revenue and expense accounts back to zero at the end of the accounting period. The idea is the same as setting the scoreboard back to zero after a football game.

Closing is a clerical procedure that is easily handled by computers. Recall that the income statement reports only one period's income. For example, net income for Vodafone or Air & Sea Travel for 2001 relates exclusively to 2001. At each year end, Vodafone accountants close the company's revenues and expenses for that year. Because revenues and expenses relate to a particular accounting period, they are called **temporary accounts.** The Dividends account is also temporary. The closing process applies only to temporary accounts (revenues, expenses, and dividends).

Let's contrast the temporary accounts with the **permanent accounts:** assets, liabilities, and stockholders' equity. The permanent accounts are not closed at the end of the period because their balances are not used to measure income. Instead, they carry over to the next period. Consider Cash, Receivables, Buildings, Accounts Payable, Notes, Common Stock, and Retained Earnings. Their ending balances at the end of one period become the beginning balances of the next period.

Closing entries transfer the revenue, expense, and dividends balances to Retained Earnings. Following are the steps to close the books of a corporation such as Vodafone or Air & Sea Travel:

① Debit each revenue account for the amount of its credit balance. Credit Retained Earnings for the sum of the revenues. Now the sum of the revenues is in Retained Earnings.

② Credit each expense account for the amount of its debit balance. Debit Retained Earnings for the sum of the expenses. The sum of the expenses is also in Retained Earnings.

③ Credit the Dividends account for the amount of its debit balance. Debit the Retained Earnings account. This entry places the dividends amount alongside expenses in the Retained Earnings account. *Remember that dividends are not expenses and do not affect net income or net loss.*

After closing the books, the Retained Earnings account appears as follows (using Air & Sea Travel actual data):

Retained Earnings

		Beginning balance	**11,250**
Expenses	**4,415**	**Revenues**	**7,400**
Dividends	**3,200**		
		Ending balance	**11,035**

Assume that Air & Sea Travel closes the books at the end of April. Exhibit 3-16 presents the complete closing process for the business. Panel A gives the closing journal entries, and Panel B shows the accounts after closing.

Closing the books
The process of preparing the accounts to begin recording the next period's transactions. Closing the accounts consists of journalizing and posting the closing entries to set the balances of the revenue, expense, and dividends accounts to zero. Also called *closing the accounts.*

Closing entries
Entries that transfer the revenue, expense, and dividends balances from these respective accounts to the Retained Earnings account.

Temporary account
Another name for a *nominal account.* The revenue and expense accounts that relate to a particular accounting period and are closed at the end of the period are temporary accounts. For a corporation, the Dividends account is also temporary.

Permanent account
Asset, liability, and stockholders' equity that are not closed at the end of the period. Also called a *real account.*

Exhibit 3-16

Journalizing and Posting the Closing Entries

PANEL A—Journalizing the Closing Entries — Page 5

Closing Entries

	Date	Accounts	Debit	Credit
①	Apr. 30	Service Revenue	7,400	
		Retained Earnings		7,400
②	30	Retained Earnings	4,415	
		Rent Expense		1,000
		Salary Expense		1,900
		Supplies Expense		300
		Depreciation Expense		275
		Utilities Expense		400
		Income Tax Expense		540
③	30	Retained Earnings	3,200	
		Dividends		3,200

✔ Check Point 3-13

PANEL B—Posting to the Accounts

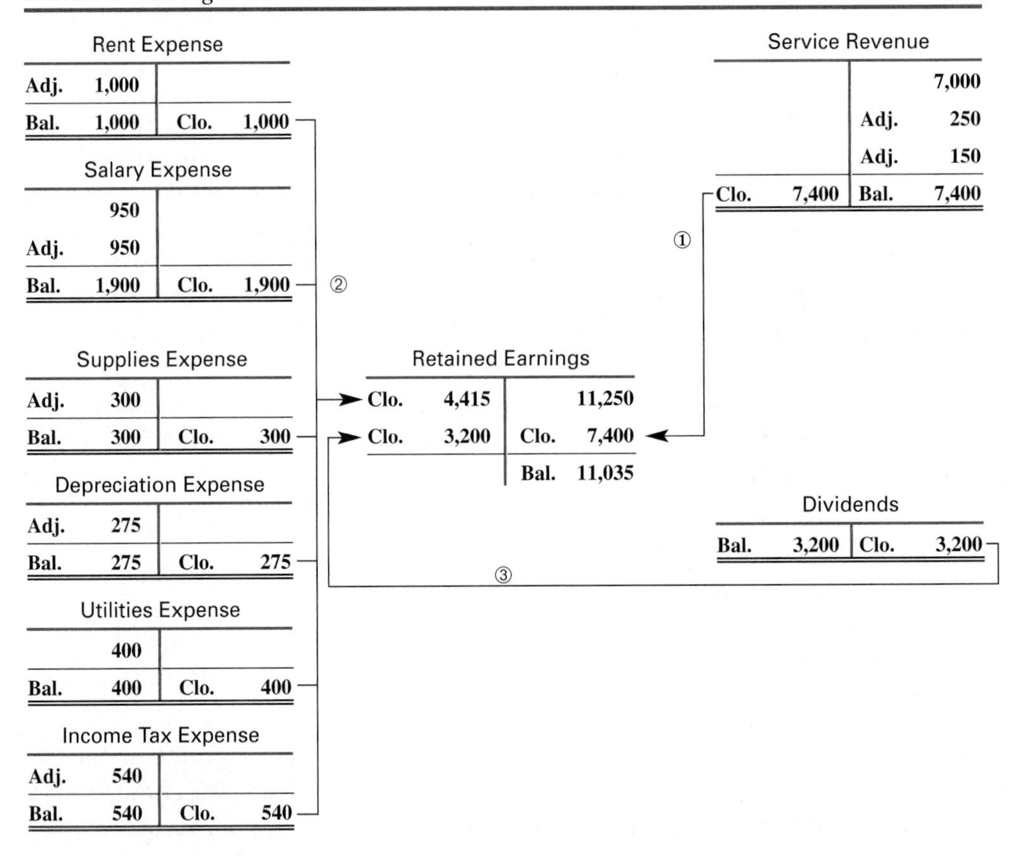

Adj. = Amount posted from an adjusting entry
Clo. = Amount posted from a closing entry
Bal. = Balance
As arrow ② in Panel B shows, it is not necessary to make a separate closing entry for each expense. In one closing entry, we record one debit to Retained Earnings and a separate credit to each expense account.

current assets, current liabilities

Liquidity
Measure of how quickly an item can be converted to cash.

Classifying Assets and Liabilities

On the balance sheet, assets and liabilities are classified as *current* or *long term* to indicate their relative liquidity. **Liquidity** measures how quickly an item can be converted to cash. Cash is the most liquid asset. Accounts receivable are relatively liquid because the business expects to collect the cash in the near future. Inventory is less liquid than accounts receivable because the company must first sell the goods. Furniture and buildings are even less liquid because these assets are held for use and not for sale.

Users of financial statements are interested in liquidity because financial problems arise from a shortage of cash. How quickly can the business convert an asset to cash and pay a debt? How soon must a liability be paid? These are questions of liquidity. A balance sheets lists assets and liabilities in the order of their relative liquidity.

CURRENT ASSETS. As we saw in Chapter 1, **current assets** are the most liquid assets. They will be converted to cash, sold, or consumed during the next 12 months or within the business's normal operating cycle if longer than a year. The **operating cycle** is the time span during which (1) cash is paid for goods and services and (2) these goods and services are sold to bring in cash. For most businesses, the operating cycle is a few months. Cash, Accounts Receivable, Merchandise Inventory, and Prepaid Expenses are current assets. Service entities such as Vodafone, America Online (AOL), and Air & Sea Travel do not hold inventory.

Current asset
An asset that is expected to be converted to cash, sold, or consumed during the next 12 months, or within the business' normal operating cycle if longer than a year.

Operating cycle
Time span during which cash is paid for goods and services that are sold to customers who pay the business in cash.

LONG-TERM ASSETS. **Long-term assets** are all assets not classified as current assets. One category of long-term assets is plant assets, often labeled Property, Plant, and Equipment. Land, Buildings, Furniture and Fixtures, and Equipment are plant assets. Of these, Air & Sea Travel has only Furniture. Long-Term Investments, Intangible Assets, and Other Assets (a catchall category for assets that are not classified more precisely) are also long term.

Long-term asset
An asset that is not a current asset.

Those who use financial statements (such as bankers and other lenders) are interested in the due dates of an entity's liabilities. The sooner a liability must be paid, the more current it is. Liabilities that must be paid immediately create the greatest strain. Therefore, the balance sheet lists liabilities in the order in which they must be paid. Balance sheets usually report two liability classifications, *current liabilities* and *long-term liabilities*.

CURRENT LIABILITIES. As we saw in Chapter 1, **current liabilities** are debts that must be paid within 1 year or within the entity's operating cycle if longer than a year. Accounts Payable, Notes Payable due within 1 year, Salary Payable, Unearned Revenue, Interest Payable, and Income Tax Payable are current liabilities.

Current liability
A debt due to be paid within one year or within the entity's operating cycle if the cycle is longer than a year.

LONG-TERM LIABILITIES. All liabilities that are not current are classified as **long-term liabilities.** Many notes payable are long term. Some notes payable are paid in installments, with the first installment due within 1 year, the second installment due the second year, and so on. In this case, the first installment would be a current liability and the remainder would be long term.

Long-term liability
A liability that is not a current liability.

Let's see how a real company reports these asset and liability categories on its balance sheet.

✔ Check Point 3-14

Reporting Assets and Liabilities: Best Buy Co.

Exhibit 3-17 shows the actual classified balance sheet, the income statement, and the statement of cash flows of Best Buy Co., Inc., the nation's largest specialty retailer of consumer electronics. A **classified balance sheet** separates current assets from long-term assets and current liabilities from long-term liabilities. You should be familiar with most of Best Buy's accounts. Study the Best Buy statements all the way through—line by line.

Classified balance sheet
A balance sheet that shows current assets separate from long-term assets, and current liabilities separate from long-term liabilities.

Exhibit 3-17

Financial Statements of Best Buy Company, Inc.

Best Buy Company, Inc.

Consolidated Balance Sheets (Adapted)

	Thousands	
Assets	***March 3, 2001***	***Feb. 26, 2000***
Current Assets		
Cash and cash equivalents	$ 746,879	$ 750,723
Receivables	209,031	189,301
Merchandise inventories	1,766,934	1,183,681
Other current assets	205,819	114,755
Total current assets	2,928,663	2,238,460
Property and Equipment		
Land and buildings	170,978	76,228
Leasehold improvements	556,534	254,767
Fixtures and equipment	1,259,880	762,476
	1,987,392	1,093,471
Less accumulated depreciation	543,220	395,387
Net property and equipment	1,444,172	698,084
Goodwill, Net	385,355	—
Other Assets	81,397	58,798
Total Assets	$4,839,587	$2,995,342
Liabilities and Shareholders' Equity		
Current Liabilities		
Accounts payable	$1,772,722	$1,313,940
Accrued compensation and related expenses payable	154,159	102,065
Accrued liabilities	545,590	287,888
Accrued income taxes payable	127,287	65,366
Current portion of long-term debt	114,940	15,790
Total current liabilities	2,714,698	1,785,049
Other Long-Term Liabilities	121,952	99,448
Long-Term Debt	181,009	14,860
Shareholders' Equity		
Common stock	597,632	267,528
Retained earnings	1,224,296	828,457
Total shareholders' equity	1,821,928	1,095,985
Total Liabilities and Shareholders' Equity	$4,839,587	$2,995,342

Best Buy Company, Inc.

Consolidated Statements of Earnings (Adapted)

	Thousands	
For the Fiscal Years Ended	*March 3, 2001*	*Feb. 26, 2000*
Revenues	$15,326,552	$12,494,023
Cost of goods sold	12,267,459	10,100,594
Gross profit	3,059,093	2,393,429
Selling, general and administrative expenses	2,454,785	1,854,170
Operating income	604,308	539,259
Interest income	37,171	23,311
Earnings before income tax expense	641,479	562,570
Income tax expense	245,640	215,500
Net earnings	$ 395,839	$ 347,070

Best Buy Company, Inc.

Consolidated Statements of Cash Flows (Adapted)

	Thousands	
For the Fiscal Years Ended	*March 3, 2001*	*Feb. 26, 2000*
Operating Activities		
Total cash provided by operating activities	$ 808,204	$ 776,448
Investing Activities		
Additions to property and equipmen.	(657,706)	(361,024)
Acquisitions of businesses, net of cash acquired	(326,077)	—
Increase in other assets	(46,019)	(55,310)
Total cash used in investing activities	(1,029,802)	(416,334)
Financing Activities		
Long-term debt payments	(17,625)	(29,946)
Issuance of common stock	235,379	32,229
Repurchase of common stock	—	(397,451)
Total cash provided by (used in) financing activities	217,754	(395,168)
(Decrease) Increase in Cash and Cash Equivalents	(3,844)	(35,054)
Cash and Cash Equivalents at Beginning of Period	750,723	785,777
Cash and Cash Equivalents at End of Period	$ 746,879	$ 750,723

Best Buy's financial statements need a few explanations:

1. *Consolidated* in the statement titles means that Best Buy owns a number of different companies, and all of those companies' financial statements are combined, or consolidated, into a single set of statements for Best Buy Co., Inc.

2. The dates of the statements may look strange. Best Buy, like many other companies, ends its accounting year on the Saturday nearest its basic year-end date, which is February 28 each year. In 2001, that date fell on March 3. In 2000, the year-end date fell on February 26.

3. Best Buy is in a major growth phase. Total assets on the balance sheet grew dramatically (from $3.0 to $4.8 billion) during the year ended March 3, 2001. Net income (net earnings) on the income statement (statement of earnings) also increased (from $347 to $395 million).

4. The statement of cash flows reports strong positive cash flow from operations ($808 million in 2001). Investing activities reveal that Best Buy is expanding (additions to property and equipment). Financing activities are strong; Best Buy was able to issue lots of new stock.

Comparing Income Statements: Vodafone and Best Buy

Let's compare the adapted income statements of Vodafone, a British company, and Best Buy, an American corporation. The chapter opener gives Vodafone's income statement, which appears with only five lines of data. Best Buy's income statement (Exhibit 3-17) fills nine lines. The biggest difference between the two income statements is in the reporting of expenses. Vodafone reports a single total for operating expenses. Best Buy reports two expense categories—cost of goods sold and selling, and general and administrative expenses.

The Best Buy data are more useful for investors and lenders because of the breakdown of expenses. True, Vodafone sells services, whereas Best Buy sells products (cost of goods sold). But many American service companies, such as Sprint and AT&T, which are similar to Vodafone, report an expense for *cost of services sold*. In general, U.S. companies report more data than foreign companies do. This is one reason that foreigners invest more in U.S. companies than Americans invest in foreign companies.

Formats for the Financial Statements

Companies can format their financial statements in different ways. Both the balance sheet and the income statement can be formatted in two basic ways.

Balance Sheet Formats

Report format
A balance-sheet format that lists assets at the top, followed by liabilities and stockholders' equity below.

Account format
A balance-sheet format that lists assets on the left and liabilities and stockholders' equity on the right.

The **report format** lists the assets at the top, followed by the liabilities and stockholders' equity below. The balance sheet of Best Buy Co., Inc., in Exhibit 3-17 illustrates the report format. Either format is acceptable. The report format is more popular, with approximately 60% of large companies using it.

The **account format** lists the assets on the left and the liabilities and stockholders' equity on the right in the same way that a T-account appears, with assets (debits) on the left and liabilities and equity (credits) on the right.

Income Statement Formats

A **multi-step income statement** contains a number of subtotals to highlight important relationships among revenues and expenses. For example, Best Buy's multi-step income statement in Exhibit 3-17 highlights gross profit (also called *gross margin*), operating income, and other income and expense (such as Interest income for Best Buy).

Multi-step income statement
An income statement that contains subtotals to highlight important relationships between revenues and expenses.

A **single-step income statement** does not show gross profit or operating income. Instead, it lists all the revenues together under a heading such as Revenues, or Revenues and Gains. The expenses are listed together in a single category titled Expenses, or Expenses and Losses. There is only one step, the subtraction of Expenses and Losses from the sum of Revenues and Gains, in arriving at net income. If Best Buy were to report its income statement in single-step format, the statement would appear as follows:

Single-step income statement
An income statement that lists all the revenues together under a heading such as Revenues or Revenues and Gains. Expenses appear in a separate category called Expenses, Costs, and Expenses, or perhaps Expenses and Losses.

Best Buy Company, Inc.
Statement of Earnings (Adapted as Single-Step)
Year Ended March 3, 2001

Revenues:	
Revenues	$15,326,552
Interest income	37,171
Total revenues	15,363,723
Expenses:	
Cost of goods sold	12,267,459
Selling, general, and administrative expenses	2,454,785
Income tax expense	245,640
Total expenses	14,967,884
Net income	$ 395,839

Most actual company income statements do not conform to either a pure single-step format or a pure multi-step format. Today, business operations are too complex for all companies to conform to rigid reporting formats.

Decision Making: Using Accounting Ratios

As we've seen, accounting provides information for decision making. A bank considering lending money must predict whether the borrower can repay the loan. If the borrower already has a lot of debt, the probability of repayment may be low. If the borrower owes little, the loan may go through. To analyze a company's financial position, decision makers use ratios computed from various items in the financial statements. Let's see exactly how this process works.

current ratio, debt ratio

Objective

6 **Use** the current ratio and the debt ratio to evaluate a business

Current Ratio

One of the most widely used financial ratios is the **current ratio**, which is the ratio of an entity's current assets to its current liabilities, taken from the balance sheet.

Current ratio
Current assets divided by current liabilities. Measures a company's ability to pay current liabilities with current assets.

$$\text{Current ratio} = \frac{\text{Total current assets}}{\text{Total current liabilities}}$$

For Best Buy (amounts in thousands for 2001):

$$\frac{\$2{,}928{,}663}{\$2{,}714{,}698} = 1.08$$

The current ratio measures the company's ability to pay current liabilities with current assets. A company prefers to have a high current ratio, which means that the business has plenty of current assets to pay current liabilities. An increasing current ratio from period to period indicates improvement in financial position.

As a rule of thumb, a strong current ratio is 1.50, which indicates that the company has $1.50 in current assets for every $1.00 in current liabilities. A company with a current ratio of 1.50 would probably have little trouble paying its current liabilities. Most successful businesses operate with current ratios between 1.20 and 1.50. A current ratio of 1.00 is considered quite low. Best Buy's current ratio of 1.08 is low and indicates a weak current position.

The Decision Guidelines feature on page 145 provides some tips for using the current ratio.

Debt Ratio

Debt ratio
Ratio of total liabilities to total assets. States the proportion of a company's assets that is financed with debt.

A second aid to decision making is the **debt ratio,** which is the ratio of total liabilities to total assets:

$$\text{Debt ratio} = \frac{\text{Total liabilities}}{\text{Total assets}}$$

For Best Buy (amounts in thousands for 2001),

$$\frac{\$2{,}714{,}698 + \$121{,}952 + \$181{,}009}{\$4{,}839{,}587} = \frac{\$3{,}017{,}659}{\$4{,}839{,}587} = .62$$

The debt ratio indicates the proportion of a company's assets that is financed with debt. This ratio measures a business's ability to pay both current and long-term debts (total liabilities).

A low debt ratio is safer than a high debt ratio. Why? Because a company with a small amount of liabilities has low required payments. This company is unlikely to get into financial difficulty. By contrast, a business with a high debt ratio may have trouble paying its liabilities, especially when sales are low and cash is scarce. Best Buy's debt ratio of 62% (0.62) is in the normal range for most companies in the United States.

When a company fails to pay its debts, the creditors can take the company away from its owners. The largest retail bankruptcy in history, Federated Department Stores (parent company of Bloomingdale's), was due largely to high debt during an industry recession. Federated was unable to weather the downturn.

✔ Check Point 3-15

Decision Guidelines

In general, a *high* current ratio is preferable to a low current ratio. *Increases* in the current ratio indicate improving financial position. By contrast, a *low* debt ratio is preferable to a high debt ratio. Improvement is indicated by a *decrease* in the debt ratio.

No single ratio gives the whole picture about a company. Therefore, lenders and investors use many ratios to evaluate a company. Now, let's apply what we have learned. Suppose you are a loan officer at Bank One, and Best Buy has asked you to lend the company, $20 million to open new stores in Columbus, Ohio. How will you make this loan decision? The Decision Guidelines show how bankers and investors use two key ratios.

USING THE CURRENT RATIO

Decision	Guidelines
How can you measure a company's ability to pay current liabilities with current assets?	$\text{Current ratio} = \dfrac{\text{Total current assets}}{\text{Total current liabilities}}$
Who uses the current ratio for decision making?	*Lenders* and other *creditors*, who must predict whether a borrower can pay its current liabilities. *Stockholders*, who know that a company that cannot pay its debts is not a good investment because it may go bankrupt. *Managers*, who must have enough cash to pay the company's current liabilities.
What is a good value of the current ratio?	Depends on the industry: A company with strong cash flow can operate successfully with a low current ratio of, say, 1.10–1.20. A company with weak cash flow needs a higher current ratio of, say, 1.30–1.50. Traditionally, a current ratio of 2.00 was considered ideal. Recently, acceptable values have decreased as companies have been able to operate more efficiently; today, a current ratio of 1.50 is considered strong.

USING THE DEBT RATIO

Decision	Guidelines
How can you measure a company's ability to pay total liabilities?	$\text{Debt ratio} = \dfrac{\text{Total liabilities}}{\text{Total assets}}$
Who uses the debt ratio for decision making?	*Lenders* and other *creditors*, who must predict whether a borrower can pay its debts. *Stockholders*, who know that a company that cannot pay its debts is not a good investment because it may go bankrupt. *Managers* who must have enough assets to pay the company's debts.
What is a good value of the debt ratio?	Depends on the industry: A company with strong cash flow can operate successfully with a high debt ratio of, say, 0.70–0.80. A company with weak cash flow needs a lower debt ratio of, say, 0.60–0.70. Traditionally, a debt ratio of 0.50 was considered ideal. Recently, values have increased as companies have been able to operate more efficiently; today, a normal value of the debt ratio is around 0.60–0.65.

Excel Application Problem

Goal: Create an Excel spreadsheet to calculate the current ratio and debt ratio for different companies, and use the results to answer questions about the companies. Requires Web research on Gap, Inc. and Pacific Sunwear.

Scenario: You are deciding whether to buy the stock of two well-known clothing retailers, Gap, Inc., and Pacific Sunwear. You know that the current ratio and the debt ratio measure whether a company has the assets to cover its liabilities.

Your task is to create a simple spreadsheet to compare the current ratio and the debt ratio for each company. When done, answer these questions:

1. Do both companies have an acceptable current ratio? How can you tell?
2. Do both companies have an acceptable debt ratio? How can you tell?
3. What is the trend (up or down) for the ratios of both companies? Is the trend for each company positive or negative? Why?
4. Which company has the "better" ending current ratio? The "better" ending debt ratio?

Step-by-step:

1. Locate the following current and prior year information for Gap, Inc. and Pacific Sunwear (found on the "Consolidated Balance Sheets"). For Gap, go to **www.gap.com**, click on "Company Info," then "Financials & Media," and then "Annual Reports." For Pacific Sunwear, go to **www.pacsun.com**, click on "Company," then "Investor Info," "SEC Filings," and then locate the latest Form 10-K.
   a. Current Assets
   b. Total Assets
   c. Current Liabilities
   d. Long-Term Liabilities (This may have to be computed on the spreadsheet.)
   e. Total Liabilities (This may have to be computed on the spreadsheet.)
   f. Total Shareholders' Equity (Investment)
   g. Total Liabilities and Shareholders' Equity (Investment)
2. Open a new Excel spreadsheet.
3. Create a bold-faced heading for your spreadsheet that contains the following:
   a. Chapter 3 Decision Guidelines
   b. The Current Ratio and Debt Ratio
   c. Gap, Inc. and Pacific Sunwear Comparison
   d. Today's date
4. Two rows down from your worksheet heading, create a column heading titled "GAP (in 000's)." Make it bold and underline the heading.
5. One row down from Gap's column heading, create a row with the following bold, underlined column titles:
   a. Account
   b. FYxx (xx = the most recent fiscal year, for example, 02)
   c. FYyy (yy = the prior fiscal year, for example, 01)
6. Starting with the "Account" column heading, enter the data found in #1, above. You should have seven rows of data, with row descriptions (for example, "Current Assets"). Format the columns as necessary.
7. Skip a row at the end of your data, and then create a row titled "Current Ratio" and another row titled "Debt Ratio."
8. Enter the formula for each ratio in the "FYxx" and "FYyy" columns. You should have four formulas. Make both rows bold.
9. Repeat steps 4–8, substituting the Pacific Sunwear title and data as appropriate.
10. Save your work to disk, and print a copy for your files.

End-of-Chapter Summary Problem

Refer to the mid-chapter summary problem that begins on page 133.

Required

1. Make State Service Company's closing entries at December 31, 20X5. Explain what the closing entries accomplish and why they are necessary.
2. Post the closing entries to Retained Earnings and compare Retained Earnings' ending balance with the amount reported on the balance sheet on page 136. The two amounts should be the same.
3. Prepare State Service Company's classified balance sheet to identify the company's current assets and current liabilities. (State has no long-term liabilities.) Then compute the company's current ratio and debt ratio at December 31, 20X5.
4. The top management of State Service Company has asked you for a $500,000 loan to expand the business. State proposes to pay off the loan over a 10-year period. Recompute State's debt ratio assuming you make the loan. Use the company financial statements plus the ratio values to decide whether to grant the loan at an interest rate of 8%, 10%, or 12%. State Service Company's cash flow is strong. Give the reasoning underlying your decision.

Answers

Requirement 1

20X5		(In thousands)	
Dec. 31	Service Revenue	330	
	Retained Earnings		330
31	Retained Earnings	259	
	Salary Expense		177
	Depreciation Expense—Furniture and Fixtures		20
	Depreciation Expense—Building		10
	Supplies Expense		4
	Income Tax Expense		35
	Miscellaneous Expense		13
31	Retained Earnings	65	
	Dividends		65

Explanation of Closing Entries

The closing entries set the balance of each revenue, expense, and Dividends account back to zero for the start of the next accounting period. We must close these accounts because their balances relate only to one accounting period.

Requirement 2

Retained Earnings

Clo.	**259**		**193**
Clo.	**65**	**Clo.**	**330**
		Bal.	**199**

The balance in the Retained Earnings account agrees with the amount reported on the balance sheet, as it should.

Requirement 3

$$\text{Current ratio} = \frac{\$582}{\$433} = 1.34 \qquad \text{Debt ratio} = \frac{\$433}{\$732} = 0.59$$

State Service Company

Balance Sheet
December 31, 20X5

(Amounts in Thousands)

Assets			Liabilities	
Current assets			Current liabilities	
Cash		$198	Accounts payable	$380
Accounts receivable		382	Salary payable	5
Supplies		2	Unearned service revenue	13
Total current assets		582	Income tax payable	35
Furniture and fixtures	$100		Total current liabilities	433
Less Accumulated depreciation	(60)	40	**Stockholders' Equity**	
Building	$250		Common stock	100
Less Accumulated depreciation	(140)	110	Retained earnings	199
			Total stockholders' equity	299
Total assets		$732	Total liabilities and stockholders' equity	$732

Requirement 4

$$\text{Debt ratio assuming the loan is made} = \frac{\$433 + \$500}{\$732 + \$500} = \frac{\$933}{\$1,232} = .76$$

Decision: Make the loan at 10%.

Reasoning: Prior to the loan, the company's financial position and cash flow are strong. The current ratio is in a middle range, and the debt ratio is not too high. Net income (from the income statement) is high in relation to total revenue. Therefore, the company should be able to repay the loan.

The loan will increase the company's debt ratio from 59% to 76%, which is more risky than the company's financial position at present. On this basis, a midrange interest rate appears reasonable—at least as the starting point for the negotiation between State Service Company and the bank.

Review
Accrual Accounting & Financial Statements

Lessons Learned

1. **Relate accrual accounting and cash flows.** *Accrual accounting* recognizes the impact of a business event as it occurs, whether or not cash is received or paid. In *cash-basis accounting*, nothing is recorded unless cash changes hands. The cash basis omits important events, such as purchases and sales on account, and distorts the financial statements. For this reason, generally accepted accounting principles require accrual-basis accounting.
2. **Apply the revenue and matching principles.** The *revenue principle* tells accountants (1) to record revenue when it has been earned, but not before, and (2) to record revenue equal to the cash value of the goods or services transferred to the customer. The *matching principle* directs accountants to identify all the expenses incurred during the accounting period,

to measure those expenses, and to match the expenses against the revenues earned during that period to measure net income.

3. **Update the financial statements by adjusting the accounts.** *Adjusting entries* assign revenues to the period in which they are earned and expenses to the period in which they are incurred. These entries, made at the end of the period, update the accounts for preparation of the financial statements. Adjusting entries fall into five categories: prepaid expenses, depreciation of plant assets, accrued expenses, accrued revenues, and unearned revenues. They are used to prepare an adjusted trial balance.
4. **Prepare the financial statements.** Accountants use the adjusted trial balance to prepare three financial statements: the income statement, statement of retained earnings, and balance sheet.

   Income, shown on the *income statement*, increases retained earnings. This increase also appears on the *statement of retained earnings*. The ending balance of retained earnings appears on the *balance sheet*.
5. **Close the books.** At the end of each accounting period accountants close the *temporary accounts*—Revenues, Expenses, and Dividends. Closing sets each account back to zero. The *permanent accounts*—assets, liabilities, and equity—are not closed. Their balances carry over to the next period.
6. **Use the current ratio and the debt ratio to evaluate a business.** The *current ratio* measures a company's ability to pay current liabilities. It is equal to total current assets divided by total current liabilities. The higher the current ratio, the stronger the company's financial position. The *debt ratio* measures a company's ability to pay its debts and equals total liabilities divided by total assets. The lower the debt ratio, the less risky the company's financial position.

Accounting Vocabulary

account format (p. 142)
accounting cycle (p. 112)
accrual (p. 119)
accrual accounting (p. 113)
accrued expense (p. 124)
accrued revenue (p. 125)
Accumulated Depreciation (p. 122)
adjusted trial balance (p. 128)
book value (of a plant asset) (p. 123)
cash-basis accounting (p. 113)
classified balance sheet (p. 139)
closing the books (p. 137)
closing entries (p. 137)
contra account (p. 122)
current assets (p. 139)
current liabilities (p. 139)
current ratio (p. 143)
debt ratio (p. 144)
deferral (p. 118)
depreciation (p. 119)
liquidity (p. 138)
long-term assets (p. 139)
long-term liabilities (p. 139)
matching principle (p. 115)
multi-step income statement (p. 143)
operating cycle (p. 139)
permanent accounts (p. 137)
plant assets (p. 121)
prepaid expense (p. 119)
report format (p. 142)
revenue principle (p. 115)
single-step income statement (p. 143)
temporary accounts (p. 137)
time-period concept (p. 114)
unearned revenue (p. 126)

Questions

1. Distinguish accrual accounting from cash-basis accounting.
2. What two questions does the revenue principle help answer?
3. Briefly explain the matching principle.
4. Name five categories of adjusting entries and give an example of each.
5. Do all adjusting entries affect the net income or net loss of the period? Include the definition of an adjusting entry.
6. Manning Supply Company pays $1,800 for an insurance policy that covers 3 years. At the end of the first year, the balance of its Prepaid Insurance account contains two elements. What are the two elements, and what is the correct amount of each?
7. The title Prepaid Expense suggests that this type of account is an expense. If it is, explain why. If it is not, what type of account is it?
8. The manager of a Quickie-Pickie convenience store presents his entity's balance sheet to a banker when applying for a loan. The balance sheet reports that the entity's plant assets have a book value of $135,000 and accumulated depreciation of $65,000. What does *book value* of a plant asset mean? What was the cost of the plant assets?
9. Why is an unearned revenue a liability? Give an example.
10. Identify the types of accounts (assets, liabilities, and so on) debited and credited for each of the five types of adjusting entries.
11. Explain the relationships among the income statement, the statement of retained earnings, and the balance sheet.
12. Bellevue Company failed to record the following adjusting entries at December 31, the end of its fiscal year: (a) accrued expenses, $500; (b) accrued revenues, $850; and (c) depreciation, $1,000. Did these omissions cause net

income for the year to be understated or overstated? By what overall amount?

13. Distinguish between permanent accounts and temporary accounts; indicate which type is closed at the end of the period. Give five examples of each type of account.

14. Why are assets classified as current or long term? On what basis are they classified? Where do the classified amounts appear?

15. Indicate which of the following accounts are current assets and which are long-term assets: Prepaid Rent, Building, Furniture, Accounts Receivable, Merchandise Inventory, Cash, Note Receivable (due within 1 year), Note Receivable (due after 1 year).

16. Identify an outside party that would be interested in whether a liability is current or long term. Why would this party be interested in this information?

17. Show how to compute the current ratio and the debt ratio. Indicate what ability each ratio measures, and state whether a high value or a low value is safer for each.

Assess Your Progress

Check Points

Linking accrual accounting and cash flows **(Obj. 1)**

CP3-1 **Pier 1 Imports, Inc.** made sales of $1,411 million during 20X1. Of this amount, Pier 1 collected cash for all but $3 million. The company's cost of goods sold was $817 million, and all other expenses for the year totaled $499 million. Also during 20X1, Pier 1 paid $863 million for its inventory and $356 million for everything else. Beginning cash was $47 million. Suppose Pier 1's top management is interviewing you for a job and you are asked two questions:

a. How much was Pier 1's net income for 20X1?
b. How much was Pier 1's cash balance at the end of 20X1?

Assume you will get the job if you answer both questions correctly.

Linking accrual accounting and cash flows **(Obj. 1)**

CP3-2 Assume **Sony Corporation** began 20X4 owing long-term debt of $5.3 billion. During 20X4 Sony borrowed $2.6 billion long-term and paid off $2.5 billion of long-term debt from prior years. Interest expense for the year was $0.7 billion, including $0.1 billion of interest expense accrued at December 31, 20X4.

As a new Sony employee, it is your job to show what Sony should report for these facts on the following financial statements:

- Income statement
- Balance sheet

Applying the revenue and the matching principles **(Obj. 2)**

CP3-3 **General Motors Corporation (GM)** sells large fleets of vehicles to auto rental companies, such as **Avis** and **Hertz**. Suppose Avis is negotiating with GM to purchase 1,000 Chevrolets. Write a short paragraph to explain to GM when the company should, and should not, record this sales revenue and the related cost of goods sold. Mention the accounting principles that provide the basis for your explanation.

Adjusting prepaid expenses **(Obj. 3)**

CP3-4 Answer the following questions about prepaid expenses:

a. Prepaid expenses are discussed beginning on page 119. Focus on the accounting for prepaid rent. Assume that Air & Sea Travel's initial $3,000 prepayment of rent of April 1 was for 1 year rather than for 3 months. Give the adjusting entry to record rent expense at April 30. Include the date of the entry and an explanation. Then post to the two accounts involved, and show their balances at April 30.
b. Refer to the supplies example on pages 120–121. Assume that Air & Sea Travel has $500 of supplies on hand (rather than $400) at April 30. Make the required journal entry. Then post to the accounts and show their balances at April 30.

Recording depreciation; cash flows
(Obj. 1, 3)

CP3-5 Refer to the discussion in Chapter 1 of the income statement and the balance sheet. **Vodafone** uses computers in its operations. Suppose that on May 1 the company paid cash of £36,000 for **Dell** computers that are expected to remain useful for 3 years. At the end of 3 years, the computers' values are expected to be zero.

1. Make journal entries to record (a) purchase of the computers on May 1 and (b) depreciation on May 31. Include dates and explanations, and use the following accounts: Computer Equipment; Accumulated Depreciation—Computer Equipment; and Depreciation Expense—Computer Equipment.
2. Post to the accounts and show their balances at May 31.
3. What is the equipment's book value at May 31?
4. Which account(s) will Vodafone report on the income statement for the month of May? Which accounts will appear on the balance sheet of May 31? Show the amount to report for each item on both financial statements.

Applying the matching principle and the time-period concept
(Obj. 2)

CP3-6 Assume that at December 31, 20X3, **Hawaiian Airlines** accrued salary expense of $2,600,000. Suppose Hawaiian Airlines paid $2,900,000 to its employees on January 3, 20X4, the company's next payday after the end of the 20X3 year. For this sequence of transactions,

Show what Hawaiian Airlines would report on its 20X3 income statement. Show what the company would report on its 20X4 income statement.

Accruing and paying interest expense
(Obj. 3)

CP3-7 Suppose Air & Sea Travel borrowed $50,000 on August 1 by signing a note payable to **Texas First Bank.** The interest expense for each month is $250. The loan agreement requires Air & Sea Travel to pay interest at the end of October.

1. Make Air & Sea Travel's adjusting entry to record interest expense and interest payable at August 31, at September 30, and at October 31. Date each entry and include its explanation.
2. Post all three entries to the Interest Payable account. You need not take the balance of the account at the end of each month.
3. Record the payment of interest at October 31.
4. Show what Air & Sea Travel will report on its balance sheet at August 31, September 30, and October 31.

Accruing and receiving cash from interest revenue
(Obj. 3)

CP3-8 Return to the situation in Check Point 3-7. Suppose you are accounting for the same transactions on the books of **Texas First Bank**, which lent the money to Air & Sea Travel. Perform all three steps of Check Point 3-7 for Texas First Bank using its own accounts.

Explaining unearned revenues
(Obj. 3)

CP3-9 Write a paragraph to explain why unearned revenues are liabilities instead of revenues. In your explanation, use the following actual example: ***USA Today***, the national newspaper, collects cash from subscribers in advance and later delivers newspapers to subscribers over a 1-year period. Explain what happens to the unearned subscription revenue over the course of a year as *USA Today* delivers papers to subscribers. Where (into what account) does the unearned subscription revenue go as USA delivers papers? Give the adjusting entry that *USA Today* would make to record earning $10,000 of Subscription Revenue. Include an explanation for the entry, as illustrated in the chapter.

Reporting prepaid expenses
(Obj. 4)

CP3-10 Study the T-accounts in Exhibit 3-10, Panel C, on page 129. Focus on the Prepaid Rent account. Which amount in the Prepaid Rent account appeared on the *unadjusted* trial balance (Exhibit 3-11, page 130)? Which amount in the Prepaid Rent account will appear on the *adjusted* trial balance? Which amount will be reported on the balance sheet at April 30? Why will the balance sheet report this amount? Under what balance sheet category will Prepaid Rent appear?

Reporting on the financial statements
(Obj. 4)

CP3-11 In the Adjustments columns of Exhibit 3-11, page 130, two adjustments affected Service Revenue.

1. Make journal entries for the two adjustments. Date the entries and include an explanation.
2. The journal entries you just made affected three accounts: Accounts Receivable, Unearned Service Revenue, and Service Revenue. Show how Air & Sea Travel will report all three accounts in its financial statements at April 30. For each account, identify its (a) financial statement, (b) category on the financial statement, and (c) balance.

Preparing the financial statements
(Obj. 4)

CP3-12 **Rawlings Sporting Goods Company** reported the following data at August 31, 20X1, with amounts adapted and in thousands:

Retained earnings, August 31, 20X0	$ 1,331	Cost of goods sold	$126,996
Accounts receivable	27,750	Cash	921
Net revenues	174,528	Property and equipment, net	7,271
Total current liabilities	53,602	Common stock	28,318
All other expenses	45,775	Inventories	33,379
Other current assets	4,883	Long-term liabilities	13,533
Other assets	24,337		

Use these data to prepare Rawlings Sporting Goods Company's income statement for the year ended August 31, 20X1; statement of retained earnings for the year ended August 31, 20X1; and classified balance sheet at August 31, 20X1. Use the report format for the balance sheet. Draw arrows linking the three statements.

Making closing entries
(Obj. 5)

CP3-13 Use the **Rawlings Sporting Goods** data in Check Point 3-12 to make the company's closing entries at August 31, 20X1. Then set up a T-account for Retained Earnings and post to that account. Compare Retained Earnings' ending balance to the amount reported on Rawlings' statement of retained earnings and balance sheet. What do you find?

Classifying assets and liabilities as current or long term
(Obj. 6)

CP3-14 **Lands' End** had sales of $1,355 million during the year ended January 31, 20X1, and total assets of $378 million at January 31, 20X1, the end of the company's fiscal year. The financial statements of Lands' End reported the following (adapted and in millions):

Sales revenue	$1,355	Land and buildings	$105
Inventory	188	Accounts payable	96
Interest revenue	2	Operating expenses	560
Receivables	19	Accumulated depreciation	132
Interest expense	1	Accrued liabilities (such as Salary payable)	41
Equipment	104		
Prepaid expenses	21	Net income	35

1. Identify the assets (including contra assets) and liabilities.
2. Classify each asset and each liability as current or long term.
3. Compute total assets, total liabilities, and stockholders' equity.

Using the current ratio and the debit ratio
(Obj. 6)

CP3-15 At December 31, 20X0, **The Coca-Cola Company** (Coke) had the following account balances (adapted) with amounts given in millions:

Property and equipment	$ 4,168	Long-term liabilities	$ 2,197
Cash	1,892	Other assets	10,046
Sales revenue	20,458	Accounts receivable	1,757
Owners' equity	9,316	Total expenses	18,281
Other current assets	2,971	Accounts payable	3,905
Short-term notes payable	4,795	Other current liabilities	621

1. How much in current assets does Coca-Cola have for each dollar of current liabilities that the company owes? Compute the current ratio to answer this question. Is Coke's current ratio high or low?
2. What percentage of Coca-Cola's total assets are financed with debt? Compute the debt ratio to answer this question.
3. What percentage of Coca-Cola's total assets do the stockholders of the company actually own free and clear of debt?

Exercises

Linking accrual accounting and cash flows
(Obj. 1)

E3-1 During 20X0 **Hershey Foods Corporation** made sales of $4,221 (assume all on account) and collected cash of $4,194 from customers. Operating expenses totaled $1,127, all paid in cash. At December 31, 20X0. Hershey customers owed the company $380. Hershey owed creditors $149 on account. All amounts are in millions.

1. For these facts, show what Hershey reported on the following financial statements:
   - Income statement
   - Balance sheet
2. Suppose Hershey had used the cash basis of accounting. What would Hershey have reported for these facts?

Linking accrual accounting and cash flows
(Obj. 1)

E3-2 At December 31, 1999, **eBay Inc.** reported income tax payable of $11 million. During 2000, eBay had income tax expense of $33 million and paid $38 to the government for income tax. Help eBay figure these amounts:

a. Income tax payable at December 31, 2000
b. What to report on eBay's:
   1. Income statement for 2000
   2. Balance sheet at December 31, 2000
c. Which of these amounts will eBay use to measure profitability and financial position?

Accrual basis of accounting, applying accounting principles
(Obj. 1, 2)

E3-3 During 20X0, **Qlogic Corporation**, which designs high-bandwidth controllers for network servers, earned revenues of $203 million. Expenses totaled $149 million. Qlogic collected all but $18 million of the revenues and paid $159 million on its expenses. Qlogic's top managers are evaluating 20X0, and they ask you the following questions:

a. Under accrual accounting, what amount of revenue should the company report for 20X0? Is the revenue the $203 million earned or is it the amount of cash actually collected? How does the revenue principle help to answer these questions?
b. Under accrual accounting, what amount of total expense should Qlogic report for 20X0—$149 million or $159 million? Which accounting principle helps to answer this question?
c. Which financial statement reports revenues and expenses? Which statement reports cash receipts and cash payments?

Applying accounting concepts and principles
(Obj. 2)

E3-4 Identify the accounting concept or principle that gives the most direction on how to account for each of the following situations:

a. A utility bill is received on December 30 and will be paid next year. When should the company record utility expense?
b. Salary expense of $35,000 is accrued at the end of the period to measure income properly.
c. March has been a particularly slow month, and the business will have a net loss for the first quarter of the year. Management is considering not following its customary practice of reporting quarterly earnings to the public.
d. A construction company is building a highway system, and construction may take 3 years. When should the company record the revenue it earns?

e. A physician performs a surgical operation and bills the patient's insurance company. It may take 3 months to collect from the insurance company. Should the physician record revenue now or wait until cash is collected?

Applying accounting concepts
(Obj. 2)

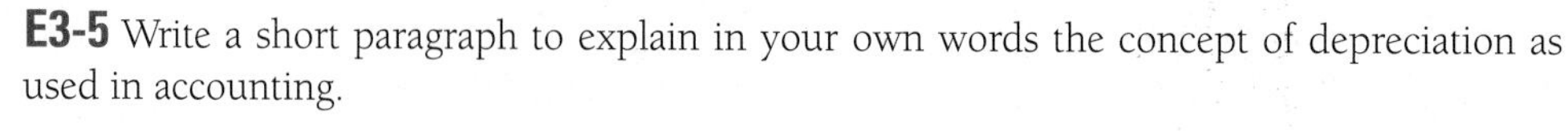

E3-5 Write a short paragraph to explain in your own words the concept of depreciation as used in accounting.

Journalizing adjusting entries and analyzing their effects on net income; accrual versus cash basis
(Obj. 1, 3)

Integrator CD general ledger

E3-6 An accountant made the following adjustments at December 31, the end of the accounting period:

a. Depreciation, $6,200.
b. Employees' salaries owed for 2 days of a 5-day work week; weekly payroll, $9,000.
c. Income before income tax expense, $100,000. Income tax rate is 40%.
d. Prepaid insurance, beginning, $600. Payments for insurance during the period, $2,000. Prepaid insurance, ending, $800.
e. Interest revenue accrued, $4,100.
f. Unearned service revenue, beginning, $800. Unearned service revenue, ending, $300.

Required

1. Journalize the adjusting entries.
2. Suppose the adjustments were not made. Compute the overall overstatement or understatement of net income as a result of the omission of these adjustments.

Allocating supplies cost to the asset and the expense
(Obj. 2, 3)

Integrator CD spreadsheet

E3-7 Assume **PepsiCo, Inc.**, experienced four situations for its supplies. Compute the amounts indicated by question marks for each situation. For situations 1 and 4, journalize the needed transaction. Consider each situation separately.

	Situation			
	1	2	3	4
Beginning supplies	$500	$ 900	$ 200	$ 900
Payments for supplies during the year	?	1,100	?	1,100
Total cost to account for	?	2,000	1,300	?
Ending supplies	400	?	400	500
Supplies expense	$700	$1,400	$ 900	$?

Linking accrual accounting and cash flows
(Obj. 1, 3)

E3-8 Return to the data in Exercise 3-7. For situation 1, show what **PepsiCo** would report on the following financial statements:

- Income statement
- Balance sheet

For each item, list the account and also give the dollar amount to report.

Journalizing adjusting entries
(Obj. 3)

Integrator CD general ledger

E3-9 Suppose **The Home Depot, Inc.** faced the following situations. Journalize the adjusting entry needed at December 31 for each situation. Consider each fact separately.

a. Equipment was purchased at the beginning of last year at a cost of $50,000. The equipment's useful life is 4 years. Record the depreciation for this year and then determine the equipment's book value.
b. On September 1, when we prepaid $1,200 for a 1-year insurance policy, we debited Prepaid Insurance and credited Cash.
c. The business will pay interest expense of $9,000 early in the next period. Of this amount, two-thirds is expense of the current year.
d. Interest revenue of $900 has been earned but not yet received. The business holds a $20,000 note receivable that it will collect, along with the interest, next year.
e. On July 1, when we collected $6,000 rent in advance, we debited Cash and credited Unearned Rent Revenue. The tenant was paying for 2 years' rent.

f. Salary expense is $1,000 per day—Monday through Friday—and the business pays employees each Friday. This year, December 31 falls on a Thursday.
g. The unadjusted balance of the Supplies account is $3,100. The total cost of supplies on hand is $800.

E3-10 Use the data in Exercise 3-9 to answer these questions. Each letter links to the same lettered item in Exercise 3-9.

Separating accrual accounting and cash flows
(Obj. 1, 3)

a. Refer to item a in Exercise 3-9. Show what Home Depot will report on its
   1. Balance sheet (show all the data items needed to report the asset's book value)
   2. Income statement
b. Refer to item c in Exercise 3-9. Show what Home Depot will report on the following financial statements:
   1. Income statement of the current year.
   2. Balance sheet at end of the current year.
   3. Income statement of the following year.
   4. Balance sheet of the following year.

E3-11 The accounting records of **Studio Art Gallery** include the following unadjusted balances at May 31: Accounts Receivable, $1,000; Supplies, $900; Salary Payable, $0; Unearned Service Revenue, $900; Service Revenue, $4,700; Salary Expense, $1,200; Supplies Expense, $0. Studio Art Gallery's accountant develops the following data for the May 31 adjusting entries:

Making adjustments in T-accounts
(Obj. 3)

general ledger

a. Supplies on hand, $200.
b. Salary owed to employee, $700.
c. Service revenue accrued, $350.
d. Unearned service revenue that has been earned, $550.

Open the foregoing T-accounts with their beginning balances. Then record the adjustments directly in the accounts, keying each adjustment amount by letter. Show each account's adjusted balance. Journal entries are not required.

E3-12 The adjusted trial balance of **The Coca-Cola Company** (adapted) follows.

Preparing the financial statements
(Obj. 4)

spreadsheet

The Coca-Cola Company
Adjusted Trial Balance (Adapted)
December 31, 20X0

(Millions)	Adjusted Trial Balance	
	Debit	Credit
Cash	1,900	
Accounts receivable	1,800	
Inventories	1,100	
Prepaid expenses	1,900	
Property, plant, equipment	6,600	
Accumulated depreciation		2,400
Other assets	9,900	
Accounts payable		8,700
Income tax payable		600

continued

	Debit	Credit
Other liabilities		2,200
Common stock		4,100
Retained earnings (beginning: December 31, 19X9)		4,700
Dividends	1,700	
Sales revenue		20,500
Cost of goods sold	6,200	
Selling, administrative, and general expense	9,100	
Income tax expense	3,000	
	43,200	43,200

Required

Prepare Coca-Cola's income statement and statement of retained earnings for the year ended December 31, 20X0, and its balance sheet on that date. Draw the arrows linking the three statements.

Measuring financial statement amounts
(Obj. 3)

E3-13 The adjusted trial balances of **Best Buy Co., Inc.**, at February 28, 20X1, and February 28, 20X0, include these amounts (adapted and in millions):

	20X1	20X0
Receivables	$209	$189
Prepaid expenses (rent, insurance)	102	42
Salary payable	154	102

Assume Best Buy completed these transactions during the year ended February 28, 20X1.

Collections from customers	$15,306
Payment of prepaid expenses	251
Cash payments for salaries	922

Compute the amount of sales revenue, rent and insurance expense (a combined total), and salary expense to report on the income statement for the year ended February 28, 20X1.

Reporting on the financial statements
(Obj. 4)

E3-14 This question deals with the items and the amounts that two entities, Hillcrest Health Maintenance Organization, Inc. (Hillcrest) and City of Denver (Denver) should report in their financial statements.

Required

1. On July 31, 20X5, Hillcrest collected $4,800 in advance from Denver, a client. Under the contract Hillcrest is obligated to perform medical exams for City of Denver employees evenly during the year ended July 31, 20X6. Assume you are Hillcrest.

   Hillcrest's income statement for the year ended December 31, 20X6, will report _____ of $_____.

   Hillcrest's balance sheet at December 31, 20X6, will report _____ of $_____.
2. Assume now that you are City of Denver (Denver). What will Denver report on its balance sheet at December 31, 20X5, and on its income statement for the year ended December 31, 20X5?

   Denver's income statement for the year ended December 31, 20X5, will report _____ of $_____.

   Denver's balance sheet at December 31, 20X5, will report _____ of $_____.

Linking deferrals and cash flows
(Obj. 1, 3)

E3-15 This exercise builds from a simple situation to a slightly more complex situation. **Vodafone**, the British wireless phone service provider, collects cash in advance from customers. All amounts are in millions.

Assume Vodafone collected £380 in advance during 20X2 and at year end still owed customers phone service worth £90.

Required

1. Show what Vodafone will report for 20X2 on its
   - Income statement
   - Balance sheet
2. Use the same facts for Vodafone as in item 1. Further, assume Vodafone reported unearned service revenue of £70 back at the end of 20X1.
   Show what Vodafone will report for 20X2 on the same financial statements. Explain why your answer differs from your answer to item 1.

Closing the accounts
(Obj. 5)

E3-16 Prepare the closing entries from the following accounts adapted from the records of Sprint Corporation at December 31, 2000 (amounts in millions):

Unearned revenues	$ 607	Service revenue	$23,613
Cost of services sold	11,620	Notes payable	17,514
Accumulated depreciation	17,799	Depreciation expense	4,144
Selling, general, and administrative expense	6,919	Other revenue	675
Other expense	396	Dividends	476
		Income tax expense	126
Retained earnings, December 31, 1999	1,961	Interest expense	990
		Income tax payable	440

How much net income did Sprint earn during 2000? Prepare a T-account for Retained Earnings to show the December 31, 2000, balance of Retained Earnings. What caused Retained Earnings to decrease during 2000?

Identifying and recording adjusting and closing entries
(Obj. 3, 5)

general ledger

E3-17 The unadjusted trial balance and income statement amounts from the March adjusted trial balance of Wall Street Workout Company are given on page 158. Wall Street Workout is a turnaround specialist.

Required

Journalize the adjusting and closing entries of Wall Street Workout Company at March 31. There was only one adjustment to Service Revenue.

Preparing a classified balance sheet and using the ratios
(Obj. 4, 6)

E3-18 Refer to Exercise 3-17.

Required

1. After solving Exercise 3-17, use the data in that exercise to prepare Wall Street Workout Company's classified balance sheet at March 31 of the current year. Use the report format.
2. Compute Wall Street Workout's current ratio and debt ratio at March 31. A year ago, the current ratio was 1.30 and the debt ratio was 0.29. Indicate whether the company's ability to pay its debts has improved or deteriorated during the current year.

Serial Exercise

Exercise 3-19 continues the Sandy Lloyd, Certified Public Accountant, P.C., situation begun in Exercise 2-14 of Chapter 2 (p. 82).

Adjusting the accounts, preparing the financial statements, closing the accounts, and evaluating the business
(Obj. 3, 4, 5, 6)

E3-19 Refer to Exercise 2-14 of Chapter 2. Start from the trial balance and the posted T-accounts that Sandy Lloyd, Certified Public Accountant, Professional Corporation (P.C.), prepared for her accounting practice at December 18. A professional corporation is not subject to income tax. Later in December, the business completed these transactions:

E3-17
(Continued)

Wall Street Workout Company

Account Title	Unadjusted Trial Balance		From the Adjusted Trial Balance	
Cash	10,200			
Supplies	2,400			
Prepaid rent	1,100			
Equipment	32,100			
Accumulated depreciation		6,200		
Accounts payable		4,600		
Salary payable				
Unearned service revenue		8,400		
Income tax payable				
Common stock		8,700		
Retained earnings		10,300		
Dividends	1,000			
Service revenue		12,800		19,100
Salary expense	3,000		3,800	
Rent expense	1,200		1,400	
Depreciation expense			300	
Supplies expense			400	
Income tax expense			1,600	
	51,000	51,000	7,500	19,100
Net income			11,600	
			19,100	19,100

E3-19
Sandy Lloyd, CPA
(Continued)

general ledger

Dec. 21	Received $900 in advance for tax work to be performed evenly over the next 30 days.
21	Hired a secretary to be paid $1,500 on the 20th day of each month.
26	Paid for the supplies purchased on December 5.
28	Collected $600 from the consulting client on December 18.
30	Declared and paid dividends of $1,600.

Required

1. Open these T-accounts: Accumulated Depreciation—Equipment, Accumulated Depreciation—Furniture, Salary Payable, Unearned Service Revenue, Retained Earnings, Depreciation Expense—Equipment, Depreciation Expense—Furniture, and Supplies Expense. Also, use the T-accounts opened for Exercise 2-14.
2. Journalize the transactions of December 21 through 30.
3. Post the December 21 to 30 transactions to the T-accounts, keying all items by date.
4. Prepare a trial balance at December 31. Also set up columns for the adjustments and for the adjusted trial balance, as illustrated in Exhibit 3-11, page 130.
5. At December 31, Lloyd gathers the following information for the adjusting entries:
   a. Accrued service revenue, $400.
   b. Earned a portion of the service revenue collected in advance on December 21.
   c. Supplies on hand, $100.
   d. Depreciation expense—equipment, $50; furniture, $60.
   e. Accrued expense for secretary's salary. Use a 30-day month to simplify the computation.

   Make these adjustments directly in the adjustments columns and complete the adjusted trial balance at December 31.

6. Journalize and post the adjusting entries. Denote each adjusting amount as Adj. and an account balance as Bal.
7. Prepare the income statement and statement of retained earnings of Sandy Lloyd, Certified Public Accountant, P.C. for the month ended December 31 and the classified balance sheet at that date. Draw arrows to link the financial statements.
8. Journalize and post the closing entries at December 31. Denote each closing amount as Clo. and an account balance as Bal.
9. Compute the current ratio and the debt ratio of Lloyd's accounting practice and evaluate these ratio values as indicative of a strong or weak financial position.

Challenge Exercises

Evaluating the current ratio
(Obj. 6)

E3-20 AOL Time Warner Inc. combines the power of the Internet with Time Warner's publishing and entertainment empire. At December 31, 1999, AOL Time Warner reported the following current accounts (adapted, and in millions):

Accounts payable	$ 68
Prepaid expenses	283
Cash	3,096
Unearned revenues	869
Accrued expenses payable	1,240
Receivables	496

Assume that during 2000, AOL Time Warner completed these transactions:

- Sold services on account, $8,555
- Depreciation expense, $444
- Paid for expenses, $7,186, which includes prepaid expenses of $150.
- Collected from customers on account, $7,586
- Accrued expenses, $256
- Purchased services on account, $477
- Paid on account, $453
- Used up prepaid expenses, $141
- Collected cash from customers in advance, $270
- Paid accrued expenses payable, $399

Compute AOL Time Warner's current ratio at December 31, 1999, and again at December 31, 2000. Did the current ratio improve or deteriorate during 2000?

Computing financial statement amounts
(Obj. 3, 4)

E3-21 The accounts of Glenapp Castle Hotel Company, prior to the year-end adjustments, follow on the next page.

Adjusting data at the end of the year include:

a. Unearned service revenue that has been earned, $1,900.
b. Accrued rent revenue, $1,200.
c. Accrued property tax expense, $900.
d. Accrued service revenue, $1,700.
e. Supplies used in operations, $600.
f. Accrued salary expense, $1,400.
g. Insurance expense, $1,800.
h. Depreciation expense—furniture, $800; building, $2,100.
i. Accrued interest expense, $500.

general ledger

Cash	$ 4,200	Note payable, long-term	$ 6,000
Accounts receivable	7,200	Common stock	10,000
Rent receivable		Retained earnings	50,100
Supplies	1,100	Dividends	16,200
Prepaid insurance	2,200	Service revenue	4,100
Furniture	15,700	Rent revenue	140,000
Accumulated depreciation—furniture	1,300	Salary expense	32,700
Building	96,800	Depreciation expense—furniture	
Accumulated depreciation—building	14,900	Depreciation expense—building	
Land	51,200	Supplies expense	
Accounts payable	6,100	Insurance expense	
Salary payable		Interest expense	
Interest payable		Advertising expense	7,800
Property tax payable		Property tax expense	
Unearned service revenue	5,300	Utilities expense	2,700

Richardson Mantooth, the principal stockholder, has received an offer to sell Glenapp Castle Hotel Company. He needs to know the following information within 1 hour:

a. Net income for the year covered by these data.
b. Total assets.
c. Total liabilities.
d. Total stockholders' equity.
e. Proof that total assets = total liabilities + total stockholders' equity after all items are updated

Required

Without opening any accounts, making any journal entries, or using a work sheet, provide Mr. Mantooth with the requested information. The business is not subject to income tax. Show all computations.

Problems

(Group A)

Linking accrual accounting and cash flows **(Obj. 1)**

P3-1A Sara Lee Corporation earned revenues of $17.7 billion during 20X1 and ended the year with net income of $2.3 billion. During 20X1, Sara Lee collected $18.0 billion from customers and paid cash for all of its expenses plus an additional $0.4 billion on 20X0 expenses left over from the preceding year. Answer these questions about Sara Lee's operating results, financial position, and cash flows during 20X1:

Required

1. How much were the company's total expenses? Show your work.
2. Identify all the items that Sara Lee will report on its 20X1 income statement. Show each amount.
3. How much cash did Sara Lee pay for expenses in 20X1?
4. Sara Lee began 20X1 with receivables of $1.8 billion. What was the company's receivables balance at the end of 20X1? Identify the appropriate financial statement, and show how Sara Lee will report ending receivables in the 20X1 annual report.
5. Sara Lee began 20X1 owing accounts payable and accrued expenses payable totaling $2.7 billion. How much in accounts payable and accrued expenses payable did the company owe at the end of the year? Identify the appropriate financial statement and show how Sara Lee will report these two items in its 20X1 annual report. (For this requirement combine accounts payable and accrued expenses payable into a single amount.)

P3-2A Lexington Image Consultants had the following selected transactions in October:

Cash basis versus accrual basis
(Obj. 1)

Oct. 1	Prepaid insurance for October through December, $900.
4	Purchased software for cash, $800 (ignore depreciation).
5	Performed service and received cash, $700.
8	Paid advertising expense, $300.
11	Performed service on account, $2,500.
19	Purchased computer on account, $1,600 (ignore depreciation).
24	Collected for the October 11 service.
26	Paid account payable from October 19.
29	Paid salary expense, $900.
31	Adjusted for October insurance expense (see Oct. 1).
31	Earned revenue of $1,300 that was collected in advance back in September.

Required

1. Show how each transaction would be handled using the cash basis and the accrual basis. Under each column, give the amount of revenue or expense for October. Journal entries are not required. Use the following format for your answer, and show your computations:

Lexington Image Consultants

Amount of Revenue (Expense) for October

Date	Cash Basis	Accrual Basis

2. Compute October income (loss) before tax under each accounting method.
3. Indicate which measure of net income or net loss is preferable. Use the transactions on October 11 and 24 to explain.

P3-3A Write a memo to explain for a new employee the difference between the cash basis of accounting and the accrual basis. Mention the roles of the revenue principle and the matching principle in accrual accounting.

Applying accounting principles
(Obj. 1, 2)

P3-4A Journalize the adjusting entry needed on December 31, end of the current accounting period, for each of the following independent cases affecting First Bancorp, Inc.

Making accounting adjustments
(Obj. 3)

general ledger

a. Details of Prepaid Insurance are shown in the account:

PREPAID INSURANCE

Jan. 1	**Bal.**	**600**	
Mar. 31		**3,000**	

First Bancorp prepays insurance each year on March 31.

b. First Bancorp pays employees each Friday. The amount of the weekly payroll is $6,000 for a 5-day work week, and the daily salary amounts are equal. The current accounting period ends on Thursday.

c. First Bancorp has loaned money, receiving notes receivable. During the current year, the entity has earned accrued interest revenue of $509 that it will receive next year.

d. The beginning balance of supplies was $2,680. During the year, First Bancorp purchased supplies costing $6,180, and at December 31 the cost of supplies on hand is $2,150.

e. First Bancorp is providing financial services for Manatee Investments, and the owner of Manatee paid First Bancorp $12,900 as the annual service fee. First Bancorp recorded this amount as Unearned Service Revenue. First Bancorp estimates that the bank has earned one-fourth of the total fee during the current year.

f. Depreciation for the current year includes Office Furniture, $700; Equipment, $2,730; and Buildings, $10,320. Make a compound entry.

Analyzing and recording adjustments
(Obj. 3)

P3-5A Western Hoteliers, Inc.'s unadjusted and adjusted trial balances at September 30, 20X1, follow:

general ledger

Western Hoteliers, Inc.
Adjusted Trial Balance
September 30, 20X1

	Trial Balance		Adjusted Trial Balance	
Account Title	Debit	Credit	Debit	Credit
Cash	8,180		8,180	
Accounts receivable	6,360		6,840	
Interest receivable			300	
Note receivable	4,100		4,100	
Supplies	980		290	
Prepaid insurance	2,480		720	
Building	66,450		66,450	
Accumulated depreciation		16,010		18,210
Accounts payable		6,920		6,920
Wages payable				170
Unearned rental revenue		670		110
Common stock		18,000		18,000
Retained earnings		42,790		42,790
Dividends	3,600		3,600	
Rental revenue		9,940		10,980
Interest revenue				300
Wage expense	1,600		1,770	
Insurance expense			1,760	
Depreciation expense			2,200	
Property tax expense	370		370	
Supplies expense			690	
Utilities expense	210		210	
	94,330	94,330	97,480	97,480

Required

1. Make the adjusting entries that account for the differences between the two trial balances. Western is not subject to income tax.
2. Compute Western's total assets, total liabilities, total equity, and net income.

Preparing the financial statements and using the debt ratio
(Obj. 4, 6)

P3-6A The adjusted trial balance of Oriental Design Studio, Inc., at December 31, 20X6, follows on the next page.

Required

1. Prepare Oriental Design's 20X6 income statement, statement of retained earnings, and balance sheet. List expenses (except for income tax) in decreasing order on the income statement and show total liabilities on the balance sheet. Draw arrows linking the three financial statements.
2. Oriental Design's lenders require that the company maintain a debt ratio no higher than 0.50. Compute Oriental Design's debt ratio at December 31, 20X6, to determine whether the company is in compliance with this debt restriction. If not, suggest a way that Oriental could have avoided this difficult situation.

spreadsheet

Oriental Design Studio, Inc.

Adjusted Trial Balance
December 31, 20X6

Cash	$ 1,320	
Accounts receivable	8,920	
Supplies	2,300	
Prepaid rent	1,600	
Equipment	37,180	
Accumulated depreciation		$ 4,350
Accounts payable		3,640
Interest payable		830
Unearned service revenue		620
Income tax payable		2,100
Note payable		18,620
Common stock		5,000
Retained earnings		1,090
Dividends	44,000	
Service revenue		127,910
Depreciation expense	1,680	
Salary expense	39,900	
Rent expense	10,300	
Interest expense	3,100	
Insurance expense	3,810	
Supplies expense	2,950	
Income tax expense	7,100	
Total	164,160	164,160

Preparing an adjusted trial balance and the financial statements; using the current ratio to evaluate the business
(Obj. 3, 4, 6)

general ledger

P3-7A The unadjusted trial balance of Colorado Valley Legal Associates at July 31, 20X2, and the related month-end adjustment data follow at the top of the next page.
Adjustment data:

a. Accrued legal service revenue at July 31, $400.
b. Prepaid rent expired during the month. The unadjusted prepaid balance of $3,600 relates to the period July through October.
c. Supplies used during July, $600.
d. Depreciation on furniture for the month. The estimated useful life of the furniture is 5 years.
e. Accrued salary expense at July 31 for Monday and Tuesday. The 5-day weekly payroll of $1,750 will be paid on Friday, August 2.

Required

1. Using Exhibit 3-11, page 130, as an example, prepare the adjusted trial balance of Colorado Valley Legal Associates, at July 31, 20X2. Key each adjusting entry by letter. The business is not subject to income tax.
2. Prepare the income statement, the statement of retained earnings, and the classified balance sheet. Draw arrows linking the three financial statements.
3. **a.** Compare the business's net income for July to the amount of dividends paid to the owners. Suppose this trend continues each month for the remainder of 20X2. What will be the effect on the business's financial position, as shown by its accounting equation?
   b. Will the trend make it easier or more difficult to borrow money if the business gets in a bind and needs cash? Why?
   c. Does either the current ratio or the cash position suggest the need for immediate borrowing? Explain.

Colorado Valley Legal Associates

Trial Balance
July 31, 20X2

Cash	$ 5,600	
Accounts receivable	11,600	
Prepaid rent	3,600	
Supplies	800	
Furniture	36,000	
Accumulated depreciation		$ 3,500
Accounts payable		10,450
Salary payable		
Common stock		26,200
Retained earnings		13,650
Dividends	4,000	
Legal service revenue		10,750
Salary expense	2,400	
Rent expense		
Utilities expense	550	
Depreciation expense		
Supplies expense		
Total	$64,550	$64,550

Preparing a classified balance sheet and using the ratios to evaluate the business **(Obj. 4, 6)**

P3-8A The accounts of Datacom Service Center, Inc., at March 31, 20X3, are listed in alphabetical order.

Accounts payable	$14,700	Furniture	$43,200
Accounts receivable	11,500	Insurance expense	600
Accumulated depreciation—building	47,300	Note payable, long-term	6,200
		Note receivable, long-term	6,900
Accumulated depreciation—furniture	7,100	Other assets	2,300
		Prepaid expenses	5,300
Advertising expense	900	Retained earnings, March 31, 20X2	30,800
Building	55,900	Salary expense	17,800
Cash	6,400	Salary payable	2,400
Common stock	9,100	Service revenue	71,100
Current portion of note payable	800	Supplies	3,800
Depreciation expense	1,900	Supplies expense	4,600
Dividends	31,200	Unearned service revenue	2,800

Required

1. All adjustments have been journalized and posted, but the closing entries have not yet been made. Prepare the company's classified balance sheet at March 31, 20X3. Use captions for total assets, total liabilities, and total liabilities and stockholders' equity. A professional corporation is not subject to income tax.
2. Compute Datacom's current ratio and debt ratio at March 31, 20X3. At March 31, 20X2, the current ratio was 1.28 and the debt ratio was 0.29. Did Datacom's ability to pay debts improve or deteriorate during 20X3? Evaluate Datacom's overall debt position as strong or weak and give your reason.

P3-9A Refer back to Problem 3-8A.

Closing the books and evaluating retained earnings
(Obj. 5)

1. Use the Datacom Service Center data in Problem 3-8A to journalize Datacom's closing entries at March 31, 20X3.
2. Set up a T-account for Retained Earnings and post to that account. What is the ending balance of Retained Earnings?
3. Did Retained Earnings increase or decrease during the year? What caused the increase or the decrease?

P3-10A This problem demonstrates the effects of transactions on the current ratio and the debt ratio of a well-known company. **Johnson & Johnson** produces Band-aids and other medical products. Johnson & Johnson's condensed and adapted balance sheet at December 31, 20X0, is:

Analyzing financial ratios
(Obj. 6)

	(In billions)
Total current assets	$15.5
Properties, plant, equipment, and other assets	15.8
	$31.3
Total current liabilities	$ 7.2
Total long-term liabilities	5.3
Total stockholders' equity	18.8
	$31.3

Assume that during the first quarter of the following year, 20X1, Johnson & Johnson completed the following transactions:

a. Paid half the current liabilities.
b. Borrowed $3 billion on long-term debt.
c. Earned revenue, $2.5 billion on account.
d. Paid selling expense of $1 billion.
e. Accrued general expense of $800 million. Credit General Expense Payable, a current liability.
f. Purchased equipment, paying cash of $1.4 billion and signing a long-term note payable for $2.8 billion.
g. Recorded depreciation expense of $600 million.

Required

1. Compute Johnson & Johnson's current ratio and debt ratio at December 31, 20X0.
2. Compute Johnson & Johnson's current ratio and debt ratio after each transaction during 20X1. Consider each transaction separately.
3. Based on your analysis, you should be able to readily identify the effects of certain transactions on the current ratio and the debt ratio. Test your understanding by completing these statements with either "increase" or "decrease":
   a. Revenues usually ______________ the current ratio.
   b. Revenues usually ______________ the debt ratio.
   c. Expenses usually ______________ the current ratio. (*Note:* Depreciation is an exception to this rule.)
   d. Expenses usually ______________ the debt ratio.
   e. If a company's current ratio is greater than 1.0, as it is for Johnson & Johnson, paying off a current liability will always ______________ the current ratio.
   f. Borrowing money on long-term debt will always ______________ the current ratio and ______________ the debt ratio.

(Group B)

Linking accrual accounting and cash flows
(Obj. 1)

P3-1B During 20X1, **Nike, Inc.**, earned revenues of $9.5 billion from the sale of shoes and clothing. Nike ended the year with net income of $0.6 billion. Nike collected cash of $9.4 billion from customers and paid cash for all 20X1 expenses plus an additional $0.3 billion for 20X0 expenses that were accrued at the end of 20X0. Answer these questions about Nike's operating results, financial position, and cash flows during 20X1:

1. How much were Nike's total expenses? Show your work.
2. Identify all the items that Nike will report on its income statement for 20X1. Show each amount.
3. How much cash did Nike pay for expenses and accrued liabilities during 20X1?
4. Nike began 20X1 with receivables of $1.6 billion. What was Nike's receivables balance at the end of 20X1? Identify the appropriate financial statement and show how Nike will report its ending receivables balance in the company's 20X1 annual report.
5. Nike began 20X1 owing accounts payable and accrued expenses payable totaling $1.2 billion. How much in accounts payable and accrued expenses payable did Nike owe at the end of 20X1? Identify the appropriate financial statement and show how Nike will report these two items in its 20X1 annual report. (For this requirement combine accounts payable and accrued expenses payable into a single amount.)

Cash basis versus accrual basis
(Obj. 1)

P3-2B Buzzard Billy's Restaurant had the following selected transactions during May:

May	1	Received $800 in advance for a banquet to be served later.
	5	Paid electricity expenses, $700.
	9	Received cash for the day's sales, $1,400.
	14	Purchased two video games, $1,800 (ignore depreciation).
	23	Served a banquet, receiving a note receivable, $1,900.
	31	Accrued salary expense, $900.
	31	Prepaid building rent for June, July, and August, $3,000.

Required

1. Show how each transaction would be handled using the cash basis and the accrual basis. Under each column, give the amount of revenue or expense for May. Journal entries are not required. Use the following format for your answer, and show your computations:

Buzzard Billy's
Amount of Revenue (Expense) for May

Date	Cash Basis	Accrual Basis

2. Compute income (loss) before tax for May under the two accounting methods.
3. Which method better measures income and assets? Use the last transaction to explain.

Applying accounting principles
(Obj. 1, 2)

P3-3B As the controller of Maribeaux Plastics, you have hired a new employee, whom you must train. He objects to making an adjusting entry for accrued salaries at the end of the period. He reasons, "We will pay the salaries soon. Why not wait until payment to record the expense? In the end, the result will be the same." Write a reply to explain to the employee why the adjusting entry is needed for accrued salary expense.

Making accounting adjustments
(Obj. 3)

Integrator CD
general ledger

P3-4B Journalize the adjusting entry needed on December 31, the end of the current accounting period, for each of the following independent cases affecting Bulova Electric, Inc. (BEI):

a. Each Friday, BEI pays employees for the current week's work. The amount of the payroll is $2,500 for a 5-day work week. The current accounting period ends on Monday.
b. BEI has received notes receivable from some clients for professional services. During the current year, BEI has earned accrued interest revenue of $2,640, which will be received next year.
c. The beginning balance of Engineering Supplies was $1,800. During the year, the entity purchased supplies costing $12,530, and at December 31 the inventory of supplies on hand is $2,970.
d. BEI is conducting tests of the strength of the steel to be used in a large building, and the client paid BEI $36,000 at the start of the project. BEI recorded this amount as Unearned Engineering Revenue. The tests will take several months to complete. BEI executives estimate that the company has earned three-fourths of the total fee during the current year.
e. Depreciation for the current year includes Office Furniture, $5,500; Engineering Equipment, $6,360; and Building, $3,790. Make a compound entry.
f. Details of Prepaid Insurance are shown in the account:

PREPAID INSURANCE			
Jan. 1	Bal.	600	
Apr. 30		2,400	

BEI pays the annual insurance premium (the payment for insurance coverage is called a *premium*) on April 30 each year.

Analyzing and recording adjustments
(Obj. 3)

P3-5B DuPont Engraving Company's unadjusted and adjusted trial balances at December 31, 20X7, are given here.

DuPont Engraving Company
Adjusted Trial Balance
December 31, 20X7

	Trial Balance		Adjusted Trial Balance	
Account Title	**Debit**	**Credit**	**Debit**	**Credit**
Cash	4,120		4,120	
Accounts receivable	11,260		12,090	
Supplies	1,090		780	
Prepaid insurance	2,600		910	
Office furniture	21,630		21,630	
Accumulated depreciation		8,220		9,360
Accounts payable		6,310		6,310
Salary payable				960
Interest payable				480
Note payable		12,000		12,000
Unearned commission revenue		1,840		1,160
Common stock		10,000		10,000
Retained earnings		3,510		3,510
Dividends	29,370		29,370	
Commission revenue		72,890		74,400
Depreciation expense			1,140	
Supplies expense			310	
Utilities expense	4,960		4,960	

(continued)

P3-5B
(Continued)

Account Title	Trial Balance Debit	Trial Balance Credit	Adjusted Trial Balance Debit	Adjusted Trial Balance Credit
Salary expense	26,660		27,620	
Rent expense	12,200		12,200	
Interest expense	880		1,360	
Insurance expense			1,690	
	114,770	114,770	118,180	118,180

general ledger

Required

1. Make the adjusting entries that account for the difference between the two trial balances. DuPont Engraving is not subject to income tax.
2. Compute DuPont's total assets, total liabilities, total equity, and net income.

Preparing the financial statements and using the debt ratio
(Obj. 4, 6)

spreadsheet

P3-6B The adjusted trial balance of Thrifty Nickel Advertising, Inc., at December 31, 20X1, follows.

Required

1. Prepare Thrifty Nickel's 20X1 income statement, statement of retained earnings, and balance sheet. List expenses in decreasing order on the income statement and show total liabilities on the balance sheet. Draw arrows linking the three financial statements.
2. Thrifty Nickel's lenders require that the company maintain a debt ratio no higher than 0.60. Compute Thrifty Nickel's debt ratio at December 31, 20X1, to determine whether the company is in compliance with this debt restriction. If not, suggest a way that Thrifty Nickel could have avoided this difficult situation.

Thrifty Nickel Advertising Inc.

Adjusted Trial Balance
December 31, 20X1

Cash	$ 11,640	
Accounts receivable	41,490	
Prepaid rent	1,350	
Equipment	75,690	
Accumulated depreciation		$ 22,240
Accounts payable		13,600
Unearned service revenue		4,520
Interest payable		2,130
Salary payable		930
Income tax payable		8,800
Note payable		36,200
Common stock		12,000
Retained earnings		20,380
Dividends	48,000	
Service revenue		187,670
Depreciation expense	11,300	
Salary expense	94,000	
Rent expense	12,000	
Interest expense	4,200	
Income tax expense	8,800	
Total	$308,470	$308,470

P3-7B Consider the unadjusted trial balance of Alpha Beta Internet Connections at October 31, 20X2, and the related month-end adjustment data.

Preparing an adjusted trial balance and the financial statements; using the current ratio to evaluate the business
(Obj. 3, 4, 6)

general ledger

Alpha Beta Internet Connections

Trial Balance
October 31, 20X2

Cash	$ 5,300	
Accounts receivable	7,000	
Prepaid rent	4,000	
Supplies	600	
Furniture	36,000	
Accumulated depreciation		$ 3,000
Accounts payable		8,800
Salary payable		
Common stock		15,000
Retained earnings		21,000
Dividends	4,600	
Advertising revenue		14,400
Salary expense	4,400	
Rent expense		
Utilities expense	300	
Depreciation expense		
Supplies expense		
Total	$62,200	$62,200

Adjustment data:

a. Accrued advertising revenue at October 31, $2,900.
b. Prepaid rent expired during the month. The unadjusted prepaid balance of $4,000 relates to the period October 20X2 through January 20X3.
c. Supplies used during October, $200.
d. Depreciation on furniture for the month. The furniture's expected useful life is 5 years.
e. Accrued salary expense at October 31 for Tuesday through Friday; the 5-day weekly payroll is $2,000.

Required

1. Using Exhibit 3-11, page 130, as an example, prepare the adjusted trial balance of Alpha Beta at October 31, 20X2. Key each adjusting entry by letter.
2. Prepare the income statement, the statement of retained earnings, and the classified balance sheet. Draw arrows linking the three financial statements.
3. **a.** Compare the business net income for October to the amount of dividends paid to the owners. Suppose this trend continues into 20X3. What will be the effect on the business financial position, as shown by its accounting equation?
   b. Will the trend make it easier or more difficult for Alpha Beta to borrow money if the business gets in a bind and needs cash? Why?
   c. Does either the current ratio or the cash position suggest the need for immediate borrowing? Explain.

P3-8B The accounts of Gay Gillen eTravel, Inc., at December 31, 20X5, are listed in alphabetical order.

Preparing a classified balance sheet and using the ratios to evaluate the business
(Obj. 4, 6)

Accounts payable	$ 5,100	Insurance expense	$ 800
Accounts receivable	6,600	Note payable, long-term	10,600
Accumulated depreciation—furniture	11,600	Note receivable, long-term	4,000
Advertising expense	2,200	Other assets	3,600
Cash	7,300	Prepaid expenses	7,700
Commission revenue	93,500	Retained earnings, December 31, 20X4	5,300
Common stock	15,000	Salary expense	24,600
Current portion of note payable	2,200	Salary payable	3,900
Depreciation expense	1,300	Supplies expense	5,700
Dividends	47,400	Unearned commission revenue	5,400
Furniture	41,400		

Required

1. All adjustments have been journalized and posted, but the closing entries have not yet been made. Prepare the company's classified balance sheet in report format at December 31, 20X5. Label total assets, total liabilities, and total liabilities and stockholders' equity. The travel agency is not subject to income tax.
2. Compute Gillen's current ratio and debt ratio at December 31, 20X5. At December 31, 20X4, the current ratio was 1.52 and the debt ratio was 0.45. Did Gillen's overall ability to pay debts improve or deteriorate during 20X5?

Closing the books and evaluating retained earnings
(Obj. 5)

P3-9B Refer back to Problem 3-8B.

1. Use the Gay Gillen eTravel data in Problem 3-8B to journalize Gillen's closing entries at December 31, 20X5.
2. Set up a T-account for Retained Earnings and post to that account. What is the ending balance of Retained Earnings?
3. Did Retained Earnings increase or decrease during the year? What caused the increase or decrease?

Analyzing financial ratios
(Obj. 6)

P3-10B This problem demonstrates the effects of transactions on the current ratio and the debt ratio of a well-known company. **Sony Corporation** is famous for its electronics products. Sony's condensed balance sheet at March 31, 20X1, is given in yen (¥), the Japanese monetary unit.

	(In trillions)
Total current assets	¥3.0
Properties, net, and other assets	3.8
	¥6.8
Total current liabilities	¥2.2
Total long-term liabilities	2.4
Total stockholders' equity	2.2
	¥6.8

Assume that during the following year, ending March 31, 20X2, Sony completed the following transactions:

a. Paid half the current liabilities.
b. Borrowed ¥3 trillion on long-term debt.

c. Earned revenue of ¥2.5 trillion on account.
d. Paid selling expense of ¥1 trillion.
e. Accrued general expense of ¥0.8 trillion. Credit General Expense Payable, a current liability.
f. Purchased equipment, paying cash of ¥1.4 trillion and signing a long-term note payable for ¥2.8 trillion.
g. Recorded depreciation expense of ¥0.6 trillion.

Required

1. Compute Sony's current ratio and debt ratio at March 31, 20X1.
2. Compute Sony's current ratio and debt ratio after each transaction during 20X2. Consider each transaction separately.
3. Based on your analysis, you should be able to readily identify the effects of certain transactions on the current ratio and the debt ratio. Test your understanding by completing these statements with either "increase" or "decrease":
   a. Revenues usually ______________ the current ratio.
   b. Revenues usually ______________ the debt ratio.
   c. Expenses usually ______________ the current ratio. (*Note:* Depreciation is an exception to this rule.)
   d. Expenses usually ______________ the debt ratio.
   e. If a company's current ratio is greater than 1.0, as for Sony, paying off a current liability will always ______________ the current ratio.
   f. Borrowing money on long-term debt will always ______________ the current ratio and ______________ the debt ratio.

Apply Your Knowledge

Decision Cases

Preparing financial statements; continue or close the business? **(Obj. 4)**

Case 1. On June 1, Billy Bob Brown opened a gourmet fried chicken restaurant named B3, Inc. After the first month of operations, Billy Bob is at a crossroads. The June financial statements paint a dismal picture of the business, and Billy Bob has asked you whether he should continue in business or shut down the restaurant. He is confused about the success or failure of the business, but he is sure of one thing: To start the business, he invested $12,000, not the $2,000 amount reported as "Investments by owner" on the income statement. The bookkeeper plugged the $2,000 "Investments by owner" amount as common stock into the balance sheet to make it come out even. Billy Bob shows you the following financial statements that the bookkeeper prepared.

Required

Prepare corrected financial statements for B3, Inc.: Income Statement, Statement of Retained Earnings, and Balance Sheet. Then, based on your corrected statements, recommend to Mr. Brown whether he should close the restaurant or continue in business.

B3, Inc.
Income Statement
Month Ended June 30, 20X4

Revenues:		
Investments by owner	$2,000	
Unearned banquet sales revenue	3,000	
		$ 5,000
Expenses:		
Wages expense	$5,000	
Rent expense	4,000	
Dividends	3,000	
Depreciation expense—fixtures	1,000	
		13,000
Net income (Net loss)		$ (8,000)

B3, Inc.
Balance Sheet
June 30, 20X4

Assets:		Liabilities:	
Cash	$ 6,000	Accounts payable	$ 5,000
Prepaid insurance	1,000	Sales revenue	32,000
Insurance expense	1,000	Accumulated depreciation—	
Food inventory	3,000	fixtures	1,000
Cost of goods sold (expense)	14,000		38,000
Fixtures (tables, chairs, etc.)	11,000	Owners' equity:	
Dishes and silverware	4,000	Common stock	2,000
	$40,000		$40,000

Valuing a business on the basis of its net income
(Obj. 3, 4)

Case 2. Angus McSwain has owned and operated McSwain Advertising, Inc. since its beginning 10 years ago. Recently, McSwain mentioned that he would consider selling the company for the right price.

Assume that you are interested in buying this business. You obtain its most recent monthly trial balance, which follows. Revenues and expenses vary little from month to month, and April is a typical month. Your investigation reveals that the trial balance does not include the effects of monthly revenues of $3,800 and expenses totaling $1,100. If you were to buy McSwain Advertising, you would hire a manager so you could devote your time to other duties. Assume that this person would require a monthly salary of $4,000.

Required

1. Assume that the most you would pay for the business is 25 times the monthly net income *you could expect to earn* from it. Compute this possible price.
2. McSwain states that the least he will take for the business is its stockholders' equity on April 30. Compute this amount.
3. Under these conditions, how much should you offer McSwain? Give your reason.

McSwain Advertising, Inc.

Trial Balance
April 30, 20XX

Cash	$ 10,000	
Accounts receivable	4,900	
Prepaid expenses	3,200	
Plant assets	221,300	
Accumulated depreciation		$189,600
Land	158,000	
Accounts payable		13,800
Salary payable		
Unearned advertising revenue		56,700
Common stock		50,000
Retained earnings		88,000
Dividends	9,000	
Advertising revenue		12,600
Rent expense		
Salary expense	3,400	
Utilities expense	900	
Depreciation expense		
Supplies expense		
Total	$410,700	$410,700

Adjusting and correcting the accounts; computing and evaluating the current ratio **(Obj. 3, 6)**

Case 3. The stockholders need to know the current ratio of Ping Technology, Inc. The unadjusted trial balance of Ping at February 28, 20X6, does not balance. In addition, the trial balance needs to be updated before the financial statements at February 28, 20X6 can be prepared.

Cash	$ 4,200
Accounts receivable	2,200
Supplies	800
Prepaid rent	1,200
Land	39,000
Accounts payable	5,400
Salary payable	0
Unearned service revenue	700
Note payable, due in 3 years	25,400
Common stock	5,000
Retained earnings	7,300
Service revenue	9,100
Salary expense	3,400
Rent expense	0
Advertising expense	900
Supplies expense	0

Required

1. How much *out of balance* is the trial balance?
2. Ping needs to make the following adjustments at February 28:
   a. Supplies of $600 were used during February.
   b. The balance of Prepaid Rent was paid on January 1 and covers the whole year 20X6.
   c. At February 28, Ping owes employees $400.
   d. Unearned service revenue of $200 was earned during February.

   Prepare a corrected, adjusted trial balance. The error is in the Accounts Receivable account.
3. After the error is corrected and after these adjustments are made, compute the current ratio of Ping Technology. If your business had this current ratio, could you sleep at night?

Completing the accounting cycle to develop the information for a bank loan
(Obj. 3, 5)

Case 4. One year ago, Jack Hewlett and Melanie Packard founded Hewlett-Packard (HP) Service Center, Inc. The business has prospered. Packard, who remembers that you majored in accounting while in college, comes to you for advice. She wishes to know how much net income the business earned during the past year. She also wants to know what the entity's total assets, liabilities, and stockholders' equity are. The business accounting records consist of the T-accounts that follow.

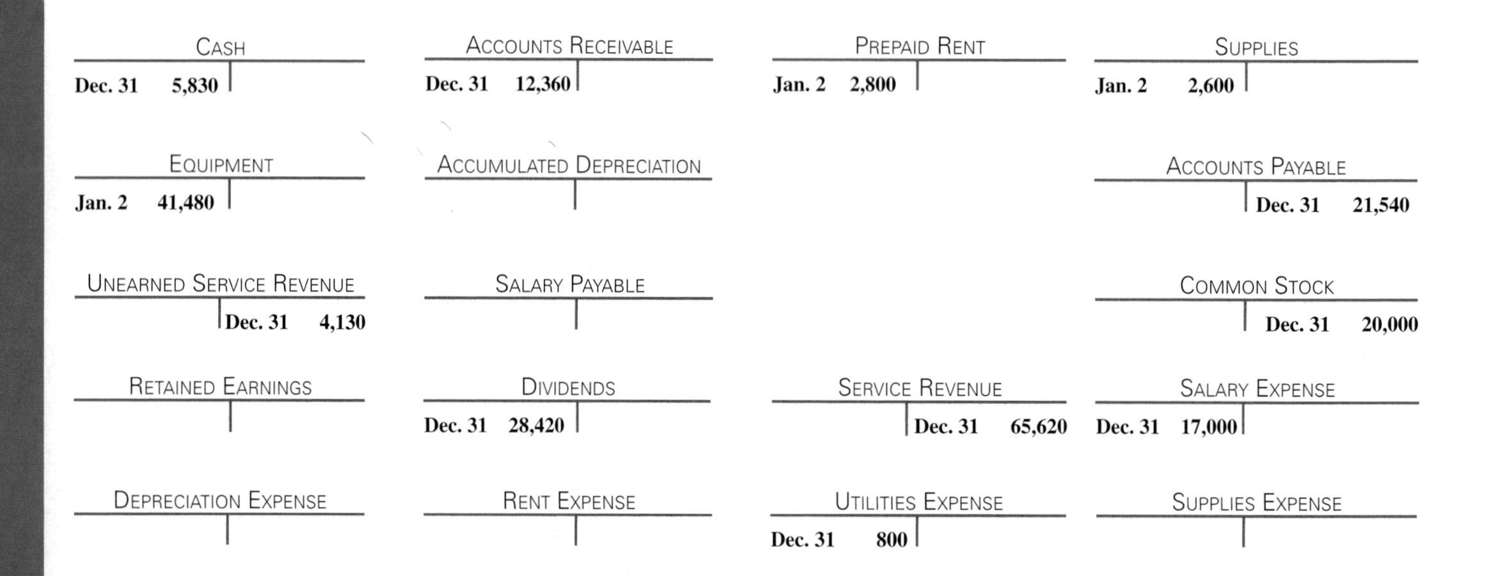

Packard indicates that at the year's end, customers owe the business $1,600 accrued service revenue, which it expects to collect early next year. These revenues have not been recorded. During the year, HP collected $4,130 service revenue in advance from customers, but it earned only $600 of that amount. Rent expense for the year was $2,400, and HP used up $2,100 in supplies. Packard estimates that depreciation on equipment was $5,900 for the year. At December 31, the business owes employees $1,200 accrued salary.

At the conclusion of your meeting, Hewlett and Packard express concern that dividends during the year might have exceeded net income. To get a loan to expand the business, HP must show the bank that total stockholders' equity has grown from its original $20,000 balance. Has it? You, Hewlett, and Packard agree that you will meet again in 1 week. You perform the analysis and prepare the financial statements to answer Packard's questions.

Ethical Issues

Issue 1. BAE, a management consulting firm, is in its third year of operations. The company was initially financed by owners' equity as the two partners each invested $50,000. The first year's slim profits were expected because new businesses often start slowly. During the second year, BAE landed a large contract and referrals from that project brought in more jobs. To expand the business, BAE borrowed $75,000 from the Bank of Kansas City. As a condition for making this loan, the bank required that BAE maintain a current ratio of at least 1.50 and a debt ratio of no more than 0.50.

Business during the third year has been less than expected. Expenses have brought the current ratio down to 1.47 and the debt ratio up to 0.51 at December 15. Stephen Hyde, the general manager, is considering the implication of reporting this current ratio to the bank.

Hyde is considering recording some revenue on account that BAE will earn next year. The contract for this job has been signed, and BAE will perform the management consulting service during January.

Required

1. Journalize the revenue transaction, and indicate how recording this revenue in December would affect the current ratio and the debt ratio.
2. State whether it is ethical to record the revenue transaction in December. Identify the accounting principle relevant to this situation.
3. Propose for BAE a course of action that is ethical.

Issue 2. The net income of Mother Earth Provision Company decreased sharply during 2003. Clay Rollins, owner of the store, anticipates the need for a bank loan in 2004. Late in 2003, he instructed the accountant to record a $50,000 sale of recreational gear to the Rollins family, even though the goods will not be shipped from the manufacturer until January 2004. Rollins also told the accountant *not* to make the following December 31, 2003 adjusting entries:

Salaries owed to employees	$1,000
Prepaid insurance that has expired	500

Required

1. Compute the overall effect of these transactions on the store's reported income for 2003. Is income overstated or understated?
2. Why did Rollins take these actions? Are they ethical? Give your reason, identifying the parties helped and the parties harmed by Rollins' action.
3. As a personal friend, what advice would you give the accountant?

Financial Statement Case

Tracing account balances to the financial statements
(Obj. 3, 6)

Fossil, Inc.—like all other businesses—adjusts accounts prior to year end to measure assets, liabilities, revenues, and expenses for the financial statements. Examine Fossil's balance sheet in Appendix A, and pay particular attention to (a) Prepaid Expenses and Other Current Assets and (b) Accrued Expenses: Compensation.

Required

1. Why aren't Prepaid Expenses "true" expenses? What word could be added to Accrued Expenses: Compensation to make the nature of this account clear?
2. Open T-accounts for the two accounts listed above. Insert Fossil's balances (in thousands) at December 30, 2000 (fiscal year 2000).
3. Journalize the following for the year ended January 5, 2002 (fiscal year 2001; consider this date the same as December 31, 2001). Key entries by letter, and show amounts in thousands. Explanations are not required.
   - **a.** Paid the beginning balance of Accrued Expenses: Compensation.
   - **b.** Paid the ending balance of Prepaid Expenses.
   - **c.** Recorded Accrued Expenses: Compensation for the ending balance. Assume this is a selling expense.
   - **d.** Recorded General Expense for the beginning balance of Prepaid Expenses.

4. Post these entries and show that the balances in Prepaid Expenses and Other Current Assets and in Accrued Expenses: Compensation agree with the corresponding amounts reported in the January 5, 2002 balance sheet.
5. Compute the current ratios and debt ratios for Fossil at January 5, 2002 and at December 30, 2000. Treat Minority Interest as a liability. Did the ratio values improve, deteriorate, or hold steady during the year ended January 5, 2002? Do the ratio values indicate financial strength or weakness?

Analytical Case

Explaining accruals and deferrals
(Obj. 3)

During 2002, **Pier 1 Imports** experienced numerous accruals and deferrals. As a new member of Pier 1's accounting and financial staff, it is your job to explain the effects of accruals and deferrals on Pier 1's net income for 2002. The accrual and deferral data follow, along with questions that Pier 1 stockholders have raised (all amounts in millions):

1. Beginning receivables for 2002 totaled $84. Ending receivables for 2002 are $51. Which of these amounts did Pier 1 earn in 2001? Which amount did Pier 1 earn in 2002? Which amount is included in Pier 1's net income for 2002?
2. Accumulated depreciation stood at $249 at the end of 2001 and at $280 at year end 2002. Depreciation expense for 2002 was $43. What other event affected accumulated depreciation during 2002? Give its amount.
3. Pier 1 reports an account titled Gift Cards, Gift Certificates, and Merchandise Credits Outstanding. This account carried credit balances of $19 at the end of 2001 and $29 at the end of 2002. What type of account is Gift Cards, Gift Certificates, and Merchandise Credits Outstanding? Make a single journal entry to show how this account increased its balance during 2002. Then explain the event in your own words.
4. Certain income-statement accounts are directly linked to specific balance-sheet accounts other than cash. Examine Pier 1's income statement in Appendix B at the end of this book. For each "Operating cost and expenses," each "Nonoperating (income) and expense," and Provision for income taxes, identify the related balance sheet account (other than cash). Use standard account titles, not necessarily the titles Pier 1 uses.

Group Project

Barron Tompkins formed a lawn service company as a summer job. To start the business on May 1, he deposited $1,000 in a new bank account in the name of the corporation. The $1,000 consisted of a $600 loan from his father and $400 of his own money. The corporation issued 400 shares of common stock to Barron.

Barron rented lawn equipment, purchased supplies, and hired high school students to mow and trim his customers' lawns. At the end of each month, Barron mailed bills to his customers. On August 31, Barron was ready to dissolve the business and return to Baylor University for the fall semester. Because he had been so busy, he had kept few records other than his checkbook and a list of amounts owed by customers.

At August 31, Barron's checkbook shows a balance of $1,190, and his customers still owe him $500. During the summer, he collected $4,750 from customers. His checkbook lists payments for supplies totaling $400, and he still has gasoline, weedeater cord, and other supplies that cost a total of $50. He paid his employees $1,900, and he still owes them $200 for the final week of the summer. Barron rented some equipment from Ludwig Tool Company. On May 1, he signed a 6-month lease on mowers and paid $600 for the full lease period. Ludwig will refund the unused portion of the prepayment if the equipment is in good shape. To get the refund, Barron has kept the mowers in excellent condition. In fact, he had to pay $300 to repair a mower that ran over a hidden tree stump. To transport employees and equipment to jobs, Barron used a trailer that he bought for $300. He figures that the summer's work used up one-third of the trailer's service potential. The business checkbook lists an expenditure of $460 for dividends paid to Barron during the summer. Barron paid his father back during the summer.

Required

1. Prepare the income statement of Tompkins Lawn Service, Inc. for the 4 months May through August. The business is not subject to income tax.
2. Prepare the classified balance sheet of Tompkins Lawn Service, Inc., at August 31.

4

Internal Control & Managing Cash

Learning Objectives

1. **Set up** an effective system of internal control
2. **Use** a bank reconciliation as a control device
3. **Apply** internal controls to cash receipts and cash payments
4. **Use** a budget to manage cash
5. **Weigh** ethical judgments in business

Need additional help? Go to the **Integrator CD** *and search these key words:* bank reconciliation, cash budget, cash disbursements, cash payments, ethics, internal control

Integrator CD

Enron Corporation

Financial Highlights (Excerpts)*

	2000	1999	1998	1997
Revenues	$100,789	$40,112	$31,260	$20,273
Net income	$ 979	$ 893	$ 703	$ 105
Total assets	$ 65,503	$33,381	$29,350	$22,552
NYSE price range—High	$ 90 $^{9}/_{16}$	$ 44 $^{7}/_{8}$	$ 29 $^{3}/_{8}$	$ 22 $^{9}/_{16}$

*Unaudited: in millions, except stock price per share
Source: Enron Corporation Annual Report 2000, p. 1.

The meltdown of Enron Corporation was one of the largest corporate bankruptcies in history. It certainly represents the biggest accounting scandal ever.

Enron, by its own admission, "outdistanced the competition." Once a stodgy gas pipeline company, Enron remade itself into the nation's leading marketer of natural gas, electric power, and bandwidth capacity. So ambitious was the company that Enron thought it could sell electricity to residential consumers over the Internet.

Revenues soared from $20 billion in 1997 to $100 billion in 2000. Profits increased 10-fold, from $100 million to nearly $1 billion. The company had such a following on Wall Street that Enron chief executive officer (CEO) Jeffrey Skilling could bluff his way around tough questions about the company's operations. What happened to bring this high-flying company down?

The answer is simple. Enron lost sight of a basic principle of internal control—Don't let your right hand know what your left hand is doing. In other words, don't invest too much power in one person.

Enron made the mistake of letting Andrew Fastow wear two hats. As chief financial officer (CFO) of Enron, Fastow set up outside partnerships to conduct Enron business. The problem was that Fastow was negotiating with the partnerships on behalf of Enron. But as the principal in the partnerships, he was also negotiating with Enron on behalf of the partnerships. The obvious question that arises is, which entity did Fastow favor in these deals? As the evidence unfolds, it appears that Enron's stockholders, creditors, and employees all came out as losers.

Sitemap

This chapter discusses *internal control*—the organizational plan that managers use to protect assets and keep the business on track. The chapter applies internal controls to cash (the most liquid asset). It also presents ethical issues in accounting and provides a framework for making ethical judgments. Later chapters discuss how managers control other assets.

Internal Control

internal control

Internal control Organizational plan and all the related measures adopted by an entity to safeguard assets, encourage adherence to company policies, promote operational efficiency, and ensure accurate and reliable accounting records.

✔ Check Point 4-1

Managers must control the operations of their business. Owners and top managers set goals, managers lead the way, and employees carry out plans. If managers don't control operations, the entity may suffer losses unnecessarily, as Enron did.

Internal control is the organizational plan and all the related measures that an entity adopts to

1. Safeguard assets
2. Encourage adherence to company policies
3. Promote operational efficiency
4. Ensure accurate and reliable accounting records

Exhibit 4-1 is an excerpt from the Report of Management Responsibility for General Mills, Inc. famous for Wheaties, Cheerios, and Betty Crocker foods. The company's top managers take responsibility for the financial statements and for the internal controls. Let's examine how companies create effective systems of internal control.

Exhibit 4-1

General Mills, Inc.—Report of Management Responsibilities (Excerpts)

GENERAL MILLS, INC.—Report of Management Responsibilities

The management of General Mills, Inc. . . . has established a system of internal controls that provides reasonable assurance that assets are adequately safeguarded and transactions are recorded accurately. . . . We maintain a strong audit program that independently evaluates the adequacy and effectiveness of internal controls. Our internal controls provide for appropriate separation of duties and responsibilities. . . . These . . . policies demand highly ethical conduct from all employees.

S. W. Sanger
Chairman of the Board and Chief Executive Officer

J. A. Lawrence
Executive Vice President and Chief Financial Officer

Source: General Mills, Inc., *Annual Report 2001*, p. 21.

Components of an Effective System

Objective

1 Set up an effective system of internal control

Whether the business is Enron, General Mills, or a local department store, an effective system of internal controls has the following characteristics.

Competent, Reliable, and Ethical Personnel. Employees should be *competent*, *reliable*, and *ethical*. Paying good salaries, training employees, and supervising their work build a competent staff. Rotating employees through various jobs makes them

Exhibit 4-2 **Organizational Chart of a Corporation**

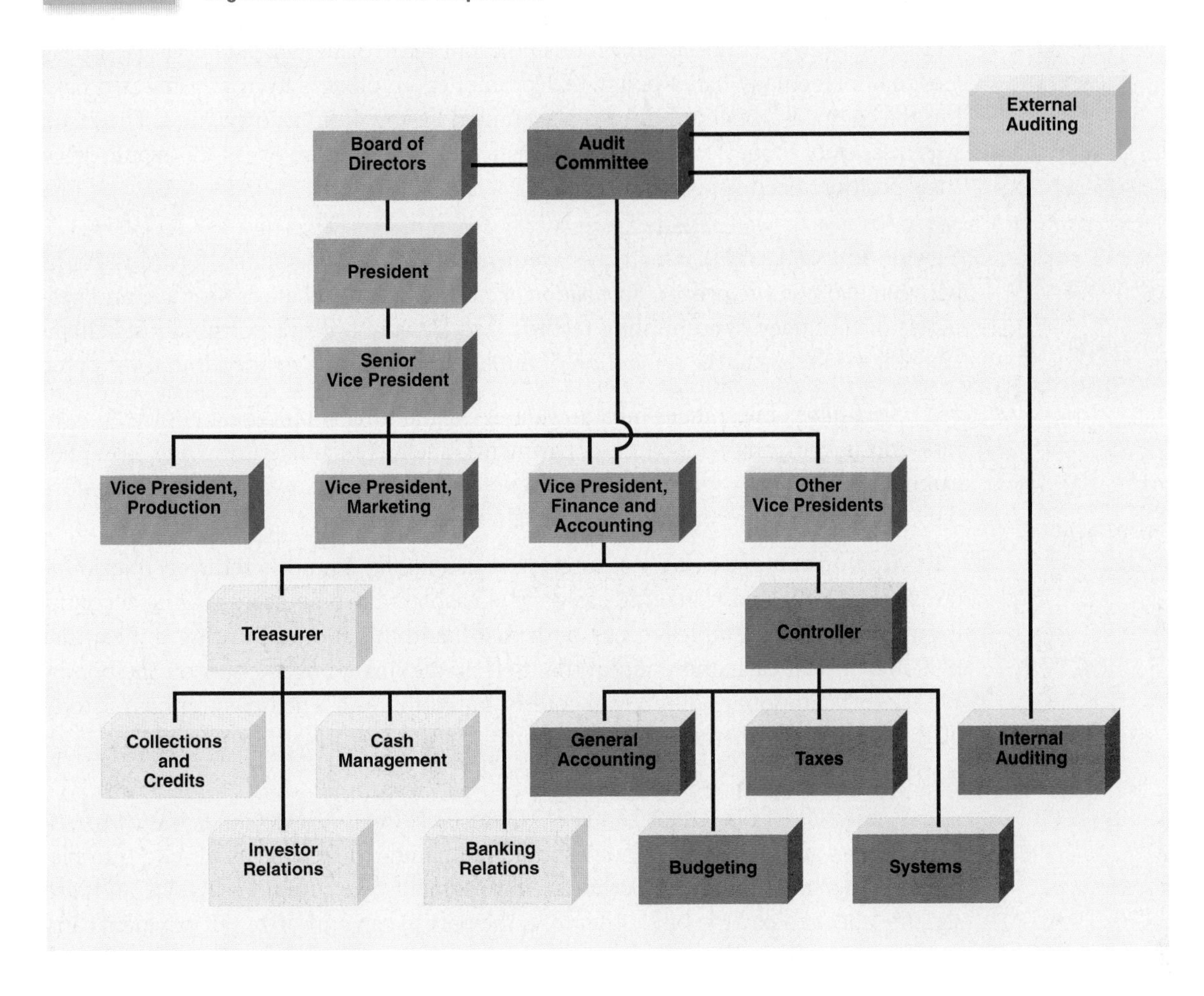

more valuable to the organization. If one employee is sick or on vacation, a second employee can step in and do the job.

Assignment of Responsibilities. A business with good internal controls oversees all important duties. Each employee is assigned certain responsibilities. A model *assignment of responsibilities* appears in Exhibit 4-2. Notice that the corporation has a vice president of finance and accounting. Two other officers, the treasurer and the controller, report to that vice president. The treasurer manages cash, and the **controller** is in charge of accounting.

Controller
The chief accounting officer of a business.

The controller may be responsible for approving invoices (bills) for payment, while the treasurer may actually sign the checks. Working under the controller, one accountant is responsible for property taxes and another, for income taxes. All duties are assigned to individuals who bear responsibility for carrying them out.

Proper Authorization. An organization generally has rules that outline approved procedures. Any deviation from standard policy requires *proper authorization*. For example, managers of retail stores must approve customer checks for amounts above the store's usual limit. Likewise, department chairs of colleges and universities must authorize juniors to enroll in senior-level courses.

SUPERVISION OF EMPLOYEES. Even the most trusted workers can be tempted to steal or defraud the company if he or she is not supervised. In the chapter-opening story, Andrew Fastow's actions as Enron CFO did not receive adequate supervision. Enron Corporation actually had a policy that prohibited employees from wearing two hats, but the company's board of directors exempted Fastow from its own rules. The result was a series of money-losing transactions for Enron. All employees, no matter what their position, need supervision.

SEPARATION OF DUTIES. Smart management divides responsibilities for transactions between two or more people. *Separation of duties* limits the chances for fraud and promotes the accuracy of accounting records. The General Mills responsibility statement (Exhibit 4-1) refers to the separation of duties, which may be divided into three parts:

1. *Separation of operations from accounting.* Accounting should be completely separate from a company's operating departments, such as manufacturing and sales. For example, computer programmers should not operate a company's computers, because they can program the computer to write checks to themselves.

2. *Separation of the custody of assets from accounting.* Fraud is reduced if accountants are not allowed to handle cash and if cashiers have no access to the accounting records. If one employee has both cash-handling and accounting duties, that person can steal cash and conceal the theft by making a bogus entry on the books. We see this component of internal control in Exhibit 4-2. The treasurer has custody of the cash while the controller accounts for the cash. Neither person has both responsibilities.

3. *Separation of the authorization of transactions from the custody of related assets.* Persons who authorize transactions should not handle the related asset. For example, the same person should not authorize the payment of a supplier's invoice and also sign the check to pay the bill. Otherwise, the person can authorize self-payments and then sign the checks.

✔ Check Point 4-2

INTERNAL AND EXTERNAL AUDITS. To guarantee the accuracy of accounting records, most companies have an audit. An **audit** is an examination by an outside party. In accounting, an auditing firm examines the company's financial statements, accounting systems, and internal controls. Auditors must be independent of the operations they examine.

Audit
A periodic examination of a company's financial statements and the accounting systems, controls, and records that produce them.

Auditors cannot examine all the transactions during a period, as they must rely on the accounting system to produce accurate records. To gauge the reliability of the accounting system, auditors evaluate its system of internal controls. Auditors offer *objectivity* in their reports; managers immersed in day-to-day operations may overlook their own weaknesses.

Audits can be internal or external. Exhibit 4-2 shows *internal auditors* as employees of the business reporting to the audit committee. Throughout the year, internal auditors examine various segments of the organization to ensure that employees follow company policies.

External auditors are entirely independent of the business. They are hired by a company such as General Mills, Intel, or General Electric to audit the entity as a whole. External auditors are concerned mainly with the financial statements.

DOCUMENTS AND RECORDS. Business *documents* and *records* vary considerably. They include invoices (bills), paid checks, and accounting journals and ledgers.

Documents should be prenumbered. A gap in the numbered sequence points to a missing document.

Prenumbering cash-sale receipts discourages theft by cashiers. The receipts can be checked against the actual amount of cash received. If the receipts are not prenumbered, the cashier can destroy a receipt and pocket the cash. But with prenumbered receipts, the missing one can be identified. Computerized systems automatically keep records of all sales.

ELECTRONIC AND COMPUTER CONTROLS. Businesses use electronic devices to safeguard assets. Retailers such as Target Stores, Bradlees, and Dillard's control inventories by attaching electronic sensors to merchandise. If a customer tries to leave the store with a sensor still attached, an alarm sounds. According to Checkpoint Systems, these electronic sensors reduce theft by as much as 50%.

Accounting systems are relying less and less on documents and more and more on digital storage devices. Computers produce accurate records, but they do not automatically safeguard assets. Computers have shifted the internal controls to computer programmers, so all the controls that apply to accountants apply to programmers as well. Programmers should not have access to the company's assets.

Computers provide dishonest employees with quirky ways to steal. We are all aware that dollar amounts get rounded to the nearest cent. A dishonest computer programmer had all the discarded third-digit amounts accumulated in a "Suspense" account (for example, $35.504; $.004 is the discarded third digit). He then programmed the computer to write him a check for each week's total. This fraud was caught when the programmer's supervisors investigated how he could afford a Lexus on his $38,000 annual salary.

The receivables department relies on computer operators to post to thousands of customer accounts. Proper posting can be ensured by devising customer account numbers so that the last digit is the sum of the previous digits (for example, 1359, where 1 + 3 + 5 = 9). Miskeying a customer account number would trigger an error message, and the computer would not accept the number.

E-Commerce, *e.fr@ud,* and Internal Controls

In an information economy, information provides access to assets. Companies must protect their assets, so a new generation of internal controls has sprung up to safeguard the information that drives e-commerce.

Most companies, including General Electric, Ford Motor Company, and Intel Corporation, use e-commerce to transact some of their business. Security issues are paramount: Companies must protect against hackers and systems failures. In a recent survey of the largest companies worldwide, KPMG, the international accounting firm, found that hackers posed the greatest threat to system security.

To prevent *e.fr@ud*, experts in information technology have devised the ***onion model*** of system security. The onion model includes several layers of devices and techniques to protect e-commerce hardware, software, and data. Exhibit 4-3 shows the model.

Encryption is the transformation of data by a mathematical process into a form that is unreadable by anyone who does not have the secret decryption key. For example, Procter and Gamble (P&G) may send encrypted messages to buy chemicals online from DuPont, the giant chemical company. A hacker who intercepts this buy

Exhibit 4-3

Onion Model of E-Commerce System Security

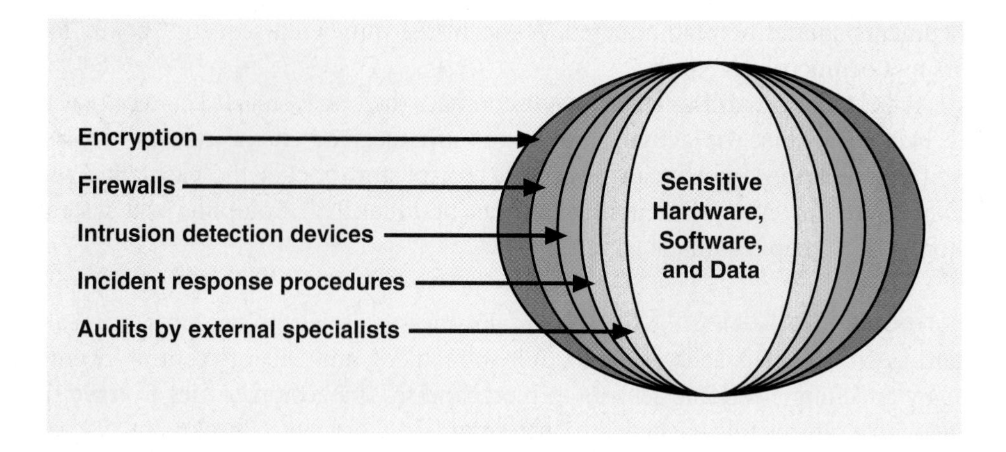

order would find it difficult to interpret P&G's message without the decryption key, as diagrammed in Exhibit 4-4.

Exhibit 4-4

Encryption

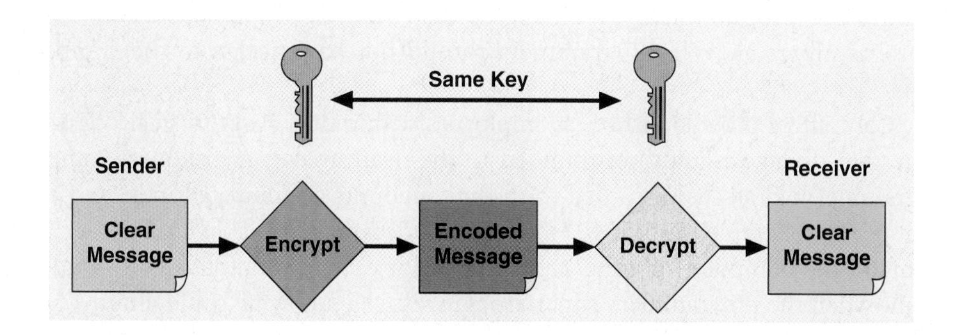

A *firewall* is a technique that limits access to hardware, software, or data to persons within a network. The challenge with designing firewalls is to allow legitimate users to enter the system while denying access to intruders. Most companies use a series of firewalls, illustrated in Exhibit 4-5.

Exhibit 4-5

How Firewalls Work

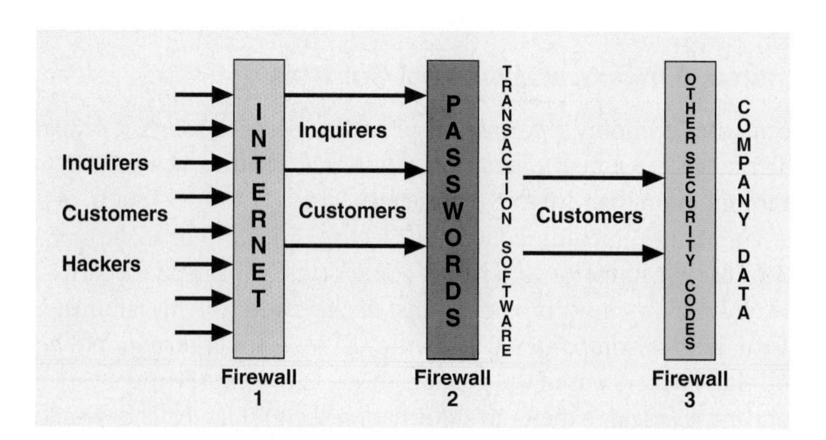

Let's return to the P&G and DuPont transaction. Suppose these two companies use the Internet to conduct e-commerce. P&G access through the first firewall may be as easy as logging onto DuPont's Web site at **www.dupont.com**. Then P&G may go to "Quick Links for Business Customers" and proceed through the next firewall using a password. This process would continue until P&G sends its encrypted order for chemicals to DuPont.

Hackers try to burrow into secure Web sites and sometimes succeed. The next layer of the onion model consists of intrusion detection devices, which are electronic monitors that identify unauthorized entries to the system. Then incident response procedures kick in to apprehend any hackers and remove them from the system. Finally, some companies pay for audits by external specialists, such as WebTrust, SysTrust, and the CPA firms, to test their e-commerce systems for availability, security, and integrity. You may see these logos on e-commerce Web sites that you frequent.

Other Controls

Businesses keep cash and important business documents such as contracts and property titles in fireproof vaults. They use burglar alarms to protect buildings and other property.

Retailers receive most of their cash from customers on the spot. To safeguard cash, they use ***point-of-sale terminals*** that serve as cash registers and record each transaction in the machine. A supervisor removes the cash often for deposit in the bank.

Credit card and bankcard sales require a different set of internal controls. With no cash changing hands at the point of sale, the clerk has no chance to steal cash. Controls such as encryption of data and firewalls provide security as the data are transmitted electronically from a Wal-Mart store to VISA or MasterCard.

Many businesses purchase ***fidelity bonds*** on cashiers. The bond is an insurance policy that reimburses the company for losses due to employee theft. Before issuing a fidelity bond, the insurance company investigates the employee's past. ***Mandatory vacations*** and ***job rotation*** require that employees be trained to do a variety of jobs. General Electric, Eastman Kodak, and other large companies move employees from job to job.

Ralph works the late movie at Galaxy Theater. Occasionally, he must both sell the tickets and take them as customers enter the theater. Standard procedure requires Ralph to tear the tickets, give one-half to the customer, and keep the other half. To control cash receipts, the theater manager compares each night's cash receipts with the number of ticket stubs on hand.

What is the internal control weakness in this situation? What might a dishonest employee do to steal cash? What additional steps should the manager take to strengthen the control over cash receipts?

Answer:

The weakness is the lack of separation of duties. Ralph not only receives cash from customers but also controls the tickets. Good internal control would require that Ralph handle either cash or the tickets, but not both. If he were dishonest, he could fail to issue a ticket and then keep the customer's cash. To control such dishonest behavior, the manager could physically count the people watching a movie and compare that number with the number of ticket stubs collected. Otherwise, a dishonest employee could destroy some ticket stubs and keep the cash received from customers. To catch that dishonest behavior, the manager could account for all ticket stubs by serial number. Missing serial numbers would raise questions and lead to investigation.

Limitations of Internal Control

Unfortunately, most internal control measures can be overcome. Systems designed to thwart one person's fraud can be beaten by two or more employees working together—*colluding*—to defraud the firm.

One of the most dramatic frauds in U.S. business history was a case of massive collusion. High-level managers of Equity Funding of America, an insurance company, okayed the writing of phony insurance policies. Equity Funding then sold the policies for cash. This scheme, like all others, was bound to fail because purchasers of the phony policies could never collect on them. Amazingly, the Equity Funding employees held "parties" to create the fictitious insurance policies. Whenever top managers are involved in a fraud, or when they fail to supervise employees, internal controls are of limited usefulness.

A system of internal control that is too complex can strangle the business with red tape. Just how tight should the internal controls be? Managers must make sensible judgments. Investments in internal control must be worth more than they cost.

Bank Account as a Control Device

bank reconciliation

Cash is the most liquid asset because it is the medium of exchange. Cash is easy to conceal and relatively easy to steal. As a result, most businesses have elaborate controls to safeguard cash.

Keeping cash in a bank account is important because banks safeguard and help control cash. Banks provide depositors with detailed records of their cash transactions. To take full advantage of these control features, the business should deposit all cash receipts in the bank account and make all cash payments through it (except petty cash disbursements, which we cover later in this chapter).

Check
Document instructing a bank to pay the designated person or business the specified amount of money.

To draw money from an account, the depositor writes a **check**, the document that instructs the bank to pay a specified amount of money. There are three parties to a check: the *maker*, who signs the check; the *payee*, to whom the check is drawn; and the *bank* on which the check is drawn. Checks are serially numbered and preprinted with the name and address of the maker and the bank. Exhibit 4-6 shows a check drawn on the bank account of Business Research, Inc. The *remittance advice* is an optional attachment that tells the payee the reason for the payment. The internal controls at Business Research require two signatures.

Check with Remittance Advice

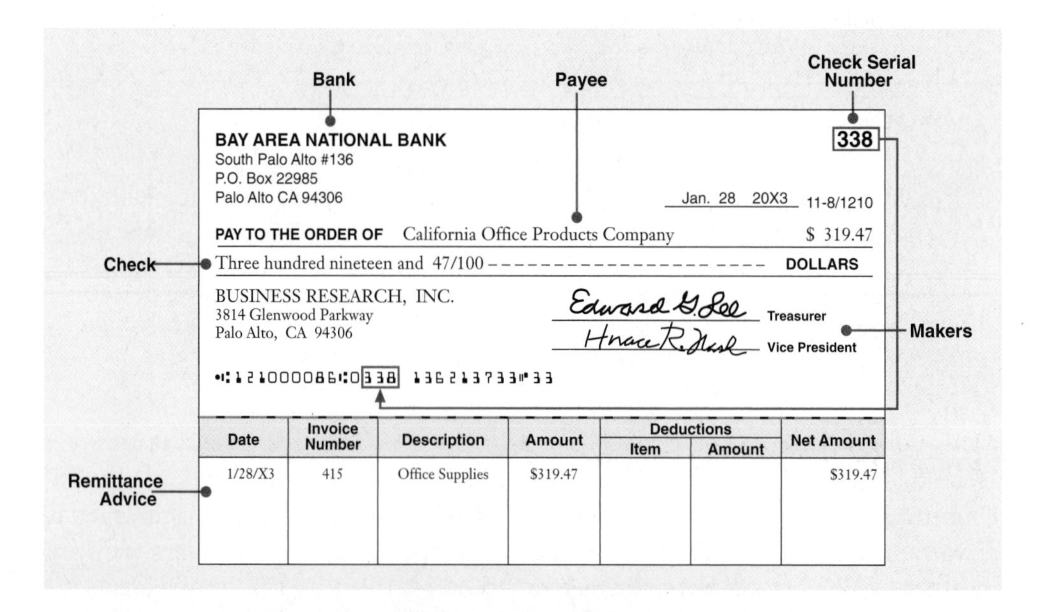

Date	Invoice Number	Description	Amount	Deductions Item	Deductions Amount	Net Amount
1/28/X3	415	Office Supplies	$319.47			$319.47

Exhibit 4-7 **Bank Statement**

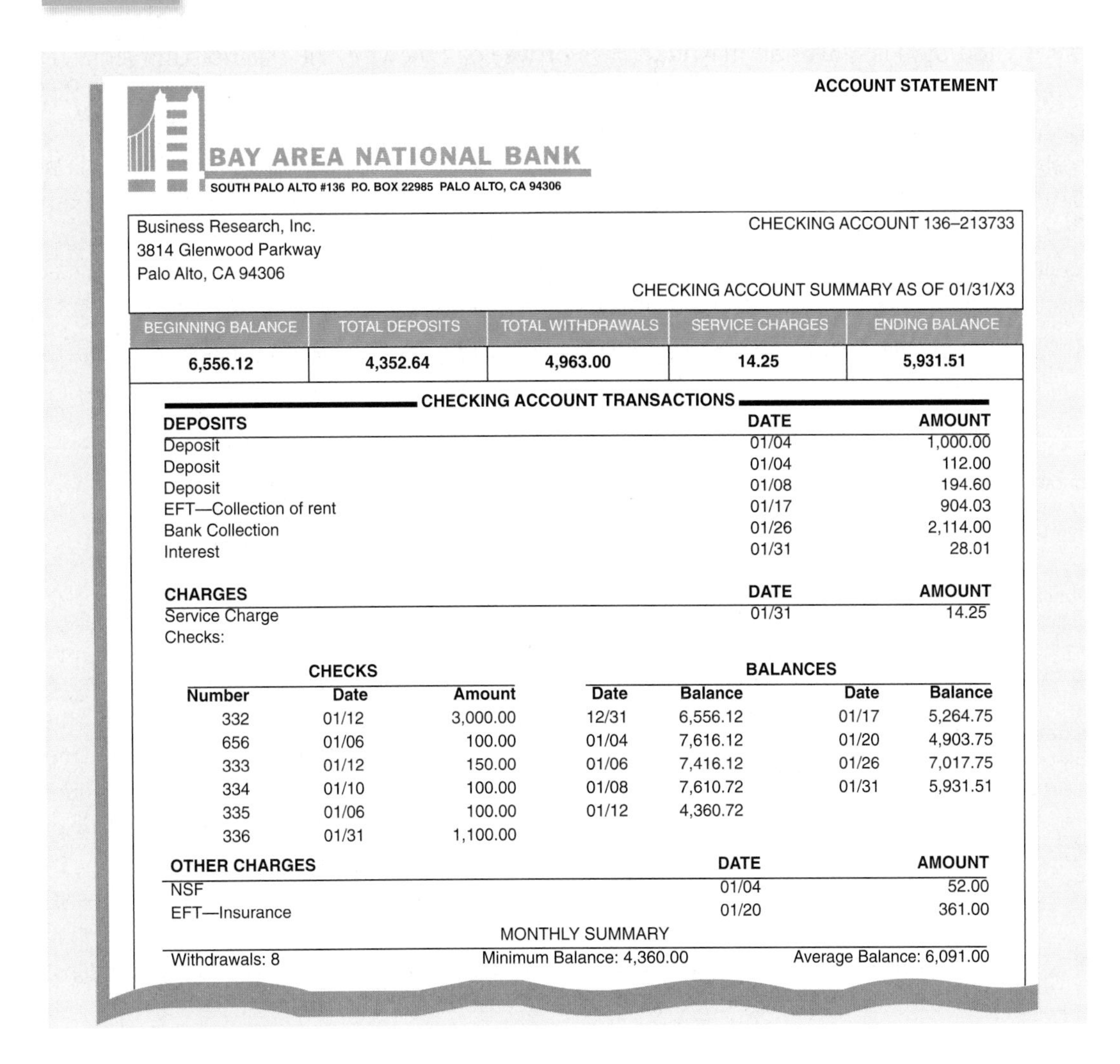

ACCOUNT STATEMENT

BAY AREA NATIONAL BANK
SOUTH PALO ALTO #136 P.O. BOX 22985 PALO ALTO, CA 94306

Business Research, Inc.
3814 Glenwood Parkway
Palo Alto, CA 94306

CHECKING ACCOUNT 136–213733

CHECKING ACCOUNT SUMMARY AS OF 01/31/X3

BEGINNING BALANCE	TOTAL DEPOSITS	TOTAL WITHDRAWALS	SERVICE CHARGES	ENDING BALANCE
6,556.12	4,352.64	4,963.00	14.25	5,931.51

CHECKING ACCOUNT TRANSACTIONS

DEPOSITS	DATE	AMOUNT
Deposit	01/04	1,000.00
Deposit	01/04	112.00
Deposit	01/08	194.60
EFT—Collection of rent	01/17	904.03
Bank Collection	01/26	2,114.00
Interest	01/31	28.01

CHARGES	DATE	AMOUNT
Service Charge	01/31	14.25
Checks:		

CHECKS			BALANCES			
Number	Date	Amount	Date	Balance	Date	Balance
332	01/12	3,000.00	12/31	6,556.12	01/17	5,264.75
656	01/06	100.00	01/04	7,616.12	01/20	4,903.75
333	01/12	150.00	01/06	7,416.12	01/26	7,017.75
334	01/10	100.00	01/08	7,610.72	01/31	5,931.51
335	01/06	100.00	01/12	4,360.72		
336	01/31	1,100.00				

OTHER CHARGES	DATE	AMOUNT
NSF	01/04	52.00
EFT—Insurance	01/20	361.00

MONTHLY SUMMARY

Withdrawals: 8 Minimum Balance: 4,360.00 Average Balance: 6,091.00

Banks send monthly **bank statements** to their depositors. Exhibit 4-7 is the bank statement of Business Research, Inc. for the month ended January 31, 20X3. We will use this bank statement to illustrate a bank reconciliation.

Bank statement
Document showing the beginning and ending balances of a particular bank account listing the month's transactions that affected the account.

Electronic funds transfer (EFT) is a system that relies on electronic communications—not paper documents—to transfer cash. EFTs are used for repetitive cash transactions. It is much cheaper for a company to pay employees by EFT (direct deposit) than by issuing payroll checks. Also, many people pay their regular bills by prior arrangement with their banks and never write checks. The bank statement lists cash receipts by EFT among the deposits and cash payments by EFT among the checks and other bank charges.

Electronic funds transfer (EFT)
System that transfers cash by electronic communication rather than by paper documents.

The Bank Reconciliation

There are two records of a business's cash: (1) the company's Cash account on its own books; and (2) the bank statement, which shows the actual amount of cash in the bank. The cash balance on the books rarely equals the balance shown on the bank statement, but both the books and the bank may be correct. Differences arise because of a time lag in recording transactions. When a firm writes a check, it immediately credits the Cash account. The bank, however, will not subtract the amount of the check from the business's balance until the bank receives the check and pays it. This step may take days or weeks. Likewise, the business immediately debits Cash for all cash receipts, but it may take a day or so for the bank to add this amount to the firm's balance.

Bank reconciliation A document explaining the reasons for the difference between a depositor's records and the bank's records about the depositor's bank account.

To ensure accurate financial records, the firm's accountant must explain why the firm's records and the bank statement figures disagree. This process creates a document called the **bank reconciliation.** The bank reconciliation ensures that the company accounts for all cash transactions and also that the bank records are correct.

✔ Check Point 4-3

ITEMS FOR RECONCILIATION. Here are some common items that cause differences between the bank balance and the book balance.

Deposit in transit A deposit recorded by the company but not yet by its bank.

Outstanding check A check issued by the company and recorded on its books but not yet paid by its bank.

Bank collection Collection of money by the bank on behalf of a depositor.

Nonsufficient funds (NSF) check A "hot" check, one for which the payer's bank account has insufficient money to pay the check. NSF checks are cash receipts that turn out to be worthless.

- ***Items recorded by the company but not yet recorded by the bank.***

  Deposits in transit (outstanding deposits). The company has recorded these cash receipts, but the bank has not.

  Outstanding checks. The company has issued these checks and recorded cash payments on its books, but the bank has not yet paid them.

- ***Items recorded by the bank but not yet recorded by the company.***

  Bank collections. Banks collect money on behalf of depositors. Many businesses have their customers pay directly to the company bank account. This practice, called a *lockbox system*, places the business's cash in circulation immediately.

  Electronic funds transfers. The bank may receive or pay cash on behalf of the depositor. The bank statement will list the EFTs.

  Service charge. This is the bank's fee for processing the depositor's transactions.

  Interest revenue earned on checking account. Depositors earn interest if they keep a large enough balance of cash in their account.

  Nonsufficient funds (NSF) checks received from customers. NSF checks are cash receipts that turn out to be worthless. Deduct NSF checks on the book side of the reconciliation. Several other items are treated in the same way as NSF checks. Banks return checks to the payee if (1) the maker's account has closed, (2) the date is stale ("void after 30 days"), (3) the signature is not authorized, or (4) the check has been altered.

  Printed checks. This charge is handled as a service charge.

- ***Errors by the company or the bank.*** For example, a bank may improperly decrease the bank balance of Business Research, Inc., for a check drawn by another company. Also the company may record a check incorrectly. All errors must be corrected, and the corrections will be a part of the bank reconciliation.

Objective 2 Use a bank reconciliation as a control device

BANK RECONCILIATION ILLUSTRATED. The bank statement in Exhibit 4-7 indicates that the January 31 bank balance of Business Research, Inc. is $5,931.51. However, Exhibit 4-8 shows that the company's Cash account on the books has a balance of $3,294.21. The following reconciling items explain why the two balances differ:

1. The January 31 deposit of $1,591.63 does not appear on the bank statement. This is a deposit in transit.
2. The bank erroneously charged to the Business Research, Inc., account a $100 check—number 656—written by Business Research Associates (Exhibit 4-7).

Exhibit 4-8

Cash Records of Business Research, Inc.

ACCOUNT Cash

Date	Item	Debit	Credit	Balance
20X3				
Jan. 1	Balance			6,556.12
2	Cash receipt	1,112.00		7,668.12
7	Cash receipt	194.60		7,862.72
31	Cash payments		6,160.14	1,702.58
31	Cash receipt	1,591.63		3,294.21

Cash Payments

Check No.	Amount	Check No.	Amount
332	$3,000.00	338	$ 319.47
333	510.00	339	83.00
334	100.00	340	203.14
335	100.00	341	458.53
336	1,100.00		
337	286.00	Total	$6,160.14

✔Check Point 4-4

This is a bank error and must be corrected on the bank side of the reconciliation.

3. Five company checks issued late in January and recorded in the journal have not been paid by the bank. These are outstanding checks.

Check No.	*Date*	*Amount*
337	Jan. 27	$ 286.00
338	28	319.47
339	28	83.00
340	29	203.14
341	30	458.53
Total		$1,350.14

4. The bank received $904.03 by EFT on behalf of Business Research, Inc. This EFT is like a bank collection.
5. The bank collected on behalf of the company a note receivable, $2,114 (including interest revenue of $214). This is another bank collection.
6. The bank statement shows interest revenue of $28.01, which the company has earned on its cash balance.
7. Check number 333 for $150 paid to Brown Company on account was recorded as a cash payment of $510, creating a $360 understatement of the Cash balance in the books. This is a book error and must be corrected on the book side of the reconciliation.
8. The bank service charge for the month was $14.25.
9. The bank statement shows an NSF check for $52, received from customer L. Ross.
10. Business Research pays insurance expense monthly by EFT. The company has not yet recorded this $361 payment.

Exhibit 4-9 is the bank reconciliation based on the preceding data. After the reconciliation, the adjusted bank balance equals the adjusted book balance. This equality is an accuracy check on both the bank and the books.

Exhibit 4-9

Bank Reconciliation

Business Research, Inc.
Bank Reconciliation
January 31, 20X3

Bank		*Books*	
Balance, January 31	$5,931.51	Balance, January 31	$3,294.21
Add:		Add:	
1. Deposit of January 30 in transit	1,591.63	4. EFT receipt of rent revenue	904.03
2. Correction of bank error—Business Research Associates check erroneously charged against company account	100.00	5. Bank collection of note receivable, including interest revenue of $214	2,114.00
		6. Interest revenue earned on bank balance	28.01
	7,623.14	7. Correction of book error—overstated amount of check no. 333	360.00
			6,700.25
3. Less: Outstanding checks:		Less:	
No. 337 .... $286.00		8. Service charge $14.25	
No. 338 .... 319.47		9. NSF check 52.00	
No. 339 .... 83.00		10. EFT payment of insurance	
No. 340 .... 203.14			
No. 341 .... 458.53	(1,350.14)	expense 361.00	(427.25)
Adjusted bank balance	$6,273.00	Adjusted book balance	$6,273.00

Amounts should agree.

✔ Check Point 4-5

Each reconciling item is treated in the same way in every situation. Here is a summary of how to treat the various reconciling items:

Bank Balance	**Book Balance**
Add deposits in transit.	*Add* bank collection items, interest revenue, and EFT receipts.
Subtract outstanding checks.	*Subtract* service charges, NSF checks, and EFT payments.
Add or *subtract* corrections of bank errors, as appropriate.	*Add* or *subtract* corrections of book errors, as appropriate.

ACCOUNTING FOR TRANSACTIONS FROM THE RECONCILIATION. The bank reconciliation does not directly affect the actual accounts (the books). The reconciliation is an accountant's tool, separate from the company's books. On the basis of the reconciliation in Exhibit 4-9, Business Research, Inc., makes the following journal entries. Numbers in parentheses correspond to the reconciling items described earlier.

		Debit	Credit
(4)	Cash	904.03	
	Rent Revenue		904.03
	Receipt of monthly rent.		
(5)	Cash	2,114.00	
	Notes Receivable		1,900.00
	Interest Revenue		214.00
	Note receivable collected by bank.		
(6)	Cash	28.01	
	Interest Revenue		28.01
	Interest earned on bank balance.		
(7)	Cash	360.00	
	Accounts Payable—Brown Company		360.00
	Correction of check no. 333.		
(8)	Miscellaneous Expense*	14.25	
	Cash		14.25
	Bank service charge.		
(9)	Accounts Receivable—L. Ross	52.00	
	Cash		52.00
	NSF customer check returned by bank.		
(10)	Insurance Expense	361.00	
	Cash		361.00
	Payment of monthly insurance.		

✔ Check Point 4-6

*Note: Miscellaneous Expense is debited for the bank service charge because the service charge pertains to no particular expense category.

The bank statement balance is $4,500 and shows a service charge of $15, interest earned of $5, and an NSF check for $300. Deposits in transit total $1,200; outstanding checks are $575. The bookkeeper recorded as $152 a check of $125 in payment of an account payable.

1. What is the adjusted bank balance?
2. What was the book balance of cash before the reconciliation?

Answers:

1. $5,125 ($4,500 + $1,200 − $575).
2. $5,408 ($5,125 + $15 − $5 + $300 − $27). The adjusted book and bank balances are the same. The answer can be determined by working backward from the adjusted balance.

Using the Bank Reconciliation to Control Cash

The bank reconciliation is a powerful control device. Randy Vaughn is a CPA in Houston, Texas. He owns several apartment complexes that are managed by his aunt. His aunt signs up tenants, collects the monthly rents, arranges custodial and maintenance work, hires and fires employees, writes the checks, and performs the bank reconciliation. In short, she does it all. This concentration of duties in one person is evidence of weak internal control. Vaughn's aunt could be stealing from him, and as a CPA he is aware of this possibility.

Vaughn trusts his aunt because she is a member of the family. Nevertheless, he exercises some controls over her management of his apartments. Vaughn periodically drops by his properties to see whether the custodial/maintenance staff is keeping the property in good condition. To control cash, Vaughn occasionally examines the bank reconciliation that his aunt has performed. Vaughn would know immediately if his aunt is writing checks to herself. By examining each check, Vaughn establishes control over cash payments.

Vaughn has a simple method for controlling cash receipts. He knows the occupancy level of his apartments. He also knows the monthly rent he charges. He multiplies the number of apartments—say 20—by the monthly rent (which averages $500 per unit) to arrive at expected monthly rent revenue of $10,000. By tracing the $10,000 revenue to the bank statement, Vaughn can tell if all his rent money went into his bank account. To keep his aunt on her toes, Vaughn lets her know that he periodically audits her work.

✔ Check Point 4–7

✔ Check Point 4–8

Control activities such as these are critical. If there are only a few employees, separation of duties may not be feasible. The manager must control operations, or the assets will slip away.

Mid-Chapter Summary Problem

The Cash account of Bain Company at February 28, 20X3, is as follows:

Cash

Feb. 1	**Balance**	**3,995**	**Feb. 3**	**400**
6		**800**	**12**	**3,100**
15		**1,800**	**19**	**1,100**
23		**1,100**	**25**	**500**
28		**2,400**	**27**	**900**
Feb. 28	**Balance**	**4,095**		

Bain Company deposits all cash receipts in the bank and makes all cash payments by check. Bain Company receives this bank statement on February 28, 20X3 (as always, negative amounts are in parentheses):

Bank Statement for February 20X3

Beginning balance		$ 3,995
Deposits:		
Feb. 7	$ 800	
15	1,800	
24	1,100	3,700
Checks (total per day):		
Feb. 8	$ 400	
16	3,100	
23	1,100	(4,600)
Other items:		
Service charge		(10)
NFS check from M. E. Crown		(700)
Bank collection of note receivable		1,000*
EFT—monthly rent expense		(330)
Interest on account balance		15
Ending balance		$ 3,070

*Includes interest of $119

Required

1. Prepare the bank reconciliation of Bain Company at February 28, 20X3.
2. Record the journal entries based on the bank reconciliation.

Answers

Requirement 1

Bain Company

Bank Reconciliation
February 28, 20X3

Bank:		
Balance, February 28, 20X3		$3,070
Add: Deposit of February 28 in transit		2,400
		5,470
Less: Outstanding checks issued on Feb 25 ($500) and Feb. 27 ($900)		(1,400)
Adjusted bank balance, February 28, 20X3		$4,070
Books:		
Balance, February 28, 20X3		$4,095
Add: Bank collection of note receivable, including interest of $119		1,000
Interest earned on bank balance		15
		5,110
Less: Service charge	$ 10	
NSF check	700	
EFT—Rent expense	330	(1,040)
Adjusted book balance, February 28, 20X3		$4,070

Requirement 2

Date	Accounts and Explanation	Debit	Credit
Feb. 28	Cash	1,000	
	Note Receivable ($1,000 − $119)		881
	Interest Revenue		119
	Note receivable collected by bank.		
28	Cash	15	
	Interest Revenue		15
	Interest earned on bank balance.		
28	Miscellaneous Expense	10	
	Cash		10
	Bank service charge.		
Feb. 28	Accounts Receivable—M. E. Crown	700	
	Cash		700
	NSF check returned by bank.		
28	Rent Expense	330	
	Cash		330
	Monthly rent expense.		

Controlling and Managing Cash

cash budget, cash disbursements, cash payments

Objective

3 **Apply** internal controls to cash receipts and cash payments

Internal Control: Receipts

Internal control over cash receipts ensures that all cash receipts are deposited in the bank and that no collections are lost. Many businesses receive cash over the counter and through the mail. Each source of cash receipts calls for its own security measures.

Over-the-Counter Receipts. The point-of-sale terminal (cash register) offers control over the cash received in a store. Consider a Macy's store. Company policy requires the issuance of a receipt to make sure that each sale is recorded by the cash register. The cash drawer opens only when the sales clerk enters an amount on the keypad, and the machine records each transaction. At the end of the day, a manager proves the cash by comparing the total amount in the cash drawer against the machine's record of the day's sales. At the end of the day, the cashier deposits the cash in the bank. The accounting record of cash receipts goes electronically to the accounting department for entry in the Cash account.

✔ Check Point 4-9

Mail Receipts. If the company does receive cash by mail, all incoming mail should be opened by a mailroom employee. This person should compare the amount of the check received with the attached remittance advice (the slip of paper that lists the amount due). The mailroom clerk keeps a running total of cash received for the day. At the end of the day, this control total is given to a responsible official, such as the controller, for verification. Cash receipts should be given to the cashier, who combines them with any cash received over the counter and prepares the bank deposit.

The mailroom employee forwards the remittance advices to the accounting department. These data are entered in the cash books and posted to customers' accounts. As a final step, the controller compares the three records of the day's cash receipts:

- The control tape total from the mailroom.
- The bank deposit amount from the cashier.
- The debit to Cash from the accounting department.

Many companies use a lockbox system for cash receipts by mail. Customers send checks directly to an address that is essentially a bank account, so company personnel do not handle incoming cash. The lockbox system improves efficiency because the cash goes to work for the company immediately.

Exhibit 4-10 summarizes the controls over cash receipts.

Exhibit 4-10

Internal Controls over Cash Receipts

Element of Internal Control	*Internal Controls over Cash Receipts*
Competent, reliable, ethical personnel	Companies carefully screen employees for honesty. They also train employees.
Proper authorization	Only designated employees can grant exceptions for customers, approve check receipts above a certain amount, and allow customers to purchase on credit.
Separation of duties	Cashiers and mailroom employees who handle cash do not have access to the accounting records. Accountants who record cash receipts do not handle cash.
Internal and external audits	Internal auditors examine company transactions for agreement with management policies. External auditors examine the internal controls over cash receipts in order to express an opinion on the financial statement.
Electronic and computer controls	Cash registers serve as transaction records. Each day's receipts are matched with customer remittance advices and with the day's deposit ticket from the bank.

Internal Control: Payments

It is critical for an organization to control cash payments, both check payments and petty cash.

Payment by Check. Payment by check is an important control over cash. First, the check provides a record of the payment. Second, to be valid, the check must be signed by an authorized official. To illustrate: suppose the business is buying inventory for sale to customers. Let's examine the process leading up to the cash payment.

The purchasing process—outlined in Exhibit 4-11—starts when the sales department identifies the need for merchandise and prepares a *purchase request* (or *requisition*). A separate purchasing department specializes in locating the best buys and sends a *purchase order* to the supplier, the outside company that sells the needed goods. When the supplier ships the goods to the purchaser, the supplier also sends the *invoice*, or bill, which indicates the need to pay.

✔ Check Point 4-10

Exhibit 4-11
Purchasing Process

Business Document	Prepared by	Sent to
Purchase request (requisition)	Sales department	Purchasing department
Purchase order	Purchasing department	Supplier
Invoice (bill)	Supplier	Accounting department
Receiving report	Receiving department	Accounting department
Disbursement packet	Accounting department	Officer who signs the check

As the goods arrive, the receiving department checks them for damage and lists the merchandise received on a document called the *receiving report*. The accounting department combines all the foregoing documents, checks them for accuracy and agreement, and forwards this *disbursement packet* to designated officers for approval and payment. The packet includes the invoice, receiving report, purchase order, and purchase request, as shown in Exhibit 4-12.

Exhibit 4-12
Disbursement Packet

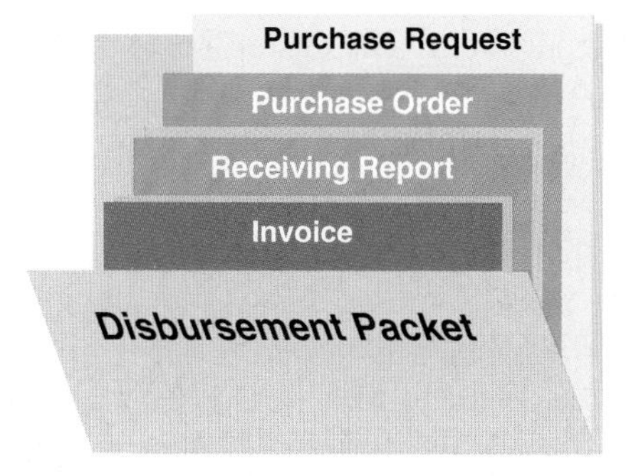

Before approving the disbursement, the controller or the treasurer should apply the following controls:

1. The invoice is compared with the purchase order and purchase request to ensure that the business pays only for the goods that it ordered.
2. The invoice is compared with the receiving report to ensure that the business pays only for the goods actually received.

After payment, the check signer can punch a hole through the disbursement packet. This hole denotes that the invoice has been paid and discourages dishonest employees from running the documents through the system for a duplicate payment. Exhibit 4-13 summarizes the internal controls over cash payments.

Exhibit 4-13

Internal Controls over Cash Payments

Element of Internal Control	*Controls over Cash Payments*
Competent, reliable, ethical personnel	Cash payments are entrusted to high-level employees, with larger amounts paid by the treasurer.
Proper authorization	Large expenditures must be authorized by top managers or the board of directors to ensure agreement with company goals.
Separation of duties	Computer operators and other employees who handle checks have no access to the accounting records. Accountants who record cash payments do not handle cash.
Internal and external audits	Internal auditors examine company transactions for agreement with management policies. External auditors examine the internal controls over cash payments to express an opinion on the financial statements.
Electronic and computer controls	Computer programmers do not operate the computers.

Petty cash Fund containing a small amount of cash that is used to pay minor expenditures.

Imprest system A way to account for petty cash by maintaining a constant balance in the petty cash account, supported by the fund (cash plus disbursement tickets) totaling the same amount.

PETTY CASH. It would be uneconomical for a business to write separate checks for an executive's taxi fare, floppy disks needed right away, or delivery of a message across town. Therefore, companies keep a small amount of cash on hand to pay such minor amounts. This fund is called **petty cash.**

The petty cash fund is opened with a particular amount of cash. A check for that amount is then issued to Petty Cash. Assume that on February 28, Cisco Systems, the worldwide leader in networks for the Internet, establishes a petty cash fund of $500 in a sales department. The custodian of the petty cash fund cashes the check and places $500 in the fund, which may be a cash box or other device.

For each petty cash payment, the custodian prepares a *petty cash ticket* to list the item purchased. The sum of the cash in the petty cash fund plus the total of the ticket amounts should equal the opening balance at all times—in this case, $500. The Petty Cash account keeps its prescribed $500 balance at all times. Maintaining the Petty Cash account at this balance, supported by the fund (cash plus tickets), is how an **imprest system** works. The control feature of an imprest system is that it clearly identifies the amount for which the custodian is responsible.

Using a Budget to Manage Cash

Objective

4 Use a budget to manage cash

Managers control their organizations with a budget. A **budget** is a financial plan that helps coordinate business activities. Cash is the item that is budgeted most often.

How, for example, does AT&T decide when to invest millions in new wireless technology? How will AT&T decide how much to spend? Will borrowing be needed, or can AT&T finance the purchase with internally generated cash? Similarly, by what process do you decide how much to spend on your education? On an automobile? On a house? All these decisions depend to some degree on the information that a cash budget provides.

Budget
A quantitative expression of a plan that helps managers coordinate the entity's activities.

A cash budget helps a company or an individual manage cash by planning the receipt and payment of cash during a future period. To prepare for the future, a company must determine how much cash it will need and then decide whether or not its operations will bring in the needed cash. Managers proceed as follows:

1. Start with the entity's cash balance at the beginning of the period, the amount left over from the preceding period.
2. Add the budgeted cash receipts and subtract the budgeted cash payments.
3. The beginning balance plus the expected receipts minus the expected payments equals the expected cash balance at the end of the period.
4. Compare the expected cash balance at the end of the period to the desired, or budgeted, cash balance at the end of the period. Managers know the minimum amount of cash they need (the budgeted balance) to keep the entity running. If there is excess cash, they can invest the excess. But if the expected cash balance falls below the budgeted balance, the company will need to obtain additional financing.

The budget period can span any length of time desired by managers—a day, a week, a month, or a year. Exhibit 4-14 shows a cash budget for Gap, Inc., for the year ended January 31, 20X3. Study it carefully, because at some point in your career or personal affairs, you will use a cash budget.

Exhibit 4-14
Cash Budget

Gap, Inc.
Cash Budget (Hypothetical)
For the Year Ended January 31, 20X3

			(In Millions)
(1)	Cash balance, February 1, 20X2		$ 202.6
	Estimated cash receipts:		
(2)	Collections from customers		2,858.3
(3)	Interest and dividends on investments		6.2
(4)	Sale of store fixtures		4.9
			3,072.0
	Estimated cash payments:		
(5)	Purchases of inventory	$1,906.2	
(6)	Operating expenses	561.0	
(7)	Expansion of existing stores	206.4	
(8)	Opening of new stores	344.6	
(9)	Payment of long-term debt	148.7	
(10)	Payment of dividends	219.0	3,385.9
(11)	Cash available (needed) before new financing		(313.9)
(12)	Budgeted cash balance, January 31, 20X3		(200.0)
(13)	Cash available for additional investments, or (New financing needed)		$ (513.9)

The cash budget has sections for cash receipts and cash payments. The budget is prepared *before* the period's transactions, and it can take any form that helps managers make decisions. Because the cash budget is an internal document, used only by the managers of the business, it is not bound by generally accepted accounting principles (GAAP).

Gap's hypothetical cash budget in Exhibit 4-14 begins with $202.6 million of cash (line 1). The year's budget calls for Gap to end the year with a *negative* cash balance of $313.9 million (line 11). Therefore, it looks like the company will need additional financing.

Assume that Gap managers wish to maintain a cash balance of at least $200 million (line 12). Because the year's activity is expected to leave the company with a negative cash balance of $313.9 million (line 11), the managers need to arrange $513.9 million of financing (line 13). Line 11 of the cash budget identifies the amount of cash available or needed. Line 12 lists the minimum cash balance to maintain at all times. Add lines 11 and 12 to arrive at the amount of new financing needed.

✔ Check Point 4-11

✔ Check Point 4-12

The cash budget helps managers arrange any new financing in an orderly manner. With enough cash, Gap can expand its stores and search out new products that keep customers coming back. Without the cash needed for these investments, Gap cannot compete with The Limited, Macy's, and other stores.

Reporting Cash on the Balance Sheet

Cash is the first current asset listed on the balance sheet of most companies. Even small businesses have numerous bank accounts, but companies usually combine all cash amounts into a single total called "Cash and Cash Equivalents" on the balance sheet. Cash equivalents include liquid assets such as time deposits and certificates of deposit, which are interest-bearing accounts that can be withdrawn with no penalty after a short period of time. Although they are slightly less liquid than cash, they are sufficiently similar to be reported along with cash. For example, the balance sheet of America Online (predecessor to AOL Time Warner Inc.), reported the following:

America Online, Inc.
Consolidated Balance Sheet (Excerpts, Adapted)
December 31,

(In Millions)	*2000*
Assets	
Current assets:	
Cash and cash equivalents	$2,610
Short-term investments	886
Accounts receivable	464

Compensating Balance Agreements

The Cash account on the balance sheet is the amount of liquid assets available for day-to-day use. None of the cash balance is restricted in any way.

Any restricted amount of cash should *not* be reported as Cash on the balance sheet. For example, banks often lend money under a compensating balance agreement.

The borrower agrees to maintain a minimum balance in a checking account at all times, so the minimum balance becomes a long-term asset and not cash in the normal sense.

Suppose Pier 1 Imports borrowed $5 million at 7% from First Interstate Bank and agreed to keep 10% ($500,000) on deposit at all times. The net result of the compensating balance agreement is that Pier 1 Imports actually borrowed only $4.5 million. And by paying 7% interest on the full $5 million, Pier 1's actual interest rate is higher than 7%.

Ethics and Accounting

Integrator CD
ethics

An article in the *Wall Street Journal* quoted a young entrepreneur in Russia as saying that he was getting ahead in business by breaking laws. He stated, "Older people have an ethics problem. By that I mean they ***have*** ethics." Conversely, Roger Smith, former chairman of General Motors, said, "Ethical practice is, quite simply, good business." First and foremost, practicing good ethics is the right thing to do. Second, unethical behavior always comes back to haunt you.

Most large companies have a code of ethics designed to encourage ethical and responsible behavior by employees. However, general guidelines may not be specific enough to identify misbehavior, and a list of dos and don'ts can lead to the false view that anything is okay if it's not specifically forbidden. Most businesses are intolerant of unethical conduct by employees. As one executive has put it. "I cannot describe all unethical behavior, but I know it when I see it." Codes of conduct are not enough: Senior management must set a high ethical tone that is steadily reinforced by management words and actions.

Accountants have additional incentives to behave ethically. As professionals, they are expected to maintain higher standards than society in general. Why? Their ability to do business depends entirely on their reputations. Most independent accountants are members of the American Institute of Certified Public Accountants (AICPA) and must abide by the *AICPA Code of Professional Conduct*. Accountants who are members of the Institute of Management Accountants are bound by the *Standards of Ethical Conduct for Management Accountants* →. Unacceptable actions can result in expulsion from the organization—a penalty that makes it difficult to remain in the accounting profession.

✔Check Point 4-13

← *Refer to Chapter 1, page 11, for further discussion of these topics.*

Ethical Issues in Accounting

Objective

5 Weigh ethical judgments in business

In many situations, the ethical choice is clear-cut. The computer programmer who bought a Lexus with discarded amounts from the computer was stealing from the company and lost his job. Equity Funding defrauded thousands of investors and went out of business. Enron got into trouble with the Securities and Exchange Commission (SEC) by putting out inaccurate financial statements. In accounting, the fundamental ethical issue is whether the accounting data that are made available to the public are complete and accurate. The Securities Exchange Act of 1934 gives investors broad powers to obtain a legal judgment against a company whose financial statements are incomplete.

The chapter-opening story about Enron Corporation illustrates a conflict of interest. A conflict of interest occurs when someone plays two roles that directly compete. A conflict of interest, therefore, poses an ethical dilemma that is best avoided. For example, a judge will not decide a lawsuit when a relative of the judge is involved in the case. Judges *recuse* themselves from the case because of the natural temptation to favor a relative.

As CFO of Enron Corporation, Andrew Fastow managed Enron's finances. In this position he was honor-bound to act in the best interest of the Enron stockholders. But in his capacity as the principal of the outside partnerships he was also honor-bound to act in the best interest of the investors who owned those partnerships. When Fastow negotiated transactions between Enron and the partnerships, he must have been torn by the competing motives to get the best deal for Enron and also the best deal for the outside partners. Exhibit 4-15 illustrates the conflict of interest:

Exhibit 4-15

Conflict of Interest

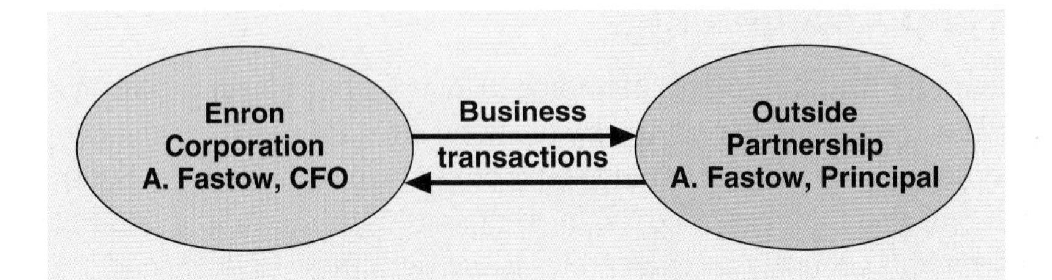

One problem that arose from Enron's transactions with the outside partnerships is that, with Andrew Fastow negotiating both sides of the deal, the values of the items bought and sold may have been rigged to come out too low or too high. Investors considering buying Enron stock received financial statements based on faulty values. Flawed income amounts could lead investors to pay unreasonable amounts for Enron stock. Then, when the truth came out, Enron's stock tumbled and a lot of people lost money.

How could the conflict of interest have been avoided? Enron's board of directors should not have let CFO Andrew Fastow transact business with partnerships that he controlled. Then the values that came out of the transactions would have been more objective. This is only one of the problems that affected Enron Corporation, but it illustrates an important ethical issue.

Decision Guidelines

ETHICAL JUDGMENTS

Suppose you are former Enron Vice President Sherron Watkins, a CPA who understood what was going on in the company. Watkins was faced with a tough decision that had an ethical dimension. For her, as for others in similar situations, weighing tough ethical judgments requires a decision framework. Consider these six steps as general guidelines. Let's apply them to Sherron Watkins.

Question	Decision Guidelines
1. What is the ethical issue, if any?	1. *Identify the ethical issues.* The root word of ethical is *ethics,* which Webster's dictionary defines as "the discipline dealing with what is good and bad and with moral duty and obligation." Watkins' ethical dilemma is to decide what she should do with the information she has uncovered.
2. What are the options?	2. *Specify the alternatives.* For Sherron Watkins, three alternatives are (a) express her concern about the outside partnerships to her boss, CFO, Andrew Fastow; (b) express her concern to Kenneth Lay, CEO of Enron; or (c) do nothing.

3. Who is involved in the situation?	**3.** *Identify the people involved.* Individuals who could be affected include all Enron employees (including Watkins), stockholders, creditors, and the SEC).
4. What are the possible consequences?	**4.** *Assess the possible outcomes.* **a.** If Watkins approaches Fastow, he might penalize her, or he might reward her for careful work. This would preserve her integrity and may lead Fastow to correct the situation and preserve Enron's public trust, but Fastow may fire Watkins for insubordination. **b.** If Watkins takes her concerns to the CEO, who is Fastow's boss—going over Fastow's head—her integrity would be preserved. Her relationship with Fastow would surely be strained and it might be difficult for them to work together in the future. Watkins might be rewarded for careful work, but if Fastow's boss has colluded with Fastow in setting up the partnership. Watkins could be penalized. If the situation is corrected and outsiders are notified, Enron could be reprimanded by the SEC if the company's financial-statement data prove inaccurate. **c.** If Watkins does nothing, she would avoid a confrontation with Fastow or Lay. But, the public may suffer if investors and creditors rely on faulty data.
5. What shall I do?	**5.** *Make the decision.* Identifying the best choice is difficult. Watkins must balance the likely effects on the various people against the dictates of her own conscience. This framework identifies the relevant factors. As it turned out, Watkins took her concerns to CEO Kenneth Lay, and he launched an investigation into the situation. Unfortunately, however, enough damage had already been done that Enron filed for Chapter 11 bankruptcy protection from its creditors. Enron fired Andrew Fastow.

Excel Application Problem

Goal: Create an Excel spreadsheet to help evaluate various options for an ethical dilemma.

Scenario: Consider the dilemma of Max Shauk, in problem P4-7A. In addition to the facts in the problem, Shauk's board is considering additional options. First, they've been told that there is a comparable site in the same general area with an appraised value of $2.9 million. It has, however, recently been found to be home to a delicate species of woodland fungus that scientists believe holds promise in the treatment of diabetes. Second, the board is considering remodeling and expanding the existing location square footage by 25%. The board has received a bid of $2.2 million on the remodel and new construction from Shauk's brother-in-law.

Assume the following: If the board makes an offer on Staas' property, it will propose a price of $2.5 million. If an offer is made on the comparable site, it will be $2.4 million. If the board chooses to remodel and expand the current location, the bid price will be accepted.

Your task is to create a spreadsheet that weights the issues associated with each scenario option and calculates the best choice.

After you have prepared your spreadsheet, answer these questions:

1. What additional issues did you include in your list?
2. Which option does your spreadsheet suggest the board choose?
3. For each option, which issue did you weight the most (in other words, which issue was most important to consider)?
4. If you were Shauk, which option would you recommend the board choose, and why?

Step-by-step:

1. Open a new Excel worksheet.
2. Create a bold-faced heading for your spreadsheet that contains the following:
   a. Chapter 4 Decision Guidelines
   b. Ethical Dilemma
   c. Today's Date
3. In row 5, create the following column headings:
   a. Issues
   b. Option 1 (Staas)
   c. Option 2 (Comp Site)
   d. Option 3 (Remodel)
   e. Option 4 (Do Nothing)
4. In the Issues column, list the issues that should be considered in making a decision. Add as many issues as you believe are relevant. Here's a starter list:
   a. Cost
   b. No potential environmental issues
   c. Absence of conflict of interest

d. No exploitation of seller's circumstances
e. Local community support

5. Next, using a range of 1–10, assign a score to each issue for each option. The higher the number, the more desirable it is for Shauk and the board. For example, if the local community response for Option 1 is unimportant, the score should be close to 1 or 2. If the local community response to Option 2 is expected to be adverse, it could be given a higher score to reflect the expected lack of support.
6. Underneath your last row of issues, create a "Total" row, and sum up the numbers for each column. This number represents the score for the option. Assuming all relevant issues have been appropriately ranked, the option with the highest score indicates the best choice. (For simplicity, this analysis assumes equal weighting for each issue.)

End-of-Chapter Summary Problem

Assume the following situation for PepsiCo, Inc.: PepsiCo ended 20X3 with total assets of $24 billion ($24,000 million), which included cash of $6.6 billion. At December 31, 20X3, PepsiCo owed $17 billion, of which it expected to pay $6.6 billion during 20X4. At the end of 20X3, Bob Detmer, the CFO of PepsiCo, is preparing the budget for the next year.

During 20X4, Detmer expects PepsiCo to collect $26.4 billion from customers and an additional $90 million in interest earned from investments. PepsiCo expects to pay $12.5 billion for its inventories and $5.4 billion for operating expenses. To remain competitive, PepsiCo plans to spend $2.2 billion to upgrade production facilities and an additional $320 million to acquire other companies. PepsiCo also plans to sell older assets for approximately $300 million and to collect $220 million of this amount in cash. Because PepsiCo certainly expects to earn a profit during 20X4 (approximately $1.8 billion), the company is budgeting dividend payments of $550 million during the year. Finally, the company is scheduled to pay off $1.2 billion of long-term debt in addition to the current liabilities left over from 20X3.

Because of the increased level of activity planned for 20X4, Detmer budgets the need for a minimum cash balance of $330 million.

Required

1. How much must PepsiCo borrow during 20X4 to keep its cash balance from falling below $330 million? Prepare the 20X4 cash budget to answer this important question.
2. Consider the company's need to borrow $2,160 million. PepsiCo can avoid the need to borrow money in 20X4 by delaying one particular cash payment until 20X5 or later. Identify the item, and state why it would nevertheless be unwise to delay its payment.

Answers

Requirement 1

Pepsico, Inc.
Cash Budget
For the Year Ended December 31, 20X4

	(In Millions)	
Cash balance, December 31, 20X3		$ 230
Estimated cash receipts:		
Collections from customers		26,400
Receipt of interest		90
Sale of assets		220
		26,940
Estimated cash payments:		
Purchases of inventory	$12,500	
Payment of operating expenses	5,400	
Upgrading of production facilities	2,200	
Acquisition of other companies	320	
Payment of dividends	550	
Payment of long-term debt and other liabilities ($1,200 + $6,600)	7,800	(28,770)
Cash available (needed) before new financing		(1,830)
Budgeted cash balance, December 31, 20X4		(330)
Cash available for additional investments, or (New financing needed)		$ (2,160)

Requirement 2

PepsiCo can eliminate the need for borrowing $2,160 million by delaying the $2,200 million payment to *upgrade the company's production facilities*. The delay would be unwise because PepsiCo needs the upgrading to remain competitive.

Review Internal Control and Cash

Lessons Learned

1. **Know how to set up an effective system of internal control.** An effective internal control system includes these features: *competent, reliable, and ethical personnel; clear-cut assignment of responsibilities; proper authorization; separation of duties; internal and external audits; documents and records;* and *electronic and computer controls*. Many companies also make use of fireproof vaults, point-of-sale terminals, fidelity bonds, mandatory vacations, and job rotation. Effective computerized internal control systems must meet the same basic standards that good manual systems do.
2. **Use a bank reconciliation as a control device.** The *bank account* helps control and safeguard cash. Businesses use the *bank statement* and the *bank reconciliation* to account for cash and banking transactions and to bring the books up to date.
3. **Apply internal controls to cash receipts and cash payments.** To control cash receipts over the counter, companies use point-of-sale terminals that customers can see and require that cashiers provide customers with receipts. As an additional control, the machine records each sale and cash transaction.

   To control cash receipts many companies use lockbox systems in which customers send their checks to a lockbox controlled by the bank. For cash receipts by mail, a mailroom employee opens the mail, compares the enclosed amount with the remittance advice, and prepares a control tape. This is an essential separation of duties—the accounting department should not open the mail. At the end of the day, the controller compares the three records of the day's cash receipts: the control tape total from the mail room, the bank deposit amount from the cashier, and the debit to Cash from the accounting department.

To control payments by check, checks should be issued and signed only when a ***disbursement packet*** including the purchase request, purchase order, invoice (bill), and receiving report (with all appropriate signatures) has been prepared.

4. **Use a budget to manage cash.** A budget is a quantitative expression of a plan that helps managers coordinate the entity's activities. To prepare for the future, a company must determine how much cash it will need and then decide whether its operations will bring in the needed cash. If not, then the company knows to arrange financing early. If operations will bring in an excess of cash, the company can be on the lookout for investment activities.
5. **Weigh ethical judgments in business.** To make ethical decisions, people should proceed in five steps: (1) Identify the ethical issues. (2) Specify the alternatives. (3) Identify the people involved. (4) Assess the possible outcomes. (5) Make the decision. Ethical business practice is simply good business.

Accounting Vocabulary

audit (p. 182)
bank collections (p. 188)
bank reconciliation (p. 188)
bank statement (p. 187)
budget (p. 197)
check (p. 186)
controller (p. 181)
deposits in transit (p. 188)
electronic funds transfer (EFT) (p. 187)
imprest system (p. 196)
internal control (p. 180)
nonsufficient funds (NSF) check (p. 188)
outstanding checks (p. 188)
petty cash (p. 196)

Questions

1. What is the goal of internal control? Why is it so important?
2. Are internal controls optional? If not, which federal law affects internal control procedures? What requirement does it place on management?
3. Identify the features of an effective system of internal control.
4. Separation of duties may be divided into three parts. What are they?
5. How can internal control systems be circumvented?
6. Are internal control systems designed to be foolproof? What is a fundamental constraint in planning and maintaining these systems?
7. Each of the items in the following list must be accounted for in the bank reconciliation. Next to each item, enter the appropriate letter from these possible treatments: (a) bank side of reconciliation—add the item; (b) bank side of reconciliation—subtract the item; (c) book side of reconciliation—add the item; (d) book side of reconciliation—subtract the item.

   _______ Outstanding check
   _______ NSF check
   _______ Bank service charge
   _______ Cost of printed checks
   _______ Bank error that decreased bank balance
   _______ Deposit in transit
   _______ Bank collection
   _______ Customer check returned because of unauthorized signature
   _______ Book error that increased balance of Cash account

8. What purpose does a bank reconciliation serve?
9. What role does a cash register play in an internal control system?
10. Describe the internal control procedures for cash received by mail.
11. What documents make up the disbursement packet? Describe two procedures that use the disbursement packet to ensure that each payment is appropriate.
12. Describe ways in which a budget helps a company manage its cash.
13. "Our managers know that they are expected to meet budgeted profit figures. We don't want excuses. We want results." Discuss the ethical implications of this policy.

Assess Your Progress

Check Points

Description of internal control
(Obj. 1)

CP4-1 Internal controls are designed to safeguard assets, encourage employees to follow company policies, promote operational efficiency, and ensure accurate records. Which of these four goals of internal controls is most important? Give your reason.

CP4-2 Explain in your own words why separation of duties is often described as the cornerstone of internal controls for safeguarding assets. Describe what can happen if the same person has custody of an asset and also accounts for it.

Characteristics of an effective system of internal control **(Obj. 1)**

CP4-3 Draw a simple diagram with three boxes and four arrows to show the relationships among (a) the accounting records, (b) the bank reconciliation, and (c) the bank statement. Use the arrows to show the flow of data.

Bank reconciliation **(Obj. 2)**

CP4-4 Compare Business Research, Inc.'s Cash account in Exhibit 4-8, page 189, with the bank statement that the company received in Exhibit 4-7, page 187.

Identifying reconciling items from bank documents **(Obj. 2)**

1. Trace each of Business Research's checks from the cash payments record in Exhibit 4-8 to the bank statement in Exhibit 4-7. List all outstanding checks by check number and dollar amount.
2. Trace each cash receipt from the Cash account (Exhibit 4-8) to a deposit on the bank statement (Exhibit 4-7). Which deposit is in transit on January 31? Give its date and dollar amount.
3. On which side of the bank reconciliation do deposits in transit and outstanding checks appear—the bank side or the book side? Are they added or subtracted on the bank reconciliation?

CP4-5 The Cash account of Cable Car Clothiers reported a balance of $1,585 at May 31. Included were outstanding checks totaling $900 and a May 31 deposit of $500 that did not appear on the bank statement. The bank statement, which came from Cornerstone Bank, listed a May 31 balance of $2,490. Included in the bank balance was a May 30 collection of $550 on account from a customer who pays the bank directly. The bank statement also shows a $20 service charge, $10 of interest revenue that Cable Car Clothiers earned on its bank balance, and an NSF check for $35.

How much cash does Cable Car Clothiers actually have at May 31?

Preparing a bank reconciliation **(Obj. 2)**

CP4-6 After preparing Cable Car Clothiers' bank reconciliation in Check Point 4-5, make the company's journal entries for transactions that arise from the bank reconciliation. Include an explanation with each entry.

Recording transactions from a bank reconciliation **(Obj. 2)**

CP4-7 Elizabeth Beck owns The Aquatic Center. She fears that a trusted employee has been stealing from the company. This employee receives cash from customers and also prepares the monthly bank reconciliation. To check up on the employee, Beck prepares her own bank reconciliation, as follows:

Using a bank reconciliation as a control device **(Obj. 2)**

The Aquatic Center
Bank Reconciliation
August 31, 20X7

Bank		Books	
Balance, August 31	$3,300	Balance, August 31	$2,150
Add		Add	
Deposits in transit	400	Bank collections	800
		Interest revenue	10
Less		Less	
Outstanding checks	(1,100)	Service charge	(30)
Adjusted bank balance	$2,600	Adjusted book balance	$2,930

Does it appear that the employee has stolen from the company? If so, how much? Explain your answer. Which side of the bank reconciliation shows the company's true cash balance?

Internal controls and the bank reconciliation
(Obj. 2)

CP4-8 Who in an organization should prepare the bank reconciliation? Should it be someone with cash-handling duties, someone with accounting duties, or someone with both duties? Does it matter? Give your reason.

Control over cash receipts
(Obj. 3)

CP4-9 Paul Krause sells memberships to The Aquatic Center in San Clemente, California. Company procedure requires Krause to write a customer receipt for all sales. The receipt forms are prenumbered. Krause is having personal financial problems and steals $500 received from a customer. To hide his theft, Krause destroys the company copy of the sales receipt he gave the customer. What will alert owner Elizabeth Beck that something is wrong? What will this knowledge lead Beck to do?

Internal control over payments by check
(Obj. 3)

CP4-10 Answer the following questions about internal control over cash payments:

1. Payment by check carries two basic controls over cash. What are they?
2. Suppose a purchasing agent receives the goods that he purchases and also approves payment for the goods. How could a dishonest purchasing agent cheat his company? How do companies avoid this internal control weakness?

Preparing cash budgets with two different outcomes
(Obj. 4)

CP4-11 Return to **Gap, Inc.**'s hypothetical cash budget in Exhibit 4-14, page 197.

1. Suppose Gap were to postpone the expansion of existing stores until 20X4. How much new financing would Gap need, or how much cash would the company have available for additional investments during the year ended January 31, 20X3?
2. Now suppose Gap were to postpone both the expansion of existing stores and the opening of new stores until 20X4. How much new financing would Gap need, or how much cash would the company have available for additional investments during the year ended January 31, 20X3?

Preparing a cash budget
(Obj. 4)

CP4-12 **California Artichoke Growers** is a major food cooperative. Suppose the organization begins 2006 with cash of $16 million. California Artichoke Growers estimates cash receipts during 2006 will total $147 million. Planned payments for the year will total $154 million. To meet daily cash needs, California Artichoke Growers must maintain a cash balance of at least $5 million. Prepare the organization's cash budget for 2006.

Making an ethical judgment
(Obj. 5)

ECP4-13 Elizabeth Grant, an accountant for Westlake Charities, discovers that her supervisor, Jules Duquet, made several errors last year. Overall, the errors overstated Westlake's cash flow by 20%. It is not clear whether the errors were deliberate or accidental. What should Grant do?

Exercises

Correcting an internal control weakness
(Obj. 1)

E4-1 Consider this story from a *Wall Street Journal* article:

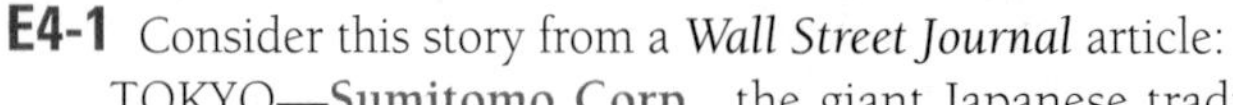

> TOKYO—**Sumitomo Corp.**, the giant Japanese trading company, said unauthorized trades by its former head of copper trading over the past decade caused it huge losses that may total $1.8 billion. The fiasco adds the flamboyant Yasuo Hamanaka to the role of all-time rogue trader. Sumitomo said it learned of the damage after Mr. Hamanaka confessed to making unauthorized trades over a 10-year period. Mr. Hamanaka, according to a Sumitomo statement, admitted to concealing the losses by falsifying Sumitomo's books and records.

What internal control weakness at Sumitomo allowed this loss to grow so large? How could the company have avoided and/or limited the size of the loss?

Identifying internal control strengths and weaknesses
(Obj. 1)

E4-2 The following situations describe two cash receipts situations and two equipment purchase situations. In each pair, one situation's internal controls are significantly better than the other's. Evaluate the internal controls in each situation as strong or weak, and give the reason for your answers.

Equipment purchases:

a. Centennial Homes policy calls for construction supervisors to request the equipment needed for construction jobs. The home office then purchases the equipment and has it shipped to the construction site.

b. Wayside Construction Company policy calls for project supervisors to purchase the equipment needed for construction jobs. The supervisors then submit the paid receipts to the home office for reimbursement. This policy enables supervisors to get the equipment they need quickly and keep construction jobs moving.

Cash receipts:

a. Cash received by mail goes straight to the accountant, who debits Cash and credits Accounts Receivable to record the collections from customers. The accountant then deposits the cash in the bank.

b. Cash received by mail goes to the mail room, where a mail clerk opens envelopes and totals the cash receipts for the day. The mail clerk forwards customer checks to the cashier for deposit in the bank and forwards the remittance slips to the accounting department for posting credits to customer accounts.

Identifying internal controls **(Obj. 1)**

E4-3 Identify the missing internal control characteristic in the following situations:

a. Barbara Shapiro manages the "Suspense" account at Texoma Oil Co. Amounts go into the "Suspense" account when Texoma needs to pay oil royalties to a property owner who cannot be identified. Some royalty amounts are unclaimed for years, so the "Suspense" account holds several million dollars. Ms. Shapiro alone is responsible for releasing amounts from "Suspense."

b. Grocery stores such as **Kroger** and **Winn Dixie** purchase large quantities of merchandise from a few suppliers. At another grocery store, the manager decides to reduce paperwork. He does not require that the receiving department prepare a report to list the items received.

c. When business is brisk, Stop-n-Shop deposits cash in the bank several times during the day. The manager at another convenience store wants to save time delivering cash to the bank, so he lets cash build up over weekends. The total is deposited on Sunday evening.

d. At Pay Less Pharmacy, the accountant orders merchandise and approves invoices for payment.

e. Business is slow at White Water Park on Tuesday, Wednesday, and Thursday nights. To reduce expenses, the owner decides not to use a ticket taker on those nights. The ticket seller (cashier) keeps the tickets as a record of the number sold.

Explaining the role of internal control **(Obj. 1)**

E4-4 Answer the following questions on internal control:

1. Separation of duties is an important consideration. Why is this so?
2. Cash may be a small item on the financial statements. Nevertheless, internal control over cash is very important. Why is this true?
3. Ling Ltd. requires that all documents supporting a check be canceled (stamped paid). Why is this practice required? What might happen if it were not?
4. Managers think safeguarding assets is the most important objective of internal control systems, while auditors emphasize internal control for ensuring reliable accounting data. Explain why managers are more concerned about safeguarding assets and why auditors are more concerned about the quality of the accounting records.

Classifying bank reconciliation items **(Obj. 2)**

E4-5 The following items may appear on a bank reconciliation:

1. Deposits in transit.
2. NSF check.
3. Bank collection of a note receivable on our behalf.
4. Book error: We debited Cash for $200. The correct debit was $2,000.
5. Outstanding checks.
6. Bank error: The bank charged our account for a check written by another customer.
7. Service charge.

Classify each item as (a) an addition to the bank balance, (b) a subtraction from the bank balance, (c) an addition to the book balance, or (d) a subtraction from the book balance.

Preparing a bank reconciliation **(Obj. 2)**

E4-6 Blakely Robinson's checkbook lists the following:

Date	Check No.	Item	Check	Deposit	Balance
10/1					$ 525
4	622	La Petite France Bakery	$ 19		506
9		Dividends		$ 116	622
13	623	General Tire Co.	43		579
14	624	ExxonMobil Oil Co.	58		521
18	625	Cash	50		471
26	626	Antioch Bible Church	25		446
28	627	Bent Tree Apartments	275		171
30		Paycheck		1,600	1,771

The October bank statement shows

Balance				$ 525
Add: Deposits				116
Deduct checks:	No.	Amount		
	622	$19		
	623	43		
	624	85*		
	625	50		(197)
Other charges:				
NSF check			$ 8	
Service charge			12	(20)
Balance				$ 424

*This is the correct amount for check number 624.

Required

Prepare Robinson's bank reconciliation at October 31, 20X6.

Preparing a bank reconciliation **(Obj. 2)**

E4-7 James VanWinkle operates four **Exxon** convenience stores. He has just received the monthly bank statement at May 31 from City National Bank, and the statement shows an ending balance of $1,840. Listed on the statement are an EFT rent collection of $300, a service charge of $12, two NSF checks totaling $74, and a $9 charge for printed checks. In reviewing his cash records, VanWinkle identifies outstanding checks totaling $603 and a May 31 deposit in transit of $1,788. During May, he recorded a $290 check for the salary of a part-time employee as $29. VanWinkle's Cash account shows a May 31 cash balance of $3,081. How much cash does VanWinkle actually have at May 31?

Making journal entries from a bank reconciliation **(Obj. 2)**

E4-8 By using the data from Exercise 4-7, make the journal entries that VanWinkle should record on May 31 to update his Cash account. Include an explanation for each entry.

Applying internal controls to the bank reconciliation **(Obj. 1, 2)**

E4-9 A court of law convicted the manager of Buzzard Billy's Armadillo Grill for stealing cash from the company. Over a 3-year period, the manager took almost $100,000 and attempted to cover the theft by manipulating the bank reconciliation.

What is the most likely way that a person would manipulate a bank reconciliation to cover a theft? Be specific. What internal control arrangement could prevent this theft?

Evaluating internal control over cash receipts **(Obj. 3)**

E4-10 Kmart stores use cash registers. The register shows the amount of each sale, the cash received from the customer, and any change returned to the customer. The machine also produces a customer receipt but keeps no record of transactions. At the end of the day, the clerk counts the cash in the register and gives it to the cashier for deposit in the company bank account.

Write a memo to convince the store manager that there is an internal control weakness over cash receipts. Identify the weakness that gives an employee the best opportunity to steal cash and state how to prevent such a theft.

Accounting for petty cash **(Obj. 3)**

general ledger

E4-11 Assume **Habitat for Humanity** in Topeka, Kansas, has created a $500 imprest petty cash fund. During July, the fund custodian authorized and signed petty cash tickets as follows:

Ticket No.	Item	Account Debited	Amount
1	Delivery of pledge cards to donors	Delivery Expense	$ 17.50
2	Mail package	Postage Expense	52.80
3	Newsletter	Supplies Expense	134.14
4	Key to closet	Miscellaneous Expense	2.85

Required

1. How much cash should the fund custodian request in order to replenish the petty cash fund?
2. Describe the items in the fund immediately before replenishment.
3. Describe the items in the fund immediately after replenishment.
4. Describe the internal control feature for this petty cash fund.

Preparing a cash budget **(Obj. 4)**

spreadsheet

E4-12 Suppose **Sprint Corporation**, the long-distance telephone company, is preparing its cash budget for 20X4. Assume the company ended 20X3 with $125.8 million, and top management foresees the need for a cash balance of at least $125 million to pay bills as they come due.

Collections from customers are expected to total $11,584.2 million during 20X4, and payments for the cost of services and products should reach $6,166 million. Operating expense payments are budgeted at $2,543.6 million.

During 20X4, Sprint expects to invest $1,825.7 million in new equipment and $275 million in the company's cellular division and to sell older assets for $115.7 million. Debt payments scheduled for 20X4 will total $597.2 million. The company forecasts net income of $890.4 million for 20X4 and plans to pay dividends of $338 million.

Prepare Sprint's cash budget for 20X4. Will the budgeted level of cash receipts leave Sprint with the desired ending cash balance of $125 million, or will the company need additional financing?

Evaluating the ethics of conduct by government legislators **(Obj. 5)**

E4-13 Approximately 300 current and former members of the U.S. House of Representatives—on a regular basis—wrote $250,000 of checks without having the cash in their accounts. Later investigations revealed that no public funds were involved. The House bank was a free-standing institution that recirculated House members' cash. In effect, the delinquent check writers were borrowing money from each other on an interest-free, no-service-charge basis. Nevertheless, the House closed its bank after the events became public.

Suppose you are a new congressional representative from your state. Apply the decision guidelines for ethical judgments outlined on pp. 200–201 to decide whether you would write NSF checks on a regular basis through the House bank.

Challenge Exercises

Internal control over cash payments, ethical considerations **(Obj. 3, 5)**

E4-14 David Chin, the owner of Chin's Imports, has delegated management of the business to Lee Phan, a friend. Chin drops by the business to meet customers and check up on cash receipts, but Phan buys the merchandise and handles cash payments. Business has been brisk lately, and cash receipts have kept pace with the apparent level of sales. However, for a year or so, the amount of cash on hand has been too low. When asked about this, Phan explains that suppliers are charging more for goods than in the past. During the past year, Phan has returned to Hong Kong twice, and Chin wonders how Phan could afford these trips on his $50,000 annual salary and commissions.

List at least three ways Phan could be defrauding Chin of cash. In each instance also identify how Chin can determine whether Phan's actions are ethical. Limit your answers to the store's cash payments. The business pays all suppliers by check (no EFTs).

Preparing and using a cash budget
(Obj. 4)

E4-15 Among its many products, **International Paper Company** makes paper for JC Penney shopping bags, the labels on Del Monte canned foods, and ***Redbook*** magazine. Marianne Parrs, the chief financial officer, is responsible for International Paper's cash budget for 20X2. The budget will help Parrs determine the amount of long-term borrowing needed to end the year with a cash balance of $100 million. Parrs' assistants have assembled budget data for 20X2, which the computer printed in alphabetical order. Not all the data items, reproduced below, are used in preparing the cash budget.

	(In Millions)
Acquisition of other companies	$ 1,315
Actual cash balance, December 31, 20X1	270
Borrowing	?
Budgeted total assets before borrowing	23,977
Budgeted total current assets before borrowing	5,873
Budgeted total current liabilities before borrowing	4,863
Budgeted total liabilities before borrowing	16,180
Budgeted total stockholders' equity before borrowing	7,797
Collections from customers	19,467
Dividend payments	237
Issuance of stock	516
Net income	1,153
Other cash receipts	111
Payment of long-term and short-term debt	950
Payment of operating expenses	2,349
Purchases of inventory items	14,345
Purchase of property and equipment	1,518

Required

1. Prepare the cash budget to determine the amount of borrowing International Paper needs during 20X2.
2. Compute International Paper's expected current ratio and debt ratio at December 31, 20X2, both before and after borrowing on a short-term note payable. Based on these figures, and on the budgeted levels of assets and liabilities, would you lend the requested amount to International Paper? Give the reason for your decision.

Compensating balance agreement
(Obj. 4)

E4-16 Assume **Compaq Computer** borrowed $10 million from **CitiBank**, agreeing to (a) pay an interest rate of 8% and (b) maintain a compensating balance amount equal to 10% of the loan. The bank will pay no interest on the compensating balance amount. Determine Compaq's actual effective interest rate on this loan.

Problems

(Group A)

Identifying the characteristics of an effective internal control system
(Obj. 1)

P4-1A Chavez Real Estate Development Company prospers during an economic expansion. When business is good, the company doesn't bother with internal controls. A recent decline in the local real estate market has caused Chavez to experience a shortage of cash. Juan Felipe Chavez, the company owner, is looking for ways to save money.

Required

As a consultant for the company, write a memorandum to convince Chavez of the company's need for a system of internal control. Be specific in telling him how an internal control system could save the company money. Include the definition of internal control, and briefly discuss each characteristic of an effective internal control system, beginning with competent, reliable, and ethical personnel.

Identifying internal control weaknesses
(Obj. 1, 3)

P4-2A Each of the following situations reveals an internal control weakness.

a. In evaluating the internal control over cash payments, an auditor learns that the purchasing agent is responsible for purchasing diamonds for use in the company's manufacturing process, approving the invoices for payment, and signing the checks. No supervisor reviews the purchasing agent's work.
b. Todd Wagoner owns a firm that performs engineering services. His staff consists of 12 professional engineers, and he manages the office. Often, his work requires him to travel to meet with clients. During the past 6 months, he has observed that when he returns from a business trip, the engineering jobs in the office have not progressed satisfactorily. He learns that when he is away, several of his senior employees take over office management and neglect their engineering duties. One employee could manage the office.
c. Leah Kestner has been an employee of A&S Shoe Store for many years. Because the business is relatively small, Kestner performs all accounting duties, including opening the mail, preparing the bank deposit, and preparing the bank reconciliation.
d. Most large companies have internal audit staffs that continuously evaluate the business internal control. Part of the auditor's job is to evaluate how efficiently the company is running. For example, is the company purchasing inventory from the least expensive wholesaler? After a particularly bad year, McGregor Cellular Company eliminates its internal audit department to reduce expenses.
e. Law firms, consulting firms, and other professional organizations use paraprofessional employees to perform routine tasks. For example, a legal paraprofessional might examine documents to assist a lawyer prepare a lawsuit. In the law firm of Dunham & Lee, Cecil Dunham, the senior partner, turns over a significant portion of his high-level legal work to his paraprofessional staff.

Required

1. Identify the missing internal control characteristic in each situation.
2. Identify each firm's possible problem.
3. Propose a solution to the problem.
4. How will what you learned by solving this problem help you manage a business?

Using the bank reconciliation as a control device
(Obj. 2)

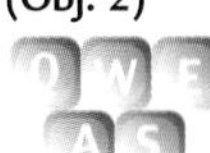

spreadsheet

P4-3A The cash data of Investors Brokerage Co. for April 20X4 follow:
The Cash account of Investors Brokerage shows the following information at April 30, 20X4:

Cash Receipts (CR)		Cash Payments (CP)	
Date	**Cash Debit**	**Check No.**	**Cash Credit**
Apr. 2	$ 4,174	3113	$ 891
8	407	3114	147
10	559	3115	1,930
16	2,187	3116	664
22	1,854	3117	1,472
29	1,060	3118	1,000
30	337	3119	632
Total	$10,578	3120	1,675
		3121	100
		3122	2,413
		Total	$10,924

Cash					
Date	Item	Jrnl. Ref.	Debit	Credit	Balance
Apr. 1	Balance				1,911
30		CR 6	10,578		12,489
30		CP 11		10,924	1,565

Investors Brokerage received the following bank statement on April 30, 20X4:

Bank Statement for April 20X4

Beginning balance		$ 1,911
Deposits and other Credits:		
Apr. 1	$ 326 EFT	
4	4,174	
9	407	
12	559	
17	2,187	
22	1,701 BC	
23	1,854	11,208
Checks and other Debits:		
Apr. 7	$ 891	
13	1,390	
14	903 US	
15	147	
18	664	
21	219 EFT	
26	1,472	
30	1,000	
30	20 SC	(6,706)
Ending balance		$ 6,413

Explanation: EFT—electronic funds transfer, BC—bank collection, US—unauthorized signature, SC—service charge

Additional data for the bank reconciliation include the following:

a. The EFT deposit was a receipt of monthly rent. The EFT debit was a monthly insurance payment.
b. The unauthorized signature check was received from S. M. Holt.
c. The $1,701 bank collection of a note receivable on April 22 included $185 interest revenue.
d. The correct amount of check number 3115, a payment on account, is $1,390. (Investors' accountant mistakenly recorded the check for $1,930.)

Required

1. Prepare the Investors Brokerage Company bank reconciliation at April 30, 20X4.
2. Describe how a bank account and the bank reconciliation help the Investors Brokerage Company control its cash.

Preparing a bank reconciliation and the related journal entries
(Obj. 2)

spreadsheet

P4-4A The August 31 bank statement of Palm Harbor Apartments has just arrived from Florida First Bank. To prepare the Palm Harbor bank reconciliation, you gather the following data:

a. Palm Harbor's Cash account shows a balance of $3,366.14 on August 31.
b. The August 31 bank balance is $4,484.22.
c. The bank statement shows that Palm Harbor earned $38.19 of interest on its bank balance during August. This amount was added to Palm Harbor's bank balance.
d. Palm Harbor pays utilities ($750) and insurance ($290) by EFT.
e. The following Palm Harbor checks did not clear the bank by August 31:

Check No.	Amount
237	$ 46.10
288	141.00
291	578.05
293	11.87
294	609.51
295	8.88
296	101.63

f. The bank statement includes a deposit of $891.17, collected by the bank on behalf of Palm Harbor Apartments. Of the total, $811.81 is collection of a note receivable, and the remainder is interest revenue.
g. The bank statement lists a $10.50 debit for the bank service charge.
h. On August 31, the Palm Harbor treasurer deposited $16.15, which will appear on the September bank statement.
i. The bank statement includes a $300.00 deposit that Palm Harbor did not make. The bank credited Palm Harbor for another company's deposit.
j. The bank statement includes two charges for returned checks from customers. One is a $395.00 check received from Shoreline Express and returned by Shoreline's bank with the imprint "Unauthorized Signature." The other is a nonsufficient funds check in the amount of $146.67 received from Lipsey, Inc.

Required

1. Prepare the bank reconciliation for Palm Harbor Apartments.
2. Journalize the August 31 transactions needed to update Palm Harbor's Cash account. Include an explanation for each entry.
3. How will your learning from solving this problem help you manage a business?

Identifying internal control weakness **(Obj. 3)**

P4-5A Altec Sound Systems makes all sales of stereo equipment on credit. Cash receipts arrive by mail, usually within 30 days of the sale. Matt Larosz opens envelopes and separates the checks from the accompanying remittance advices. Larosz forwards the checks to another employee, who makes the daily bank deposit but has no access to the accounting records. Larosz sends the remittance advices, which show the amount of cash received, to the accounting department for entry in the accounts. Larosz's only other duty is to grant sales allowances to customers. (A *sales allowance* decreases the amount that the customer must pay.) When Larosz receives a customer check for less than the full amount of the invoice, he records the sales allowance and forwards the document to the accounting department.

Required

You are a new employee of Altec Sound Systems. Write a memo to the company president identifying the internal control weakness in this situation. State how to correct the weakness.

Preparing a cash budget and using cash-flow information **(Obj. 4)**

P4-6A Louis Lipschitz, executive vice president and chief financial officer of **Toys "Я" Us, Inc.**, is responsible for the company's budgeting process. Suppose Lipschitz's staff is preparing the Toys "Я" Us cash budget for 20X2. A key input to the budgeting process is last year's statement of cash flows, reproduced in an adapted format as follows:

Toys "Я" Us Inc., and Subsidiaries

Consolidated Statement of Cash Flows (Adapted)

(In Millions)	20X1
Cash Flows from Operating Activities	
Collections from customers	$9,412
Interest received	17
Purchases of inventory	(6,750)
Operating expenses	(2,035)
Restructuring costs	(394)
Net cash provided by operating activities	250
Cash Flows from Investing Activities	
Capital expenditures	(468)
Purchases of other assets	(67)
Net cash used in investing activities	(535)
Cash Flows from Financing Activities	
Short-term borrowings	210
Long-term borrowings	82
Long-term debt repayments	(9)
Issuance of stock	16
Share repurchases	(200)
Net cash provided by financing activities	99
Effect of foreign-currency exchange rate changes on cash and cash equivalents	19
Cash and Cash Equivalents	
(Decrease)/increase during year	(167)
Beginning of year	370
End of year	$ 203

Required

1. Prepare the Toys "Я" Us cash budget for 20X2. Date the budget simply "20X2" and denote the beginning and ending cash balances as "beginning" and "ending." Assume the company expects 20X2 to be the same as 20X1, but with the following changes:
   a. In 20X2, the company expects a 15% increase in collections from customers and a 10% increase in purchases of inventory.
   b. The company expects to incur no restructuring costs in 20X2.
   c. The amount of any borrowings and the issuances of stock needed in 20X2 will be determined as a result of the cash budget and thus are not causal factors for the preparation of the budget (but scheduled long-term debt repayments and share repurchases should be the same in 20X2 as they were in 20X1).
   d. Lipschitz plans to end the year with a cash balance of $200 million.

You will find these explanations helpful:

"Capital expenditures" are purchases of property and equipment.

Toys "Я" Us does not pay cash dividends. Instead the company *repurchases* its stock from its stockholders. This is another way for a corporation to return cash to the stockholders.

2. Answer these questions about the company. Explain your reasoning for each answer.
   a. Does the company's cash budget for 20X2 suggest that Toys "Я" Us is growing, holding steady, or decreasing in size?
   b. Do the statement of cash flows for 20X1 and the cash budget for 20X2 suggest that operating activities are generating enough cash?

Making an ethical judgment
(Obj. 5)

P4-7A Max Shauk is executive vice president of Bluegrass Investments of Lexington, Kentucky. Active in community affairs, Shauk serves on the board of directors of **Army–Navy Surplus** stores. Army–Navy Surplus is expanding rapidly and is considering relocating its Lexington store. At a recent meeting, Army–Navy board members decided to buy 200 acres of land on the edge of town. The owner of the property is Jerry Staas, a client of Bluegrass Investments. Staas is completing a bitter divorce, and Shauk knows that Staas is eager to sell his property. In view of Staas's difficult situation, Shauk believes Staas would accept a low offer for the land. Realtors have appraised the property at $3.6 million.

Required

Apply the ethical judgment framework outlined in the chapter Decision Guidelines to help Shauk decide what role he should play in Army–Navy Surplus's attempt to buy the land from Staas.

(Group B)

Identifying the characteristics of an effective internal control system
(Obj. 1)

P4-1B An employee of Crisis Management, Inc. recently stole thousands of dollars of the company's cash. The company has decided to install a new system of internal controls.

Required

As a consultant for Crisis Management, write a memo to the president explaining how a separation of duties helps to safeguard company assets.

Identifying internal control weaknesses
(Obj. 1, 3)

P4-2B Each of the following situations has an internal control weakness:

a. Dick Monroe, who has no known sources of outside income, has been a trusted employee of Stone Products Company for 20 years. He performs all cash-handling and accounting duties, including opening the mail, preparing the bank deposit, accounting for cash and accounts receivable, and preparing the bank reconciliation. Monroe has just purchased a new home in an expensive suburb. Lou Dobbs, owner of the company, wonders how Monroe can afford the new home on his salary.
b. Ashley Webb employs three professional interior designers in her design studio. She is located in an area with a lot of new construction, and her business is booming. Ordinarily, Webb does all the purchasing of furniture, draperies, carpets, and other materials needed to complete jobs. During the summer, she takes a long vacation, and in her absence she allows each designer to purchase materials and labor. On her return, Webb reviews operations and observes that expenses are much higher and net income much lower than in the past.
c. Discount stores such as **Wal-Mart** and **Kmart** receive a large portion of their sales revenue in cash, with the remainder in credit card sales. To reduce expenses, a store manager ceases purchasing fidelity bonds on the cashiers.
d. The office supply company from which Haught Air Conditioning Service purchases cash receipt forms recently notified Haught that the last-shipped receipts were not prenumbered. Jerry Haught, the owner, replied that he did not use the receipt numbers, so the omission is not important.
e. Digital Graphics is a software company that specializes in programs with accounting applications. The company's most popular program prepares all the accounting records and financial statements. In the company's early days, the owner and eight employees wrote the computer programs, lined up production of the diskettes, sold the products to ComputerLand and ComputerCraft, and performed the general management and accounting of the company. As Digital has grown, the number of employees has increased dramatically. Recently, the development of a new software program stopped while the programmers redesigned Digital's accounting system. Digital's own accountants could have performed this task.

Required

1. Identify the missing internal control characteristics in each situation.
2. Identify each firm's possible problem.
3. Propose a solution to the problem.
4. How will what you learned by solving this problem help you manage a business?

Using the bank reconciliation as a control device
(Obj. 2)

P4-3B The cash data of Town & Country Builders for March 20X5 follow:

Cash

Date	Item	Jrnl. Ref.	Debit	Credit	Balance
Mar. 1	Balance				10,188
31		CR 10	9,106		19,294
31		CP 16		11,353	7,941

Cash Receipts (CR)

Date	Cash Debit
Mar. 4	$2,716
9	544
11	1,655
14	896
17	367
25	890
31	2,038
Total	$9,106

Cash Payments (CP)

Check No.	Cash Credit
1413	$ 1,465
1414	1,004
1415	450
1416	8
1417	775
1418	88
1419	4,126
1420	970
1421	200
1422	2,267
Total	$11,353

On March 31, 20X5, Town & Country received this bank statement:

Bank Statement for March 20X5

Beginning balance		$10,188
Deposits and other Credits:		
Mar. 1	$ 625 EFT	
5	2,716	
10	544	
11	1,655	
15	896	
18	367	
25	890	
31	1,400 BC	9,093
Checks and other Debits:		
Mar. 8	$ 441 NSF	
9	1,465	
13	1,004	
14	450	
15	8	
19	340 EFT	
22	775	
29	88	
31	4,216	
31	25 SC	(8,812)
Ending balance		$10,469

Explanation: BC—bank collection, EFT—electronic funds transfer, NSF—nonsufficient fund check, SC—service charge

Additional data for the bank reconciliation:

a. The EFT deposit was for monthly rent revenue. The EFT debit was for monthly insurance expense.
b. The NSF check was received late in February from Jay Andrews.
c. The $1,400 bank collection of a note receivable on March 31 included $122 interest revenue.
d. The correct amount of check number 1419, a payment on account, is $4,216. (The Town & Country accountant mistakenly recorded the check for $4,126.)

Required

1. Prepare the bank reconciliation of Town & Country Builders at March 31, 20X5.
2. Describe how a bank account and the bank reconciliation help managers control a firm's cash.

P4-4B The May 31 bank statement of Teletouch Answering Service has just arrived from New Orleans National Bank. To prepare the Teletouch bank reconciliation, you gather the following data:

Preparing a bank reconciliation and the related journal entries
(Obj. 2)

spreadsheet

a. The May 31 bank balance is $9,530.82.
b. Teletouch Cash account shows a balance of $8,521.55 on May 31.
c. The following Teletouch checks are outstanding at May 31:

Check No.	Amount
616	$403.00
802	74.02
806	36.60
809	161.38
810	229.05
811	48.91

d. The bank statement includes two special deposits: $899.14, which is the amount of dividend revenue the bank collected from **General Electric Company** on behalf of TeleTouch, and $16.86, the interest revenue TeleTouch earned on its bank balance during May.
e. The bank statement lists a $6.25 debit for the bank service charge.
f. On May 31 the TeleTouch treasurer deposited $381.14, which will appear on the June bank statement.
g. The bank statement includes a $410.00 deduction for a check drawn by Telemann Music Company.
h. The bank statement includes two charges for returned checks from customers. One is a nonsufficient funds check in the amount of $67.50 received from Harley Doherty. The other is a $195.03 check received from Maria Shell. It was returned by Shell's bank with the imprint "Unauthorized Signature."
i. A few customers pay monthly bills by EFT. The May bank statement lists an EFT deposit for service revenue of $200.23.

Required

1. Prepare the bank reconciliation for TeleTouch Answering Service at May 31.
2. Journalize the transactions needed to update the Cash account. Include an explanation for each entry.
3. How will your learning from solving this problem help you manage a business?

P4-5B Pacific Irrigation Co. makes all sales on credit. Cash receipts arrive by mail, usually within 30 days of the sale. Liz Galeano opens envelopes and separates the checks from the accompanying remittance advices. Galeano forwards the checks to another employee, who makes the daily bank deposit but has no access to the accounting records. Galeano sends the remittance advices, which show the amount of cash received, to the accounting department

Identifying internal control weakness
(Obj. 3)

for entry in the accounts. Galeano's only other duty is to grant sales allowances to customers. (A *sales allowance* decreases the amount that the customer must pay.) When Galeano receives a customer check for less than the full amount of the invoice, she records the sales allowance and forwards the document to the accounting department.

Required

You are a new employee of Pacific Irrigation. Write a memo to the company president identifying the internal control weakness in this situation. Explain how to correct the weakness.

Preparing a cash budget and using cash-flow information
(Obj. 4)

P4-6B Louis Lipschitz, executive vice president and chief financial officer of Toys "Я" Us, Inc., is responsible for the company's budgeting process. Suppose Lipschitz's staff is preparing the Toys "Я" Us cash budget for 20X4. Assume the starting point is the statement of cash flows of the current year, 20X3, reproduced in an adapted format as follows:

Toys "Я" Us, Inc., and Subsidiaries

Consolidated Statement of Cash Flows (Adapted)

(In Millions)	20X3
Cash Flows from Operating Activities	
Collections from customers	$8,089
Interest received	24
Purchases of inventory	(5,597)
Operating expenses	(1,858)
Net cash provided by operating activities	658
Cash Flows from Investing Activities	
Capital expenditures, net	(555)
Purchases of other assets	(58)
Net cash used in investing activities	(613)
Cash Flows from Financing Activities	
Short-term borrowings, net	119
Long-term borrowings	40
Long-term debt repayments	(1)
Issuance of stock	29
Share repurchases	(183)
Net cash provided by financing activities	4
Effect of foreign-currency exchange rate changes on cash and cash equivalents	(20)
Cash and Cash Equivalents	
(Decrease)/increase during year	29
Beginning of year	763
End of year	$ 792

Required

1. Prepare the Toys "Я" Us cash budget for 20X4. Date the budget simply "20X4" and denote the beginning and ending cash balances as "beginning" and "ending." Assume the company expects 20X4 to be the same as 20X3, but with the following changes:
   a. In 20X4, the company expects a 10% increase in collections from customers, an 11% increase in purchases of inventory, and a doubling of capital expenditures.
   b. The amount of borrowings and issuances of stock needed in 20X4 will be determined by the cash budget and thus does not appear on the cash budget (but scheduled

long-term debt repayments and share repurchases should be the same in 20X4 as they were in 20X3).

c. Lipschitz hopes to end the year with a cash balance of $200 million.

You will find these explanations helpful:

"Capital expenditures" are purchases of property and equipment.

Toys "Я" Us does not pay cash dividends. Instead the company *repurchases* its stock from its stockholders. This is another way for a corporation to return cash to the stockholders.

2. Answer these questions about the company. Explain your reasoning for each answer.
   a. Does the company's cash budget for 20X4 suggest that Toys "Я" Us is growing, holding steady, or decreasing in size?
   b. Do the statement of cash flows for 20X3 and the cash budget for 20X4 suggest that operating activities are generating enough cash?

Making an ethical judgment
(Obj. 5)

P4-7B Yuma Bank in Yuma, Arizona, has a loan receivable from Wilsonart Plastics Company. Wilsonart is 6 months late in making payments to the bank, and Leon Hess, a Yuma Bank vice president, is assisting Wilsonart to restructure its debt.

Hess learns that Wilsonart is depending on landing a job with Binswanger Glass Company, another Yuma Bank client. Hess also serves as Binswanger's loan officer at the bank. In this capacity, he is aware that Binswanger is considering bankruptcy. No one else outside Binswanger Glass knows this. Hess has been a great help to Wilsonart and Wilsonart's owner is counting on Hess's expertise in loan workouts to advise the company through this difficult process. To help the bank collect on this large loan, Hess has a strong motivation to help Wilsonart to survive.

Required

Apply the ethical judgment framework outlined in the chapter to help Leon Hess plan his next action.

Apply Your Knowledge

Decision Cases

Using the bank reconciliation to detect a theft
(Obj. 2)

Case 1. Heart Strings Craft Shop has poor internal control. Recently Marie Duarte, the owner, has suspected the cashier of stealing. Here are some details of the business's cash position at April 30.

a. The Cash account shows a balance of $20,102. This amount includes an April 30 deposit of $3,794 that does not appear on the April 30 bank statement.
b. The April 30 bank statement shows a balance of $16,624. The bank statement lists a $200 credit for a bank collection, an $8 debit for the service charge, and a $36 debit for an NSF check. The Heart Strings accountant has not recorded any of these items.
c. At April 30, the following checks are outstanding:

Check No.	Amount
154	$116
256	150
278	853
291	990
292	206
293	145

d. The cashier handles all incoming cash and makes bank deposits. He also reconciles the monthly bank statement. Here is his April 30 reconciliation:

Balance per books, April 30		$20,102
Add: Outstanding checks		160
Bank collection		200
Subtotal		20,462
Less: Deposits in transit	$3,794	
Service charge	8	
NSF check	36	3,838
Balance per bank, April 30		$16,624

Required

Duarte has requested that you determine whether the cashier has stolen cash from the business and, if so, how much. She also asks you to explain how the cashier has attempted to conceal the theft. To make this determination, you perform your own bank reconciliation. There are no bank or book errors. Duarte also asks you to evaluate the internal controls and to recommend any changes needed to improve them.

Correcting an internal control weakness
(Obj. 1, 3)

Case 2. This case is based on an actual situation experienced by one of the authors. Centennial Homes, headquartered in Charlotte, North Carolina, built a motel in Raleigh. The construction foreman, whose name was Dirk Dirksen, moved into Raleigh in May to hire the 40 workers needed to complete the project. Dirk Dirksen hired the construction workers, had them fill out the necessary tax forms, and sent the employment documents to the home office, which opened a payroll file for each employee.

Work on the motel began on June 1 and ended in October. Each Thursday evening, Dirk Dirksen filled out a time card that listed the hours worked for each employee during the 5-day work week ended at 5 P.M. on Thursday. Dirksen faxed the time sheets to the home office, which prepared the payroll checks on Friday morning. Dirksen drove to the home office after lunch on Friday, picked up the payroll checks, and returned to the construction site. At 5 P.M. on Friday, Dirksen distributed the payroll checks to the workers.

a. Describe in detail the internal control weakness in this situation. Specify what negative result could occur because of the internal control weakness.
b. Describe what you would do to correct the internal control weakness.

Ethical Issue

Jim Sirbasku owns apartment complexes in St. Louis and Kansas City. Each property has a manager who collects rent, arranges for repairs, and runs advertisements in the local newspaper. The property managers transfer cash to Sirbasku monthly and prepare their own bank reconciliations. The manager in St. Louis has been stealing large sums of money. To cover the theft, he understates the amount of the outstanding checks on the monthly bank reconciliation. As a result, each monthly bank reconciliation appears to balance. However, the balance sheet reports more cash than Sirbasku actually has in the bank. While negotiating the sale of the St. Louis property, Sirbasku shows the balance sheet to prospective investors.

Required

1. Identify two parties other than Sirbasku who can be harmed by this theft. In what ways can they be harmed?
2. Discuss the role accounting plays in this situation.

Financial Statement Case

Cash and internal control
(Obj. 1, 3)

Refer to the **Fossil, Inc.**, financial statements in Appendix A at the end of this book. Suppose Fossil's year-end bank statement, dated January 5, 2002, has just arrived at company headquarters. Further assume the bank statement shows Fossil's cash balance at $68,193 thousand. Fossil's Cash and Cash Equivalents account has a balance of $67,647 thousand.

1. In deciding how much to report for cash and cash equivalents on the January 5, 2002, balance sheet, suppose you uncover these items (all amounts are assumed and in thousands):
   a. Interest earned on bank balance, $360.
   b. Bank service fees and other charges, $9.
   c. Outstanding checks, $2,758.
   d. Bank collections of various items, $400.
   e. Deposits in transit, $2,056.
   f. Book error—Fossil overstated cash by $907.

   Show how Fossil arrived at the correct amount of cash and cash equivalents to report on its January 5, 2002, balance sheet. Indicate how you can prove that your answer is the actual amount that Fossil reported.
2. Study Fossil's Report of Management, and indicate how that report links to specific items of internal control discussed in this chapter.

Analytical Case

Analyzing cash flows
(Obj. 5)

Refer to **Pier 1 Imports**' financial statements in Appendix B at the end of this book.

1. Focus on cash, including temporary investments—this is the same as cash and cash equivalents. Did this item increase or decrease during 2002, and by how much?
2. Why did cash change so much during 2002? The statement of cash flows holds the answer to this question. Analyze the seven largest individual items on the statement of cash flows (not the summary subtotals such as "net cash provided by operating activities"). For each of the seven individual items, state how Pier 1's action affected cash.
3. Total up the amount of the seven cash-flow items that you analyzed. These seven items are important to most companies. What is their total? How much of the total change in cash during 2002 is not accounted for by these seven items?

Group Project

You are promoting a rock concert in your area. Assume you organize as a corporation, with each member of your group purchasing $10,000 of the corporation's stock. Therefore, each of you is risking some hard-earned money on this venture. Assume it is April 1 and that the concert will be performed on June 30. Your promotional activities begin immediately, and ticket sales start on May 1. You expect to sell all the firm's assets, pay all the liabilities, and distribute all remaining cash to the group members by July 31.

Required

Write an internal control manual that will help to safeguard the assets of the business. The manual should address the following aspects of internal control:

1. Assigning responsibilities among the group members
2. Authorizing individuals, including group members and any outsiders that you need to hire, to perform specific jobs
3. Separating duties among the group and any employees
4. Describing all documents needed to account for and safeguard the business's assets

5

Receivables & Short-Term Investments

Learning Objectives

1. **Understand** short-term investments
2. **Apply** internal controls to receivables
3. **Use** the allowance method for uncollectible receivables
4. **Account** for notes receivable
5. **Use** days' sales in receivables and the acid-test ratio to evaluate financial position

Integrator CD

Need additional help? Go to the **Integrator CD** *and search these key words:* acid-test ratio, accounts receivable, estimating uncollectibles, cash flow, days' sales, notes receivable, quick ratio, short-term investments

Oracle Corporation

Condensed Balance Sheets (Adapted)
May 31, 2001 and 2000

(Dollars in Millions)	May 31, 2001	May 31, 2000
Assets		
Current Assets		
Cash and cash equivalents	$ 4,449	$ 7,429
Short-term investments	1,438	333
Trade receivables, net of allowance for doubtful accounts of $403 in 2001 and $272 in 2000	2,432	2,534
Prepaid expenses and other current assets	644	587
Total current assets	8,963	$10,883
Long-term investments	—	110
Property, net	975	935
Other assets	1,092	1,149
Total assets	$11,030	$13,077
Liabilities and Stockholders' Equity		
Total current liabilities	$ 3,916	$ 5,862
Long-term debt	301	301
Other long-term liabilities	535	452
Stockholders' equity	6,278	6,462
Total liabilities and stockholders' equity	$11,030	$13,077

What do a professional football team and a billion-dollar software company have in common? The answer is more than you might think. New York Jets linemen must learn which opposing player to block, and that depends on the formation the opposing team is using. In the information age, the Jets use software, not playbooks with *X* and *O* diagrams, to map out plays. With help from Oracle Corporation, an interactive multimedia show turns football formations into live animation.

Using Developer/2000 and multimedia software, Carl Banks, director of player development for the Jets, has a state-of-the-art teaching model. Says Banks, "By the time [the players] hit the practice field, [they] lose the ability to visualize *X*'s and *O*'s as actual plays. Oracle has helped create [a] learning environment that increases [players'] retention by as much as 250%."

Oracle is the world's second largest software company. With annual revenues exceeding $10 billion, the company offers products and services to clients around the world. As Oracle's balance sheet shows, Trade receivables (another name for Accounts receivable) are a significant asset.

Receivables present a challenge: How much of a company's receivables will it be able to collect in cash? This chapter shows how to answer this and other questions about receivables. It also covers short-term investments, Oracle's second most liquid asset, which is listed immediately after cash on the balance sheet.

Sitemap

Before getting into short-term investments and receivables, we need to define some key terms.

- **Creditor.** The party to whom money is owed. The creditor has a receivable.
- **Debtor.** The party who owes money. The debtor has a payable.
- **Debt instrument.** A payable, usually some form of note or bond payable. The maker (issuer) of a debt instrument is the *debtor*. The holder of a debt instrument is the *creditor* (or investor) to whom the instrument is a receivable (or an investment).
- **Equity securities.** Stock certificates that represent the investor's ownership in a corporation.
- **Maturity.** The date on which a debt instrument must be paid.
- **Securities.** Notes payable or stock certificates that entitle the owner to the benefits of an investment.
- **Term.** The length of time from inception to maturity.

Creditor
The party to whom money is owed.

Debtor
The party who owes money.

Debt instrument
A payable, usually some form of note or bond payable.

Equity securities
Stock certificates that represent the investor's ownership in a corporation.

Short-Term Investments

short-term investments

Objective

1 Understand short-term investments

Maturity
The date on which a debt instrument must be paid.

Securities
Notes payable or stock certificates that entitle the owner to the benefits of an investment.

Term
The length of time from inception to maturity.

Short-term investments
Investments that a company plans to hold for one year or less. Also called *marketable securities.*

Held-to-maturity investments
Bonds and notes that an investor intends to hold until maturity.

Trading investments
Stock investments that are to be sold in the near future with the intent of generating profits on the sale.

Available-for-sale investments
All investments not classified as held-to-maturity or trading securities.

Short-term investments, also called **marketable securities,** are investments that a company plans to hold for 1 year or less. These investments allow the company to "park" cash temporarily and earn a modest return until the cash is needed. Short-term investments fall into three categories:

1. **Held-to-maturity investments,** which the investor expects to hold until the securities' maturity date
2. **Trading investments,** which the investor holds to generate a gain by selling the securities within a few weeks or months
3. **Available-for-sale investments,** which are all investments other than held-to-maturity investments and trading investments[1]

All trading investments are short-term because companies intend to hold them for a few months or less. Held-to-maturity investments and available-for-sale investments may be short- or long-term, depending on the length of time management intends to hold them.

A held-to-maturity investment earns interest revenue for the investor. Accounting for a held-to-maturity investment is the same as accounting for a note receivable, as discussed starting on page 227 of this chapter.

Trading Investments

The investor intends to hold a trading investment for a very short time—a few months at most. The purpose of owning a trading investment is to sell it for more than its cost. For most companies, trading investments are minor because they invest

[1]Available-for-sale investments are included here for completeness. Chapter 10 discusses the accounting for these investments.

any excess cash in their own businesses. Oracle, Intel, and other high-tech companies are exceptions to this rule. They often have vast amounts of cash invested in short-term securities.

Trading investments can be the stock of another company. Suppose Oracle Corporation purchases Ford Motor Company stock, intending to sell the stock within a few months. If the market value of the Ford stock increases, Oracle will have a gain; if the price of the Ford stock drops, Oracle will have a loss. Along the way, Oracle will receive dividend revenue from Ford Motor Company.

Suppose Oracle buys the Ford stock on May 18, paying $100,000 cash. Oracle records the purchase of the investment at cost:

May 18	Short-Term Investment	100,000	
	Cash		100,000
	Purchased investment.		

ASSETS	=	LIABILITIES	+	STOCKHOLDERS' EQUITY
+100,000 −100,000	=	0	+	0

Assume on May 27 Oracle receives a cash dividend of $4,000 from Ford. Oracle records the receipt of the dividend as follows:

May 27	Cash	4,000	
	Dividend Revenue		4,000
	Received cash dividend.		

ASSETS	=	LIABILITIES	+	STOCKHOLDERS' EQUITY	+	REVENUES
+4,000	=				+	4,000

Oracle's fiscal year ends on May 31, and Oracle prepares a balance sheet and an income statement. Assume the Ford stock has risen in value, and on May 31 Oracle's investment has a current market value of $102,000. Market value is the amount the owner can receive when selling the investment. Oracle has an *unrealized gain* on the investment:

- *Gain* because the market value ($102,000) is greater than Oracle's cost of the investment ($100,000). A gain has the same effect as a revenue.
- *Unrealized gain* because Oracle has not yet sold the investment.

Trading investments are reported on the balance sheet at their current market value. The relevant measure for an investment is its current market value because that is the amount the investor can receive by selling the investment. Prior to preparing financial statements on May 31, Oracle adjusts the Ford investment to its current market value with this journal entry:

✔ Check Point 5-1

May 31	Short-Term Investment	2,000	
	Unrealized Gain on Investment		2,000
	Adjusted investment to market value.		

ASSETS	=	LIABILITIES	+	STOCKHOLDERS' EQUITY	+	GAINS
+2,000	=	0	+	0	+	2,000

After the adjustment, Oracle's investment account appears as follows:

Short-Term Investment		
Cost	**100,000**	
Adjustment to market value	**2,000**	
Balance	**102,000**	

Now the Short-term Investment account is ready to be reported on the balance sheet—at current market value of $102,000.

If Oracle's investment in Ford stock had decreased in value, say to $95,000, then Oracle would have had an unrealized loss. A *loss* has the same effect as an expense. In that case, Oracle would have made a different entry at May 31. For an *unrealized loss*:

- *Debit* an Unrealized Loss account for $5,000 ($100,000 − $95,000).
- *Credit* the Short-term Investment account for $5,000 to reduce its balance to a market value of $95,000.

Report a short-term investment at current market value.

Reporting Short-Term Investments on the Balance Sheet and Revenues, Gains, and Losses on the Income Statement

THE BALANCE SHEET. Short-term investments are current assets. They appear on the balance sheet immediately after cash because short-term investments are almost as liquid as cash. (In business, *liquid* means close to cash.) Report trading investments at their current market value.

INCOME STATEMENT. Investments earn interest revenue and dividend revenue. Investments also create gains and losses. For trading investments these items are reported on the income statement as Other revenue, gains, and (losses), as shown in Exhibit 5-1.

Exhibit 5-1

Reporting Short-Term Investments and the Related Revenues, Gains, and Losses (Amounts from the Preceding Example)

Balance sheet		**Income statement**	
Current assets:		Revenues	$ XXX
Cash	$ XXX	Expenses	XXX
Short-term trading investments, at market value	102,000	Other revenue, gains, and (losses):	
Accounts receivable	XXX	Interest revenue	XXX
		Dividend revenue	4,000
		Unrealized gain on investment	2,000
		⋮	⋮
		Net income	$ XXX

✔ Check Point 5-2

✔ Check Point 5-3

Mid-Chapter Summary Problem

Humana, Inc., is one of the largest U.S. managed health-care companies. It provides a full array of health plans, including health maintenance organizations (HMOs) and other plans. The largest current asset on Humana's balance sheet is Marketable Securities (short-term investments). Their cost is $1,144 million, and their market value is $1,116 million.

If Humana holds the marketable securities in the hope of selling them at a profit within a short time, how will it classify the investment? What will Humana report on the balance sheet at December 31, 20X6? What will Humana report on its 20X6 income statement?

Answers

Trading investments, reported on the balance sheet as follows (amounts in millions):

	(In millions)
Current assets	
Cash	$ XX
Marketable securities (or short-term investments), at market value	1,116

Humana's income statement will report:

	(In millions)
Other revenue and expense:	
Unrealized gain (loss) on investments ($1,116 − $1,144 million)	$ (28)

Accounts and Notes Receivable

accounts receivable, notes receivable

Receivables are the third most liquid asset—after cash and short-term investments. Receivables are assets because they are claims to someone else's cash. But a receivable can be bad news if the business cannot collect it. In the remainder of the chapter, we discuss how companies control and manage their receivables.

Types of Receivables

Receivables
Monetary claims against a business or an individual, acquired mainly by selling goods and services and by lending money.

Receivables are monetary claims against others. They are acquired mainly by selling goods and services and by lending money.

The two major types of receivables are accounts receivable and notes receivable. A business's *accounts receivable* are the amounts collectible from customers from the sale of goods and services. Accounts receivable, which are *current assets*, are sometimes called *trade receivables*, as Oracle Corporation does on its balance sheet.

The Accounts Receivable account in the general ledger serves as a *control account* that summarizes the total amount receivable from all customers. Companies also keep a *subsidiary record* of accounts receivable with a separate account for each customer, illustrated as follows:

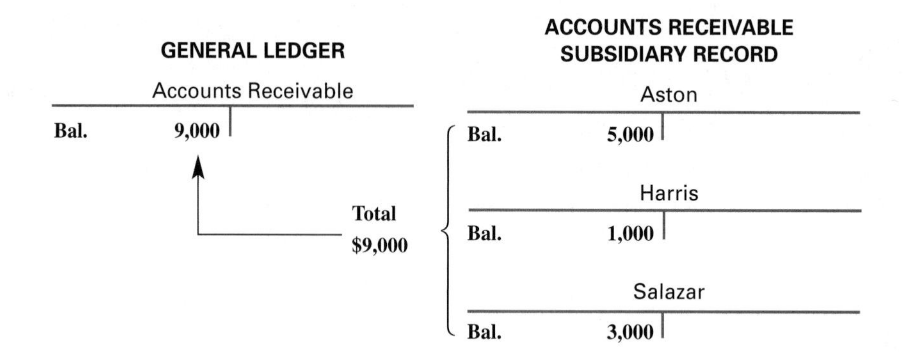

Notes receivable are more formal contracts than accounts receivable. The debtor signs a written promise to pay the creditor a definite sum at the *maturity* date. The note may require the debtor to pledge *security* for the loan. This means that the borrower gives the lender permission to claim certain assets, called *collateral*, if the borrower fails to pay the amount due.

Notes receivable due within 1 year or less are current assets. Notes due beyond 1 year are *long-term receivables* and are reported as Long-term Investments. Oracle Corporation also reports long-term investments on its balance sheet.

Some notes receivable are collected in installments. The portion due within 1 year is a current asset and the remainder is long term. General Motors (GM) may hold a $6,000 note receivable from you, but only the $1,500 you must pay within 1 year is a current asset.

Other receivables is a miscellaneous category that includes loans to employees and subsidiary companies. Some companies report other receivables under the heading Other Assets on the balance sheet, as shown for Oracle Corporation.

Establishing Internal Control over Collections

Objective

2 **Apply** internal controls to receivables

Businesses that sell on credit receive most of their cash receipts by mail. Internal control over collections is important. Chapter 4 discusses control procedures for cash receipts, but a critical element of internal control deserves emphasis here—the separation of cash-handling and cash-accounting duties. Consider the following case:

> *Butler Supply Co. is a small, family-owned business that takes pride in the loyalty of its workers. Most employees have been with the Butlers for at least 5 years. The company makes 90% of its sales on account.*
>
> *The office staff consists of a bookkeeper and a supervisor. The bookkeeper maintains the general ledger and the accounts receivable subsidiary ledger. He also makes the daily bank deposit. The supervisor prepares monthly financial statements and any special reports the Butlers require. She also takes sales orders from customers and serves as office manager.*

Can you identify the internal control weakness here? The problem is that the bookkeeper has access to the accounts and the cash. The bookkeeper could steal an incoming customer check and write off the customer's account as uncollectible. (The bookkeeper would need to forge the endorsements of the checks and deposit them in a bank account that he controls.) The customer doesn't complain because Butler has written the account off the books and no longer pursues collection.

How can this weakness be corrected? The supervisor could open incoming mail and make the daily bank deposit. The bookkeeper should *not* be allowed to handle cash. Only the remittance advices would be forwarded to the bookkeeper to credit customer accounts. Removing cash handling from the bookkeeper and keeping the accounts away from the supervisor separates duties and strengthens internal control.

✔ Check Point 5-4

Using a bank lockbox achieves the same separation of duties. Customers send their payments directly to Butler Supply's bank, which records and deposits the cash into Butler's account. The bank then forwards the remittance advice to Butler's bookkeeper, who credits the appropriate customer accounts.

DECISION: How Do We Manage the Risk of Not Collecting?

In Chapters 1 to 4, we use many different companies to illustrate how to account for a business. Chapter 1 began with Fossil, a retailer of watches. Chapter 2 featured Frito-Lay and PepsiCo, which are food concerns Chapter 3 used Vodafone, which provides telephone service in England. All these companies sell on credit and thus hold accounts receivable.

By selling on account, all companies run the risk of not collecting some receivables. Unfortunately, customers sometimes do not pay the amounts they owe. The prospect that we may fail to collect from a customer provides the biggest challenge in accounting for receivables. The Decision Guidelines address this challenge.

Decision Guidelines

MANAGING AND ACCOUNTING FOR RECEIVABLES

The Decision Guidelines feature identifies the management and accounting issues that a business faces when it extends credit to customers. For each issue, it proposes a plan of action. Let's look at a business situation: Suppose you and a friend open a health club near your college. Assume you will let customers use the club and charge bills to their accounts. What challenges will you encounter by extending credit to customers?

The main issues in *managing* receivables, along with a plan of action, are:

Issues	Plan of Action
1. What are the benefits of extending credit to customers? What is the cost?	**1.** Benefit—Increase in sales. Cost—Risk of not collecting.
2. Extend credit only to creditworthy customers.	**2.** Run a credit check on prospective customers.
3. Separate cash-handling and accounting duties to keep employees from stealing the cash collected from customers.	**3.** Design the internal control system to separate duties.
4. Pursue collection from customers to maximize cash flow.	**4.** Keep a close eye on customer pay habits. Send second, and third, statements to slow-paying customers, if necessary.

The main issues in *accounting* for receivables, and the related plans of action, are

Issues	Plan of Action
1. Measure and report receivables on the balance sheet at their *net realizable value*, the amount we expect to collect. This is the appropriate amount to report for receivables.	1. Report receivables at their net realizable value: **Balance sheet** Receivables . . . . $1,000 Less: Allowance for uncollectibles . . . . (80) Receivables, net . . . . $ 920
2. Measure and report the expense associated with failure to collect receivables. This expense is called *uncollectible-account expense* and is reported on the income statement.	2. Measure the expense of not collecting from customers: **Income statement** Sales (or service) revenue . . . . . . $8,000 Expenses: Uncollectible-account expense 190

Excel Application Problem

Goal: Create a worksheet that shows accounts receivable activity for a company.

Scenario: You are the summer intern at Fossil headquarters in Richardson, Texas. Assume that one day shortly into your employment, your supervisor asks you to prepare an Excel spreadsheet that breaks down the month's accounts receivable by customer. She gives you the following data (all dollars are in thousands):

Customer ID	*Customer Name*	*Beginning Balance*	*Purchases*	*Payments*	*Credits*
F01-235-00	Macy's	$10,500	$2,500	$ 4,500	$ 295
F07-988-45	Federated Stores	$ 8,760	$1,592	$ 2,980	$ 600
W40-860-91	Bloomingdale's	$12,287	$4,765	$ 4,000	$ 325
W35-672-45	May Dept. Stores	$20,469	$7,650	$ 6,584	$ 675
L25-723-04	International Traders	$18,752	$8,542	$10,678	$1,400
L10-567-80	Saks Fifth Avenue	$ 5,437	$1,250	$ 4,000	$ 500
X99-013-77	Nieman Marcus	$ 2,594	$1,000	$ 1,250	$ 0

Assume net sales are $430,985,000, credit terms are net 60, and a service charge of 2.25% is assessed for net outstanding balances, calculated as 2.25% times the net amount of (beginning balance – payments – credits).

When you have finished creating your worksheet, answer the following questions:

1. How much cash did Fossil collect this month?
2. How much is still receivable by Fossil?
3. What recommendations would you make to Fossil regarding its credit terms?

Step-by-step:

1. Open a new Excel spreadsheet.
2. Create a bold-faced heading for your spreadsheet that contains the following:
   a. Chapter 5 Decision Guidelines
   b. Fossil Accounts Receivable (in 000's)
   c. Today's Date
3. Two rows down from your heading, create a row containing the following column headings:
   a. Customer ID
   b. Customer Name
   c. Beginning Balance
   d. Purchases
   e. Payments
   f. Credits
   g. Service Charge
   h. New Balance
4. Enter the data from the scenario into the spreadsheet. At the end of the entries, create a row for "Totals" and calculate totals for all financial columns.
5. Format your work. Experiment with the AutoFormat feature found by clicking "Format" on the menu bar. (Be sure to highlight the entire chart before doing so.)
6. Save your worksheet and print a copy for your files.

Accounting for Uncollectible Receivables

Integrator CD
estimating uncollectibles

Selling on credit creates both a benefit and a cost:

- *Benefit*: Customers who cannot pay cash immediately can buy on credit, so company profits rise as sales increase.
- *Cost*: The company will be unable to collect from some credit customers. Accountants label this cost **uncollectible-account expense, doubtful-account expense**, or **bad-debt expense.**

Uncollectible-account expense
Cost to the seller of extending credit. Arises from the failure to collect from credit customers. Also called *doubtful-account expense* or *bad-debt expense*.

The extent of uncollectible-account expense varies from company to company. At Albany Ladder, a construction firm headquartered in Albany, New York, 85% of company sales are on account. Bad debts cost Albany Ladder about $100,000 a year, or about 1% to 1 1/2% of total sales. It takes Albany Ladder an average of 70 days to collect its receivables. **Wal-Mart Stores**, on the other hand, sells for cash and on credit cards and therefore has no bad-debt expense.

Uncollectible-account expense is an operating expense along with salary expense, rent expense, and utilities expense. To measure uncollectible-account expense, accountants use the allowance method or, in certain limited cases, the direct write-off method (which we discuss on page 235).

Allowance Method

Objective

3 **Use** the allowance method for uncollectible receivables

The best way to measure bad debts is by the **allowance method.** This method records collection losses on the basis of estimates. It does not wait to see which customers will not pay. Managers estimate bad-debt expense on the basis of the company's collection experience. The business records the estimated amount as Uncollectible-Account Expense and sets up **Allowance for Uncollectible Accounts** (or **Allowance for Doubtful Accounts**). This is a contra account to Accounts Receivable. It shows the amount of the receivables that the business expects *not* to collect.

Allowance method
A method of recording collection losses based on estimates of how much money the business will not collect from its customers.

Accounts Receivable minus the Allowance for Uncollectibles yields the net amount the company *does* expect to collect, as shown here (using assumed numbers):

Allowance for Uncollectible Accounts
A contra account, related to accounts receivable, that holds the estimated amount of collection losses. Another name for *Allowance for Doubtful Accounts*.

Balance sheet (partial):	
Accounts receivable	$10,000
Less Allowance for uncollectible accounts	(900)
Accounts receivable, net	$ 9,100

Customers owe this company $10,000, of which it expects to collect $9,100. The net realizable value of the receivables is, therefore, $9,100. The company estimates that it will not collect $900 of its accounts receivable.

Another way to report these receivables follows the pattern used by Oracle Corporation, as follows:

Accounts receivable, net of allowance of $900	$9,100

✔ Check Point 5-5

An investor can work backward to determine the full amount of the receivable, $10,000 (net realizable value of $9,100 plus the allowance of $900).

The income statement reports Uncollectible-account expense among the operating expenses, as follows (using assumed figures):

Income statement (partial):	
Expenses:	
Uncollectible-account expense	$2,000

Refer to the Oracle balance sheet on page 223. At May 31, 2001, how much did customers owe Oracle Corporation? How much did Oracle expect *not* to collect? How much of the receivables did Oracle expect to collect? What was the net realizable value of Oracle's receivables?

Answer:

	Millions
Customers owed Oracle	$2,835
Oracle expected not to collect	(403)
Oracle expected to collect—net realizable value	$2,432

The most logical way to estimate uncollectibles uses the business's history of collections from customers. There are two basic ways to estimate uncollectibles:

- Percentage-of-sales method
- Aging-of-receivables method

Percentage-of-sales method Computes uncollectible-account expense as a percentage of net sales. Also called the *income statement approach* because it focuses on the amount of expense to be reported on the income statement.

PERCENTAGE-OF-SALES. The **percentage-of-sales method** computes uncollectible-account expense as a percentage of revenue. This method is also called the **income-statement approach** because it focuses on the amount of expense to be reported on the income statement. Uncollectible-account expense is recorded at the end of the period. Assume it is December 31, 20X1 and Oracle Corporation's accounts have these balances *before the year-end adjustments* (the following discussion expresses all amounts in millions):

Accounts Receivable		Allowance for Uncollectible Accounts	
2,835			73

Customers owe Oracle $2,835, and the Allowance amount is $73. But the economy is in a recession, and Oracle's top managers know that the company will fail to collect more than $73. Suppose Oracle's credit department estimates that uncollectible-account expense is 3% of total revenues, which were $11,000 for 20X1. The entry to record bad-debt expense for the year also updates the allowance as follows:

20X1			
Dec. 31	Uncollectible-Account Expense ($11,000 × .03)	330	
	Allowance for Uncollectible Accounts		330
	Recorded expense for the year.		

The expense decreases assets, as shown by the accounting equation:

ASSETS	=	LIABILITIES	+	STOCKHOLDERS' EQUITY	−	EXPENSES
−330	=	0			−	330

Now the accounts are ready for reporting in the financial statements.

✔ Check Point 5-6

Accounts Receivable		Allowance for Uncollectible Accounts	
2,835			73
			330
			403

Net accounts receivable, $2,432

Compare these amounts to the preceding Stop and Think answer. They should be the same.

Customers still owe Oracle $2,835, but now the Allowance for Uncollectibles balance is realistic. Oracle's balance sheet actually reported accounts receivable at their net realizable value amount of $2,432 ($2,835 − $403). Oracle's income statement included uncollectible-account expense among the operating expenses for the period.

AGING OF RECEIVABLES. The other popular method for estimating uncollectibles is called **aging-of-receivables.** This method is a **balance-sheet approach** because it focuses on accounts receivable. In the aging method, individual receivables from specific customers are analyzed based on how long they have been outstanding.

Aging-of-accounts receivable A way to estimate bad debts by analyzing individual accounts receivable according to the length of time they have been receivable from the customer. Also called the *balance-sheet approach.*

Computerized accounting packages are programmed to age the company's accounts receivable. Exhibit 5-2 shows an aging of receivables for Oracle Corporation at May 31, 20X1. Oracle's receivables total $2,835. Of this amount, the aging schedule shows that the company will *not* collect $403, but the allowance for uncollectible accounts is not yet up-to-date. Suppose Oracle's accounts are as follows *before the year-end adjustment* (in millions):

Accounts Receivable			Allowance for Uncollectible Accounts	
2,835				120

Exhibit 5-2

Aging the Accounts Receivable of Oracle Corporation

	Age of Account Dollar Amounts (in Millions)				
Customer	***1–30 Days***	***31–60 Days***	***61–90 Days***	***Over 90 Days***	***Total Balance***
IBM	$ 30				$ 30
City of San Francisco	20				20
Sarasota Pipe Corporation		$ 50	$ 11		61
Oneida, Inc.				$ 39	39
Other accounts*	1,505	700	300	180	2,685
Totals	$1,555	$750	$311	$219	$2,835
Estimated percent uncollectible	× 6%	×10%	× 20%	×79%	
Allowance for Uncollectible Accounts balance should be	$ 93 +	$ 75 +	$ 62 +	$173 =	$ 403

*Each of the "other accounts" would appear individually.

The aging method will bring the balance of the allowance account ($120) to the needed amount ($403) as determined by the aging schedule in Exhibit 5-2. The lower right corner gives the needed balance in the allowance account. To update the allowance, Oracle would make this entry:

20X1			
Dec. 31	Uncollectible-Account Expense	283	
	Allowance for Uncollectible Accounts ($403 − $120)		283
	Recorded expense for the year.		

The expense decreases assets, as shown by the accounting equation.

ASSETS	=	LIABILITIES	+	STOCKHOLDERS' EQUITY	−	EXPENSES
−283	=	0			−	283

Now the balance sheet can report the amount that Oracle actually expects to collect from customers: $2,432 ($2,835 − $403). This is the net realizable value of Oracle's trade receivables. Oracle's accounts are now ready for the balance sheet, as follows:

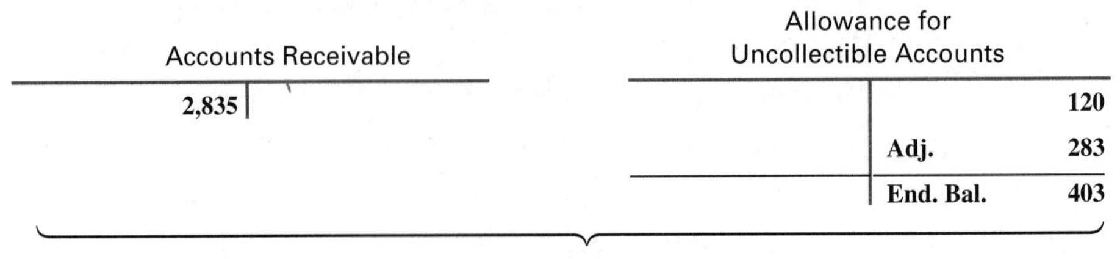

Net accounts receivable, $2,432

WRITING OFF UNCOLLECTIBLE ACCOUNTS. Suppose that early in 20X2, Oracle's credit department determines that Oracle cannot collect from customers Sarasota Pipe and Oneida. Oracle then writes off the receivables from these two delinquent customers with the following entry (in millions):

20X2			
Mar. 31	Allowance for Uncollectible Accounts	100	
	Accounts Receivable—Sarasota Pipe		61
	Accounts Receivable—Oneida, Inc.		39
	Wrote off uncollectible receivables.		

The accounting equation shows that the write-off of uncollectibles has no effect on total assets. There is no effect on net income either.

✔ Check Point 5-7

✔ Check Point 5-8

ASSETS	=	LIABILITIES	+	STOCKHOLDERS' EQUITY
+100 −100	=	0	+	0

In the preceding accounting equation (for the write-off of uncollectible receivable), why is there no effect on total assets? Why is there no effect on net income?

Answer:
There is no effect on total assets because the write-off of an uncollectible receivable decreases both Accounts Receivable and the Allowance for Uncollectibles, a contra account. Both accounts are part of net receivables, so one effect offsets the other. The result is no effect on net receivables and no effect on total assets. There is no effect on net income because the write off of uncollectibles affects no expense account.

COMBINING THE PERCENTAGE-OF-SALES AND THE AGING METHODS. In practice, companies use the percentage-of-sales and aging-of-accounts methods together, as follows:

- For *interim statements* (monthly or quarterly), companies use the percent-of-sales method because it is easier to apply. The percent-of-sales method focuses on the uncollectible-account *expense*, but that is not enough.
- At the end of the year, companies use the aging method to ensure that Accounts Receivable is reported at *net realizable value*—that is, the amount the company expects to collect. The aging method focuses on the amount of the receivables—the *asset*—that is uncollectible.
- Using the two methods together provides good measures of both the expense and the asset. Exhibit 5-3 compares the two methods.

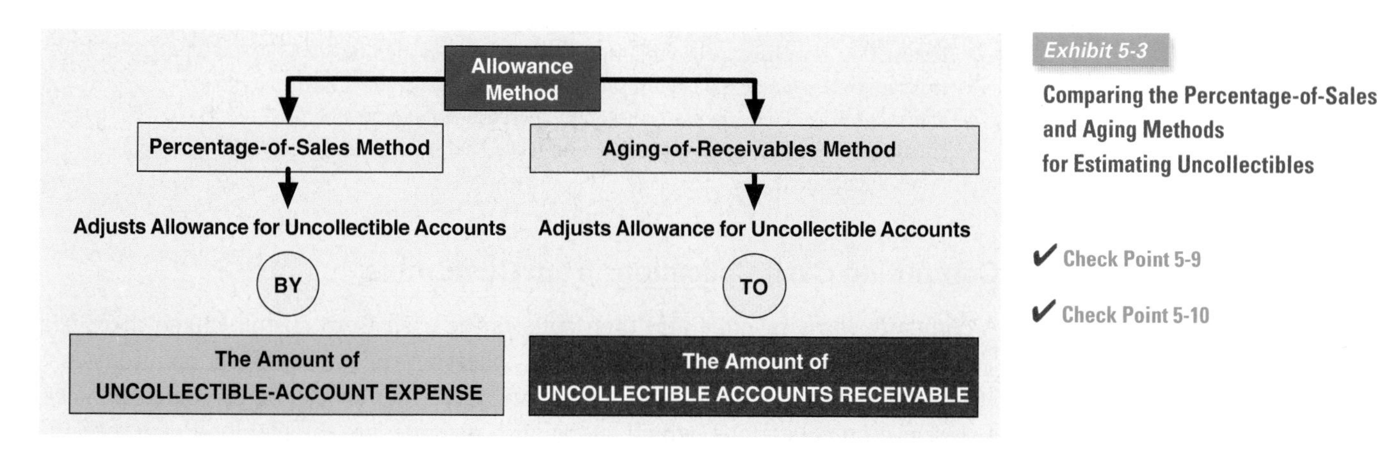

Exhibit 5-3

Comparing the Percentage-of-Sales and Aging Methods for Estimating Uncollectibles

✔ Check Point 5-9

✔ Check Point 5-10

Direct Write-Off Method

A less preferable way to account for uncollectible receivables exists. Under the **direct write-off method**, the company waits until it decides that a specific customer's receivable is uncollectible. Then the accountant records Uncollectible-Account Expense and writes off the customer's Account Receivable as follows (using assumed data):

Direct write-off method
A method of accounting for bad debts in which the company waits until the credit department decides that a customer's account receivable is uncollectible and then debits Uncollectible-Account Expense and credits the customer's Account Receivable.

20X4			
Jan. 2	Uncollectible-Account Expense	2,000	
	Accounts Receivable—Jones		2,000
	Wrote off a bad account by direct write-off method.		

This method is defective for two reasons:

1. The direct write-off method does not set up an allowance for uncollectibles. As a result, receivables are always reported at their full amount, which is more than the business expects to collect. *Assets on the balance sheet are overstated.*
2. The direct write-off method causes a poor matching of uncollectible-account expense against revenue. In this example, the company made the sale to Jones in 20X3 and should have recorded the expense during 20X3. By recording the expense in 20X4, *the company overstates net income in 20X3.* Then by recording the expense when it writes off the receivable in 20X4, the company understates net income in 20X4.

According to the matching principle, expenses should be matched against the revenue of the same period. Thus the direct write-off method is acceptable only when uncollectibles are so low that there is no significant difference between bad-debt expense by the allowance method and the direct write-off method.

1. Under the allowance method, there are only two transactions to record. What are they?
2. Which transaction affects net income?
3. Which transaction affects net receivables?
4. Which transaction affects total assets?
5. Which transaction leaves net income, net receivables, and total assets unchanged?

Answers:

1. Transaction 1—Record uncollectible-account expense and set up the allowance for uncollectible accounts.
   Transaction 2—Write off uncollectible receivables.

2. Transaction 1—The expense transaction decreases net income.
3. Transaction 1—The expense transaction decreases net receivables.
4. Transaction 1—The expense transaction decreases total assets.
5. Transaction 2—The write-off transaction leaves net income, net receivables, and total assets unchanged.

Computing Cash Collections from Customers

A company earns revenue and then collects the cash from customers, so there is a time lag between earning the revenue to collecting the cash. Collections from customers are the single most important source of cash for any business. Managers keep a close eye on collections, which, along with revenue, are the lifeblood of an organization. You can compute a company's collections from customers by analyzing its Accounts Receivable account. Receivables typically hold only five items, as follows (amounts assumed):

Accounts Receivable

Beg. balance (left over from the preceding period)	**200**	**Collections from customers**	**X = 1,500****
Sales (or service) revenue	**1,800***	**Write-offs of uncollectibles**	**100†**
End. balance (carries over to the next period)	**400**		

Often write-offs are not known and must be omitted. Then the computation of collections becomes an approximation.

Notes Receivable

cash flow, notes receivable

Objective

4 **Account** for notes receivable

As stated earlier, notes receivable are more formal than accounts receivable. There are two parties to a note:

- The *creditor* has a note receivable.
- The *debtor* has a note payable.

The debtor signs the note and thereby creates a contract with the creditor. Exhibit 5-4 is a typical promissory note.

Principal
The amount borrowed by a debtor and lent by a creditor.

Interest
The borrower's cost of renting money from a lender. Interest is revenue for the lender, expense for the borrower.

The **principal** amount of the note is the amount borrowed by the debtor, lent by the creditor. The term of the note runs from August 31, 20X5, to February 28, 20X6, when Lauren Holland (the maker) promises to pay Continental Bank (the payee) the principal of $1,000 plus 9% interest for the year. **Interest** is revenue to be earned by the lender (Continental Bank, in this case) and expense for the borrower (Lauren Holland).

---

*The journal entry that places revenue into the receivable account is

Accounts Receivable	1,800	
Sales (or Service) Revenue		1,800

**The journal entry that places collections into the receivable account is

Cash	1,500	
Accounts Receivable		1,500

†The journal entry for write-offs is

Allowance for Uncollectibles	100	
Accounts Receivable		100

Exhibit 5-4 A Promissory Note

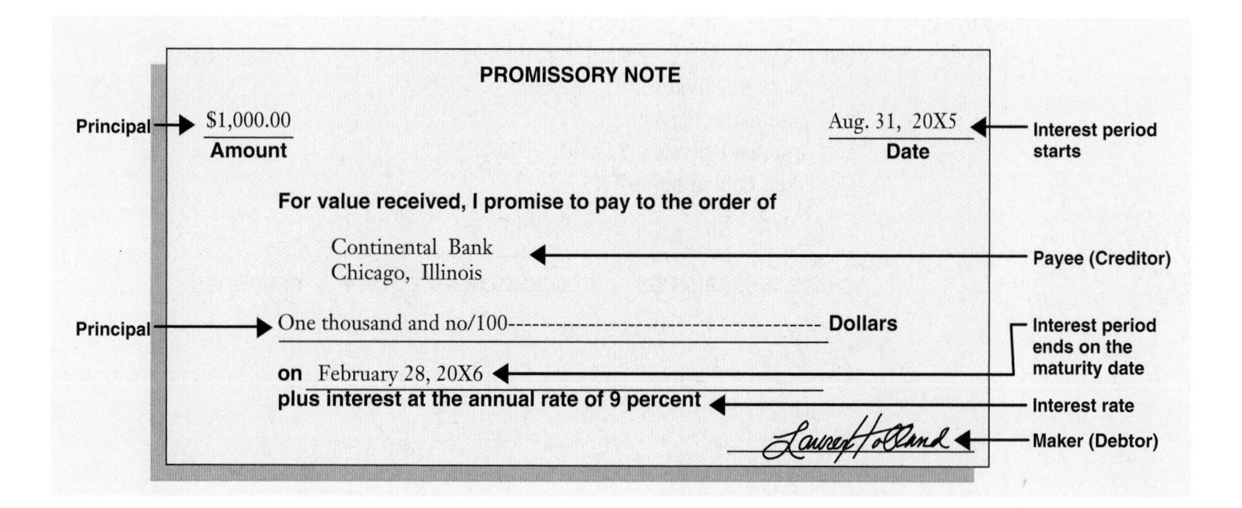

Accounting for Notes Receivable

Consider the promissory note shown in Exhibit 5-4. After Lauren Holland signs the note, Continental Bank gives her $1,000 cash. The bank's entries follow, assuming a December 31 year end for Continental Bank:

20X5			
Aug. 31	Note Receivable—L. Holland	1,000	
	Cash		1,000
	Made a loan.		

The bank gave one asset, cash, in return for another asset, a note receivable, so the bank's total assets did not change.

ASSETS	=	LIABILITIES	+	STOCKHOLDERS' EQUITY
+1,000 −1,000	=	0	+	0

Continental Bank earns interest revenue during September, October, November, and December. At December 31, the bank accrues interest revenue for 4 months as follows:

Dec. 31	Interest Receivable ($1,000 × .09 × 4/12)	30	
	Interest Revenue		30
	Accrued interest revenue.		

This transaction increased both the bank's assets and its revenues:

ASSETS	=	LIABILITIES	+	STOCKHOLDERS' EQUITY	+	REVENUES
30	=	0			+	30

The bank collects the note on February 28, 20X6, and records

20X6			
Feb. 28	Cash	1,045	
	Note Receivable—L. Holland		1,000
	Interest Receivable		30
	Interest Revenue ($1,000 × .09 × 2/12)		15
	Collected note at maturity.		

Check Point 5-11

ASSETS	=	LIABILITIES	+	STOCKHOLDERS' EQUITY	+	REVENUES
+1,045						
−1,000	=	0			+	15
− 30						

Two aspects of these entries deserve mention:

1. Interest rates are always for an annual period unless stated otherwise. In this example, the annual interest rate is 9%. At December 31, 20X5, Continental Bank accrues interest revenue for the 4 months the bank has held the note. The interest computation is

Principal	×	Interest rate	× Time	= Amount of Interest
$1,000	×	.09	× 4/12 =	$30

Check Point 5-12

Check Point 5-13

Check Point 5-14

2. The time element in the interest computation in the portion of the year that the note has been in force.

Some companies sell goods and services on notes receivable (versus selling on accounts receivable). This often occurs when the payment term extends beyond the customary accounts receivable period of 30 to 60 days.

Suppose that on March 20, 20X6, General Electric (GE) sells household appliances for $15,000 to Dorman Builders. GE receives Dorman's 90-day promissory note at 10% annual interest. The entries to record the sale and collection from Dorman follow the pattern illustrated previously for Continental Bank and Lauren Holland, with one exception. At the outset, GE would credit Sales Revenue (instead of Cash) because GE is making a sale (and not lending money to Dorman).

A company may accept a note receivable from a trade customer whose account receivable is past due. The customer signs a note payable, and the company then credits the accounts receivable and debits a note receivable. We would say the company "received a note receivable from a customer on account."

DECISION: How to Speed Up Cash Flow?

All companies want speedy cash receipts. Rapid cash flow improves profits because the business has cash to invest in new technology, research, and development. Thus, companies find ways to collect cash immediately. Three common strategies generate cash more quickly than waiting to collect from customers.

Credit Card or Bankcard Sales. The merchant sells merchandise and lets the customer pay with a credit card, such as Discover or American Express, or with a bankcard, such as VISA or MasterCard. This strategy may dramatically increase sales, but the added revenue comes at a cost. Let's see how credit cards and bankcards work from the seller's perspective. To record a $100,000 sale on a VISA card, the seller records this entry:

Cash	97,000	
Financing Expense	3,000	
Sales Revenue		100,000
Recorded bankcard sales.		

ASSETS	=	LIABILITIES	+	STOCKHOLDERS' EQUITY	+	REVENUES	−	EXPENSES
+97,000	=	0	+		+	$100,000	−	$3,000

The merchant deposits the VISA slip in its bank and immediately receives a discounted portion, say $97,000, of the $100,000 sale amount. VISA gets 3%, or $3,000 ($100,000 × .03 = $3,000). To the merchant, the financing expense is an operating expense similar to interest expense.

Selling Receivables. The company makes a normal sale on account, debiting Accounts Receivable and crediting Sales Revenue for the full $100,000. The company can then sell its accounts receivable to another business, called a *factor*. The factor earns revenue by paying a discounted price for the receivable, say $95,000, and then hopefully collecting the full $100,000 from the customer. The benefit to the company is the immediate receipt of cash.

To illustrate selling, or factoring, accounts receivable, let's return to the Oracle Corporation balance sheet at the beginning of the chapter (page 223). Locate Oracle's Trade receivables. Suppose Oracle wishes to speed up cash flow and therefore sells $100,000 of trade receivables, receiving cash of $95,000. Oracle would record the sale of the receivables as follows:

Cash	95,000	
Financing Expense	5,000	
Trade (Accounts) Receivable		100,000
Sold accounts receivable.		

ASSETS	=	LIABILITIES	−	STOCKHOLDERS' EQUITY	−	EXPENSES
+95,000	=	0			−	5,000
−100,000						

Again, financing expense is an operating expense.

Discounting Notes Receivable. A company holding a note receivable may need cash immediately. The company can sell its note receivable at a discount. This arrangement, called *discounting a note receivable*, is similar to selling an account receivable, as in the foregoing example. However, the credit is to Notes Receivable (instead of Accounts Receivable or Trade Receivables).

acid-test ratio, day's sales in receivables, quick ratio

Decision Making: Using Ratios

Investors and creditors use ratios to evaluate the financial health of a company. A prominent example is the current ratio that we introduced in Chapter 3. Other ratios, including the quick (or acid-test) ratio and the number of days' sales in receivables, help investors measure the liquidity of firms. Liquidity relates to how quickly a company can obtain and pay cash. These measures help to build a picture of the strength of a business.

Objective

5 **Use** days' sales in receivables and the acid-test ratio to evaluate financial position

Days' Sales in Receivables

Days' sales in receivables Ratio of average net accounts receivable to one day's sale. Indicates how many days' sales remain in Accounts Receivable awaiting collection. Also called the *collection period*.

After a business makes a credit sale, the *next* critical event in the business cycle is collecting the receivable. Several financial ratios center on receivables. **Days' sales in receivables**, also called the *average collection period*, indicates how long it takes to collect the average level of receivables. A shorter collection period is better because cash is coming in quickly. The longer the collection period, the less cash is available to pay bills and expand. Days' sales in receivables can be computed in two logical steps, as follows. First, compute one day's sales (or total revenues). Then divide one day's sales into average receivables for the period.

For Oracle Corporation (Millions)

1. $$\text{One day's sales} = \frac{\text{Net sales}}{\text{365 days}} \qquad \frac{\$10,860^*}{365} = \$29.75 \text{ per day}$$

2. $$\begin{array}{c}\text{Days' sales in}\\ \text{average accounts}\\ \text{receivable}\end{array} = \frac{\text{Average net accounts receivable}}{\text{One day's sales}} = \frac{\left(\text{Beginning net receivables} + \text{Ending net receivables}\right) \div 2}{\text{One day's sales}}$$

$$= \frac{(\$2,534 + \$2,432)/2}{\$29.75} = 83 \text{ days}$$

*Taken from Oracle Corporation's 2001 income statement. Courtesy of Oracle Corporation.

The length of the collection period depends on the credit terms of the company's sales. For example, sales on net 30 terms should be collected within approximately 30 days. When we offer a 2% discount for payment within 10 days, the collection period may be shorter. Terms of net 45 or net 60 result in longer collection periods.

Companies watch their collection periods closely. Whenever the collections get slow, the business must find other sources of financing, such as borrowing or factoring receivables. During recessions, customers pay more slowly, and a longer collection period may be unavoidable.[2]

[2]Another ratio, **accounts receivable turnover**, captures the same information as days' sales in receivables. Receivable turnover is computed as follows: Net sales ÷ Average net accounts receivable. During 2001, Oracle had a receivable turnover rate of 4.4 times {$10,860 ÷ [($2,534 + $2,432)/2]}. The authors prefer days' sales in receivables because it is easier to interpret. Days' sales in receivables can be compared directly to the company's credit sale terms.

Acid-Test (or Quick) Ratio

The balance sheet lists assets in the order of relative liquidity:

- Cash and cash equivalents
- Short-term investments
- Accounts (or trade) receivables

Oracle Corporation's balance sheet in the chapter-opening story shows the ordering of these accounts.

Owners and managers care about the liquidity of assets. In Chapter 3, for example, we saw the current ratio, which measures the ability to pay current liabilities with current assets. A more stringent measure of ability to pay current liabilities is the **acid-test** (or **quick**) **ratio**→:

← *The acid-test ratio is similar to the current ratio introduced in Chapter 3 (page 143), but it excludes inventory and prepaid expenses.*

For Oracle Corporation, 2001* (Millions)

$$\text{Acid-test ratio} = \frac{\text{Cash} + \begin{matrix}\text{Short-term} \\ \text{investments}\end{matrix} + \begin{matrix}\text{Net current} \\ \text{receivables}\end{matrix}}{\text{Total current liabilities}} = \frac{\$4,449 + \$1,438 + \$2,432}{\$3,916} = 2.12$$

*Taken from Oracle Corporation's 2001 balance sheet, page 25. Courtesy of Oracle Corporation.

The higher the acid-test ratio, the easier it is to pay current liabilities. Oracle Corporation's acid-test ratio of 2.12 means that Oracle has $2.12 of quick assets to pay each $1 of current liabilities. This ratio value is extremely high; it indicates great liquidity for Oracle.

Acid-test ratio
Ratio of the sum of cash plus short-term investments plus net current receivables to total current liabilities. Tells whether the entity can pay all its current liabilities if they come due immediately. Also called the *quick ratio*.

Inventory is excluded from the acid-test ratio because inventory is not a liquid asset. A company with lots of inventory may have an acceptable current ratio but find it hard to pay its bills.

What is an acceptable acid-test ratio? The answer depends on the industry. Auto dealers can operate smoothly with an acid-test ratio of 0.20, roughly one-tenth of Oracle's ratio value. How can auto dealers survive with so low an acid-test ratio? GM, Toyota, and the other auto manufacturers help finance their dealers' inventory. GM can always loosen credit terms when a Chevy dealer's cash gets tight. Most dealers, therefore, have a financial safety net. Even with a low acid-test ratio, an auto dealer can spend heavily on advertising and promotions in order to move cars off its lot. Nike, the sports manufacturer, has a quick ratio of around 1.0. In general, an acid-test ratio of 1.00 is considered safe.

✔ Check Point 5-15

✔ Check Point 5-16

Reporting on the Statement of Cash Flows

Receivables and short-term investments appear on the balance sheet as assets. We saw these in Oracle Corporation's balance sheet at the beginning of the chapter, and we've also seen how to report the related revenues, gains, and losses on the income statement. Because receivables and investment transactions affect cash, their effects must also be reported on the statement of cash flows.

Receivables bring in cash when the business collects from customers. These transactions are reported as *operating activities* on the statement of cash flows because they result from sales. Investment transactions show up as *investing activities* on the statement of cash flows. Chapter 12 shows how companies report their cash flows to the public on the statement of cash flows. In that chapter we will see exactly how to report cash flows related to receivables and investment transactions.

End-of-Chapter Summary Problem

CPC International, Inc., is the food-products company that produces Skippy peanut butter, Hellmann's mayonnaise, and Mazola corn oil. The company balance sheet at December 31, 20X7, reported:

	(In millions)
Notes and accounts receivable [total]	$549.9
Allowance for doubtful accounts	(12.5)

Required

1. How much of the December 31, 20X7 balance of notes and accounts receivable did CPC expect to collect? Stated differently, what was the expected realizable value of these receivables?
2. Journalize, without explanations, 20X8 entries for CPC International, assuming
   a. Estimated Doubtful-Account Expense of $19.2 million, based on the percentage-of-sales method, all during the year
   b. Write-offs of uncollectible accounts receivable totaling $23.6 million
   c. December 31, 20X8, aging of receivables, which indicates that $15.3 million of the total receivables of $582.7 million is uncollectible at year end
3. Show how CPC International's receivables and related allowance will appear on the December 31, 20X8 balance sheet.
4. Show what CPC International's income statement will report for the foregoing transactions.

Answers

Requirement 1

	(In millions)
Expected realizable value of receivables ($549.9 − $12.5)	$537.4

Requirement 2

a. Doubtful-Account Expense	19.2	
Allowance for Doubtful Accounts		19.2
b. Allowance for Doubtful Accounts	23.6	
Accounts Receivable		23.6

Allowance for Doubtful Accounts

20X8 Write-offs	**23.6**	**Dec. 31, 20X7**	**12.5**
		20X8 Expense	**19.2**
		20X8 Balance prior to December 31, 20X8	**8.1**

c. Doubtful-Account Expense ($15.3 − $8.1)	7.2	
Allowance for Doubtful Accounts		7.2

Allowance for Doubtful Accounts

	8.1
	7.2
	15.3

Requirement 3

	(In millions)
Notes and accounts receivable	$582.7
Allowance for doubtful accounts	(15.3)

Requirement 4

	(In millions)
Expenses: Doubtful-account expense for 20X8 ($19.2 + $7.2)	$26.4

Review Receivables and Investments

Lessons Learned

1. **Understand short-term investments.** Short-term investments, also called *marketable securities*, are investments that a company plans to hold for 1 year or less. There are three types of short-term investments: held-to-maturity investments, trading investments, and available-for-sale investments. Trading investments are reported on the balance sheet at market value.
2. **Apply internal controls to receivables.** Businesses that sell on credit receive most of their cash receipts by mail. To ensure internal control, cash-handling duties must be separated from cash-accounting duties. A bank lockbox is often used to achieve this separation.
3. **Use the allowance method for uncollectible receivables.** In the *percentage-of-sales* method, uncollectible-account expense is estimated as a percentage of the company's net sales. Under the *aging-of-accounts-receivable* method, individual accounts are analyzed according to the length of time they have been receivable from the customer. The aging method adjusts Allowance for Uncollectible Accounts to the proper amount of uncollectible accounts receivable.
4. **Account for notes receivable.** *Notes receivable* are formal receivable arrangements in which the debtor signs a promissory note, agreeing to pay back both the principal borrowed plus a stated amount of interest on a certain date. To increase their cash flow, companies may sell on credit cards or factor or discount their receivables.
5. **Use days' sales in receivables and the acid-test ratio to evaluate financial position.** Day's sales in receivables tell how long it takes to collect receivables. The *acid-test ratio* measures ability to pay current liabilities with the most liquid current assets.

Accounting Vocabulary

acid-test ratio (p. 241)
accounts receivable turnover (p. 240)
aging-of-accounts receivable (p. 233)
Allowance for Doubtful Accounts (p. 231)
Allowance for Uncollectible Accounts (p. 231)
allowance method (p. 231)
available-for-sale investments (p. 224)
bad-debt expense (p. 231)
balance-sheet approach (p. 233)
creditor (p. 224)
days' sales in receivables (p. 240)
debt instrument (p. 224)
debtor (p. 224)
direct write-off method (p. 235)
doubtful-account expense (p. 231)
equity securities (p. 224)
held-to-maturity investments (p. 224)
income-statement approach (p. 232)
interest (p. 236)
marketable securities (p. 224)
maturity (p. 224)
percentage-of-sales method (p. 232)
principal (p. 236)
quick ratio (p. 241)
receivables (p. 227)
securities (p. 224)
short-term investments (p. 224)
term (p. 224)
trading investments (p. 224)
uncollectible-account expense (p. 231)

Questions

1. Suppose you are the president of Lands' End, Inc. Would you be most inclined to make large investments in U.S. Treasury bills, the stock of eBay, or new lines of merchandise in your main line of business? Explain your choice.
2. Describe the three categories of short-term investments. Indicate the amount to report on the balance sheet for trading investments.
3. MFS Communication, Inc., pays $100,000 to purchase Oracle stock as a short-term investment. MFS plans to hold the stock no longer than 1 month and hopes to sell at a profit. Show how MFS will report the investment on its balance sheet, including the dollar amount, if at year end the market value of the Oracle stock is

   a. $90,000 b. $107,000

   Identify the category of assets in which the investment is reported and the accounts that come before and after the investment on the balance sheet.
4. Many businesses receive most of their cash on credit sales through the mail. Suppose you own a business in which you must hire employees to handle cash receipts and perform the related accounting duties. What internal control feature should you use to ensure that the cash received from customers is not taken by a dishonest employee?
5. Which of the two methods of accounting for uncollectible accounts—the allowance method or the direct write-off method—is preferable? Why?
6. Identify the accounts debited and credited to account for uncollectibles under (a) the allowance method and (b) the direct write-off method.
7. Identify and briefly describe the two ways to estimate bad-debt expense and uncollectible accounts under the allowance method.
8. Briefly describe how a company may combine both the percentage-of-sales method and the aging method to account for uncollectibles.
9. For each of the following notes receivable, compute the amount of interest revenue earned during 20X2:

	Principal	Interest Rate	Interest Period	Maturity Date
a. Note 1	$ 10,000	9%	60 days	11/30/20X2
b. Note 2	50,000	10%	3 months	9/30/20X2
c. Note 3	100,000	8%	18 months	12/31/20X3
d. Note 4	15,000	12%	90 days	1/15/20X3

10. Why does the payee of a note receivable usually need to record interest at the end of the accounting period?
11. Show two ways to report Accounts Receivable of $100,000 and Allowance for Uncollectible Accounts of $2,800 on the balance sheet or in the related notes.
12. Why is the acid-test ratio a more stringent measure of the ability to pay current liabilities than the current ratio?
13. Which measure of days' sales in receivables is preferable, 30 or 40? Give your reason.
14. Which comes first, revenue or collections from customers? Are these items the same? If not, what causes them to differ? Which item affects the income statement? Which affects the balance sheet?

Assess Your Progress

Check Points

Classifying investments as current or long-term
(Obj. 1)

CP5-1 Answer these questions about investments.

1. Why is a trading investment always a current asset? Explain.
2. What is the amount to report for a trading investment on the balance sheet?

Accounting for a trading investment
(Obj. 1)

CP5-2 Assume Intel Corporation holds short-term trading investments. Suppose that on November 16, Intel paid $80,000 for a short-term trading investment in Coca-Cola stock. At December 31, the market value of Coca-Cola stock is $84,000. For this situation, show everything that Intel would report on its December 31 balance sheet and on its income statement for the year ended December 31.

Accounting for a trading investment
(Obj. 1)

CP5-3 Return to page 225 and the example of Oracle Corporation's short-term trading investment in Ford Motor Company stock.

1. How much did Oracle pay for the short-term investment in Ford stock? Stated differently, what was Oracle's cost of the Ford stock?
2. Suppose the Ford stock had decreased in value to $95,000 at May 31. Make the Oracle journal entry to adjust the Short-Term Investment account to market value.

3. Show how Oracle would report the short-term investment on its balance sheet and the unrealized loss on its income statement.

Internal control over the collection of receivables
(Obj. 2)

CP5-4 Return to the Accounts Receivable T-accounts on page 232. Suppose Gary Bauer is the accountant responsible for these records. What duty will a good internal control system withhold from Bauer? Why?

Applying the allowance method to account for uncollectibles
(Obj. 3)

CP5-5 The allowance method of accounting for uncollectible receivables uses two accounts in addition to Accounts Receivable. Identify the two accounts and indicate which financial statement reports each account. Which of these is a contra account? Make up reasonable amounts to show how to report the contra account under its companion account on the balance sheet.

Applying the allowance method (percentage-of-sales) to account for uncollectibles
(Obj. 3)

CP5-6 During its first year of operations, Quartz Microchip Manufacturers had net sales of $800,000, all on account. Industry experience suggests that Quartz's had debts will amount to 1% of net credit sales. At December 31, 20X4, Quartz's accounts receivable total $90,000. The company uses the allowance method to account for uncollectibles.

1. Make Quartz's journal entry for uncollectible-account expense using the percent-of-sales method.
2. Show how Quartz should report accounts receivable on its balance sheet at December 31, 20X4. Follow the reporting format illustrated in the middle of page 231.

Applying the allowance method (percentage-of-sales) to account for uncollectibles
(Obj. 3)

CP5-7 This exercise continues the situation of Check Point 5-6, in which Quartz Microchip Manufacturers ended the year 20X4 with accounts receivable of $90,000 and an allowance for uncollectible accounts of $8,000.

During 20X5, Quartz completed the following transactions:

1. Net credit sales, $800,000
2. Collections on account, $780,000
3. Write-offs of uncollectibles, $5,000
4. Uncollectible-account expense, 1% of net credit sales

Journalize the 20X5 transactions for Quartz Microchip Manufacturers. Explanations are not required.

Applying the allowance method (percentage-of-sales) to account for uncollectibles
(Obj. 3)

CP5-8 Use the solution to Check Point 5-7 to answer these questions about Quartz Microchip Manufacturers.

1. Start with Accounts Receivable's beginning balance ($90,000) and then post to the Accounts Receivable T-account. How much do Quartz's customers owe the company at December 31, 20X5?
2. Start with the Allowance account's beginning credit balance ($8,000) and then post to the Allowance for Uncollectible Accounts T-account. How much of the receivables at December 31, 20X5, does Quartz expect *not* to collect?
3. At December 31, 20X5, how much cash does Quartz expect to collect on its accounts receivable?
4. Show what Quartz should report on its 20X5 balance sheet and income statement.

Applying the allowance method (aging-of-accounts-receivable) to account for uncollectibles
(Obj. 3)

CP5-9 Corwin & Corwin, a law firm, started 20X6 with accounts receivable of $100,000 and an allowance for uncollectible accounts of $8,000. The 20X6 revenues totaled $700,000, and cash collections on account totaled $720,000. During 20X6, Corwin wrote off uncollectible accounts receivable of $6,000. At December 31, 20X6, the aging of accounts receivable indicated that Corwin will *not* collect $5,000 of its accounts receivable.

Journalize Corwin's (a) credit sales, (b) cash collections on account, (c) write-offs of uncollectible receivables, and (d) uncollectible-account expense for the year. Explanations are not required. Prepare a T-account for Allowance for Uncollectible Accounts to show your computation of uncollectible-account expense for the year.

Applying the allowance method (aging-of-accounts-receivable) to account for uncollectibles
(Obj. 3)

CP5-10 Perform the following operations for the receivables of Corwin & Corwin, a law firm, at December 31, 20X6.

1. Start with the beginning balances for these T-accounts:
   - Accounts Receivable, $100,000
   - Allowance for Uncollectible Accounts, $8,000

   Post the following 20X6 transactions to the T-accounts:
   a. Service revenue of $700,000
   b. Collections on account, $720,000
   c. Write-offs of uncollectible accounts, $6,000
   d. Uncollectible-account expense (allowance method), $5,000
2. What are the ending balances of Accounts Receivable and Allowance for Uncollectible Accounts?
3. Show how Corwin & Corwin will report accounts receivable on its balance sheet at December 31, 20X6. Follow the reporting format on page 231.

Accounting for a note receivable
(Obj. 4)

CP5-11 Capitol Bank lent $100,000 to Roane Lacy on a 6-month, 7% note. Record the following for Capitol Bank:

a. Lending the money on May 19.
b. Collecting the principal and interest at maturity. Specify the date.

Explanations are not required.

Computing note receivable amounts
(Obj. 4)

CP5-12

1. Compute the amount of interest during 20X7, 20X8, and 20X9 for the following note receivable: On April 30, 20X7, Synergy Bank lent $500,000 to Lane Fusilier on a 2-year, 9% note.
2. Which party has a
   a. Note receivable?
   b. Note payable?
   c. Interest revenue?
   d. Interest expense?
3. How much in total would Synergy Bank collect if Fusilier paid off the note early—say, on November 30, 20X7?

Accruing interest receivable and collecting a note receivable
(Obj. 4)

CP5-13 Return to the promissory note in Exhibit 5-4, page 237. Assume the accounting year of Continental Bank ends on September 30, 20X5. Journalize Continental Bank's (a) lending money on the note receivable at August 31, 20X5, (b) accrual of interest at September 30, 20X5, and (c) collection of principal and interest at February 28, 20X6, the maturity date of the note. Carry amounts to the nearest cent.

Reporting receivables amounts
(Obj. 6)

CP5-14 Using your answers to Check Point 5-13 for Continental Bank, show how the bank will report the following (carry amounts to the nearest cent):

a. Whatever needs to be reported on its classified balance sheet at September 30, 20X5.
b. Whatever needs to be reported on its income statement for the year ended September 30, 20X5.
c. Whatever needs to be reported on its classified balance sheet at September 30, 20X6. You may ignore Cash.
d. Whatever needs to be reported on its income statement for the year ended September 30, 20X6.

Using the acid-test ratio and days' sales in receivables to evaluate an actual company
(Obj. 5)

CP5-15 Cabletron Systems, a cable TV company, reported the following items, as adapted, at February 28, 20X1 (amounts in millions, with 20X0 amounts also given as needed):

Accounts payable	$469	Accounts receivable:	
Cash	215	February 28, 20X1	$ 235
Allowance for uncollectible accounts:		February 29, 20X0	160
February 28, 20X1	15	Cost of goods sold	575
February 29, 20X0	7	Short-term investments	165
Inventories:		Other current assets	93
February 28, 20X1	198	Other current liabilities	145
February 29, 20X0	161	Net service revenue	1,706
Long-term liabilities	11	Long-term assets	416

Compute Cabletron's (a) acid-test ratio and (b) days' sales in average receivables for 20X1. Evaluate each ratio value as strong or weak. Assume Cabletron sells its goods on terms of net 30.

Reporting receivables and other accounts in the financial statements **(Obj. 5)**

CP5-16 **Sprint Corporation**, the telecommunications company, reported the following items, as adapted (amounts in millions):

Service revenue	$23,613	Unearned revenues	$ 607
Other assets	1,767	Allowance for doubtful accounts	389
Property, plant, and equipment	25,316	Other expenses	12,569
Cost of services sold	11,620	Accounts receivable	4,417
Cash	239	Accounts payable	2,285
Notes payable	18,719		

1. Classify each item as (a) income statement or balance sheet and as (b) debit balance or credit balance.
2. How much net income (or net loss) did Sprint report for the year?
3. Show how Sprint reported receivables on its classified balance sheet. Follow the reporting format on page 231.

Exercises

Accounting for a trading investment **(Obj. 1)**

E5-1 **ExxonMobil**, the giant oil company, often has extra cash to invest. Suppose the Exxon Division buys 5,000 shares of **Xerox Corporation** stock at $60 per share. Assume Exxon expects to hold the Xerox stock for 1 month and then sell it. The purchase occurs on December 20, 20X1. At December 31, the market price of a share of Xerox stock is $63 per share.

Required

1. What type of investment is this to Exxon? Give the reason for your answer.
2. Record Exxon's purchase of the Xerox stock on December 20, and the adjustment to market value on December 31.
3. Show how Exxon would report this investment on its balance sheet at December 31, and any gain or loss on its income statement for the year ended December 31, 20X1.

Reporting a trading investment **(Obj. 1)**

E5-2 On November 16, a company paid $98,000 for a trading investment in the stock of **Hewlett-Packard Company**. On December 12, the company received a $900 cash dividend from Hewlett-Packard. It is now December 31, and the market value of the Hewlett-Packard stock is $91,000. For this investment, show what the company should report in its income statement and balance sheet.

Accounting for a trading investment **(Obj. 1)**

general ledger

E5-3 **Curtiss-Wright Corporation** developed the Wankel engine that thrust Mazda automobiles into prominence. Curtiss-Wright reports short-term investments on its balance sheet. Suppose Curtiss-Wright completed the following short-term investment transactions during 20X3:

20X3	
Nov 6	Purchased 2,000 shares of Titan Corporation stock for $67,000. Curtiss-Wright plans to sell the stock at a profit in the near future.
27	Received a quarterly cash dividend of $0.85 per share on the Titan stock.
Dec. 31	Adjusted the investment in Titan stock. Current market value is $81,000. Curtiss-Wright still plans to sell the stock in early 20X4.
20X4	
Jan. 11	Sold the Titan stock for $82,000.

Required

1. Prepare T-accounts for Cash; Short-Term Investment; Dividend Revenue; Unrealized Gain on Investment; and Gain on Sale of Investment, to show the effects of Curtiss-Wright's investment transactions. Start with a cash balance of $110,000; all the other accounts start at zero.
2. Show how Curtiss-Wright would report this investment on its balance sheets at December 31, 20X3 and 20X4, and the related items on the 20X3 and 20X4 income statements.

Controlling cash receipts from customers
(Obj. 2)

E5-4 As a recent college graduate, you land your first job in the customer collections department of Vivendi Party Productions. LaTanya Davis, one of the owners, has asked you to propose a system to ensure that cash received by mail from customers is handled properly. Draft a short memorandum identifying the essential element in your proposed plan and state why this element is important. Refer to Chapter 4 if necessary.

Reporting bad debts by the allowance method
(Obj. 3)

E5-5 At December 31, 20X3, assume **Payless Shoes** has an accounts receivable balance of $61,000. Sales revenue for 20X3 is $600,000. Allowance for Doubtful Accounts has a credit balance of $900 before the year-end adjustment. Payless estimates that doubtful-account expense for the year is 1/2 of 1% of sales. Prepare the year-end entry to record doubtful-account expense. Show how the accounts receivable and the allowance for doubtful accounts are reported on the balance sheet. Use the reporting format of Oracle Corporation on page 223.

Using the allowance method for bad debts
(Obj. 3)

E5-6 On September 30, a Salvation Army Thrift Store had a $28,000 balance in Accounts Receivable and a $1,600 credit balance in Allowance for Uncollectible Accounts. During October, the store made credit sales of $100,000. October collections on account were $91,000, and write-offs of uncollectible receivables totaled $1,700. Uncollectible-account expense is estimated as 2% of revenue.

Required

1. Journalize sales, collections, write-offs of uncollectibles, and uncollectible-account expense by the allowance method during October. Explanations are not required.
2. Show the ending balances in Accounts Receivable, Allowance for Uncollectible Accounts, and *Net* Accounts Receivable at October 31. How much does the store expect to collect?
3. Show how the store will report Accounts Receivable on its October 31 balance sheet. Use the Oracle Corporation format on page 223.

Using the direct write-off method for bad debts
(Obj. 3)

E5-7 Refer to Exercise 5-6.

Required

1. Record uncollectible-account expense for October by the direct write-off method.
2. What amount of accounts receivable would the Salvation Army Thrift Store report on its October 31 balance sheet under the direct write-off method? Does the store expect to collect the full amount?

Using the aging approach to estimate bad debts
(Obj. 3)

E5-8 At December 31, 20X3, the accounts receivable balance of Peak's Unique Boutique is $269,000. The allowance for doubtful accounts has a $5,900 credit balance. Peak's prepares the following aging schedule for accounts receivable:

Total Balance	Age of Accounts			
	1–30 Days	31–60 Days	61–90 Days	Over 90 Days
$269,000$106,000	$78,000	$70,000	$15,000	
Estimated uncollectible	.5%	1.5%	6.0%	50%

Integrator CD
spreadsheet

Required

1. Based on the aging of accounts receivable, does the balance of the allowance account appear adequate? Too high? Too low?
2. Make any entry required by the aging schedule. Show the T-account for the allowance.
3. Show how Peak's will report Accounts Receivable on its December 31 balance sheet. Include the two accounts that come before receivables on the balance sheet, using assumed amounts.

Measuring and accounting for uncollectibles
(Obj. 3)

E5-9 Assume Kellogg's, the breakfast cereal company, experienced the following sales and accounts receivable write-offs (in millions).

Year	Sales	Accounts Receivable Write-Offs in Year				
		20X1	20X2	20X3	20X4	Total
20X1	$ 6,800	$53	$ 86			$139
20X2	7,000		105	$ 33		138
20X3	7,100			110	$34	144
	$20,900	$53	$191	$143	$34	$421

Suppose Kellogg's estimates that 2% of sales will become uncollectible.

Required

1. Is the 2% estimate reasonable, too high, or too low? Give your reason.
2. Journalize sales (all on account), bad-debt expense, and write-offs for 20X3. Include explanations.

Recording notes receivable and accruing interest revenue
(Obj. 4)

general ledger

E5-10 Record the following transactions in the journal of Van Diuvendyk Capital Management. Round interest amounts to the nearest dollar. How much interest revenue did Van Diuvendyk earn this year? → Int Revenue of $645 this year.

Nov.	1	Loaned $40,000 cash to Sara Phillips on a 1-year, 9% note.
Dec.	3	Sold goods to SMU, Inc., receiving a 90-day, 12% note for $3,750.
	16	Received a $2,000, 6-month, 12% note on account from McMaster Company.
	31	Accrued interest revenue for the year.

Reporting the effects of note receivable transactions on the balance sheet and income statement
(Obj. 4)

general ledger

E5-11 Assume Canon Copiers completed these transactions:

20X3	
Apr. 1	Loaned $50,000 to Lee Franz on a 1-year, 10% note.
Dec. 31	Accrued interest revenue on the Franz note.
20X4	
Apr. 1	Collected the maturity value of the note (principal plus interest) from Franz.

Show what Canon would report for these transactions on its 20X3 and 20X4 balance sheets and income statements.

Practical questions about receivables
(Obj. 3, 4)

E5-12 Answer these questions about receivables and uncollectibles. For the true–false questions, explain why the statement is false:

1. True or false? Credit sales increase receivables. Collections and write-offs decrease receivables.
2. Which receivables figure, the *total* amount that customers *owe* the company or the *net* amount the company expects to collect, is more interesting to investors as they consider buying the company's stock? Give your reason.
3. Show how to determine net accounts receivable. State exactly where this item is reported in the financial statements. Be very specific: statement, classification, position.

4. True or false? The direct write-off method of accounting for uncollectibles overstates assets.
5. Stockton Bank lent $100,000 to California Company on a 6-month, 6% note. Which party has interest receivable? Which party has interest payable? Interest expense? Interest revenue? How much interest will these organizations record 1 month after California signs the note?
6. When Stockton Bank accrues interest on the California Company note, show the directional effects on the bank's assets, liabilities, and equity (increase, decrease, or no effect). Also show the effects on California Company's assets, liabilities, and equity. For each company, indicate why its equity is affected.

Evaluating the acid-test ratio and days' sales in receivables
(Obj. 5)

E5-13 **Salesman's Sample Company** reported the following amounts in its 20X6 financial statements. The 20X5 figures are given for comparison.

	20X6		20X5	
Current assets				
Cash		$ 4,000		$ 9,000
Short-term investments		15,000		11,000
Accounts receivable	$80,000		$74,000	
Less allowance for uncollectibles	(7,000)	73,000	(6,000)	68,000
Inventory		188,000		189,000
Prepaid insurance		2,000		2,000
Total current assets		282,000		279,000
Total current liabilities		101,000		107,000
Net sales		743,000		732,000

Required

1. Determine whether the acid-test ratio improved or deteriorated from 20X5 to 20X6. How does Salesman's Sample's acid-test ratio compare with the industry average of 0.90?
2. Compare the days' sales in receivables measure for 20X6 with the company's credit terms of net 30. What action, if any, should Salesman's Sample Company take?

Analyzing a company's financial statements
(Obj. 5)

E5-14 **America Online, Inc. (AOL)** reported these figures in millions of dollars:

	2000	1999
Total Revenues	$7,703	$5,724
Receivables at end of year	464	385

Required

1. Compute AOL's average collection period during 2000.
2. Is AOL's collection period long or short? **Compaq Computer** takes 53 days to collect its average level of receivables. **Kellogg's** the breakfast cereal company, takes 36 days. What causes AOL's collection period to be so different?

Challenge Exercises

Determining whether to sell on bank cards
(Obj. 2)

E5-15 Barry's Coffee Company, an importer of Colombian coffee, sells on credit and manages its own receivables. Average experience for the past 3 years has been as follows:

	Cash	Credit	Total
Sales	$200,000	$200,000	$400,000
Cost of goods sold	120,000	90,000	210,000
Uncollectible-account expense	—	4,000	4,000
Other expenses	34,000	27,000	61,000

Barry Christian, the owner, is considering whether to accept bankcards (VISA, MasterCard). He expects total sales to increase by 10%, but cash sales remain unchanged. If Barry's switches to bankcards, the business can save $2,000 on accounting and other expenses, but VISA and MasterCard charge 2% on bankcard sales. Christian figures that the increase in sales will be due to the increased volume of bankcard sales.

Required

Should Barry's Coffee Company start selling on bankcards? Show the computations of net income under the present plan and under the bankcard plan.

Reconstructing receivables and bad-debt amounts
(Obj. 3)

E5-16 **Compaq Computer Corporation** reported net trade receivables of $5,600 million and $6,700 million at December 31, 19X9 and 20X0, after subtracting allowances of $200 million and $300 million at these respective dates. Assume Compaq recorded doubtful-account expense of $800 million (1.90476% of total revenue) for 20X0. (All amounts are adapted from Compaq financial statements.)

Required

Use this information to measure the following amounts for 20X0:

a. Write-offs of uncollectible receivables.
b. Total revenue.
c. Collections from customers.

Selling receivables
(Obj. 4)

E5-17 Aussie Wear, Inc., sells hiking gear to foreign retailers on account. Sales for the year have totaled $820,000 thus far. Because the economy is in a recession, cash collections have been very slow, and the company is facing a cash squeeze. Receivables at the beginning of the year were $80,000, and Aussie Wear must limit receivables to no higher than $90,000.

Aussie Wear is considering selling its receivables to a factoring company. The negotiation with the factor boils down to the discount to be charged. If the two parties reach an agreement, the factor will collect Aussie Wear's receivables and then pay Aussie Wear the amount collected, minus the discount. What percentage discount should Aussie Wear be willing to absorb to get cash immediately and also keep receivables within the company's prescribed boundary? *Hint*: A T-account for Receivables helps answer this question.

Problems

(Group A)

Accounting for a trading investment
(Obj. 1)

general ledger

P5-1A During the fourth quarter of 20X3, Four Seasons, Inc., generated excess cash, which the company invested in securities, as follows:

Oct. 3	Purchased 5,000 shares of common stock as a trading investment, paying $9.25 per share.
14	Received cash dividend of $0.32 per share on the trading investment.
Dec. 31	Adjusted the trading investment to its market value of $7.40 per share

Required

1. Prepare T-accounts for: Cash, balance of $400,000; Short-Term Investment; Dividend Revenue; Unrealized Gain (Loss) on Investment.
2. Journalize the foregoing transactions and post to the T-accounts.
3. Show how to report the short-term investment on the Four Seasons balance sheet at December 31.
4. Show how to report whatever should appear on Four Seasons' income statement.

Controlling cash receipts from customers
(Obj. 2)

P5-2A Tony the Tiger, Inc., manufactures toys and sells to Toys "Я" Us, Levine's, and other toy stores. All sales are made on account. Joy Loudermilk, accountant for the company, receives and opens the mail. Company procedure requires Loudermilk to separate customer checks from the remittance slips, which list the amounts that Loudermilk posts as credits to customer accounts receivable. Loudermilk deposits the checks in the bank. At the end of each day she computes the day's total amount posted to customer accounts and matches this total to the bank deposit slip. This procedure ensures that all receipts are deposited in the bank.

Required

As a consultant hired by Tony the Tiger, Inc., write a memo to management evaluating the company's internal controls over cash receipts from customers. If the system is effective, identify its strong features. If the system has flaws, propose a way to strengthen the controls.

Accounting for revenue, collections, and uncollectibles; percent-of-sales method **(Obj. 3)**

P5-3A This problem takes you through the accounting for sales, receivables, and uncollectibles for **Nike, Inc.**, the sports manufacturer. By selling on credit, Nike cannot expect to collect 100% of its accounts receivable. At May 31, 2001, and 2000, respectively, Nike reported the following on its balance sheet (adapted and in millions of dollars):

	May 31, 2001	May 31, 2000
Accounts receivable	$1,693	$1,635
Less Allowance for uncollectibles	(72)	(65)
Accounts receivable, net	$1,621	$1,570

During the year ended May 31, 2001, Nike earned sales revenue and collected cash from customers. Assume uncollectible-account expense for the year was 1% of sales revenue and that Nike wrote off uncollectible receivables. At year end Nike ended with the foregoing May 31, 2001, balances.

Required

1. Prepare T-accounts for Accounts Receivable and Allowance for Uncollectibles and insert the May 31, 2000, balances as given.
2. Journalize the following assumed transactions of Nike, Inc. for the year ended May 31, 2001 (explanations are not required):
   a. Sales revenue on account, $9,489 million.
   b. Collections on account, $9,343 million.
   c. Uncollectible-account expense, 1% of sales revenue (round to the nearest $1 thousand).
   d. Write-offs of uncollectible accounts receivable, $? You must solve for the amount of write-offs.
3. Post your entries to the Accounts Receivable and Allowance for Uncollectibles T-accounts.
4. Compute the ending balances for the two T-accounts and compare your balances to the actual May 31, 2001 amounts. They should be the same.
5. At May 31, 2001, how much did customers owe Nike? How much did Nike expect to collect from customers?
6. Show what Nike would report on its income statement for the year ended May 31, 2001.

Using the aging approach for uncollectibles **(Obj. 3)**

P5-4A The September 30, 20X4, records of Precision Tool Company include these accounts:

Accounts Receivable	$143,000
Allowance for Doubtful Accounts	(3,200)

During the year, Precision Tool estimates doubtful-account expense at 1 1/2% of credit sales. At year end, the company ages its receivables and adjusts the balance in Allowance for Doubtful Accounts to correspond to the aging schedule. During the last quarter of 20X4, the company completed the following selected transactions:

20X4	
Nov. 18	Wrote off as uncollectible the $700 account receivable from Bliss Company and the $400 account receivable from Micro Data.
Dec. 31	Adjusted the Allowance for Doubtful Accounts and recorded doubtful-account expense at year end, based on the aging of receivables:

Total Balance	Age of Accounts			
	1–30 Days	31–60 Days	61–90 Days	Over 90 Days
$163,000	$100,000	$40,000	$14,000	$9,000
Estimated uncollectible	.1%	.5%	5.0%	30.0%

Required

1. Record the transactions in the journal. Explanations are not required.
2. Prepare a T-account for Allowance for Doubtful Accounts and post to that account.
3. Show how Precision Tool Company will report its accounts receivable on a comparative balance sheet for 20X4 and 20X3. Use the reporting format on page 231. At December 31, 20X3, the company's Accounts Receivable balance was $112,000 and the Allowance for Doubtful Accounts stood at $2,200.

Short-term investments, uncollectibles, notes, and the ratios
(Obj. 1, 3, 4, 5)

P5-5A Ciliotta, Inc. is hoping to offer its stock to the public and seeks the advice of **Pricewaterhouse Coopers (PWC)**, the accounting firm. Assume PWC advises Ciliotta that its financial statements must be changed to conform to GAAP. At December 31, 20X3, Ciliotta's accounts include the following:

Cash	$ 21,000
Short-term trading investments, at cost	19,000
Accounts receivable	37,000
Note receivable	50,000
Inventory	61,000
Prepaid expenses	14,000
Total current assets	$202,000
Accounts payable	$ 62,000
Other current liabilities	41,000
Total current liabilities	$103,000

PWC advised Ciliotta that

- Cash includes $10,000 that is deposited in a compensating balance account that is tied up until 20X6.
- The market value of the short-term trading investments is $7,000. Ciliotta purchased the investments in November.
- Ciliotta has been using the direct write-off method to account for uncollectible receivables. During 20X3, Ciliotta wrote off bad receivables of $6,000. PWC states that uncollectible-account expense should be 2.5% of service revenue, which totaled $600,000 in 20X3. PWC's aging of Ciliotta's receivables at year end indicated uncollectibles of $5,000.
- The notes receivable are scheduled to be collected in 20X5.
- Ciliotta reported net income of $72,000 in 20X3.

Required

1. Restate Ciliotta's current accounts to conform to GAAP.
2. Compute Ciliotta's current ratio and acid-test ratio both before and after your corrections.
3. Determine Ciliotta's correct net income for 20X3.
4. Evaluate the overall effect of PWC's suggestions on Ciliotta's financial appearance.

Notes receivable and accrued interest revenue
(Obj. 4)

P5-6A Assume that **Green Giant Foods**, famous for canned and frozen fruits and vegetables, completed the following selected transactions:

general ledger

20X5	
Oct. 31	Sold goods to **Kroger, Inc.**, receiving a $30,000, 3-month, 6% note.
Dec. 31	Made an adjusting entry to accrue interest on the Kroger note.
20X6	
Jan. 31	Collected the Kroger note.
23	Received a 90-day, 15%, $4,000 note from Bliss Company on account.
Mar. 31	Sold the Bliss Company note to Lakewood Bank, receiving cash of $3,800.
Nov. 16	Loaned $45,000 cash to McNeil, Inc., receiving a 90-day, 12% note.
Dec. 31	Accrued the interest on the McNeil, Inc. note.

Required

1. Record the transactions in the journal. Explanations are not required.
2. Show what Green Giant will report on its comparative classified balance sheet at December 31, 20X6, and December 31, 20X5.

Using ratio data to evaluate a company's financial position
(Obj. 5)

Integrator CD spreadsheet

P5-7A The comparative financial statements of Braswell-Davis Organic Gardening Supply for 2001, 2000, and 1999 included the following selected data.

	2001	2000	1999
		(In millions)	
Balance sheet:			
Current assets:			
Cash	$ 36	$ 80	$ 60
Short-term investments	140	154	122
Receivables, net of allowance for doubtful accounts of $27, $21, and $15, respectively	297	285	178
Inventories	319	341	342
Prepaid expenses	21	27	46
Total current assets	813	887	748
Total current liabilities	603	528	413
Income statement:			
Net sales	$4,989	$ 5,295	$4,206
Cost of sales	2,734	2,636	2,418

Required

1. Compute these ratios for 2001 and 2000:
   a. Current ratio b. Acid-test ratio c. Days' sales in receivables
2. Write a memo explaining to top management which ratio values improved from 2000 to 2001 and which ratio values deteriorated. State whether this trend is favorable or unfavorable and give the reason for your evaluation.

(Group B)

Accounting for a trading investment
(Obj. 1)

P5-1B During the fourth quarter of 20X4, the operations of York Air Conditioning Company generated excess cash, which the company invested in securities, as follows:

general ledger

Oct. 2	Purchased 2,000 shares of common stock as a trading investment, paying $12.75 per share.
21	Received semiannual cash dividend of $0.45 per share on the trading investment.
Dec. 31	Adjusted the trading investment to its market value of $31,000.

Required

1. Prepare T-accounts for Cash, balance of $400,000; Short-Term Investment; Dividend Revenue; and Unrealized Gain (Loss) on Investment.

2. Journalize the foregoing transactions and post to the T-accounts.
3. Show how to report the short-term investments on York's balance sheet at December 31.
4. Show how to report whatever should appear on York's income statement.

Controlling cash receipts from customers **(Obj. 2)**

P5-2B Ingall's Custom Lamps distributes merchandise to furniture stores. All sales are on credit, so virtually all cash receipts arrive in the mail. Akbar Kuwaja, the company president, has just returned from a trade association meeting with new ideas for the business. Among other things, Kuwaja plans to institute stronger internal controls over cash receipts from customers.

Required

Take the role of Akbar Kuwaja, the company president. Write a memo to employees outlining procedures to ensure that all cash receipts are deposited in the bank and that the total amounts of each day's cash receipts are posted to customer accounts receivable.

Accounting for revenue, collections, and uncollectibles; percentage-of-sales method **(Obj. 3)**

P5-3B This problem takes you through the accounting for revenue, receivables, and uncollectibles for **America Online, Inc.**, the Internet service company. AOL sells for cash and on account. By selling on credit, AOL cannot expect to collect 100% of its accounts receivable. At December 31, 2000 and 1999, respectively, AOL reported the following on its balance sheet (all amounts adapted and in millions of dollars):

	December 31,	
	2000	1999
Accounts receivable	$561	$443
Less Allowance for uncollectibles	(97)	(58)
Accounts receivable, net	$464	$385

During the year ended December 31, 2000, AOL earned service revenue and collected cash from customers. Assume uncollectible-account expense for the year was 4% of service revenue and that AOL wrote off uncollectible accounts receivable. At year end AOL ended with the foregoing December 31, 2000, balances.

Required

1. Prepare T-accounts for Accounts Receivable and Allowance for Uncollectibles, and insert the December 31, 1999, balances as given.
2. Journalize the following assumed transactions of AOL for the year ended December 31, 2000 (explanations are not required):
   a. Service revenue on account, $7,703 million.
   b. Collections from customers on account, $7,316 million.
   c. Uncollectible-account expense, 4% of service revenue (rounded to the nearest $1 million).
   d. Write-offs of uncollectible accounts receivable, $? You must solve for the amount of write-offs.
3. Post to the Accounts Receivable and Allowance for Uncollectibles T-accounts.
4. Compute the ending balances for the two T-accounts and compare to the actual December 31, 2000, amounts. They should be the same.
5. At December 31, 2000, how much did customers owe AOL? How much did AOL expect to collect from customers?
6. Show what AOL would report on its income statement for the year ended December 31, 2000.

Using the aging approach for uncollectibles **(Obj. 3)**

P5-4B The September 30, 20X2, records of DodgeRam Auto Supply include these accounts:

Accounts Receivable	$265,000
Allowance for Doubtful Accounts	(7,100)

During the year DodgeRam estimates doubtful-account expense at 2% of credit sales. At year end, the company ages its receivables and adjusts the balance in Allowance for Doubtful Accounts to correspond to the aging schedule. During the last quarter of 20X2, DodgeRam completed the following selected transactions:

20X2	
Nov. 22	Wrote off the following accounts receivable as uncollectible: Monet Corporation $1,300; Blocker, Inc., $2,100; and M Street Plaza, $700.
Dec. 31	Adjusted the Allowance for Doubtful Accounts and recorded doubtful-account expense at year end, based on the aging of receivables:

	Age of Accounts			
Total Balance	1–30 Days	31–60 Days	61–90 Days	Over 90 Days
$289,000	$160,000	$80,000	$34,000	$15,000
Estimated uncollectible	.5%	1.0%	5.0%	50.0%

Required

1. Record the transactions in the journal. Explanations are not required.
2. Prepare a T-account for Allowance for Doubtful Accounts and post to that account.
3. Show how DodgeRam Auto Supply will report its accounts receivable in a comparative balance sheet for 20X2 and 20X1. Use the reporting format on page 231. At December 31, 20X1, the company's Accounts Receivable balance was $271,000 and the Allowance for Doubtful Accounts stood at $8,700.

Short-term investments, uncollectibles, notes, and the ratios
(Obj. 1, 3, 4, 5)

P5-5B Bzensky Corporation is preparing for an initial public offering of the company's stock. Top managers of Bzensky seek the counsel of **KPMG**, the accounting firm, and learn that Bzensky must make some changes to bring its financial statements into conformity with generally accepted accounting principles (GAAP). At December 31, 20X5, Bzensky's accounts include the following:

Cash	$ 18,000
Short-term trading investments, at cost	34,000
Accounts receivable	49,000
Notes receivable	42,000
Inventory	54,000
Prepaid expenses	5,000
Total current assets	$202,000
Accounts payable	$ 76,000
Other current liabilities	69,000
Total current liabilities	$145,000

Assume KPMG drew the following conclusions:

- Cash includes $8,000 that is deposited in a compensating balance account that will be tied up until 20X8.
- The market value of the short-term trading investments is $22,000. Bzensky purchased the investments in early December.
- Bzensky has been using the direct write-off method to account for uncollectibles. During 20X5, the company wrote off bad receivables of $7,000. KPMG believes uncollectible-account expense should be 3% of sales, which for 20X5 totaled $400,000. An aging of receivables at year end indicated uncollectibles of $4,000.
- The notes receivable will be collected in installments starting in 20X8.
- Bzensky reported net income of $65,000 for 20X5.

Required

1. Restate all current accounts to conform to GAAP.
2. Compute Bzensky's current ratio and acid-test ratio both before and after your corrections.
3. Determine Bzensky's correct net income for 20X5.
4. Evaluate the overall effect of KPMG's suggestions on Bzensky's financial appearance.

Notes receivable and accrued interest revenue
(Obj. 4)

general ledger

P5-6B Assume that **Sherwin-Williams**, the paint company, completed the following selected transactions:

20X4	
Nov. 30	Sold goods to **Kelly Moore Paint Company**, receiving a $60,000, 3-month, 10% note.
31	Made an adjusting entry to accrue interest on the Kelly Moore note.
20X5	
Feb. 18	Received a 90-day, 10%, $5,000 note from Altex Company on account.
28	Collected the Kelly Moore note.
Mar. 8	Sold the Altex note to First State Bank, receiving cash of $4,600.
Nov. 11	Loaned $50,000 cash to Consolidated, Inc., receiving a 90-day, 9% note.
Dec. 31	Accrued the interest on the Consolidated, Inc. note.

Required

1. Record the transactions in the journal. Explanations are not required.
2. Show what Sherwin-Williams will report on its comparative classified balance sheet at December 31, 20X5, and December 31, 20X4.

Using ratio data to evaluate a company's financial position
(Obj. 5)

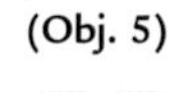

spreadsheet

P5-7B The comparative financial statements of Crain's Stationary Company for 2001, 2000, and 1999 included the following selected data:

	2001	2000	1999
		(In Millions)	
Balance sheet:			
Current assets:			
Cash	$ 27	$ 26	$ 22
Short-term investments	93	101	69
Receivables, net of allowance for doubtful accounts of $7, $6, and $4, respectively	206	154	127
Inventories	408	383	341
Prepaid expenses	32	31	25
Total current assets	766	695	584
Total current liabilities	540	446	388
Income statement:			
Net sales	$2,671	$2,505	$1,944
Cost of sales	1,380	1,360	963

Required

1. Compute these ratios for 2001 and 2000:
   a. Current ratio b. Acid-test ratio c. Days' sales in receivables

2. Write a memo explaining to top management which ratio values showed improvement from 2000 to 2001 and which ratio values deteriorated. State whether this trend is favorable or unfavorable for the company and give the reason for your evaluation.

Decision Cases

Revenues, collections, and bad debts on receivables
(Obj. 3)

Case 1. Central Florida Baptist Medical Clinic (CFBMC) serves the area around Orlando. The clinic extends credit to indigent patients and collects cash from individuals, Medicare, Medicaid, and various insurance companies. The rising population of Central Florida has caused the need for expansion, and the clinic needs a loan to finance new construction.

After opening in 20X1, CFBMC earned service revenue of $800,000 and collected $600,000 during the remainder of the year. The clinic's accountant estimated (bad debts) uncollectible receivables at 8% of revenue, and write-offs for the year totaled $30,000. There was no aging of receivables at December 31, 20X1.

At December 31, 20X2, the chief executive of CFBMC is astonished to learn that the clinic's revenue records and most expense records are missing. The bank requires at least a summary income statement to support the loan. The only accounting data for 20X2 that CFBMC can come up with follow—all balances at December 31, 20X2:

Accounts receivable	$260,000
Less Allowance for bad debts	(52,000)*
Total expenses, excluding bad-debt expense	870,000
Collections from customers	950,000
Write-offs of bad receivables	40,000

*Determined by aging of receivables

Prepare a summary income statement for Central Florida Baptist Medical Clinic for the year ended December 31, 20X2. Was the clinic profitable in 20X2?

Uncollectible accounts and evaluating a business
(Obj. 3, 4)

Case 2. Shaker Health Foods sells to health food stores either for cash or on notes receivable. The business uses the direct write-off method to account for bad debts. Margaret Durham, the owner, has prepared the company's financial statements. The most recent comparative income statements, for 20X2 and 20X1, follow:

	20X2	20X1
Total revenue	$220,000	$195,000
Total expenses	150,000	143,000
Net income	$ 70,000	$ 52,000

On the basis of the increase in net income, Durham seeks to expand operations. She asks you to invest $50,000 in the business. From Durham you learn that notes receivable from customers were $200,000 at the end of 20X0 and $400,000 at the end of 20X1. Also, total revenues for 20X2 and 20X1 include interest at 10% on the year's beginning notes receivable balance. Total expenses include doubtful-account expense of $2,000 each year, based on the direct write-off method. Durham estimates that doubtful-account expense would be 5% of sales revenue if the allowance method were used.

Required

1. Prepare for Shaker Health Foods a comparative single-step income statement that identifies sales revenue, interest revenue, doubtful-account expense, and other expenses, all computed in accordance with GAAP.
2. Consider whether sales revenue or interest revenue caused net income to increase during 20X2. Is Shaker's future as promising as Durham's income statement makes it appear? Give the reason for your answer.

Estimating the collectibility of accounts receivable
(Obj. 3)

Case 3. Assume that you work in the corporate loan department of Nations First Bank. Rudy Martinez, owner of Fleetwood Mobile Homes, has come to you seeking a loan for $1 million to expand operations. Martinez proposes to use accounts receivable as collateral for the loan and has provided you with the following information from the company's most recent financial statements:

	20X4	20X3	20X2
		(In Thousands)	
Sales	$1,475	$1,589	$1,502
Cost of goods sold	876	947	905
Gross profit	599	642	597
Other expenses	518	487	453
Net profit or (loss) before taxes	$ 81	$ 155	$ 144
Accounts receivable	$ 458	$ 387	$ 374
Allowance for doubtful accounts	23	31	29

Required

1. What analysis would you perform on the information Martinez has provided? Would you grant the loan on the basis of this information? Give your reason.
2. What additional information would you request from Martinez? Give your reason.
3. Assume that Martinez provided you with the information requested in requirement 2. What would make you change the decision you made in requirement 1?

Ethical Issue

Bellmead Credit Company is in the consumer loan business. It borrows from banks and loans out the money at higher interest rates. Bellmead's bank requires Bellmead to submit quarterly financial statements to keep its line of credit. Bellmead's main asset is Notes Receivable. Therefore, Uncollectible-Account Expense and Allowance for Uncollectible Accounts are important accounts.

Grant Mandrell, the company's owner, prefers for net income to increase in a smooth pattern, rather than increase in some periods and decrease in other periods. To report smoothly increasing net income, Mandrell underestimates Uncollectible-Account Expense in some periods. In other periods, Mandrell overestimates the expense. He reasons that the income overstatements roughly offset the income understatements over time.

Required

Is Bellmead Credit's practice of smoothing income ethical? Why or why not?

Financial Statement Case

Short-term investments and accounts receivable
(Obj. 1, 3)

Refer to the **Fossil, Inc.**, financial statements in Appendix A at the end of this book.

1. What types of securities does Fossil classify as short-term marketable investments? How long before these investments mature?

2. During the year ended January 5, 2002 (fiscal year 2001), Fossil sold some short-term marketable securities. The balance sheet provides the data to compute the cost of the investments sold. The statement of cash flows tells how much cash Fossil received from selling the investments. Did the sale of short-term investments result in a gain or a loss, and how much was the gain or loss? Assume that Fossil purchased no new short-term investments during the year.
3. Note 1, "Significant Accounting Policies," reports the amounts of Fossil's accounts receivable allowances (one for estimated customer returns and the other for doubtful accounts). Use these data, plus Fossil's balance sheet, to show Fossil's *gross* accounts receivable and *net* accounts receivable at the end of fiscal year 2001. At the end of 2001, how much did Fossil expect to collect from customers?

Analytical Case

Analyzing accounts receivable **(Obj. 3)**

This case is based on the **Pier 1 Imports** financial statements in Appendix B at the end of this book.

1. Consider only Pier 1's "Other accounts receivable." How much did Pier 1's customers owe the company at the end of 2002? Of this amount, how much did Pier 1 expect to collect? How much did Pier 1 expect *not* to collect?
2. What is the most likely reason Pier 1's allowance for doubtful accounts decreased in 2002?
3. Would you predict that Pier 1's doubtful-account expense increased or decreased during 2002? Indicate how you formed your opinion.
4. Were Pier 1's "Other accounts receivable" of higher quality at the end of 2002 or at the end of 2001? How can you tell?

Group Project

Jillian Michaels and Dee Childress worked for several years as sales representatives for **Xerox Corporation.** During this time, they became close friends as they acquired expertise with the company's full range of copier equipment. Now they see an opportunity to put their experience to work and fulfill lifelong desires to establish their own business. Navarro Community College, located in their city, is expanding, and there is no copy center within 5 miles of the campus. Business in the area is booming, office buildings and apartments are springing up, and the population of the Navarro section of the city is growing.

Michaels and Childress want to open a copy center, similar to a **Kinko's**, near the Navarro campus. A small shopping center across the street from the college has a vacancy that would fit their needs. Michaels and Childress each have $35,000 to invest in the business, but they forecast the need for $200,000 to renovate the store and purchase some of the equipment they will need. Xerox Corporation will lease two large copiers to them at a total monthly rental of $6,000. With enough cash to see them through the first 6 months of operation, they are confident they can make the business succeed. The two women work very well together, and both have excellent credit ratings. Michaels and Childress must borrow $130,000 to start the business, advertise its opening, and keep it running for its first 6 months.

Required

Assume two roles: (1) Michaels and Childress, the partners who will own Navarro Copy Center; and (2) loan officers at Synergy Bank.

1. As a group, visit a copy center to familiarize yourselves with its operations. If possible, interview the manager or another employee. Then write a loan request that Michaels and Childress will submit to Synergy Bank with the intent of borrowing $130,000 to be paid back over 3 years. The loan will be a personal loan to the partnership of Michaels and

Childress, not to Navarro Copy Center. The request should specify all the details of Michaels' and Childress's plan that will motivate the bank to grant the loan. Include a budget for each of the first 6 months of operation of the proposed copy center.

2. As a group, interview a loan officer in a bank. Write Synergy Bank's reply to the loan request. Specify all the details that the bank should require as conditions for making the loan.
3. If necessary, modify the loan request or the bank's reply in order to reach agreement between the two parties.

Merchandise Inventory, Cost of Goods Sold, and Gross Profit

Learning Objectives

1. **Use** the cost-of-goods-sold model
2. **Account** for inventory transactions
3. **Analyze** the various inventory methods
4. **Identify** the income and the tax effects of the inventory methods
5. **Show** how inventory errors affect cost of goods sold and income
6. **Use** the gross profit percentage and inventory turnover to evaluate a business
7. **Estimate** inventory by the gross profit method

Integrator CD

Need additional help? Go to the **Integrator CD** *and search these key words:* average cost, cost of goods sold, FIFO, gross profit method, inventory turnover, LIFO, lower of cost or market, periodic, perpetual, weighted-average methods

General Motors Corporation

Consolidated Statements of Income (Adapted)
Years Ended December 31,

	(Billions)	
	2000	1999
Net sales	$185	$177
Cost of sales	146	141
Selling, general and other expenses	22	19
Interest expense	10	8
Total expenses	178	168
Income before income taxes	7	9
Income tax expense	3	3
Net income	$ 4	$ 6

"Zero, zero, zero" said the ad. "Zero down, zero percent financing, zero payments for one year." Campaigns like these have sold lots of cars, but companies like General Motors (GM), Ford, and Mitsubishi have not realized massive profits as a result. Why? Among other things, letting buyers string out their payments with no interest charges decreased revenues. At times, revenue barely covered cost. Why would auto companies sell this way? Because competition is getting fiercer all the time.

Macy's, Bloomingdale's, and other high-end retailers have suffered a similar fate—high sales but low profits. Yet other retailers are doing fine—take Yahoo!, for example. The sales volume on Yahoo's Internet shopping site jumped 86% in 2001. Because people are staying home and shopping on the Web, traditional businesses are finding it harder and harder to compete with online retailers who keep prices low. Competition again.

Sitemap

Inventory
The merchandise that a company sells to customers.

Cost of goods sold
The cost of the inventory that the business has sold to customers. Also called *cost of sales*.

Managing inventory (the goods the company sells) and managing costs are at the heart of earning profits for a merchandising company. This chapter covers the purchase and sale of merchandise inventory—usually referred to simply as **inventory**—which includes everything from software and fax machines in an Office Depot store to Chevy trucks sitting on a car lot. Inventory is the asset, and **cost of goods sold (cost of sales)** is the expense. GM's income statement shows that cost of sales is the most important expense for a company that sells goods instead of services. During 2000, GM's cost of goods sold was $146 billion, far more than all other expenses. Examine GM's income statement and you will see that sales revenue rose during 2000. But net income dropped, because expenses rose faster than revenue.

The chapter will introduce you to a number of key concepts that will help you do business in a global economy marked by intense competition. We begin by showing how the financial statements of a merchandiser such as GM or Macy's differ from those of the service entities we have discussed so far.[1] The following financial statements demonstrate how service entities differ from merchandisers.

Service Company
Century 21 Real Estate
Income Statement
Year Ended December 31, 20XX

Service revenue	$XXX
Expenses	
Salary expense	X
Depreciation expense	X
Income tax expense	X
Net income	$ X

Merchandising Company
General Motors Corporation
Income Statement
Year Ended December 31, 20XX

Sales revenue	$185
Cost of goods sold	146
Gross profit	39
Operating *expenses*	
Salary expense	X
Depreciation expense	X
Income tax expense	X
Net income	$ 4

Century 21 Real Estate
Balance Sheet
December 31, 20XX

Assets	
Current assets	
Cash	$X
Short-term investments	X
Accounts receivable, net	X
Prepaid expenses	X

General Motors Corporation
Balance Sheet
December 31, 20XX

Assets	
Current assets	
Cash	$X
Short-term investments	X
Accounts receivable, net	X
Inventory	11
Prepaid expenses	X

Merchandisers have two accounts that service entities don't need: cost of goods sold on the income statement and inventory on the balance sheet.

[1]Adapted from Erin White, Amy Merrick, and Gary McWilliams, "Retailers Finish Holidays with Sales Surge," *The Wall Street Journal* (December 27, 2001), p. A3.

Accounting for Inventory

cost of goods sold, periodic method, perpetual method

The basic concept of accounting for merchandise inventory can be illustrated with a simple example. Suppose General Motors (GM) makes three Silverado pickups for $15,000 each, marks them up by $5,000, and sells two of the trucks for $20,000 each. GM's balance sheet reports the truck that the company still holds in inventory, and the income statement reports the cost of the two trucks sold, as follows:

Balance Sheet (partial)		***Income Statement (partial)***	
Current assets:		Sales revenue	
Cash	$ XXX	(2 trucks @ $20,000)	$40,000
Short-term investments	XXX	Cost of goods sold	
Accounts receivable	XXX	(2 trucks @ $15,000)	30,000
Inventory (1 truck @ $15,000)	15,000	Gross profit	$10,000
Prepaid expenses	XXX		

Gross margin
Sales revenue minus cost of goods sold. Also called *gross profit*.

Gross profit, also called **gross margin**, is the excess of sales revenue over cost of goods sold. It is called *gross profit* because operating expenses have not yet been subtracted. Exhibit 6-1 shows actual inventory and cost of goods sold data from the financial statements of General Motors Corporation, as adapted.

✔ Check Point 6-1

Exhibit 6-1

General Motors Corporation Inventory and Cost of Goods Sold (Cost of Sales)

General Motors Corporation
Balance Sheets (Adapted)
December 31, 2000 and 1999

	(Billions)	
Assets	***2000***	***1999***
Current assets		
Cash and cash equivalents	$ 9	$ 9
Short-term investments	1	2
Accounts and notes receivable	6	5
Inventories	11	11

General Motors Corporation
Statements of Income (Adapted)
Years Ended December 31, 2000 and 1999

	(Billions)	
	2000	***1999***
Net sales	$185	$177
Cost of sales (same as cost of goods sold)	146	141
Gross profit	39	36

GM's inventory of $11 billion represents

$$\textbf{Inventory (balance sheet)} = \textbf{Number of units of inventory } \textbf{\textit{on hand}} \times \textbf{Cost per unit of inventory}$$

GM's cost of goods sold ($146 billion) represents

$$\text{Cost of goods sold (income statement)} = \text{Number of units of inventory } \textit{sold} \times \text{Cost per unit of inventory}$$

NUMBER OF UNITS OF INVENTORY. The number of inventory units on hand is determined from accounting records, backed up by a physical count of the goods at year end. Companies do not include in their inventory any goods that they hold on *consignment* because those goods belong to another company, but they do include their own inventory that is out on consignment and held by another company.

COST PER UNIT OF INVENTORY. The cost per unit of inventory poses a challenge because companies purchase goods at different prices throughout the year. Which unit costs go into ending inventory for the balance sheet? Which unit costs should be used for cost of goods sold on the income statement?

The next section shows how the different accounting methods determine ending inventory on the balance sheet and cost of goods sold for the income statement. First, however, you need to understand the cost-of-goods-sold model and how managers decide how much inventory to purchase.

Cost-of-Goods-Sold Model

Objective

1 **Use** the cost-of-goods-sold model

Cost-of-goods-sold model Brings together all the inventory data for the entire accounting period: Beginning inventory + Purchases = Cost of goods available for sale. Then, cost of goods available − Ending inventory = Cost of goods sold.

The **cost-of-goods-sold model** brings together all the inventory data for the entire accounting period:

- Beginning inventory (the balance of inventory left over from the preceding period)
- Purchases of inventory during the current period
- Ending inventory (balance of inventory on hand at the end of the current period)

We begin by illustrating the model for a situation in which the unit cost of inventory remains unchanged. Exhibit 6-2 presents the basic cost-of-goods-sold model, with all data assumed for the illustration.

Exhibit 6-2

Cost of Goods Sold (Data Assumed for the Illustration)

Cost of goods sold:	
Beginning inventory (2 units @ $10 each)	$ 20
+ Purchases (10 units @ $10 each)	100
= Cost of goods available (12 units @ $10 each)	120
− Ending inventory (3 units @ $10 each)	(30)
= Cost of goods sold (9 units @ $10 each)	$ 90

The logic behind the model is this: You start with some goods (2 units of beginning inventory). Then you buy some more goods (purchase 10 units). The sum of these two amounts equals the goods available for sale (12 units). At the end of the period, you have some goods left over (ending inventory of 3 units). The excess of goods available over ending inventory measures the cost of goods sold during the period, based on the 9 units you sold.

Exhibit 6-3 diagrams the cost-of-goods-sold model. Beginning inventory and Purchases go into goods available. Ending inventory and Cost of goods sold come out. The sum of what goes in equals the sum of what comes out.

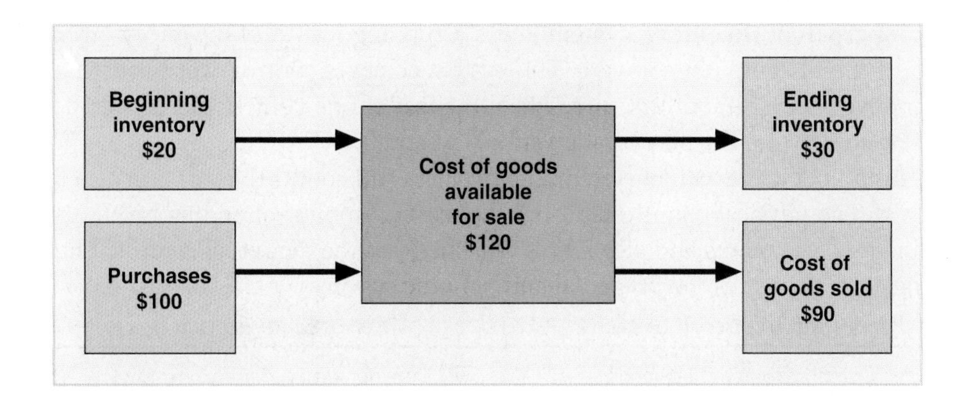

Exhibit 6-3

Diagram of the Cost-of-Goods-Sold Model

DECISION: How Much Inventory Should We Purchase?

Suppose you are the buyer for a Macy's store. You are moving into the next period and planning your buying of Tommy Hilfiger sportswear. You have decided on several different lines of Hilfiger clothing. What is your next decision? You must decide how much to buy. If you buy too much inventory, you may be unable to sell it and you may lose money. If you buy too little, you cannot satisfy your customers, and they may take their business elsewhere. That would be unfortunate because it is much easier to keep a customer than it is to lure a new customer away from a competitor.

How will you make the buying decision? The amount of inventory to purchase is computed as follows:

$$\text{Purchases} = \begin{matrix}\text{Budgeted}\\\text{cost of}\\\text{goods sold}\end{matrix} + \begin{matrix}\text{Budgeted}\\\text{ending}\\\text{inventory}\end{matrix} - \begin{matrix}\text{Actual}\\\text{beginning}\\\text{inventory}\end{matrix}$$

To stay in business, managers must keep tabs on these items. A rearrangement of the cost-of-goods-sold formula helps a manager determine how much inventory to buy, as follows (all amounts assumed):

1	Cost of goods sold (based on the budget for the next period)	$6,000
2	+ Ending inventory (based on the budget for the next period)	1,500
3	= Cost of goods available for sale, as budgeted	7,500
4	− Beginning inventory (actual amount left over from the prior period)	(1,200)
5	= Purchases (how much inventory managers need to buy)	$6,300

Managers use this formula to decide how much to spend on inventory. The power of the cost-of-goods-sold model lies in the vast amount of information it captures: beginning and ending inventory levels, purchases, and cost of goods sold. Now let's examine the different inventory costing methods, beginning with what goes into inventory cost.

Accounting for Inventory in the Perpetual System

Objective

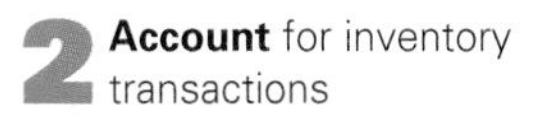
2 **Account** for inventory transactions

There are two main types of inventory accounting systems: the periodic system and the perpetual system. The **periodic inventory system** is used by businesses that sell inexpensive goods. A fabric store or a lumber yard may not keep a running record of every bolt of fabric and every two-by-four. Instead, these stores count their inventory periodically—at least once a year—to determine the quantities on hand. Businesses such as restaurants and hometown nurseries also use the periodic inventory system because the accounting cost is low.

Periodic inventory system
An inventory system in which the business does not keep a continuous record of the inventory on hand. Instead, at the end of the period, the business makes a physical count of the inventory on hand and applies the appropriate unit costs to determine the cost of the ending inventory.

Perpetual inventory system An inventory system in which the business keeps a continuous record for each inventory item to show the inventory on hand at all times.

A **perpetual inventory system** keeps a running record of inventory on hand, with the use of computer software. This system achieves control over goods such as automobiles, jewelry, and furniture, where the loss of one item would be significant. Most businesses use the perpetual inventory system.

Even under a perpetual system, the business still counts the inventory on hand annually. The physical count establishes the correct amount of ending inventory for the financial statements and also serves as a check on the perpetual records. The following chart compares the perpetual and periodic systems:

Perpetual Inventory System	*Periodic Inventory System*
■ Keeps a running record of all goods bought and sold	■ Does not keep a running record of all goods bought and sold
■ Inventory counted at least once a year	■ Inventory counted at least once a year
■ Used for all types of goods	■ Used for inexpensive goods

WHAT THE PERPETUAL SYSTEM DOES. How does a perpetual inventory system work? Let's use an everyday situation. When you check out of a Foot Locker, a Best Buy, or a Target store, the clerk scans the bar codes on the product labels of the items you buy. Exhibit 6-4 illustrates a typical bar code. Suppose you are buying a pair of Nike cross-trainer shoes from Foot Locker. The bar code on the shoe box holds lots of information. The optical scanner reads the bar code, and the electronic signal activates the computer to perform the following operations:

Exhibit 6-4

Bar Code for Electronic Scanner

- Record the sale, debiting cash and crediting Sales Revenue.
- Update the perpetual inventory record for Nike cross-trainers, debiting Cost of Goods Sold and crediting Inventory. As you can see, this entry records cost of goods sold and keeps a running record of inventory on hand.

RECORDING TRANSACTIONS IN THE PERPETUAL SYSTEM. In the perpetual system, the business records the purchase of inventory by debiting the Inventory account. When the business makes a sale, two entries are needed. The company records the sale—debits Cash or Accounts Receivable and credits Sales Revenue for the sale price of the goods. The company must remove the goods sold from the Inventory account, so it debits Cost of Goods Sold and credits Inventory for cost. The debit to Inventory (for purchases) and the credit to Inventory (for sales) keep the perpetual record of inventory at cost.

Exhibit 6-5 page 269, shows the accounting for inventory in a perpetual system. Panel A gives the journal entries and the T-accounts, and Panel B presents the income statement and the balance sheet. All amounts are assumed. (The chapter appendix illustrates the accounting for these transactions in a periodic inventory system.)

In Exhibit 6-5, Panel A, the first entry to Inventory summarizes a lot of detail. The cost of the inventory, $560,000, is the *net* amount of the purchases, determined as follows (using assumed amounts):

Purchase price of the inventory from the seller	$600,000
+ **Freight-in** (Transportation cost to move the goods from the seller to the buyer)	4,000
− **Purchase returns** for unsuitable goods returned to the seller	(25,000)
− **Purchase allowances** granted by the seller	(5,000)
− **Purchase discounts** for early payment	(14,000)
= Net purchases of inventory	$560,000

Freight-in, purchase returns and allowances, and purchase discounts are explained starting at the bottom of page 269.

Exhibit 6-5 Recording and Reporting Inventory—Perpetual System (Amounts Assumed)

Perpetual System

PANEL A—Recording Transactions and the T-accounts

1. Purchase of inventory on account, $560,000:

Inventory	560,000	
Accounts Payable		560,000

ASSETS	=	LIABILITIES	+	STOCKHOLDERS' EQUITY
560,000	=	560,000	+	0

2. Sale of goods on account, $900,000 (cost $540,000):

Accounts Receivable	900,000	
Sales Revenue		900,000

ASSETS	=	LIABILITIES	+	STOCKHOLDERS' EQUITY	+	REVENUES
900,000	=	0			+	900,000

Cost of Goods Sold	540,000	
Inventory		540,000

ASSETS	=	LIABILITIES	+	STOCKHOLDERS' EQUITY	−	EXPENSES
−540,000	=	0			−	540,000

The T-accounts show the following:

Inventory

Debit	Credit
100,000*	540,000
560,000	
120,000	

Cost of Goods Sold

Debit	Credit
540,000	

*Beginning inventory was $100,000.

✔ Check Point 6-2

✔ Check Point 6-3

PANEL B—Reporting in the Financial Statements

Income Statement (Partial)

Sales revenue	$900,000
Cost of goods sold	540,000
Gross profit	$360,000

Ending Balance Sheet (Partial)

Current assets:	
Cash	$ XXX
Short-term investments	XXX
Accounts receivable	XXX
Inventory	120,000
Prepaid expenses	XXX

Freight-in is the transportation cost, paid by the buyer, to move goods from the seller to the buyer. Freight-in is accounted for as part of the cost of inventory.

A **purchase return** is a decrease in the cost of inventory because the buyer returned the goods to the seller. A **purchase allowance** also decreases the cost of inventory because the buyer got an allowance (a deduction) from the amount owed. Throughout this book, we often refer to net purchases simply as Purchases, as in Exhibits 6-2 and 6-3 (pp. 266 and 267).

Purchase return
A decrease in the cost of purchases because the buyer returned the goods to the seller.

Purchase allowance
A decrease in the cost of purchases because the seller has granted the buyer a subtraction (an allowance) from the amount owed.

Purchase discount
A decrease in the cost of purchases earned by making an early payment to the vendor.

A **purchase discount** is a decrease in the cost of inventory that is earned by paying quickly. A common arrangement states payment terms of 2/10 n/30. This means the buyer can take a 2% discount for payment within 10 days, with the final amount due within 30 days. In summary,

Net purchases = Purchases
− Purchase returns and allowances
− Purchase discounts
+ Freight-in

Net sales are computed exactly the same as net purchases, but with no freight-in.

Net sales = Sales revenue
− Sales returns and allowances
− Sales discounts

Freight-out paid by the seller is not part of the cost of inventory. Instead, freight-out is the expense of delivering merchandise to customers. It is Delivery Expense. (The chapter appendix shows the accounting for these same transactions in a periodic accounting system.)

Inventory Costing

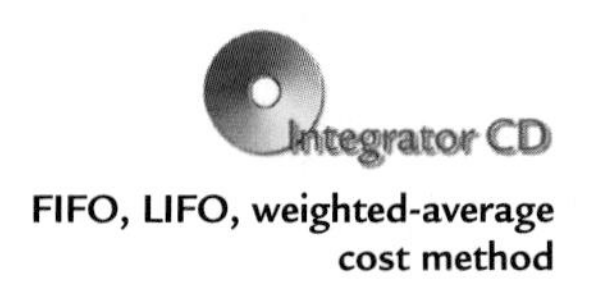

FIFO, LIFO, weighted-average cost method

Inventory provides the first situation we have studied in which a manager can decide which accounting method to use. And, as we shall see, the accounting method affects the profits to be reported and also the amount of income tax. This is why inventory is such an important topic: Inventory affects profits, taxes, and cash flow.

What Goes into Inventory Cost?

The $11 billion cost of inventory on GM's Balance sheet represents all the costs that GM incurred to bring automobiles to the point of sale. GM's cost of a Chevy Malibu would include the following costs:

- Steel
- Glass
- Plastics
- Tires
- Labor
- Factory overhead
- Shipping cost of materials purchased
- Insurance on materials while in transit

The following cost principle applies to all assets:

The cost of any asset, such as inventory, is the sum of all the costs incurred to bring the asset to its intended use.

For merchandise inventory, such as a Chevy truck, the intended use is readiness for sale. After the auto is sitting on a car lot, other costs, such as advertising and sales commissions, are expensed. These are *not* included as the cost of inventory.

DECISION: Which Inventory Method Will Help Us Accomplish Our Objectives?

Objective

3 Analyze the various inventory methods

Determining the cost of inventory is easy when the unit cost remains constant, as in Exhibit 6-2. But the unit cost usually changes. For example, prices often rise. The Hilfiger shirts that cost Macy's $30 in January may cost $32 in June and $34 in October. Suppose Macy's sells 1,000 shirts in November. How many of the Tommy shirts cost $30, how many cost $32, and how many cost $34?

To compute cost of goods sold and the cost of ending inventory still on hand, we must assign unit cost to the items. The four generally accepted inventory methods are:

1. **Specific unit cost**
2. **Weighted-average cost**
3. **First-in, first-out (FIFO) cost**
4. **Last-in, first-out (LIFO) cost**

A company can use any of these methods. As we shall see, these methods can have very different effects on reported profits, income taxes, and cash flow. Therefore, companies select their inventory method with great care.

FIFO (first-in, first-out) method Inventory costing method by which the first costs into inventory are the first costs out to cost of goods sold. Ending inventory is based on the costs of the most recent purchases.

LIFO (last-in, first-out) method Inventory costing method by which the last costs into inventory are the first costs out to cost of goods sold. This method leaves the oldest costs—those of beginning inventory and the earliest purchases of the period—in ending inventory.

SPECIFIC UNIT COST. Some businesses deal in unique inventory items, such as antique furniture, jewels, and real estate. These businesses cost their inventories at the specific cost of the particular unit. For instance, a Chevrolet dealer may have two vehicles in the showroom—a "stripped-down" model that cost $14,000 and a "loaded" model that cost $17,000. If the dealer sells the loaded model, cost of goods sold is $17,000. The stripped-down auto will be the only unit left in inventory, and so ending inventory is $14,000.

The **specific-unit-cost method** is also called the *specific identification* method. This method is too expensive to use for inventory items that have common characteristics, such as bushels of wheat, gallons of paint, or automobile tires.

Specific-unit-cost method Inventory cost method based on the specific cost of particular units of inventory.

The other inventory accounting methods—weighted-average, FIFO, and LIFO—are fundamentally different. These other methods do not use the specific cost of a particular unit. Instead, they assume different flows of costs into and out of inventory.

WEIGHTED-AVERAGE COST. The **weighted-average cost method,** often called the *average-cost method,* is based on the weighted-average cost of inventory during the period. Weighted-average cost is determined as follows:

Weighted-average cost method Inventory costing method based on the weighted average cost of inventory during the period. Weighted-average cost is determined by dividing the cost of goods available for sales by the number of units available. Also called the *average-cost method.*

$$\text{Weighted-average unit cost} = \frac{\text{Cost of goods available*}}{\text{Number of units available*}}$$

$$\begin{matrix}\text{Cost of} \\ \text{ending} \\ \text{inventory}\end{matrix} = \begin{matrix}\text{Number of units} \\ \text{on hand at the} \\ \text{end of the period}\end{matrix} \times \begin{matrix}\text{Weighted-} \\ \text{average} \\ \text{unit cost}\end{matrix}$$

Consider Deckers Outdoor Corporation, maker of the Teva sandals popular with students. Suppose Deckers has 60 units of inventory, such as hiking socks, available for sale. Ending inventory consists of 20 units, and cost of goods sold is 40 units. Panel A of Exhibit 6-6 gives the data for computing ending inventory and cost of goods sold for hiking socks.

*Beginning inventory + purchases

Note the question marks for ending inventory and cost of goods sold in Panel A. **We must compute ending inventory and cost of goods sold**. Panel B shows the computations for the various accounting methods.

Exhibit 6-6

Inventory and Cost of Goods Sold under Weighted-Average, FIFO, and LIFO Cost

PANEL A—Illustrative Data		
Beginning inventory (10 units @ $10 per unit)		$100
Purchases:		
No. 1 (25 units @ $14 per unit)	$350	
No. 2 (25 units @ $18 per unit)	450	
Total purchases		800
Cost of goods available for sale (60 units)		900
Ending inventory (20 units @ $? per unit)		?
Cost of goods sold (40 units @ $? per unit)		$?

PANEL B—Ending Inventory and Cost of Goods Sold		
Weighted-Average Cost Method		
Cost of goods available for sale—see Panel A (60 units @ average cost of $15* per unit)		$900
Ending inventory (20 units @ $15 per unit)		(300)
Cost of goods sold (40 units @ $15 per unit)		$600
FIFO Cost Method		
Cost of goods available for sale (60 units—see Panel A)		$900
Ending inventory (cost of the *last* 20 units available):		
20 units @ $18 per unit (from purchase No. 2)		(360)
Cost of goods sold (cost of the *first* 40 units available):		
10 units @ $10 per unit (all of beginning inventory)	$100	
25 units @ $14 per unit (all of purchase No. 1)	350	
5 units @ $18 per unit (from purchase No. 2)	90	
Cost of goods sold		$540
LIFO Cost Method		
Cost of goods available for sale (60 units—see Panel A)		$900
Ending inventory (cost of the *first* 20 units available):		
10 units @ $10 per unit (all of beginning inventory)	$100	
10 units @ $14 per unit (from purchase No. 1)	140	
Ending inventory		(240)
Cost of goods sold (cost of the *last* 40 units available):		
25 units @ $18 per unit (all of purchase No. 2)	$450	
15 units @ $14 per unit (from purchase No. 1)	210	
Cost of goods sold		$660

*Cost of goods available for sale, $900 / Number of units available for sale, 60 = Average cost per unit, $15

✔ Check Point 6-4

✔ Check Point 6-5

✔ Check Point 6-6

✔ Check Point 6-7

FIFO COST. Under the FIFO method, the first costs into inventory are the first costs out to cost of goods sold—hence, the name *first-in, first-out*. Ending inventory is always based on the latest costs of purchases. In Exhibit 6-6, the FIFO cost of ending inventory is $360. Cost of goods sold is, therefore, $540 because the cost of goods available is $900. Panel A gives the data, and Panel B shows the FIFO computation.

LIFO COST. The LIFO method is the opposite of FIFO. Under LIFO, the last costs into inventory are always the first costs out to cost of goods sold. LIFO, therefore, leaves in ending inventory the oldest costs—beginning inventory *plus* the earliest purchases. In Exhibit 6-6, the LIFO cost of ending inventory is $240. Cost of goods sold is, therefore, $660.

Income Effects of FIFO, LIFO, and Weighted-Average Cost

In our Deckers example, the cost of inventory rose from $10 to $14 to $18 during the period. When inventory unit costs change this way, the various inventory methods (FIFO, LIFO, average) produce different cost-of-goods-sold and ending inventory figures, as Exhibit 6-6 shows. ***When inventory unit costs are increasing,***

- FIFO ending inventory is *highest* because it is priced at the most recent costs, which are the highest.
- LIFO ending inventory is *lowest* because it is priced at the oldest costs, which are the lowest.

When inventory unit costs are decreasing,

- FIFO ending inventory is *lowest.*
- LIFO ending inventory is *highest.*

Exhibit 6-7 summarizes the income effects (sales − cost of goods sold = gross profit) of the three inventory methods, using the data from Exhibit 6-6 (remember that prices are rising). Study the exhibit carefully, focusing on ending inventory, cost of goods sold, and gross profit.

Exhibit 6-7

Income Effects of the FIFO, LIFO, and Weighted-Average Inventory Methods (Data from Exhibit 6–6)

	FIFO		LIFO		Weighted Average	
Sales revenue (assumed)		$1,000		$1,000		$1,000
Cost of goods sold:						
Goods available for sale	$900		$900		$900	
Ending inventory	(360)		(240)		(300)	
Cost of goods sold		540		660		600
Gross profit		$ 460		$ 340		$ 400

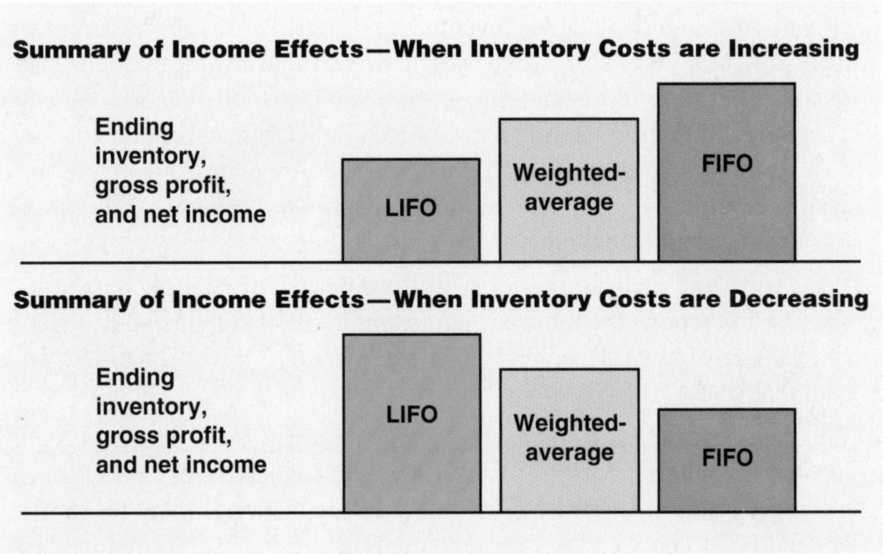

Summary of Income Effects—When Inventory Costs are Increasing

Ending inventory, gross profit, and net income	LIFO	Weighted-average	FIFO

Summary of Income Effects—When Inventory Costs are Decreasing

Ending inventory, gross profit, and net income	LIFO	Weighted-average	FIFO

Tax Advantage of LIFO

Objective

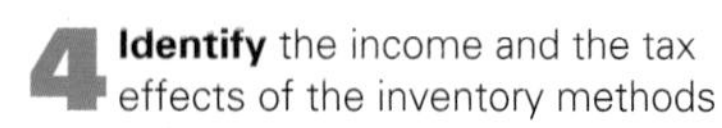

4 **Identify** the income and the tax effects of the inventory methods

Inventory methods directly affect income taxes, which must be paid and thus affect cash flow. When prices are rising, LIFO results in the *lowest taxable income* and thus the *lowest income taxes*. Let's use the gross profit data of Exhibit 6-7 to illustrate.

	FIFO	*LIFO*
Gross profit	$460	$340
Operating expenses (assumed)	260	260
Income before income tax	$200	$ 80
Income tax expense (40%)	$ 80	$ 32

✔ Check Point 6-7

Income tax expense is lowest under LIFO ($32) and highest under FIFO ($80). The most attractive feature of LIFO is low income tax payments, which is why about one-third of all companies use this method. During periods of inflation, many companies prefer LIFO for its tax and cash-flow advantage. Exhibit 6-8, based on an American Institute of Certified Public Accountants (AICPA) survey of 600 companies, indicates that FIFO remains the most popular inventory method.

If LIFO is so popular because it saves on income tax, then why do more companies use the FIFO method (see Exhibit 6-8)? There are two main reasons: What are they?

Answer:

1. Some companies prefer to report higher profits, which FIFO provides when prices are rising.
2. Some companies are in declining-cost industries. These companies, therefore, use FIFO to save on income taxes.

Actually there's also a third reason for FIFO's popularity. When prices aren't changing much, FIFO, LIFO, and average cost all produce similar results. FIFO is much less expensive to apply in actual practice.

Exhibit 6-8

Use of the Various Inventory Methods

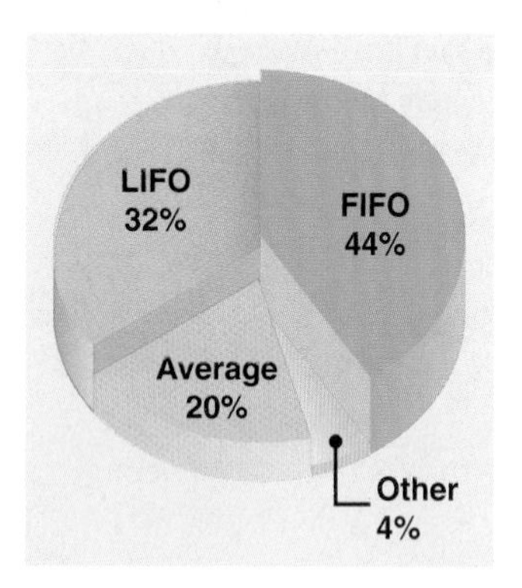

Comparison of the Inventory Methods

Let's compare the weighted-average, FIFO, and LIFO inventory methods.

1. How well does each method measure income by matching inventory expense—cost of goods sold—against revenue? LIFO results in the most realistic net income figure. LIFO best matches the current value of cost of goods sold with revenue because it assigns the most recent inventory costs to expense. Therefore, LIFO produces the cost-of-goods-sold figure closest to what it would cost to replace these goods. In contrast, FIFO matches old inventory costs against revenue—a poor matching of expense with revenue. FIFO income is less realistic than income under LIFO.
2. Which method reports the most up-to-date inventory cost on the balance sheet? FIFO reports the most current inventory cost on the balance sheet. LIFO can value inventory at very old costs because LIFO leaves the oldest prices in ending inventory.
3. What effects do the methods have on income taxes? LIFO results in the lowest income tax when prices are *rising*. Taxes are highest under FIFO, but when inventory prices are *decreasing*, income taxes are highest under LIFO and lowest under FIFO. The weighted-average method produces amounts between the extremes of LIFO and FIFO.

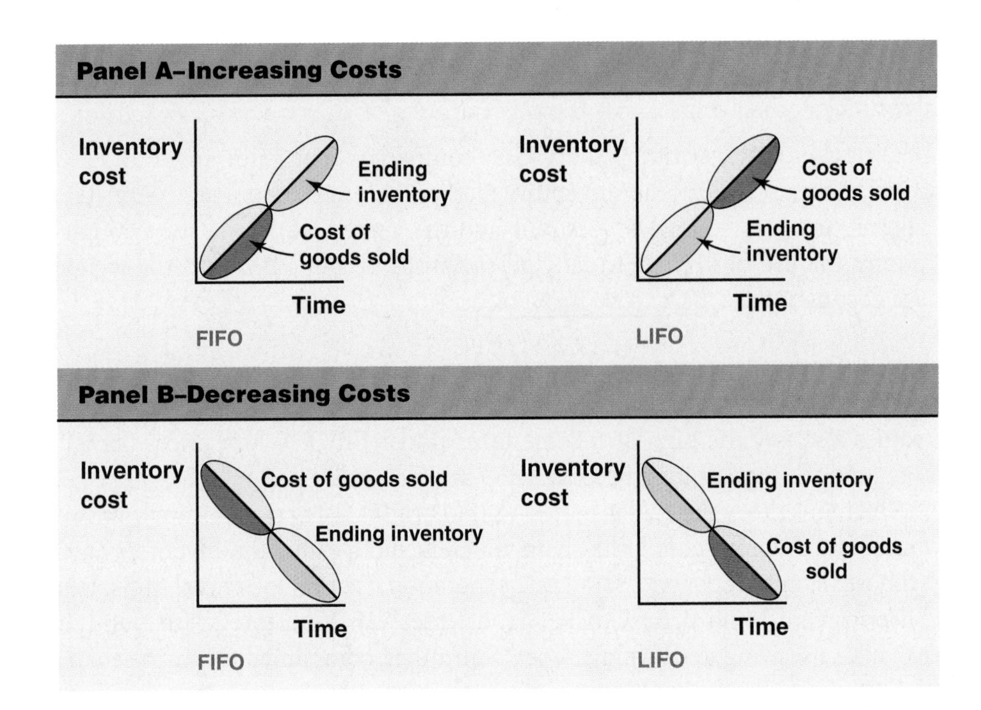

Exhibit 6-9

Cost of Goods Sold and Ending Inventory—FIFO and LIFO Increasing Costs and Decreasing Costs

Exhibit 6-9 graphs the flow of costs under FIFO and LIFO during both increasing costs (Panel A) and decreasing costs (Panel B). Study this exhibit carefully; it will help you *really* understand FIFO and LIFO.

FIFO PRODUCES INVENTORY PROFITS. FIFO overstates income by so-called inventory profit during periods of inflation. **Inventory profit** is the difference between gross profit figured on the FIFO basis and gross profit under LIFO. Exhibit 6-7 (p. 273) illustrates inventory profit. The $120 difference between FIFO and LIFO gross profits ($460 − $340) is called *FIFO inventory profit*. It is viewed as misleading because the replacement cost of the merchandise sold is closer to LIFO ($660) than to the FIFO amount ($540).

Inventory profit
Difference between gross margin figured on the FIFO basis and gross margin figured on the LIFO basis.

LIFO AND MANAGING REPORTED INCOME. LIFO allows managers to manipulate net income by timing their purchases of inventory. When inventory prices are rising rapidly and a company wants to show less income (to pay less taxes), managers can buy a large amount of inventory near the end of the year. Under LIFO, these high inventory costs become cost of goods sold immediately. As a result, net income is decreased. If the business is having a bad year, management may need to report higher income. They can delay the purchase of high-cost inventory until next year and avoid decreasing the current year's reported income. In the process, the company draws down inventory quantities, a practice known as *LIFO inventory liquidation*.

✔ Check Point 6-8

LIFO LIQUIDATION. When LIFO is used and inventory quantities fall below the level of the previous period, the situation is called *LIFO liquidation*. To compute cost of goods sold, the company must dip into older layers of inventory cost. Under LIFO and when prices are rising, that action shifts older, lower costs into cost of goods sold. The result is higher net income. Managers try to avoid LIFO liquidation because it increases income taxes.

Owens-Corning, the world's leading supplier of glass fiber materials, reported that LIFO liquidations added $2.7 million to its net income. As a result,

Owens-Corning had to pay more income tax. For this reason, companies that use LIFO try to avoid inventory liquidations.

INTERNATIONAL PERSPECTIVE. Many U.S. companies that value inventory by the LIFO method must use another inventory method in foreign countries. Why? LIFO is not allowed in some countries. Australia and the United Kingdom, for example, do not permit the use of LIFO. Virtually all countries permit FIFO and the weighted-average cost method.

HIGHER INCOME OR LOWER TAXES? Most companies want to report the highest income, and (as we've seen) FIFO meets this need when prices are rising. But those companies also pay the highest income taxes under FIFO. When prices are falling, LIFO reports the highest income, and FIFO saves on taxes.

Which inventory method is better—LIFO or FIFO? There is no single answer to this question. Different companies have different motives for the inventory method they choose. Home Depot and Sara Lee Corporation use FIFO. General Mills, famous for Cheerios cereal and Betty Crocker foods, uses LIFO. Motorola, Inc., and Texas Instruments use weighted-average cost. Still other companies use more than one method. PepsiCo, Inc. uses all three.

Mid-Chapter Summary Problem

Suppose a division of IBM Corporation that handles computer components has these inventory records for January 20X6:

Date	Item	Quantity	Unit Cost
Jan. 1	Beginning inventory	100 units	$ 8
6	Purchase	60 units	9
21	Purchase	150 units	9
27	Purchase	90 units	10

Company accounting records reveal that operating expense for January was $1,900, and sales of 310 units generated sales revenue of $6,770.

Required

1. Prepare the January income statement, showing amounts for FIFO, LIFO, and weighted-average cost. Label the bottom line "Operating income." (Round figures to whole-dollar amounts.) Show your computations, and use the model in Exhibit 6-2, page 266, to compute cost of goods sold.
2. Suppose you are the financial vice president of IBM. Which inventory method will you use if your motive is to
   a. Minimize income taxes?
   b. Report the highest operating income?
   c. Report operating income between the extremes of FIFO and LIFO?
   d. Report inventory on the balance sheet at the most current cost?
   e. Attain the best measure of net income for the income statement?

   State the reason for each of your answers.

Answers

Requirement 1

IBM Corporation

Income Statement for Component
Month Ended January 31, 20X6

	FIFO		LIFO		Weighted Average	
Sales revenue		$6,770		$6,770		$6,770
Cost of goods sold:						
Beginning inventory	$ 800		$ 800		$ 800	
Purchases	2,790		2,790		2,790	
Cost of goods available for sale	3,590		3,590		3,590	
Ending inventory	(900)		(720)		(808)	
Cost of goods sold		2,690		2,870		2,782
Gross profit		4,080		3,900		3,988
Operating expenses		1,900		1,900		1,900
Operating income		$2,180		$2,000		$2,088

Computations

Beginning inventory: 100 × $8 = $800

Purchases: (60 × $9) + (150 × $9) + (90 × $10) = $2,790

Ending inventory—FIFO: 90* × $10 = $900

LIFO: 90 × $8 = $720

Weighted-average: 90 × $8.975** = $808 (rounded from $807.75)

*Number of units in ending inventory = 100 + 60 + 150 + 90 − 310 = 90
**$3,590/400 units† = $8.975 per unit
†Number of units available = 100 + 60 + 150 + 90 = 400

Requirement 2

a. Use LIFO to minimize income taxes. Operating income under LIFO is lowest when inventory unit costs are increasing, as they are in this case (from $8 to $10). (If inventory costs were decreasing, income under FIFO would be lowest.)
b. Use FIFO to report the highest operating income. Income under FIFO is highest when inventory unit costs are increasing, as in this situation.
c. Use weighted-average cost to report an operating income amount between the FIFO and LIFO extremes. This is true in this situation and in others when inventory unit costs are increasing or decreasing.
d. Use FIFO to report inventory on the balance sheet at the most current cost. The oldest inventory costs are expensed as cost of goods sold, leaving in ending inventory the most recent (most current) costs of the period.
e. Use LIFO to attain the best measure of net income. LIFO produces the best matching of current expense with current revenue. The most recent (most current) inventory costs are expensed as cost of goods sold.

Accounting Principles and Inventories

lower of cost or market

Several accounting principles have special relevance to inventories:

- Consistency
- Disclosure
- Materiality
- Conservatism

Consistency Principle

Consistency principle
A business must use the same accounting methods and procedures from period to period.

The **consistency principle** states that businesses should use the same accounting methods and procedures from period to period. Consistency enables investors to compare a company's financial statements from one period to the next.

Suppose you are analyzing Interfax Corporation's net income pattern over a 2-year period. Suppose Interfax switched from LIFO to FIFO during that time. Its net income increased dramatically, but only because of the change in inventory method. If you did not know of the change, you might believe that Interfax's income increased due to improved operations, which is not the case.

The consistency principle does not mean that a company may never change its accounting methods. However, a company making an accounting change must disclose the effect of the change on net income. American-Saudi Oil Company, Inc., disclosed the following in a note to its annual report:

EXCERPT FROM NOTE 6 OF THE FINANCIAL STATEMENTS
. . . American-Saudi changed its method of accounting for the cost of crude oil . . . from the FIFO method to the LIFO method. The company believes that the LIFO method better matches current costs with current revenues. . . . The change decreased the 20X1 net income . . . by $3 million. . . .

Answer these questions about American-Saudi's accounting change. Assume there was no effect on American-Saudi's beginning inventory. Give your reason for each answer.

1. Did the accounting change (from FIFO to LIFO) increase or decrease ending inventory, cost of goods sold? gross profit? income taxes?
2. Were inventory costs increasing or decreasing at the time of American-Saudi's accounting change?

Answers:

1. The change in inventory method
   a. Decreased ending inventory
   b. Increased cost of goods sold
   c. Decreased gross profit
   d. Decreased income taxes

Effects of the Accounting Change

Sales revenue	No effect
Cost of goods sold	
Beginning inventory	No effect
+ Purchases	No effect
= Goods available for sale	No effect
− Ending inventory	↓
= Cost of goods sold	↑
Gross profit	↓
Income tax expense	↓
Net income	↓

For reasons, see "The Effects of the Accounting Change" above. Start with ending inventory and work your way down the income statement.

2. Inventory costs were rising at the time of the change from FIFO to LIFO. We know this because net income decreased. This can occur only when prices are rising (see Exhibit 6-9, Panel A, under LIFO).

Disclosure principle
A business's financial statements must report enough information for outsiders to make knowledgeable decisions about the business. The company should report relevant, reliable, and comparable information about its economic affairs.

Disclosure Principle

The **disclosure principle** holds that a company's financial statements should report enough information for outsiders to make informed decisions about the company.

The company should report *relevant, reliable*, and *comparable* information about itself. That means disclosing inventory accounting methods. Without knowledge of the accounting method, for example, a banker could make an unwise lending decision. Suppose the banker is comparing two companies—one using LIFO and the other, FIFO. The FIFO company reports higher net income, but only because it uses the FIFO method. Without knowing this, the banker could loan money to the wrong business.

Materiality Concept

The **materiality concept** states that a company must perform strictly proper accounting only for items that are significant to the business. Information is significant—or, in accounting terms, *material*—when knowledge of the information would change a decision. Immaterial items justify less-than-perfect accounting because they would not affect anything significantly. The materiality concept frees accountants from having to report every last item in detail and reduces the cost of accounting.

Materiality concept
A company must perform strictly proper accounting only for items and transactions that are significant to the business's financial statements.

How does a business draw the line between the material and the immaterial? This decision depends on how large the business is. Take Wendy's, the fast-food chain. Wendy's has over $500 million in assets. Wendy's management would likely treat as immaterial a $100 loss of food due to theft. Wendy's would of course try to prevent the theft, but the company wouldn't report such a small loss in its financial statements.

Accounting Conservatism

Conservatism in accounting means reporting financial statement amounts that paint the gloomiest immediate picture of the company. This happens when there are alternative ways to account for an item. What advantage does conservatism give a business? Managers must look on the bright side; for example, company press releases often highlight successes but don't focus on problem areas. Many accountants regard conservatism as a counterbalance to management's optimistic tendencies. The goal is to present reliable data.

Conservatism
The accounting concept by which the least favorable figures are presented in the financial statements.

Conservatism appears in accounting guidelines such as "anticipate no gains, but provide for all probable losses" and "if in doubt, record an asset at the lowest reasonable amount and report a liability at the highest reasonable amount." Conservatism directs accountants to decrease the accounting value of an asset if it appears unrealistically high. Assume that Texas Instruments paid $35,000 for inventory that has become outdated and whose current value is only $12,000. Conservatism dictates that Texas Instruments record a $23,000 loss immediately and write the inventory down to $12,000.

Lower-of-Cost-or-Market Rule

The **lower-of-cost-or-market rule** (abbreviated as **LCM**) is based on accounting conservatism. LCM requires that inventory be reported in the financial statements at whichever is lower—its historical cost or its market value. Applied to inventories, *market value* generally means *current replacement cost* (that is, how much the business would have to pay now to replace its inventory.) If the replacement cost of inventory falls below its historical cost, the business must write down the value of its goods to market value. The business reports ending inventory at its LCM value on the balance sheet. All this can be done automatically by a computerized accounting system. How is the write-down accomplished?

Lower-of-cost-or-market (LCM) rule
Requires that an asset be reported in the financial statements at whichever is lower—its historical cost or its market value (current replacement cost for inventory).

Suppose Intel Corporation paid $3,000 for inventory on September 26. By December 31, its value has fallen. The inventory can now be replaced for $2,200. Intel's December 31 balance sheet must report this inventory at LCM value of $2,200. Exhibit 6-10 presents the effects of LCM on the balance sheet and the income statement. The exhibit shows that the *lower* of cost ($3,000) or market value ($2,200) is the relevant amount for valuing inventory on the balance sheet. An LCM write-down decreases the Inventory account and increases Cost of Goods Sold.

Exhibit 6-10

Lower-of-Cost-or-Market (LCM) Effects

Balance Sheet

Current assets:	
Cash	$ XXX
Short-term investments	XXX
Accounts receivable	XXX
Inventories, at market (which is lower than $3,000 cost)	2,200
Prepaid expenses	XXX
Total current assets	$X,XXX

Income Statement

Sales revenue		$20,000
Cost of goods sold:		
Beginning inventory (LCM = Cost)	$ 2,800	
Purchases	11,000	
Cost of goods available for sale	13,800	
Ending inventory—		
Cost = $3,000; Replacement cost (market value) = $2,200		
LCM = Market	(2,200)	
Cost of goods sold		11,600
Gross profit		$ 8,400

✔ Check Point 6-9

Companies disclose LCM in notes to their financial statements, as shown here for Intel:

NOTE 1: ACCOUNTING POLICIES

■ **Inventories.** Inventories are stated at the *lower of cost* or *market*. [Emphasis added.]

LCM is not optional. It is required by GAAP.

Effects of Inventory Errors

Objective

5 **Show** how inventory errors affect cost of goods sold and income

Businesses count their inventories at the end of the period, and errors may occur. The period 1 segment of Exhibit 6-11 shows that an error in the ending inventory creates, errors for cost of goods sold and gross profit. Examine period 1, in which ending inventory is overstated by $5,000. Cost of goods sold is understated by $5,000. Then compare period 1 with period 3, which is correct. *Period 1 should look exactly like period 3.*

Recall that period 1's ending inventory becomes period 2's beginning amount. Thus, the error in period 1 carries over into period 2. Trace the ending inventory of $15,000 from period 1 to period 2. Then compare periods 2 and 3. *Period 2 should also look exactly like period 3.* All the amounts in color in Exhibit 6-11 are incorrect.

Exhibit 6-11 **Inventory Errors: An Example**

	Period 1		Period 2		Period 3	
	Ending Inventory Overstated by $5,000		*Beginning Inventory Overstated by $5,000*		*Correct*	
Sales revenue		$100,000		$100,000		$100,000
Cost of goods sold:						
Beginning inventory	$10,000		$ 15,000		$10,000	
Purchases	50,000		50,000		50,000	
Cost of goods available for sale	60,000		65,000		60,000	
Ending inventory	(15,000)		(10,000)		(10,000)	
Cost of goods sold		45,000		55,000		50,000
Gross profit		$ 55,000		$ 45,000		$ 50,000
			$ 100,000			

Source: The authors thank Carl High for this example.

Beginning inventory and ending inventory have opposite effects on cost of goods sold (beginning is added; ending is subtracted). Therefore, after two periods, an inventory accounting error washes out of the financial statements (counterbalances) as illustrated in Exhibit 6-11. Notice that total gross profit for periods 1 and 2 combined is correct ($100,000) even though each year's gross profit is wrong by $5,000.

✔ Check Point 6-10

✔ Check Point 6-11

Inventory errors cannot be ignored simply because they counterbalance. Suppose you are analyzing trends in Intel's operations. Exhibit 6-11 shows a drop in gross profit from period 1 to period 2, followed by an increase in period 3. Did Intel really get worse and then better again? No, that picture of operations is inaccurate because of the accounting error. The correct gross profit is $50,000 for each period. We must have accurate information for all periods. Exhibit 6-12 summarizes the effects of inventory accounting errors.

Exhibit 6-12 **Effects of Inventory Errors**

	Period 1		Period 2	
Inventory Error	*Cost of Goods Sold*	*Gross Profit and Net Income*	*Cost of Goods Sold*	*Gross Profit and Net Income*
Period 1 Ending inventory overstated	Understated	Overstated	Overstated	Understated
Period 1 Ending inventory understated	Overstated	Understated	Understated	Overstated

Inventory and the Financial Statements

Detailed Income Statement

inventory turnover

Exhibit 6-13 brings the chapter together by providing an example of a detailed income statement. This example fits all the pieces of the inventory puzzle together. Study it carefully.

Analyzing Financial Statements

Objective

6 **Use** the gross profit percentage and inventory turnover to evaluate a business

Owners, managers, and investors use ratios to evaluate a business. Two ratios relate directly to inventory: the gross profit percentage and inventory turnover.

Exhibit 6-13

Detailed Income Statement

Silicon Valley Software Company

Income Statement
Year Ended December 31, 20XX

Sales revenue		$100,000	
Less: Sales discounts		(2,000)	
Sales returns and allowances		(3,000)	
Net sales			$95,000*
Cost of goods sold:			
Beginning inventory		$ 10,000	
Purchases	$49,000		
Less: Purchase discounts	(1,000)		
Purchase returns and allowances	(4,000)		
Freight-in	3,000		
Net purchases		47,000	
Cost of goods available for sale		57,000	
Ending inventory		(12,000)	
Cost of goods sold			45,000**
Gross profit			50,000
Operating expenses:			
Selling:			
Sales commission expense		$ 5,000	
Freight-out (delivery expense)		1,000	
Other expenses (detailed)		6,000	12,000
Administrative:			
Salary expense		$ 2,000	
Depreciation expense		2,000	
Other expenses (detailed)		4,000	8,000
Income before income tax			30,000
Income tax expense (40%)			12,000
Net income			$18,000

*Most companies report only the net sales figure, $95,000.
**Most companies report only the cost of goods sold total, $45,000.

Gross margin percentage Gross margin divided by net sales revenue. Also called the *gross profit percentage*.

GROSS PROFIT PERCENTAGE. Gross profit—sales minus cost of goods sold—is a key indicator of a company's ability to sell its inventory at a profit. Merchandisers strive to increase their **gross profit percentage**, also called the **gross margin percentage**, which is computed as follows for General Motors Corporation. Data (in billions) are taken from Exhibit 6-1, page 265.

$$\text{Gross profit percentage} = \frac{\text{Gross profit}}{\text{Net sales revenue}} = \frac{\$39}{\$185} = .211 = 21.1\%$$

The gross profit (or gross margin) percentage is a measure of profitability. It is one of the most carefully watched profitability measures by both managers and investors. A 21% gross margin means that each dollar of sales generates 21 cents of gross profit. On average, cost of goods sold by GM consumes 79 cents of each sales dollar. For most firms, the gross profit percentage changes little from year to year, so a small downturn may signal an important drop in net income.

GM's gross profit percentage of 21% compares favorably with other automakers. By contrast, the average gross profit percentage is 48% for Texas Instruments, which makes computer chips and 61% for PepsiCo the soft drink and snack food company. Exhibit 6-14 compares General Motors' gross profit percentage to that of PepsiCo, Inc.

Exhibit 6-14

Gross Profit on $1.00 of Sales for Two Merchandisers

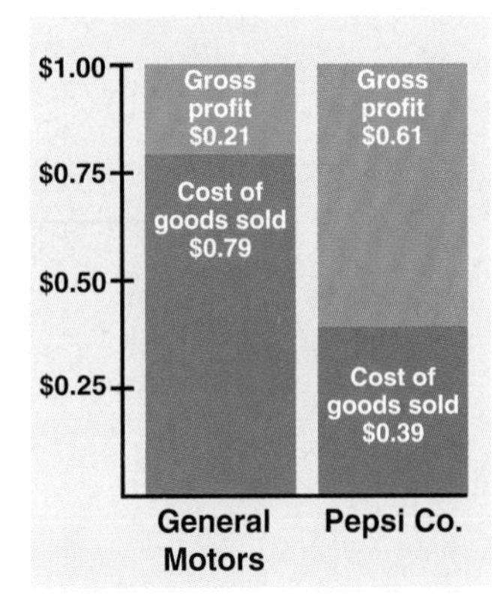

INVENTORY TURNOVER GM strives to sell its inventory as quickly as possible because automobiles generate no profit until they are sold. The faster the sales, the higher the company's income, and vice versa for slow-moving goods. Ideally, a business could operate with zero inventory, but most businesses must keep some goods on hand. **Inventory turnover,** the ratio of cost of goods sold to average inventory, indicates how rapidly inventory is sold. Its computation for GM follows (data in billions from Exhibit 6-1, page 265):

$$\text{Inventory turnover} = \frac{\text{Cost of goods sold}}{\text{Average inventory}} = \frac{\text{Cost of goods sold}}{\left(\begin{array}{c}\text{Beginning} \\ \text{inventory}\end{array} + \begin{array}{c}\text{Ending} \\ \text{inventory}\end{array}\right) \div 2}$$

$$= \frac{\$146}{(\$11 + 11)/2} = \begin{array}{c}\text{13.3 times per year} \\ \text{(every 27 days)}\end{array}$$

Inventory turnover
Ratio of cost of goods sold to average inventory. Indicates how rapidly inventory is sold.

The inventory turnover statistic shows how many times the company sold (or turned over) its average level of inventory during the year. Inventory turnover varies from industry to industry.

GM and the other automakers turn their inventory over rapidly. When sales of Saturns are hot, GM can manufacture a car and get it to a dealer in less than a month. When sales are slow, GM halts production for a while. This flexibility is possible because the automakers use just-in-time production systems.

In a **just-in-time system,** suppliers bring body frames, windshields, and other components to the GM assembly plant hours (or minutes) before production begins. The just-in-time system enables GM to keep inventories low, and that speeds up turnover, keeps expenses low, and beefs up profits.

Just-in-time system
A system in which a company schedules production just in time to satisfy needs. Materials are purchased and finished goods are completed only as needed to satisfy customer demand.

Department stores such as Lord and Taylor, specialty retailers such as Pier 1 Imports, and discounters Wal-Mart and Target must keep lots of inventory on hand. As a result, their inventory turnover is slower than GM's. Wal-Mart, the largest retail chain in the United States, has a turnover rate of 7 times per year, and for Pier 1, turnover is around 3 times a year.

✔ Check Point 6-12

Calculate inventory turnover for Pier 1 Imports (amounts in millions):

Beginning inventory	$ 269
Ending inventory	311
Purchases	859
Sales	1,411

Answer:

$$\text{Inventory turnover} = \frac{\text{Cost of goods sold*}}{\text{Average inventory**}}$$

$$= \frac{\$817}{\$290} = \text{2.8 times per year}$$

*$269 + $859 − $311 = $817

**($269 + $311) ÷ 2 = $290

Note: Sales revenue is not used to compute inventory turnover.

Reporting Transactions on the Statement of Cash Flows

Let's return once again to the GM example. In addition to the income statement and the balance sheet, GM publishes a statement of cash flows at the end of the year. Examine the GM income statement and balance sheet data on page 263. The income statement shows GM's revenues, cost of sales, and gross profit. The balance sheet reports the company's assets.

But how much cash did GM spend on inventory during the year? How much cash did the company collect from customers? Did operations provide a net cash inflow, as they should for a successful company, or were operating activities a drain on cash? Only the statement of cash flows answers these questions.

Inventory transactions are *operating activities* because the purchase and sale of merchandise drive a company's operations. The purchase of inventory requires a cash payment, and a sale results in a cash receipt. In Chapter 12 we will see how to compute cash receipts and cash payments for inventory transactions.

Additional Inventory Issues

gross profit method

Estimating Inventory: Gross Profit Method

Often a business must *estimate* the value of its goods. A fire may destroy inventory, and to file an insurance claim the business must estimate the value of its loss. In this case, the business must estimate the value of ending inventory because it cannot count it.

Gross margin method
A way to estimate inventory based on a rearrangement of the cost-of-goods-sold model: Beginning inventory + net purchases = Cost of goods available for sale. Cost of goods sold = Ending inventory. Also called *gross profit method.*

The **gross profit method**, also known as the **gross margin method**, is a widely used way to estimate ending inventory. This method uses the familiar cost-of-goods-sold model.

Beginning inventory
+ Purchases
= Cost of goods available for sale
− Ending inventory
= Cost of goods sold

We rearrange *ending inventory* and *cost of goods sold* as follows. Exhibit 6-15 gives a visual picture of the gross profit method.

Exhibit 6-15

Estimating Ending Inventory

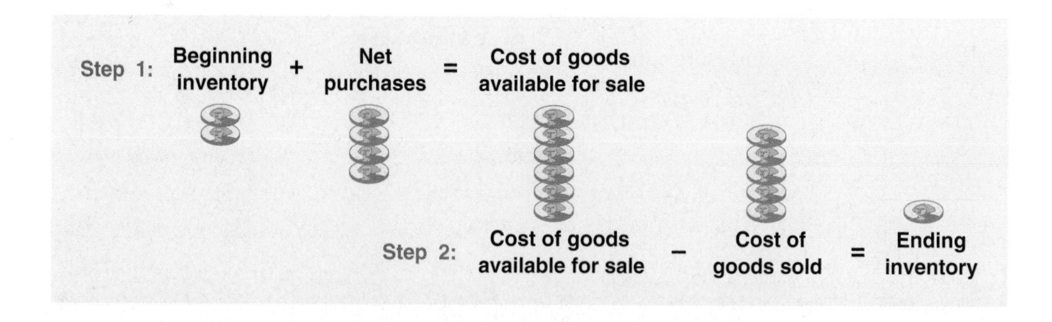

Suppose a fire destroys some of Sara Lee Corporation's food inventory. To collect insurance, Sara Lee must estimate the cost of the ending inventory. Beginning inventory, net purchases, and net sales up to the date of the fire can be taken directly from the accounting records. Using Sara Lee's actual *gross profit rate* of 42% (that is, gross profit divided by net sales), you can estimate cost of goods sold. Then subtract cost of goods sold from goods available to estimate ending inventory. Exhibit 6-16 shows the calculations for the gross profit method.

Exhibit 6-16

Gross Profit Method of Estimating Inventory (amounts assumed)

Beginning inventory		$14,000
Purchases		66,000
Cost of goods available for sale		80,000
Cost of goods sold:		
Net sales revenue	$100,000	
Less estimated gross profit of 42%	(42,000)	
Estimated cost of goods sold		58,000
Estimated cost of *ending inventory*		$22,000

✔ Check Point 6-13

Accountants, managers, and auditors use the gross profit method to test the reasonableness of an ending inventory amount determined by a physical count. This method also helps to detect large errors.

Beginning inventory is $70,000, net purchases total $365,000, and net sales are $500,000. With a normal gross profit rate of 30% of sales, how much is ending inventory?

Answer:

$85,000 = [$70,000 + $365,000 − (0.70 × $500,000)]

Ethical Considerations

No area of accounting has a deeper ethical dimension than inventory. Managers of companies whose profits do not meet stockholder expectations are sometimes tempted to "cook the books" to increase reported income. The increase in reported income may lead investors and creditors into thinking the business is more successful than it really is.

What do managers hope to gain from fraudulent accounting? In some cases, they are trying to keep their jobs. In other cases, their bonuses are tied to reported income: the higher the company's net income, the higher the managers' bonuses. There are two main schemes for cooking the books. The easiest is simply to overstate ending inventory. The upward-pointing arrows in the accounting equation indicate an overstatement—reporting more assets and equity than are actually present:

ASSETS	=	LIABILITIES	+	STOCKHOLDERS' EQUITY
↑	=	0	+	↑

The second way of using inventory to cook the books involves sales revenue. Sales schemes are more complex than overstating ending inventory. Consider two examples of real companies. Datapoint Corporation and MiniScribe, both computer-related companies, were charged with creating fictitious sales to boost reported profits. Datapoint is alleged to have hired drivers to transport its inventory around San Antonio so that the goods could not be physically counted. Datapoint tried to show that the goods had been sold. The scheme fell apart when the trucks returned the goods to Datapoint's warehouse, and Datapoint had unrealistic amounts of sales returns. What would you think of a company with $10 million in sales and $3 million of sales returns? No company produces that many defective computers.

MiniScribe is alleged to have shipped boxes of bricks labeled as computer parts to customers right before year end. The bogus transactions increased the company's sales by $4 million—but only temporarily. The scheme boomeranged when MiniScribe had to record the returns. In virtually every area, accounting imposes a discipline that brings frauds to light.

✔ Check Point 6-14

The Decision Guidelines feature summarizes the situations that call for a particular inventory accounting system and the motivation for using each costing method.

Decision Guidelines

INVENTORY MANAGEMENT

PetSmart Tropical Fish stocks two basic categories of merchandise:

- Tropical fish, which are unique
- Prepackaged pet foods and supplies

Jacob Stiles, the owner of PetSmart, is considering how accounting will affect the business. Let's examine several decisions that Stiles must make to achieve his goals for PetSmart.

Decision	Guidelines	System or Method
Which inventory system to use?	• Expensive merchandise • Cannot control inventory by visual inspection	Perpetual system for the prepackaged pet foods and supplies
	• Can control inventory by visual inspection	Periodic system for the tropical fish
Which costing method to use?	• Unique inventory items	Specific unit cost for the tropical fish because they are unique
	• Most current cost of ending inventory • Maximizes reported income when costs are rising	FIFO (Pick one of these methods for prepackaged inventory)
	• Most current measure of cost of goods sold and net income • Minimizes income tax when costs are rising	LIFO (Pick one of these methods for prepackaged inventory)
	• Middle-of-the-road approach for income tax and reported income	Weighted-average (Pick one of these methods for prepackaged inventory)

Excel Application Problem

Goal: Create an Excel spreadsheet that will compare gross profit, ending inventory, and cost of goods sold under the LIFO, FIFO, and weighted-average methods of inventory valuation.

Scenario: John Kalinich, Chief Operations Officer at Teva Sport Sandals in Flagstaff, Arizona, has a decision to make. He's in charge of Teva's online store, and is responsible for the inventory sold through the Web. John must decide which inventory method to use for the business.

Your task is to create a spreadsheet and embedded graph that compares gross profit, ending inventory, and cost of goods sold under three methods: weighted-average, FIFO, and LIFO. John has provided the following data from the most recent month of operations for your use in creating the spreadsheet:

July 1	Beginning inventory	2,000 units @ $30.00 cost per unit
July 6	Purchase	600 units @ $31.25 cost per unit
July 17	Purchase	400 units @ $33.50 cost per unit
July 28	Purchase	200 units @ $34.75 cost per unit
Sales for July:		1,800 pairs of sandals sold @ $69.00 each

After you have prepared your spreadsheet, answer these questions:

1. Which method produces the lowest cost of goods sold? Why?
2. Which method produces the lowest ending inventory? Why?
3. If John Kalinich wants to maximize gross profit for Teva, which method should he choose? Does this method do a good job of matching inventory expense (cost of goods sold) to sales revenue?

Step-by-step:

1. Open a new Excel spreadsheet.
2. Create a heading for your spreadsheet that contains the following:
   a. Chapter 6 Decision Guidelines
   b. Inventory Management
   c. Teva Sport Sandals
   d. Today's date
3. At the top of your spreadsheet, create a "Data Section" for the July data provided by John Kalinich. Set up columns for Date, Activity ("Beginning Inventory," "Purchases," "Goods Available for Sale," "Sales," and "Ending Inventory"), Units, Unit Cost, and Total Cost. Compute goods available for sale and ending inventory.
4. Include the calculation for "average unit cost" on a separate row in this section.
5. Next, create a section titled "Inventory Method Comparison" in bold print and underlined. Include one column for each method (weighted-average, FIFO, and LIFO). Include rows for Ending Inventory, Cost of Goods Sold, and Gross Profit. Format as necessary. Be sure your calculations are based on the "Data Section" figures. Do not "hard code" any amounts in this section.
6. When done, create an embedded bar chart underneath the "Inventory Method Comparison" section that compares Gross Profit, Ending Inventory, and Cost of Goods Sold for all three methods. (Hint: use the Chart Wizard button on the Standard Excel toolbar.)
7. Save your spreadsheet, and print a copy for your files.

End-of-Chapter Summary Problem

Mesa Hardware Company began 20X4 with 60,000 units of inventory that cost $36,000. During 20X2, Mesa purchased merchandise on account for $352,500 as follows:

Purchase 1	(100,000 units costing)	$ 65,000
Purchase 2	(270,000 units costing)	175,500
Purchase 3	(160,000 units costing)	112,000

Cash payments on account totaled $326,000 during the year.

Mesa's sales during 20X4 consisted of 520,000 units of inventory for $660,000, all on account. The company uses the FIFO inventory method.

Cash collections from customers were $630,000. Operating expenses totaled $240,500, of which Mesa paid $211,000 in cash. Mesa credited Accrued Liabilities for the remainder. At December 31, Mesa accrued income tax expense at the rate of 35% of income before tax.

Required

1. Make summary journal entries to record Mesa Hardware's transactions for the year, assuming the company uses a perpetual inventory system.
2. Determine the FIFO cost of Mesa's ending inventory at December 31, 20X4 two ways:
   a. Use a T-account.
   b. Multiply the number of units on hand by the unit cost.
3. Show how Mesa would compute cost of goods sold for 20X4. Follow Exhibit 6-2 (page 266).
4. Prepare Mesa Hardware's income statement for 20X4. Show totals for the gross profit and income before tax.
5. Determine Mesa's gross profit percentage, rate of inventory turnover, and net income as a percentage of sales for the year. In the hardware industry, a gross profit percentage of 40%, an inventory turnover of six times per year, and a net income percentage of 7% are considered excellent. How well does Mesa compare to these industry averages?

Answers

Requirement 1

	Debit	Credit
Inventory ($65,000 + $175,500 + $112,000)	352,500	
Accounts Payable		352,500
Accounts Payable	326,000	
Cash		326,000
Accounts Receivable	660,000	
Sales Revenue		660,000
Cost of Goods Sold	339,500	
Inventory		339,500
[$36,000 + $65,000 + $175,500 + $63,000 (90,000 units × $0.70)] ($112,000 ÷ 160,000 units = $0.70 per unit)		
Cash	630,000	
Accounts Receivable		630,000
Operating Expenses	240,500	
Cash		211,000
Accrued Liabilities		29,500
Income Tax Expense	28,000	
Income Tax Payable		28,000
($660,000 − $339,500 − $240,500) × .35 = $28,000		

Requirement 2

a.

Inventory	
36,000	339,500
352,500	
49,000	

b.

Number of units in ending inventory (60,000 + 100,000 + 270,000 + 160,000 − 520,000)		70,000
Unit cost of ending inventory at FIFO ($112,000 ÷ 160,000)	×	$ 0.70
FIFO cost of ending inventory		$49,000

Requirement 3

Cost of goods sold:	
Beginning inventory	$ 36,000
Purchases	352,500
Cost of goods available for sale	388,500
Ending inventory	(49,000)
Cost of goods sold	$339,500

Requirement 4

Mesa Hardware Company
Income Statement
Year Ended December 31, 20X4

Sales revenue	$660,000
Cost of goods sold	339,500
Gross profit	320,500
Operating expenses	240,500
Income before tax	80,000
Income tax expense	28,000
Net Income	$ 52,000

Requirement 5

Gross profit percentage: $\$320{,}500 \div \$660{,}000 = 48.6\%$

Inventory turnover: $\dfrac{\$339{,}500}{(\$36{,}000 + \$49{,}000)/2} = 8 \text{ times}$

Net income as a percentage of sales: $\$52{,}000 \div \$660{,}000 = 7.9\%$

Mesa's statistics are better than the industry averages.

Review Merchandise Inventory

Lessons Learned

1. **Use the cost-of-goods-sold model.** This model captures data on: Beginning inventory + Purchases − Ending inventory = Cost of goods sold. It helps managers determine how much inventory to buy.
2. **Account for inventory transactions.** Merchandisers can choose between two inventory systems. In a *perpetual inventory system*, the business keeps a continuous record for each inventory item to show the inventory on hand for control purposes. In a periodic system, there is no running record of inventory on hand. Instead, the company must count the goods on hand to determine ending inventory and cost of goods sold.
3. **Analyze the various inventory methods.** Businesses multiply the quantity of inventory items by their unit cost to determine inventory cost. There are four inventory costing methods: *specific unit cost; weighted-average cost; first-in, first-out (FIFO) cost;* and *last-in, first-out (LIFO) cost*. The specific identification method is used for unique items. Most other companies use the other methods. FIFO reports ending inventory at the most current cost. LIFO reports cost of goods sold at the most current cost.
4. **Identify the income and the tax effects of the inventory methods.** When inventory costs are increasing, LIFO produces the highest cost of goods sold and the lowest income, thus minimizing income taxes. FIFO results in the highest income. The weighted-average method gives results between the extremes of FIFO and LIFO.
5. **Show how inventory errors affect cost of goods sold and net income.** Inventory overstatements in one period are counterbalanced by inventory understatements in the next period.
6. **Use the gross profit percentage and inventory turnover to evaluate a business.** Two key decision aids for merchandising companies are (1) the *gross profit percentage* (gross profit divided by net sales revenue), which measures the percentage of gross profit on each dollar of sales, and (2) *inventory turnover* (cost of goods sold divided by average inventory), which indicates how rapidly the company is selling its inventory. Increases in these measures usually signal an increase in profits.
7. **Estimate inventory by the gross profit method.** The *gross profit method* is a technique for estimating the cost of inventory. It comes in handy for preparing interim financial statements and for estimating the cost of inventory destroyed by fire or other casualties.

Accounting Vocabulary

average-cost method (p. 271)
conservatism (p. 279)
consistency principle (p. 278)
cost of goods sold (p. 264)
cost-of-goods-sold model (p. 266)
cost of sales (p. 264)
disclosure principle (p. 278)
first-in, first-out (FIFO) cost (method) (p. 271)
gross margin (p. 265)
gross margin method (p. 284)
gross margin percentage (p. 282)
gross profit (p. 265)
gross profit method (p. 284)
gross profit percentage (p. 282)
inventory (p. 264)
inventory profit (p. 275)
inventory turnover (p. 283)
just-in-time system (p. 283)
last-in, first-out (LIFO) cost (method) (p. 271)
lower-of-cost-or-market (LCM) rule (p. 279)
materiality concept (p. 279)
periodic inventory system (p. 267)
perpetual inventory system (p. 268)
purchase allowances (p. 269)
purchase discounts (p. 270)
purchase returns (p. 269)
specific-unit-cost method (p. 271)
weighted-average cost method (p. 271)

Questions

1. Suppose your company deals in expensive jewelry. Which inventory system should you use to achieve good internal control over the inventory? If your business is a hardware store that sells low-cost goods, which inventory system would you be likely to use? Why would you choose this system?
2. What is the role of the physical count of inventory in the perpetual inventory system?
3. a. If beginning inventory is $10,000, purchases total $85,000, and ending inventory is $12,700, how much is cost of goods sold?
   b. If beginning inventory is $32,000, purchases total $119,000, and cost of goods sold is $127,000, how much is ending inventory?
4. Briefly describe the four generally accepted inventory cost methods. During a period of rising prices, which method produces the highest reported income? Which produces the lowest reported income?
5. Which inventory costing method produces the ending inventory valued at the most current cost? Which method produces the cost-of-goods-sold amount valued at the most current cost?
6. What is the most attractive feature of LIFO? Does LIFO have this advantage during periods of increasing prices or during periods of decreasing prices? Why has LIFO had this advantage recently?
7. What is inventory profit? Which method produces it?
8. Identify the chief criticism of LIFO.
9. How does the consistency principle affect accounting for inventory?
10. Briefly describe the influence that the concept of conservatism has on accounting for inventory.
11. Manley Company's inventory has a cost of $45,000 at the end of the year, and the current replacement cost of the inventory is $47,000. At which amount should the company report the inventory on its balance sheet? Now suppose the current replacement cost of the inventory is $42,000 instead of $47,000. At which amount should Manley report the inventory? What rule governs your answers to these questions?
12. Gabriel Company accidentally overstated its ending inventory by $40,000 at the end of period 1. Is gross profit of period 1 overstated or understated? Is gross profit of period 2 overstated, understated, or unaffected by the period 1 error? Is total gross profit for the two periods overstated, understated, or correct? Give the reason for your answers.
13. Identify an important method of estimating inventory amounts. What familiar model underlies this estimation method?
14. A fire destroyed the inventory of Olivera Company, but the accounting records were saved. The beginning inventory was $22,000, purchases for the period were $71,000, and sales were $140,000. Olivera's customary gross profit is 40% of sales. Use the gross profit method to estimate the cost of the inventory destroyed by the fire.

Assess Your Progress

Check Points

Basic concept of accounting for inventory **(Obj. 1)**

CP6-1 Suppose Toyota Motor Company, North America (Toyota) purchased 1,000 door handles as units of inventory for $60 each and marked up the goods by $40 per unit. Toyota then sold 700 units. For these transactions, show what Toyota would report on its balance sheet at December 31, 20X0 and on its income statement for the year ended December 31, 20X0 for these items. Include a complete heading for each statement.

CP6-2 Auto Max Used Cars purchased inventory costing $100,000 and sold 70% of the automobiles for $120,000. All purchases were on account. Sales were for notes receivable, with Auto Max collecting 20% up front.

Accounting for inventory transactions **(Obj. 2)**

1. Journalize these two transactions for Auto Max, which uses the perpetual inventory system.
2. For these transactions, show what Auto Max will report for inventory, revenues, and expenses on its financial statements. Report gross profit on the appropriate statement.

CP6-3

Journalize the following transactions for **The Coca-Cola Company**:

Accounting for inventory transactions **(Obj. 2)**

- Cash purchases of inventory, $5.9 billion
- Sales on account, $20.5 billion
- Cost of goods sold (perpetual inventory system), $6.2 billion
- Collections on account, $20.3 billion

CP6-4 Study Exhibit 6-6, page 272, and answer these questions.

Applying the FIFO, LIFO, and weighted-average inventory methods **(Obj. 1, 3)**

1. In Panel A, are the company's inventory costs stable, increasing, or decreasing during the period? Cite specific figures to support your answer.
2. Which inventory method results in the *highest* amount for ending inventory (give this figure)? Explain why this method produces the highest amount for ending inventory. Does this method result in the highest, or the lowest, cost of goods sold? Explain why this occurs. Does this method result in the highest, or the lowest, gross profit? Explain your answer.
3. Which inventory method results in the *lowest* amount for ending inventory (give this figure)? Explain why this method produces the lowest amount for ending inventory. Does this method result in the highest or the lowest cost of goods sold? Explain why this occurs. Does this method result in the highest, or the lowest, gross profit? Explain your answer.

CP6-5 Return to Exhibit 6-6, page 272, and assume that the business sold 50 units of inventory during the period (instead of 40 units as in the exhibit). Compute ending inventory and cost of goods sold for each of the following costing methods:

Applying the weighted-average, FIFO, and LIFO methods **(Obj. 1, 3)**

a. Weighted average b. FIFO c. LIFO

Follow the computational format illustrated in the exhibit.

CP6-6 Ink Jet, Inc. markets the ink used in laser printers. Ink Jet started the year with 100 containers of ink (weighted-average cost of $9.14 each, FIFO cost of $9 each, LIFO cost of $8 each). During the year, Ink Jet purchased 700 containers of ink at $13 and sold 600 units for $20 each. Ink Jet paid operating expenses throughout the year, a total of $4,000. Assume Ink Jet is not subject to income tax.

Applying the weighted-average, FIFO, and LIFO methods **(Obj. 3)**

Prepare Ink Jet's income statement for the current year ended December 31 under the weighted-average, FIFO, and LIFO inventory costing methods. Include a complete statement heading. Round unit cost to the nearest cent.

CP6-7 This check point should be used in conjunction with Check Point 6-6. Ink Jet in Check Point 6-6 is a corporation subject to a 40% income tax. Compute Ink Jet's income tax expense under the weighted-average, FIFO, and LIFO inventory costing methods. Which method would you select to (a) maximize reported income and (b) minimize income tax expense? Format your answer as shown on page 272.

Income tax effects of the inventory costing methods **(Obj. 4)**

CP6-8 **Nike, Inc.** uses the LIFO method to account for inventory. Suppose Nike is having an unusually bad year, with net income below expectations. Assume Nike inventory costs are rising rapidly. What can Nike's managers do immediately before the end of the year to increase reported profits? Explain how this action increases reported income.

Income and tax effects of LIFO **(Obj. 3)**

CP6-9 Return to the **General Motors** data in Exhibit 6-1, page 265. At December 31, 2000, the controller of the company applied the lower-of-cost-or-market rule to GM inventories. Suppose

Applying the lower-of-cost-or-market rule to inventory
(Obj. 5)

the controller determined that the current replacement cost (current market value) of the inventory was $10 billion. Show what GM would report for inventory and cost of goods sold.

Assessing the effect of an inventory error—1 year only
(Obj. 5)

CP6-10 Examine the **General Motors** financial data in Exhibit 6-1, on page 265. Suppose GM's inventory at December 31, 2000, as reported, is overstated by $3 billion. What are correct amounts for GM (a) inventory, (b) net sales, (c) cost of goods sold, and (d) gross profit?

Assessing the effect of an inventory error on 2 years of statements
(Obj. 5)

CP6-11 Fran Bailey, staff accountant of an **Office Max** store, learned that Office Max's $4 million cost of inventory at the end of last year was understated by $1.5 million. She notified the company president of the accounting error and the need to alert Office Max's lenders that last year's reported net income was incorrect. Michael LeVan, president of Office Max, explained to Bailey that there is no need to report the error to lenders because the error will counterbalance this year. Even with no correction, LeVan reasons, gross profit for both years combined will be the same whether or not Office Max corrects its error.

1. Was last year's reported gross profit of $6.0 million overstated, understated, or correct? What was the correct amount of gross profit last year?
2. Is this year's gross profit of $6.8 million overstated, understated, or correct? What is the correct amount of gross profit for the current year?
3. Whose perspective is better, Bailey's or LeVan's? Give your reason. Consider the trend of reported gross profit both without the correction and with the correction.

Using ratio data to evaluate operations
(Obj. 6)

CP6-12 Use the data in Exhibits 6-6 and 6-7, pages 272 and 273, to compute the company's gross profit percentage and rate of inventory turnover under

1. FIFO
2. LIFO

Which method makes the company look better on

3. Gross profit percentage?
4. Inventory turnover?

Estimating ending inventory by the gross profit method
(Obj. 7)

CP6-13 Answer the following questions:

1. BXI Software began the year with inventory of $400,000. Inventory purchases for the year totaled $1,600,000. BXI managers estimate that cost of goods sold for the year will be $1,800,000. How much is BXI's estimated cost of ending inventory? Use the gross profit method.
2. BXI Systems, a related company, began the year with inventory of $400,000 and purchased $1,600,000 of goods during the year (the same as in question 1). Sales for the year are $3,000,000, and BXI's gross profit percentage is 40% of sales. Compute BXI's estimated cost of ending inventory by the gross profit method. Compare this answer to your answer in question 1; they should be the same.

Ethical implications of inventory actions
(Obj. 4, 5)

CP6-14 Determine whether each of the following actions in buying, selling, and accounting for inventories is ethical or unethical. Give your reason for each answer.

1. Brazos Corporation consciously overstated purchases to produce a high figure for cost of goods sold (low amount of net income). The real reason was to decrease the company's income tax payments to the government.
2. In applying the lower-of-cost-or-market rule to inventories, Fort Wayne Industries recorded an excessively low market value for ending inventory. This allowed the company to keep from paying income tax for the year.
3. DTE Photo Film purchased lots of inventory shortly before year end to increase the LIFO cost of goods sold and decrease reported income for the year.
4. Edison Electrical Products delayed the purchase of inventory until after December 31, 20X4, to keep 20X3's cost of goods sold from growing too large. The delay in purchasing inventory helped net income of 20X4 to reach the level of profit demanded by the company's investors.
5. Dover Sales Company deliberately overstated ending inventory in order to report higher profits (net income).

Exercises

E6-1 Supply the missing income statement amounts for each of the following companies (amounts adapted, and in millions):

Determining amounts for the income statement
(Obj. 1)

Company	Net Sales	Beginning Inventory	Purchases	Ending Inventory	Cost of Goods Sold	Gross Profit
Coca-Cola	$ 20,458	$ (a)	$ 6,194	$ 1,066	$6,204	$ (b)
Wal-Mart	191,329	19,793	(c)	21,442	(d)	41,074
Intel	33,726	1,478	13,413	2,241	(e)	21,076
Estée Lauder	(f)	513	1,005	(g)	972	3,395

Prepare the income statement for Estée Lauder Companies, showing the computation of cost of goods sold. Estée Lauder's operating expenses for the year were $2,896, and its income tax rate is 37%. Net income, $314 million

Note: Exercise 6-14 builds on Exercise 6-1 with a profitability analysis of these four actual companies.

E6-2 Toys "Я" Us is budgeting for the fiscal year ended January 31, 20X4. During the preceding year ended January 31, 20X3, sales totaled $9,400 million and cost of goods sold was $6,500 million. Inventory stood at $1,700 million at January 31, 20X2; and at January 31, 20X3, inventory stood at $1,900 million.

Budgeting inventory purchases
(Obj. 1)

During the upcoming 20X4 year, suppose Toys "Я" Us expects sales and cost of goods sold to increase by 10%. The company budgets next year's ending inventory at $2,200 million.

Required

How much inventory should Toys "Я" Us purchase during the upcoming year to reach its budgeted figures?

E6-3 Accounting records for Firestone, Inc. yield the following data for the year ended December 31, 20X5 (amounts in thousands):

Accounting for inventory transactions
(Obj. 2, 3)

Inventory, December 31, 20X4	$ 370
Purchases of inventory (on account)	2,900
Sales of inventory—80% on account; 20% for cash (cost $2,600)	3,500
Inventory at FIFO cost, December 31, 20X5 (market value = $ 690)	?

Required

1. Journalize Firestone's inventory transactions for the year under the perpetual system. Show all amounts in thousands. Use Exhibit 6-5 as a model.
2. Report ending inventory, sales, cost of goods sold, and gross profit on the appropriate financial statement (amounts in thousands). Show the computation of cost of goods sold.

E6-4 Suppose **Intel Corporation's** inventory records for a particular computer chip show the following at October 31:

Analyzing inventory transactions
(Obj. 2, 3)

Oct. 1	Beginning inventory	5 units @ $160
8	Purchase	4 units @ 160
15	Purchase	11 units @ 170
26	Purchase	5 units @ 180

At October 31, eight of these computer chips are on hand. Journalize for Intel:

1. Total October purchases in one summary entry. All purchases were on credit.
2. Total October sales and cost of goods sold in two summary entries. The selling price was $500 per unit, and all sales were on credit. Intel uses the FIFO inventory method.
3. How much gross profit did Intel earn on these transactions? What is the cost of Intel's ending inventory?

Determining ending inventory and cost of goods sold by four methods
(Obj. 3)

spreadsheet

E6-5 Use the **Intel Corporation** data in Exercise 6-4 to answer the following questions.

Required COGS: wtd. avg. $2863; FIFO $2800; LIFO $2930

1. Compute ending inventory and cost of goods sold, using each of the following methods:
   a. Specific unit cost, assuming four $160 units and four $170 units are on hand
   b. Weighted-average cost
   c. First-in, first-out
   d. Last-in, first-out
2. Which method produces the highest cost of goods sold? Which method produces the lowest cost of goods sold? What causes the difference in cost of goods sold?

Computing the tax advantage of LIFO over FIFO
(Obj. 4)

E6-6 Use the data in Exercise 6-4 to illustrate Intel's income tax advantage from using LIFO over FIFO. Sales revenue is $6,000, operating expenses are $1,100, and the income tax rate is 40%. How much in taxes would Intel save by using the LIFO method?

Determining ending inventory and cost of goods sold
(Obj. 1, 3)

E6-7 Minolta Prints, Inc. specializes in printing equipment. Because each inventory item is expensive, Minolta uses a perpetual inventory system. Company records indicate the following data for a line of printers:

Date	Item	Quantity	Unit Cost
May 1	Balance	5	$90
6	Sale	3	
8	Purchase	12	95
17	Sale	4	
30	Sale	3	

Required

1. Determine the amounts that Minolta should report for ending inventory and cost of goods sold two ways:
   a. FIFO
   b. LIFO (Use the computational approach illustrated in Exhibit 6-6 because that is the way LIFO is applied in practice.)
2. Report inventory and cost of goods sold at FIFO in the financial statements. Include the names of all the current asset accounts on the balance sheet, and prepare the income statement through gross profit.

Measuring gross profit
(Obj. 1, 3)

E6-8 Suppose a **Wal-Mart** store in Branson, Missouri, ended May 20X4 with 800,000 units of merchandise that cost an average of $7 each. Suppose the store then sold 600,000 units of merchandise for $4.9 million during June 20X4. Further, assume the store made two large purchases during June as follows:

June 6	100,000 units @ $6 =	$ 600,000
21	400,000 units @ $5 =	2,000,000

1. At June 30, the store manager needs to know the store's gross profit under both FIFO and LIFO. Supply this information.

2. What caused the FIFO and LIFO gross profit figures to differ? Does the difference go in the direction you would predict? Explain in detail.

Change from LIFO to FIFO
(Obj. 4)

spreadsheet

E6-9 Sea-N-Ski Sports is considering a change from the LIFO inventory method to the FIFO method. Managers are concerned about the effect of this change on income tax expense and reported net income. If the change is made, it will become effective on March 1. Inventory on hand at February 28 is $63,000. During March, Sea-N-Ski managers expect sales of $260,000; net purchases between $159,000 and $182,000; and operating expenses, excluding income tax, of $83,000. The income tax rate is 40%. Inventories at March 31 are budgeted as follows: FIFO, $85,000; LIFO, $78,000.

	A	B	C	D	E
1	**Sea-N-Ski Sports**				
2	**Estimated Income under FIFO and LIFO**				
3	**March 20XX**				
4					
5		FIFO	LIFO	FIFO	LIFO
6					
7	Sales	$260,000	$260,000	$260,000	$260,000
8					
9	Cost of goods sold				
10	Beginning inventory	63,000	63,000	63,000	63,000
11	Purchases	159,000	159,000	182,000	182,000
12					
13	Cost of goods available				
14	Ending inventory	(85,000)	(78,000)	(85,000)	(78,000)
15					
16	Cost of goods sold				
17					
18	Gross profit				
19	Operating expenses	83,000	83,000	83,000	83,000
20					
21	Income from operations				
22	Income tax expense				
23					
24	Net income	$24000	$19800	$10,200	$6000
25					

Required

Create a spreadsheet model to compute estimated net income for March under FIFO and LIFO. Format your answer as shown here.

Managing income taxes under the LIFO method
(Obj. 4)

E6-10 Fellingham, Inc. is nearing the end of its best year ever. With 3 weeks until year end, it appears that net income for the year will have increased by 70% over last year. John Fellingham, the principal stockholder and president, is pleased with the year's success but unhappy about the huge increase in income taxes that the business will have to pay.

Fellingham asks you, the financial vice president, to come up with a way to decrease the business's income tax burden. Inventory quantities are a little lower than normal because sales have been especially strong during the last few months. Fellingham uses the LIFO inventory method, and inventory costs have risen dramatically during the latter part of the year.

Required

Write a memorandum to John Fellingham to explain how the company can decrease its income taxes for the current year. Fellingham is a man of integrity, so your plan must be completely honest and ethical.

Identifying income, tax, and other effects of the inventory methods
(Obj. 4)

E6-11 This exercise tests your understanding of the various inventory methods. In the space provided, write the name of the inventory method that best fits the description. Assume that the cost of inventory is rising.

_________ 1. Matches the most current cost of goods sold against sales revenue.
_________ 2. Results in an old measure of the cost of ending inventory.
___LIFO___ 3. Generally associated with saving income taxes.
_________ 4. Results in a cost of ending inventory that is close to the current cost of replacing the inventory.
Specific Unit Cost 5. Used to account for automobiles, jewelry, and art objects.
_________ 6. Associated with inventory profits.
Weighted Average Cost Method 7. Provides a middle-ground measure of ending inventory and cost of goods sold.
_________ 8. Maximizes reported income.
_________ 9. Enables a company to buy high-cost inventory at year end and thereby decrease reported income.
_________ 10. Enables a company to keep reported income from dropping lower by liquidating older layers of inventory.

Correcting an inventory error
(Obj. 5)

E6-12 Photo Unique, maker of photographic developing solutions, reported the following comparative income statement for the years ended September 30, 20X5 and 20X4:

Photo Unique
Income Statement
Years Ended September 30, 20X5 and 20X4

	20X5		20X4	
Sales revenue		$149,000		$122,000
Cost of goods sold:				
Beginning inventory	$18,000		$12,000	
Purchases	72,000		66,000	
Cost of goods available	90,000		78,000	
Ending inventory	(16,000)		(18,000)	
Cost of goods sold		74,000		60,000
Gross profit		75,000		62,000
Operating expenses		30,000		20,000
Net income		$ 45,000		$ 42,000

Photo Unique's president and shareholders are thrilled by the company's boost in sales and net income during 20X5. Then they discover that ending 20X4 inventory was understated by $6,000. Prepare the corrected comparative income statement for the 2-year period. How well did Photo Unique really perform in 20X5, as compared with 20X4? What caused the evaluation of 20X5 to change so dramatically? Discuss in detail.

Correcting an inventory error
(Obj. 5)

E6-13 **Pharmacia Corporation** uses a perpetual inventory system and reports inventory at the lower of cost or market. Assume that prior to releasing its December 2000 financial statements, the Pharmacia preliminary income statement is as follows:

Income Statement (Partial)

Sales revenue	$18,144
Cost of goods sold	5,456
Gross profit	$12,688

general ledger

During the year, Pharmacia purchased inventory at a cost of $5,798 million. Assume that the company has learned that beginning inventory was understated by $200 million and that ending inventory at December 31, 2000, is $2,927 million with this amount overstated by $100 million.

Show how Pharmacia should report the preceding data on its 2000 income statement, and the company's inventory on its December 31 balance sheet.

Measuring profitability
(Obj. 6)

E6-14 Refer to the data in Exercise 6-1 (p. 265). Which company has the highest, and the lowest, gross profit percentage? Which company has the highest, and the lowest rate of inventory turnover? Explain how your answers to these questions describe the merchandising philosophies of these companies. Be specific. Based on your figure, which company appears to be the most profitable?

Applying the lower-of-cost-or-market rule to inventories
(Obj. 1, 4)

E6-15 Sloan Corporation, which uses a perpetual inventory system, has these account balances at December 31, 20X4, prior to releasing the financial statements for the year:

Inventory

Beg. bal.	12,400	
End. bal.	18,000	

Cost of Goods Sold

Bal.	110,000	

Sales Revenue

	Bal.	225,000

A year ago, when Sloan prepared its 20X3 financial statements, the replacement cost of ending inventory was $13,050. Sloan has determined that the replacement cost of the December 31, 20X4, ending inventory is $17,600.

Required

Prepare Sloan Corporation's 20X4 income statement through gross profit to show how the company would apply the lower-of-cost-or-market rule to its inventories.

Measuring gross profit and reporting cash flows
(Obj. 1, 6)

E6-16 The Home Depot made sales of $45.7 billion in the year ended January 31, 2001. Collections from customers totaled $45.5 billion. The company began the year with $5.5 billion in inventories and ended with $6.6 billion. During the year purchases of inventory added up to $33.2 billion. Of the purchases, Home Depot paid $35.2 billion to suppliers.

As an investor searching for a good investment, suppose you identify several critical pieces of information about Home Depot's operations during the year:

Compute Home Depot's gross profit, gross profit percentage, and rate of inventory turnover during 2001.

Estimating inventory by the gross profit method
(Obj. 7)

spreadsheet

E6-17 Atlanta Technologies began January with inventory of $39,000. The business made net purchases of $136,000 and had net sales of $200,000 before a fire destroyed its merchandise inventory. For the past several years, Atlanta's gross profit percentage has been 40%. Estimate the cost of the inventory destroyed by the fire. Identify another reason managers use the gross profit method to estimate inventory cost on a regular basis.

Challenge Exercises

Inventory policy decisions
(Obj. 3, 5)

E6-18 For each of the following situations, identify the inventory method that you would use or, given the use of a particular method, state the strategy that you would follow to accomplish your goal:

a. Your inventory turns over slowly. Inventory costs are increasing, and the company prefers to report high income.
b. Inventory costs have been stable for several years, and you expect costs to remain stable for the indefinite future. (Give the reason for your choice of method.)
c. Company management, like that of **IBM**, prefers a middle-of-the-road inventory policy that avoids extremes.
d. Suppliers of your inventory are threatening a labor strike, and it may be difficult for your company to obtain inventory. This situation could increase your income taxes.
e. Inventory costs are decreasing, and your company's board of directors wants to minimize income taxes.
f. Inventory costs are increasing. Your company uses LIFO and is having an unexpectedly good year. It is near year end, and you need to keep net income from increasing too much.

Measuring the effect of a LIFO liquidation
(Obj. 3, 4, 5)

E6-19 Suppose **Neiman Marcus**, the specialty retailer, had these records for ladies' evening gowns during 20X4.

Beginning inventory (40 @ $1,000)	$ 40,000
Purchase in February (20 @ $1,100)	22,000
Purchase in June (50 @ $1,200)	60,000
Purchase in December (30 @ $1,300)	39,000
Cost of goods available	$161,000

Assume sales of evening gowns totaled 130 units during 20X4 and that Neiman Marcus uses the LIFO method to account for inventory. The income tax rate is 40%.

Required

1. Compute Neiman Marcus's cost of goods sold for evening gowns in 20X4.
2. Compute what cost of goods sold would have been if Neiman Marcus had purchased enough inventory in December—at $1,300 per evening gown—to keep year-end inventory at the same level it was at the beginning of the year.
3. How much did the LIFO liquidation boost Neiman Marcus's gross profit and net income? How much did the LIFO liquidation cost the company in income tax? Was the LIFO liquidation good or bad for the company? State the reason for your answer.

Evaluating a company's profitability
(Obj. 6)

E6-20 **Kmart Corporation** declared bankruptcy. Let's see why. Kmart reported these figures:

Kmart Corporation
Statement of Income (Adapted)
Years Ended December 31, 2000, 1999, and 1998

Billions	2000	1999	1998
Sales	$37.0	$35.9	$33.7
Cost of sales	29.7	28.1	26.3
Selling, general and administrative expenses	7.4	6.5	6.2
Other expenses	0.1	0.9	0.7
Net income (net loss)	$ (0.2)	$ 0.4	$ 0.5

Required

Evaluate the trend of Kmart's results of operations during 1998 through 2000. Consider the trends of sales, gross profit, and net income. Track the gross profit percentage (to three decimal places) and the rate of inventory turnover (to one decimal place) in each year. Kmart inventories at December 31, 1997, 1998, 1999, and 2000 were $6.4, $6.5, $7.1, and $6.4 billion, respectively. Also discuss the role that selling expenses must have played in Kmart difficulties.

Problems

(Group A)

P6-1A Assume condensed versions of a **Shell** convenience store's most recent income statement and balance sheet reported as follows. Because the business is organized as a proprietorship, it pays no corporate income tax.

Using the cost-of-goods-sold model to budget operations
(Obj. 1)

Shell Convenience Store
Income Statement
Year Ended December 31, 20X4

Sales	$900,000
Cost of sales	690,000
Gross profit	210,000
Operating expenses	80,000
Net income	$130,000

Shell Convenience Store
Balance Sheet
December 31, 20X4

Assets		Liabilities and Capital	
Cash	$ 70,000	Accounts payable	$ 35,000
Inventories	35,000	Note payable	280,000
Land and		Total liabilities	315,000
buildings, net	360,000	Owner, capital	150,000
		Total liabilities	
Total assets	$465,000	and capital	$465,000

The owner is budgeting for 20X5. He expects sales to increase by 10% and the gross profit *percentage* to remain unchanged. To meet customer demand for the increase in sales, ending inventory will need to be $45,000 at December 31, 20X5. He hopes to earn a net income of $150,000 next year.

Required

1. A key variable the owner can control is the amount of inventory he purchases. Show how to determine the amount of purchases he should make in 20X5.
2. Prepare the store's budgeted income statement for 20X5 to reach the target net income of $150,000.

P6-2A Toys "Я" Us purchases inventory in crates of merchandise; each unit of inventory is a crate of toys. The fiscal year of Toys "Я" Us ends each January 31.

Accounting for inventory in a perpetual system
(Obj. 2, 3)

Assume you are dealing with a single Toys "Я" Us store in San Antonio, Texas, and that the store experienced the following: The San Antonio store began fiscal year 20X5 with an inventory of 20,000 units that cost a total of $1,200,000. During the year, the store purchased merchandise on account as follows:

April (30,000 units @ $65)	$ 1,950,000
August (50,000 units @ $65)	3,250,000
November (90,000 units @ $70)	6,300,000
Total purchases	$11,500,000

Cash payments on account during the year totaled $11,390,000.

During fiscal year 20X5, the store sold 180,000 units of merchandise for $16,400,000, of which $5,300,000 was for cash and the balance was on account. Toys "Я" Us uses the LIFO method for inventories.

Operating expenses for the year were $4,000,000. The store paid 80% in cash and accrued the rest. The store accrued income tax at the rate of 40%.

Required

1. Make summary journal entries to record the store's transactions for the year ended January 31, 20X5. Toys "Я" Us uses a perpetual inventory system.

2. Determine the LIFO cost of the store's ending inventory at January 31, 20X5. Use a T-account.
3. Prepare the store's income statement for the year ended January 31, 20X5. Show totals for the gross profit, income before tax, and net income.

Measuring cost of goods sold and ending inventory
(Obj. 1, 3)

P6-3A Assume a **Reebok** outlet store began August 20X0 with 50 pairs of hiking boots that cost $40 each. The sale price of these boots was $70. During August, the store completed these inventory transactions:

		Units	Unit Cost	Unit Sale Price
Aug. 3	Sale	16	$40	$70
8	Purchase	80	41	72
11	Sale	34	40	70
19	Sale	9	41	72
24	Sale	32	41	72
30	Purchase	18	42	73
31	Sale	8	41	72

Required

1. The preceding data are taken from the store's inventory records. Which cost method does the store use? Explain how you arrived at your answer.
2. Determine the store's cost of goods sold for August. Also compute gross profit for August.
3. What is the cost of the store's August 31 inventory of hiking boots?

Computing inventory by three methods
(Obj. 3, 4)

P6-4A Calico Corners, an upscale fabric store, began March with 73 yards of fabric that cost $23 per yard. During the month, Calico Corners made the following purchases:

March 4	113 yards @ $27
12	81 yards @ 29
19	167 yards @ 32
25	44 yards @ 35

At March 31 the ending inventory consists of 60 yards of fabric.

Required

1. Determine the ending inventory and cost-of-goods-sold amounts for March under (1) weighted-average cost, (2) FIFO cost, and (3) LIFO cost. Round weighted-average cost per unit to the nearest cent and round all other amounts to the nearest dollar.
2. Explain why cost of goods sold is highest under LIFO. Be specific.
3. How much income tax would Calico Corners save during the month by using LIFO versus FIFO? The income tax rate is 40%.

Applying the different inventory costing methods
(Obj. 3, 4)

P6-5A The records of Schlosstein Restaurant Supply include the following accounts for cases of cups at December 31 of the current year:

Inventory

Jan. 1	**Balance (700 units @ $7.00)**	**4,900**		
Jan. 6	**Purchase 300 units @ $7.05**	**2,115**		
Mar. 19	**Purchase 1,100 units @ 7.35**	**8,085**		
June 22	**Purchase 8,400 units @ 7.50**	**63,000**		
Oct. 4	**Purchase 500 units @ 8.50**	**4,250**		

Sales Revenue

		Dec. 31	**10,000 units**	**134,970**

Required

1. Prepare a partial income statement through gross profit under the weighted-average, FIFO, and LIFO methods. Use the cost-of-goods-sold model.
2. Which inventory method would you use to minimize income tax? Explain why this method causes income tax to be the lowest.

Applying the lower-of-cost-or-market rule to inventories **(Obj. 4)**

P6-6A Rebecca Arden Cosmetics has recently been plagued with lackluster sales. The rate of inventory turnover has dropped, and some of the company's merchandise is gathering dust. At the same time, competition has forced Arden's suppliers to lower the prices that the company will pay when it replaces its inventory. It is now December 31, 20X4, and the current replacement cost of Arden's ending inventory is $1,600,000 below what Arden actually paid for the goods, which was $4,900,000. Before any adjustments at the end of the period, the Cost of Goods Sold account has a balance of $29,600,000.

What action should Arden take in this situation? Give any journal entry required. At what amount should Arden report Inventory on the balance sheet? At what amount should the company report Cost of Goods Sold on the income statement? Discuss the accounting principle or concept that is most relevant to this situation.

Correcting inventory errors over a 3-year period **(Obj. 5)**

P6-7A Target Corporation reported these data (adapted, in billions):

	2000		1999		1998	
Net sales revenue		$36		$33		$30
Cost of goods sold:						
Beginning inventory	$ 4		$ 3		$ 2	
Purchases	25		24		22	
Cost of goods available	29		27		24	
Less ending inventory	(4)		(4)		(3)	
Cost of goods sold		25		23		21
Gross profit		11		10		9
Total operating expenses		10		9		8
Net income		$ 1		$ 1		$ 1

Assume that in early 2001, internal auditors discovered that the ending inventory for 1998 was overstated by $1 billion and that the ending inventory for 1999 was understated by $1 billion. The ending inventory at year-end 2000 was correct.

Required

1. Show corrected income statements for the 3 years.
2. State whether each year's net income as reported here and the related owners' equity amounts are understated or overstated. For each incorrect figure, indicate the amount of the understatement or overstatement.
3. How much did these assumed corrections add to or take away from the Target total net income over the 3-year period? How did the corrections affect the trend of net income?

Using the gross profit percentage and the inventory turnover ratio to evaluate two retailers **(Obj. 6)**

P6-8A Pier 1 Imports, the specialty retailer, and Wal-Mart Stores, the discount merchandiser, reported these figures, which have been disguised to hide the companies' identities.

Required

1. Compute the gross profit percentage and the inventory turnover ratio for Company A and for Company B during 2001.
2. Is Company A Pier 1 Imports, or is it Wal-Mart? Is Company B Pier 1 or Wal-Mart? State the reasoning for your answer, based solely on the ratios you computed.

Company A

Consolidated Statement of Income (Adapted)

(Amounts in billions)	Fiscal Years Ended January 31, 2001	2000
Revenues:		
Net sales	$191	$165
Other income—net	2	2
	193	167
Costs and Expenses:		
Cost of sales	150	130
Operating, selling, and general and administrative expenses	32	27

Company A

Consolidated Balance Sheet (Adapted)

(Amounts in billions)	January 31, 2001	2000
Assets		
Current assets:		
Cash and cash equivalents	$ 2	$ 2
Receivables	2	1
Inventories	21	20
Prepaid expenses and other	1	1
Total Current Assets	$26	$24

Company B

Consolidated Statement of Operations (Adapted)

(Amounts in millions)	Year Ended 2001	2000
Net sales	$1,412	$1,231
Cost of sales	817	719
Selling, general and administrative expenses	400	349

Company B

Consolidated Balance Sheet (Adapted)

(Amounts in millions)	Year End 2001	2000
Assets		
Current assets:		
Cash and temporary investments	$ 47	$ 50
Accounts receivable, net	84	59
Inventories	311	269

P6-9A Assume **Procter & Gamble Company** lost some Pringle Potato Chips inventory in a fire. To file an insurance claim, Procter & Gamble must estimate its inventory by the gross profit method. Assume that for the past 2 years, the gross profit has averaged 40% of net sales. Suppose the company's inventory records reveal the following data:

Estimating inventory by the gross profit method; preparing the income statement
(Obj. 7)

spreadsheet

Inventory, July 1	$ 367,000
Transactions during July:	
Purchases	5,789,000
Purchase discounts	26,000
Purchase returns	12,000
Sales	6,430,000
Sales returns	25,000

Required

1. Estimate the cost of the lost inventory, using the gross profit method.
2. Prepare the July income statement for this product through gross profit. Show the detailed computation of cost of goods sold in a separate schedule.

(Group B)

P6-1B Assume condensed versions of a **Texaco** convenience store's income statement and balance sheet reported the following. The business is organized as a proprietorship, so it pays no corporate income tax.

Using the cost-of-goods-sold model to budget operations
(Obj. 1)

The owner is budgeting for 20X4. He expects sales to increase by 5% and the gross profit percentage to remain unchanged. To meet customer demand for the increase in sales, ending inventory will need to be $80,000 at December 31, 20X4. The owner can lower operating expenses by doing some of the work himself. He hopes to earn a net income of $150,000 next year.

Texaco Convenience Store
Income Statement
Year Ended December 31, 20X3

Sales	$960,000
Cost of sales	720,000
Gross profit	240,000
Operating expenses	110,000
Net income	$130,000

Texaco Convenience Store
Balance Sheet
December 31, 20X3

Assets		Liabilities and Capital	
Cash	$ 40,000	Accounts payable	$ 30,000
Inventories	70,000	Note payable	190,000
Land and		Total liabilities	220,000
buildings net	270,000	Owner, capital	160,000
		Total liabilities	
Total assets	$380,000	and capital	$380,000

Required

1. A key variable the owner can control is the amount of inventory he purchases. Show how to determine the amount of purchases the owner should make in 20X4.
2. Prepare the store's budgeted income statement for 20X4 to reach the target net income of $150,000.

P6-2B The **May Department Stores Company** operates over 300 department stores in the United States, including Lord & Taylor, Hecht's, Foleys, Robinson-May, Kaufmann's, and Filene's Basement. The company's fiscal year ends each January 31.

Accounting for inventory in a perpetual system
(Obj. 2, 3)

Assume you are dealing with a single Lord & Taylor store that experienced the following: The Lord & Taylor store in Atlanta began fiscal year 20X0 with an inventory of 50,000 units that cost $1,500,000. During the year the store purchases merchandise on account as follows:

March (60,000 units @ $32)	$1,920,000
August (40,000 units @ $34)	1,360,000
October (180,000 units @ $35)	6,300,000
Total purchases	$9,580,000

Cash payments on account during the year totaled $9,110,000.

During fiscal year 20X0, the store sold 290,000 units of merchandise for $13,400,000, of which $4,700,000 was for cash and the balance was on account. Lord & Taylor uses the LIFO method for inventories.

Operating expenses for the year were $2,130,000. Lord & Taylor paid two-thirds in cash and accrued the rest. The store accrued income tax at the rate of 40%.

Required

1. Make summary journal entries to record the Lord & Taylor store's transactions for the year ended January 31, 20X0. The company uses a perpetual inventory system.
2. Determine the LIFO cost of the store's ending inventory at January 31, 20X0. Use a T-account.
3. Prepare the Lord & Taylor store's income statement for the year ended January 31, 20X0. Show totals for the gross profit, income before tax, and net income.

Measuring cost of goods sold and ending inventory
(Obj. 1, 3)

P6-3B Assume an **Eddie Bauer** store began March with 50 backpacks that cost $19 each. The sale price of each backpack was $36. During March, Eddie Bauer completed these inventory transactions:

		Units	Unit Cost	Unit Sale Price
March 2	Purchase	12	$20	$37
8	Sale	27	19	36
13	Sale	23	19	36
	Sale	1	20	37
17	Purchase	24	20	37
22	Sale	25	20	37
29	Purchase	24	21	39

Required

1. The preceding data are taken from the store's inventory records. Which cost method does Bauer use? How can you tell?
2. Determine the store's cost of goods sold for March. Also compute gross profit for March.
3. What is the cost of the store's March 31 inventory of backpacks?

Computing inventory by three methods
(Obj. 3, 4)

P6-4B Hot Wheels Motorcycles began December with 140 racing helmets that cost $76 each. During December, the store made the following purchases:

Dec. 3	217 @ $81
12	95 @ 82
18	210 @ 84
24	248 @ 87

Hot Wheels' ending inventory consists of 214 helmets.

Required

1. Determine the ending inventory and cost-of-goods-sold amounts under the weighted-average, FIFO, and LIFO cost methods. Round weighted-average cost per unit to the nearest cent and round all other amounts to the nearest dollar.
2. Explain why cost of goods sold is highest under LIFO. Be specific.
3. How much income tax would Hot Wheels save during December for this one store by using LIFO versus FIFO? The income tax rate is 40%.

P6-5B The records of Blockbuster Digital Images include the following for a line of compact discs at December 31 of the current year:

Applying the different inventory costing methods
(Obj. 3, 4)

INVENTORY

Jan. 1	**Balance** { **300 units @ $3.00**	**1,215**	
	100 units @ 3.15		
Feb. 6	**Purchase 800 units @ 3.15**	**2,520**	
May 19	**Purchase 600 units @ 3.35**	**2,010**	
Aug. 12	**Purchase 400 units @ 3.50**	**1,400**	
Oct. 4	**Purchase 700 units @ 3.70**	**2,590**	

SALES REVENUE

	Dec. 31	**2,500 units**	**11,200**

Required

1. Prepare a partial income statement through gross profit under the weighted-average, FIFO, and LIFO cost methods. Round weighted-average cost to the nearest cent and all other amounts to the nearest dollar. Use the cost-of-goods-sold model.
2. Which inventory method would you use to report the highest net income? Explain why this method produces the highest reported income.

P6-6B LM Electronics has recently been plagued with lackluster sales. The rate of inventory turnover has dropped, and some of the company's merchandise is gathering dust. At the same time, competition has forced some of LM's suppliers to lower the prices that LM will pay when it replaces its inventory. It is now December 31, 20X4. The current replacement cost of LM's ending inventory is $1,500,000 below what the company paid for the goods, which was $8,900,000. Before any adjustments at the end of the period, LM's Cost of Goods Sold account has a balance of $27,400,000.

Applying the lower-of-cost-or-market rule to inventories
(Obj. 4)

What action should LM take in this situation? Give any journal entry required. At what amount should LM report Inventory on the balance sheet? At what amount should the company report Cost of Goods Sold on the income statement? Discuss the accounting principle or concept that is most relevant to this situation.

P6-7B The accounting records of **Pier 1 Imports, Inc.** (top of page 306) show these data (adapted, in millions):

Correcting inventory errors over a 3-year period
(Obj. 5)

Assume that in early 2002 internal auditors discovered that the ending inventory for 1999 was understated by $50 million and that the ending inventory for 2000 was overstated by $20 million. The ending inventory at December 31, 2001, was correct.

Pier 1 Imports

(Amounts in millions)	2001		2000		1999	
Net sales revenue		$1,412		$1,231		$1,138
Cost of goods sold:						
Beginning inventory	$ 269		$259		$234	
Purchases	859		729		663	
Cost of goods available	1,128		988		897	
Less ending inventory	(311)		(269)		(259)	
Cost of goods sold		817		719		638
Gross profit		595		512		500
Total operating expenses		500		437		420
Net income		$ 95		$ 75		$ 80

Required

1. Show corrected income statements for the 3 years.
2. State whether each year's net income as reported here and the related owners' equity amounts are understated or overstated. For each incorrect figure, indicate the amount of the understatement or overstatement.
3. How much did these assumed corrections add to, or take away from Pier 1's total net income over the 3-year period? How did the corrections affect the trend of net income?

Using the gross profit percentage and the inventory turnover ratio to evaluate two leading companies
(Obj. 6)

P6-8B Hershey Foods Corporation, famous for chocolate, and Target Corporation, the discount retailer, reported these amounts:

Hershey Foods Corporation

Consolidated Statement of Income (Adapted)

(Amounts in millions)	Years Ended December 31, 2000	1999
Net Sales	$4,221	$3,971
Costs and Expenses:		
Cost of sales	2,471	2,355
Selling, marketing, and administrative expenses	1,127	1,058

Hershey Foods Corporation

Consolidated Balance Sheet (Adapted)

(Amounts in millions)	December 31, 2000	1999
Assets		
Cash and cash equivalents	$ 32	$118
Accounts receivable—trade	380	353
Inventories	605	602

Target Corporation

Consolidated Statement of Operations (Adapted)

(Amounts in millions)	Year Ended 2000	1999
Sales	$36,362	$33,212
Cost of sales	25,295	23,029
Selling, general and administrative expenses	8,190	7,490

Target Corporation

Consolidated Financial Position (Adapted)

(Amounts in millions)	Year End 2000	1999
Cash and cash equivalents	$ 356	$ 220
Receivable-backed securities	1,941	1,724
Inventory	4,248	3,798

Required

1. Compute both companies' gross profit percentage and their rate of inventory turnover during 2000.
2. Can you tell from these statistics which company should be more profitable in percentage terms? Why? What important category of expenses do the gross profit percentage and the inventory turnover ratio fail to consider?

Estimating inventory by the gross profit method; preparing the income statement **(Obj. 7)**

spreadsheet

P6-9B Assume **Kinko's**, the copy center, lost some paper supplies inventory in a fire. To file an insurance claim, Kinko's must estimate its inventory by the gross profit method. Assume for the past 2 years, Kinko's gross profit has averaged 40% of net sales. Suppose the company's inventory records reveal the following data:

Inventory, March 1	$1,292,000
Transactions during March:	
Purchases	6,585,000
Purchase discounts	149,000
Purchase returns	8,000
Sales	8,657,000
Sales returns	17,000

Required

1. Estimate the cost of the lost inventory using the gross profit method.
2. Prepare Kinko's March income statement for this inventory through gross profit. Show the detailed computation of cost of goods sold in a separate schedule.

Apply Your Knowledge

Decision Cases

Assessing the impact of a year-end purchase of inventory
(Obj. 3, 4)

Case 1. Caledonia Corporation is nearing the end of its first year of operations. The company made inventory purchases of $745,000 during the year, as follows:

January	1,000 units @ $100.00 =		$100,000
July	4,000	121.25	485,000
November	1,000	160.00	160,000
Totals	6,000		$745,000

Sales for the year will be 5,000 units for $1,200,000 of revenue. Expenses other than cost of goods sold and income taxes will be $200,000. The president of the company is undecided about whether to adopt the FIFO method or the LIFO method for inventories.

The company has storage capacity for 5,000 additional units of inventory. Inventory prices are expected to stay at $160 per unit for the next few months. The president is considering purchasing 1,000 additional units of inventory at $160 each before the end of the year. He wishes to know how the purchase would affect net income under both FIFO and LIFO. The income tax rate is 40%.

Required

1. To aid company decision making, prepare income statements under FIFO and under LIFO, both *without* and *with* the year-end purchase of 1,000 units of inventory at $160 per unit.
2. Compare net income under FIFO *without* and *with* the year-end purchase. Make the same comparison under LIFO. Under which method does the year-end purchase have the greater effect on net income?
3. Under which method can a year-end purchase be made in order to manage net income?

Assessing the impact of the inventory costing method on the financial statements
(Obj. 3, 4, 5)

Case 2. The inventory costing method a company chooses can affect the financial statements and thus the decisions of the people who use those statements.

Required

1. A leading accounting researcher stated that one inventory costing method reports the most recent costs in the income statement, whereas another method reports the most recent costs in the balance sheet. In this person's opinion, the result is that one or the other of the statements is "inaccurate" when prices are rising. What did the researcher mean?
2. Conservatism is an accepted accounting concept. Would you want management to be conservative in accounting for inventory if you were (a) a shareholder or (b) a prospective shareholder? Give your reason.
3. Outback Cycle Company follows conservative accounting and writes the value of its inventory of bicycles down to market, which has declined below cost. The following year, an unexpected cycling craze results in a demand for bicycles that far exceeds supply, and the market price increases above the previous cost. What effect will conservatism have on the income of Outback over the 2 years?

Ethical Issue

During 20X5, Balmoral Corporation changed to the LIFO method of accounting for inventory. Suppose that during 20X6, Balmoral changes back to the FIFO method and the following year switches back to LIFO again.

Required

1. What would you think of a company's ethics if it changed accounting methods every year?
2. What accounting principle would changing methods every year violate?
3. Who can be harmed when a company changes its accounting methods too often? How?

Financial Statement Case

Analyzing inventories
(Obj. 2, 3)

The notes are part of the financial statements. They give details that would clutter the statements. This case will help you learn to use a company's inventory notes. Refer to Fossil's statements and related notes in Appendix A at the end of the book and answer the following questions:

1. How much was Fossil's merchandise inventory at January 5, 2002? At December 30, 2000?
2. How does Fossil value its inventories? Which cost method does the company use?
3. How much were Fossil's inventory purchases during the year ended January 5, 2002?

Analytical Case

Measuring critical inventory amounts
(Obj. 3, 6)

Refer to the **Pier 1 Imports** financial statements in Appendix B at the end of this book.

1. Three important pieces of inventory information are (a) the cost of inventory on hand, (b) the cost of goods sold, and (c) the cost of inventory purchases. Identify or compute each of these items for Pier 1 at the end of 2002.
2. Which item in requirement 1 is most directly related to cash flow? Why?
3. Assume that all inventory purchases were made on account, and that only inventory purchases increased Accounts Payable. Compute Pier 1's cash payments for inventory during 2002. The amount of Accounts Payable is reported in Pier 1's "Notes to Consolidated Financial Statements."
4. How does Pier 1 value its inventories? Which costing method does Pier 1 use?
5. Did Pier 1's gross profit percentage and rate of inventory turnover improve or deteriorate in 2002 (versus 2001)? Consider the overall effect of these two ratios. Did Pier 1 improve during 2002? Pier 1's inventories totaled $268,906 thousand at the end of 2000.

Group Project

Comparing companies' inventory turnover ratios
(Obj. 6)

Obtain the annual reports of 10 companies, 2 from each of five different industries. Most companies' financial statements can be downloaded from their Web sites.

1. Compute each company's gross profit percentage and rate of inventory turnover for the most recent 2 years. If annual reports are unavailable or do not provide enough data for multiple-year computations, you can gather financial statement data from *Moody's Industrial Manual*.
2. For the industries of the companies you are analyzing, obtain the industry averages for gross profit percentage and inventory turnover from Robert Morris Associates, *Annual*

Statement Studies; Dun and Bradstreet, *Industry Norms and Key Business Ratios;* or Leo Troy, *Almanac of Business and Industrial Financial Ratios.*

3. How well does each of your companies compare to the other company in its industry? How well do your companies compare to the average for their industry? What insight about your companies can you glean from these ratios?
4. Write a memo to summarize your findings, stating whether your group would invest in each of the companies it has analyzed.

Appendix A to Chapter 6

Accounting for Inventory in the Periodic System

In the periodic inventory system, the business keeps no running record of the inventory on hand. Instead, at the end of the period, the business counts inventory on hand and applies the unit costs to determine the cost of ending inventory. This inventory figure appears on the balance sheet and is used to compute cost of goods sold.

Recording Transactions in the Periodic System

In the periodic system, the business records purchases of inventory in the Purchases account (an expense). Throughout the period, the Inventory account carries the beginning balance left over from the preceding period. At the end of the period, the Inventory account must be updated for the financial statements. A journal entry removes the beginning balance by crediting Inventory and debiting Cost of Goods Sold. A second journal entry sets up the ending inventory balance, based on the physical count. The final entry in this sequence transfers the amount of Purchases to Cost of Goods Sold. These end-of-period entries can be made during the closing process.

Exhibit 6A-1 illustrates the accounting in the periodic system. After the process is complete, Inventory has its correct ending balance of $120,000, and Cost of Goods Sold shows $540,000.

Check Points

Recording inventory transactions in the periodic system

CP6-1A Parkland Technologies began the year with inventory of $20,000. During the year, Parkland purchased inventory costing $100,000 and sold goods for $140,000, with all transactions on account. Parkland ended the year with inventory of $30,000. Journalize all the necessary transactions under the periodic inventory system.

Computing cost of goods sold and preparing the income statement

CP6-2A Use the data in Check Point 6-1A to do the following for Parkland Technologies:

1. Post to the Inventory and Cost of Goods Sold accounts.
2. Compute cost of goods sold by the cost-of-goods-sold model.
3. Prepare the income statement of Parkland Technologies through gross profit.

Exercises

Computing amounts for the GAAP inventory methods

E6-1A Suppose **Intel Corporation's** inventory records for a particular computer chip indicate the following at October 31:

Oct. 1	Beginning inventory	5 units @ $160
8	Purchase	4 units @ 160
15	Purchase	11 units @ 170
26	Purchase	5 units @ 180

The physical count of inventory at October 31 indicates that eight units of inventory are on hand, and there are no consignment goods.

Required

Compute ending inventory and cost of goods sold, using each of the following methods. Round, all amounts to the nearest dollar:

1. Specific unit cost, assuming four $160 units and four $170 units are on hand
2. Weighted-average cost
3. First-in, first-out
4. Last-in, first-out

Exhibit 6A-1 **Recording and Reporting Inventories—Periodic System (Amounts Assumed)**

PANEL A—Recording Transactions and the T-accounts

1. Purchase of inventory on account, $560,000

Purchases	560,000	
Accounts Payable		560,000

ASSETS	=	LIABILITIES	+	STOCKHOLDERS' EQUITY	−	EXPENSES
0	=	560,000			−	560,000

2. Sales of goods on account, $900,000

Accounts Receivable	900,000	
Sales Revenue		900,000

ASSETS	=	LIABILITIES	+	STOCKHOLDERS' EQUITY	+	REVENUES
900,000	=	0			+	900,000

3. End-of-period entries to update Inventory and record Cost of Goods Sold:

a. Transfer beginning inventory ($100,000) to Cost of Goods Sold.

Cost of Goods Sold	100,000	
Inventory (beginning balance)		100,000

b. Set up ending inventory ($120,000) based on a physical count.

Inventory (ending balance)	120,000	
Cost of Goods Sold		120,000

c. Transfer the cost of purchases to Cost of Goods Sold.

Cost of Goods Sold	560,000	
Purchases		560,000

The T-accounts show the following:

Inventory	
100,000*	100,000
120,000	

Cost of Goods Sold	
100,000	120,000
560,000	
540,000	

PANEL B—Reporting in the Financial Statements

Income Statement (Partial)

Sales revenue		$900,000
Cost of goods sold:		
Beginning inventory	$100,000	
Purchases	560,000	
Cost of goods available	660,000	
Ending inventory	(120,000)	
Cost of goods sold		540,000
Gross profit		$360,000

Ending Balance Sheet (Partial)

Current assets:	
Cash	$ XXX
Short-term investments	XXX
Accounts receivable	XXX
Inventory	120,000
Prepaid expenses	XXX

*Beginning Inventory was $100,000.

E6-2A Use the data in Exercise 6-1A to journalize the following for the periodic system:

Journalizing inventory transactions in the periodic system; computing cost of goods sold

1. Total October purchases in one summary entry. All purchases were on credit.
2. Total October sales in a summary entry. Assume that the selling price was $300 per unit and that all sales were on credit. Intel uses LIFO.
3. October 31 entries for inventory. Intel uses LIFO. Post to the Cost of Goods Sold T-account to show how this amount is determined. Label each item in the account.
4. Show the computation of cost of goods sold by the cost-of-goods-sold model.

Problems

P6-1A Assume a **Ralph Lauren Polo** outlet store began August 20X4 with 50 units of inventory that cost $40 each. The sale price of these units was $70. During August, the store completed these inventory transactions:

Computing cost of goods sold and gross profit on sales

		Units	Unit Cost	Unit Sale Price
Aug. 3	Sale	16	$40	$70
8	Purchase	80	41	72
11	Sale	34	40	70
19	Sale	9	41	72
24	Sale	35	41	72
30	Purchase	18	42	73
31	Sale	10	41	72

Required

1. Determine the store's cost of goods sold for August under the periodic inventory system. Assume the FIFO method.
2. Compute gross profit for August.

P6-2A Accounting records for Total Desserts, Inc. yield the following data for the year ended December 31, 20X5 (amounts in thousands):

Recording transactions in the periodic system; reporting inventory items in the financial statements

Inventory, December 31, 20X4	$ 370
Purchases of inventory (on account)	2,900
Sales of inventory—80% on account; 20% for cash	4,390
Inventory at the lower of FIFO cost or market, December 31, 20X5	560

Required

1. Journalize Total Desserts' inventory transactions for the year under the periodic system. Show all amounts in thousands. Use Exhibit 6A-1 as a model.
2. Report ending inventory, sales, cost of goods sold, and gross profit on the appropriate financial statement (amounts in thousands). Show the computation of cost of goods sold.

Appendix B to Chapter 6

The LIFO Reserve—Converting a LIFO Company's Income to the FIFO Basis

Suppose you are a financial analyst, and it is your job to recommend stocks for your clients to purchase as investments. You have narrowed your choice to **Wal-Mart Stores, Inc.**, and **Gap Inc.** Wal-Mart uses the LIFO method for inventories and the Gap uses FIFO. The two companies' net incomes are not comparable because they use different inventory methods. To compare the two companies, you need to place them on the same footing.

The Internal Revenue Service allows companies to use LIFO for income tax purposes only if they use LIFO for financial reporting, but companies may also report an alternative inventory amount in the financial statements. Doing so presents a rare opportunity to convert a company's net income from the LIFO basis to what the income would have been if the business had used FIFO. Fortunately, you can convert Wal-Mart's income from the LIFO basis, as reported in the company's financial statements, to the FIFO basis. Then you can compare Wal-Mart and Gap.

Like many other companies that use LIFO, Wal-Mart reports the FIFO cost, a LIFO Reserve, and the LIFO cost of ending inventory. The **LIFO Reserve**[1] is the difference between the LIFO cost of an inventory and what the cost of that inventory would be under FIFO. Assume that Wal-Mart reported the following amounts:

Wal-Mart Uses LIFO

	(In millions) 20X4	20X3
From the Wal-Mart balance sheet:		
Inventories (approximate FIFO cost)	$ 7,856	$6,207
Less LIFO reserve	(572)	(399)
LIFO cost	7,284	5,808
From the Wal-Mart income statement:		
Cost of goods sold	$34,786	
Net income	1,608	
Income tax rate	37%	

Converting Wal-Mart's 20X4 net income to the FIFO basis focuses on the LIFO Reserve because the reserve captures the difference between Wal-Mart's ending inventory costed at LIFO and at FIFO. Observe that during each year, the FIFO cost of ending inventory exceeded the LIFO cost. During 20X4, the LIFO Reserve increased by $173 million ($572 million − $399 million). *The LIFO Reserve can increase only when inventory costs are rising.* Recall that during a period of rising costs, LIFO produces the highest cost of goods sold and the lowest net income. Therefore, for 20X4, Wal-Mart's cost of goods sold would have been lower if the company had used the FIFO method for inventories. Wal-Mart's net income would have been higher, as the following computations show:

[1]The LIFO Reserve account is widely used in practice even though the term *reserve* is poor terminology.

If Wal-Mart Had Used FIFO in 20X4

	(In Millions)
Cost of goods sold, as reported under LIFO	$34,786
− Increase in LIFO Reserve ($572 − $399)	(173)
= Cost of goods sold, if Wal-Mart had used FIFO	$34,613
Lower cost of goods sold → Higher pretax income by	$ 173
Minus income taxes (37%)	(64)
Higher net income under FIFO	109
Net income as reported under LIFO	1,608
Net income Wal-Mart would have reported for 20X4 if using FIFO	$ 1,717

Now you can compare Wal-Mart's net income with that of Gap, Inc. All the ratios used for the analysis—current ratio, inventory turnover, and so on—can be compared between the two companies as though they both used the FIFO inventory method.

The LIFO Reserve provides another opportunity for managers and investors to answer a key question about a company:

How much income tax has the company saved over its lifetime by using the LIFO method to account for inventory?

Using Wal-Mart as an example, the computation at the end of 20X4 is (amounts in millions):

Income tax saved by using LIFO	=	**LIFO Reserve**	×	**Income tax rate**
$211.6	=	**$572**	×	**.37**

With these price changes by the end of 20X4, Wal-Mart has saved a total of $211.6 million by using the LIFO method to account for its merchandise inventory. Had Wal-Mart used the FIFO method, Wal-Mart would have almost $212 million less cash to invest in the opening of new stores.

In recent years many companies have experienced decreases in the cost of their inventory. When prices decline, cost of goods sold under FIFO is greater (LIFO cost of goods sold is less). This makes gross profit and net income less under FIFO.

7

Plant Assets, Intangibles, Related Expenses

Learning Objectives

1. **Determine** the cost of a plant asset
2. **Account** for depreciation
3. **Select** the best depreciation method
4. **Analyze** the effect of a plant asset disposal
5. **Account** for natural resources and depletion
6. **Account** for intangible assets and amortization
7. **Report** plant asset transactions on the statement of cash flows

Integrator CD

Need additional help? Go to the **Integrator CD** *and search these key words:*
accelerated depreciation, amortization, depletion, double-declining balance, goodwill, intangibles, MACRS, plant asset, straight-line, units-of-production

FedEx Corporation

Consolidated Balance Sheets (Assets Only, Adapted)

In millions	May 31, 2001	May 31, 2000
Assets		
Current Assets		
1 Cash and cash equivalents	$ 121	$ 68
2 Receivables, less allowances of $95,815 and $85,972	2,506	2,547
3 Spare parts, supplies and fuel	269	255
4 Prepaid expenses and other	553	415
5 Total current assets	3,449	3,285
6 **Property and Equipment, at Cost**		
7 Flight equipment	5,313	4,960
8 Package-handling and ground support equipment and vehicles	4,621	4,204
9 Computer and electronic equipment	2,637	2,416
10 Other	3,841	3,162
11	16,412	14,742
12 Less Accumulated depreciation and amortization	8,312	7,659
13 Net property and equipment	8,100	7,083
14 **Other Assets**		
15 Goodwill	1,082	501
16 Other assets	709	658
17 Total other assets	1,791	1,159
18	$13,340	$11,527

A merger specialist in Zurich, Switzerland, is putting together the acquisition of a software company in North Carolina. The merger documents have been agreed on but must be signed—tomorrow.

An artist in Cincinnati, Ohio, is scheduled to exhibit her lithographs in a museum in Santa Fe, New Mexico, and the curator of the museum needs the prints—by noon tomorrow.

Three hundred immigrants entered the United States at Miami, Florida, and the U.S. Customs officer must get copies of their passports to U.S. Customs in Seattle. Alas, the Seattle fax machine is not working, so the officer must find another way to get the documents there.

What do these three situations have in common? In each, someone has to get some information to another place absolutely, positively on time and with no chance for error. Where do they turn? To FedEx Corporation, the overnight delivery service. FedEx uses a wide variety of assets to move packages, from a few documents to a shipment of computers, around the world, usually overnight. What are FedEx's most important assets? The company's balance sheets show that FedEx has lots of airplanes (line 7), package-handling equipment (line 8), and computers (line 9). These are its plant assets.

Sitemap

- Types of Assets
- Measuring Plant Asset Depreciation
- Other Issues in Accounting for Plant Assets
- Accounting for Natural Resources
- Accounting for Intangible Assets
- Reporting Plant Asset Transactions: The Statement of Cash Flows

This chapter examines the category of long-term plant assets. It also covers natural resources such as oil and coal; and intangibles, which are assets with no physical form, like goodwill.

Chapter 7 concludes our coverage of assets, except for long-term investments, which we discuss in Chapter 10. The two key decisions about any asset are (1) buying the right assets at the right price and (2) using those assets to accomplish the organization's goals. Let's begin by examining the various types of long-term assets.

Types of Assets

intangibles, plant assets

Long-lived assets used in a business and not held for sale are divided into two categories in Exhibit 7-1.

Exhibit 7-1

Plant Asset Terminology

Asset Account (Balance Sheet)	*Related Expense Account (Income Statement)*
Plant Assets	
Land	None
Buildings, Machinery and Equipment, Furniture and Fixtures, and Land Improvements	Depreciation
Natural Resources	Depletion
Intangibles	Amortization

Plant asset
Long-lived assets, such as land, buildings, and equipment, used in the operation of the business. Also called *fixed assets*.

→ *We introduced the concept of depreciation in Chapter 3.*

✔ **Check Point 7-1**

- **Plant assets,** or *fixed assets,* are long-lived assets that are tangible—for instance, land, buildings, and equipment. The expense associated with plant assets is called *depreciation* ←. Of the plant assets, land is unique. Land is not expensed over time because its usefulness does not decrease. Most companies report plant assets as Property, plant, and equipment on the balance sheet. FedEx labels its plant assets as Property and equipment (line 6).
- **Intangible assets** are useful because of the special rights they carry. They have no physical form. Patents, copyrights, and trademarks are intangible assets; so is goodwill. Accounting for intangibles is similar to accounting for plant assets. FedEx reports the intangible asset Goodwill on its balance sheet (line 15).

Intangible asset
An asset with no physical form, a special right to current and expected future benefits.

Ex: a copyright
tangible - a patent is the exclusive to produce an item; meeting such a criteria (20 yrs.)

Accounting for plant assets and intangibles has its own terminology. Different names apply to the individual plant assets and their corresponding expense accounts, as shown in Exhibit 7-1.

Unless stated otherwise, we describe accounting in accordance with generally accepted accounting principles for financial-statement reporting to outsiders, as distinguished from reporting to the IRS for income tax purposes.

DECISION: How to Value Plant Assets—At Cost or at Market Value?

The accounting profession is moving toward market value accounting, which would report assets at their current value on the date of the balance sheet. **Market value** is the price the asset could be sold for. But the business community is not yet ready to apply market value accounting to tangible plant assets. Market values are too hard to determine for most plant assets because there is no established market to determine their prices. Consider a General Motors (GM) assembly plant. How much are all the robots worth? No one but Ford or DaimlerChrysler could use GM robots, and they may not want them. This is why we report plant assets at their historical cost. Historical cost is the price the company actually paid to acquire the asset. It is an objective but often outdated measure of a plant asset.

Here is a basic working rule for determining the cost of an asset: **The cost of any asset is the sum of all the costs incurred to bring the asset to its intended use.**

The cost of a plant asset includes purchase price, plus any taxes, commissions, and other amounts paid to make the asset ready for use. Because the specific costs differ for the various categories of plant assets, we discuss the major groups individually.

Objective

1 **Determine** the cost of a plant asset

Land

The cost of land includes its purchase price (cash plus any note payable given), brokerage commission, survey fees, legal fees, and any back property taxes that the purchaser pays. Land cost also includes expenditures for grading and clearing the land and for demolishing or removing unwanted buildings.

The cost of land does *not* include the cost of fencing, paving, sprinkler systems, and lighting. These are separate plant assets—called *land improvements*—and they are subject to depreciation.

Suppose FedEx signs a $300,000 note payable to purchase 20 acres of land for a new shipping site. FedEx also pays $10,000 for real estate commission, $8,000 of back property tax, $5,000 for removal of an old building, a $1,000 survey fee, and $260,000 to pave the parking lot—all in cash. What is FedEx's cost of this land?

Purchase price of land		$300,000
Add related costs:		
Real estate commission	$10,000	
Back property tax	8,000	
Removal of building	5,000	
Survey fee	1,000	
Total related costs		24,000
Total cost of land		$324,000

✔ Check Point 7-2

Note that the cost to pave the parking lot, $260,000, is *not* included in the land's cost, because the pavement is a land improvement. FedEx would record the purchase of this land as follows:

Land	324,000	
Note Payable		300,000
Cash		24,000

ASSETS	=	LIABILITIES	+	STOCKHOLDERS' EQUITY
+324,000 −24,000	=	+300,000	+	0

The purchase increases both assets and liabilities. There is no effect on equity.

Buildings, Machinery, and Equipment

The cost of constructing a building includes architectural fees, building permits, contractors' charges, and payments for material, labor, and overhead. If the company constructs its own building, the cost will also include the cost of interest on money borrowed to finance the construction.

When an existing building (new or old) is purchased, its cost includes the purchase price, brokerage commission, sales and other taxes paid, and all expenditures to repair and renovate the building for its intended purpose.

The cost of machinery and equipment includes its purchase price (less any discounts), plus transportation, insurance while in transit, sales and other taxes, purchase commission, installation costs, and any expenditures to test the asset before it is placed in service. The equipment cost will also include the cost of any special platforms used to support the equipment. After the asset is up and running, insurance, taxes, and maintenance costs are recorded as expenses, not as part of the asset's cost.

Land Improvements and Leasehold Improvements

For a FedEx shipping terminal, the cost to pave a parking lot ($260,000) would be recorded in a separate account entitled Land Improvements. This account includes costs for such other items as driveways, signs, fences, and sprinkler systems. Although these assets are located on the land, they are subject to decay, and their cost should therefore be depreciated. Also, the cost of a new building constructed on the land is an addition to the asset account Building.

FedEx leases some of its airplanes and other assets. The company customizes these assets to meet its special needs. For example, FedEx paints its logo on airplanes and delivery trucks. These improvements are assets of FedEx Corporation even though the company does not own the airplane or truck. The cost of improvements to leased assets appears on the company's balance sheet under other property and equipment (see line 10 of the FedEx balance sheet on page 317). The cost of leasehold improvements should be depreciated over the term of the lease. Most companies call the depreciation on leasehold improvements *amortization,* which is the same concept as *depreciation.*

Lump-Sum (or Basket) Purchases of Assets

Businesses often purchase several assets as a group, or in a "basket," for a single lump-sum amount. For example, a company may pay one price for land and a building. The company must identify the cost of each asset. The total cost is divided among the assets according to their relative sales (or market) values. This technique is called the *relative-sales-value method.*

Suppose Xerox Corporation purchases land and a building in Kansas City for a midwestern sales office. The building sits on two acres of land, and the combined purchase price of land and building is $2,800,000. An appraisal indicates that the land's market value is $300,000 and that the building's market value is $2,700,000.

Xerox first figures the ratio of each asset's market value to the total market value. Total appraised value is $2,700,000 + $300,000 = $3,000,000. Thus, the land, valued at $300,000, is 10% of the total market value. The building's appraised value is 90% of the total. These percentages are then used to determine the cost of each asset, as follows:

* On Test

Asset	Market (Sales) Value		Total Market Value		Percentage of Total Market Value	Total Cost		Cost of Each Asset
Land	$ 300,000	÷	$3,000,000	=	10%	× $2,800,000	=	$ 280,000
Building	2,700,000	÷	3,000,000	=	90%	× $2,800,000	=	2,520,000
Total	$3,000,000				100%			$2,800,000

If Xerox pays cash, the entry to record the purchase of the land and building is

Land	280,000	
Building	2,520,000	
Cash		2,800,000

✔ Check Point 7-3

ASSETS	=	LIABILITIES	+	STOCKHOLDERS' EQUITY
+280,000	=			
+2,520,000	=	0	+	0
−2,800,000	=			

How would FedEx Corporation divide a $120,000 lump-sum purchase price for land, building, and equipment with estimated market values of $40,000, $95,000, and $15,000, respectively?

Answer:

	Estimated Market Value	Percentage of Total Market Value	×	Total Cost	=	Cost of Each Asset
Land	$ 40,000	26.7%*	×	$120,000	=	$ 32,040
Building	95,000	63.3%	×	120,000	=	75,960
Equipment	15,000	10.0%	×	120,000	=	12,000
	$150,000	100.0%				$120,000

*$40,000/$150,000 = 0.267, and so on

DECISION: Capital Expenditure versus an Immediate Expense

When a company spends money on a plant asset, it must decide whether to record an asset or an expense. Examples of these expenditures range from FedEx's purchase of package-handling equipment to replacing the windshield wipers on a FedEx delivery van.

Expenditures that increase the asset's capacity or extend its useful life are called **capital expenditures.** For example, the cost of a major overhaul that extends the useful life of a FedEx delivery van is a capital expenditure. Capital expenditures are said to be *capitalized*, which means the cost is added to an asset account and not expensed immediately.

Capital expenditure
Expenditure that increases an asset's capacity or efficiency or extends its useful life. Capital expenditures are debited to an asset account.

Costs that do not extend the asset's capacity or its useful life, but merely maintain the asset, or restore it to working order, are recorded as expenses. For example,

Repair Expense is reported on the income statement and matched against revenue. The costs of repainting a FedEx delivery truck, repairing a dented fender, and replacing tires are also expensed immediately. Exhibit 7-2 illustrates the distinction between capital expenditures and immediate expenses for delivery truck expenditures.

Exhibit 7-2

Capital Expenditure or Immediate Expense for Costs Associated with a Delivery Truck

Record an Asset for Capital Expenditures	***Record Repair and Maintenance Expense, and not an Asset, for an Expense***
Extraordinary repairs:	*Ordinary repairs:*
Major engine overhaul	Repair of transmission or other mechanism
Modification of body for new use of truck	Oil change, lubrication, and so on
	Replacement tires, windshield, or a paint job
Addition to storage capacity of truck	

A major decision in accounting for plant assets is whether to capitalize or to expense a certain cost. The distinction between a capital expenditure and an expense requires judgment: Does the cost extend the asset's usefulness or its useful life? If so, record an asset. If the cost merely repairs or maintains the asset or returns it to its prior condition, then record an expense.

A company such as FedEx or Home Depot, wanting to look good to investors and creditors, has an incentive to capitalize the cost and add to the assets it reports to the public. But these companies have a competing incentive. They also want an immediate tax deduction, which they can have by expensing the cost immediately. They can't have it both ways.

Most companies expense all small costs, say, below $1,000. For higher costs, they follow the rule we gave above: they capitalize costs that extend the asset's usefulness or its useful life, and they expense all other costs. A conservative policy that avoids overstating assets and profits is safe. Companies that overstate their assets may get into trouble and have to defend themselves in court. Whenever investors lose money because a company overstated its profits or its assets, the investors file a lawsuit. The courts tend to be sympathetic to investor losses caused by shoddy accounting. The Enron debacle is an example.

✔ Check Point 7-4

Measuring Plant Asset Depreciation

accelerated depreciation, double-declining balance, straight-line, units of production

Plant assets wear out, grow obsolete, and lose value over time. To account for this process, we allocate a plant asset's cost to expense over its life—a process called *depreciation*. The depreciation process matches the asset's expense against revenue to measure income, as the matching principle directs ←. Exhibit 7-3 illustrates the depreciation process for the purchase of a Boeing 737 jet by FedEx Corporation.

→ *See Chapter 3 for a discussion of the matching principle.*

Exhibit 7-3

Depreciation and the Matching of Expense with Revenue

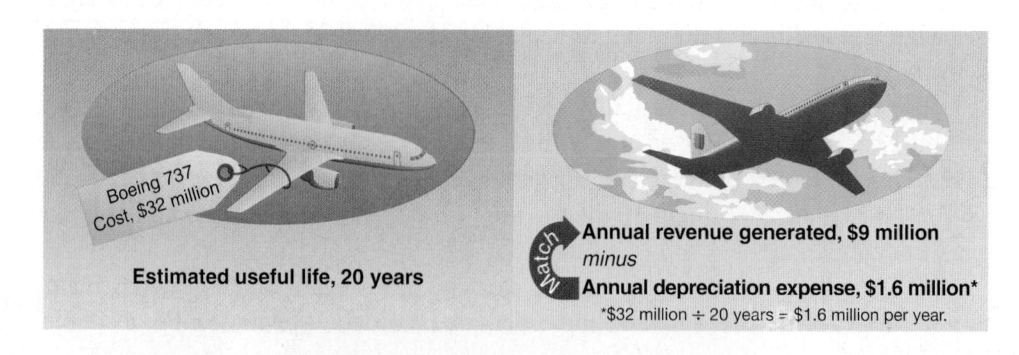

Only land has an unlimited life. For most plant assets, depreciation is caused by

- *Physical wear and tear.* For example, physical deterioration takes its toll on the usefulness of FedEx airplanes, delivery trucks, and buildings.
- *Obsolescence.* Computers and other electronic equipment may be *obsolete* before they deteriorate. An asset is obsolete when another asset can do the job more efficiently. An asset's useful life may be shorter than its physical life. Companies depreciate their computers over a short period of time—perhaps 4 years—even though the computers will remain in working condition much longer.

Suppose FedEx buys a computer for use in tracking packages. FedEx believes it will get 4 years of service from the computer, which will then be worthless. Under straight-line depreciation, FedEx expenses one-quarter of the asset's cost in each of its 4 years of use.

Let's contrast what depreciation accounting is with what it is *not*.

1. ***Depreciation is not a process of valuation.*** Businesses do not record depreciation based on changes in the market value of their plant assets. Instead, businesses allocate the asset's cost to the periods of its useful life based on a specific depreciation method.
2. ***Depreciation does not mean setting aside cash to replace assets as they wear out.*** Any cash fund is entirely separate from depreciation.

How to Measure Depreciation

To measure depreciation for a plant asset, we must know its

1. Cost
2. Estimated useful life
3. Estimated residual value

We have already discussed cost—that is, the purchase price of the asset—which is a known amount. The other two factors must be estimated.

Estimated useful life is the length of service expected from using the asset. Useful life may be expressed in years, units of output, miles, or some other measure. For example, the useful life of a building is stated in years. The useful life of a FedEx airplane or delivery truck may be expressed as the total number of miles the vehicle is expected to travel. Companies base such estimates on past experience and information from industry and government publications.

Estimated useful life
Length of a service that a business expects to get from an asset. May be expressed in years, units of output, miles, or other measures.

Estimated residual value—also called *scrap value* or *salvage value*—is the expected cash value of an asset at the end of its useful life. For example, FedEx may believe that a package-handling machine will be useful for 7 years. After that time, FedEx may expect to sell the machine as scrap metal. The amount FedEx believes it can get for the machine is the estimated residual value. In computing depreciation, the asset's estimated residual value is *not* depreciated because FedEx expects to receive this amount from selling the asset. If there's no expected residual value, the full cost of the asset is depreciated. A plant asset's **depreciable cost** is measured as follows:

Estimated residual value
Expected cash value of an asset at the end of its useful life. Also called *residual value, scrap value,* or *salvage value.*

Depreciable cost
The cost of a plant asset minus its estimated residual value.

Depreciable cost = Asset's cost − Estimated residual value

Depreciation Methods

Objective

2 Account for depreciation

There are three main depreciation methods:

- Straight-line
- Units-of-production
- Double-declining-balance—
  an accelerated depreciation method
- SYD - Some of the years digits

These methods allocate different amounts of depreciation to each period. However, they all result in the same total amount of depreciation, which is the asset's depreciable cost. Exhibit 7-4 presents the data we use to illustrate depreciation computations for a FedEx truck.

Exhibit 7-4

Data for Depreciation Computations—A FedEx Truck

Data Item	*Amount*
Cost of truck	$41,000
Less Estimated residual value	(1,000)
Depreciable cost	$40,000
Estimated useful life:	
Years	5 years
Units of production	100,000 units [miles]

Straight-line (SL) method Depreciation method in which an equal amount of depreciation expense is assigned to each year (or period) of asset use.

STRAIGHT-LINE METHOD. In the **straight-line (SL) method**, an equal amount of depreciation is assigned to each year (or period) of asset use. Depreciable cost is divided by useful life in years to determine the annual depreciation expense. Applied to the FedEx truck data from Exhibit 7-4, SL depreciation is

$$\textbf{Straight-line depreciation per year} = \frac{\textbf{Cost} - \textbf{Residual value}}{\textbf{Useful life, in years}}$$

$$= \frac{\$41,000 - \$1,000}{5}$$

$$= \$8,000$$

The entry to record depreciation is

Depreciation Expense	8,000	
Accumulated Depreciation		8,000

ASSETS	=	LIABILITIES	+	STOCKHOLDERS' EQUITY	–	EXPENSES
–8,000	=	0			–	8,000

Observe that depreciation decreases the asset (through Accumulated Depreciation) and also decreases equity (through Depreciation Expense). Let's assume that FedEx purchased this truck on January 1, 20X3, and that FedEx's fiscal year ends on December 31. Exhibit 7-5 gives a *straight-line depreciation schedule* for the truck. The final column of the exhibit shows the *asset's book value*, which is its cost less accumulated depreciation ←.

→ *We introduced the concept of book value in Chapter 3.*

Exhibit 7-5 **Straight-Line Depreciation for a FedEx Truck**

		Depreciation for the Year						
Date	**Asset Cost**	**Depreciation Rate**		**Depreciable Cost**		**Depreciation Expense**	**Accumulated Depreciation**	**Asset Book Value**
1- 1-20X3	$41,000							$41,000
12-31-20X3		.20*	×	$40,000	=	$8,000	$ 8,000	33,000
12-31-20X4		.20	×	40,000	=	8,000	16,000	25,000
12-31-20X5		.20	×	40,000	=	8,000	24,000	17,000
12-31-20X6		.20	×	40,000	=	8,000	32,000	9,000
12-31-20X7		.20	×	40,000	=	8,000	40,000	1,000

* $^1/_5$ years = .20 per year

As an asset is used in operations, accumulated depreciation increases, and the book value of the asset decreases. An asset's final book value is its *residual value* ($1,000 in Exhibit 7-5). At the end of its useful life, the asset is said to be *fully depreciated.*

A FedEx sorting machine that cost $10,000, has a useful life of 5 years and residual value of $2,000, was purchased on January 1. What is SL depreciation for each year?

Answer: $1,600 = ($10,000 − $2,000)/5

Units-of-production (UOP) method Depreciation method by which a fixed amount of depreciation is assigned to each unit of output produced by the plant asset.

UNITS-OF-PRODUCTION METHOD. In the **units-of-production (UOP) method**, a fixed amount of depreciation is assigned to each *unit of output,* or service, produced by the asset. Depreciable cost is divided by useful life, in units of production, to determine this amount. This per-unit depreciation expense is then multiplied by the number of units produced each period to compute depreciation. The UOP depreciation for the FedEx truck data in Exhibit 7-4 (page 324) is

$$\textbf{Units-of-production depreciation per unit of output} = \frac{\textbf{Cost} - \textbf{Residual value}}{\textbf{Useful life, in units of production}}$$

$$= \frac{\$41,000 - \$1,000}{100,000 \text{ miles}} = \$0.40 \text{ per mile}$$

Assume that the truck is expected to be driven 20,000 miles during the first year, 30,000 during the second, 25,000 during the third, 15,000 during the fourth, and 10,000 during the fifth. Exhibit 7-6 shows the UOP depreciation schedule.

Exhibit 7-6 **Units-of-Production Depreciation for a FedEx Truck**

		Depreciation for the Year						
Date	**Asset Cost**	**Depreciation Per Unit**		**Number of Units**		**Depreciation Expense**	**Accumulated Depreciation**	**Asset Book Value**
1- 1-20X3	$41,000							$41,000
12-31-20X3		$0.40*	×	20,000	=	$ 8,000	$ 8,000	33,000
12-31-20X4		0.40	×	30,000	=	12,000	20,000	21,000
12-31-20X5		0.40	×	25,000	=	10,000	30,000	11,000
12-31-20X6		0.40	×	15,000	=	6,000	36,000	5,000
12-31-20X7		0.40	×	10,000	=	4,000	40,000	1,000

*($41,000 − $1,000)/100,000 miles = $0.40 per mile.

The amount of UOP depreciation varies with the number of units the asset produces. In our example, the total number of units produced is 100,000. UOP depreciation does not depend directly on time, as do the other methods.

Accelerated depreciation method A depreciation method that writes off a relatively larger amount of the asset's cost nearer the start of its useful life than the straight-line method does.

Double-declining-balance (DDB) method An accelerated depreciation method that computes annual depreciation by multiplying the asset's decreasing book value by a constant percentage, which is 2 times the straight-line rate.

DOUBLE-DECLINING-BALANCE METHOD. An **accelerated depreciation method** writes off a larger amount of the asset's cost near the start of its useful life than the straight-line method does. Double-declining-balance is the main accelerated depreciation method. **Double-declining-balance (DDB) depreciation** computes annual depreciation by multiplying the asset's declining book value by a constant percentage, which is two times the straight-line depreciation rate. DDB amounts are computed as follows:

- *First*, compute the straight-line depreciation rate per year. A 5-year truck has a straight-line depreciation rate of 1/5, or 20% each year. A 10-year asset has a straight-line rate of 1/10, or 10%, and so on.
- *Second*, multiply the straight-line rate by 2 to compute the DDB rate. For a 5-year asset, the DDB rate is 40% (20% × 2). A 10-year asset has a DDB rate of 20% (10% × 2).
- *Third*, multiply the DDB rate by the period's beginning asset book value (cost less accumulated depreciation). Under the DDB method, ignore the residual value of the asset in computing depreciation, except during the last year. The DDB rate for the FedEx truck in Exhibit 7-4 (page 324) is

$$\textbf{DDB depreciation rate per year} = \frac{1}{\textbf{Useful life, in years}} \times 2$$

$$= \frac{1}{\textbf{5 years}} \times 2$$

$$= 20\% \times 2 = 40\%$$

✔ Check Point 7-5

- *Fourth*, determine the final year's depreciation amount—that is, the amount needed to reduce asset book value to its residual value. In Exhibit 7-7, the fifth and final year's DDB depreciation is $4,314—book value of $5,314 less the $1,000 residual value. *The residual value should not be depreciated* but should remain on the books until the asset is disposed.

Exhibit 7-7

Double-Declining-Balance Depreciation for a FedEx Truck

		Depreciation for the Year							
Date	**Asset Cost**	**DDB Rate**		**Asset Book Value**		**Depreciation Expense**	**Accumulated Depreciation**	**Asset Book Value**
1- 1-20X3	$41,000							$41,000
12-31-20X3		.40	×	$41,000	=	$16,400	$16,400	24,600
12-31-20X4		.40	×	24,600	=	9,840	26,240	14,760
12-31-20X5		.40	×	14,760	=	5,904	32,144	8,856
12-31-20X6		.40	×	8,856	=	3,542	35,686	5,314
12-31-20X7						4,314*	40,000	1,000

*Last-year depreciation is the amount needed to reduce asset book value to the residual value ($5,314 − $1,000 = $4,314).

The DDB method differs from the other methods in two ways:

1. Residual value is ignored initially; in the first year, depreciation is computed on the asset's full cost.
2. Depreciation expense in the final year is whatever amount is needed to reduce the asset's book value to its residual value.

What is the DDB depreciation of the asset in the Stop & Think on page 325 for each year?

Answers:

Yr. 1: \$4,000 (\$10,000 × 40%)
Yr. 2: \$2,400 (\$6,000 × 40%)
Yr. 3: \$1,440 (\$3,600 × 40%)
Yr. 4: \$160 (\$10,000 − \$4,000 − \$2,400 − \$1,440 − \$2,000)*
Yr. 5: \$0

*The asset is not depreciated below residual value.

Comparing Depreciation Methods

Let's compare the three methods in terms of the yearly amount of depreciation. The yearly amount of depreciation varies by method, but the total \$40,000 depreciable cost is the same under all methods.

	Amount of Depreciation Per Year		
			Accelerated Method
Year	*Straight-Line*	*Units-of-Production*	*Double-Declining-Balance*
1	\$ 8,000	\$ 8,000	\$16,400
2	8,000	12,000	9,840
3	8,000	10,000	5,904
4	8,000	6,000	3,542
5	8,000	4,000	4,314
Total	\$40,000	\$40,000	\$40,000

✔ Check Point 7-6

Generally accepted accounting principles (GAAP) direct a business to match an asset's depreciation against the revenue the asset produces. For a plant asset that generates revenue evenly over time, the straight-line method best meets the matching principle. The units-of-production method best fits those assets that wear out because of physical use rather than obsolescence. The accelerated method (DDB) applies best to assets that generate greater amounts of revenue earlier in their useful lives.

Exhibit 7-8 graphs annual depreciation amounts for the straight-line, units-of-production, and accelerated depreciation (DDB) methods. The graph of straight-line depreciation is flat through time because annual depreciation is the same in all periods. Units-of-production depreciation follows no particular pattern because annual depreciation depends on the use of the asset. Accelerated depreciation is greatest in the first year and less in the later years.

Exhibit 7-8

Depreciation Patterns Through Time

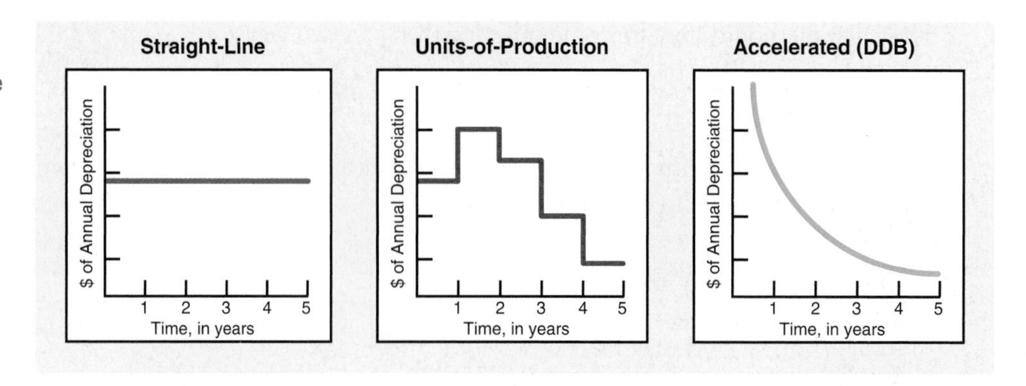

A recent survey of 600 companies conducted by the American Institute of CPAs indicates that the straight-line method is most popular. Exhibit 7-9 shows the percentages of companies that use each of the depreciation methods.

Exhibit 7-9

Depreciation Methods Used by 600 Companies

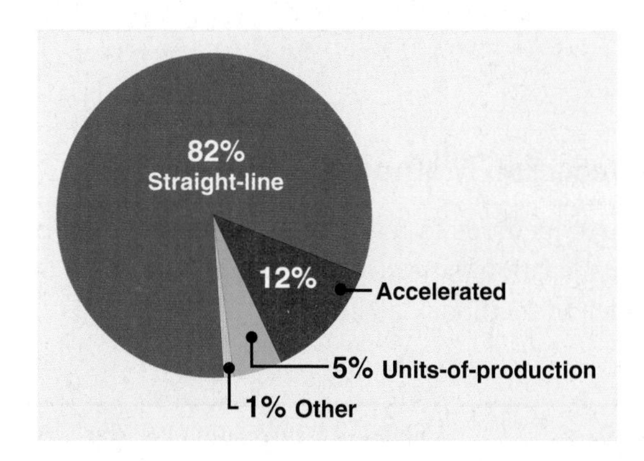

Mid-Chapter Summary Problem

Suppose FedEx Corporation purchased equipment on January 1, 20X3, for $44,000. The expected useful life of the equipment is 10 years or 100,000 units of production, and its residual value is $4,000. Under three depreciation methods, the annual depreciation expense and the balance of accumulated depreciation at the end of 20X3 and 20X4 are as follows:

	Method A		Method B		Method C	
Year	Annual Depreciation Expense	Accumulated Depreciation	Annual Depreciation Expense	Accumulated Depreciation	Annual Depreciation Expense	Accumulated Depreciation
20X3	$4,000	$4,000	$8,800	$ 8,800	$1,200	$1,200
20X4	4,000	8,000	7,040	15,840	5,600	6,800

Required

1. Identify the depreciation method used in each instance, and show the equation and computation for each. (Round off to the nearest dollar.)

2. Assume continued use of the same method through year 20X5. Determine the annual depreciation expense, accumulated depreciation, and book value of the equipment for 20X3 through 20X5 under each method, assuming 12,000 units of production in 20X5.

Answers

Requirement 1

Method A: Straight-Line

Depreciable cost = $40,000 ($44,000 − $4,000)
Each year: $40,000/10 years = $4,000

Method B: Double-Declining-Balance

$$\text{Rate} = \frac{1}{10 \text{ years}} \times 2 = 10\% \times 2 = 20\%$$

20X3: .20 × $44,000 = $8,800

20X4: .20 × ($44,000 − $8,800) = $7,040

Method C: Units-of-Production

$$\text{Depreciation per unit} = \frac{\$44{,}000 - \$4{,}000}{100{,}000 \text{ units}} = \$0.40$$

20X3: $0.40 × 3,000 units = $1,200

20X4: $0.40 × 14,000 units = $5,600

Requirement 2

Method A: Straight-Line

Year	Annual Depreciation Expense	Accumulated Depreciation	Book Value
Start			$44,000
20X3	$4,000	$ 4,000	40,000
20X4	4,000	8,000	36,000
20X5	4,000	12,000	32,000

Method B: Double-Declining-Balance

Year	Annual Depreciation Expense	Accumulated Depreciation	Book Value
Start			$44,000
20X3	$8,800	$ 8,800	35,200
20X4	7,040	15,840	28,160
20X5	5,632	21,472	22,528

Method C: Units-of-Production

Year	Annual Depreciation Expense	Accumulated Depreciation	Book Value
Start			$44,000
20X3	$1,200	$ 1,200	42,800
20X4	5,600	6,800	37,200
20X5	4,800	11,600	32,400

Computations for 20X5	
Straight-line	\$40,000/10 years = \$4,000
Double-declining-balance	.20 × \$28,160 = \$5,632
Units-of-production	\$0.40 × 12,000 units = \$4,800

MACRS

Other Issues in Accounting for Plant Assets

Plant Assets are complex because of their long lives. Depreciation affects income taxes, and companies may have gains or losses when they sell plant assets.

Depreciation for Tax Purposes

Objective

3 **Select** the best depreciation method.

Most companies use straight-line depreciation for reporting to their stockholders and creditors on their financial statements. They also keep a separate set of depreciation records for computing their income taxes. For tax purposes, most companies use an accelerated depreciation method.

Suppose you are a business manager. The IRS allows an accelerated depreciation method, which most managers prefer to straight-line depreciation. Why? Because it provides the fastest depreciation deductions, thus decreasing your immediate tax payments. You can then reinvest the cash back into your business.

To understand the relationships between cash flow, depreciation, and income tax, recall our earlier depreciation example for a FedEx truck:

- First-year depreciation is \$8,000 under straight-line and \$16,400 under double-declining-balance (DDB).
- DDB is permitted for income tax reporting.

Assume that this FedEx office has \$400,000 in revenue and \$300,000 in cash operating expenses during the truck's first year and an income tax rate of 30%. The cash flow analysis appears in Exhibit 7-10.

Exhibit 7-10

The Cash-Flow Advantage of Accelerated Depreciation over Straight-Line Depreciation for Income Tax Purposes

		SL	*Accelerated*
1	Cash revenues	\$400,000	\$400,000
2	Cash operating expenses	300,000	300,000
3	Cash provided by operations before income tax	100,000	100,000
4	Depreciation expense (a noncash expense)	8,000	16,400
5	Income before income tax	92,000	83,600
6	Income tax expense (30%)	\$ 27,600	\$ 25,080
	Cash-flow analysis:		
7	Cash provided by operations before tax	\$100,000	\$100,000
8	Income tax expense	27,600	25,080
9	Cash provided by operations	\$ 72,400	\$ 74,920
10	Extra cash available for investment if DDB is used (\$74,920 − \$72,400)		\$ 2,520

✔ Check Point 7-7

Exhibit 7-10 highlights an important fact: The higher the depreciation expense, the lower the income before tax and thus the lower the tax payment. Therefore, accelerated depreciation helps conserve cash for use in the business. Exhibit 7-10 shows that FedEx will have $2,520 (line 10) more cash at the end of the first year if it uses accelerated depreciation instead of SL.

Which depreciation method makes FedEx look better to its stockholders? How much better? Show how you arrive at your answer.

Answer:
Straight-line depreciation makes FedEx look better. Net income under

- Straight-line depreciation is $64,400 ($92,000 − $27,600).
- Accelerated depreciation is $58,520 ($83,600 − $25,080).

Under straight-line depreciation, FedEx reports $5,880 ($64,400 − $58,520) more net income. Therefore, most managers prefer to use straight-line depreciation for their financial statements.

There is a special depreciation method—used only for income tax purposes—called the **Modified Accelerated Cost Recovery System (MACRS).** Under this method, assets are grouped into one of eight classes identified by asset life (Exhibit 7-11). Depreciation for the first four classes is computed by the double-declining-balance method. Depreciation for 15-year assets and 20-year assets is computed by the 150%-declining-balance method. Under this method, the annual depreciation rate is computed by multiplying the straight-line rate by 1.50 (instead of 2.00, as for DDB). For a 20-year asset, the straight-line rate is .05 per year (1/20 = .05), so the annual MACRS depreciation rate is .075 (.05 × 1.50 = .075). The taxpayer computes annual depreciation by multiplying asset book value by .075, in a manner similar to the way the DDB method works. Most real estate is depreciated by the straight-line method (see the last two categories in Exhibit 7-11).

Modified Accelerated Cost Recovery System (MACRS)
A special depreciation method used only for income tax purposes. Assets are grouped into classes, and for a given class depreciation is computed by the double-declining-balance method, the 150%-declining balance method, or, for most real estate, the straight-line method.

Exhibit 7-11

Details of the Modified Accelerated Cost Recovery System (MACRS) Depreciation Method

Class Identified by Asset Life (years)	*Representative Assets*	*Depreciation Method*
3	Race horses	DDB
5	Automobiles, light trucks	DDB
7	Equipment	DDB
10	Equipment	DDB
15	Sewage-treatment plants	150% DB
20	Certain real estate	150% DB
$27\frac{1}{2}$	Residential rental property	SL
39	Nonresidential rental property	SL

Depreciation for Partial Years

Companies purchase plant assets whenever they need them. They do not wait until the beginning of a year or a month. Therefore, companies must compute *depreciation for partial years*. Suppose the County Line Bar-B-Q restaurant in Denver purchases a building on April 1 for $500,000. The building's estimated life is 20 years, and its estimated residual value is $80,000. The restaurant's fiscal year ends on December 31. Let's consider how the company computes depreciation for April through December:

- First compute depreciation for a full year.
- Then multiply the full year's depreciation by the fraction of the year that you held the asset. Assuming the straight-line method, the year's depreciation for County Line's building is $15,750, as follows:

$$\text{Full-year depreciation } \frac{\$500{,}000 - \$80{,}000}{20} = \$21{,}000$$

$$\text{Partial year depreciation } \$21{,}000 \times 9/12 = \$15{,}750$$

What if County Line bought the asset on April 18? Many businesses record no monthly depreciation on assets purchased after the 15th of the month, and they record a full month's depreciation on an asset bought on or before the 15th.

✔ Check Point 7-8

Most companies use computerized systems to account for fixed assets. Each asset has a unique identification number that links to the asset's cost, estimated life, residual value, and depreciation method. The system will automatically calculate the depreciation expense for each period. Both Accumulated Depreciation and book value are automatically updated.

Changing the Useful Life of a Depreciable Asset

As we've discussed, managers must decide on an asset's useful life to compute its depreciation. After the asset is put into use, managers may refine its estimate on the basis of experience and new information. The Walt Disney Company made such a change, called a *change in accounting estimate*. Disney recalculated depreciation on the basis of revised useful lives of several of its theme park assets. The following note in Walt Disney's financial statements reports this change in accounting estimate:

> *Note 5*
> *. . . [T]he Company extended the estimated useful lives of certain theme park ride and attraction assets based upon historical data and engineering studies. The effect of this change was to decrease depreciation by approximately $8 million (an increase in net income of approximately $4.2 million . . .).*

Assume that a Disney hot dog stand cost $40,000 and that the company originally believed the asset had an 8-year useful life with no residual value. Using the straight-line method, the company would record $5,000 depreciation each year ($40,000/8 years = $5,000). Suppose Disney used the asset for 2 years. Accumulated depreciation reached $10,000, leaving a remaining depreciable book value (cost *less* accumulated depreciation *less* residual value) of $30,000 ($40,000 − $10,000). From its experience, management believes the asset will remain useful for an additional 10 years. The company would spread the remaining depreciable book value over the asset's remaining life as follows:

Asset's remaining depreciable book value	÷	(New) Estimated useful life remaining	=	(New) Annual depreciation
$30,000	÷	**10 years**	=	**$3,000**

The yearly depreciation entry based on the new estimated useful life is

Depreciation Expense—Hot Dog Stand	3,000	
Accumulated Depreciation—Hot Dog Stand		3,000

✔ Check Point 7-9

ASSETS	=	LIABILITIES	+	STOCKHOLDERS' EQUITY	−	EXPENSES
−3,000	=	0			−	3,000

1. Suppose Walt Disney Company was having a bad year—net income is well below expectations and lower than last year's income. For depreciation purposes, Disney extended the estimated useful lives of its depreciable assets. How would this accounting change affect Disney's (a) depreciation expense, (b) net income, and (c) owners' equity?
2. Suppose that Disney's accounting change turned a loss year into a profitable year. Without the accounting change, the company would have reported a net loss for the year. The accounting change enabled Disney to report net income. Under GAAP, Disney's annual report must disclose the accounting change and its effect on net income. Would investors evaluate Disney as better or worse for having made this accounting change?

Answers:

1. An accounting change that lengthens the estimated useful lives of depreciable assets (a) decreases depreciation expense and (b, c) increases net income and owners' equity.
2. Investor reactions are not always predictable. There is research to indicate that companies cannot fool investors. In this case, investment advisers would *probably* subtract from Disney's reported net income the amount added by the accounting change. Investors could then use the remaining net *loss* figure to evaluate Disney's lack of progress during the year. Investors would probably view Disney as worse for having made this accounting change.

DECISION: Is It Ethical to Keep Two Sets of Depreciation Records?

Is it ethical for FedEx Corporation, Home Depot, and GM to keep two sets of depreciation records—one for its financial statements and the other for reporting to the IRS? Yes, that's perfectly okay because the two sets of depreciation records serve two very different purposes.

The depreciation records illustrated in this chapter are designed for the income statement and the balance sheet. The purpose here is to measure accounting income and asset values for reporting to stockholders and creditors. Accounting theory is the driving force behind these depreciation amounts to provide relevant information for investment and credit decisions.

Depreciation amounts for income tax purposes march to the beat of a different drummer. Congress designs tax depreciation to raise tax revenue for the government. Political considerations enter the world of taxes, so tax depreciation is a little different from basic accounting depreciation.

Fully Depreciated Assets

A *fully depreciated asset* is an asset that has reached the end of its estimated useful life. Suppose FedEx has fully depreciated equipment with zero residual value (cost was $50,000). FedEx accounts will appear as follows:

Equipment			Accumulated Depreciation	
50,000				**50,000**

The equipment's book value is zero, but that doesn't mean the equipment is worthless. FedEx may continue using the equipment for a few more years, but will not take any more depreciation.

When FedEx disposes of the equipment, FedEx will remove both the asset's cost ($50,000) and its accumulated depreciation ($50,000) from the books. The next section shows how to account for plant asset disposals.

Accounting for Disposal of Plant Assets

Objective

4 **Analyze** the effect of a plant asset disposal

Eventually, a plant asset ceases to serve a company's needs. The asset may wear out, become obsolete, or for some other reason cease to be useful. Before accounting for the disposal of the asset, the business should bring depreciation up to date to measure the asset's final book value.

To account for disposal remove the asset and its related accumulated depreciation from the books. Suppose the final year's depreciation expense has just been recorded for a machine that cost $50,000 and is estimated to have zero residual value. The machine's accumulated depreciation thus totals $50,000. Assuming that this asset is junked, the entry to record its disposal is:

Accumulated Depreciation—Machinery	50,000	
Machinery		50,000
To dispose of fully depreciated machine.		

ASSETS	=	LIABILITIES	+	STOCKHOLDERS' EQUITY
+150,000 −150,000	=	0	+	0

There is no gain or loss on this disposal, so there is no effect on equity.

If assets are junked before being fully depreciated, the company incurs a loss on the disposal. Suppose Wal-Mart disposes of store fixtures that cost $4,000 in this manner. Accumulated depreciation is $3,000, and book value is, therefore, $1,000. Junking these store fixtures results in a loss as follows:

Accumulated Depreciation—Store Fixtures	3,000	
Loss on Disposal of Store Fixtures	1,000	
Store Fixtures		4,000
To dispose of store fixtures.		

ASSETS	=	LIABILITIES	+	STOCKHOLDERS' EQUITY	−	LOSSES
+3,000 −4,000	=	0			−	1,000

Wal-Mart got rid of an asset with $1,000 book value and received nothing. The result is a $1,000 loss, which decreases equity.

The Loss on Disposal of Store Fixtures is reported as Other income (expense) on the income statement. Losses decrease net income exactly as expenses do. Gains increase net income in the same manner as revenues.

SELLING A PLANT ASSET. Suppose FedEx sells equipment on September 30, 20X4, for $5,000 cash. The equipment cost $10,000 when purchased on January 1, 20X1, and has been depreciated on a straight-line basis. FedEx originally estimated a

10-year useful life and no residual value. Prior to recording the sale, the FedEx accountants must update the asset's depreciation. Suppose the business uses the calendar year as its accounting period. Partial-year depreciation must be recorded for the asset's expense from January 1, 20X4, to the sale date. The straight-line depreciation entry at September 30, 20X4, is

Sept. 30	Depreciation Expense ($10,000/10 years × 9/12)	750	
	Accumulated Depreciation—Fixtures		750
	To update depreciation.		

ASSETS	=	LIABILITIES	+	STOCKHOLDERS' EQUITY	−	EXPENSES
−750	=	0			−	750

The Fixtures account and the Accumulated Depreciation—Fixtures account appear as follows. Observe that the fixtures' book value is $6,250 ($10,000 − $3,750).

Fixtures			
Jan. 1, 20X1	10,000		

Accumulated Depreciation—Fixtures			
		Dec. 31, 20X1	1,000
		Dec. 31, 20X2	1,000
		Dec. 31, 20X3	1,000
		Sep. 30, 20X4	750
		Balance	3,750

Suppose FedEx sells the fixtures for $5,000 cash. The loss on the sale is $1,250, determined as follows:

Cash received from sale of the asset		$5,000
Book value of asset sold:		
Cost	$10,000	
Less accumulated depreciation	(3,750)	6,250
Gain (loss) on sale of the asset		($1,250)

The entry to record sale of the fixtures for $5,000 cash is

Sept. 30	Cash	5,000	
	Accumulated Depreciation—Fixtures	3,750	
	Loss on Sale of Fixtures	1,250	
	Fixtures		10,000
	To sell fixtures.		

✔ Check Point 7-10

ASSETS	=	LIABILITIES	−	STOCKHOLDERS' EQUITY	−	LOSSES
+ 5,000						
+ 3,750	=	0			−	1,250
− 10,000						

If the sale price had been $7,000, the business would have had a gain of $750 (Cash, $7,000 − asset book value, $6,250). Gains are recorded as credits, in the same manner as revenues. Gains and losses on asset disposals appear on the income statement as other income (expense).

Suppose FedEx Corporation's comparative income statement for 2 years included these items:

	(In billions)	
	20X2	20X1
Net revenues	$30.2	$28.0
Income from operations	2.7	3.2
Other income (expense)		
Gain on sale of store facilities	.8	
Income before income taxes	$ 3.5	$ 3.2

Which was a better year for FedEx—20X2 or 20X1?

Answer:

From a revenue standpoint, 20X2 was better because revenues were higher. But from an *income* standpoint, 20X1 was better.

In 20X1, shipping operations—the company's core business—generated $3.2 billion of income from operations. In 20X2, operations produced only $2.7 billion of operating income. Almost $1 billion of the company's income in 20X2 came from selling store facilities (gain of $0.8 billion). A business cannot hope to continue on this path very long. This example shows why investors and creditors care about the sources of a company's profits, not just the final amount of net income.

EXCHANGING PLANT ASSETS. Managers often trade in old plant assets for new ones. For example, a pizzeria may trade in a 5-year-old delivery car for a newer model. In many cases, the business simply transfers the book value of the old asset plus any cash payment into the new asset account. For example, assume Mazzio Pizzeria's old delivery car cost $9,000 and has accumulated depreciation of $8,000. The old car's book value is $1,000. If Mazzio trades in the old automobile and pays cash of $10,000, the cost of the new delivery car is $11,000 (book value of the old asset, $1,000, plus cash given, $10,000). The pizzeria records the exchange transaction as follows:

Delivery Auto (new)	11,000	
Accumulated Depreciation (old)	8,000	
Delivery Auto (old)		9,000
Cash		10,000
Traded in old delivery car for new auto.		

ASSETS	=	LIABILITIES	+	STOCKHOLDERS' EQUITY
+ 11,000				
+ 8,000	=	0	+	0
− 9,000				
− 10,000				

There was no gain or loss on this exchange, so there was no effect on equity.

Accounting for Natural Resources

depletion

Natural resources are plant assets of a special type, such as iron ore, petroleum (oil), and timber. As plant assets are expensed through depreciation, so natural resource assets are expensed through *depletion*. **Depletion expense** is that portion of the cost of a natural resource that is used up in a particular period. Depletion expense is computed in the same way as units-of-production depreciation.

Objective

5 **Account** for natural resources and depletion

Depletion expense
That portion of a natural resource's cost that is used up in a particular period. Depletion expense is computed in the same way as units-of-production depreciation.

An oil lease may cost Exxon Mobil $100,000 and contain an estimated 10,000 barrels of oil. The depletion rate would be $10 per barrel ($100,000/10,000 barrels). If 3,000 barrels are extracted, depletion expense is $30,000 (3,000 barrels × $10 per barrel). The depletion entry is

Depletion Expense (3,000 barrels × $10)	30,000	
Accumulated Depletion—Oil		30,000

ASSETS	=	LIABILITIES	+	STOCKHOLDERS' EQUITY	−	EXPENSES
− 30,000	=	0			−	30,000

Both assets and equity decrease. Why equity? Because the depletion expense decreases net income and then also decreases retained earnings.

If 4,500 barrels are removed the next year, that period's depletion is $45,000 (4,500 barrels × $10 per barrel). Accumulated Depletion is a contra account similar to Accumulated Depreciation.

Natural resource assets can be reported on ExxonMobil's balance sheet as follows (amounts assumed):

Property, Plant, and Equipment:		
Equipment	$960,000	
Less: Accumulated depreciation	(410,000)	$550,000
Oil	$340,000	
Less: Accumulated depletion	(70,000)	270,000
Total property, plant, and equipment		$820,000

✔ Check Point 7-11

Accounting for Intangible Assets

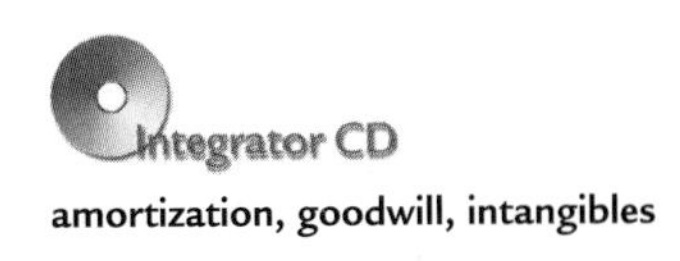

amortization, goodwill, intangibles

As we saw earlier, *intangible assets* are long-lived assets with no physical form. Intangibles are valuable because they carry special rights from patents, copyrights, trademarks, franchises, leaseholds, and goodwill. Like buildings and equipment, an intangible asset is recorded at its acquisition cost. Cost is then systematically expensed through **amortization** over the intangible estimated useful life unless the asset is determined to have an indefinite life.

Objective

6 **Account** for intangible assets and amortization

Amortization
The systematic reduction of a lump-sum amount. Expense that applies to intangible assets in the same way depreciation applies to plant assets and depletion applies to natural resources.

Amortization is the same concept as depreciation, but applied to intangibles it is called amortization. Amortization is often computed on a straight-line basis. Amortization expense for an intangible asset can be written off directly against the asset account rather than held in an accumulated amortization account. The residual value of most intangibles is zero.

Assume that Sony purchases a patent on a new DVD process. Legally, the patent may run for 20 years. But Sony realizes that new technologies will limit the process's life to 4 years. If the patent cost $80,000, each year of amortization expense is $20,000 ($80,000/4). The balance sheet reports the patent at its acquisition cost less amortization expense to date. After 1 year, the patent has a $60,000 balance ($80,000 − $20,000), after 2 years a $40,000 balance, and so on.

Types of Intangible Assets

Each type of intangible asset is unique, and the accounting can vary from one intangible to another.

Patent
A federal government grant giving the holder the exclusive right for 20 years to produce and sell an invention.

PATENTS. **Patents** are federal government grants giving the holder the exclusive right for 20 years to produce and sell an invention. The invention may be a product or a process—for example, Sony compact disk players and the Dolby noise-reduction process. Like any other asset, a patent may be purchased. Suppose a company pays $170,000 to acquire a patent on January 1, and the business believes the expected useful life of the patent is 5 years. Amortization expense is $34,000 per year ($170,000/5 years). Sony records the acquisition and amortization for this patent as follows:

Jan. 1	Patents	170,000	
	Cash		170,000
	To acquire a patent.		

ASSETS	=	LIABILITIES	+	STOCKHOLDERS' EQUITY
+ 170,000 − 170,000	=	0	+	0

Dec. 31	Amortization Expense—Patents ($170,000/5)	34,000	
	Patents		34,000
	To amortize the cost of a patent.		

ASSETS	=	LIABILITIES	+	STOCKHOLDERS' EQUITY	−	EXPENSES
− 34,000	=	0			−	34,000

Both assets and equity decrease because of the amortization expense.

Copyright
Exclusive right to reproduce and sell a book, musical composition, film, other work of art, or computer program. Issued by the federal government, copyrights extend 50 years beyond the author's life.

COPYRIGHTS. **Copyrights** are exclusive rights to reproduce and sell a book, musical composition, film, or other work of art. Copyrights also protect computer software programs, such as Microsoft's Windows® and Excel's spreadsheet. Issued by the federal government, copyrights extend 50 years beyond the author's (composer's, artist's, or programmer's) life. The cost of obtaining a copyright from the government is low, but a company may pay a large sum to purchase an existing copyright from the owner. For example, a publisher may pay the author of a popular novel $1 million or more for the book copyright. Because the useful life of a copyright is usually no longer than 2 or 3 years, each period's amortization amount is a high proportion of the copyright cost.

Trademark, trade name
A distinctive identification of a product or service. Also called a *brand name*.

TRADEMARKS AND TRADE NAMES. **Trademarks** and **trade names** (or **brand names**). These are distinctive identifications of products or services. The "eye" symbol that flashes across our television screens is the trademark that identifies the CBS television network. You are probably also familiar with NBC's peacock. Seven-Up, Pepsi, Egg McMuffin, and Rice-a-Roni are everyday trade names. Advertising slogans that are legally protected include United Airlines' "Fly the friendly skies" and Avis Rental Car's "We try harder."

The cost of a trademark or trade name may be amortized over its useful life. But if the trademark is expected to generate cash flow for the indefinite future, the business should not amortize the trademark's cost.

Franchises and licenses Privileges granted by a private business or a government to sell product or service in accordance with specified conditions.

FRANCHISES AND LICENSES. **Franchises** and **licenses** are privileges granted by a private business or a government to sell a product or service in accordance with specified conditions. The Dallas Cowboys football organization is a franchise granted to its owner by the National Football League. McDonald's restaurants and Holiday Inns are popular franchises. Consolidated Edison Company (ConEd) holds a New York City franchise right to provide electricity to residents. The useful lives of many franchises and licenses are indefinite and, therefore, are not amortized.

Goodwill Excess of the cost of an acquired company over the sum of the market values of its net assets (assets minus liabilities).

GOODWILL. In accounting, **goodwill** has a very specific meaning. It is defined as the excess of the cost of purchasing another company over the sum of the market values of its net assets (assets minus liabilities). A purchaser is willing to pay for goodwill when it buys another company with abnormal earning power.

Wal-Mart Stores has expanded into Mexico and other countries. Suppose Wal-Mart acquires Mexana Company at a cost of $10 million. The sum of the market values of Mexana's assets is $9 million, and its liabilities total $1 million so Mexana's *net* assets total $8 million at current market value. In this case, Wal-Mart paid $2 million for goodwill, computed as follows:

Purchase price paid for Mexana Company		$10 million
Sum of the market values of Mexana Company's assets	$9 million	
Less: Mexana Company's liabilities	(1 million)	
Market value of Mexana Company's net assets		8 million
Excess is called *goodwill*		$ 2 million

Wal-Mart's entry to record the acquisition of Mexana Company, including its goodwill, would be

Assets (Cash, Receivables, Inventories, Plant Assets, all at market value)	9,000,000	
Goodwill	2,000,000	
Liabilities		1,000,000
Cash		10,000,000

✔ Check Point 7-12

ASSETS	=	LIABILITIES	+	STOCKHOLDERS' EQUITY
+9,000,000				
+2,000,000	=	+1,000,000	+	0
−10,000,000				

Note that Wal-Mart has acquired both Mexana's assets *and* its liabilities.

Goodwill has special features, as follows:

1. Goodwill is recorded *only* when it is purchased in the acquisition of another company. A purchase transaction provides objective evidence of the value of goodwill. Companies never record goodwill that they create for their own business.
2. According to generally accepted accounting principles (GAAP), goodwill is not amortized because the goodwill of many entities increases in value.

Accounting for the Impairment of an Intangible Asset

Some intangibles—such as goodwill, licenses, and some trademarks—have indefinite lives and, therefore, are not subject to amortization. But all intangibles are subject to a write-down when their value decreases. PepsiCo is a major company with vast amounts of purchased goodwill due to its acquisition of other companies.

Each year, PepsiCo determines whether the goodwill it has purchased has increased or decreased in value. If PepsiCo's goodwill is worth more at the end of the year than at the beginning, no increase in the asset is permitted. But if PepsiCo's goodwill has decreased in value, say from $500 million to $470 million, then PepsiCo will record a $30 million loss as follows (in millions):

20X2			
Dec. 31	Loss on Goodwill ($500 − $470)	30	
	Goodwill		30

ASSETS	=	LIABILITIES	+	STOCKHOLDERS' EQUITY	−	EXPENSES
−30	=	0			−	30

PepsiCo's financial statements will report the following (in millions):

	20X2	*20X1*
Balance sheet		
Intangible assets:		
Goodwill	$470	$500
Income statement		
(Loss) on goodwill	(30)	—

Valuing Intangibles: Why Did the Dot-Com Bubble Burst?

Many wonder why the dot-com bubble burst. For one thing, investors were valuing companies such as Mother Nature.Com and Dr. Koop.Com based on expected future earnings. Overeager investors looked at the dot-coms' revenues and reasoned that they must earn a profit someday. Unfortunately, in too many cases, that day never arrived.

An examination of the balance sheets of most dot-coms reveals very little in the way of assets. Investors were paying prices for the dot-coms' stocks as though the companies were profitable and asset-rich. But about all they had were an enterprising idea and a slot on the Internet—both of which are intangible. Like all other assets, intangibles are only as valuable as the profits and the cash flow they generate. Some intangibles are immensely valuable, but they have an inherent disadvantage compared to plant and equipment: If the company fails, the owners can sell buildings and equipment. Intangibles are almost always worthless. So, in the final analysis, many dot-com investors spent and lost billions buying "blue sky."

Accounting for Research and Development Costs

Accounting for research and development (R&D) costs is one of the most difficult issues the accounting profession has faced. R&D is the lifeblood of companies such as Procter & Gamble, General Electric, Intel, and Boeing. It can be argued that R&D is one of these companies' most valuable (intangible) assets. But, in general, companies do not report R&D assets on their balance sheets.

GAAP requires companies to expense R&D costs as they incur them. Only in limited circumstances may the company capitalize R&D cost as an asset. For example, a company may incur R&D cost under a contract guaranteeing that the company will recover the costs from a customer. This R&D cost is an asset, and the company records an intangible R&D asset when it incurs the cost. But this is the exception to the general rule.

✔ Check Point 7-13

Reporting Plant Asset Transactions on the Statement of Cash Flows

Objective

7 Report plant asset transactions on the statement of cash flows

Three main types of plant asset transactions appear on the statement of cash flows: acquisitions, sales, and depreciation (including amortization and depletion).

Acquisitions and sales are *investing* activities. A company invests in plant assets by paying cash or by incurring a liability. The cash payments for plant and equipment are investing activities that appear on the statement of cash flows. The sale of plant assets results in a cash receipt, as illustrated in Exhibit 7-12, which excerpts data from the cash-flow statement of FedEx Corporation. The acquisitions, sales, and depreciation of plant assets are denoted in color (lines 5, 6, and 2).

Exhibit 7-12

Reporting Plant Asset Transactions on FedEx's Statement of Cash Flows

FedEx Corporation

Statement of Cash Flows (partial, adapted)
Year Ended May 31, 2001

		(In millions)
	Operating activities:	
1	Net income	$ 584
	Adjustments to reconcile net income to cash provided by operating activities:	
2	Depreciation and amortization	1,276
3	Other items (summarized)	184
4	Cash provided by operating activities	2,044
	Investing Activities:	
5	Purchases of property and equipment	(1,893)
6	Proceeds from dispositions of property and equipment	237
7	Other items (summarized)	(457)
8	Cash used in investing activities	(2,113)
	Financing Activities:	
9	Cash provided by financing activities	122
10	Net increase (decrease) in cash and cash equivalents	53
11	Cash and cash equivalents at beginning of year	68
12	Cash and cash equivalents at end of year	$ 121

✔ Check Point 7-14

Let's examine the investing activities first. During the fiscal year ended May 31, 2001, FedEx paid $1,893 million for plant assets (line 5). FedEx also sold property and equipment, receiving cash of $237 million (line 6). FedEx labels the cash received as Proceeds from dispositions of property and equipment. The $237 million is the amount of cash received from the sale of plant assets. A gain or loss on the sale of plant assets is not reported as an investing activity on the statement of cash flows. The gain or loss is reported on the income statement.

FedEx's statement of cash flows reports Depreciation and amortization in the operating activities section (line 2). Observe that "Depreciation and amortization" is listed as a positive item under Adjustments to reconcile net income to Cash provided by operating activities. You may be wondering why depreciation appears on the cash-flow statement. After all, depreciation does not affect cash.

In this format, the operating activities section of the cash-flow statement starts with net income (line 1) and reconciles to cash provided by operating activities (line 4). Depreciation decreases net income in the same way that all other expenses do. But depreciation does not affect cash. Depreciation is therefore added back to net income to measure cash flow from operations. The add-back of depreciation to net income offsets the earlier subtraction of the expense. The sum of net income plus depreciation, therefore, helps to reconcile net income (on the accrual basis) to cash flow from operations (a cash-basis amount). We revisit this topic in the full context of the statement of cash flows in Chapter 12.

Incidentally, FedEx's cash flows are exceptionally strong. Operations generated $2,044 million of cash and FedEx spent $1,893 million on new property and equipment. The company is not standing still.

Test your ability to use the cash-flow statement.

1. Make an entry in the journal to record FedEx's purchases of property and equipment during the year.
2. Suppose the book value of the property and equipment that FedEx sold was $51 million (cost of $72 million minus accumulated depreciation of $21 million). Record the company's transaction to sell the property and equipment. Also write a sentence to explain why the sale transaction resulted in a gain for FedEx Corporation.
3. Where would FedEx report any gain or loss on the sale of the property and equipment—on which financial statement, under what heading?

Answers:

	(In millions)	
1. Property and Equipment	1,893	
Cash		1,893
Made capital expenditures.		
2. Cash	237	
Accumulated Depreciation	21	
Property and Equipment		72
Gain on Sale of Property and Equipment		186

Sold property and equipment.
The company sold for $237 million assets that had book value of $51 million. The result of the sale was a gain of $186 million ($237 million received − $51 million given up).

3. Report the gain on the *income statement* under the heading *Other income (expense).*

Decision Guidelines

PLANT ASSETS AND RELATED EXPENSES

FedEx Corporation, like all other companies, must make some decisions about how to account for its plant assets and intangibles. Let's review some of these decisions.

Decision	Guidelines
Capitalize or expense a cost?	General rule: Capitalize all costs that provide *future* benefit for the business, such as a new package-handling system. Expense all costs that provide *no future* benefit, such as a repair to an airplane.
Capitalize or expense:	
• Cost associated with a new asset?	Capitalize all costs that bring the asset to its intended use, including asset purchase price, transportation charges, and taxes paid to acquire the asset.
• Cost associated with an existing asset?	Capitalize only those costs that add to the asset's usefulness or to its useful life. Expense all other costs as maintenance or repairs.
• Interest cost incurred to finance the asset's acquisition?	Capitalize interest cost only on assets constructed by the business for its own use. Expense all other interest cost.
Which depreciation method to use	
• For financial reporting?	Use the method that best matches depreciation expense against the revenues produced by the asset. Most companies use the straight-line method.
• For income tax?	Use the method that produces the fastest tax deductions (MACRS). A company can use different depreciation methods for financial reporting and for income tax purposes. In the United States, this practice is considered both legal and ethical.
• How to account for natural resources?	Capitalize the asset's acquisition cost and all later costs that add to the natural resource's future benefit. Then record depletion expense, as computed by the units-of-production method.
• How to account for intangibles?	Capitalize acquisition cost and all later costs that add to the asset's future benefit. For intangibles with finite lives, record amortization expense. For intangibles with indefinite lives, do not record amortization. But if an intangible asset loses value, then record a loss in the amount of the decrease in asset value.

Excel Application Problem

Goal: To create an Excel worksheet that calculates the net income on an investment in a proposed plant asset under different depreciation methods.

Scenario: Suppose FedEx is considering investing in a new computerized parcel-sorting machine for its primary distribution center in Memphis, Tennessee. The following information is related to the acquisition and operation of the machine:

Initial investment	$1,000,000
Salvage value	$100,000
Useful life	6 years
Annual revenue attributable to the investment	$420,000
Annual operating expenses associated with the investment	$140,000

The machine will be in use for 5,840 hours in year one, 4,380 hours each in years two and four, 3,650 hours in year five, and 2,920 hours each in years three and six.

When done with your worksheet, answer these questions:

1. Which depreciation method produces the highest net income in year 1? In year 6? If it's not the same method for each year, why not?
2. Which method would FedEx choose for tax purposes? Why?
3. Which method would FedEx choose for reporting to stockholders and creditors? Why? What if the company wanted to change methods after two years?

Step-by-step:

1. Open a new Excel worksheet.
2. Prepare a bold-faced heading with the following information:
   a. Chapter 7 Decision Guidelines
   b. FedEx Depreciation Schedule
   c. Today's Date
3. Two rows under your heading, prepare four sections in your worksheet:
   a. Section 1 needs to contain the information listed in the table above, plus a line item for depreciation per unit.
   b. Section 2 will calculate net income from the investment using straight-line depreciation calculated using the SLN spreadsheet function. This section will have the following format:

Section 2: Straight-Line Depreciation

	Year						
	0	1	2	3	4	5	6
Annual Operating Revenue							
Annual Operating Expenses							
Annual Depreciation							
Annual Net Income							

   c. Section 3 will calculate net income from the investment using double-declining-balance depreciation calculated using the DDB spreadsheet function. This section will have a format like that of Section 2.
   d. Section 4 will calculate net income from the investment using units-of-production depreciation (there is no Excel formula for this depreciation method). This section will have a format like that of Section 2, with the addition of a row for the annual units of production.
4. Format all cells appropriately, save your worksheet, and print a copy for your files.

End-of-Chapter Summary Problem

Problem 1

The figures that follow appear in the *Answers to the Mid-Chapter Summary Problem*, Requirement 2, on page 329.

	Method A: Straight-Line			Method B: Double-Declining-Balance		
Year	Annual Depreciation Expense	Accumulated Depreciation	Book Value	Annual Depreciation Expense	Accumulated Depreciation	Book Value
Start			$44,000			$44,000
20X3	$4,000	$ 4,000	40,000	$8,800	$ 8,800	35,200
20X4	4,000	8,000	36,000	7,040	15,840	28,160
20X5	4,000	12,000	32,000	5,632	21,472	22,528

Required

Suppose the income tax authorities permitted a choice between these two depreciation methods. Which method would FedEx Corporation select for income tax purposes? Why?

Problem 2

Suppose FedEx purchased the equipment described in the table on January 1, 20X3.

Management has depreciated the equipment by using the double-declining-balance method. On July 1, 20X5, FedEx sold the equipment for $27,000 cash.

Required

Record depreciation for 20X5 and the sale of the equipment on July 1, 20X5.

Answers

Problem 1

For tax purposes, most companies select the accelerated method because it results in the most depreciation in the earliest years of the equipment's life. Accelerated depreciation minimizes taxable income and income tax payments in the early years of the asset's life, thereby maximizing the business's cash at the earliest possible time.

Problem 2

To record depreciation to date of sale, and then the sale of the equipment:

20X5			
July 1	Depreciation Expense—Equipment ($5,632 × 1/2 year)	2,816	
	Accumulated Depreciation—Equipment		2,816
	To update depreciation.		
July 1	Cash	27,000	
	Accumulated Depreciation—Equipment ($15,840 + $2,816)	18,656	
	Equipment		44,000
	Gain on Sale of Equipment		1,656
	To record sale of equipment.		

Review Plant Assets and Intangibles

Lessons Learned

1. **Determine the cost of a plant asset.** Plant assets are long-lived tangible assets, such as land, buildings, and equipment, used in the operation of a business. The cost of a plant asset is the purchase price plus applicable taxes, purchase commissions, and all other amounts paid to acquire the asset and to prepare it for its intended use.
2. **Account for depreciation.** Most businesses account for depreciation (the allocation of a plant asset's cost to expense over its useful life) by three methods: *straight-line, units-of-production,* or the *double-declining-balance method.*
3. **Select the best depreciation method.** Most companies use an accelerated depreciation method for income tax purposes. Accelerated depreciation results in higher expenses, lower taxable income, and lower tax payments early in the asset's life.
4. **Analyze the effect of a plant asset disposal.** Before disposing of, selling, or trading in a plant asset, the company updates the asset's depreciation. Then remove the book balances of the asset account and its related accumulated depreciation. Sales often result in a gain or loss, which is reported on the income statement. When exchanging a plant asset, the cost of the new asset is the book value of the old asset plus any cash payment.
5. **Account for natural resources and depletion.** The cost of natural resources, a special category of long-lived assets is expensed through *depletion*, which is computed on a units-of-production basis. Accumulated Depletion is a contra account similar to Accumulated Depreciation.
6. **Account for intangible assets and amortization.** Intangible assets have no physical form. They give their owners a special right to current and expected future benefits. The major types of intangible assets are patents, copyrights, trademarks, franchises and licenses, leaseholds, and goodwill.

   The cost of intangibles except goodwill is expensed through *amortization*. Amortization on intangibles is computed on a straight-line basis over the asset's useful life.
7. **Report plant asset transactions on the statement of cash flows.** Three main plant asset transactions appear on the statement of cash flows. Acquisitions and sales of plant assets are investing activities. Depreciation, depletion, and amortization appear among operating activities as add-backs to net income.

Accounting Vocabulary

accelerated depreciation method (p. 326)
amortization (p. 337)
brand name (p. 338)
capital expenditure (p. 321)
copyright (p. 338)
depletion expense (p. 337)
depreciable cost (p. 323)
double-declining-balance (DDB) method (p. 326)
estimated residual value (p. 323)
estimated useful life (p. 323)
franchises and licenses (p. 339)
goodwill (p. 339)
intangible assets (p. 318)
Modified Accelerated Cost Recovery System (MACRS) (p. 331)
patent (p. 338)
plant assets (p. 318)
straight-line (SL) method (p. 324)
trademark, trade name (p. 338)
units-of-production (UOP) method (p. 325)

Questions

1. To what types of long-lived assets do the following expenses apply: depreciation, depletion, and amortization?
2. Describe how to measure the cost of a plant asset. Would an ordinary cost of repairing the asset after it is placed in service be included in the asset's cost? Give your reason.
3. When assets are purchased as a group for a single price and no individual asset cost is given, how is each asset's cost determined?
4. Distinguish a capital expenditure from an immediate expense. What is the fundamental difference between these two costs?
5. Define depreciation. Present the common misconceptions about depreciation.
6. Explain the concept of accelerated depreciation. Which other depreciation method is used in the definition of double-declining-balance depreciation? Which depreciation method results in the most depreciation in the first year of the asset's life?
7. The level of business activity fluctuates widely for Harwood Delivery Service, reaching its peak around Christmas each year. At other times, business is slow. Which depreciation method is most appropriate for the company's fleet of Ford Aerostar minivans?
8. **Kinko's** uses the most advanced copy machines available to keep a competitive edge over other copy centers. To maintain this advantage, Kinko's replaces its machines before they are worn out. Describe the major factors affecting the useful lives of Kinko's copy machines.
9. Which type of depreciation method is best from an income tax standpoint? Why? How does depreciation affect income taxes? How does depreciation affect cash provided by operations?
10. What expense applies to natural resources? By which depreciation method is this expense computed?
11. How do intangible assets differ from most other assets? Why are they assets at all? What type of expense applies to intangible assets? Under what condition is this expense recorded? Under what condition is the expense not recorded?
12. Why is the cost of patents and other intangible assets often expensed over a shorter period than the legal life of the asset?
13. Your company has just purchased another company for $400,000. The market value of the other company's net assets is $325,000. What is the $75,000 excess called? What type of asset is it? How is this asset accounted for over its useful life?
14. **Microsoft** is recognized as a world leader in the development of software. The company's past success created vast amounts of business goodwill. Would you expect to see this goodwill reported on Microsoft's financial statements? Why or why not?
15. Describe the three types of plant asset transactions reported on a statement of cash flows. Indicate where and how each type of transaction appears on the statement.

Assess Your Progress

Check Points

Cost and book value of a company's plant assets
(Obj. 1)

CP7-1 Examine the balance sheet of **FedEx Corporation** at the beginning of this chapter. Answer these questions about the company:

1. When does FedEx's fiscal year end? Why does the company's fiscal year end on this date?
2. What is FedEx's largest category of assets?
3. What was FedEx's cost of property and equipment at May 31, 2001? What was the book value of property and equipment on this date? Why is book value less than cost?

CP7-2 Page 319 of this chapter lists the costs included for the acquisition of land. First is the purchase price of the land, which is obviously included in the cost of the land. The reasons for including the related costs are not so obvious. For example, property tax is ordinarily an expense, not part of the cost of an asset. State why the related costs listed on page 319 are included as part of the cost of the land. After the land is ready for use, will these related costs be capitalized or expensed?

Measuring the cost of a plant asset
(Obj. 1)

CP7-3 Return to the **FedEx** Stop & Think feature on page 321. Suppose at the time of your acquisition, the land has a current market value of $80,000, the building's market value is $60,000, and the equipment's market value is $20,000. Journalize FedEx's lump-sum purchase of the three assets for a total cost of $140,000. You sign a note payable for this amount.

Lump-sum purchase of assets
(Obj. 1)

CP7-4 Assume **Delta Airlines** repaired one of its Boeing 777 aircraft at a cost of $1 million, which Delta paid in cash. Further, assume the Delta accountant erroneously capitalized this cost as part of the cost of the plane.

Show the effects of the accounting error on Delta Airlines' income statement and balance sheet. To answer this question, determine whether plant assets, total expenses, net income, total assets, and owners' equity would be overstated or understated by the accounting error.

Capitalizing versus expensing plant asset costs
(Obj. 1)

CP7-5 Assume that at the beginning of 20X0, **UPS**, the package shipping company, purchased a used Boeing 737 aircraft at a cost of $21,000,000. UPS expects the plane to remain useful for 5 years (5 million miles) and to have a residual value of $6,000,000. UPS expects the plane to be flown 750,000 miles the first year and 1,250,000 miles the last year.

1. Compute UPS's first-year depreciation on the plane using the following methods:
   a. Straight-line b. Units-of-production c. Double-declining-balance
2. Show the airplane's book value at the end of the first year under each depreciation method.

Computing depreciation by three methods—first year only
(Obj. 2)

CP7-6 Use the assumed **UPS** data in Check Point 7-5 to compute UPS's fifth-year depreciation on the plane using the following methods:
a. Straight-line b. Units-of-production c. Double-declining-balance

Computing depreciation by three methods—final year only
(Obj. 2)

CP7-7 This exercise uses the assumed **UPS** data from Check Point 7-6. Assume UPS is trying to decide which depreciation method to use for income tax purposes.

1. Which depreciation method offers the tax advantage for the first year? Describe the nature of the tax advantage.
2. How much income tax will UPS save for the first year of the airplane's use as compared with using the straight-line depreciation method? UPS's income tax rate is 35%. Ignore any earnings from investing the extra cash.

Selecting the best depreciation method for income tax purposes
(Obj. 3)

CP7-8 Assume that on March 31, 20X4, **Lufthansa**, the German airline, purchased a used Airbus aircraft at a cost of €45,000,000 (€ is the symbol for the euro). Lufthansa expects the plane to remain useful for 5 years (5,000,000 miles) and to have a residual value of €5,000,000. Lufthansa expects the plane to be flown 500,000 miles during the remainder of the first year ended December 31, 20X4. Compute Lufthansa's depreciation on the plane for the year ended December 31, 20X4, using the following methods:
a. Straight-line b. Units-of-production c. Double-declining-balance

Which method would produce the highest net income for 20X4? Which method produces the lowest net income?

Partial-year depreciation
(Obj. 2)

Computing and recording depreciation after a change in useful life of the asset
(Obj. 2)

CP7-9 Return to the example of the Disney World hot dog stand on page 332. Suppose that after using the hot dog stand for 4 years, **The Walt Disney Company** determines that the asset will remain useful for only 3 more years. Record Disney's depreciation on the hot dog stand for year 5 by the straight-line method.

Recording a gain or loss on disposal under two depreciation methods
(Obj. 4)

CP7-10 Return to the **FedEx** delivery-truck depreciation example in Exhibit 7-5 (page 325) and 7-7 (page 326). Suppose FedEx sold the truck on January 1, 20X5, for $15,000 cash, after using the truck for two full years.

1. Record FedEx's sale of the truck under
   a. Straight-line depreciation (Exhibit 7-5, page 325).
   b. Double-declining-balance depreciation (Exhibit 7-7, page 326).
2. Why is there such a big difference between the gain or loss on disposal under the two depreciation methods?

Accounting for the depletion of a company's natural resources
(Obj. 5)

CP7-11 **Texaco**, the giant oil company, holds reserves of oil and gas assets. At the end of 20X4, assume the cost of Texaco's mineral assets totaled approximately $44 billion, representing 4.4 billion barrels of oil in the ground.

1. Which depreciation method do Texaco and other oil companies use to compute their annual depletion expense for the minerals removed from the ground?
2. Suppose Texaco removed 0.6 billion barrels of oil during 20X5. Record Texaco's depletion expense for the year.
3. At December 31, 20X4, Texaco's Accumulated Depletion account stood at $25.0 billion. If Texaco did not add any new oil and gas reserves during 20X5, what would be the book value of the company's oil and gas reserves at December 31, 20X5? Cite a specific figure from your answer to illustrate why exploration activities are so important for companies such as Texaco.

Analyzing a company's goodwill
(Obj. 6)

CP7-12 Examine the balance sheet of **FedEx Corporation** at the beginning of this chapter. Answer these questions about the company:

1. Assume that during the year ended May 31, 2001, FedEx experienced no write-downs due to loss in the value of goodwill. How much new goodwill did FedEx purchase during 2001?
2. What event during 2001 caused FedEx to record additional goodwill?
3. Assume FedEx wrote off $300 million of goodwill during fiscal year 2001. How much new goodwill did FedEx purchase during the year?

Accounting for patents and research and development cost
(Obj. 6)

CP7-13 This exercise summarizes the accounting for patents, which like copyrights, trademarks, and franchises, provide the owner with a special right or privilege. It also covers research and development costs.

Suppose **Oracle Software** paid $500,000 to research and develop a new software program. Oracle also paid $300,000 to acquire a patent on the new software. After readying the software for production, Oracle's sales revenue for the first year totaled $1,300,000. Cost of goods sold was $200,000, and operating (chiefly selling) expenses were $400,000. All these transactions occurred during 20X4. Oracle expects the patent to have a useful life of 3 years.

1. Prepare Oracle Software's income statement for the year ended December 31, 20X4, complete with a heading.
2. What should Oracle's outlook for future profits be on the new software program?

Reporting investing activities on the statement of cash flows
(Obj. 7)

CP7-14 During 20X5, **Pegasus Communications** purchased two other companies for $153 million. Assume Pegasus financed this purchase by paying cash of $100 million and borrowing the remainder. Also during fiscal 20X5, Pegasus made capital expenditures of $45 million to expand its transmission capabilities. During the year, Pegasus sold cable operations, receiving cash of $167 million and experienced a gain of $87 million on the disposal. Overall, Pegasus reported a net loss of $1.4 million during 20X5.

Show what Pegasus would report for cash flows from investing activities on its statement of cash flows for 20X5. Report a total amount for net cash provided by (used in) investing activities.

Exercises

Determining the cost of plant assets **(Obj. 1)**

E7-1 Hankamer Enterprises purchased land, paying $100,000 cash as a down payment and signing a $150,000 note payable for the balance. Hankamer also had to pay delinquent property tax of $2,000, title insurance costing $2,500, and $5,500 to level the land and to remove an unwanted building. The company paid $50,000 to remove earth for the foundation and then constructed an office building at a cost of $1,400,000. It also paid $72,000 for a fence around the property, $10,400 for the company sign near the property entrances, and $6,000 for lighting of the grounds. Determine the cost of the company's land, land improvements, and building.

Allocating costs to assets acquired in a lump-sum purchase; disposing of a plant asset **(Obj. 1, 4)**

E7-2 Assume **Schlotzky Deli** bought three used machines in a $40,000 lump-sum purchase. An independent appraiser valued the machines as follows:

Machine No.	Appraised Value
1	$12,000
2	20,000
3	16,000

Schlotzky paid one-fourth in cash and signed a note payable for the remainder. What is each machine's individual cost? Immediately after making this purchase Schlotzky sold machine 2 for its appraised value. What is the result of the sale? Round decimals to three places.

Distinguishing capital expenditures from expenses **(Obj. 1)**

E7-3 Assume **Intel Corporation** purchased a piece of manufacturing machinery. Classify each of the following expenditures as a capital expenditure or an immediate expense related to machinery: (a) purchase price, (b) sales tax paid on the purchase price, (c) transportation and insurance while machinery is in transit from seller to buyer, (d) installation, (e) training of personnel for initial operation of the machinery, (f) special reinforcement to the machinery platform, (g) income tax paid on income earned from the sale of products manufactured by the machinery, (h) major overhaul to extend useful life by 3 years, (i) ordinary repairs to keep the machinery in good working order, (j) lubrication of the machinery before it is placed in service, and (k) periodic lubrication after the machinery is placed in service.

Measuring, depreciating, and reporting plant assets **(Obj. 1, 2)**

E7-4 During 20X4, Barclay International (BI) paid $200,000 for land and built a store in Madison, Wisconsin. Prior to construction, the city of Madison charged BI $1,000 for a building permit, which BI paid. BI also paid $10,000 for architect's fees. The construction cost of $530,000 was financed by a long-term note payable, with interest cost of $39,000 paid at December 31, 20X4. The building was completed September 30, 20X4. BI depreciates the building by the straight-line method over 40 years, with estimated residual value of $100,000.

1. Journalize transactions for
   a. Purchase of the land
   b. All the costs chargeable to the building in a single entry
   c. Depreciation on the building

   Explanations are not required.
2. Report BI's plant assets on the company's balance sheet at December 31, 20X4.
3. What will BI's income statement for the year ended December 31, 20X4 report for the building?

Explaining the concept of depreciation
(Obj. 2)

E7-5 Melanie Byrd has just slept through the class in which Professor Baldwin explained the concept of depreciation. Because the next test is scheduled for Wednesday, Byrd telephones Gretchen Webb to get her notes from the lecture. Webb's notes are concise: "Depreciation—Sounds like Greek to me." Byrd next tries Trent Lewis, who says he thinks depreciation is what happens when an asset wears out. Lisa Altenau is confident that depreciation is the process of building up a cash fund to replace an asset at the end of its useful life. Explain the concept of depreciation for Byrd. Evaluate the explanations of Lewis and Altenau. Be specific.

Determining depreciation amounts by three methods
(Obj. 2, 3)

spreadsheet

E7-6 Superior Bank, Inc., bought a delivery van on January 2, 20X4, for $15,000. The van was expected to remain in service 4 years (100,000 miles). At the end of its useful life, Superior Bank officials estimated that the van's residual value would be $3,000. The van traveled 34,000 miles the first year, 28,000 the second year, 18,000 the third year, and 20,000 in the fourth year. Prepare a schedule of *depreciation expense* per year for the van under the three depreciation methods. Show your computations.

Which method tracks the wear and tear on the van most closely? Which method would the bank prefer to use for income tax purposes? Explain in detail why Superior Bank prefers this method.

Reporting plant assets, depreciation, and cash flow
(Obj. 1, 2, 7)

E7-7 In January 20X2, Chilli's Restaurant purchased an old building, paying $50,000 cash and signing a $100,000 note payable. The restaurant paid another $50,000 to remodel the building. Furniture and fixtures cost $30,000, and dishes and supplies—a current asset—were obtained for $9,000.

Chilli's Restaurant is depreciating the building over 20 years by the straight-line method, with estimated residual value of $40,000. The furniture and fixtures will be replaced at the end of 5 years; these assets are being depreciated by the double-declining-balance method, with zero residual value. At the end of the first year, the restaurant still has dishes and supplies worth $2,000.

Show what the restaurant will report for supplies, plant assets, and cash flows at the end of the first year on its

- Income statement
- Balance sheet
- Statement of cash flows (investing only)

Show all computations.

Note: The purchase of dishes and supplies is an operating cash flow because supplies are a current asset.

Units-of-production depreciation
(Obj. 2)

E7-8 Nautilus Gym purchased Cybex exercise equipment at a cost of $100,000. In addition, Nautilus paid $2,000 for a special platform on which to stabilize the equipment for use. Freight costs of $1,200 to ship the equipment were borne by Cybex. Nautilus will depreciate the equipment by the units-of-production method, based on an expected useful life of 50,000 hours of exercise. The estimated residual value of the equipment is $10,000. How many hours of usage can Nautilus Gym expect from the machine if depreciation expense is $5,520 for the year 20X5?

Selecting the best depreciation method for income tax purposes
(Obj. 3)

E7-9 On June 30, 20X6, Air-Bag Safety Corp. paid $210,000 for equipment that is expected to have a 7-year life. In this industry, the residual value of equipment is approximately 10% of the asset's cost. Air-Bag Safety cash revenues for the year are $100,000 and cash expenses total $60,000.

Select the appropriate MACRS depreciation method for income tax purposes. Then determine the extra amount of cash that Air-Bag Safety Corp. can invest by using MACRS depreciation, versus straight-line, for the year ended December 31, 20X6. The income tax rate is 30%.

Changing a plant asset's useful life
(Obj. 2)

E7-10 Baptist Charities, Inc. purchased a building for $900,000 and depreciated it on a straight-line basis over 40 years. The estimated residual value was $100,000. After using the building for 10 years. Baptist Charities realized that the building will remain useful only 20 more years. Starting with the 11th year, Baptist Charities began depreciating the building over the newly revised total life of 30 years and decreased the estimated residual value to $50,000. Record depreciation expense on the building for years 11 and 12.

Analyzing the effect of a sale of a plant asset; DDB depreciation
(Obj. 4)

E7-11 Assume that on January 2, 20X4, a **Marriott Hotel** purchased fixtures for $8,700 cash, expecting the fixtures to remain in service 5 years. The hotel has depreciated the fixtures on a double-declining-balance basis, with $1,000 estimated residual value. On September 30, 20X5, Marriot sold the fixtures for $2,500 cash. Record both the depreciation expense on the fixtures for 20X5 and then the sale of the fixtures. Apart from your journal entry, also show how to compute the gain or loss on Marriott's disposal of these fixtures.

Measuring a plant asset's cost, using UOP depreciation, and trading in a used asset
(Obj. 1, 2, 4)

E7-12 Overland Express is a large trucking company that operates throughout the midwestern United States. Overland uses the units-of-production (UOP) method to depreciate its trucks because its managers believe UOP depreciation best measures the wear and tear.

Overland Express trades in its trucks often to keep driver morale high and to maximize fuel efficiency. Consider these facts about one **Freightliner** truck in the company's fleet: When acquired in 20X2, the tractor-trailer rig cost $285,000 and was expected to remain in service for 5 years or 1,000,000 miles. Estimated residual value was $35,000. During 20X2, the truck was driven 75,000 miles; during 20X3, 120,000 miles; and during 20X4, 210,000 miles. After 40,000 miles in 20X5, the company traded in the Freightliner truck for a **Peterbilt** rig. Overland Express paid cash of $120,000. Determine Overland Express's cost of the new truck. Journal entries are not required.

Recording natural resource assets and depletion
(Obj. 5)

E7-13 Shoshone Mines paid $398,500 for the right to extract ore from a 200,000-ton mineral deposit. In addition to the purchase price, Shoshone also paid a $500 filing fee, a $1,000 license fee to the state of Utah, and $60,000 for a geologic survey of the property. Because the company purchased the rights to the minerals only, it expected the asset to have zero residual value when fully depleted. During the first year of production, Shoshone Mines removed 40,000 tons of ore. Make journal entries to record (a) purchase of the mineral rights, (b) payment of fees and other costs, and (c) depletion for first-year production. What is the mineral asset's book value at the end of the year?

Recording intangibles, amortization, and a change in the asset's useful life
(Obj. 6)

E7-14 Magnetic Imaging, Inc. (MII) has recently purchased for $400,000 a patent for the design of a new X-ray machine. Although it gives legal protection for 20 years, the patent is expected to provide MII with a competitive advantage for only 8 years. Assuming the straight-line method of amortization, make journal entries to record (a) the purchase of the patent and (b) amortization for year 1.

After using the patent for 4 years, Magnetic Imaging's research director learns at a professional meeting that **Honeywell** is designing a more efficient machine. On the basis of this new information, MII determines that the patent's total useful life is only 6 years. Record amortization for year 5.

Business acquisitions and cash flows
(Obj. 6, 7)

E7-15 Assume **Campbell Soup Company's** 20X3 statement of cash flows reported:

	20X3
Cash Flows from Investing Activities:	Millions
Businesses acquired	$(1,255)

Assume Campbell Soup's balance sheet reported:

	20X3	20X2
Intangible assets:	Millions	
Purchase price in excess of net assets		
of businesses acquired	$1,583	$452

Required

Answer these questions:

1. What is the popular title of the account that Campbell Soup labels as "Purchase price in excess of net assets of businesses acquired"?
2. Explain the meaning of the (a) $1,255 million that Campbell Soup reported on the statement of cash flows, and (b) $1,583 million on the balance sheet.
3. Assume $1,200 million of the $1,255 purchase price was for goodwill. What must have happened in 20X3 to cause $452 million + $1,200 million to not equal $1,583 million? Describe the transaction and give its dollar amount.

Measuring and recording goodwill
(Obj. 6)

E7-16 PepsiCo, Inc. dominates the snack-food industry with its Frito-Lay brand. Assume that PepsiCo, Inc. purchased Hot Chips, Inc., for $8.5 million cash. The market value of Hot Chips' assets is $14 million, and Hot Chips has liabilities of $11 million.

Required

1. Compute the cost of the goodwill purchased by PepsiCo.
2. Record the purchase by PepsiCo.
3. Explain how PepsiCo will account in future years for any goodwill that PepsiCo purchased.

Interpreting a cash-flow statement
(Obj. 7)

E7-17 The following items are excerpted from an annual report of Pier 1 Imports, Inc.:

Pier 1 Imports, Inc.

Consolidated Statement of Cash Flows
(Partial, Adapted)

(Millions of Dollars)	20X1
Cash flow from operating activities:	
Net income	$ 95
Adjustments for noncash [expenses] included in net income:	
Depreciation and amortization	43
Cash flow from investing activities:	
Capital expenditures	$(45)
Acquisitions of businesses	(4)
Proceeds from dispositions of properties	353

Required

Answer these questions:

1. Why are depreciation and amortization listed on the statement of cash flows?
2. Explain in detail each investing activity.

Reporting cash flows for property and equipment
(Obj. 7)

E7-18 Assume Pier 1 Imports, Inc., completed the following transactions. For each transaction, show what Pier 1 would report for investing activities on its statement of cash flows. Show negative amounts in parentheses.

a. Sold a building for $500,000. The building had cost Pier 1, $2,000,000 and at the time of the sale its accumulated depreciation totaled $1,500,000.
b. Lost a store building in a fire. The warehouse cost $5,000,000 and had accumulated depreciation of $2,000,000. The insurance proceeds received by Pier 1 were $2,500,000.
c. Renovated a store at a cost of $800,000, paying $300,000 cash and borrowing the remainder on a 3-year note payable.
d. Traded in a delivery truck on a new one. The list price of the new truck was $55,000. Pier 1's old truck cost $45,000 and had accumulated depreciation of $42,000. Pier gave the old truck plus $47,000 cash.
e. Purchased store fixtures for $135,000. The fixtures are expected to remain in service for 10 years and then be sold for $15,000. Pier 1 uses the straight-line depreciation method.

Challenge Exercises

E7-19 Target Corporation, the discount chain, reported the following for property and equipment (in millions):

Determining the sale price of property and equipment
(Obj. 4)

	Year End	
	20X1	20X0
Property and equipment	$15,759	$13,824
Accumulated depreciation	(4,341)	(3,925)

During 20X1, Target paid $2,528 million for new property and equipment. Depreciation for the year totaled $940 million. Assume that during 20X1, Target sold property and equipment at a gain of $31 million. For how much did Target sell the property and equipment?

E7-20 Fossil, Inc., the company known for its popular lines of wristwatches and sunglasses, reported net income of $55.9 million for 20X3. Depreciation expense for the year totaled $6.4 million. Assume Fossil depreciates plant assets over approximately 8 years using the straight-line method and no residual value. The company's income tax rate is 40%.

Determining net income after a change in depreciation method
(Obj. 2)

Assume that Fossil's plant assets are 3 years old and that Fossil switches over to double-declining-balance (DDB) depreciation at the start of 20X4. Further, assume that 20X4 is expected to be the same as 20X3 except for the change in depreciation method. How much net income can Fossil, Inc., expect to earn during 20X4?

E7-21 Agence France Press (AFP) is a major French telecommunication conglomerate. Assume that early in year 1, AFP purchased equipment at a cost of 4 million euros (€4 million). Management expects the equipment to remain in service 5 years and estimated residual value to be negligible. AFP uses the straight-line depreciation method. *Through an accounting error, AFP expensed the entire cost of the equipment at the time of purchase.* Because the company is operated as a partnership, it pays no income tax.

Capitalizing versus expensing; measuring the effect of an error
(Obj. 1)

Required

Prepare a schedule to show the overstatement or understatement in the following items at the end of each year over the 5-year life of the equipment:

1. Total current assets
2. Equipment, net
3. Net income
4. Owners' equity

Problems

(Group A)

P7-1A Assume Road Runner High-Speed Online, Inc. incurred the following costs in acquiring land, making land improvements, and constructing and furnishing its own sales building:

Identifying the elements of a plant asset's cost
(Obj. 1, 2)

a. Purchase price of four acres of land, including an old building that will be used for a garage (land market value is $240,000; building market value is $80,000)	$250,000
b. Landscaping (additional dirt and earth moving)	8,100
c. Fence around the land	17,650
d. Attorney fee for title search on the land	600
e. Delinquent real estate taxes on the land to be paid by Road Runner	5,900

(continued)

f. Company signs at front of the company property	$ 1,800
g. Building permit for the sales building	350
h. Architect fee for the design of the sales building	19,800
i. Masonry, carpentry, roofing, and other labor to construct the sales building	709,000
j. Concrete, wood, and other materials used in the construction of the sales building	214,000
k. Renovation of the garage building	41,800
l. Interest cost on construction loan for sales building	9,000
m. Landscaping (trees and shrubs)	6,400
n. Parking lot and concrete walks on the property	52,300
o. Lights for the parking lot, walkways, and company signs	7,300
p. Supervisory salary of construction supervisor (85% to sales building; 9% to fencing, parking lot, and concrete walks; and 6% to garage building renovation)	40,000
q. Office furniture for the sales building	107,100
r. Transportation and installation of furniture	1,800

Road Runner depreciates buildings over 40 years, land improvements over 20 years, and furniture over 8 years, all on a straight-line basis with zero residual value.

Required

1. Set up columns for Land, Land Improvements, Sales Building, Garage Building, and Furniture. Show how to account for each of Road Runner's costs by listing the cost under the correct account. Determine the total cost of each asset.
2. Assuming that all construction was complete and the assets were placed in service on May 4, record depreciation for the year ended December 31. Round to the nearest dollar.
3. How will what you learned in this problem help you manage a business?

Recording plant asset transactions; reporting on the balance sheet
(Obj. 2)

P7-2A Oriental Rugs, Inc. reported the following on its balance sheet at December 31, 20X5:

Property, plant, and equipment, at cost:	
Land	$ 90,000
Buildings	200,000
Less Accumulated depreciation	(40,000)
Equipment	700,000
Less Accumulated depreciation	(260,000)

In early July 20X6, Oriental Rugs expanded operations and purchased additional equipment at a cost of $500,000. The company depreciates buildings by the straight-line method over 20 years with residual value of $80,000. Due to obsolescence, the equipment has a useful life of only 10 years and is being depreciated by the double-declining-balance method with zero residual value.

Required

1. Journalize Oriental Rugs, Inc.'s plant asset purchase and depreciation transactions for 20X6.
2. Report plant assets on the December 31, 20X6, balance sheet.

Recording plant asset transactions, exchanges, changes in useful life
(Obj. 1, 2, 4)

general ledger

P7-3A **Consolidated Freightways** provides cross-country freight service. Assume that the company's balance sheet includes the following assets under Property, Plant, and Equipment: Land, Buildings, and Motor-Carrier Equipment. Consolidated has a separate accumulated depreciation account for each of these assets except land. Further, assume that Consolidated completed the following transactions:

Jan. 2	Traded in motor-carrier equipment with book value of $47,000 (cost of $130,000) for similar new equipment with a cash cost of $176,000. Consolidated received a trade-in allowance of $70,000 on the old equipment and paid the remainder in cash.
July 3	Sold a building that had cost $550,000 and had accumulated depreciation of $247,500 through December 31 of the preceding year. Depreciation is computed on a straight-line basis. The building has a 30-year useful life and a residual value of $55,000. Consolidated received $100,000 cash and a $400,000 note receivable.
Oct. 29	Purchased land and a building for a single price of $300,000. An independent appraisal valued the land at $160,000 and the building at $200,000.
Dec. 31	Recorded depreciation as follows: Motor-carrier equipment has an expected useful life of 5 years and an estimated residual value of 5% of cost. Depreciation is computed on the double-declining-balance method. Depreciation on buildings is computed by the straight-line method. The new building carries a 40-year useful life and a residual value equal to 10% of its cost.

Required

Record the transactions in Consolidated Freightways' journal.

P7-4A The board of directors of Manatee Pleasure Boats, Inc., is reviewing the 20X7 annual report. A new board member—a professor with little business experience—questions the company accountant about the depreciation amounts. The professor wonders why depreciation expense has decreased from $200,000 in 20X6 to $184,000 in 20X7 to $172,000 in 20X8. She states that she could understand the decreasing annual amounts if the company had been disposing of properties each year, but that has not occurred. Further, she notes that growth in the city is increasing the values of company properties. Why is the company recording depreciation when the property values are increasing?

Explaining the concept of depreciation **(Obj. 2)**

Required

Write a paragraph or two to explain the concept of depreciation to the professor and to answer her questions.

P7-5A On January 3, 20X5, Ahmadi Distribution Co. paid $224,000 for a computer system. In addition to the basic purchase price, the company paid a setup fee of $6,200, $6,700 sales tax, and $3,100 for a special platform on which to place the computer. Ahmadi management estimates that the computer will remain in service 5 years and have a residual value of $20,000. The computer will process 50,000 documents the first year, with annual processing decreasing by 5,000 documents during each of the next 4 years (that is, 45,000 documents in 20X6; 40,000 documents in 20X7; and so on). In trying to decide which depreciation method to use, the company president has requested a depreciation schedule for each of three depreciation methods (straight-line, units-of-production, and double-declining-balance).

Computing depreciation by three methods and the cash-flow advantage of accelerated depreciation for tax purposes **(Obj. 2, 3)**

spreadsheet

Required

1. For each of the generally accepted depreciation methods, prepare a depreciation schedule showing asset cost, depreciation expense, accumulated depreciation, and asset book value.
2. Ahmadi reports to stockholders and creditors in the financial statements using the depreciation method that maximizes reported income in the early years of asset use. For income tax purposes, however, the company uses the depreciation method that minimizes income tax payments in those early years. Consider the first year Ahmadi uses the computer. Identify the depreciation methods that meet Ahmadi's objectives, assuming the income tax authorities would permit the use of any of the methods.

(continued)

3. Assume that cash provided by operations before income tax is $200,000 for the computer's first year. The combined federal and state income tax rate is 35%. For the two depreciation methods identified in Requirement 2, compare the net income and cash provided by operations (cash flow). Show which method gives the net-income advantage and which method gives the cash-flow advantage.

Analyzing plant asset transactions from a company's financial statements
(Obj. 2, 4, 7)

P7-6A Fossil, Inc. features high-fashion wristwatches and sunglasses. The company's motto is "Never a dull moment." The excerpts that follow are adapted from Fossil's financial statements for 2000.

Balance Sheet (dollars in millions)	December 31, 2000	1999
Assets		
Total current assets	$253	$231
Property, plant, and equipment	66	47
Less Accumulated depreciation	(24)	(19)
Intangibles	5	6

Statement of Cash Flows (dollars in millions)	Year Ended December 31, 2000	1999
Operating activities:		
Net income	$56	$52
Noncash items affecting net income:		
Depreciation	6	5
Amortization	1	1
Investing activities:		
Additions to property, plant, and equipment	(20)	(10)
Sale of property, plant, and equipment	1*	—

*There was no gain or loss on these dispositions.

Required

Answer these questions about Fossil's plant assets:

1. How much was Fossil's cost of plant assets at December 31, 2000? How much was the book value of plant assets? Show computations.
2. The financial statements give two evidences that Fossil purchased plant assets during 2000. What are they?
3. Prepare T-accounts for Property, Plant, and Equipment; Accumulated Depreciation, and Intangibles. Then show all the activity in these accounts during 2000. Label each increase or decrease and give its dollar amount.
4. Why are depreciation and amortization added to net income on the statement of cash flows?

Accounting for intangibles, natural resources, and the related expenses
(Obj. 5, 6)

P7-7A *Part 1.* Collins Foods International, Inc., is the majority owner of Sizzler Restaurants. The company's balance sheet reports the asset Cost in Excess of Net Assets of Purchased Businesses. Assume that Collins purchased this asset as part of the acquisition of another company, which carried these figures:

Book value of assets	$2.4 million
Market value of assets	5.1 million
Liabilities	2.2 million

Required

1. What is another title for the asset Cost in Excess of Net Assets of Purchased Businesses?
2. Record a journal entry for Collins' purchase of the other company for $6.1 million cash.
3. Assume that Collins Foods determined that Cost in Excess of Net Assets of Purchased Businesses increased in value by $800,000. Make whatever journal entry is needed to record this transaction. Then, suppose Cost in Excess of Net Assets of Purchased Businesses decreased in value by $800,000. Make the needed journal entry for this transaction.

Part 2. Georgia-Pacific Corporation is one of the world's largest forest products companies. The company's balance sheet includes the assets Natural Gas, Oil, and Coal.

Suppose Georgia-Pacific paid $3.8 million cash for a lease giving the firm the right to work a mine that contained an estimated 100,000 tons of coal. Assume that the company paid $60,000 to remove unwanted buildings from the land and $45,000 to prepare the surface for mining. Further assume that Georgia-Pacific signed a $30,000 note payable to a landscaping company to return the land surface to its original condition after the lease ends. During the first year, Georgia-Pacific removed 35,000 tons of coal, which it sold on account for $67 per ton. Operating expenses for the first year totaled $240,000, all paid in cash. In addition, the company accrued income tax at the tax rate of 30%.

Required

1. Record all of Georgia-Pacific's transactions for the year.
2. Prepare the company's income statement for its coal operations for the first year. Evaluate the profitability of the coal operations.

Reporting plant asset transactions on the statement of cash flows
(Obj. 7)

P7-8A At the end of 20X0, The Coca-Cola Company had total assets of $20.8 billion and total liabilities of $11.5 billion. Included among the assets were property, plant, and equipment with a cost of $6.6 billion and accumulated depreciation of $2.4 billion.

Assume that Coca-Cola completed the following selected transactions during 20X1: The company earned total revenues of $20.5 billion and incurred total expenses of $18.3 billion, which included depreciation of $0.7 billion. During the year, Coca-Cola paid $0.7 billion for new property, plant, and equipment and sold old plant assets for $0.5 billion. The cost of the assets sold was $0.8 billion, and their accumulated depreciation was $0.4 billion.

Required

1. Explain how to determine whether Coca-Cola had a gain or loss on the sale of old plant assets during the year. What was the amount of the gain or loss, if any?
2. Show how Coca-Cola would report property, plant, and equipment on the balance sheet at December 31, 20X1. What was the book value of property, plant, and equipment?
3. Show how Coca-Cola would report operating activities and investing activities on its statement of cash flows for 20X1. The company's cash-flow statement starts with net income.

(Group B)

Identifying the elements of a plant asset's cost
(Obj. 1, 2)

P7-1B Assume that Cisco Systems, Inc. incurred the following costs in acquiring land and a garage, making land improvements, and constructing and furnishing a district office building.

a. Purchase price of 3 1/2 acres of land, including a building that will be used as a garage (land market value is $750,000; building market value is $50,000)	$720,000
b. Delinquent real estate taxes on the land to be paid by Cisco Systems	3,700
c. Landscaping (additional dirt and earth moving)	3,550
d. Title insurance on the land acquisition	1,000
e. Fence around the land	44,100
f. Building permit for the office building	200
g. Architect fee for the design of the office building	45,000

(continued)

h. Company signs near front and rear approaches to the company property	$ 53,550
i. Renovation of the garage	23,800
j. Concrete, wood, and other materials used in the construction of the office building	414,000
k. Masonry, carpentry, roofing, and other labor to construct the office building	734,000
l. Interest cost on construction loan for office building	3,400
m. Parking lots and concrete walks on the property	17,450
n. Lights for the parking lot, walkways, and company signs	8,900
o. Supervisory salary of construction supervisor (90% to office building; 6% to fencing, parking lot, and concrete walks; and 4% to garage renovation)	55,000
p. Office furniture for the office building	123,500
q. Transportation of furniture from seller to the office building	1,300
r. Landscaping (trees and shrubs)	9,100

Cisco Systems depreciates buildings over 40 years, land improvements over 20 years, and furniture over 8 years, all on a straight-line basis with zero residual value.

Required

1. Set up columns for Land, Land Improvements, District Office Building, Garage, and Furniture. Show how to account for each of Cisco's costs by listing the cost under the correct account. Determine the total cost of each asset.
2. Assuming that all construction was complete and the assets were placed in service on March 19, record depreciation for the year ended December 31. Round figures to the nearest dollar.
3. How will what you learned in this problem help you manage a business?

Recording plant asset transactions; reporting on the balance sheet **(Obj. 2)**

P7-2B Diebold Security Systems, Inc. has a hefty investment in security equipment, as reported in the company's balance sheet at December 31, 20X5:

Property, plant, and equipment, at cost:	
Land	$ 120,000
Buildings	110,000
Less Accumulated depreciation	(40,000)
Security equipment	520,000
Less Accumulated depreciation	(170,000)

In early July 20X6, Diebold purchased additional security equipment at a cost of $180,000. Diebold depreciates buildings by the straight-line method over 20 years with residual value of $30,000. Due to obsolescence, security equipment has a useful life of only 10 years and is being depreciated by the double-declining-balance method with zero residual value.

Required

1. Journalize Diebold's plant asset purchase and depreciation transactions for 20X6.
2. Report plant assets on the company's December 31, 20X6, balance sheet.

Recording plant asset transactions, exchanges, changes in useful life **(Obj. 1, 2, 4)**

P7-3B Polling Associates surveys American television-viewing trends. The company's balance sheet reports the following assets under Property and Equipment: Land, Buildings, Office Furniture, Communication Equipment, and Televideo Equipment. The company has a separate accumulated depreciation account for each of these assets except land. Assume that Polling Associates completed the following transactions:

Integrator CD
general ledger

Jan. 2	Traded in communication equipment with book value of $11,000 (cost of $96,000) for similar new equipment with a cash cost of $88,000. The seller gave Polling Associates a trade-in allowance of $15,000 on the old equipment, and Polling Associates paid the remainder in cash.
Aug. 31	Sold a building that had cost $475,000 and had accumulated depreciation of $353,500 through December 31 of the preceding year. Depreciation is computed on a straight-line basis. The building has a 30-year useful life and a residual value of $47,500. Polling Associates received $150,000 cash and a $450,000 note receivable.
Nov. 4	Purchased used communication and televideo equipment from the **Gallup** polling organization. Total cost was $80,000 paid in cash. An independent appraisal valued the communication equipment at $75,000 and the televideo equipment at $25,000.
Dec. 31	Recorded depreciation as follows: Equipment is depreciated by the double-declining-balance method over a 5-year life with zero residual value. Record depreciation separately on the equipment purchased on January 2 and on November 4

Required

Record the transactions in the journal of Polling Associates.

Explaining the concept of depreciation
(Obj. 2)

P7-4B The board of directors of Scottish Life Magazine is having its regular quarterly meeting. Accounting policies are on the agenda, and depreciation is being discussed. A new board member, an attorney, has some strong opinions about two aspects of depreciation policy. Martin Luther, a professor of theology, argues that depreciation must be coupled with a fund to replace company assets. Otherwise, there is no substance to depreciation, he argues. He also challenges the 5-year estimated life over which Scottish Life Magazine is depreciating company computers. He notes that the computers will last much longer and should be depreciated over at least 10 years.

Required

Write a paragraph or two to explain the concept of depreciation to Martin Luther and to answer his arguments.

Computing depreciation by three methods and the cash-flow advantage of accelerated depreciation for tax purposes
(Obj. 2, 3)

spreadsheet

P7-5B On January 2, 20X4, Centex Insurance Company purchased a computer at a cost of $63,000. Before placing the computer in service, the company spent $2,200 for special chips, $800 for a keyboard, and $4,000 for four-color monitors. Centex management estimates that the computer will remain in service for 6 years and have a residual value of $16,000. The computer can be expected to process 18,000 documents in each of the first 4 years and 14,000 documents in each of the next 2 years. In trying to decide which depreciation method to use, Grant Taft, the general manager, requests a depreciation schedule for each method (straight-line, units-of-production, and double-declining-balance).

Required

1. Prepare a depreciation schedule for each of the depreciation methods, showing asset cost, depreciation expense, accumulated depreciation, and asset book value.
2. Centex reports to creditors in the financial statements using the depreciation method that maximizes reported income in the early years of asset use. For income tax purposes, however, the company uses the depreciation method that minimizes income tax payments in those early years. Consider the first year that Centex uses the computer. Identify the depreciation methods that meet the general manager's objectives, assuming the income tax authorities would permit the use of any of the methods.
3. Cash provided by operations before income tax is $150,000 for the computer's first year. The combined federal and state income tax rate is 40%. For the two depreciation methods

identified in Requirement 2, compare the net income and cash provided by operations (cash flow). Show which method gives the net-income advantage and which method gives the cash-flow advantage.

Analyzing plant asset transactions from a company's financial statements **(Obj. 2, 4, 7)**

P7-6B Estée Lauder Companies, Inc., features several popular brands of cosmetics, including Estée Lauder, Clinique, and Tommy. The excerpts that follow are adapted from Estée Lauder's financial statements for fiscal year 2000.

Balance Sheet (dollars in millions)	June 30, 2000	1999
Assets		
Total current assets	$1,619	$1,570
Property, plant, and equipment	974	800
Less Accumulated depreciation	(494)	(416)
Intangibles	31	51

Statement of Cash Flows (dollars in millions)	Year Ended June 30, 2000	1999
Cash Flows from Operating Activities:		
Net income	$ 314	$ 273
Noncash items affecting net income:		
Depreciation	109	92
Amortization	20	8
Cash Flows from Investing Activities:		
Capital expenditures	$(205)	$(118)
Proceeds from dispositions of plant assets	31*	1

*There was no gain or loss on these dispositions.

Required

Answer these questions about Estée Lauder's plant assets:

1. How much was Estée Lauder's cost of plant assets at June 30, 2000? How much was the book value of plant assets? Show computations.
2. The financial statements give two evidences that Estée Lauder purchased plant assets during 2000. What are they?
3. Prepare T-accounts for Property, Plant, and Equipment; Accumulated Depreciation; and Intangibles. Then show all the activity in these accounts during 2000. Label each increase or decrease and give its dollar amount.
4. Why are depreciation and amortization added to net income on the statement of cash flows?

Accounting for intangibles, natural resources, and the related expenses **(Obj. 5, 6)**

P7-7B *Part 1.* United Telecommunications, Inc. (United Telecom) provides communication services in Florida, North Carolina, New Jersey, Texas, and other states. The company's balance sheet reports the asset Cost of Acquisitions in Excess of the Fair Market Value of the Net Assets of Subsidiaries. Assume that United Telecom purchased this asset as part of the acquisition of another company, which carried these figures:

Book value of assets	$640,000
Market value of assets	920,000
Liabilities	405,000

Required

1. What is another title for the asset Cost of Acquisitions in Excess of the Fair Market Value of the Net Assets of Subsidiaries?

2. Make the journal entry to record United Telecom's purchase of the other company for $800,000 cash.
3. Assume United Telecom determined that Cost of Acquisitions in Excess of the Fair Value of the Net Assets of Subsidiaries *increased* in value by $80,000. Make whatever journal entry is needed to record this transaction. Then suppose "Cost of Acquisitions in Excess . . . of Subsidiaries" *decreased* in value by $80,000. Make the needed journal entry for this transaction.

Part 2. Continental Pipeline Company operates a pipeline that provides natural gas to Atlanta; Washington, DC; Philadelphia; and New York City. The company's balance sheet includes the asset Oil Properties.

Suppose Continental paid $7 million cash for petroleum reserves that contained an estimated 500,000 barrels of oil. Assume that the company paid $350,000 for additional geologic tests of the property and $110,000 to prepare the surface for drilling. Prior to production, the company signed a $65,000 note payable to have a building constructed on the property. Because the building provides on-site headquarters for the drilling effort and will be abandoned when the oil is depleted, its cost is debited to the Oil Properties account and included in depletion charges. During the first year of production, Continental removed 82,000 barrels of oil, which it sold on credit for $18 per barrel. Operating expenses related to this project totaled $185,000 for the first year, all paid in cash. In addition, Continental accrued income tax at the rate of 30%.

Required

1. Record all of Continental's transactions for the year.
2. Prepare the company's income statement for this oil and gas project for the first year. Evaluate the profitability of the project.

Reporting plant asset transactions on the statement of cash flows
(Obj. 7)

P7-8B Assume that at the end of 20X2, Sprint Corporation, the telecommunications company, had total assets of $15.2 billion and total liabilities of $10.5 billion. Included among the assets were property, plant, and equipment with a cost of $19.9 billion and accumulated depreciation of $10.2 billion.

Assume that Sprint completed the following selected transactions during 20X3: The company earned total revenues of $13.9 billion and incurred total expenses of $13.2 billion, which included depreciation of $1.1 billion. During the year, Sprint paid $2.8 billion for new property, plant, and equipment and sold old plant assets for $0.8 billion. The cost of the assets sold was $0.6 billion, and their accumulated depreciation was $0.4 billion.

Required

1. Explain how to determine whether Sprint had a gain or a loss on the sale of old plant assets. What was the amount of the gain or loss, if any?
2. Show how Sprint Corporation would report property, plant, and equipment on the balance sheet at December 31, 20X3.
3. Show how Sprint would report operating activities and investing activities on its statement of cash flows for 20X3. The company's cash-flow statement starts with net income.

Apply Your Knowledge

Decision Cases

Measuring profitability based on different inventory and depreciation methods
(Obj. 2, 3)

Case 1. Suppose you are considering investing in two businesses, 360 Communications and Beepers Unlimited. The two companies are virtually identical, and both began operations at the beginning of the current year. Assume that during the year, each company purchased inventory as follows:

Jan. 4	10,000	units at $4 =	$ 40,000
Apr. 6	5,000	units at 5 =	25,000
Aug. 9	7,000	units at 6 =	42,000
Nov. 27	10,000	units at 7 =	70,000
Totals	32,000		$177,000

During the first year, both companies sold 25,000 units of inventory.

In early January, both companies purchased equipment costing $150,000 that had a 10-year estimated useful life and a $20,000 residual value. 360 uses the inventory and depreciation methods that maximize reported income. By contrast, Beepers uses the inventory and depreciation methods that minimize income tax payments. Assume that both companies' trial balances at December 31 included the following:

Sales revenue	$370,000
Operating expenses	50,000

The income tax rate is 35%.

Required

1. Prepare both companies' income statements.
2. Write an investment newsletter to address the following questions for your clients: Which company appears to be more profitable? Which company has more cash to invest in promising projects? If prices continue rising over the long term, which company would you prefer to invest in? Why?

Plant assets and intangible assets
(Obj. 1, 6)

Case 2. The following questions are unrelated except that they all apply to fixed assets and intangible assets:

1. It has been suggested that because many intangible assets have no value except to the company that owns them, they should be valued at $1.00 or zero on the balance sheet. Many accountants disagree with this view. Which view do you support? Why?
2. The manager of Horizon Software regularly buys plant assets and debits the cost to Repairs and Maintenance Expense. Why would he do that, since he knows this action violates GAAP?
3. The manager of Central Transportation Systems regularly debits the cost of repairs and maintenance of plant assets to Plant and Equipment. Why would she do that, since she knows she is violating GAAP?

Ethical Issue

United Kansas Bank of Topeka purchased land and a building for the lump sum of $4.3 million. To get the maximum tax deduction, the bank's managers allocated 80% of the purchase price to the building and only 20% to the land. A more realistic allocation would have been 60% to the building and 40% to the land.

Required

1. Explain the tax advantage of allocating too much to the building and too little to the land.
2. Was United Kansas Bank's allocation ethical? If so, state why. If not, why not? Identify who was harmed.

Financial Statement Case

Analyzing plant assets
(Obj. 2, 3, 6, 7)

Refer to **Fossil's** financial statements in Appendix A at the end of the book, and answer the following questions:

a. Which depreciation method does Fossil use for reporting to stockholders and creditors in the financial statements? What type of depreciation method does the company probably use for income tax purposes? Why is this method preferable for tax purposes?
b. Depreciation expense is embedded in the expense amounts listed on the income statement. It is reported elsewhere in the financial statements. How much was Fossil's depreciation and

amortization expense during fiscal year 2001? How much was Fossil's accumulated depreciation and amortization at the end of year 2001? Explain why accumulated depreciation and amortization exceeds depreciation and amortization expense for the current year.

c. Explain why Fossil adds depreciation and amortization expenses back to net income in the computation of net cash from operating activities.

d. How much did Fossil spend on property, plant, and equipment during 2002? Evaluate the trend in these expenditures as to whether it conveys good news or bad news for Fossil. Explain.

e. Fossil describes three intangible assets. What are they? How does Fossil account for each of these intangibles over its lifetime?

Analytical Case

Explaining plant asset activity **(Obj. 2, 4, 7)**

Refer to the **Pier 1 Imports** financial statements in Appendix B at the end of this book. This case leads you through a comprehensive analysis of Pier 1's long-term assets. The object of the case is to show you how to account for all of an actual company's plant asset (properties) transactions in summary form.

1. How much did Pier 1 pay for capital expenditures during 2002? How much cash did Pier 1 receive from the disposal of plant assets (fixed assets) during 2002? Consider the loss on disposal of fixed assets reported under Cash Flow from Operating Activities, and determine the book value of plant assets sold during 2002.
2. Use the answer to requirement 1, plus the amount of depreciation and amortization reported on the statement of cash flows, to explain all the activity in the Properties, Net account during 2002. Of the total depreciation and amortization for 2002, $3,671 thousand related to Other Noncurrent Assets and not to Properties. Use either a T-account or an equation for your analysis.
3. Which depreciation method does Pier 1 use?
4. Make the following assumptions:
   a. Pier 1 uses no residual values for depreciation computations.
   b. Pier 1 depreciates the beginning costs of buildings over 30 years and of equipment, furniture and fixtures over 6 years.
   c. All capital expenditures occur at year end.
   d. Depreciation and amortization for 2002 totaled $42,821 thousand, as reported on the statement of cash flows.

   What amount of amortization did Pier 1 record for leasehold interests and improvements during 2002?
5. During 2002, Pier 1 added $57,925 thousand of new plant assets. Therefore, it is possible that the company's plant assets at the end of 2002 were proportionately newer than the assets the company held at the end of 2001. Were plant assets proportionately newer or older at the end of 2002 (versus 2001)?

Group Project

Visit a local business.

Required

1. List all its plant assets.
2. If possible, interview the manager. Gain as much information as you can about the business's plant assets. For example, try to determine the assets' costs, the depreciation method the company is using, and the estimated useful life of each asset category. If an interview is impossible, then develop your own estimates of the assets' costs, useful lives, and book values, assuming an appropriate depreciation method.
3. Determine whether the business has any intangible assets. If so, list them and gain as much information as possible about their nature, cost, and estimated useful lives.
4. Write a detailed report of your findings and be prepared to present your results to the class.

8

Current & Long-Term Liabilities

Learning Objectives

1. **Account** for current liabilities and contingent liabilities
2. **Account** for bonds-payable transactions
3. **Measure** interest expense
4. **Understand** the advantages and disadvantages of borrowing
5. **Report** liabilities on the balance sheet

Integrator CD

Need additional help? Go to the ***Integrator CD*** *and search these key words:* amortizing bonds, bond pricing, capital lease, contingent liability, current liabilities, discount, effective interest rate, EPS, premium, present value, short-term note payable

The Home Depot, Inc.

Consolidated Balance Sheet (Adapted, with Amounts in Millions)
January 31,

	2001	2000
Assets		
Total current assets	$ 7,777	$ 6,390
Property and equipment, net	13,068	10,227
Other assets	540	464
Total Assets	**$21,385**	**$17,081**
Liabilities		
Current liabilities:		
Accounts payable	$ 1,976	$ 1,993
Accrued salaries and related expenses	627	541
Sales taxes payable	298	269
Other accrued expenses	1,402	763
Income taxes payable	78	61
Current installments of long-term debt	4	29
Total current liabilities	4,385	3,656
Long-term debt, excluding current installments	1,545	750
Other long-term liabilities	451	334
Stockholders' Equity	**15,004**	**12,341**
Total Liabilities and Equity	**$21,385**	**$17,081**

H.J. Heinz Company

Consolidated Balance Sheet (Adapted, with Amounts in Millions)
April 30,

	2001	2000
Assets		
Total current assets	$3,117	$3,170
Property and equipment, net	2,168	2,359
Other assets	3,750	3,322
Total Assets	**$9,035**	**$8,851**
Liabilities		
Current liabilities:		
Short-term debt	$1,556	$ 151
Portion of long-term debt due within one year	315	25
Accounts payable	962	1,027
Salaries and wages	54	48
Accrued marketing	146	201
Accrued restructuring costs	135	126
Other accrued liabilities	389	359
Income taxes	98	189
Total current liabilities	3,655	2,126
Long-term debt	3,015	3,936
Other long-term liabilities	991	1,193
Stockholders' Equity	**1,374**	**1,596**
Total Liabilities and Equity	**$9,035**	**$8,851**

Home Depot is the leading home-improvement warehouse in the United States. H.J. Heinz sets the worldwide standard for ketchup. Both companies have assets, both are profitable, and both owe money. Let's examine the liabilities (or debts) that Home Depot and H.J. Heinz report on their balance sheets.

continued

Current liabilities exert more pressure on Heinz than on Home Depot. This may come as a surprise because Home Depot owes more current liabilities than Heinz does ($4.4 billion for Home Depot; $3.7 billion for Heinz). But that's not the end of the story. Home Depot has over twice as much in current assets than Heinz. This is why analysts are interested in a company's current ratio; it reveals the ability to cover current liabilities with current assets, and thus gives an indication of ability to pay debts.

The key question about a company's liabilities—whether it's Home Depot, H.J. Heinz, or any other entity—is whether the company can pay them when they come due. Current liabilities are more pressing than long-term debt because the current liabilities must be paid sooner.

Liabilities are a popular way to finance operations. Managers love debt financing because it's great to run a business with other people's money. But lenders and stockholders worry when a company's debts pile up. Why? Because of the risk that the business cannot pay its debts when they come due. Walking this tightrope is one of the biggest challenges that managers face. The notorious Enron case underscores the importance of management decisions about the size and the timing of liabilities. ■

Sitemap

- **Current Liabilities** ■
- **Long-Term Liabilities: Bonds** ■
- **Long-Term Liabilities: Leases and Pensions** ■
- **Reporting Liabilities** ■

Focus on the balance sheets of Home Depot and H.J. Heinz. Both companies report current liabilities (those due within 1 year or less) and both report long-term liabilities.

Home Depot and Heinz report essentially the same current liabilities, but they list them in slightly different order. (Exceptions are: Heinz has *short-term debt*, which is a note payable due within 1 year or less; *accrued marketing*, which is a payable for advertising or other marketing costs; and *accrued restructuring* costs, a liability that Heinz has recorded for a future payment to restructure something within the company.)

These minor variations are common in practice. By familiarizing yourself with the varying formats used by real companies, you will be able to deal with the actual financial statements you will encounter in your career.

Liabilities are debts, and borrowing is one of the ways a company finances its operations. By focusing on liabilities, this chapter covers debt financing. Let's start with current liabilities.

Current Liabilities

contingent liabilities, current liabilities, short-term note payable

Current liabilities are obligations due within 1 year or within the company's normal operating cycle if longer than a year. Obligations due beyond that period of time are classified as *long-term liabilities* ←.

→ *Current liabilities and long-term liabilities were discussed in Chapter 3, page 139.*

Current liabilities are of two kinds: known amounts and estimated amounts. We look first at current liabilities of a known amount.

Current Liabilities of Known Amount

Objective

1 Account for current liabilities and contingent liabilities

Current liabilities of known amount include accounts payable, short-term notes payable, sales tax payable, current portion of long-term debt, accrued expenses payable, payroll liabilities, and unearned revenues.

ACCOUNTS PAYABLE. Amounts owed for products or services purchased on account are *accounts payable*. We have seen many accounts payable examples in preceding chapters. For example, Home Depot purchases inventories on an account payable. The company reported Accounts Payable of $1,976 million at January 31, 2001 (see the Home Depot balance sheet on page 365).

One of a merchandiser's most common transactions is the credit purchase of inventory. A computer integrates the accounts payable and inventory systems. When merchandise dips below a certain level, the computer prints a purchase order. The goods are received and the computer increases Inventory and Accounts Payable.

SHORT-TERM NOTES PAYABLE. **Short-term notes payable,** a common form of financing, are notes payable due within 1 year. H.J. Heinz company lists its short-term notes payable as *short-term debt*. Heinz may issue short-term notes payable to borrow cash or to purchase assets. On its notes payable, Heinz must accrue interest expense and interest payable at the end of the period →. The following sequence of entries covers the purchase of inventory, accrual of interest expense, and payment of a short-term note payable.

Short-term note payable
Note payable due within one year.

←Recall from Chapter 3, page 124, that all adjusting entries for accrued expenses require a debit to an expense and a credit to a payable.

20X5			
Jan. 30	Inventory	8,000	
	Note Payable, Short-Term		8,000
	Purchase of inventory by issuing a 1-year 10% note payable.		

This transaction increases both an asset and a liability.

ASSETS	=	LIABILITIES	+	STOCKHOLDERS' EQUITY
8,000	=	8,000	+	0

The H.J. Heinz fiscal year ends each April 30. At year end, Heinz must accrue interest expense.

Apr. 30	Interest Expense ($8,000 × .10 × 3/12)	200	
	Interest Payable		200
	Adjusting entry to accrue interest expense at year end.		

ASSETS	=	LIABILITIES	+	STOCKHOLDERS' EQUITY	−	EXPENSES
0	=	200			−	200

The balance sheet at year end will report the Note Payable of $8,000 and the related Interest Payable of $200 as current liabilities. The income statement will report interest expense of $200.

The following entry records the note's payment at maturity:

✔ Check Point 8-1

✔ Check Point 8-2

20X6			
Jan. 30	Note Payable, Short-Term	8,000	
	Interest Payable	200	
	Interest Expense ($8,000 × 0.10 × 9/12)	600	
	Cash [$8,000 + ($8,000 × .10)]		8,800
	Payment of a note payable and interest at maturity.		

ASSETS	=	LIABILITIES	+	STOCKHOLDERS' EQUITY	−	EXPENSES
−8,800	=	−8,000			−	600
		− 200				

The debits to the two payables zero out those accounts. The entry also records the interest expense of year 20X6.

SALES TAX PAYABLE. Most states levy a sales tax on retail sales. Retailers charge their customers the sales tax and thus owe the state the sales tax collected. Home Depot reported sales tax payable of $298 million at January 31, 2001. See Home Depot's balance sheet on page 365.

Suppose one Saturday's sales at a Home Depot Store totaled $200,000. The business collected an additional 5% in sales tax, which would equal $10,000 ($200,000 × .05). The store would record that day's sales as follows:

Cash ($200,000 × 1.05)	210,000	
Sales Revenue		200,000
Sales Tax Payable ($200,000 × .05)		10,000
To record cash sales and the related sales tax.		

ASSETS	=	LIABILITIES	+	STOCKHOLDERS' EQUITY	+	REVENUES
210,000	=	10,000			+	200,000

Current installment of long-term debt The amount of the principal that is payable within one year.

CURRENT PORTION OF LONG-TERM DEBT. Some long-term debt must be paid in installments. The **current installment of long-term debt** (also called *current portion*) is the amount of the principal that is payable within 1 year. At the end of each year, a company reclassifies (from long-term debt to a current liability) the amount of its long-term debt that must be paid during the upcoming year.

The Home Depot balance sheet (page 365) reports Current Installments of Long-Term Debt as the last current liability. It also reports Long-Term Debt, excluding current installments, immediately after total current liabilities. *Long-term debt*

Study H.J. Heinz's balance sheet and answer these questions about the company's current and long-term debt:

1. At April 30, 2001, how much in total did Heinz owe on current and long-term debt?
2. How much of the long-term debt did Heinz expect to pay during the year ended April 30, 2002? How much was the company scheduled to pay during later years?

Answers:

1. $3,330 million ($315 + $3,015)
2. Pay next year—$315 million. Pay later—$3,015 million

refers to the notes payable and bonds payable that we cover in the second half of this chapter. H.J. Heinz also reports these two liabilities labeling the current liability as *Portion of long-term debt due within 1 year.*

The liabilities for the Current Installments of Long-Term Debt and for the long-term debt do *not* include any accrued interest payable. The two accounts, Current Installments of Long-Term Debt and Long-Term Debt represent only the principal amounts owed. Interest Payable is a separate current liability. Home Depot reports interest payable under the Current Liability caption Other Accrued Expenses; Heinz reports Other Accrued Liabilities, which we discuss next.

Accrued expense
An expense incurred but not yet paid in cash. Also called *accrued liability.*

ACCRUED EXPENSES (ACCRUED LIABILITIES). An **accrued expense** is an expense the business has incurred but not yet paid. Therefore, an accrued expense is also a liability, which explains why it is also called an **accrued liability.** Many accrued expenses, such as Home Depot's interest payable on its long-term debt, occur with the passage of time. Home Depot reports several categories of accrued expenses on its balance sheet:

- Accrued Salaries and Related Expenses
- Other Accrued Expenses
- Income Taxes Payable

Accrued Salaries and Related Expenses are the company's liabilities for salaries, wages, and related payroll expenses not yet paid at the end of the period. This caption also includes payroll taxes withheld from employee paychecks. Other Accrued Liabilities include the company's interest payable and property tax payable. Income Taxes Payable is the amount of income tax The Home Depot still owes at year end.

H.J. Heinz Company reports accrued liabilities for Accrued Marketing and Accrued Restructuring Costs.

Payroll
Employee compensation, a major expense of many businesses.

PAYROLL LIABILITIES. **Payroll,** also called *employee compensation,* is a major expense. For service organizations—such as law firms, real estate brokers, and travel agents—compensation is *the* major expense, just as cost of goods sold is the largest expense for a merchandising company.

Employee compensation takes different forms. A *salary* is pay stated at a yearly or monthly rate. *Wages* are pay stated at an hourly rate. Sales employees earn a *commission,* which is a percentage of the sales the employee has made. A *bonus* is an amount over and above regular compensation. Accounting for all forms of compensation follows the same pattern, as illustrated in Exhibit 8-1 (using assumed figures).

Exhibit 8-1

Accounting for Payroll Expenses and Liabilities

Salary Expense	10,000	
Employee Income Tax Payable		1,200
FICA Tax Payable		800
Salary Payable to Employees [take-home pay]		8,000
To record salary expense.		

ASSETS	=	LIABILITIES	+	STOCKHOLDERS' EQUITY	−	EXPENSES
		1,200			−	10,000
0	=	+800				
		+8,000				

Salary expense represents *gross pay* (that is, pay before subtractions for taxes and other deductions). Salary expense creates several payroll liabilities:

- *Salary payable* to employees is their net (take-home) pay.
- *Employee Income Tax Payable* is the employees' income tax that has been withheld from paychecks.
- *FICA Tax Payable* includes the employees' Social Security tax and Medicare tax, which also are withheld from paychecks. (FICA stands for the Federal Insurance Contributions Act, which created the Social Security tax.)

Companies also must pay some *employer* payroll taxes and expenses for employee benefits. Accounting for these expenses is similar to the illustration in Exhibit 8-1.

UNEARNED REVENUES. *Unearned revenues* are also called *deferred revenues* and *revenues collected in advance*. All these account titles indicate that the business has received cash from customers before earning the revenue. The company has an obligation to provide goods or services to the customer. Let's consider an example.

The Dun & Bradstreet (D&B) Corporation provides credit evaluation services to subscribers. When a company pays in advance to have D&B investigate a potential customer's credit history D&B collects cash and incurs a liability called Unearned Subscription Revenue.

Assume that D&B charges a client $750 for a 3-year subscription. D&B's entries would be as follows:

20X1			
Jan. 1	Cash	750	
	Unearned Subscription Revenue		750
	To receive cash for a 3-year subscription.		

D&B assets and liabilities increase equally. There is no revenue yet.

ASSETS	=	LIABILITIES	+	STOCKHOLDERS' EQUITY
750	=	750	+	0

20X1, 20X2, 20X3			
Dec. 31	Unearned Subscription Revenue	250	
	Subscription Revenue ($750/3)		250
	To record revenue earned at the end of each year.		

The liability decreases as D&B earns the revenue.

YEAR	ASSETS	=	LIABILITIES	+	STOCKHOLDERS' EQUITY	+	REVENUES
20X1	0	=	−250			+	250
20X2	0	=	−250			+	250
20X3	0	=	−250			+	250

D&B financial statements would report the following:

Balance Sheet	Year 1	December 31 Year 2	Year 3
Current liabilities:			
Unearned subscription revenue	$250	$250	$0
Long-term liabilities:			
Unearned subscription revenue	$250	$ 0	$0
Income Statement	**Year 1**	**Year 2**	**Year 3**
Revenues:			
Subscription revenue	$250	$250	$250

Current Liabilities That Must Be Estimated

A business may know that a liability exists and not know the exact amount. But the business must report the liability on the balance sheet. Estimated liabilities vary among companies. Let's look first at Estimated Warranty Payable, a liability account that most merchandisers have.

ESTIMATED WARRANTY PAYABLE. Many companies guarantee their products under *warranty* agreements. The warranty period may extend for 90 days to a year for consumer products. Automobile companies—BMW, General Motors, and Toyota—accrue liabilities for vehicle warranties.

Whatever the warranty's life, the matching principle demands that the company record the *warranty expense* in the same period that the business records sales revenue →. After all, the warranty motivates customers to buy products, so the company must record warranty expense. At the time of the sale, however, the company does not know which products are defective. The exact amount of warranty expense cannot be known with certainty, so the business must estimate warranty expense and the related warranty liability.

← *For a review of the matching principle, see Chapter 3, page 115.*

Assume that Black & Decker, which manufactures products sold in Home Depot, Wal-Mart, and Target stores, made sales of \$200,000,000 subject to product warranties. If, in past years, between 2% and 4% of products proved defective, Black & Decker could estimate that 3% of the products it sells this year will require repair or replacement. The company would estimate warranty expense of \$6,000,000 (\$200,000,000 × 0.03) for the period and make the following entry:

Warranty Expense	6,000,000	
Estimated Warranty Payable		6,000,000
To accrue warranty expense.		

ASSETS	=	LIABILITIES	+	STOCKHOLDERS' EQUITY	−	EXPENSES
0	=	6,000,000			−	6,000,000

Assume that defective merchandise totals $5,800,000. Black & Decker will replace the defective products and record the following:

Estimated Warranty Payable	5,800,000	
Inventory		5,800,000
To replace defective products sold under warranty.		

If Black & Decker paid cash to satisfy the warranty, then the credit would be to the Cash account rather than to Inventory.

✔ Check Point 8-3

✔ Check Point 8-4

ASSETS	=	LIABILITIES	+	STOCKHOLDERS' EQUITY
−5,800,000	=	−5,800,000	+	0

In the preceding sequence, what would Black & Decker report on its income statement and balance sheet?

Answer:

Income statement:	Warranty expense	$6,000,000
Balance sheet:	Estimated warranty payable ($6,000,000 − $5,800,000)	$ 200,000

The warranties discussed here are not the extended warranties companies sell on certain products. Those warranties involve a revenue stream and are not illustrated here.

CONTINGENT LIABILITIES. A *contingent liability* is not an actual liability. Instead, it is a potential liability that depends on a *future* event arising out of past events. The Financial Accounting Standards Board (FASB) provides these guidelines to account for contingent losses (or expenses) and their related liabilities:

1. Record an actual liability if it is *probable* that the loss (or expense) will occur and the *amount can be reasonably estimated.* Warranty expense is an example.
2. Report the contingency in a financial statement note if it is *reasonably possible* that a loss (or expense) will occur. Lawsuits in progress are a prime example. Microsoft Corporation includes a lengthy note on its financial statements to report contingent liabilities.
3. There is no need to report a contingent loss that is *remote*—unlikely to occur. Instead, wait until an actual transaction clears up the situation. For example, suppose Del Monte Foods grows vegetables in Nicaragua, and the Nicaraguan government issues a mild threat to confiscate the assets of all foreign companies. Del Monte will report nothing about the contingency if the probability of a loss is considered remote.

Home Depot reported its contingencies (type 2 above) in the following note:

Note 8, Commitments and Contingencies

1. *At January 31, 2000, the Company was contingently liable for approximately $442 million under outstanding letters of credit issued primarily in connection with purchase commitments.*

2. *The Company is involved in litigation arising from the normal course of business. In management's opinion, this litigation is not expected to materially impact the Company's results of operation or financial condition.*

Contingency 1 arises because Home Depot has committed to purchase assets and has promised to pay for the goods when delivered. When the other company ships the assets to Home Depot, the other company can deposit the letters of credit into its bank account. If the other company never ships the goods, then Home Depot has no liability and will pay nothing.

Contingency 2 arises from lawsuits that claim wrongdoing by Home Depot and seek damages through the courts. If the court rules in favor of Home Depot, there is no liability. But if the ruling favors the plaintiff, then Home Depot has an actual liability.

It would be unethical to omit these disclosures from the financial statements. Investors need this information to properly evaluate Home Depot's stock.

✔ Check Point 8-5

Mid-Chapter Summary Problem

Assume that the Estée Lauder Companies, Inc. faced the following liability situations at June 30, 20X4, the end of the company's fiscal year:

a. Long-term debt totals $100 million and is payable in annual installments of $10 million each. The interest rate on the debt is 7%, and interest is paid each December 31.

b. The company pays royalties on its purchased trademarks. Royalties for the trademarks are equal to a percentage of Estée Lauder's sales. Assume that sales in 20X4 were $400 million and were subject to a royalty rate of 3%. At June 30, 20X4, Estée Lauder owes two-thirds of the year's royalty, to be paid in July.

c. Salary expense for the last payroll period of the year was $900,000. Of this amount, employees' withheld income tax totaled $88,000 and FICA taxes were $61,000. These payroll amounts will be paid early in July.

d. On fiscal year 20X4 sales of $400 million, management estimates warranty expense of 2%. One year ago, at June 30, 20X3, Estimated Warranty Liability stood at $3 million. Warranty payments were $9 million during the year ended June 30, 20X4.

Show how Estée Lauder would report these liabilities on its balance sheet at June 30, 20X4.

Answer

a. Current liabilities:	
Current installment of long-term debt	$10,000,000
Interest payable ($100,000,000 × .07 × 6/12)	3,500,000
Long-term debt ($100,000,000 − $10,000,000)	90,000,000
b. Current liabilities:	
Royalties payable ($400,000,000 × .03 × 2/3)	8,000,000
c. Current liabilities:	
Salary payable ($900,000 − $88,000 − $61,000)	751,000
Employee income tax payable	88,000
FICA tax payable	61,000
d. Current liabilities:	
Estimated warranty payable	2,000,000
[$3,000,000 + ($400,000,000 × .02) − $9,000,000]	

amortizing bonds, bond pricing, discount, effective interest rate, EPS, premium, present value of money

Bonds payable
Groups of notes payable (bonds) issued to multiple lenders called *bondholders.*

Long-Term Liabilities: Bonds

Large companies such as The Home Depot, H.J. Heinz, and Daimler-Chrysler Corporation cannot borrow billions from a single lender. So how do large corporations borrow huge amounts? They issue (sell) bonds to the public. **Bonds payable** are groups of notes payable issued to multiple lenders, called *bondholders*. Chrysler, a division of Daimler-Chrysler, can borrow large amounts by issuing bonds to thousands of individual investors, who each lend a modest amount to Chrysler. Chrysler receives what it needs, and each investor limits his or her risk by diversifying investments—not putting all the investors' "eggs in one basket." In the pages that follow, we treat bonds payable and long-term notes payable together because their accounting is the same.

Bonds: An Introduction

Each bond payable is, in effect, a long-term note payable. Bonds payable are debts of the issuing company.

Purchasers of bonds receive a bond certificate, which carries the issuing company's name. The certificate also states the *principal*, which is typically stated in units

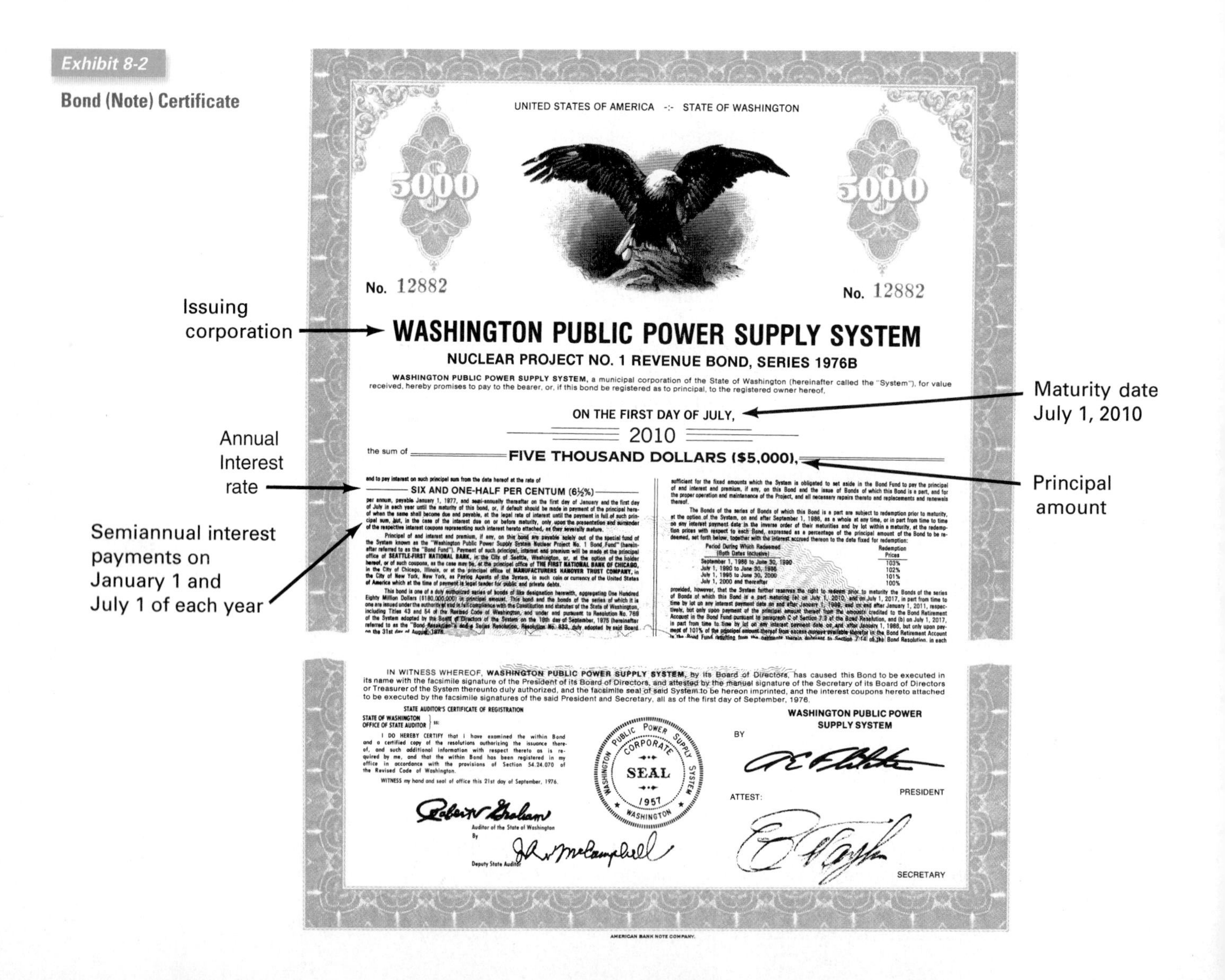

Exhibit 8-2
Bond (Note) Certificate

of $1,000; principal is also called the bond *face value, maturity value*, or *par value*. The bond obligates the issuing company to pay the debt at a specific future time called the *maturity date*.

Bondholders loan their money to companies for a price: *interest*. Interest is the rental fee on money borrowed. The bond certificate states the interest rate that the issuer will pay the holder and the dates that the interest payments are due (generally twice a year). Exhibit 8-2 shows an actual bond certificate.

Issuing bonds usually requires the services of a securities firm, such as Merrill Lynch, to act as the underwriter of the bond issue. The **underwriter** purchases the bonds from the issuing company and resells them to its clients, or it may sell the bonds to its clients and earn a commission on the sale.

Underwriter
Organization that purchases the bonds from an issuing company and resells them to its clients or sells the bonds for a commission, agreeing to buy all unsold bonds.

TYPES OF BONDS. All the bonds in a particular issue may mature at a specified time (**term bonds**), or in installments over a period of time (**serial bonds**). Serial bonds are like installment notes payable. Both Home Depot's and H.J. Heinz's long-term debts are serial in nature because they come due in installments.

Secured, or *mortgage, bonds* give the bondholder the right to take specified assets of the issuer if the company *defaults*—that is, fails to pay interest or principal. *Unsecured bonds*, called **debentures,** are backed only by the good faith of the borrower. Debentures carry a higher rate of interest than secured bonds because debentures are riskier investments.

Term bonds
Bonds that all mature at the same time for a particular issue.

Serial bonds
Bonds that mature in installments over a period of time.

Debentures
Unsecured bonds—bonds backed only by the good faith of the borrower.

BOND PRICES AND THE TIME VALUE OF MONEY. Investors may buy and sell bonds through bond markets. The most famous bond market is the *New York Exchange*, which lists several thousand bonds. Bond prices are quoted at a percentage of their maturity value. For example, a $1,000 bond quoted at 100 is bought or sold for $1,000, which is 100% of its face value. The same bond quoted at $101^1/_2$ has a market price of $1,015 (101.5% of face value = $1,000 × 1.015). Prices are quoted to one-eighth of 1%. A $1,000 bond quoted at $88^3/_8$ is priced at $883.75 ($1,000 × .88375).

Exhibit 8-3 contains actual price information for the bonds of Ohio Edison Company, taken from *The Wall Street Journal*. On this particular day, 12 of Ohio Edison's $9^1/_2$%, $1,000 face-value bonds maturing in the year 2006 (indicated by 06) were traded. The bonds' highest price on this day was $795 ($1,000 × .795). The lowest price of the day was $785 ($1,000 × .785). The closing price (last sale price of the day) was $795. This price was 2 points higher than the closing price of the preceding day. What was the bonds' closing price the preceding day? It was $77^1/_2$ ($79^1/_2 - 2$).

Bonds	Volume	High	Low	Close	Net Change
OhEd $9^1/_2$ 06	12	$79^1/_2$	$78^1/_2$	$79^1/_2$	+2

Exhibit 8-3
Bond Price Information for Ohio Edison Company (OhEd)

A bond issued at a price above its face (par) value is said to be issued at a **premium,** and a bond issued at a price below face (par) value has a **discount.** As a bond nears maturity, its market price moves toward par value. On the maturity date, a bond's market value exactly equals its par value because the company that issued the bond pays that amount to retire the bond.

Premium (on a bond)
Excess of a bond's issue price over its maturity (par) value.

Discount (on a bond)
Excess of a bond's maturity (par value) over its issue price.

✔ Check Point 8-6

A dollar received today is worth more than a dollar to be received in the future. You may invest today's dollar immediately and earn income from it. But if you must wait to receive the dollar, you forgo the interest revenue. Money earns income over time, a fact called the *time value of money*. Let's examine how the time value of money affects the pricing of bonds.

Assume that a bond with a face value of $1,000 reaches maturity 3 years from today and carries no interest. Would you pay $1,000 to purchase the bond? No, because the payment of $1,000 today to receive the same amount in the future provides you with no income on the investment. You would not be taking advantage of the time value of money. Just how much would you pay today to receive $1,000 at the end of 3 years? The answer is some amount *less* than $1,000. Let's suppose that you feel $750 is a good price. By investing $750 now to receive $1,000 later, you earn $250 interest revenue over the 3 years. The issuing company sees the transaction this way: It pays you $250 interest for the use of your $750 for 3 years.

Present value
Amount a person would invest now to receive a greater amount at a future date.

The amount that a person would invest *at the present time* to receive a greater amount at a future date is called the **present value** of a future amount. In our example, $750 is the present value of the $1,000 amount to be received 3 years later.

Our $750 bond price is a reasonable estimate. The exact present value of any future amount depends on

1. The amount of the future payment (or receipt)
2. The length of time from the investment to the date when the future amount is to be paid (or received)
3. The interest rate during the period

Present value is always less than the future amount. We discuss how present value is computed in Appendix D at the end of the book (page 689). We need to be aware of the present-value concept in our discussion of bond prices.

HOW BOND INTEREST RATES DETERMINE BOND PRICES. Bonds are always sold at their *market price*, which is the amount investors are willing to pay. Market price is the bond's present value, which equals the present value of the principal payment plus the present value of the cash interest payments (which are made semiannually [twice a year], annually, or quarterly over the term of the bond).

Two interest rates work to set the price of a bond.

Contract interest rate
Interest rate that determines the amount of cash interest the borrower pays and the investor receives each year. Also called *stated interest rate.*

- The **contract interest rate**, or **stated interest rate**, is the interest rate that determines the amount of cash interest the borrower pays—and the investor receives—each year. For example, Chrysler Corporation's 9% bonds have a contract interest rate of 9%. Thus, Chrysler pays $9,000 of interest annually on each $100,000 bond. Each semiannual interest payment is $4,500 ($100,000 $\times$ 0.09 $\times$ $^1/_2$).

Market interest rate
Interest rate that investors demand for loaning their money. Also called *effective interest rate.*

- The **market interest rate**, or **effective-interest rate**, is the rate that investors demand for loaning their money. The market rate varies by the minute. A company may issue bonds with a contract interest rate that differs from the prevailing market interest rate.

Exhibit 8-4 shows how the contract (stated) interest rate and the market interest rate interact to determine the issuance price of a bond payable for three separate

Exhibit 8-4

How the Contract Interest Rate and the Market Interest Rate Interact

Issuance Price of Bonds Payable

Case A:				
Contract (stated) interest rate on a bond payable	equals	Market interest rate	implies	Price of par (face, or maturity) value
Example: 9%	=	9%	→	*Par: $1,000 bond issued for $1,000*
Case B:				
Contract (stated) interest rate on a bond payable	less than	Market interest rate	implies	Discount (price *below* par)
Example: 9%	<	10%	→	*Discount: $1,000 bond issued below $1,000*
Case C:				
Contract (stated) interest rate on a bond payable	greater than	Market interest rate	implies	Premium (price *above* par)
Example: 9%	>	8%	→	*Premium: $1,000 bond issued above $1,000*

✔ Check Point 8-7

cases. Chrysler, for example, may issue its 9% bonds when the market rate has risen to 10%. Will the Chrysler bonds attract investors in this market? No, because investors can earn 10% on other bonds of similar risk. Therefore, investors will purchase Chrysler bonds only at a price less than their par value. The difference between the lower price and face value is a *discount* (Exhibit 8-4). Conversely, if the market interest rate is 8%, Chrysler's 9% bonds will be so attractive that investors will pay more than face value for them. The difference between the higher price and face value is a *premium*.

Issuing Bonds Payable at Par Value

Objective 2 **Account** for bonds payable transactions

Suppose Chrysler Corporation has $50 million in 9% bonds that mature in 5 years. Assume that Chrysler issues these bonds at par on January 1, 2004. The issuance entry is

2004			
Jan. 1	Cash	50,000,000	
	Bonds Payable		50,000,000
	To issue 9%, 5-year bonds at par.		

ASSETS	=	LIABILITIES	+	STOCKHOLDERS' EQUITY
50,000,000	=	50,000,000	+	0

Chrysler, the borrower, makes a one-time entry to record the receipt of cash and the issuance of bonds. Afterward, investors buy and sell the bonds through the bond markets. These buy-and-sell transactions between outside investors do *not* involve Chrysler at all.

Interest payments occur each January 1 and July 1. Chrysler's entry to record the first semiannual interest payment is:

2004			
July 1	Interest Expense		
	($50,000,000 × .09 × 6/12)	2,250,000	
	Cash		2,250,000
	To pay semiannual interest.		

ASSETS	=	LIABILITIES	+	STOCKHOLDERS' EQUITY	−	EXPENSES
−2,250,000	=	0	+			− 2,250,000

At year end, Chrysler must accrue interest expense and interest payable for 6 months (July through December), as follows:

2004			
Dec. 31	Interest Expense		
	($50,000,000 × .09 × 6/12)	2,250,000	
	Interest Payable		2,250,000
	To accrue interest		

ASSETS	=	LIABILITIES	+	STOCKHOLDERS' EQUITY	−	EXPENSES
0	=	2,250,000	+			− 2,250,000

At maturity, Chrysler will pay off the bonds as follows:

2009			
Jan. 1	Bonds Payable	50,000,000	
	Cash		50,000,000
	To pay bonds payable at maturity.		

✔ Check Point 8-8

ASSETS	=	LIABILITIES + STOCKHOLDERS' EQUITY
−50,000,000	=	−50,000,000

Issuing Bonds Payable at a Discount

We know that market conditions may force a company to issue bonds at a discount. Suppose Chrysler Corporation issues $100,000 of its 9%, 5-year bonds when the market interest rate is 10%. The market price of the bonds drops, and Chrysler receives $96,149[1] at issuance. The transaction is recorded as follows:

2004			
Jan. 1	Cash	96,149	
	Discount on Bonds Payable	3,851	
	Bonds Payable		100,000
	To issue 9%, 5-year bonds at a discount.		

[1]Appendix D at the end of this book shows how to determine the price of this bond.

ASSETS	=	LIABILITIES	+	STOCKHOLDERS' EQUITY
+96,149	=	−3,851	+	0
		+100,000		

Now the bond accounts have these balances:

Bonds Payable		Discount on Bonds Payable	
	100,000	**3,851**	

Chrysler's balance sheet immediately after issuance of the bonds would report the following:

Total current liabilities		$ XXX
Long-term liabilities		
Bonds payable, 9%, due 2009	$100,000	
Less: Discount on bonds payable	(3,851)	96,149

Discount on Bonds Payable is a contra account to Bonds Payable, a decrease in the company's liabilities. Subtracting the discount from Bonds Payable yields the *carrying amount* of the bonds. Thus, Chrysler's liability is $96,149, which is the amount the company borrowed.

DECISION: How Much Is Chrysler's Interest Expense on These Bonds Payable?

Objective 3 **Measure** interest expense

Chrysler pays interest on its bonds semiannually, which is common practice. Each semiannual interest *payment* remains the same over the life of the bonds:

$$\text{Semiannual interest payment} = \$100{,}000 \times .09 \times 6/12 = \$4{,}500$$

This payment amount is fixed by the bond contract. But Chrysler's interest *expense* increases from period to period as the bonds march toward maturity because these bonds were issued at a discount.

Panel A of Exhibit 8-5 repeats the Chrysler bond data we've been using so far. Panel B provides an amortization table that

- Determines the periodic interest expense
- Shows the bond carrying amount

Study the exhibit carefully because the amounts we will be using come directly from the amortization table →. This exhibit is an example of the *effective-interest method of amortization*, which is the correct way to measure interest expense.

← *Recall from Chapter 7, page 337, that amortization is the systematic reduction of a particular amount—in this case, the Discount on Bonds Payable.*

Interest Expense on Bonds Issued at a Discount

In Exhibit 8-5, Chrysler Corporation borrowed $96,149 cash but must pay $100,000 when the bonds mature. What happens to the $3,851 balance of the discount account over the life of the bond issue?

(continued on page 380 after Exhibit 8-5)

Exhibit 8-5 **Debt Amortization for a Bond Discount**

PANEL A—Bond Data

Issue date—January 1, 2004	Market interest rate at time of issue—10% annually, 5% semiannually
Maturity (face, or par) value—$100,000	Issue price—$96,149
Contract interest rate—9%	Maturity date—January 1, 2009

Interest paid—$4\frac{1}{2}$% semiannually, $4,500 = $100,000 × .09 × 6/12

PANEL B—Amortization Table

	A	B	C	D	E
Semiannual Interest Date	***Interest Payment ($4^1/_2$% of Maturity Value)***	***Interest Expense (5% of Preceding Bond Carrying Amount)***	***Discount Amortization (B − A)***	***Discount Account Balance (Preceding D − C)***	***Bond Carrying Amount ($100,000 − D)***
Jan. 1, 2004				$3,851	$ 96,149
July 1	$4,500	$4,807	$307	3,544	96,456
Jan. 1, 2005	4,500	4,823	323	3,221	96,779
July 1	4,500	4,839	339	2,882	97,118
Jan. 1, 2006	4,500	4,856	356	2,526	97,474
July 1	4,500	4,874	374	2,152	97,848
Jan. 1, 2007	4,500	4,892	392	1,760	98,240
July 1	4,500	4,912	412	1,348	98,652
Jan. 1, 2008	4,500	4,933	433	915	99,085
July 1	4,500	4,954	454	461	99,539
Jan. 1, 2009	4,500	4,961*	461	-0-	100,000

*Adjusted for effect of rounding

Notes

- Column A The semiannual interest payments are constant—fixed by the bond contract.
- Column B The interest expense each period = the preceding bond carrying amount × the market interest rate. Interest expense increases as the bond carrying amount (E) increases.
- Column C The excess of interest expense (B) over interest payment (A) is the discount amortization (C) for the period.
- Column D The discount balance (D) decreases when amortized.
- Column E The bond carrying amount (E) increases from $96,149 at issuance to $100,000 at maturity.

The $3,851 is really additional interest expense to Chrysler—interest expense over and above the stated interest that Chrysler pays each 6 months. Exhibit 8-6 graphs the interest expense and the interest payment on the Chrysler bonds over their lifetime. Observe that the semiannual interest payment is fixed—by contract—at $4,500 (column A). But the amount of interest expense (column B) increases each period as the bond carrying amount moves upward toward maturity.

The discount is not paid until the bonds are paid off at maturity. The discount is, therefore allocated to interest expense through amortization each period over the term of the bonds. Exhibit 8-7 illustrates the amortization of the bonds' carrying value from $96,149 at issuance to $100,000 at maturity. These amounts come from Exhibit 8-5, column E. Now let's see how to account for the Chrysler bonds issued at a discount.

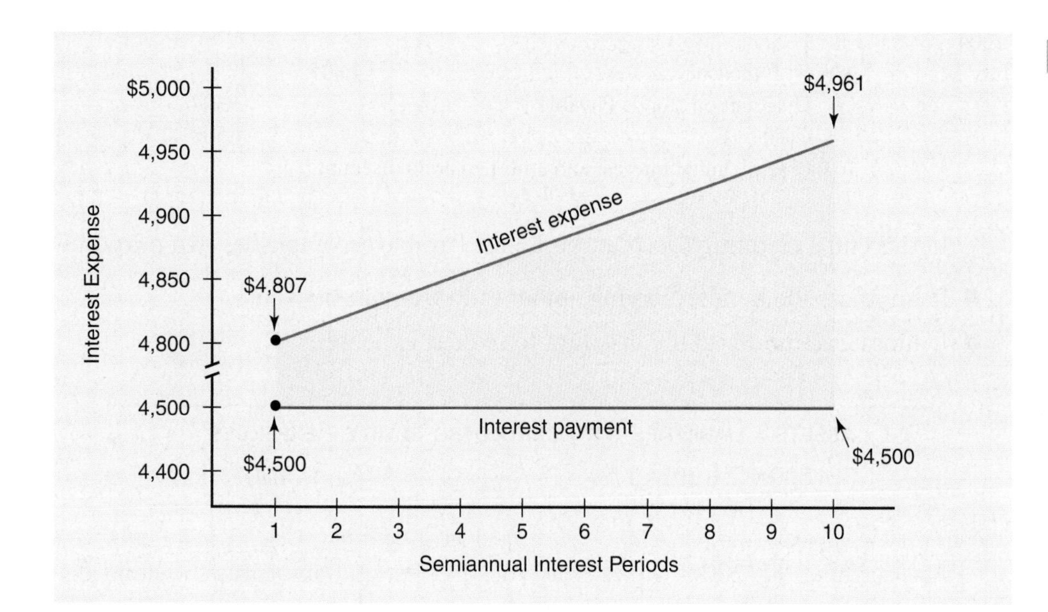

Exhibit 8-6

Interest Expense on Bonds Payable Issued at a Discount

What explains the difference between interest expense and the cash payment of interest for bonds issued at a discount? Why is interest expense always greater than the cash payment?

Answer:

Amortization of the bond discount is the difference between interest expense and the cash payment of interest. Interest expense exceeds the interest payment because Chrysler borrowed $96,149 but must pay $100,000 at maturity.

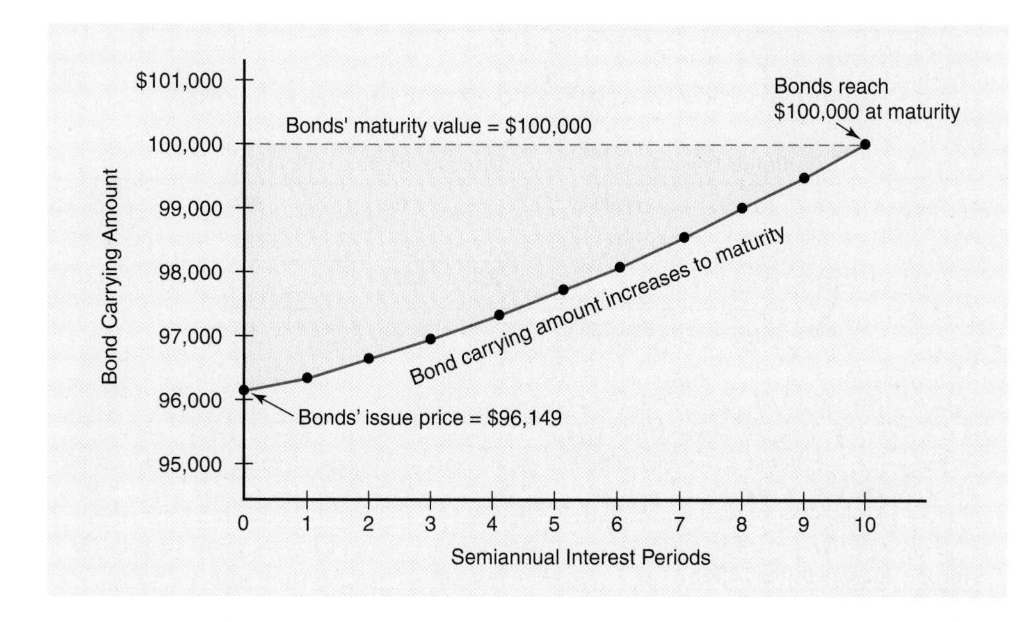

Exhibit 8-7

Amortizing Bonds Payable Issued at a Discount

Chrysler issued its bonds on January 1, 2004. On July 1, Chrysler made the first $4,500 semiannual interest payment. But Chrysler's interest expense is greater than $4,500. Chrysler's journal entry to record interest expense and the interest payment for the first 6 months follows (with all amounts taken from Exhibit 8-5):

2004			
July 1	Interest Expense	4,807	
	Discount on Bonds Payable		307
	Cash		4,500
	To pay semiannual interest and amortize bond discount.		

In this entry, crediting Discount on Bonds Payable accomplishes two purposes:

- It amortizes the bonds' carrying amount toward maturity value.
- It allocates (amortizes) the discount to interest expense.

ASSETS	=	LIABILITIES	+	STOCKHOLDERS' EQUITY	−	EXPENSES
−4,500	=	+ 307			−	4,807

✔ Check Point 8-9

At December 31, 2004, Chrysler accrues interest and amortizes the bond discount for July through December with this entry (amounts from Exhibit 8-5):

2004			
Dec. 31	Interest Expense	4,823	
	Discount on Bonds Payable		323
	Interest Payable		4,500
	To accrue semiannual interest and amortize bond discount.		

ASSETS	=	LIABILITIES	+	STOCKHOLDERS' EQUITY	−	EXPENSES
0	=	+ 323			−	4,823
		+ 4,500				

At December 31, 2004 Chrysler's bond accounts appear as follows:

Bonds Payable		Discount on Bonds Payable	
	100,000	**3,851**	**307**
			323
		Bal. 3,221	

Bond carrying amount, $96,779 = ($100,000 − $3,221) from Exhibit 8-5

What would Chrysler Corporation's 2004 income statement and year-end balance sheet report for these bonds?

Answer:

Income Statement for 2004

Interest expense ($4,807 + $4,823)		$ 9,630

Balance Sheet at December 31, 2004

Current liabilities:		
Interest payable		$ 4,500
Long-term liabilities:		
Bonds payable	$100,000	
Less: Discount on bonds payable	(3,221)	96,779

✔ Check Point 8-10

At the bonds' maturity on January 1, 2009, the discount will have been amortized to zero, and the bonds' carrying amount will be $100,000. Chrysler will retire the bonds by making a $100,000 payment to the bondholders.

Issuing Bonds Payable at a Premium

Let's modify the Chrysler bond example to illustrate issuance of the bonds at a premium. Assume that Chrysler Corporation issues $100,000 of 5-year, 9% bonds that pay interest semiannually. If the bonds are issued when the market interest rate is 8%, their issue price is $104,100.[2] The premium on these bonds is $4,100, and Exhibit 8-8 shows how to amortize the bonds by the effective-interest method. In practice,

(continued on page 384)

Exhibit 8-8 **Debt Amortization for a Bond Premium**

PANEL A—Bond Data

Issue date—January 1, 2004
Maturity (face, or par) value—$100,000
Contract interest rate—9%
Interest paid—$4\frac{1}{2}$% semiannually, $4,500 = $100,000 × .09 × 6/12
Market interest rate at time of issue—8% annually, 4% semiannually
Issue price—$104,100
Maturity date—January 1, 2009

PANEL B—Amortization Table

	A	B	C	D	E
Semiannual Interest Date	***Interest Payment ($4\frac{1}{2}$% of Maturity Value)***	***Interest Expense (4% of Preceding Bond Carrying Amount)***	***Premium Amortization (A − B)***	***Premium Account Balance (Preceding D − C)***	***Bond Carrying Amount ($100,000 + D)***
Jan. 1, 2004				$4,100	$104,100
July 1	$4,500	$4,164	$336	3,764	103,764
Jan. 1, 2005	4,500	4,151	349	3,415	103,415
July 1	4,500	4,137	363	3,052	103,052
Jan. 1, 2006	4,500	4,122	378	2,674	102,674
July 1	4,500	4,107	393	2,281	102,281
Jan. 1, 2007	4,500	4,091	409	1,872	101,872
July 1	4,500	4,075	425	1,447	101,447
Jan. 1, 2008	4,500	4,058	442	1,005	101,005
July 1	4,500	4,040	460	545	100,545
Jan. 1, 2009	4,500	3,955*	545	-0-	100,000

*Adjusted for effect of rounding

Notes

- Column A — The semiannual interest payments are constant—fixed by the bond contract.
- Column B — The interest expense each period = the preceding bond carrying amount × the market interest rate. Interest expense decreases as the bond carrying amount (E) decreases.
- Column C — The excess of each interest payment (A) over interest expense (B) is the premium amortization for the period (C).
- Column D — The premium balance (D) decreases when amortized (C).
- Column E — The bond carrying amount (E) decreases from $104,100 at issuance to $100,000 at maturity.

[2] Again, Appendix D at the end of the book shows how to determine the price of this bond.

bond premiums are rare because few companies issue their bonds to pay cash interest above the market interest rate.

Chrysler's entries to record issuance of the bonds on January 1, 2004, and to make the first interest payment and amortize the bonds on July 1, are as follows:

2004			
Jan. 1	Cash	104,100	
	Bonds Payable		100,000
	Premium on Bonds Payable		4,100
	To issue 9% bonds at a premium.		

ASSETS	=	LIABILITIES	+	STOCKHOLDERS' EQUITY
104,100	=	100,000	+	0
		+4,100		

2004			
July 1	Interest Expense	4,164	
	Premium on Bonds Payable	336	
	Cash		4,500
	To pay semiannual interest and amortize bond premium.		

ASSETS	=	LIABILITIES	+	STOCKHOLDERS' EQUITY	–	EXPENSES
−4,500	=	−336			–	4,164

Immediately after issuing the bonds at a premium on January 1, 2004, Chrysler would report the bonds payable on the balance sheet as follows:

Total current liabilities		$ XXX
Long-term liabilities:		
Bonds payable	$100,000	
Premium on bonds payable	4,100	104,100

Note that the premium on bonds payable is *added* to the balance of bonds payable to determine the carrying amount.

In Exhibit 8-8 Chrysler Corporation borrowed $104,100 cash but must pay only $100,000 at maturity. The $4,100 premium on the bonds is a reduction in Chrysler's interest expense over the term of the bonds. Exhibit 8-9 graphs Chrysler's interest payments (column A from Exhibit 8-8) and interest expense (column B).

The premium is allocated as a subtraction of interest expense through amortization each period over the term of the bonds. Exhibit 8-10 diagrams the amortization of the bond carrying amount from the issue price of $104,100 to maturity value of $100,000. All amounts are taken from Exhibit 8-8.

A Quick and Dirty Way to Measure Interest Expense

A less precise method can be used to develop estimates and perform quick analyses. Called the *straight-line amortization method*, it divides a bond discount (or premium)

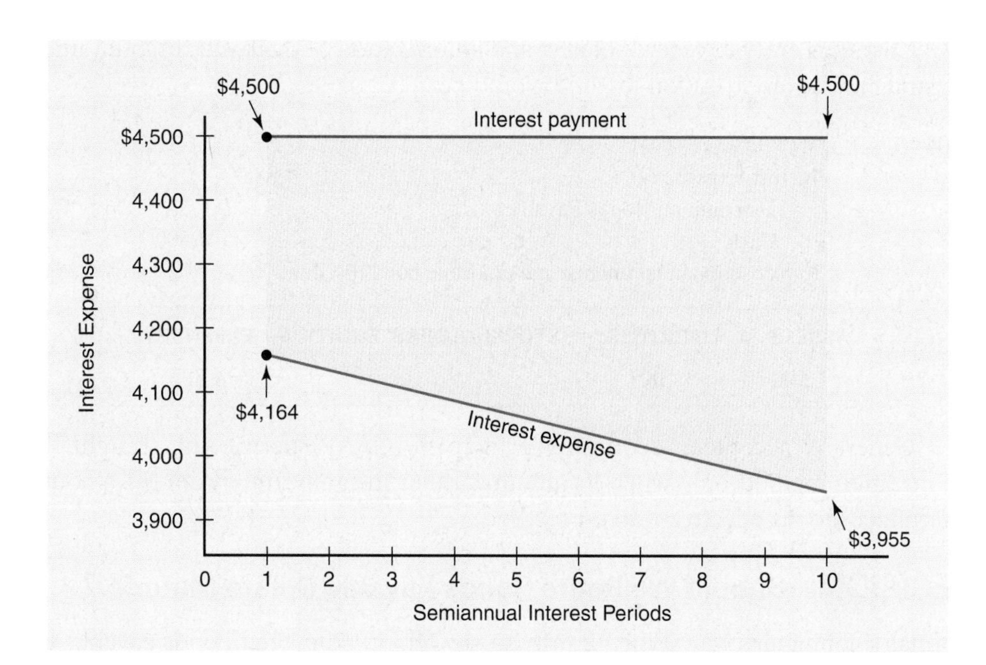

Exhibit 8-9

Interest Expense on Bonds Payable Issued at a Premium

into equal periodic amounts over the bond's term. The amount of interest expense is thus the same for each interest period.

Let's apply the straight-line method to the Chrysler bonds issued at a discount and illustrated in Exhibit 8-5 (p. 380). Suppose Chrysler's financial vice president is considering issuing the 9% bonds at $96,149. To estimate semiannual interest expense on the bonds, the executive can use the straight-line amortization method for the bond discount.

Semiannual cash interest payment ($100,000 × .09 × 6/12)	$4,500
+ Semiannual amortization of discount ($3,851 ÷ 10)	385
= Estimated semiannual interest expense	$4,885

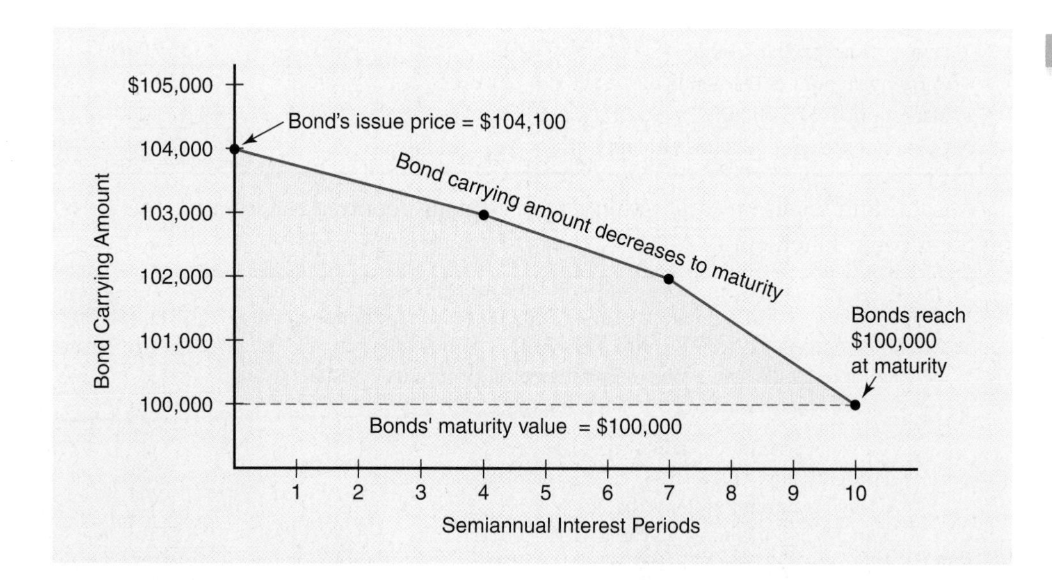

Exhibit 8-10

Amortizing Bonds Payable Issued at a Premium

Chrysler's entry to record interest and amortization of the bond discount under the straight-line amortization method would be

2004			
July 1	Interest Expense	4,885	
	Discount on Bonds Payable		385
	Cash		4,500
	To pay semiannual interest and amortize bond discount.		

✔ Check Point 8-11

✔ Check Point 8-12

ASSETS	=	LIABILITIES	+	STOCKHOLDERS' EQUITY	−	EXPENSES
− 4,500	=	+ 385			−	4,885

Generally accepted accounting principles (GAAP) permit the straight-line amortization method only when its amounts differ insignificantly from the amounts determined by the effective-interest method.

DECISION: Should We Retire Bonds Payable Before Maturity?

Normally, companies wait until maturity to pay off, or *retire*, their bonds payable. But companies sometimes retire their bonds payable before maturity. The main reason for retiring bonds early is to relieve the pressure of making interest payments. Interest rates fluctuate, and the company may be able to borrow at a lower interest rate.

Callable bonds Bonds that the issuer may call (pay off) at a specified price whenever the issuer wants.

Some bonds are **callable,** which means that the bonds' issuer may *call*, or pay off, those bonds at a specified price whenever the issuer so chooses. The call price is usually a few percentage points above the par value, perhaps 102 or 103. Callable bonds give the issuer the benefit of being able to pay off the bonds whenever it is most favorable to do so. The alternative to calling the bonds is to purchase them in the open market at their current market price.

Air Products and Chemicals, Inc., a producer of industrial gases and chemicals, has $70 million of debenture bonds outstanding with unamortized discount of $350,000. Lower interest rates in the market may convince management to pay off these bonds now. Assume that the bonds are callable at 103. If the market price of the bonds is $99^1/_4$ will Air Products and Chemicals call the bonds or purchase them in the open market? Market price is the better choice because the market price is lower than the call price. Retiring the bonds at $99^1/_4$ results in a gain of $175,000, computed as follows:

Par value of bonds being retired	$70,000,000
Less: Unamortized discount	(350,000)
Carrying amount of the bonds	69,650,000
Market price ($70,000,000 × .9925)	69,475,000
Gain on retirement of bonds payable	$ 175,000

Gains and losses on early retirement of debt are reported as Other income (loss) on the income statement.

Several years ago Quill Corporation issued $300,000 of 10-year bonds at a discount. The carrying value of the bonds is $299,000. Quill retires half the bonds by paying the call price of 101. What is the amount of Quill's gain or loss on retirement of the bonds payable?

Answer:

Carrying amount of Quill Corp.'s bonds payable	$299,000
Portion being retired	× .50
Carrying amount of bonds being retired	$149,500
Call price of the bonds ($150,000 × 1.01)	151,500
Loss on retirement of bonds payable	$ 2,000

Convertible Bonds and Notes

Many corporate bonds and notes payable may be converted into the issuing company's common stock →. These bonds and notes are called **convertible bonds** (or **notes**). For investors they combine the safety of assured receipt of interest and principal on the bonds with the opportunity for gains on the stock. The conversion feature is so attractive that investors usually accept a lower interest rate than they would on nonconvertible bonds. The lower cash interest payments benefit the issuer. If the market price of the issuing company's stock gets high enough, the bondholders will convert the bonds into stock.

Convertible bonds (or notes) Bonds (or notes) that may be converted into the issuing company's common stock at the investor's option.

← *For a review of common stock, see Chapter 1, page 17.*

Texas Instruments Inc., a leading microchip manufacturer, has convertible notes payable of $250 million. If Texas Instruments stock rises significantly, the noteholders will convert the notes into the company's common stock. Conversion of the notes payable into stock will decrease Texas Instruments' debt and increase its equity.

Assume the noteholders convert half the notes into 4 million shares of Texas Instruments common stock ($1 par) on May 14. Texas Instruments makes the following entry in its accounting records:

May 14	Notes Payable ($250,000,000 × $^1/_2$)	125,000,000	
	Common Stock (4,000,000 × $1 par)		4,000,000
	Paid-in Capital in Excess of Par-Common		121,000,000
	To record conversion of notes payable.		

ASSETS	=	LIABILITIES	+	STOCKHOLDERS' EQUITY
0	=	−125,000,000	+	4,000,000 + 121,000,000

The carrying amount of the notes (125 million) becomes stockholders' equity as the notes payable account is zeroed out. Common Stock is recorded at its *par value,* which is a dollar amount assigned to each share of stock. In this case, the credit to Common Stock is $4,000,000 (4,000,000 shares × $1 par value per share). Any extra carrying amount of the notes payable is credited to another stockholders' equity account, Paid in Capital in Excess of Par—Common.

DECISION: Financing Operations with Bonds or Stock?

Objective

4 **Understand** the advantages and disadvantages of borrowing

Managers must decide how to acquire assets. The money to purchase an asset may be financed by retained earnings, by issuing stock, or by borrowing on bonds payable. Each strategy has its advantages:

1. ***Issuing stock*** creates no liabilities or interest expense and is less risky to the issuing corporation.
2. ***Issuing notes or bonds payable*** does not dilute stock ownership or control of the corporation. It results in higher earnings per share because the earnings on borrowed money usually exceed interest expense.

Earnings per share (EPS) is the amount of a company's net income for each share of its stock. EPS is perhaps the single most important statistic used to evaluate

Earnings per share (EPS) Amount of a company's net income per share of its outstanding common stock.

companies because it is a standard measure of operating performance for comparing companies of different sizes and from different industries.

Suppose Athens Corporation needs $500,000 for expansion. Athens has net income of $300,000 and 100,000 shares of common stock outstanding. Management is considering two financing plans. Plan 1 is to issue $500,000 of 10% bonds payable, and plan 2 is to issue 50,000 shares of common stock for $500,000. Management believes the new cash can be invested in operations to earn income of $200,000 before interest and taxes.

Exhibit 8-11 shows the earnings-per-share advantage of borrowing. As you can see, Athens Corporation's EPS amount is higher if the company borrows by issuing bonds. Athens earns more on the investment ($90,000) than the interest it pays on the bonds ($50,000). Earning more income on borrowed money than the related interest expense increases the earnings for common stockholders and is called **trading on the equity.** It is widely used to increase earnings per share of common stock.

Trading on the equity
Earning more income on borrowed money than the related interest expense, thereby increasing the earnings for the owners of the business. Also called *leverage.*

Exhibit 8-11 Earnings-Per-Share Advantage of Borrowing

	Plan 1 Borrow $500,000 at 10%		Plan 2 Issue 50,000 Shares of Common Stock for $500,000	
Net income before expansion		$300,000		$300,000
Expected project income before interest and income tax	$200,000		$200,000	
Less interest expense ($500,000 × .10)	(50,000)		0	
Expected project income before income tax	150,000		200,000	
Less income tax expense (40%)	(60,000)		(80,000)	
Expected project net income		90,000		120,000
Total company net income		$390,000		$420,000
Earnings per share after expansion:				
Plan 1 ($390,000/100,000 shares)		$3.90		
Plan 2 ($420,000/150,000 shares)				$2.80

In this case borrowing results in higher earnings per share than issuing stock. Borrowing has its disadvantages, however. Interest expense may be high enough to eliminate net income and lead to a cash crisis or even bankruptcy. Also, borrowing creates liabilities that accrue during bad years as well as good years. In contrast, a company that issues stock can omit its dividends during a bad year. The Decision Guidelines feature provides some guidance to help decide how to finance operations.

✔ Check Point 8-13

Decision Guidelines

FINANCING WITH DEBT OR WITH STOCK

El Chico is the leading chain of Tex-Mex restaurants in the United States, begun by the Cuellar family in the Dallas area. Suppose El Chico is expanding into neighboring states. Take the role of Miguel Cuellar and assume you must make some key decisions about how to finance the expansion.

Decision	Guidelines
How will you finance El Chico's expansion?	Your financing plan depends on El Chico's ability to generate cash flow, your willingness to give up some control of the business, the amount of financing risk you are willing to take, and El Chico's credit rating.
Do El Chico's operations generate enough cash to meet all its financing needs?	If yes, the business needs little outside financing. There is no need to borrow. If no, the business will need to issue additional stock or borrow the money.
Are you willing to give up some of your control of the business?	If yes, then issue stock to other stockholders, who can vote their shares to elect the company's directors. If no, then borrow from bondholders, who have no vote in the management of the company.
How much financing risk are you willing to take?	If much, then borrow as much as you can, and you may increase El Chico's earnings per share. But this will increase the business's debt ratio and the risk of being unable to pay its debts. If little, then borrow sparingly. This will hold the debt ratio down and reduce the risk of default on borrowing agreements. But El Chico's earnings per share may be lower than if you were to borrow.
How good is the business's credit rating?	The better the credit rating, the easier it is to borrow on favorable terms. A good credit rating also makes it easier to issue stock. Neither stockholders nor creditors will entrust their money to a company with a bad credit rating.

Excel Application Problem

Goal: Create an Excel worksheet to compare earnings per share under two financing scenarios: borrowing and issuing stock.

Scenario: El Chico is thinking about building a new distribution warehouse to serve its growing restaurant operations. In order to finance the warehouse, managers must recommend whether to borrow the funds for construction or issue stock. Construction costs are estimated at $5 million. If borrowing is chosen, long-term bonds payable will be issued at 8% to raise the $5 million. If stock is chosen, 80,000 shares will be issued to cover the $5 million cost. Managers expect sales to increase by $700,000 in the first year. Income tax expense is 40%. Net income before construction is $4 million, and shares outstanding before construction total 500,000.

Your task is to create a spreadsheet that compares earnings per share under the two scenarios described above. After completing the spreadsheet, answer these questions:

1. Which plan generates the higher earnings per share? Why?
2. Under what circumstances would El Chico consider using debt to finance its new warehouse?
3. Under what circumstances would El Chico consider the use of equity to finance its new warehouse?
4. Which option do you recommend for El Chico? Why? Does your recommendation change if the bond interest rate changes to 10%?

Step-by-step:

1. Open a new Excel worksheet.
2. Create a heading for your worksheet that contains the following:
   a. Chapter 8 Decision Guidelines
   b. Financing with Debt or Stock
   c. El Chico
   d. Today's date
3. Use Exhibit 8-11 as a model for the layout of your spreadsheet. Label the long-term bonds as "Plan 1," and the issuance of common stock as "Plan 2." Be sure to set up the spreadsheet so that you can change variables, such as the interest rate on the bonds, without retyping any formulas in the body of the spreadsheet.
4. When finished, your spreadsheet should show earnings per share under both plans, and be capable of recomputing earnings per share simply by changing the interest rate on the bonds.
5. Save your work and print a copy of the worksheet (in landscape mode) for your files.

DECISION: How much Debt Can We Manage— The Times-Interest-Earned Ratio

We have just seen how the wise use of borrowing can increase EPS. But too much debt can lead to bankruptcy if the business cannot pay liabilities as they come due. Managers and lenders use ratios to determine how much credit risk they are taking.

Times-interest-earned ratio
Ratio of income from operations to interest expense. Measures the number of times that operating income can cover interest expense. Also called the *interest-coverage ratio.*

The debt ratio measures the effect of debt on the company's *financial position* but says nothing about the ability to pay interest expense. Analysts use a second ratio—the **times-interest-earned ratio**—to relate income to interest expense. To compute this ratio, we divide *income from operations* (also called *operating income*) by interest expense. This ratio measures the number of times that operating income can *cover* interest expense. The ratio is also called the *interest-coverage ratio.* A high times-interest-earned ratio indicates ease in paying interest expense; a low value suggests difficulty. Let's see how Home Depot and H.J. Heinz compare on the times-interest-earned ratio (dollar amounts in billions).

				Home Depot	**H.J. Heinz Company**
Times-interest-earned ratio	=	Operating income / Interest expense	=	$4,191 / $93 = 45 times	$982 / $333 = 3 times

Home Depot's income from operations covers its interest expense 45 times. Heinz's interest-coverage ratio is 3 times. Home Depot is much less risky on this ratio than H.J. Heinz.

✔ Check Point 8-14

Which company, Home Depot or Heinz, would you expect to have the higher debt ratio? Examine the two companies' balance sheets at the beginning of the chapter to confirm your opinion.

Answer:
Heinz has a much higher debt ratio than Home Depot, as follows (dollar amounts in billions):

				Home Depot	H.J. Heinz
Debt ratio	=	Total liabilities / Total assets	=	$6.4 / $21.4 = .30	$7.7 / $9.0 = .86

Heinz operates in the food industry, which is more stable than the cyclical home-improvements industry. Therefore, Heinz can manage a higher debt ratio than Home Depot can.

Lease
Rental agreement in which the tenant (lessee) agrees to make rent payments to the property owner (lessor) in exchange for the use of the asset.

capital lease

Long-Term Liabilities: Leases and Pensions

Lessee
Tenant in a lease agreement.

Lessor
Property owner in a lease agreement.

A **lease** is a rental agreement in which the tenant **(lessee)** agrees to make rent payments to the property owner **(lessor)** in exchange for the use of the asset. Leasing allows the lessee to acquire the use of a needed asset without having to make the large initial cash down payment that purchase agreements require. Accountants distinguish between two types of leases: operating and capital.

Types of Leases

Operating lease
Usually a short-term or cancelable rental agreement.

Operating leases are often short-term or cancelable. They give the lessee the right to use the asset but provide the lessee with no continuing rights to the asset. The lessor retains the usual risks and rewards of owning the leased asset. To account for an operating lease, the lessee debits Rent Expense (or Lease Expense) and credits Cash for the amount of the lease payment. The lessee's books do not report the leased asset or any lease liability. Nevertheless, operating leases require the lessee to make rent payments. Therefore, an operating lease creates a liability even though the liability does not appear on the balance sheet.

Most businesses use capital leasing to finance the acquisition of some assets. A **capital lease** is a long-term and noncancelable financing obligation that is a form of debt. How do you distinguish a capital lease from an operating lease? *FASB Statement No. 13* provides the guidelines. To be classified as a capital lease, a particular lease agreement must meet any *one* of the following criteria:

Capital lease
Lease agreement that meets any one of four criteria: (1) The lease transfers title of the leased asset to the lessee. (2) The lease contains a bargain purchase option. (3) The lease term is 75% or more of the estimated useful life of the leased asset. (4) The present value of the lease payments is 90% or more of the market value of the leased asset.

1. The lease transfers title of the leased asset to the lessee at the end of the lease term. Thus, the lessee becomes the legal owner of the leased asset.
2. The lease contains a *bargain purchase option*. The lessee can be expected to purchase the leased asset and become its legal owner.
3. The lease term is 75% or more of the estimated useful life of the leased asset. The lessee uses up most of the leased asset's service potential.
4. The present value of the lease payments is 90% or more of the market value of the leased asset. In effect, the lease payments are the same as installment payments for the leased asset.

Accounting for a capital lease is much like accounting for the purchase of an asset by the lessee. The lessee enters the asset into its own accounts and records a lease liability at the beginning of the lease term. Thus, the lessee capitalizes the asset in its own financial statements even though it may never take legal title to the property.

Most companies lease some of their plant assets. The Home Depot leases store buildings under capital leases. At January 31, 2001, Home Depot reported its capital leases in Note 5 of its financial statements, excerpted as follows:

Note 5 Leases (partial)

The approximate future minimum lease payments under capital [. . .] leases at January 31, 2001 were as follows (in millions):

Fiscal Year	Capital Leases	
2001	$ 38	
2002	38	
2003	38	
2004	38	
2005	39	
Thereafter	519	
	710	
Less: Imputed interest	(480)	
Net present value of capital lease obligations	230	← *This is Home Depot's total liability under the leases.*
Less: Current installments	(3)	← *Current liability*
Long-term capital lease obligations, excluding current installments	$ 227	← *Long-term liability*

The note reveals that Home Depot must pay a total of $710 million on its capital leases. The present value of this liability is $230 million, of which $3 million is a current liability and $227 million is long-term debt. These amounts are included in the liability figures reported on Home Depot's balance sheet.

DECISION: Do Lessees Prefer Operating Leases or Capital Leases?

Suppose you were the chief financial officer (CFO) of H.J. Heinz Co. Assume Heinz is leasing assets valued at close to $1 billion. Heinz is the lessee (the renter) in the transaction. The lease can be structured either as an operating lease or as a capital lease. Which type of lease would you prefer for H.J. Heinz Co.? Why? Computing Heinz's debt ratio two ways (new lease as an operating lease; new lease as a capital lease) will make your decision clear:

(dollar amounts in billions)	*Operating Lease*	*Capital Lease*
$\text{Debt ratio} = \dfrac{\text{Total liabilities}}{\text{Total assets}} =$	$\dfrac{\$7.3}{\$8.9} = 0.82$	$\dfrac{\$7.3 + \$1.0}{\$8.9 + \$1.0} = \dfrac{\$8.3}{\$9.9} = 0.84$

Heinz would prefer an operating lease because an operating lease adds no assets and no liabilities to the balance sheet. By contrast, a capital lease forces Heinz to capitalize the leased asset and record a lease liability as though it had purchased the asset with long-term debt. As a result, a capital lease would increase Heinz's debt ratio and might increase Heinz's interest expense on new borrowings. For this reason, lessees generally prefer operating leases.

Pensions and Postretirement Liabilities

Pension
Employee compensation that will be received during retirement.

Most companies have pension plans for their employees. A **pension** is employee compensation that will be received during retirement. Companies also provide postretirement benefits, such as medical insurance for retired former employees. Because employees earn these benefits by their service, the company records pension and retirement-benefit expense while employees work for the company.

Pensions are one of the most complex areas of accounting. As employees earn their pensions and the company pays into the pension plan, the plan's assets grow. The obligation for future pension payments to employees also accumulates. At the end of each period, the company compares

- The fair market value of the assets in the pension plan—cash and investments—with
- The plan's accumulated benefit obligation. The *accumulated benefit obligation* is the present value of promised future pension payments to retirees.

If the plan assets exceed the accumulated benefit obligation, the plan is said to be *overfunded*. In this case, the asset and obligation amounts are to be reported only in the notes to the financial statements. However, if the accumulated benefit obligation (the pension liability) exceeds plan assets, the plan is *underfunded*, and the company must report the excess liability amount as a long-term pension liability on the balance sheet.

At April 30, 2001, the pension plan of H.J. Heinz Company was underfunded. It had

- Assets with a fair market value of $215 million
- Accumulated pension benefit obligations totaling $359 million

Heinz's balance sheet, therefore, included a Long-Term Pension Liability of $144 million ($359 − $215). This amount is included among Other long-term liabilities.

Reporting Liabilities

Reporting on the Balance Sheet

Objective

5 Report liabilities on the balance sheet

This chapter began with the liabilities reported on the balance sheets of The Home Depot, Inc. and H.J. Heinz Company. Exhibit 8-12 repeats the liabilities section of Home Depot's balance sheet.

Exhibit 8-12 **Reporting Liabilities of The Home Depot, Inc.**

The Home Depot, Inc.

Balance Sheet (Partial, Adapted)

Amounts in millions	
Liabilities	
Current liabilities:	
Accounts payable	$1,976
Accrued salaries and related expenses	627
Sales taxes payable	298
Other accrued expenses	1,402
Income taxes payable	78
Current installments of long-term debt (note 2)	4
Total current liabilities	4,385
Long-term debt, excluding current installments (note 2)	1,545
Other long-term liabilities	451

Note 2 Long-Term Debt (adapted)

The company's long-term debt at January 31, 2001 consisted of the following:

Amounts in millions	
Commercial Paper; weighted average interest rate of 6.1%	$ 754
$6\frac{1}{2}$% Senior Notes; due September 15, 2004	500
Capital Lease Obligations	230
Installment Notes Payable; interest rates between 7.2% and 10.0%, in varying installments through 2018	41
Other	24
Total long-term debt	1,549
Less current installments	4
Long-term debt, excluding current installments	$1,545

Exhibit 8-12 includes Note 2 from Home Depot's financial statements, which gives additional details about the company's liabilities. Note 2 shows the interest rates and the maturity dates of Home Depot's long-term debt. Investors need these data to evaluate the company. The note also reports

- Capital lease obligations of $230 million included among the long-term debt
- Current installments of long-term debt ($4 million) as a current liability
- Long-term debt, excluding current installments, of $1,545 million

Trace these amounts from Note 2 to the company's balance sheet. Working back and forth between the financial statements and the related notes is an important part of financial analysis. You now have the tools to understand the liabilities reported on an actual balance sheet.

✔ Check Point 8-15

Reporting the Fair Market Value of Long-Term Debt

FASB Statement Number 107 requires companies to report the fair market value of their long-term debt. At January 31, 2001, Home Depot's Note 2 included this excerpt:

> *The estimated fair value of commercial paper borrowings approximate their carrying value [of $754 million]. The estimated fair value of all other long-term borrowings was approximately $67 million compared to the carrying value of $65 million [$41 + $24].*

Overall, the fair market value of Home Depot's long-term debt is about the same as its carrying amount on Home Depot's books.

Reporting Financing Activities on the Statement of Cash Flows

The Home Depot's balance sheet shows that the company finances most of its operations with equity. In fact, the company's debt ratio is only 30% (total liabilities of $6.4 billion ÷ total assets of $21.4 billion). Let's examine Home Depot's financing activities as reported on its statement of cash flows. Exhibit 8-13 is an excerpt from the company's cash-flow statement.

Exhibit 8-13

Statement of Cash Flows (Adapted) for the Home Depot, Inc.

The Home Depot, Inc.

Statement of Cash Flows

(In millions)	*Year Ended January 31, 2001*
Cash Flow from Operating Activities:	
Net cash provided by operating activities	$ 2,796
Cash Flow from Investing Activities:	
Net cash used in investing activities	$(3,530)
Cash Flow from Financing Activities:	
Borrowing by issuing commercial paper	$ 754
Proceeds from long-term borrowings	32
Payments of long-term debt	(29)

During the year ended January 31, 2001, The Home Depot borrowed $786 million by issuing commercial paper and other long-term debt. The company paid $29 million on its long-term debt. These were the only financing transactions that affected the company's liabilities during the year. Home Depot is able to finance most of its asset purchases with cash generated by operations—a healthy $2,796 million. This is an indication of strong cash flows and a stable financial position.

End-of-Chapter Summary Problem

The **Cessna Aircraft Company** has outstanding an issue of 8% convertible bonds that mature in 2018. Suppose the bonds are dated October 1, 1998, and pay interest each April 1 and October 1.

Required

1. Complete the following effective-interest amortization table through October 1, 2000:

Bond Data

Maturity value—$100,000
Contract interest rate—8%
Interest paid—4% semiannually, $4,000 ($100,000 × .08 × 6/12)
Market interest rate at the time of issue—9% annually, $4^1/_2$% semiannually
Issue price—$90^3/_4$

Amortization Table

	A	B	C	D	E
Semiannual Interest Date	Interest Payment (4% of Maturity Amount)	Interest Expense ($4^1/_2$% of Preceding Bond Carrying Amount)	Discount Amortization (B − A)	Discount Account Balance (Preceding D − C)	Bond Carrying Amount ($100,000 − D)
10-1-98					
4-1-99					
10-1-99					
4-1-00					
10-1-00					

2. Using the amortization table, record the following transactions:
   a. Issuance of the bonds on October 1, 1998.
   b. Accrual of interest and amortization of the bonds on December 31, 1998.
   c. Payment of interest and amortization of the bonds on April 1, 1999.
   d. Conversion of one-third of the bonds payable into no-par stock on October 2, 2000. For no-par stock, transfer the bond carrying amount into the Common Stock account. There is No Additional Paid-in Capital.
   e. Retirement of two-thirds of the bonds payable on October 2, 2000. Purchase price of the bonds was based on their call price of 102.

Answers

Requirement 1

	A	B	C	D	E
Semiannual Interest Date	Interest Payment (4% of Maturity Amount)	Interest Expense ($4^1/_2$% of Preceding Bond Carrying Amount)	Discount Amortization (B − A)	Discount Account Balance (Preceding D − C)	Bond Carrying Amount ($100,000 − D)
10-1-98				$9,250	$90,750
4-1-99	$4,000	$4,084	$84	9,166	90,834
10-1-99	4,000	4,088	88	9,078	90,922
4-1-00	4,000	4,091	91	8,987	91,013
10-1-00	4,000	4,096	96	8,891	91,109

Requirement 2

Date	Accounts	Debit	Credit
a. 1998			
Oct. 1	Cash ($100,000 × 0.9075)	90,750	
	Discount on Bonds Payable	9,250	
	Bonds Payable		100,000
	To issue 8%, 20-year bonds at a discount.		
b. Dec. 31	Interest Expense ($4,084 × 3/6)	2,042	
	Discount on Bonds Payable ($84 × 3/6)		42
	Interest Payable ($4,000 × 3/6)		2,000
	To accrue interest and amortize the bonds.		
c. 1999			
Apr. 1	Interest Expense	2,042	
	Interest Payable	2,000	
	Discount on Bonds Payable ($84 × 3/6)		42
	Cash		4,000
	To pay semiannual interest, part of which was accrued, and amortize the bonds.		
d. 2000			
Oct. 2	Bonds Payable ($100,000 × 1/3)	33,333	
	Discount on Bonds Payable ($8,891 × 1/3)		2,964
	Common Stock ($91,109 × 1/3)		30,369
	To record conversion of bonds payable.		
e. Oct. 2	Bonds Payable ($100,000 × 2/3)	66,667	
	Loss on Retirement of Bonds	7,260	
	Discount on Bonds Payable ($8,891 × 2/3)		5,927
	Cash ($100,000 × 2/3 × 1.02)		68,000
	To retire bonds payable before maturity.		

Review Liabilities

Lessons Learned

1. **Account for current liabilities and contingent liabilities.** *Current liabilities* are obligations due within 1 year or within the company's normal operating cycle if it is longer than 1 year. Obligations beyond that term are classified as *long-term liabilities.*

   Contingent liabilities are potential liabilities that depend on a future event arising out of a past transaction.
2. **Account for bonds-payable transactions.** Corporations may borrow by issuing long-term notes or bonds payable. A bond contract specifies the *maturity value* of the bonds, the *principal* (amount borrowed from the lender), a *contract interest rate*, and dates for the payment of interest and principal. Bonds issued above par are issued at a *premium*, and bonds issued below par are issued at a *discount*.
3. **Measure interest expense.** When a bond's contract interest rate differs from the market interest rate, the company's interest expense differs from period to period. For bonds issued at a discount, the amount of interest expense each period increases as the bond carrying amount increases. For bonds issued at a premium, the amount of interest expense each period decreases as the bond carrying amount decreases.

4. **Understand the advantages and disadvantages of borrowing.** A key advantage of borrowing versus issuing stock is that interest expense on debt is tax-deductible. Thus, selling bonds is less costly than issuing stock. Bonds also lead to a higher earnings per share than stock issues do. The key disadvantage of borrowing: The company must repay the loan and interest, in good times and in bad.

5. **Report liabilities on the balance sheet.** Many companies report additional categories of liabilities on the balance sheet. *Deferred income taxes* are income tax liabilities that the company has deferred and will pay later. *Deferred gains* and *deferred credits* are long-term unearned revenues.

Accounting Vocabulary

accrued expense (p. 369)
accrued liability (p. 369)
bonds payable (p. 374)
callable bonds (p. 386)
capital lease (p. 391)
contract interest rate (p. 376)
convertible bonds (or **notes**) (p. 387)
current installment of long-term debt (p. 368)
debentures (p. 375)
discount (on a bond) (p. 375)
earnings per share (EPS) (p. 387)
effective-interest rate (p. 376)
interest-coverage ratio (p. 390)
lease (p. 390)
lessee (p. 390)
lessor (p. 390)
leverage (p. 388)
market interest rate (p. 376)
operating lease (p. 391)
payroll (p. 369)
pension (p. 392)
premium (on a bond) (p. 375)
present value (p. 376)
serial bonds (p. 375)
short-term notes payable (p. 367)
stated interest rate (p. 376)
term bonds (p. 375)
times-interest-earned ratio (p. 390)
trading on the equity (p. 388)
underwriter (p. 375)

Questions

1. What distinguishes a current liability from a long-term liability? What distinguishes a contingent liability from an actual liability?
2. A company purchases a machine by signing a $60,000, 10%, 1-year note payable on July 31. Interest is to be paid at maturity. What two current liabilities related to this purchase does the company report on its December 31 balance sheet? What is the amount of each current liability?
3. At the beginning of the school term, what type of account is the tuition that your college or university collects from students? What type of account is the tuition at the end of the school term?
4. Patton Company warrants its products against defects for 3 years from date of sale. During the current year, the company made sales of $300,000. Store management estimated that warranty costs on those sales would total $21,000 over the 3-year warranty period. Ultimately, the company paid $22,000 cash on warranties. What was the company's warranty expense for the year? What accounting principle governs this answer?
5. How does a contingent liability differ from a regular liability? Identify three things that create contingent liabilities.
6. Compute the price to the nearest dollar for the following bonds with a face value of $10,000:

   a. 100
   b. 93
   c. $88\frac{3}{4}$
   d. $101\frac{3}{8}$
   e. $122\frac{1}{2}$
7. In which of the following situations will bonds sell at par, at a premium, and at a discount?

   a. 9% bonds sold when the market interest rate is 9%
   b. 9% bonds sold when the market interest rate is 8%
   c. 9% bonds sold when the market interest rate is 10%
8. A company retires 10-year bonds payable of $100,000 after 5 years. The business issued the bonds at 104 and called them at 101. Compute the dollar amount of the gain or loss on retirement.
9. Why are convertible bonds attractive to investors? Why are they popular with borrowers?
10. Contrast the effects on a company of financing operations by issuing bonds versus issuing stock.
11. Identify the ratio that measures the ability to pay interest expense. Show how to compute this ratio. What other ratio measures the ability to pay total liabilities? Show how to compute this ratio also.
12. What characteristics distinguish a capital lease from an operating lease?
13. Distinguish an overfunded pension plan from an underfunded plan. Which situation requires the company to report a pension liability on the balance sheet? How is this liability computed?
14. What are the two main financing cash flows related to long-term debt?

Assess Your Progress

Check Points

Accounting for a note payable
(Obj. 1)

CP8-1 Return to the $8,000 purchase of inventory on a short-term note payable that begins on page 367. Assume that the purchase of inventory occurred on May 31, 20X5, instead of January 30, 20X5. Journalize the company's (a) purchase of inventory, (b) accrual of interest expense on December 31, 20X5, and (c) payment of the note plus interest on May 31, 20X6.

Reporting a short-term note payable and the related interest in the financial statements
(Obj. 1)

CP8-2 This check point should be done in conjunction with Check Point 8-1.

1. Refer to the data in Check Point 8-1. Show what the company would report for the note payable on its balance sheet at December 31, 20X5, and on its income statement for the year ended on that date.
2. What one item will the financial statements for the year ended December 31, 20X6 report? Identify the financial statement, the item, and its amount.

Accounting for warranty expense and estimated warranty payable
(Obj. 1)

CP8-3 **Daimler-Chrysler Corporation** guarantees some of its automobiles against defects for 4 years or 50,000 miles, whichever comes first. Suppose Chrysler's experience indicates that the company can expect warranty costs during the 4-year period to add up to 6% of sales.

Assume that Four Corners Dodge in Durango, Colorado, made sales of $500,000 during 20X0. Four Corners Dodge received cash for 10% of the sales and took notes receivable for the remainder. Payments to satisfy customer warranty claims totaled $26,000 during 20X0.

1. Record the sales, warranty expense, and warranty payments for Four Corners Dodge. Ignore any reimbursement Four Corners Dodge may receive from Daimler-Chrysler Corporation.
2. Post to the Estimated Warranty Payable T-account. The beginning balance was $7,000. At the end of 20X0, how much in estimated warranty payable does Four Corners Dodge owe its customers? Why must the warranty payable amount be estimated?

Applying GAAP; reporting warranties in the financial statements
(Obj. 1)

CP8-4 Refer to the data given in Check Point 8-3. What amount of warranty expense will Four Corners Dodge report during 20X0? Which accounting principle addresses this situation? Does the warranty expense for the year equal the year's cash payments for warranties? Explain how the accounting principle works for measuring warranty expense.

Interpreting a company's contingent liabilities
(Obj. 1)

CP8-5 **Harley-Davidson, Inc.**, the motorcycle manufacturer, included the following note in its annual report:

NOTES TO CONSOLIDATED FINANCIAL STATEMENTS
7 (In Part): Commitments and Contingencies

> *The Company self-insures its product liability losses in the United States up to $3 million (catastrophic coverage is maintained for individual claims in excess of $3 million up to $25 million). Outside the United States, the Company is insured for product liability up to $25 million per individual claim and in the aggregate.*

1. Why are these *contingent* (versus *real*) liabilities?
2. In the United States, how can the contingent liability become a real liability for Harley-Davidson? What are the limits to the company's product liabilities in the United States? Explain how these limits work.
3. How can a contingency outside the United States become a real liability for the company? How does Harley-Davidson's potential liability differ for claims outside the United States?

Pricing bonds
(Obj. 2)

CP8-6 Compute the price of the following bonds:

a. $2,000,000 quoted at $89\frac{3}{4}$
b. $500,000 quoted at $110\frac{3}{8}$
c. $100,000 quoted at $97\frac{1}{2}$
d. $400,000 quoted at $102\frac{5}{8}$

CP8-7 Determine whether the following bonds payable will be issued at par value, at a premium, or at a discount:

Determining bond prices at par, discount, or premium
(Obj. 2)

a. The market interest rate is 9%. Corinth, Inc., issues bonds payable with a stated rate of $8\frac{1}{2}$%.
b. Macedonia Corporation issued $7\frac{1}{2}$% bonds payable when the market rate was $7\frac{1}{2}$%.
c. Sparta Corporation issued 8% bonds when the market interest rate was $6\frac{7}{8}$%.
d. Athens Company issued bonds payable that pay cash interest at the contract rate of 7%. At the date of issuance, the market interest rate was $8\frac{1}{4}$%.

CP8-8 Suppose **Washington Public Power Supply System (WPPSS)** issued the 10-year bond in Exhibit 8-2, page 374, when the market interest rate was $6\frac{1}{2}$%. Assume that the accounting year of WPPSS ends on December 31. Journalize the following transactions for WPPSS, including an explanation for each entry:

Journalizing basic bond payable transactions; bonds issued at par
(Obj. 2)

a. Issuance of the bond payable on July 1, 2000.
b. Accrual of interest expense on December 31, 2000. (rounded to the nearest dollar)
c. Payment of cash interest on January 1, 2001.
d. Payment of the bonds payable at maturity. (Give the date.)

CP8-9 Guaranty Mortgage Company issued \$500,000 of 7%, 10-year bonds payable at a price of 87 on January 31, 20X4. The market interest rate at the date of issuance was 9%, and the Guaranty Mortgage bonds pay interest semiannually.

Issuing bonds payable and amortizing the bonds effective-interest method
(Obj. 3)

1. Prepare an effective-interest amortization table for the bonds through the first three interest payments. Use Exhibit 8-5, page 380, as a guide and round amounts to the nearest dollar.
2. Record Guaranty Mortgage's issuance of the bonds on January 31, 20X4, and, on July 31, 20X4, payment of the first semiannual interest amount and amortization of the bonds. Explanations are not required.

CP8-10 Use the amortization table that you prepared for Guaranty Mortgage Company in Check Point 8-9 to answer these questions about the company's long-term debt:

Analyzing data on long-term debt
(Obj. 3)

1. How much cash did Guaranty Mortgage borrow on January 31, 20X4? How much cash will Guaranty pay back at maturity on March 31, 20X14?
2. How much cash interest will Guaranty Mortgage pay each 6 months?
3. How much interest expense will Guaranty Mortgage report on July 31, 20X4 and on January 31, 20X5? Why does the amount of interest expense increase each period? Explain in detail.

CP8-11 **WPPSS** borrowed money by issuing the bond payable in Exhibit 8-2, page 374. Assume the issue price was $95\frac{3}{4}$ on July 1, 2000.

Determining bonds payable amounts; amortizing the bonds by the straight-line method
(Obj. 3)

1. How much cash did WPPSS receive when it issued the bond payable?
2. How much must WPPSS pay back at maturity? When is the maturity date?
3. How much cash interest will WPPSS pay each 6 months? Carry the interest amount to the nearest cent.
4. How much interest expense will WPPSS report each 6 months? Assume the straight-line amortization method and carry the interest amount to the nearest cent.

CP8-12 Return to the **WPPSS** bond in Exhibit 8-2, page 374. Assume that WPPSS issued the bond payable on July 1, 2000, at a price of 96. Also assume that WPPSS's accounting year ends on December 31. Journalize the following transactions for WPPSS, including an explanation for each entry:

Issuing bonds payable, accruing interest, and amortizing the bonds by the straight-line method
(Obj. 3)

a. Issuance of the bonds on July 1, 2000.
b. Accrual of interest expense and amortization of bonds on December 31, 2000. (Use the straight-line amortization method, and round amounts to the nearest dollar.)
c. Payment of the first semiannual interest amount on January 1, 2001.

Earnings-per-share effects of financing with bonds versus stock
(Obj. 4)

CP8-13 Manatech Health Foods needs $1 million to expand the company. Manatech is considering the issuance of either

- $1,000,000 of 8% bonds payable to borrow the money
- 100,000 shares of common stock at $10 per share

Before any new financing, Manatech expects to earn net income of $400,000, and the company already has 200,000 shares of common stock outstanding. Manatech believes the expansion will increase income before interest and income tax by $200,000. Manatech's income tax rate is 40%.

Prepare an analysis similar to Exhibit 8-11, page 388, to determine which plan is likely to result in the higher earnings per share. Based solely on the earnings-per-share comparison, which financing plan would you recommend for Manatech? Why does the plan with the lower net income result in higher earnings per share?

Computing the times-interest-earned ratio
(Obj. 4)

CP8-14 **Sprint Corporation** reported the following data in 2000 (adapted, in billions):

Net operating revenues	$23.6
Operating expenses	23.1
Operating income	0.5
Nonoperating items:	
Interest expense	(1.0)
Other	.6
Net income	$ 0.1

Compute Sprint's times-interest-earned ratio, and write a sentence to explain what the ratio value means. Would you be willing to lend Sprint $1 billion? State your reason.

Reporting liabilities, including capital lease obligations
(Obj. 5)

CP8-15 Drexel Furniture Company has the following selected accounts at December 31, 20X5:

Current obligation under capital lease	$ 8,000	Bonds payable	$350,000
Accounts payable	27,000	Equipment under capital lease	114,000
Long-term capital lease liability	56,000	Interest payable (due March 1, 20X6)	7,000
Discount on bonds payable (all long-term)	6,000	Current portion of bonds payable	50,000
Accounts receivable	31,000	Notes payable, long-term	60,000

Prepare the liabilities section of Drexel Furniture Company's balance sheet at December 31, 20X5, to show how Drexel would report these items. Report total current liabilities.

Exercises

Accounting for warranty expense and the related liability
(Obj. 1)

E8-1 Assume the accounting records of **Jerry Stevens Car Care Center** included the following balances at the end of the period:

ESTIMATED WARRANTY PAYABLE		SALES REVENUE		WARRANTY EXPENSE	
	Beg. bal 8,100		170,000		

In the past, Stevens' warranty expense has been 6% of sales. During the current period, the business paid $9,400 to satisfy the warranty claims of customers.

Required

1. Record Stevens' warranty expense for the period and the company's cash payments to satisfy warranty claims. Explanations are not required.
2. Show what Stevens will report on its income statement and balance sheet for this situation.
3. Which data item from requirement 2 will affect Stevens' current ratio? Will Stevens' current ratio increase or decrease as a result of this item?

E8-2 Assume **The Houston Post** publishing company completed the following transactions during 20X6:

Recording and reporting current liabilities **(Obj. 1)**

Nov. 1	Sold a 1-year subscription, collecting cash of $300, plus sales tax of 8%.
Dec. 15	Remitted (paid) the sales tax to the state of Texas.
31	Made the necessary adjustment at year end.

Journalize these transactions (explanations not required). Then report any liability on the company's balance sheet.

E8-3 A **Wells Fargo Bank** has an annual payroll of $800,000. In addition, the bank incurs payroll tax expense of 9%. At December 31, the end of the bank's accounting year, Wells Fargo owes salaries of $7,000 and FICA and other payroll tax of $2,000. The bank will pay these amounts early next year.

Reporting payroll expense and liabilities **(Obj. 1)**

Show what the Wells Fargo Bank will report for the foregoing on its income statement and year-end balance sheet.

E8-4 Assume that **Allen Samuels Mercedes-Benz** completed the following note-payable transactions.

Recording note payable transactions **(Obj. 1)**

general ledger

20X4	
May 1	Purchased wheel-balancing equipment costing $60,000 by issuing a 1-year, 8% note payable.
Dec. 31	Accrued interest on the note payable.
20X5	
May 1	Paid the note payable at maturity.

Answer these questions for Allen Samuels:

1. How much interest expense must be accrued at December 31, 20X4?
2. Determine the amount of Samuels' final payment on May 1, 20X5.
3. How much interest expense will Samuels report for 20X4 and for 20X5?

E8-5 Assume the following for **Campbell Soup Company**. At December 31, 20X1, Campbell Soup Company reported a current liability for income tax payable of $195 million. During 20X2, Campbell Soup earned income of $987 million before income tax. The company's income tax rate during 20X2 was 34%. Also during 20X2, Campbell Soup paid income taxes of $341 million.

Accounting for income tax **(Obj. 1)**

How much income tax payable did Campbell Soup Company report on its balance sheet at December 31, 20X2? How much income tax expense did Campbell Soup report on its 20X2 income statement? Round amounts to the nearest $1 million.

E8-6 **Temple Industries** is a large holding company with major interests in paper, packaging, building products, and timber resources. Assume Temple's 20X4 revenues totaled $2,794 million, and at December 31, 20X4, the company had $653 million in current assets. The December 31, 20X4, balance sheet reported the liabilities and stockholders' equity, as adapted on the next page.

Analyzing liabilities **(Obj. 1, 5)**

Required

1. Describe each of Temple Industries' liabilities and state how the liability arose.
2. How much were Temple's total assets at December 31, 20X4? Was the company's debt ratio high, low, or in a middle range?

At year end (In millions)	20X4	20X3
Liabilities and Shareholders' Equity		
Current Liabilities		
Accounts payable	$ 138	$ 176
Accrued expenses	157	178
Employee compensation and benefits	37	25
Current portion of long-term debt	5	14
Total Current Liabilities	337	393
Long-Term Debt	1,489	1,316
Deferred Income Taxes	259	229
Postretirement Benefits Payable	132	126
Other Liabilities	21	17
Shareholders' Equity	2,021	1,783
Total Liabilities and Shareholders' Equity	$4,259	$3,864

Reporting a contingent liability
(Obj. 1)

E8-7 **American Home Products Corporation (AHP)** is a global leader in pharmaceuticals and consumer health-care products such as Advil and Dimetapp. Revenues for 2000 totaled $13.2 billion. As with most pharmaceutical companies, AHP is a defendant in lawsuits related to its products. Note 10 of AHP's Annual Report for 2000 reported:

> **10. Contingencies and Litigation Charges**
>
> *The Company has been named as a defendant in numerous legal actions relating to the diet drugs* Redux *or* Pondimin, *which the Company estimated were used in the United States, [. . .], by approximately 5.8 million people. These actions allege, among other things, that the use of* Redux *and/or* Pondimin, *independently or in combination with the prescription drug phentermine (which the Company did not manufacture, distribute or market), caused certain serious conditions, including valvular heart disease.*

Required

1. Suppose AHP's lawyers believe that a significant legal judgment against the company is reasonably possible. Should AHP disclose this situation in its financial statements? If so, how?
2. Suppose AHP's lawyers believe it is probable that a $400 million judgment will be rendered against the company. Report this situation in AHP's financial statements. Journalize any entry required by GAAP. Explanations are not required.

Reporting current liabilities
(Obj. 1, 5)

E8-8 Assume the top management of **CVS Corporation**, the drugstore chain, examines company accounting records at December 24, immediately before the end of the year (amounts in billions):

Total current assets.	$4.9
Noncurrent assets	3.0
	$7.9
Total current liabilities	$3.0
Noncurrent liabilities	0.6
Owners' equity.	4.3
	$7.9

Suppose CVS's borrowing agreements with banks require CVS to keep a current ratio of 1.8 or better. How much in current liabilities should CVS pay off within the next week to comply with its borrowing agreements?

Reporting current and long-term liabilities
(Obj. 1, 5)

E8-9 Assume that **Callaway Golf Corporation** completed these selected transactions during December 20X4:

a. **Sport Spectrum**, a chain of sporting goods stores, ordered $100,000 of golf equipment. With its order, Sport Spectrum sent a check for $100,000, and Callaway shipped $70,000 of the goods. Callaway will ship the remainder of the goods on January 3, 20X5.

b. The December payroll of $120,000 is subject to employee withheld income tax of 9% and FICA tax of 8%. On December 31, Callaway pays employees their take-home pay and accrues all tax amounts.

c. Sales of $2,000,000 are subject to estimated warranty cost of 3%. The estimated warranty payable at the beginning of the year was $18,000, and warranty payments for the year totaled $55,000.

d. On December 1, Callaway signed a $100,000 note payable that requires annual payments of $20,000 plus 9% interest on the unpaid balance each December 1.

Required

Classify each liability as current or long-term and report the amount that would appear for these items on the Callaway Golf Corporation balance sheet at December 31, 20X4. Show a total for current liabilities.

Issuing bonds payable, paying and accruing interest, and amortizing the bonds by the straight-line method
(Obj. 2)

E8-10 On January 31, Leeds Luggage issues 10-year, 8% bonds payable with a face value of $1,000,000. The bonds were issued at 98 and pay interest on January 31 and July 31. Leeds amortizes bonds by the straight-line method. Record (a) issuance of the bonds on January 31, (b) the semiannual interest payment on July 31, and (c) the interest accrual on December 31.

Measuring cash amounts for a bond; amortizing the bonds by the straight-line method
(Obj. 2, 3)

E8-11 Campbell Soup Company has $200 million of 8.88% debenture bonds outstanding. The bonds mature in 2021. Assume the bonds were issued at 102 in 2001.

Required

1. How much cash did Campbell Soup receive when it issued these bonds?
2. How much cash in *total* will Campbell Soup pay the bondholders through the maturity date of the bonds?
3. Take the difference between your answers to Requirements 1 and 2. This difference represents Campbell Soup's total interest expense over the life of the bonds.
4. Compute Campbell Soup's annual interest expense by the straight-line amortization method. Multiply this amount by 20. Your 20-year total should be the same as your answer to Requirement 3.

Issuing bonds payable; recording interest payments and the related bond amortization
(Obj. 2, 3)

E8-12 Norrell Smartpages.com is authorized to issue $500,000 of 7%, 10-year bonds payable. On December 31, 20X4, when the market interest rate is 8%, the company issues $400,000 of the bonds and receives cash of $372,660. Norrell amortizes bonds by the effective-interest method. The semiannual interest dates are June 30 and December 31.

Required

1. Prepare a bond amortization table for the first four semiannual interest periods.
2. Record the semiannual interest payment on December 31, 20X5, and the payment on December 31, 20X6.

spreadsheet

Issuing bonds payable; recording interest accrual and payment and the related bond amortization
(Obj. 2, 3)

E8-13 On July 31, 2003, the market interest rate is 7%. Altex Cable, Inc. issues $300,000 of 8%, 20-year bonds payable at $110^{5}/_{8}$. The bonds pay interest on January 31 and July 31. Altex amortizes bonds by the effective-interest method.

Required

1. Prepare a bond amortization table for the first four semiannual interest periods.
2. Record issuance of the bonds on July 31, 2003, the accrual of interest at December 31, 2003, and the semiannual interest payment on January 31, 2004.

spreadsheet

Debt payment and bond amortization schedule
(Obj. 3)

E8-14 Richland Mall, Inc. issued $600,000 of $8^{3}/_{8}$% (.08375), 5-year bonds payable on January 1, 20X5, when the market interest rate was $9^{1}/_{2}$% (.095). The mall pays interest annually at year end. The issue price of the bonds was $574,082.

Required

Create a spreadsheet model to prepare a schedule to amortize the bonds. Use the effective-interest method of amortization. Round to the nearest dollar and format your answer as shown here.

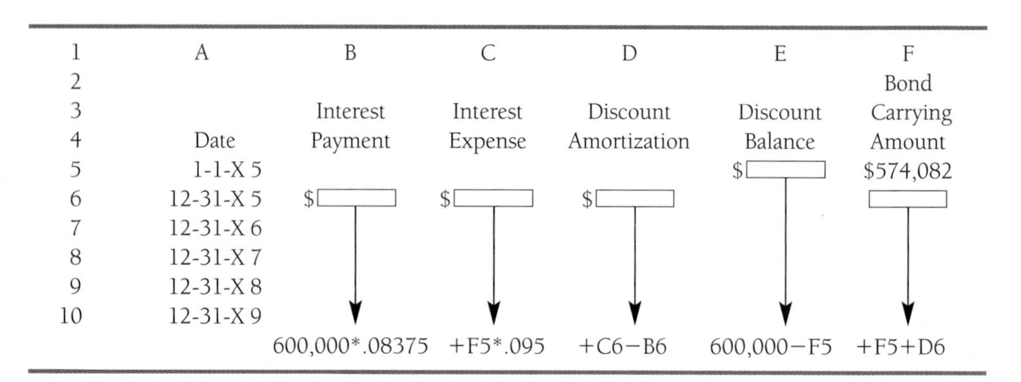

1	A	B	C	D	E	F
2						Bond
3		Interest	Interest	Discount	Discount	Carrying
4	Date	Payment	Expense	Amortization	Balance	Amount
5	1-1-X 5				$	$574,082
6	12-31-X 5	$	$	$		
7	12-31-X 6					
8	12-31-X 7					
9	12-31-X 8					
10	12-31-X 9					
		600,000*.08375	+F5*.095	+C6−B6	600,000−F5	+F5+D6

Recording conversion of notes payable
(Obj. 2)

E8-15 Ping Techology Corp. issued $400,000 of $8^1/_2$% notes payable on December 31, 20X5, at a price of $98^1/_2$. The notes' term to maturity is 10 years. After 3 years, the notes may be converted into the company's common stock. Each $1,000 face amount of notes is convertible into 40 shares of $1 par stock. On December 31, 20X9, noteholders exercised their right to convert the notes into common stock.

Required

1. What would cause the noteholders to convert their notes into common stock?
2. Without making journal entries, compute the carrying amount of the notes payable at December 31, 20X9, immediately before the conversion. Ping Technology uses the straight-line method to amortize bonds.
3. All amortization has been recorded properly. Journalize the conversion transaction at December 31, 20X9.
4. Identify the two ratios affected most directly in the future by the conversion transaction. Will the conversion increase or decrease each ratio? After the conversion, will Ping look more or less risky?

Recording early retirement and conversion of bonds payable
(Obj. 2)

E8-16 National Flower Transporters, Inc. reported the following at September 30, immediately after the quarterly accounting adjustments:

Long-term liabilities:		
Convertible bonds payable, 9%, 8 years to maturity	$300,000	
Discount on bonds payable..........................	(6,000)	$294,000

Required

1. Record retirement of half the bonds on October 1 at the call price of 104.
2. Record conversion of the other half of the bonds into 10,000 shares of National's $1-par common stock on October 1. What would cause the bondholders to convert their bonds into stock?

Measuring the times-interest-earned ratio
(Obj. 4)

E8-17 Companies that operate in different industries may look very different on their financial ratios. These differences may grow even wider when we compare companies located in different countries.

Let's compare three leading companies on their current ratio, debt ratio, and times-interest-earned ratio. Compute these three ratios for **Safeway** (the U.S. grocery chain), **Sony** (the Japanese electronics manufacturer), and **Nokia** (the telecommunications company from Finland).

Income data (Amounts in millions or billions)	Safeway	Sony	Nokia
Total revenues	$34,301	¥7,315	€ 6,047
Total operating expenses	31,712	7,090	2,187
Interest expense	447	43	59
Net income	$ 1,254	¥ 17	€ 4,065

Asset and liability data (Amounts in millions or billions)	Safeway	Sony	Nokia
Total current assets	$ 3,312	¥3,477	€ 8,669
Long-term assets	14,151	4,351	5,886
Total current liabilities	3,883	2,647	4,425
Long-term liabilities	7,690	2,866	90
Stockholders' equity	5,890	2,315	10,040

Note: ¥ is the symbol for a Japanese yen; € for a euro. In April 2002, ¥1 = $0.075; €1 = $0.881.

Based on your computed ratio values, which company looks the most risky? Least risky?

Analyzing alternative plans for raising money
(Obj. 4)

E8-18 Common Grounds Coffee Shops is considering two plans for raising $500,000 to expand operations. Plan A is to borrow at 9%, and plan B is to issue 100,000 shares of common stock. Before any new financing, Common Grounds has net income of $600,000 and 100,000 shares of common stock outstanding. Assume you own most of Common Grounds' existing stock. Management believes the company can use the new funds to earn additional income of $420,000 before interest and taxes. The income tax rate is 40%.

Required

1. Analyze Common Grounds situation to determine which plan will result in higher earnings per share. Use Exhibit 8-11 (page 388) as a model.
2. Which plan results in the higher earnings per share? Which plan allows you to retain control of the company? Which plan creates more financial risk for the company? Which plan do you prefer? Why? Present your conclusion in a memo to Common Grounds' board of directors.

Challenge Exercises

Refinancing old bonds payable with new bonds
(Obj. 2, 3, 5)

E8-19 United Brands, famous for Chiquita bananas, completed one of the most famous debt refinancings in history. A debt refinancing occurs when a company issues new bonds payable to retire old bonds.

United had $125 million of $5^3/_8$% bonds payable outstanding, with 21 years to maturity. United retired these old bonds by issuing $75 million of new 9% bonds payable to the holders of the old bonds, and paying the bondholders $13 million in cash. United issued both groups of bonds at par. At the time of the debt refinancing, United Brands had total assets of $500 million and total liabilities of $360 million. Net income for the most recent year was $6.5 million on sales of $1 billion.

Required

1. Journalize the debt refinancing transaction.
2. Compute annual interest expense for both the old and the new bond issues.
3. Why did United Brands refinance the old $5^3/_8$% bonds payable with the new 9% bonds? Consider interest expense, net income, and the debt ratio.

Analyzing bond transactions
(Obj. 2, 3)

E8-20 This (updated) advertisement appeared in *The Wall Street Journal*. (*Note*: A *subordinated debenture* is one whose rights are subordinated to the rights of other bondholders.)

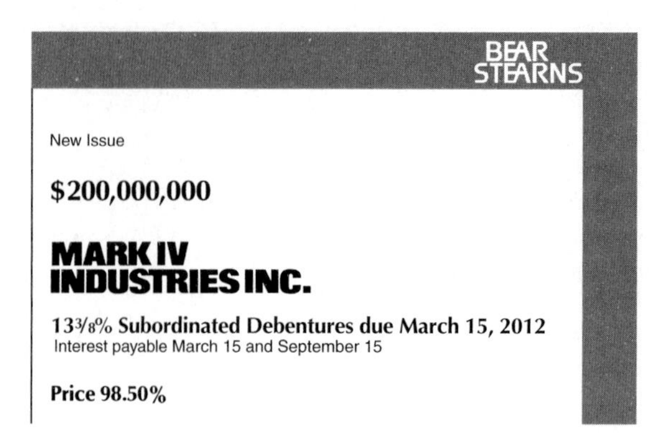
BEAR STEARNS

New Issue

$200,000,000

MARK IV INDUSTRIES INC.

13⅜% Subordinated Debentures due March 15, 2012
Interest payable March 15 and September 15

Price 98.50%

Required

Answer these questions.

1. Suppose investors purchased these securities at their offering price on March 15, 2002. Describe the transaction in detail, indicating who received cash, who paid cash, and how much.
2. Why is the contract interest rate on these bonds so high?
3. Compute the annual cash interest payment on the bonds.
4. Compute the annual interest expense under the straight-line amortization method.
5. Compute both the first-year (from March 15, 2002, to March 15, 2003) and the second-year interest expense (March 15, 2003, to March 15, 2004) under the effective-interest amortization method. The market rate of interest at the date of issuance was approximately 13.65%. Why is interest expense greater in the second year?

Problems

(Group A)

Measuring current liabilities
(Obj. 1)

P8-1A Following are five pertinent facts about events during the current year at Mathers & Mathers Air Conditioning:

a. On August 31, Mathers & Mathers signed a 6-month, 7% note payable to purchase a graphics computer costing $80,000. The note requires payment of principal and interest at maturity.
b. On October 31, Mathers & Mathers received cash of $2,400 in advance for service revenue. This revenue will be earned evenly over 6 months.
c. December revenue totaled $104,000, and in addition, Mathers & Mathers collected sales tax of 6%. This amount will be sent to the state of Illinois early in January.
d. Mathers & Mathers owes $100,000 on a long-term note payable. At December 31, 6% interest for the year plus $20,000 of this principal are payable within 1 year.
e. Revenue of $909,000 were covered by Mathers & Mathers' service warranty. At January 1, estimated warranty payable was $11,300. During the year, Mathers & Mathers recorded warranty expense of $31,100 and paid warranty claims of $28,100.

Required

For each item, indicate the account and the related amount to be reported as a current liability on the Mathers & Mathers December 31 balance sheet.

Recording liability-related transactions
(Obj. 1)

P8-2A Assume the following transactions of Suzuki Piano Company occurred during 20X5 and 20X6:

general ledger

20X5	
Feb. 3	Purchased a machine for \$47,000, signing a 6-month, 8% note payable.
Apr. 30	Borrowed \$100,000 on a 9% note payable that calls for annual installment payments of \$25,000 principal plus interest. Record the short-term note payable in a separate account from the long-term note payable.
Aug. 3	Paid the 6-month, 8% note at maturity.
Dec. 31	Accrued warranty expense, which is estimated at 2% of sales of \$145,000.
31	Accrued interest on the outstanding note payable.
20X6	
Apr. 30	Paid the first installment and interest for 1 year on the outstanding note payable.

Required

Record the transactions in Suzuki's journal. Explanations are not required.

Recording bond transactions (at par) and reporting bonds payable on the balance sheet
(Obj. 2)

P8-3A The board of directors of Synex Communications authorizes the issue of \$3 million of 7%, 10-year bonds payable. The semiannual interest dates are May 31 and November 30. The bonds are issued through an underwriter on May 31, 20X5, at par.

general ledger

Required

1. Journalize the following transactions:
   a. Issuance of the bonds on May 31, 20X5.
   b. Payment of interest on November 30, 20X5.
   c. Accrual of interest on December 31, 20X5.
   d. Payment of interest on May 31, 20X6.
2. Report interest payable and bonds payable as they would appear on the Synex balance sheet at December 31, 20X5.

Issuing bonds at a discount, amortizing by the straight-line method, and reporting bonds payable on the balance sheet
(Obj. 2, 5)

P8-4A On February 28, 20X4, Village Green Apartments issues $8\frac{1}{2}\%$, 20-year bonds payable with a face value of \$500,000. The bonds pay interest on February 28 and August 31. Village Green amortizes bonds by the straight-line method.

general ledger

Required

1. If the market interest rate is $8\frac{7}{8}\%$ when Village Green issues its bonds, will the bonds be priced at par, at a premium, or at a discount? Explain.
2. If the market interest rate is $7\frac{3}{8}\%$ when Village Green issues its bonds, will the bonds be priced at par, at a premium, or at a discount? Explain.
3. Assume that the issue price of the bonds is 97. Journalize the following bond transactions:
   a. Issuance of the bonds on February 28, 20X4.
   b. Payment of interest and amortization of the bonds on August 31, 20X4.
   c. Accrual of interest and amortization of the bonds on December 31, 20X4.
   d. Payment of interest and amortization of the bonds on February 28, 20X5.
4. Report interest payable and bonds payable as they would appear on the Village Green balance sheet at December 31, 20X4.

Accounting for bonds payable at a discount and amortizing by the straight-line method
(Obj. 2)

P8-5A

1. Journalize the following transactions of Oak Cliff Country Club:

2007	
Jan. 1	Issued $1,000,000 of 8%, 10-year bonds payable at 97.
July 1	Paid semiannual interest and amortized bonds by the straight-line method on the 8% bonds payable.
Dec. 31	Accrued semiannual interest expense and amortized bonds by the straight-line method on the 8% bonds payable.
2017	
Jan. 1	Paid the 8% bonds at maturity.

2. At December 31, 2007, after all year-end adjustments, determine the carrying amount of Oak Cliff Country Club bonds payable, net.
3. For the 6 months ended July 1, 2007, determine for Oak Cliff Country Club:
   a. Interest expense   b. Cash interest paid

   What causes interest expense on the bonds to exceed cash interest paid?

Analyzing a company's long-term debt and reporting long-term debt on the balance sheet (effective-interest method)
(Obj. 2, 3, 5)

spreadsheet

P8-6A The notes to Oasis Landscaping financial statements reported the following data on September 30, year 1 (the end of the fiscal year):

Note 4. Indebtedness

Long-term debt at September 30, year 1, included the following:	
5.00% bonds payable due year 21 with an effective interest rate of 9.66%, net of discount of $81,223,000	$118,777,000
Other indebtedness with an interest rate of 8.30%, due $9,300,000 in year 5 and $19,257,000 in year 6	28,557,000

Oasis amortizes bonds by the effective-interest method.

Required

1. Answer the following questions about Oasis's long-term liabilities:
   a. What is the maturity value of the 5.00% bonds?
   b. What are Oasis's annual cash interest payments on the 5.00% bonds?
   c. What is the carrying amount of the 5.00% bonds at September 30, year 1?
2. Prepare an amortization table through September 30, year 4, for the 5.00% bonds. Round all amounts to the nearest thousand dollars and assume that Oasis pays interest annually on September 30. How much is Oasis's interest expense on the 5.00% bonds for the year ended September 30, year 4? Round interest to the nearest thousand dollars.
3. Show how Oasis Landscaping would report the bonds payable and other indebtedness at September 30, year 4.

Issuing convertible bonds at a discount, amortizing by the effective-interest method, retiring bonds early, converting bonds, and reporting the bonds payable on the balance sheet
(Obj. 2, 3, 5)

general ledger

P8-7A On December 31, 20X4, Mobil Technology issues 8%, 10-year convertible bonds with a maturity value of $500,000. The semiannual interest dates are June 30 and December 31. The market interest rate is 9%, and the issue price of the bonds is 94. Mobil Technology amortizes bonds by the effective-interest method.

Required

1. Prepare an effective-interest-method amortization table for the first four semiannual interest periods.
2. Journalize the following transactions:
   a. Issuance of the bonds on December 31, 20X4. Credit Convertible Bonds Payable.
   b. Payment of interest and amortization of the bonds on June 30, 20X5.
   c. Payment of interest and amortization of the bonds on December 31, 20X5.
   d. Retirement of bonds with face value of $200,000 July 1, 20X6. Mobil purchases the bonds at 102 in the open market.
   e. Conversion by the bondholders on July 1, 20X6, of bonds with face value of $200,000 into 50,000 shares of Mobil's $1-par common stock.

3. Show how Mobil Technology would report the remaining bonds payable on its balance sheet at December 31, 20X6.

Financing operations with debt or with stock
(Obj. 4)

P8-8A Marketing studies have shown that consumers prefer upscale restaurants, and recent trends in industry sales have supported the research. To capitalize on this trend, assume that **Pappadeaux's Restaurant, Inc.** is embarking on a massive expansion. Assume plans call for opening 20 new restaurants during the next 2 years. Each restaurant is scheduled to be 50% larger than the company's existing locations, furnished more elaborately, and with upgraded menus. Management estimates that company operations will provide $3 million of the cash needed for expansion. Pappadeaux's must raise the remaining $9.5 million from outsiders. The board of directors is considering obtaining the $9.5 million either through borrowing or by issuing common stock.

Required

1. Write a memo to Pappadeaux's management discussing the advantages and disadvantages of borrowing and of issuing common stock to raise the needed cash. Which method of raising the funds would you recommend?
2. How will what you learned in this problem help you manage a business?

Reporting liabilities on the balance sheet, times-interest-earned ratio
(Obj. 5)

P8-9A Assume the accounting records of Mirage Casino Corp. include the following items at December 31, 20X5:

Capital lease liability, long-term	$ 81,000	Accumulated depreciation, equipment	$ 46,000
Discount on bonds payable (all long-term)	7,000	Capital lease liability, current	18,000
Operating income	315,000	Mortgage note payable, current	39,000
Equipment acquired under capital lease	137,000	Accumulated pension benefit obligation	419,000
Pension plan assets (market value)	382,000	Bonds payable, long-term	675,000
Interest payable	9,000	Mortgage note payable, long-term	82,000
Interest expense	57,000	Bonds payable, current portion	75,000

Required

1. Show how these items would be reported on the Mirage Casino Corp. classified balance sheet, including headings and totals for current liabilities, long-term liabilities, and so on.
2. Answer the following questions about Mirage's financial position at December 31, 20X5:
   a. What is the carrying amount of the bonds payable?
   b. During what year will Mirage make the last payment on the bonds?
   c. Why is the interest-payable amount so much less than the amount of interest expense?
3. How many times did Mirage cover its interest expense during 20X5? Do you consider this ratio value safe or risky. Why?

(Group B)

Measuring current liabilities
(Obj. 1)

P8-1B Following are five pertinent facts about events during the current year at *7th* Avenue Appliances, Inc.:

a. December sales totaled $38,000, and *7th* Avenue collected an additional state sales tax of 7%. This amount will be sent to the state of New York early in January.
b. On November 30, *7th* Avenue received rent of $5,400 in advance for a lease on unused store space. This rent will be earned evenly over 3 months.
c. On September 30, *7th* Avenue signed a 6-month, 9% note payable to purchase store fixtures costing $12,000. The note requires payment of principal and interest at maturity.

d. Sales of $430,000 were covered by 7th Avenue Appliances' product warranty. At January 1, estimated warranty payable was $12,400. During the year, 7th Avenue recorded warranty expense of $22,300 and paid warranty claims of $20,600.
e. 7th Avenue Appliances owes $100,000 on a long-term note payable. At December 31, 6% interest since July 31 and $20,000 of this principal are payable within 1 year.

Required

For each item, indicate the account and the related amount to be reported as a current liability on the 7th Avenue Appliances balance sheet at December 31.

Recording liability-related transactions
(Obj. 1)

P8-2B Assume the following transactions of **Park Cities Ford** occurred during 20X4 and 20X5.

general ledger

Required

Record the transactions in the company's journal. Explanations are not required.

20X4	
Jan. 9	Purchased a machine at a cost of $52,000, signing an 8%, 6-month note payable for that amount.
Feb. 28	Borrowed $200,000 on a 9% note payable that calls for annual installment payments of $50,000 principal plus interest. Record the short-term note payable in a separate account from the long-term note payable.
July 9	Paid the 6-month, 8% note at maturity.
Dec. 31	Accrued warranty expense, which is estimated at 3% of sales of $650,000.
31	Accrued interest on the outstanding note payable.
20X5	
Feb. 28	Paid the first installment and interest for one year on the outstanding note payable.

Recording bond transactions (at par) and reporting bonds payable on the balance sheet
(Obj. 2)

P8-3B Assume the board of directors of **Rose Bowl Pasadena, Inc.**, authorizes the issue of $2 million of 8%, 20-year bonds payable. The semiannual interest dates are March 31 and September 30. The bonds are issued through an underwriter on March 31, 20X3, at par.

general ledger

Required

1. Journalize the following transactions:
   a. Issuance of the bonds on March 31, 20X3.
   b. Payment of interest on September 30, 20X3.
   c. Accrual of interest on December 31, 20X3.
   d. Payment of interest on March 31, 20X4.
2. Report interest payable and bonds payable as they would appear on the Rose Bowl Pasadena, Inc. balance sheet at December 31, 20X3.

Issuing notes at a premium, amortizing by the straight-line method, and reporting notes payable on the balance sheet
(Obj. 2, 5)

P8-4B On February 28, 20X3, Malibu Race Track Amusement Park, Inc. issues $7^3/_4$%, 10-year notes payable with a face value of $300,000. The notes pay interest on February 28 and August 31, and Malibu amortizes bonds by the straight-line method.

general ledger

Required

1. If the market interest rate is $8^1/_2$% when Malibu issues its notes, will the notes be priced at par, at a premium, or at a discount? Explain.
2. If the market interest rate is 7% when Malibu issues its notes, will the notes be priced at par, at a premium, or at a discount? Explain.

3. Assume that the issue price of the notes is 102. Journalize the following note payable transactions:
   a. Issuance of the notes on February 28, 20X3.
   b. Payment of interest and amortization of the bonds on August 31, 20X3.
   c. Accrual of interest and amortization of the bonds on December 31, 20X3.
   d. Payment of interest and amortization of the bonds on February 28, 20X4.
4. Report interest payable and notes payable as they would appear on the Malibu balance sheet at December 31, 20X3.

P8-5B

Accounting for bonds payable at a discount and amortizing by the straight-line method
(Obj. 2)

1. Journalize the following transactions of Stoneleigh Hotels, Inc.:

2004	
Jan. 1	Issued $500,000 of 8%, 10-year bonds payable at 94.
July 1	Paid semiannual interest and amortized the bonds by the straight-line method on our 8% bonds payable.
Dec. 31	Accrued semiannual interest expense and amortized the bonds by the straight-line method on our 8% bonds payable.
2014	
Jan. 1	Paid the 8% bonds at maturity.

2. At December 31, 2004, after all year-end adjustments, determine the carrying amount of Stoneleigh Hotels' bonds payable, net.
3. For the 6 months ended July 1, 2004, determine for Stoneleigh Hotels, Inc.:
   a. Interest expense
   b. Cash interest paid

   What causes interest expense on the bonds to exceed cash interest paid?

P8-6B The notes to the www.Eyesite.com financial statements reported the following data on September 30, year 1 (the end of the fiscal year):

Analyzing a company's long-term debt and reporting the long-term debt on the balance sheet (effective-interest method)
(Obj. 2, 3, 5)

spreadsheet

Note E—Long-Term Debt	
5% bonds payable, due year 14, net of discount of $31,645,000 (effective interest rate of 7.50%)	$119,855,000
Notes payable, interest rate of 8.67%, principal due in annual amounts of $26,000,000 in years 5 through 10.	156,000,000

Eyesite amortizes bonds by the effective-interest method.

Required

1. Answer the following questions about Eyesite's long-term liabilities:
   a. What is the maturity value of the 5% bonds?
   b. What is Eyesite's annual cash interest payment on the 5% bonds?
   c. What is the carrying amount of the 5% bonds at September 30, year 1?
2. Prepare an amortization table through September 30, year 4, for the 5% bonds. Round all amounts to the nearest thousand dollars. Eyesite pays interest annually on September 30. How much is Eyesite's interest expense on the 5% bonds for the year ended September 30, year 4?
3. Show how Eyesite would report the 5% bonds payable and notes payable at September 30, year 4.

P8-7B On Decsember 31, 20X1, Minneapolis Gold & Silver Exchange issues 9%, 10-year convertible bonds with a maturity value of $300,000. The semiannual interest dates are June 30 and December 31. The market interest rate is 8%, and the issue price of the bonds is 106. Minneapolis amortizes bonds by the effective-interest method.

Issuing convertible bonds at a premium, amortizing by the effective-interest method, retiring bonds early, converting bonds, and reporting the bonds payable on the balance sheet
(Obj. 2, 3, 5)

general ledger

Required

1. Prepare an effective-interest-method amortization table for the first four semiannual interest periods.
2. Journalize the following transactions:
   a. Issuance of the bonds on December 31, 20X1. Credit Convertible Bonds Payable.
   b. Payment of interest and amortization of the bonds on June 30, 20X2.
   c. Payment of interest and amortization of the bonds on December 31, 20X2.
   d. Retirement of bonds with face value of $100,000 on July 1, 20X3. Minneapolis Gold & Silver Exchange pays the market price of 104.
   e. Conversion by the bondholders on July 1, 20X3, of bonds with face value of $100,000 into 10,000 shares of Minneapolis $1-par common stock.
3. Show how Minneapolis would report the remaining bonds payable on its balance sheet at December 31, 20X3.

Financing operations with debt or with stock
(Obj. 4)

P8-8B Two businesses in very different circumstances are pondering how to raise $10 million.

Callnotes Voice Message Service is in the midst of its most successful period since it began operations in 1992. For each of the past 10 years, net income and earnings per share have increased by 25%. The outlook for the future is equally bright with new markets opening up and competitors unable to compete with Callnotes. As a result Callnotes is planning a large-scale expansion.

Lincoln Property Management Company has fallen on hard times. Net income has remained flat for 5 of the last 6 years, even falling by 10% from last year's level of profits, and cash flow also took a nose dive. Top management has experienced some turnover and has stabilized only recently. To become competitive again, Lincoln needs $10 million to invest in new real estate.

Required

1. Propose a plan for each company to raise the needed cash. Which company should borrow? Which company should issue stock? Consider the advantages and the disadvantages of raising money by borrowing and by issuing stock and discuss them in your answer.
2. How will what you learned in this problem help you manage a business?

Reporting liabilities on the balance sheet; times-interest-earned ratio
(Obj. 5)

P8-9B The accounting records of L'Image Beauty Salons, Inc. include the following items at December 31, 20X6:

Interest expense	$ 47,000	Premium on bonds payable (all long-term)	$ 13,000
Pension plan assets (market value)	402,000	Interest payable	6,200
Bonds payable, current portion	60,000	Operating income	71,000
Accumulated depreciation, building	88,000	Capital lease liability, long-term	73,000
Mortgage note payable, long term	467,000	Accumulated pension benefit obligation	436,000
Bonds payable, long-term	180,000	Building acquired under capital lease	190,000

Required

1. Show how these items would be reported on L'Image's classified balance sheet, including headings and totals for current liabilities, long-term liabilities, and so on.
2. Answer the following questions about the financial position of L'Image Beauty Salons at December 31, 20X6:
   a. What is the carrying amount of the bonds payable?
   b. During what year will L'Image make its final payment on the bonds?
   c. Why is the interest payable amount so much less than the amount of interest expense?
3. How many times did L'Image cover its interest expense during 20X6? Do you consider this ratio value safe or risky? Why?

Apply Your Knowledge

Decision Cases

Analyzing alternative ways of raising $5 million
(Obj. 4)

Case 1. Business is going well for Park 'N Fly, the company that operates remote parking lots near major airports. The board of directors of this family-owned company believes that Park 'N Fly could earn an additional $1.5 million income before interest and taxes by expanding into new markets. However, the $5 million that the business needs for growth cannot be raised within the family. The directors, who strongly wish to retain family control of the company, must consider issuing securities to outsiders. They are considering three financing plans.

Plan A is to borrow at 6%. Plan B is to issue 100,000 shares of common stock. Plan C is to issue 100,000 shares of nonvoting, $3.75 preferred stock ($3.75 is the annual dividend paid on each share of preferred stock).* Park 'N Fly presently has net income of $2.5 million and 1 million shares of common stock outstanding. The company's income tax rate is 40%.

Required

1. Prepare an analysis to determine which plan will result in the highest earnings per share of common stock.
2. Recommend one plan to the board of directors. Give your reasons.

Exploring an actual bankruptcy
(Obj. 2)

Case 2. In 2002, Enron Corporation filed for Chapter 11 bankruptcy protection, shocking the business community: How could a company this large and this successful go bankrupt? This case explores the causes and the effects of Enron's bankruptcy.

At December 31, 2000, and for the 4 years ended on that date, Enron reported the following (amounts in millions):

Balance Sheet (summarized)				
Total assets				$65,503
Total liabilities				54,033
Total stockholders' equity				11,470
Income Statements (Excerpts)				
	2000	**1999**	**1998**	**1997**
Net income	$979*	$893	$703	$105

*Operating income = $1,953
Interest expense = $838

Unknown to investors and lenders, Enron also controlled hundreds of partnerships that owed vast amounts of money. These special-purpose entities (SPEs) did not appear on the Enron financial statements. Assume that the SPEs' assets totaled $7,000 million and their liabilities stood at $6,900 million; assume a 10% interest rate on the debt.

During the 4-year period of 1997 to 2000, Enron's stock price shot up from $17.50 to $90.56. Enron used its escalating stock price to finance the SPEs by guaranteeing lenders that Enron would give them Enron stock if the SPEs could not pay their loans.

In 2001, the SEC launched an investigation into Enron's accounting practices. It was alleged that Enron should have been including the SPEs in its financial statements all along. Enron then restated net income for 1997 to 2000, wiping out nearly $600 million of total net income (and total assets) for this 4-year period. Enron's stock price tumbled, and the guarantees to the SPEs' lenders added millions to Enron's liabilities (assume the full amount of the

*For a discussion of preferred stock, see Chapter 9.

SPEs' debt). To make matters worse, the assets of the SPEs lost much of their value; assume that their market value is only $500 million.

Required

1. Compute the debt ratio that Enron reported at the end of 2000. Recompute this ratio after including the SPEs in Enron's financial statements. Also compute Enron's times-interest-earned ratio both ways for 2000. Assume that the changes to Enron's financial position occurred during 2000.
2. Why does it appear that Enron failed to include the SPEs in its financial statements? How do you view Enron after including the SPEs in the financial statements?

Ethical Issue 1

The Boeing Company, manufacturer of jet aircraft, was the defendant in numerous lawsuits claiming unfair trade practices. Boeing has strong incentives not to disclose these contingent liabilities. However, GAAP requires that companies report their contingent liabilities.

Required

1. Why would a company prefer not to disclose its contingent liabilities?
2. Describe how a bank could be harmed if a company seeking a loan did not disclose its contingent liabilities.
3. What is the ethical tightrope that companies must walk when they report their contingent liabilities?

Ethical Issue 2

SolarTech, manufacturer of solar energy panels, borrowed heavily to exploit the advantage of financing operations with debt. At first, SolarTech was able to earn operating income much higher than its interest expense and was therefore quite profitable. However, cheaper energy sources emerged, and SolarTech's debt burden pushed the company to the brink of bankruptcy. Operating income was less than interest expense.

Required

Is it unethical for managers to saddle a company with a high level of debt? Or is it just risky? Who could be hurt by a company's taking on too much debt? Discuss.

Financial Statement Case

Analyzing current and contingent liabilities
(Obj. 1, 5)

Refer to Fossil, Inc.'s, financial statements in Appendix A at the end of this book.

1. What caused Fossil's Note payable to increase during the year ended January 5, 2002? (Fossil calls this fiscal year 2001).
2. What was the disposition of Fossil's January 5, 2002, balance of Accrued expenses for co-op advertising? How can you tell? Give a full explanation.
3. Provision for income taxes is another title for income tax expense. Why is Fossil's provision for income tax larger than income taxes payable at the end of each year?
4. How would experienced analysts rate Fossil's overall debt position—risky, safe, or average? Compute the ratio at January 5, 2002, that answers this question.
5. Does Fossil have any contingent liabilities (commitments)? If so, what are they?

Analytical Case

Analyzing current liabilities and long-term debt
(Obj. 1, 2, 3, 5)

Pier 1 Imports' financial statements in Appendix B at the end of this book report a number of liabilities.

1. How would experienced analysts rate Pier 1's overall debt position—risky, safe, or average? Compute the ratio that enables you to answer this question.

2. During 2002, Pier 1 completed two long-term debt transactions.

   Use two T-accounts to show all the company's activity in long-term debt and the current portion of long-term debt during 2002. Then explain the two transactions in your own words.

3. Use the data on the faces of Pier 1's 2002 income statement and balance sheet to estimate Pier 1's average interest rate during 2002 on all company borrowings. For this calculation, combine all long-term liabilities into a single amount, and use the beginning balance for 2002. Then compare your estimated interest rate to Pier 1's actual interest rates on borrowings that were outstanding during 2002. Are the estimated and the actual interest rates similar or different?

Group Projects

Project 1. Consider three different businesses:

1. A bank
2. A magazine publisher
3. A department store

For each business, list all of its liabilities—both current and long-term. Then compare the three lists to identify the liabilities that the three businesses have in common. Also identify the liabilities that are unique to each type of business.

Project 2. Alcenon Corporation leases the majority of the assets that it uses in operations. Alcenon prefers operating leases (versus capital leases) in order to keep the lease liability off its balance sheet and maintain a low debt ratio.

Alcenon is negotiating a 10-year lease on an asset with an expected useful life of 15 years. The lease requires Alcenon to make 10 annual lease payments of $20,000 each, with the first payment due at the beginning of the lease term. The leased asset has a market value of $135,180. The lease agreement specifies no transfer of title to the lessee and includes no bargain purchase option.

Write a report for Alcenon's management to explain what condition must be present for Alcenon to be able to account for this lease as an operating lease.

9

Stockholders' Equity

Learning Objectives

1. **Explain** the advantages and disadvantages of a corporation
2. **Measure** the effect of issuing stock on a company's financial position
3. **Describe** how treasury stock transactions affect a company
4. **Account** for dividends and measure their impact on a company
5. **Use** different stock values in decision making
6. **Evaluate** a company's return on assets and return on stockholders' equity
7. **Report** stockholders' equity transactions on the statement of cash flows

Need additional help? Go to the **Integrator CD** *and search these key words:* book value, cash flows, common stock, dividends, preferred stock, return on assets (ROA), return on equity (ROE), stock split, stockholders' equity, treasury stock

Integrator CD

IHOP Corp.

Consolidated Balance Sheets (Adapted)

		December 31,	
	(In thousands, except share amounts)	2000	1999
	Assets		
	Current assets		
	Total current assets	$ 51,102	$ 47,885
	Long-term receivables	287,346	265,983
	Property and equipment, net	193,624	177,743
	Other assets	30,140	28,791
	Total assets	$562,212	$520,402
	Liabilities and Shareholders' Equity		
	Current liabilities		
	Total current liabilities	$ 49,973	$ 46,187
	Long-term debt	36,363	41,218
	Other long-term liabilities	215,881	206,517
1	Shareholders' equity		
2	Preferred stock, $1 par value, 10,000,000 shares authorized; shares issued and outstanding: 2000 and 1999, none	—	—
3	Common stock, $.01 par value, 40,000,000 shares authorized: 2000; 20,299,091 shares issued and 20,011,341 shares outstanding; 1999; 20,117,314 shares issued and outstanding	203	201
4	Additional paid-in capital	69,655	66,485
5	Retained earnings	193,632	158,294
6	Treasury stock, at cost (2000; 287,750 shares; 1999; none)	(5,170)	—
7	Other	1,675	1,500
8	Total shareholders' equity	259,995	226,480
	Total liabilities and shareholders' equity	$562,212	$520,402

Forget the dot-com flashes and return to basics, Wall Street. There are plenty of businesses out there that can actually turn a profit. Corporate mergers and gigabytes may capture the headlines, but people still have to eat. Consider IHOP Corp., the world's greatest supplier of pancakes.

IHOP has grown the old-fashioned way—one pancake at a time. IHOP started in California and expanded into neighboring states. Along the way, management saw the need for more capital and faced a critical decision: Do we remain small and retain control, or do we go outside and raise the money to expand? For the men and women who birthed a company and made it go, this can be a gut-wrenching decision. IHOP managers took the plunge and went public.

In its initial public offering of stock, IHOP sought to issue 6.2 million common shares at $10 each. The shares got off to a good start and the stock has traded at $34.50 lately. And, yes, the company is still profitable, a real American success story.

Sitemap

What does it mean to "go public," as IHOP did? A corporation *goes public* when it sells its stock to the general public. A common reason for going public is to raise money for expansion. By offering its stock to the public, a company can raise more money than if the stockholders remain private. The IHOP Corporation balance sheet (lines 3 and 4) indicates that through the end of 2000, the company had received almost $70 million from its stockholders.

Chapters 4 to 8 discussed accounting for the assets and the liabilities of a company. By this time, you should be familiar with all the assets and liabilities listed on IHOP's balance sheet. Let's focus now on the last part of the balance sheet—IHOP's stockholders' equity, which the company labels as *shareholders' equity.* In this chapter, we discuss some of the decisions a company faces when issuing and buying back its stock and when declaring and paying dividends. In the process we cover the elements of stockholders' equity in detail. Let's begin by reviewing how a corporation is organized.

DECISION: What Is the Best Way to Organize a Business?

Objective

1 Explain the advantages and disadvantages of a corporation

Anyone starting a business must decide whether to organize the entity as a proprietorship, a partnership, or a corporation. Many businesses choose the corporation. Why is the corporate form of business so attractive? The ways in which corporations differ from proprietorships and partnerships provide some reasons.

Stockholder A person who owns stock in a corporation. Also called a *shareholder.*

SEPARATE LEGAL ENTITY. A corporation is a business entity formed under state law. A corporation is a distinct entity, an artificial person that exists apart from its owners, who are called **stockholders** or **shareholders.** The corporation has many of the rights that a person has. For example, a corporation may buy, own, and sell property. Assets and liabilities in the business belong to the corporation rather than to its owners. The corporation may enter into contracts, sue, and be sued.

Nearly all well-known companies, such as IHOP, CBS, Gap, and IBM, are corporations. Their full names may include *Corporation* or *Incorporated* (abbreviated *Corp.* and *Inc.*) to indicate that they are corporations, for example, CBS, Inc., and IHOP Corp.

CONTINUOUS LIFE AND TRANSFERABILITY OF OWNERSHIP. Corporations have *continuous lives* regardless of changes in the ownership of their stock. The stockholders of IHOP or any corporation may transfer stock as they wish. They may sell or trade the stock to another person, give it away, bequeath it in a will, or dispose of it in any other way. The transfer of the stock does not affect the continuity of the corporation. In contrast, proprietorships and partnerships terminate when ownership changes.

Limited liability No personal obligation of a stockholder for corporation debts. A stockholder can lose no more on an investment in a corporation's stock than the cost of the investment.

LIMITED LIABILITY. Stockholders have **limited liability** for the corporation's debts. They have no personal obligation for corporate liabilities. The most that a stockholder can lose on an investment in a corporation's stock is the cost of the investment. In contrast, proprietors and partners are personally liable for all the debts of their businesses. Limited liability is one of the most attractive features of the corporate form of organization. It enables corporations to raise more capital from a wider group of investors than proprietorships and partnerships can.

SEPARATION OF OWNERSHIP AND MANAGEMENT. Stockholders own the corporation, but a *board of directors*—elected by the stockholders—appoints officers to manage the business. Thus, stockholders may invest $1,000 or $1 million in the corporation without having to manage the business or disrupt their personal affairs.

Management's goal is to maximize the firm's value for the stockholders. But the separation between owners and managers may create problems. Corporate officers may run the business for their own benefit and not for the stockholders. For example, the chief financial officer (CFO) of Enron Corporation set up outside partnerships and paid himself millions to manage the partnerships—unknown to Enron stockholders.

CORPORATE TAXATION. Corporations are separate taxable entities. They pay a variety of taxes not borne by proprietorships or partnerships, including an annual franchise tax levied by the state. The franchise tax is paid to keep the corporate charter in force and enables the corporation to continue in business. Corporations also pay federal and state income taxes.

Corporate earnings are subject to **double taxation** of their income. First, corporations pay income taxes on their corporate income. Then stockholders pay personal income tax on the cash dividends that they receive from corporations. Proprietorships and partnerships pay no business income tax. Instead, the tax falls solely on the owners.

Double taxation
Corporations pay income taxes on corporate income. Then, the stockholders pay personal income tax on the cash dividends that they receive from corporations.

GOVERNMENT REGULATION. Because stockholders have only limited liability for corporation debts, outsiders doing business with the corporation can look no further than the corporation if it fails to pay. To protect the creditors and the stockholders of a corporation, both federal and state governments monitor corporations. This government regulation consists mainly of ensuring that corporations disclose the information that investors and creditors need to make informed decisions. Accounting provides much of this information.

Exhibit 9-1 summarizes the advantages and disadvantages of the corporate form of business organization.

Exhibit 9-1

Advantages and Disadvantages of a Corporation

Advantages	*Disadvantages*
1. Can raise more capital than a proprietorship or partnership can	1. Separation of ownership and management
2. Continuous life	2. Corporate taxation
3. Ease of transferring ownership	3. Government regulation
4. Limited liability of stockholders	

Organizing a Corporation

stockholders' equity

The process of creating a corporation begins when its organizers, called the *incorporators*, obtain a charter from the state. The charter includes the authorization for the corporation to issue a certain number of shares of stock. The incorporators pay fees, sign the charter, and file documents with the state. They agree to a set of **bylaws,** which act as the constitution for governing the corporation. The corporation then comes into existence.

Bylaws
Constitution for governing a corporation.

Ultimate control of the corporation rests with the stockholders. The stockholders elect a **board of directors,** which sets policy and appoints officers. The board

Board of directors
Group elected by the stockholders to set policy for a corporation and to appoint its officers.

Chairperson
Elected by a corporation's board of directors, usually the most powerful person in the corporation.

President
Chief operating officer in charge of managing the day-to-day operations of a corporation.

elects a **chairperson,** who usually is the most powerful person in the organization. The board also designates the **president,** who is the chief operating officer in charge of day-to-day operations. Most corporations also have vice presidents in charge of sales, manufacturing, accounting and finance (the chief financial officer, or CFO), and other key areas. Exhibit 9-2 shows the authority structure in a corporation.

Exhibit 9-2

Authority Structure in a Corporation

✔ Check Point 9-1

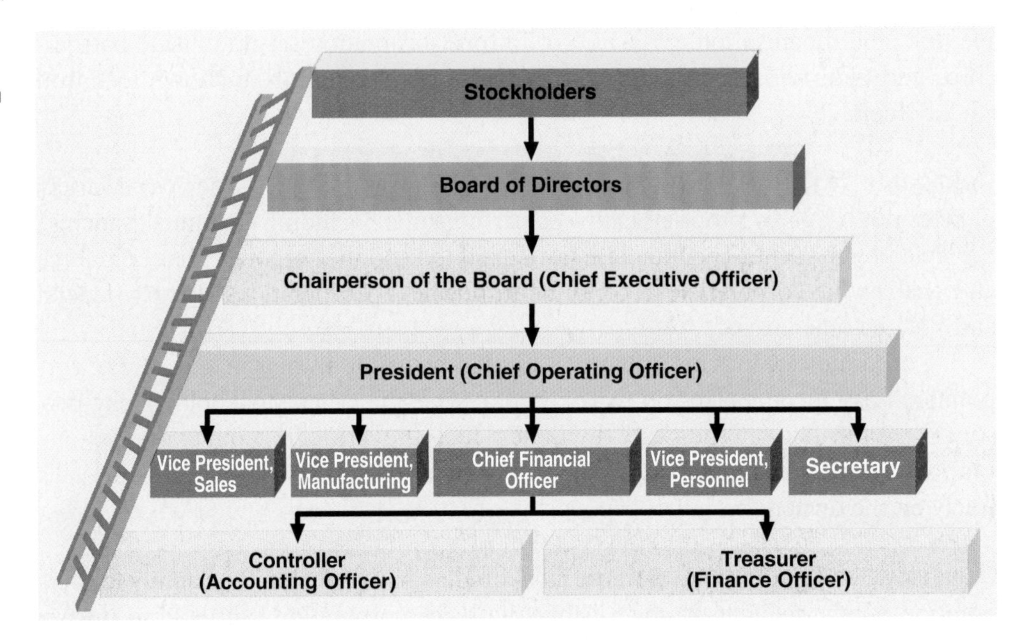

Stockholders' Rights

Ownership of stock entitles stockholders to four basic rights, unless specific rights are withheld by agreement with the stockholders:

1. *Vote.* The right to participate in management by voting on matters that come before the stockholders. This is the stockholder's sole voice in the management of the corporation. A stockholder is entitled to one vote for each share of stock owned.
2. *Dividends.* The right to receive a proportionate part of any distributed payment, or dividend. Each share of stock in a particular class receives an equal dividend.
3. *Liquidation.* The right to receive a proportionate share (based on number of shares held) of any assets remaining after the corporation pays its liabilities in liquidation. Liquidation means to go out of business, sell the entity's assets, pay its liabilities, and distribute any remaining cash to the owners.
4. *Preemption.* The right to maintain one's proportionate ownership in the corporation. Suppose you own 5% of a corporation's stock. If the corporation issues 100,000 new shares, it must offer you the opportunity to buy 5% (5,000) of the new shares. This right, called the *preemptive right,* is usually withheld from the stockholders.

Stockholders' Equity

Stockholders' equity
The stockholders' ownership interest in the assets of a corporation.

As we saw in Chapter 1, **stockholders' equity** represents the stockholders' ownership interest in the assets of a corporation. Stockholders' equity is divided into two main parts:

1. **Paid-in capital**, also called **contributed capital.** This is the amount of stockholders' equity the stockholders have contributed to the corporation. Paid-in capital includes the stock accounts and any additional paid-in capital.
2. **Retained earnings.** This is the amount of stockholders' equity the corporation has earned through profitable operations and has not used for dividends.

Paid-in capital
The amount of stockholders' equity that stockholders have contributed to the corporation. Also called *contributed capital.*

Retained earnings
The amount of stockholders' equity that the corporation has earned through profitable operation of the business and has not given back to stockholders.

Companies report stockholders' equity by source. They report paid-in capital separately from retained earnings because most states prohibit the declaration of cash dividends from paid-in capital. Thus, cash dividends are declared from retained earnings.

The owners' equity of a corporation is divided into shares of **stock.** A corporation issues *stock certificates* to its owners in exchange for their investment in the business. Because stock represents the corporation's capital, it is often called *capital stock.* The basic unit of capital stock is called a *share*. A corporation may issue a stock certificate for any number of shares it wishes—one share, 100 shares, or any other number—but the total number of *authorized* shares is limited by charter. Exhibit 9-3 shows an actual stock certificate for 288 shares of Central Jersey Bancorp common stock.

Stock
Shares into which the owners' equity of a corporation is divided.

Exhibit 9-3 **Stock Certificate**

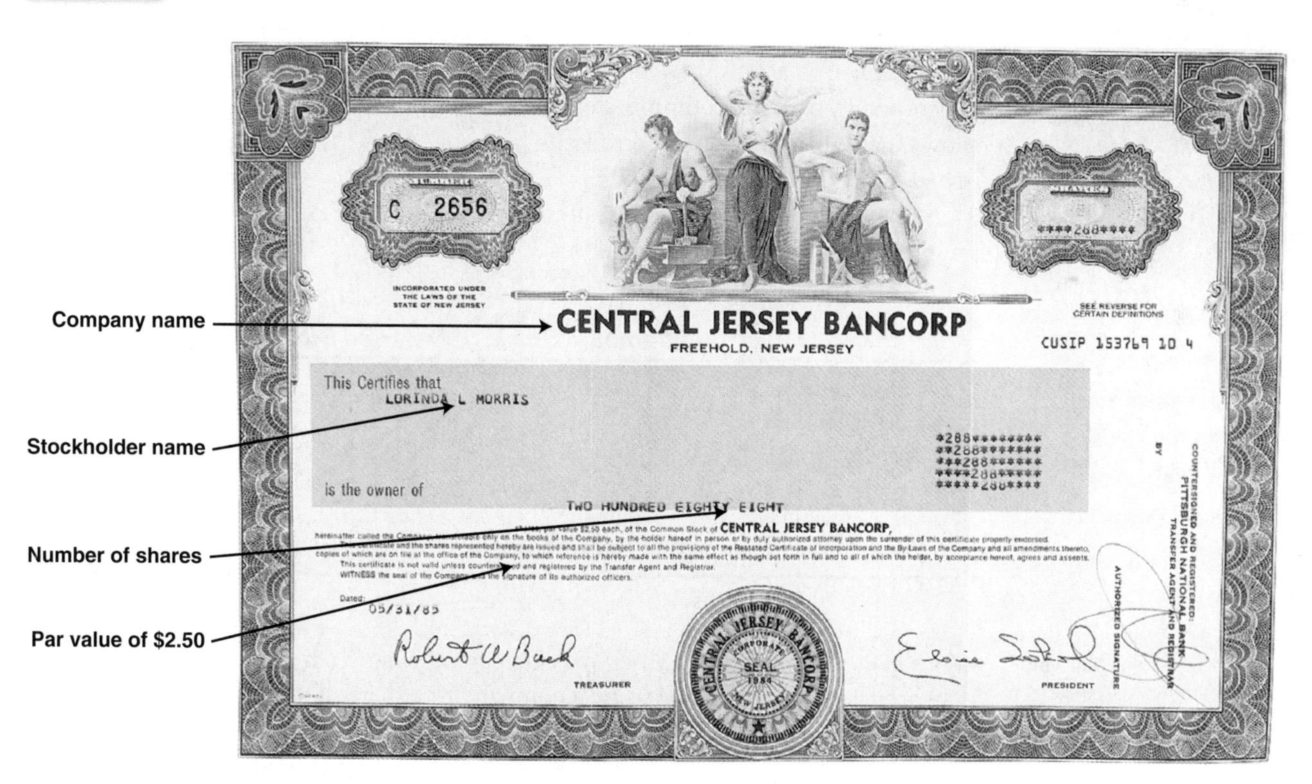

Stock in the hands of a stockholder is said to be **outstanding.** The total number of shares of stock outstanding at any time represents 100% ownership of the corporation.

Outstanding stock
Stock in the hands of stockholders.

Classes of Stock

Corporations issue different types of stock to appeal to a variety of investors. The stock of a corporation may be either

- Common or preferred
- Par or no-par

Common stock
The most basic form of capital stock. Common stockholders own a corporation.

Preferred stock
Stock that gives its owners certain advantages, such as the priority to receive dividends before the common stockholders and the priority to receive assets before the common stockholders if the corporation liquidates.

COMMON AND PREFERRED. Every corporation issues **common stock,** the basic form of capital stock. Unless designated otherwise, the word *stock* is understood to mean "common stock." Common stockholders have the four basic rights of stock ownership, unless a right is specifically withheld. For example, some companies issue Class A common stock, which usually carries the right to vote, and Class B common stock, which may be nonvoting. In describing a corporation, we would say the common stockholders are the owners of the business.

Preferred stock gives its owners certain advantages over common stockholders. Preferred stockholders receive dividends before the common stockholders and receive assets before the common stockholders if the corporation liquidates. Owners of preferred stock also have the four basic stockholder rights, unless a right is specifically denied. Companies may issue different classes of preferred stock (Class A and Class B or Series A and Series B, for example). Each class is recorded in a separate account.

✔ Check Point 9-2

Exhibit 9-4

Preferred Stock

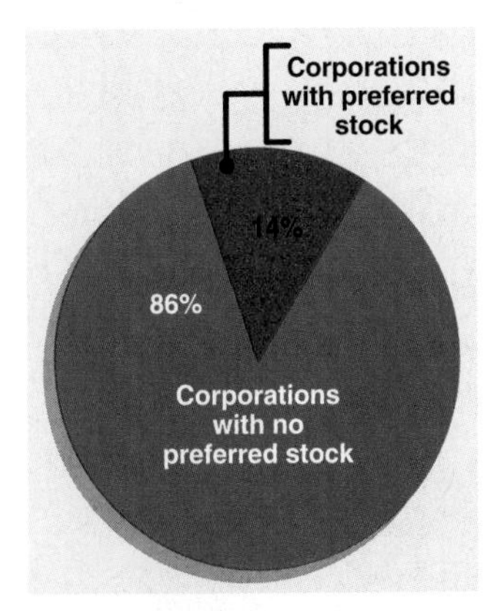

Preferred stock is a hybrid between common stock and long-term debt. Like debt, preferred stock pays a fixed dividend amount to the investor. But like stock, the dividend is not required to be paid unless the board of directors has declared the dividend. Also, companies have no obligation to pay back true preferred stock. Preferred stock that must be redeemed (paid back) by the corporation is a liability masquerading as a stock.

Preferred stock is rarer than you might think. A recent survey of 600 corporations revealed that only 14% of them had preferred stock outstanding (Exhibit 9-4). All corporations have common stock. The balance sheet of IHOP Corp (page 417) shows that IHOP is authorized to issue preferred stock. To date, however, IHOP has issued none of the preferred stock.

Exhibit 9-5 summarizes the similarities and differences among common stock, preferred stock, and long-term debt.

Exhibit 9-5

Comparison of Common Stock, Preferred Stock, and Long-Term Debt

	Common Stock	Preferred Stock	Long-Term Debt
Corporate obligation to repay principal	No	No	Yes
Dividends/interest	Dividends not tax-deductible	Dividends not tax-deductible	Tax-deductible interest expense
Corporate obligation to pay dividends/interest	Only after declaration	Only after declaration	At fixed dates

Par value
Arbitrary amount assigned by a company to a share of its stock.

Legal capital
Minimum amount of stockholders' equity that a corporation must maintain for the protection of creditors. For corporation's with par-value stock, legal capital is the par value of the stock issued.

Stated value
An arbitrary amount assigned to no-par stock; similar to par value.

PAR VALUE AND NO-PAR. Stock may be par value stock or no-par stock. **Par value** is an arbitrary amount assigned by a company to a share of its stock. Most companies set the par value of their common stock low to avoid legal difficulties from issuing their stock below par. Most states require companies to maintain a minimum amount of stockholders' equity for the protection of creditors, and this minimum is often called the corporation's legal capital. For corporations with par value stock, **legal capital** is the par value of the shares issued.

The par value of Coca-Cola Company common stock is $0.25 per share. Amazon.com common stock, like that of IHOP, carries a par value of $0.01 per share, and Pier 1 Imports common stock par value is $1 per share. Par value of preferred stock is sometimes higher.

No-par stock does not have par value. But some no-par stock has a **stated value,** which makes it similar to par-value stock. The stated value is an arbitrary amount similar to par value. In a recent survey, only 11% of the companies had no-par stock outstanding.

Issuing Stock

Integrator CD
common stock, preferred stock

Large corporations such as Coca-Cola, IHOP, and Microsoft need huge quantities of money to operate. Corporations may sell stock directly to the stockholders or use the service of an *underwriter,* such as the brokerage firms Merrill Lynch and Saloman Smith Barney. Companies often advertise the issuance of their stock to attract investors. The *Wall Street Journal* is the most popular medium for such advertisements, which are also called *tombstones.* Exhibit 9-6 is a reproduction of IHOP's tombstone, which appeared in the *Wall Street Journal.*

Objective

2 Measure the effect of issuing stock on a company's financial position

The lead underwriter of IHOP's public offering was the First Boston group of Credit Suisse First Boston. Several other domestic brokerage firms and investment bankers sold IHOP stock to their clients. In its initial public offering in 1991 (illustrated in Exhibit 9-6), IHOP sought to raise $62 million of capital.

Common Stock

COMMON STOCK AT PAR. Suppose IHOP's common stock carried a par value of $10 per share. The entry for issuance of 6.2 million shares of stock at par would be

Jan. 8	Cash (6,200,000 × $10)	62,000,000	
	Common Stock		62,000,000
	To issue common stock.		

IHOP's assets and stockholders' equity increase by the same amount.

ASSETS	=	LIABILITIES	+	STOCKHOLDERS' EQUITY
62,000,000	=	0	+	62,000,000

COMMON STOCK ABOVE PAR. Most corporations set par value at a low amount, then issue common stock for a price above par. IHOP's common stock has a par value of $0.01 (1 cent) per share. The $9.99 difference between issue price ($10) and par value ($0.01) is additional paid-in capital. Both the par value of the stock and the additional amount are part of paid-in capital.

✔ Check Point 9-3

Because the entity is dealing with its own stockholders, a sale of stock is not gain, income, or profit to the corporation. This situation illustrates one of the fundamentals of accounting: *A company neither earns a profit nor incurs a loss when it sells its stock to, or buys its stock from, its own stockholders.*

With a par value of $0.01, IHOP's entry to record the issuance of the stock is

July 23	Cash (6,200,000 × $10).	62,000,000	
	Common Stock (6,200,000 × $0.01) . . .		62,000
	Paid-in Capital in Excess of Par—Common (6,200,000 × $9.99)		61,938,000
	To issue common stock.		

ASSETS	=	LIABILITIES	+	STOCKHOLDERS' EQUITY
62,000,000	=	0		+62,000
				+61,938,000

Exhibit 9-6

Announcement of Public Offering of IHOP Stock (Adapted)

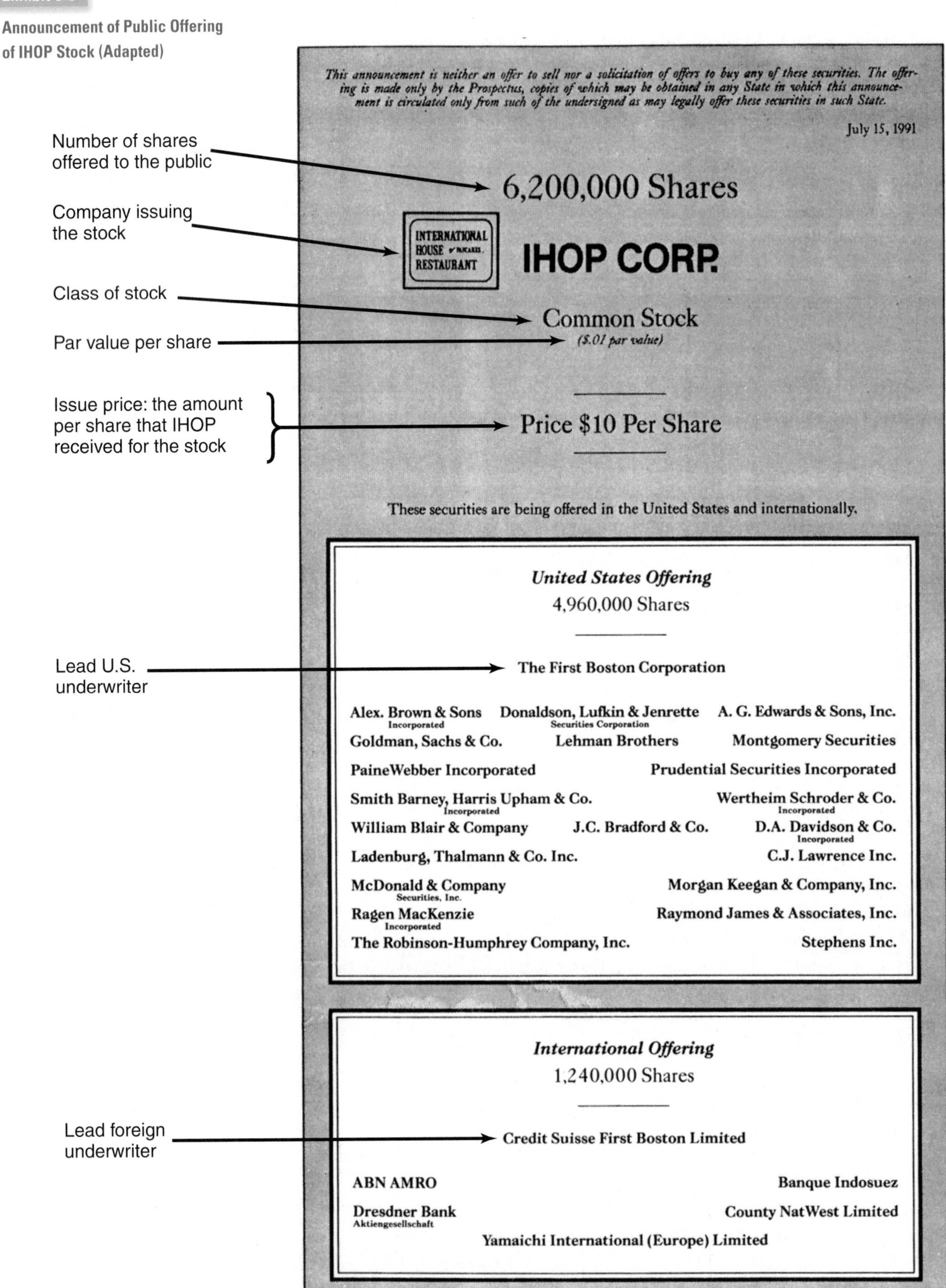

Another title for Paid-in Capital in Excess of Par—Common is Additional Paid-in Capital—Common, as used by IHOP Corporation. At the end of the year, IHOP would report stockholders' equity on its balance sheet as follows:

Stockholders' Equity

Common stock, $0.01 par, 40 million shares authorized, 6.2 million shares issued	$ 62,000
Paid-in capital in excess of par	61,938,000
Total paid-in capital	62,000,000
Retained earnings	194,000,000
Total stockholders' equity	$256,000,000

✔ **Check Point 9-4**

All the transactions recorded in this section include a receipt of cash by the corporation as it issues *new* stock. These transactions are different from those reported in the financial press. In those transactions, one stockholder sells stock to another investor, and the corporation makes no journal entry.

STOP & THINK

Examine IHOP's balance sheet at December 31, 2000, given at the beginning of the chapter (page 417). Answer these questions about IHOP's actual stock transactions (amounts in thousands, except per share):

1. What was IHOP's total paid-in capital at December 31, 2000? At December 31, 1999?
2. How many shares of common stock had IHOP issued through the end of 2000? Through the end of 1999?
3. What was the average issue price of the IHOP stock that the company issued during 2000?

Answers:

	December 31 2000	December 31 1999
1. Total paid-in capital	$203 + $69,655 = $69,858	$201 + $66,485 = $66,686
2. Number of shares issued	20,299	20,117

3. $$\text{Average issue price of stock issued in 2000} = \frac{\text{Total received from issuance of stock}}{\text{New shares issued}} = \frac{\$69{,}858 - \$66{,}686}{20{,}299 - 20{,}117}$$

$$= \$17.43 \text{ per share}$$

The IHOP stock has risen in value from its initial price of $10 per share.

NO-PAR COMMON STOCK. To record the issuance of no-par stock, the company debits the asset received and credits the stock account for the market value of the asset received. Glenwood Corporation, which manufactures skateboards, issues 3,000 shares of no-par common stock for $20 per share. The stock issuance entry is

Aug. 14	Cash (3,000 × $20)	60,000	
	Common Stock		60,000
	To issue no-par common stock.		

ASSETS	=	LIABILITIES	+	STOCKHOLDERS' EQUITY
60,000	=	0	+	60,000

Glenwood Corporation's charter authorizes Glenwood to issue 100,000 shares of no-par stock, and the company has $46,000 in retained earnings. The corporation reports stockholders' equity on the balance sheet as follows:

Stockholders' Equity

Common stock, no par, 10,000 shares authorized, 3,000 shares issued	$ 60,000
Retained earnings	46,000
Total stockholders' equity	$106,000

NO-PAR COMMON STOCK WITH A STATED VALUE. Accounting for no-par stock with a stated value is identical to accounting for par value stock. The excess over stated value is credited to Additional Paid-in Capital.

COMMON STOCK ISSUED FOR ASSETS OTHER THAN CASH. When a corporation issues stock in exchange for assets other than cash, it records the assets received at their current market value and credits the capital accounts accordingly. The assets' prior book value does not matter because the stockholder will demand stock equal to the market value of the asset given. Kahn Corporation issued 15,000 shares of its $1 par common stock for equipment worth $4,000 and a building worth $120,000. Kahn's entry is

✔ Check Point 9-5

Nov. 12	Equipment	4,000	
	Building	120,000	
	Common Stock (15,000 × $1)		15,000
	Paid-in Capital in Excess of Par—Common ($124,000 − $15,000)		109,000
	To issue common stock in exchange for equipment and a building.		

ASSETS	=	LIABILITIES	+	STOCKHOLDERS' EQUITY
+4,000 +120,000	=	0	+	+15,000 +109,000

Preferred Stock

Accounting for preferred stock follows the pattern we illustrated for common stock. The company records a Preferred Stock account at its par value, with any excess credited to Paid-in Capital in Excess of Par—Preferred. This is an entirely separate account from Paid-in Capital in Excess of Par—Common. The two accounts are not combined. Accounting for no-par preferred stock follows the pattern for no-par common stock. When reporting stockholders' equity on the balance sheet, a corporation lists preferred stock, common stock, and retained earnings—in that order, as illustrated for IHOP on page 417.

Ethical Considerations

Issuance of stock for *cash* poses no serious ethical challenge. The company simply receives cash and records the stock at the amount received, as illustrated in the preceding sections of this chapter. There is no difficulty in valuing stock issued for cash because the value of the cash—and the stock—is obvious.

Issuing stock for assets other than cash can pose an ethical challenge. The company issuing the stock often wishes to record a large amount for the noncash asset received (such as land or a building) and for the stock that it is issuing. Why? Because large asset and stockholders' equity amounts on the balance sheet make the business look more prosperous and more creditworthy.

A company is supposed to record an asset received at its current market value. But one person's perception of a particular asset's market value can differ from another person's opinion. One person may appraise land at a market value of $400,000. Another may honestly believe the land is worth only $300,000. A company receiving land in exchange for its stock must decide whether to record the land received and the stock issued at $300,000, at $400,000, or at some amount in between.

The ethical course of action is to record the asset at its current fair market value, as determined by a good-faith estimate of market value from independent appraisers. It is rare for a public corporation to be found guilty of *understating* the asset values on its balance sheet, but companies have been embarrassed by *overstating* these values. Investors who rely on the financial statements may be able to prove in a court of law that an overstatement of asset values caused them to pay too much for the company's stock. In this case, the court may render a judgment against the company. For this reason, companies often value assets conservatively.

Mid-Chapter Summary Problems

1. Test your understanding of the first half of this chapter by deciding whether each of the following statements is true or false.
   a. The policy-making body in a corporation is called the board of directors.
   b. The owner of 100 shares of preferred stock has greater voting rights than the owner of 100 shares of common stock.
   c. Par value stock is worth more than no-par stock.
   d. Issuance of 1,000 shares of $5 par value stock at $12 increases contributed capital by $12,000.
   e. The issuance of no-par stock with a stated value is fundamentally different from issuing par value stock.
   f. A corporation issues its preferred stock in exchange for land and a building with a combined market value of $200,000. This transaction increases the corporation's owners' equity by $200,000 regardless of the assets' prior book values.
   g. Preferred stock is a riskier investment than common stock.
2. The brewery Adolph Coors Company has two classes of common stock. Only the Class A common stockholders are entitled to vote. The company's balance sheet included the following presentation:

Stockholders' Equity

Capital stock	
Class A common stock, voting, $1 par value, authorized and issued 1,260,000 shares	$ 1,260,000
Class B common stock, nonvoting, no par value, authorized and issued 46,200,000 shares	11,000,000
	12,260,000
Additional paid-in capital	2,011,000
Retained earnings	872,403,000
	$886,674,000

✔ Check Point 9-6

✔ Check Point 9-7

Required

a. Record the issuance of the Class A common stock. Use the Coors account titles.
b. Record the issuance of the Class B common stock. Use the Coors account titles.
c. How much of Coors's stockholders' equity was contributed by the stockholders? How much was provided by profitable operations? Does this division of equity suggest that the company has been successful? Why or why not?
d. Write a sentence to describe what Coors' stockholders' equity means.

Answers

1. a. True b. False c. False d. True e. False f. True g. False

2. a.

	Debit	Credit
Cash	3,271,000	
Class A Common Stock		1,260,000
Additional Paid-in Capital		2,011,000
To record issuance of Class A common stock.		

b.

	Debit	Credit
Cash	11,000,000	
Class B Common Stock		11,000,000
To record issuance of Class B common stock.		

c. Contributed by the stockholders: $14,271,000 ($12,260,000 + $2,011,000).
Provided by profitable operations: $872,403,000.
This division suggests that the company has been very successful because most of its stockholders' equity has come from profitable operations.

d. A Coors stockholders' equity of $886,674,000 means that the company's stockholders own $886,674,000 of the business's assets.

treasury stock

Treasury Stock Transactions

Objective

3 **Describe** how treasury stock transactions affect a company

Treasury stock
A corporation's own stock that it has issued and later reacquired.

A company's own stock that it has issued and later reacquired is called **treasury stock.**[1] In effect, the corporation holds the stock in its treasury. Corporations may purchase their own stock for several reasons:

1. The company has issued all its authorized stock and needs the stock for distributions to employees under stock purchase plans.
2. The business is trying to increase net assets by buying its shares low and hoping to resell them for a higher price.
3. Management wants to avoid a takeover by an outside party.

DECISION: Should a Company Buy Back Its Own Stock?

Let's illustrate the accounting for treasury stock by using the actual data of IHOP Corp. in the chapter opener (page 417). If IHOP had not purchased any treasury stock, the company would have reported the following stockholders' equity (adapted) at December 31, 2000 (amounts in thousands):

(Before Purchase of Treasury Stock)

Common Stock	$ 203
Paid-in capital in excess of par—common	69,655
Retained earnings	193,632
Total equity	$263,490

[1]In this text, we illustrate the *cost* method of accounting for treasury stock because it is used most widely. Other methods are presented in intermediate accounting courses.

During 2000, IHOP paid $5,170,000 to purchase 288,000 shares of its common stock as treasury stock. IHOP recorded the treasury stock as follows (in thousands):

2000			
Nov. 12	Treasury Stock	5,170	
	Cash		5,170
	Purchased treasury stock.		

The Treasury Stock account has a debit balance, which is the opposite of the other owners' equity accounts. Therefore, *Treasury Stock is contra stockholders' equity*. Treasury stock is recorded at cost and is reported beneath Retained Earnings on the balance sheet. Treasury Stock's balance is subtracted from equity as follows (amounts in thousands):

(After Purchase of Treasury Stock)

Common stock	$ 203
Paid-in capital in excess of par—common	69,655
Retained earnings	193,632
Less: Treasury stock (288 shares at cost)	(5,170)
Total equity	$258,320

Compare IHOP's total equity before the purchase of treasury stock ($263,490) and after ($258,320). You will see that IHOP's total equity decreased by $5,170, the amount the company paid to buy back its own stock. The purchase of treasury stock has the opposite effect of issuing stock:

- Issuing stock *grows* a company's assets and equity.
- Purchasing treasury stock *shrinks* assets and equity.

If treasury stock shrinks a company, then why do managers spend hard-earned cash to buy it? Usually in the hope of reselling the treasury stock at a higher price. That's why it is called Treasury stock—because the company holds the stock in its treasury awaiting resale. Now let's see how to account for the sale of treasury stock.

Sale of Treasury Stock

Selling treasury stock grows a company exactly as issuing new stock does. Suppose IHOP resells its treasury stock in 2002 for $5,300,000. The sale of treasury stock increases assets and equity by the full amount of cash received from the sale. IHOP would record this sale of treasury stock as follows (in thousands):

2002			
July 22	Cash	5,300	
	Treasury Stock		5,170
	Paid-in Capital from Treasury Stock Transactions (or Additional Paid-in Capital—Common)		130
	Sold treasury stock.		

Retirement of Stock

A corporation may purchase its own stock and *retire* it by canceling the stock certificates. Retirements of preferred stock occur more often than retirements of common stock, as companies seek to avoid having to pay dividends on the preferred stock.

The retired stock cannot be reissued. When a company retires its stock, the journal entry debits the stock account and any additional paid-in capital on the stock and credits Cash.

Report IHOP's stockholders' equity after selling the treasury stock for $5,300.

Answer:

	Thousands
Common stock	$ 203
Paid-in capital in excess of par—common ($69,655 + $130)	69,785
Retained earnings	193,632
Total equity	$263,620

Now compare total equity after selling treasury stock to total equity before IHOP purchased the treasury stock. What was the net effect of buying and reselling treasury stock?

Answer:

✔ Check Point 9-8

✔ Check Point 9-9

	Thousands
Total equity after purchase and resale of treasury stock	$263,620
Total equity before purchase of treasury stock	263,490
Increase in stockholders' equity	$ 130

Retained Earnings, Dividends, and Splits

dividends, stock splits

We have seen that the equity section of the corporation balance sheet is called *stockholders' equity* or *shareholders' equity*. The paid-in capital accounts and retained earnings make up the stockholders' equity section.

The Retained Earnings account carries the balance of the business's net income less its net losses and less any declared dividends accumulated over the corporation's lifetime. *Retained* means "held onto." Successful companies grow by reinvesting back into the business the assets they generate through profitable operations. IHOP Corp. is an example; the majority of its equity comes from retained earnings.

Deficit Debit balance in the Retained Earnings account.

The Retained Earnings account is not a reservoir of cash waiting for the board of directors to pay dividends to the stockholders. In fact, the corporation may have a large balance in Retained Earnings but not have the cash to pay a dividend. Cash and Retained Earnings are two separate accounts with no particular relationship. A $500,000 balance in Retained Earnings simply means that $500,000 of owners' equity has been created by profits reinvested in the business. It says nothing about the company's Cash balance.

A *credit* balance in Retained Earnings is normal, indicating that the corporation's lifetime earnings exceed its lifetime losses and dividends. A *debit* balance in Retained Earnings arises when a corporation's lifetime losses and dividends exceed its lifetime earnings. Called a **deficit**, this amount is subtracted from the sum of the other equity accounts to determine total stockholders' equity. In a recent survey, 75 of 600 companies (12.5%) had a retained earnings deficit (Exhibit 9-7).

Exhibit 9-7

Retained Earnings of the *Accounting Trends & Techniques 600* Companies

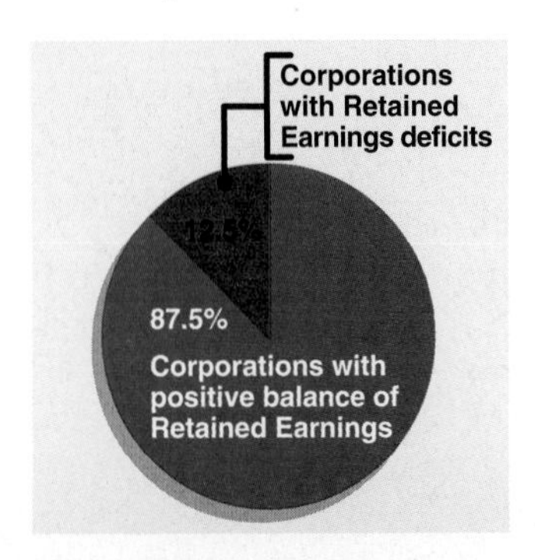

DECISION: Should the Company Declare and Pay Cash Dividends?

A **dividend** is a corporation's return to its stockholders of some of the benefits of earnings, commonly in the form of cash payments. Corporate finance courses address the question of how a company decides on its dividend policy. Accounting tells a company if it has the wherewithal to pay cash dividends. To do so, a company must have sufficient:

Dividend
Distribution (usually cash) by a corporation to its stockholders.

- Retained earnings to *declare* the dividend
- Cash to *pay* the dividend

A corporation declares a dividend before paying it. Only the board of directors has the authority to declare a dividend. The corporation has no obligation to pay a dividend until the board declares one, but once declared, the dividend becomes a legal liability of the corporation. Three relevant dates for dividends are as follows:

1. ***Declaration date, June 19.*** On the declaration date, the board of directors announces the intention to pay the dividend. The declaration creates a liability for the corporation. Declaration is recorded by debiting Retained Earnings and crediting Dividends Payable. Assume a $50,000 dividend.

June 19	Retained Earnings	50,000	
	Dividends Payable		50,000
	Declared a cash dividend.		

2. ***Date of record, July 1.*** As part of the declaration, the corporation announces the record date, which follows the declaration date by a few weeks. There is no entry to record. The stockholders as of the record date will receive the dividend.
3. ***Payment date; July 10.*** Payment of the dividend usually follows the record date by a week or two. Payment is recorded by debiting Dividends Payable and crediting Cash.

July 10	Dividends Payable	50,000	
	Cash		50,000
	Paid cash dividend.		

On Test

Dividends on Preferred Stock

Objective

4 **Account** for dividends and measure their impact on a company

When a company has issued both preferred and common stock, the preferred stockholders receive their dividends first. The common stockholders receive dividends only if the total declared dividend is large enough to pay the preferred stockholders first.

In addition to its common stock, Pinecraft Industries, Inc., a furniture manufacturer, has 100,000 shares of $1.50 preferred stock outstanding. This designation means that preferred dividends are paid at the annual rate of $1.50 per share. Assume that in 20X4, Pinecraft declares an annual dividend of $1,000,000. The allocation to preferred and common stockholders is as follows:

Preferred dividend (100,000 shares × $1.50 per share)	$ 150,000
Common dividend (remainder: $1,500,000 − $150,000)	850,000
Total dividend	$1,000,000

If Pinecraft declares only a $200,000 dividend, preferred stockholders receive $150,000, and the common stockholders receive the remainder, $50,000 ($200,000 − $150,000).

EXPRESSING THE DIVIDEND RATE ON PREFERRED STOCK. Dividends on preferred stock are stated either as a

- Percentage rate or
- Dollar amount

For example, preferred stock may be "6% preferred," which means that owners of the preferred stock receive an annual dividend of 6% of the stock's par value. If par value is $100 per share, preferred stockholders receive an annual cash dividend of $6 per share (6% of $100), or the preferred stock may be "$3 preferred," which means that stockholders receive an annual dividend of $3 per share regardless of the preferred stock's par value. The dividend rate on no-par preferred stock is stated in a dollar amount per share.

Cumulative preferred stock Preferred stock whose owners must receive all dividends in arrears before the corporation can pay dividends to the common stockholders.

DIVIDENDS ON CUMULATIVE AND NONCUMULATIVE PREFERRED STOCK. The allocation of dividends may be complex if the preferred stock is *cumulative*. Corporations sometimes fail to pay a dividend to preferred stockholders. This is called *passing the dividend*, and the passed dividends are said to be *in arrears*. The owners of **cumulative preferred stock** must receive all dividends in arrears plus the current year's dividend before the corporation can pay dividends to the common stockholders. *The law considers preferred stock cumulative unless it is specifically labeled as noncumulative.*

The preferred stock of Pinecraft Industries is cumulative. Suppose the company passed the 20X4 preferred dividend of $150,000. Before paying dividends to its common stockholders in 20X5, the company must first pay preferred dividends of $150,000 for both 20X4 and 20X5, a total of $300,000.

Assume that Pinecraft Industries passes its 20X4 preferred dividend. In 20X5, the company declares a $500,000 dividend. The entry to record the declaration is

✔ Check Point 9-10

✔ Check Point 9-11

Sept. 6	Retained Earnings	500,000	
	Dividends Payable, Preferred ($150,000 × 2)		300,000
	Dividends Payable, Common ($500,000 − $300,000)		200,000
	To declare a cash dividend.		

If the preferred stock is *noncumulative*, the corporation is not obligated to pay dividends in arrears. A liability for dividends arises only when the board of directors declares the dividend.

DECISION: Why Issue a Stock Dividend?

Stock dividend A proportional distribution by a corporation of its own stock to its stockholders.

A **stock dividend** is a proportional distribution by a corporation of its own stock to its stockholders. Stock dividends increase the stock account and decrease Retained Earnings. Total equity is unchanged, and no asset or liability is affected.

The corporation distributes stock dividends to stockholders in proportion to the number of shares they already own. If you own 300 shares of IHOP common stock and IHOP distributes a 10% common stock dividend, you will receive 30 (300 × .10) additional shares. You would then own 330 shares of the stock. All other IHOP stockholders would also receive additional shares equal to 10% of their prior holdings.

In distributing a stock dividend, the corporation gives up no assets. Why, then, do companies issue stock dividends? A corporation may choose to distribute stock dividends for the following reasons:

1. ***To continue dividends but conserve cash.*** A company may want to keep cash for operations and yet wish to continue dividends in some form. So the corporation may distribute a stock dividend. Stockholders pay no tax on stock dividends.
2. ***To reduce the per-share market price of its stock.*** Distribution of a stock dividend may cause the market price of a share of the company's stock to fall

because of the increased supply of the stock. The objective is to make the stock less expensive and thus more attractive to a wider range of investors.

Suppose IHOP declared a 10% stock dividend in 2001. At the time, assume IHOP had 20,000,000 shares of common stock outstanding. Generally accepted accounting principles (GAAP) label a stock dividend of 25% or less as *small* and suggest that the dividend be accounted for at the market value of the shares distributed. At the time of the stock dividend, assume IHOP's stock is trading for $15 per share. IHOP would record this stock dividend as follows:

2001			
May 19	Retained Earnings (20,000,000 shares of common outstanding × .10 stock dividend × $15 market value per share of common)	30,000,000	
	Common Stock (20,000,000 × .10 × $0.01 par value per share)		20,000
	Paid-in Capital in Excess of Par—Common		29,980,000
	Distributed a 10% stock dividend.		

GAAP identifies stock dividends above 25% as *large* and permit them to be accounted for at par value. For a large stock dividend, therefore, IHOP would debit Retained Earnings and credit Common Stock for the par value of the shares distributed in the dividend.

A corporation issued 1,000 shares of its $15-par common as a stock dividend when the stock's market price was $25 per share. Assume that the 1,000 shares issued are (1) 10% of the outstanding shares and (2) 100% of the outstanding shares. Which stock dividend decreases total stockholders' equity?

Answer:
Neither a large stock dividend nor a small stock dividend affects total stockholders' equity. Why? Because all the accounts affected by a stock dividend are part of stockholders' equity.

✔ Check Point 9-12

Stock Splits

A **stock split** is an increase in the number of authorized, issued, and outstanding shares of stock, coupled with a proportionate reduction in the stock's par value. For example, if the company splits its stock 2 for 1, the number of outstanding shares is doubled and each share's par value is halved. A stock split, like a large stock dividend, decreases the market price of the stock—with the intention of making the stock more attractive in the market. Most leading companies in the United States—IBM, Ford Motor Company, Giant Food, Inc., and others—have split their stock.

Stock split
An increase in the number of authorized, issued, and outstanding shares of stock coupled with a proportionate reduction in the stock's par value.

The market price of a share of Quaker Oats common stock has been approximately $25. Assume that Quaker Oats wishes to decrease the market price to approximately $12.50. Quaker may decide to split its common stock 2 for 1. A 2-for-1 stock split means that the company would have twice as many shares of stock outstanding after the split as it had before and that each share's par value would be cut in half. Before the split, Quaker had approximately 170 million shares of $5 par common stock issued and outstanding. Compare Quaker Oats stockholders' equity before and after a 2-for-1 stock split:

Quaker Oats Stockholders' Equity (Adapted)

Before 2-for-1 Stock Split:	(In millions)	After 2-for-1 Stock Split	(In millions)
Common stock, $5 par, 400 million shares authorized, 170 million shares issued	$ 850	Common stock $2.50 par, 800 million shares authorized, 340 million shares issued	$ 850
Additional paid-in capital	136	Additional paid-in capital	136
Retained earnings	1,062	Retained earnings	1,062
Other	(1,683)	Other	(1,683)
Total stockholders' equity	$ 365	Total stockholders' equity	$ 365

All account balances are the same after the stock split, as before. Only the par value per share of common, the number of shares authorized, and the number of shares issued are affected. Total equity does not change.

Measuring the Value of Stock

book value, return on assets (ROA), return on equity (ROE)

The business community measures *stock values* in various ways, depending on the purpose of the measurement. These values include market value, redemption value, liquidation value, and book value.

Objective

5 **Use** different stock values in decision making

Market, Redemption, Liquidation, and Book Value

Market value (of a stock) Price for which a person could buy or sell a share of stock.

A stock's **market value,** or *market price*, is the price a person can buy or sell a share of the stock for. The issuing corporation's net income, financial position, and future prospects and the general economic conditions determine market value. *In almost all cases, stockholders are more concerned about the market value of a stock than about any of the other values discussed next*. In the chapter opening story, IHOP's most recent stock price was quoted at $34.50. Therefore, if IHOP were issuing 1,000 shares of its common stock, IHOP would receive $34,500 (1,000 shares × $34.50 per share).

Preferred stock that requires the company to redeem (pay to retire) the stock at a set price is called **redeemable preferred stock**. The company is *obligated* to redeem the preferred stock, so redeemable preferred stock is really not stockholders' equity but instead is a liability. The price the corporation agrees to pay for the stock, which is set when the stock is issued, is called the *redemption value.* **Liquidation value** is the amount that a company must pay a preferred stockholder in the event the company liquidates (sells out) and closes its doors.

Book value (of a stock) Amount of owners' equity on the company's books for each share of its stock.

The **book value** per share of common stock is the amount of owners' equity on the company's books for each share of its stock. If the company has only common stock outstanding, its book value is computed by dividing total equity by the number of shares of common *outstanding*. For example, a company with stockholders' equity of $180,000 and 5,000 shares of common stock outstanding has a book value of $36 per share ($180,000 ÷ 5,000 shares).

If the company has both preferred stock and common stock outstanding, the preferred stockholders have the first claim to owners' equity. Preferred stock often has a specified liquidation or redemption value. The preferred equity is its redemption value plus any cumulative preferred dividends in arrears. Book value per share of common is then computed as follows:

$$\text{Book value per share of common stock} = \frac{\text{Total stockholders' equity} - \text{Preferred equity}}{\text{Number of shares of common stock outstanding}}$$

Assume that the company balance sheet reports the following amounts:

Stockholders' Equity	
Preferred stock, 6%, $100 par, 400 shares issued, redemption value $130 per share	$ 40,000
Additional paid-in capital—preferred	4,000
Common stock, $10 par, 5,500 shares issued	55,000
Additional paid-in capital—common	72,000
Retained earnings	85,000
Treasury stock—common, 500 shares at cost	(15,000)
Total stockholders' equity	$241,000

Suppose that 4 years (including the current year) of cumulative preferred dividends are in arrears and observe that preferred stock has a redemption value of $130 per share. The book-value-per-share computations for this corporation are as follows:

Preferred equity	
Redemption value (400 shares × $130)	$ 52,000
Cumulative dividends ($40,000 × .06 × 4 years)	9,600
Preferred equity	$ 61,600*
Common equity	
Total stockholders' equity	$241,000
Less preferred equity	(61,600)
Common equity	$179,400
Book value per share [$179,400 ÷ 5,000 shares outstanding (5,500 shares issued minus 500 treasury shares)]	$ 35.88

*If the preferred stock had no redemption value, then preferred equity would be $40,000 + $4,000 + preferred dividends in arrears.

DECISION MAKING: Using Book Value Per Share

Companies negotiating the purchase of a corporation may wish to know the book value of its stock. The book value of stockholders' equity may figure into the negotiated purchase price. Corporations—especially those whose stock is not publicly traded—may buy out a retiring executive, agreeing to pay the book value of the person's stock in the company.

Some investors compare the book value of a company's stock with the stock's market value. The idea is that a share selling below its book value is underpriced and thus a good buy. Let's compare two companies, IHOP and Intel:

		Book Value Per Share		
Company	***Recent Stock Price***	***(Common stockholders' equity) /***	***(Number of shares of common stock outstanding)***	***Book Value***
IHOP	$34.50	$259,995/	20,011	= $ 12.99
Intel	$29.26	$37,322,000/	6,721,000	= $ 5.55

Neither company's stock is selling below its book value. But IHOP's book value per share is closer to its market value than Intel's. Does this mean IHOP's stock is the better investment? Not necessarily. Investment decisions should be based on more than one ratio. Let's turn now to two widely used measures of operating performance.

✔ **Check Point 9-13**

DECISION MAKING: How to Relate Profitability to a Company's Stock

Objective

6 **Evaluate** a company's return on assets and return on stockholders' equity

Investors and creditors are constantly evaluating managers' ability to earn profits. Investors search for companies whose stocks are likely to increase in value. Investment decisions often include a comparison of companies. But a comparison of IHOP Corp.'s net income with the net income of a new dot-com startup is not meaningful. IHOP's profits may run into the millions of dollars, which far exceed a new company's net income. Does this automatically make IHOP a better investment? Not necessarily. To make relevant comparisons among companies of different size, investors use some standard profitability measures. Two prominent measures of profitability are return on assets and return on equity.

Rate of return on total assets Net income plus interest expense, divided by average total assets. This ratio measures a company's success in using its assets to earn income for the persons who finance the business. Also called *return on assets.*

RETURN ON ASSETS. The **rate of return on total assets,** or simply **return on assets,** measures a company's success in using its assets to earn income for the two groups who finance the business:

- Creditors to whom the corporation owes money and who, therefore, earn interest
- Stockholders who own the corporation's stock and expect it to earn net income

The sum of interest expense and net income is the return to the two groups who finance a corporation and this is the numerator of the return-on-assets ratio. The denominator is average total assets. Return on assets is computed as follows, using actual data from the 2000 annual report of IHOP Corp. (dollar amounts in thousands):

$$\text{Rate of return on total assets} = \frac{\text{Net income} + \text{Interest expense}}{\text{Average total assets}}$$

$$= \frac{\$35{,}338 + \$21{,}751}{(\$520{,}402 + \$562{,}212)/2} = \frac{\$57{,}089}{\$541{,}307} = 0.105$$

Net income and interest expense are taken from the income statement. Average total assets is computed from the beginning and ending balance sheets.

What is a good rate of return on total assets? Ten percent is considered strong for most companies. However, rates of return vary widely by industry. For example, high-technology companies earn much higher returns than do utility companies, groceries, and manufacturers of consumer goods such as toothpaste and paper towels.

Rate of return on common stockholders' equity Net income minus preferred dividends, divided by average common stockholders' equity. A measure of profitability. Also called *return on equity.*

RETURN ON EQUITY. **Rate of return on common stockholders' equity,** often called **return on equity,** shows the relationship between net income and average common stockholders' equity. Return on equity is computed only on common stock because the return to preferred stockholders is their specified dividend.

The numerator of return on equity is net income minus preferred dividends, information taken from the income statement. The denominator is *average common stockholders' equity*—total stockholders' equity minus preferred equity. IHOP Corp.'s rate of return on common stockholders' equity for 2000 is computed as follows (dollar amounts in thousands):

$$\text{Rate of return on common stockholders' equity} = \frac{\text{Net income} - \text{Preferred dividends}}{\text{Average common stockholders' equity}}$$

$$= \frac{\$35,338 - \$0}{(\$226,480 + \$259,995)/2} = \frac{\$35,338}{\$243,238} = 0.145$$

Because IHOP Corp. has no preferred stock, preferred dividends are zero. With no preferred stock outstanding, average *common* stockholders' equity is the same as average *total* equity—the average of the beginning and ending amounts.

✔ Check Point 9-14

✔ Check Point 9-15

IHOP's return on equity (14.5%) is higher than its return on assets (10.5%). This difference results from the interest-expense component of return on assets. Companies such as IHOP borrow at one rate (say, 7%) and invest the funds to earn a higher rate (say, 15%). Borrowing at a lower rate than the company's return on investments is called *using leverage*. Leverage increases net income as long as operating income exceeds the interest expense from borrowing.

Investors and creditors use return on common stockholders' equity in much the same way they use return on total assets—to compare companies. The higher the rate of return, the more successful the company. In most industries, 15% is considered good. Therefore, the IHOP's 14.5% return on common stockholders' equity is quite good.

The Decision Guidelines feature (page 439) offers suggestions for what to consider when investing in stock.

Reporting Stockholders' Equity Transactions

Integrator CD

cash flows

Statement of Cash Flows

Objective

7 **Report** stockholders' equity transactions on the statement of cash flows

Many of the transactions discussed in this chapter are reported on the statement of cash flows. Stockholders' equity transactions are *financing activities* because the company is dealing with its owners, the stockholders—the basic group of people who finance the company. Financing transactions that affect stockholders' equity and cash (and thus appear on the statement of cash flows) fall into three main categories: issuances of stock, repurchases of stock, and dividends.

ISSUANCES OF STOCK. *Issuances of stock* include basic transactions in which a company issues its stock for cash. During 2000, IHOP Corp. issued stock, as shown by the increases in Common stock and Additional paid-in capital on the company's balance sheet (page 417, lines 3 and 4). IHOP's statement of cash flows (Exhibit 9-8) reports the cash received from issuing stock as a financing activity.

Exhibit 9-8

IHOP Corp's Financing Activities (Adapted)

✔ Check Point 9-16

Cash Flows from Financing Activities	*(In thousands)*
Proceeds from issuance of common stock	$ 3,172
Purchase of treasury stock	(5,170)
Net cash used by financing activities	$(1,998)

REPURCHASES OF STOCK. As we discussed earlier, a company can repurchase its stock as treasury stock. During 2000, IHOP purchased treasury stock and reported the payment as a financing activity.

DIVIDENDS. Most companies pay cash dividends to their stockholders. Dividend payments are a type of financing transaction because the company is paying its stockholders for the use of their money. Stock dividends are not reported on the statement of cash flows because the company pays no cash. IHOP paid no dividends during 2000.

In Exhibit 9-8, cash receipts appear as positive amounts and cash payments as negative amounts, denoted by parentheses.

Prepare T-accounts for common stock, Additional Paid-in Capital, and Treasury Stock to show the effects of IHOP's financing activities reported in Exhibit 9-8. Insert the beginning and ending balances of these accounts, taken from the IHOP balance sheet on page 000. Then post the debits and credits that arose from the issuance of stock and the purchase of treasury stock.

Answer (amounts in thousands):

Common Stock (Dr.)	Common Stock (Cr.)	Additional Paid-in Capital (Dr.)	Additional Paid-in Capital (Cr.)	Treasury Stock (Dr.)	Treasury Stock (Cr.)
	201		**66,485**	**0**	
	Issuance 2		Issuance 3,170	Purchase 5,170	
	203		**69,655**	**5,170**	

$2 + $3,170 = $3,172

Variations in Reporting Stockholders' Equity

Businesses often use terminology and formats in reporting stockholders' equity that differ from our examples. We use a more detailed format in this book to help you learn all the components of stockholders' equity. Companies assume that readers of their statements already understand the details.

One of the most important skills you will learn in this course is the ability to understand the financial statements of real companies. Exhibit 9-9 presents a side-by-side comparison of our general teaching format and the format you are more likely to encounter in real-world balance sheets.

Exhibit 9-9

Formats for Reporting Stockholders' Equity

General Teaching Format

Stockholders' equity	
Paid-in capital:	
Preferred stock, 8%, $10 par, 30,000 shares authorized and issued	$ 300,000
Paid-in capital in excess of par—preferred	10,000
Common stock, $1 par, 100,000 shares authorized, 60,000 shares issued	60,000
Paid-in capital in excess of par—common	2,140,000
Paid-in capital from treasury stock transactions, common	9,000
Paid-in capital from retirement of preferred stock	11,000
Total paid-in capital	2,530,000
Retained earnings	1,565,000
Subtotal	4,095,000
Less treasury stock, common (1,400 shares at cost)	(42,000)
Total stockholders' equity	$4,053,000

Real-World Format

Stockholders' equity	
Preferred stock, 8%, $10 par, 30,000 shares authorized and issued	$ 310,000
Common stock, $1 par, 100,000 shares authorized, 60,000 shares issued	60,000
Additional paid-in capital	2,160,000
Retained earnings	1,565,000
Less treasury stock, common (1,400 shares at cost)	(42,000)
	$4,053,000

Decision Guidelines

INVESTING IN STOCK

Suppose you've saved $5,000 to invest. You visit a nearby Edward Jones office, where the broker probes you for your risk capability. Are you investing mainly for dividends, or for growth in the stock price? You must make some key decisions.

Investor Decision	Guidelines
Which category of stock to buy for:	
• A safe investment?	Preferred stock is safer than common, but for even more safety, invest in high-grade corporate bonds or government securities.
• Steady dividends?	Cumulative preferred stock. However, the company is not obligated to declare preferred dividends, and the dividends are unlikely to increase.
• Increasing dividends?	Common stock, as long as the company's net income is increasing and the company has adequate cash flow to pay a dividend after meeting all obligations and other cash demands.
• Increasing stock price?	Common stock, but again only if the company's net income and cash flow are increasing.
How to identify a good stock to buy?	There are many ways to pick stock investments. One strategy that works reasonably well is to invest in companies that consistently earn higher rates of return on assets and on equity than competing firms in the same industry. Also, select industries that are expected to grow.

Excel Application Problem

Goal: Create an Excel worksheet that compares financial performance of several publicly traded stocks.

Scenario: Your task is to create an Excel worksheet that compares the historical performance of Abercrombie & Fitch; Gap, Inc.; and The Limited on three key financial measures. Embedded graphs of each financial dimension also must be created. All data used in your spreadsheet will come from Morningstar's Web site.

When done, answer these questions:

1. Which of the three companies, if any, has earned a consistently higher return on equity than the others?
2. Which of the three companies, if any, has earned a consistently higher return on assets than the others?
3. Increasing cash flow from operations is a good sign for investing. Which of the companies, if any, has experienced increasing cash flows over the past five years?
4. Based on these very limited data, would you invest in any of these companies? Why or why not?

Step-by-step:

1. Locate **www.morningstar.com** on the Web.
2. Under the "Morningstar Quicktake Reports" section, enter the ticker symbol for each company. Gap's ticker is GPS, The Limited's ticker is LTD, and Abercrombie & Fitch's ticker is ANF. To locate the required information, look under "Financials—Balance Sheet" and "Morningstar Stock Grades—Financial Health." (Note: If the Web site differs from these headings, you may have to search other areas of the Web site.) Print out the pages used for each company.
3. Open a new Excel worksheet.
4. Create a bold-faced heading for your spreadsheet that contains the following:
   a. Chapter 9 Decision Guidelines
   b. Investing in Stock
   c. Stock Performance Analysis
   d. Today's date
5. Under the heading, create a bold-faced, underlined section titled "Return on Equity %." Move down one row. Create one column each for the last four years (e.g., "2001," "2000," and so on). Create one row each for Gap, The Limited, and Abercrombie & Fitch.
6. Enter the "Return on Equity %" data for the past four years for each company.
7. Repeat Steps 5 and 6 for "Return on Assets %" and "Operating Cash Flow (in millions)."
8. Using the Excel Chart Wizard, create separate graphs for Return on Equity %, Return on Assets %, and Operating Cash Flow. Resize and position each graph to the right of the data so that everything appears on one page when you print.
9. Save your work, and print your worksheet in landscape mode (with graphs) for your files.

End-of-Chapter Summary Problems

1. The balance sheet of Trendline Corp. reported the following at December 31, 20X5:

Stockholders' Equity	
Preferred stock, 4%, $10 par, 10,000 shares authorized and issued (redemption value, $110,000)	$100,000
Common stock, no-par, $5 stated value, 100,000 shares authorized	250,000
Paid-in capital in excess of par or stated value:	
Common stock	239,500
Retained earnings	395,000
Less: Treasury stock, common (1,000 shares)	(8,000)
Total stockholders' equity	$976,500

Required

a. Is the preferred stock cumulative or noncumulative? How can you tell?
b. What is the total amount of the annual preferred dividend?
c. How many shares of common stock has the company issued? How many shares are outstanding?
d. Compute the book value per share of the common stock. No preferred dividends are in arrears, and Trendline has not yet declared the 20X5 dividend.

2. Use the following accounts and related balances to prepare the classified balance sheet of Whitehall, Inc., at September 30, 20X4. Use the account format of the balance sheet.

Common stock, $1 par, 50,000 shares authorized, 20,000 shares issued	$ 20,000	Long-term note payable	$ 80,000
Dividends payable	4,000	Inventory	85,000
Cash	9,000	Property, plant, and equipment, net	226,000
Accounts payable	28,000	Accounts receivable, net	23,000
Paid-in capital in excess of par—common	115,000	Preferred stock, $3.75, no-par, 10,000 shares authorized, 2,000 shares issued	24,000
Treasury stock, common, 1,000 shares at cost	6,000	Accrued liabilities	3,000
		Retained earnings	75,000

Answers

1. a. The preferred stock is cumulative because it is not specifically labeled otherwise.
   b. Total annual preferred dividend: $4,000 ($100,000 × 0.04).
   c. Common stock issued: 50,000 shares ($250,000 ÷ $5 stated value). Common shares outstanding: 49,000 (50,000 issued − 1,000 treasury).
   d. Book value per share of common stock:

Common:	
Total stockholders' equity	$976,500
Less stockholders' equity allocated to preferred	(114,000)*
Stockholders' equity allocated to common	$862,500
Book value per share ($862,500 ÷ 49,000 shares)	$17.60

*Redemption value	$110,000
Cumulative dividend ($100,000 × .04)	4,000
Stockholders' equity allocated to preferred	$114,000

2.

Whitehall, Inc.
Balance Sheet
September 30, 20X4

Assets		Liabilities		
Current		Current		
Cash	$ 9,000	Accounts payable	$ 28,000	
Accounts receivable, net	23,000	Dividends payable	4,000	
Inventory	85,000	Accrued liabilities	3,000	
Total current assets	117,000	Total current liabilities	35,000	
Property, plant, and equipment, net	226,000	Long-term note payable	80,000	
		Total liabilities	115,000	
		Stockholders' Equity		
		Preferred stock, $3.75, no par, 10,000 shares authorized, 2,000 shares issued	$ 24,000	
		Common stock, $1 par, 50,000 shares authorized, 20,000 shares issued	20,000	
		Paid-in capital in excess of par—common	115,000	
		Retained earnings	75,000	
		Treasury stock, common, 1,000 shares at cost	(6,000)	
		Total stockholders' equity		228,000
Total assets	$343,000	Total liabilities and stockholders' equity		$343,000

Review Stockholders' Equity

Lessons Learned

1. **Explain the advantages and disadvantages of a corporation.** Corporations are legal entities that exist apart from their owners. The advantages of corporations are their ability to raise capital, continuous life, transferability of ownership, and limited liability of owners. The disadvantages are the separation of ownership from management, double taxation, and government regulation.
2. **Measure the effect of issuing stock on a company's financial position.** Corporations may issue common or preferred stock. Regardless of the type of stock, its issuance increases assets and equity.
3. **Describe how treasury stock transactions affect a company.** *Treasury stock* is a corporation's own stock that it has issued and later reacquired. The purchase of treasury stock decreases the company's assets and equity. The sale of treasury stock increases assets and equity. Treasury stock is a contra element of stockholders' equity.
4. **Account for dividends and measure their impact on a company.** Companies may issue dividends in cash or stock. Preferred stock has priority over common. All cash dividends decrease assets and equity.

   A *stock dividend* is a proportional distribution by a corporation of its own stock to its stockholders. Stock dividends increase the stock account and decrease Retained Earnings. Total stockholders' equity is unchanged.
5. **Use different stock values in decision making.** A stock's *market value* is the price for which a person could buy or sell a share of the stock. The price a company agrees to pay for a stock when buying it back is the stock's *redemption value. Liquidation value* is the amount the corporation agrees to pay the preferred stockholders per share if the corporation liquidates. *Book value* is the amount of owners' equity

on the company's books for each share of the stock outstanding.

6. **Evaluate a company's return on assets and return on stockholders' equity.** Return on assets and return on equity are two measures of profitability. *Return on assets* measures a company's success in using assets to earn income for both creditors and the stockholders. *Return on equity* measures success in earning net income for the common stockholders. A healthy company's return on equity will exceed its return on assets.
7. **Report stockholders' equity transactions on the statement of cash flows.** Three main *financing* categories that affect stockholders' equity are issuances of stock, repurchases of stock, and dividends.

Accounting Vocabulary

board of directors (p. 419)
book value (of a stock) (p. 434)
bylaws (p. 419)
chairperson (p. 420)
common stock (p. 422)
contributed capital (p. 421)
cumulative preferred stock (p. 432)
deficit (p. 430)
dividends (p. 431)
double taxation (p. 419)
legal capital (p. 422)
limited liability (p. 418)
market value (of a stock) (p. 434)
outstanding stock (p. 421)
paid-in capital (p. 421)
par value (p. 422)
preferred stock (p. 422)
president (p. 420)
rate of return on common stockholders' equity (p. 436)
rate of return on total assets (p. 436)
retained earnings (p. 421)
return on assets (p. 436)
return on equity (p. 436)
shareholders (p. 418)
stated value (p. 422)
stock (p. 421)
stock dividend (p. 432)
stockholders (p. 418)
stockholders' equity (p. 420)
stock split (p. 433)
treasury stock (p. 428)

Questions

1. Why is a corporation called a "creature of the state"? Briefly outline the steps in the organization of a corporation.
2. Identify the characteristics of a corporation and explain why corporations face a tax disadvantage.
3. Suppose **Verizon Communications Inc.** issued 1,000 shares of its 3.65%, $100-par preferred stock for $120 per share. How much would this transaction increase the company's paid-in capital? How much would it increase Verizon's retained earnings? How much would it increase Verizon's annual cash dividend payments?
4. Rank the following accounts in the order they would appear on the balance sheet: Common Stock, Equipment, Preferred Stock, Retained Earnings, Dividends Payable. Also, give each account's balance sheet classification.
5. What effect does the purchase of treasury stock have on the (a) assets, (b) issued stock, and (c) outstanding stock of the corporation?
6. What is the normal balance of the Treasury Stock account? What type of account is Treasury Stock? Where is Treasury Stock reported on the balance sheet?
7. What effects do the purchase and retirement of common stock have on the (a) assets, (b) issued stock, and (c) outstanding stock of the corporation?
8. Briefly discuss the three important dates for a dividend.
9. As a preferred stockholder, would you rather own cumulative or noncumulative preferred? If all other factors are the same, would the corporation rather the preferred stock be cumulative or noncumulative? Give your reason.
10. **Ametek, Inc.**, reported a cash balance of $73 million and a retained earnings balance of $162.5 million. Explain how Ametek can have so much more retained earnings than cash. In your answer, identify the nature of retained earnings and state how it relates to cash.
11. A friend of yours receives a stock dividend on an investment. He believes that stock dividends are the same as cash dividends. Explain why the two are not the same.
12. Distinguish between the market value of stock and the book value of stock. Which is more important to investors?
13. Why should a healthy company's rate of return on stockholders' equity exceed its rate of return on total assets?
14. Which financing activities (that affect stockholders' equity) increase cash, and which activities decrease cash?

Assess Your Progress

Check Points

CP9-1 Consider the authority structure in a corporation, as diagrammed in Exhibit 9-2, page 420.

Authority structure in a corporation
(Obj. 1)

1. Who is in charge of day-to-day operations?
2. Who is the most powerful person in the corporation?
3. What group holds the ultimate power in a corporation?
4. Who manages the accounting?
5. Who has primary responsibility for the corporation's cash?

CP9-2 Answer the following questions about the characteristics of a corporation's stock:

Characteristics of preferred and common stock
(Obj. 1)

1. Which right clearly distinguishes a stockholder from a creditor (who has lent money to the corporation)?
2. What privileges do preferred stockholders enjoy that common stockholders do not have?
3. Which stockholders are the real owners of a corporation?
4. Which class of stockholders would expect to reap greater benefits from a highly profitable corporation? Why?

CP9-3 Study **IHOP's** July 23 stock issuance entry given on page 423 and answer these questions about the nature of the IHOP transaction.

Effect of a stock issuance on net income
(Obj. 2)

1. IHOP received $62,000,000 for the issuance of its stock. The par value of the IHOP stock was only $62,000. Was the excess amount of $61,938,000 a profit to IHOP? If not, what was it?
2. Suppose the par value of the IHOP stock had been $1 per share, $5 per share, or $10 per share. Would a change in the par value of the company's stock affect IHOP's total paid-in capital? Give the reasons for your answer.

CP9-4 At December 31, 2000, **The Coca-Cola Company** reported the following on its comparative balance sheet, which included 1999 amounts for comparison (adapted, with all amounts except par value in millions):

Issuing stock and analyzing retained earnings
(Obj. 2)

	December 31, 2000	1999
Common stock $0.25 par value		
Authorized: 5,600 shares		
Issued: 3,480 shares in 2000	$ 870	
3,466 shares in 1999		$ 867
Paid-in capital in excess of par	3,196	2,584
Retained earnings	21,265	20,773

1. How much did Coca-Cola's total paid-in capital increase during 2000? What caused total paid-in capital to increase? How can you tell?
2. Journalize Coca-Cola's issuance of stock for cash during 2000.
3. Did Coca-Cola have a profit or a loss for 2000? How can you tell?

CP9-5 This Check Point shows the similarity and the difference between two ways to acquire plant assets.

Issuing stock to finance the purchase of assets
(Obj. 2)

Case A—Issue stock and buy the assets in separate transactions:	*Case B—Issue stock to acquire the assets:*
Burrows Corporation issued 10,000 shares of its $5 par common stock for cash of $900,000. In a separate transaction, Burrows used the cash to purchase a warehouse building for $600,000 and equipment for $300,000. Journalize the two transactions.	Burrows Corporation issued 10,000 shares of its $5 par common stock to acquire a warehouse building valued at $600,000 and equipment worth $300,000. Journalize this transaction.

Compare the balances in all accounts after making both sets of entries. Are the account balances similar or different?

Preparing the stockholders' equity section of a balance sheet
(Obj. 2)

CP9-6 **Paychex, Inc.** provides employer services for small- to medium-size businesses. The financial statements of Paychex, Inc. reported the following accounts (adapted, dollar amounts in millions except for par value):

Net revenues	$ 870	Paid-in capital in excess of par	$140
Accounts payable	16	Other stockholders' equity	13
Retained earnings	601	Common stock $0.01 par;	
Other current liabilities	2,128	400 million shares issued	4
Operating expenses	615	Long-term liabilities	5

Prepare the stockholders' equity section of the Paychex, Inc. balance sheet. Net income has already been closed to Retained Earnings.

Using stockholders' equity data
(Obj. 2)

CP9-7 Use the **Paychex, Inc.**, data in Check Point 9-6 to compute Paychex's

a. Net income
b. Total liabilities
c. Total assets (use the accounting equation)

Accounting for purchase and sale of treasury stock
(Obj. 3)

CP9-8 **General Dynamics Corporation**, manufacturer of fighter aircraft, Army tanks, and Navy ships, reported the following stockholders' equity (adapted, in millions):

Common stock	$ 243
Additional paid-in capital	297
Retained earnings	2,159
Treasury stock	(691)
Total stockholders' equity	$2,008

During the next year, General Dynamics purchased treasury stock at a cost of $28 million and resold treasury stock for $7 million (this treasury stock had cost General Dynamics $3 million).

Record the purchase and resale of General Dynamics treasury stock. Overall, how much did stockholders' equity increase or decrease as a result of the two treasury stock transactions?

Explaining treasury stock transactions
(Obj. 3)

CP9-9 Return to the **General Dynamics** data of Check Point 9-8. Explain how General Dynamics can have a larger balance of Treasury Stock than the sum of Common Stock and Additional Paid-In Capital. Does it mean that General Dynamics has more treasury stock than the amount of stock the company has issued?

Accounting for cash dividends
(Obj. 4)

CP9-10 Augusta National Company earned net income of $90,000 during the year ended December 31, 20X6. On December 15, Augusta declared the annual cash dividend on its $4\frac{1}{2}$% preferred stock (10,000 shares with total par value of $100,000) and a $0.50 per share cash dividend on its common stock (50,000 shares with total par value of $250,000). Augusta then paid the dividends on January 4, 20X7.

Journalize for Augusta National Company:

a. Declaring the cash dividends on December 15, 20X6.
b. Paying the cash dividends on January 4, 20X7.

Did Retained Earnings increase or decrease during 20X6? By how much?

Dividing cash dividends between preferred and common stock **(Obj. 4)**

CP9-11 Refer to the allocation of dividends for Pinecraft Industries on page 431. Answer these questions about Pinecraft's cash dividends.

1. How much in dividends must Pinecraft declare each year before the common stockholders receive cash dividends for the year?
2. Suppose Pinecraft declares cash dividends of $200,000 for 20X4. How much of the dividends go to preferred? How much goes to common?
3. Is Pinecraft's preferred stock cumulative or noncumulative? How can you tell?
4. Suppose Pinecraft passed the preferred dividend in 20X3 and 20X4. In 20X5, Pinecraft declares cash dividends of $550,000. How much of the dividends go to preferred? How much goes to common?

Recording a small stock dividend **(Obj. 4)**

CP9-12 **Oracle Corporation** has 6 billion shares of $0.01 par common stock outstanding. Suppose Oracle distributes a 5% stock dividend when the market value of its stock is $11.50 per share.

1. Journalize Oracle's distribution of the Oracle's stock dividend on March 19. An explanation is not required.
2. What was the overall effect of the stock dividend on Oracle's total assets? On total liabilities? On total stockholders' equity?

Computing book value per share **(Obj. 5)**

CP9-13 Refer to the Real-World Format of Stockholders' Equity in Exhibit 9-9, page 438. That company has passed its preferred dividends for the current year and the preceding year. Compute the book value of a share of the company's common stock.

Computing and explaining return on assets and return on equity **(Obj. 6)**

CP9-14 Give the formula for computing (a) rate of return on total assets and (b) rate of return on common stockholders' equity. Then answer these questions about the rate-of-return computations.

1. Why is interest expense added to net income to compute return on assets?
2. Why are preferred dividends subtracted from net income to compute return on common stockholders' equity? Why are preferred dividends *not* subtracted from net income to compute return on assets?

Computing return on assets and return on equity for a leading company **(Obj. 6)**

CP9-15 **Sara Lee's** 2001 financial statements reported the following items, with 2000 figures given for comparison (adapted, in millions). Compute Sara Lee's return on assets and on common equity for 2001. Evaluate the rates of return as strong or weak.

	20X1	20X0
Balance sheet		
Total assets	$10,167	$11,611
Total liabilities	$ 9,045	$10,377
Total stockholders' equity (all common)	1,122	1,234
Total liabilities and equity	$10,167	$11,611
Income statement		
Net sales	$17,747	
Operating expense	15,874	
Interest expense	270	
Other income	663	
Net income	$ 2,266	

Measuring cash flows from financing activities **(Obj. 7)**

CP9-16 During fiscal year 2001 **Kmart Corporation** incurred a net loss of $244 million. The company borrowed $397 million and paid off $151 million of debt. Kmart raised $53 million by issuing common stock and paid $139 million to purchase treasury stock. Determine the amount of Kmart's *net cash flow from financing activities* during 2001.

Exercises

Organizing a corporation
(Obj. 1)

E9-1 Celia Bastis and Kathryn Bentson are opening a deli to be named The Red Tomato. They need outside capital, so they plan to organize the business as a corporation. Because your office is in the same building, they come to you for advice. Write a memorandum informing them of the steps in forming a corporation. Identify specific documents used in this process, and name the different parties involved in the ownership and management of a corporation.

Issuing stock and reporting stockholders' equity
(Obj. 2)

general ledger

E9-2 Bird-Kultgen Auto Sales, Inc., obtained a corporate charter that authorized the issuance of 100,000 shares of common stock and 5,000 shares of preferred stock. During its first year, the business completed the following stock issuance transactions:

Feb. 19	Issued 1,000 shares of $2.50 par common stock for cash of $6.50 per share.
Mar. 3	Sold 500 shares of $1.50 no-par preferred stock for $6,000 cash.
11	Received inventory valued at $11,000 and equipment with market value of $8,500 for 3,300 shares of the $2.50 par common stock.

Required

1. Journalize the transactions. Explanations are not required.
2. Prepare the stockholders' equity section of Bird-Kultgen's balance sheet. The ending balance of retained earnings is a deficit of $12,000.

Stockholders' equity section of a balance sheet
(Obj. 2)

E9-3 Assume that the charter of **Spenco Medical Corporation** authorizes the issuance of 5,000 shares of class A preferred stock, 1,000 shares of class B preferred stock, and 10,000 shares of common stock. Assume further that during a 2-month period, Spenco completed these stock-issuance transactions:

June 23	Issued 1,000 shares of $1 par common stock for cash of $12.50 per share.
July 2	Sold 300 shares of $4.50, no-par class A preferred stock for $20,000 cash.
12	Received inventory valued at $25,000 and equipment with market value of $16,000 for 3,300 shares of the $1 par common stock.

Required

Prepare the stockholders' equity section of the Spenco balance sheet for the transactions given in this exercise. Retained earnings has a balance of $88,000. Journal entries are not required.

Measuring the paid-in capital of a corporation
(Obj. 2)

E9-4 TeleTouch Wireless Corporation was recently organized. The company issued common stock to an attorney who gave legal services of $20,000 to help organize the corporation. TeleTouch issued common stock to an inventor in exchange for his patent with a market value of $120,000. In addition, TeleTouch received cash both for the issuance of 1,000 shares of its preferred stock at $110 per share and for the issuance of 26,000 shares of its common stock at $15 per share. During the first year of operations, TeleTouch earned net income of $85,000 and declared a cash dividend of $26,000. Without making journal entries, determine the total paid-in capital created by these transactions.

Stockholders' equity section of a balance sheet
(Obj. 2, 3)

spreadsheet

E9-5 **Avon Products, Inc.**, the cosmetic's company, had the following selected account balances at December 31, 20X3 (adapted, in millions, except par value per share). Prepare the stockholders' equity section of Avon's balance sheet (in millions).

Common stock, $0.25 par per share, 800 shares authorized, 356 shares issued	$ 89	Inventory	$ 613
Retained earnings	1,390	Property, plant, and equipment, net	775
Accounts receivable, net	520	Paid-in capital in excess of par	938
Notes payable	1,325	Treasury stock, common, 120 shares at cost	2,002

How can Avon have a larger balance of treasury stock than the sum of Common Stock and Paid-in Capital in Excess of Par?

Recording treasury stock transactions and measuring their effects on stockholders' equity
(Obj. 2, 3)

general ledger

E9-6 Journalize the following assumed transactions of **Johnson & Johnson:**

Jan. 19	Issued 10,000 shares of $1 par common stock at $5 per share.
Oct. 22	Purchased 900 shares of treasury stock at $7 per share.
Dec. 11	Sold 200 shares of treasury stock at $12 per share.

What was the overall effect of these transactions on Johnson & Johnson's stockholders' equity?

Issuing stock; dividends
(Obj. 2, 4)

E9-7 The balance sheet of aircraft manufacturer **Lockheed Martin Corporation** (as adapted) reported the following stockholders' equity. All amounts, except for par value per share, are given in millions.

Lockheed Martin Corporation

Stockholders Equity

	December 31, 2001	2000
Common stock, $1 par, shares issued and outstanding: 441 and 431, respectively	$ 441	$ 431
Additional paid-in capital	2,142	1,789
Retained earnings	3,961	5,199

Required

1. Through the end of 2001, at what average price per share was the common stock issued? Lockheed Martin's stock has traded recently around $60 per share. Comparing the two per-share values, when do you think the company issued most of its stock?
2. Lockheed Martin lists no treasury stock. How else can you tell that the company holds no treasury stock?
3. Lockheed Martin declared and paid cash dividends of $192 million during 2001. Did the company have a net income or a net loss for 2001? Determine which it is, and compute the amount.

Recording stock issuance, treasury stock, and dividend transactions
(Obj. 2, 3, 4)

E9-8 At December 31, 20X1, **Sprint Corporation** reported the stockholders' equity accounts shown here (as adapted, with dollar amounts in millions, except par value per share).

Common stock $1.50 par value per share, 1,829 million shares issued	$ 2,744
Capital in excess of par value	10,076
Retained earnings (deficit)	(261)
Treasury stock, at cost	-0-
Total stockholders' equity	$12,559

Assume that Sprint's 20X2 transactions included the following:

a. Net income, $440 million.
b. Issuance of 6 million shares of common stock for $13.50 per share.
c. Purchase of 1 million shares of treasury stock for $14 million.
d. Declaration and payment of cash dividends of $30 million.

Journalize Sprint's transactions in b, c, and d. Explanations are not required.

Reporting stockholders' equity after a sequence of transactions
(Obj. 2, 3, 4)

E9-9 Use the **Sprint Corporation** data in Exercise 9-8 to prepare the stockholders' equity section of the company's balance sheet at December 31, 20X2.

Inferring transactions from a company's stockholders' equity
(Obj. 2, 3, 4, 5)

E9-10 Krisler Corporation reported the following shareholders' equity on its balance sheet:

Shareholders' Equity (Dollars and shares in millions)	December 31, 20X4	20X3
Preferred stock—$1 per share par value; authorized 20.0 shares; Series A Convertible Preferred Stock; issued and outstanding: 20X4 and 20X3—0.1 and 1.7 shares, respectively (aggregate liquidation preference $68 million and $863 million, respectively)	$ *	$ 2
Common stock—$1 per share par value; authorized 1,000.0 shares; issued: 20X4 and 20X3—408.2 and 364.1 shares, respectively	408	364
Additional paid-in capital	5,506	5,536
Retained earnings	6,280	5,006
Treasury stock, common—at cost 20X4—29.9 shares; 20X3—9.0 shares	(1,235)	(214)
Total Shareholders' Equity	10,959	10,694
Total Liabilities and Shareholders' Equity	$53,756	$49,539

*Less than $1 million

Required

1. What caused Krisler's preferred stock to decrease during 20X4? Cite all the causes.
2. What caused Krisler's common stock to increase during 20X4? Identify all the causes.
3. How many shares of Krisler common stock were outstanding at December 31, 20X4?
4. Assume that during 20X4, Krisler sold no treasury stock. What average price per share did Krisler pay for the treasury stock the company purchased during the year? During 20X4, the market price of Krisler's common stock ranged from a low of $38.25 to a high of $58.13. Compare the average price Krisler paid for its treasury stock during 20X4 to the range of market prices during the year.
5. Krisler's net income during 20X4 was $1,680 million. How much were Krisler's dividends during the year?

Computing dividends on preferred and common stock
(Obj. 4)

E9-11 The following elements of stockholders' equity are adapted from the balance sheet of **Gulf Resources & Chemical Corporation.** All dollar amounts, except the dividends per share, are given in thousands.

Gulf Resources & Chemical Corporation

Stockholders' Equity

Preferred stock, cumulative, $1 par (Note 7)	
Series A, 58,000 shares issued	$ 58
Series B, 376,000 shares issued	376
Common stock, $0.10 par, 9,130,000 shares issued	913

Note 7. Preferred Stock:

	Designated Annual Cash Dividend per Share
Series A	$0.20
Series B	1.00

Assume that the Series A preferred has preference over the Series B preferred and that the company has paid all preferred dividends through 20X3.

Required

Compute the dividends to both series of preferred and to common for 20X4 and 20X5 if total dividends are $0 in 20X4 and $800,000 in 20X5. Round to the nearest dollar.

E9-12 The stockholders' equity for **Electronic Data Systems Corporation (EDS)** on December 31, 2001, follows (adapted in millions, except for par value per share):

Recording a stock dividend and reporting stockholders' equity
(Obj. 4)

Stockholders' Equity	
Common stock, $0.01 par, 2,000 shares authorized, 500 shares issued	$ 5
Paid-in capital in excess of par—common	962
Retained earnings	7,122
Other	(1,643)
Total stockholders' equity	$6,446

On April 15, 2002, the market price of EDS common stock was $51.55 per share. Assume EDS distributed a 20% stock dividend on this date.

Required

1. Journalize the distribution of the stock dividend.
2. Prepare the stockholders' equity section of the balance sheet after the stock dividend.
3. Why is total stockholders' equity unchanged by the stock dividend?
4. Suppose EDS had a cash balance of $3,000 million on April 16, 2002. What is the maximum amount of cash dividends EDS can declare?

E9-13 Identify the effects—both the direction and the dollar amount—of these assumed transactions on the total stockholders' equity of **Pier 1 Imports, Inc.** Each transaction is independent.

Measuring the effects of stock issuance, dividends, and treasury stock transactions
(Obj. 2, 3, 4)

a. Purchase of 2,000 shares of treasury stock (par value $1) at $4.25 per share.
b. 10% stock dividend. Before the dividend, 69 million shares of $1 par common stock were outstanding; the market value was $7.625 at the time of the dividend.
c. Sale of 600 shares of $1 par treasury stock for $5.00 per share. Cost of the treasury stock was $4.25 per share.
d. A 3-for-1 stock split. Prior to the split, 69 million shares of $1 par common were outstanding.
e. A 50% stock dividend. Before the dividend, 69 million shares of $1 par common stock were outstanding; the market value was $13.75 at the time of the dividend.

E9-14 **Gap, Inc.**, had the following stockholders' equity (adapted) at January 31 (dollars in millions):

Reporting stockholders' equity after a stock split
(Obj. 4)

Common stock, $0.05 par, 500 million shares authorized, 440 million shares issued	$ 22
Additional paid-in capital	318
Retained earnings	2,393
Other	(1,149)
Total stockholders' equity	$1,584

Assume that on March 7, Gap split its $0.05 par common stock 4 for 1. Prepare the stockholders' equity section of the balance sheet immediately after the split. (Note: A stock split also increases the number of authorized shares.)

E9-15 The balance sheet of Chesapeake Investment Bankers reported the following, with all amounts, including shares, in thousands:

Measuring the book value per share of common stock
(Obj. 5)

Redeemable preferred stock, 6%, redemption value $6,362; outstanding 100 shares	$ 4,860
Common stockholders' equity	
11,120 shares issued and outstanding	114,200
Total stockholders' equity	$119,060

Required

1. Compute the book value per share for the common stock, assuming all preferred dividends are fully paid up (none in arrears).
2. Compute the book value per share of the common stock, assuming that 3 years' preferred dividends including the current year, are in arrears.
3. Chesapeake's common stock recently traded at market value of $8.75. Does this mean that Chesapeake stock is a good buy at $8.75?

Evaluating profitability
(Obj. 6)

E9-16 PepsiCo, Inc., reported these figures for 20X1 and 20X0 (adapted, in millions):

	20X1	20X0
Income statement:		
Operating income	$ 4,021	$ 3,818
Interest expense	219	272
Net income	2,662	2,543
Balance sheet:		
Total assets	21,695	20,757
Common stock and additional paid-in capital	43	388
Retained earnings	11,519	16,510
Other equity	(2,914)	(9,294)

Compute PepsiCo's return on assets and return on common stockholders' equity for 20X1. Do these rates of return suggest strength or weakness? Give your reason.

Evaluating profitability
(Obj. 6)

E9-17 Kraft Foods, Inc., included the following items in its financial statements for 20X1, the current year (amounts in millions):

Borrowings	$6,582	Payment of long-term debt	$17,055
Dividends paid	225	Proceeds from issuance	
Interest expense:		of common stock	8,425
Current year	1,437	Total liabilities:	
Preceding year	597	Current year end	32,320
Net income:		Preceding year end	38,023
Current year	1,882	Total stockholders' equity:	
Preceding year	2,001	Current year end	23,478
Operating income:		Preceding year end	14,048
Current year	4,884		
Preceding year	4,012		

Compute Kraft's return on assets and return on common equity during 20X1 (the current year). Kraft has no preferred stock outstanding. Do Kraft's rates of return look strong or weak? Give your reason.

Challenge Exercises

Reporting cash flows from financing activities
(Obj. 7)

E9-18 Use the Kraft Foods data in Exercise 9-17 to show how Kraft reported cash flows from financing activities during 20X1 (the current year). List items in descending order from largest to smallest dollar amount.

E9-19 Chilton Corporation began operations on January 1 and immediately issued its stock, receiving cash. Chilton's balance sheet at December 31 reported the following stockholders' equity:

Reconstructing transactions from the financial statements
(Obj. 2, 3, 4)

Common stock, $1 par	$ 50,000
Additional paid-in capital	100,600
Retained earnings	18,000
Treasury stock, 500 shares	(2,000)
Total stockholders' equity	$166,600

During the year Chilton

a. Issued stock for $3 per share.
b. Reacquired 800 shares of its own stock for the corporate treasury.
c. Resold some of the treasury shares.
d. Earned net income of $ 26,000, and declared and paid dividends.

Required

Journalize all of Chilton's stockholders' equity transactions during the year. Chilton's entry to close net income to the Retained Earnings account was:

Revenues	141,000	
Expenses		115,000
Retained Earnings		26,000

E9-20 **DoubleTree Corporation** reported the following stockholders' equity data (adapted):

Explaining the changes in stockholders' equity
(Obj. 2, 3, 4)

(In millions, except par value per share)	December 31, 20X3	20X2
Preferred stock	$ 665	$ 686
Common stock, $1 par value	894	891
Additional paid-in capital	1,549	1,468
Retained earnings	20,661	19,108
Treasury stock, common	(3,158)	(2,643)

DoubleTree earned net income of $3,604 during 20X3. For each account except Retained Earnings, one transaction explains the change from the December 31, 20X2, balance to the December 31, 20X3, balance. Two transactions affected Retained Earnings. Give a full explanation, including the dollar amount, for the change in each account.

E9-21 DigiTech Group, Inc., began 20X6 with 8 million shares of $1 par common stock issued and outstanding. Beginning additional paid-in capital was $13 million, and retained earnings totaled $40 million. In March 20X6, DigiTech issued 2 million shares of common stock at a price of $2 per share. In May, the company distributed a 10% stock dividend at a time when DigiTech's common stock had a market value of $3 per share. Then in October, DigiTech's stock price dropped to $1 per share and the company purchased 2 million shares of treasury stock. For the year, DigiTech earned net income of $26 million and declared cash dividends of $5 million.

Complete the following tabulation to show what DigiTech should report for stockholders' equity at December 31, 20X6. Journal entries are not required.

Accounting for changes in stockholders' equity
(Obj. 2, 3, 4)

spreadsheet

(Amounts in millions)	Common Stock	Additional Paid-In Capital	Retained Earnings	Treasury Stock	Total
Balance, Dec. 31, 20X5	$8	$13	$40		$61
Issuance of stock					
Stock dividend					
Purchase of treasury stock				$	
Net income					
Cash dividends					
Balance, Dec. 31, 20X6	$	$	$	$	$

Problems

(Group A)

Explaining the features of a corporation's stock
(Obj. 1, 2, 5)

P9-1A Grabow & Eisenbarth, an engineering firm, is conducting a special meeting of its board of directors to address some concerns raised by its stockholders. Stockholders have submitted the following questions. Answer each question.

1. Why are capital stock and retained earnings shown separately in the shareholders' equity section of the balance sheet?
2. Ann Martinelli, a shareholder of Grabow & Eisenbarth, proposes to give some land she owns to the company in exchange for shares of the company stock. How should Grabow & Eisenbarth determine the number of shares of our stock to issue for the land?
3. Preferred shares generally are preferred with respect to dividends and in the event of our liquidation. Why would investors buy our common stock when preferred stock is available?
4. What does the redemption value of our preferred stock require us to do?
5. One of our stockholders owns 100 shares of Grabow & Eisenbarth stock and someone has offered to buy his shares for their book value. Our stockholder asks us the formula for computing the book value of *his* stock.

Recording corporate transactions and preparing the stockholders' equity section of the balance sheet
(Obj. 2)

general ledger

P9-2A The partners who own Bhanapol & Cink (B&C) wished to avoid the unlimited personal liability of the partnership form of business, so they incorporated as B&C Exploration, Inc. The charter from the state of Wyoming authorizes the corporation to issue 10,000 shares of 6%, $100 par preferred stock and 250,000 shares of no-par common stock with a stated value of $5 per share. In its first month. B&C Exploration completed the following transactions:

Dec. 3	Issued 500 shares of common stock to the promoter for assistance with issuance of the common stock. The promotional fee was $5,000. Debit the asset account Organization Cost.
3	Issued 5,100 shares of common stock to Bhanapol and 3,800 shares to Cink in return for cash equal to the stock's market value of $10 per share.
12	Issued 1,000 shares of preferred stock to acquire a patent with a market value of $110,000.
22	Issued 1,500 shares of common stock for $10 cash per share.

Required

1. Record the transactions in the journal.
2. Prepare the stockholders' equity section of the B&C Exploration, Inc., balance sheet at December 31. The ending balance of Retained Earnings is $89,000.

Preparing the stockholders' equity section of the balance sheet
(Obj. 2, 4)

P9-3A Srixon Inc. has the following stockholders' equity information:

Srixon's charter authorizes the company to issue 10,000 shares of $2.50 preferred stock with par value of $100 and 120,000 shares of no-par common stock. The company issued 1,000 shares of the preferred stock at $104 per share. It issued 40,000 shares of the common stock for a total of $220,000. The company's retained earnings balance at the beginning of 20X3 was $40,000, and net income for the year was $90,000. During 20X3, Srixon declared the specified dividend on preferred and a $0.50 per-share dividend on common. Preferred dividends for 20X2 were in arrears.

Required

Prepare the stockholders' equity section of Srixon Inc.'s balance sheet at December 31, 20X3. Show the computation of all amounts. Journal entries are not required.

Purchasing treasury stock to fight off a takeover of the corporation
(Obj. 3)

P9-4A Yuma Corporation is positioned ideally in its line of business. Located in Nogales, Arizona, Yuma is the only company between Texas and California with reliable sources for its imported gifts. The company does a brisk business with specialty stores such as **Pier 1 Imports.** Yuma's recent success has made the company a prime target for a takeover. An investment group from Mexico City is attempting to buy 51% of Yuma's outstanding stock against the wishes of Yuma's board of directors. Board members are convinced that the Mexico City investors would sell the most desirable pieces of the business and leave little of value.

At the most recent board meeting, several suggestions were advanced to fight off the hostile takeover bid. The suggestion with the most promise is to purchase a huge quantity of treasury stock. Yuma has the cash to carry out this plan.

Required

1. Suppose you are a significant stockholder of Yuma Corporation. Write a memorandum to explain to the board how the purchase of treasury stock would make it more difficult for the Mexico City group to take over Yuma. Include in your memo a discussion of the effect that purchasing treasury stock would have on stock outstanding and on the size of the corporation.
2. Suppose Yuma management is successful in fighting off the takeover bid and later sells the treasury stock at prices greater than the purchase price. Explain what effect these sales will have on assets, stockholders' equity, and net income.

Measuring the effects of stock issuance, treasury stock, and dividend transactions on stockholders' equity
(Obj. 2, 3, 4)

P9-5A The corporate charter of Hebrides Woolens, Inc., granted by the state of Delaware, authorizes the company to issue 1,000,000 shares of $1 par common stock and 100,000 shares of $50 par preferred stock.

In its initial public offering during 20X2, Hebrides issued 200,000 shares of its $1 par common stock for $6.50 per share. Over the next 5 years, Hebrides' common stock price increased in value, and the company issued 100,000 more shares at prices ranging from $7 to $11. The average issue price of these shares was $9.25.

During 20X4, the price of Hebrides' common stock dropped to $8, and Hebrides purchased 30,000 shares of its common stock for the treasury. After the market price of the common stock increased in 20X5, Hebrides sold 20,000 shares of the treasury stock for $9 per share.

During the 5 years 20X2 to 20X6, Hebrides' earned net income of $295,000 and declared and paid cash dividends of $119,000. Stock dividends of $110,000 were distributed to the stockholders in 20X3, with $14,000 transferred to common stock and $96,000 transferred to additional paid-in capital. At December 31, 20X6, total assets of the company are $5,365,000, and liabilities add up to $3,024,000.

Required

Show the computation of Hebrides Woolens' total stockholders' equity at December 31, 20X6. Present detailed computations of each element of stockholders' equity.

Analyzing the stockholders' equity and dividends of a corporation
(Obj. 2, 4)

P9-6A U and I Group, which makes food products and livestock feeds, included the following stockholders' equity on its year-end balance sheet at February 28:

Stockholders' Equity	(In thousands)
Voting Preferred stock, 5.5% cumulative—par value $23 per share; authorized 100,000 shares in each class:	
Class A—issued 75,473 shares	$ 1,736
Class B—issued 92,172 shares	2,120
Common stock—par value $5 per share; authorized 5,000,000 shares; issued 2,870,950 shares	14,355
[Additional] Paid-in capital	5,548
Retained earnings	8,336
	$32,095

Required

1. Identify the different issues of stock U and I has outstanding.
2. Give the summary entries to record issuance of all the U and I stock. Assume that all the stock was issued for cash and that the additional paid-in capital applies to the common stock. Explanations are not required.
3. Suppose U and I passed its preferred dividends for 3 years. Would the company have to pay those dividends in arrears before paying dividends to the common stockholders? Give your reason.
4. What amount of preferred dividends must U and I declare and pay each year to avoid having preferred dividends in arrears?
5. Assume that preferred dividends are in arrears for 20X4. Record the declaration of an $800,000 dividend in the year ended February 28, 20X5. An explanation is not required.

Accounting for stock issuance, dividends, and treasury stock
(Obj. 2, 3, 4)

P9-7A Yankee Internet Corporation reported the following summarized balance sheet at December 31, 20X2:

Assets	
Current assets	$18,200
Property and equipment, net	34,700
Total assets	$52,900
Liabilities and Equity	
Liabilities	$ 6,200
Stockholders' equity:	
$5 cumulative preferred stock, $100 par	1,800
Common stock, $1 par	2,400
Paid-in capital in excess of par, common	23,500
Retained earnings	19,000
Total liabilities and equity	$52,900

During 20X3, Yankee completed these transactions that affected stockholders' equity:

Jan. 22	Issued 1,000 shares of common stock for $14 per share.
Aug. 4	Declared the regular cash dividend on the preferred stock.
24	Paid the cash dividend.

Oct. 9	Distributed a 10% stock dividend on the common stock. Market price of the common stock, was $15 per share.
Nov. 19	Reacquired 800 shares of common stock as treasury stock, paying $12 per share.
Dec. 8	Sold 600 shares of the treasury stock for $15 per share.

Required

1. Journalize Yankee's transactions. Explanations are not required.
2. Report Yankee's stockholders' equity at December 31, 20X3. Net income for 20X3 was $39,000.

Measuring the effects of dividend and treasury stock transactions on a company **(Obj. 3, 4)**

general ledger

P9-8A Assume **Steak & Shake, Inc.** completed the following transactions during 20X6:

Jan. 18	Purchased 2,000 shares of the company's own common stock at $12 per share.
Mar. 22	Sold 700 shares of treasury common stock for $16 per share.
July 6	Declared a cash dividend on the 10,000 shares of $1.70 no-par preferred stock.
Aug. 1	Paid the cash dividends.
Nov. 18	Distributed a 10% stock dividend on the 30,000 shares of $1 par common stock outstanding. The market value of the common stock was $15 per share.

Required

Analyze each transaction in terms of its effect on the accounting equation of Steak & Shake, Inc.

Preparing a corporation's balance sheet; measuring profitability **(Obj. 3, 6)**

spreadsheet

P9-9A The following accounts and related balances of Air Control Specialists, Inc., as of September 30, 20X5, are arranged in no particular order.

Interest expense	$ 6,100	Cash	$13,000
Property, plant, and equipment, net	357,000	Accounts receivable, net	24,000
Common stock, $1 par, 500,000 shares authorized, 115,000 shares issued	115,000	Paid-in capital in excess of par—common	19,000
Prepaid expenses	10,000	Accrued liabilities	26,000
Common stockholders' equity, September 30, 20X4	192,000	Long-term note payable	72,000
Net income	31,000	Inventory	59,000
Total assets, September 30, 20X4	404,000	Dividends payable	9,000
Treasury stock, common 18,000 shares at cost	22,000	Retained earnings	?
Goodwill, net	14,000	Accounts payable	31,000
		Trademark, net	9,000
		Preferred stock, $0.20, no-par, 10,000 shares authorized and issued	27,000

Required

1. Prepare the company's classified balance sheet in the account format at September 30, 20X5.

2. Compute rate of return on total assets and rate of return on common stockholders' equity for the year ended September 30, 20X5.
3. Do these rates of return suggest strength or weakness? Give your reason.

Analyzing the statement of cash flows
(Obj. 7)

P9-10A The statement of cash flows of **PepsiCo, Inc.** reported the following (adapted) for the year ended December 31, 20X1:

Cash flows from financing activities—*amounts in millions*	
Cash dividends paid	$ (994)
Issuance of common stock	623
Proceeds from issuance of long-term debt	324
Purchases of treasury stock	(1,731)
Payments of long-term debt	(573)
Reissuance of treasury stock (cost, $374)	524

Required

1. Make the journal entry that PepsiCo used to record each of these transactions.
2. From these transactions, would you expect PepsiCo's total liabilities, total stockholders' equity, and total assets to have grown or shrunk during 20X1? PepsiCo's net income for 20X1 was $2,662 million. Show your work.

(Group B)

Explaining the features of a corporation's stock
(Obj. 1, 3, 4)

P9-1B The board of directors of Akin & Gump, Inc., investment bankers, is meeting to address the concerns of stockholders. Stockholders have submitted the following questions for discussion at the board meeting. Answer each question.

1. Why did Akin & Gump organize as a corporation if a corporation must pay an additional layer of income tax?
2. How is preferred stock similar to common stock? How is preferred stock similar to debt?
3. Akin & Gump purchased treasury stock for $50,000 and a year later sold it for $65,000. Explain to the stockholders why the $15,000 excess is not profit to be reported on the company's income statement.
4. Would our investors prefer to receive cash dividends or stock dividends? Explain your reasoning.

Recording corporate transactions and preparing the stockholders' equity section of the balance sheet
(Obj. 2)

general ledger

P9-2B The partnership of Grant and Hoffman needed additional capital to expand into new markets, so the business incorporated as GH, Inc. The charter from the state of Illinois authorizes GH, Inc. to issue 10,000 shares of 6%, $100 par preferred stock and 100,000 shares of no-par common stock with a stated value of $5 per share. In its first month, GH, Inc. completed the following transactions:

Feb. 2	Issued 300 shares of common stock to the promoter for assistance with issuance of the common stock. The promotional fee was $1,800. Debit the asset account Organization Cost.
2	Issued 9,000 shares of common stock to Grant and 12,000 shares to Hoffman in return for cash equal to the stock's market value of $6 per share.
10	Issued 400 shares of preferred stock to acquire a patent with a market value of $40,000.
16	Issued 2,000 shares of common stock for cash of $12,000.

Required

1. Record the transactions in the journal.
2. Prepare the stockholders' equity section of the GH, Inc. balance sheet at February 28. The ending balance of Retained Earnings is $119,000.

P9-3B The following summary provides the information needed to prepare the stockholders' equity section of the Eli Jackson Company balance sheet:

Preparing the stockholders' equity section of the balance sheet
(Obj. 2, 4)

> *Jackson's charter authorizes the company to issue 5,000 shares of 5%, $100 par preferred stock and 500,000 shares of no-par common stock. Jackson issued 1,000 shares of the preferred stock at $105 per share. It issued 100,000 shares of the common stock for $519,000. The company's retained earnings balance at the beginning of 20X4 was $61,000. Net income for 20X4 was $80,000, and the company declared a 5% cash dividend on preferred stock for 20X4. Preferred dividends for 20X3 were in arrears.*

Required

Prepare the stockholders' equity section of Eli Jackson Company's balance sheet at December 31, 20X4. Show the computation of all amounts. Journal entries are not required.

P9-4B Guilford Distributing Company is positioned ideally in the clothing business. Located in Concord, New Hampshire, Guilford is the only company with a distribution network for its imported goods. The company does a brisk business with specialty stores such as **Bloomingdale's, I. Magnin,** and **Bonwit Teller.** Guilford's recent success has made the company a prime target for a takeover. Against the wishes of Guilford's board of directors, an investment group from Cincinnati is attempting to buy 51% of Guilford's outstanding stock. Board members are convinced that the Cincinnati investors would sell off the most desirable pieces of the business and leave little of value. At the most recent board meeting, several suggestions were advanced to fight off the hostile takeover bid.

Fighting off a takeover of the corporation
(Obj. 3)

Required

Suppose you are a significant stockholder of Guilford Distributing Company. Write a short memo to the board to propose an action that would make it difficult for the investor group to take over Guilford. Include, in your memo a discussion of the effect your proposed action would have on the company's assets, liabilities, and total stockholders' equity.

P9-5B The corporate charter of House of Carpets, granted by the state of Georgia, authorizes the company to issue 5,000,000 shares of $1 par common stock and 50,000 shares of $50 par preferred stock.

Measuring the effects of stock issuance, treasury stock, and dividend transactions on stockholders' equity
(Obj. 2, 3, 4)

In its initial public offering during 20X4, House of Carpets issued 500,000 shares of its $1 par common stock for $5.00 per share. Over the next 5 years, House of Carpets' stock price increased in value and the company issued 400,000 more shares at prices ranging from $6 to $10.75. The average issue price of these shares was $8.50.

During 20X6, the price of House of Carpets' common stock dropped to $7, and the company purchased 60,000 shares of its common stock for the treasury. After the market price of the common stock rose in 20X7, House of Carpets sold 40,000 shares of the treasury stock for $8 per share.

During the 5 years 20X4 to 20X8, House of Carpets earned net income of $1,020,000 and declared and paid cash dividends of $640,000. Stock dividends of $220,000 were distributed to the stockholders in 20X7, with $35,000 transferred to common stock and $185,000 transferred to additional paid-in capital. At December 31, 20X8, the company has total assets of $13,100,000 and total liabilities of $6,920,000.

Required

Show the computation of House of Carpets' total stockholders' equity at December 31, 20X8. Present detailed computations of each element of stockholders' equity.

Analyzing the stockholders' equity and dividends of a corporation
(Obj. 2, 4)

P9-6B Bethlehem Steel Corporation is the nation's largest steel company. Bethlehem included the following stockholders' equity on its balance sheet:

Stockholders' Equity	($ Millions)
Preferred stock—	
Authorized 20,000,000 shares in each class; issued:	
$5.00 Cumulative Convertible Preferred Stock,	
at $50.00 stated value, 2,500,000 shares	$ 125
$2.50 Cumulative Convertible Preferred Stock,	
at $25.00 stated value, 4,000,000 shares	100
Common stock—$8 par value—	
Authorized 80,000,000 shares, issued 48,308,516 shares	621
Retained earnings	529
	$1,375

Observe that Bethlehem reports no Paid-in Capital in Excess of Par or Stated Value. Instead, the company reports those items in the stock accounts.

Required

1. Identify the different issues of stock Bethlehem has outstanding.
2. Which class of stock did Bethlehem issue at par or stated value, and which class did it issue above par or stated value?
3. Suppose Bethlehem passed its preferred dividends for 1 year. Would the company have to pay these dividends in arrears before paying dividends to the common stockholders? Why?
4. What amount of preferred dividends must Bethlehem declare and pay each year to avoid having preferred dividends in arrears?
5. Assume preferred dividends are in arrears for 20X2. Journalize the declaration of a $61 million dividend for 20X3. No explanation is needed.

Accounting for stock issuance, dividends, and treasury stock
(Obj. 2, 3, 4)

P9-7B Dixie Network Corporation reported the following summarized balance sheet at December 31, 20X3:

Assets	
Current assets	$33,400
Property and equipment, net	51,800
Total assets	$85,200
Liabilities and Equity	
Liabilities	$37,800
Stockholders' equity	
$0.50 cumulative preferred stock, $5 par	2,000
Common stock, $1 par	6,000
Paid-in capital in excess of par, common	17,400
Retained earnings	22,000
Total liabilities and equity	$85,200

During 20X4, Dixie Network Corporation completed these transactions that affected stockholders' equity:

Mar. 13	Issued 2,000 shares of common stock for $4 per share.
July 7	Declared the regular cash dividend on the preferred stock.
24	Paid the cash dividend.
Sept. 9	Distributed a 10% stock dividend on the common stock. Market price of the common stock was $5 per share.

(continued)

Oct. 26	Reacquired 500 shares of common stock as treasury stock, paying $7 per share.
Nov. 20	Sold 200 shares of the treasury stock for $8 per share.

Required

1. Journalize Dixie Network's transactions. Explanations are not required.
2. Report Dixie Network's stockholders' equity at December 31, 20X4. Net income for 20X4 was $27,000.

Measuring the effects of dividend and treasury stock transactions on a company **(Obj. 3, 4)**

general ledger

P9-8B Assume that IHOP Corporation completed the following selected transactions during the current year:

April 18	Distributed a 10% stock dividend on the 9.7 million shares of common stock outstanding. The market value of the common stock was $25 per share.
May 23	Declared a cash dividend on the 5%, $100 par preferred stock (1,000 shares outstanding).
July 30	Paid the cash dividends.
Oct. 26	Purchased 2,500 shares of the company's own common stock at $24 per share.
Nov. 8	Sold 1,000 shares of treasury common stock for $27 per share.

Required

Analyze each transaction in terms of its effect on the accounting equation of IHOP.

Preparing a corporation's balance sheet; measuring profitability **(Obj. 3, 6)**

Integrator CD

spreadsheet

P9-9B The following accounts and related balances of InterMax Graphics, Inc., are arranged in no particular order.

Accounts payable	$ 31,000	Dividends payable	$ 3,000
Retained earnings	?	Total assets, November 30, 20X2	481,000
Common stock, $5 par; 100,000 shares authorized, 42,000 shares issued	210,000	Net income	36,200
Inventory	170,000	Common stockholders' equity November 30, 20X2	383,000
Property, plant, and equipment, net	181,000	Interest expense	12,800
Goodwill, net	6,000	Treasury stock, common 1,600 shares at cost	11,000
Preferred stock, 4%, $10 par, 25,000 shares authorized, 3,700 shares issued	37,000	Prepaid expenses	13,000
		Patent, net	31,000
		Accrued liabilities	17,000
Cash	32,000	Long-term note payable	7,000
Additional paid-in-capital— common	140,000	Accounts receivable, net	102,000

Required

1. Prepare InterMax's classified balance sheet in the account format at November 30, 20X3.
2. Compute rate of return on total assets and rate of return on common stockholders' equity for the year ended November 30, 20X3.
3. Do these rates of return suggest strength or weakness? Give your reason.

Analyzing the statement of cash flows
(Obj. 7)

P9-10B Assume the statement of cash flows of **Reebok International Ltd.** reported the following for the year ended December 31, 20X0:

Cash flows from financing activities—*amounts in millions*	
Dividends [declared and] paid	$ (28.3)
Proceeds from issuance of common stock	14.1
Payments of short-term notes payable	(36.9)
Repayments of long-term debt	(1.3)
Proceeds from long-term debt	632.1
Repurchases of common stock	(686.3)

Required

1. Make the journal entry that Reebok used to record each of these transactions.
2. From these transactions, would you expect Reebok's total liabilities, total stockholders' equity, and total assets to have grown or shrunk during 20X0? Reebok's net income for 20X0 was $135 million. Show your work.

Apply Your Knowledge

Decision Cases

Evaluating the financial position and profitability of a real company
(Obj. 2, 3, 4, 5)

Case 1. At December 31, 2000, **Enron Corporation** reported the following data (condensed, in millions):

Stockholders' equity	$11,470	Total current liabilities	$ 28,406
Long-term liabilities	25,627	Investments and other assets	23,379
Property, plant, equipment, net	11,743	Total current assets	30,381
Total expenses for 2000	99,810	Total revenues for 2000	100,789

During 2001, Enron restated company financial statements for 1997 to 2000, after reporting that some data had been omitted from those prior-year statements. Assume that the startling events of 2001 included the following:

- Several related companies should have been, but were not, included in the Enron statements for 2000. These companies had revenues of $90 million, total assets of $5,700 million, expenses of $220 million, and liabilities totaling $5,600 million.
- In January 2001, Enron's stockholders got the company to exchange $2,000 million of 12% long-term notes payable for their common stock. Interest is accrued at year end.

Take the role of an analyst with **Moody's Investor Services.** It is your job to analyze Enron Corporation and rate the company's long-term debt.

Required

1. Measure Enron's expected net income for 2001 two ways:
   a. Assume 2001's net income should be approximately the same as the amount of net income that Enron actually reported for 2000.
   b. Recompute expected net income for 2001 taking into account all the new developments of 2001.
   c. Evaluate Enron's likely trend of net income for the future. Discuss *why* this trend is developing. Ignore income tax.

2. Write Enron's accounting equation two ways:
   a. As actually reported at December 31, 2000.
   b. As adjusted for the events of 2001.
3. Measure Enron's debt ratio as reported at December 31, 2000, and after making the adjustments for the events of 2001.
4. Based on your analysis, make a recommendation to the Debt-Rating Committee of Moody's Investor Services. Would you recommend upgrading, downgrading, or leaving Enron's debt rating undisturbed (currently, it is "high-grade").

Evaluating alternative ways of raising capital
(Obj. 2)

Case 2. Jerry Weygandt and Belverd Needles have written a computer program for a video game that they believe will rival Playstation 2 and XBox. They need additional capital to market the product, and they plan to incorporate their partnership. They are considering alternative capital structures for the corporation. Their primary goal is to raise as much capital as possible without giving up control of the business. The partners plan to receive 110,000 shares of the corporation's common stock in return for the net assets of the partnership. After the partnership books are closed and the assets adjusted to current market value, Weygandt's capital balance will be $60,000, and Needles' balance will be $50,000.

The corporation's plans for a charter include an authorization to issue 5,000 shares of preferred stock and 500,000 shares of $1 par common stock. Weygandt and Needles are uncertain about the most desirable features for the preferred stock. Prior to incorporating, the partners are discussing their plans with two investment groups. The corporation can obtain capital from outside investors under either of the following plans:

- Plan 1. Group 1 will invest $160,000 to acquire 1,400 shares of 6%, $100 par nonvoting, noncumulative preferred stock.
- Plan 2. Group 2 will invest $105,000 to acquire 1,000 shares of $5, no-par preferred stock and $70,000 to acquire 70,000 shares of common stock. Each preferred share receives 50 votes on matters that come before the stockholders.

Required

Assume that the corporation is chartered.

1. Journalize the issuance of common stock to Weygandt and Needles. Debit each partner's capital account for its balance.
2. Journalize the issuance of stock to the outsiders under both plans.
3. Assume that net income for the first year is $120,000 and total dividends are $19,000. Prepare the stockholders' equity section of the corporation's balance sheet under both plans.
4. Recommend one of the plans to Weygandt and Needles. Give your reasons.

Analyzing cash dividends and stock dividends
(Obj. 4)

Case 3. United Parcel Service (UPS), Inc. had the following stockholders' equity amounts on December 31, 2000 (adapted, in millions):

Common stock and additional paid-in capital; 1,135 shares issued	$ 278
Retained earnings	9,457
Total stockholders' equity	$9,735

During 2000, UPS paid a cash dividend of $0.68 per share. Assume that, after paying the cash dividends, UPS distributed a 10% stock dividend. Assume further that the following year UPS declared and paid a cash dividend of $0.62 per share.

Suppose you own 10,000 shares of UPS common stock, acquired 3 years ago, prior to the 10% stock dividend. The market price of UPS stock was $61.02 per share before the stock dividend.

Required

1. How does the stock dividend affect your proportionate ownership in UPS? Explain.
2. What amount of cash dividends did you receive last year? What amount of cash dividends will you receive after the above dividend action?
3. Assume that immediately after the stock dividend was distributed, the market value of UPS stock decreased from $61.02 per share to $55.47 per share. Does this decrease represent a loss to you? Explain.
4. Suppose UPS announces at the time of the stock dividend that the company will continue to pay the annual $0.68 *cash* dividend per share, even after distributing the *stock* dividend. Would you expect the market price of the stock to decrease to $55.47 per share as in Requirement 3? Explain.

Ethical Issues

Ethical Issue 1. *Note: This case is based on a real situation*

George Campbell paid $50,000 for a franchise that entitled him to market Success Associates software programs in the countries of the European Union. Campbell intended to sell individual franchises for the major language groups of western Europe—German, French, English, Spanish, and Italian. Naturally, investors considering buying a franchise from Campbell asked to see the financial statements of his business.

Believing the value of the franchise to be greater than $50,000, Campbell sought to capitalize his own franchise at $500,000. The law firm of McDonald & LaDue helped Campbell form a corporation chartered to issue 500,000 shares of common stock with par value of $1 per share. Attorneys suggested the following chain of transactions:

a. A third party borrows $500,000 and purchases the franchise from Campbell.
b. Campbell pays the corporation $500,000 to acquire all its stock.
c. The corporation buys the franchise from the third party, who repays the loan.

In the final analysis, the third party is debt-free and out of the picture. Campbell owns all the corporation's stock, and the corporation owns the franchise. The corporation balance sheet lists a franchise acquired at a cost of $500,000. This balance sheet is Campbell's most valuable marketing tool.

Required

1. What is unethical about this situation?
2. Who can be harmed? How can they be harmed? What role does accounting play here?

Ethical Issue 2. St. Genevieve Petroleum Company is an independent oil producer in Baton Parish, Louisiana. In February, company geologists discovered a pool of oil that tripled the company's proven reserves. Prior to disclosing the new oil to the public, St. Genevieve quietly bought most of its stock as treasury stock. After the discovery was announced, the company's stock price increased from $6 to $27.

Required

1. Did St. Genevieve managers behave ethically? Explain your answer.
2. Identify the accounting principle relevant to this situation.
3. Who was helped and who was harmed by management's action?

Financial Statement Case

Analyzing common stock, additional paid-in capital, and retained earnings
(Obj. 2, 6)

Fossil's financial statements appear in Appendix A at the end of this book.

1. During the year ended January 5, 2002 (fiscal year 2001), Fossil issued some common stock and bought back some of its own stock for retirement. Fossil's statement of stockholders' equity provides the data needed to analyze these transactions. Journalize the

a. Issuance of common stock upon exercise of stock options (Fossil received cash).
b. Issuance of common stock in connection with acquisitions of other companies (assume Fossil acquired buildings and store fixtures).
c. Repurchases and retirement of common stock.

2. Prove that only one item affected Fossil's retained earnings during fiscal year 2001. Identify the item and its amount.
3. How much had Fossil stockholders paid into the company through January 5, 2002 (the end of fiscal year 2001), net of amounts paid back to retire company stock?
4. Compute Fossil's return on equity and return on assets for 2001. Which is larger? Is this a sign of financial strength or weakness? Explain.

Analytical Case

Analyzing treasury stock and retained earnings
(Obj. 2, 3, 4)

This case is based on the financial statements of **Pier 1 Imports**, given in Appendix B at the end of this book. In particular, this case uses Pier 1's statement of shareholders' equity for the year ended March 2, 2002.

1. During the year ended March 2, 2002, Pier 1 purchased treasury stock and also sold treasury stock under the company's stock option plan and stock purchase plan. Was Pier 1's average price per share higher for the treasury stock purchased or for the treasury stock sold? What was the difference in price per share between the two transactions?
2. Journalize the purchase of treasury stock and the sale of treasury stock during the year ended March 2, 2002. Also journalize the restricted stock amortization transaction (it was for executive compensation expense).
3. Prepare a T-account to show the beginning and ending balances, plus all the activity in Retained Earnings for the year ended March 2, 2002.

Group Project

Competitive pressures are the norm in business. **Lexus** automobiles (made in Japan) have cut into the sales of **Mercedes-Benz** (a German company), **Jaguar Motors** (a British company), **General Motors' Cadillac Division**, and **Ford's Lincoln Division** (both U.S. companies). **Dell**, **Gateway**, and **Compaq** computers have siphoned business away from **Apple** and **IBM**. Foreign steelmakers have reduced the once-massive U.S. steel industry to a fraction of its former size.

Indeed, corporate downsizing has occurred on a massive scale. Each company or industry mentioned here has pared down plant and equipment, laid off employees, or restructured operations.

Required

1. Identify all the stakeholders of a corporation. A *stakeholder* is a person or a group who has an interest (that is, a stake) in the success of the organization.
2. Identify several measures by which a company may be considered deficient and in need of downsizing. How can downsizing help to solve this problem?
3. Debate the downsizing issue. One group of students takes the perspective of the company and its stockholders, and another group of students takes the perspective of other stakeholders of the company.

10

Long-Term Investments & International Operations

Learning Objectives

1. **Account** for available-for-sale investments
2. **Use** the equity method for investments
3. **Understand** consolidated financial statements
4. **Account** for long-term investments in bonds
5. **Account** for international operations
6. **Report** investing transactions on the statement of cash flows

Need additional help? Go to the **Integrator CD** *and search these key words:* available-for-sale investments, bond investments, cash flows, consolidation, equity method, foreign currency, minority interest, trading investments

Integrator CD

General Electric Company and Consolidated Subsidiaries (Adapted)

Statement of Financial Position

At December 31 (in billions)	2001	2000
Assets		
Cash and equivalents	$ 9	$ 8
Investment securities	101	91
Inventories	9	8
Financing, insurance, and other receivables	222	189
Property, plant, and equipment, net	42	40
Goodwill and other intangibles	32	27
Other assets	80	74
Total assets	$495	$437
Liabilities		
Total liabilities	$435	$382
Minority interest in consolidated entities	5	5
Equity		
Common stock and other capital	17	16
Retained earnings	69	62
Accumulated gains (losses):		
Unrealized gains (losses) on investments	(1)	—
Currency translation adjustments	(3)	(3)
Hedges	(1)	—
Less Treasury stock	(26)	(25)
Total liabilities and equity	$495	$437

Year in and year out, General Electric Company (GE) manages an incredible portfolio of businesses—ranging from aircraft engines to household refrigerators to the NBC television network. GE also finances golf resorts, Wal-Mart and Home Depot credit cards, and home mortgages. When you take out a home loan from your bank, you may wind up making the monthly mortgage payments to a GE company because GE Capital buys up mortgage loans and services the accounts.

GE has been called the best company in the world. Why? Because GE is an employee-friendly place to work, and because the company consistently churns out exceptional rates of return on equity. GE has mastered the art of change management like no other worldwide conglomerate. Whatever shift appears on the horizon, GE stays ahead of the curve. GE's experiences illustrate virtually every topic covered in this chapter on accounting for investments and international operations.

How does GE succeed so consistently? For one thing, GE gives operating managers lots of responsibility—and then holds them accountable for performance. The company's philosophy was molded in large part by former chief executive officer (CEO) Jack Welch, who groomed others to take over the company. In their words, Jack Welch is ". . . first and foremost, a teacher." Time will tell if Welch's students learned their lessons.

Sitemap

Throughout this course, you have become increasingly familiar with the financial statements of companies such as GE, Fossil, and IHOP. You have seen most of the items that appear in a set of financial statements. One of your learning goals for this course should be to develop the ability to interpret virtually everything you will encounter in real-company statements. Only a few items remain. This chapter, which discusses long-term investments and international operations, continues your education in how to use financial statements.

available-for-sale investments, trading investments

Stock Investments: A Review

Investments come in all sizes and shapes—from a few shares of stock to the acquisition of an entire company. In earlier chapters, we discussed stocks and bonds from the perspective of the company that issued the securities. In Chapter 5, we covered *short-term* investments. In this chapter, we examine *long-term* investments. First, however, let's review how investment transactions take place.

Stock Prices, Investors, and Investees

Investors buy more stock in transactions among themselves than from large companies such as GE. Each share of stock is issued only once, but it may be traded among investors many times thereafter. You may log onto the Internet or consult a newspaper to learn GE's current stock price.

Exhibit 10-1 presents information on GE common stock. During the previous 52 weeks, GE common stock reached a high price of $53.55 and a low price of $28.50 per share. The annual cash dividend is $0.72 per share. During the previous day, 19,596,000 (195,960 × 100) shares of GE common stock were traded. At day's end the price of the stock closed at $33.70 down $0.10 from the closing price of the preceding day's.

Exhibit 10-1

Stock Price Information for General Electric Company

52-Week				Volume		Net
Hi	*Lo*	*Stock (sym)*	*Div*	*100s*	*Close*	*Change*
$53.55	$28.50	Gen Elec **GE**	$0.72	195,960	$33.70	–$0.10

To move further into investments, we need to define two key terms. The entity that owns stock in a corporation is the *investor*. The corporation that issued the stock is the *investee*. If you own shares of GE common stock, you are an investor and GE is the investee.

Reporting Short- and Long-Term Investments

Short-term investment
Investment that a company plans to hold for one year or less. Also called *marketable securities.*

An investment in stock is an asset to the investor. The investment may be short-term or long-term. **Short-term investments**—sometimes called **marketable securities**—are current assets. To be listed on the balance sheet as short-term, the investment must be *liquid* (readily convertible to cash). Also, the investor must intend either to convert the investment to cash within 1 year or to use it to pay a current liability. We saw how to account for short-term investments in Chapter 5.

Investments not meeting both requirements of short-term investments are classified as **long-term investments,** a category of noncurrent assets. Long-term investments include stocks and bonds that the investor expects to hold for longer than 1 year. Exhibit 10-2 shows the positions of short-term and long-term investments on the balance sheet. In this chapter, we focus on long-term investments.

Long-term investment
Any investment that does not meet the criteria of a short-term investment; any investment that the investor expects to hold longer than a year or that is not readily marketable.

Exhibit 10-2

Reporting Investments on the Balance Sheet

Current Assets:		
Cash	$X	
Short-term investments	X	
Accounts receivable	X	
Inventories	X	
Prepaid expenses	X	
Total current assets		$X
Long-term investments [or simply Investments]		X
Property, plant, and equipment		X
Intangible assets		X
Other assets		X

We report assets in the order of liquidity. Long-Term Investments are less liquid than Current Assets but more liquid than Property, Plant, and Equipment. GE reports investment securities immediately after cash.

Trading and Available-for-Sale Investments

We begin our discussion of stock investments with those situations in which the investor holds less than a 20% interest in the investee company. These investments are classified as either trading investments or available-for-sale investments.

Trading investments are expected to be sold in the very near future—days, weeks, or only a few months—with the intent of generating a profit on the sale. Trading investments are therefore classified as *current assets.*

Trading investments
Stock investments that are to be sold in the near future with the intent of generating profits on the sale.

Available-for-Sale Investments

available-for-sale investments

Objective

1 Account for available-for-sale investments

Available-for-Sale Investments are stock investments other than trading securities. They are classified as current assets if the business expects to sell them within the next year. All other available-for-sale investments are classified as long term (Exhibit 10-2).

Accounting for Available-for-Sale Investments

Available-for-sale investments
All investments not classified as held-to-maturity or trading securities.

The market value method is used to account for available-for-sale investments in stock because the company expects to resell the stock at its market value. Under the **market value method,** *cost* is used only as the initial amount for recording the investments. These investments are reported on the balance sheet at their *current market value.*

Market value method of accounting (for investments)
Used to account for all available-for-sale securities. These investments are reported at their current market value.

Suppose GE purchases 1,000 shares of Hewlett-Packard common stock at the market price of $35.75. GE intends to hold this investment for longer than a year and therefore classifies it as an available-for-sale investment. GE's entry to record the investment is:

20X4			
Feb. 23	Long-Term Investment (1,000 × $35.75)	35,750	
	Cash		35,750
	Purchased investment.		

ASSETS	=	LIABILITIES	+	STOCKHOLDERS' EQUITY
+35,750 −35,750	=	0	+	0

Assume that GE receives a $0.22 per share cash dividend on the Hewlett-Packard stock. GE's entry to record receipt of the dividend is

20X4			
July 14	Cash (1,000 × $0.22)	220	
	Dividend Revenue		220
	Received cash dividend.		

ASSETS	=	LIABILITIES	+	STOCKHOLDERS EQUITY	+	REVENUES
220	=	0	+		+	220

→ For a review of stock dividends, see Chapter 9, page 432.

Receipt of a *stock* dividend is different from receipt of a cash dividend ←. For a stock dividend, the investor records no dividend revenue. Instead, the investor makes a memorandum entry in the accounting records to denote the new number of shares of stock held as an investment. Because the number of shares of stock held has increased, the investor's cost per share of the stock decreases. For example, suppose GE receives a 5% stock dividend from Hewlett-Packard Company. GE would receive 50 shares (5% of 1,000 shares previously held) and make this memorandum entry in its accounting records:

MEMORANDUM—Receipt of stock dividend: Received 50 shares of Hewlett-Packard common stock in 5% stock dividend. New cost per share is $34.05 (cost of $35,750 ÷ 1,050 shares).

In all of GE's future transactions that affect the Hewlett-Packard investment, GE will use the new cost per share of $34.05.

DECISION: What Value of an Investment Is Most Relevant?

Market value is the amount that one can buy or sell an investment for. Market value thus governs the amount of cash to be received or paid for an investment. Because of the relevance of market values for decision making, available-for-sale investments in stock are reported on the balance sheet at their market value. This reporting requires an adjustment of the investments from their last carrying amount to current market value. Assume that the market value of GE's investment in Hewlett-Packard common stock is $36,400 on December 31, 20X4. In this case, GE makes the following entry to bring the investment to market value.

20X4			
Dec. 31	Allowance to Adjust Investment to Market ($36,400 − $35,750)	650	
	Unrealized Gain on Investment		650
	Adjusted investment to market value.		

The increase in the investment's market value creates new stockholders' equity for the investor.

ASSETS	=	LIABILITIES	+	STOCKHOLDERS' EQUITY
650	=	0	+	650

Allowance to Adjust Investment to Market is a companion account used in conjunction with the Long-Term Investment account to bring the investment's carrying amount to current market value. In this case, the investment's cost ($35,750) plus the Allowance ($650) equals the investment carrying amount ($36,400).

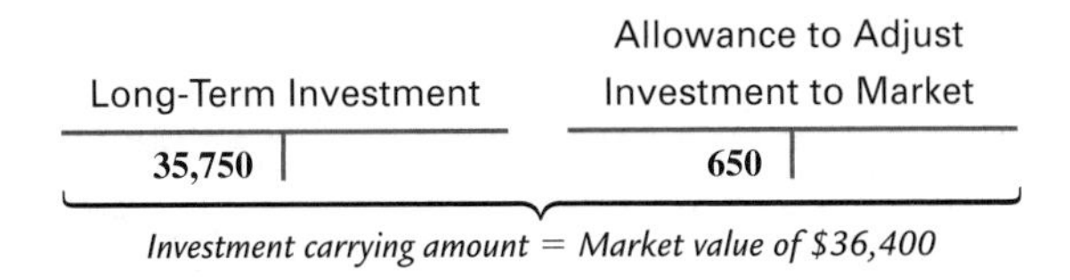

Here the Allowance has a debit balance because the market value of the investment increased. If the investment's market value declines, the Allowance is credited, and the investment carrying amount is its cost minus the Allowance.

The other side of the adjustment entry (bottom of page 468) is a credit to Unrealized Gain on Investment. If the market value of the investment declines, the company debits Unrealized Loss on Investment. An *unrealized* gain or loss results from a change in the investment's market value, not from the sale of the investment. For available-for-sale investments, the Unrealized Gain account or the Unrealized Loss account is reported in two places in the financial statements:

- *Other comprehensive income*, which can be reported on the *income statement* in a separate section below net income or in a separate statement of comprehensive income
- *Accumulated other comprehensive income*, which is a separate section of stockholders' equity, below retained earnings, on the *balance sheet*

The following display shows how GE could report its investment and the related unrealized gain in its financial statements at the end of 20X4 (all other figures are assumed for illustration in context):

Income statement		
Revenues		$10,000
Expenses, including income tax		6,000
Net income		$ 4,000
Other comprehensive income:		
Unrealized gain on investments	$650	
Less Income tax (40%)	(260)	390
Comprehensive income		$ 4,390

Balance sheet	
Assets	
Total current assets	$ XXX
Long-term investments—at market value ($35,750 + $650)	36,400
Property, plant, and equipment, net	XXX
Stockholders' equity	
Common stock	$ 1,000
Retained earnings	2,000
Accumulated other comprehensive income:	
Unrealized gain on investments	390
Total stockholders' equity	$ 3,390

✔ Check Point 10-1

The unrealized gain is not part of net income. The unrealized gain is reported at its net-of-tax amount ($390) because it comes after net income, which also is an after-tax figure. The investments appear on the balance sheet at current market value. The balance sheet also reports the unrealized gain in a separate section of stockholders' equity, Accumulated other comprehensive income, which comes after Retained Earnings. At December 31, 2001, GE reported a $1 billion unrealized loss on investments, as shown on page 465.

Selling an Available-for-Sale Investment

The sale of an available-for-sale investment can result in a *realized* gain or loss. Realized gains and losses measure the difference between the amount received from the sale of the investment and the cost of the investment.

Suppose GE sells its investment in Hewlett-Packard stock for $34,000 during 20X6. GE would record the sale as follows:

20X6			
May 19	Cash	34,000	
	Loss on Sale of Investment	1,750	
	Long-Term Investment (cost)		35,750
	Sold investment.		

ASSETS	=	LIABILITIES	+	STOCKHOLDERS' EQUITY	−	LOSSES
34,000 −35,750	=	0	+		−	1,750

GE would report the Loss on Sale of Investments as an "Other" item on the income statement. Then at December 31, 20X6, GE must update the Allowance to Adjust Investment to Market and the Unrealized Gain on Investment accounts to their current balances. These adjustments are covered in intermediate accounting courses.

✔ Check Point 10-2

Suppose Intel Corporation holds the following available-for-sale securities as long-term investments at December 31, 20X9:

Stock	Cost	Current Market Value
The Coca-Cola Company	$ 85,000	$71,000
Eastman Kodak Company	16,000	12,000
	$101,000	$83,000

Show how Intel will report long-term investments on its December 31, 20X9, balance sheet.

Answer:

Assets	
Long-term investments, at market value	$83,000

equity method

Equity-Method Investments

We use the **equity method** to account for investments in which the investor owns 20% to 50% of the investee's stock.

DECISION: Why Buy a Large Stake in Another Company?

An investor who holds less than 20% of the investee's voting stock usually plays no important role in the investee's operations. But an investor with a larger stock holding—between 20% and 50% of the investee's voting stock—may significantly influence how the investee operates the business. Such an investor can probably affect the investee's decisions on dividend policy, product lines, sources of supply, and other important matters.

Equity method for investments The method used to account for investments in which the investor has 20–50% of the investee's voting stock and can significantly influence the decisions of the investee.

This is one reason why companies commonly buy between 20% to 50% of another company's stock. General Motors (GM), for example, owns nearly 40% of Isuzu Motors Overseas Distribution Corporation. These investee companies are often referred to as affiliates; thus Isuzu is an affiliate of GM. And because GM has a voice in shaping the policy and operations of Isuzu, some measure of Isuzu's success or failure should be included in GM's accounting for the investment.

Accounting for Equity Method Investments

Objective

2 **Use** the equity method for investments

Investments accounted for by the equity method are recorded initially at cost. Suppose Phillips Petroleum Company pays $400 million for 30% of the common stock of White Rock Natural Gas Corporation. Phillips' entry to record the purchase of this investment follows (in millions):

Jan. 6	Long-Term Investment	400	
	Cash..............................		400
	To purchase equity-method investment.		

ASSETS	=	LIABILITIES	+	STOCKHOLDERS' EQUITY
+400 −400	=	0	+	0

The Investor's Percentage of Investee Income. Under the equity method, Phillips, as the investor, applies its percentage of ownership—30%, in our example—in recording its share of the investee's net income and dividends. If White Rock reports net income of $250 million for the year, Phillips records 30% of this amount as follows (in millions):

Dec. 31	Long-Term Investment ($250 × .30)	75	
	Equity-Method Investment Revenue......		75
	To record investment revenue.		

ASSETS	=	LIABILITIES	+	STOCKHOLDERS' EQUITY	+	REVENUES
75	=	0	+		+	75

Because of the close relationship between the two companies, the investor increases the Investment account and records Investment Revenue when the investee reports income. As the investee's owners' equity increases, so does the Investment account on the investor's books.

RECEIVING DIVIDENDS UNDER THE EQUITY METHOD. Phillips records its proportionate part of cash dividends received from White Rock. When White Rock declares and pays a cash dividend of $100 million, Phillips receives 30% of this dividend and records this entry (in millions):

Dec. 31	Cash ($100 × .30)	30	
	Long-Term Investment.		30
	To receive cash dividend on equity-method investment.		

ASSETS	=	LIABILITIES	+	STOCKHOLDERS' EQUITY
30				
−30	=	0	+	0

The Investment account is *decreased* for the receipt of a dividend on an equity-method investment. Why? Because the dividend decreases the investee's owners' equity and thus the investor's investment.

After the preceding entries are posted, Phillips' Investment account reflects its equity in the net assets of White Rock (in millions):

Long-Term Investment

Jan. 6	**Purchase**	**400**	**Dec. 31**	**Dividends**	**30**
Dec. 31	**Net income**	**75**			
Dec. 31	**Balance**	**445**			

✔ Check Point 10-3

Phillips would report the long-term investment on the balance sheet and the equity-method investment revenue on the income statement as follows:

	Millions
Balance sheet (partial):	
Assets	
Total current assets	$XXX
Long-term investments, at equity	445
Property, plant, and equipment, net	XXX
Income statement (partial):	
Income from operations	$XXX
Other revenue:	
Equity-method investment revenue	75
Net income	$XXX

Gain or loss on the sale of an equity-method investment is measured as the difference between the sale proceeds and the carrying amount of the investment. For example, sale of 20% of the White Rock common stock for $81 million would be recorded as follows:

Feb. 13	Cash.	81	
	Loss on Sale of Investment	8	
	Long-Term Investment ($445,000 × .20).		89
	Sold 20% of investment.		

✔ Check Point 10-4

ASSETS	=	LIABILITIES	+	STOCKHOLDERS' EQUITY	−	LOSSES
81 −89	=	0	+		−	8

SUMMARY OF THE EQUITY METHOD. The following T-account illustrates the accounting for equity-method investments:

Equity-Method Investment	
Original cost	**Share of losses**
Share of income	**Share of dividends**
Balance	

Consolidated Subsidiaries

consolidation, minority interest

Objective

3 Understand consolidated financial statements

In the preceding section, we saw that companies buy a significant stake in another company in order to *influence* the other company's operations. In this section we cover the situation in which a corporation buys enough of another company to actually *control* that company.

Controlling (majority) interest Ownership of more than 50% of an investee company's voting stock.

Parent company An investor company that owns more than 50% of the voting stock of a subsidiary company.

Subsidiary company An investee company in which a parent company owns more than 50% of the voting stock.

DECISION: Why Buy Another Company?

Most large corporations own controlling interests in other companies. A **controlling** (or **majority**) **interest** is the ownership of more than 50% of the investee's voting stock. Such an investment enables the investor to elect a majority of the members of the investee's board of directors and thus control the investee. The investor is called the **parent company**, and the investee company is called the **subsidiary.** For example, NBC is a subsidiary of GE, the parent. Therefore, the stockholders of GE control NBC, as diagrammed in Exhibit 10-3.

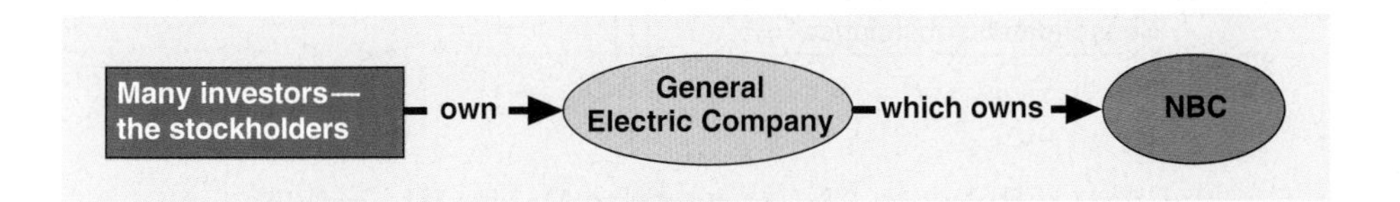

Exhibit 10-3

Ownership Structure of General Electric and NBC

Exhibit 10-4 shows some of the more interesting subsidiaries of GE Company.

GE Aircraft Engines	GE Appliances
GE Plastics	GE Lighting
NBC	GE Transportation Systems

Exhibit 10-4

Selected Subsidiaries of General Electric

Consolidation Accounting

Consolidation accounting is a method of combining the financial statements of all the companies that are controlled by the same stockholders. This method reports a single

Exhibit 10-5

Accounting Methods for Stock Investment by Percentage of Ownership

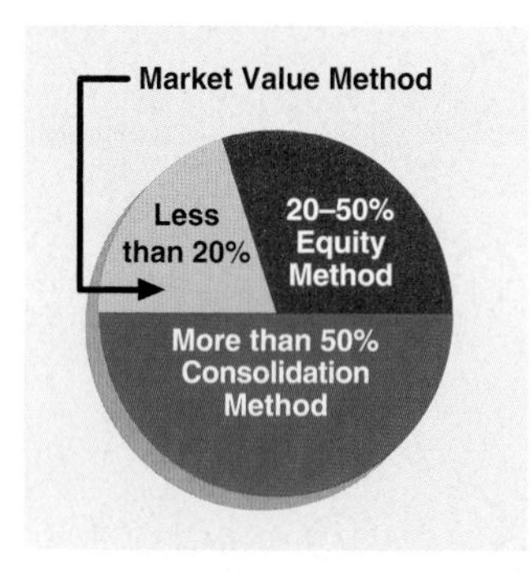

set of financial statements for the consolidated entity, which carries the name of the parent company. Exhibit 10-5 summarizes the accounting methods used for stock investments.

Because almost all published financial reports include consolidated statements, you need to know the basic concepts underlying consolidation accounting. **Consolidated statements** combine the balance sheets, income statements, and other financial statements of the parent company with those of majority-owned subsidiaries into an overall set of statements as if the parent and its subsidiaries were a single entity. The goal is to provide a better perspective on total operations than could be obtained by examining the separate reports of each individual company.

Consolidated statements Financial statements of the parent company plus those of majority-owned subsidiaries as if the combination were a single legal entity.

The consolidated financial statements present the combined account balances of the parent company and its subsidiary companies. The assets, liabilities, revenues, and expenses of each subsidiary are added to the parent's accounts. For example, the balance in the Cash account of NBC is added to the balance in the GE Cash account, and the sum of the two amounts is presented as a single amount in the GE consolidated balance sheet at the beginning of the chapter. Each account balance of a subsidiary loses its identity in the consolidated statements, which bear the name of the parent company.

Exhibit 10-6 diagrams a corporate structure whose parent corporation owns controlling interests in five subsidiary companies and an equity-method investment in another investee company.

✔ Check Point 10-5

Exhibit 10-6

Parent Company with Consolidated Subsidiaries and an Equity-Method Investment

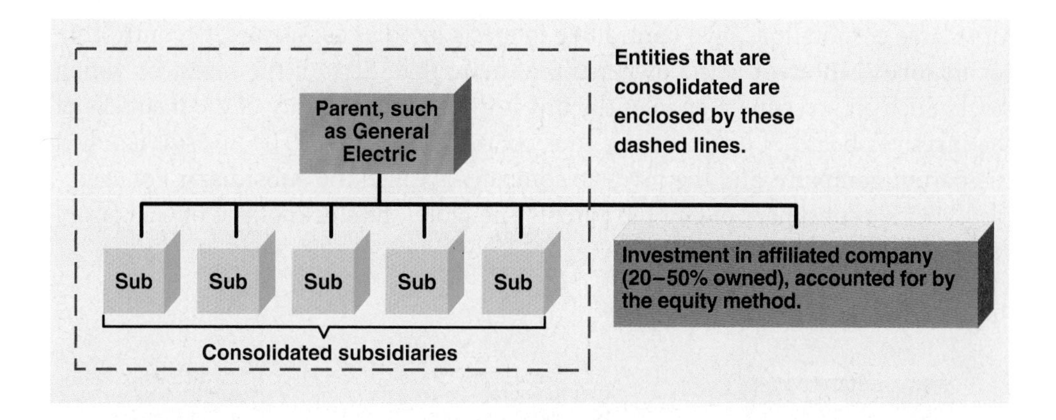

The Consolidated Balance Sheet and the Related Work Sheet

GE has purchased all (100%) the outstanding common stock of NBC. Both GE and NBC keep separate sets of books. GE, the parent company uses a work sheet to prepare the consolidated statements of GE and its consolidated subsidiaries. GE's consolidated balance sheet shows the combined assets and liabilities of both GE and all its subsidiaries.

Exhibit 10-7 shows the work sheet for consolidating the balance sheets of Parent Corporation and Subsidiary Corporation, hypothetical entities that we use to illustrate the consolidation process. Consider elimination entry (a) for the parent-subsidiary ownership accounts. Entry (a) credits the parent's Investment account to eliminate its debit balance. Entry (a) also eliminates the subsidiary's stockholders' equity accounts by debiting the subsidiary's Common Stock and Retained Earnings for their full balances. Without this elimination, the consolidated financial statements

Exhibit 10-7 **Work Sheet for Consolidated Balance Sheet**

	Parent Corporation	Subsidiary Corporation	Eliminations		Parent and Subsidiary Consolidated Amounts
			Debit	Credit	
Assets					
Cash	12,000	18,000			30,000
Note receivable from Subsidiary	80,000	—		(b) 80,000	—
Inventory	104,000	91,000			195,000
Investment in Subsidiary	150,000	—		(a) 150,000	—
Other assets	218,000	138,000			356,000
Total	564,000	247,000			581,000
Liabilities and Stockholders' Equity					
Accounts payable	43,000	17,000			60,000
Notes payable	190,000	80,000	(b) 80,000		190,000
Common stock	176,000	100,000	(a) 100,000		176,000
Retained earnings	155,000	50,000	(a) 50,000		155,000
Total	564,000	247,000	230,000	230,000	581,000

would include both the parent company's investment in the subsidiary and the subsidiary company's equity. But these accounts represent the same thing—Subsidiary's equity—and so they must be eliminated from the consolidated totals. If they weren't, the same item would be counted twice.

The resulting Parent and Subsidiary consolidated balance sheet (far right column) reports no Investment in Subsidiary account, and the consolidated totals for Common Stock and Retained Earnings are those of Parent Corporation only. Study the final column of the consolidation work sheet.

In this example, Parent Corporation has an $80,000 note receivable from Subsidiary, and Subsidiary has a note payable to Parent. The parent's receivable and the subsidiary's payable represent the same resources—all entirely within the consolidated entity. Both, therefore, must be eliminated. Entry (b) accomplishes this. The $80,000 credit in the elimination column of the work sheet zeros out Parent's Note Receivable from Subsidiary. The $80,000 debit in the elimination column zeros out the Subsidiary's Note Payable to Parent. The resulting consolidated amount for notes payable is the amount owed to creditors outside the consolidated entity, which is appropriate. After the work sheet is complete, the consolidated amount for each account represents the total asset, liability, and equity amounts controlled by Parent Corporation.

Examine Exhibit 10-7. Why does the consolidated stockholders' equity ($176,000 + $155,000) exclude the equity of Subsidiary Corporation?

Answer:
The stockholders' equity of the consolidated entity is that of the parent only. Also, the subsidiary's equity and the parent company's investment balance represent the same resources. Including both would amount to double counting.

Goodwill and Minority Interest

Goodwill and Minority Interest are two accounts that only a consolidated entity can have. **Goodwill**, which we studied in Chapter 7, arises when a parent company pays more to acquire a subsidiary company than the market value of the subsidiary's net assets ←. As we saw in Chapter 7, goodwill is the intangible asset that represents the parent company's excess payment to acquire the subsidiary. GE reports goodwill on its balance sheet at the beginning of the chapter.

→ *For a review of goodwill, see Chapter 7, pp. 339–340.*

Minority interest
A subsidiary company's equity that is held by stockholders other than the parent company.

✔ Check Point 10-6

Minority interest arises when a parent company purchases less than 100% of the stock of a subsidiary company. For example, GE owns less than 100% of some of the companies it controls. The remainder of the subsidiaries' stock is minority interest to GE. Minority Interest is included along with the liabilities on the balance sheet of the parent company. GE reports minority interest on its balance sheet.

Income of a Consolidated Entity

The income of a consolidated entity is the net income of the parent plus the parent's proportion of the subsidiaries' net income. Suppose Parent Company owns all the stock of Subsidiary S-1 and 60% of the stock of Subsidiary S-2. During the year just ended, Parent earned net income of $330,000, S-1 earned $150,000, and S-2 had a net loss of $100,000. Parent Company would report net income of $420,000, computed as follows:

	Net Income (Net Loss) of Each Company		*Parent's Ownership of Each Company*		*Parent's Consolidated Net Income (Net Loss)*
Parent Company	$ 330,000	×	100%	=	$330,000
Subsidiary S-1	150,000	×	100%	=	150,000
Subsidiary S-2	(100,000)	×	60%	=	(60,000)
Consolidated net income .					$420,000

Long-Term Investments in Bonds and Notes

Integrator CD
bond investments

Objective

4 Account for long-term investments in bonds

The major investors in bonds are financial institutions—pension plans, mutual funds, and insurance companies such as GE Financial Assurance. The relationship between the issuing corporation and the investor (bondholder) may be diagrammed as follows:

Investor (Bondholder)		*Issuing Corporation*
Investment in bonds	←——→	Bonds payable
Interest revenue	←——→	Interest expense

An investment in bonds is classified either as short-term (a current asset) or as long-term. Short-term investments in bonds are rare. Here, we focus on long-term investments called **held-to-maturity investments** ←.

Held-to-maturity investments
Bonds and notes that an investor intends to hold until maturity.

→ *We first encountered held-to-maturity investments in Chapter 5, page 224.*

Bond investments are recorded at cost. Years later, at maturity, the investor will receive the bonds' face value. Often bond investments are purchased at a premium or a discount. When there is a premium or discount, held-to-maturity investments are amortized to account for interest revenue and the bonds' carrying amount. Held-to-maturity investments are reported at their *amortized cost*, which determines the carrying amount.

Suppose an investor purchases $10,000 of 6% CBS bonds at a price of 95.2 on April 1, 20X5. The investor intends to hold the bonds as a long-term investment until their maturity. Interest dates are April 1 and October 1. Because these bonds mature on April 1, 20X9, they will be outstanding for 4 years (48 months). In this case the investor paid a discount price for the bonds (95.2% of face value). The investor must amortize the bonds' carrying amount from cost of $9,520 up to $10,000 over their term to maturity. Assume amortization of the bonds by the straight-line method →. The following are the entries for this long-term investment:

← Straight-line amortization of a bond investment is calculated the same way as it is calculated for bonds payable (see Chapter 8, page 381).

20X5			
Apr. 1	Long-Term Investment in Bonds ($10,000 × 0.952)	9,520	
	Cash		9,520
	To purchase bond investment.		
Oct. 1	Cash ($10,000 × .06 × 6/12)	300	
	Interest Revenue		300
	To receive semiannual interest.		
Oct. 1	Long-Term Investment in Bonds [($10,000 − $9,520)/48] ×6	60	
	Interest Revenue		60
	To amortize bond investment.		

At December 31, the year-end adjustments are

20X5			
Dec. 31	Interest Receivable ($10,000 × .06 × 3/12)	150	
	Interest Revenue		150
	To accrue interest revenue.		
Dec. 31	Long-Term Investment in Bonds [($10,000 − $9,520)/48] × 3	30	
	Interest Revenue		30
	To amortize bond investment.		

This amortization entry has two effects:

1. It increases the Long-Term Investment account on its march toward maturity value.
2. It records the interest revenue earned from the increase in the carrying amount of the investment.

✔ **Check Point 10-7**

✔ **Check Point 10-8**

The financial statements at December 31, 20X5 report the following for this investment in bonds:

Balance sheet at December 31, 20X5:	
Current assets:	
Interest receivable	$ 150
Long-term investments in bonds ($9,520 + $60 + $30)	9,610
Property, plant, and equipment	X,XXX
Income statement for the year ended December 31, 20X5:	
Other revenues:	
Interest revenue ($300 + $60 + $150 + $30)	$ 540

Decision Guidelines

This chapter has illustrated how to account for various types of long-term investments. The Decision Guidelines feature shows which accounting method to use for each type of long-term investment.

General Electric Company has all types of investments—stocks, bonds, 25% interests, controlling interests. How should GE account for its various investments?

ACCOUNTING METHOD TO USE FOR EACH TYPE OF LONG-TERM INVESTMENT

Type of Long-Term Investment	Accounting Method
GE owns less than 20% of investee stock (Available-for-sale investment classified as noncurrent asset)	Market value
GE owns between 20% and 50% of investee/affiliate stock	Equity
GE owns more than 50% of investee stock	Consolidation
GE owns long-term investment in bonds (held-to-maturity investment)	Amortized cost

Excel Application Problem

Goal: Create an Excel worksheet showing the total amounts for key balance sheet accounts.

Scenario: Suppose General Electric (GE) paid $25 billion for all the common stock of its various subsidiaries, and that GE owes the subsidiaries a total of $4 billion in notes payable. Your task is to create a worksheet that calculates the combined amounts GE would report on its financial statements for the period. Assume any amounts from foreign subsidiaries conform to GAAP and that currency translation has been performed.

Data are as follows (all amounts are in billions):

	Parent	*Subsidiaries*
Cash	$ 8	$ 2
Receivables	22	13
Inventories	$ 7	$ 4
Investment in Subsidiaries	$ 25	$ 0
Other assets	$158	$106
Total liabilities, not including notes payable above	$175	$100
Common stock	$ 20	$ 10
Retained earnings	$ 25	$ 15

(Note: amounts listed are not actual results)

When done, answer these questions:

1. What accounting method is being used in this situation? What type of interest does General Electric have in its subsidiaries?
2. What amount would be reported for combined total assets?
3. Does the combined stockholders' equity include the equity of the subsidiary companies? Why or why not?

Step-by-step:

1. Open a new Excel worksheet.
2. Create a heading for your worksheet that contains the following:
   a. Chapter 10 Decision Guideline
   b. General Electric (in billions)
   c. Today's Date
3. Use the Mid-Chapter Summary problem, part 4, as the model for your worksheet format. Fill in the required entries from the data given in the scenario. (Hint: Use the "Merge and Center" formatting tool to center the text "Eliminations" across the debit and credit columns.)
4. When finished, save your work and print a copy for your files.

Mid-Chapter Summary Problems

1. Identify the appropriate accounting method for each of the following situations:
   a. Investment in 25% of investee's stock
   b. Available-for-sale investment in stock
   c. Investment in more than 50% of investee's stock
2. At what amount should the following available-for-sale investment portfolio be reported on the December 31 balance sheet? All the investments are less than 5% of the investee's stock.

Stock	Investment Cost	Current Market Value
DuPont	$ 5,000	$ 5,500
ExxonMobil	61,200	53,000
Procter & Gamble	3,680	6,230

   Journalize any adjusting entry required by these data.
3. Investor paid $67,900 to acquire a 40% equity-method investment in the common stock of Investee. At the end of the first year, Investee's net income was $80,000, and Investee declared and paid cash dividends of $55,000. What is Investor's ending balance in its Equity-Method Investment account?
4. Parent Company paid $85,000 for all the common stock of Subsidiary Company, and Parent owes Subsidiary $20,000 on a note payable. Complete the consolidation work sheet below.

	Parent Company	Subsidiary Company	Eliminations		Consolidated Amounts
			Debit	Credit	
Assets					
Cash	7,000	4,000			
Note receivable from Parent	—	20,000			
Investment in Subsidiary	85,000	—			
Other assets	108,000	99,000			
Total	200,000	123,000			
Liabilities and Stockholders' Equity					
Accounts payable	15,000	8,000			
Notes payable	20,000	30,000			
Common stock	120,000	60,000			
Retained earnings	45,000	25,000			
Total	200,000	123,000			

Answers

1. a. Equity b. Market value c. Consolidation
2. Report the investments at market value: $64,730.

Stock	Investment Cost	Current Market Value
DuPont	$ 5,000	$ 5,500
ExxonMobil	61,200	53,000
Procter & Gamble	3,680	6,230
Totals	$69,880	$64,730

Adjusting entry:

	Debit	Credit
Unrealized Loss on Investments ($69,880 − $64,730)	5,150	
Allowance to Adjust Investment to Market		5,150
To adjust investments to current market value.		

3.

Equity-Method Investment

Cost	67,900	Dividends	22,000**
Income	32,000*		
Balance	77,900		

*$80,000 × .40 = $32,000
**$55,000 × .40 = $22,000

4. Consolidation work sheet:

	Parent Company	Subsidiary Company	Eliminations Debit	Eliminations Credit	Consolidated Amounts
Assets					
Cash	7,000	4,000			11,000
Note receivable from Parent	—	20,000		(a) 20,000	—
Investment in Subsidiary	85,000	—		(b) 85,000	—
Other assets	108,000	99,000			207,000
Total	200,000	123,000			218,000
Liabilities and Stockholders' Equity					
Accounts payable	15,000	8,000			23,000
Notes payable	20,000	30,000	(a) 20,000		30,000
Common stock	120,000	60,000	(b) 60,000		120,000
Retained earnings	45,000	25,000	(b) 25,000		45,000
Total	200,000	123,000	105,000	105,000	218,000

Accounting for International Operations

foreign currency

Did you know that The Coca-Cola Company earns most of its revenue outside the United States? It is common for U.S. companies to do a large part of their business abroad. Coca-Cola, Intel, and General Electric, among many others, are very active in other countries. Exhibit 10-8 shows the percentages of international sales for these companies.

Exhibit 10-8

Extent of international Business

Company	*Percentage of International Sales*
Coca-Cola	62%
Intel	56
General Electric	29

Accounting for business activities across national boundaries is called *international accounting*. Electronic communication makes international accounting more important because as the world grows smaller, investors around the world need the same data to make decisions. Therefore, the accounting in Australia needs to be the same as in Brazil and the United States. The International Accounting

Standards Board (IASB) is working on a uniform set of accounting standards for the whole world.

The business environment varies widely across the globe. New York reflects the diversity of the market-driven economy of the United States. Japan's economy is similar to that of the United States, although Japanese business activity focuses more on imports and exports. International accounting deals with such differences in economic structures.

Foreign Currencies and Exchange Rates

Most countries use their own national currency. An exception is a group of European nations (the European Union)—France, Germany, Italy, Belgium, and so on—most of which use a common currency, the *euro*, whose symbol is €. If GE, a U.S.-owned company, sells jet engines to Air France, will GE receive U.S. dollars or euros? If the transaction takes place in dollars, Air France must exchange its euros for dollars to pay GE in U.S. currency. If the transaction takes place in euros, GE must exchange euros for dollars. In either case, a step has been added to the transaction: One of the companies must convert domestic currency into foreign currency.

The price of one nation's currency may be stated in terms of another country's monetary unit. This measure of one currency against another is called the **foreign-currency exchange rate.** In Exhibit 10-9, the dollar value of a euro is $0.89. This means that one euro can be bought for 89 cents. Other currencies, such as the British pound and the Japanese yen (also listed in Exhibit 10-9), are similarly bought and sold.

Foreign-currency exchange rate The measure of one country's currency against another country's currency.

Exhibit 10-9

Foreign-Currency Exchange Rates

Country	Monetary Unit	U.S. Dollar Value	Country	Monetary Unit	U.S. Dollar Value
Brazil	Real (R)	$0.43	United Kingdom	Pound (£)	$1.45
Canada	Dollar ($)	0.64	Italy	Euro (€)	0.89
France	Euro (€)	0.89	Japan	Yen (¥)	0.0077
Germany	Euro (€)	0.89	Mexico	Peso (P)	0.108

Source: *The Wall Street Journal* (April 23, 2002), p. C12.

We use the exchange rate to convert the cost of an item given in one currency to its cost in a second currency. We call this conversion a *translation*. Suppose an item costs 200 euros. To compute its cost in dollars, we multiply the amount in euros by the conversion rate: 200 euros × $0.89 = $178.

Two main factors determine the supply and demand for a particular currency:

1. **The ratio of a country's imports to its exports.**
2. **The rate of return available in the country's capital markets.**

THE IMPORT/EXPORT RATIO. Japanese exports often surpass Japan's imports. Customers of Japanese companies must buy yen (the Japanese unit of currency) in the international currency market to pay for their purchases. This strong demand drives up the price—the foreign exchange rate—of the yen. In contrast, France imports more goods than it exports. French businesses must sell euros to buy the foreign currencies needed to acquire the foreign goods. As the supply of the euro increases, its price decreases.

The Rate of Return. The rate of return available in a country's capital markets affects the amount of investment funds flowing into the country. When rates of return are high in a politically stable country such as the United States, international investors buy stocks, bonds, and real estate in that country. This activity increases the demand for the nation's currency and drives up its exchange rate.

Currencies are often described as "strong" or "weak." The exchange rate of a **strong currency** is rising relative to other nations' currencies. The exchange rate of a **weak currency** is falling relative to other currencies.

Strong currency
A currency whose exchange rate is rising relative to other nations' currencies.

Weak currency
A currency whose exchange rate is falling relative to that of other nations.

Suppose *The Wall Street Journal* listed the exchange rate for the British pound as \$1.45 on April 23. On April 25, that rate may change to \$1.40. We would say that the dollar has risen against—is stronger than—the British pound. Because the pound has become less expensive, the dollar now buys more pounds. A stronger dollar would make travel to England more attractive to Americans.

Objective

5 Account for international operations

Managing Cash in International Transactions. Because international transactions are common, more companies are realizing the need to manage cash transactions conducted in foreign currencies. D.E. Shipp Belting, a small family-owned company in Waco, Texas, provides an example. Shipp makes conveyor belts used in a variety of industries. Farmers in the Rio Grande Valley along the Texas–Mexico border use Shipp conveyor belts to process vegetables. Because some of these customers are on the Mexican side of the border, Shipp conducts some of its business in pesos, the Mexican monetary unit. Conversely, the Swiss have developed some of the leading technologies for manufacturing high-grade conveyor belts. Shipp Belting, therefore, purchases inventory from Swiss companies. Some of these transactions are conducted in Swiss francs.

DECISION: Do We Collect Cash in Dollars or in a Foreign Currency?

Consider Shipp Belting's sale of conveyor belts to Artes de Mexico, a vegetable grower in Matamoros, Mexico. The sale can be conducted in dollars or in pesos. If Artes de Mexico agrees to pay in dollars, Shipp avoids the complication of dealing in a foreign currency, and the transaction is the same as selling to M&M Mars across town. But suppose Artes de Mexico orders 1 million pesos (approximately \$130,000) worth of conveyor belts from Shipp. Further suppose that Artes demands to pay in pesos and that Shipp agrees to receive pesos instead of dollars.

Because Shipp will need to convert the pesos to dollars, the transaction poses a challenge. What if the peso loses value—weakens, taking more pesos to obtain each dollar—before Shipp collects from Artes? In this case, Shipp will not earn as much as expected on the sale. The following example shows how to account for international transactions that result in the receipt of a foreign currency. It also shows how to measure the effects of such transactions on a company's cash position and profits.

Shipp Belting sells goods to Artes de Mexico for a price of 1 million pesos on July 28. On that date, a peso was worth \$0.107, as quoted in exchange rate tables of *The Wall Street Journal*. One month later, on August 28, the peso has weakened against the dollar so that a peso is worth only \$0.104. Shipp receives 1 million pesos from Artes on August 28, but the dollar value of Shipp's cash receipt is \$3,000 less than expected. Shipp ends up earning less than hoped for on the transaction. The following journal entries show how Shipp would account for these transactions:

July 28	Accounts Receivable—Artes (1,000,000 pesos × $0.107)	107,000	
	Sales Revenue		107,000
	Sale on account.		

ASSETS	=	LIABILITIES	+	STOCKHOLDERS' EQUITY	+	REVENUES
107,000	=	0	+		+	107,000

Aug. 28	Cash (1,000,000 pesos × $0.104)	104,000	
	Foreign-Currency Transaction Loss	3,000	
	Accounts Receivable—Artes		107,000
	Collection on account.		

ASSETS	=	LIABILITIES	+	STOCKHOLDERS' EQUITY	−	LOSSES
104,000 −107,000	=	0	+		−	3,000

✔ Check Point 10-9

If Shipp had required Artes to pay at the time of the sale, Shipp would have received pesos worth $107,000. But by waiting the normal 30-day collection period to receive cash, Shipp exposed itself to *foreign-currency exchange risk*, the risk of loss in an international transaction. In this case, Shipp experienced a $3,000 foreign-currency transaction loss and received $3,000 less cash than expected, as shown in the collection entry.

If the peso had increased in value, Shipp would have experienced a foreign-currency transaction gain. When a company holds a receivable denominated in a foreign currency, it wants the foreign currency to remain strong so that it can be converted into more dollars. Unfortunately, that did not occur for Shipp Belting. One way of managing foreign-currency exchange risk is for the seller to simply quote a higher price for its goods in foreign markets. If the buyer accepts, the seller has protected itself against the risk of loss.

DECISION: Do We Pay in Dollars or in a Foreign Currency?

Purchasing from a foreign company may also expose a company to foreign-currency exchange risk. To illustrate, assume Shipp Belting buys inventory from Gesellschaft Ltd., a Swiss company. After lengthy negotiations, the two companies decide on a price of 20,000 Swiss francs. On September 15, when Shipp receives the goods, the Swiss franc is quoted in international currency markets at $0.799. When Shipp pays 2 weeks later, on September 29, the Swiss franc has weakened against the dollar—decreased in value to $0.781. Shipp would record the purchase and payment as follows:

Sept. 15	Inventory (20,000 Swiss francs × $0.799)	15,980	
	Accounts Payable—Gesellschaft Ltd.		15,980
	Purchase on account.		

ASSETS	=	LIABILITIES	+	STOCKHOLDERS' EQUITY
15,980	=	15,980	+	0

Sept. 29	Accounts Payable—Gesellschaft Ltd.	15,980	
	Cash (20,000 Swiss francs × $0.781)		15,620
	Foreign-Currency Transaction Gain		360
	Payment on account.		

ASSETS	=	LIABILITIES	+	STOCKHOLDERS' EQUITY	+	GAINS
−15,620	=	−15,980	+		+	360

✔ Check Point 10-10

The Swiss franc could have strengthened against the dollar, in which case Shipp would have had a foreign-currency transaction loss. A company with a payable denominated in a foreign currency hopes that the dollar gets stronger: When the payment date arrives, the company can use fewer dollars to purchase the foreign currency and thereby reduce its cost.

Reporting Gains and Losses on the Income Statement

The Foreign-Currency Transaction Gain account is the record of the gains on transactions settled in a currency other than the dollar. Likewise, the Foreign-Currency Transaction Loss account shows the amount of the losses on transactions conducted in foreign currencies. The company reports the *net amount* of these two accounts on the income statement as Other Revenues and Gains, or Other Expenses and Losses, as the case may be. For example, Shipp Belting would combine the $3,000 foreign-currency loss and the $360 gain and report the net loss of $2,640 on the income statement as follows:

Other Expenses and Losses:	
Foreign-currency transaction loss, net	$2,640

These gains and losses fall into the "Other" category because they arise from buying and selling foreign currencies, not from the main line of the company's business (in the case of D.E. Shipp Belting, selling conveyor belts). Companies seek to minimize their foreign-currency losses by a strategy called *hedging*. **Hedging** means to protect oneself from losing money in one transaction by engaging in a counterbalancing transaction.

Hedging
To protect oneself from losing money in one transaction by engaging in a counterbalancing transaction.

DECISION: Should We Hedge Our Foreign-Currency-Transaction Risk?

One way for U.S. companies to avoid foreign-currency transaction losses is to insist that international transactions be settled in dollars. This requirement puts the burden of currency translation on the foreign party. But this approach may alienate customers and decrease sales. Another way for a company to protect itself is by hedging.

A U.S. company selling goods to be collected in Mexican pesos expects to receive a fixed number of pesos in the future. If the peso is losing value, the U.S. company would expect the pesos to be worth fewer dollars than the amount of the receivable—an expected loss situation, as we saw for Shipp Belting.

The U.S. company may have accumulated payables stated in a foreign currency in the normal course of its business, such as the amount payable by Shipp to the Swiss company. Losses on the receipt of pesos may be offset by gains on the payment of Swiss francs to Gesellschaft Ltd. Most companies do not have equal amounts of receivables and payables in foreign currency. To obtain a more precise hedge, some companies buy *futures contracts*, which are contracts for foreign currencies to be received in the future. Futures contracts can effectively create a payable to exactly offset a receivable, and vice versa. Many companies that do business internationally use hedging techniques. GE, for example, reported a $1 billion loss on securities purchased as hedges (see the GE balance sheet at the beginning of the chapter).

Consolidation of Foreign Subsidiaries

A U.S. company, such as GE, with a foreign subsidiary must consolidate the subsidiary's financial statements into its own statements for reporting to the public. The consolidation of a foreign subsidiary poses two special challenges:

1. Many countries outside the United States specify accounting treatments that differ from American accounting principles. For reporting to the American public, accountants must first bring the subsidiary's statements into conformity with American generally accepted accounting principles (GAAP).
2. The second accounting challenge arises when the subsidiary statements are expressed in a foreign currency. One step in the consolidation process is to translate the subsidiary statements into dollars. Then the dollar-value statements of the subsidiary can be combined with the parent's statements in the usual manner, as illustrated in the first part of this chapter.

The process of translating a foreign subsidiary's financial statements into dollars usually creates a *foreign-currency translation adjustment*. This item appears in the financial statements of most multinational companies and is reported as part of other comprehensive income on the income statement and as part of stockholders' equity on the consolidated balance sheet. GE's balance sheet on page 465 gives a concrete example.

A translation adjustment arises due to changes in the foreign exchange rate over time. In general, *assets* and *liabilities* in the foreign subsidiaries' financial statements are translated into dollars at the exchange rate in effect on the date of the statements. *Stockholders' equity* is translated into dollars at older, historical exchange rates. This difference in exchange rates creates an out-of-balance condition on the balance sheet. The translation adjustment amount brings the balance sheet back into balance. Let's use an example to see how the translation adjustment works.

U.S. Express Corporation owns Italian Imports, Inc., whose financial statements are expressed in euros (the European currency). U.S. Express must consolidate the Italian subsidiary's financial statements into its own statements. When U.S. Express acquired Italian Imports in 20X2, 1 euro was worth $1.04. When Italian Imports earned its retained income during 20X2–20X6, the average exchange rate was $0.92. On the balance sheet date in 20X6, a euro is worth only $0.89. Exhibit 10-10 shows how to translate Italian Imports' balance sheet into dollars and shows how the translation adjustment arises.

The **foreign-currency translation adjustment** is the balancing amount that brings the dollar amount of the total liabilities and stockholders' equity of a foreign subsidiary into agreement with the dollar amount of its total assets (in Exhibit 10-10, total assets equal $712,000). Only after the translation adjustment of $21,000 do total liabilities and stockholders' equity equal total assets stated in dollars.

Foreign-currency translation adjustment
The balancing figure that brings the dollar amount of the total liabilities and stockholders' equity of the foreign subsidiary into agreement with the dollar amount of its total assets.

What in the economic environment caused the negative translation adjustment? A weakening of the euro since the acquisition of Italian Imports brought about the

Exhibit 10-10

Translation of a Foreign-Currency Balance Sheet into Dollars

Italian Imports, Inc., Amounts	*Euros*	*Exchange Rate*	*Dollars*
Assets	800,000	$0.89	$712,000
Liabilities	500,000	0.89	$445,000
Stockholders' equity			
Common stock	100,000	1.04	104,000
Retained earnings	200,000	0.92	184,000
Accumulated other comprehensive income:			
Foreign-currency translation adjustment			(21,000)
	800,000		$712,000

need for this adjustment. When U.S. Express acquired the foreign subsidiary in 20X2, a euro was worth $1.04. When Italian Imports earned its retained income during 20X2 through 20X6, the average exchange rate was $0.92. On the balance sheet date in 20X6, a euro is worth only $0.89. Thus, Italian Imports' equity (assets minus liabilities) are translated into only $267,000 ($712,000 − $445,000).

To bring stockholders' equity to $267,000 requires a $21,000 negative amount. In a sense, a negative translation adjustment is like a loss. And it is reported as a contra item in the stockholders' equity section of the balance sheet, as shown in Exhibit 10-10. The interpretation of a negative translation adjustment is this: Measured in today's dollars, the book value of U.S. Express Corporation's investment in Italian Imports, Inc., is less than the amount U.S. Express invested to acquire the company.

The Italian Imports dollar figures in Exhibit 10-10 are the amounts that U.S. Express Corporation would include in its consolidated balance sheet. The consolidation procedures would follow those illustrated beginning on page 473.

International Accounting Standards

In this text, we focus on the accounting principles that are generally accepted in the United States. Most accounting methods are consistent throughout the world. Double-entry accounting, the accrual system, and the basic financial statements are used worldwide. Differences, however, do exist among countries, as shown in Exhibit 10-11.

Exhibit 10-11

Some International Accounting Differences

Country	*Inventories*	*Goodwill*	*Research and Development Costs*
United States	Specific unit cost, FIFO, LIFO, weighted-average	Record any loss in value of goodwill	Expensed as incurred
Germany	Similar to U.S.	Amortized over 5 years	Expensed as incurred
Japan	Similar to U.S.	Amortized over 5 years	May be capitalized and amortized over 5 years
United Kingdom	LIFO is unacceptable for tax purposes and is not widely used	Amortized over useful life or not amortized if life indefinite	Expense research costs. Some development costs may be capitalized

In discussing depreciation (Chapter 7), we emphasized that in the United States, the methods used for reporting to tax authorities differ from the methods used for reporting to shareholders. However, tax reporting and shareholder reporting are identical in many countries. For example, France has a "Plan Compatible" which specifies that a National Uniform Chart of Accounts be used for both tax returns and reporting to shareholders. German financial reporting is also determined primarily by tax laws. In Japan, certain methods are allowed for tax purposes only if they are also used for shareholder reporting.

For inventory, goodwill, and research and development costs, German accounting practices are more similar to those of the United States than to those of other countries. Despite the common heritage of the United States and the United Kingdom, U.S. and British accounting practices vary widely.

A company that sells its stock through a foreign stock exchange must follow the accounting principles of the foreign country. For example, because Sony stock is available through the New York Stock Exchange, Sony financial statements issued in the United States follow American GAAP.

The globalization of business enterprises and capital markets is creating much interest in establishing common, worldwide accounting standards. There are probably too many cultural, social, and political differences to expect complete worldwide standardization in the near future. However, the number of differences is decreasing.

✔ Check Point 10-11

Several organizations are working to achieve worldwide harmony of accounting standards. Chief among these is the *IASB*, created in 2001. The IASB operates much as the Financial Accounting Standards Board (FASB) in the United States. It has the support of the accounting professions in the United States, most of the British Commonwealth countries, Japan, France, Germany, the Netherlands, and Mexico. However, the IASB has no authority to require compliance with its standards. It must rely on cooperation by the various national accounting professions. The IASB goal is worldwide accounting standards in 2005.

Using the Statement of Cash Flows

cash flows

Objective

6 **Report** investing transactions on the statement of cash flows

Investing activities include many types of transactions. In Chapter 7, we covered investing transactions in which companies purchase and sell long-term assets such as plant and equipment. In this chapter, we examined another type of investing activity actually called *investment*. The purchase and sale of investments in stocks and bonds of other companies are also investing activities reported on the cash-flow statement.

Investing activities are usually reported on the statement of cash flows as the second category, after operating activities and before financing activities. Exhibit 10-12 provides excerpts from General Electric's statement of cash flows. During 2001, GE spent $15 billion on plant assets and $12 billion to acquire other companies. The company loaned $14 billion of cash. Overall, GE invested $40 billion more than it received from selling assets. This is one reason GE stays ahead of competitors: it invests in the future.

✔ Check Point 10-12

Exhibit 10-12

General Electric Company Consolidated Statement of Cash Flows (Partial, Adapted)

General Electric Company

Statement of Cash Flows

(In billions)	***2001***
Cash flows—investing activities	
Additions to property, plant, and equipment	$(15)
Dispositions of property, plant, and equipment	7
Loans to others	(14)
Payments for other companies	(12)
All other investing activities	(6)
Cash used for investing activities	(40)

End-of-Chapter Summary Problem

Translate the balance sheet of the Brazilian subsidiary of **Wrangler Corporation**, a U.S. company, into dollars. When Wrangler acquired this subsidiary, the exchange rate of the Brazilian currency, the real, was $0.48. The average exchange rate applicable to retained earnings is $0.41. The real's current exchange rate is $0.43.

Before performing the translation, predict whether the translation adjustment will be positive or negative. Does this situation generate a foreign-currency translation gain or loss? Give your reasons.

	Reals
Assets	900,000
Liabilities	600,000
Stockholders' equity:	
Common stock	30,000
Retained earnings	270,000
	900,000

Answers

Translation of foreign-currency balance sheet:

This situation will generate a *positive* translation adjustment, which is like a gain. The gain occurs because the real's current exchange rate, which is used to translate net assets (assets minus liabilities), exceeds the historical exchange rates used for stockholders' equity.

The calculation follows.

	Reals	Exchange Rate	Dollars
Assets	900,000	0.43	$387,000
Liabilities	600,000	0.43	$258,000
Stockholders' equity:			
Common stock	30,000	0.40	12,000
Retained earnings	270,000	0.41	110,700
Accumulated other comprehensive income:			
Foreign-currency translation adjustment	—		6,300
	900,000		$387,000

Review Long-Term Investments and International

Lessons Learned

1. **Account for available-for-sale investments.** *Available-for-sale securities* are stock investments other than trading securities. Most available-for-sale securities are classified as long-term investments. These investments are reported at current market value on the balance sheet and unrealized gains or losses are shown as an element of stockholders' equity.

2. **Use the equity method for investments.** The *equity method* is used when an investor owns 20% to 50% of the stock of an investee. The investor applies its percentage of ownership in recording its share of the investee's net income and dividends. Equity-method investment revenue is reported under Other revenues on the income statement.

3. **Understand consolidated financial statements.** Ownership of more than 50% of a company's voting stock

creates a *parent–subsidiary* relationship, and the parent company must use the *consolidation method* to account for its subsidiaries. The subsidiary's financial statements are included in the parent's consolidated financial statements.

4. **Account for long-term investments in bonds.** *Held-to-maturity investments* are bonds and notes the investor intends to hold until maturity. The *amortized-cost method* is used to account for held-to-maturity investments.
5. **Account for international operations.** Foreign-currency gains and losses are reported on the income statement as Other gains and losses. Consolidating a foreign subsidiary's financial statements into the parent company's statements requires translating the foreign-company statements into U.S. dollars. The translation process creates a *translation adjustment*, which is an element of stockholders' equity.
6. **Report investing transactions on the statement of cash flows.** Investing activities are the second major category of transactions reported on the statement of cash flows (after operating activities and before financing activities).

Accounting Vocabulary

available-for-sale investments (p. 467)
consolidated statements (p. 474)
controlling interest (p. 473)
equity method (p. 471)
foreign-currency exchange rate (p. 481)
foreign-currency translation adjustment (p. 485)
hedging (p. 484)
held-to-maturity investments (p. 476)
long-term investments (p. 467)
majority interest (p. 473)
marketable securities (p. 466)
market value method (p. 467)
minority interest (p. 476)
parent company (p. 473)
short-term investments (p. 466)
strong currency (p. 482)
subsidiary company (p. 473)
trading investments (p. 467)
weak currency (p. 482)

Questions

1. How are stock prices quoted in the securities market? What is the investor's cost of 1,000 shares of Ford Motor Company stock at 55.75 with a brokerage commission of $1,350?
2. Show the positions of short-term investments and long-term investments on the balance sheet.
3. Outline the accounting methods for the different types of investments.
4. How does an investor record the receipt of a cash dividend on an available-for-sale investment? How does this investor record receipt of a stock dividend?
5. An investor paid $11,000 for 1,000 shares of stock—a trading investment—and later received a 10% stock dividend. At December 31, the investment's market value is $11,800. Compute the unrealized gain or loss on the investment.
6. When is an investment accounted for by the equity method? Explain how to apply the equity method. Mention how to record the purchase of the investment, the investor's proportion of the investee's net income, and receipt of a cash dividend from the investee. Describe how to measure gain or loss on the sale of this investment.
7. Why are intercompany items eliminated from consolidated financial statements? Name two intercompany items that are eliminated.
8. Name the account that expresses the excess of the cost of an investment over the market value of the subsidiary's owners' equity. What type of account is this, and where in the financial statements is it reported?
9. When a parent company buys more than 50% but less than 100% of a subsidiary's stock, a new category of ownership must appear on the balance sheet. What is this category called, and under what heading do most companies report it?
10. How would you measure the net income of a parent company with three subsidiaries? Assume that two subsidiaries are wholly (100%) owned and that the parent owns 60% of the third subsidiary.
11. McVey, Inc. acquired a foreign subsidiary when the foreign currency's exchange rate was $0.32. Over the years, the foreign currency has steadily risen against the dollar. Will McVey's balance sheet report a positive or a negative foreign-currency translation adjustment?
12. Describe the computation of a foreign-currency translation adjustment.

Check Points

Accounting for an available-for-sale investment; unrealized loss
(Obj. 1)

CP10-1 Assume Intel Corporation completed these long-term available-for-sale investment transactions during 20X4:

20X4	
Jan. 14	Purchased 300 shares of **Sysco** stock, paying $19.75 per share. Intel intends to hold the investment for the indefinite future.
Aug. 22	Received a cash dividend of $1.25 per share on the Sysco stock.
Dec. 31	Adjusted the Sysco investment to its current market value of $5,174.

1. Journalize Intel's investment transactions. Explanations are not required.
2. Show how to report the investment and any unrealized gain or loss on Intel's balance sheet at December 31, 20X4. Ignore income tax.

Accounting for the sale of an available-for-sale investment
(Obj. 1)

CP10-2 Use the data given in Check Point 10-1. On August 4, 20X5 Intel sold its investment in Sysco stock for $20.75 per share.

1. Journalize the sale. No explanation is required.
2. How does the gain or loss that you recorded differ from the gain or loss that was recorded at December 31, 20X4?

Accounting for a 40% investment in another company
(Obj. 2)

CP10-3 Suppose on January 6, 20X3, **General Motors** paid $150 million for its 40% investment in **Isuzu Motors.** Assume Isuzu earned net income of $12.5 million and paid cash dividends of $10 million during 20X3.

1. What method should General Motors use to account for the investment in Isuzu? Give your reason.
2. Journalize these three transactions on the books of General Motors. Show all amounts in millions of dollars and include an explanation for each entry.
3. Post to the Long-Term Investment T-account. What is its balance after all the transactions are posted?

Accounting for the sale of an equity-method investment
(Obj. 2)

CP10-4 Use the data given in Check Point 10-3. Assume that in January 20X4, General Motors sold half its investment in Isuzu to **Toyota.** The sale price was $62 million. Compute General Motors' gain or loss on the sale.

Understanding consolidated financial statements
(Obj. 3)

CP10-5 Answer these questions about consolidation accounting:

1. Define a parent company. Define a subsidiary company.
2. How do consolidated financial statements differ from the financial statements of a single company?
3. Which company's name appears on the consolidated financial statements? How much of the subsidiary's stock must the parent own before reporting consolidated statements?

Understanding goodwill and minority interest
(Obj. 3)

CP10-6 Two accounts that arise from consolidation accounting are minority interest and goodwill.

1. What is minority interest, and which company reports it, the parent or the subsidiary? Where is minority interest reported?
2. What is goodwill, and how does it arise? Which company reports goodwill, the parent or the subsidiary? Where is goodwill reported?

Working with a bond investment
(Obj. 4)

CP10-7 **GMAC**, the financing subsidiary of **General Motors Corporation**, owns vast amounts of corporate bonds. Suppose GMAC buys $1,000,000 of **E.I. DuPont** bonds at a price of 101. The DuPont bonds pay cash interest at the annual rate of 7% and mature at the end of 5 years.

1. How much did GMAC pay to purchase the bond investment? How much will GMAC collect when the bond investment matures?
2. How much cash interest will GMAC receive each year from DuPont?
3. Will GMAC's annual interest revenue on the bond investment be more or less than the amount of cash interest received each year? Give your reason.
4. Compute GMAC's annual interest revenue on this bond investment. Use the straight-line method to amortize the investment.

CP10-8 Return to Check Point 10-7, the **GMAC** investment in **DuPont** bonds. Journalize on GMAC's books:

Recording bond investment transactions **(Obj. 4)**

a. Purchase of the bond investment on January 2, 20X4. GMAC expects to hold the investment to maturity.
b. Receipt of annual cash interest on December 31, 20X4.
c. Amortization of the bonds on December 31, 20X4.
d. Collection of the investment's face value at the maturity date on January 2, 20X9. (Assume the receipt of 20X8 interest and the amortization of bonds for 20X8 have already been recorded, so ignore these entries.)

CP10-9 Suppose **PepsiCo** sells soft drink syrup to a Russian company on March 14. PepsiCo agrees to accept 200,000 Russian rubles. On the date of sale, the ruble is quoted at $0.32. PepsiCo collects half the receivable on April 19, when the ruble is worth $0.31. Then on May 10, when the foreign-exchange rate of the ruble is $0.34, PepsiCo collects the final amount.

Accounting for transactions stated in a foreign currency **(Obj. 5)**

Journalize these three transactions for PepsiCo.

CP10-10 Page 483 includes a sequence of **Shipp Belting** journal entries for transactions denominated in Mexican pesos. Suppose the foreign-exchange rate for a peso is $0.117 on August 28. Record Shipp Belting's collection of cash on August 28.

Accounting for transactions stated in a foreign currency **(Obj. 5)**

On page 000, Shipp Belting buys inventory for which Shipp must pay Swiss francs. Suppose a Swiss franc costs $0.811 on September 29. Record Shipp Belting's payment of cash on September 29.

CP10-11 Exhibit 10–11, page 486, outlines some differences between accounting in the United States and accounting in other countries. American companies transact more business with British companies than with any other. Interestingly, however, there are several important differences between American and British accounting. In your own words, describe those differences for inventories, goodwill, and research and development.

International accounting differences **(Obj. 5)**

CP10-12 Companies divide their cash flows into three categories for reporting on the statement of cash flows.

Reporting cash flows **(Obj. 7)**

1. List the three categories of cash flows in the order they appear on the statement of cash flows. Which category of cash flows is most closely related to this chapter?
2. Identify two types of transactions that companies report as cash flows from investing activities.

Exercises

E10-1 Journalize the following long-term available-for-sale investment transactions of Gaudino Securities:

Journalizing transactions for an available-for-sale investment **(Obj. 1)**

general ledger

a. Purchased 400 shares of **AOL Time Warner** common stock at $19.87 per share, with the intent of holding the stock for the indefinite future.
b. Received cash dividend of $1 per share on the AOL investment.
c. At year end, adjusted the investment account to current market value of $21.20 per share.
d. Sold the AOL stock for the market price of $23.14 per share.

E10-2 Suppose **Oracle Corporation** bought 3,000 shares of **Xerox** common stock at $37.375; 600 shares of **Coca-Cola** stock at $46.75; and 1,400 shares of **Panasonic** stock at $79—all as available-for-sale investments. At December 31, ***The Wall Street Journal*** reports Xerox stock at $26.125, Coca-Cola at $48.50, and Panasonic at $68.25.

Accounting for long-term investments **(Obj. 1)**

Required

1. Determine the cost and the market value of the long-term investment portfolio at December 31.

2. Record any adjusting entry needed at December 31.
3. What would Oracle report on its income statement and balance sheet for the information given? Make the necessary disclosures. Ignore income tax.

Accounting for transactions under the equity method
(Obj. 2)

E10-3 **J.C. Penney Company** owns equity-method investments in several companies. Suppose Penney paid $1,600,000 to acquire a 25% investment in Thai Imports Company. Assume that Thai Imports reported net income of $640,000 for the first year and declared and paid cash dividends of $420,000. Record the following in Penney's journal: (a) purchase of the investment, (b) Penney's proportion of Thai Imports' net income, and (c) receipt of the cash dividends. What is the ending balance in Penney's investment account?

Measuring gain or loss on the sale of an equity-method investment
(Obj. 2)

E10-4 Without making journal entries, record the transactions of Exercise 10-3 directly in the **J.C. Penney** account, Long-Term Investment in Thai Imports. Assume that after all the noted transactions took place, Penney sold its entire investment in Thai Imports for cash of $1,400,000. How much is Penney's gain or loss on the sale of the investment?

Applying the appropriate accounting method for a 30% investment
(Obj. 2)

E10-5 Network Investors, Limited, paid $160,000 for a 30% investment in the common stock of eTrav, Inc. For the first year, eTrav reported net income of $84,000 and at year end declared and paid cash dividends of $46,000. On the balance sheet date, the market value of Network Investors' investment in eTrav stock was $184,000.

Required

1. Which method is appropriate for Network Investors to use in accounting for its investment in eTrav? Why?
2. Show everything that Network Investors would report for the investment and any investment revenue in its year-end financial statements.

Preparing a consolidated balance sheet
(Obj. 3)

spreadsheet

E10-6 Mercedes, Inc., owns Benz Corp. The two companies' individual balance sheets follow.

	Mercedes	Benz
Assets		
Cash	$ 49,000	$ 14,000
Accounts receivable, net	82,000	53,000
Note receivable from Mercedes	—	12,000
Inventory	55,000	77,000
Investment in Benz	100,000	—
Plant assets, net	486,000	129,000
Other assets	22,000	8,000
Total	$794,000	$293,000
Liabilities and Stockholders' Equity		
Accounts payable	$ 44,000	$ 26,000
Notes payable	47,000	36,000
Other liabilities	82,000	131,000
Common stock	210,000	80,000
Retained earnings	411,000	20,000
Total	$794,000	$293,000

Required

1. Prepare the consolidated balance sheet of Mercedes, Inc. It is sufficient to complete the consolidation work sheet.
2. What is the amount of stockholders' equity of the consolidated entity?

Recording bond investment transactions
(Obj. 4)

E10-7 Assume that on March 31, 20X3, **Hyundai, Inc.**, paid 97 for 7% bonds of **Daewoo Corporation** as a long-term held-to-maturity investment. The maturity value of the bonds will be $20,000 on March 31, 20X8. The bonds pay interest on March 31 and September 30.

Required

1. What method should Hyundai use to account for its investment in the Daewoo bonds?
2. Using the straight-line method of amortizing the bonds, journalize all of Hyundai's transactions on the bonds for 20X3.
3. Show how Hyundai would report everything related to the bond investment on its balance sheet at December 31, 20X3.

Managing and accounting for foreign-currency transactions
(Obj. 5)

general ledger

E10-8 Assume that **Sears** completed the following foreign-currency transactions:

Nov. 17	Purchased DVD players as inventory on account from **Sony**. The price was 200,000 yen, and the exchange rate of the yen was $0.0077.
Dec. 16	Paid Sony when the exchange rate was $0.0082.
19	Sold merchandise on account to **Cartier**, a French company, at a price of 60,000 euros. The exchange rate was $0.88.
30	Collected from Cartier when the exchange rate was $0.91.

1. Journalize these transactions for Sears. Focus on the gains and losses caused by the changes in foreign-currency exchange rates.
2. On November 18, immediately after the purchase, and on December 20, immediately after the sale, which currencies did Sears want to strengthen? Which currencies did in fact strengthen? Explain your reasoning in detail.

Translating a foreign-currency balance sheet into dollars
(Obj. 5)

spreadsheet

E10-9 Translate into dollars the balance sheet of **Olive Garden's** Italian subsidiary. When Olive Garden acquired the foreign subsidiary, a euro was worth $1.01. The current exchange rate is $0.89. During the period when retained earnings were earned, the average exchange rate was $0.94 per euro.

	Euros
Assets	500,000
Liabilities	300,000
Stockholders' equity:	
Common stock	50,000
Retained earnings	150,000
	500,000

During the period covered by this situation, which currency was stronger, the dollar or the euro?

Preparing and using the statement of cash flows
(Obj. 6)

E10-10 During fiscal year 20X1, **The Home Depot, Inc.**, reported net income of $2,581 million and paid $26 million to acquire other businesses. Home Depot made capital expenditures of $3,558 million to open new stores and sold property, plant, and equipment for $95 million. The company purchased long-term investments in stocks and bonds at a cost of $39 million and sold other long-term investments for $30 million.

Required

Prepare the investing activities section of The Home Depot's statement of cash flows. Based solely on Home Depot's investing activities, does it appear that the company is growing or shrinking? How can you tell?

Using the statement of cash flows
(Obj. 6)

E10-11 **SunWest Corporation** earns approximately 15% of its net income from financial services through its wholly-owned subsidiary, SunWest Financial Corporation. As a result, Finance Receivables is the largest single long-term asset on SunWest's balance sheet. At the end of a recent year, SunWest's statement of cash flows reported the following for investing activities:

SunWest Corporation

Consolidated Statement of Cash Flows (Partial)

	(In millions)
Cash Flows from Investing Activities	
Finance receivables collected	$ 4,192
Purchases of short-term investments	(3,457)
Proceeds from sales of [intangible] assets	1,409
Proceeds from sales of investments	461
Expenditures for property and equipment	(1,761)
Net cash provided by investing activities	$ 844

Required

For each item listed, make the journal entry that placed the item on SunWest's statement of cash flows. The intangible assets that SunWest sold had a book value equal to their sale price. The cost of the investments that SunWest sold was $419 million.

Challenge Exercises

Accounting for various types of investments
(Obj. 1, 2, 3, 5)

E10-12 This exercise summarizes the accounting for investments. Suppose **Motorola, Inc.** owns the following investments at December 31, 20X1:

a. 100% of the common stock of Motorola United Kingdom, which holds assets of £800 million and owes a total of £600 million. At December 31, 20X1, the current exchange rate of the pound (£) is £1 = $1.50. The translation rate of the pound applicable to stockholders' equity is £1 = $1.80. During 20X1, Motorola United Kingdom earned net income of £100 million, and the average exchange rate for the year was £1 = $1.45. Motorola United Kingdom paid cash dividends of £40 million during 20X1.
b. 25% of the common stock of Motorola Financing Associates. During 20X1, Motorola Financing earned net income of $300 million and declared and paid cash dividends of $80 million. The carrying amount of this investment was $700 million at December 31, 20X0.
c. Available-for-sale investments that cost $900 million. These investments declined in value by $400 million during 20X1, but they paid cash dividends of $16 million to Motorola. At December 31, 20X0, the market value of these investments was $1,100 million.

Required

1. Which method is used to account for each investment?
2. By how much did these investments increase or decrease Motorola's net income during 20X1?
3. For investments b and c, show how Motorola would report these investments on its balance sheet at December 31, 20X1.

Explaining and analyzing accumulated other comprehensive income
(Obj. 1, 6)

E10-13 **FedEx Corporation** reported stockholders' equity on its balance sheet at May 31, as shown at the top of the next page.

Required

1. Identify the two components that make up Accumulated other comprehensive income.
2. For each component of Accumulated other comprehensive income, describe the event that can cause a *positive* balance. Also describe the events that can cause a *negative* balance for each component.
3. During 20X1, FedEx had a foreign-currency translation adjustment (debit balance) of $19 million and an unrealized loss of $1 million on available-for-sale investments. What was FedEx's balance of Accumulated other comprehensive income 1 year ago, at May 31, 20X0?
4. How does FedEx's Accumulated other comprehensive income affect net income? How does it affect total stockholders' equity?

FedEx Corporation

Balance Sheet (Partial)

	(In millions) May 31, 20X1
Shareholders' Equity	
Common stock, $0.10 par value—	
Authorized 800 million shares,	
issued 299 million shares	$ 30
Additional paid-in capital	1,121
Retained earnings	4,880
Accumulated other comprehensive income	(56)
Less Treasury stock, at cost	(74)

Problems

(Group A)

Reporting investments on the balance sheet and the related revenue on the income statement
(Obj. 1, 2)

general ledger

P10-1A Wells Fargo & Company, headquartered in San Francisco, owns banks in most states west of the Mississippi River. Wells Fargo owns numerous investments in the stock of other companies. Assume that Wells Fargo completed the following long-term investment transactions during 20X6:

20X6	
Feb. 12	Purchased 20,000 shares, which make up 35% of the common stock of Demski Corporation at total cost of $490,000.
Aug. 9	Received annual cash dividend of $1.26 per share on the Demski investment.
Oct. 16	Purchased 800 shares of Busy Beaver, Inc., common stock as an available-for-sale investment, paying $41.50 per share.
Nov. 30	Received semiannual cash dividend of $0.60 per share on the Busy Beaver investment.
Dec. 31	Received annual report from Demski Corporation. Net income for the year, was $510,000.

At year end the current market value of the Busy Beaver stock is $29,800. The market value of the Demski stock is $652,000.

Required

1. For which investment is current market value used in the accounting? Why is market value used for one investment and not the other?
2. Show what Wells Fargo & Company would report on its year-end balance sheet and income statement for these investment transactions. It is helpful to use a T-account for the investment in Demski stock. Ignore income tax.

Accounting for available-for-sale and equity-method investments
(Obj. 1, 2)

P10-2A The beginning balance sheet of Montgomery Investment Corporation included the following:

general ledger

Long-Term Investments in UPS, Inc. (equity-method investment)	$344,000

Montgomery completed the following investment transactions during the year:

Apr.	2	Purchased 2,000 shares of ATI, Inc. common stock as a long-term available-for-sale investment, paying $12.25 per share.
June	21	Received cash dividend of $0.75 per share on the ATI investment.
Nov.	17	Received cash dividend of $81,000 from UPS, Inc.
Dec.	31	Received annual report from UPS, Inc.; total net income for the year was $550,000. Of this amount, Montgomery's proportion is 22%.

At year end the market values of Montgomery's investments are ATI, $26,800; UPS, Inc., $500,000.

Required

1. Record the transactions in the journal of Montgomery Investment Corporation.
2. Post entries to the Long-Term Investments in UPS, Inc., T-account and determine its balance at December 31.
3. Show how to report the Long-Term Available-for-Sale Investments and the Long-Term Investments in UPS accounts on Montgomery's balance sheet at December 31.

Analyzing consolidated financial statements **(Obj. 3)**

P10-3A This problem demonstrates the dramatic effect that consolidation accounting can have on a company's ratios. **Ford Motor Company** (Ford) owns 100% of **Ford Motor Credit Corporation (FMCC)**, its financing subsidiary. Ford's main operations consist of manufacturing automotive products. FMCC mainly helps people finance the purchase of automobiles from Ford and its dealers. The two companies' individual balance sheets are adapted and summarized as follows (amounts in billions):

	Ford (Parent)	FMCC (Subsidiary)
Total assets	$89.6	$170.5
Total liabilities	$65.1	$156.9
Total stockholders' equity	24.5	13.6
Total liabilities and equity	$89.6	$170.5

Assume that FMCC's liabilities include $1.6 billion owed to Ford, the parent company.

Required

1. Compute the debt ratio of Ford Motor Company considered alone.
2. Determine the consolidated total assets, total liabilities, and stockholders' equity of Ford Motor Company after consolidating the financial statements of FMCC into the totals of Ford, the parent company.
3. Recompute the debt ratio of the consolidated entity. Why do companies prefer not to consolidate their financing subsidiaries into their own financial statements?

Consolidating a wholly-owned subsidiary **(Obj. 3)**

P10-4A Assume **Tejas Logistics, Inc.**, paid $266,000 to acquire all the common stock of Volunteer Corporation, and Volunteer owes Tejas $81,000 on a note payable. Immediately after the purchase on September 30, 20X8, the two companies' balance sheets follow on the next page.

spreadsheet

Required

1. Prepare the consolidated balance sheet for Tejas Logistics, Inc. (It is sufficient to complete a consolidation work sheet.)
2. Why aren't total assets of the consolidated entity equal to the sum of total assets for both companies combined? Why isn't consolidated equity equal to the sum of the two companies' stockholders' equity amounts?

	Tejas	Volunteer
Assets		
Cash	$ 24,000	$ 20,000
Accounts receivable, net	91,000	42,000
Note receivable from Volunteer	81,000	—
Inventory	145,000	214,000
Investment in Volunteer	266,000	—
Plant assets, net	278,000	219,000
Total	$885,000	$495,000
Liabilities and Stockholders' Equity		
Accounts payable	$ 57,000	$ 49,000
Notes payable	177,000	149,000
Other liabilities	129,000	31,000
Common stock	274,000	118,000
Retained earnings	248,000	148,000
Total	$885,000	$495,000

Accounting for a bond investment purchased at a premium
(Obj. 4)

P10-5A Financial institutions such as insurance companies and pension plans hold large quantities of bond investments. Suppose **Farm Bureau Insurance and Financial Services** purchases $600,000 of 6% bonds of Eaton, Inc., for 103 on March 1, 20X4. These bonds pay interest on March 1 and September 1 each year. They mature on March 1, 20X8. At December 31, 20X4, the market price of the bonds is 103 1/2.

Required

1. Journalize Farm Bureau's purchase of the bonds as a long-term investment on March 1, 20X4 (to be held to maturity), receipt of cash interest, and amortization of the bond investment at December 31, 20X4. The straight-line method is appropriate for amortizing the bond investment.
2. Show all financial statement effects of this long-term bond investment on Farm Bureau Insurance and Financial Services' balance sheet and income statement at December 31, 20X4.

Recording foreign-currency transactions and reporting the transaction gain or loss
(Obj. 5)

general ledger

P10-6A Suppose **Goodyear Tire & Rubber Company** completed the following international transactions:

Feb.	1	Sold inventory on account to **Fiat**, the Italian automaker, for €82,000. The exchange rate of the euro is $0.90, and Fiat demands to pay in euros.
	10	Purchased supplies on account from a Canadian company at a price of Canadian $50,000. The exchange rate of the Canadian dollar is $0.70, and payment will be in Canadian dollars.
	17	Sold inventory on account to an English firm for 100,000 British pounds. Payment will be in pounds, and the exchange rate of the pound is $1.50.
	22	Collected from Fiat. The exchange rate is €1 = $0.93.
Mar.	18	Paid the Canadian company. The exchange rate of the Canadian dollar is $0.67.
	24	Collected from the English firm. The exchange rate of the British pound is $1.47.

Required

1. Record these transactions in Goodyear's journal and show how to report the transaction gain or loss on the income statement.
2. How will what you learned in this problem help you structure international transactions?

Measuring and explaining the foreign-currency translation adjustment
(Obj. 5)

P10-7A Assume **Texas Instruments** (TI) has a semiconductor subsidiary company based in Japan.

Required

1. Translate into dollars the foreign-currency balance sheet of the Japanese subsidiary of TI. When TI acquired this subsidiary, the Japanese yen was worth \$0.0064. The current exchange rate is \$0.0086. During the period when the subsidiary earned its income, the average exchange rate was \$0.0070 per yen.

	Yen
Assets	300,000,000
Liabilities	80,000,000
Stockholders' equity:	
Common stock	20,000,000
Retained earnings	200,000,000
	300,000,000

Before you perform the foreign-currency translation calculations, indicate whether TI has experienced a positive or a negative translation adjustment. State whether the adjustment is a gain or a loss, and show where it is reported in the financial statements.

2. To which company does the foreign-currency translation adjustment "belong"? In which company's financial statements will the translation adjustment be reported?
3. How will what you learned in this problem help you understand published financial statements?

Using a cash-flow statement
(Obj. 6)

P10-8A Excerpts from **Intel Corporation's** statement of cash flows, as adapted, appear as follows:

Intel Corporation
Consolidated Statement of Cash Flows (Adapted, Partial)
Years Ended December 31

(In Millions)	20X1	20X0
Cash and cash equivalents, beginning of year	\$ 2,976	\$ 3,695
Net cash provided by operating activities	8,654	12,827
Cash flows provided by (used for) investing activities:		
Additions to property, plant, and equipment	(7,309)	(6,674)
Acquisitions of other companies	(883)	(2,317)
Purchases of available-for-sale investments	(7,141)	(17,188)
Sales of available-for-sale investments	15,138	16,144
Net cash (used for) investing activities	(195)	(10,035)
Cash flows provided by (used for) financing activities:		
Borrowing	329	215
Retirement of long-term debt	(10)	(46)
Proceeds from issuance of stock	762	797
Repurchase and retirement of common stock	(4,008)	(4,007)
Payment of dividends to stockholders	(538)	(470)
Net cash (used for) financing activities	(3,465)	(3,511)
Net increase (decrease) in cash and cash equivalents	4,994	(719)
Cash and cash equivalents, end of year	\$ 7,970	\$ 2,976

Required

As the chief executive officer of Intel Corporation, your duty is to write the management letter to your stockholders to explain Intel's investing activities during 20X1. Compare the company's level of investment with preceding years and indicate the major way the company financed its investments during 20X1. Net income for 20X1 was $1,291 million.

(Group B)

Reporting investments on the balance sheet and the related revenue on the income statement
(Obj. 1, 2)

P10-1B Jefferson-Pilot Corporation, a financial service concern headquartered in Greensboro, North Carolina, owns numerous investments in the stock of other companies. Assume that Jefferson-Pilot completed the following long-term investment transactions:

20X4	
May 1	Purchased 8,000 shares, which make up 25% of the common stock of Venus Company at total cost of $640,000.
Sep. 15	Received semiannual cash dividend of $1.40 per share on the Venus investment.
Oct. 12	Purchased 1,000 shares of Mercury Corporation common stock as an available-for-sale investment paying $22.50 per share.
Dec. 14	Received semiannual cash dividend of $0.75 per share on the Mercury investment.
Dec. 31	Received annual report from Venus Company. Net income for the year was $350,000.

At year end the current market value of the Mercury stock is $20,700. The market value of the Venus stock is $740,000.

Required

1. For which investment is current market value used in the accounting? Why is market value used for one investment and not the other?
2. Show what Jefferson-Pilot would report on its year-end balance sheet and income statement for these investment transactions. (It is helpful to use a T-account for the investment in Venus stock.) Ignore income tax.

Accounting for available-for-sale and equity-method investments
(Obj. 1, 2)

P10-2B The beginning balance sheet of Charter Investment Bankers, Ltd. included the following:

Long-Term Investments in Affiliates (equity-method investments) . . .	$657,000

Charter completed the following investment transactions during the year:

Feb. 16	Purchased 5,000 shares of BCM Software common stock as a long-term available-for-sale investment, paying $9.25 per share.
May 14	Received cash dividend of $0.82 per share on the BCM investment.
Oct. 15	Received cash dividend of $29,000 from an affiliated company.
Dec. 31	Received annual reports from affiliated companies. Their total net income for the year was $620,000. Of this amount, Charter's proportion is 25%.

The market values of Charter's investments are BCM, $45,100; affiliated companies, $947,000.

Required

1. Record the transactions in the journal of Charter Investment Bankers.
2. Post entries to the Long-Term Investments in Affiliates T-account and determine its balance at December 31.
3. Show how to report the Long-Term Available-for-Sale Investments and the Long-Term Investments in Affiliates on Charter's balance sheet at December 31.

Analyzing consolidated financial statements
(Obj. 3)

P10-3B This problem demonstrates the dramatic effect that consolidation accounting can have on a company's ratios. **General Motors Corporation (GM)** owns 100% of **General Motors Acceptance Corporation (GMAC)**, its financing subsidiary. GM's main operations consist of manufacturing automotive products. GMAC mainly helps people finance the purchase of automobiles from GM and its dealers. The two companies' individual balance sheets are summarized as follows (amounts in billions):

	General Motors (Parent)	GMAC (Subsidiary)
Total assets	$132.6	$94.6
Total liabilities	$109.3	$86.3
Total stockholders' equity	23.3	8.3
Total liabilities and equity	$132.6	$94.6

Assume that GMAC's liabilities include $5.1 billion owed to General Motors, the parent company.

Required

1. Compute the debt ratio of GM Corporation considered alone.
2. Determine the consolidated total assets, total liabilities, and stockholders' equity of GM after consolidating the financial statements of GMAC into the totals of GM, the parent company.
3. Recompute the debt ratio of the consolidated entity. Why do companies prefer not to consolidate their financing subsidiaries into their own financial statements?

Consolidating a wholly-owned subsidiary
(Obj. 3)

spreadsheet

P10-4B Water Resources Corporation paid $179,000 to acquire all the common stock of Hydra Park, Inc., and Hydra Park owes Water Resources $55,000 on a note payable. Immediately after the purchase on June 30, 20X6, the two companies' balance sheets were as follows:

	Water Resources	Hydra Park
Assets		
Cash	$ 18,000	$ 32,000
Accounts receivable, net	264,000	43,000
Note receivable from Hydra Park	55,000	—
Inventory	193,000	153,000
Investment in Hydra Park	179,000	—
Plant assets, net	305,000	138,000
Total	$1,014,000	$366,000
Liabilities and Stockholders' Equity		
Accounts payable	$ 76,000	$ 37,000
Notes payable	118,000	123,000
Other liabilities	144,000	27,000
Common stock	282,000	90,000
Retained earnings	394,000	89,000
Total	$1,014,000	$366,000

Required

1. Prepare Water Resources' consolidated balance sheet. (It is sufficient to complete a consolidation work sheet.)
2. Why aren't total assets of the consolidated entity equal to the sum of total assets for both companies combined? Why isn't consolidated equity equal to the sum of the two companies' stockholders' equity combined?

Accounting for a bond investment purchased at a discount **(Obj. 4)**

P10-5B Financial institutions such as investment companies and pension plans hold large quantities of bond investments. Suppose **Paine Webber** purchases $500,000 of 6% bonds of **General Motors Corporation** for 92 on January 31, 20X0. These bonds pay interest on January 31 and July 31 each year. They mature on July 31, 20X8. At December 31, 20X0, the market price of the bonds is 93.

Required

1. Journalize Paine Webber's purchase of the bonds as a long-term investment on January 31, 20X0 (to be held to maturity), receipt of cash interest and amortization of the bond investment on July 31, 20X0, and accrual of interest revenue and amortization at December 31, 20X0. The straight-line method is appropriate for amortizing the bond investment.
2. Show all financial statement effects of this long-term bond investment on Paine Webber's balance sheet and income statement at December 31, 20X0.

Recording foreign-currency transactions and reporting the transaction gain or loss **(Obj. 5)**

general ledger

P10-6B Suppose **Big Red Company**, which features a strawberry soda, completed the following international transactions:

June 4	Sold soft-drink syrup on account to a Mexican company for $43,000. The exchange rate of the Mexican peso is $0.101, and the customer agrees to pay in dollars.
13	Purchased inventory on account from a Canadian company at a price of Canadian $100,000. The exchange rate of the Canadian dollar is $0.65, and payment will be in Canadian dollars.
20	Sold goods on account to an English firm for 70,000 British pounds. Payment will be in pounds; and exchange rate of the pound is $1.50.
27	Collected from the Mexican company.
July 21	Paid the Canadian company. The exchange rate of the Canadian dollar is $0.62.
Aug. 17	Collected from the English firm. The exchange rate of the British pound is $1.40.

Required

1. Record these transactions in Big Red's journal and show how to report the transaction gain or loss on the income statement.
2. How will what you learned in this problem help you structure international transactions?

Measuring and explaining the foreign-currency translation adjustment **(Obj. 5)**

P10-7B International Pastries, Inc. owns a subsidiary based in Denmark.

Required

1. Translate the foreign-currency balance sheet of the Danish subsidiary of International Pastries, Inc. into dollars. When International Pastries acquired this subsidiary, the Danish krone was worth $0.17. The current exchange rate is $0.12. During the period when the subsidiary earned its income, the average exchange rate was $0.16 per krone.

	Kroner
Assets	3,000,000
Liabilities	1,000,000
Stockholders' equity:	
Common stock	300,000
Retained earnings	1,700,000
	3,000,000

Before you perform the foreign-currency translation calculation, indicate whether International Pastries, Inc. has experienced a positive or a negative foreign-currency translation adjustment. State whether the adjustment is a gain or loss, and show where it is reported in the financial statements.

2. To which company does the translation adjustment "belong"? In which company's financial statements will the translation adjustment be reported?
3. How will what you learned in this problem help you understand published financial statements?

Using a cash-flow statement **(Obj. 6)**

P10-8B Excerpts from The Coca-Cola Company statement of cash flows, as adapted, appear as follows:

The Coca-Cola Company and Subsidiaries

Consolidated Statements of Cash Flows (Adapted)

(In Millions)	Years Ended December 31, 20X1	20X0
Operating Activities		
Net cash provided by operating activities	$ 4,110	$ 1,165
Investing Activities		
Acquisitions and investments, principally trademarks and bottling companies	(651)	(397)
Purchases of investments	(456)	(508)
Proceeds from disposals of investments	455	290
Purchases of property, plant, and equipment	(769)	(733)
Proceeds from disposals of property, plant, and equipment	91	45
Other investing activities	142	138
Net cash used in investing activities	(1,188)	(1,165)
Financing Activities		
Issuances of debt (borrowing)	3,011	3,671
Payments of debt	(3,937)	(4,256)
Issuances of stock	164	331
Purchases of stock for treasury	(277)	(133)
Dividends	(1,791)	(1,685)
Net cash used in financing activities	(2,830)	(2,072)

Required

As the chief executive officer of The Coca-Cola Company, your duty is to write the management letter to your stockholders explaining Coca-Cola's major investing activities during 20X1. Compare the company's level of investment with previous years and indicate how the company financed its investments during 20X1. Net income for 20X1 was $3,969 million.

Apply Your Knowledge

Decision Cases

Making an investment sale decision
(Obj. 1, 2, 4)

Case 1. Shelly Herzog is the general manager of McNamara Service Company, which provides data-management services for physicians in the Orlando, Florida, area. McNamara Service Company is having a rough year. Net income trails projections for the year by almost $75,000. This shortfall is especially important. McNamara plans to issue stock early next year and needs to show investors that the company can meet its earnings targets.

McNamara holds several investments purchased a few years ago. Even though investing in stocks is outside McNamara's core business of data-management services, Herzog thinks these investments may hold the key to helping the company meet its net income goal for the year. She is considering what to do with the following investments:

1. McNamara owns 50% of the common stock of Mid-Florida Office Systems, which provides the company's business forms that McNamara uses. Mid-Florida has lost money for the past 2 years but still has a retained earnings balance of $550,000. Herzog thinks she can get Mid-Florida's treasurer to declare a $160,000 cash dividend, half of which would go to McNamara.
2. McNamara owns a bond investment purchased 8 years ago for $250,000. The purchase price represents a discount from the bonds' maturity value of $400,000. These bonds mature 2 years from now, and their current market value is $380,000. Herzog has checked with an **Edward Jones** investment representative, and Ms. Herzog is considering selling the bonds. Edward Jones would charge a 1% commission on the sale transaction.
3. McNamara owns 5,000 shares of **Microsoft** stock valued at $53 per share. One year ago, Microsoft stock was worth only $28 per share because the company was involved in a major antitrust lawsuit. McNamara purchased the Microsoft stock for $37 per share. Herzog wonders whether McNamara should sell the Microsoft stock.

Required

Evaluate all three actions as a way for McNamara Service Company to generate the needed amount of income. Recommend the best way for McNamara to achieve its net income goal.

Making an investment decision
(Obj. 1, 5)

Case 2. **United Technologies (UT)** may not be an everyday name in American households, but millions of people ride on **Otis** elevators, keep cool with **Carrier** air conditioners, and travel on airplanes powered by **Pratt & Whitney** engines. All these companies are subsidiaries of United Technologies. UT's consolidated sales for 2000 were $26.6 billion, and expenses totaled $24.8 billion. UT operates worldwide and conducts 37% of its business outside the United States. During 2000, UT reported the following items in its financial statements:

Foreign-currency translation adjustments	$(202)
Unrealized holding ______ on available-for-sale investments	(328)

As you consider an investment in UT stock, some concerns arise. Answer each of the following questions:

1. What do the parentheses around these items signify?
2. Are these items reported as assets, liabilities, stockholders' equity, revenues, or expenses? Are they normal-balance accounts, or are they contra accounts?
3. Are these items reason for rejoicing or sorrow at UT? Are UT's emotions about these items deep or only moderate? Why?

(continued)

4. Did UT include these items in net income? in retained earnings? In the final analysis, how much net income did UT report for 2000?
5. Should these items scare you away from investing in UT stock? Why or why not?

Ethical Issue

Media One owns 18% of the voting stock of Web Talk, Inc. The remainder of the Web Talk stock is held by numerous investors with small holdings. Austin Cohen, president of Media One and a member of Web Talk's board of directors, heavily influences Web Talk's policies.

Under the market value method of accounting for investments, Media One's net income increases as it receives dividend revenue from Web Talk. Media One pays President Cohen a bonus computed as a percentage of Media One's net income. Therefore, Cohen can control his personal bonus to a certain extent by influencing Web Talk's dividends.

A recession occurs in 20X4, and Media One's income is low. Cohen uses his power to have Web Talk pay a large cash dividend. The action requires Web Talk to borrow in order to pay the dividend.

Required

1. In getting Web Talk to pay the large cash dividend, is Cohen acting within his authority as a member of the Web Talk board of directors? Are Cohen's actions ethical? Whom can his actions harm?
2. Discuss how using the equity method of accounting for investments would decrease Cohen's potential for manipulating his bonus.

Financial Statement Case

Analyzing goodwill, consolidated subsidiaries, and international operations **(Obj. 3, 5)**

This case is based on the financial statements of **Pier 1 Imports**, given in Appendix B at the end of this book.

1. During 2001, Pier 1 completed the acquisition of Cargo Furniture, Inc. How much goodwill did Pier 1 purchase in this acquisition? Which account (on which financial statement) includes the goodwill? How much amortization expense will Pier 1 record on the goodwill during 2003?
2. What is Pier 1's percentage ownership of its consolidated subsidiaries? How can you tell? Which financial statement provides the evidence?
3. Does Pier 1 have any foreign subsidiaries? What evidence answers this question? Which financial statement provides the evidence?
4. Which monetary currency was stronger, the U.S. dollar or Pier 1's foreign currencies, during 2000, 2001, and 2002? Give the basis for your answers.

Analytical Case

Analyzing investments, consolidated statements, and international operations **(Obj. 1, 2, 3, 5)**

This case is based on the financial statements of **Fossil, Inc.**, given in Appendix A at the end of this book.

1. Fossil accounts for investments in joint ventures by the equity method. Fiscal year 2001 saw lots of activity in Fossil's joint-venture investments. Details appear on the balance sheet, the income statement, the statement of cash flows, and in Notes 3 and 8. Use these data to explain how Fossil moved from its beginning balance of Investments in Joint Ventures to its ending balance during the year ended January 5, 2002 (fiscal year 2001). You may use either a T-account or an equation. Assume the net income of Fossil Spain are not included in any other income or loss figure. Note: It is impossible to account for $3 thousand of the year's activity.
2. Identify the three items that comprise other comprehensive income (ignore the cumulative effect of . . . SFAS 133). Then answer these questions about the individual items during fiscal year 2001?

a. Did the foreign currencies of Fossil's non-U.S. subsidiaries rise or fall relative to the U.S. dollar?

b. Did Fossil's marketable investments increase or decrease in value? By how much? At January 5, 2002, was the current market value of Fossil's marketable investments above or below cost? By how much? The statement of stockholders' equity provides the data.

c. Briefly describe Fossil's forward-contract hedging activities. Were the hedging activities successful or unsuccessful during the year? How can you tell?

3. What evidence appears on Fossil's balance sheet to indicate that Fossil owns less than 100% of some of its consolidated subsidiaries? Did those subsidiaries experience profits or losses during fiscal year 2001? Fossil sold no companies in which a minority interest existed. Explain how you formed your answer.

Group Project

Pick a stock from *The Wall Street Journal* or other database or publication. Assume that your group purchases 1,000 shares of the stock as a long-term investment and that your 1,000 shares are less than 20% of the company's outstanding stock. Research the stock in *Value Line, Moody's Investor Record*, or other source to determine whether the company pays cash dividends and, if so, how much and at what intervals.

Required

1. Track the stock for a period assigned by your professor. Over the specified period, keep a daily record of the price of the stock to see how well your investment has performed. Each day, search the Corporate Dividend News in *The Wall Street Journal* to keep a record of any dividends you've received. End the period of your analysis with a month end, such as September 30 or December 31.
2. Journalize all transactions that you have experienced, including the stock purchase, dividends received (both cash dividends and stock dividends), and any year-end adjustment required by the accounting method that is appropriate for your situation. Assume you will prepare financial statements on the ending date of your study.
3. Show what you will report on your company's balance sheet, income statement, and statement of cash flows as a result of your investment transactions.

11

The Income Statement & The Statement of Stockholders' Equity

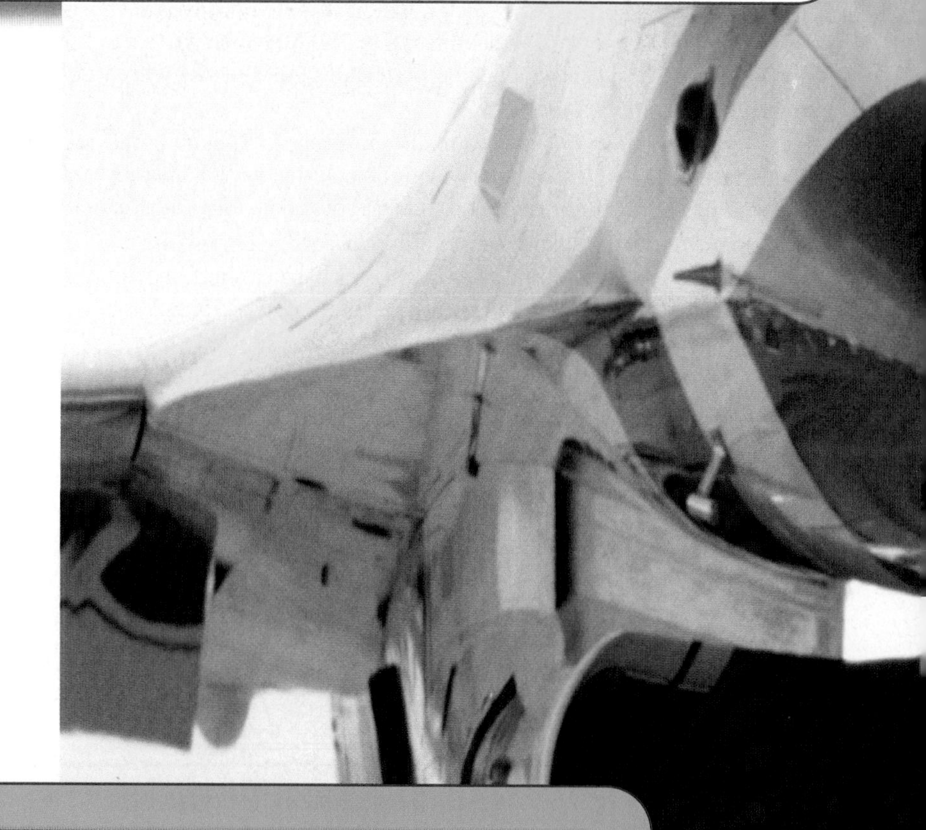

Learning Objectives

1. **Analyze** a complex income statement
2. **Account** for a corporation's income tax
3. **Analyze** a statement of stockholders' equity
4. **Understand** managers' and auditors' responsibilities for the financial statements

Integrator CD

Need additional help? Go to the **Integrator CD** *and search these key words:* comprehensive income statement, earnings per share (EPS), extraordinary gain/loss, prior period adjustment, statement of stockholders' equity, taxable income

Lockheed Martin Corporation

Consolidated Statement of Operations (adapted)

	(In millions, except per share data)	2001	2000	1999
		Year ended December 31,		
1	*Net sales*	$23,990	$24,541	$24,999
2	Cost of sales	22,447	22,881	23,346
3	Earnings from operations	1,543	1,660	1,653
4	Other income and expenses, net	(655)	(409)	344
5		888	1,251	1,997
6	Interest expense	700	919	809
7	Earnings from continuing operations before income taxes, extraordinary items and cumulative effect of change in accounting	188	332	1,188
8	Income tax expense	109	714	459
9	Earnings (loss) from continuing operations before extraordinary items and cumulative effect of change in accounting	79	(382)	729
10	Discontinued operations	(1,089)	(42)	8
11	Extraordinary loss	(36)	(95)	—
12	Cumulative effect of change in accounting	—	—	(355)
13	*Net (loss) earnings*	$ (1,046)	$ (519)	$ 382
14	*Earnings (loss) per common share:*			
	Basic			
	Continuing operations before extraordinary items and cumulative effect of change in accounting	$ 0.18	$ (0.95)	$ 1.91
	Discontinued operations	(2.55)	(0.10)	0.02
	Extraordinary loss	(0.08)	(0.24)	—
	Cumulative effect of change in accounting	—	—	(0.93)
		$ (2.45)	$ (1.29)	$ 1.00

Lockheed Martin's PAC-3 Missile Intercepts Tactical Ballistic Missile . . . .
Second PAC-3 Missile Did Not Launch Against Storm Target.

> DALLAS, April 25, 2002—A Patriot Advanced Capability-3 (PAC-3) Missile successfully intercepted and destroyed an incoming tactical ballistic missile (TBM). . . . The PAC-3 Missile destroyed a Patriot-As-A-Target missile.
>
> A second PAC-3 Missile, slated to defend against an incoming Storm TBM, did not launch. An investigation is being conducted to determine the cause of that anomaly.
>
> "We're pleased that the PAC-3 Missile succeeded in its mission, though there are some system issues requiring further refinement," said Steve Graham, PAC-3 Missile program director for Lockheed Martin Missiles and Fire Control. "Today's test is an example of why aggressive flight tests are necessary to perfect all aspects of the system. . . ."

Watching a PAC missile test or a space shuttle launch may not point you to accounting, but it should. Lockheed Martin Corporation's financial statements report on the activities of a key military contractor. Underlying the statement are Patriot missiles, Joint Strike fighter planes, and Atlas launchers. Lockheed Martin also helps European countries manage their nuclear stockpiles and air defenses. Japan gets help defending its shorelines.

You might think Lockheed Martin would have no problems, that its far-flung empire would automatically generate profits. Not always—2001 was a tough year for the company, mainly because it sold off money-losing segments. These discontinued operations, plus an extraordinary event, combined for over $1 billion of losses and wiped out Lockheed Martin's profits for the year.

Source: Lockheed Martin Corporation Press Release (April 25, 2002), at www.lockheedmartin.com/news/articles/042502_z.html.

Sitemap

This chapter shows how to interpret the discontinued operations and extraordinary items that you will encounter. We begin by examining one of the most important decisions an analyst faces: how to evaluate the quality of a company's earnings.

Evaluating the Quality of Earnings

comprehensive income statement, earnings per share (EPS), extraordinary gain/loss

Objective

1 Analyze a complex income statement

A corporation's net income (net earnings) receives more attention than any other item in the financial statements. To stockholders, the larger the corporation's profit, the greater the likelihood of dividends. To creditors, the larger the profit, the better the ability to pay debts.

Suppose you are considering investing in the stock of two Internet sales companies. In reading their annual reports, you learn that the companies earned the same net income last year and that each company has increased its net income by 15% annually over the last 5 years.

The two companies, however, have generated income in different ways:

- Company A's income has resulted from central operations (Internet sales).
- Company B's Internet sales have struggled. Its growth in net income resulted from selling off land acquired years earlier.

In which company would you invest?

Company A holds the promise of better earnings in the future. This corporation earns profits from *continuing operations*. We may expect Company A to match its past earnings in the future. Company B shows no growth from operations. Its net income results from *one-time transactions*—the selling off of assets. Sooner or later, Company B will run out of assets to sell. So your decision is to invest in the stock of Company A. Investors would say that Company A's earnings are of *higher quality* than Company B's earnings.

Another factor to consider in evaluating the quality of a company's earnings is how early the business records revenue. A company that records all revenue up front may be trying to hide bad operating results. Likewise, a company that capitalizes costs that should be expensed may not be as profitable as its financial statements show. WorldCom admitted doing this.

Lockheed Martin's earnings have turned into losses (line 13). But continuing operations generated a profit in 2001 after losing money in 2000 (see line 9). To explore the makeup of net income, let's examine the various sources of income. Exhibit 11-1 provides a comprehensive example that we will use throughout the chapter. It is the income statement of Allied Electronics Corporation, which produces electronic-control instruments.

Continuing Operations

In the income statement in Exhibit 11-1, the topmost section reports income from continuing operations (lines 1 to 10). This part of the business is expected to

Exhibit 11-1

Allied Electronics Corporation Income Statement

Allied Electronics Corporation

Income Statement
Year Ended December 31, 20X5

Continuing operations	1	Sales revenue	$500,000
	2	Cost of goods sold	240,000
	3	Gross margin	260,000
	4	Operating expenses (detailed)	181,000
	5	Operating income	79,000
		Other gains (losses):	
	6	Loss on restructuring operations	(8,000)
	7	Gain on sale of machinery	19,000
	8	Income from continuing operations before income tax	90,000
	9	Income tax expense	36,000
	10	Income from continuing operations	54,000
Special items	11	Discontinued operations, $35,000, less income tax of $14,000	21,000
	12	Income before extraordinary item and cumulative effect of change in depreciation method	75,000
	13	Extraordinary flood loss, $20,000, less income tax saving of $8,000	(12,000)
	14	Cumulative effect of change in depreciation method, $10,000, less income tax of $4,000	6,000
	15	Net income	$ 69,000
Earnings per share		Earnings per share of common stock (20,000 shares outstanding):	
	16	Income from continuing operations	$2.70
	17	Income from discontinued operations	1.05
	18	Income before extraordinary item and cumulative effect of change in depreciation method	3.75
	19	Extraordinary loss	(0.60)
	20	Cumulative effect of change in depreciation method	0.30
	21	Net income	$3.45

✔ Check Point 11-1

✔ Check Point 11-2

✔ Check Point 11-3

continue from period to period. We may use this information to predict that Allied Electronics will earn income of approximately $54,000 next year.

The continuing operations of Allied Electronics include three new items:

- During 20X5, the company restructured operations at a loss of $8,000 (line 6). Restructuring costs include severance pay to laid-off workers and moving expenses for employees transferred to other locations. The restructuring loss is part of continuing operations because Allied Electronics is remaining in the same line of business. But the restructuring loss is an "Other" item on the income statement because restructuring the business falls outside Allied's core activity, which is selling electronics products.
- Allied had a gain on the sale of machinery (line 7), also outside the company's core business activity. This explains why the gain is reported separately from Allied's operating income (lines 1 to 5).
- Income tax expense (line 9) is subtracted in arriving at income from continuing operations. Corporate income tax is a significant expense. The current

maximum federal income tax rate for corporations is 35%. State income taxes run about 5% in many states. Thus, we use an income tax rate of 40% in our illustrations. The $36,000 income tax expense in Exhibit 11-1 equals the pre-tax income from continuing operations multiplied by the tax rate ($90,000 .40 = $36,000).

How much was Allied Electronics' *total* income tax expense during 20X5? Consider lines, 9, 11, 13, and 14 of the income statement in Exhibit 11-1.

Answer:
$46,000 = ($36,000 + $14,000 − $8,000 + $4,000)

DECISION: Which Income Number to Use for Predicting Future Profits?

How is income from continuing operations used in investment analysis? Suppose Laney Gibbs, an analyst with Prudential Securities in Atlanta, is estimating the value of Allied Electronics' common stock. Gibbs and her staff may believe that Allied Electronics can earn annual income of $54,000 each year for the indefinite future, based on Allied's 20X5 income from continuing operations.

To estimate the value of Allied's common stock, financial analysts determine the present value (present value means the value *today*) of Allied's stream of future income. Gibbs must use some interest rate to compute the present value ←. Assume that an appropriate interest rate (*i*) for the valuation of Allied Electronics is 12%. This rate is determined subjectively, based on the risk that Allied might not be able to earn annual income of $54,000 for the indefinite future. The rate is also called the **investment capitalization rate** because it is used to estimate the value of an investment in a company. The higher the risk, the higher the rate, and vice versa. The computation of the estimated value of a stock is

→ *See Appendix B for a review of present value.*

Investment capitalization rate An earnings rate used to estimate the value of an investment in the capital stock of another company.

$$\begin{array}{c}\text{Estimated value of}\\\text{Allied Electronics}\\\text{common stock}\end{array} = \frac{\begin{array}{c}\text{Estimated annual}\\\text{income in the future}\end{array}}{\begin{array}{c}\text{Investment}\\\text{capitalization rate}\end{array}} = \frac{\$54,000}{.12} = \$450,000^{*}$$

Gibbs thus estimates that Allied Electronics Corporation is worth $450,000. She would then compare this estimate to the current market value of Allied Electronics' stock, which is $513,000. Allied Electronics' balance sheet reports that Allied has 108,000 shares of common stock outstanding, and *The Wall Street Journal* reports that Allied common stock is selling for $4.75 per share. The current market value of Allied Stock is thus

Current market value of the company	=	Number of shares of common stock outstanding	×	Current market price per share
$513,000	=	108,000	×	$4.75

*This valuation model has many forms, which are covered in finance classes. Here we introduce the basic form of a widely used valuation model to illustrate how accounting income can be used in actual practice.

The investment decision rule may take this form:

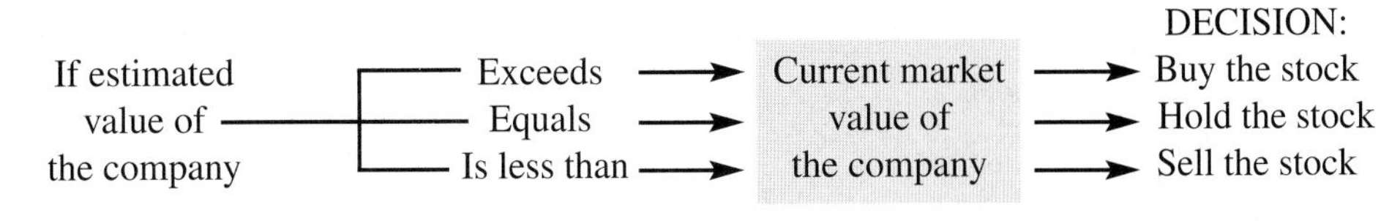

In this case,

Estimated value of the company		Current market value of the company	DECISION:
$450,000	Is less than	$513,000	→ Sell the stock

Gibbs believes the stock price should fall below its current market value of 513,000 to somewhere in a range near $450,000. Based largely on its income from continuing operations, Gibbs thinks that Allied's stock would be more fairly valued at $450,000. Based on this analysis, Prudential would recommend that investors holding Allied Electronics stock should sell it.

Investors often make their decisions based on the value of a single share of stock. They can estimate the value of one share of stock with a variation of the valuation computation that uses earnings per share (EPS) of common stock, as follows:

$$\text{Estimated value of one share of common stock} = \frac{\text{Estimated annual earnings per share}}{\text{Investment capitalization rate}}$$

✔ Check Point 11-4

The analysis based on one share of stock follows the pattern illustrated for the company as a whole.

Discontinued Operations

Most large corporations engage in several lines of business. For example, Lockheed Martin has four business segments: aeronautics, space systems, technology services, and systems integration. Sears, Roebuck & Company has a real-estate development company (Homart) and an insurance company (Allstate) in addition to its retail stores. We call each identifiable division of a company a **segment of the business.**

Segment of the business
One of various separate divisions of a company.

A company may sell a segment of its business. Lockheed Martin sold its global telecommunications services business during 2001. The sale of a business segment is viewed as a one-time transaction. Lockheed's income statement for 2001 reports on the segment that has been disposed of under the heading Discontinued Operations (line 10 on page 507).

Let's return to the Allied Electronics example in Exhibit 11-1 (page 509). The discontinued operations are taxed at the 40% rate. Therefore, discontinued operations are reported along with their income tax effect by Allied Electronics Corporation as follows (line 11, page 509):

Discontinued operations, $35,000, less income tax of $14,000	$21,000

Discontinued operations relate to an identifiable segment of the business. Gains and losses on normal asset dispositions are *not* reported as discontinued operations. They can be reported in the "Other" section of the income statement (Exhibit 11-1, lines 6 and 7).

Financial analysts typically do *not* include discontinued operations in predictions of future corporate income because the discontinued segments will not continue to generate income for the company.

Extraordinary Gains and Losses (Extraordinary Items)

Extraordinary gains and losses Also called *extraordinary items*, these gains and losses are both unusual for the company and infrequent.

Extraordinary gains and losses, also called **extraordinary items,** are both *unusual* for the company and *infrequent*. Losses from natural disasters (such as earthquakes, floods, and tornadoes) and the taking of company assets by a foreign government (expropriation) are extraordinary. Lockheed Martin reports an extraordinary loss (see page 507, line 11).

Extraordinary items are reported along with their income tax effect. During 20X5, Allied Electronics Corporation lost $20,000 of inventory in a flood (Exhibit 11-1, line 13). This flood loss, which reduced income, also reduced Allied's income tax. The tax effect decreases the net amount of the loss in the same way that income tax reduces the amount of net income. Another way to report an extraordinary loss along with its tax effect is as follows:

Extraordinary flood loss.	$(20,000)
Less income tax saving.	8,000
Extraordinary flood loss, net of tax	(12,000)

Trace this item to the income statement in Exhibit 11-1 (line 13). An extraordinary gain is reported in the same way, net of its income tax.

Gains and losses due to lawsuits, restructuring, and the sale of plant assets are *not* extraordinary items. They are considered normal business occurrences. However, because they are outside the business's central operations, they are reported on the income statement as Other gains and losses. Examples include losses due to labor strikes, the gain on sale of machinery, and the restructuring loss in the Other gains (losses) section of Exhibit 11-1 (page 509, lines 6 and 7).

Cumulative Effect of a Change in Accounting Principle

→ For a review of depreciation methods, see Chapter 7. For a review of inventory methods, see Chapter 6.

Companies sometimes change from one accounting method to another, such as from double-declining-balance (DDB) to straight-line depreciation, or from first-in, first-out (FIFO) to weighted-average cost for inventory ←. An accounting change makes it difficult to compare one period's financial statements with those of preceding periods. Without detailed information, investors and creditors can be misled into thinking that the current year is better or worse than the preceding year when in fact the only difference is a change in accounting method.

To help investors separate the effects of regular business operations from those caused by a change in accounting method, companies report the effect of the accounting change in a special section of the income statement. This section usually appears after extraordinary items. Exhibit 11-1, line 14 gives an example for Allied Electronics.

Allied Electronics Corporation changed from DDB to straight-line depreciation at the beginning of 20X5. How did this change in depreciation affect the 20X5 financial statements? First, it decreased depreciation expense for 20X5 and thereby increased 20X5 income from continuing operations. Second, the change affected the cumulative amounts from previous years. If Allied had been using straight-line depreciation in previous years, depreciation expense would have been less, and net income would have been $6,000 higher ($10,000 minus the additional income tax of $4,000). Exhibit 11-1 reports the cumulative effect of this accounting change on line 14.

Earnings per Share of Common Stock

The final segment of a corporation's income statement presents the company's earnings per share. **Earnings per share (EPS)** is the amount of a company's net income per share of its *outstanding common stock*. EPS is a key measure of a business's success, computed as follows:

Earnings per share (EPS) Amount of a company's net income per share of its outstanding common stock.

$$\text{Earnings per share} = \frac{\text{Net income} - \text{Preferred dividends}}{\text{Average number of shares of common stock outstanding}}$$

Just as the corporation lists its various sources of income separately from continuing operations, discontinued operations, and so on—it also lists the EPS figure separately for each significant element of net income. Consider the EPS calculations for Allied Electronics Corporation. The final section (lines 16 to 21) of Exhibit 11-1 shows how the EPS figures are reported on the income statement:

	Earnings per share of common stock (20,000 shares outstanding):	
16	Income from continuing operations ($54,000/20,000)	$2.70
17	Income from discontinued operations ($21,000/20,000)	1.05
18	Income before extraordinary item and cumulative effect of change in depreciation method ($75,000/20,000)	3.75
19	Extraordinary loss ($12,000/20,000)	(0.60)
20	Cumulative effect of change in depreciation method ($6,000/20,000)	0.30
21	Net income ($69,000/20,000)	$3.45

EFFECT OF PREFERRED DIVIDENDS ON EARNINGS PER SHARE. Recall that EPS is earnings per share of *common* stock. Holders of preferred stock have first claim on dividends →. Therefore, preferred dividends affect EPS and must be subtracted in the computation of EPS. Preferred dividends are not subtracted from discontinued operations, extraordinary items, or the cumulative effect of accounting changes.

← *Chapter 9, page 422, provide detailed information on preferred stock.*

If Allied Electronics Corporation had 10,000 shares of preferred stock outstanding, each with a $1.00 dividend, the annual preferred dividend would be $10,000 (10,000 × $1.00). The $10,000 would be subtracted from each of the different income subtotals, resulting in the following EPS computations:

Earnings per share of common stock (20,000 shares outstanding);	
Income from continuing operations ($54,000 − $10,000)/20,000	$2.20
Income from discontinued operations ($21,000/20,000)	1.05
Income before extraordinary item and cumulative effect of change in depreciation method ($75,000 − $10,000)/20,000	3.25
Extraordinary loss ($12,000/20,000)	(0.60)
Cumulative effect of change in depreciation method ($6,000/20,000)	0.30
Net income ($69,000 − $10,000)/20,000	$2.95

✔ Check Point 11-5
✔ Check Point 11-6

Earnings per Share Dilution. Some corporations make their preferred stock attractive by offering convertible preferred. The holders of convertible preferred may exchange the preferred for common stock. When preferred is converted to common, the EPS is *diluted*—reduced—because more common shares are divided into net income. Corporations with complex capital structures present two sets of EPS figures:

- EPS based on actual outstanding common shares (*basic* EPS)
- EPS based on outstanding common shares plus the additional common shares that would arise from conversion of the preferred stock into common (*diluted* EPS)

DECISION: Can You Believe Pro Forma Earnings?

Investors cannot wait until December 31 to get a company's earnings figures. They make investment decisions throughout the year. To meet the need for timely data, companies report their forecasted (or *pro forma*) earnings. This often comes in a press release, such as the following from eBay, October 29, 2001:

> *Based on eBay's current outlook..., 2002 pro forma earnings per share could range between $0.70 and $0.73 per [...] share.*

Investors can compare the pro forma earnings for 2002 to the comparable earnings per share figure for 2001, which was $0.32. The higher expected earnings for 2002 may cause investors to buy eBay stock.

Astute investors take pro forma earnings with a grain of salt because pro forma means "as if." In short, reader beware! As 2002 unfolds, eBay may or may not be able to earn net income of $0.73 per share.

Another feature of pro forma earnings is that the amounts are not audited by independent accountants. There is no generally accepted accounting principles (GAAP) definition of pro forma earnings, so managers are free to report whatever figures they wish. Unfortunately, some over-optimistic managers have conveniently omitted some losses and thus increased the pro forma earnings they released to the public.

By contrast, GAAP provides an objective way to measure net income and its components. And the income figures in annual reports are audited by outside accountants. GAAP is designed to provide reliable information, so astute investors also examine the income figures reported in the audited statements.

Using the Price/Earnings Ratio

The price/earnings (P/E) ratio is the ratio of the price of a company's stock to its EPS. P/E ratios are quoted widely in the business press. A popular investment strategy is to buy low P/E stocks under the theory that a company with a low P/E ratio must be a better buy than a company whose P/E ratio is high.

Let's consider eBay's P/E ratio, computed two ways—based on:

- 2001 actual earnings per share of $0.32
- 2002 pro forma earnings per share of $0.73

At the time of this writing, eBay's stock sold for $54.06 per share. Therefore, eBay's

- P/E based on 2001 actual earnings = 169 ($54.06/$0.32), which is sky high.
- P/E based on 2002 pro forma earnings = 74 ($54.06/$0.73), which is considerably lower (but still high by stock market standards).

Do you see the incentive to report a high pro forma earnings figure? The higher the pro forma earnings, the lower the P/E ratio, and thus the more attractive the stock to investors. The lesson to take away from this discussion: Be aware that pro forma earnings may be biased. Ask the company how it computed pro forma earnings. Did it include all gains and losses, or did it pick and choose items for inclusion in pro forma EPS?

Reporting of Comprehensive Income

All companies report net income or net loss on their income statements. As we saw in Chapter 10, companies with unrealized gains and losses on certain investments, and foreign-currency translation adjustments also report another income figure. **Comprehensive income** is the company's change in total stockholders' equity from all sources other than from the owners of the business. Comprehensive income includes net income plus:

Comprehensive income
A company's change in total stockholders' equity from all sources other than from the owners of the business.

- Unrealized gains (losses) on available-for-sale investments
- Foreign-currency translation adjustments

These items do not enter into the determination of net income but instead can be reported as Other comprehensive income, as shown in Exhibit 11-2. Assumed figures are used for all items.

Exhibit 11-2

Reporting Comprehensive Income

Allied Electronics Corporation

Statement of Comprehensive Income (Partial)
Year Ended December 31, 20X5

Net income			$69,000
Other comprehensive income:			
Unrealized gain on investment	$ 6,500		
Less income tax (40%)	2,600	$3,900	
Foreign-currency translation adjustment (loss)	$(9,000)		
Less income tax saving (40%)	3,600	(5,400)	
Other comprehensive income			(1,500)
Comprehensive income			$67,500

✔ Check Point 11-7

Earnings per share is reported only for net income and its components (continuing operations, discontinued operations, and so on). EPS is *not* reported for comprehensive income.

DECISION: What Should You Analyze to Gain an Overall Picture of a Company?

Two key figures used in financial analysis are

- Net income
- Cash flow from operations

For any one period, Allied Electronics' net income and net cash flow from operating activities may chart different paths. Accounting income arises from the accrual process as follows:

$$\text{Total revenues and gains} - \text{Total expenses and losses} = \text{Net income (or Net loss)}$$

As we have seen, revenues and gains are recorded when they occur, regardless of when the company receives or pays cash.

Net cash flow, on the other hand, is based solely on cash receipts and cash payments. During any particular period, a company may have lots of revenues and expenses and a hefty net income. But the company may have weak cash flow because it has not yet collected from customers. The reverse may also be true: The company may have abundant cash but little income.

The income statement and the cash-flow statement often paint different pictures of the company. Which one provides better information? Neither: Not just one but both statements are needed, along with the balance sheet and statement of stockholders' equity, for an overall view of the business.

Over long periods of time, a business's net income will equal its net cash flow because ultimately all revenues are realized in cash and all expenses are paid in cash. But until that happens, people will continue analyzing both net income and cash flow to make investment, credit, and management decisions.

Accounting for Corporate Income Taxes

taxable income

2 Account for a corporation's income tax

Corporations pay income tax in the same way individuals do. Corporate and personal tax rates differ, however. The current federal tax rate on most corporate income is 35%. Because most states also levy income taxes on corporations, most corporations have a combined federal and state income tax rate of approximately 40%.

To account for income tax, the corporation measures for each period:

- *Income tax expense*, an expense on the income statement
- *Income tax payable*, a liability on the balance sheet

Pretax accounting income Income before tax on the income statement.

Accounting for income tax by a corporation follows the principles of accrual accounting. Suppose in 20X4 that Nike, Inc., reported income before tax (also called **pretax accounting income**) of $900 million. Assume Nike's combined income tax rate is 40%. To begin this discussion let's assume income tax expense and income tax payable are the same. Then Nike would record income tax for the year as follows (amounts in millions):

20X4			
Dec. 31	Income Tax Expense ($900 × .40)	360	
	Income Tax Payable		360
	Recorded income tax for the year.		

ASSETS	=	LIABILITIES	+	STOCKHOLDERS' EQUITY	−	EXPENSES
0	=	360	+		−	360

Nike's 20X4 financial statements would report these figures (partial, in millions):

Income statement		Balance sheet	
Income before income tax	$900	Current liabilities:	
Income tax expense	(360)	Income tax payable	$360
Net income	$540		

In general, income tax expense and income tax payable can be computed as follows:*

Income tax *expense*	=	Income before income tax (from the *income statement*)	×	Income tax rate

Income tax *payable*	=	Taxable income (from the *income tax return* filed with the IRS)	×	Income tax rate

The income statement and the income tax return are entirely separate documents:

- The *income statement* reports the results of operations we have been working with throughout this course.
- The *income tax return* is filed with the Internal Revenue Service (IRS) to determine how much tax the company must pay the government.

For most companies, income tax expense and income tax payable differ. Certain revenues and expenses affect income differently for accounting purposes and for tax purposes. The most important difference between accounting income and **taxable income** occurs when a corporation uses straight-line depreciation for the financial statements and accelerated depreciation (modified accelerated cost recovery system [MACRS]→ for the tax return. For any 1 year, tax depreciation usually differs from accounting depreciation on the income statement.

Taxable income
The basis for computing the amount of tax to pay the government.

← *We learned in Chapter 7 that the MACRS depreciation method is similar to the double-declining-balance method.*

Continuing with the Nike illustration, suppose for 20X5 that Nike, Inc., has:

- Pretax accounting income of $900 million on the income statement
- Taxable income of $800 million on the company's income tax return

Taxable income is $100 million less than accounting income because Nike, Inc., like many other companies, uses straight-line depreciation for accounting purposes and accelerated depreciation for income tax purposes. Nike will record income tax for 20X5 as follows (dollar amounts in millions and an income tax rate of 40%):

20X5			
Dec. 31	Income Tax Expense ($900 × .40)	360	
	Income Tax Payable ($800 × .40)		320
	Deferred Tax Liability		40
	Recorded income tax for the year.		

ASSETS	=	LIABILITIES	+	STOCKHOLDERS' EQUITY	−	EXPENSES
0	=	320 + 40	+		−	$360

Income tax expense is reported on the income statement, and income tax payable and deferred tax liability on the balance sheet, as follows for Nike, Inc., at the end of 20X5:

Income statement		**Balance sheet**	
Income before income tax	$900	Current liabilities:	
Income tax expense	(360)	Income tax payable	$320
Net income	$540	Long-term liabilities:	
		Deferred tax liability	40**

**Assumes the beginning balance of Deferred tax liability was zero.

✔ Check Point 11-8

*The authors thank Jean Marie Hudson for suggesting this presentation.

Early in 20X6, Nike would pay its income tax payable of $320 million because this is a current liability. Deferred tax liability, however, is usually long-term, and the company may pay this liability over a longer period.

For a given year, Income Tax Payable can exceed Income Tax Expense. When that occurs, the company records a Deferred Tax Asset.

At year end 2001, Nike reported liabilities as shown in Exhibit 11-3.

Exhibit 11-3

Nike's Liabilities

Nike, Inc.

Consolidated Balance Sheet (Partial, Adapted)

(In millions)	*May 31, 2001*
Liabilities	
Current Liabilities:	
Current portion of long-term debt	$ 5.4
Notes payable	855.3
Accounts payable	432.0
Accrued liabilities	472.1
Income taxes payable	21.9
Total current liabilities	1,786.7
Long-term debt	435.9
Deferred tax liability	102.2

At the end of fiscal year 2001, how much income tax did Nike expect to pay within 1 year or less, and after a year? What was Nike's total income tax liability?

	(In millions)
Payable within 1 year	$ 21.9
Payable after a year	102.2
Total income tax liability	$124.1

prior-period adjustment

Analyzing Retained Earnings

Prior-Period Adjustments

What happens when a company records revenues or expenses incorrectly? If the error occurs in one period and is corrected in a later period, the balance of Retained Earnings will be wrong until the error is corrected.

Prior-period adjustment A correction to beginning balance of retained earnings for an error of an earlier period.

Corrections to the beginning balance of Retained Earnings for errors of an earlier period are called **prior-period adjustments.** The prior-period adjustment appears on the corporation's statement of retained earnings to correct the Retained Earnings balance.

Assume that CNN Corporation recorded 20X4 income tax expense as $30,000. The correct amount was $40,000. This error understated 20X4 expenses by $10,000 and overstated net income by $10,000. A bill from the government in 20X5 for the additional $10,000 alerted CNN to the mistake.

Prior-period adjustments are not reported on the income statement because they relate to an earlier accounting period. This prior-period adjustment would appear on the statement of retained earnings, as shown in Exhibit 11-4, with all amounts assumed:

CNN Corporation

Statement of Retained Earnings
Year Ended December 31, 20X5

Retained earnings balance, December 31, 20X4, as originally reported	$390,000
Prior-period adjustment—debit to correct error in recording income tax expense of 20X4	(10,000)
Retained earnings balance, December 31, 20X4, as adjusted	380,000
Net income for 20X5	114,000
	494,000
Dividends for 20X5	(41,000)
Retained earnings balance, December 31, 20X5	$453,000

Exhibit 11-4

Reporting a Prior-Period Adjustment

✔ **Check Point 11-9**

Restrictions on Retained Earnings

Dividends and purchases of treasury stock require payments by the corporation to its stockholders →. These outlays decrease the corporation's assets, so fewer assets are available to pay debts. Therefore, a company's creditors may restrict a corporation's dividend payments and treasury stock purchases. For example, a bank may agree to loan $500,000 only if the corporation limits dividend payments and its purchases of treasury stock. These restrictions focus on the balance of retained earnings.

← *For a review of treasury stock transactions, see Chapter 9, pages 428 to 430.*

Companies report any retained earnings restrictions in notes to the financial statements. Alberto-Culver Company—maker of Alberto VO5 hair products—had restrictions on retained earnings, as reported in Note 3:

> ***Notes to Consolidated Financial Statements***
> *Note 3: Long-Term Debt*
> *Various borrowing arrangements impose restrictions on such items as . . . dividend payments, treasury stock purchases, and interest expense. At September 30, 19X8, . . . $73 million of retained earnings was not restricted as to the payment of dividends and purchases of treasury stock.*

Why would a borrower such as Alberto-Culver Company agree to restrict dividends as a condition for receiving a loan?

Answer:
To get a lower interest rate. The greater the borrower's concessions are, the more favorable the terms of the loan.

Analyzing the Statement of Stockholders' Equity

statement of stockholders' equity

Objective

3 **Analyze** a statement of stockholders' equity

Most companies report a statement of stockholders' equity, which includes the statement of retained earnings. The statement of stockholders' equity is formatted in a manner similar to a statement of retained earnings but with columns for each element of stockholders' equity. The **statement of stockholders' equity** thus reports the changes in all categories of equity during the period.

Statement of stockholders' equity Reports the changes in all categories of stockholders' equity during the period.

Exhibit 11-5 is the 20X5 statement of stockholders' equity for Allied Electronics Corporation. Study its format. There is a column for each element of equity, with the far right column reporting total stockholders' equity. The top row (line 1) reports the beginning balance of each element, taken directly from last period's ending balance sheet. Each row of the statement reports the effect of a different transaction, starting with Issuance of stock (line 2). After explaining all the changes in equity, the statement ends with the December 31, 20X5, balances (line 10), which appear on the ending balance sheet, given in Exhibit 11-6.

Exhibit 11-5

Statement of Stockholders' Equity

Allied Electronics Corporation

Statement of Stockholders' Equity
Year Ended December 31, 20X5

					Accumulated Other Comprehensive Income		
	Common Stock, $1 Par	Additional Paid-in Capital	Retained Earnings	Treasury Stock	Unrealized Gain (Loss) on Investments	Foreign-Currency Translation Adjustment	Total Stockholders' Equity
1 Balance, December 31, 20X4	$ 80,000	$160,000	$130,000	$(25,000)	$6,000	$(10,000)	$341,000
2 Issuance of stock	20,000	65,000					85,000
3 Net income			69,000				69,000
4 Cash dividends			(21,000)				(21,000)
5 Stock dividends—8%	8,000	26,000	(34,000)				0
6 Purchase of treasury stock				(9,000)			(9,000)
7 Sale of treasury stock		7,000		4,000			11,000
8 Unrealized gain on investments					1,000		1,000
9 Foreign-currency translation adjustment						2,000	2,000
10 Balance, December 31, 20X5	$108,000	$258,000	$144,000	$(30,000)	$7,000	$ (8,000)	$479,000

Exhibit 11-6

Stockholders' Equity Section of the Balance Sheet

Allied Electronics Corporation

Balance Sheet (Partial)
December 31, 20X5

	20X5
Total assets	$939,000
Total liabilities	$460,000
Stockholders' Equity	
Common stock, $1 par, shares issued—108,000 and 80,000, respectively	108,000
Additional paid-in capital	258,000
Retained earnings	144,000
Treasury stock	(30,000)
Accumulated other comprehensive income:	
Unrealized gain on investments	7,000
Foreign-currency translation adjustment	(8,000)
Total stockholders' equity	479,000
Total liabilities and stockholders' equity	$939,000

The statement of stockholders' equity provides information about a company's transactions, such as

1. Net income
2. Issuance of stock
3. Declaration of cash dividends
4. Distribution of stock dividends
5. Purchase and sale of treasury stock
6. Accumulated other comprehensive income:
   a. Unrealized gains (losses) on available-for-sale investments
   b. Foreign-currency translation adjustment

Let's delve more deeply into the transactions that affected Allied Electronics' stockholders' equity during 20X5. Only after we understand what the business did can we decide whether we approve or disapprove. Let's use Exhibit 11-5 to analyze all the effects on Allied Electronics' stockholders' equity during 20X5.

ISSUANCE OF STOCK (LINE 2). During 20X5, Allied issued common stock for $85,000. Of this total, $20,000 (par value) went into the Common Stock account, and $65,000 increased Additional Paid-in Capital. The issuance of stock increased Allied's total equity by $85,000.

NET INCOME (LINE 3). During 20X5, Allied Electronics earned net income of $69,000, which increased Retained Earnings. Trace net income from the income statement (Exhibit 11-1 page 509) to the statement of stockholders' equity (Exhibit 11-5). Then trace the ending amount of Retained Earnings to the balance sheet in Exhibit 11-6. Moving back and forth among the financial statements is an important part of financial analysis.

DECLARATION OF CASH DIVIDENDS (LINE 4). The statement of stockholders' equity reports the amount of cash dividends the company declared during the year →. Allied Electronics' cash dividends were $21,000, approximately one-third of net income. Exhibit 11-5 reports the decrease in retained earnings from the declaration of the cash dividends.

← *See Chapter 9, pages 430 to 433, for a review of dividends.*

DISTRIBUTION OF STOCK DIVIDENDS (LINE 5). During 20X5, Allied Electronics distributed stock dividend to its stockholders. Prior to the stock dividend, Allied's Common Stock account had a balance of $100,000 (beginning balance of $80,000 + new issue of $20,000). The 8% stock dividend then added 8,000 shares of $1-par common stock, or $8,000, to the Common Stock account. This is how we can determine the percentage of the stock dividend.

But there was more to this stock dividend. Allied decreased (debited) Retained Earnings for the market value of the new shares issued in the stock dividend. This market value, $34,000, is reported under Retained Earnings in Exhibit 11-5. The difference between the market value of the dividend ($34,000) and the par value of the stock dividend ($8,000) was credited to Additional Paid-in Capital ($26,000).

PURCHASE AND SALE OF TREASURY STOCK (LINES 6 AND 7). The statement of stockholders' equity reports the purchases and sales of treasury stock. Recall from Chapter 9 that treasury stock is recorded at its cost. During 20X5, Allied Electronics paid

$9,000 to buy treasury stock (line 6). This transaction decreased stockholders' equity by $9,000. Allied later sold some treasury stock during the year (line 7). The sale of treasury stock brought in $11,000 cash and increased total stockholders' equity by $11,000. The treasury stock that Allied sold had cost the company $4,000, and the extra $7,000 was added to Additional Paid-in Capital. At year end (line 10), Allied still owned treasury stock that cost the company $30,000 when it was purchased. The parentheses around the treasury stock figures in Exhibit 11-5 mean that treasury stock is a negative element of stockholders' equity. Trace treasury stock's ending balance to the balance sheet in Exhibit 11-6.

ACCUMULATED OTHER COMPREHENSIVE INCOME (LINES 8 AND 9). Two categories of other comprehensive income are unrealized gains and losses on available-for-sale investments and the foreign-currency translation adjustment.

At December 31, 20X4, Allied Electronics held available-for-sale investments, that were worth $6,000 more than Allied paid for them. This explains the $6,000 beginning balance of the unrealized gain (line 1) in Exhibit 11-5 ←. Then, during 20X5, the market value of the investments increased by another $1,000 (line 8). At December 31, 20X5, Allied's portfolio of available-for-sale investments had a market value that exceeded Allied's cost by the accumulated amount of $7,000 (line 10). An unrealized loss on investments would appear on the statement of stockholders' equity as a negative amount.

→ *See Chapter 10, pages 469 to 470, for a review of unrealized gains (losses) on available-for-sale investments.*

At December 31, 20X4, Allied had a negative foreign-currency translation adjustment of $10,000 (see the beginning balance on line 1) ←. During 20X5, the foreign currency strengthened against the dollar and decreased the negative amount of the translation adjustment by $2,000 (line 9). At December 31, 20X5, Allied's cumulative foreign-currency translation adjustment stood at $8,000—a negative amount that resembles an unrealized loss (line 10).

→ *See Chapter 10, pages 485 to 486, for a review of the foreign-currency translation adjustment.*

✔ **Check Point 11-10**

Responsibility for the Financial Statements

Management's Responsibility

Objective

4 Understand managers' and auditors' responsibilities for the financial statements

Management issues a *statement of responsibility* along with the company's financial statements. Exhibit 11-7 is an excerpt from the statement of management's responsibility included in the annual report of Lockheed Martin Corporation.

Exhibit 11-7

Excerpt from Management's Responsibility for Financial Reporting—Lockheed Martin Corporation

Management's Responsibility for Financial Reporting

Lockheed Martin Corporation

The management of Lockheed Martin prepared and is responsible for the consolidated financial statements and all related financial information contained in this Annual Report. The consolidated financial statements, which include amounts based on estimates and judgments, have been prepared in accordance with accounting principles generally accepted in the United States.

Management declares its responsibility for the financial statements and states that they conform to GAAP. As we've seen throughout this book, GAAP is the standard for preparing the financial statements and are designed to produce relevant, reliable, and useful information for making investment and credit decisions.

Auditor Report

The Securities Exchange Act of 1934 requires companies that issue their stock publicly to file audited financial statements with the Securities and Exchange Commission (SEC), a governmental agency. To comply with this requirement, companies engage outside auditors who are certified public accountants to examine their statements. The independent auditors decide whether the company's financial statements comply with GAAP and then issue an audit report. Exhibit 11-8 is the audit report on the financial statements of Lockheed Martin Corporation.

Exhibit 11-8

Excerpts from the Audit Report on the Financial Statements of Lockheed Martin Corporation

Report of Ernst & Young LLP, Independent Auditors

Lockheed Martin Corporation

Board of Directors and Stockholders
Lockheed Martin Corporation

We have audited the accompanying consolidated balance sheet of Lockheed Martin Corporation as of December 31, 2001 and 2000, and the related consolidated statements of operations, stockholders' equity, and cash flows for each of the three years in the period ended December 31, 2001.

We conducted our audits in accordance with auditing standards generally accepted in the United States. We believe that our audits provide a reasonable basis for our opinion.

In our opinion, the consolidated financial statements referred to above present fairly, in all material respects, the consolidated financial position of Lockheed Martin Corporation at December 31, 2001 and 2000, and the consolidated results of its operations and its cash flows for each of the three years in the period ended December 31, 2001, in conformity with accounting principles generally accepted in the United States.

Ernst + Young LLP

McLean, Virginia
January 21, 2002

The audit report is addressed to the board of directors and shareowners of the company. The auditing firm signs its name, in this case the McLean, Virginia, office of Ernst & Young LLP (LLP is the abbreviation for limited liability partnership).

The audit report typically contains three paragraphs:

- The first paragraph identifies the audited financial statements.
- The second paragraph describes how the audit was performed, mentioning that generally accepted auditing standards are the benchmark for evaluating the audit's quality.
- The third paragraph states Ernst & Young's opinion that Lockheed's financial statements conform to GAAP and that people can rely on them for decision making. Lockheed's audit report contains a **clean opinion,** more properly called an *unqualified* opinion. Audit reports usually fall into one of four categories:
  1. **Unqualified (clean).** The statements are reliable.
  2. **Qualified.** The statements are reliable, except for one or more items for which the opinion is said to be qualified.
  3. **Adverse.** The statements are unreliable.
  4. **Disclaimer.** The auditor was unable to reach a professional opinion.

Unqualified (clean) opinion
An audit opinion stating that the financial statements are reliable.

Qualified opinion
An audit opinion stating that the financial statements are reliable, except for one or more items for which the opinion is said to be qualified.

Adverse opinion
An audit opinion stating that the financial statements are unreliable.

Disclaimer
An audit opinion stating that the auditor was unable to reach a professional opinion regarding the quality of the financial statements.

The independent audit adds credibility to the financial statements. It is no accident that financial reporting and auditing are more advanced in the United States and Canada than anywhere else in the world and that these two countries' capital markets are the envy of the world.

Decision Guidelines

In the Decision Guidelines, we'll revisit the decision setting in which investors use accounting information to make investment decisions. You have completed your studies, taken a job, and been fortunate to save $10,000. Now you are ready to start investing. These guidelines provide a framework for using accounting information for investment analysis.

USING THE INCOME STATEMENT AND THE RELATED NOTES IN INVESTMENT ANALYSIS

Decision	Factors to Consider		Decision Variable or Model
Which measure of profitability should be used for investment analysis?	Are you interested in accounting income? →	Income, including all revenues, expenses, gains, and losses?	Net income (bottom line)
	→	Income that can be expected to repeat from year to year?	Income from continuing operations
	Are you interested in cash flows? →		Cash flows from operating activities (Chapter 12)

Note: A conservative strategy may use both income and cash flows and compare the two sets of results.

Decision	Factors to Consider	Decision Variable or Model
What is the estimated value of the stock?	If you believe the company can earn the income (or cash flow) indefinitely →	$\text{Estimated value} = \dfrac{\text{Annual income}}{\text{Investment capitalization rate}}$
	If you believe the company can earn the income (or cash flow) for a finite number of years →	$\text{Estimated value} = \text{Annual income} \times \text{Present value of annuity}$ (See Appendix D)
How does risk affect the value of the stock?	If the investment is high risk →	Increase the investment capitalization rate
	If the investment is low risk →	Decrease the investment capitalization rate

Excel Application Problem

Goal: Create an Excel worksheet to assist with an investment decision.

Scenario: In this chapter's Decision Guidelines, you have saved $10,000 to invest in the stock market. The company you are considering is Fossil, maker of fashion watches and leather accessory goods. The Excel worksheet created in this exercise will help you determine whether to invest in Fossil.

Use the results of your completed worksheet to answer these questions:

1. Suppose that investors believe Fossil can maintain its fiscal year net income indefinitely. Assuming an interest capitalization rate of 8%, what is the estimated total value of outstanding Fossil stock? What is the per-share amount?
2. Suppose that investors believe Fossil can maintain its fiscal year net income for the next 10 years. Now what is the estimated value of Fossil's stock? What is the per-share amount? (Hint: Use the Excel PV function and multiply the income value by minus 1 to get a positive dollar amount.)
3. How do your answers for questions 1 and 2 change if investors believe investment in Fossil is high-risk? Low risk? (Hint: Change the 8% investment capitalization rate.)
4. As of January 4, 2002, Fossil's common stock was quoted at the market price of $13.67 per share. Calculate Fossil's actual market value as of this date. What does this tell you about the market's value of Fossil stock? Would you invest? Why or why not?

Step-by-step:

1. Locate the Fossil annual report (an online copy may be found at **www.fossil.com**).
2. Open a new Excel worksheet.
3. Create a bold-faced heading for your spreadsheet that contains the following:
   a. Chapter 11 Decision Guidelines
   b. Fossil
   c. Investment Analysis
   d. Today's date
4. Two rows under your heading in the first column, create a data section to include the following items:
   a. Fossil Net Income FY 2001
   b. Years
   c. Investment Capitalization Rate
   d. Number of Shares Outstanding
   e. Market Price of Common Stock on 1/4/02
5. Two rows under the data section, in Column A, enter the heading "Estimated Market Value." In Column C, enter the heading "Per-Share Outstanding." Make both headings bold and underlined.
6. Then, in Column A, enter the following two rows and calculate the amounts for total estimated market value and per-share outstanding.
   a. Indefinite Time Period
   b. Fixed Time Period
7. Two rows under the calculations in #6, enter a row labeled "Current Market Value," and calculate the amount.
8. Format all cells, save your work, and print a copy for your files.

End-of-Chapter Summary Problem

The following information was taken from the ledger of **Kraft Corporation:**

Prior-period adjustment— credit to Retained Earnings	$ 5,000	Treasury stock, common (5,000 shares at cost)	$ 25,000
Gain on sale of plant assets	21,000	Selling expenses	78,000
Cost of goods sold	380,000	Common stock, no par, 45,000 shares issued	180,000
Income tax expense (saving):		Sales revenue	620,000
Continuing operations	32,000	Interest expense	30,000
Discontinued operations	8,000	Extraordinary gain	26,000
Extraordinary gain	10,000	Income from discontinued operations	20,000
Cumulative effect of change in inventory method		Loss due to lawsuit	11,000
Preferred stock, 8%, $100 par,	(4,000)	General expenses	62,000
500 shares issued		Retained earnings, beginning, as originally reported	103,000
Paid-in capital in excess of	50,000		
par—preferred	7,000	Cumulative effect of change	
Dividends	16,000	in inventory method (debit)	(10,000)

Required

Prepare a single-step income statement (with all revenues grouped together) and a statement of retained earnings for Kraft Corporation for the current year ended December 31, 20XX. Include the earnings-per-share presentation and show computations. Assume no changes in the stock accounts during the year.

Answers

Kraft Corporation

Income Statement
Year Ended December 31, 20XX

Revenue and gains:		
Sales revenue		$620,000
Gain on sale of plant assets		21,000
Total revenues and gains		641,000
Expenses and losses:		
Cost of goods sold	$380,000	
Selling expenses	78,000	
General expenses	62,000	
Interest expense	30,000	
Loss due to lawsuit	11,000	
Income tax expense	32,000	
Total expenses and losses		593,000
Income from continuing operations		48,000
Discontinued operations, $20,000, less income tax, $8,000		12,000
Income before extraordinary item and cumulative effect of change in inventory method		60,000
Extraordinary gain, $26,000, less income tax, $10,000		16,000
Cumulative effect of change in inventory method, $10,000, less income tax saving, $4,000		(6,000)
Net income		$ 70,000
Earnings per share:*		
Income from continuing operations [($48,000 − $4,000)/40,000 shares]		$ 1.10
Income from discontinued operations ($12,000/40,000 shares)		0.30
Income before extraordinary item and cumulative effect of change in inventory method [($60,000 − $4,000)/40,000 shares]		1.40
Extraordinary gain ($16,000/40,000 shares)		0.40
Cumulative effect of change in inventory method ($6,000/40,000)		(0.15)
Net income [($70,000 − $4,000)/40,000 shares]		$ 1.65

*Computations:

$$\text{EPS} = \frac{\text{Income} - \text{Preferred dividends}}{\text{Common shares outstanding}}$$

Preferred dividends: $50,000 × .08 = $4,000

Common shares outstanding:
45,000 shares issued − 5,000 treasury shares = 40,000 shares outstanding

Kraft Corporation

Statement of Retained Earnings
Year Ended December 31, 20XX

Retained earnings balance, beginning, as originally reported	$103,000
Prior-period adjustment—credit	5,000
Retained earnings balance, beginning, as adjusted	108,000
Net income for current year	70,000
	178,000
Dividends for current year	(16,000)
Retained earnings balance, ending	$162,000

Review The Income Statement

Lessons Learned

1. **Analyze a complex income statement.** A company's income statement reports on (1) continuing operations, (2) discontinued operations, (3) extraordinary gains and losses, and (4) cumulative effect of accounting changes. It also reports income tax expense and earnings per share (EPS) for each of these categories.
2. **Account for a corporation's income tax.** Corporations pay income tax and must account for both income tax expense and income tax payable. *Income tax expense* is based on pretax accounting income. *Income tax payable* is based on taxable income. A difference between the expense and the payable creates another account, Deferred Tax Asset or Deferred Tax Liability.
3. **Analyze a statement of stockholders' equity.** A statement of stockholders' equity reports the changes in all categories of a company's equity during a period, including details about the company's (1) issuance of stock, (2) declaration of cash dividends, (3) distribution of stock dividends, (4) purchase and sale of treasury stock, (5) unrealized gains and losses on available-for-sale investments, and (6) foreign-currency translation adjustment.
4. **Understand managers' and auditors' responsibilities for the financial statements.** The top managers of a company are responsible for the preparation and integrity of the company's financial statements. Independent CPAs audit the financial statements, then offer an objective opinion on whether the statements meet GAAP standards.

Accounting Vocabulary

adverse opinion (p. 523)
clean opinion (p. 523)
comprehensive income (p. 515)
disclaimer (p. 523)
earnings per share (EPS) (p. 513)
extraordinary gains and losses (p. 512)
extraordinary items (p. 512)
investment capitalization rate (p. 510)
pretax accounting income (p. 516)
prior-period adjustment (p. 518)
qualified opinion (p. 523)
segment of the business (p. 511)
statement of stockholders' equity (p. 520)
taxable income (p. 517)
unqualified (clean) opinion (p. 523)

Questions

1. Why is it important for a corporation to report income from continuing operations separately from discontinued operations and extraordinary items?
2. Explain how an investor can use income from continuing operations to estimate the value of a stock. Give the equation, using amounts of your own choosing.
3. Give two examples of extraordinary gains and losses and three examples of gains and losses that are *not* extraordinary.
4. Why is it important for companies to report the effects of their changes in accounting principles (accounting methods)? What appears on the income statement to alert investors that the company has made an accounting change?
5. What is the most widely used of all accounting statistics? Compute the price-to-earnings ratio for a company with EPS of $2 and market price of $12 per share of common stock.
6. What is the earnings per share of a company with net income of $5,500, issued common stock of 12,000 shares, and treasury common stock of 1,000 shares?
7. Identify three subtotals on the income statement that generate income tax expense. What is an income tax saving? How does it arise?

8. Explain the difference between the income tax expense and the income tax payable of a corporation. How is the amount of each item determined, and where does each item appear in the financial statements?
9. Why do creditors wish to restrict a corporation's payment of cash dividends and purchases of treasury stock?
10. What information does the statement of stockholders' equity report? Which other financial statement (besides the balance sheet and the notes) reports on the transactions that appear on the statement of stockholders' equity?
11. Who bears primary responsibility for the financial statements? What role do the independent auditors play? Of what value is the audit?

Assess Your Progress

Check Points

Preparing a complex income statement
(Obj. 1)

CP11-1 List the major parts of a complex corporate income statement for Harley-Davis Corporation for the year ended December 31, 20X4. Include all the major parts of the income statement, starting with net sales revenue and ending with net income (net loss). You may ignore dollar amounts and earnings per share.

Explaining the items on a complex income statement
(Obj. 1)

CP11-2 Study the income statement of Allied Electronics Corporation in Exhibit 11-1 (page 509) and answer these questions about the company:

1. How much gross profit did Allied earn on the sale of its products—before deducting any operating expenses? How does Allied label gross profit on the income statement?
2. Why are the loss on restructuring and the gain on sale of machinery reported as "Other gains (losses)"?
3. What dollar amount of net income would most sophisticated investors predict for Allied Electronics to earn during 20X6 and beyond? Name this item, give its amount, and state your reason.
4. How do the discontinued operations differ from the extraordinary loss?

Preparing a complex income statement
(Obj. 1)

CP11-3 International Cosmetics, Inc. reported the following items, listed in no particular order, at December 31, 20X5 (in thousands):

Extraordinary loss	$(5,000)	Other gains (losses)	$ (2,000)
Cost of goods sold	71,000	Net sales revenue	182,000
Operating expenses	64,000	Gain on discontinued operations	15,000
Accounts receivable	19,000		

Income tax of 40% applies to all items.

Prepare International Cosmetics' income statement for the year ended December 31, 20X5. Omit earnings per share.

Valuing a company's stock
(Obj. 1)

CP11-4 **Target Corporation** reported net sales of $39,176 million, net income of $1,368 million, and no significant discontinued operations, extraordinary items, or accounting changes for 20X1.

Earnings per share was $1.52. At a capitalization rate of 6%, how much should one share of Target stock be worth? Compare your estimated stock price to Target's actual stock price as quoted in *The Wall Street Journal*, in your newspaper, or over the Internet. Based on your estimated market value, should you buy, hold, or sell Target stock?

CP11-5 Return to the International Costmetics data in CP11-3. The company had 10,000 shares of common stock outstanding during 20X5. International Cosmetics declared and paid preferred dividends of $3,000 during 20X5.

Reporting earnings per share **(Obj. 1)**

Show how International Cosmetics reported earnings per share on its 20X5 income statement.

CP11-6 A corporation has preferred stock outstanding and issued additional common stock during the year.

Interpreting earnings-per-share data **(Obj. 1)**

1. Give the basic equation to compute earnings per share of common stock for net income.
2. List the income items for which the corporation must report earnings-per-share data.
3. What makes earnings per share so useful as a business statistic?

CP11-7 Use the International Cosmetics data in Check Point 11-3. In addition, International Cosmetics had unrealized losses of $1,000 on investments and a $2,000 foreign-currency translation adjustment (a gain) during 20X5. Both amounts are net of tax. Start with International's net income from CP11-3 and show how the company could report other comprehensive income on its 20X5 income statement.

Reporting comprehensive income **(Obj. 1)**

Should International report earnings per share for other comprehensive income? State why or why not.

CP11-8 Pappadeaux Pizza had income before income tax of $100,000 and taxable income of $90,000 for 20X5, the company's first year of operations. The income tax rate is 40%.

Accounting for a corporation's income tax **(Obj. 2)**

1. Make the entry to record Pappadeaux's income taxes for 20X5.
2. Show what Pappadeaux Pizza will report on its 20X5 income statement starting with income before income tax. Also show what Pappadeaux will report for current and long-term liabilities on its December 31, 20X5, balance sheet.

CP11-9 Examine **CNN Corporation's** statement of retained earnings on page 519. Suppose instead that CNN had overpaid 20X4 income tax expense by $7,000. Show how CNN would report this prior-period adjustment on the statement of retained earnings for 20X5.

Reporting a prior-period adjustment **(Obj. 3)**

CP11-10 Use the statement of stockholders' equity in Exhibit 11-5 (page 520) to answer the following questions about Allied Electronics Corporation:

Using the statement of stockholders' equity **(Obj. 4)**

1. At December 31, 20X5, Allied had total liabilities of $514,000. How much were the company's total assets?
2. How much cash did the issuance of common stock bring in during 20X5?
3. What was the cost of the treasury stock that Allied purchased during 20X5? What was Allied's cost of the treasury stock that Allied sold during the year? For how much did Allied sell the treasury stock during 20X5?
4. What was the stock dividend's effect on Allied's retained earnings? on total paid-in capital? on total stockholders' equity? on total assets?

Exercises

E11-1 **Pharmacia Corporation** is a global pharmaceutical company. Pharmacia reported a number of special items on its income statement. The following data, listed in no particular order, were adapted from Pharmacia's financial statements (amounts in millions):

Preparing and using a complex income statement **(Obj. 1)**

Net sales	$13,837	Income tax expense (saving):	
Foreign-currency translation adjustment	368	Continuing operations	$296
Extraordinary loss	14	Discontinued operations	54
Income from discontinued operations	275	Extraordinary loss	(3)
Dividends declared and paid	683	Unrealized net gain on investments	41
Total operating expenses	12,250	Short-term investments	35

Required

Show how the Pharmacia Corporation income statement for 20X1 should appear. Omit earnings per share.

Preparing and using a complex income statement
(Obj. 1)

E11-2 **ChevronTexaco Corporation's** accounting records contain the following information for 20X1 (in millions):

spreadsheet

Extraordinary loss	$ 787
Sales revenue	104,409
Total operating expenses	97,954
Other revenues	1,836
Income tax saving—extraordinary loss	144
Income tax expense—income from operations	4,360

Required

1. Prepare ChevronTexaco's single-step income statement for the year ended December 31, 20X1, including EPS. ChevronTexaco had 1,060 million shares of common stock and no preferred outstanding during the year.
2. Assume investors capitalize ChevronTexaco earnings at 5%. Estimate the price of one share of the company's stock.

Using an actual income statement
(Obj. 1)

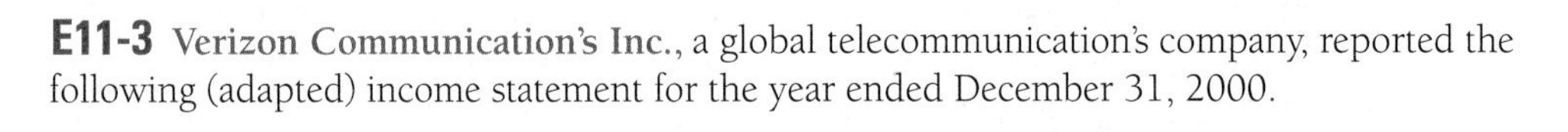

E11-3 **Verizon Communication's Inc.**, a global telecommunication's company, reported the following (adapted) income statement for the year ended December 31, 2000.

	Millions
Operating revenues	$64,707
Operating expenses	47,949
Operating income	16,758
Other revenue (expense), net	(5,948)
Income before extraordinary item and cumulative effect of accounting change	10,810
Extraordinary item, net of tax	1,027
Cumulative effect of accounting change, net of tax	(40)
Net income	$11,797

Verizon's extraordinary item resulted from selling businesses as required by U.S. federal regulatory agencies. The accounting change also resulted from U.S. government action; the SEC required Verizon to expense immediately some costs that the company had been capitalizing as assets and amortizing as expense over future periods.

Required

1. Were Verizon's extraordinary item and the cumulative effect of the accounting change more like an expense or a revenue? How can you tell?

2. Should the extraordinary item and the cumulative effect of Verizon's accounting change be included in or excluded from net income? State your reason.
3. Suppose you are working as a financial analyst and your job is to predict Verizon's net income for 2001 and beyond. Which item from the income statement will you use for your prediction? Why will you use this item?

Using income data for investment analysis
(Obj. 1)

E11-4 During 20X1, **PepsiCo, Inc.** had sales of $26.9 billion, operating profit of $4.0 billion, and net income of $2.7 billion. Earnings per share (EPS) were $1.51. At May 1, 20X2, the market price of a share of PepsiCo's common stock closed at $52.92 on the New York Stock Exchange.

What investment capitalization rate did investors appear to be using to determine the value of one share of PepsiCo stock? The formula for the value of one share of stock uses EPS in the calculation. Does this capitalization rate suggest high risk or low risk? What about PepsiCo's line of business is consistent with your evaluation of the company's risk?

Computing earnings per share
(Obj. 1)

E11-5 **Fannie Mae** is a leading provider of low-cost mortgages. During 20X1, Fannie Mae earned net income of $5,894 million. Fannie Mae's financial statements also report the following figures (in millions):

Preferred stock, $50 stated value, 6%, 46 million shares issued and outstanding	$2,303
Common stock, $0.525 par, 1,129 million shares issued	593
Treasury stock, common, 132 million shares at cost	5,539

Required

Compute Fannie Mae's EPS for 20X1.

Computing and using earnings per share
(Obj. 1)

E11-6 **Cendant Corporation** operates numerous businesses, including Days Inn, Travelodge, and Ramada motels; Avis rent-a-car; and Coldwell Banker and Century 21 real-estate companies. Year 20X0 was interesting for Cendant, which reported the following on its income statement (in millions):

Net revenues	$3,930
Total expenses and other	3,354
Income from continuing operations	576
Discontinued operations, net of tax	84
Income before extraordinary item and cumulative effect of accounting change, net of tax	660
Extraordinary loss, net of tax	(2)
Cumulative effect of accounting change, net of tax	(56)
Net income	$ 602

During 20X0, Cendant had the following (adapted, in millions, except for par value per share):

Mandatorily redeemable preferred stock (no dividends because the preferred stock is really debt)	$2,058
Common stock, $0.01 par value, 917 shares issued	9
Treasury stock, 197 shares at cost	(3,568)

Required

1. Show how Cendant should report its earnings per share for 20X0.
2. At the end of 20X0, Cendant's common stock was quoted at the market price of $9.64 per share. To arrive at this price, the stock market was capitalizing Cendant's earnings at 8.3%. After computing Cendant's EPS, show how the stock market arrived at the price of $9.64 per share for Cendant stock.

Accounting for income tax by a corporation
(Obj. 2)

E11-7 For 20X6, its first year of operations, Pinnacle Capital Inc. has pre-tax accounting income (on the income statement) of $420,000. Taxable income (on the tax return filed with the Internal Revenue Service) is $300,000. The income tax rate is 40%. Record Pinnacle Capital's income taxes for the year. What is the balance in the Deferred Tax Liability account at the end of the year? Show what Pinnacle will report on its 20X6 income statement and balance sheet for this situation. Start the income statement with income before tax.

Accounting for the income tax of a major corporation
(Obj. 2)

E11-8 **Raytheon Company** competes with **Lockheed Martin Corporation** (the featured company in this chapter) in a number of electronic, aircraft, and defense markets. During 20X0, Raytheon's income statement reported income of $877 million before income tax. Assume that the company's income tax return filed with the IRS reported taxable income of only $214 million. During 20X0, Raytheon was subject to an income tax rate of 43%.

Required

1. Journalize Raytheon's income taxes for 20X0.
2. How much income tax did Raytheon have to pay currently for the year 20X0?
3. At the beginning of 20X0, Raytheon's balance of Deferred Tax Liability was $488 million. How much Deferred Tax Liability did Raytheon report on its balance sheet at December 31, 20X0?

Reporting a prior-period adjustment on the statement of retained earnings
(Obj. 3)

spreadsheet

E11-9 Upper 10, Inc., a soft drink company, reported a prior-period adjustment in 20X3. An accounting error caused net income of prior years to be understated by $3.8 million. Retained earnings at December 31, 20X2, as previously reported, stood at $395.3 million. Net income for 20X3 was $92.1 million, and dividends were $61.8 million.

Required

Prepare the company's statement of retained earnings for the year ended December 31, 20X3. How does the prior-period adjustment affect Upper 10's net income for 20X3?

Preparing a statement of stockholders' equity
(Obj. 3)

E11-10 At December 31, 20X4, Acura Corporation reported stockholders' equity as follows:

Common stock, $5 par, 500,000 shares authorized, 300,000 shares issued	$1,500,000
Additional paid-in capital	3,100,000
Retained earnings	1,700,000
Treasury stock, 2,500 shares at cost	(78,000)
	$6,222,000

During 20X5, Acura completed these transactions and events (listed in chronological order):

a. Declared and issued a 10% stock dividend. At the time, Acura's stock was quoted at a market price of $31 per share.
b. Sold 1,000 shares of treasury stock for $36 per share (cost was $31).

(continued)

c. Issued 500 shares of common stock to employees at the price of $28 per share.
d. Net income for the year, $340,000.
e. Declared cash dividends of $180,000, to be paid early in 20X6.

Required

Prepare Acura Corporation's statement of stockholders' equity for 20X5, using the format of Exhibit 11-5 (page 520) as a model. Then use the statement you prepared to answer the following questions:

1. Did Acura's retained earnings increase or decrease during 20X5? What caused retained earnings to change during the year?
2. How did the stock dividend affect total stockholders' equity? How did it affect total assets? Total liabilities?
3. How would creditors feel about Acura's sale of treasury stock? Acura's issuance of common stock? Why?

Using an actual company's statement of stockholders' equity
(Obj. 3)

E11-11 Lowe's Companies, Inc., with home-improvement stores in 44 states, reported the following items on its statement of shareholders' equity for the year ended February 1, 20X2 (adapted, in millions):

	$0.50 Par Common Stock	Capital in Excess of Par Value	Retained Earnings	Accumulated Other Comprehensive Income	Total Shareholders' Equity
Balance, Feb. 2, 20X1	$383.2	$1,595.1	$3,518.4	$0.5	$5,497.2
Net earnings			1,023.2		
Unrealized gain on investments				0.2	
Issuance of stock	4.6	209.1			
Cash dividends			(59.9)		
Balance, Feb. 1, 20X2					

Required

1. Determine the February 1, 20X2, balances in Lowe's shareholders' equity accounts and total shareholders' equity on this date.
2. Lowe's total liabilities on February 1, 20X2 are $7,061.8 million. What is Lowe's debt ratio on this date?
3. Was there a profit or a loss for the year ended February 1, 20X2? How can you tell?
4. At what price per share did Lowe's issue common stock during 20X2?
5. What suggests that all Lowe's stores are located in the United States?

Identifying responsibility and standards for the financial statements
(Obj. 4)

E11-12 The annual report of The Gap, Inc. included the following reports:

The Gap, Inc.
Management's Report on Financial Information (Excerpts)

Management is responsible for the . . . financial information presented in the Annual Report. The financial statements have been prepared in accordance with accounting principles generally accepted in the United States of America . . . .

In fulfilling its responsibility for the reliability of financial information, Management has established and maintains accounting systems . . . supported by internal accounting controls. Management believes that the internal accounting controls in use provide reasonable assurance that assets are safeguarded . . . , transactions are executed in accordance with Management's authorization, and . . . the financial records are reliable for preparing financial statements. . . . The financial statements of the Company have been audited by Deloitte & Touche LLP, independent auditors, whose report appears below.

Independent Auditors' Report
To the Shareholders and Board of Directors of The Gap, Inc.:

We have audited the accompanying consolidated balance sheets of The Gap, Inc. and subsidiaries as of February 2, 2002, and February 3, 2001, and the related consolidated statements of operations, shareholders' equity and cash flows for each of the three fiscal years in the period ended February 2, 2002. These financial statements are the responsibility of the Company's management. Our responsibility is to express an opinion on these financial statements based on our audits.

We conducted our audits in accordance with auditing standards generally accepted in the United States of America. Those standards require that we plan and perform the audit to obtain reasonable assurance about whether the financial statements are free of material misstatement. An audit includes examining, on a test basis, evidence supporting the amounts and disclosures in the financial statements. An audit also includes assessing the accounting principles used and significant estimates made by management, as well as evaluating the overall financial statement presentation. We believe that our audits provide a reasonable basis for our opinion.

In our opinion, such consolidated financial statements present fairly, in all material respects, the financial position of the Company and its subsidiaries as of February 2, 2002, and February 3, 2001, and the results of their operations and their cash flows for each of the three fiscal years in the period ended February 2, 2002, in conformity with accounting principles generally accepted in the United States of America.

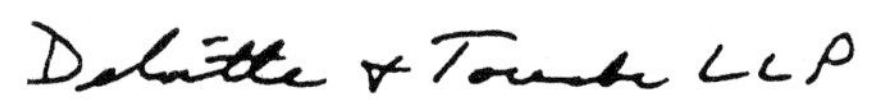

San Francisco, California
March 12, 2002

1. Who is responsible for Gap's financial statements? Is it Gap's management, or is it the auditor?
2. By what accounting standard are the financial statements prepared? Give the abbreviation of this standard.
3. Identify one concrete action that Gap management takes to fulfill its responsibility for the reliability of the company's financial information. List three objectives of this management action.
4. Which entity gave an outside, independent opinion on the Gap financial statement? Where was this entity located, and when did it release its opinion to the public?
5. Exactly what did the audit cover? Give names and dates.
6. By what standard did the auditor conduct the audit?
7. By what standard did the auditor evaluate Gap's financial statements?
8. What was the auditor's opinion of Gap's financial statements?

Problems

(Group A)

Preparing a complex income statement **(Obj. 1)**

P11-1A The following information was taken from the records of Motors Unlimited, which specializes in engines for antique sports cars, at December 31, 20X3.

Dividends on common stock	$31,000	Prior-period adjustment—debit to Retained Earnings	$ 4,000
Interest expense	23,000	Income tax expense (saving):	
Gain on settlement of lawsuit	8,000	Continuing operations	28,000
Paid-in capital from retirement of preferred stock	16,000	Income from discontinued operations	2,000
Dividend revenue	11,000	Extraordinary gain	10,800
Treasury stock, common (2,000 shares at cost)	28,000	Cumulative effect of change in depreciation method	3,000
General expenses	71,000		

Sales revenue	$567,000	Loss on sale of plant assets	$ 10,000
Retained earnings, beginning, as originally reported	63,000	Income from discontinued operations	7,000
Selling expenses	87,000	Dividends on preferred stock	?
Common stock, no par, 22,000 shares authorized and issued	350,000	Preferred stock, 6%, $25 par, 20,000 shares authorized, 4,000 shares issued	100,000
Extraordinary gain	27,000	Cumulative effect of change in depreciation method (credit)	7,600
		Cost of goods sold	319,000

Required

1. Prepare Motors Unlimited's single-step income statement, which lists all revenues together and all expenses together, for the fiscal year ended December 31, 20X3. Include earnings-per-share data.
2. Evaluate income for the year ended December 31, 20X3, in terms of the outlook for 20X4. 20X3 was a typical year, and Motors Unlimited top managers hoped to earn income from continuing operations equal to 10% of sales.

Preparing a statement of retained earnings **(Obj. 3)**

P11-2A Use the data in Problem 11-1A to prepare the Motors Unlimited statement of retained earnings for the year ended December 31, 20X3.

Using income data to make an investment decision **(Obj. 1)**

P11-3A Motors Unlimited in Problem 11-1A holds significant promise for carving a niche in the antique auto parts industry and a group of Canadian investors is considering purchasing the company. Motors Unlimited's stock is currently selling for $42 per share.

A *Business Today* magazine story predicted the company's income is bound to grow. It appears that the company can earn at least its current level of income for the indefinite future. Based on this information, the investors think that an appropriate investment capitalization rate for estimating the value of Motors Unlimited's common stock is 6%. Any capitalization rate below 6% would overvalue the stock. How much will this belief lead the investors to offer for Motors Unlimited? Will the existing stockholders of Motors Unlimited be likely to accept this offer? Explain your answers.

Computing earnings per share and estimating the price of a stock **(Obj. 1)**

P11-4A Wall Street Workout, Inc. (WSWO) specializes in turning around underperforming companies. WSWO's capital structure at December 31, 20X5 included 5,000 shares of $2.50 preferred stock and 120,000 shares of common stock. During 20X6, WSWO issued stock and ended the year with 127,000 shares of common outstanding. Average common shares outstanding during 20X6 were 123,500. Income from continuing operations during 20X6 was $371,885. The company discontinued a segment of the business at a gain of $69,160, and an extraordinary item generated a loss of $49,510.

Required

1. Compute WSWO's earnings per share. Start with income from continuing operations. Income and loss amounts are net of income tax.
2. Analysts believe WSWO can earn its current level of income for the indefinite future. Estimate the market price of a share of WSWO common stock at investment capitalization rates of 5%, 7%, and 9%. The formula for estimating the value of one share of stock uses earnings per share. Which estimate presumes an investment in WSWO is the most risky? How can you tell?

Preparing a corrected income statement, including comprehensive income **(Obj. 1)**

P11-5A Blake Willis, accountant for Willis Jeep Sales, Inc., was injured in a skiing accident. Another employee prepared the following income statement for the fiscal year ended June 30, 20X4:

Willis Jeep Sales, Inc.

Income Statement
June 30, 20X4

Revenue and gains:		
Sales		$733,000
Paid-in capital in excess of par—common		100,000
Total revenues and gains		833,000
Expenses and losses:		
Cost of goods sold	$383,000	
Selling expenses	103,000	
General expenses	74,000	
Sales returns	22,000	
Unrealized loss on available-for-sale investments	4,000	
Dividends paid	15,000	
Sales discounts	10,000	
Income tax expense	56,400	
Total expenses and losses		667,400
Income from operations		165,600
Other gains and losses:		
Extraordinary loss	$ (30,000)	
Loss on discontinued operations	(15,000)	
Total other gains (losses)		(45,000)
Net income		$120,600
Earnings per share		$6.03

The individual *amounts* listed on the income statement are correct. However, some *accounts* are reported incorrectly, and one does not belong on the income statement at all. Also, income tax (40%) has not been applied to all appropriate figures. Willis issued 24,000 shares of common stock in 20X1 and held 4,000 shares as treasury stock during the fiscal year 20X4.

Required

Prepare a corrected statement of income (single-step, which lists all revenues together and all expenses together), including comprehensive income, for fiscal year 20X4; include earnings per share.

Accounting for a corporation's income tax **(Obj. 2)**

P11-6A The accounting (not the income tax) records of British Wire Wheels, Inc. provide the comparative income statement for 20X5 and 20X6, respectively:

	20X5	20X6
Total revenue	$600,000	$720,000
Expenses:		
Cost of goods sold	$290,000	$310,000
Operating expenses	180,000	190,000
Total expenses before tax	470,000	500,000
Pretax accounting income	$130,000	$220,000

Total revenue in 20X6 includes rent of $10,000 for cash that was received late in 20X5. This rent is included in 20X6 total revenue because the rent was earned in 20X6.

However, rent revenue that is collected in advance is included in taxable income when the cash is received. In calculating taxable income on the tax return, this rent revenue belongs in 20X5.

In addition, operating expenses for each year include depreciation of $40,000 computed under the straight-line method. In calculating taxable income on the tax return, British Wire Wheels uses the modified accelerated cost recovery system (MACRS). MACRS depreciation was $60,000 for 20X5 and $20,000 for 20X6. The income tax rate is 35%.

Required

1. Compute British Wire Wheels' taxable income for 20X5.
2. Journalize the corporation's income taxes for 20X5.
3. Prepare the corporation's income statement for 20X5.

P11-7A Pricewaterhouse Coopers (PwC), Inc., an English company, reported the following statement of stockholders' equity for the year ended June 30, 20X4:

Using a statement of stockholders' equity **(Obj. 3)**

Pricewaterhouse Coopers, Inc.
Statement of Stockholders' Equity
Year Ended June 30, 20X4

(In millions)	Common Stock	Additional Paid-in Capital	Retained Earnings	Treasury Stock	Total
Balance, June 30, 20X3	£173	£2,118	£1,702	£(18)	£3,975
Net income			520		520
Cash dividends			(117)		(117)
Issuance of stock (5,000,000 shares)	7	46			53
Stock dividend	18	272	(290)		—
Sale of treasury stock		22		11	33
Balance, June 30, 20X4	£198	£2,458	£1,815	£ (7)	£4,464

Required

Answer these questions about PwC's stockholders' equity transactions.

1. The income tax rate is 35%. How much income before income tax did PwC report on the income statement?
2. What is the par value of the company's common stock?
3. At what price per share did PwC issue its common stock during the year?
4. What was the cost of treasury stock sold during the year? What was the selling price of the treasury stock sold? What was the increase in total stockholders' equity?
5. PwC's statement of stockholders' equity lists the stock transactions in the order in which they occurred. What was the percentage of the stock dividend? Round to the nearest percentage.

(Group B)

P11-1B The following information was taken from the records of Otis Systems, Inc., at September 30, 20X3. Otis manufactures electronic control devices for elevators.

Preparing a complex income statement **(Obj. 1)**

Treasury stock, common (1,000 shares at cost)	$11,000	Dividends	$ 15,000
Prior-period adjustment— debit to Retained Earnings	6,000	Interest revenue	4,000
Contributed capital from treasury stock transactions	7,000	Extraordinary loss	30,000
Interest expense	11,000	Income from discontinued operations	5,000
Cost of goods sold	424,000	Loss on insurance settlement	12,000
Cumulative effect of change in depreciation method (debit)	(18,000)	General expenses	113,000
Loss on sales of plant assets	8,000	Preferred stock—5%, $40 par, 10,000 shares authorized, 5,000 shares issued	200,000
Income tax expense (saving):		Paid-in capital in excess of par—common	20,000
Continuing operations	72,000	Retained earnings, beginning, as originally reported	88,000
Discontinued operations	2,000	Selling expenses	136,000
Extraordinary loss	(12,000)	Common stock, $10 par, 25,000 shares authorized and issued	250,000
Cumulative effect of change in depreciation method	(7,000)		
Sales revenue	833,000		

Required

1. Prepare Otis Systems' single-step income statement, which lists all revenues together and all expenses together, for the fiscal year ended September 30, 20X3. Include earnings-per-share data.
2. Evaluate income for the year ended September 30, 20X3, in terms of the outlook for 20X4; 20X3 was a typical year, and Otis's top managers hoped to earn income from continuing operations equal to 10% of sales.

Preparing a statement of retained earnings
(Obj. 3)

P11-2B Use the data in Problem 11-1B to prepare Otis Systems, Inc.'s statement of retained earnings for the year ended September 30, 20X3.

Using income data to make an investment decision
(Obj. 1)

P11-3B Otis Systems in Problem 11-1B holds significant promise for carving a niche in the electronic control device industry, and a group of Swiss investors is considering purchasing the company. Otis's common stock is currently selling for $33.75 per share.

A *Business Today* magazine story predicts that Otis's income is bound to grow. It appears that the company can earn at least its current level of income for the indefinite future. Based on this information, the investors think an appropriate investment capitalization rate for estimating the value of Otis common stock is 8%. Any capitalization rate below 8% would overvalue the stock. How much will this belief lead the investors to offer for Otis Systems? Will the existing stockholders of Otis be likely to accept this offer? Explain your answers.

Computing earnings per share and estimating the price of a stock
(Obj. 1)

P11-4B The capital structure of Wells Cargo Trailer Corporation, at December 31, 20X5, included 20,000 shares of $1.25 preferred stock and 44,000 shares of common stock. During 20X6, Wells Cargo issued stock and ended the year with 58,000 shares. The average number of common shares outstanding for the year was 51,000. Income from continuing operations during 20X6 was $81,100. The company discontinued a segment of the business at a gain of $6,630, and an extraordinary item generated a gain of $16,000.

Required

1. Compute Wells Cargo's earnings per share. Start with income from continuing operations. Income and loss amounts are net of income tax.

2. Analysts believe Wells Cargo can earn its current level of income for the indefinite future. Estimate the market price of a share of Wells Cargo common stock at investment capitalization rates of 8%, 10%, and 12%. The formula for estimating the value of one share of stock uses earnings per share. Which estimate presumes an investment in Wells Cargo stock is the most risky? How can you tell?

Preparing a corrected income statement, including comprehensive income **(Obj. 1)**

P11-5B Colin Thatcher, accountant for British Telecom, Inc., was injured in a motorcycle accident. Another employee prepared the accompanying income statement for the year ended December 31, 20X3.

The individual *amounts* listed on the income statement are correct. However, some *accounts* are reported incorrectly, and one does not belong on the income statement at all. Also, income tax (40%) has not been applied to all appropriate figures. British Telecom issued 52,000 shares of common stock in 20X1 and held 2,000 shares as treasury stock during 20X3.

British Telecom, Inc.
Income Statement
20X3

Revenue and gains:		
Sales		£362,000
Unrealized gain on available-for-sale investments		10,000
Paid-in capital in excess of par—common		80,000
Total revenues and gains		452,000
Expenses and losses:		
Cost of goods sold	£103,000	
Selling expenses	56,000	
General expenses	61,000	
Sales returns	11,000	
Dividends paid	7,000	
Sales discounts	6,000	
Income tax expense	50,000	
Total expenses and losses		294,000
Income from operations		158,000
Other gains and losses:		
Extraordinary gain	£ 20,000	
Loss on discontinued operations	(3,000)	
Total other gains, net		17,000
Net income		£175,000
Earnings per share		£3.50

Required

Prepare a corrected statement of income (single-step, which lists all revenues together and all expenses together), including comprehensive income, for 20X3; include earnings per share.

Accounting for a corporation's income tax **(Obj. 2)**

P11-6B The accounting (not the income tax) records of Yoeman Corporation provide the following comparative income statement for 20X4 and 20X5, respectively:

	20X4	20X5
Total revenue	$900,000	$990,000
Expenses:		
Cost of goods sold	$430,000	$460,000
Operating expenses	270,000	280,000
Total expenses before tax	700,000	740,000
Pretax accounting income	$200,000	$250,000

Total revenue of 20X5 includes $15,000 for cash that was received late in 20X4. This revenue is included in 20X5 total revenue because it was earned in 20X5. However, revenue collected in advance is included in the taxable income of the year when the cash is received. In calculating taxable income on the tax return, this revenue belongs in 20X4. Also, the operating expenses of each year include depreciation of $50,000 computed under the straight-line method. In calculating taxable income on the tax return, Yoeman uses the modified accelerated cost recovery system (MACRS). MACRS depreciation was $80,000 for 20X4 and $20,000 for 20X5. The income tax rate is 35%.

Required

1. Compute Yoeman Corporation's taxable income for 20X4.
2. Journalize the corporation's income taxes for 20X4.
3. Prepare the corporation's income statement for 20X4.

Using a statement of stockholders' equity **(Obj. 3)**

P11-7B Transpacific Communication, Inc., reported the following statement of stockholders' equity for the year ended October 31, 20X4:

Transpacific Communication, Inc.

Statement of Stockholders' Equity
Year Ended October 31, 20X4

(In millions)	Common Stock	Additional Paid-in Capital	Retained Earnings	Treasury Stock	Total
Balance, Oct. 31, 20X3	$427	$1,622	$904	$(117)	$2,836
Net income			336		336
Cash dividends			(194)		(194)
Issuance of stock					
(10,000,000 shares)	13	36			49
Stock dividend	22	61	(83)		—
Sale of treasury stock		9		19	28
Balance, Oct. 31, 20X4	$462	$1,728	$963	$ (98)	$3,055

Required

Answer these questions about Transpacific's stockholders' equity transactions:

1. The income tax rate is 40%. How much income before income tax did Transpacific report on the income statement?
2. What is the par value of the company's common stock?
3. At what price per share did Transpacific issue its common stock during the year?
4. What was the cost of treasury stock sold during the year? What was the selling price of the treasury stock sold? What was the increase in total stockholders' equity?
5. Transpacific's statement lists the stock transactions in the order they occurred. What was the percentage of the stock dividend? Round to the nearest percentage.

Apply Your Knowledge

Decision Cases

Evaluating the components of income
(Obj. 1)

Case 1. Magnetic Imaging, Inc., is having its initial public offering (IPO) of company stock. To create public interest in its stock, Magnetic's chief financial officer has blitzed the media with press releases. One, in particular, caught your eye. On November 19, Magnetic announced pro forma earnings per share (EPS) of \$3.15, up 20% from last year's EPS of \$2.63. A 20% increase in EPS is very good.

Before deciding to buy Magnetic Imaging stock, you investigated further and found that the company omitted several items from the determination of pro forma EPS, as follows:

- Unrealized loss on available-for-sale investments, \$0.05 per share
- Gain on sale of building, \$0.05 per share
- Cumulative effect of change in method of recognizing service revenue, increase in retained earnings, \$1.10 per share
- Restructuring expenses, \$0.19 per share
- Loss on settlement of lawsuit begun 5 years ago, \$0.12 per share
- Lost income due to employee labor strike, \$0.14 per share
- Income from discontinued operations, \$0.07 per share

Wondering how to treat these "special items," you called your stockbroker at **Merrill Lynch**. She thinks that these items are nonrecurring and outside Magnetic's core operations. Furthermore, she suggested that you ignore the items and consider Magnetic's earnings of \$3.15 per share to be a good estimate of long-term profitability.

Required

What EPS number will you use to predict Magnetic Imaging's future profits? Show your work, and explain your reasoning for each item.

Using the financial statements in investment analysis
(Obj. 1)

Case 2. **Clayton Homes, Inc.** manufactures and sells houses across the southern part of the United States. Clayton's annual report includes Note 1—Summary of Significant Accounting Policies, as follows:

> **Income Recognition**
> [S]ales are recognized when cash payment is received or, in the case of credit sales, which represent the majority of . . . sales, when a down payment is received and the customer enters into an installment sales contract. Most of these installment sales contracts . . . are normally [collectible] over 36 to 180 months. . . .
>
> [Revenue] from . . . insurance policies [sold to customers] are recognized as income over the terms of the contracts. [E]xpenses are matched to recognize profits over the life of the contracts.

Magnuson Home Builders, Inc., a competitor of Clayton, includes the following note in its Summary of Significant Accounting Policies:

> **Accounting Policies for Revenues**
> Sales are recognized when cash payment is received or, in the case of credit sales, which represent the majority of . . . sales, when the customer enters into an installment sales contract. Customer down payments on credit sales are rare. Most of these installment sales contracts are normally [collectible] over 36 to 180 months. . . . Revenue from insurance policies sold to customers are recognized when the customer signs an insurance contract. Expenses are recognized over the life of the insurance contracts.

Suppose you have decided to invest in the stock of a home builder and you've narrowed your choices to Clayton and Magnuson. Which company's earnings are of higher quality? Why?

Will their accounting policies affect your investment decision? If so, how? Mention specific accounts in the financial statements that will differ between the two companies.

Ethical Issue

The income statement of **General Cinema Corporation** reported the following results of operations:

Earnings before income taxes, extraordinary gain, and cumulative effect of accounting change	$187,046
Income tax expense	72,947
Earnings before extraordinary gain and cumulative effect of accounting change	114,099
Extraordinary gain, net of income tax	419,557
Cumulative effect of change in accounting, net of income tax	(39,196)
Net earnings	$494,460

Suppose General Cinema's management had reported the company's results of operations in this manner:

Earnings before income taxes	$847,111
Income tax expense	352,651
Net earnings	$494,460

Required

1. Does it really matter how a company reports its operating results? Why? Who could be helped by management's action? Who could be hurt?
2. Suppose General Cinema's management decides to report its operating results in the second manner. Evaluate the ethics of this decision.

Financial Statement Case

Analyzing income, investments, and income taxes
(Obj. 1, 2)

Refer to the **Fossil, Inc.**, financial statements in Appendix A at the end of this book.

1. Fossil's net income includes only one large "special" item. Identify the special item and its amount. Also state what about the related asset motivated Fossil to complete the transaction.
2. How much income from continuing operations did Fossil earn in 2001? How can you be certain of your answer?
3. Take the role of an investor, and suppose you are determining the price you are willing to pay for a share of Fossil stock at the end of 2001. Assume you are considering three investment capitalization rates that depend on the risk of an investment in Fossil: 6%, 9%, and 12%. Compute your estimated value of a share of Fossil stock using each of the three capitalization rates. Which estimated value would you base your investment strategy on if you rate Fossil as a rather risky investment? Which estimated value would you use if you consider Fossil a safe investment?
4. How much income tax expense did Fossil report for 2001? Did the company pay more or less cash for income tax during the year, in comparison to the amount of income tax expense for the year? Also consider two other accounts: Deferred Income Tax Liability and Income Taxes Payable. Explain how you can be certain of your answer.

Analytical Case

Evaluating the quality of earnings, valuing investments, and analyzing stock outstanding
(Obj. 1, 3)

This case is based on the **Pier 1 Imports** financial statements in Appendix B at the end of this book.

1. What is your evaluation of the quality of Pier 1's earnings? State how you formed your opinion.

2. How much would you be willing to pay at the end of 2002 for one share of Pier 1 stock if you rate the investment as high risk? as low risk? Use even-numbered investment capitalization rates in the range of 6%–12% for your analysis.
3. During 2002, Pier 1's average shares of common stock outstanding changed from the preceding year. But the balance sheet and the statement of shareholders' equity report the same amount for common stock at the end of each year. What event during 2002 altered the number of Pier 1 shares outstanding? Did this event increase or decrease the number of shares outstanding? Why didn't this event affect the Common Stock account as reported on the balance sheet?

Group Project

Select a company and research its business. Search the business press for articles about this company. Obtain its annual report by requesting it directly from the company or from the company's Web site or from *Moody's Industrial Manual* (the exercise will be most meaningful if you obtain an actual copy and do not have to use *Moody's*).

Required

1. Based on your group's analysis, come to class prepared to instruct the class on six interesting facts about the company that can be found in its financial statements and the related notes. Your group can mention only the obvious, such as net sales or total revenue, net income, total assets, total liabilities, total stockholders' equity, and dividends, in conjunction with other terms. Once you use an obvious item, you may not use that item again.
2. The group should write a paper discussing the facts that it has uncovered. Limit the paper to two double-spaced, word-processed pages.

12

The Statement of Cash Flows

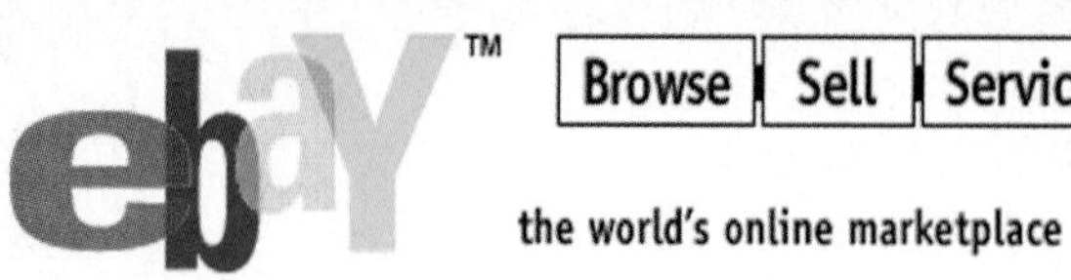

Learning Objectives

1 **Identify** the purposes of the statement of cash flows

2 **Distinguish** among operating, investing, and financing cash flows

3 **Prepare** a statement of cash flows by the indirect method

4 **Prepare** a statement of cash flows by the direct method

Need additional help? Go to the **Integrator CD** *and search these key words:* direct method, financing activities, indirect method, investing activities, operating activities, statement of cash flows

Integrator CD

eBay Inc.

Consolidated Statement of Cash Flows (Adapted) (In Thousands)

	Year Ended December 31,	
Operating	2000	2001
Cash flows from **operating** activities:		
Net income	$ 48,294	$ 90,448
Adjustments to reconcile net income to net cash provided by operating activities:		
Depreciation and amortization	38,050	86,641
Changes in assets and liabilities, net of acquired businesses		
Accounts receivable	(48,862)	(50,221)
Other current assets	(20,530)	11,607
Accounts payable	(408)	(4,087)
Accrued expenses and other liabilities	31,167	6,790
Unearned revenue	6,659	1,516
Income taxes payable	4,637	9,499
Other	41,141	99,919
Net cash provided by operating activities	100,148	252,112
Investing		
Cash flows from **investing** activities:		
Purchases of property and equipment	(49,753)	(57,420)
Purchases of investments	(398,998)	(602,485)
Sales of investments	248,547	738,989
Purchases of other non-current assets	(5,850)	(1,733)
Proceeds from sale of property and equipment	—	4,560
Acquisitions, net of cash acquired	—	(111,730)
Net cash used in investing activities	(206,054)	(29,819)
Financing		
Cash flows from **financing** activities:		
Proceeds from issuance of common stock, net	45,530	123,710
Proceeds from (principal payments on) long-term debt	2,869	(21,886)
Other	37,579	(319)
Net cash provided by financing activities	85,978	101,505
Effect of exchange rate changes on cash and cash equivalents	—	(1,702)
Net increase (decrease) in cash and cash equivalents	(19,928)	322,096
Cash and cash equivalents at beginning of year	221,801	201,873
Cash and cash equivalents at end of year	$ 201,873	$ 523,969

eBAY Inc. Outlines Global Business Strategy

San Jose, Calif., October 29, 2001—eBay Inc. (NASDAQ: eBay www.ebay.com), the world's online marketplace, today . . . outlined its strategy for growth through 2005. eBay executives highlighted key areas of growth, both domestically and abroad. "The depth, breadth and potential of our business gives us great confidence in the future," said Meg Whitman, president and CEO of eBay. "The eBay marketplace is thriving across geographies . . . user growth, and the services we offer our community."

While many dot.coms came and went, eBay was revolutionizing commerce and is still thriving. The company is in the enviable position of being both profitable and cash rich. In 2001, operations provided a quarter billion dollars of cash—quite an accomplishment for so new a company.

This chapter is devoted to the analysis of cash flows. It shows how to prepare the statement of cash flows and also how to interpret the information reported on the statement. Understanding cash flows is vital for making good business decisions.

Sitemap

In preceding chapters, we included cash-flow analysis as it related to the topics covered: receivables, plant assets, and so on. In this chapter, we discuss the statement of cash flows. Our goals are to give you the tools for cash-flow analysis and to show you how to prepare the statement of cash flows. We begin by explaining the statement format used by the vast majority of companies, called the *indirect approach*. We end the chapter with the alternate format of the statement of cash flows, the *direct approach*. After working through this chapter, you will be able to analyze the cash flows of any company you encounter.

This chapter has three distinct sections:

- Introduction, beginning on this page
- Preparing the Statement of Cash Flows by the Indirect Method, which begins on page 549
- Preparing the Statement of Cash Flows by the Direct Method, which begins on page 562

The chapter ends with a brief discussion of free cash flow and Decision Guidelines that show how to use cash-flow and income data for investment and credit analysis.

The introduction applies to all the cash-flow topics. To cover only the indirect method, instructors can assign the first two parts of the chapter. Those interested only in the direct method can cover just the Introduction and then go directly to the section on the Direct Method.

Basic Concepts: Statement of Cash Flows

financing activities, investing activities, operating activities, statement of cash flows

The balance sheet reports financial position at a given date. By examining balance sheets from two periods, you can tell whether cash increased or decreased. However, the balance sheet does not indicate *why* the cash balance changed. The income statement reports revenues, expenses, and net income—clues about the sources and uses of cash—but the income statement does not tell *why* cash increased or decreased.

Statement of cash flows
Reports cash receipts and cash disbursements classified according to the entity's major activities: operating, investing, and financing.

Cash flows
Cash receipts and cash payments (disbursements).

The **statement of cash flows** reports the entity's **cash flows**—cash receipts and cash payments—during the period. In other words, it shows where cash came from and how it was spent. It explains the *causes* of the change in the entity's cash balance during any given time period. The statement of cash flows covers a span of time and therefore is dated "Year Ended December 31, 20X2" or "Month Ended June 30, 20X3." Exhibit 12-1 illustrates the relative timing of the financial statements.

The statement of cash flows serves the following purposes:

Objective

1 **Identify** the purposes of the statement of cash flows

1. ***Predict future cash flows.*** Past cash receipts and payments are good predictors of future cash flows.
2. ***Evaluate management decisions.*** If managers make wise investment decisions, their business prospers. If they make unwise investments, the business suffers. The statement of cash flows reports cash flows from operations and also the investments the company is making. This gives investors and creditors cash-flow information for evaluating managers' decisions.

3. ***Determine the company's ability to pay dividends to stockholders and interest and principal to creditors.*** Stockholders are interested in receiving dividends on their investments. Creditors want to collect interest and principal. The statement of cash flows helps investors and creditors predict whether the business can make these payments.
4. ***Show the relationship of net income to the business's cash flows.*** Usually, cash and net income move together. High levels of income tend to lead to increases in cash, and vice versa. However, a company's cash flow can suffer even when net income is high.

✔ Check Point 12-1

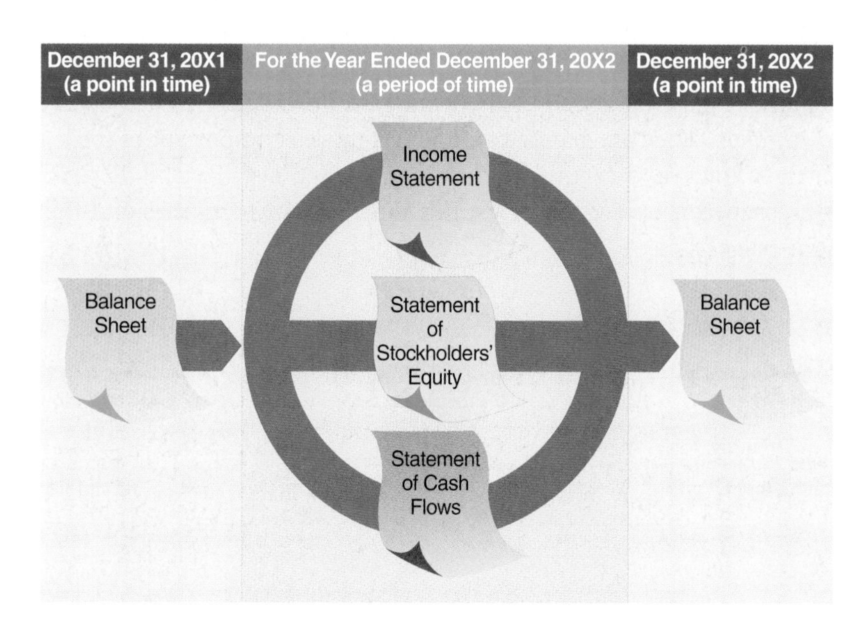

Exhibit 12-1

Timing of the Financial Statements

On a statement of cash flows, *Cash* means more than just cash on hand and cash in the bank. It includes **cash equivalents,** which are highly liquid short-term investments that can be converted into cash with little delay. Examples of cash equivalents are money-market investments and investments in U.S. Government Treasury bills. Businesses invest extra cash in liquid assets rather than let the cash remain idle. Throughout this chapter, the term *cash* refers to cash and cash equivalents.

Cash equivalents
Highly liquid short-term investments that can be converted into cash with little delay.

Operating, Investing, and Financing Activities

Objective

2 **Distinguish** among operating, investing, and financing cash flows

A business engages in three types of business activities:

- Operating activities
- Investing activities
- Financing activities

On Test

The statement of cash flows reports cash flows under these three headings, as shown for eBay on page 545.

Operating activities create revenues, expenses, gains, and losses. They affect *net income* on the income statement, which is a product of accrual-basis accounting. The operating section of the statement of cash flows reports the cash effects of operating activities. Operating activities also affect *current assets* and *current liabilities* on

Nature of the Business

Operating activities
Activities that create revenue or expense in the entity's major line of business; a section of the statement of cash flows. Operating activities affect the income statement.

the balance sheet. For example, a sale on account increases Sales Revenue on the income statement and Accounts Receivable, a current asset, on the balance sheet. Operating activities are the most important of the three categories because they are at the heart of every organization. A successful business must generate most of its cash from customers through day-to-day operations.

Investing activities
Activities that increase or decrease the long-term assets available to the business; a section of the statement of cash flows.

Financing activities
Activities that obtain from investors and creditors the cash needed to launch and sustain the business; a section of the statement of cash flows.

Investing activities increase and decrease *long-term assets*, such as computers and software, land, buildings, equipment, and investments in other companies. The purchases and the sales of these assets are investing activities. Loans to others and collections of loans are also investing activities. Investing activities are important because they acquire assets, but they are less critical than operating activities.

Financing activities obtain cash from investors and creditors to launch a business and keep it running. These activities include issuing stock, borrowing money, buying and selling treasury stock, and paying dividends to stockholders. Paying off a loan is another financing activity. Financing cash flows relate to *long-term liabilities* and *owners' equity*. They are generally viewed as the least important of the three categories of cash flows, and that's why they are reported last. Exhibit 12-2 shows the relationship between operating, investing, and financing activities and the various parts of the balance sheet.

Exhibit 12-2

Operating, Investing, and Financing Cash Flows and the Balance-Sheet Accounts

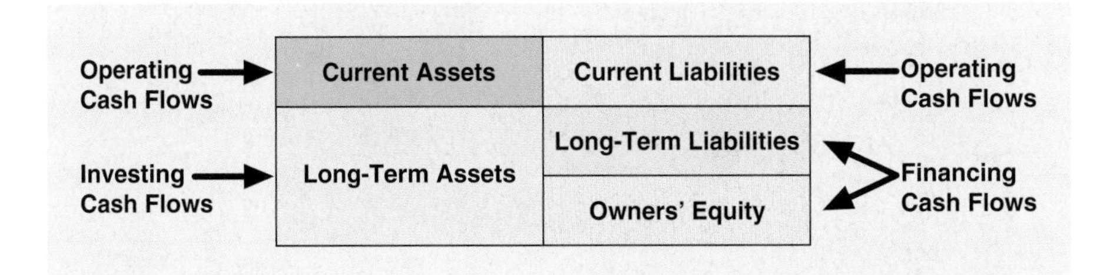

Examine eBay's statement of cash flows on page 545. Focus on the final line of each section: Operating, Investing, and Financing. eBay has very strong cash flows. During 2001, eBay's operating activities provided over $252 million of net cash inflow. eBay spent almost $30 million on investing activities, and the company received over $100 million from people willing to finance the company. These figures represent almost textbook-perfect relationships, as follows:

- *Operations* are eBay's largest source of cash.
- The company is *investing* in the future.
- People are willing to *finance* eBay.

✔ Check Point 12-2

Two Formats for Operating Activities

Indirect method
Format of the operating activities section of the statement of cash flows; starts with net income and reconciles to cash flows from operating activities. Also called the *reconciliation method*.

Direct method
Format of the operating activities section of the statement of cash flows; lists the major categories of operating cash receipts (collections from customers and receipts of interest and dividends) and cash disbursements (payments to suppliers, to employees, for interest and income taxes).

There are two ways to format operating activities on the statement of cash flows:

- **Indirect method,** which reconciles from net income to net cash provided by operating activities.
- **Direct method,** which reports all cash receipts and cash payments from operating activities.

The two methods use different computations, but they produce the same amount of cash from operations. The two methods have no effect on investing or financing activities.

The following table summarizes the differences between the approaches for operating activities:

Indirect Method		*Direct Method*	
Net income.	$XXX	Collections from customers	$XXX
Adjustments:		*Deductions:*	
Depreciation, etc.	XXX	Payments to suppliers, etc..	XXX
Net income provided by operating activities	$XXX	Net income provided by operating activities	$XXX

Let's begin with the indirect method because the vast majority of companies use it.

Preparing the Statement of Cash Flows by the Indirect Method

indirect methods, financing activities, investing activities, operating activities

The preparation of the statement of cash flows uses data from both the income statement and the comparative balance sheet. Consider Anchor Corporation, a dealer in auto parts for older British sports cars such as MG, Triumph, and Austin Healy. Proceed as follows to prepare the statement of cash flows by the indirect method:

Objective

3 **Prepare** a statement of cash flows by the indirect method

Exhibit 12-3

Template of the Statement of Cash Flows: Indirect Method

Anchor Corporation

Statement of Cash Flows
Year Ended December 31, 20X2

Cash flows from operating activities:

Net income

Adjustments to reconcile net income to net cash provided by operating activities:

+ Depreciation / amortization expense
+ Loss on sale of long-term assets
− Gain on sale of long-term assets
− Increases in current assets other than cash
+ Decreases in current assets other than cash
+ Increases in current liabilities
− Decreases in current liabilities

Net cash provided by operating activities

Cash flows from investing activities:

Sales of long-term assets (investments, land, building, equipment, and so on)
− Purchases of long-term assets
+ Collections of long-term receivables
− Long-term loans to others

Net cash provided by (used for) investing activities

Cash flows from financing activities:

Issuance of stock
+ Sale of treasury stock
− Purchase of treasury stock
+ Borrowing (issuance of notes or bonds payable)
− Payment of notes or bonds payable
− Payment of dividends

Net cash provided by (used for) financing activities

Net increase (decrease) in cash during the year

+ Cash at December 31, 20X1
= Cash at December 31, 20X2

(continued)

Exhibit 12-3 *(Cont.)* **Positive and Negative Items on the Statement of Cash Flows: Indirect Method**

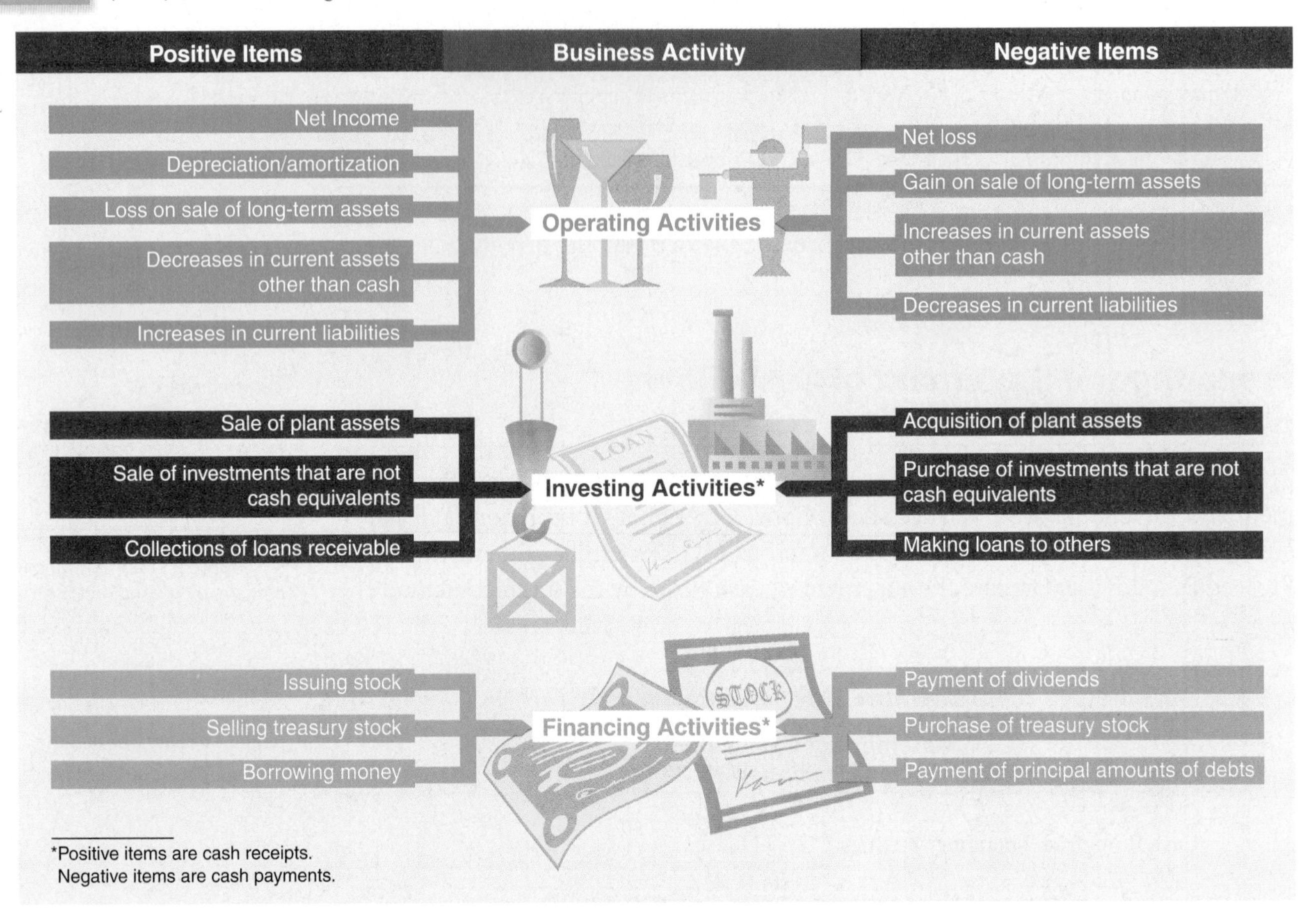

STEP 1 Lay out the template as shown in Exhibit 12-3. The exhibit is comprehensive. Study it carefully because you will be using it throughout your career in business. Part 2 of the exhibit gives a more visual picture of the statement. Steps 2 to 4 provide the data to complete the statement of cash flows.

STEP 2 Use the comparative balance sheet to determine the increase or decrease in cash during the period. The change in cash is the "check figure" for the statement of cash flows. Exhibit 12-4 gives the comparative balance sheet of Anchor Corporation at December 31, 20X2 and 20X1, with cash highlighted. Anchor's cash decreased by $20,000 during 20X2. This fact is interesting, but it begs a more important question: *Why* did Anchor's cash fall during the year? The statement of cash flows explains.

STEP 3 From the income statement, take net income, depreciation, depletion, and amortization expense, and any gains or losses on the sale of long-term assets. These amounts are needed for the statement of cash flows. Exhibit 12-5 gives the income statement of Anchor Corporation for the year ended December 31, 20X2, with relevant items highlighted.

STEP 4 Use the data from the income statement and the balance sheet to prepare the statement of cash flows. You can be confident that the statement of cash flows is complete only after explaining the year-to-year changes in all the balance sheet accounts.

Exhibit 12-4

Comparative Balance Sheet

Anchor Corporation

Comparative Balance Sheet
December 31, 20X2 and 20X1

(In thousands)	*20X2*	*20X1*	*Increase (Decrease)*	
Assets				
Current:				
Cash	$ 22	$ 42	$ (20)	*Changes in current assets—Operating*
Accounts receivable	93	80	13	
Interest receivable	3	1	2	
Inventory	135	138	(3)	
Prepaid expenses	8	7	1	
Long-term receivable from another company	11	—	11	*Changes in noncurrent assets—Investing*
Plant assets, net of depreciation	453	219	234	
Total	$725	$487	$238	
Liabilities				
Current:				
Accounts payable	$ 91	$ 57	$ 34	*Changes in current liabilities—Operating*
Salary and wage payable	4	6	(2)	
Accrued liabilities	1	3	(2)	
Long-term debt	160	77	83	*Changes in long-term liabilities and paid-in capital accounts—Financing*
Stockholders' Equity				
Common stock	359	258	101	
Retained earnings	110	86	24	*Change due to net income—Operating and change due to dividends—Financing*
Total	$725	$487	$238	

Exhibit 12-5

Income Statement

Anchor Corporation

Income Statement
Year Ended December 31, 20X2

	(In thousands)	
Revenues and gains:		
Sales revenue	$284	
Interest revenue	12	
Dividend revenue	9	
Gain on sale of plant assets	8	
Total revenues and gains		$313
Expenses:		
Cost of goods sold	$150	
Salary and wage expense	56	
Depreciation expense	18	
Other operating expense	17	
Interest expense	16	
Income tax expense	15	
Total expenses		272
Net income		$ 41

Exhibit 12-6

Statement of Cash Flows—Operating Activities by the Indirect Method

Anchor Corporation

Statement of Cash Flows
For the Year Ended December 31, 20X2

		(In thousands)	
	Cash flows from operating activities:		
	Net income		$41
	Adjustments to reconcile net income to net cash provided by operating activities:		
Ⓐ	Depreciation	$ 18	
Ⓑ	Gain on sale of plant assets	(8)	
Ⓒ	Increase in accounts receivable	(13)	
	Increase in interest receivable	(2)	
	Decrease in inventory	3	
	Increase in prepaid expenses	(1)	
	Increase in accounts payable	34	
	Decrease in salary and wage payable	(2)	
	Decrease in accrued liabilities	(2)	27
	Net cash provided by operating activities		$68

Let's apply Step 3 to prepare the operating activities section of Anchor Corporation's statement of cash flows for 20X2, which is in Exhibit 12-6.

Cash Flows from Operating Activities

The operating section of the cash-flow statement begins with net income, taken from the income statement (Exhibit 12-5). Additions and subtractions, which follow, are labeled "Adjustments to reconcile net income to net cash provided by operating activities."

Operating Activities Are Related to the Transactions That Make Up Net Income.[1]

Ⓐ **DEPRECIATION, DEPLETION, AND AMORTIZATION EXPENSES.** These expenses are added back to net income when we go from net income to cash flow. Let's see why. Depreciation is recorded as follows:

Depreciation Expense	18,000	
Accumulated Depreciation		18,000

This entry shows that depreciation expense has no effect on cash. However, depreciation expense, like all other expenses, is deducted from revenues to compute net income. Therefore, in going from net income to cash flows, we add depreciation back to net income. The add-back cancels the earlier deduction.

Example: Suppose you had only two transactions during the period, a $1,000 cash sale and depreciation expense of $300. Net income is $700 ($1,000 − $300). Cash flow from operations is $1,000. To reconcile from net income ($700) to cash flow ($1,000), we must add back the depreciation amount of $300. Depletion and amortization are also added back.

Ⓑ **GAINS AND LOSSES ON THE SALE OF ASSETS.** Sales of long-term assets are *investing* activities. On the statement of cash flows, a gain or loss on the sale is an adjustment to net income. Exhibit 12-6 above includes an adjustment for a gain. During 20X2,

[1]The authors thank Alfonso Oddo for suggesting this summary.

Anchor sold equipment for $62,000. Because the equipment's book value was $54,000, there was a gain of $8,000.

The $62,000 cash sale is an investing activity; the $62,000 includes the $8,000 gain on the sale. If the $8,000 gain is not removed from cash provided by operations, it will be counted twice. That is, the $8,000 will be included in both operating and investing cash flows. Hence, the $8,000 gain is removed from net income and thus excluded from cash flows from operations, as shown in Anchor Corporation's complete statement of cash flows in Exhibit 12-7. (We explain investing activities in the next section.)

A loss on the sale of plant assets also creates an adjustment to net income in the operating section of the cash-flow statement. However, a loss is *added back* to income to compute cash flow from operations. The cash received from selling the plant assets is then reported under investing activities.

Ⓒ **CHANGES IN THE CURRENT ASSET AND CURRENT LIABILITY ACCOUNTS.** Most current assets and current liabilities result from operating activities. For example, accounts receivable result from sales, inventory relates to cost of goods sold, and so on. Changes in the current accounts are reported as adjustments to net income on the cash-flow statement. The reasoning follows:

1. ***An increase in a current asset other than cash indicates a decrease in cash.*** The reason is because it takes cash to acquire assets. Suppose a company makes a sale on account. Accounts receivable are increased, but cash receipts are zero. Exhibit 12-4 (page 551) reports that Anchor Corporation's Accounts Receivable increased by $13,000 during 20X2. To compute the impact of revenue on Anchor's cash-flow amount, we must subtract the $13,000 increase in Accounts Receivable from net income in Exhibit 12-6. The reason is this: We have *not* collected this $13,000 in cash. The same logic applies to the other current assets. If they increase during the period, subtract the increase from net income to compute cash flow.
2. ***A decrease in a current asset other than cash indicates an increase in cash.*** Suppose Anchor's Accounts Receivable balance decreased by $4,000. Because cash receipts caused Accounts Receivable to decrease, add decreases in Accounts Receivable and the other current assets to net income.
3. ***A decrease in a current liability indicates a decrease in cash.*** The payment of a current liability causes both cash and the liability to decrease, so we subtract decreases in current liabilities from net income. In Exhibit 12-6, the $2,000 decrease in Accrued Liabilities is *subtracted* from net income to compute net cash provided by operating activities.

✔ **Check Point 12-3**

4. ***An increase in a current liability indicates an increase in cash.*** Anchor's Accounts Payable increased during the year. This increase can occur only if cash is not spent to pay this liability. In that case, cash payments are less than the related expense and Anchor has more cash on hand. Thus, increases in current liabilities are *added* to net income.

✔ **Check Point 12-4**

EVALUATING CASH FLOWS FROM OPERATING ACTIVITIES. During 20X2, Anchor Corporation's operations provided net cash flow of $68,000. This amount exceeds net income, as it should because of the add-back of depreciation. However, to fully evaluate a company's cash flows, analysts also examine its investing and financing activities. Let's see how to account for those cash flows, as reported in Exhibit 12-7.

Exhibit 12-7

Statement of Cash Flows—Indirect Method

Anchor Corporation

Statement of Cash Flows
For the Year Ended December 31, 20X2

			(In thousands)
	Cash flows from operating activities:		
	Net income		$ 41
	Adjustments to reconcile net income to net cash provided by operating activities:		
Ⓐ	Depreciation	$ 18	
Ⓑ	Gain on sale of plant assets	(8)	
Ⓒ	Increase in accounts receivable	(13)	
Ⓒ	Increase in interest receivable	(2)	
Ⓒ	Decrease in inventory	3	
Ⓒ	Increase in prepaid expenses	(1)	
Ⓒ	Increase in accounts payable	34	
Ⓒ	Decrease in salary and wage payable	(2)	
Ⓒ	Decrease in accrued liabilities	(2)	27
	Net cash provided by operating activities		68
	Cash flows from investing activities:		
	Acquisition of plant assets	$ (306)	
	Loan to another company	(11)	
	Proceeds from sale of plant assets	62	
	Net cash used for investing activities		(255)
	Cash flows from financing activities:		
	Proceeds from issuance of common stock	$ 101	
	Proceeds from issuance of long-term debt	94	
	Payment of long-term debt	(11)	
	Payment of dividends	(17)	
	Net cash provided by financing activities		167
	Net decrease in cash		**$ (20)**
	Cash balance, December 31, 20X1		42
	Cash balance, December 31, 20X2		$ 22

✔ Check Point 12-5
✔ Check Point 12-6
✔ Check Point 12-7

Cash Flows from Investing Activities

Investing activities affect long-term asset accounts, such as Plant Assets, Investments, and Notes Receivable. Most data for the computations of cash payments and receipts are taken directly from the income statement and the balance sheet.

COMPUTING ACQUISITIONS AND SALES OF PLANT ASSETS. Companies keep separate accounts for Land, Buildings, Equipment, and other plant assets. But for computing investing cash flows, it is helpful to combine these accounts into a single summary account. Also, we subtract accumulated depreciation from the assets' cost and get a net figure for plant assets. This approach allows us to work with a single plant asset account.

To illustrate, observe that Anchor Corporation's

- Balance sheet reports beginning plant assets, net of depreciation, of $219,000 and an ending net amount of $453,000 (Exhibit 12-4).
- Income statement shows a depreciation expense of $18,000 and an $8,000 gain on sale of plant assets (Exhibit 12-5).

Further, the acquisitions of plant assets total $306,000 (see Exhibit 12-7). How much, then, are the proceeds from the sale of plant assets? First, we must determine the book value of plant assets sold, as follows:

Plant Assets (net)

Beginning balance	+	Acquisitions	−	Depreciation	−	Book value of assets sold	=	Ending balance
$219,000	+	$306,000	−	$18,000		−X	=	$453,000
						−X	=	$453,000 − $219,000 − $306,000 + $18,000
						X	=	$54,000

Now we can compute the sale proceeds:

Sale proceeds	=	Book value of assets sold	+	Gain	−	Loss
	=	$54,000	+	$8,000	−	$0
	=	$62,000				

Trace the sale proceeds of $62,000 to the statement of cash flows in Exhibit 12-7. If the sale resulted in a loss of $3,000, the sale proceeds would be $51,000 ($54,000 − $3,000), and the statement would report $51,000 as a cash receipt from this investing activity.

The Plant Assets T-account provides another look at the computation of the book value of the assets sold.

Plant Assets (Net)

Beginning balance	**219,000**	**Depreciation**	**18,000**
Acquisitions	**306,000**	Book value of assets sold	54,000
Ending balance	**453,000**		

Proceeds from the sale of an asset can be computed as follows:

$$\text{Proceeds} = \text{Book value sold} + \text{Gain, or} - \text{Loss}$$

The book-value information comes from the balance sheet; the gain or loss comes from the income statement.

COMPUTING ACQUISITIONS AND SALES OF INVESTMENTS; AND LOANS AND THEIR COLLECTIONS. The cash amounts of transactions involving investments can be computed in the manner illustrated for plant assets. Investments are easier because there is no depreciation to account for, as shown in the following equation:

Investments (amounts assumed for illustration only)

Beginning balance	+	Purchases	−	Book value of investments sold	=	Ending balance
$100,000	+	$50,000		−X	=	$140,000
				−X	=	$140,000 − $100,000 − $50,000
				X	=	$10,000

If you prefer T-accounts, the Investments account holds these amounts:

Investments

Beginning balance	**100**		
Purchases	**50**	Book value of investments sold	10
Ending balance	**140**		

✔ Check Point 12-8

Apart from the Anchor Corporation example: Cash flows from loan transaction can be determined as follows:

Loans and Notes Receivable (amounts assumed for illustration only)

Beginning balance	+	New loans made	−	Collections	=	Ending balance
$90,000	+	$10,000		−X	=	$30,000
				−X	=	$30,000 − $90,000 − $10,000
				X	=	$70,000

Loans and Notes Receivable

Beginning balance	**90**		
New loans made	**10**	Collections	70
Ending balance	**30**		

Exhibit 12-8 summarizes the computation of cash flows from investing activities, highlighted in color.

Exhibit 12-8 **Computing Cash Flows from Investing Activities**

Receipts

From sale of plant assets	Beginning plant assets (net) + Acquisition cost − Depreciation − Book value of assets sold = Ending plant assets (net)
	Cash received = Book value of assets sold + Gain on sale or − Loss on sale
From sale of investments	Beginning investments + Purchase cost of investments − Cost of investments sold = Ending investments
	Cash received = Cost of investments sold + Gain on sale or − Loss on sale
From collection of loans and notes receivable	Beginning loans or notes receivable + New loans made − Collections = Ending loans or notes receivable

Payments

For acquisition of plant assets	Beginning plant assets (net) + Acquisition cost − Depreciation − Book value of assets sold = Ending plant assets (net)
For purchase of investments	Beginning investments + Purchase cost of investments − Cost of investments sold = Ending investments
For new loans made	Beginning loans or notes receivable + New loans made − Collections = Ending loans or notes receivable

Cash Flows from Financing Activities

Financing activities affect liability and stockholders' equity accounts, such as Notes Payable, Bonds Payable, Long-Term Debt, Common Stock, Paid-in Capital in Excess of Par, and Retained Earnings.

COMPUTING ISSUANCES AND PAYMENTS OF LONG-TERM DEBT. The beginning and ending balances of Long-Term Debt, Notes Payable, or Bonds Payable are taken from the balance sheet. If either the amount of new issuances or the payments is known, the other amount can be computed. For Anchor Corporation, new debt issuances total $94,000 (Exhibit 12-7). The computation of debt payments uses the Long-Term Debt account, with amounts from Anchor Corporation's balance sheet in Exhibit 12-4:

Long-Term Debt

Beginning balance	+	Issuance of new debt	−	Payments of debt	=	Ending balance
$77,000	+	$94,000		−X	=	$160,000
				−X	=	$160,000 − $77,000 − $94,000
				X	=	$11,000

Long-Term Debt

		Beginning balance	**77,000**
Payments	11,000	**Issuance of new debt**	**94,000**
		Ending balance	**160,000**

COMPUTING ISSUANCES OF STOCK AND PURCHASES OF TREASURY STOCK. The cash effects of these financing activities can be determined by analyzing the stock accounts. For example, the amount of a new issuance of common stock is determined from the Common Stock and Capital in Excess of Par. It is convenient to work with a single summary account for stock as we do for plant assets. Using data from Exhibits 12-4 and 12-7, we have

Common Stock

Beginning balance	+	Issuance of new stock	=	Ending balance
$258,000	+	$101,000	=	$359,000

Common Stock

		Beginning balance	**258,000**
		Issuance of new stock	101,000
		Ending balance	**359,000**

Apart from the Anchor Corporation example: Cash flows affecting Treasury Stock can be analyzed as follows:

Treasury Stock (amounts assumed for illustration only)

Beginning balance	+	Purchase of treasury stock	=	Ending balance
$16,000	+	$3,000	=	$19,000

Treasury Stock

Beginning balance	**16,000**		
Purchases of treasury stock	3,000		
Ending balance	**19,000**		

COMPUTING DIVIDEND PAYMENTS. If dividend payments are not given elsewhere, they can be computed. The following computations show how to determine Anchor Corporation's dividend payments:

Retained Earnings

Beginning balance	+	Net income	−	Dividend declarations and payments	=	Ending balance
\$86,000	+	\$41,000		−X	=	\$110,000
				−X	=	\$110,000 − \$86,000 − \$41,000
				X	=	\$17,000

The T-accounts provide another view of the dividand computation.

✔ Check Point 12-9

Retained Earnings

Dividend declarations and payments	**17,000**	**Beg. bal.**	**86,000**
		Net income	**41,000**
		End. bal.	**110,000**

Exhibit 12-9 summarizes the computation of cash flows from financing activities, highlighted in color.

Exhibit 12-9 **Computing Cash Flows from Financing Activities**

Receipts	
From issuance of long-term debt	Beginning long-term debt + Cash received from issuance of long-term debt − Payment of debt = Ending long-term debt
From issuance of stock	Beginning stock + Cash received from issuance of new stock = Ending stock
Payments	
Of long-term debt	Beginning long-term debt + Cash received from issuance of long-term debt − Payment of debt = Ending long-term debt
To purchase treasury stock	Beginning treasury stock + Purchase cost of treasury stock = Ending treasury stock
Of dividends	Beginning retained earnings + Net income − Dividend declarations and payments = Ending retained earnings

Classify each of the following as an operating activity, an investing activity, or a financing activity:

a. Issuance of stock
b. Borrowing
c. Sales revenue
d. Payment of dividends
e. Purchase of land
f. Purchase of treasury stock
g. Paying bonds payable
h. Interest expense
i. Sale of equipment
j. Cost of goods sold
k. Purchase of another company
l. Making a loan

Answer:

a. Financing
b. Financing
c. Operating
d. Financing
e. Investing
f. Financing
g. Financing
h. Operating
i. Investing
j. Operating
k. Investing
l. Investing

Noncash Investing and Financing Activities

Companies make investments that do not require cash. They also obtain financing other than cash. Our examples thus far have included none of these transactions. Now suppose that Anchor Corporation issued common stock valued at $320,000 to acquire a warehouse. Anchor would journalize this transaction as follows:

Warehouse Building	320,000	
Common Stock		320,000

This transaction would not be reported on the cash-flow statement because Anchor paid no cash. But the investment in the warehouse and the issuance of stock are important. Noncash investing and financing activities like this transaction can be reported in a separate schedule that accompanies the statement of cash flows. Exhibit 12-10 illustrates noncash investing and financing activities (all amounts are assumed). This information follows the cash-flow statement or can be disclosed in a note.

Exhibit 12-10

Noncash Investing and Financing Activities (All Amounts Assumed)

	Thousands
Noncash Investing and Financing Activities:	
Acquisition of building by issuing common stock	$320
Acquisition of land by issuing note payable	72
Payment of long-term debt by transferring investments to the creditor	104
Acquisition of equipment by issuing short-term note payable	37
Total noncash investing and financing activities	$533

Now let's put into practice what you have learned about the statement of cash flows prepared by the indirect method.

Mid-Chapter Summary Problem

Robins Corporation reported the following income statement and comparative balance sheet for 20X5, along with transaction data for 20X5:

Robins Corporation

Income Statement
Year Ended December 31, 20X5

Sales revenue		$662,000
Cost of goods sold		560,000
Gross profit		102,000
Operating expenses		
Salary expenses	$46,000	
Depreciation expense, equipment	7,000	
Amortization expense, patent	3,000	
Rent expense	2,000	
Total operating expenses		58,000
Income from operations		44,000
Other items:		
Loss on sale of equipment		(2,000)
Income before income tax		42,000
Income tax expense		16,000
Net income		$ 26,000

Robins Corporation

Balance Sheet
December 31,

Assets	20X5	20X4	Liabilities	20X5	20X4
Current:			Current:		
Cash and equivalents	$ 19,000	$ 3,000	Accounts payable	$ 35,000	$ 26,000
Accounts receivable	22,000	23,000	Accrued liabilities	7,000	9,000
Inventories	34,000	31,000	Income tax payable	10,000	10,000
Prepaid expenses	1,000	3,000	Total current liabilities	52,000	45,000
Total current assets	76,000	60,000	Long-term note payable	44,000	—
Long-term investments	18,000	10,000	Bonds payable	40,000	53,000
Equipment, net	67,000	52,000	**Owners' Equity**		
Patent, net	44,000	10,000	Common stock	52,000	20,000
Total assets	$205,000	$132,000	Retained earnings	27,000	19,000
			Less: Treasury stock	(10,000)	(5,000)
			Total liabilities and equity	$205,000	$132,000

Transaction Data for 20X5:	
Purchase of equipment	$98,000
Payment of cash dividends	18,000
Issuance of common stock to retire bonds payable	13,000
Purchase of long-term investment	8,000
Issuance of long-term note payable to purchase patent	37,000
Issuance of long-term note payable to borrow cash	7,000
Issuance of common stock for cash	19,000
Sale of equipment (book value, $76,000)	74,000
Purchase of treasury stock	5,000

Required

Prepare Robins Corporation's statement of cash flows for the year ended December 31, 20X5. Format operating cash flows by the indirect method. Follow the four steps outlined below. For Step 4, prepare a T-account to show the transaction activity in each long-term balance sheet account. For each plant asset, use a single account, net of accumulated depreciation (for example: Equipment, net).

Requirement 1

STEP 1 Lay out the template of the statement of cash flows.

STEP 2 From the comparative balance sheet, determine the increase in cash during the year, $16,000.

STEP 3 From the income statement, take net income, depreciation, amortization, and the loss on sale of equipment, to the statement of cash flows.

STEP 4 Complete the statement of cash flows. Account for the year-to-year change in each balance sheet account.

Answer

Robins Corporation
Statement of Cash Flows
Year Ended December 31, 20X5

Cash flows from operating activities:		
Net income		$26,000
Adjustments to reconcile net income to net cash provided by operating activities:		
Depreciation	$ 7,000	
Amortization	3,000	
Loss on sale of equipment	2,000	
Decrease in accounts receivable	1,000	
Increase in inventories	(3,000)	
Decrease in prepaid expenses	2,000	
Increase in accounts payable	9,000	
Decrease in accrued liabilities	(2,000)	19,000
Net cash provided by operating activities		45,000
Cash flows from investing activities:		
Purchase of equipment	$(98,000)	
Sale of equipment	74,000	
Purchase of long-term investment	(8,000)	
Net cash used for investing activities		(32,000)
Cash flows from financing activities:		
Issuance of common stock	$ 19,000	
Payment of cash dividends	(18,000)	
Issuance of long-term note payable	7,000	
Purchase of treasury stock	(5,000)	
Net cash provided by financing activities		3,000
Net increase in cash		$16,000
Cash balance, December 31, 20X4		3,000
Cash balance, December 31, 20X5		$19,000
Noncash investing and financing activities:		
Issuance of long-term note payable to purchase patent		$37,000
Issuance of common stock to retire bonds payable		13,000
Total noncash investing and financing activities		$50,000

Long-Term Investments

	Debit		Credit
Bal.	10,000		
	8,000		
Bal.	18,000		

Equipment, Net

	Debit		Credit
Bal.	52,000		
	98,000		76,000
			7,000
Bal.	67,000		

Patent, Net

	Debit		Credit
Bal.	10,000		
	37,000		3,000
Bal.	44,000		

Long-term Note Payable

	Debit		Credit
		Bal.	0
			37,000
			7,000
		Bal.	44,000

Bonds Payable

	Debit		Credit
		Bal.	53,000
	13,000		
		Bal.	40,000

Common Stock

	Debit		Credit
		Bal.	20,000
			13,000
			19,000
		Bal.	52,000

Retained Earnings

	Debit		Credit
		Bal.	19,000
	18,000		26,000
		Bal.	27,000

Treasury Stock

	Debit		Credit
Bal.	5,000		
	5,000		
Bal.	10,000		

direct method, financing activities, investing activities, operating activities

Preparing the Statement of Cash Flows by the Direct Method

Objective

4 **Prepare** a statement of cash flows by the direct method

The Financial Accounting Standards Board (FASB) has expressed a preference for the direct method of reporting cash flows from operating activities. Unfortunately, very few companies use this method because it takes more computations than the indirect method. But the direct method provides clearer information about the sources and uses of a company's operating cash. Investing and financing cash flows are unaffected by the method of formatting operating cash flows; they are the same under both methods.

To illustrate the statement of cash flows, we will be using Anchor Corporation, a dealer in auto parts for older British sports cars such as MG, Triumph, and Austin Healy. To prepare the statement of cash flows by the direct method, proceed as follows:

STEP 1 Lay out the template of the statement of cash flows by the direct method, as shown in Exhibit 12-11. Part 2 of Exhibit 12-11 gives a more visual picture of the statement. Steps 2 and 3 will provide the data to complete the statement of cash flows.

Exhibit 12-11

Part 1 Template of the Statement of Cash Flows: Direct Method

Anchor Corporation

Statement of Cash Flows
Year Ended December 31, 20X2

Cash flows from operating activities:
Receipts:
Collections from customers
Interest received on notes receivable
Dividends received on investments in stock
Total cash receipts
Payments:
To suppliers
To employees
For interest
For income tax
Total cash payments
Net cash provided by operating activities
Cash flows from investing activities:
Sales of long-term assets (investments, land, building, equipment, and so on)
− Purchases of long-term assets
+ Collections of long-term receivables
− Long-term loans to others
Net cash provided by (used for) investing activities
Cash flows from financing activities:
Issuance of stock
+ Sale of treasury stock
− Purchase of treasury stock
+ Borrowing (issuance of notes or bonds payable)
− Payment of notes or bonds payable
− Payment of dividends
Net cash provided by (used for) financing activities
Net increase (decrease) in cash during the year
+ Cash at December 31, 20X1
= Cash at December 31, 20X2

Exhibit 12-11 **Part 2 Cash Receipts and Cash Payments on the Statement of Cash Flows—Direct Method**

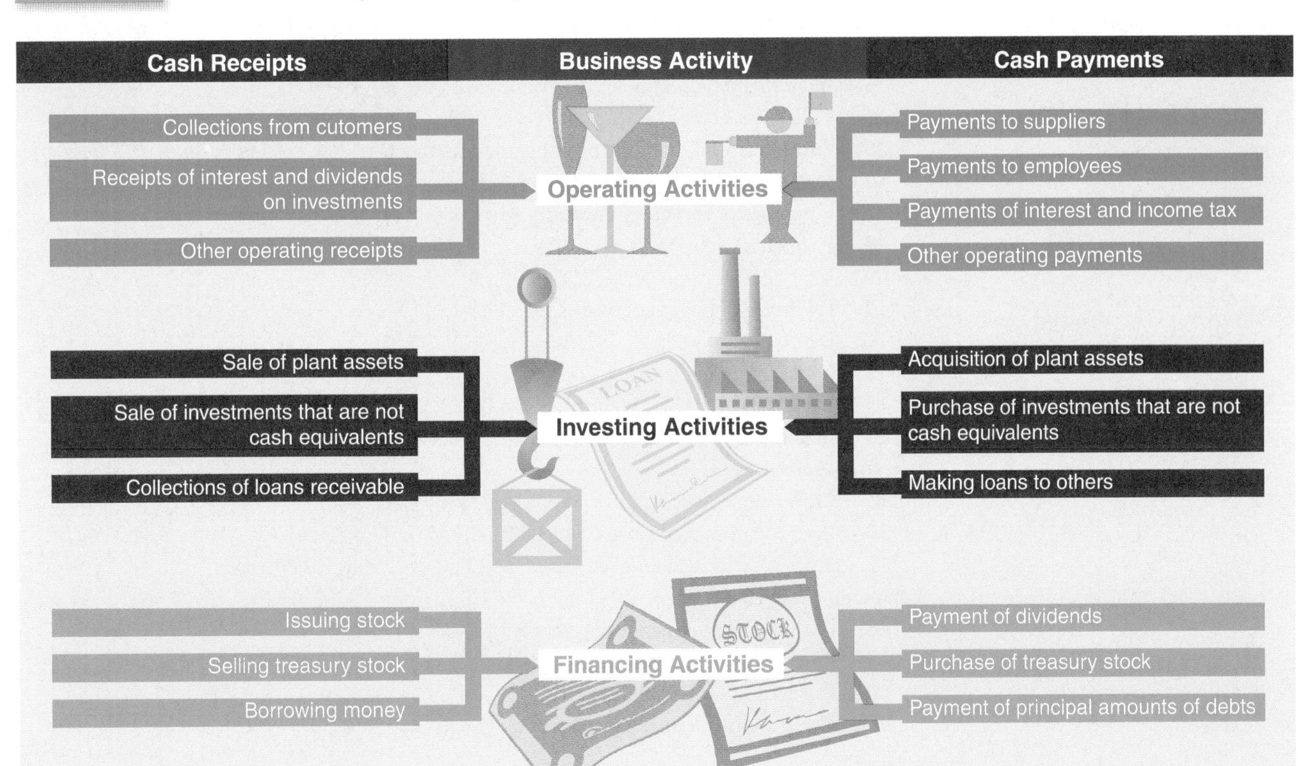

STEP 2 Use the comparative balance sheet to determine the increase or decrease in cash during the period. The change in cash is the "check figure" for the statement of cash flows. The comparative balance sheet of Anchor Corporation at December 31, 20X2 and 20X1 indicates that Anchor's cash decreased by $20,000 during 20X2. See Exhibit 12-4, page 551. This fact is interesting, but it begs a more important question: *Why* did Anchor's cash fall during 20X2? The statement of cash flows explains *why* cash changed.

STEP 3 Use the available data to prepare the statement of cash flows. Suppose Anchor has assembled the summary of 20X2 transactions in Exhibit 12-12. These transactions give the data for both the income statement (see Exhibit 12-5, page 551) and the statement of cash flows. Some transactions affect one statement and some, the other. For example, sales (item 1) are reported on the income statement, and cash collections (item 2) on the statement of cash flows. Other transactions, such as the cash receipt of dividend revenue (item 5) affect both statements. *The statement of cash flows reports only those transactions with cash effects* (those with an asterisk in Exhibit 12-12). Exhibit 12-13 gives Anchor Corporation's statement of cash flows for 20X2.

Cash Flows from Operating Activities

Operating cash flows are listed first because they are the largest and most important source of cash for most businesses. Exhibit 12-13 shows that Anchor is sound; its operating activities were the largest source of cash receipts, $290,000.

Exhibit 12-12

Summary of Anchor Corporation's 20X2 Transactions

Operating Activities

1. Sales on credit, $284,000
*2. Collections from customers, $271,000
3. Interest revenue on notes receivable, $12,000
*4. Collection of interest receivable, $10,000
*5. Cash receipt of dividend revenue on investments in stock, $9,000
6. Cost of goods sold, $150,000
7. Purchases of inventory on credit, $147,000
*8. Payments to suppliers, $133,000
9. Salary and wage expense, $56,000
*10. Payments of salary and wages, $58,000
11. Depreciation expense, $18,000
12. Other operating expense, $17,000
*13. Interest expense and payments, $16,000
*14. Income tax expense and payments, $15,000

Investing Activities

*15. Cash payments to acquire plant assets, $306,000
*16. Loan to another company, $11,000
*17. Proceeds from sale of plant assets, $62,000, including $8,000 gain

Financing Activities

*18. Proceeds from issuance of common stock, $101,000
*19. Proceeds from issuance of long-term debt, $94,000
*20. Payment of long-term debt, $11,000
*21. Declaration and payment of cash dividends, $17,000

*Indicates a cash flow to be reported on the statement of cash flows
Note: Income statement data are taken from Exhibit 12-16, page 569.

CASH COLLECTIONS FROM CUSTOMERS. Cash sales bring in cash immediately, and collections of accounts receivable take longer. Both are reported on the statement of cash flows as "Collections from customers . . . $271,000" in Exhibit 12-13.

CASH RECEIPTS OF INTEREST. Interest revenue is earned on notes receivable. The income statement reports interest revenue. Only the cash receipts of interest appear on the statement of cash flows—$10,000 in Exhibit 12-13.

CASH RECEIPTS OF DIVIDENDS. Dividends are earned on investments in stock. Dividend revenue is reported on the income statement, and this cash receipt is reported on the statement of cash flows—$9,000 in Exhibit 12-13. (Dividends *received* are part of operating activities, but dividends *paid* constitute a financing activity.)

PAYMENTS TO SUPPLIERS. Payments to suppliers include all payments for inventory and operating expenses except employee compensation, interest, and income taxes. *Suppliers* are those entities that provide the business with its inventory and essential services. For example, a clothing store's suppliers may include Levi Strauss, Liz Claiborne, and Reebok. Other suppliers provide advertising, utility, and various services that are operating expenses. In Exhibit 12-13, Anchor Corporation reports payments to suppliers of $133,000.

PAYMENTS TO EMPLOYEES. This category includes payments for salaries, wages, commissions, and other forms of employee compensation. Accrued amounts are excluded because they have not yet been paid. The statement of cash flows in Exhibit 12-13 reports only the cash payments ($58,000).

Exhibit 12-13

Statement of Cash Flows—Direct Method

Anchor Corporation

Statement of Cash Flows
Year Ended December 31, 20X2

	(In thousands)	
Cash flows from operating activities:		
Receipts:		
Collections from customers	$ 271	
Interest received on notes receivable	10	
Dividends received on investments in stock	9	
Total cash receipts		$290
Payments:		
To suppliers	$(133)	
To employees	(58)	
For interest	(16)	
For income tax	(15)	
Total cash payments		(222)
Net cash provided by operating activities		68
Cash flows from investing activities:		
Acquisition of plant assets	$(306)	
Loan to another company	(11)	
Proceeds from sale of plant assets	62	
Net cash used for investing activities		(255)
Cash flows from financing activities:		
Proceeds from issuance of common stock	$ 101	
Proceeds from issuance of long-term debt	94	
Payment of long-term debt	(11)	
Payment of dividends	(17)	
Net cash provided by financing activities		167
Net decrease in cash		**$ (20)**
Cash balance, December 31, 20X1		42
Cash balance, December 31, 20X2		$ 22

PAYMENTS FOR INTEREST EXPENSE AND INCOME TAX EXPENSE. These cash payments are reported separately from the other expenses. In the Anchor Corporation example, interest and income tax expenses equal their cash payments amounts. Therefore, the same amount appears on the income statement and the statement of cash flows. The cash-flow statement reports the cash payments for interest ($16,000) and income tax ($15,000). Interest payments are operating cash flows because the interest is an expense.

DEPRECIATION, DEPLETION, AND AMORTIZATION EXPENSE. These expenses are *not* listed on the statement of cash flows in Exhibit 12-13 because they do not affect cash.

Cash Flows from Investing Activities

Investing is critical because a company's investments determine its future course. Large purchases of plant assets signal expansion. Low levels of investing over a lengthy period indicate that the business is not replenishing assets.

Purchases of Plant Assets; Investments in and Loans to Other Companies. These cash payments acquire a long-term asset. The first investing activity reported by Anchor Corporation in Exhibit 12-13 is the purchase of plant assets ($306,000). In the second transaction, Anchor makes an $11,000 loan and thus obtains a note receivable. These are investing activities because the company is investing in long-term assets.

Proceeds from the Sale of Plant Assets and Investments; and the Collections of Loans. These cash receipts are also investing activities. The sale of the plant assets needs explanation. The statement of cash flows in Exhibit 12-13 reports that Anchor Corporation received $62,000 cash from the sale of plant assets. The income statement shows an $8,000 gain on this transaction. What is the appropriate amount to show on the cash-flow statement? It is $62,000, the cash proceeds from the sale, not the $8,000 gain. Because a gain occurred, you may wonder why this cash receipt is not reported as part of operations. Operations consist of buying and selling *merchandise* or rendering *services* to earn revenue. Investing activities refer to the acquisition and disposition of long-term assets. Therefore, the FASB views the sale of plant assets and the sale of investments as cash inflows from investing activities.

Investors and creditors are often critical of a company that sells large amounts of its plant assets. That may signal an emergency. For example, budget cuts in the defense industry required the defense contractor Northrup-Grumman Corporation to shed almost one-third of its facilities worldwide. Grumman could no longer compete and was taken over by Martin Marietta.

In other situations, selling off fixed assets may be good news if, for example, the company is selling off an unprofitable division. Whether sales of plant assets are good news or bad news should be evaluated in light of a company's operating and financing characteristics.

Cash Flows from Financing Activities

Cash flows from financing activities include the following:

Proceeds from Issuance of Stock and Debt. Readers of financial statements want to know how the entity obtains its financing. Issuing stock and borrowing money are two common ways to finance operations. In Exhibit 12-13, Anchor Corporation issued common stock and received cash of $101,000. Anchor also issued long-term debt to borrow $94,000.

Payment of Debt and Purchases of the Company's Own Stock. The payment of debt decreases cash, which is the opposite effect of borrowing. Anchor Corporation reports long-term debt payments of $11,000. Other transactions in this category include the purchase of treasury stock.

✔ Check Point 12-10

✔ Check Point 12-11

✔ Check Point 12-12

Payment of Cash Dividends. The payment of cash dividends decreases cash and is therefore a financing cash payment, as illustrated by Anchor's $17,000 payment in Exhibit 12-13. A *stock* dividend has no effect on Cash and is *not* reported on the cash-flow statement.

Noncash Investing and Financing Activities

Companies make investments that do not require cash. They also obtain financing other than cash. Our examples thus far have included none of these transactions. Now suppose that Anchor Corporation issued common stock valued at $320,000 to acquire a warehouse. Anchor would journalize this transaction as follows:

Warehouse Building	320,000	
Common Stock		320,000

This transaction would not be reported on the cash-flow statement because Anchor paid no cash. But the investment in the warehouse and the issuance of stock are important. Noncash investing and financing activities like this transaction can be reported in a separate schedule that accompanies the statement of cash flows. Exhibit 12-14 illustrates noncash investing and financing activities (all amounts are assumed). This information follows the cash-flow statement or can be disclosed in a note.

Exhibit 12-14

Noncash Investing and Financing Activities (All Amounts Assumed)

	Thousands
Noncash Investing and Financing Activities:	
Acquisition of building by issuing common stock	$320
Acquisition of land by issuing note payable	72
Payment of long-term debt by transferring investments to the creditor . .	104
Acquisition of equipment by issuing short-term note payable	37
Total noncash investing and financing activities	$533

Classify each of the following as an operating activity, an investing activity, or a financing activity, Also identify those items that are not reported on the statement of cash flows prepared by the direct method.

a. Net income
b. Payment of dividends
c. Borrowing
d. Payment of cash to suppliers
e. Making a loan
f. Sale of treasury stock
g. Depreciation expense
h. Purchase of equipment
i. Issuance of stock
j. Purchase of another company
k. Payment of a note payable
l. Payment of income taxes
m. Collections from customers
n. Accrual of interest revenue
o. Expiration of prepaid expense
p. Receipt of cash dividends

Answer:

a. Not reported	e. Investing	i. Financing	m. Operating
b. Financing	f. Financing	j. Investing	n. Not reported
c. Financing	g. Not reported	k. Financing	o. Not reported
d. Operating	h. Investing	l. Operating	p. Operating

Now let's see how to compute the amounts of the operating cash flows by the direct method.

Computing Operating Cash Flows by the Direct Method

How do we compute the operating cash flows for the direct method? We can use the income statement and the *changes* in the related balance sheet accounts, as diagrammed in Exhibit 12-15.

Exhibit 12-15

Direct Method of Computing Cash Flows from Operating Activities

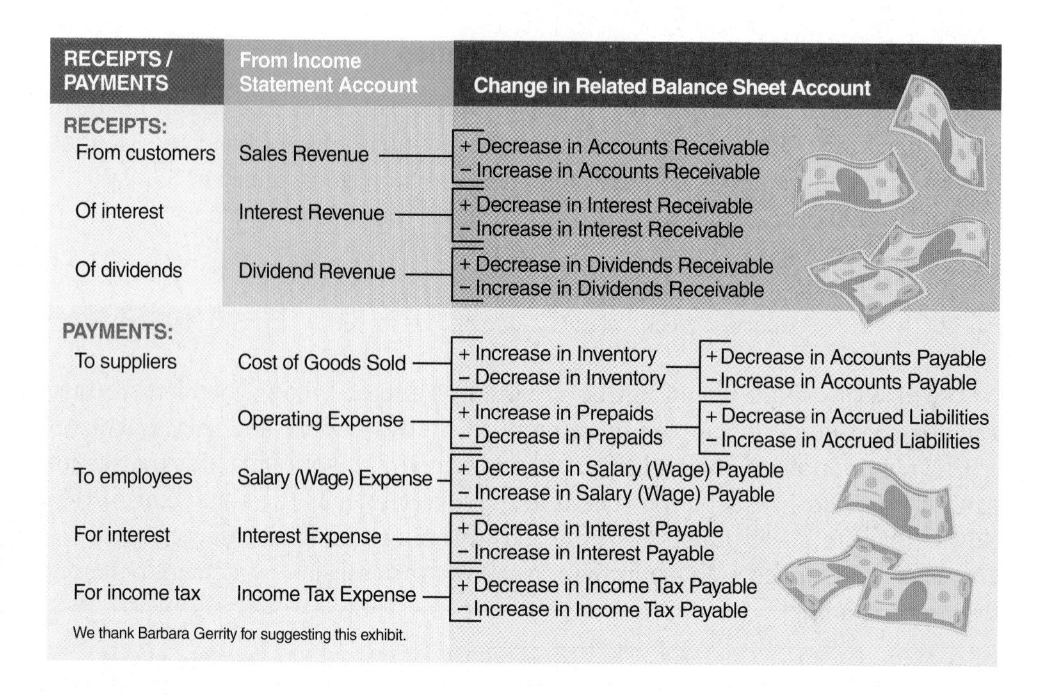

RECEIPTS / PAYMENTS	From Income Statement Account	Change in Related Balance Sheet Account	
RECEIPTS:			
From customers	Sales Revenue	+ Decrease in Accounts Receivable − Increase in Accounts Receivable	
Of interest	Interest Revenue	+ Decrease in Interest Receivable − Increase in Interest Receivable	
Of dividends	Dividend Revenue	+ Decrease in Dividends Receivable − Increase in Dividends Receivable	
PAYMENTS:			
To suppliers	Cost of Goods Sold	+ Increase in Inventory − Decrease in Inventory	+ Decrease in Accounts Payable − Increase in Accounts Payable
	Operating Expense	+ Increase in Prepaids − Decrease in Prepaids	+ Decrease in Accrued Liabilities − Increase in Accrued Liabilities
To employees	Salary (Wage) Expense	+ Decrease in Salary (Wage) Payable − Increase in Salary (Wage) Payable	
For interest	Interest Expense	+ Decrease in Interest Payable − Increase in Interest Payable	
For income tax	Income Tax Expense	+ Decrease in Income Tax Payable − Increase in Income Tax Payable	

We thank Barbara Gerrity for suggesting this exhibit.

Data for computing Anchor Corporation's operating cash flows are provided by the company's income statement (Exhibit 12-16) and comparative balance sheet (Exhibit 12-17).

COMPUTING CASH COLLECTIONS FROM CUSTOMERS. Collections can be computed by converting sales revenue (an accrual-basis amount) to the cash basis. Anchor Corporation's income statement (Exhibit 12-16) reports sales of $284,000. Exhibit 12-17 shows that Accounts Receivable increased from $80,000 at the beginning of the year to $93,000 at year end, a $13,000 increase. Based on those amounts, Cash Collections equal $271,000, as shown in the following equation and the related T-account for Accounts Receivable. We must solve for cash collections (X).

Accounts Receivable

Beginning balance	+	Sales	−	Collections	=	Ending balance
$80,000	+	$284,000		−X	=	$93,000
				−X	=	$93,000 − $80,000 − $284,000
				Collections	=	$271,000

Accounts Receivable			
Beginning balance	**80,000**		
Sales	**284,000**	Collections	271,000
Ending balance	**93,000**		

If Accounts Receivable increased, then collections must be less than sales.

All collections of receivables are computed in the same way. In our example, Anchor Corporation earned interest revenue of $12,000 (Exhibit 12-16). Interest Receivable's balance increased $2,000 (Exhibit 12-17). Cash receipts of interest must be $10,000 (Interest Revenue of $12,000 minus the $2,000 increase in Interest Receivable). Exhibit 12-15 shows how to make this computation.

Exhibit 12-16

Income Statement

Anchor Corporation

Income Statement
Year Ended December 31, 20X2

	(In thousands)	
Revenues and gains:		
Sales revenue	$284	
Interest revenue	12	
Dividend revenue	9	
Gain on sale of plant assets	8	
Total revenues and gains		$313
Expenses:		
Cost of goods sold	$150	
Salary and wage expense	56	
Depreciation expense	18	
Other operating expense	17	
Interest expense	16	
Income tax expense	15	
Total expenses		272
Net income		$ 41

Exhibit 12-17 **Comparative Balance Sheet**

Anchor Corporation

Comparative Balance Sheet
December 31, 20X2 and 20X1

(In thousands)	*20X2*	*20X1*	*Increase (Decrease)*	
Assets				
Current:				
Cash	$ 22	$ 42	$(20)	
Accounts receivable	93	80	13	*Changes in current assets—Operating*
Interest receivable	3	1	2	
Inventory	135	138	(3)	
Prepaid expenses	8	7	1	
Long-term receivable from another company	11	—	11	*Changes in noncurrent assets—Investing*
Plant assets, net of depreciation	453	219	234	
Total	$725	$487	$238	
Liabilities				
Current:				
Accounts payable	$ 91	$ 57	$ 34	*Changes in current liabilities—Operating*
Salary and wage payable	4	6	(2)	
Accrued liabilities	1	3	(2)	
Long-term debt	160	77	83	*Changes in long-term liabilities and paid-in capital accounts—Financing*
Stockholders' Equity				
Common stock	359	258	101	
Retained earnings	110	86	24	*Change due to net income—Operating and change due to dividends—Financing*
Total	$725	$487	$238	

Computing Payments to Suppliers. This computation includes two parts:

- Payments for inventory
- Payments for operating expenses (other than interest and income tax)

Payments for inventory are computed by converting cost of goods sold to the cash basis. We accomplish this process by analyzing Cost of Goods Sold from the income statement and Accounts Payable from the balance sheet. The computation of Anchor Corporation's cash payments for inventory is given by the following equations. First, we must solve for purchases, \$147,000. Then, we insert purchases into Accounts Payable and solve for *payments for inventory* \$113,000. Throughout, all amounts come from Exhibits 12-16 and 12-17.

Cost of Goods Sold

Beginning inventory	+	Purchases	−	Ending inventory	=	Cost of goods sold
\$138,000	+	X	−	\$135,000	=	\$150,000
		X			=	\$150,000 − \$138,000 + \$135,000
		Purchases			=	\$147,000

Now we can insert the amount of purchases into Accounts Payable to determine the amount of cash payments for inventory (Y), as follows:

Accounts Payable

Beginning balance	+	Purchases	−	Payments for inventory	=	Ending balance
\$57,000	+	\$147,000		−Y	=	\$91,000
				−Y	=	\$91,000 − \$57,000 − \$147,000
				Payments	=	\$113,000

The T-accounts show where the data come from.

Cost of Goods Sold

Beg. inventory	138,000	End. inventory	135,000
Purchases	147,000		
Cost of goods sold	150,000		

Accounts Payable

Payments for inventory	113,000	Beg. bal.	57,000
		Purchases	147,000
		End bal.	91,000

✔ Check Point 12-13

If Accounts Payable increased, then payments must be less than purchases.

Computing Payments for Operating Expenses. Payments for operating expenses other than interest and income tax can be computed as plug figures by analyzing three accounts: Prepaid Expenses, Accrued Liabilities, and Other Operating Expenses, as follows for Anchor Corporation (again, all numbers are taken from Exhibits 12-16 and 12-17): For each account the purpose is to determine cash payments for operating expenses.

Prepaid Expenses

Beginning balance	+	Payments	−	Expiration of prepaid expense	=	Ending balance
$7,000	+	X	−	$7,000	=	$8,000
		X			=	$8,000 − $7,000 + $7,000
		Payments			=	$8,000

Accrued Liabilities

Beginning balance	+	Accrual of expense at year end	−	Payments	=	Ending balance
$3,000	+	$1,000		−X	=	$1,000
				−X	=	$1,000 − $3,000 − $1,000
				Payments	=	$3,000

Other Operating Expenses (other than Salaries, Wages, Depreciation)

Accrual of expense at year end	+	Expiration of prepaid expense	+	Payments	=	Ending balance
$1,000	+	$7,000	+	X	=	$17,000
				X	=	$17,000 − $1,000 − $7,000
				Payments	=	$9,000

Total payments for operating expenses = $20,000
$8,000 + $3,000 + $9,000 = $20,000

The T-accounts give another picture of the same data.

Prepaid Expenses

Beg. bal.	7,000	Expiration of prepaid expense	7,000
Payments	8,000		
End. bal.	8,000		

Accrued Liabilities

Payment	3,000	Beg. bal.	3,000
		Accrual of expense at year end	1,000
		End. bal.	1,000

Operating Expenses (other than Salaries, Wages, and Depreciation)

Accrual of expense at year end	1,000		
Expiration of prepaid expense	7,000		
Payments	9,000		
End. bal.	17,000		

Payments to suppliers ($133,000) = payments for inventory ($113,000) + payments for operating expenses ($20,000).

COMPUTING PAYMENTS TO EMPLOYEES. It is convenient to combine all payments to employees into one account. We adjust Salary and Wage Expense for the change in Salary and Wage Payable, as shown here, backed up by the Salary and Wage Payable T-account:

Salary and Wage Payable

Beginning balance	+	Salary and wage expense	−	Payments	=	Ending balance
$6,000	+	$56,000		−X	=	$4,000
				−X	=	$4,000 − $6,000 − $56,000
				Payments	=	$58,000

Salary and Wage Payable

		Beginning balance	**6,000**
Payments to employees	58,000	**Salary and wage expense**	**56,000**
		Ending balance	**4,000**

✔ Check Point 12-14

Exhibit 12-15 (page 568) summarizes this computation under Payments to Employees.

Computing Payments of Interest and Income Taxes. In our example, the expense and payment amounts are the same for interest and income tax. Therefore, no analysis is required to determine these payment amounts. If the expense and the payment differ, the payment can be computed by analyzing the related liability account (Interest Payable and Income Tax Payable, respectively), as illustrated for payments to employees; Exhibit 12-15 summarizes the procedure.

Computing Investing and Financing Cash Flows

Detailed computations of investing and financing cash flows are given on pages 554–558.

Viacom Inc., the company that owns Paramount Pictures, Blockbuster Video, and MTV Music Television, reported the following for 2001 and 2000 (adapted, in millions):

At December 31,	2001	2000
Receivables, net	$ 3,582	$ 3,964
Inventory	5,224	5,035
Accounts payable	945	1,261
Income taxes payable	865	901

Year ended December 31,	2001	2000
Revenues	$23,223	$20,044
Cost of goods and services sold	14,137	11,707
Income tax expense	923	730

Based on these figures, how much cash did

- Viacom collect from customers during 2001?
- Viacom pay for inventory and related services during 2001?
- Viacom pay for income taxes during 2001?

Answers (in millions):

		Beginning Receivables	+ Revenues	− Collections	= Ending Receivables
Collections from customers	= $23,605	$3,964	+ $23,223	− $23,605	= $3,582

		Cost of Goods Sold	+ Increase in Inventory	+ Decrease in Accounts Payable	= Payments
Payments for inventory and related services	= $14,642	$14,137	+ ($5,224 − $5,035)	+ ($1,261 − $945)	= $14,642

		Beginning Income Taxes Payable	+ Income Tax Expense	− Payment	= Income Taxes Payable
Payment of income taxes	= $959	$901	+ $923	− $959	= $865

Measuring Cash Adequacy: Free Cash Flow

Throughout this chapter, we have focused on cash flows from operating, investing, and financing activities. Some investors, creditors, and managers make a further distinction. They seek to measure the amount of cash flow that a company can "free up" for opportunities that arise unexpectedly. The business world changes so quickly that new possibilities arise daily. The company with the most free cash flow is best able to respond to new opportunities. **Free cash flow** is the amount of cash available from operations after paying for planned investments in plant, equipment, and other long-term assets. Free cash flow can be computed as follows:

Free cash flow
The amount of cash available from operations after paying for planned investments in plant, equipment, and other long-term assets.

Free cash flow	=	Net cash flow from operating activities	−	Cash outflow earmarked for investments in plant, equipment, and other long-term assets

PepsiCo, Inc. uses free cash flow to manage its operations. Suppose PepsiCo expects net cash inflow of $2.3 billion from operations. Assume PepsiCo plans to spend $1.9 billion to modernize its bottling plants. In this case, PepsiCo's free cash flow would be $0.4 billion ($2.3 billion − $1.9 billion). If a good investment opportunity comes along, PepsiCo should have $0.4 billion to invest in the other company. The managers of Shell Oil Company, AT&T, and Briggs & Stratton also use free-cash-flow analysis to manage their businesses.

A large amount of free cash flow is preferable because it means that a lot of cash is available for new investments. High-tech software companies such as Intel, Microsoft, and America Online (AOL) depend on technological breakthroughs for their competitive edge. These companies' investment opportunities may arise more quickly than those of older companies like General Motors and Consolidated Edison, the electric utility. For Intel, Microsoft, and AOL, free cash flow may be more important.

The Decision Guidelines feature shows some ways to use cash-flow and income data for investment and credit analysis.

Decision Guidelines

INVESTORS' AND CREDITORS' USE OF CASH-FLOW AND RELATED INFORMATION

Anne Gray is a private investor. Through years of experience she has devised some guidelines for evaluating both stock investments and bond investments. Gray uses a combination of accrual-accounting data and cash-flow information. Here are her decision guidelines for both investors and creditors.

Investors

Question	Factors to Consider*	Financial Statement Predictor/Decision Model*
1. How much in dividends can I expect to receive from an investment in stock?	Expected future net income	Income from continuing operations**
	Expected future cash balance	Net cash flows from (in order): • Operating activities • Investing activities • Financing activities
	Future dividend policy	Current and past dividend policy

2. Is the stock price likely to increase or decrease?	Expected future net income	Income from continuing operations**
	Expected future cash flows from operating activities	Income from continuing operations** Net cash flow from operating activities
3. What is the future stock price likely to be?	Expected future income from • continuing operations, *and* • net cash flow from operating activities	Expected future price of a share of stock = Expected future earnings per share** / Investment capitalization rate or Expected future price of a share of stock = Net cash flow from operations per share / Investment capitalization rate

Creditors

Question	Factors to Consider	Financial Statement Predictor
Can the company pay the interest and principal at the maturity of a loan?	Expected future net cash flow from operating activities	Income from continuing operations** Net cash flow from • Operating activities

*There are many other factors to consider for making these decisions. These are some of the more common.
**See Chapter 11.

Excel Application Problem

Goal: To create an Excel work sheet that computes cash flows from operating activities using the indirect method.

Scenario: As an accountant at Ochoa, Inc., you have been asked to compute the net cash provided by operating activities using the indirect method for the month of March. Using Excel and the information provided in Exercise 12-5, determine the cash flows from operating activities. When done, answer these questions:

1. Does Ochoa have trouble collecting receivables? How can you tell?
2. Does the company have difficulty selling inventory? How can you tell?
3. Based on the Decision Guidelines for this chapter, what decisions might investors make with this information?

Step-by-step:

1. Open a new Excel work sheet.
2. Create a heading for your work sheet that contains the following:
   a. Chapter 12 Decision Guideline
   b. Ochoa, Inc.
   c. Statement of Cash Flows—Operating Activities
   d. For the Month Ended March 31, 20X3
3. Follow the statement of cash flows format in Exhibit 12-6 and use formulas for all computations.
4. Save your work and print a copy for your files.

End-of-Chapter Summary Problem

Granite Shoals Corporation reported the following comparative balance sheet and income statement for 20X6.

Granite Shoals Corporation

Balance Sheet
December 31,

	20X6	20X5
Cash	$ 19,000	$ 3,000
Accounts receivable	22,000	23,000
Inventories	34,000	31,000
Prepaid expenses	1,000	3,000
Equipment (net)	90,000	79,000
Intangible assets	9,000	9,000
	$ 175,000	$ 148,000
Accounts payable	$ 14,000	$ 9,000
Accrued liabilities	16,000	19,000
Income tax payable	14,000	12,000
Long-term debt	45,000	50,000
Common stock	31,000	20,000
Retained earnings	64,000	40,000
Treasury stock	(9,000)	(2,000)
	$ 175,000	$ 148,000

Granite Shoals Corporation

Income Statement
Year Ended December 31,

	20X6	20X5
Sales revenue	$ 190,000	$ 165,000
Gain or sale of equipment	6,000	—
Total revenue and gains	196,000	165,000
Cost of goods sold	$ 85,000	$ 70,000
Depreciation expense	19,000	17,000
Other operating expenses	36,000	33,000
Total expenses	140,000	120,000
Income before income tax	56,000	45,000
Income tax expense	18,000	15,000
Net income	$ 38,000	$ 30,000

Assume that Berkshire Hathaway is considering buying Granite Shoals Corporation. Berkshire Hathaway analysts need the following Granite Shoals cash-flow data for 20X6. There were no noncash investing and financing activities.

a. Collections from customers
b. Cash payments for inventory
c. Cash payments for operating expenses
d. Cash payment for income tax

e. Cash received from the sale of equipment, with Granite Shoals paying $40,000 for new equipment during the year.
f. Issuance of common stock.
g. Issuance of long-term debt, with Granite Shoals paying off $20,000 of long-term debt during the year.
h. Cash dividends, with no stock dividends.

Provide the analysts with the needed data. Show your work.

Answer

a. Analyze Accounts Receivable (let X = Collections from customers):

Beginning	+	Sales	−	Collections	=	Ending
$23,000	+	$190,000	−	X	=	$22,000
				X		= $191,000

b. Analyze Inventory and Accounts Payable (let X = Purchases, and let Y = Payments for inventory):

Beginning inventory	+	Purchases	−	Ending inventory	=	Cost of Goods Sold
$31,000	+	X	−	$34,000	=	$85,000
		X				= $88,000

Beginning Accounts Payable	+	Purchases	−	Payments	=	Ending Accounts Payable
$9,000	+	$88,000	−	Y	=	$14,000
				Y		= $83,000

c. Start with Other Operating Expenses, and adjust for the changes in Prepaid Expenses and Accrued Liabilities:

Other Operating Expenses	+ Increase, or − Decrease in Prepaid Expenses	− Increase, or + Decrease in Accrued Liabilities	=	Payments for Operating Expenses
$36,000	− $2,000	+ 3,000	=	$37,000

d. Analyze Income Tax Payable (let X = Payments of income tax):

Beginning	+	Income Tax Expense	−	Payments	=	Ending
$12,000	+	$18,000	−	X	=	$14,000
				X		= $16,000

e. Analyze Equipment (Net) (let X = Book value of equipment sold. Then combine with gain or loss on sale to compute cash received from sale.)

Beginning	+	Acquisitions	−	Depreciation	−	Book Value Sold	=	Ending
$79,000	+	$40,000	−	$19,000	−	X	=	$90,000
						X	=	$10,000

Cash received from sale	=	Book Value Sold	+ Gain, or	− Loss on Sale
$16,000	=	$10,000	+ $6,000	

f. Analyze Common Stock (let X = issuance)

Beginning	+ Issuance	= Ending
$20,000	+ X	= $31,000
	X	= $11,000

g. Analyze Long-Term Debt (let X = issuance):

Beginning	+ Issuance	− Payment	= Ending
$50,000	+ X	− $20,000	= $45,000
	X		= $15,000

h. Analyze Retained Earnings (let X = dividends)

Beginning	+ Net Income	− Dividends	= Ending
$40,000	+ $38,000	− X	= $64,000
		X	= $14,000

Review Statement of Cash Flows

Lessons Learned

1. **Identify the purposes of the statement of cash flows.** The *statement of cash flows* reports a business's cash receipts, cash payments, and net change in cash for the accounting period. It shows *why* cash increased or decreased during the period. It gives a different view of the business from that given by accrual-basis statements. The cash-flow statement helps financial statement users predict the future cash flows of the entity and evaluate management decisions, determine the company's ability to pay dividends and interest, and ascertain the relationship of net income to cash flows. Cash includes cash and *cash equivalents*.
2. **Distinguish among operating, investing, and financing cash flows.** The cash-flow statement is divided into *operating activities, investing activities*, and *financing activities*. Operating activities create revenues and expenses and thus relate to the components of net income. Investing activities increase and decrease long-term assets. Financing activities obtain the cash needed to launch and sustain the business. Each section of the statement includes increases and decreases in cash and concludes with a net cash increase or decrease.
3. **Prepare a statement of cash flows by the indirect method.** Two formats are used to report cash flows from operating activities—the indirect method and the direct method. The indirect method is used by the vast majority of companies. The *indirect method* starts with net income and reconciles to cash flow from operations.
4. **Prepare a statement of cash flows by the direct method.** The *direct method* lists the major categories of operating cash receipts (collections from customers and receipts of interest and dividends) and cash payments (payments to suppliers, payments to employees, and payments for interest and income taxes).

Accounting Vocabulary

cash equivalents (p. 547)
cash flows (p. 546)
direct method (p. 548)
financing activities (p. 548)
free cash flow (p. 573)
indirect method (p. 548)
investing activities (p. 548)
operating activities (p. 547)
statement of cash flows (p. 546)

Questions

1. What information does the statement of cash flows report that is not shown on the balance sheet, the income statement, or the statement of retained earnings?
2. Identify four purposes of the statement of cash flows.
3. Identify and briefly describe the three types of activities that are reported on the statement of cash flows.
4. How is the statement of cash flows dated, and why?
5. What is the check figure for the statement of cash flows? (In other words, which figure do you check to make sure you've done your work correctly?) Where is it obtained, and how is it used?
6. What is the most important source of cash for most successful companies?
7. How can cash decrease during a year when income is high? How can cash increase during a year when income is low? How can investors and creditors learn such facts about a company?
8. DeBerg, Inc., prepares its statement of cash flows by the *indirect* method for operating activities. Identify the section of DeBerg's statement of cash flows where each of the following transactions will appear.
   a. Issuance of note payable
   b. Decrease in accounts payable
   c. Net income
   d. Amortization expense
   e. Purchase of building
9. Identify the cash effects (plus or minus) of increases and decreases in current assets other than cash. What are the cash effects of increases and decreases in current liabilities?
10. Milano Corporation earned net income of $38,000 and had depreciation expense of $22,000. Also, noncash current assets decreased $13,000, and current liabilities decreased $9,000. What was Milano's net cash provided by operating activities?
11. An investment that cost $65,000 was sold for $80,000, resulting in a $15,000 gain. Show how to report this transaction on a statement of cash flows prepared by the indirect method.
12. Marshall Corporation's beginning plant asset balance, net of accumulated depreciation, was $193,000, and the ending amount was $176,000. Marshall recorded depreciation of $37,000 and sold plant assets with a book value of $9,000. How much cash did Marshall pay to purchase plant assets during the period? Where on the statement of cash flows should Marshall report this item?
13. How should issuance of a note payable to purchase land be reported in the financial statements? Identify three other transactions that fall into this same category.
14. Summarize the major cash receipts and cash payments in the three categories of activities that appear on the cash-flow statement (direct method for operating cash flows).
15. Why are depreciation, depletion, and amortization expenses *not* reported on a cash-flow statement that reports operating activities by the direct method? Why and how are these expenses reported on a statement prepared by the indirect method?
16. Mainline Distributing Company collected cash of $92,000 from customers and $6,000 interest on notes receivable. Cash payments included $24,000 to employees, $13,000 to suppliers, $6,000 as dividends to stockholders, and $5,000 as a loan to another company. How much was Mainline's net cash provided by operating activities?
17. Kirchner, Inc., recorded salary expense of $51,000 during a year when the balance of Salary Payable decreased from $10,000 to $2,000. How much cash did Kirchner pay to employees during the year? Where on the statement of cash flows should Kirchner report this item?
18. What is free cash flow?

Assess Your Progress

Check Points

Purposes of the statement of cash flows **(Obj. 1)**

CP12-1 How does the statement of cash flows help investors and creditors perform each of the following functions?

1. Predict future cash flows.
2. Evaluate management decisions.
3. Predict the company's ability to pay dividends and interest.

Using an actual statement of cash flows **(Obj. 1)**

CP12-2 Examine the statement of cash flows of **eBay Inc.** on page 545. Identify three strong points about the company's cash flows.

CP12-3 Return to the eBay Inc. cash-flow statement on page 000. Suppose eBay's operating activities *used*, rather than *provided*, rather than cash. Identify three things under the indirect method that could cause operating cash flows to be negative.

Evaluating operating cash flows
(Obj. 2)

CP12-4 Grisham Publishing Company began 20X6 with accounts receivable, inventory, and prepaid expenses totaling $65,000. At the end of the year, the company had a total of $78,000 for these current assets. At the beginning of 20X6, Grisham owed current liabilities of $42,000, and at year end current liabilities totaled $40,000.

Reporting cash flows from operating activities—indirect method
(Obj. 3)

Net income for the year was $81,000, after including all revenues and gains and after subtracting all expenses and losses. Included in the computation of net income were a $4,000 gain on the sale of land and depreciation expense of $9,000.

Show how Grisham should report cash flows from operating activities for 20X6. Grisham uses the *indirect* method. Use Exhibit 12-6 (page 552) as a guide.

CP12-5 Post Corporation is preparing its statement of cash flows for the year ended September 30, 20X4. Post reports cash flows from operating activities by the *indirect* method. The company's head bookkeeper has provided the following list of items for you to consider in preparing the company's statement of cash flows. Identify each item as an operating activity—addition to net income (O+), or subtraction from net income (O−); an investing activity (I); a financing activity (F); or an activity that is not used to prepare the cash-flow statement by the indirect method (N). Answer by placing the appropriate symbol in the blank space.

Identifying items for reporting cash flows from operations—indirect method
(Obj. 2)

______	a. Loss on sale of land	______	h. Increase in accounts payable
______	b. Depreciation expense	______	i. Sales revenue
______	c. Increase in inventory	______	j. Payment of dividends
______	d. Decrease in prepaid expense	______	k. Decrease in accrued liabilities
______	e. Decrease in accounts receivable	______	l. Issuance of common stock
______	f. Purchase of equipment	______	m. Gain on sale of building
______	g. Collection of cash from customers	______	n. Retained earnings

CP12-6 (Check Point 12-7 is an alternative exercise.) Mid-America Resources, Inc. accountants have assembled the following data for the year ended June 30, 20X5.

Computing operating cash flows—indirect method
(Obj. 3)

Payment of dividends	$ 6,000	Cost of goods sold	$100,000
Proceeds from issuance of common stock	20,000	Other operating expenses	35,000
Sales revenue	210,000	Purchase of equipment	40,000
Increase in current assets other than cash	30,000	Decrease in current liabilities	5,000
Purchase of treasury stock	5,000	Payment of note payable	30,000
		Proceeds from sale of land	60,000
		Depreciation expense	15,000

Prepare the *operating* activities section of Mid-America's statement of cash flows for the year ended June 30, 20X5. Mid-America uses the *indirect* method for operating cash flows.

CP12-7 Use the data in Check Point 12-6 to prepare Mid-America's statement of cash flows for the year ended June 30, 20X5. Mid-America uses the *indirect* method for operating activities. Use Exhibit 12-7, page 554, as a guide, but you may stop after determining the net increase (or decrease) in cash.

Preparing a statement of cash flows—indirect method
(Obj. 3)

CP12-8 Grace Chemical Company reported the following financial statements for 20X6:

Computing investing cash flows
(Obj. 3)

Grace Chemical Company

Income Statement
Year Ended December 31, 20X6

(In thousands)	
Sales revenue	$710
Cost of goods sold	$340
Depreciation expense	60
Salary expense	50
Other expenses	150
Total expenses	600
Net income	$110

Grace Chemical Company

Comparative Balance Sheet
December 31, 20X6 and 20X5

(In thousands)					
Assets	20X6	20X5	**Liabilities**	20X6	20X5
Current			Current		
Cash	$ 19	$ 16	Accounts payable	$ 47	$ 42
Accounts receivable	54	48	Salary payable	23	21
Inventory	80	84	Accrued liabilities	8	11
Prepaid expenses	3	2	Long-term notes payable	66	68
Long-term investments	75	90			
Plant assets, net	225	185	**Stockholders' Equity**		
			Common stock	40	37
			Retained earnings	272	246
Total	$456	$425	Total	$456	$425

Compute the following investing cash flows:

a. Acquisitions of plant assets (all were for cash), with Grace selling no plant assets
b. Proceeds from the sale of investments, with Grace purchasing no investments

Computing financing cash flows
(Obj. 3)

CP12-9 Use the Grace Chemical Company data in Check Point 12-8 to compute

a. New borrowing or payment of long-term notes payable, with Grace having only one long-term note payable transaction during the year
b. Issuance of common stock or retirement of common stock, with Grace having only one common stock transaction during the year
c. Payment of cash dividends (same as dividends declared)

Preparing a statement of cash flows—direct method
(Obj. 4)

CP12-10 Wellness Health Laboratories began 20X4 with cash of $104,000. During the year, Wellness earned service revenue of $600,000 and collected $590,000 from customers. Expenses for the year totaled $420,000, of which Wellness paid $410,000 in cash to suppliers and employees. Wellness also paid $140,000 to purchase equipment and a cash dividend of $50,000 to its stockholders during 20X4.

Prepare the company's statement of cash flows for the year. Format operating activities by the direct method.

Computing operating cash flows—direct method
(Obj. 4)

CP12-11 Mid-America Resources, Inc. accountants have assembled the following data for the year ended June 30, 20X5.

Payment of dividends	$ 6,000	Cost of goods sold	$100,000
Proceeds from issuance of common stock	20,000	Payments to suppliers	80,000
		Purchase of equipment	40,000
Sales revenue	210,000	Payments to employees	70,000
Collections from customers	200,000	Payment of note payable	30,000
Payment of income tax	10,000	Proceeds from sale of land	60,000
Purchase of treasury stock	5,000	Depreciation expense	15,000

Prepare the *operating* activities section of Mid-America's statement of cash flows for the year ended June 30, 20X5. Mid-America uses the direct method for operating cash flows.

Preparing a statement of cash flows—direct method **(Obj. 4)**

CP12-12 Use the data in Check Point 12-11 to prepare Mid-America's statement of cash flows for the year ended June 30, 20X5. Mid-America uses the *direct* method for operating activities. Use Exhibit 12-13, page 000, as a guide, but you may stop after determining the net increase (or decrease) in cash.

Computing operating cash flows—direct method **(Obj. 4)**

CP12-13 Use the Grace Chemical Company data in Check Point 12-8 to compute the following:

a. Collections from customers
b. Payments for inventory

Computing operating cash flows—direct method **(Obj. 4)**

CP12-14 Use the Grace Chemical Company data in Check Point 12-8 to compute the following:

a. Payments to employees
b. Payments of other expenses

Exercises

Identifying the purposes of the statement of cash flows **(Obj. 1)**

E12-1 Biz Mart Stores, Inc., has experienced an unbroken string of 10 years of growth in net income. Nevertheless, the business is facing bankruptcy. Creditors are calling all of Biz Mart's outstanding loans for immediate payment, and the cash is simply not available. Attempts to explain where Biz Mart went wrong make it clear that managers placed undue emphasis on net income and gave too little attention to cash flows.

Required

Write a brief memo, in your own words, to explain to the managers of Biz Mart Stores the purposes of the statement of cash flows.

Identifying activities for the statement of cash flows—indirect method **(Obj. 2)**

E12-2 Identify each of the following transactions as an operating activity (O), an investing activity (I), a financing activity (F), a noncash investing and financing activity (NIF), or a transaction that is not reported on the statement of cash flows (N). For each cash flow, indicate whether the item increases (+) or decreases (−) cash. The indirect method is used to report cash flows from operating activities.

______	a. Amortization of intangible assets	______	k. Acquisition of equipment by issuance of note payable
______	b. Issuance of long-term note payable to borrow cash	______	l. Payment of long-term debt
______	c. Depreciation of equipment	______	m. Acquisition of building by issuance of common stock
______	d. Purchase of treasury stock	______	n. Accrual of salary expense
______	e. Issuance of common stock for cash	______	o. Purchase of long-term investment
______	f. Increase in accounts payable	______	p. Decrease in merchandise inventory
______	g. Net income	______	q. Increase in prepaid expenses
______	h. Payment of cash dividend	______	r. Cash sale of land
______	i. Sale of long-term investment	______	s. Decrease in accrued liabilities
______	j. Loss on sale of land		

Classifying transactions for the statement of cash flows—indirect method
(Obj. 2)

E12-3 Indicate whether each of the following transactions would result in an operating activity, an investing activity, or a financing activity for a statement of cash flows prepared by the *indirect* method and the accompanying schedule of noncash investing and financing activities.

Account	Debit	Credit
a. Equipment	18,000	
Cash		18,000
b. Cash	7,200	
Long-Term Investment		7,200
c. Bonds Payable	45,000	
Cash		45,000
d. Building	164,000	
Note Payable, Long-Term		164,000
e. Loss on Disposal of Equipment	1,400	
Equipment Net		1,400
f. Dividends Payable	16,500	
Cash		16,500
g. Furniture and Fixtures	22,100	
Note Payable, Short-Term		22,100
h. Cash	81,000	
Common Stock		12,000
Capital in Excess of Par		69,000
i. Treasury Stock	13,000	
Cash		13,000
j. Cash	60,000	
Accounts Receivable	10,000	
Sales Revenue		70,000
k. Salary Expense	22,000	
Cash		22,000
l. Land	87,000	
Cash		87,700
m. Depreciation Expense	9,000	
Accumulated Depreciation		9,000

Computing cash flows from operating activities—indirect method
(Obj. 3)

E12-4 The accounting records of Auto Chef Corporation reveal the following:

Net income	$22,000	Depreciation	$12,000
Collection of dividend revenue	7,000	Decrease in current liabilities	20,000
Payment of interest	16,000	Increase in current assets other than cash	27,000
Sales revenue	9,000	Payment of dividends	7,000
Loss on sale of land	5,000	Payment of income tax	13,000
Acquisition of land	37,000		

Required

Compute cash flows from operating activities by the indirect method. Use the format of the operating activities section of Exhibit 12-7 (page 554). Also evaluate the operating cash flow of Auto Chef Corporation. Give the reason for your evaluation.

Computing cash flows from operating activities—indirect method
(Obj. 3)

E12-5 The accounting records of Ochoa, Inc. include these accounts:

CASH

Mar. 1	5,000		
Receipts	447,000	Payments	448,000
Mar. 31	4,000		

ACCOUNTS RECEIVABLE

Mar. 1	18,000		
Sales	443,000	Collections	447,000
Mar. 31	14,000		

INVENTORY

Mar. 1	19,000		
Purchases	337,000	Cost of sales	335,000
Mar. 31	21,000		

EQUIPMENT

Mar. 1	93,000		
Acquisition	6,000		
Mar. 31	99,000		

ACCUMULATED DEPRECIATION—EQUIPMENT

		Mar. 1	52,000
		Depreciation	3,000
		Mar. 31	55,000

ACCOUNTS PAYABLE

		Mar. 1	14,000
Payments	332,000	Purchases	337,000
		Mar. 31	19,000

ACCRUED LIABILITIES

		Mar. 1	9,000
Payments	14,000	Expenses	11,000
		Mar. 31	6,000

RETAINED EARNINGS

Quarterly		Mar. 1	64,000
dividend	18,000	Net income	69,000
		Mar. 31	115,000

Compute Ochoa's net cash provided by (used for) operating activities during March. Use the indirect method. Does Ochoa have trouble collecting receivables or selling inventory? How can you tell?

E12-6 The income statement and additional data of Crawford Properties, Inc. follow:

Preparing the statement of cash flows—indirect method
(Obj. 3)

Crawford Properties, Inc.
Income Statement
Year Ended June 30, 20X6

Revenues:		
Sales revenue	$229,000	
Dividend revenue	8,000	$237,000
Expenses:		
Cost of goods sold	$103,000	
Salary expense	45,000	
Depreciation expense	29,000	
Advertising expense	11,000	
Interest expense	2,000	
Income tax expense	9,000	199,000
Net income		$ 38,000

Additional data:

a. Acquisition of plant assets is $116,000. Of this amount, $101,000 is paid in cash and $15,000, by signing a note payable.
b. Proceeds from sale of land total $24,000.
c. Proceeds from issuance of common stock total $30,000.
d. Payment of long-term note payable is $15,000.
e. Payment of dividends is $11,000.
f. From the balance sheet:

	June 30,	
	20X6	20X5
Current Assets:		
Cash	$27,000	$20,000
Accounts receivable	43,000	58,000
Inventory	83,000	77,000
Prepaid expenses	9,000	8,000
Current Liabilities:		
Accounts payable	$35,000	$22,000
Accrued liabilities	13,000	21,000

Required

1. Prepare Crawford Properties, Inc.'s statement of cash flows for the year ended June 30, 20X6, using the indirect method.
2. Evaluate Crawford Properties' cash flows for the year. In your evaluation, mention all three categories of cash flows and give the reason for your evaluation.

E12-7 Consider three independent cases for the cash-flow data of Ken Nall & Associates. For each case, identify from the cash-flow statement how Nall generated the cash to acquire new plant assets. Rank the three cases from the most healthy financially to the least healthy.

Interpreting a cash-flow statement—indirect method
(Obj. 3)

	Case A	Case B	Case C
Cash flows from operating activities:			
Net income	$ 30,000	$ 30,000	$ 30,000
Depreciation and amortization	11,000	11,000	11,000
Increase in current assets	(7,000)	(1,000)	(19,000)
Decrease in current liabilities	(8,000)	0	(6,000)
	$ 26,000	$ 40,000	$ 16,000
Cash flows from investing activities:			
Acquisition of plant assets	$ (91,000)	$(91,000)	$(91,000)
Sales of plant assets	4,000	8,000	97,000
	$ (87,000)	$(83,000)	$ 6,000
Cash flows from financing activities:			
Issuance of stock	$104,000	$ 50,000	$ 16,000
Payment of debt	(29,000)	(9,000)	(21,000)
	$ 75,000	$ 41,000	$ (5,000)
Net increase (decrease) in cash	$ 14,000	$ (2,000)	$ 17,000

Computing investing and financing amounts for the statement of cash flows
(Obj. 3)

E12-8 Compute the following items for the statement of cash flows:

a. Beginning and ending Retained Earnings are $45,000 and $73,000, respectively. Net income for the period is $62,000, and stock dividends are $8,000. How much are cash dividends?

b. Beginning and ending Plant Assets, net, are $103,000 and $107,000, respectively. Depreciation for the period is $16,000, and acquisitions of new plant assets are $27,000. Plant assets were sold at a $1,000 loss. What were the cash proceeds of the sale?

Identifying activities for the statement of cash flows—direct method
(Obj. 4)

E12-9 Identify each of the following transactions as an operating activity (O), an investing activity (I), a financing activity (F), a noncash investing and financing activity (NIF), or a transaction that is not reported on the statement of cash flows (N). For each cash flow, indicate whether the item increases (+) or decreases (−) cash. Assume that the direct method is used to report cash flows from operating activities.

_____ a. Collection of account receivable
_____ b. Issuance of long-term note payable to borrow cash
_____ c. Depreciation of equipment
_____ d. Purchase of treasury stock
_____ e. Issuance of common stock for cash
_____ f. Payment of account payable
_____ g. Issuance of preferred stock for cash
_____ h. Payment of cash dividend
_____ i. Sale of long-term investment
_____ j. Amortization of bond discount
_____ k. Acquisition of equipment by issuance of note payable
_____ l. Payment of long-term debt
_____ m. Acquisition of building by issuance of common stock
_____ n. Accrual of salary expense
_____ o. Purchase of long-term investment
_____ p. Payment of wages to employees
_____ q. Collection of cash interest
_____ r. Cash sale of land
_____ s. Distribution of stock dividend

Classifying transactions for the statement of cash flows—direct method
(Obj. 4)

E12-10 Indicate where, if at all, each of the following transactions would be reported on a statement of cash flows prepared by the *direct* method and the accompanying schedule of noncash investing and financing activities.

a. Equipment	18,000	
Cash		18,000
b. Cash	7,200	
Long-Term Investment		7,200
c. Bonds Payable	45,000	
Cash		45,000
d. Building	164,000	
Note Payable, Long-Term		164,000
e. Cash	1,400	
Accounts Receivable		1,400
f. Dividends Payable	16,500	
Cash		16,500

(continued)

g. Furniture and Fixtures	22,100	
Note Payable, Short-Term		22,100
h. Salary Expense	4,300	
Cash		4,300
i. Cash	81,000	
Common Stock		12,000
Paid-in Capital in Excess of Par—Common		69,000
j. Treasury Stock	13,000	
Cash		13,000
k. Retained Earnings	36,000	
Common Stock		36,000
l. Cash	2,000	
Interest Revenue		2,000
m. Land	87,700	
Cash		87,700
n. Accounts Payable	8,300	
Cash		8,300

E12-11 The accounting records of Auto Chef Corporation reveal the following:

Computing cash flows from operating activities—direct method
(Obj. 4)

Net income	$22,000	Payment of salaries and wages	$34,000
Payment of income tax	13,000	Depreciation	12,000
Collection of dividend revenue	7,000	Decrease in current liabilities	20,000
Payment of interest	16,000		
Cash sales	9,000	Increase in current assets other than cash	27,000
Loss on sale of land	5,000		
Acquisition of land	37,000	Payment of dividends	7,000
Payment of accounts payable	54,000	Collection of accounts receivable	93,000

Required

Compute cash flows from operating activities by the direct method. Use the format of the operating activities section of Exhibit 12-13 (page 565). Also evaluate the operating cash flow of Auto Chef Corporation. Give the reason for your evaluation.

E12-12 Selected accounts of Crossroads Clinic, Inc. show the following:

Identifying items for the statement of cash flows—direct method
(Obj. 4)

DIVIDENDS RECEIVABLE

Beginning balance	**9,000**	**Cash receipts of dividends**	**38,000**
Dividend revenue	**40,000**		
Ending balance	**11,000**		

INVESTMENT IN LAND

Beginning balance	**90,000**	**Book value of investments sold**	**109,000**
Acquisitions	**127,000**		
Ending balance	**108,000**		

LONG-TERM DEBT

Payments	**69,000**	**Beginning balance**	**273,000**
		Issuance of debt for cash	**83,000**
		Ending balance	**287,000**

Required

For each account, identify the item or items that should appear on a statement of cash flows prepared by the direct method. State where to report the item.

Preparing the statement of cash flows—direct method
(Obj. 4)

E12-13 The income statement and additional data of Crawford Properties, Inc., follow:

Crawford Properties, Inc.
Income Statement
Year Ended June 30, 20X6

Revenues:		
Sales revenue	$229,000	
Dividend revenue	8,000	$237,000
Expenses:		
Cost of goods sold	$103,000	
Salary expense	45,000	
Depreciation expense	29,000	
Advertising expense	11,000	
Interest expense	2,000	
Income tax expense	9,000	199,000
Net income		$ 38,000

Additional data:

a. Collections from customers are $15,000 more than sales.
b. Payments to suppliers are $1,000 more than the sum of cost of goods sold plus advertising expense.
c. Payments to employees are $1,000 more than salary expense.
d. Dividend revenue, interest expense, and income tax expense equal their cash amounts.
e. Acquisition of plant assets is $116,000. Of this amount, $101,000 is paid in cash and $15,000, by signing a note payable.
f. Proceeds from sale of land total $24,000.
g. Proceeds from issuance of common stock total $30,000.
h. Payment of long-term note payable is $15,000.
i. Payment of dividends is $11,000.
j. Cash balance, June 30, 20X5, was $ 20,000.

Required

1. Prepare Crawford Properties' statement of cash flows and accompanying schedule of noncash investing and financing activities. Report operating activities by the *direct* method.
2. Evaluate Crawford's cash flows for the year. In your evaluation, mention all three categories of cash flows and give the reason for your evaluation.

Computing amounts for the statement of cash flows—direct method
(Obj. 4)

E12-14 Compute the following items for the statement of cash flows:

a. Beginning and ending Accounts Receivable are $22,000 and $18,000, respectively. Credit sales for the period total $81,000. How much are cash collections?
b. Cost of goods sold is $90,000. Beginning Inventory balance is $25,000, and ending Inventory balance is $21,000. Beginning and ending Accounts Payable are $11,000 and $8,000, respectively. How much are cash payments for inventory?

Challenge Exercises

Computing cash-flow amounts
(Obj. 3, 4)

E12-15 Walgreen Company, the nationwide pharmacy chain, reported the following in its financial statements for the year ended August 31, 20X1 (adapted, in millions):

	20X1	20X0
Income Statement		
Net sales	$24,623	$21,207
Cost of sales	18,048	15,466
Depreciation	269	230
Other operating expenses	4,883	4,248
Income tax expense	537	486
Net income	$ 886	$ 777
Balance Sheet		
Cash and equivalents	$ 17	$ 13
Accounts receivable	798	615
Inventories	3,482	2,831
Property and equipment, net	4,345	3,428
Accounts payable	$ 1,547	$ 1,364
Accrued liabilities	938	848
Income tax payable	224	194
Long-term liabilities	478	464
Common stock	676	446
Retained earnings	4,531	3,788

Determine the following for Walgreen during 20X1:

a. Collections from customers
b. Payments for inventory
c. Payments of operating expenses
d. Payment of income tax
e. Acquisitions of property and equipment (no sales during 20X1)
f. Borrowing, with Walgreen paying no long-term liabilities
g. Proceeds from issuance of common stock
h. Payment of cash dividends

For operating cash flows, follow the approach outlined in Exhibit 12-15, page 568.

E12-16 Motorola, Inc., reported the following at December 31, 20X1 (adapted, in millions):

Using the balance sheet and the cash-flow statement together
(Obj. 3)

	20X1	20X0
From the comparative balance sheet:		
Property and equipment, net	$11,157	$9,591
Long-term debt	4,293	3,089
Common stock	6,574	6,418
Additional paid-in capital	1,188	—
From the statement of cash flows:		
Depreciation	$2,352	
Capital expenditures	(4,131)	
Proceeds from dispositions of property and equipment	174	
Proceeds from issuance of long-term debt	1,190	
Repayment of long-term debt	(5)	
Issuance of common stock	383	

Determine the following items for Motorola during 20X1:

1. Gain or loss on the sale of property and equipment
2. Amount of long-term debt issued for something other than cash
3. Amount of total paid-in capital issued for something other than cash

Problems

(Group A)

Using cash-flow information to evaluate performance
(Obj. 1, 2)

P12-1A Top managers of Oasis Water, Inc., are reviewing company performance for 20X7. The income statement reports a 20% increase in net income over 20X6. However, most of the increase resulted from an extraordinary gain on insurance proceeds from storm damage to a building. The balance sheet shows a large increase in receivables. The cash-flow statement, in summarized form, reports the following:

Net cash used for operating activities	$(80,000)
Net cash provided by investing activities	40,000
Net cash provided by financing activities	50,000
Increase in cash during 20X7	$ 10,000

Required

Write a memo giving Oasis Water managers your assessment of 20X7 operations and your outlook for the future. Focus on the information content of the cash-flow data.

Preparing an income statement, balance sheet, and statement of cash flows—indirect method
(Obj. 2, 3)

P12-2A Scott Corporation, a furniture store, was formed on January 1, 20X8, when Scott issued its no-par common stock for $300,000. Early in January, Scott made the following cash payments:

a. $150,000 for equipment
b. $120,000 for inventory (1,000 pieces of furniture)
c. $20,000 for 20X8 rent on a store building

In February, Scott purchased 2,000 units of furniture inventory on account from a Mexican company. Cost of this inventory was $260,000. Before year end, Scott paid $208,000 of this debt. Scott uses the FIFO method to account for inventory.

During 20X8, Scott sold 2,500 units of inventory for $200 each. Before year end, Scott collected 80% of this amount.

The store employs three people. The combined annual payroll is $95,000, of which Scott owes $4,000 at year end. At the end of the year, Scott paid income tax of $10,000.

Late in 20X8, Scott declared and paid cash dividends of $11,000.

For equipment, Scott uses the straight-line depreciation method, over 5 years, with zero residual value.

Required

1. Prepare Scott Corporation's income statement for the year ended December 31, 20X8. Use the single-step format, with all revenues listed together and all expenses together.
2. Prepare Scott's balance sheet at December 31, 20X8.
3. Prepare Scott's statement of cash flows for the year ended December 31, 20X8. Format cash flows from operating activities by the indirect method.

Preparing the statement of cash flows—indirect method
(Obj. 2, 3)

P12-3A Datex Corporation accountants have assembled the following data for the year ended December 31, 20X7.

Required

Prepare Datex Corporation's statement of cash flows using the *indirect* method to report operating activities. Include an accompanying schedule of noncash investing and financing activities.

	December 31, 20X7	December 31, 20X6
Current Accounts:		
Current assets:		
Cash and cash equivalents	$50,700	$22,700
Accounts receivable	69,700	64,200
Inventories	88,600	83,000
Prepaid expenses	5,300	4,100
Current liabilities:		
Accounts payable	$57,200	$55,800
Income tax payable	18,600	16,700
Accrued liabilities	15,500	27,200

Transaction Data for 20X7:

Acquisition of land by issuing long-term note payable	$107,000	Purchase of treasury stock	$14,300
Stock dividends	31,800	Loss on sale of equipment	11,700
Collection of loan	8,700	Payment of cash dividends	18,300
Depreciation expense	21,800	Issuance of long-term note payable to borrow cash	34,400
Acquisition of building	125,300	Net income	57,100
Retirement of bonds payable by issuing common stock	65,000	Issuance of common stock for cash	41,200
Acquisition of long-term investment	31,600	Sale of equipment	58,000
		Amortization expense	5,300

P12-4A The comparative balance sheet of Southern Bell Company at March 31, 20X9, reported the following:

Preparing the statement of cash flows—indirect method
(Obj. 2, 3)

spreadsheet

	March 31, 20X9	March 31, 20X8
Current Assets:		
Cash and cash equivalents	$19,900	$ 4,000
Accounts receivable	14,900	21,700
Inventories	63,200	60,600
Prepaid expenses	1,900	1,700
Current Liabilities:		
Accounts payable	$30,300	$27,600
Accrued liabilities	10,700	11,100
Income tax payable	8,000	4,700

Southern Bell's transactions during the year ended March 31, 20X9, included the following:

Acquisition of land by issuing note payable	$76,000	Sale of long-term investment	$13,700
Amortization expense	2,000	Depreciation expense	15,300
Payment of cash dividend	30,000	Cash acquisition of building	47,000
Cash acquisition of equipment	78,700	Net income	70,000
Issuance of long-term note payable to borrow cash	50,000	Issuance of common stock for cash	11,000
		Stock dividend	18,000

Required

1. Prepare Southern Bell's statement of cash flows for the year ended March 31, 20X9, using the *indirect* method to report cash flows from operating activities. Report noncash investing and financing activities in an accompanying schedule.
2. Evaluate Southern Bell's cash flows for the year. Mention all three categories of cash flows and give the reason for your evaluation.

Preparing the statement of cash flows—indirect method
(Obj. 2, 3)

spreadsheet

P12-5A The 20X5 comparative balance sheet and income statement of Town East Press follow.

Town East had no noncash investing and financing transactions during 20X5. During the year, there were no sales of land or equipment, no issuances of notes payable, no retirements of stock, and no treasury stock transactions.

Required

1. Prepare the 20X5 statement of cash flows, formatting operating activities by the indirect method.
2. How will what you learned in this problem help you evaluate an investment?

Town East Press

Comparative Balance Sheet

	December 31, 20X5	December 31, 20X4	Increase (Decrease)
Current assets:			
Cash and cash equivalents	$ 10,500	$ 5,300	$ 5,200
Accounts receivable	25,300	26,900	(1,600)
Interest receivable	1,900	700	1,200
Inventories	83,600	87,200	(3,600)
Prepaid expenses	2,500	1,900	600
Plant assets:			
Land	89,000	60,000	29,000
Equipment, net	53,500	49,400	4,100
Total assets	$266,300	$231,400	$34,900
Current liabilities:			
Accounts payable	$ 31,400	$ 28,800	$ 2,600
Interest payable	4,400	4,900	(500)
Salary payable	3,100	6,600	(3,500)
Other accrued liabilities	13,700	16,000	(2,300)
Income tax payable	8,900	7,700	1,200
Long-term liabilities:			
Notes payable	75,000	100,000	(25,000)
Stockholders' equity:			
Common stock, no-par	88,300	64,700	23,600
Retained earnings	41,500	2,700	38,800
Total liabilities and stockholders' equity	$266,300	$231,400	$34,900

Town East Press

Income Statement for 20X5

Revenues:		
Sales revenue.		$213,000
Interest revenue.		8,600
Total revenues		221,600
Expenses:		
Cost of goods sold.	$70,600	
Salary expense.	27,800	
Depreciation expense	4,000	
Other operating expense	10,500	
Interest expense	11,600	
Income tax expense.	29,100	
Total expenses		153,600
Net income		$ 68,000

Preparing the statement of cash flows—direct method
(Obj. 2, 4)

P12-6A Accountants for Triad Associates, Inc. have developed the following data from the company's accounting records for the year ended April 30, 20X5:

a. Credit sales, $583,900
b. Loan to another company, $12,500
c. Cash payments to acquire plant assets, $59,400
d. Cost of goods sold, $382,600
e. Proceeds from issuance of common stock, $8,000
f. Payment of cash dividends, $48,400
g. Collection of interest, $4,400
h. Acquisition of equipment by issuing short-term note payable, $16,400
i. Payments of salaries, $93,600
j. Proceeds from sale of plant assets, $22,400, including $6,800 loss
k. Collections on accounts receivable, $448,600
l. Interest revenue, $3,800
m. Cash receipt of dividend revenue on stock investments, $4,100
n. Payments to suppliers, $368,500
o. Cash sales, $171,900
p. Depreciation expense, $59,900
q. Proceeds from issuance of short-term debt, $19,600
r. Payments of long-term debt, $50,000
s. Interest expense and payments, $13,300
t. Salary expense, $95,300
u. Loan collections, $12,800
v. Proceeds from sale of investments, $9,100, including $2,000 gain
w. Payment of short-term note payable by issuing long-term note payable, $63,000
x. Amortization expense, $2,900
y. Income tax expense and payments, $37,900
z. Cash balance: April 30, 20X4, $39,300; April 30, 20X5, $?

Required

1. Prepare Triad Associates' statement of cash flows for the year ended April 30, 20X5. Use the direct method for cash flows from operating activities. Follow the format of Exhibit 12-13, but do *not* show amounts in thousands. Include an accompanying schedule of noncash investing and financing activities.
2. Evaluate 20X5 from a cash-flow standpoint. Give your reasons.

Preparing an income statement, balance sheet, and statement of cash flows—direct method
(Obj. 5)

P12-7A Use the Scott Corporation data from Problem 12-2A.

Required

1. Prepare Scott Corporation's income statement for the year ended December 31, 20X8. Use the single-step format, with all revenues listed together and all expenses together.
2. Prepare Scott's balance sheet at December 31, 20X8.
3. Prepare Scott's statement of cash flows for the year ended December 31, 20X8. Format cash flows from operating activities by the direct method.

Preparing the statement of cash flows—direct method
(Obj. 2, 4)

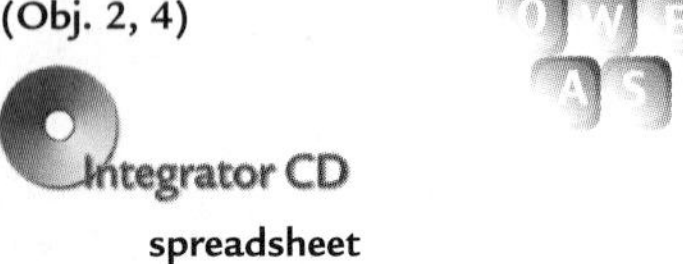

P12-8A Use the Town East Press data from Problem 12-5A.

Required

1. Prepare the 20X5 statement of cash flows by the direct method.
2. How will what you learned in this problem help you evaluate an investment?

Preparing the statement of cash flows—direct and indirect methods
(Obj. 3, 4)

P12-9A To prepare the statement of cash flows, accountants for Internet Guide, Inc., have summarized 20X8 activity in two accounts as follows:

CASH

Debits		Credits	
Beginning balance	53,600	Payments on accounts payable	399,100
Collection of loan	13,000	Payments of dividends	27,200
Sale of investment	8,200	Payments of salaries and wages	143,800
Receipts of interest	12,600	Payments of interest	26,900
Collections from customers	673,700	Purchase of equipment	31,400
Issuance of common stock	47,300	Payments of operating expenses	34,300
Receipts of dividends	4,500	Payment of long-term debt	41,300
		Purchase of treasury stock	26,400
		Payment of income tax	18,900
Ending balance	63,600		

COMMON STOCK

Beginning balance	84,400
Issuance for cash	47,300
Issuance to acquire land	80,100
Issuance to retire long-term debt	19,000
Ending balance	230,800

Required

1. Prepare the statement of cash flows of Internet Guide, Inc., for the year ended December 31, 20X8, using the *direct* method to report operating activities. Also prepare the accompanying schedule of noncash investing and financing activities.
2. Use the following data from Internet Guide's 20X8 income statement and balance sheet to prepare a supplementary schedule showing cash flows from operating activities by the *indirect* method.

Internet Guide, Inc.
Income Statement
Year Ended December 31, 20X8

Revenues:		
Sales revenue		$701,300
Interest revenue		12,600
Dividend revenue		4,500
Total revenues		718,400
Expenses and losses:		
Cost of goods sold	$402,600	
Salary and wage expense	150,800	
Depreciation expense	19,300	
Other operating expense	44,100	
Interest expense	28,800	
Income tax expense	16,200	
Loss on sale of investments	1,100	
Total expenses		662,900
Net income		$ 55,500

Internet Guide, Inc.

Selected Balance Sheet Data

	20X8 Increase (Decrease)
Current assets:	
Cash and cash equivalents	$ 10,000
Accounts receivable	27,600
Inventories	(11,800)
Prepaid expenses	600
Loan receivable	(13,000)
Long-term investments	(9,300)
Equipment, net	12,100
Land	80,100
Current liabilities:	
Accounts payable	$ (8,300)
Interest payable	1,900
Salary payable	7,000
Other accrued liabilities	10,400
Income tax payable	(2,700)
Long-term debt	(60,300)
Common stock, no-par	146,400
Retained earnings	28,300
Treasury stock	26,400

Preparing the statement of cash flows—indirect and direct methods
(Obj. 3, 4)

P12-10A The comparative balance sheet of Safeco Defensive Driving, Inc., at June 30, 20X9, included the amounts given on the next page.

Transaction data for the year ended June 30, 20X9:

a. Net income, $56,200
b. Depreciation expense on equipment, $13,400
c. Purchased long-term investment, $4,900
d. Sold land for $46,900, including $6,700 loss
e. Acquired equipment by issuing long-term note payable, $14,300
f. Paid long-term note payable, $61,000
g. Received cash for issuance of common stock, $3,900
h. Paid cash dividends, $38,100
i. Paid short-term note payable by issuing common stock, $4,700

Required

1. Prepare the statement of cash flows of Safeco Defensive Driving, Inc., for the year ended June 30, 20X9, using the *indirect* method to report operating activities. Also prepare the accompanying schedule of noncash investing and financing activities. All current accounts except short-term notes payable result from operating transactions.
2. Prepare a supplementary schedule showing cash flows from operations by the *direct* method. The income statement reports the following: sales, $245,300; interest revenue, $10,600; cost of goods sold, $82,800; salary expense, $38,800; other operating expenses, $42,000; depreciation expense, $5,400; income tax expense, $9,900; loss on sale of land, $6,700; and interest expense, $6,100.

Safeco Defensive Driving, Inc.
Balance Sheet
June 30, 20X9 and 20X8

	20X9	20X8	Increase (Decrease)
Current assets:			
Cash	$ 24,500	$ 8,600	$ 15,900
Accounts receivable	45,900	48,300	(2,400)
Interest receivable	2,900	3,600	(700)
Inventories	68,600	60,200	8,400
Prepaid expenses	3,700	2,800	900
Long-term investment	10,100	5,200	4,900
Equipment, net	74,500	73,600	900
Land	42,400	96,000	(53,600)
	$272,600	$298,300	$(25,700)
Current liabilities:			
Notes payable, short-term	$ 13,400	$ 18,100	$ (4,700)
Accounts payable	42,400	40,300	2,100
Income tax payable	13,800	14,500	(700)
Accrued liabilities	8,200	9,700	(1,500)
Interest payable	3,700	2,900	800
Salary payable	900	2,600	(1,700)
Long-term note payable	47,400	94,100	(46,700)
Common stock	59,800	51,200	8,600
Retained earnings	83,000	64,900	18,100
	$272,600	$298,300	$(25,700)

(Group B)

Using cash-flow information to evaluate performance
(Obj. 1, 2)

P12-1B Top managers of Internet Solutions, Inc., are reviewing company performance for 20X4. The income statement reports a 15% increase in net income, the fifth consecutive year with an income increase above 10%. The income statement includes a nonrecurring loss without which net income would have increased by 16%. The balance sheet shows modest increases in assets, liabilities, and stockholders' equity. The assets posting the largest increases are plant and equipment because the company is halfway through a 5-year expansion program. No other assets and no liabilities are increasing dramatically. A summarized version of the cash-flow statement reports the following:

Net cash provided by operating activities	$310,000
Net cash used for investing activities	(290,000)
Net cash provided by financing activities	70,000
Increase in cash during 20X4	$ 90,000

Required

Write a memo giving top managers of Internet Solutions your assessment of 20X4 operations and your outlook for the future. Focus on the information content of the cash-flow data.

Preparing an income statement, balance sheet, and statement of cash flows—indirect method
(Obj. 2, 3)

P12-2B Dohn Corporation, a discounter of men's suits, was formed on January 1, 20X6, when Dohn issued its no-par common stock for $200,000. Early in January, Dohn made the following cash payments:

a. For store fixtures, $50,000
b. For inventory (1,000 men's suits), $120,000
c. For rent on a store building, $12,000

In February, Dohn purchased 2,000 men's suits on account from a Chinese company. Cost of this inventory was $160,000. Before year end, Dohn paid $140,000 of this debt. Dohn uses the FIFO method to account for inventory.

During 20X6, Dohn sold 2,800 units of inventory for $200 each. Before year end, Dohn collected 90% of this amount.

The store employs three people. The combined annual payroll is $90,000, of which Dohn owes $3,000 at year end. At the end of the year, Dohn paid income tax of $64,000.

Late in 20X6, Dohn declared and paid cash dividends of $40,000.

For equipment, Dohn uses the straight-line depreciation method, over 5 years, with zero residual value.

Required

1. Prepare Dohn Corporation's income statement for the year ended December 31, 20X6. Use the single-step format, with all revenues listed together and all expenses together.
2. Prepare Dohn's balance sheet at December 31, 20X6.
3. Prepare Dohn's statement of cash flows for the year ended December 31, 20X6. Format cash flows from operating activities by the indirect method.

Preparing the statement of cash flows—indirect method **(Obj. 2, 3)**

P12-3B Accountants for WWW.Smart, Inc. have assembled the following data for the year ended December 31, 20X4:

	December 31, 20X4	December 31, 20X3
Current Accounts:		
Current assets:		
Cash and cash equivalents	$48,600	$34,800
Accounts receivable	70,100	73,700
Inventories	90,600	96,500
Prepaid expenses	3,200	2,100
Current liabilities:		
Accounts payable	$71,600	$67,500
Income tax payable	5,900	6,800
Accrued liabilities	28,300	23,200

Transaction Data for 20X4:

Stock dividends	$ 12,600	Payment of cash dividends	$48,300
Collection of loan	10,300	Issuance of long-term debt to borrow cash	71,000
Depreciation expense	29,200	Net income	50,500
Acquisition of equipment	69,000	Issuance of preferred stock for cash	36,200
Payment of long-term debt by issuing common stock	89,400	Sale of long-term investment	12,200
Acquisition of long-term investment	44,800	Amortization expense	1,100
Acquisition of building by issuing long-term note payable	118,000	Payment of long-term debt	47,800
		Gain on sale of investment	3,500

Required

Prepare WWW.Smart's statement of cash flows using the *indirect* method to report operating activities. Include an accompanying schedule of noncash investing and financing activities.

Preparing the statement of cash flows—indirect method **(Obj. 2, 3)**

P12-4B The comparative balance sheet of CNA Leasing, Inc., at December 31, 20X5, reported the following:

	December 31, 20X5	20X4
Current Assets:		
Cash and cash equivalents	$ 8,400	$12,500
Accounts receivable	28,600	29,300
Inventories	51,600	53,000
Prepaid expenses	4,200	3,700
Current Liabilities:		
Accounts payable	$31,100	$28,000
Accrued liabilities	14,300	16,800
Income tax payable	11,000	14,300

CNA's transactions during 20X5 included the following:

Amortization expense	$ 5,000	Cash acquisition of building	$124,000
Payment of cash dividends	17,000	Net income	31,600
Cash acquisition of equipment	55,000	Issuance of common stock for cash	105,600
Issuance of long-term note payable to borrow cash	32,000	Stock dividend	13,000
Retirement of bonds payable by issuing common stock	55,000	Sale of long-term investment	6,000
		Depreciation expense	12,800

Required

1. Prepare the statement of cash flows of CNA Leasing, Inc., for the year ended December 31, 20X5. Use the *indirect* method to report cash flows from operating activities. Report non-cash investing and financing activities in an accompanying schedule.
2. Evaluate CNA's cash flows for the year. Mention all three categories of cash flows and give the reason for your evaluation.

Preparing the statement of cash flows—indirect method
(Obj. 2, 3)

P12-5B The 20X8 comparative balance sheet and income statement of Genie Marketing, Inc., follows.

Genie had no noncash investing and financing transactions during 20X8. During the year, there were no sales of land or equipment, no issuances of notes payable, no retirements of stock, and no treasury stock transactions.

Required

1. Prepare the 20X8 statement of cash flows, formatting operating activities by the indirect method.
2. How will what you learned in this problem help you evaluate an investment?

Genie Marketing, Inc.
Comparative Balance Sheet

	December 31, 20X8	20X7	Increase (Decrease)
Current assets:			
Cash and cash equivalents	$ 8,700	$ 15,600	$(6,900)
Accounts receivable	46,500	43,100	3,400
Interest receivable	600	900	(300)
Inventories	94,300	89,900	4,400
Prepaid expenses	1,700	2,200	(500)

(continued)

Plant assets:			
Land	$ 35,100	$ 10,000	$ 25,100
Equipment, net	100,900	93,700	7,200
Total assets	$287,800	$255,400	$ 32,400
Current liabilities:			
Accounts payable	$ 16,400	$ 17,900	$ (1,500)
Interest payable	6,300	6,700	(400)
Salary payable	2,100	1,400	700
Other accrued liabilities	18,100	18,700	(600)
Income tax payable	6,300	3,800	2,500
Long-term liabilities:			
Notes payable	55,000	65,000	(10,000)
Stockholders' equity:			
Common stock, no-par	131,100	122,300	8,800
Retained earnings	52,500	19,600	32,900
Total liabilities and stockholders' equity	$287,800	$255,400	$ 32,400

Genie Marketing, Inc.

Income Statement for 20X8

Revenues:		
Sales revenue		$438,000
Interest revenue		11,700
Total revenues		449,700
Expenses:		
Cost of goods sold	$205,200	
Salary expense	76,400	
Depreciation expense	15,300	
Other operating expense	49,700	
Interest expense	24,600	
Income tax expense	16,900	
Total expenses		388,100
Net income		$ 61,600

Preparing the statement of cash flows—direct method
(Obj. 2, 4)

P12-6B Data Solutions, Inc., accountants have developed the following data from the company's accounting records for the year ended July 31, 20X5:

a. Salary expense, $105,300
b. Cash payments to purchase plant assets, $181,000
c. Proceeds from issuance of short-term debt, $44,100
d. Payments of long-term debt, $18,800
e. Proceeds from sale of plant assets, $59,700, including $10,600 gain
f. Interest revenue, $12,100
g. Cash receipt of dividend revenue on stock investments, $2,700
h. Payments to suppliers, $673,300
i. Interest expense and payments, $37,800
j. Cost of goods sold, $481,100
k. Collection of interest revenue, $11,700
l. Acquisition of equipment by issuing short-term note payable, $35,500
m. Payments of salaries, $104,000
n. Credit sales, $608,100
o. Loan to another company, $35,000
p. Income tax expense and payments, $56,400
q. Depreciation expense, $27,700
r. Collections on accounts receivable, $681,100
s. Loan collections, $74,400
t. Proceeds from sale of investments, $34,700, including $3,800 loss
u. Payment of long-term debt by issuing preferred stock, $107,300

(continued)

v. Amortization expense, $23,900
w. Cash sales, $146,000
x. Proceeds from issuance of common stock, $116,900
y. Payment of cash dividends, $50,500
z. Cash balance: July 31, 20X4—$53,800; July 31, 20X5—$?

Required

1. Prepare Data Solutions' statement of cash flows for the year ended July 31, 20X5. Use the direct method for cash flows from operating activities. Follow the format of Exhibit 12-13, but do *not* show amounts in thousands. Include an accompanying schedule of noncash investing and financing activities.
2. Evaluate 20X5 in terms of cash flow. Give your reasons.

Preparing an income statement, balance sheet, and statement of cash flows—direct method
(Obj. 2, 4)

P12-7B Use the Dohn Corporation data from Problem 12-2B.

Required

1. Prepare Dohn Corporation's income statement for the year ended December 31, 20X6. Use the single-step format, with all revenues listed together and all expenses together.
2. Prepare Dohn's balance sheet at December 31, 20X6.
3. Prepare Dohn's statement of cash flows for the year ended December 31, 20X6. Format cash flows from operating activities by the direct method.

Preparing the statement of cash flows—direct method
(Obj. 2, 4)

spreadsheet

P12-8B Use the Genie Marketing, Inc., data from Problem 12-5B.

Required

1. Prepare the 20X8 statement of cash flows by the direct method.
2. How will what you learned in this problem help you evaluate an investment?

Preparing the statement of cash flows—direct and indirect methods
(Obj. 3, 4)

P12-9B To prepare the statement of cash flows, accountants for Rolex Paper Company have summarized 20X8 activity in two accounts as follows:

CASH

Beginning balance	87,100	Payments of operating expenses	46,100
Issuance of common stock	34,600	Payment of long-term debt	78,900
Receipts of dividends	1,900	Purchase of treasury stock	10,400
Collection of loan	18,500	Payment of income tax	8,000
Sale of investments	9,900	Payments on accounts payable	101,600
Receipts of interest	12,200	Payment of dividends	1,800
Collections from customers	308,100	Payments of salaries and wages	67,500
Sale of treasury stock	26,200	Payments of interest	21,800
		Purchase of equipment	79,900
Ending balance	82,500		

COMMON STOCK

		Beginning balance	103,500
		Issuance for cash	34,600
		Issuance to acquire land	62,100
		Issuance to retire long-term debt	21,100
		Ending balance	221,300

Required

1. Prepare Rolex's statement of cash flows for the year ended December 31, 20X8, using the *direct* method to report operating activities. Also prepare the accompanying schedule of noncash investing and financing activities. Rolex's 20X8 income statement and selected balance sheet data follow.

2. Use these data to prepare a supplementary schedule showing cash flows from operating activities by the *indirect* method.

Rolex Paper Company

Income Statement
Year Ended December 31, 20X8

Revenues and gains:		
Sales revenue		$291,800
Interest revenue		12,200
Dividend revenue		1,900
Gain on sale of investments		700
Total revenues and gains		306,600
Expenses:		
Cost of goods sold	$103,600	
Salary and wage expense	66,800	
Depreciation expense	20,900	
Other operating expense	44,700	
Interest expense	24,100	
Income tax expense	2,600	
Total expenses		262,700
Net income		$ 43,900

Rolex Paper Company

Selected Balance Sheet Data

	20X8 Increase (Decrease)
Current assets:	
Cash and cash equivalents	$ (4,600)
Accounts receivable	(16,300)
Inventories	5,700
Prepaid expenses	(1,900)
Loan receivable	(18,500)
Investments	(9,200)
Equipment, net	59,000
Land	62,100
Current liabilities:	
Accounts payable	$ 7,700
Interest payable	2,300
Salary payable	(700)
Other accrued liabilities	(3,300)
Income tax payable	(5,400)
Long-term debt	(100,000)
Common stock	117,800
Retained earnings	42,100
Treasury stock	(15,800)

Preparing the statement of cash flows—indirect and direct methods
(Obj. 3, 4)

P12-10B Heart O'Texas Optical Corporation's comparative balance sheet at September 30, 20X4 included the following balances:

Heart O'Texas Optical

Balance Sheet
September 30, 20X4 and 20X3

	20X4	20X3	Increase (Decrease)
Current assets:			
Cash	$ 11,700	$ 17,600	$ (5,900)
Accounts receivable	41,900	44,000	(2,100)
Interest receivable	4,100	2,800	1,300
Inventories	121,700	116,900	4,800
Prepaid expenses	8,600	9,300	(700)
Long-term investments	51,100	13,800	37,300
Equipment, net	131,900	92,100	39,800
Land	47,100	74,300	(27,200)
	$418,100	$370,800	$ 47,300
Current liabilities:			
Notes payable, short-term	$ 22,000	$ 0	$ 22,000
Accounts payable	61,800	70,300	(8,500)
Income tax payable	21,800	24,600	(2,800)
Accrued liabilities	17,900	29,100	(11,200)
Interest payable	4,500	3,200	1,300
Salary payable	1,500	1,100	400
Long-term note payable	123,000	121,400	1,600
Common stock	113,900	62,000	51,900
Retained earnings	51,700	59,100	(7,400)
	$418,100	$370,800	$ 47,300

Transaction data for the year ended September 30, 20X4:

a. Net income, $56,900
b. Depreciation expense on equipment, $8,500
c. Acquired long-term investments, $37,300
d. Sold land for $38,100, including $10,900 gain
e. Acquired equipment by issuing long-term note payable, $26,300
f. Paid long-term note payable, $24,700
g. Received cash of $51,900 for issuance of common stock
h. Paid cash dividends, $64,300
i. Acquired equipment by issuing short-term note payable, $22,000

Required

1. Prepare Heart O'Texas Optical's statement of cash flows for the year ended September 30, 20X4 using the *indirect* method to report operating activities. Also prepare the accompanying schedule of noncash investing and financing activities. All current accounts except short-term notes payable result from operating transactions.
2. Prepare a supplementary schedule showing cash flows from operations by the *direct* method. The income statement reports the following: sales, $333,600; gain on sale of land, $10,900; interest revenue, $7,300; cost of goods sold, $161,500; salary expense, $63,400; other operating expenses, $29,600; income tax expense, $18,400; interest expense, $13,500; and depreciation expense, $8,500.

Apply Your Knowledge

Decision Cases

Preparing and using the statement of cash flows to evaluate operations
(Obj. 3)

Case 1. The 20X6 comparative income statement and the 20X6 comparative balance sheet of Tennis, Tennis, Tennis!, Inc. have just been distributed at a meeting of the company's board of directors. The members of the board of directors raise a fundamental question: Why is the cash balance so low? This question is especially troublesome to the board members because 20X6 showed record profits. As the controller of the company, you must answer the question.

Tennis, Tennis, Tennis!, Inc.
Comparative Income Statement
Years Ended December 31, 20X6 and 20X5

(In thousands)	20X6	20X5
Revenues and gains:		
Sales revenue	$444	$310
Gain on sale of equipment (sale price, $33)	—	18
Totals	$444	$328
Expenses and losses:		
Cost of goods sold	$221	$162
Salary expense	48	28
Depreciation expense	46	22
Interest expense	13	20
Amortization expense on patent	11	11
Loss on sale of land (sale price, $61)	—	35
Total expenses and losses	339	278
Net income	$105	$ 50

Tennis, Tennis, Tennis!, Inc.
Comparative Balance Sheet
December 31, 20X6 and 20X5

(In thousands)	20X6	20X5
Assets		
Cash	$ 25	$ 63
Accounts receivable, net	72	61
Inventories	194	181
Long-term investments	31	0
Property, plant, and equipment	369	259
Accumulated depreciation	(244)	(198)
Patents	177	188
Totals	$624	$554
Liabilities and Owners' Equity		
Accounts payable	$ 63	$ 56
Accrued liabilities	12	17
Notes payable, long-term	179	264
Common stock, no-par	149	61
Retained earnings	221	156
Totals	$624	$554

Required

1. Prepare a statement of cash flows for 20X6 in the format that best shows the relationship between net income and operating cash flow. The company sold no plant assets or long-term investments and issued no notes payable during 20X6. There were *no* noncash investing and financing transactions during the year. Show all amounts in thousands.
2. Answer the board members' question: Why is the cash balance so low? In explaining the business's cash flows, identify two significant cash receipts that occurred during 20X5 but not in 20X6. Also point out the two largest cash payments during 20X6.
3. Considering net income and the company's cash flows during 20X6, was it a good year or a bad year? Give your reasons.

Using cash-flow data to evaluate an investment
(Obj. 1, 2)

Case 2. Carolina Technology, Inc., and Northwest Electric Power Corporation are asking you to recommend their stock to your clients. Because Carolina and Northwest earn about the same net income and have similar financial positions, your decision depends on their cash-flow statements, summarized as follows:

	Carolina		Northwest	
Net cash provided by operating activities:		$ 70,000		$ 30,000
Cash provided by (used for) investing activities:				
Purchase of plant assets	$(100,000)		$(20,000)	
Sale of plant assets	10,000	(90,000)	40,000	20,000
Cash provided by (used for) financing activities:				
Issuance of common stock		30,000		—
Paying off long-term debt		—		(40,000)
Net increase in cash		$ 10,000		$ 10,000

Based on their cash flows, which company looks better? Give your reasons.

Ethical Issue

Victoria British Auto Parts is having a bad year. Net income is only $37,000. Also, two important overseas customers are falling behind in their payments to Victoria, and Victoria's accounts receivable are ballooning. The company desperately needs a loan. The Victoria board of directors is considering ways to put the best face on the company's financial statements. Victoria's bank closely examines cash flow from operations. Daniel Peavey, Victoria's controller, suggests reclassifying as long-term the receivables from the slow-paying clients. He explains to the board that removing the $80,000 rise in accounts receivable from current assets will increase net cash provided by operations. This approach may help Victoria get the loan.

Required

1. Using only the amounts given, compute net cash provided by operations, both without and with the reclassification of the receivables. Which reporting makes Victoria look better?
2. Under what condition would the reclassification of the receivables be ethical? Unethical?

Using the statement of cash flows
(Obj. 1, 2, 3, 4, 5)

Financial Statement Case

Use Fossil, Inc.'s statement of cash flows along with the company's other financial statements, all in Appendix A at the end of the book, to answer the following questions.

Required

1. By which method does Fossil report net cash flows from *operating* activities? How can you tell?
2. Suppose Fossil reported net cash flows from operating activities by the direct method. Compute these amounts for the year ended January 5, 2002 (ignore the statement of cash flows):
   a. Collections from customers
   b. Payments for inventory
3. Prepare a T-account for Property, Plant, and Equipment—Net and show all activity in this account for the year ended January 5, 2002 (fiscal year 2001). Assume that 10% of the cash paid for business acquisitions obtained plant assets and that $538 thousand of depreciation and amortization related to intangible and other assets.
4. Evaluate the year ended January 5, 2002 (fiscal year 2001) in terms of net income, total assets, stockholders' equity, the debt ratio, cash flows, and overall results. Be specific.

Analytical Case

Analyzing cash flows
(Obj. 2, 3)

Refer to the Pier 1 Imports financial statements in Appendix B at the end of this book.

1. What is Pier 1's main source of cash? Is this good news or bad news to Pier 1 managers, stockholders, and creditors? What is Pier 1's main use of cash? Good news or bad news? Explain all answers in detail.
2. Explain in detail the three main reasons why net cash provided by operations exceeds net income. Are these effects real or imaginary? Over which of these three items does Pier 1 have the most control from year to year? Explain.
3. "Proceeds from stock options exercised, stock purchase plan, and other, net" from the statement of cash flows does not agree with the amount reported for these transactions on the statement of shareholders' equity. What explains the $878,000 difference?

The following question uses the financial statements of ***Fossil, Inc.****, given in Appendix A at the end of this book.*

4. Fossil's balance sheet reports asset and liability balances at the end of each year. The statement of cash flows reports the changes in Fossil's current accounts as part of operating activities. For example, on Fossil's comparative balance sheet, accounts receivable—net increased from $62,876 thousand to $74,035 thousand. But the statement of cash flows reports a $7,340 change in receivables. Similar discrepancies occur for the other current accounts. What explains these discrepancies? The statement of cash flows provides the explanation. What is it?

Group Projects

Project 1. Each member of the group should obtain the annual report of a different company. Select companies in different industries. Evaluate each company's trend of cash flows for the most recent 2 years. In your evaluation of the companies' cash flows, you may use any other information that is publicly available—for example, the other financial statements (income statement, balance sheet, statement of stockholders' equity, and the related notes) and news stories from magazines and newspapers. Rank the companies' cash flows from best to worst and write a two-page report on your findings.

Project 2. Select a company and obtain its annual report, including all the financial statements. Focus on the statement of cash flows and, in particular, the cash flows from operating activities. Specify whether the company uses the direct method or the indirect method to report operating cash flows. As necessary, use the other financial statements (income statement, balance sheet, and statement of stockholders' equity) and the notes to prepare the company's cash flows from operating activities by the *other* method.

13

Financial Statement Analysis

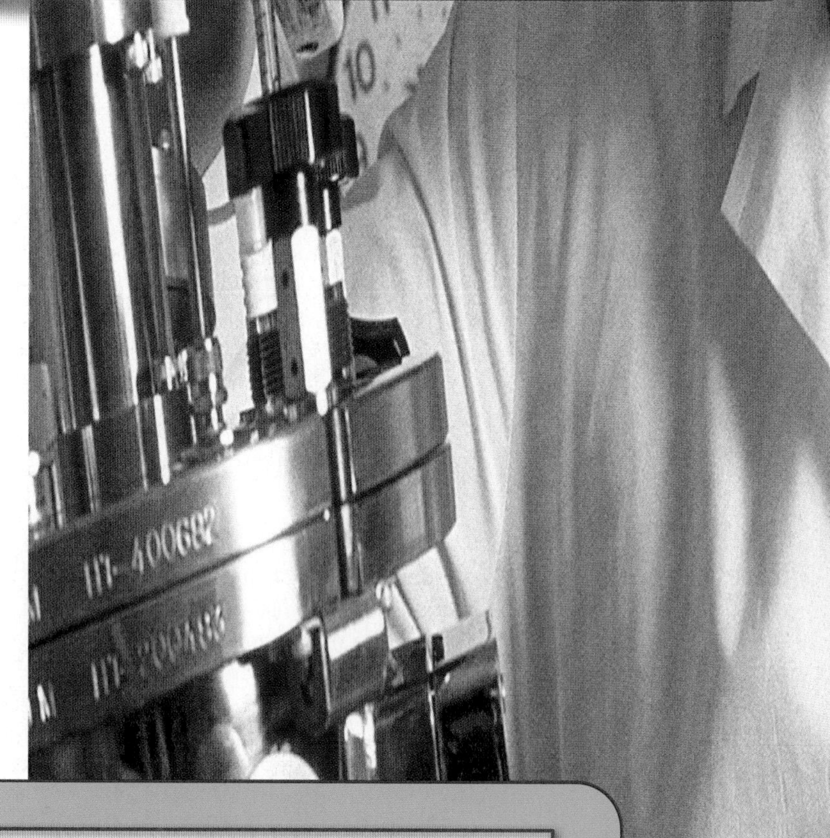

Learning Objectives

1 **Perform** a horizontal analysis of comparative financial statements

2 **Perform** a vertical analysis of financial statements

3 **Prepare** and use common-size financial statements

4 **Use** the statement of cash flows for decisions

5 **Compute** the standard financial ratios

6 **Use** ratios in decision making

7 **Measure** the economic value added by operations

Integrator CD

Need additional help? Go to the **Integrator CD** *and search these key words:* Common-size, current, acid-test ratios; day's sales, inventory turnover, profitability ratios; horizontal, trend, vertical analysis; P/E, EVA, debt ratio; times-interest-earned, return on assets, sales; dividend yield

Bristol-Myers Squibb Company

Consolidated Statement of Earnings (Adapted)

(In millions)		Year Ended December 31, 2001	2000
Earnings			
1	**Net sales**	$19,423	$18,216
2	**Expenses:**		
3	Cost of products sold	5,575	4,759
4	Marketing, selling and administrative	3,903	3,860
5	Advertising and product promotion	1,433	1,672
6	Research and development	5,003	1,939
7	**Operating income**	3,509	5,986
8	Other expense, net	523	508
9	**Earnings from continuing operations before income tax**	2,986	5,478
10	Income taxes	459	1,382
11	**Earnings from continuing operations**	2,527	4,096
12	Discontinued operations	2,718	615
13	**Net earnings**	$ 5,245	$ 4,711

Peter R. Dolan, chief executive officer (CEO) of Bristol-Myers Squibb (BMS) Company, wrote the following for "Mr. Dolan's Neighborhood," which appeared in the company's 2001 Annual Report:

> Like any chief executive of a large corporation, I get my share of critical letters . . . , and I've pretty much learned to take them in stride. But the pencil-smudged notes that I received this past spring from a bunch of third graders were something very different.
>
> "*Somebody in my class brought in a tape about sleeping sickness in Africa,*" read one. "*People are dying and I would help them, but I don't have the medicine. You can help them, please. If you don't, I think that's selfish and mean.*"
>
> The third graders had watched a TV newsmagazine segment that criticized Bristol-Myers Squibb for making a cosmetic product, *VANIQA*, that contains . . . a treatment for sleeping sickness that is in desperately short supply in Africa. The show incorrectly portrayed our company as being indifferent to the plight of Africans . . . , despite the fact that we have led other companies in an effort to secure a [cure for the disease]. In fact, we . . . help support the World Health Organization's efforts in treating this disease.
>
> But there was another reason the letters got to me. The school was in the town where I live—in fact, both my sons had gone there, and . . . the third-grade teacher . . . [was] one of my younger son's favorite teachers from three years before.
>
> I guess you could say I took it personally. So much so, in fact, that last June . . . I visited her classroom and spoke to her third graders myself.

CEOs of large companies have to satisfy lots of people—from third graders to Wall Street analysts.

Study BMS's 2001 income statement at the beginning of this chapter. You'll see that 2001 was a tough year for the company. Yes, net earnings (line 13) were up from year 2000, but only because BMS sold off some discontinued operations (line 12). Both operating income (line 7) and earnings from continuing operations (line 11) were down.

Wall Street wasn't happy about these results because the predictor of future profits—income from continuing operations—was down in 2001. This chapter covers some of the analytical tools people use to make investment and credit decisions.

Source: Bristol-Myers Squibb Company Annual Report (2001), p. 6.

Sitemap

- Horizontal Analysis ■
- Vertical Analysis ■
- Benchmarking ■
- Using Ratios to Make Decisions ■
- The Limitations of Financial Analysis ■

DECISION: How Does an Investor Evaluate a Company?

Investors and creditors cannot evaluate a company by examining only 1 year's data. This is why most financial statements cover at least 2 periods, like the Bristol-Myers Squibb (BMS) income statement that begins this chapter. In fact, most financial analysis covers trends of 3, 5, or even 10 years. This chapter illustrates some of the analytical tools we use to chart a company's progress through time. What is the goal of financial analysis? To predict the future.

The graphs in Exhibit 13-1 show some important data about BMS. The graphs depict BMS's 3-year trend of net sales from continuing operations and research and development (R&D). How relevant are these facts for making decisions about BMS or competitor Procter & Gamble (P&G)? They are very relevant because they help managers, investors, and creditors chart the company's future.

Exhibit 13-1

Representative Financial Data of Bristol-Myers Squibb Company (Adapted)

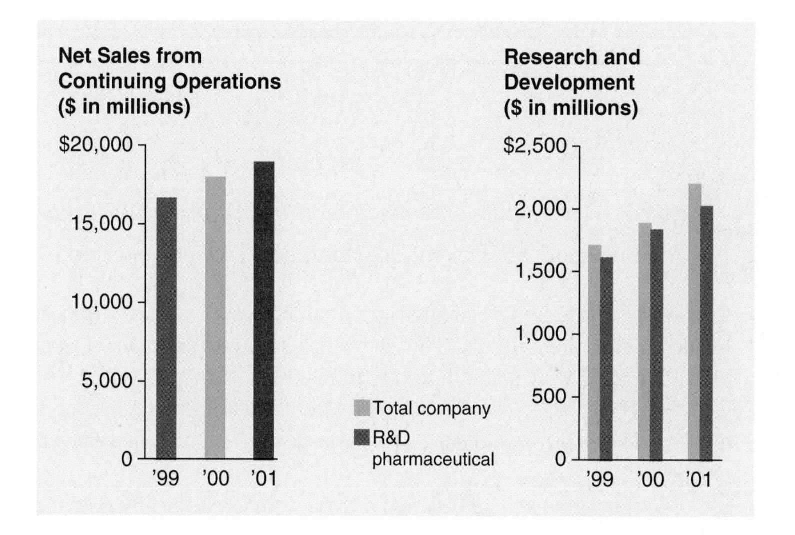

Both sales from continuing operations and R&D increased during 2001. These are good signs for the future. Consider what you would predict for BMS's sales in 2002 and 2003. Based on the recent past, you would probably extend the sales line upward. And the increase in R&D lays a foundation for the development of new products.

Investors who purchase stock want dividends, and they hope the stock's value will increase. Investors bear the risk that they will not receive a good return on their investment. They use financial statement analysis to (1) predict their expected returns and (2) assess the risks associated with those returns. Let's examine some of the tools of financial analysis: we begin with horizontal analysis.

Horizontal Analysis

Integrator CD
horizontal analysis, trend analysis

Objective

1 **Perform** a horizontal analysis of comparative financial statements

Horizontal analysis
Study of percentage changes in comparative financial statements.

Many decisions hinge on whether the numbers—in sales, income, expenses, and so on—are increasing or decreasing over time. Has the sales figure risen from last year? By how much? We may find that sales have increased by $20,000. Considered alone this fact is not very informative. The *percentage change* in sales over time enhances our understanding. It is more useful to know that sales have increased by 20% than to know that the increase in sales is $20,000.

The study of percentage changes in comparative statements is called **horizontal analysis.** Computing a percentage change in comparative statements requires two steps:

1. Compute the dollar amount of the change from the base (earlier) period to the later period.
2. Divide the dollar amount of change by the base-period amount.

Illustration: Bristol-Myers Squibb

Horizontal analysis is illustrated for Bristol-Myers Squibb (BMS) as follows (dollar amounts in millions):

			Increase (Decrease)	
	2001	***2000***	***Amount***	***Percentage***
Sales	$19,423	$18,216	$1,207	6.6%

BMS's sales increased by 6.6% during 2001, computed as follows:

STEP 1 Compute the dollar amount of change in sales from 2000 to 2001:

2001		2000		Increase
$19,423	−	$18,216	=	$1,207

STEP 2 Divide the dollar amount of change by the base-period amount. This computes the percentage change for the period:

$$\text{Percentage change} = \frac{\text{Dollar amount of change}}{\text{Base-year amount}}$$

$$= \frac{\$1{,}207}{\$18{,}216} = 6.6\%$$

Detailed horizontal analyses are shown in the two right-hand columns of Exhibits 13-2 and 13-3, the financial statements of BMS Company. The income statements (statements of earnings) reveal that net sales increased by 6.6% during 2001. But cost of goods sold grew by 17.1%, so gross profit grew by only 2.9%—not a good sign.

✔ Check Point 13-1

Exhibit 13-2

Comparative Income Statement—Horizontal Analysis

Bristol-Myers Squibb Company

Statement of Earnings (Adapted)
Years Ended December 31, 2001 and 2000

			Increase (Decrease)	
(Dollar amounts in millions)	***2001***	***2000***	***Amount***	***Percentage***
Net sales	$19,423	$18,216	$ 1,207	6.6%
Cost of products sold	5,575	4,759	816	17.1
Gross profit	13,848	13,457	391	2.9
Operating expenses:				
Marketing, selling, and administrative	3,903	3,860	43	1.1
Advertising and product promotion	1,433	1,672	(239)	(14.3)
Research and development	5,003	1,939	3,064	158.0
Operating income	3,509	5,986	(2,477)	(41.4)
Other expense net	523	508	15	3.0
Earnings from continuing operations before income tax	2,986	5,478	(2,492)	(45.5)
Income taxes	459	1,382	(923)	(66.8)
Earnings from continuing operations	2,527	4,096	(1,569)	(38.3)
Discontinued operations	2,718	615	2,103	342.0
Net earnings	$ 5,245	$ 4,711	$ 534	11.3

Note: Any increase from zero to a positive number is treated as an increase of 100%.

← *We introduced the income statement and the balance sheet in Chapter 1.*

Exhibit 13-3

Comparative Balance Sheet—Horizontal Analysis

Bristol-Myers Squibb Company

Balance Sheet (Adapted)
December 31, 2001 and 2000

(Dollar amounts in millions)	*2001*	*2000*	Increase (Decrease) *Amount*	*Percentage*
Assets				
Current Assets:				
Cash and cash equivalents	$ 5,500	$ 3,182	$2,318	72.8%
Time deposits and marketable securities	154	203	(49)	(24.1)
Receivables, net	3,949	3,662	287	7.8
Inventories	1,487	1,831	(344)	(18.8)
Prepaid expenses	1,259	946	313	33.1
Total current assets	12,349	9,824	2,525	25.7
Property, plant, and equipment—net	4,879	4,548	331	7.3
Goodwill	5,200	1,436	3,764	262.1
Intangible assets, net	2,247	384	1,863	485.2
Other assets	2,382	1,386	996	71.9
Total assets	$27,057	$17,578	$9,479	53.9
Liabilities				
Current Liabilities:				
Short-term borrowings	$ 174	$ 162	$ 12	7.4%
Accounts payable	1,587	1,702	(115)	(6.8)
Accrued expenses payable	4,207	3,067	1,140	37.2
U.S. and foreign income taxes payable	2,858	701	2,157	307.7
Total current liabilities	8,826	5,632	3,194	56.7
Other liabilities	1,258	1,430	(172)	(12.0)
Long-term debt	6,237	1,336	4,901	366.8
Total liabilities	16,321	8,398	7,923	94.3
Stockholders' Equity				
Common stock	220	220	—	0.0
Capital in excess of par value of stock	2,336	2,002	334	16.7
Other accumulated comprehensive income (loss)	(1,117)	(1,103)	(14)	(1.3)
Retained earnings	20,686	17,781	2,905	16.3
Less cost of treasury stock	(11,389)	(9,720)	(1,669)	17.2
Total stockholders' equity	10,736	9,180	1,556	16.9
Total liabilities and stockholders' equity	$27,057	$17,578	$9,479	53.9

We have seen that BMS sales and gross profit both increased during 2001. But operating income and earnings from continuing operations for the year were down sharply. Examine the horizontal analysis of BMS's income statement in Exhibit 13-2. What one item is most responsible for the decrease in operating income? Evaluate the long-run implication of the item that caused operating income to decrease. Does that item point to a positive or a negative outlook for the future?

Answer:

R&D expense increased by 158% in 2001, and that was the main reason operating income was down for the year. The long-run implication of BMS's heavy expenditure for R&D is positive because R&D often produces successful new products. Without R&D, companies such as BMS and P&G would lose their competitive edge.

The comparative balance sheet in Exhibit 13-3 shows that 2001 was a year of expansion for BMS. Total assets increased by 53.9%. The bulk of this growth occurred in goodwill and intangible assets such as patents, technology, and licenses →. These items increased by 262% and 485%, respectively.

← Chapter 7 covered intangible assets.

The horizontal analysis of BMS's balance sheet reveals how the company financed its purchases of these assets. Long-term debt grew by 367% during 2001. This means that BMS borrowed most of the money that it invested in 2001. The vertical analysis that we will perform in the next section will help determine whether BMS is borrowing too heavily.

Trend Percentages

Trend percentages are a form of horizontal analysis. Trends indicate the direction a business is taking. How have sales changed over a 5-year period? What trend does income from continuing operations show? These questions can be answered by trend percentages over a representative period, such as the most recent 5 or 10 years.

Trend percentages are computed by selecting a base year whose amounts are set equal to 100%. The amounts for each following year are expressed as a percentage of the base amount. To compute trend percentages, divide each item for following years by the corresponding amount during the base year:

$$\text{Trend \%} = \frac{\text{Any year \$}}{\text{Base year \$}}$$

BMS Company showed income from continuing operations for the past 6 years as follows:

(In millions)	*2001*	*2000*	*1999*	*1998*	*1997*	*1996*
Earnings from continuing operations	$2,527	$4,096	$3,789	$2,750	$2,744	$2,484

We want trend percentages for the 5-year period 1997 to 2001. The base year is 1996. Trend percentages are computed by dividing each year's amount by the 1996 amount. The resulting trend percentages follow (1996, the base year = 100%):

	2001	*2000*	*1999*	*1998*	*1997*	*1996*
Earnings from continuing operations	102%	165%	153%	111%	110%	100%

✔ Check Point 13-2

Continuing operations were increasingly profitable through 2000. Then, as we have already seen, profits dropped in 2001.

You can perform a trend analysis on any item you consider important. We selected earnings from continuing operations because it is a good predictor of future profits. Trend analysis is widely used for predicting the future.

vertical analysis, common size statement

Objective

2 Perform a vertical analysis of financial statements

Vertical Analysis

Horizontal analysis highlights changes in an item over time. However, no single technique gives a complete picture of a business.

Vertical analysis of a financial statement reveals the relationship of each statement item to a specified base, which is the 100% figure. Every other item on the financial statement is then reported as a percentage of that base. When an income statement is analyzed, net sales is usually the base. Suppose under normal conditions a company's gross profit is 70% of net sales. A drop to 60% may cause the company to suffer a loss. Management, investors, and creditors view a large decline in gross profit and operating income with alarm.

Vertical analysis
Analysis of a financial statement that reveals the relationship of each statement item to a specified base, which is the 100% figure.

Illustration: Bristol-Myers Squibb

Exhibit 13-4 shows the vertical analysis of BMS's income statement as a percentage of net sales. In this case,

$$\textbf{Vertical analysis \%} = \frac{\textbf{Each income statement item}}{\textbf{Net sales}}$$

Exhibit 13-4

Comparative Income Statement—Vertical Analysis

Bristol-Myers Squibb Company
Statement of Earnings (Adapted)
Years Ended December 31, 2001 and 2000

	2001		2000	
(Dollar amounts in millions)	*Amount*	*Percentage of Total*	*Amount*	*Percentage of Total*
Net sales	$19,423	100.0%	$18,216	100.0%
Cost of products sold	5,575	28.7	4,759	26.1
Gross profit	13,848	71.3	13,457	73.9
Operating expenses:				
Marketing, selling, and administrative	3,903	20.1	3,860	21.2
Advertising and product promotion	1,433	7.4	1,672	9.2
Research and development	5,003	25.7	1,939	10.6
Operating income	3,509	18.1	5,986	32.9
Other expense net	523	2.7	508	2.8
Earnings from continuing operations before income tax	2,986	15.4	5,478	30.1
Income taxes	459	2.4	1,382	7.6
Earnings from continuing operations	2,527	13.0	4,096	22.5
Discontinued operations	2,718	14.0	615	3.4
Net earnings	$ 5,245	27.0%	$ 4,711	25.9%

So, for example, the vertical-analysis percentage for Cost of products sold for 2001 is 28.7% ($5,575/$19,423 = .287). Unfortunately for BMS, this percentage increased during 2001. Look further. R&D expense's percentage also increased. Consequently, the percentages for operating income and earnings from continuing operations were down from their 2000 levels.

Exhibit 13-5 shows the vertical analysis of BMS's balance sheet. The base amount (100%) is total assets.

Exhibit 13-5

Comparative Balance Sheet—Vertical Analysis

Bristol-Myers Squibb Company

Balance Sheet (Adapted)
December 31, 2001 and 2000

(Dollar amounts in millions)	2001 Amount	2001 Percent of Total	2000 Amount	2000 Percent of Total
Assets				
Current Assets:				
Cash and cash equivalents	$ 5,500	20.3%	$ 3,182	18.1%
Time deposits and marketable securities	154	0.6	203	1.2
Receivables, net of allowances	3,949	14.6	3,662	20.8
Inventories	1,487	5.5	1,831	10.4
Prepaid expenses	1,259	4.7	946	5.4
Total current assets	12,349	45.7	9,824	55.9
Property, plant, and equipment—net	4,879	18.0	4,548	25.9
Goodwill	5,200	19.2	1,436	8.1
Intangible assets, net	2,247	8.3	384	2.2
Other assets	2,382	8.8	1,386	7.9
Total assets	$ 27,057	100.0%	$17,578	100.0%
Liabilities				
Current Liabilities:				
Short-term borrowings	$ 174	0.6%	$ 162	0.9%
Accounts payable	1,587	5.9	1,702	9.7
Accrued expenses payable	4,207	15.5	3,067	17.4
U.S. and foreign income taxes payable	2,858	10.6	701	4.0
Total current liabilities	8,826	32.6	5,632	32.0
Other Liabilities	1,258	4.6	1,430	8.1
Long-Term Debt	6,237	23.1	1,336	7.6
Total liabilities	16,321	60.3	8,398	47.7
Stockholders' Equity				
Common stock	220	0.8	220	1.3
Capital in excess of par value of stock	2,336	8.6	2002	11.4
Other accumulated comprehensive income (loss)	(1,117)	(4.1)	(1,103)	(6.3)
Retained earnings	20,686	76.5	17,781	101.2
Less cost of treasury stock	(11,389)	(42.1)	(9,720)	(55.3)
Total stockholders' equity	10,736	39.7	9,180	52.3
Total liabilities and stockholders' equity	$ 27,057	100.0%	$17,578	100.0%

The vertical analysis of BMS's balance sheet reveals several things about the company's financial position:

✔ Check Point 13-3

- Current assets make up a smaller percentage of total assets (45.7% in 2001, compared to 55.9% in 2000). This is good because current assets earn a low rate of return.
- Intangibles, including goodwill, increased as a percentage of total assets. Lenders will dislike the buildup of intangibles because, in a liquidation of the company, intangibles are often worthless. But in the information-driven economy of the 2000s, intangible assets are more important.
- Long-term debt increased to 23.1% of total assets, and total liabilities climbed to 60.3%→. Overall, the creditworthiness of BMS declined a bit in 2001.

← Long-term debt is covered in Chapter 8.

DECISION: How Do We Compare One Company to Another?

Objective

3 **Prepare** and use common-size financial statements

Common-size statement
A financial statement that reports only percentages (no dollar amounts).

The percentages in Exhibits 13-4 and 13-5 can be presented as a separate statement that reports only percentages (no dollar amounts). Such a statement is called a **common-size statement.**

On a common-size income statement, each item is expressed as a percentage of the net sales amount. Net sales is the *common size* to which we relate the other amounts. In the balance sheet, the common size is total assets. A common-size statement eases the comparison of different companies because their amounts are stated in percentages.

Common-size statements may identify the need for corrective action. Exhibit 13-6 gives an example. In 2000, BMS had almost 56% of its resources tied up in current assets. As we have mentioned, cash, receivables, and inventories earn low rates of return, as compared to plant and equipment and intangibles. It appears that the top management of BMS made a serious shift during 2001. BMS invested heavily in other companies, purchasing goodwill, patents, technology, and licenses. These investments increased the company's long-term assets to 54.3% of total resources in 2001.

Exhibit 13-6

Common-Size Analysis of Current Assets

Bristol-Myers Squibb Company
Common-Size Analysis of Current and Long-Term Assets
December 31, 2001 and 2000

	Percent of Total Assets	
	2001	**2000**
Current Assets	45.7%	55.9%
Long-Term Assets	54.3	44.1
Total Assets	100.0%	100.0%

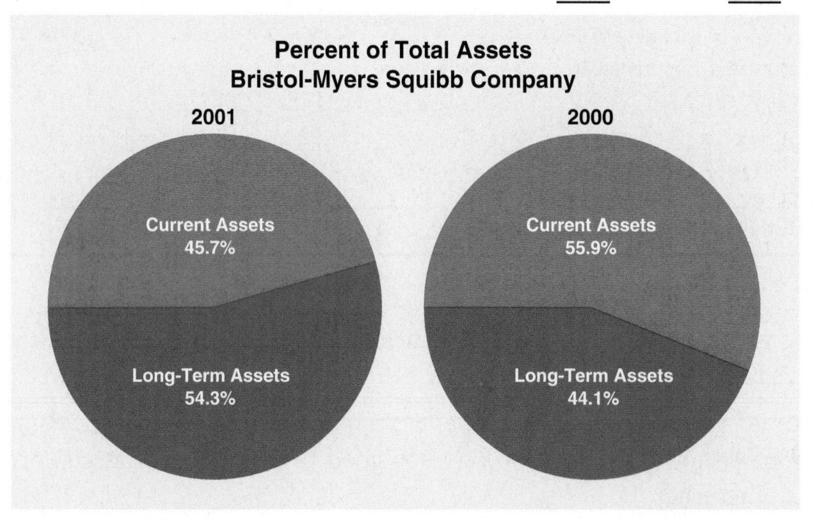

Benchmarking

Benchmarking
The practice of comparing a company to a standard set by other companies, with a view toward improvement.

Benchmarking is the practice of comparing a company to a standard set by other companies, with a view toward improvement.

Calculate the common-size percentages for the following income statement:

Net sales	$150,000
Cost of goods sold	60,000
Gross profit	90,000
Operating expense	40,000
Operating income	50,000
Income tax expense	15,000
Net income	$ 35,000

Answer:

Net sales	100%	(= $150,000 ÷ $150,000)
Cost of goods sold	40	(= $ 60,000 ÷ $150,000)
Gross profit	60	(= $ 90,000 ÷ $150,000)
Operating expense	27	(= $ 40,000 ÷ $150,000)
Operating income	33	(= $ 50,000 ÷ $150,000)
Income tax expense	10	(= $ 15,000 ÷ $150,000)
Net income	23%	(= $ 35,000 ÷ $150,000)

Benchmarking Against the Industry Average

We study a company to gain insight into its past results and future performance. Still, that knowledge is limited to the one company. We may learn that gross profit has decreased and that net income has increased steadily for the last 10 years. This information is helpful, but it does not consider how other companies have fared over the same time period. Have competitors profited even more? Managers, investors, and creditors need to know how a company compares with others in the same line of business. For example, during 2001, P&G also experienced a downturn in profits.

Exhibit 13-7 gives the common-size income statement of BMS compared with the average for the pharmaceuticals (health-care) industry. This analysis compares BMS with all other companies in its line of business. The industry averages were adapted from Risk Management Association's *Annual Statement Studies*. Analysts at Merrill Lynch, Edward Jones, and other financial institutions specialize in a particular industry and compare companies to decide which stocks to buy and sell. For example, Merrill Lynch has health-care specialists, airline-industry specialists, and so on. They compare a company with others in the same industry. Exhibit 13-7 shows that BMS compares favorably with competing companies in its industry. Its gross profit percentage is much higher than the industry average. Even though 2001 was not a great year, BMS's percentage of income from continuing operations is significantly higher than the industry average.

Benchmarking Against a Key Competitor

Common-size statements are also used to compare two or more companies. Suppose you are a financial analyst for Edward Jones Company. You are considering an investment in the stock of a health-care company, and you are choosing between BMS and P&G. A direct comparison of their financial statements in dollar amounts is not meaningful because the amounts are so different. However, you can convert the two companies' income statements to common size and compare the percentages.

Exhibit 13-7

Common-Size Income Statement Compared with the Industry Average

Bristol-Myers Squibb Company

Common-Size Income Statement for Comparison with Industry Average
Year Ended December 31, 2001

	Bristol-Myers Squibb	*Industry Average*
Net sales	100.0%	100.0%
Cost of products sold	28.7	51.6
Gross profit	71.3	48.4
Operating and other expenses	55.9	39.2
Earnings from continuing operations before income tax	15.4	9.2
Income tax expense	2.4	2.8
Earnings from continuing operations	13.0	6.4
Special items (discontinued operations, extraordinary gains and losses, and effects of accounting changes)	14.0	1.3
Net earnings	27.0%	5.1%

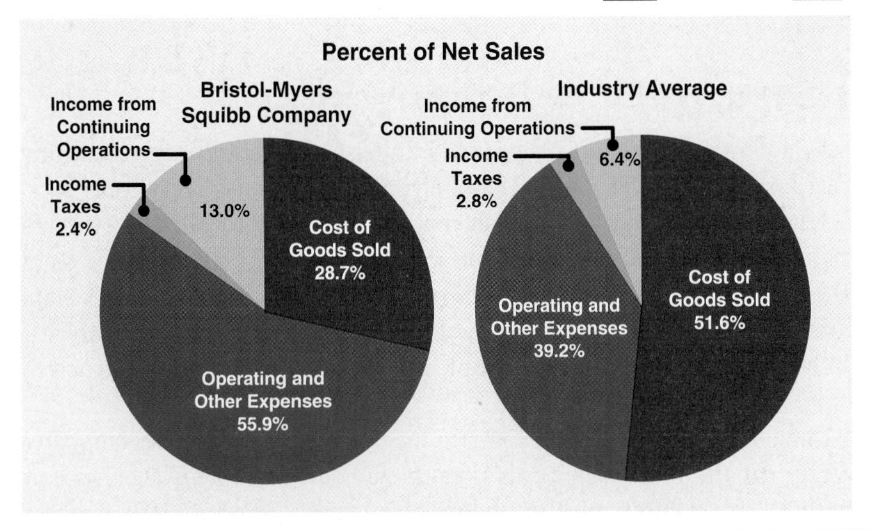

Exhibit 13-8 presents the common-size income statements of BMS and P&G. P&G serves as an excellent benchmark because most of its products are market leaders. In this comparison, BMS has higher percentages of gross profit, earnings from continuing operations, and net earnings.

✔ Check Point 13-4

DECISION MAKING: Using the Statement of Cash Flows

Objective

4 **Use** the statement of cash flows for decisions

The chapter has thus far focused on the income statement and balance sheet. We may also perform horizontal and vertical analysis on the statement of cash flows. In Chapter 12, we discussed how to prepare the statement. To continue our discussion of its role in decision making, let's use Exhibit 13-9 (p. 616), the statement of cash flows of Unix Corporation.

Analysts find the statement of cash flows more helpful for spotting weakness than for gauging success. Why? Because a *shortage* of cash can throw a company into bankruptcy, but an abundance of cash doesn't necessarily mean success. The statement of cash flows in Exhibit 13-9 reveals at least two weaknesses in Unix Corporation:

(continued on page 615 after Exhibit 13-8)

Exhibit 13-8

Common-Size Income Statement Compared with a Key Competitor

Bristol-Myers Squibb Company

Common-Size Income Statement for Comparison with Key Competitor
Year Ended During 2001

	Bristol-Myers Squibb	*Procter & Gamble*
Net sales	100.0%	100.0%
Cost of products sold	28.7	56.3
Gross profit	71.3	43.7
Operating and other expenses	55.9	31.9
Earnings from continuing operations before income tax	15.4	11.8
Income tax expense	2.4	4.3
Earnings from continuing operations	13.0	7.5
Special items (discontinued operations, extraordinary gains and losses, and effects of accounting changes)	14.0	—
Net earnings	27.0%	7.5%

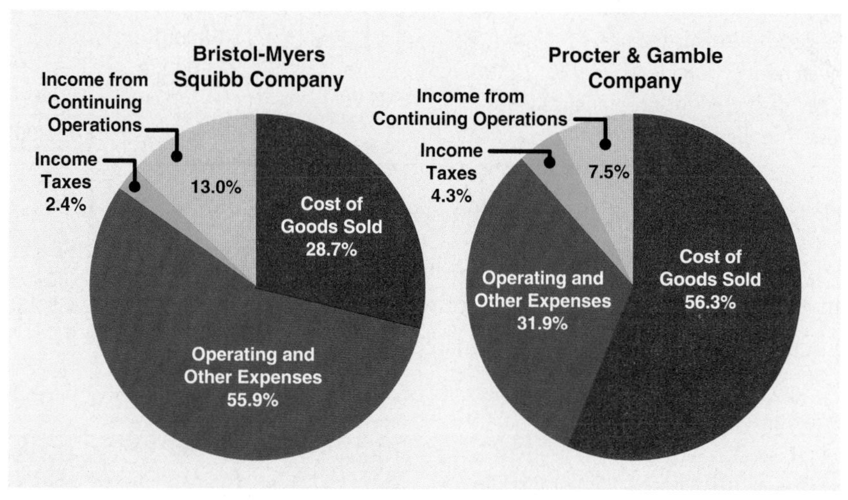

- Operations provide less cash than net income. Ordinarily, cash provided by operations exceeds net income because of the add-back of depreciation. The increases in current assets and current liabilities should cancel out over time, leaving the depreciation amount to push cash flow above net income. For Unix Corporation, current assets increased far more than current liabilities during fiscal year 2002. This may be harmless, or it may signal difficulty in collecting receivables or selling inventory. Either event may cause trouble. An analyst should examine cash flow from operations to determine why it is less than net income.
- The sale of plant assets is Unix's major source of cash. This may be a one-time situation for Unix. For example, Unix may be shifting from one line of business to another, and the company may be selling off old, unproductive assets. That may be okay. But, if the sale of plant assets continues to be the major source of cash, then the company will ultimately face a cash shortage. A company cannot continue to sell off its plant assets, or it will go out of business.

The only strength shown by the statement of cash flows is that Unix paid off more long-term debt than new borrowing. This will improve its debt ratio and credit standing.

Exhibit 13-9

Statement of Cash Flows

Unix Corporation

Statement of Cash Flows
Year Ended June 30, 2002

		Millions
Operating activities:		
Net Income		$ 35,000
Adjustments for noncash items:		
Depreciation	$ 14,000	
Net increase in current assets other than cash	(24,000)	
Net increase in current liabilities	8,000	(2,000)
Net cash provided by operating activities		33,000
Investing activities:		
Sale of property, plant, and equipment	$ 91,000	
Net cash provided by investing activities		91,000
Financing activities:		
Borrowing	$ 22,000	
Payment of long-term debt	(90,000)	
Purchase of treasury stock	(9,000)	
Payment of dividends	(23,000)	
Net cash used for financing activities		(100,000)
Increase (decrease) in cash		$ 24,000

Here are some cash-flow signs of a healthy company:

- Operations are a major source (not a use) of cash.
- Investing activities include more purchases than sales of long-term assets.
- Financing activities are not dominated by borrowing.

Mid-Chapter Summary Problem

Perform a horizontal analysis and a vertical analysis of the comparative income statement of TRE Corporation, which makes metal detectors. State whether 20X3 was a good year or a bad year, and give your reasons.

TRE Corporation

Comparative Income Statement
Months Ended December 31, 20X3 and 20X2

	20X3	20X2
Total revenues	$275,000	$225,000
Expenses:		
Cost of products sold	$194,000	$165,000
Engineering, selling, and administrative expenses	54,000	48,000
Interest expense	5,000	5,000
Income tax expense	9,000	3,000
Other expense (income)	1,000	(1,000)
Total expenses	263,000	220,000
Net earnings	$ 12,000	$ 5,000

Answer

The horizontal analysis shows that total revenues increased 22.2%. This was greater than the 19.5% increase in total expenses, resulting in a 140% increase in net earnings.

TRE Corporation

Horizontal Analysis of Comparative Income Statement
Months Ended December 31, 20X3 and 20X2

			Increase (Decrease)	
	20X3	20X2	Amount	Percent
Total revenues	$275,000	$225,000	$50,000	22.2%
Expenses:				
Cost of products sold	$194,000	$165,000	$29,000	17.6
Engineering, selling, and administrative expenses	54,000	48,000	6,000	12.5
Interest expense	5,000	5,000	—	—
Income tax expense	9,000	3,000	6,000	200.0
Other expense (income)	1,000	(1,000)	2,000	—*
Total expenses	263,000	220,000	43,000	19.5
Net earnings	$ 12,000	$ 5,000	$ 7,000	140.0%

*Percentage changes are typically not computed for shifts from a negative to a positive amount, and vice versa.

The vertical analysis shows decreases in the percentages of net sales consumed by the cost of products sold (from 73.3% to 70.5%) and by the engineering, selling, and administrative expenses (from 21.3% to 19.6%). Because these two items are TRE's largest dollar expenses, their percentage decreases are quite important. The relative reduction in expenses raised December 20X3 net earnings to 4.4% of sales, compared with 2.2% the preceding December. The overall analysis indicates that December 20X3 was significantly better than December 20X2.

TRE Corporation

Vertical Analysis of Comparative Income Statement
Months Ended December 31, 20X3 and 20X2

	20X3		20X2	
	Amount	Percent	Amount	Percent
Total revenues	$275,000	100.0%	$225,000	100.0%
Expenses:				
Cost of products sold	$194,000	70.5	$165,000	73.3
Engineering, selling, and administrative expenses	54,000	19.6	48,000	21.3
Interest expense	5,000	1.8	5,000	2.2
Income tax expense	9,000	3.3	3,000	1.4**
Other expense (income)	1,000	0.4	(1,000)	(0.4)
Total expenses	263,000	95.6	220,000	97.8
Net earnings	$ 12,000	4.4%	$ 5,000	2.2%

**Number rounded up.

Using Ratios to Make Business Decisions

current ratio, acid-test (quick) ratio, inventory turnover, days' sales in receivables, debt ratio, times-interest-earned, return on sales, return on assets, price/earnings ratio, dividend yield

Ratios are a major tool of financial analysis. A ratio expresses the relationship of one number to another. For example, if the balance sheet shows current assets of $100,000 and current liabilities of $50,000, the ratio of current assets to current liabilities is

Objective

5 Compute the standard financial ratios

$100,000 to $50,000. We can express this ratio as 2 to 1, or 2:1. Other ways to describe this ratio are (1) "current assets are 200% of current liabilities," (2) "the business has $2 in current assets for every dollar of current liabilities," or, simply, (3) "the current ratio is 2.0."

A manager, lender, or financial analyst may use any ratio that is relevant to a particular decision. Many companies include ratios in a special section of their annual financial reports. RubberMate Corporation displays ratio data in the consolidated financial summary section of its annual report. Exhibit 13-10 shows data adapted from that summary section. Investment services—Moody's, Standard & Poor's, Risk Management Association, and others—report these ratios for companies and industries.

Exhibit 13-10

Consolidated Financial Summary of RubberMate Corporation (Dollar Amounts in Millions Except per-Share Amounts)

Years Ended December 31	*20X2*	*20X1*	*20X0*
Operating Results			
Net earnings	$ 211	$ 164	$ 163
Per common share	$1.32	$1.02	$1.02
Percent of sales	10.8%	9.1%	9.8%
Return on average shareholders' equity	20.0%	17.5%	19.7%
Financial Position			
Current assets	$ 830	$ 700	$ 664
Current liabilities	$ 259	$ 223	$ 245
Working capital	$ 571	$ 477	$ 419
Current ratio	3.20	3.14	2.71

The widely used ratios we discuss in this chapter may be classified as follows:

1. Ratios that measure ability to pay current liabilities
2. Ratios that measure ability to sell inventory and collect receivables
3. Ratios that measure ability to pay long-term debt
4. Ratios that measure profitability
5. Ratios used to analyze stock as an investment

How much can a computer help in analyzing financial statements for investment purposes? Time yourself as you perform one of the financial-ratio problems in this chapter. Multiply your efforts by, say, 100 companies that you are comparing by means of this ratio. Now consider ranking these 100 companies on the basis of four or five additional ratios.

Online financial databases, such as Lexis/Nexis and the Dow Jones News Retrieval Service, offer quarterly financial figures for thousands of public corporations going back as far as 10 years. Assume that you want to compare companies' recent earnings histories. You might have the computer compare hundreds of companies on the basis of price/earnings (P/E) ratio and rates of return on stockholders' equity and total assets. The computer could then give you the names of the 20 (or however many) companies that appear most favorable in terms of these ratios. Alternatively, you could have the computer download financial statement data to your spreadsheet and compute the ratios yourself.

Measuring Ability to Pay Current Liabilities

Working capital
Current assets minus current liabilities; measures a business's ability to meet its short-term obligations with its current assets.

Working capital is defined as follows:

Working capital = Current assets − Current liabilities

Working capital measures the ability to meet short-term obligations with current assets. In general, the larger the working capital, the better able is the business to pay its debts. Recall that capital, or owners' equity, is total assets minus total liabilities. Working capital is like a "current" version of total capital. The working-capital amount alone does not give a complete picture of the entity's working-capital position, however. Consider two companies with equal working capital:

	Company A	Company B
Current assets	$100,000	$200,000
Current liabilities	50,000	150,000
Working capital	$ 50,000	$ 50,000

Both companies have working capital of $50,000, but Company A's working capital is as large as its current liabilities. Company B's working capital is only one-third as large as its current liabilities. Which business has a better working-capital position? Company A does, because its working capital is a higher percentage of current assets and current liabilities.

To use working-capital data in decision making, it is helpful to develop ratios. Two decision-making tools based on working-capital data are the *current ratio* and the *acid-test ratio.*

CURRENT RATIO. The most common ratio using current assets and current liabilities is the **current ratio**, which is current assets divided by current liabilities →. A company's current assets and current liabilities represent the core of its day-to-day operations. The current ratio measures the company's ability to pay current liabilities with current assets.

← *We introduced the current ratio in Chapter 3 (page 143).*

Current ratio
Current assets divided by current liabilities. Measures a company's ability to pay current liabilities with current assets.

Exhibit 13-11 gives the comparative income statement and balance sheet of Palisades Furniture, Inc. The current ratios of Palisades Furniture, Inc., at December 31, 20X5 and 20X4, follow, along with the average for the retail furniture industry:

	Palisades' Current Ratio		Industry
Formula	20X5	20X4	Average
$\text{Current ratio} = \frac{\text{Current assets}}{\text{Current liabilities}}$	$\frac{\$262{,}000}{\$142{,}000} = 1.85$	$\frac{\$236{,}000}{\$126{,}000} = 1.87$	1.50

The current ratio decreased slightly during 20X5. Lenders, stockholders, and managers closely monitor changes in a company's current ratio. In general, a higher current ratio indicates a stronger financial position. A higher current ratio suggests that the business has sufficient liquid assets to maintain normal business operations. Compare Palisades Furniture's current ratio of 1.85 with the industry average of 1.50 and with the current ratios of some well-known companies:

✔ Check Point 13-5

Company	Current Ratio
Chesebrough-Pond's Inc.	2.50
Wal-Mart Stores, Inc.	1.51
General Mills, Inc.	1.05

(continued at the bottom of the next page)

Exhibit 13-11

Comparative Financial Statements

Palisades Furniture, Inc.

Comparative Income Statement
Years Ended December 31, 20X5 and 20X4

	20X5	*20X4*
Net sales	$858,000	$803,000
Cost of goods sold	513,000	509,000
Gross profit	345,000	294,000
Operating expenses:		
Selling expenses	126,000	114,000
General expenses	118,000	123,000
Total operating expenses	244,000	237,000
Income from operations	101,000	57,000
Interest revenue	4,000	—
Interest expense	24,000	14,000
Income before income taxes	81,000	43,000
Income tax expense	33,000	17,000
Net income	$ 48,000	$ 26,000

Palisades Furniture, Inc.

Comparative Balance Sheet
December 31, 20X5 and 20X4

	20X5	*20X4*
Assets		
Current Assets:		
Cash	$ 29,000	$ 32,000
Accounts receivable, net	114,000	85,000
Inventories	113,000	111,000
Prepaid expenses	6,000	8,000
Total current assets	262,000	236,000
Long-term investments	18,000	9,000
Property, plant, and equipment, net	507,000	399,000
Total assets	$787,000	$644,000
Liabilities		
Current Liabilities:		
Notes payable	$ 42,000	$ 27,000
Accounts payable	73,000	68,000
Accrued liabilities	27,000	31,000
Total current liabilities	142,000	126,000
Long-term debt	289,000	198,000
Total liabilities	431,000	324,000
Stockholders' Equity		
Common stock, no par	186,000	186,000
Retained earnings	170,000	134,000
Total stockholders' equity	356,000	320,000
Total liabilities and stockholders' equity	$787,000	$644,000

What is an acceptable current ratio? The answer depends on the nature of the industry. The norm for companies in most industries is around 1.50, as reported by the Risk Management Association. Palisades Furniture's current ratio of 1.85 is within the range of those values. In most industries, a current ratio of 2.0 is considered good.

ACID-TEST RATIO. The **acid-test** (or **quick**) **ratio** tells us whether the entity could pay all its current liabilities if they came due immediately →. That is, could the company pass this *acid test*? To do so, the company would have to convert its most liquid assets to cash.

← *We saw In Chapter 5 (page 241) that the higher the acid-test ratio, the better able is the business to pay its current liabilities.*

To compute the acid-test ratio, we add cash, short-term investments, and net current receivables (accounts and notes receivable, net of allowances) and divide by current liabilities. Inventory and prepaid expenses are the two current assets *not* included in the acid-test computations because they are the least liquid of the current assets. A business may not be able to convert them to cash immediately to pay current liabilities. The acid-test ratio uses a narrower asset base to measure liquidity than the current ratio does.

Acid-test ratio
Ratio (of the sum of cash plus short-term investments plus net current receivables) to (total current liabilities). Tells whether the entity can pay all its current liabilities if they come due immediately. Also called the *quick ratio*.

Palisades Furniture's acid-test ratios for 20X5 and 20X4 follow:

Formula	Palisades' Acid-Test Ratio 20X5	Palisades' Acid-Test Ratio 20X4	Industry Average
Acid-test ratio = (Cash + short-term investments + net current receivables) / Current liabilities	($29,000 + $0 + $114,000) / $142,000 = 1.01	($32,000 + $0 + $85,000) / $126,000 = 0.93	0.40

The company's acid-test ratio improved considerably during 20X5 and is significantly better than the industry average. Compare Palisades' 1.01 acid-test ratio with the acid-test values of some well-known companies.

Company	Acid-Test Ratio
Chesebrough-Pond's Inc.	1.25
Wal-Mart Stores, Inc.	0.08
General Motors, Inc.	0.91

✔ Check Point 13-6

How can a leading company such as Wal-Mart function with such a low acid-test ratio? Wal-Mart has almost no receivables. Its inventory is priced low to turn over very quickly. The norm ranges from 0.20 for shoe retailers to 1.00 for manufacturers of equipment, as reported by the Risk Management Association. An acid-test ratio of 0.90 to 1.00 is acceptable in most industries.

Palisades Furniture's current ratio is 1.85, which looks strong, whereas the company's acid-test ratio is 1.01, also strong. Suppose Palisades' acid-test ratio were low, say 0.48. What would be the most likely reason for the discrepancy between a high current ratio and a weak acid-test ratio?

Answer:
It would appear that the company is having difficulty selling its inventory. The level of inventory must be relatively high, and the inventory is propping up the current ratio. The rate of inventory turnover may be low.

Measuring Ability to Sell Inventory and Collect Receivables

The ability to sell inventory and collect receivables is fundamental to business success. Recall the operating cycle of a merchandiser: cash to inventory to receivables and back to cash. In this section, we discuss three ratios that measure the company's ability to sell inventory and collect receivables.

Inventory turnover
Ratio of cost of goods sold to average inventory. Indicates how rapidly inventory is sold.

→ We introduced inventory turnover in Chapter 6, page 283. Average inventory is computed as follows: (Beginning inventory + Ending inventory)/2.

INVENTORY TURNOVER. Companies generally seek to achieve the quickest possible return on their investments, including their investments in inventory. The faster inventory sells, the sooner the business collects cash.

Inventory turnover is a measure of the number of times a company sells its average level of inventory during a year ←. A high rate of turnover indicates ease in selling inventory; a low turnover indicates difficulty in selling. In general, companies prefer a high inventory turnover. A value of 6 means that the company's average level of inventory has been sold six times during the year. This is generally better than a turnover of 3 or 4. However, a high value can mean that the business is not keeping enough inventory on hand, and inadequate inventory can result in lost sales if the company cannot fill a customer's order. Therefore, a business strives for the most *profitable* rate of inventory turnover, not necessarily the *highest* rate.

To compute the inventory turnover ratio, we divide cost of goods sold by the average inventory for the period. We use the cost of goods sold—not sales—in the computation because both cost of goods sold and inventory are stated *at cost*. Sales are stated at the sales value of inventory and therefore are not comparable with inventory cost.

Palisades Furniture's inventory turnover for 20X5 is

Formula	*Palisades' Inventory Turnover*	*Industry Average*
$\text{Inventory turnover} = \dfrac{\text{Cost of goods sold}}{\text{Average inventory}}$	$\dfrac{\$513{,}000}{\$112{,}000} = 4.6$	3.4

Cost of goods sold comes from the income statement (Exhibit 13-11). Average inventory is figured by averaging the beginning inventory ($111,000) and ending inventory ($113,000). (See the balance sheet, Exhibit 13-11.) If inventory levels vary greatly from month to month, compute the average by adding the 12 monthly balances and dividing the sum by 12.

Inventory turnover varies widely with the nature of the business. For example, most manufacturers of farm machinery have an inventory turnover close to three times a year. In contrast, companies that remove natural gas from the ground hold their inventory for a very short period of time and have an average turnover of 30. Palisades Furniture's turnover of 4.6 times a year is high for its industry, which has an average turnover of 3.4. Palisades' high inventory turnover results from its policy of keeping little inventory on hand. The company takes customer orders and has its suppliers ship directly to some customers.

Inventory turnover rates can vary greatly within a company. At Toys "Я" Us, diapers and formula turn over more than 12 times a year, while seasonal toys turn over less than 3 times a year. The entire Toys "Я" Us inventory turns over an average of 3 times a year. The company's inventory is at its lowest point on January 31 and at its highest point around October 31.

To evaluate fully a company's inventory turnover, we must compare the ratio over time. A sharp decline in the rate of inventory turnover or a steady decline over a long period suggests the need for corrective action.

Accounts receivable turnover
Measures a company's ability to collect cash from credit customers. To compute accounts receivable turnover, divide net credit sales by average net accounts receivable.

ACCOUNTS RECEIVABLE TURNOVER. **Accounts receivable turnover** measures a company's ability to collect cash from credit customers. In general, the higher the ratio, the more successfully the business collects cash and the better off its operations. However, a receivable turnover that is too high may indicate that credit is too tight, causing the loss of sales to good customers. To compute the accounts receivable turnover, we divide net credit sales by average net accounts receivable. The resulting ratio indicates how many times during the year the average level of receivables was turned into cash.

Palisades Furniture's accounts receivable turnover ratio for 20X5 is computed as follows:

Formula	*Palisades' Accounts Receivable Turnover*	*Industry Average*
$\text{Accounts receivable turnover} = \dfrac{\text{Net credit sales}}{\text{Average net accounts receivable}}$	$\dfrac{\$858{,}000}{\$99{,}500} = 8.6$	51.0

Palisades Furniture makes all sales on credit. If the company makes both cash and credit sales, this ratio is best computed by using only net credit sales. Average net accounts receivable is figured by adding the beginning accounts receivable balance ($85,000) and the ending balance ($114,000), then dividing by 2. If the accounts receivable balances exhibit a seasonal pattern, compute the average by using the 12 monthly balances.

Palisades' receivable turnover of 8.6 times per year is much slower than the industry average. The explanation is simple: Palisades is a hometown store that sells to local people who tend to pay their bills over a period of time. Many larger furniture stores sell their receivables to other companies called *factors*, a practice that keeps receivables low and receivable turnover high. But companies that factor (sell) their receivables receive less than face value of the receivables. Palisades Furniture follows a different strategy.

The sales of Comptronix, a manufacturer of computerized metering equipment, grew far faster than its receivables. Would this situation create an unusually high or an unusually low accounts receivable turnover?

Answer:
Receivable turnover would be unusually high. This high ratio would look strange in relation to the company's past measures of receivable turnover.

Days' sales in receivables
Ratio of average net accounts receivable to one day's sale. Indicates how many days' sales remain in Accounts Receivable awaiting collection. Also called the *collection period.*

DAYS' SALES IN RECEIVABLES. Businesses must convert accounts receivable to cash. All else equal, the lower the Accounts Receivable balance, the more successful the business has been in converting receivables into cash, and the better off the business is.

The **days'-sales-in-receivables** ratio tells us how many days' sales remain in Accounts Receivable →. To compute the ratio, we follow a two-step process:

← *Recall from Chapter 5 (page 240) that days' sales in receivables indicates how many days it takes to collect the average level of receivables.*

First, divide net sales by 365 days to figure the average sales amount for one day. *Second*, divide this average day's sales amount into average net accounts receivable.

The data to compute this ratio for Palisades Furniture, Inc. for 20X5 are taken from the income statement and the balance sheet (Exhibit 13-11):

Formula	Palisades' Days' Sales in Accounts Receivable	Industry Average
Days' Sales in *average* Accounts Receivable:		
1. One day's sales $= \frac{\text{Net sales}}{\text{365 days}}$	$\frac{\$858{,}000}{\text{365 days}} = \$2{,}351$	
2. Days' sales in average accounts receivable $= \frac{\text{Average net accounts receivable}}{\text{One day's sales}}$	$\frac{\$99{,}500}{\$2{,}351} = \text{42 days}$	7 days

✔ Check Point 13-7

Days' sales in average receivables can also be computed in a single step: $99,500/($858,000/365 days) = 42 days.

Palisades' ratio tells us that 42 average days' sales remain in accounts receivable and need to be collected. The company will increase its cash flow if it can decrease this ratio. To detect any changes over time in the firm's ability to collect its receivables, let's compute the days'-sales-in-receivables ratio at the beginning and the end of 20X5:

Days' Sales in ENDING 20X4 Accounts Receivable:

$$\text{One day's sales} = \frac{\$803{,}000}{\text{365 days}} = \$2{,}200 \qquad \begin{array}{c}\text{Days' sales in}\\ \textit{ENDING 20X4}\\ \text{accounts receivable}\end{array} = \frac{\$85{,}000}{\$2{,}200} = \begin{array}{c}\text{39 days at the}\\ \text{beginning of 20X5}\end{array}$$

Days' Sales in ENDING 20X5 Accounts Receivable:

$$\text{One day's sales} = \frac{\$858{,}000}{\text{365 days}} = \$2{,}351 \qquad \begin{array}{c}\text{Days' sales in}\\ \textit{ENDING 20X5}\\ \text{accounts receivable}\end{array} = \frac{\$114{,}000}{\$2{,}351} = \begin{array}{c}\text{48 days at the}\\ \text{end of 20X5}\end{array}$$

This analysis shows a slowdown in Palisades Furniture's collection of receivables; days' sales in accounts receivable have increased from 39 at the beginning of the year to 48 at year end. The credit and collection department should strengthen its collection efforts. Otherwise, the company may experience a cash shortage in 20X6 and beyond.

The days' sales in receivables measure for Palisades is much higher (worse) than the industry average because Palisades collects its own receivables. Many other furniture stores sell their receivables and carry fewer days' sales in receivables. Palisades Furniture remains competitive because of its personal relationship with its customers. Without their good paying habits, the company's cash flow would suffer.

Measuring Ability to Pay Long-Term Debt

The ratios discussed so far give us insight into current assets and current liabilities. They help us measure a business's ability to sell inventory, to collect receivables, and to pay current liabilities. Most businesses also have long-term debt. Two key indicators of a business's ability to pay long-term liabilities are the *debt ratio* and the *times-interest-earned ratio*.

Debt Ratio. Suppose you are a loan officer at a bank and you are evaluating loan applications from two companies with equal sales and total assets. Both companies have asked to borrow $500,000 and have agreed to repay the loan over a 10-year period. The first firm already owes $600,000 to another bank. The second owes only $250,000. Other things equal, to which company are you more likely to lend money at a lower interest rate? Company 2, because the bank faces less risk by loaning to Company 2. That company owes less to creditors than Company 1 owes.

Debt ratio
Ratio of total liabilities to total assets. States the proportion of a company's assets that is financed with debt.

This relationship between total liabilities and total assets—called the **debt ratio**—tells us the proportion of the company's assets that it has financed with debt →. If the debt ratio is 1, then debt has been used to finance all the assets. A debt ratio of 0.50 means that the company has used debt to finance half its assets and that the owners of the business have financed the other half. The higher the debt ratio, the higher the strain of paying interest each year and the principal amount at maturity. The lower the ratio, the lower the business's future obligations. Creditors view a high debt ratio with caution. If a business seeking financing already has large liabilities, then additional debt payments may be too much for the business to handle. To help protect themselves, creditors generally charge higher interest rates on new borrowing to companies with an already high debt ratio.

← *We introduced the debt ratio in Chapter 3, page 144.*

The debt ratios for Palisades Furniture at the end of 20X5 and 20X4 follow:

Formula	Palisades' Debt Ratio 20X5	Palisades' Debt Ratio 20X4	Industry Average
Debt ratio = $\frac{\text{Total liabilities}}{\text{Total assets}}$	$\frac{\$431,000}{\$787,000} = 0.55$	$\frac{\$324,000}{\$644,000} = 0.50$	0.64

Palisades Furniture expanded operations by financing the purchase of property, plant, and equipment through borrowing, which is a common practice. This expansion explains the firm's increased debt ratio. Even after the increase in 20X5, the company's debt is not very high. Risk Management Association reports that the average debt ratio for most companies ranges around 0.57 to 0.67, with relatively little variation from company to company. Palisades' 0.55 debt ratio indicates a fairly low-risk debt position compared with the retail furniture industry average of 0.64.

Times-Interest-Earned Ratio. The debt ratio says nothing about the ability to pay interest expense. Analysts use a second ratio—the **times-interest-earned ratio**—to relate income to interest expense. To compute this ratio, we divide income from operations (operating income) by interest expense. This ratio measures the number of times that operating income can *cover* interest expense. This ratio is also called the *interest-coverage ratio*. A high times-interest-earned ratio indicates ease in paying interest expense; a low value suggests difficulty.

Times-interest-earned ratio
Ratio of income from operations to interest expense. Measures the number of times that operating income can cover interest expense. Also called the *interest-coverage ratio*.

Calculation of Palisades' times-interest-earned ratios is as follows:

Formula	Palisades' Times-Interest-Earned Ratio 20X5	Palisades' Times-Interest-Earned Ratio 20X4	Industry Average
Times-interest-earned ratio = $\frac{\text{Income from operations}}{\text{Interest expense}}$	$\frac{\$101,000}{\$24,000} = 4.21$	$\frac{\$57,000}{\$14,000} = 4.07$	2.80

The company's times-interest-earned ratio increased in 20X5. This is a favorable sign, especially because the company's short-term notes payable and long-term debt rose substantially during the year. We can conclude that Palisades Furniture's new plant assets have earned more than they have cost the business in interest expense.

✔ Check Point 13-8

The company's times-interest-earned ratio of around 4.00 is significantly better than the 2.80 average for furniture retailers. The norm for U.S. business, as reported by Risk Management Association, falls in the range of 2.0 to 3.0 for most companies. On the basis of its debt ratio and its times-interest-earned ratio, Palisades Furniture appears to have little difficulty *servicing its debt*, that is, paying its liabilities.

Measuring Profitability

The fundamental goal of business is to earn a profit. Ratios that measure profitability are reported in the business press, by investment services, and in companies' annual financial reports.

Suppose you are a personal financial planner who helps clients select stock investments. One client invests in new software. Over the next few years, you expect eBay to earn higher rates of return on its investments than analysts are forecasting for Yahoo! Which company's stock will you recommend? Probably eBay's—for reasons that you will better understand after studying four rate-of-return measurements.

Rate of return on net sales Ratio of net income to net sales. A measure of profitability. Also called *return on sales.*

RATE OF RETURN ON NET SALES. In business, the term *return* is used broadly and loosely as an evaluation of profitability. Consider a ratio called the **rate of return on net sales,** or simply *return on sales*. (The word *net* is usually omitted for convenience, even though the net sales figure is used to compute the ratio.) This ratio shows the percentage of each sales dollar earned as net income. The rate-of-return-on-sales ratios for Palisades Furniture are calculated as follows:

	Palisades' Rate of Return on Sales		
Formula	***20X5***	***20X4***	***Industry Average***
$\text{Rate of return on sales} = \frac{\text{Net income}}{\text{Net sales}}$	$\frac{\$48{,}000}{\$858{,}000} = 0.056$	$\frac{\$26{,}000}{\$803{,}000} = 0.032$	0.008

Companies strive for a high rate of return. The higher the rate of return, the more sales dollars are providing income to the business and the fewer sales dollars are absorbed by expenses. The increase in Palisades Furniture's return on sales is significant and identifies the company as more successful than the average furniture store. Compare Palisades' rate of return on sales to the rates of some other companies:

Company	***Rate of Return on Sales***
eBay	.121
Bristol-Myers Squibb	.270
Wal-Mart	.031

One strategy for increasing the rate of return on sales is to develop a product that commands a premium price, such as Häagen-Dazs ice cream, Mercedes-Benz automobiles, and Maytag appliances. Another strategy is to control costs. If successful, either strategy converts a higher proportion of sales into net income and increases the rate of return on net sales.

A return measure can be computed on any revenue or sales amount. Return on net sales, as we have seen, is net income divided by net sales. *Return on total revenues* is net income divided by total revenues. A company can compute a return on any portion of revenue as its information needs dictate.

Rate of return on total assets
Net income plus interest expense, divided by average total assets. This ratio measures a company's success in using its assets to earn income for the persons who finance the business. Also called *return on assets*.

RATE OF RETURN ON TOTAL ASSETS. The **rate of return on total assets,** or simply *return on assets*, measures a company's success in using its assets to earn a profit →. Creditors have loaned money to the company, and the interest they receive is the return on their investment. Shareholders have invested in the company's stock, and net income is their return.

← *We first discussed the rate of return on total assets in Chapter 9, page 436.*

The sum of interest expense and net income is thus the return to the two groups that have financed the company's operations. This sum is the numerator of the return-on-assets ratio. Average total assets is the denominator. Computation of the return-on-assets ratio for Palisades Furniture is as follows:

Formula	Palisades' 20X5 Rate of Return on Total Assets	Industry Average
$\text{Rate of return on assets} = \dfrac{\text{Net income} + \text{Interest expense}}{\text{Average total assets}}$	$\dfrac{\$48{,}000 + \$24{,}000}{\$715{,}500} = 0.101$	0.078

To compute average total assets, we take the average of beginning and ending total assets from the comparative balance sheet. Compare Palisades Furniture's rate of return on assets to the rates of some other companies:

Company	Rate of Return on Assets
General Electric	0.053
Procter & Gamble	0.108
Dell Computer	0.175

Rate of return on common stockholders' equity
Net income minus preferred dividends, divided by average common stockholders' equity. A measure of profitability. Also called *return on equity*.

RATE OF RETURN ON COMMON STOCKHOLDERS' EQUITY. A popular measure of profitability is **rate of return on common stockholders' equity,** which is often shortened to **return on stockholders' equity,** or simply *return on equity* →. This ratio shows the relationship between net income and common stockholders' investment in the company—how much income is earned for every $1 invested by the common shareholders.

← *We examined this ratio in detail in Chapter 9. For a review, see page 436.*

To compute this ratio, we first subtract preferred dividends from net income. This calculation provides net income available to the common stockholders, which we need to compute the ratio. We then divide net income available to common stockholders by the average stockholders' equity during the year. Common stockholders' equity is total stockholders' equity minus preferred equity. The 20X5 rate of return on common stockholders' equity for Palisades Furniture is calculated as follows:

Formula	Palisades' 20X5 Rate of Return on Common Stockholders' Equity	Industry Average
$\text{Rate of return on common stockholders' equity} = \dfrac{\text{Net income} - \text{Preferred dividends}}{\text{Average common stockholders' equity}}$	$\dfrac{\$48{,}000 - \$0}{\$338{,}000} = 0.142$	0.121

We compute average equity by using the beginning and ending balances [($356,000 + $320,000)/2 = $338,000]. Common stockholders' equity is total equity minus preferred equity.

Observe that Palisades' return on equity (0.142) is higher than its return on assets (0.101). This difference results from borrowing at one rate—say, 8%—and investing the funds to earn a higher rate, such as the firm's 14.2% return on stockholders' equity. This practice is called **trading on the equity**, or using **leverage** ←. It is directly related to the debt ratio. The higher the debt ratio, the higher the leverage. Companies that finance operations with debt are said to *leverage* their positions.

→ *For a review of trading on the equity, see Chapter 8, page 388.*

Trading on the equity
Earning more income on borrowed money than the related interest expense, thereby increasing the earnings for the owners of the business. Aslo called *leverage*.

For Palisades Furniture and for many other companies, leverage increases profitability. This is not always the case, however. Leverage can have a negative impact on profitability. If revenues drop, debt and interest expense still must be paid. Therefore, leverage is a double-edged sword, increasing profits during good times but compounding losses during bad times.

Compare Palisades Furniture's rate of return on common stockholders' equity with the rates of some leading companies:

Company	*Rate of Return on Common Equity*
General Electric	0.26
Procter & Gamble	0.24
Dell Computer	0.40

✔ **Check Point 13-9**

Palisades Furniture is not as profitable as these leading companies—perhaps because the larger companies must satisfy millions of stockholders worldwide. Palisades Furniture, on the other hand, is a much smaller company with stockholders who do not demand so high a return on their equity.

EARNINGS PER SHARE OF COMMON STOCK. *Earnings per share of common stock*, or simply ← **earnings per share (EPS)**, is perhaps the most widely quoted of all financial statistics. EPS is the only ratio that must appear on the face of the income statement. EPS is the amount of net income per share of the company's outstanding *common* stock.

→ *Chapter 11, pages 513–514, provide detailed treatment of EPS.*

Earnings per share (EPS)
Amount of a company's net income per share of its outstanding common stock.

Earnings per share is computed by dividing net income available to common stockholders by the number of common shares outstanding during the year. Preferred dividends are subtracted from net income because the preferred stockholders have a prior claim to their dividends. Palisades Furniture, Inc., has no preferred stock outstanding and thus has no preferred dividends. Computation of the firm's EPS for 20X5 and 20X4 follows (the company had 10,000 shares of common stock outstanding throughout 20X4 and 20X5):

Formula	Palisades' Earnings per Share *20X5*	*20X4*
Earnings per share of common stock $= \dfrac{\text{Net income} - \text{Preferred dividends}}{\text{Number of shares of common stock outstanding}}$	$\dfrac{\$48{,}000 - \$0}{10{,}000} = \$4.80$	$\dfrac{\$26{,}000 - \$0}{10{,}000} = \$2.60$

Palisades Furniture's EPS increased 85%. Its stockholders should not expect such a significant boost in EPS every year. Most companies strive to increase EPS by

10% to 15% annually, and the more successful companies do so. But even the most dramatic upward trends include an occasional bad year.

Analyzing Stock Investments

Investors purchase stock to earn a return on their investment. This return consists of two parts: (1) gains (or losses) from selling the stock at a price above or below purchase price, and (2) dividends. The ratios we examine in this section help analysts evaluate stock in terms of market price or dividend payments.

PRICE/EARNINGS RATIO. The **price/earnings ratio** is the ratio of the market price of a share of common stock to the company's earnings per share. This ratio, abbreviated P/E, appears in *The Wall Street Journal* stock listings. P/E ratios play an important part in decisions to buy, hold, and sell stocks. They indicate the market price of $1 of earnings.

Price/earnings ratio
Ratio of the market price of a share of common stock to the company's earnings per share. Measures the value that the stock market places on $1 of a company's earnings.

Calculations for the P/E ratios of Palisades Furniture, Inc. follow. The market price of its common stock was $60 at the end of 20X5 and $35 at the end of 20X4. These prices can be obtained from a financial publication, a stockbroker, or the company's Web site.

	Palisades' Price/Earnings Ratio	
Formula	***20X5***	***20X4***
$\text{P/E ratio} = \dfrac{\text{Market price per share of common stock}}{\text{Earnings per share}}$	$\dfrac{\$60.00}{\$4.80} = 12.5$	$\dfrac{\$35.00}{\$2.60} = 13.5$

Given Palisades Furniture's 20X5 P/E ratio of 12.5, we would say that the company's stock is selling at 12.5 times earnings. The decline from the 20X5 P/E ratio of 13.5 is no cause for alarm because the market price of the stock is not under Palisades Furniture's control. Net income is more controllable, and it increased during 20X5.

Like most other ratios, P/E ratios vary from industry to industry. P/E ratios range from 8 to 10 for electric utilities (Pennsylvania Power and Light, for example) to 40 or more for "glamour stocks" such as Auto Zone, an auto parts chain, and Oracle Systems, which develops computer software. The P/E ratios of many Internet stocks have reached into the hundreds.

✔ Check Point 13-10

The higher a stock's P/E ratio, the higher its *downside risk*—the risk that the stock's market price will fall. Many investors interpret a sharp increase in a stock's P/E ratio as a signal to sell the stock.

DIVIDEND YIELD. **Dividend yield** is the ratio of dividends per share of stock to the stock's market price per share. This ratio measures the percentage of a stock's market value that is returned annually as dividends, an important concern of stockholders. *Preferred* stockholders, who invest primarily to receive dividends, pay special attention to this ratio.

Dividend yield
Ratio of dividends per share of stock to the stock's market price per share. Tells the percentage of a stock's market value that the company returns to stockholders as dividends.

Palisades Furniture paid annual cash dividends of $1.20 per share of common stock in 20X5 and $1.00 in 20X4, and market prices of the company's common stock were $60 in 20X5 and $35 in 20X4. Calculation of the firm's dividend yields on common stock is as follows:

Formula	Dividend Yield on Palisades' Common Stock 20X5	20X4
$\text{Dividend yield on common stock}^* = \dfrac{\text{Dividend per share of common stock}}{\text{Market price per share of common stock}}$	$\dfrac{\$1.20}{\$60.00} = .020$	$\dfrac{\$1.00}{\$35.00} = .029$

*Dividend yields may also be calculated for preferred stock.

An investor who buys Palisades Furniture common stock for $60 can expect to receive almost 2% of the investment annually in the form of cash dividends. Dividend yields vary widely, from 5% to 8% for older, established firms (such as P&G and General Motors) down to the range of 0% to 3% for young, growth-oriented companies. Intel Corporation, for example, pays a cash dividend of only $0.08 per share, for a dividend yield of .003. Oracle and eBay do not pay cash dividends.

Book value per share of common stock Common stockholders' equity divided by the number of shares of common stock outstanding. The recorded amount for each share of common stock outstanding.

BOOK VALUE PER SHARE OF COMMON STOCK. **Book value per share of common stock** is simply common stockholders' equity divided by the number of shares of common stock outstanding. Common shareholders' equity equals total stockholders' equity less preferred equity. Palisades Furniture has no preferred stock outstanding. Calculations of its book-value-per-share-of-common-stock ratios follow. Recall that 10,000 shares of common stock were outstanding at the end of years 20X5 and 20X4.

Formula	Book Value per Share of Palisades' Common Stock 20X5	20X4
$\text{Book value per share of common stock} = \dfrac{\text{Total stockholders' equity} - \text{Preferred equity}}{\text{Number of shares of common stock outstanding}}$	$\dfrac{\$356{,}000 - \$0}{10{,}000} = \$35.60$	$\dfrac{\$320{,}000 - \$0}{10{,}000} = \$32.00$

➔ Recall from Chapter 9, pages 434 to 435, that book value depends on historical costs, while market value depends on investors' outlook for dividends and an increase in the stock's value.

Book value indicates the recorded accounting amount for each share of common stock outstanding. Many experts argue that book value is not useful for investment analysis ←. It bears no relationship to market value and provides little information beyond stockholders' equity reported on the balance sheet. But some investors base their investment decisions on book value. For example, some investors rank stocks on the basis of the ratio of market price to book value. To these investors, the lower the ratio, the more attractive the stock. These investors are called "value" investors, as contrasted with "growth" investors, who focus more on trends in a company's net income.

The Limitations of Financial Analysis

EVA

Business decisions are made in a world of uncertainty. As useful as ratios are, they have limitations. We may liken their use in decision making to a physician's use of a thermometer. A reading of 101.6 Fahrenheit indicates that something is wrong with the patient, but the temperature alone does not indicate what the problem is or how to cure it.

In financial analysis, a sudden drop in a company's current ratio signals that *something* is wrong, but this change does not identify the problem or show how to correct it. The business manager must analyze the figures that go into the ratio to determine whether current assets have decreased, current liabilities have increased, or both. If current assets have dropped, is the problem a cash shortage? Are accounts receivable down? Are inventories too low? Only by analyzing the individual items that make up the ratio can the manager determine how to solve the problem. The manager must evaluate data on all ratios in the light of other information about the company and about its particular line of business, such as increased competition or a slowdown in the economy.

Objective

6 **Use** ratios in decision making

✔ Check Point 13-11

✔ Check Point 13-12

Legislation, international affairs, competition, scandals, and many other factors can turn profits into losses, and vice versa. To be most useful, ratios should be analyzed over a period of years to take into account a representative group of these factors. Any 1 year, or even any 2 years, may not be representative of the company's performance over the long term.

Another way to evaluate company performance is with EVA®, a measure of change in stockholder wealth.

Economic Value Added

Objective

7 **Measure** the economic value added by operations

The top managers of Coca-Cola, Quaker Oats, and other leading companies use **economic value added (EVA®)** to evaluate a company's operating performance. EVA® combines the concepts of accounting income and corporate finance to measure whether the company's operations have increased stockholder wealth. EVA® can be computed as follows:

Economic value added (EVA) Used to evaluate a company's operating performance. EVA combines the concepts of accounting income and corporate finance to measure whether the company's operations have increased stockholder wealth. EVA = Net income + Interest expense − Capital charge.

$$\text{EVA}^{®} = \text{Net income} + \text{Interest expense} - \text{Capital charge}$$

where

$$\text{Capital charge} = \left(\begin{array}{c}\text{Notes}\\\text{payable}\end{array} + \begin{array}{c}\text{Loans}\\\text{payable}\end{array} + \begin{array}{c}\text{Long-term}\\\text{debt}\end{array} + \begin{array}{c}\text{Stockholders'}\\\text{equity}\end{array}\right) \times \begin{array}{c}\text{Cost of}\\\text{capital}\end{array}$$

All amounts for the EVA® computation, except the cost of capital, are taken from the financial statements. The **cost of capital** is a weighted average of the returns demanded by the company's stockholders and lenders. The cost of capital varies with the company's level of risk. For example, stockholders would demand a higher return from a start-up computer software company than from Coca-Cola because the new company is untested and therefore more risky. Lenders would also charge the new company a higher interest rate because of this greater risk. Thus, the new company has a higher cost of capital than Coca-Cola.

Cost of capital A weighted average of the returns demanded by the company's stockholders and lenders.

The cost of capital is a major topic in finance classes. In the following discussions we assume a value for the cost of capital (such as 10%, 12%, or 15%) to illustrate the computation of EVA® and its use in decision making.

The idea behind EVA® is that the returns to the company's stockholders (net income) and to its creditors (interest expense) should exceed the company's capital charge. The **capital charge** is the amount that stockholders and lenders *charge* a company for the use of their money. A positive EVA® amount indicates an increase in stockholder wealth, and the company's stock should remain attractive to investors. If the EVA® measure is negative, stockholders will probably be unhappy with the company and sell its stock, resulting in a decrease in the stock's price. Different companies tailor the EVA® computation to meet their own needs.

Capital charge The amount that stockholders and lenders charge a company for the use of their money. Calculated as (Notes payable + Loans payable + Long-term debt + Stockholders' equity) × Cost of capital.

The Coca-Cola Company is a leading user of EVA®. Coca-Cola's EVA® for 2001 can be computed as follows, assuming a 10% cost of capital for the company (dollar amounts in millions):

$$\text{Coca-Cola's EVA}^{®} = \text{Net income} + \text{Interest expense} - \left(\text{Loans and notes payable} + \text{Long-term debt} + \text{Stockholders' equity}\right) \times \text{Cost of capital}$$

$$= \$3{,}969 + \$289 - [(\$3{,}743 + \$1{,}375 + \$11{,}366) \times 0.12]$$

$$= \$4{,}258 - \$16{,}484 \times 0.12$$

$$= \$4{,}258 - \$1{,}978$$

$$= \$2{,}280$$

By this measure, Coca-Cola's operations during 2001 added $2.28 billion ($2,280 million) of value to its stockholders' wealth after meeting the company's capital charge. This performance is outstanding.

✔ Check Point 13-13

DECISION: Red Flags in Financial Statement Analysis

The accounting scandals of 2002 highlighted the importance of *red flags* that may signal financial trouble. If the following conditions are present, the company may be too risky.

- **Earnings Problems.** Have income from continuing operations and net income decreased significantly for several years in a row? Has income turned into a loss? This may be okay for a company in a cyclical industry, such as an airline or a home builder, but many companies cannot survive consecutive loss years.
- **Decreased Cash Flow.** Cash flow validates earnings. Is cash flow from operations consistently lower than net income? Are the sales of plant assets a major source of cash? If so, the company may face a cash shortage.
- **Too Much Debt.** How does the company's debt ratio compare to that of major competitors and to the industry average? If the debt ratio is much higher than average, the company may be unable to pay debts during tough times.
- **Inability to Collect Receivables.** Are days' sales in receivables growing faster than for other companies in the industry? A cash shortage may be looming.
- **Buildup of Inventories.** Is inventory turnover slowing down? If so, the company may be unable to move products, or it may be overstating inventory. Recall from the cost-of-goods-sold model that one of the easiest ways to overstate net income is to overstate ending inventory.
- **Movement of Sales, Inventory, and Receivables.** Sales, receivables, and inventory generally move together. Increased sales lead to higher receivables and require more inventory in order to meet demand. Strange movements among these items may spell trouble.

Efficient Markets

Efficient capital market A capital market in which market prices fully reflect all information available to the public.

An **efficient capital market** is one in which market prices fully reflect all information available to the public. Because stocks are priced in full recognition of all publicly accessible data, it can be argued that the stock market is efficient. Market efficiency has implications for management action and for investor decisions. It means that managers cannot fool the market with accounting gimmicks. If the information is available, the market as a whole can translate accounting data into a "fair" price for the company's stock.

Suppose you are the president of Anacomp corporation. Reported earnings per share are $4, and the stock price is $40—so the P/E ratio is 10. You believe the corporation's stock is underpriced in comparison with other companies in the same industry. To correct this situation, you are considering changing your depreciation method from accelerated to straight-line. The accounting change will increase earnings per share to $5. Will the stock price then rise to $50? Probably not, the company's stock price will probably remain at $40 because the market can understand the accounting change. After all, the company merely changed its method of computing depreciation. There is no effect on the company's cash flows, and its economic position is unchanged. An efficient market interprets data in light of their true underlying meaning.

In an efficient market, the search for "underpriced" stock is fruitless unless the investor has relevant private information. Moreover, it is unlawful to invest on the basis of *inside* information. For outside investors, an appropriate strategy seeks to manage risk, diversify, and minimize transaction costs. The role of financial statement analysis consists mainly of identifying the risks of various stocks to manage the risk of the overall investment portfolio.

The Decision Guidelines summarize the most widely used ratios. The Excel Application Problem provides an opportunity to apply your understanding of the ratios.

Decision Guidelines

USING RATIOS IN FINANCIAL STATEMENT ANALYSIS

Lane and Kay Collins operate a financial services firm. They manage other people's money and do most of their own financial-statement analysis. How do they measure companies' ability to pay bills, sell inventory, collect receivables, and so on? They use the standard ratios we have covered throughout this book.

Ratio	Computation	Information Provided
Measuring ability to pay current liabilities:		
1. Current ratio	$\frac{\text{Current assets}}{\text{Current liabilities}}$	Measures ability to pay current liabilities with current assets
2. Acid-test (quick) ratio	$\frac{\text{Cash} + \text{Short-term investments} + \text{Net current receivables}}{\text{Current liabilities}}$	Shows ability to pay all current liabilities if they come due immediately
Measuring ability to sell inventory and collect receivables:		
3. Inventory turnover	$\frac{\text{Cost of goods sold}}{\text{Average inventory}}$	Indicates saleability of inventory—the number of times a company sells its average inventory level during a year
4. Accounts receivable turnover	$\frac{\text{Net credit sales}}{\text{Average net accounts receivable}}$	Measures ability to collect cash from credit customers
5. Days' sales in receivables	$\frac{\text{Average net accounts receivable}}{\text{One day's sales}}$	Shows how many days' sales remain in Accounts Receivable—how many days it takes to collect the average level of receivables
Measuring ability to pay long-term debt:		
6. Debt ratio	$\frac{\text{Total liabilities}}{\text{Total assets}}$	Indicates percentage of assets financed with debt

7. Times-interest-earned ratio	$\frac{\text{Income from operations}}{\text{Interest expense}}$	Measures the number of times operating income can cover interest expense
Measuring profitability:		
8. Rate of return on net sales	$\frac{\text{Net income}}{\text{Net sales}}$	Shows the percentage of each sales dollar earned as net income
9. Rate of return on total assets	$\frac{\text{Net income + Interest expense}}{\text{Average total assets}}$	Measures how profitably a company uses its assets
10. Rate of return on common stockholders' equity	$\frac{\text{Net income – Preferred dividends}}{\text{Average common stockholders' equity}}$	Gauges how much income is earned with the money invested by common shareholders
11. Earnings per share of common stock	$\frac{\text{Net income – Preferred dividends}}{\text{Number of shares of common stock outstanding}}$	Gives the amount of net income per one share of the company's common stock
Analyzing stock as an investment:		
12. Price/earnings ratio	$\frac{\text{Market price per share of common stock}}{\text{Earnings per share}}$	Indicates the market price of $1 of earnings
13. Dividend yield	$\frac{\text{Dividend per share of common (or preferred) stock}}{\text{Market price per share of common (or preferred) stock}}$	Shows the percentage of a stock's market value returned as dividends to stockholders each period
14. Book value per share of common stock	$\frac{\text{Total stockholders' equity – Preferred equity}}{\text{Number of shares of common stock outstanding}}$	Indicates the recorded accounting amount for each share of common stock outstanding

Excel Application Problem

Goal: Create an Excel worksheet that calculates financial ratios to compare Fossil and The Movado Group. Then use the results to determine which company has the stronger financial performance.

Scenario: You've saved $5,000 from your summer internship at Fossil. You'd like to invest your savings in the stock of your employer, but your parents think the better investment would be stock in The Movado Group, which has watch brands such as ESQ, Concord, Coach, Tommy Hilfiger, and of course, Movado. Before making your purchase, you decide to create an Excel worksheet that compares both companies on several key financial ratios.

Your task is to create an Excel worksheet to compare the following ratios for Fossil and The Movado Group.

1. Acid-test (quick) ratio
2. Inventory turnover
3. Debt ratio
4. Return on net sales
5. Price/earnings ratio

When done with the worksheet, answer the following questions:

1. Which company is in a better position to pay all current liabilities if they come due immediately?
2. Which company's inventory is more "saleable?"
3. Which company is financing more of its assets with debt?
4. Which company earned more profit, as a percentage, on each sales dollar?
5. Which company's earnings have a higher market price per dollar of earnings?

Step-by-step:

1. Locate the data required for each ratio in the annual reports of Fossil (www.fossil.com) and The Movado Group (www.movadogroupinc.com). Note: For fiscal year-end stock prices, go to www.morningstar.com.
2. Open a new Excel worksheet.
3. Create a bold-faced heading for your spreadsheet that contains the following:

a. Chapter 13 Decision Guidelines
b. Using Ratios in Financial Statement Analysis
c. Fossil and The Movado Group Comparison
d. Today's date

4. In the first column, enter the names of all five ratios. Skip a row between each ratio name.
5. Create bold-faced, underlined column headings for Fossil and The Movado Group. Underneath, enter the "As Of" date for the financial statements used in the analysis (fiscal year-ends may not match exactly).
6. Enter the data located in step 1, using the correct ratio formulas found in the Decision Guidelines. For the P/E ratio, use basic EPS in the denominator. Format all cells as necessary.
7. Save your work, and print a copy for your files.

End-of-Chapter Summary Problem

The following financial data are adapted from the annual reports of **Gap Inc.**, which operates Gap, Banana Republic, and Old Navy clothing stores:

Gap Inc.

Five-Year Selected Financial Data for Years Ended January 31,

Operating Results*	2002	2001	2000	1999
Net sales	$13,848	$13,673	$11,635	$9,054
Cost of goods sold and occupancy expenses excluding depreciation and amortization	9,704	8,599	6,775	5,318
Interest expense	109	75	45	46
Income from operations	338	1,445	1,817	1,333
Net earnings (net loss)	(8)	877	1,127	824
Cash dividends	76	75	76	77
Financial Position				
Merchandise inventory	1,677	1,904	1,462	1,056
Total assets	7,591	7,012	5,189	3,963
Current ratio	1.48:1	0.95:1	1.25:1	1.20:1
Stockholders' equity	3,010	2,928	2,630	1,574
Average number of shares of common stock outstanding (in thousands)	860	879	895	576

*Dollar amounts are in thousands.

Required

Compute the following ratios for 2000 through 2002, and evaluate Gap's operating results. Are operating results strong or weak? Did they improve or deteriorate during the 4-year period? Your analysis will reveal a clear trend.

1. Gross profit percentage
2. Net income as a percentage of sales
3. Earnings per share
4. Inventory turnover
5. Times-interest-earned ratio
6. Rate of return on stockholders' equity

Answer

	2002	2001	2000
1. Gross profit percentage	$\frac{\$13{,}848 - \$9{,}704}{\$13{,}848} = 29.9\%$	$\frac{\$13{,}673 - \$8{,}599}{\$13{,}673} = 37.1\%$	$\frac{\$11{,}635 - \$6{,}775}{\$11{,}635} = 41.8\%$
2. Net income as a percentage of sales	$\frac{\$(8)}{\$13{,}848} = (.05\%)$	$\frac{\$877}{\$13{,}673} = 6.4\%$	$\frac{\$1{,}127}{\$11{,}635} = 9.7\%$
3. Earnings per share	$\frac{\$(8)}{860} = \$(0.01)$	$\frac{\$877}{879} = \$1.00$	$\frac{\$1{,}127}{895} = \$1.26$
4. Inventory turnover	$\frac{\$9{,}704}{(\$1{,}677 + \$1{,}904)/2} = 5.4$ times	$\frac{\$8{,}599}{(\$1{,}904 + \$1{,}462)/2} = 5.1$ times	$\frac{\$6{,}775}{(\$1{,}462 + \$1{,}056)/2} = 5.4$ times
5. Times-interest-earned ratio	$\frac{\$338}{\$109} = 3.1$ times	$\frac{\$1{,}455}{\$75} = 19.4$ times	$\frac{\$1{,}817}{\$45} = 40.4$ times
6. Rate of return on stockholders' equity	$\frac{\$(8)}{(\$3{,}010 + \$2{,}928)/2} = (0.3\%)$	$\frac{\$877}{(\$2{,}928 + \$2{,}630)/2} = 31.6\%$	$\frac{\$1{,}127}{(\$2{,}630 + \$1{,}574)/2} = 53.6\%$

Evaluation: During this period, Gap's operating results deteriorated on all these measures except inventory turnover. The gross margin percentage is down sharply, as are the times-interest-earned ratio and all the return measures. From these data it is clear that Gap could sell its merchandise, but not at the markups the company enjoyed in the past. The final result, in 2002, was a net loss for the year.

Review Financial Statement Analysis

Lesson Learned

1. **Perform a horizontal analysis of comparative financial statements.** *Horizontal analysis* is the study of percentage changes in financial statement items from one period to the next. To compute these percentage changes, (1) calculate the dollar amount of the change from the base (earlier) period to the later period, and (2) divide the dollar amount of change by the base-period amount. *Trend percentages* are a form of horizontal analysis.
2. **Perform a vertical analysis of financial statements.** *Vertical analysis* of a financial statement reveals the relationship of each statement item to a specified base, which is the 100% figure. In an income statement, net sales is usually the base. On a balance sheet, the base is the total assets figure.
3. **Prepare and use common-size financial statements.** A form of vertical analysis, *common-size statements* report only percentages, no dollar amounts. Common-size statements ease the comparison of different companies and may signal the need for corrective action.
4. *Benchmarking* is the practice of comparing a company to a standard set by other companies, with a view toward improvement.
5. **Use the statement of cash flows for decisions.** Analysts use cash-flow analysis to identify danger signals about a company's financial situation. The most important information provided by the cash-flow statement is the net cash flow from operating activities.
6. **Compute the standard financial ratios.** A ratio expresses the relationship of one item to another. The most important financial ratios measure a company's ability to pay current liabilities; ability to sell inventory and collect receivables; ability to pay long-term debt; profitability; and its value as an investment.
7. **Use ratios in decision making.** Analysis of financial ratios over time is an important way to track a company's progress. A change in one of the ratios over time may reveal a problem. It is up to the company's managers to find the source of this problem and take actions to correct it.
8. **Measure economic value added by operations.** *Economic value added (EVA)* measures whether a company's operations have increased its stockholders' wealth. EVA can be defined as the excess of net income and interest expense over the company's capital charge, which is the amount that the company's stockholders and lenders charge for the use of their money.

Accounting Vocabulary

accounts receivable turnover (p. 623)
acid-test ratio (p. 621)
benchmarking (p. 612)
book value per share of common stock (p. 630)
capital charge (p. 631)
common-size statement (p. 612)
cost of capital (p. 631)
current ratio (p. 619)

days' sales in receivables (p. 623)
debt ratio (p. 625)
dividend yield (p. 629)
earnings per share (EPS) (p. 628)
economic value added (EVA)® (p. 631)
efficient capital market (p. 632)
horizontal analysis (p. 606)
inventory turnover (p. 622)
leverage (p. 628)
price/earnings ratio (p. 629)
quick ratio (p. 621)
rate of return on common stockholders' equity (p. 627)
rate of return on net sales (p. 626)
rate of return on total assets (p. 627)
return on stockholders' equity (p. 627)
times-interest-earned ratio (p. 625)
trading on the equity (p. 628)
trend percentages (p. 609)
vertical analysis (p. 610)
working capital (p. 618)

Questions

1. Name the three broad categories of analytical tools that are based on accounting information.
2. Briefly describe horizontal analysis. How do decision makers use this analytical tool?
3. What is vertical analysis, and what is its purpose?
4. What is the purpose of common-size statements?
5. State how an investor might analyze the statement of cash flows. How might the investor analyze investing-activities data?
6. Identify two ratios used to measure the ability to pay current liabilities. Show how they are computed.
7. Why is the acid-test ratio given that name?
8. What does the inventory turnover ratio measure?
9. Suppose the days'-sales-in-receivables ratio of Gomez, Inc. increased from 36 at January 1 to 43 at December 31. Is this a good sign or a bad sign? What might Gomez management do in response to this change?
10. Company A's debt ratio has increased from 0.50 to 0.70. Identify a decision maker to whom this increase is important, and state how the increase affects this party's decisions about the company.
11. Which ratio measures the *effect of debt* on (a) financial position (the balance sheet) and (b) the company's ability to pay interest expense (the income statement)?
12. Company A is a chain of grocery stores, and Company B is a computer manufacturer. Which company is likely to have the higher (a) current ratio, (b) inventory turnover, and (c) rate of return on sales? Give your reasons.
13. Identify four ratios used to measure a company's profitability. Show how to compute these ratios and state what information each ratio provides.
14. The price/earnings ratio of Bank of New York was 20, and the price/earnings ratio of American Express was 40. Which company did the stock market favor? Explain.
15. McDonald's Corporation paid cash dividends of $0.23 per share when the market price of the company's stock was $30.15. What was the dividend yield on McDonald's stock? What does dividend yield measure?
16. Hold all other factors constant and indicate whether each of the following situations generally signals good or bad news about a company:
    a. Increase in current ratio
    b. Decrease in inventory turnover
    c. Increase in debt ratio
    d. Decrease in interest-coverage ratio
    e. Increase in return on sales
    f. Decrease in earnings per share
    g. Increase in price/earnings ratio
    h. Increase in book value per share
17. What is EVA®, and how is it used in financial analysis?

Assess Your Progress

Check Points

Horizontal analysis of revenues and gross profit
(Obj. 1)

CP13-1 Nike, Inc., reported the following amounts on its 2001 comparative income statement:

(In millions)	2001	2000	1999
Revenues	$9,489	$8,995	$8,777
Cost of sales	5,785	5,404	5,494

Perform a horizontal analysis of revenues and gross profit—both in dollar amounts and in percentages—for 2001 and 2000.

Trend analysis of revenues and net income
(Obj. 1)

CP13-2 Nike, Inc., reported the following revenues and net income amounts:

(In millions)	2001	2000	1999	1998	1997	1996
Revenues	$9,489	$8,995	$8,777	$9,553	$9,187	$6,471
Net income	590	579	451	400	796	553

1. Show Nike's trend percentages for revenues and net income. Use 1996 as the base year.
2. Which year shows the sharpest change in trend for Nike? Give the reason for your answer.

Vertical analysis to correct a cash shortage
(Obj. 2)

CP13-3 Perfect 10 Sporting Goods reported the following amounts on its balance sheets at December 31, 20X6, 20X5, and 20X4:

	20X6	20X5	20X4
Cash	$ 6,000	$ 6,000	$ 5,000
Receivables, net	30,000	22,000	19,000
Inventory	48,000	36,000	24,000
Prepaid expenses	2,000	2,000	1,000
Property, plant, and equipment, net	96,000	88,000	87,000
Total assets	$182,000	$154,000	$136,000

1. Sales and profits are high. Nevertheless, the company is experiencing a cash shortage. Perform a vertical analysis of Perfect 10 assets at the end of years 20X6, 20X5, and 20X4. Use the analysis to explain the reason for the cash shortage.
2. Suggest a way for Perfect 10 to generate more cash.

Common-size income statements of two leading companies
(Obj. 3)

CP13-4 Nike, Inc., and the Home Depot are leaders in their respective industries. Compare the two companies by converting their income statements (adapted) to common size.

(In millions)	Nike	Home Depot
Net sales	$9,489	$19,536
Cost of goods sold	5,785	14,101
Selling and administrative expenses	2,690	3,846
Interest expense	59	16
Other expense	34	38
Income tax expense	331	597
Net income	$ 590	$ 938

Which company earns more net income? Which company's net income is a higher percentage of its net sales? Which company is more profitable? Explain your answer.

Evaluating the trend in a company's current ratio
(Obj. 5, 6)

CP13-5 Examine the financial data of RubberMate Corporation in Exhibit 13-10. Show how to compute RubberMate's current ratio for each year 20X0 through 20X2. Is the company's ability to pay its current liabilities improving or deteriorating?

Evaluating a company's acid-test ratio
(Obj. 5, 6)

CP13-6 Use the Bristol-Myers Squibb balance sheet data in Exhibit 13-3.

1. Compute the company's acid-test ratio at December 31, 2001 and 2000.
2. Compare Bristol-Myers Squibb's ratio values to those of Chesebrough-Pond's, Wal-Mart, and General Motors on page 621. Is Bristol-Myers Squibb's acid-test ratio strong or weak? Explain.

Computing inventory turnover and days' sales in receivables
(Obj. 5)

CP13-7 Use the Bristol-Myers Squibb 2001 income statement (page 607) and balance sheet (page 608) to compute the following:

a. The rate of inventory turnover for 2001.
b. Days' sales in average receivables during 2001. All sales are made on account. (Round dollar amounts to one decimal place.)

Which of these measures looks weak? Give the reason for your answer.

CP13-8 Use the actual financial statements of Bristol-Myers Squibb Company (pages 607 and 608).

Measuring ability to pay long-term debt
(Obj. 5, 6)

1. Compute the company's debt ratio at December 31, 2001.
2. Compute the company's times-interest-earned ratio for 2001. Interest expense is not reported separately in the financial statements. Assume interest expense for 2001 was 7% of the sum of average Short-term borrowings and average Long-term debt for the year ended December 31, 2001. Round interest expense to the nearest million dollars.
3. Is Bristol-Myers Squibb's ability to pay its liabilities and interest expense strong or weak? Comment on the value of each ratio computed for requirements 1 and 2.

CP13-9 Use the financial statements of Bristol-Myers Squibb Company (pages 607 and 608) to determine or, if necessary, to compute these profitability measures for 2001:

Measuring profitability
(Obj. 5, 6)

a. Rate of return on net sales.
b. Rate of return on total assets. Assume interest expense for 2001 was $277 million.
c. Rate of return on common stockholders' equity. Are these rates of return strong or weak? Explain.

CP13-10 The annual report of **Dell Computer Corporation** for the year ended February 1, 2002, included the following items (in millions):

Computing EPS and the price/earnings ratio
(Obj. 5)

Preferred stock outstanding	$0
Net earnings (net income)	$1,246
Number of shares of common stock outstanding	2,602

1. Compute earnings per share (EPS) and the price/earnings ratio for Dell's stock. Round to the nearest cent. The price of a share of Dell stock is $26.85.
2. How much does the stock market say $1 of Dell's net income is worth?

CP13-11 A skeleton of **Campbell Soup Company's** income statement (as adapted) appears as follows (amounts in millions):

Using ratio data to reconstruct an income statement
(Obj. 5)

Income Statement

Net sales	$7,278
Cost of goods sold	(a)
Selling expenses	1,390
Administrative expenses	326
Interest expense	(b)
Other expenses	151
Income before taxes	1,042
Income tax expense	(c)
Net income	$ (d)

Use the following ratio data to complete Campbell Soup's income statement:

a. Inventory turnover was 5.53 (beginning inventory was $787; ending inventory was $755).
b. Rate of return on sales is 0.0959.

CP13-12 A skeleton of **Campbell Soup Company's** balance sheet (as adapted) appears as follows (amounts in millions):

Using ratio data to reconstruct a balance sheet
(Obj. 5)

Balance Sheet

Cash	$ 53	Total current liabilities	$2,164
Receivables	(a)	Long-term debt	(e)
Inventories	755	Other long-term liabilities	826
Prepaid expenses	(b)		
Total current assets	(c)	Common stock	185
Plant assets, net	(d)	Retained earnings	2,755
Other assets	2,150	Other stockholders' equity	(472)
Total assets	$6,315	Total liabilities and equity	$ (f)

Use the following ratio data to complete Campbell Soup's balance sheet:

a. Debt ratio is 0.6092.
b. Current ratio is 0.7306.
c. Acid-test ratio is 0.3161.

Measuring economic value added
(Obj. 7)

CP13-13 Use the financial statements of **Bristol-Myers Squibb** (pages 607 and 608).

1. Compute economic value added (EVA®) by the company's operations during 2001. Use beginning-of-year amounts to compute the capital charge. Assume that the company's cost of capital is 12% and that interest expense for 2001 was $277 million. Round all amounts to the nearest million dollars.
2. Should the company's stockholders be happy with the EVA® for 2001?

Exercises

Computing year-to-year changes in working capital
(Obj. 1)

E13-1 What were the dollar amount of change and the percentage of change in Micron Electronics' working capital during 2005 and 2006? Is this trend favorable or unfavorable?

	2006	2005	2004
Total current assets	$302,000	$290,000	$280,000
Total current liabilities	150,000	157,000	140,000

Horizontal analysis of an income statement
(Obj. 1)

E13-2 Prepare a horizontal analysis of the following comparative income statement of Newsletter E-Mail, Inc. Round percentage changes to the nearest one-tenth percent (three decimal places):

spreadsheet

Newsletter E-Mail, Inc.
Comparative Income Statement
Years Ended December 31, 2005 and 2004

	2005	2004
Total revenue	$430,000	$373,000
Expenses:		
Cost of goods sold	$202,000	$188,000
Selling and general expenses	98,000	93,000
Interest expense	7,000	4,000
Income tax expense	42,000	37,000
Total expenses	349,000	322,000
Net income	$ 81,000	$ 51,000

Why did net income increase by a higher percentage than total revenues during 2005?

E13-3 Compute trend percentages for Metro Graphics' net revenues and net income for the following 5-year period, using year 1 as the base year. Round to the nearest full percent.

Computing trend percentages
(Obj. 1)

(In thousands)	Year 5	Year 4	Year 3	Year 2	Year 1
Total revenue	$1,418	$1,187	$1,106	$1,009	$1,043
Net income	132	114	83	71	85

Which grew faster during the period, total revenue or net income?

E13-4 Consolidated Water System of Sierra Nevada has requested that you perform a vertical analysis of its balance sheet to determine the component percentages of its assets, liabilities, and stockholders' equity.

Vertical analysis of a balance sheet
(Obj. 2)

Consolidated Water System of Sierra Nevada
Balance Sheet
December 31, 20X5

Assets	
Total current assets	$ 42,000
Property, plant, and equipment, net	247,000
Other assets	35,000
Total assets	$324,000
Liabilities	
Total current liabilities	$ 48,000
Long-term debt	108,000
Total liabilities	156,000
Stockholders' Equity	
Total stockholders' equity	168,000
Total liabilities and stockholders' equity	$324,000

E13-5 Prepare a comparative common-size income statement for Newsletter E-Mail, Inc., using the 2005 and 2004 data of Exercise 13-2 and rounding percentages to one-tenth percent (three decimal places). To an investor, how does 2005 compare with 2004? Explain your reasoning.

Preparing a common-size income statement
(Obj. 3)

spreadsheet

E13-6 Identify any weaknesses revealed by the statement of cash flows of Ambassador Pacific, Inc.

Analyzing the statement of cash flows
(Obj. 4)

Ambassador Pacific, Inc.
Statement of Cash Flows
For the Current Year

Operating activities:		
Income from operations		$ 32,000
Add (subtract) noncash items:		
Depreciation	$ 23,000	
Net increase in current assets other than cash ..	(45,000)	
Net decrease in current liabilities exclusive of short-term debt	(7,000)	(29,000)
Net cash provided by operating activities		3,000
Investing activities:		
Sale of property, plant, and equipment		101,000

(continued)

Financing activities:		
Issuance of bonds payable	$102,000	
Payment of short-term debt	(159,000)	
Payment of long-term debt	(79,000)	
Payment of dividends	(42,000)	
Net cash used for financing activities		(178,000)
Increase (decrease) in cash		$ (74,000)

Computing five ratios
(Obj. 5)

E13-7 The financial statements of Cunningham Financial Group include the following items:

	Current Year	Preceding Year
Balance sheet:		
Cash	$ 17,000	$ 22,000
Short-term investments	11,000	26,000
Net receivables	64,000	73,000
Inventory	77,000	71,000
Prepaid expenses	16,000	8,000
Total current assets	185,000	200,000
Total current liabilities	131,000	91,000
Income statement:		
Net credit sales	$454,000	
Cost of goods sold	297,000	

Required

Compute the following ratios for the current year:

a. Current ratio
b. Acid-test ratio
c. Inventory turnover
d. Accounts receivable turnover
e. Days' sales in average receivables

Analyzing the ability to pay current liabilities
(Obj. 5, 6)

E13-8 Pinnacle Market Research Corporation has asked you to determine whether the company's ability to pay its current liabilities and long-term debts has improved or deteriorated during 20X4. To answer this question, compute the following ratios for 20X4 and 20X3:

a. Current ratio
b. Acid-test ratio
c. Debt ratio
d. Times-interest-earned ratio

Summarize the results of your analysis in a written report.

	20X4	20X3
Cash	$ 61,000	$ 47,000
Short-term investments	28,000	—
Net receivables	102,000	116,000
Inventory	226,000	263,000
Prepaid expenses	11,000	9,000
Total assets	543,000	489,000
Total current liabilities	275,000	221,000
Long-term debt	46,000	52,000
Income from operations	165,000	158,000
Interest expense	48,000	39,000

E13-9 Compute four ratios that measure ability to earn profits for Save the Planet's Air, Inc., whose comparative income statement follows:

Analyzing profitability **(Obj. 5, 6)**

Save the Planet's Air, Inc.
Comparative Income Statement
Years Ended December 31, 20X6 and 20X5

Dollars in thousands	20X6	20X5
Net sales	$174,000	$158,000
Cost of goods sold	93,000	86,000
Gross profit	81,000	72,000
Selling and general expenses	46,000	41,000
Income from operations	35,000	31,000
Interest expense	9,000	10,000
Income before income tax	26,000	21,000
Income tax expense	8,000	8,000
Net income	$ 18,000	$ 13,000

Additional data:

	20X6	20X5	20X4
Total assets	$204,000	$191,000	$171,000
Common stockholders' equity	$ 96,000	$ 89,000	$ 79,000
Preferred dividends	$ 3,000	$ 3,000	$ 0
Common shares outstanding during the year	20,000	20,000	18,000

Did the company's operating performance improve or deteriorate during 20X6?

E13-10 Evaluate the common stock of Friedman Energy Company as an investment. Specifically, use the three stock ratios to determine whether the common stock has increased or decreased in attractiveness during the past year.

Evaluating a stock as an investment **(Obj. 5, 6)**

	20X4	20X3
Net income	$ 58,000	$ 55,000
Dividends	20,000	20,000
Total stockholders' equity at year end (includes 80,000 shares of common stock)	580,000	500,000
Preferred stock, 6%	200,000	200,000
Market price per share of common stock at year end	$ 11.50	$ 7.75

E13-11 Two companies with very different economic-value-added (EVA®) profiles are **Oracle Corporation**, the world's second-largest software company, and **Wells Fargo & Company**, the nationwide banking conglomerate. Adapted versions of the two companies' 2001 financial statements are presented here (in millions):

Using economic value added to measure corporate performance **(Obj. 7)**

	Oracle	Wells Fargo
Balance sheet data:		
Total assets	$11,030	$307,569
Interest-bearing debt	$ 304	$195,781
All other liabilities	4,448	84,574
Stockholders' equity	6,278	27,214
Total liabilities and equity	$11,030	$307,569

(continued)

	Oracle	Wells Fargo
Income statement data:		
Total revenue	$10,860	$ 26,891
Interest expense	24	6,741
All other expenses	8,275	16,727
Net income	$ 2,561	$ 3,423

Required

1. Before performing any calculations, which company do you think represents the better investment? Give your reason.
2. Compute the EVA® for each company and then decide which company's stock you would rather hold as an investment. Assume Oracle's cost of capital is 15%, and Wells Fargo's is 5%.

Challenge Exercises

Using ratio data to reconstruct a company's balance sheet **(Obj. 2, 3, 5)**

E13-12 The following data (dollar amounts in millions) are adapted from the financial statements of Wal-Mart Stores, Inc., the largest retailer in the world:

Total liabilities	$ 11,806
Preferred stock	$ 0
Total current assets	$ 10,196
Accumulated depreciation	$ 1,448
Debt ratio	60.342%
Current ratio	1.51

Required

Complete the following condensed balance sheet. Report amounts to the nearest million dollars.

Current assets		$?
Property, plant, and equipment	$?	
Less Accumulated depreciation	(?)	?
Total assets		$?
Current liabilities		$?
Long-term liabilities		?
Stockholders' equity		?
Total liabilities and stockholders' equity		$?

Using ratio data to reconstruct a company's income statement **(Obj. 2, 3, 5)**

E13-13 The following data (dollar amounts in millions) are from the financial statements of McDonald's Corporation, the restaurant chain.

Average stockholders' equity	$3,605
Interest expense	$ 413
Preferred stock	$ 0
Operating income as a percent of sales	24.04%
Rate of return on stockholders' equity	21.89%
Income tax rate	33.30%

Required

Complete the following condensed income statement. Report amounts to the nearest million dollars.

Sales	$?
Operating expense	?
Operating income	?
Interest expense	?
Pretax income	?
Income tax expense	?
Net income	$?

Problems

(Group A)

Trend percentages, return on sales, and comparison with the industry **(Obj. 1, 5, 6)**

P13-1A Net sales, net income, and total assets for XT Communications, Inc., for a 4-year period follow:

(In thousands)	20X8	20X7	20X6	20X5
Net sales	$357	$313	$266	$281
Net income	29	21	11	18
Total assets	286	254	209	197

Required

1. Compute trend percentages for each item for 20X6 through 20X8. Use 20X5 as the base year and round to the nearest percent.
2. Compute the rate of return on net sales for 20X6 through 20X8, rounding to three decimal places. In the telecommunications industry, rates above 5% are considered good, and rates above 7% are outstanding.
3. How does XT Communications' return on net sales compare with that of the industry?

Common-size statements, analysis of profitability, and comparison with the industry **(Obj. 2, 3, 5, 6)**

P13-2A Top managers of Escalade Technology Corporation have asked your help in comparing the company's profit performance and financial position with the average for the cell phone industry. The accountant has given you the company's income statement and balance sheet and also the following data for the industry:

Escalade Technology Corporation

Income Statement Compared with Industry Average
Year Ended December 31, 20X5

	Escalade	Industry Average
Net sales	$957,000	100.0%
Cost of goods sold	652,000	65.9
Gross profit	305,000	34.1
Operating expenses	204,000	28.1
Operating income	101,000	6.0
Other expenses	13,000	0.4
Net income	$ 88,000	5.6%

Escalade Technology Corporation

Balance Sheet Compared with Industry Average
December 31, 20X5

	Escalade	Industry Average
Current assets	$486,000	74.4%
Fixed assets, net	117,000	20.0
Intangible assets, net	24,000	0.6
Other assets	3,000	5.0
Total	$630,000	100.0%
Current liabilities	$246,000	45.6%
Long-term liabilities	136,000	19.0
Stockholders' equity	248,000	35.4
Total	$630,000	100.0%

Required

1. Prepare a common-size income statement and balance sheet for Escalade. The first column of each statement should present Escalade's common-size statement, and the second column should show the industry averages.
2. For the profitability analysis, compute Escalade's (a) ratio of gross profit to net sales, (b) ratio of operating income to net sales, and (c) ratio of net income to net sales. Compare these figures with the industry averages. Is Escalade's profit performance better or worse than the average for the industry?
3. For the analysis of financial position, compute Escalade's (a) ratios of current assets and current liabilities to total assets and (b) ratio of stockholders' equity to total assets. Compare these ratios with the industry averages. Is Escalade's financial position better or worse than average for the industry?

Using the statement of cash flows for decision making
(Obj. 4)

P13-3A You are evaluating two companies as possible investments. The two companies, similar in size, are commuter airlines that fly passengers from San Francisco to smaller cities in California. All other available information has been analyzed and your investment decision depends on cash flows.

Required

Discuss the relative strengths and weaknesses of Calair and San Fernando Airways. Conclude your discussion by recommending one of the company's stocks as an investment.

Calair Corporation

Statement of Cash Flows
Years Ended November 30, 20X9 and 20X8

	20X9		20X8	
Operating activities:				
Net income (net loss)		$(67,000)		$154,000
Adjustments for noncash items:				
Total		84,000		(23,000)
Net cash provided by operating activities		17,000		131,000
Investing activities:				
Purchase of property, plant, and equipment	$ (50,000)		$ (91,000)	
Sale of long-term investments	52,000		4,000	
Net cash provided by (used for) investing activities		2,000		(87,000)
Financing activities:				
Issuance of short-term notes payable	$122,000		$143,000	
Payment of short-term notes payable	(179,000)		(134,000)	
Payment of cash dividends	(45,000)		(64,000)	
Net cash used for financing activities		(102,000)		(55,000)
Increase (decrease) in cash		$(83,000)		$ (11,000)
Cash balance at beginning of year		92,000		103,000
Cash balance at end of year		$ 9,000		$ 92,000

San Fernando Airways, Inc.

Statement of Cash Flows
Years Ended November 30, 20X9 and 20X8

	20X9		20X8	
Operating activities:				
Net income		$184,000		$ 131,000
Adjustments for noncash items:				
Total		64,000		62,000
Net cash provided by operating activities		248,000		193,000
Investing activities:				
Purchase of property, plant, and equipment	$(303,000)		$(453,000)	
Sale of property, plant, and equipment	46,000		72,000	
Net cash used for investing activities		(257,000)		(381,000)
Financing activities:				
Issuance of long-term notes payable	$ 174,000		$ 118,000	
Payment of short-term notes payable	(66,000)		(18,000)	
Net cash provided by financing activities		108,000		100,000
Increase (decrease) in cash		$ 99,000		$ (88,000)
Cash balance at beginning of year		116,000		204,000
Cash balance at end of year		$215,000		$ 116,000

P13-4A Financial statement data on Thunderbird Medical Supply include the following items:

Effects of business transactions on selected ratios
(Obj. 5, 6)

Accounts payable	$ 96,000	Cash	$ 47,000
Accrued liabilities	50,000	Short-term investments	21,000
Long-term notes payable	146,000	Accounts receivable, net	102,000
Other long-term liabilities	78,000	Inventories	274,000
Net income	119,000	Prepaid expenses	15,000
Number of common		Total assets	933,000
shares outstanding	22,000	Short-term notes payable	72,000

Required

1. Compute Thunderbird's current ratio, debt ratio, and earnings per share. Use the following format for your answer:

Requirement 1

Current ratio	Debt ratio	Earnings per share

2. Compute the three ratios after evaluating the effect of each transaction that follows. Consider each transaction *separately*.
   a. Borrowed $27,000 on a long-term note payable.
   b. Issued 10,000 shares of common stock, receiving cash of $108,000.
   c. Paid short-term notes payable, $51,000.
   d. Purchased merchandise of $48,000 on account, debiting Inventory.
   e. Received cash on account, $6,000.

   Format your answer as follows:

Requirement 2

Transaction letter	Current ratio	Debt ratio	Earnings per share

Using ratios to evaluate a stock investment
(Obj. 5, 6)

P13-5A Comparative financial statement data of Advanced Automotive Company follow:

Advanced Automotive Company
Comparative Income Statement
Years Ended December 31, 20X6 and 20X5

	20X6	20X5
Net sales	$667,000	$599,000
Cost of goods sold	378,000	283,000
Gross profit	289,000	316,000
Operating expenses	129,000	147,000
Income from operations	160,000	169,000
Interest expense	57,000	41,000
Income before income tax	103,000	128,000
Income tax expense	34,000	53,000
Net income	$ 69,000	$ 75,000

Advanced Automotive Company
Comparative Balance Sheet
December 31, 20X6 and 20X5

	20X6	20X5	20X4*
Current assets:			
Cash	$ 37,000	$ 40,000	
Current receivables, net	208,000	151,000	$138,000
Inventories	352,000	286,000	184,000
Prepaid expenses	5,000	20,000	
Total current assets	602,000	497,000	
Property, plant, and equipment, net	287,000	276,000	
Total assets	$889,000	$773,000	707,000
Total current liabilities	$286,000	$267,000	
Long-term liabilities	245,000	235,000	
Total liabilities	531,000	502,000	
Preferred stockholders' equity, 4%, $20 par	50,000	50,000	
Common stockholders' equity, no par	308,000	221,000	148,000
Total liabilities and stockholders' equity	$889,000	$773,000	

*Selected 20X4 amounts.

Other information:

1. Market price of Advanced Automotive's common stock: $36.75 at December 31, 20X6, and $50.50 at December 31, 20X5.
2. Common shares outstanding: 15,000 during 20X6 and 14,000 during 20X5.
3. All sales on credit.

Required

1. Compute the following ratios for 20X6 and 20X5:
   a. Current ratio
   b. Inventory turnover
   c. Times-interest-earned ratio
   d. Return on assets
   e. Return on common stockholders' equity
   f. Earnings per share of common stock
   g. Price/earnings ratio

2. Decide whether (a) Advanced's financial position improved or deteriorated during 20X6 and (b) the investment attractiveness of its common stock appears to have increased or decreased.
3. How will what you learned in this problem help you evaluate an investment?

Using ratios to decide between two stock investments; measuring economic value added
(Obj. 5, 6, 7)

P13-6A Assume that you are considering purchasing stock in a company in the music industry. You have narrowed the choice to Blues Inc. and Sonic Sound Corporation and have assembled the following data:

Selected income statement data for current year:

	Blues	Sonic
Net sales (all on credit)	$603,000	$519,000
Cost of goods sold	454,000	387,000
Income from operations	93,000	72,000
Interest expense	—	8,000
Net income	56,000	38,000

Selected balance sheet and market price data at *end* of current year:

	Blues	Sonic
Current assets:		
Cash	$ 25,000	$ 39,000
Short-term investments	6,000	13,000
Current receivables, net	189,000	164,000
Inventories	211,000	183,000
Prepaid expenses	19,000	15,000
Total current assets	450,000	414,000
Total assets	974,000	938,000
Total current liabilities	366,000	338,000
Total liabilities	667,000*	691,000*
Preferred stock, 4%, $100 par		25,000
Common stock, $1 par (150,000 shares)	150,000	
$5 par (20,000 shares)		100,000
Total stockholders' equity	307,000	247,000
Market price per share of common stock	$ 9	$ 47.50

*Includes notes and bonds payable: Blues $4,000, and Sonic $303,000

Selected balance sheet data at *beginning* of current year:

	Blues	Sonic
Current receivables, net	$142,000	$193,000
Inventories	209,000	197,000
Total assets	842,000	909,000
Preferred stock, 4%, $100 par		25,000
Common stock, $1 par (150,000 shares)	150,000	
$5 par (20,000 shares)		100,000
Total stockholders' equity	263,000	215,000

Your strategy is to invest in companies that have low price/earnings ratios but appear to be in good shape financially. Assume that you have analyzed all other factors and that your decision depends on the results of ratio analysis.

Required

1. Compute the following ratios for both companies for the current year and decide which company's stock better fits your investment strategy.
   a. Acid-test ratio
   b. Inventory turnover
   c. Days' sales in average receivables
   d. Debt ratio
   e. Times-interest-earned ratio
   f. Return on common stockholders' equity
   g. Earnings per share of common stock
   h. Price/earnings ratio
2. Compute each company's economic-value-added (EVA®) measure and determine whether their EVA®s confirm or alter your investment decision. Each company's cost of capital is 10%. Round all amounts to the nearest $1,000.

Analyzing a company based on its ratios **(Obj. 6)**

P13-7A Take the role of an investment analyst at Edward Jones Company. It is your job to recommend investments for your client. The only information you have are the following ratio values for two companies in the graphics software industry.

Ratio	GraphTech Inc.	Core Software Company
Days' sales in receivables	51	43
Inventory turnover	9	7
Gross profit percentage	62%	71%
Net income as a percent of sales	16%	14%
Times-interest earned	12	18
Return on equity	29%	36%
Return on assets	19%	14%

Write a report to the Edward Jones investment committee. Recommend one company's stock over the other. State the reasons for your recommendation.

(Group B)

Trend percentages, return on common equity, and comparison with the industry **(Obj. 1, 5, 6)**

P13-1B Net revenues, net income, and common stockholders' equity for xCel Corporation, a manufacturer of contact lenses, for a 4-year period follow.

(In thousands)	2008	2007	2006	2005
Net revenues	$781	$714	$641	$662
Net income	51	45	32	48
Ending common stockholders' equity	366	354	330	296

Required

1. Compute trend percentages for each item for 2006 through 2008. Use 2005 as the base year. Round to the nearest percent.
2. Compute the rate of return on common stockholders' equity for 2006 through 2008, rounding to three decimal places. In the contact lens industry, rates of 13% are average, rates above 16% are good, and rates above 20% are outstanding. xCel has no preferred stock outstanding.
3. How does xCel's return on common stockholders' equity compare with the industry?

Common-size statements, analysis of profitability, and comparison with the industry **(Obj. 2, 3, 5, 6)**

P13-2B Bose Stereo Shops has asked you to compare the company's profit performance and financial position with the average for the stereo industry. The proprietor has given you the company's income statement and balance sheet as well as the industry average data for retailers.

Bose Stereo Shops

Income Statement Compared with Industry Average
Year Ended December 31, 20X6

	Bose	Industry Average
Net sales	$781,000	100.0%
Cost of goods sold	497,000	65.8
Gross profit	284,000	34.2
Operating expenses	163,000	19.7
Operating income	121,000	14.5
Other expenses	6,000	0.4
Net income	$115,000	14.1%

Bose Stereo Shops

Balance Sheet Compared with Industry Average
December 31, 20X6

	Bose	Industry Average
Current assets	$350,000	70.9%
Fixed assets, net	74,000	23.6
Intangible assets, net	4,000	0.8
Other assets	22,000	4.7
Total	$450,000	100.0%
Current liabilities	$207,000	48.1%
Long-term liabilities	62,000	16.6
Stockholders' equity	181,000	35.3
Total	$450,000	100.0%

Required

1. Prepare a common-size income statement and balance sheet for Bose. The first column of each statement should present Bose's common-size statement, and the second column, the industry averages.
2. For the profitability analysis, compute Bose's (a) ratio of gross profit to net sales, (b) ratio of operating income to net sales, and (c) ratio of net income to net sales. Compare these figures with the industry averages. Is Bose's profit performance better or worse than the industry average?
3. For the analysis of financial position, compute Bose's (a) ratio of current assets to total assets, and (b) ratio of stockholders' equity to total assets. Compare these ratios with the industry averages. Is Bose's financial position better or worse than the industry averages?

Using the statement of cash flows for decision making
(Obj. 4)

P13-3B You have been asked to evaluate two companies as possible investments. The two companies, America Roofing, Inc. and Imagine Time Software Corporation are similar in size. Assume that all other available information has been analyzed, and the decision concerning which company's stock to purchase depends on their cash-flow data (page 652).

Required

Discuss the relative strengths and weaknesses of each company. Conclude your discussion by recommending one company's stock as an investment.

America Roofing, Inc.

Statement of Cash Flows
Years Ended September 30, 20X7 and 20X6

	20X7		20X6	
Operating activities:				
Net income		$17,000		$44,000
Adjustments for noncash items:				
Total		(14,000)		(4,000)
Net cash provided by operating activities		3,000		40,000
Investing activities:				
Purchase of property, plant, and equipment	$ (13,000)		$ (3,000)	
Sale of property, plant, and equipment	86,000		79,000	
Net cash provided by investing activities		73,000		76,000
Financing activities:				
Issuance of short-term notes payable	$ 43,000		$ 19,000	
Payment of short-term notes payable	(101,000)		(108,000)	
Net cash used for financing activities		(58,000)		(89,000)
Increase in cash		$18,000		$27,000
Cash balance at beginning of year		31,000		4,000
Cash balance at end of year		$49,000		$31,000

Imagine Time Software Corporation

Statement of Cash Flows
Years Ended September 30, 20X7 and 20X6

	20X7		20X6	
Operating activities:				
Net income		$ 89,000		$ 71,000
Adjustments for noncash items:				
Total		19,000		—
Net cash provided by operating activities		108,000		71,000
Investing activities:				
Purchase of property, plant, and equipment	$(121,000)		$(91,000)	
Net cash used for investing activities		(121,000)		(91,000)
Financing activities:				
Issuance of long-term notes payable	$ 46,000		$ 43,000	
Payment of short-term notes payable	(15,000)		(40,000)	
Payment of cash dividends	(12,000)		(9,000)	
Net cash provided by (used for) financing activities		19,000		(6,000)
Increase (decrease) in cash		$ 6,000		$(26,000)
Cash balance at beginning of year		54,000		80,000
Cash balance at end of year		$ 60,000		$ 54,000

Effects of business transactions on selected ratios
(Obj. 5, 6)

P13-4B Financial statement data of Biz Mart Discount Center include the following items (dollars in thousands):

Cash	$ 22,000
Short-term investments	19,000
Accounts receivable, net	83,000
Inventories	141,000
Prepaid expenses	8,000

(continued)

Total assets	$657,000
Short-term notes payable	49,000
Accounts payable	103,000
Accrued liabilities	38,000
Long-term notes payable	160,000
Other long-term liabilities	31,000
Net income	71,000
Number of common shares outstanding	40,000

Required

1. Compute Biz Mart's current ratio, debt ratio, and earnings per share. Use the following format for your answer:

Requirement 1

Current ratio	Debt ratio	Earnings per share

2. Compute the three ratios after evaluating the effect of each transaction that follows. Consider each transaction *separately*.
   a. Purchased store supplies of $46,000 on account.
   b. Borrowed $125,000 on a long-term note payable.
   c. Issued 5,000 shares of common stock, receiving cash of $120,000.
   d. Paid short-term notes payable, $32,000.
   e. Received cash on account, $19,000.

   Format your answer as follows:

Requirement 2

Transaction (letter)	Current ratio	Debt ratio	Earnings per share

P13-5B Comparative financial statement data of i2 Networks, Inc. follow.

Using ratios to evaluate a stock investment **(Obj. 5, 6)**

i2 Networks, Inc.

Comparative Income Statement
Years Ended December 31, 20X9 and 20X8

	20X9	20X8
Net sales	$462,000	$427,000
Cost of goods sold	229,000	218,000
Gross profit	233,000	209,000
Operating expenses	136,000	134,000
Income from operations	97,000	75,000
Interest expense	11,000	12,000
Income before income tax	86,000	63,000
Income tax expense	30,000	27,000
Net income	$ 56,000	$ 36,000

i2 Networks, Inc.

Comparative Balance Sheet
December 31, 20X9 and 20X8

	20X9	20X8	20X7*
Current assets:			
Cash	$ 96,000	$ 97,000	
Current receivables, net	112,000	116,000	$103,000

(continued)

Inventories	$147,000	$162,000	$207,000
Prepaid expenses	16,000	7,000	
Total current assets	371,000	382,000	
Property, plant, and equipment, net	214,000	178,000	
Total assets	$585,000	$560,000	598,000
Total current liabilities	$206,000	$223,000	
Long-term liabilities	119,000	117,000	
Total liabilities	325,000	340,000	
Preferred stockholders' equity, 6%, $100 par	100,000	100,000	
Common stockholders' equity, no par	160,000	120,000	90,000
Total liabilities and stockholders' equity	$585,000	$560,000	

*Selected 20X7 amounts.

Other information:

1. Market price of i2 Networks' common stock: $53 at December 31, 20X9, and $32.50 at December 31, 20X8.
2. Common shares outstanding: 10,000 during 20X9 and 9,000 during 20X8.
3. All sales on credit.

Required

1. Compute the following ratios for 20X9 and 20X8:
   a. Current ratio
   b. Inventory turnover
   c. Times-interest-earned ratio
   d. Return on common stockholders' equity
   e. Earnings per share of common stock
   f. Price/earnings ratio
2. Decide (a) whether i2 Networks' financial position improved or deteriorated during 20X9 and (b) whether the investment attractiveness of its common stock appears to have increased or decreased.
3. How will what you learned in this problem help you evaluate an investment?

Using ratios to decide between two stock investments; measuring economic value added
(Obj. 5, 6, 7)

P13-6B Assume that you are purchasing an investment and have decided to invest in a company in the air-conditioning/heating business. You have narrowed the choice to Caremark Laboratories and AmeriCorp, Inc., and have assembled the following data:

Selected income statement data for current year:

	Caremark	AmeriCorp
Net sales (all on credit)	$371,000	$497,000
Cost of goods sold	209,000	258,000
Income from operations	79,000	138,000
Interest expense	—	19,000
Net income	48,000	72,000

Selected balance sheet data at *beginning* of current year:

	Caremark	AmeriCorp
Current receivables, net	$ 40,000	$ 48,000
Inventories	93,000	88,000
Total assets	259,000	270,000
Preferred stock, 5%, $100 par	—	20,000
Common stock, $1 par (10,000 shares)	10,000	
$2.50 par (5,000 shares)		12,500
Total stockholders' equity	118,000	126,000

Selected balance sheet and market price data at *end* of current year:

	Caremark	AmeriCorp
Current assets:		
Cash	$ 22,000	$ 19,000
Short-term investments	20,000	18,000
Current receivables, net	42,000	46,000
Inventories	87,000	100,000
Prepaid expenses	2,000	3,000
Total current assets	173,000	186,000
Total assets	265,000	328,000
Total current liabilities	108,000	98,000
Total liabilities	108,000*	131,000*
Preferred stock: 5%, $100 par		20,000
Common stock, $1 par (10,000 shares)	10,000	
$2.50 par (5,000 shares)		12,500
Total stockholders' equity	157,000	197,000
Market price per share of common stock	$ 51	$ 112

*Includes notes payable: Caremark $1,000 and AmeriCorp $86,000

Your strategy is to invest in companies that have low price/earnings ratios but appear to be in good shape financially. Assume that you have analyzed all other factors and that your decision depends on the results of ratio analysis.

Required

1. Compute the following ratios for both companies for the current year, and decide which company's stock better fits your investment strategy.
   a. Acid-test ratio
   b. Inventory turnover
   c. Days' sales in average receivables
   d. Debt ratio
   e. Times-interest-earned ratio
   f. Return on common stockholders' equity
   g. Earnings per share of common stock
   h. Price/earnings ratio
2. Compute each company's economic-value-added (EVA®) measure and determine whether their EVA®s confirm or alter your investment decision. Each company's cost of capital is 12%. Round all amounts to the nearest $1,000.

P13-7B Take the role of an investment analyst at Goldman Sachs. It is your job to recommend investments for your clients. The only information you have are the following ratio values for two companies in the pharmaceuticals industry.

Analyzing a company based on its ratios **(Obj. 6)**

Ratio	Pratt Corp.	Jacobs, Inc.
Days' sales in receivable	36	42
Inventory turnover	6	8
Gross profit percentage	49%	51%
Net income as a percentage of sales	7.2%	8.3%
Times-interest-earned	16	9
Return on equity	32.3%	21.5%
Return on assets	12.1%	16.4%

Write a report to Goldman Sachs' investment committee. Recommend one company's stock over the other. State the reasons for your recommendation.

Apply Your Knowledge

Decision Cases

Analyzing the effects of an accounting difference on the ratios
(Obj. 5, 6)

Case 1. Gap Inc. uses the first-in, first-out (FIFO) method to account for its inventory, and Lands' End uses last-in, first-out (LIFO). Analyze the effect of this difference in accounting method on the two companies' ratio values. For each ratio discussed in this chapter, indicate which company will have the higher (and the lower) ratio value. Also identify those ratios that are unaffected by the FIFO/LIFO difference. Ignore the effects of income taxes, and assume inventory costs are increasing. Then, based on your analysis of the ratios, summarize your conclusions as to which company looks better overall.

Assessing the effects of transactions on a company
(Obj. 5, 6)

Case 2. AOL Time Warner Inc. had a bad year in 2001; the company suffered a $4.9 billion net loss. The loss pushed most of the return measures into the negative column and the current ratio dropped below 1.0. The company's debt ratio is still only 0.27. Assume top management of AOL Time Warner is pondering ways to improve the company's ratios. In particular, management is considering the following transactions:

1. Sell off the cable television segment of the business for $30 million (receiving half in cash and half in the form of a long-term note receivable). Book value of the cable television business is $27 million.
2. Borrow $100 million on long-term debt.
3. Purchase treasury stock for $500 million cash.
4. Write off one-fourth of goodwill carried on the books at $128 million.
5. Sell advertising at the normal gross margin of 60%. The advertisements run immediately.
6. Purchase trademarks from NBC, paying $20 million cash and signing a 1-year note payable for $80 million.

Required

1. Top management wants to know the effects of these transactions (increase, decrease, or no effect) on the following ratios of AOL Time Warner:
   a. Current ratio
   b. Debt ratio
   c. Times-interest-earned ratio (measured as [net income + interest expense]/interest expense)
   d. Return on equity
   e. Book value per share of common stock
2. Some of these transactions have an immediately positive effect on the company's financial condition. Some are definitely negative. Others have an effect that cannot be judged as clearly positive or negative. Evaluate each transaction's effect as positive, negative, or unclear.

Identifying action to cut losses and establish profitability
(Obj. 2, 5, 6)

Case 3. Suppose you manage Outward Bound, Inc., a Vermont sporting goods store that lost money during the past year. To turn the business around, you must analyze the company and industry data for the current year to learn what is wrong. The company's data follow.

Outward Bound, Inc.

Common-Size Balance Sheet Data

	Outward Bound	Industry Average
Cash and short-term investments	3.0%	6.8%
Trade receivables, net	15.2	11.0
Inventory	64.2	60.5
Prepaid expenses	1.0	0.0
Total current assets	83.4%	78.3%

Fixed assets, net	12.6%	15.2%
Other assets	4.0	6.5
Total assets	100.0%	100.0%
Notes payable, short-term, 12%	17.1%	14.0%
Accounts payable	21.1	25.1
Accrued liabilities	7.8	7.9
Total current liabilities	46.0	47.0
Long-term debt, 11%	19.7	16.4
Total liabilities	65.7	63.4
Common stockholders' equity	34.3	36.6
Total liabilities and stockholders' equity	100.0%	100.0%

Outward Bound, Inc.

Common-Size Income Statement Data

	Outward Bound	Industry Average
Net sales	100.0%	100.0%
Cost of sales	(68.2)	(64.8)
Gross profit	31.8	35.2
Operating expense	(37.1)	(32.3)
Operating income (loss)	(5.3)	2.9
Interest expense	(5.8)	(1.3)
Other revenue	1.1	0.3
Income (loss) before income tax	(10.0)	1.9
Income tax (expense) saving	4.4	(0.8)
Net income (loss)	(5.6)%	1.1%

Required

On the basis of your analysis of these figures, suggest four courses of action Outward Bound might take to reduce its losses and establish profitable operations. Give your reasons for each suggestion.

Understanding the components of accounting ratios **(Obj. 5, 6)**

Case 4. Consider the following business situations:

a. Pinehurst Corporation's owners are concerned because the number of days' sales in receivables has increased over the previous 2 years. Explain why the ratio might have increased.

b. Sara Fulton has asked you about the stock of a particular company. She finds it attractive because it has a high dividend yield relative to another stock she is also considering. Explain to her the meaning of the ratio and the danger of making a decision based on dividend yield alone.

c. Nathanael Smith is the controller of Saturn Ltd., a dance club whose year end is December 31. Smith prepares checks for suppliers in December and posts them to the appropriate accounts in that month. However, he holds on to the checks and mails them to the suppliers in January. What financial ratio(s) are most affected by the action? What is Smith's purpose in undertaking this activity?

Ethical Issue

Balmoral Golf Corporation's long-term debt agreements make certain demands on the business. For example, Balmoral may not purchase treasury stock in excess of the balance of retained earnings. Also, long-term debt may not exceed stockholders' equity, and the current ratio may not fall below 1.50. If Balmoral fails to meet any of these requirements, the company's lenders have the authority to take over management of the company.

Changes in consumer demand have made it hard for Balmoral to attract customers. Current liabilities have mounted faster than current assets, causing the current ratio to fall to 1.47. Before releasing financial statements, Balmoral management is scrambling to improve the current ratio. The controller points out that an investment can be classified as either long-term or short-term, depending on management's intention. By deciding to convert an investment to cash within 1 year, Balmoral can classify the investment as short-term—a current asset. On the controller's recommendation, Balmoral's board of directors votes to reclassify long-term investments as short-term.

Required

1. What effect will reclassifying the investments have on the current ratio? Is Balmoral's financial position stronger as a result of reclassifying the investments?
2. Shortly after the financial statements are released, sales improve; so, too, does the current ratio. As a result, Balmoral management decides not to sell the investments it had reclassified as short term. Accordingly, the company reclassifies the investments as long term. Has management behaved unethically? Give the reasoning underlying your answer.

Financial Statement Case

Measuring profitability and analyzing stock as an investment
(Obj. 1, 5, 6)

Use the financial statements and the data in **Fossil, Inc.'s**, Financial Highlights that appear before the Fossil financial statements (Appendix A at the end of the book) to answer the following questions.

Required

1. Use 1997 as the base year, and perform a trend analysis of Fossil's sales, gross profit, and net income for each year 1998 through 2001.
2. Compute these ratios for Fossil, Inc., for each year 1998 through 2001:
   a. Gross profit percentage
   b. Inventory turnover
   c. Days' sales in average receivables
   d. Return on stockholders' equity

   You will need the following data (in thousands) at each year end:

	1999	1998	1997
Accounts receivable—net	$51,399	$42,582	$34,238
Inventories	63,029	57,295	51,382

   Ignore any ratio values that Fossil reports in its Financial Highlights.
3. Evaluate Fossil's performance record during 1998 through 2001. Comment on each item computed.

Analytical Case

Analyzing trend data
(Obj. 1, 4, 5, 6)

Use the **Pier 1 Imports** financial statements in Appendix B at the end of this book to address the following questions. Study the Financial Summary that precedes the financial statements.

1. What item kept Pier 1's net income from growing as fast as sales?
2. The data in the Financial Summary convey a clear message about Pier 1's debt ratio during the five-year period covered by the Financial Summary. Did the debt ratio increase or decrease? How can you tell?
3. Are you worried about the drop in Pier 1's current ratio? Why or why not?
4. The performance figures in the Financial Summary indicate a growing company. And yet Pier 1's shares of common stock outstanding decreased consistently during the five-year period. What caused the decrease? Confirm your answer with evidence from elsewhere in Pier 1's financial statements.

5. Consider your answer to item 4. What caused Pier 1's shareholders' equity to grow during this period? Is this healthy or unhealthy for Pier 1?

Group Projects

Project 1. Select an industry you are interested in, and use the leading company in that industry as the benchmark. Then select two other companies in the same industry. For each category of ratios in the Decision Guidelines feature on pages 000 and 000, compute at least two ratios for all three companies. Write a two-page report that compares the two companies with the benchmark company.

Project 2. Select a company and obtain its financial statements. Convert the income statement and the balance sheet to common size and compare the company you selected to the industry average. Risk Management Association's *Annual Statement Studies*, Dun & Bradstreet's *Industry Norms & Key Business Ratios*, and Prentice Hall's *Almanac of Business and Industrial Financial Ratios* by Leo Troy, publish common-size statements for most industries.

Appendix A Fossil Annual Report

FINANCIAL HIGHLIGHTS

Fiscal Year *IN THOUSANDS, EXCEPT PER SHARE DATA*	2001	2000	1999	1998	1997
Net sales	$ 545,541	$ 504,285	$ 418,762	$ 304,743	$ 244,798
Gross profit	271,850	255,746	212,887	150,504	117,528
Operating income	76,854	93,821	87,449	55,370	34,610
Income before income taxes	72,804	94,717	87,841	54,729	32,151
Net income	43,683	55,883	51,826	32,161	18,942
Pro forma net income (1)	46,548	n/a	n/a	n/a	n/a
Earnings per share: (2)					
Basic	1.45	1.76	1.63	1.04	0.63
Diluted	1.40	1.71	1.55	0.99	0.61
Pro forma earnings per share: (1)(2)					
Basic	1.54	n/a	n/a	n/a	n/a
Diluted	1.49	n/a	n/a	n/a	n/a
Weighted average common shares outstanding: (2)					
Basic	30,167	31,689	31,900	31,054	30,203
Diluted	31,240	32,675	33,428	32,586	31,250
Working capital	$ 163,280	$ 169,792	$ 155,198	$ 109,040	$ 70,603
Total assets	380,863	307,591	269,364	194,078	139,570
Long-term debt	–	–	–	–	–
Stockholders' equity	264,023	220,699	191,197	134,919	95,263
Return on average stockholders' equity	18.3%	26.9%	32.2%	29.3%	23.1%

(1) Pro forma information excludes a $4.8 million one-time pre-tax charge in fiscal 2001 which reflects the write-off of the carrying value of the Company's investment in SII Marketing International, Inc. as a result of the Company's decision to terminate its equity participation in the joint venture.
(2) All share and per share data has been adjusted to reflect three-for-two stock splits effected in the form of a stock dividend paid on April 8, 1998 and August 17, 1999.

STOCK INFORMATION

The Company's common stock prices are published daily in The Wall Street Journal and other publications under the Nasdaq National Market Listing. The stock is traded under the ticker symbol "FOSL." The following are the high and low sale prices of the Company's stock per the Nasdaq National Market. Stock prices have been adjusted in certain cases to the nearest traded amount.

	2001		2000	
	High	*Low*	*High*	*Low*
First quarter	$ 20.250	$ 13.750	$ 26.750	$ 15.813
Second quarter	23.350	16.510	25.125	16.625
Third quarter	22.300	14.110	20.500	11.563
Fourth quarter	22.600	16.150	16.438	10.500

FINANCIAL INFORMATION

INDEPENDENT AUDITORS' REPORT

To the Directors and Stockholders of Fossil, Inc.:

We have audited the accompanying consolidated balance sheets of Fossil, Inc. and subsidiaries as of January 5, 2002 and December 30, 2000, and the related consolidated statements of income and comprehensive income, stockholders' equity and cash flows for each of the three years in the period ended January 5, 2002. These financial statements are the responsibility of the Company's management. Our responsibility is to express an opinion on these financial statements based on our audits.

We conducted our audits in accordance with auditing standards generally accepted in the United States of America. Those standards require that we plan and perform the audit to obtain reasonable assurance about whether the financial statements are free of material misstatement. An audit includes examining, on a test basis, evidence supporting the amounts and disclosures in the financial statements. An audit also includes assessing the accounting principles used and significant estimates made by management, as well as evaluating the overall financial statement presentation. We believe that our audits provide a reasonable basis for our opinion.

In our opinion, such consolidated financial statements present fairly, in all material respects, the financial position of Fossil, Inc. and subsidiaries at January 5, 2002 and December 30, 2000, and the results of their operations and their cash flows for each of the three years in the period ended January 5, 2002, in conformity with accounting principles generally accepted in the United States of America.

Deloitte & Touche LLP
Dallas, Texas
February 25, 2002

REPORT OF MANAGEMENT

The accompanying consolidated financial statements and other information contained in this Annual Report have been prepared by management. The financial statements have been prepared in accordance with accounting principles generally accepted in the United States of America and include amounts that are based upon our best estimates and judgements.

To help assure that financial information is reliable and that assets are safeguarded, management maintains a system of internal controls and procedures which it believes is effective in accomplishing these objectives. These controls and procedures are designed to provide reasonable assurance, at appropriate costs, that transactions are executed and recorded in accordance with management's authorization. The consolidated financial statements and related notes thereto have been audited by Deloitte & Touche LLP, independent auditors. The accompanying auditors' report expresses an independent professional opinion on the fairness of presentation of management's financial statements.

The Audit Committee of the Board of Directors is composed of certain of the Company's outside directors, and is responsible for selecting the independent auditing firm to be retained for the coming year. The Audit Committee meets periodically with the independent auditors, as well as with management, to review internal accounting controls and financial reporting matters. The independent auditors also meet privately on occasion with the Audit Committee, to discuss the scope and results of their audits and any recommendations regarding the system of internal accounting controls.

Kosta Kartsotis
President and
Chief Executive Officer

Mike L. Kovar
Senior Vice President,
Chief Financial Officer
and Treasurer

CONSOLIDATED BALANCE SHEETS

DOLLARS IN THOUSANDS

	January 5, 2002	*December 30, 2000*
Assets		
Current assets:		
Cash and cash equivalents	$ 67,491	$ 79,501
Short-term marketable investments	5,360	11,312
Accounts receivable–net	74,035	62,876
Inventories	103,662	81,118
Deferred income tax benefits	8,718	7,779
Prepaid expenses and other current assets	10,251	10,245
Total current assets	269,517	252,831
Investments in joint ventures	1,099	5,935
Property, plant and equipment–net	90,036	42,252
Intangible and other assets–net	20,211	6,573
Total assets	$ 380,863	$ 307,591
Liabilities and Stockholders' Equity		
Current liabilities:		
Note payable	$ 15,955	$ 5,107
Accounts payable	21,266	18,325
Accrued expenses:		
Co-op advertising	14,838	14,320
Compensation	8,594	6,179
Other	27,679	19,145
Income taxes payable	17,905	19,964
Total current liabilities	106,237	83,040
Deferred income tax liability	7,318	–
Commitments (Note 10)		
Minority interest in subsidiaries	3,285	3,852
Stockholders' equity:		
Common stock, 30,284,369 and 30,136,824 shares issued and outstanding, respectively	303	301
Additional paid-in capital	15,241	14,214
Retained earnings	252,112	208,429
Accumulated other comprehensive loss	(3,633)	(2,245)
Total stockholders' equity	264,023	220,699
Total liabilities and stockholders' equity	$ 380,863	$ 307,591

See notes to consolidated financial statements.

CONSOLIDATED STATEMENTS OF INCOME AND COMPREHENSIVE INCOME

AMOUNTS IN THOUSANDS, EXCEPT PER SHARE DATA

Fiscal Year	2001	2000	1999
Net sales	$ 545,541	$ 504,285	$ 418,762
Cost of sales	273,691	248,539	205,875
Gross profit	271,850	255,746	212,887
Operating expenses:			
Selling and distribution	149,807	126,239	95,349
General and administrative	45,189	35,686	30,089
Total operating expenses	194,996	161,925	125,438
Operating income	76,854	93,821	87,449
Interest expense	319	128	117
Write-off of investment in joint venture	(4,776)	–	–
Other income (expense)-net	1,045	1,024	509
Income before income taxes	72,804	94,717	87,841
Provision for income taxes	29,121	38,834	36,015
Net income	$ 43,683	$ 55,883	$ 51,826
Other comprehensive income:			
Currency translation adjustment	(1,374)	827	(1,658)
Unrealized (loss) gain on marketable investments	(35)	187	(564)
Forward contracts as hedge of intercompany foreign currency payments:			
Cumulative effect of implementing SFAS No.133	(400)	–	–
Change in fair values	421	–	–
Total comprehensive income	$ 42,295	$ 56,897	$ 49,604
Earnings per share:			
Basic	$ 1.45	$ 1.76	$ 1.63
Diluted	$ 1.40	$ 1.71	$ 1.55
Weighted average common shares outstanding:			
Basic	30,167	31,689	31,900
Diluted	31,240	32,675	33,428

See notes to consolidated financial statements.

CONSOLIDATED STATEMENTS OF STOCKHOLDERS' EQUITY

AMOUNTS IN THOUSANDS

	common stock				accumulated other comprehensive income (loss)			treasury stock		
	shares	par value	additional paid-in capital	retained earnings	cumulative translation adjustment	unrealized gain (loss) on marketable investments	unrealized gain (loss) on forward contracts	shares	share cost	total stockholders' equity
Balance, January 2, 1999	20,932	$ 209	$ 34,345	$ 102,858	$ (1,037)	$ –	$ –	(104)	$ (1,456)	$ 134,919
Common stock issued upon exercise of stock options	709	7	3,632	–	–	–	–	–	–	3,639
Tax benefit derived from exercise of stock options	–	–	3,902	–	–	–	–	–	–	3,902
Purchase of treasury shares	–	–	–	–	–	–	–	(90)	(1,994)	(1,994)
Reissuance of treasury stock upon exercise of stock options	–	–	–	(1,115)	–	–	–	135	2,242	1,127
Three-for-two-stock split	10,466	105	(105)	–	–	–	–	–	–	–
Net income	–	–	–	51,826	–	–	–	–	–	51,826
Unrealized loss on marketable investments	–	–	–	–	–	(564)	–	–	–	(564)
Currency translation adjustment	–	–	–	–	(1,658)	–	–	–	–	(1,658)
Balance, January 1, 2000	32,107	321	41,774	153,569	(2,695)	(564)	–	(59)	(1,208)	191,197
Common stock issued upon exercise of stock options	56	–	384	–	–	–	–	–	–	384
Tax benefit derived from exercise of stock options	–	–	470	–	–	–	–	–	–	470
Purchase of treasury shares	–	–	–	–	–	–	–	(13)	(268)	(268)
Reissuance of treasury stock upon exercise of stock options	–	–	–	(1,023)	–	–	–	72	1,476	453
Repurchase and retirement of common stock	(2,026)	(20)	(28,414)	–	–	–	–	–	–	(28,434)
Net income	–	–	–	55,883	–	–	–	–	–	55,883
Unrealized gain on marketable investments	–	–	–	–	–	187	–	–	–	187
Currency translation adjustment	–	–	–	–	827	–	–	–	–	827
Balance, December 30, 2000	30,137	301	14,214	208,429	(1,868)	(377)	–	–	–	220,699
Common stock issued upon exercise of stock options	307	3	2,622	–	–	–	–	–	–	2,625
Tax benefit derived from exercise of stock options	–	–	1,160	–	–	–	–	–	–	1,160
Common stock issued in connection with acquisitions	46	1	786	–	–	–	–	–	–	787
Repurchase and retirement of common stock	(206)	(2)	(3,541)	–	–	–	–	–	–	(3,543)
Net income	–	–	–	43,683	–	–	–	–	–	43,683
Unrealized loss on marketable investments	–	–	–	–	–	(35)	–	–	–	(35)
Currency translation adjustment	–	–	–	–	(1,374)	–	–	–	–	(1,374)
Forward contracts as hedge of intercompany foreign currency payments:										
Cumulative effect of implementing SFAS No.133	–	–	–	–	–	–	(400)	–	–	(400)
Change in fair values	–	–	–	–	–	–	421	–	–	421
Balance, January 5, 2002	30,284	$ 303	$ 15,241	$ 252,112	$ (3,242)	$ (412)	$ 21	–	$ –	$ 264,023

See notes to consolidated financial statements.

CONSOLIDATED STATEMENTS OF CASH FLOWS

DOLLARS IN THOUSANDS

Fiscal Year	2001	2000	1999
Operating Activities:			
Net income	$ 43,683	$ 55,883	$ 51,826
Noncash items affecting net income:			
Write-off of investment in joint venture	4,776	–	–
Minority interest in subsidiaries	1,430	1,786	1,484
Equity in losses of joint ventures	933	381	151
Depreciation and amortization	9,627	6,436	5,889
Tax benefit derived from exercise of stock options	1,160	470	3,902
Loss on disposal of assets	316	420	19
Increase in allowance for doubtful accounts	1,811	1,523	1,044
Increase in allowance for returns–net of related inventory in transit	268	742	2,098
Deferred income taxes	6,378	(1,010)	(1,114)
Changes in operating assets and liabilities, net of effects of acquisitions:			
Accounts receivable	(7,340)	(15,983)	(11,355)
Inventories	(15,776)	(15,993)	(3,014)
Prepaid expenses and other current assets	712	(2,509)	(4,733)
Accounts payable	(1,886)	7,842	(5,056)
Accrued expenses	4,998	(2,274)	13,544
Income taxes payable	(2,184)	2,574	6,909
Net cash from operating activities	48,906	40,288	61,594
Investing Activities:			
Business acquisitions, net of cash acquired	(15,787)	–	(2,732)
Effect of de-consolidating former subsidiary	(747)	–	–
Additions to property, plant and equipment	(55,610)	(20,341)	(10,568)
Sale (purchase) of marketable investments	5,951	(442)	(10,870)
Investment in joint ventures	(373)	(2,196)	(4,000)
Increase in intangible and other assets	(810)	(818)	(1,505)
Net cash used in investing activities	(67,376)	(23,797)	(29,675)
Financing Activities:			
Common stock issued upon exercise of stock options	2,625	838	4,766
Net purchase of treasury stock	–	(268)	(1,994)
Acquisition and retirement of common stock	(3,543)	(27,806)	–
Distribution of minority interest earnings	(1,116)	(492)	(790)
Increase in notes payable–banks	8,904	64	505
Net cash from (used in) financing activities	6,870	(27,664)	2,487
Effect of exchange rate changes on cash and cash equivalents	(410)	(234)	(761)
Net (decrease) increase in cash and cash equivalents	(12,010)	(11,407)	33,645
Cash and cash equivalents:			
Beginning of year	79,501	90,908	57,263
End of year	$ 67,491	$ 79,501	$ 90,908

See notes to consolidated financial statements.

NOTES TO CONSOLIDATED FINANCIAL STATEMENTS

1. Significant Accounting Policies

Consolidated Financial Statements include the accounts of Fossil, Inc., a Delaware corporation and its subsidiaries (the "Company"). The Company reports on a fiscal year reflecting the retail-based calendar (containing 4-4-5 week calendar quarters). During 2001, the retail-based calendar contained 53 weeks instead of 52 weeks in the prior year. The additional week did not have a material impact on comparability to prior periods. References to 2001, 2000, and 1999 are for the fiscal years ended January 5, 2002, December 30, 2000 and January 1, 2000, respectively. Significant intercompany balances and transactions are eliminated in consolidation. The Company is a leader in the design, development, marketing and distribution of contemporary, high quality fashion watches, accessories and apparel. The Company's products are sold primarily through department stores and specialty retailers worldwide.

The preparation of financial statements in conformity with accounting principles generally accepted in the United States of America requires management to make estimates and assumptions that affect the reported amounts of assets and liabilities and the disclosure of contingent assets and liabilities at the date of the financial statements and the reported amounts of revenues and expenses during the reporting period. Actual results could differ from those estimates.

Cash Equivalents are considered all highly liquid investments with original maturities at date of purchase of three months or less.

Short–term Marketable Investments consist of liquid investments with original maturities exceeding three months and mutual fund investments. By policy, the Company invests primarily in high-grade marketable securities. Securities of $5.4 million and $5.1 million for fiscal years 2001 and 2000, respectively, are classified as available for sale and stated at fair value, with unrealized holding gains (losses) included in accumulated other comprehensive income (loss) as a component of stockholders' equity. At the end of 2001, there were no securities classified as held-to-maturity. Securities of $6.2 million for fiscal 2000 are classified as held-to-maturity and are stated at amortized cost.

Accounts Receivable are stated net of allowances of approximately $22.5 million and $21.2 million for estimated customer returns and approximately $11.7 million and $9.5 million for doubtful accounts at the close of fiscal years 2001 and 2000, respectively.

Inventories are stated at the lower of average cost, including any applicable duty and freight charges, or market.

Property, Plant and Equipment is stated at cost less accumulated depreciation and amortization. Depreciation is provided using the straight-line method over the estimated useful lives of the assets of three to ten years for equipment and thirty years for buildings. Leasehold improvements are amortized over the shorter of the lease term or the asset's useful life.

Intangible and Other Assets include the cost in excess of tangible assets acquired, noncompete agreements and trademarks. Non-compete agreements and trademarks are amortized using the straight-line method over the estimated useful lives of generally three and ten years, respectively. During 2001, cost in excess of tangible assets acquired, relative to business combinations occurring prior to July 1, 2001, have been amortized using the straight-line method over 20 years. In accordance with SFAS No. 142, "Goodwill and Other Intangible Assets", issued in July 2001, future cost in excess of tangible assets acquired and other indefinite-lived intangible assets, related to business combinations occuring on or after July 1, 2001, will be tested for impairment rather than amortized beginning January 2002.

Cumulative Translation Adjustment is included in accumulated other comprehensive income (loss) as a component of stockholders' equity and reflects the unrealized adjustments resulting from translating the financial statements of foreign subsidiaries. The functional currency of the Company's foreign subsidiaries is the local currency of the country. Accordingly, assets and liabilities of the foreign subsidiaries are translated to U.S. dollars at year-end exchange rates. Income and expense items are translated at the average rates prevailing during the year. Changes in exchange rates that affect cash flows and the related receivables or payables are recognized as transaction gains and losses in the determination of net income. The Company incurred net foreign currency transaction gains of approximately $0.3 million and losses of $0.4 million and $1.2 million for fiscal years 2001, 2000 and 1999, respectively, which have been included in other income (expense)–net.

Forward Contracts are entered into by the Company principally to hedge the future payment of intercompany inventory transactions with its non-U.S. subsidiaries. Beginning in fiscal year 2001 these cash flow hedges are stated at estimated fair value and changes in fair value are reported as a component of other comprehensive income. At January 5, 2002, the Company had hedge contracts to sell (i) 16.7 million Euro for approximately $14.9 million, expiring through June 2002, and (ii) approximately 0.4 million British Pounds for approximately $0.6 million, expiring through January 2002. If the Company were to settle its Euro and British Pound based contracts at fiscal year-end 2001, the net result would be a gain of approximately $21,000, net of taxes. This unrealized gain is recognized in other comprehensive income. The Company adopted SFAS No. 133, "Accounting for Derivative Instruments and Hedging Activities," effective December 31, 2000, and recognized an unrealized loss for forward contracts open at that date of $400,000, net of taxes, in other comprehensive income. The net increase in fair value of $421,000, is reported as other comprehensive income during fiscal 2001. This net increase consisted of net gains from these hedges of $1.0 million, less $584,000 of net gains reclassified into earnings.

Revenues are recognized as sales when merchandise is shipped and title transfers to the customer. The Company permits the return of damaged or defective products and accepts limited amounts of product returns in certain other instances. Accordingly, the Company provides allowances for the estimated amounts of these returns at the time of revenue recognition.

Advertising Costs for in-store and media advertising as well as co-op advertising, internet portal costs and promotional allowances are expensed as incurred. Advertising expenses for fiscal years 2001, 2000 and 1999 were approximately $32.9 million, $32.3 million and $27.1 million, respectively.

New Accounting Standards. In July 2001, the Financial Accounting Standards Board ("FASB") issued SFAS No. 141, "Business Combinations," and SFAS No. 142, "Goodwill and Other Intangible Assets." These standards were adopted by the Company on July 1, 2001. Under SFAS No. 142, all goodwill and intangible assets with indefinite lives will not be amortized in fiscal 2002 (amortization expense of $185,000 recognized in 2001) but will be tested for impairment annually and also in the event of an impairment indication. The Company does not expect the adoption of these standards to have a material effect on its financial statements.

The FASB also issued SFAS No. 144, "Accounting for the Impairment or the Disposal of Long-Lived Assets," which is effective January 6, 2002 for the Company. SFAS No. 144 supersedes SFAS No.121 "Accounting for the Impairment of Long-Lived Assets and for Long-Lived Assets to be Disposed of." The Company has evaluated the impact of the provisions of SFAS No. 144, and believes the results of such evaluation would not result in any material adjustments to the carrying value of its long-lived assets as of the balance sheet date.

Minority Interest in Subsidiaries, included within other income (expense)—net represents the minority stockholders' share of the net income (loss) of various consolidated subsidiaries. The minority interest in the consolidated balance sheets reflects the proportionate interest in the equity of the various consolidated subsidiaries.

Earnings Per Share ("EPS"). Basic EPS is based on the weighted average number of common shares outstanding during each period. Diluted EPS includes the effects of dilutive stock options outstanding during each period using the treasury stock method.

2. Acquisitions

In May 2001, Fossil UK Holdings, Ltd., an indirect wholly owned subsidiary of the Company, acquired 100% of the capital stock of The Avia Watch Company Ltd. ("Avia") as well as certain trademarks utilized by Avia from Roventa-Henex S.A. for a cash purchase price of approximately $5.0 million. The acquisition was recorded as a purchase and, in connection therewith, the Company recorded goodwill of approximately $3.3 million.

In July 2001, the Company acquired 80% of the capital stock of FSLA, Pty. Limited, the Company's distributor in Australia, for a cash purchase price of approximately $300,000. This acquisition was recorded as a purchase and, in connection therewith, the Company recorded goodwill of approximately $200,000.

Effective July 2001, Fossil (East) Limited ("Fossil East") increased its equity interest in Pulse Time, Ltd. to 90% by acquiring an additional 30% of the capital stock from its minority holders in exchange for approximately 24,000 shares of the Company's common stock, par value $0.1 per share (the "Common Stock") valued at $450,000. Additionally, on July 3, 2001, Fossil East increased its equity interest in Trylink, Ltd. to 85% by acquiring an additional 34% of the capital stock from its minority holders in exchange for $225,000 in cash and approximately 14,000 shares of the Company's Common Stock valued at $225,000. Both of these acquisitions have been accounted for as a purchase and no goodwill was recorded in connection with either transaction.

Effective August 2001, the Company acquired 99.6% of the outstanding capital stock of Vedette Industries, SA, the Company's distributor in France, for a cash purchase price of approximately $5.3 million. The terms of this transaction include a future earnout payment of an amount up to $1.5 million in the event that defined sales and operating income objectives are achieved. The acquisition was recorded as a purchase and, in connection therewith, the Company recorded goodwill of approximately $2.5 million, including amounts relating to the earnout provision.

In August 2001, the Company acquired the worldwide rights to the ZODIAC brand name and related inventory for a cash purchase price of approximately $4.7 million. This acquisition was recorded as a purchase and $0.2 million of goodwill was recorded in connection with this transaction.

In October 2001, the Company acquired the outstanding stock of two separate companies and certain assets of a third, all located in Switzerland, for a combined cash purchase price of approximately $2.3 million. The terms of these transactions include future earnout payments for amounts up to approximately

$750,000, in the event certain earnings thresholds are met. This acquisition was recorded as a purchase and, in connection therewith, the Company recorded goodwill of approximately $1.5 million, including amounts relating to the earnout provision.

The results of these business combinations are included in the accompanying consolidated financial statements since the dates of their acquisition. The proforma effects, as if transactions had occurred at the beginning of the years presented, are not significant.

3. Investments in Joint Ventures

During 1999, the Company acquired a 20% interest in SII Marketing International, Inc. ("SMI"), and since that time has invested $6.0 million in the venture. SMI, a joint venture between the Company and SII, was formed to design, market and distribute watches in the mass-market distribution channel. The investment of $5.4 million and $3.8 million at fiscal year-end 2000 and 1999, respectively, had been carried on the equity basis. The Company's equity in SMI's net loss of $1,100,000, $409,000 and $151,000 for fiscal 2001, 2000 and 1999, respectively, is included in other income (expense)—net. Subsequent to fiscal year-end 2001, the Company entered into an agreement to transfer its 20% interest in SMI to SII for no additional consideration in exchange for SII's agreement to indemnify the Company from certain existing and any future losses in connection with SMI. The write-off of the Company's remaining investment in SMI and recognition of certain transition cost of $4.8 million is reported as a separate item as other expense for fiscal year 2001.

Effective July 2001, the Company sold 50% of the equity of its wholly-owned subsidiary in Japan to Seiko Instruments Incorporated ("SII") pursuant to a joint venture agreement for the marketing, distribution and sale of the Company's products in Japan. The Company has accounted for this investment based upon the equity method from the effective date of the transaction.

In August 2000, the Company sold 50% of the equity of its former wholly-owned subsidiary ("Fossil Spain") pursuant to a joint venture agreement with Sucesores de A. Cardarso for the marketing, distribution and sale of the Company's products in Spain. The Company has accounted for the investment based upon the equity method from the effective date of the transaction. The Company's equity in Fossil Spain's net income was $497,000 and $28,000 for fiscal 2001 and 2000, respectively, and is included in other income (expense)—net.

4. Inventories

Inventories consist of the following:

Fiscal Year-End *IN THOUSANDS*	2001	2000
Components and parts	$ 4,659	$ 6,258
Work-in-process	3,855	1,182
Finished merchandise on hand	70,547	48,113
Merchandise at Company stores	11,365	13,296
Merchandise in-transit from customer returns	13,236	12,269
	$ 103,662	$ 81,118

5. Property, Plant and Equipment

Property, plant and equipment consist of the following:

Fiscal Year-End *IN THOUSANDS*	2001	2000
Land	$ 7,757	$ 2,525
Buildings	15,949	11,142
Furniture and fixtures	33,348	24,977
Computer equipment and software	18,536	11,883
Leasehold improvements	19,579	13,494
Construction in progress	27,549	1,817
	122,718	65,838
Less accumulated depreciation and amortization	32,682	23,586
	$ 90,036	$ 42,252

6. Intangible and Other Assets

Intangibles and other assets consist of the following:

Fiscal Year-End *IN THOUSANDS*	2001	2000
Costs in excess of tangible net assets acquired	$ 13,401	$ 5,200
Noncompete agreement	475	475
Trademarks	5,168	1,030
Deposits	2,320	1,458
Cash surrender value of life insurance	900	783
Other	978	290
	23,242	9,236
Less accumulated amortization	3,031	2,663
	$ 20,211	$ 6,573

8. Other Income (Expense) – Net

Other income (expense)—net consists of the following:

Fiscal Year *IN THOUSANDS*	2001	2000	1999
Interest income	$ 1,549	$ 3,480	$ 2,650
Minority interest in subsidiaries	(1,430)	(1,786)	(1,484)
Equity in losses of joint ventures	(933)	(381)	(151)
Currency gain (loss)	336	(412)	(1,181)
Royalty income	740	770	353
Insurance proceeds above book value	–	–	52
Other income (expense)	783	(647)	270
	$ 1,045	$ 1,024	$ 509

9. Income Taxes

Deferred income tax benefits reflect the net tax effects of deductible temporary differences between the carrying amounts of assets and liabilities for financial reporting purposes and the amounts used for income tax purposes. The tax effects of significant items comprising the Company's net deferred tax benefits, consist of the following:

Fiscal Year-End *IN THOUSANDS*	2001	2000
Current assets:		
Deferred tax assets:		
Bad debt allowance	$ 3,709	$ 3,163
Returns allowance	6,772	6,537
263( ) capitalization of inventory	878	704
Miscellaneous tax asset items	1,260	1,060
Deferred tax liabilities:		
In-transit returns inventory	(3,901)	(3,685)
Net current deferred tax benefits	8,718	7,779
Long-term deferred tax liability:		
Tax on certain undistributed earnings of foreign subsidiaries	(7,318)	–
Net deferred tax benefit	$ 1,400	$ 7,779

10. Commitments

License Agreements. The Company has various license agreements to market watches bearing certain trademarks owned by various entities. In accordance with these agreements, the Company incurred royalty expense of approximately $11.2 million, $9.6 million and $4.7 million in fiscal years 2001, 2000 and 1999, respectively. These amounts are included in the Company's cost of sales and selling expenses. The Company had several agreements in effect at the end of fiscal year 2001 which expire on various dates from February 2002 through December 2007 and require the Company to pay royalties ranging from 6% to 20.5% of defined net sales. Future minimum royalty commitments under such license agreements at the close of fiscal year 2001 are as follows (amounts in thousands):

2002	$ 11,122
2003	11,420
2004	5,551
2005	1,360
2006	1,863
Thereafter	1,855
	$ 33,171

Leases. The Company leases its retail and outlet store facilities as well as certain of its office facilities and equipment under non-cancelable operating leases. Most of the retail store leases provide for contingent rental based on operating results and require the payment of taxes, insurance and other costs applicable to the property. Generally, these leases include renewal options for various periods at stipulated rates. Rent expense under these agreements was approximately $17.5 million, $10.9 million, and $6.8 million for fiscal years 2001, 2000 and 1999, respectively. Contingent rent expense has been immaterial in each of the last three fiscal years. Future minimum rental commitments under non-cancelable such leases at the close of fiscal year 2001 are as follows (amounts in thousands):

2002	$ 14,428
2003	14,622
2004	14,245
2005	13,753
2006	13,115
Thereafter	50,382
	$ 120,545

Appendix B Pier 1 Imports Annual Report

Pier 1 Imports, Inc.

FINANCIAL SUMMARY
($ in millions except per share amounts)

	4-Year Compound Annual Growth Rate	Year Ended 2002	2001 (1)	2000	1999	1998
SUMMARY OF OPERATIONS:						
Net sales	9.5%	$ 1,548.6	1,411.5	1,231.1	1,138.6	1,075.4
Gross profit	8.9%	$ 649.8	594.5	512.5	500.4	461.5
Selling, general and administrative expenses	9.1%	$ 448.1	399.8	349.4	334.6	315.8
Depreciation and amortization	15.7%	$ 42.8	43.2	40.0	31.1	23.9
Operating income	6.9%	$ 158.8	151.5	123.2	134.7	121.7
Nonoperating (income) and expenses, net (2)		$ (0.2)	1.3	4.6	5.0	(2.3)
Income before income taxes	6.4%	$ 159.0	150.2	118.6	129.6	124.0
Net income	6.5%	$ 100.2	94.7	74.7	80.4	78.0
PER SHARE AMOUNTS (ADJUSTED FOR STOCK SPLITS AND DIVIDENDS):						
Basic earnings	8.3%	$ 1.06	.98	.78	.82	.77
Diluted earnings	9.6%	$ 1.04	.97	.75	.77	.72
Cash dividends declared	15.5%	$ .16	.15	.12	.12	.09
Shareholders' equity	12.4%	$ 6.20	5.52	4.60	4.12	3.89
OTHER FINANCIAL DATA:						
Working capital (3)	9.0%	$ 396.8	333.0	239.3	252.1	280.8
Current ratio (3)	(3.2%)	2.9	3.3	2.4	2.9	3.3
Total assets	7.2%	$ 862.7	735.7	670.7	654.0	653.4
Long-term debt (3)	(31.4%)	$ 25.4	25.0	25.0	96.0	114.9
Shareholders' equity	10.5%	$ 585.7	531.9	440.7	403.9	392.7
Weighted average diluted shares outstanding (millions)		96.2	98.0	103.3	108.9	112.9
Effective tax rate		37.0%	37.0	37.0	38.0	37.1
Return on average shareholders' equity		17.9%	19.5	17.7	20.2	21.8
Return on average total assets		12.5%	13.5	11.3	12.3	12.8
Pre-tax return on sales		10.3%	10.6	9.6	11.4	11.5

(1) Fiscal 2001 consisted of a 53-week year. All other fiscal years presented reflect 52-week years.
(2) Nonoperating (income) and expenses, net, were comprised of interest expense and interest and investment income in each fiscal year presented, and in addition, included net recoveries associated with trading activities in fiscal 1998.
(3) The reduction in fiscal 2000 working capital, current ratio and long-term debt was the result of the Company's call of its outstanding $5\frac{3}{4}$% convertible subordinated notes. The notes were primarily converted into shares of the Company's common stock in March 2000. Excluding the reclassification of the $5\frac{3}{4}$% notes from long-term to short-term, working capital would have been $278.5 million with a current ratio of 3.0 to 1 at fiscal 2000 year-end.

Pier 1 Imports, Inc.

REPORT OF INDEPENDENT AUDITORS

To the Board of Directors of Pier 1 Imports, Inc.

We have audited the accompanying consolidated balance sheets of Pier 1 Imports, Inc. as of March 2, 2002 and March 3, 2001, and the related consolidated statements of operations, shareholders' equity and cash flows for each of the three years in the period ended March 2, 2002. These financial statements are the responsibility of the Company's management. Our responsibility is to express an opinion on these financial statements based on our audits.

We conducted our audits in accordance with auditing standards generally accepted in the United States. Those standards require that we plan and perform the audit to obtain reasonable assurance about whether the financial statements are free of material misstatement. An audit includes examining, on a test basis, evidence supporting the amounts and disclosures in the financial statements. An audit also includes assessing the accounting principles used and significant estimates made by management, as well as evaluating the overall financial statement presentation. We believe that our audits provide a reasonable basis for our opinion.

In our opinion, the financial statements referred to above present fairly, in all material respects, the consolidated financial position of Pier 1 Imports, Inc. at March 2, 2002 and March 3, 2001, and the consolidated results of its operations and its cash flows for each of the three years in the period ended March 2, 2002, in conformity with accounting principles generally accepted in the United States.

Ernst & Young LLP

Fort Worth, Texas
April 8, 2002

REPORT OF MANAGEMENT

To our shareholders:

Management is responsible for the preparation and the integrity of the accompanying consolidated financial statements and related notes, which have been prepared in accordance with accounting principles generally accepted in the United States and include amounts based upon our estimates and judgments, as required. The consolidated financial statements have been audited by Ernst & Young LLP, independent certified public accountants. The accompanying independent auditors' report expresses an independent professional opinion on the fairness of presentation of management's financial statements.

The Company maintains a system of internal controls over financial reporting. We believe this system provides reasonable assurance that transactions are executed in accordance with management authorization and that such transactions are properly recorded and reported in the financial statements, that assets are properly safeguarded and accounted for, and that records are maintained so as to permit preparation of financial statements in accordance with accounting principles generally accepted in the United States. The Company also has instituted policies and guidelines, which require employees to maintain a high level of ethical standards.

In addition, the Board of Directors exercises its oversight role with respect to the Company's internal control systems primarily through its Audit Committee. The Audit Committee consists solely of outside directors and meets periodically with management, the Company's internal auditors and the Company's independent auditors to review internal accounting controls, audit results, financial reporting, and accounting principles and practices. The Company's independent and internal auditors have full and free access to the Audit Committee with and without management's presence. Although no cost-effective internal control system will preclude all errors and irregularities, we believe our controls as of and for the year ended March 2, 2002 provide reasonable assurance that the consolidated financial statements are reliable.

Marvin J. Girouard
Chairman of the Board
and Chief Executive Officer

Charles H. Turner
Executive Vice President,
Chief Financial Officer
and Treasurer

Pier 1 Imports, Inc.

CONSOLIDATED STATEMENTS OF OPERATIONS
(in thousands except per share amounts)

	Year Ended		
	2002	2001	2000
Net sales	$ 1,548,556	$ 1,411,498	$ 1,231,095
Operating costs and expenses:			
Cost of sales (including buying and store occupancy costs)	898,795	817,043	718,547
Selling, general and administrative expenses	448,127	399,755	349,394
Depreciation and amortization	42,821	43,184	39,973
	1,389,743	1,259,982	1,107,914
Operating income	158,813	151,516	123,181
Nonoperating (income) and expenses:			
Interest and investment income	(2,484)	(1,854)	(2,349)
Interest expense	2,300	3,130	6,918
	(184)	1,276	4,569
Income before income taxes	158,997	150,240	118,612
Provision for income taxes	58,788	55,590	43,887
Net income	$ 100,209	$ 94,650	$ 74,725
Earnings per share:			
Basic	$ 1.06	$ .98	$ .78
Diluted	$ 1.04	$ .97	$ .75
Dividends declared per share	$ .16	$ .15	$ .12
Average shares outstanding during period:			
Basic	94,414	96,306	95,766
Diluted	96,185	97,952	103,297

The accompanying notes are an integral part of these financial statements.

Pier 1 Imports, Inc.

CONSOLIDATED BALANCE SHEETS

(in thousands except share amounts)

	2002	2001
ASSETS		
Current assets:		
Cash, including temporary investments of $213,488 and $31,142, respectively	$ 235,609	$ 46,841
Beneficial interest in securitized receivables	44,620	75,403
Other accounts receivable, net of allowance for doubtful accounts of $275 and $295, respectively	6,205	8,370
Inventories	275,433	310,704
Prepaid expenses and other current assets	43,286	35,748
Total current assets	605,153	477,066
Properties, net	209,954	212,066
Other noncurrent assets	47,565	46,578
	$ 862,672	$ 735,710
LIABILITIES AND SHAREHOLDERS' EQUITY		
Current liabilities:		
Current portion of long-term debt	$ 356	$ –
Accounts payable and accrued liabilities	208,040	144,110
Total current liabilities	208,396	144,110
Long-term debt	25,356	25,000
Other noncurrent liabilities	43,264	34,721
Shareholders' equity:		
Common stock, $1.00 par, 500,000,000 shares authorized, 100,779,000 issued	100,779	100,779
Paid-in capital	140,190	139,424
Retained earnings	429,910	344,809
Cumulative other comprehensive income	(4,702)	(3,115)
Less – 7,362,000 and 4,619,000 common shares in treasury, at cost, respectively	(80,521)	(49,933)
Less – unearned compensation	–	(85)
	585,656	531,879
Commitments and contingencies	–	–
	$ 862,672	$ 735,710

The accompanying notes are an integral part of these financial statements.

Pier 1 Imports, Inc.

CONSOLIDATED STATEMENTS OF CASH FLOWS
(in thousands except share amounts)

	Year Ended		
	2002	2001	2000
CASH FLOW FROM OPERATING ACTIVITIES:			
Net income	$ 100,209	$ 94,650	$ 74,725
Adjustments to reconcile to net cash provided by operating activities:			
Depreciation and amortization	42,821	43,184	39,973
Loss on disposal of fixed assets	4,205	6,514	5,828
Deferred compensation	3,697	2,072	1,543
Deferred taxes	(2,238)	735	1,724
Other	(1,707)	(184)	1,938
Change in cash from:			
Inventories	34,804	(39,127)	(10,133)
Other accounts receivable and other current assets	(2,983)	(5,847)	586
Accounts payable and accrued expenses	66,048	6,280	8,962
Other noncurrent assets	(32)	(378)	(2,382)
Other noncurrent liabilities	(500)	(390)	(911)
Net cash provided by operating activities	244,324	107,509	121,853
CASH FLOW FROM INVESTING ACTIVITIES:			
Capital expenditures	(57,925)	(42,745)	(48,219)
Proceeds from disposition of properties	16,682	353	19,425
Net cost from disposition of Sunbelt Nursery Group, Inc. properties	–	–	(439)
Acquisitions, net of cash acquired	–	(3,917)	–
Beneficial interest in securitized receivables	30,783	(21,583)	(12,820)
Net cash used in investing activities	(10,460)	(67,892)	(42,053)
CASH FLOW FROM FINANCING ACTIVITIES:			
Cash dividends	(15,134)	(14,494)	(11,504)
Purchases of treasury stock	(44,137)	(34,270)	(31,806)
Proceeds from stock options exercised, stock purchase plan and other, net	13,463	5,627	4,148
Borrowings under long-term debt	712	82,500	4,035
Repayments of long-term debt	–	(82,515)	(36,242)
Net cash used in financing activities	(45,096)	(43,152)	(71,369)
Change in cash and cash equivalents	188,768	(3,535)	8,431
Cash and cash equivalents at beginning of year	46,841	50,376	41,945
Cash and cash equivalents at end of year	$ 235,609	$ 46,841	$ 50,376
Supplemental cash flow information:			
Interest paid	$ 2,493	$ 3,171	$ 7,137
Income taxes paid	$ 35,951	$ 58,302	$ 40,883

During fiscal 2001, the Company issued 4,764,450 shares of its common stock upon the conversion of $39,164,000 principal amount of $5\frac{3}{4}$% convertible subordinated notes.

The accompanying notes are an integral part of these financial statements.

Pier 1 Imports, Inc.

CONSOLIDATED STATEMENTS OF SHAREHOLDERS' EQUITY
(in thousands except per share amounts)

	Common Stock Shares	Common Stock Amount	Paid-in Capital	Retained Earnings	Cumulative Other Comprehensive Income	Treasury Stock	Unearned Compensation	Total Shareholders' Equity
Balance February 27, 1999	97,672	$ 100,779	$ 159,631	$ 201,457	$ (1,850)	$ (54,654)	$ (1,469)	$ 403,894
Comprehensive income:								
Net income	–	–	–	74,725	–	–	–	74,725
Other comprehensive income, net of tax:								
Currency translation adjustments	–	–	–	–	314	–	–	314
Comprehensive income								75,039
Purchases of treasury stock	(4,393)	–	–	–	–	(31,806)	–	(31,806)
Restricted stock forfeits and amortization	(83)	–	709	–	–	(1,392)	1,168	485
Exercise of stock options, stock purchase plan and other	625	–	(4,629)	–	–	9,184	–	4,555
Cash dividends ($.12 per share)	–	–	–	(11,504)	–	–	–	(11,504)
Balance February 26, 2000	93,821	100,779	155,711	264,678	(1,536)	(78,668)	(301)	440,663
Comprehensive income:								
Net income	–	–	–	94,650	–	–	–	94,650
Other comprehensive income, net of tax:								
Currency translation adjustments	–	–	–	–	(1,579)	–	–	(1,579)
Comprehensive income								93,071
Purchases of treasury stock	(3,269)	–	–	–	–	(34,270)	–	(34,270)
Restricted stock amortization	–	–	–	–	–	–	216	216
Exercise of stock options, stock purchase plan and other	825	–	(1,774)	(25)	–	9,119	–	7,320
Cash dividends ($.15 per share)	–	–	–	(14,494)	–	–	–	(14,494)
Conversion of $5^{3}/_{4}$% convertible debt	4,764	–	(14,513)	–	–	53,886	–	39,373
Balance March 3, 2001	96,141	100,779	139,424	344,809	(3,115)	(49,933)	(85)	531,879
Comprehensive income:								
Net income	–	–	–	100,209	–	–	–	100,209
Other comprehensive income, net of tax:								
Currency translation adjustments	–	–	–	–	(1,587)	–	–	(1,587)
Comprehensive income								98,622
Purchases of treasury stock	(4,021)	–	–	–	–	(44,137)	–	(44,137)
Restricted stock amortization	–	–	–	–	–	–	85	85
Exercise of stock options, stock purchase plan and other	1,269	–	766	26	–	13,549	–	14,341
Cash dividends ($.16 per share)	–	–	–	(15,134)	–	–	–	(15,134)
Balance March 2, 2002	93,389	$ 100,779	$ 140,190	$ 429,910	$ (4,702)	$ (80,521)	$ –	$ 585,656

The accompanying notes are an integral part of these financial statements.

Pier 1 Imports, Inc.

NOTES TO CONSOLIDATED FINANCIAL STATEMENTS

NOTE 1 - SUMMARY OF SIGNIFICANT ACCOUNTING POLICIES

Organization - Pier 1 Imports, Inc. is one of North America's largest specialty retailers of imported decorative home furnishings, gifts and related items, with retail stores located in the United States, Canada, Puerto Rico, the United Kingdom and Mexico. Concentrations of risk with respect to sourcing the Company's inventory purchases are limited due to the large number of vendors or suppliers and their geographic dispersion around the world. The Company sells merchandise imported from over 40 different countries, with 35% of its sales derived from merchandise produced in China, 11% derived from merchandise produced in India and 29% derived from merchandise produced in Indonesia, Thailand, Brazil, Italy, the Philippines and Mexico. The remaining 25% of sales was from merchandise produced in various Asian, European, Central American, South American and African countries or was obtained from U.S. manufacturers.

Basis of consolidation - The consolidated financial statements of Pier 1 Imports, Inc. and its consolidated subsidiaries (the "Company") include the accounts of all subsidiary companies except Pier 1 Funding, LLC, which is a non-consolidated, bankruptcy remote, securitization subsidiary. *See Note 2 of the Notes to Consolidated Financial Statements.* Material intercompany transactions and balances have been eliminated.

Acquisitions - The Company completed its acquisition of certain assets and assumption of certain liabilities of Cargo Furniture, Inc. and formed New Cargo Furniture, Inc. ("Cargo") for $3,931,000, including cash acquired, on February 21, 2001. These assets and liabilities were included in the Company's consolidated balance sheet as of March 3, 2001; however, this acquisition had no effect on the Company's fiscal 2001 operations. Cargo is a retailer and wholesaler of casual lifestyle furniture, gifts and home décor with a focus on children's furniture. This acquisition was accounted for under the purchase method of accounting, and ultimately resulted in goodwill of $4,386,000, which has been amortized using the straight-line method over 20 years through fiscal 2002, at which time amortization ceases due to the adoption of Statement of Financial Accounting Standards ("SFAS") No. 142. The pro forma effect on the Company's results of operations, as if the acquisition had been completed at the beginning of fiscal 2001, was not significant. Cargo's operations for fiscal 2002 are fully consolidated with the Company's results.

Use of estimates - Preparation of the financial statements in conformity with accounting principles generally accepted in the United States requires management to make estimates and assumptions that affect the amounts reported in the financial statements and accompanying notes. Actual results could differ from those estimates.

Reclassifications - Certain reclassifications have been made in the prior years' consolidated financial statements to conform to the fiscal 2002 presentation.

Fiscal periods - The Company utilizes 5-4-4 (week) quarterly accounting periods with the fiscal year ending on the Saturday nearest the last day of February. Fiscal 2002 and 2000 consisted of 52-week years and fiscal 2001 was a 53-week year. Fiscal 2002 ended March 2, 2002, fiscal 2001 ended March 3, 2001 and fiscal 2000 ended February 26, 2000.

Cash and cash equivalents - The Company considers all highly liquid investments with an original maturity date of three months or less to be cash equivalents. The effect of foreign currency exchange rate fluctuations on cash is not material.

Translation of foreign currencies - Assets and liabilities of foreign operations are translated into U.S. dollars at fiscal year-end exchange rates. Income and expense items are translated at average exchange rates prevailing during the year. Translation adjustments arising from differences in exchange rates from period to period are included as a separate component of shareholders' equity and are included in comprehensive income.

Financial instruments - The fair value of financial instruments is determined by reference to various market data and other valuation techniques as appropriate. There were no significant assets or liabilities with a fair value different from the recorded value as of March 2, 2002 and March 3, 2001.

Risk management instruments: The Company may utilize various financial instruments to manage interest rate and market risk associated with its on- and off-balance sheet commitments.

The Company hedges certain commitments denominated in foreign currencies through the purchase of forward contracts. The forward contracts are purchased only to cover specific commitments to buy merchandise for resale. The Company also uses contracts to hedge its exposure associated with the repatriation of funds from its Canadian

Pier 1 Imports, Inc.

NOTES TO CONSOLIDATED FINANCIAL STATEMENTS
(continued)

operations. At March 2, 2002, the notional amount of the Company's forward foreign currency exchange contracts and contracts to hedge its exposure associated with repatriation of Canadian funds totaled approximately $3.9 million and $12.2 million, respectively. For financial accounting purposes, the Company has not designated such contracts as hedges. Thus, changes in the fair value of both of these forward contracts are included in the Company's consolidated statements of operations.

The Company enters into forward foreign currency exchange contracts with major financial institutions and continually monitors its positions with, and the credit quality of, these counterparties to such financial instruments. The Company does not expect non-performance by any of the counterparties, and any losses incurred in the event of non-performance would not be material.

Beneficial interest in securitized receivables - In February 1997, the Company sold all of its proprietary credit card receivables to a special-purpose wholly-owned subsidiary, Pier 1 Funding, Inc., predecessor to Pier 1 Funding, LLC ("Funding"), which transferred the receivables to the Pier 1 Imports Credit Card Master Trust (the "Master Trust"). The Master Trust is not consolidated by the Company as it meets the requirements of a qualifying special-purpose entity under SFAS No. 140. The Master Trust issues beneficial interests that represent undivided interests in the assets of the Master Trust consisting of the transferred receivables and all cash flows from collections of such receivables. The beneficial interests include certain interests retained by Funding, which are represented by Class B Certificates, and the residual interest in the Master Trust (the excess of the principal amount of receivables held in the Master Trust over the portion represented by the certificates sold to investors and the Class B Certificates).

Gain or loss on the sale of receivables depends in part on the previous carrying amount of the financial assets involved in the transfer, allocated between the assets sold and the retained interests based on their relative fair value at the date of transfer. A servicing asset or liability was not recognized in the Company's credit card securitizations (and thus was not considered in the gain or loss computation) since the Company received adequate compensation relative to current market servicing prices to service the receivables sold. Initial transaction costs for credit card securitizations were deferred and are being amortized over the expected life of the securitization.

The beneficial interest in the Master Trust is accounted for as an available-for-sale security. The Company estimates fair value of its beneficial interest in the Master Trust, both upon initial securitization and thereafter, based on the present value of future expected cash flows estimated using management's best estimates of key assumptions including credit losses and timeliness of payments. As of March 2, 2002, the Company's assumptions included credit losses of 5% of the outstanding balance and expected payment within a six-month period using a discount rate of 15% to calculate the present value of the future cash flows. A sensitivity analysis was performed assuming a hypothetical 20% adverse change in both interest rates and credit losses, which had an immaterial impact on the fair value of the Company's beneficial interest.

Inventories - Inventories are comprised of finished merchandise and are stated at the lower of average cost or market; cost is determined on a weighted average method.

Properties, maintenance and repairs - Buildings, equipment, furniture and fixtures, and leasehold interests and improvements are carried at cost less accumulated depreciation. Depreciation is computed using the straight-line method over estimated remaining useful lives of the assets, generally thirty years for buildings and three to seven years for equipment, furniture and fixtures. Amortization of improvements to leased properties is based upon the shorter of the remaining primary lease term or the estimated useful lives of such assets. Depreciation costs were $41,047,000, $41,882,000 and $38,672,000 in fiscal 2002, 2001 and 2000, respectively.

Expenditures for maintenance, repairs and renewals, which do not materially prolong the original useful lives of the assets, are charged to expense as incurred. In the case of disposals, assets and the related depreciation are removed from the accounts and the net amount, less proceeds from disposal, is credited or charged to income.

Revenue recognition - Revenue is recognized upon customer receipt or delivery for retail sales, including sales under deferred payment promotions on the Company's proprietary credit card. An allowance has been established to provide for estimated merchandise returns. Revenue from gift cards, gift certificates and merchandise credits is deferred until redemption.

Pier 1 Imports, Inc.

NOTES TO CONSOLIDATED FINANCIAL STATEMENTS
(continued)

In the initial sale of the Receivables, the Company sold all of its Receivables and received cash and beneficial interests in the Master Trust. The Master Trust sold to third parties $50.0 million of Series 1997-1 Class A Certificates, which bore interest at 6.74% and were scheduled to mature in May 2002. Funding retained $14.1 million of Series 1997-1 Class B Certificates, which were subordinated to the Class A Certificates. Funding also retained the residual interest in the Master Trust.

In September 2001, the Master Trust negotiated the purchase of all of the Series 1997-1 Class A Certificates from their holders. Subsequently the Master Trust retired both the Series 1997-1 Class A and Class B Certificates in connection with the issuance of $100 million in 2001-1 Class A Certificates to a third party. The 2001-1 Class A Certificates bear interest at a floating rate equal to the rate on commercial paper issued by the third party. As of March 2, 2002, this rate was 1.81%. Funding continued to retain the residual interest in the Master Trust and $9.3 million in 2001-1 Class B Certificates, which are subordinated to the 2001-1 Class A Certificates. As a result of this securitization transaction, the Company effectively sold a portion of its beneficial interest for net proceeds of $49.2 million. As of March 2, 2002 and March 3, 2001, the Company had $44.6 million and $75.4 million, respectively, in beneficial interests (comprised primarily of principal and interest related to the underlying Receivables) in the Master Trust.

Under generally accepted accounting principles, if the structure of the securitization meets certain requirements, these transactions are accounted for as sales of receivables. As the Company's securitizations met such requirements as discussed above, they were accounted for as sales. Gains or losses from sales of these receivables were not material during fiscal 2002, 2001 and 2000. The Company expects no material impact on net income in future years as a result of the sales of receivables, although the precise amounts will be dependent on a number of factors such as interest rates and levels of securitization.

NOTE 3 - PROPERTIES

Properties are summarized as follows at March 2, 2002 and March 3, 2001 (in thousands):

	2002	2001
Land	$ 16,458	$ 22,353
Buildings	51,747	59,716
Equipment, furniture and fixtures	238,454	207,956
Leasehold interests and improvements	183,676	171,021
	490,335	461,046
Less accumulated depreciation and amortization	280,381	248,980
Properties, net	$ 209,954	$ 212,066

NOTE 4 - ACCOUNTS PAYABLE AND ACCRUED LIABILITIES/OTHER NONCURRENT LIABILITIES

The following is a summary of accounts payable and accrued liabilities and other noncurrent liabilities at March 2, 2002 and March 3, 2001 (in thousands):

	2002	2001
Trade accounts payable	$ 78,961	$ 52,637
Accrued payroll and other employee-related liabilities	36,999	33,685
Accrued taxes, other than income	16,815	15,576
Gift cards, gift certificates and merchandise credits outstanding	29,288	18,989
Accrued income taxes payable	29,738	7,786
Other	16,239	15,437
Accounts payable and accrued liabilities	$ 208,040	$ 144,110
Accrued average rent	$ 19,230	$ 17,590
Other	24,034	17,131
Other noncurrent liabilities	$ 43,264	$ 34,721

NOTE 5 - LONG-TERM DEBT AND AVAILABLE CREDIT

Long-term debt is summarized as follows at March 2, 2002 and March 3, 2001 (in thousands):

	2002	2001
Industrial revenue bonds	$ 25,000	$ 25,000
Other	712	–
	25,712	25,000
Less – portion due within one year	356	–
Long-term debt	$ 25,356	$ 25,000

Pier 1 Imports, Inc.

NOTES TO CONSOLIDATED FINANCIAL STATEMENTS
(continued)

In fiscal 1987, the Company entered into industrial revenue development bond loan agreements aggregating $25 million. Proceeds were used to construct three warehouse distribution facilities. The loan agreements and related tax-exempt bonds mature in the year 2026. The Company's interest rates on the loans are based on the bond interest rates, which are market driven, reset weekly and are similar to other tax-exempt municipal debt issues. The Company's weighted average interest rates were 3.8% and 5.7% for fiscal 2002 and 2001, respectively.

In September 1996, the Company issued $86.3 million principal amount of $5^3/_4$% convertible subordinated notes due October 1, 2003. The notes were convertible at any time prior to maturity, unless previously redeemed or repurchased, into shares of common stock of the Company at a conversion price of $8.22 per share, adjusted for stock splits. The Company had the option to redeem the notes, in whole or in part, on or after October 2, 1999, at a redemption price (expressed as a percentage of principal amount) of 103% of par value which was scheduled to decline annually to 100% of par value at the maturity date. Interest on the notes was payable semiannually on April 1 and October 1 of each year. In February 2000, the Company announced its intention to call the remaining $39.2 million outstanding principal amount of these notes for redemption on March 23, 2000. The notes were convertible into common stock of the Company at any time prior to the close of business on March 22, 2000, at a conversion price of $8.22 per share. During March 2000, the Company converted $39,164,000 of the notes into 4,764,450 shares of the Company's common stock and redeemed $15,000 of the notes for cash at a redemption price of 103% of par value. The conversion and redemption of these notes during fiscal 2001 reduced the Company's debt by $39.2 million and increased its capitalization by $39.4 million. Accordingly, these notes are not detailed in the above schedule as the notes were fully redeemed at fiscal 2001 year-end.

In November 2001, the Company executed a note payable in the original principal amount of £500,000. The note bears interest at 4.0% per annum and has a maturity date of April 2003. Interest is payable in semiannual installments and principle is payable in two installments, June 2002 and April 2003. At March 2, 2002, this note was valued at $712,000.

Long-term debt matures as follows (in thousands):

Fiscal Year	Long-term Debt
2003	$ 356
2004	356
2005	–
2006	–
2007	–
Thereafter	25,000
Total long-term debt	$ 25,712

The Company has a $125 million unsecured credit facility available, which expires in November 2003. The interest rate on borrowings against this facility is determined based upon a spread from LIBOR that varies depending upon either the Company's senior debt rating or leverage ratio. All of the $125 million revolving credit facility was available at fiscal 2002 year-end. The Company had no borrowings under this facility during fiscal 2002. The weighted average interest rate on borrowings outstanding for fiscal 2001 was 7.2%.

The Company has a $120 million short-term line of credit, which is primarily used to issue merchandise letters of credit. At fiscal 2002 year-end, approximately $64.6 million had been utilized for letters of credit, leaving $55.4 million available. The Company also has $28.7 million in credit lines used to issue other special-purpose letters of credit, all of which were fully utilized at fiscal 2002 year-end. Of the $28.7 million in special-purpose letters of credit, $25.6 milllion related to the Company's industrial revenue bonds.

Most of the Company's loan agreements require that the Company maintain certain financial ratios and limit specific payments and equity distributions including cash dividends, loans to shareholders and repurchases of common stock. The Company is in compliance with all debt covenants.

NOTE 6 - EMPLOYEE BENEFIT PLANS

The Company offers a qualified, defined contribution employee retirement plan to all its full- and part-time personnel who are at least 18 years old and have been employed for a minimum of six months. Employees contributing 1% to 5% of their compensation receive a matching Company contribution of up to 3%. Company contributions to the plan were $1,734,000, $1,790,000 and $1,753,000 in fiscal 2002, 2001 and 2000, respectively.

Pier 1 Imports, Inc.

NOTES TO CONSOLIDATED FINANCIAL STATEMENTS
(continued)

NOTE 8 - INCOME TAXES

The provision for income taxes for each of the last three fiscal years consists of (in thousands):

	2002	2001	2000
Federal:			
Current	$ 56,207	$ 50,455	$ 39,463
Deferred	(2,110)	583	355
State:			
Current	3,909	3,368	1,890
Deferred	(128)	152	1,370
Foreign:			
Current	910	1,032	809
	$ 58,788	$ 55,590	$ 43,887

Deferred tax assets and liabilities at March 2, 2002 and March 3, 2001 are comprised of the following (in thousands):

	2002	2001
Deferred tax assets:		
Inventory	$ 2,166	$ 1,727
Deferred compensation	9,129	7,292
Accrued average rent	8,476	7,784
Losses on a foreign subsidiary	3,948	3,301
Self insurance reserves	2,408	910
Fixed assets, net	–	795
Other	2,470	2,326
	28,597	24,135
Valuation allowance	(3,948)	(3,301)
Total deferred tax assets	24,649	20,834
Deferred tax liabilities:		
Fixed assets, net	(1,577)	–
Total deferred tax liabilities	(1,577)	–
Net deferred tax assets	$ 23,072	$ 20,834

The Company has settled and closed all Internal Revenue Service ("IRS") examinations of the Company's tax returns for all years through fiscal 1999. An IRS audit of fiscal years 2000 and 2001 is expected to begin in the first quarter of fiscal year 2003. For financial reporting purposes, a valuation allowance exists at March 2, 2002 to offset the deferred tax asset relating to the losses of a foreign subsidiary.

Undistributed earnings of the Company's non-U.S. subsidiaries amounted to approximately $22.6 million at March 2, 2002. These earnings are considered to be indefinitely reinvested and, accordingly, no additional U.S. income taxes or non-U.S. withholding taxes have been provided. Determination of the amount of additional taxes that would be payable if such earnings were not considered indefinitely reinvested is not practical.

The difference between income taxes at the statutory federal income tax rate of 35% in fiscal 2002, 2001 and 2000, and income tax reported in the consolidated statements of operations is as follows (in thousands):

	2002	2001	2000
Tax at statutory federal income tax rate	$ 55,649	$ 52,584	$ 41,514
State income taxes, net of federal benefit	3,387	3,200	2,526
Work opportunity tax credit, foreign tax credit and R&E credit	(202)	(207)	(283)
Net foreign income taxed at lower rates	(101)	(1,048)	(960)
Other, net	55	1,061	1,090
	$ 58,788	$ 55,590	$ 43,887

NOTE 9 - COMMITMENTS AND CONTINGENCIES

Leases - The Company leases certain property consisting principally of retail stores, warehouses and material handling and office equipment under leases expiring through the year 2021. Most retail store locations are leased for initial terms of 10 to 15 years with varying renewal options and rent escalation clauses. Certain leases provide for additional rental payments based on a percentage of sales in excess of a specified base. The Company's lease obligations are considered operating leases, and all payments are reflected in the accompanying consolidated statements of operations.

During fiscal 2002, the Company sold certain store properties for $12.6 million. These stores were leased back from unaffiliated third parties for periods of approximately ten years. The resulting leases are being accounted for as operating leases.

Appendix C Typical Charts of Accounts for Different Types of Businesses

A Simple Service Corporation

Assets	*Liabilities*	*Stockholders' Equity*
Cash	Accounts Payable	Common Stock
Accounts Receivable	Notes Payable, Short-Term	Retained Earnings
Allowance for Uncollectible Accounts	Salary Payable	Dividends
Notes Receivable, Short Term	Wages Payable	
Interest Receivable	Payroll Taxes Payable	***Revenues and Gains***
Supplies	Employee Benefits Payable	Service Revenue
Prepaid Rent	Interest Payable	Interest Revenue
Prepaid Insurance	Unearned Service Revenue	Gain on Sale of Land (Furniture,
Notes Receivable, Long-Term	Notes Payable, Long-Term	Equipment, or Building)
Land		
Furniture		***Expenses and Losses***
Accumulated Depreciation—Furniture		Salary Expense
Equipment		Payroll Tax Expense
Accumulated Depreciation—Equipment		Employee Benefits Expense
Building		Rent Expense
Accumulated Depreciation—Building		Insurance Expense
		Supplies Expense
		Uncollectible Account Expense
		Depreciation Expense—Furniture
		Depreciation Expense—Equipment
		Depreciation Expense—Building
		Property Tax Expense
		Interest Expense
		Miscellaneous Expense
		Loss on Sale (or Exchange) of Land (Furniture, Equipment, or Building)

Service Partnership

	Owners' Equity
Same as service corporation, except for owners' equity	Partner 1, Capital
	Partner 2, Capital
	⋮
	Partner *N*, Capital
	Partner 1, Drawing
	Partner 2, Drawing
	⋮
	Partner *N*, Drawing

A Complex Merchandising Corporation

Assets

- Cash
- Short-Term Investments
- Accounts Receivable
- Allowance for Uncollectible Accounts
- Notes Receivable, Short-Term
- Interest Receivable
- Inventory
- Supplies
- Prepaid Rent
- Prepaid Insurance
- Notes Receivable, Long-Term
- Investments in Subsidiaries
- Investments in Stock (Available-for-Sale Securities)
- Investments in Bonds (Held-to-Maturity Securities)
- Other Receivables, Long-Term
- Land
- Land Improvements
- Furniture and Fixtures
- Accumulated Depreciation—Furniture and Fixtures
- Equipment
- Accumulated Depreciation—Equipment
- Buildings
- Accumulated Depreciation—Buildings
- Organization Cost
- Franchises
- Patents
- Leaseholds
- Goodwill

Liabilities

- Accounts Payable
- Notes Payable, Short-Term
- Current Portion of Bonds Payable
- Salary Payable
- Wages Payable
- Payroll Taxes Payable
- Employee Benefits Payable
- Interest Payable
- Income Tax Payable
- Unearned Sales Revenue
- Notes Payable, Long-Term
- Bonds Payable
- Lease Liability
- Minority Interest

Stockholders' Equity

- Preferred Stock
- Paid-in Capital in Excess of Par—Preferred
- Common Stock
- Paid-in Capital in Excess of Par—Common
- Paid-in Capital from Treasury Stock Transactions
- Paid-in Capital from Retirement of Stock
- Retained Earnings
- Foreign Currency Translation Adjustment
- Treasury Stock

Revenues and Gains

- Sales Revenue
- Interest Revenue
- Dividend Revenue
- Equity-Method Investment Revenue
- Unrealized Holding Gain on Trading Investments
- Gain on Sale of Investments
- Gain on Sale of Land (Furniture and Fixtures, Equipment, or Buildings)
- Discontinued Operations—Gain
- Extraordinary Gains

Expenses and Losses

- Cost of Goods Sold
- Salary Expense
- Wage Expense
- Commission Expense
- Payroll Tax Expense
- Employee Benefits Expense
- Rent Expense
- Insurance Expense
- Supplies Expense
- Uncollectible Account Expense
- Depreciation Expense—Land Improvements
- Depreciation Expense—Furniture and Fixtures
- Depreciation Expense—Equipment
- Depreciation Expense—Buildings
- Organization Expense
- Amortization Expense—Franchises
- Amortization Expense—Leaseholds
- Amortization Expense—Goodwill
- Income Tax Expense
- Unrealized Holding Loss on Trading Investments
- Loss on Sale of Investments
- Loss on Sale (or Exchange) of Land (Furniture and Fixtures, Equipment, or Buildings)
- Discontinued Operations—Loss
- Extraordinary Losses

A Manufacturing Corporation

Same as merchandising corporation, except for Assets

Assets

- Inventories:
  - Materials Inventory
  - Work-in-Process Inventory
  - Finished Goods Inventory
- Factory Wages
- Factory Overhead

Appendix D Time Value of Money: Future Value and Present Value

The following discussion of future value lays the foundation for our explanation of present value in Chapter 8 but is not essential. For the valuation of long-term liabilities, some instructors may wish to begin on page 692.

The term *time value of money* refers to the fact that money earns interest over time. *Interest* is the cost of using money. To borrowers, interest is the expense of renting money. To lenders, interest is the revenue earned from lending. We must always recognize the interest we receive or pay. Otherwise, we overlook an important part of the transaction. Suppose you invest $4,545 in corporate bonds that pay 10% interest each year. After one year, the value of your investment has grown to $5,000. The difference between your original investment ($4,545) and the future value of the investment ($5,000) is the amount of interest revenue you will earn during the year ($455). If you ignored the interest, you would fail to account for the interest revenue you have earned. Interest becomes more important as the time period lengthens because the amount of interest depends on the span of time the money is invested.

Let's consider a second example, this time from the borrower's perspective. Suppose you purchase a machine for your business. The cash price of the machine is $8,000, but you cannot pay cash now. To finance the purchase, you sign an $8,000 note payable. The note requires you to pay the $8,000 plus 10% interest one year from the date of purchase. Is your cost of the machine $8,000, or is it $8,800 [$8,000 plus interest of $800 ($8,000 × 0.10)]? The cost is $8,000. The additional $800 is interest expense and not part of the cost of the machine.

Future Value

The main application of future value is the accumulated balance of an investment at a future date. In our first example above, the investment earned 10% per year. After one year, $4,545 grew to $5,000, as shown in Exhibit D-1.

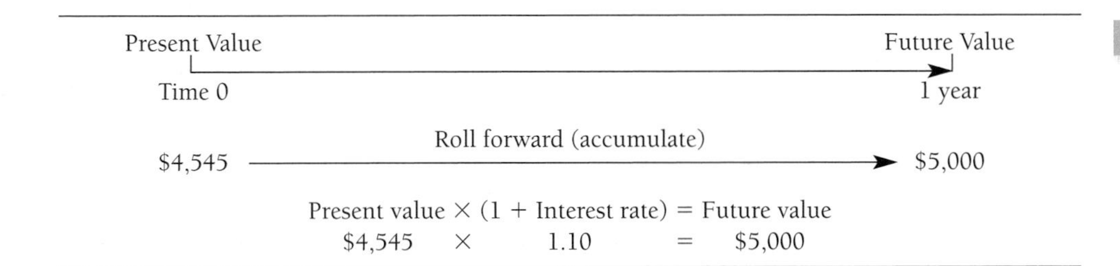

Exhibit D-1

Future Value: An Example

If the money were invested for five years, you would have to perform five such calculations. You would also have to consider the compound interest that your investment is earning. *Compound interest* is not only the interest you earn on your principal amount, but also the interest you receive on the interest you have already earned. Most business applications include compound interest. The following table shows the interest revenue earned on the original $4,545 investment each year for five years at 10%:

End of Year	Interest	Future Value
0	—	$4,545
1	$4,545 × 0.10 = $455	5,000
2	5,000 × 0.10 = 500	5,500
3	5,500 × 0.10 = 550	6,050
4	6,050 × 0.10 = 605	6,655
5	6,655 × 0.10 = 666	7,321

Earning 10%, a $4,545 investment grows to $5,000 at the end of one year, to $5,500 at the end of two years, and $7,321 at the end of five years. Throughout this appendix we round off to the nearest dollar.

Future-Value Tables

The process of computing a future value is called *accumulating* because the future value is *more* than the present value. Mathematical tables ease the computational burden. Exhibit D-2, Future Value of $1, gives the future value for a single sum (a present value), $1, invested to earn a particular interest rate for a specific number of periods. Future value depends on three factors: (1) the amount of the investment, (2) the length of time between investment and future accumulation, and (3) the interest rate. Future-value and present-value tables are based on $1 because unity (the value 1) is so easy to work with.

Exhibit D-2

Future Value of $1

Future Value of $1

Periods	4%	5%	6%	7%	8%	9%	10%	12%	14%	16%
1	1.040	1.050	1.060	1.070	1.080	1.090	1.100	1.120	1.140	1.160
2	1.082	1.103	1.124	1.145	1.166	1.188	1.210	1.254	1.300	1.346
3	1.125	1.158	1.191	1.225	1.260	1.295	1.331	1.405	1.482	1.561
4	1.170	1.216	1.262	1.311	1.360	1.412	1.464	1.574	1.689	1.811
5	1.217	1.276	1.338	1.403	1.469	1.539	1.611	1.762	1.925	2.100
6	1.265	1.340	1.419	1.501	1.587	1.677	1.772	1.974	2.195	2.436
7	1.316	1.407	1.504	1.606	1.714	1.828	1.949	2.211	2.502	2.826
8	1.369	1.477	1.594	1.718	1.851	1.993	2.144	2.476	2.853	3.278
9	1.423	1.551	1.689	1.838	1.999	2.172	2.358	2.773	3.252	3.803
10	1.480	1.629	1.791	1.967	2.159	2.367	2.594	3.106	3.707	4.411
11	1.539	1.710	1.898	2.105	2.332	2.580	2.853	3.479	4.226	5.117
12	1.601	1.796	2.012	2.252	2.518	2.813	3.138	3.896	4.818	5.936
13	1.665	1.886	2.133	2.410	2.720	3.066	3.452	4.363	5.492	6.886
14	1.732	1.980	2.261	2.579	2.937	3.342	3.798	4.887	6.261	7.988
15	1.801	2.079	2.397	2.759	3.172	3.642	4.177	5.474	7.138	9.266
16	1.873	2.183	2.540	2.952	3.426	3.970	4.595	6.130	8.137	10.748
17	1.948	2.292	2.693	3.159	3.700	4.328	5.054	6.866	9.276	12.468
18	2.026	2.407	2.854	3.380	3.996	4.717	5.560	7.690	10.575	14.463
19	2.107	2.527	3.026	3.617	4.316	5.142	6.116	8.613	12.056	16.777
20	2.191	2.653	3.207	3.870	4.661	5.604	6.728	9.646	13.743	19.461

In business applications, interest rates are always stated for the annual period of one year unless specified otherwise. In fact, an interest rate can be stated for any period, such as 3% per quarter or 5% for a six-month period. The length of the period is arbitrary. For example, an investment may promise a return (income) of 3% per quarter for six months (two quarters). In that case, you would be working with 3% interest for two periods. It would be incorrect to use 6% for one period because the interest is 3% compounded quarterly, and that amount differs from 6% compounded semiannually. *Take care in studying future-value and present-value problems to align the interest rate with the appropriate number of periods.*

Let's see how a future-value table like the one in Exhibit D-2 is used. The future value of $1.00 invested at 8% for one year is $1.08 ($1.00 × 1.080, which appears at the junction of the 8% column and row 1 in the Periods column). The figure 1.080 includes both the principal (1.000) and the compound interest for one period (0.080).

Suppose you deposit $5,000 in a savings account that pays annual interest of 8%. The account balance at the end of one year will be $5,400. To compute the future value of $5,000 at 8% for one year, multiply $5,000 by 1.080 to get $5,400. Now suppose you invest in a 10-year, 8% certificate of deposit (CD). What will be the future value of the CD at maturity? To compute the future value of $5,000 at 8% for 10 periods, multiply $5,000 by 2.159 (from Exhibit D-2) to get $10,795. This future value of $10,795 indicates that $5,000, earning 8% interest compounded annually, grows to $10,795 at the end of 10 years. Using Exhibit D-2, you can find any present amount's future value at a particular future date. Future value is especially helpful for computing the amount of cash you will have on hand for some purpose in the future.

Future Value of an Annuity

In the preceding example, we made an investment of a single amount. Other investments, called *annuities*, include multiple investments of an equal periodic amount at fixed intervals over the duration of the investment. Consider a family investing for a child's education. The Dietrichs can invest $4,000 annually to accumulate a college fund for 15-year-old Helen. The investment can earn 7% annually until Helen turns 18—a three-year investment. How much will be available for Helen on the date of the last investment? Exhibit D-3 shows the accumulation—a total future value of $12,860.

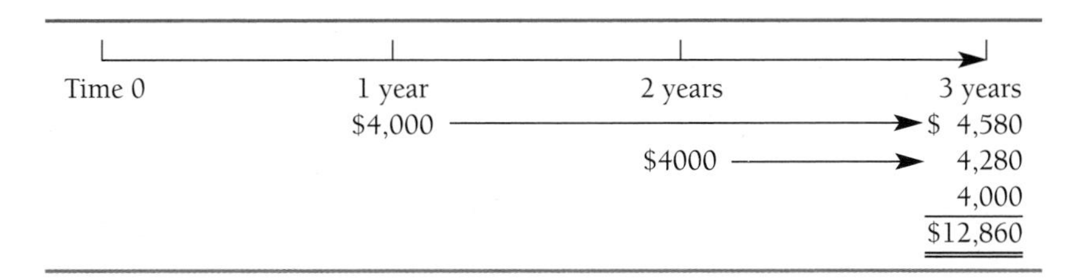

Exhibit D-3

Future Value of an Annuity

The first $4,000 invested by the Dietrichs grows to $4,580 over the investment period. The second amount grows to $4,280, and the third amount stays at $4,000 because it has no time to earn interest. The sum of the three future values ($4,580 + $4,280 + $4,000) is the future value of the annuity ($12,860), which can also be computed as follows:

End of Year	*Annual Investment*	*Interest*	*Increase for the Year*	*Future Value of Annuity*
0	—	—	—	0
1	$4,000	—	$4,000	$ 4,000
2	4,000	+ ($4,000 × 0.07 = $280) =	4,280	8,280
3	4,000	+ ($8,280 × 0.07 = $580) =	4,580	12,860

These computations are laborious. As with the Future Value of $1 (a lump sum), mathematical tables ease the strain of calculating annuities. Exhibit D-4, Future Value of Annuity of $1, gives the future value of a series of investments, each of equal amount, at regular intervals.

What is the future value of an annuity of three investments of $1 each that earn 7%? The answer, 3.215, can be found at the junction of the 7% column and row 3 in Exhibit D-4. This amount can be used to compute the future value of the investment for Helen's education, as follows:

Amount of each periodic investment	×	**Future value of annuity of $1 (Exhibit D-4)**	=	**Future value of investment**
$4,000	×	**3.215**	=	**$12,860**

Exhibit D-4 **Future Value of Annuity of $1**

					Future Value of Annuity of $1					
Periods	4%	5%	6%	7%	8%	9%	10%	12%	14%	16%
1	1.000	1.000	1.000	1.000	1.000	1.000	1.000	1.000	1.000	1.000
2	2.040	2.050	2.060	2.070	2.080	2.090	2.100	2.120	2.140	2.160
3	3.122	3.153	3.184	3.215	3.246	3.278	3.310	3.374	3.440	3.506
4	4.246	4.310	4.375	4.440	4.506	4.573	4.641	4.779	4.921	5.066
5	5.416	5.526	5.637	5.751	5.867	5.985	6.105	6.353	6.610	6.877
6	6.633	6.802	6.975	7.153	7.336	7.523	7.716	8.115	8.536	8.977
7	7.898	8.142	8.394	8.654	8.923	9.200	9.487	10.089	10.730	11.414
8	9.214	9.549	9.897	10.260	10.637	11.028	11.436	12.300	13.233	14.240
9	10.583	11.027	11.491	11.978	12.488	13.021	13.579	14.776	16.085	17.519
10	12.006	12.578	13.181	13.816	14.487	15.193	15.937	17.549	19.337	21.321
11	13.486	14.207	14.972	15.784	16.645	17.560	18.531	20.655	23.045	25.733
12	15.026	15.917	16.870	17.888	18.977	20.141	21.384	24.133	27.271	30.850
13	16.627	17.713	18.882	20.141	21.495	22.953	24.523	28.029	32.089	36.786
14	18.292	19.599	21.015	22.550	24.215	26.019	27.975	32.393	37.581	43.672
15	20.024	21.579	23.276	25.129	27.152	29.361	31.772	37.280	43.842	51.660
16	21.825	23.657	25.673	27.888	30.324	33.003	35.950	42.753	50.980	60.925
17	23.698	25.840	28.213	30.840	33.750	36.974	40.545	48.884	59.118	71.673
18	25.645	28.132	30.906	33.999	37.450	41.301	45.599	55.750	68.394	84.141
19	27.671	30.539	33.760	37.379	41.446	46.018	51.159	63.440	78.969	98.603
20	29.778	33.066	36.786	40.995	45.762	51.160	57.275	72.052	91.025	115.380

This one-step calculation is much easier than computing the future value of each annual investment and then summing the individual future values. In this way, you can compute the future value of any investment consisting of equal periodic amounts at regular intervals. Businesses make periodic investments to accumulate funds for equipment replacement and other uses—an application of the future value of an annuity.

Present Value

Often a person knows a future amount and needs to know the related present value. Recall Exhibit D-1, in which present value and future value are on opposite ends of the same time line. Suppose an investment promises to pay you $5,000 at the *end* of one year. How much would you pay *now* to acquire this investment? You would be willing to pay the present value of the $5,000 future amount.

Like future value, present value depends on three factors: (1) the *amount of payment (or receipt)*, (2) the length of *time* between investment and future receipt (or *payment*), and (3) the *interest rate*. The process of computing a present value is called *discounting* because the present value is *less* than the future value.

In our investment example, the future receipt is $5,000. The investment period is one year. Assume that you demand an annual interest rate of 10% on your investment. With all three factors specified, you can compute the present value of $5,000 at 10% for one year:

$$\textbf{Present value} = \frac{\textbf{Future value}}{\textbf{1 + Interest rate}} = \frac{\$5{,}000}{1.10} = \$4{,}545$$

By turning the data around into a future-value problem, we can verify the present-value computation:

Amount invested (present value)	$4,545
Expected earnings ($4,545 × 0.10)	455
Amount to be received one year from now (future value)	$5,000

This example illustrates that present value and future value are based on the same equation:

$$\textbf{Future value} = \textbf{Present value} \times (1 + \textbf{Interest rate})$$

$$\textbf{Present value} = \frac{\textbf{Future value}}{1 + \textbf{Interest rate}}$$

If the $5,000 is to be received two years from now, you will pay only $4,132 for the investment, as shown in Exhibit D-5. By turning the data around, we verify that $4,132 accumulates to $5,000 at 10% for two years:

Amount invested (present value)	$4,132
Expected earnings for first year ($4,132 × 0.10)	413
Value of investment after one year	4,545
Expected earnings for second year ($4,545 × 0.10)	455
Amount to be received two years from now (future value)	$5,000

You would pay $4,132—the present value of $5,000—to receive the $5,000 future amount at the end of two years at 10% per year. The $868 difference between the amount invested ($4,132) and the amount to be received ($5,000) is the return on the investment, the sum of the two interest receipts: $413 + $455 = $868.

Exhibit D-5

Present Value: An Example

Present-Value Tables

We have shown the simple formula for computing present value. However, figuring present value "by hand" for investments spanning many years is time-consuming and presents too many opportunities for arithmetic errors. Present-value tables ease our work. Let's reexamine our examples of present value by using Exhibit D-6: Present Value of $1 given at the top of the next page.

For the 10% investment for one year, we find the junction of the 10% column and row 1 in Exhibit D-6. The figure 0.909 is computed as follows: 1/1.10 = 0.909. This work has been done for us, and only the present values are given in the table. To figure the present value for $5,000, we multiply 0.909 by $5,000. The result is $4,545, which matches the result we obtained by hand.

For the two-year investment, we read down the 10% column and across row 2. We multiply 0.826 (computed as 0.909/1.10 = 0.826) by $5,000 and get $4,130, which confirms our earlier computation of $4,132 (the difference is due to rounding in the present-value table). Using the table, we can compute the present value of any single future amount.

Exhibit D-6

Present Value of $1

				Present Value of $1					
Periods	4%	5%	6%	7%	8%	10%	12%	14%	16%
1	0.962	0.952	0.943	0.935	0.926	0.909	0.893	0.877	0.862
2	0.925	0.907	0.890	0.873	0.857	0.826	0.797	0.769	0.743
3	0.889	0.864	0.840	0.816	0.794	0.751	0.712	0.675	0.641
4	0.855	0.823	0.792	0.763	0.735	0.683	0.636	0.592	0.552
5	0.822	0.784	0.747	0.713	0.681	0.621	0.567	0.519	0.476
6	0.790	0.746	0.705	0.666	0.630	0.564	0.507	0.456	0.410
7	0.760	0.711	0.665	0.623	0.583	0.513	0.452	0.400	0.354
8	0.731	0.677	0.627	0.582	0.540	0.467	0.404	0.351	0.305
9	0.703	0.645	0.592	0.544	0.500	0.424	0.361	0.308	0.263
10	0.676	0.614	0.558	0.508	0.463	0.386	0.322	0.270	0.227
11	0.650	0.585	0.527	0.475	0.429	0.350	0.287	0.237	0.195
12	0.625	0.557	0.497	0.444	0.397	0.319	0.257	0.208	0.168
13	0.601	0.530	0.469	0.415	0.368	0.290	0.229	0.182	0.145
14	0.577	0.505	0.442	0.388	0.340	0.263	0.205	0.160	0.125
15	0.555	0.481	0.417	0.362	0.315	0.239	0.183	0.140	0.108
16	0.534	0.458	0.394	0.339	0.292	0.218	0.163	0.123	0.093
17	0.513	0.436	0.371	0.317	0.270	0.198	0.146	0.108	0.080
18	0.494	0.416	0.350	0.296	0.250	0.180	0.130	0.095	0.069
19	0.475	0.396	0.331	0.277	0.232	0.164	0.116	0.083	0.060
20	0.456	0.377	0.312	0.258	0.215	0.149	0.104	0.073	0.051

Present Value of an Annuity

Return to the investment example on page 693. That investment provided the investor with only a single future receipt ($5,000 at the end of two years). *Annuity investments* provide multiple receipts of an equal amount at fixed intervals over the investment's duration.

Consider an investment that promises *annual* cash receipts of $10,000 to be received at the end of each of three years. Assume that you demand a 12% return on your investment. What is the investment's present value? That is, what would you pay today to acquire the investment? The investment spans three periods, and you would pay the sum of three present values. The computation is as follows:

Year	*Annual Cash Receipt*	*Present Value of $1 at 12% (Exhibit D-6)*	*Present Value of Annual Cash Receipt*
1	$10,000	0.893	$ 8,930
2	10,000	0.797	7,970
3	10,000	0.712	7,120
Total present value of investment			$24,020

The present value of this annuity is $24,020. By paying this amount today, you will receive $10,000 at the end of each of the three years while earning 12% on your investment.

This example illustrates repetitive computations of the three future amounts, a time-consuming process. One way to ease the computational burden is to add the three present values of $1 (0.893 + 0.797 + 0.712) and multiply their sum (2.402) by the annual cash receipt ($10,000) to obtain the present value of the annuity ($10,000 × 2.402 = $24,020).

An easier approach is to use a present value of an annuity table. Exhibit D-7 shows the present value of $1 to be received periodically for a given number of periods. The present value of a three-period annuity at 12% is 2.402 (the junction of row 3 and the 12% column). Thus, $10,000 received annually at the end of each of three years, discounted at 12%, is $24,020 ($10,000 × 2.402), which is the present value.

Exhibit D-7

Present Value of Annuity of $1

Present Value Annuity of $1

Periods	4%	5%	6%	7%	8%	10%	12%	14%	16%
1	0.962	0.952	0.943	0.935	0.926	0.909	0.893	0.877	0.862
2	1.886	1.859	1.833	1.808	1.783	1.736	1.690	1.647	1.605
3	2.775	2.723	2.673	2.624	2.577	2.487	2.402	2.322	2.246
4	3.630	3.546	3.465	3.387	3.312	3.170	3.037	2.914	2.798
5	4.452	4.329	4.212	4.100	3.993	3.791	3.605	3.433	3.274
6	5.242	5.076	4.917	4.767	4.623	4.355	4.111	3.889	3.685
7	6.002	5.786	5.582	5.389	5.206	4.868	4.564	4.288	4.039
8	6.733	6.463	6.210	5.971	5.747	5.335	4.968	4.639	4.344
9	7.435	7.108	6.802	6.515	6.247	5.759	5.328	4.946	4.607
10	8.111	7.722	7.360	7.024	6.710	6.145	5.650	5.216	4.833
11	8.760	8.306	7.887	7.499	7.139	6.495	5.938	5.453	5.029
12	9.385	8.863	8.384	7.943	7.536	6.814	6.194	5.660	5.197
13	9.986	9.394	8.853	8.358	7.904	7.103	6.424	5.842	5.342
14	10.563	9.899	9.295	8.745	8.244	7.367	6.628	6.002	5.468
15	11.118	10.380	9.712	9.108	8.559	7.606	6.811	6.142	5.575
16	11.652	10.838	10.106	9.447	8.851	7.824	6.974	6.265	5.669
17	12.166	11.274	10.477	9.763	9.122	8.022	7.120	6.373	5.749
18	12.659	11.690	10.828	10.059	9.372	8.201	7.250	6.467	5.818
19	13.134	12.085	11.158	10.336	9.604	8.365	7.366	6.550	5.877
20	13.590	12.462	11.470	10.594	9.818	8.514	7.469	6.623	5.929

Present Value of Bonds Payable

The present value of a bond—its market price—is the present value of the future principal amount at maturity plus the present value of the future contract interest payments. The principal is a *single amount* to be paid at maturity. The interest is an *annuity* because it occurs periodically.

Let's compute the present value of the 9% five-year bonds of Chrysler Corporation (discussed on page 377). The face value of the bonds is $100,000, and they pay $4\frac{1}{2}$% contract (cash) interest semiannually (that is, twice a year).[1] At issuance, the market interest rate is expressed as 10% annually, but it is computed at 5% semiannually. Therefore, the effective interest rate for each of the 10 semiannual periods is 5%. We thus use 5% in computing the present value (PV) of the maturity and of the interest. The market price of these bonds is $96,149, as follows:

	Effective annual interest rate ÷ 2	*Number of semiannual interest payments*	
PV of principal:	↓	↓	
$100,000 × PV of single amount at 5%		for 10 periods	
$100,000 × 0.614 (Exhibit D-6)			$61,400
PV of contract (cash) interest:	↓	↓	
$100,000 × 0.045 × PV of annuity at 5%		for 10 periods	
$4,500 × 7.722 (Exhibit D-7)			34,749
PV (market price) of bonds			$96,149

The market price of the Chrysler bonds shows a discount because the contract interest rate on the bonds (9%) is less than the market interest rate (10%). We discuss these bonds in more detail on pages 377–380.

[1]For a definition of contract interest rate, see page 376.

Let's consider a premium price for the 9% Chrysler bonds. Assume that the market interest rate is 8% (rather than 10%) at issuance. The effective interest rate is thus 4% for each of the 10 semiannual periods:

	Effective annual interest rate ÷ 2	*Number of semiannual interest payments*	
PV of principal:			
$100,000 × PV of single amount at 4%		for 10 periods	
$100,000 × 0.676 (Exhibit D-6)			$ 67,600
PV of contract (cash) interest:			
$100,000 × 0.045 × PV of annuity at 4%		for 10 periods	
$4,500 × 8.111 (Exhibit D-7)			36,500
PV (market price) of bonds			$104,100

We discuss accounting for these bonds on pages 383–384. It may be helpful for you to reread this section ("Present Value of Bonds Payable") after you've studied those pages.

Capital Leases

How does a lessee compute the cost of an asset acquired through a capital lease? (See page 391 for a definition of capital leases.) Consider that the lessee gets the use of the asset but does *not* pay for the leased asset in full at the beginning of the lease. A capital lease is therefore similar to an installment purchase of the leased asset. The lessee must record the leased asset at the present value of the lease liability. The time value of money must be weighed.

The cost of the asset to the lessee is the sum of any payment made at the beginning of the lease period plus the present value of the future lease payments. The lease payments are equal amounts occurring at regular intervals—that is, they are annuity payments.

Consider a 20-year building lease that requires 20 annual payments of $10,000 each, with the first payment due immediately. The interest rate in the lease is 10%, and the present value of the 19 future payments is $83,650 ($10,000 × PV of annuity at 10% for 19 periods, or 8.365 from Exhibit D-7). The lessee's cost of the building is $93,650 (the sum of the initial payment, $10,000, plus the present value of the future payments, $83,650). The lessee would base its accounting for the leased asset (and the related depreciation) and for the lease liability (and the related interest expense) on the cost of the building that we have just computed.

Appendix Problems

PD-1 For each situation, compute the required amount.

a. Kellogg Corporation is budgeting for the acquisition of land over the next several years. Kellogg can invest $100,000 today at 9%. How much cash will Kellogg have for land acquisitions at the end of 5 years? At the end of 6 years?

b. Davidson, Inc. is planning to invest $50,000 each year for 5 years. The company's investment adviser believes that Davidson can earn 6% interest without taking on too much risk. What will be the value of Davidson's investment on the date of the last deposit if Davidson can earn 6%? If Davidson can earn 8%?

PD-2 For each situation, compute the required amount.

a. Intel, Inc. operations are generating excess cash that will be invested in a special fund. During 20X2, Intel invests $5,643,341 in the fund for a planned advertising campaign on a new product to be released 6 years later, in 20X8. If Intel's investments can earn 10% each year, how much cash will the company have for the advertising campaign in 20X8?

b. Intel, Inc. will need $10 million to advertise a new type of chip in 20X8. How much must Intel invest in 20X2 to have the cash available for the advertising campaign? Intel's investments can earn 10% annually.

c. Explain the relationship between your answers to *a* and *b*.

PD-3 Determine the present value of the following notes and bonds:

1. Ten-year bonds payable with maturity value of $500,000 and contract interest rate of 12%, paid semiannually. The market rate of interest is 12% at issuance.
2. Same bonds payable as in number 2, but the market interest rate is 14%.
3. Same bonds payable as in number 2, but the market interest rate is 10%.

PD-4 On December 31, 20X1, when the market interest rate is 8%, Libby, Libby, & Short, a partnership, issues $400,000 of 10-year, 7.25% bonds payable. The bonds pay interest semiannually.

Required

1. Determine the present value of the bonds at issuance.
2. Assume that the bonds are issued at the price computed in Requirement 1. Prepare an effective-interest-method amortization table for the first 2 semiannual interest periods.
3. Using the amortization table prepared in Requirement 2, journalize issuance of the bonds and the first 2 interest payments and amortization of the bonds.

PD-5 St. Mere Eglise Children's Home needs a fleet of vans to transport the children to singing engagements throughout Normandy. Renault offers the vehicles for a single payment of 630,000 French francs due at the end of 4 years. Peugeot prices a similar fleet of vans for 4 annual payments of 150,000 francs at the end of each year. The children's home could borrow the funds at 6%, so this is the appropriate interest rate. Which company should get the business, Renault or Peugeot? Base your decision on present value, and give your reason.

PD-6 American Family Association acquired equipment under a capital lease that requires 6 annual lease payments of $40,000. The first payment is due when the lease begins, on January 1, 20X6. Future payments are due on January 1 of each year of the lease term. The interest rate in the lease is 16%.

Required

Compute the association's cost of the equipment.

Appendix E Summary of Generally Accepted Accounting Principles (GAAP)

Every technical area has professional associations and regulatory bodies that govern the practice of the profession. Accounting is no exception. In the United States, generally accepted accounting principles (GAAP) are influenced most by the Financial Accounting Standards Board (FASB). The FASB has seven full-time members and a large staff. Its financial support comes from professional associations such as the American Institute of Certified Public Accountants (AICPA).

The FASB is an independent organization with no government or professional affiliation. The FASB's pronouncements, called *Statements of Financial Accounting Standards*, specify how to account for certain business transactions. Each new *Standard* becomes part of GAAP, the "accounting law of the land." In the same way that our laws draw authority from their acceptance by the people, GAAP depends on general acceptance by the business community. Throughout this book, we refer to GAAP as the proper way to do financial accounting.

The U.S. Congress has given the Securities and Exchange Commission (SEC), a government organization that regulates the trading of investments, ultimate responsibility for establishing accounting rules for companies that are owned by the general investing public. However, the SEC has delegated much of its rule-making power to the FASB. Exhibit E-1 outlines the flow of authority for developing GAAP.

Exhibit E-1

Flow of Authority for Developing GAAP

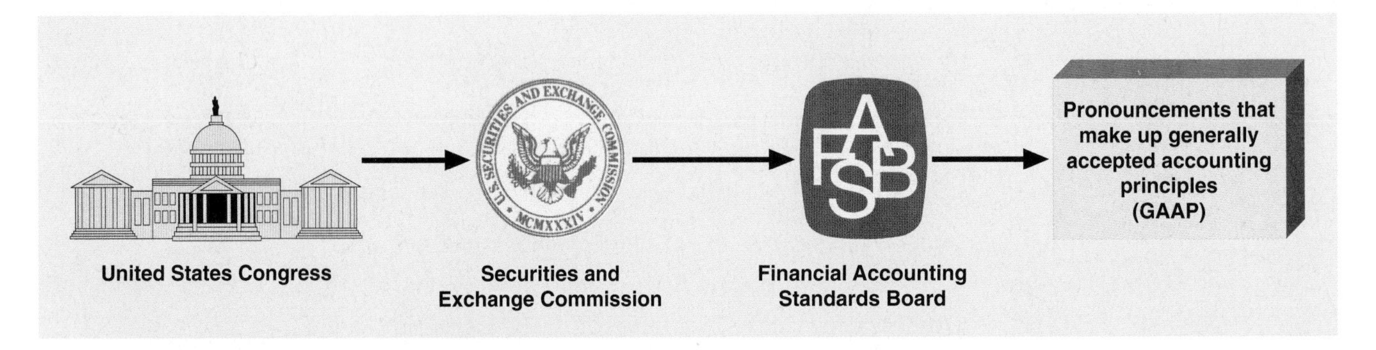

The Objective of Financial Reporting

The basic objective of financial reporting is to provide information that is useful in making investment and lending decisions. The FASB believes that accounting information can be useful in decision making only if it is *relevant, reliable, comparable*, and *consistent*.

Relevant information is useful in making predictions and for evaluating past performance—that is, the information has feedback value. For example, PepsiCo's disclosure of the profitability of each of its lines of business is relevant for investor evaluations of the company. To be relevant, information must be timely. *Reliable* information is free from significant error—that is, it has validity. Also, it is free from the bias of a particular viewpoint—that is, it is verifiable and neutral. *Comparable* and *consistent* information can be compared from period to period to help investors and creditors track the entity's progress through time. These characteristics combine to shape the concepts and principles that make up GAAP. Exhibit E-2 summarizes the concepts and principles that accounting has developed to provide useful information for decision making.

Exhibit E-2 **Summary of Important Accounting Concepts, Principles, and Financial Statements**

Concepts, Principles and Financial Statements	*Quick Summary*	*Text Reference*
Concepts		
Entity concept	Accounting draws a boundary around each organization to be accounted for.	Chapter 1, page 14
Going-concern concept	Accountants assume the business will continue operating for the foreseeable future.	Chapter 1, page 15
Stable-monetary-unit concept	Accounting information is expressed primarily in monetary terms that ignore the effects of inflation.	Chapter 1, page 15
Time-period concept	Ensures that accounting information is reported at regular intervals.	Chapter 3, page 114
Conservatism concept	Accountants report items in the financial statements in a way that avoids overstating assets, owners' equity, and revenues and avoids understating liabilities and expenses.	Chapter 6, page 279
Materiality concept	Accountants perform strictly proper accounting only for items that are significant to the company's financial statements.	Chapter 6, page 279
Principles		
Reliability (objectivity) principle	Accounting records and statements are based on the most reliable data available.	Chapter 1, page 14
Cost principle	Assets and services, revenues and expenses are recorded at their actual historical cost.	Chapter 1, page 14
Revenue principle	Tells accountants when to record revenue (only after it has been earned) and the amount of revenue to record (the cash value of what has been received).	Chapter 3, page 115
Matching principle	Directs accountants to (1) identify and measure all expenses incurred during the period and (2) match the expenses against the revenues earned during the period. The goal is to measure net income.	Chapter 3, page 115
Consistency principle	Businesses should use the same accounting methods from period to period.	Chapter 6, page 278
Disclosure principle	A company's financial statements should report enough information for outsiders to make informed decisions about the company.	Chapter 6, page 278
Financial Statements		
Balance sheet	Assets = Liabilities + Owners' Equity at a point in time.	Chapter 1
Income statement	Revenues and gains − Expenses and losses = Net income or net loss for the period.	Chapters 1 and 11
Statement of cash flows	Cash receipts − Cash payments = Increase or decrease in cash during the period, grouped under operating, investing, and financing activities.	Chapters 1 and 12
Statement of retained earnings	Beginning retained earnings + Net income (or − Net loss) − Dividends = Ending retained earnings.	Chapters 1 and 11
Statement of stockholders' equity	Shows the reason for the change in each stockholders' equity account, including retained earnings.	Chapter 11
Financial statement notes	Provide information that cannot be reported conveniently on the face of the financial statements. The notes are an integral part of the statements.	Chapter 11

Appendix F Check Figures *

Chapter 1

Check Points

CP1-1 NCF
CP1-2 NCF
CP1-3 NCF
CP1-4 NCF
CP1-5 NCF
CP1-6 NCF
CP1-7 NCF
CP1-8 NCF
CP1-9 2000 49.2%
CP1-10 RE, end. $2,391 mil.
CP1-11 Total assets $175,000
CP1-12 Net cash provided by operations $60,000
CP1-13 NCF

Exercises

E1-1 NCF
E1-2 NCF
E1-3 NCF
E1-4 3M Total assets $14.5 bil.
E1-5 2. $863 mil.
E1-6 1. Net inc. $1 bil.
E1-7 1. Total assets $7.595 bil.
E1-8 NCF
E1-9 2. Total assets $26,394 mil.
E1-10 1. Net inc. $3,044 mil.
E1-11 Net cash provided by operations $2, 729 mil.
E1-12 RE, 7/31/06 $500
E1-13 Total assets $37,700
E1-14 Net cash provided by operations $2,500
E1-15 NCF
E1-16 NCF

Problems

P1-1A NCF
P1-2A 1. Net inc. $5.1 bil.
P1-3A Best Buy issuance of stock $0.3 bil.
P1-4A 1. Total assets $150,000
P1-5A 1. Total assets $164,000
P1-6A 2. RE, end. $27,000
3. Total assets $81,000
P1-7A 1. Net increase in cash $2,310 mil.
P1-8A 1.b.$1,396 thou.
g. $4,043 thou.
m. $598 thou.
s. $13,216 thou.
P1-1B NCF
P1-2B 1. Net inc. $14 bil.
P1-3B FedEx issuance of stock $1 bil.
P1-4B 1. Total assets $82, 000
P1-5B 1. Total assets $164,000
P1-6B 2. RE, end. $88,000
3. Total assets $293,000
P1-7B 1. Net increase in cash $183 mil.
P1-8B 1. b. $7,681 thou.
g. $17,213 thou.
m. $2,740 thou.
s. $42,541 thou.

Cases

DC1 2. Net inc. $0
Total assets $55,000
DC2 NCF
DC3 NCF
FSC Amt. owed $117 mil.
AC 1. Total liab. $277 mil.

Chapter 2

Check Points

CP2-1 NCF
CP2-2 d. 5,800
CP2-3 Cash bal. $20,000
CP2-4 NCF
CP2-5 NCF
CP2-6 2. A/P bal. $1,000
CP2-7 3. Total assets $800
CP2-8 T/B total $39 mil.
CP2-9 1. $53,800
4. $5,800
CP2-10 NCF
CP2-11 NCF
CP2-12 Total debits $700,000

Exercises

E2-1 Total assets $360,000
E2-2 NCF
E2-3 NCF
E2-4 2. a. $50,800
d. $5,300
E2-5 NCF
E2-6 1. $4 mil.
3. $2 mil.
E2-7 2. Cash, end. $5,600
Net inc. $1,700
E2-8 2. T/B total $21,900
3. Total assets $20,400
E2-9 Cash bal. $12,800
E2-10 1. T/B total $145,100
2. Net inc. $11,650
E2-11 T/B total $88,100
E2-12 Cash bal. $2,300
E2-13 1. T/B total $22,500
2. Net loss $1,600
E2-14 4. T/B total $13,400
E2-15 a. Net inc. $20,100
b. Cash paid $80,400
E2-16 1. T/B out of balance by $1,700
2. T/B total $141,200
E2-17 NCF

Problems

P2-1A NCF
P2-2A 2. Net inc. $7,900
4. Total assets 26,850
P2-3A 3. Cash bal. $10,450
A/P bal. $4,000
P2-4A 2. Total assets $26,500
P2-5A 2. Cash bal. $24,000
Amt. owed $45,200
P2-6A 3. T/B total $37,600
4. Net inc. $2,560
P2-7A 3. T/B total $83,200
4. Net loss $1,400
P2-1B NCF
P2-2B 2. Net inc. $7,240
4. Total assets $75,920
P2-3B 3. Cash bal. $44,610
A/P bal. $4,720
P2-4B 2. Total assets $35,100
P2-5B 2. Cash bal. $115,400
Amt. owed 130,900
P2-6B 3. T/B total $28,300
4. Net inc. $1,670
P2-7B 3. T/B total $165,300
4. Net loss $700

Cases

DC1 3. T/B total $27,550
4. Net inc. $7,000

*NCF = No check figure

DC2 2. Net inc. $20,000
Total assets $66,000

FSC Cash $68 mil; A/R $74 mil.

AC NCF

Chapter 3

Check Points

CP3-1 Net inc. $95 mil.

CP3-2 NCF

CP3-3 NCF

CP3-4 1. Prepaid Rent bal. $2,750

CP3-5 3. £35,000

CP3-6 20X3 $2,600,000
20X4 $300,000

CP3-7 4. Interest Payable Oct. 31 bal. $750

CP3-8 4. Interest Receivable Oct. 31 bal. $750

CP3-9 NCF

CP3-10 Prepaid Rent at Apr. 30 $2,000

CP3-11 2. Income state. Service rev. $7,400

CP3-12 Net inc. $1,757 thou.
Total assets $98,541 thou.

CP3-13 R/E bal. $3,088

CP3-14 3. Total assets $305 mil.

CP3-15 Current ratio 0.71
Debt ratio 0.55

Exercises

E3-1 NCF

E3-2 a. $6 mil.

E3-3 NCF

E3-4 NCF

E3-5 NCF

E3-6 2. Net inc. overstated by $47,000

E3-7 1. Payments for supplies $600

E3-8 NCF

E3-9 NCF

E3-10 NCF

E3-11 Service Rev. $5,600

E3-12 Net inc. $2,200 mil.
Total assets $20,800 mil.

E3-13 Sales rev. $15,326 mil.
Salary exp. $974 mil.

E3-14 Hillcrest B/S: Unearned service rev. 2,800

E3-15 1. B/S: Unearned service rev. £90 mil.

E3-16 Dec. 31, 2000, bal. of R/E $1,578 mil.

E3-17 NCF

E3-18 1. Total assets $38,700
2. Debt ratio Current Yr. 0.24

E3-19 7. Net inc. $1,690
Total assets $11,790

E3-20 Current ratio at Dec. 31, 1999 1.78

E3-21 a. Net inc. $97,600
b. Total assets $159,800

Problems

P3-1A 1. $15.4 bil.
4. End. rec. $1.5 bil.

P3-2A 2. Cash basis—loss $1,300
Accrual basis—inc. $3,000

P3-3A NCF

P3-4A a. Insurance Exp. $2,850
d. Supplies Exp. $6,710

P3-5A 2. Total assets $68,670
Net inc. $4,280

P3-6A 1. Net inc. $59,070
Total assets $46,970

P3-7A 2. Net inc. $5,400
Total assets $52,400

P3-8A 1. Total assets $80,900
2. Current ratio 20X3 1.30

P3-9A 2. Mar. 31, 20X3 bal. of R/E $44,900

P3-10A 2. a. Current ratio 3.31
Debt ratio 0.32

P3-1B 1. $8.9 bil.
4. End. rec. $1.7 bil.

P3-2B 2. Cash basis—loss $3,300
Accrual basis—inc. $1,700

P3-3B NCF

P3-4B c. Engineer. Supplies Exp. $11,360
f. Insurance Exp. $2,200

P3-5B 2. Total assets $30,170
Net inc. $25,120

P3-6B 1. Net inc. $57,370
Total assets $107,930

P3-7B 2. Net inc. $9,200
Total assets $51,000

P3-8B 1. Total assets $59,000
2. Current ratio 20X5 1.30

P3-9B 2. Dec. 31, 20X5 bal. of R/E $16,800

P3-10B 2. a. Current ratio 1.73
Debt ratio 0.61

Cases

DC1 Net inc. $7,000
Total assets $24,000

DC2 1. $175,000
2. $140,000

DC3 1. $1,200
3. Current ratio 1.40

DC4 Net inc. $38,420
Total assets $56,270

FSC 5. Debt ratio 2001 0.31

AC NCF

Chapter 4

Check Points

CP4-1 NCF

CP4-2 NCF

CP4-3 NCF

CP4-4 NCF

CP4-5 Adj. bal. $2,090

CP4-6 NCF

CP4-7 NCF

CP4-8 NCF

CP4-9 NCF

CP4-10 NCF

CP4-11 1. New financing needed $307.5 mil.

CP4-12 Cash available to invest $4 mil.

CP4-13 NCF

Exercises

E4-1 NCF

E4-2 NCF

E4-3 NCF

E4-4 NCF

E4-5 NCF

E4-6 Adj. bal. $1,724

E4-7 Adj. bal. $3,025

E4-8 NCF

E4-9 NCF

E4-10 NCF

E4-11 1. $207.29

E4-12 New financing needed $44.8 mil.

E4-13 NCF

E4-14 NCF

E4-15 1. New financing needed $450 mil.
2. Current ratio after borrowing 1.19

E4-16 8.89%

Problems

P4-1A NCF

P4-2A NCF

P4-3A 1. Adj. bal. $2,990

P4-4A 1. Adj. bal. $2,703.33

P4-5A NCF

P4-6A 1. Cash available to invest $659 mil.

P4-7A NCF

P4-1B NCF

P4-2B NCF

P4-3B 1. Adj. bal. $9,070

P4-4B 1. Adj. bal. $9,369.00

P4-5B NCF

P4-6B Cash available to invest $71 mil.

P4-7B NCF

Cases

DC1 Cashier stole $2,300

DC2 NCF

FSC 1. Adj. bal. $67,491 thou.

AC 3. Total effect on cash of top 7 items $172,603 thou.

Chapter 5

Check Points

CP5-1 NCF
CP5-2 NCF
CP5-3 NCF
CP5-4 NCF
CP5-5 Accts. rec., net $900
CP5-6 2. Accts. rec., net $82,000
CP5-7 NCF
CP5-8 3. and 4. Accts. rec., net $94,000
CP5-9 d. Uncollectible-Acct.Exp. $3,000
CP5-10 3. Accts. rec., net $69,000
CP5-11 b. Dr. Cash $103,500
CP5-12 3. $526,250
CP5-13 c. Dr. Cash $1,045
CP5-14 d. Interest rev. $37.50
CP5-15 a. 0.98
b. 40 days
CP5-16 2. $(576)mil.
3. Accts. rec., net $4,028 mil.

Exercises

E5-1 NCF
E5-2 NCF
E5-3 2. Unrealized gain of $14,000 in 20X3; Gain of $1,000 on sale in 20X4
E5-4 NCF
E5-5 Accts. rec., net $57,100
E5-6 3. Accts. rec., net $33,400
E5-7 Acct. rec., end. $35,300
E5-8 3. Accts. rec., net $255,600
E5-9 NCF
E5-10 Dec. 31 Interest Rev. $645
E5-11 Interest rev,
20X3 $3,750
20X4 $1,250
E5-12 NCF
E5-13 20X6 ratios: Acid-test 0.91; Days' sales in rec. 35 days
E5-14 1. 20 days
E5-15 Expected net inc. with bank cards $145,200
E5-16 c. $40,100
E5-17 10%

Problems

P5-1A 3. Short-term investment $37,000
4. Unrealized loss $9,250
P5-2A NCF
P5-3A 2. d. Write offs $88 mil.
P5-4A 3. Accts. rec., net 20X4 $159,300
P5-5A 2. Current ratio-corrected 1.21
3. Net inc.-corrected $51,000
P5-6A 2. Dec. 31, 20X6 Interest rec. $666
P5-7A 1. 2001 ratios:
a. Current 1.35
b. Acid-test 0.78
c. Days' sales 21 days
P5-1B 3. Short-term investment $31,000
4. Unrealized gain $5,500
P5-2B NCF
P5-3B 2. d. Write offs $269 mil.
P5-4B 3. Accts. rec., net 20X2 $278,200
P5-5B 2. Current ratio-corrected 0.94
3. Net inc.-corrected $48,000
P5-6B 2. Dec. 31, 20X5 Interest rec. $616
P5-7B 1. 2001 ratios:
a. Current 1.42
b. Acid-test 0.60
c. Days' sales 25 days

Cases

DC1 Net inc. $152,000
DC2 1. Net inc.: $63,000 in 20X2; $45,250 in 20X1
DC3 NCF
FSC 2. Loss $1 thou.
3. Accts. Rec., gross, $108,235 thou.
AC 1. Customers owed Pier 1 $6,480 thou.
4. % doubtful 2002 4.2%

Chapter 6

Check Points

CP6-1 Invy. $18,000; Gross profit $28,000
CP6-2 2. Gross profit $50,000
CP6-3 NCF
CP6-4 NCF
CP6-5 COGS: a. $750; b. $720; c. $800
CP6-6 Net inc.: Wtd.-avg. $488; FIFO $600; LIFO $200
CP6-7 Inc. tax exp.: Wtd.-avg. $195; FIFO $240; LIFO $80
CP6-8 NCF
CP6-9 COGS $142 bil.
CP6-10 Gross profit $36 bil.
CP6-11 1. $7.5 mil.
2. $5.3 mil.
CP6-12 NCF
CP6-13 GP%: FIFO 46%; LIFO 34%
Turnover: FIFO 2.3 times; LIFO 3.9 times
CP6-14 2. $200,000

Exercises

E6-1 a. $1,076 mil
c. $151,904 mil.
Estée Lauder net inc. $314 mil.
E6-2 Purchase $7,450 mil.
E6-3 3. Gross profit $900 thou.
E6-4 3. Gross profit $5,700
E6-5 1. COGS: Wtd.-avg. $2,863; FIFO $2,800; LIFO $2,930
E6-6 LIFO tax advantage $52
E6-7 1. COGS: FIFO $925 LIFO $950
E6-8 1. Gross profit: FIFO $0.7 mil.; LIFO $1.6 mil.
E6-9 Net inc., in sequence: $24,000; $19,800; $10,200; $6,000
E6-10 NCF
E6-11 NCF
E6-12 Net inc.: 20X5 $39,000; 20X4 $48,000
E6-13 Gross profit $12,388 mil.
Inventory $2,827 mil.
E6-14 GP%: Coca-Cola 69.7%
Turnover: Coca-Cola 5.8 times
E6-15 Gross profit: $114,600
E6-16 GP% 29.8%; Turnover 5.3 times
E6-17 Est. cost of invy. destroyed $55,000
E6-18 NCF
E6-19 1. $151,000 2. $160,000
E6-20 2000 ratios:
GP% 19.7%; Turnover 4.4 times

Problems

P6-1A 1. Purchase $769,000
2. Net inc. $150,000
P6-2A 2. Invy. $600,000
3. Net inc. $180,000
P6-3A 2. Gross profit $3,019
3. Invy. $2,027
P6-4A 1. COGS: Wtd.-avg. $12,210; FIFO $11,911; LIFO $12,583
P6-5A 1. Gross profit: Wtd.-avg. $60,110; FIFO $60,620; LIFO $59,635
P6-6A NCF
P6-7A 1. Correct net inc.: 2000 $-0-; 1999 $3 bil.; 1998 $-0-
P6-8A 1. Company A: GP% 21.5%
Turnover 7.3 times
P6-9A 1. Est. cost of end. invy. $2,275,000
2. Gross profit $2,562,000
P6-1B Purchase $766,000
Net inc. $150,000
P6-2B 2. Invy. $1,200,000
3. Net inc. $834,000
P6-3B 2. Gross profit $1,292
3. Invy. $704
P6-4B 1. COGS: Wtd.-avg. $57,534; FIFO $56,605; LIFO $58,589
P6-5B 1. Gross profit: Wtd.-avg. $2,809; FIFO $2,945; LIFO $2,680
P6-6B NCF
P6-7B 1. Correct net inc. (mil.) 2001 $115; 2000 $5; 1999 $130
P6-8B 1. Hershey GP% 41.5%
Turnover 4.1 times

P6-9B 1. Est. cost of end. invy. $2,536,000
2. Gross profit $3,456,000

Cases

DC1 Net inc. w/o year-end pur.:
FIFO $249,000; LIFO $213,000
Net inc. w/ year-end pur.:
FIFO $249,000; LIFO $189,750

DC2 NCF

FSC 3. Purchases $296,235 thou.

AC 1. c. Purchases $863,524 thou.
3. Cash payments $837,200 thou.
5. 2002 ratios: GP% 42.0%;
Turnover 3.1 times

Appendix

CP6-1A NCF

CP6-2A 3. Gross profit $50,000

E6-1A COGS: Wtd.-avg. $2,863;
FIFO $2,800; LIFO $2,930

E6-2A 4. COGS $2,930

P6-1A 2. Gross profit $3,174

P6-2A 2. Gross profit $1,680 thou.

Chapter 7

Check Points

CP7-1 3. Book value $8,100 mil.

CP7-2 NCF

CP7-3 Building cost $52,500

CP7-4 Net inc. overstated

CP7-5 2. Book value: SL $18 mil.;
DDB $12.6 mil.

CP7-6 Depr.: UOP yr.5 $3.75 mil; DDB yr. 3 $1.56 mil.

CP7-7 2. Save $1.89 mil.

CP7-8 a. € 6 mil.
b. € 4 mil.
c. € 13.5 mil.

CP7-9 Depr. Exp. $6,667

CP7-10 1. a. Loss $10,000
b. Gain $240

CP7-11 3. Book value $13.0 bil.

CP7-12 1. Goodwill purchased $581 mil

CP7-13 1. Net inc. $100,000

CP7-14 1. Net cash provided by investing $22 mil.

Exercises

E7-1 Land $260,000 Building $1,450,000

E7-2 Machine 1 $10,000;
2 $16,680; 3 $13,320

E7-3 NCF

E7-4 2. Building, net $577,000

E7-5 NCF

E7-6 Depr. 20X7: SL $3,000;
UOP $2,400; DDB $0

E7-7 I/S: Depr. exp.-building $8,000;
B/S: Bldg., net $192,000

E7-8 3,000 hours

E7-9 DDB saves $4,950

E7-10 Depr. yr. 12 $32,500

E7-11 Loss on sale $1,154

E7-12 Cost of new truck $293,750

E7-13 c. Depletion Exp $92,000

E7-14 2. Amortiz. yr. 5 $100,000

E7-15 NCF

E7-16 1. Cost of goodwill $5,500,000

E7-17 NCF

E7-18 NCF

E7-19 Sale price $100 mil.

E7-20 Expected net inc. for 20X4 $56.3 mil.

E7-21 Yr. 4 Effects on:
2. Equip. €0.8 mil. under
3. Net inc. €0.8 mil over
4. Equity €0.8 mil under

Problems

P7-1A 1. Land $202,100; Land Improve. $89,050; Sales Bldg. $986,150

P7-2A 2. A/Depr-Bldg. $46,000
A/Depr-Equip. $398,000

P7-3A 12/31 Depr. Exp.-Motor Carrier Equip. $61,200;
Depr. Exp.-Bldgs. $625

P7-4A NCF

P7-5A Cash-flow advantage of DDB $18,200

P7-6A 1. Book value $42 mil.

P7-7A Part 1. 2. Goodwill $3,200,000
Part 2. 2. Net inc. $509,425

P7-8A 1. Gain on sale $0.1 bil.
2. PPE, net $3.8 bil.

P7-1B 1. Land $683,250; Land Improve. $136,400; Dist. Office Bldg. $1,246,100

P7-2B 2. A/Depr–Bldg. $44,000
A/Depr–Equip. $258,000

P7-3B 12/31 Depr. Exp.–Comm. Equip. $4,000; Depr. Exp.–Televideo Equip. $1,333

P7-4B NCF

P7-5B 3. Cash-flow advantage of DDB $5,733

P7-6B 1. Book value $480 mil.

P7-7B Part 1. 2. Goodwill $285,000
Part 2. 2. Net inc. $39,830

P7-8B 1. Gain on sale $0.6 bil.
2. PPE, net $11.2 bil.

Cases

DC1 1. Net inc.: 360 $116,350;
Beepers $91,650

DC2 NCF

FSC NCF

AC 1. Book value sold $20,887 thou.
4. Deprec. and amortiz.-leasehold improve. $6,171 thou.

Chapter 8

Check Points

CP8-1 5/31/X6 Debits include Interest Exp. $333

CP8-2 2. Interest exp. $333

CP8-3 2. End. bal. $11,000

CP8-4 NCF

CP8-5 NCF

CP8-6 a. $1,795,000
b. $551,875

CP8-7 NCF

CP8-8 12/31/00 Interest Exp. $163

CP8-9 1. Bond carry. amt.
7/31/X5 $441,509

CP8-10 3. Interest exp.:
1/31/X5 $19,668

CP8-11 3. $162.50
4. $173.13

CP8-12 b. Interest Exp. $173

CP8-13 EPS-Plan A $2.36
Plan B $1.73

CP8-14 Times-interest-earned ratio 0.50

CP8-15 Total current liabilities $92,000

Exercises

E8-1 2. Est. warranty pay. $8,900

E8-2 Unearned subscription rev. bal. $250

E8-3 NCF

E8-4 1. $3,200
3. Interest exp. for 20X5 $1,600

E8-5 Income tax pay. $190 mil.

E8-6 2. Debt ratio 0.53

E8-7 NCF

E8-8 Pay $0.625 bil. of current liabilities

E8-9 Total current liab. $94,150

E8-10 12/31 Interest Exp. $34,166

E8-11 3. Total interest exp.
$351,200,000

E8-12 12/31/X6 1. Bond carry. amt. $376,509; 2. Interest exp. $15,020

E8-13 7/31/04 1. Bond carry. amt. $331,093 2. Interest exp. $1,936

E8-14 12/31/X9 Bond carry. amt. $600,000

E8-15 2. $396,400
3. Cr. C/S $16,000 and PIC in Excess $380,400

E8-16 1. Loss on Retirement $9,000
2. PIC in Excess $137,000

E8-17 Safeway: Current ratio 0.85;
Debt ratio 0.66;
Times-interest-earned 5.8 times

E8-18 1. EPS: Plan A $8.25; Plan B $4.26

E8-19 Debt ratio after 0.64

E8-20 5. Bond carry. amt.
3/15/04 $197,311

Problems

P8-1A b. Unearned rev. $1,600
e. Est. warr. pay. $14,300

P8-2A 12/31/X5 Warranty Exp. $2,900

P8-3A 2. Interest pay. $17,500
Bonds pay. $3,000,000

P8-4A 4. Interest pay. $14,167
Bonds pay., net $485,625

P8-5A 2. Bond carry. amt. 12/31/07
$973,000

P8-6A 2. Bond carry. amt. 9/30/Yr. 4
$123,639

P8-7A 1. Bond carry. amt. 12/31/X6
$474,920
3. Convertible bonds pay., net $94,984

P8-8A NCF

P8-9A 1. Total current liab. $141,000
Total long-term liab. $868,000
3. Times-interest-earned 5.5 times

P8-1B b. Unearned rev. $3,600
d. Est. warr. pay. $14,100

P8-2B 12/31/X4 Warranty Exp. $19,500

P8-3B 2. Interest pay. $40,000
Bonds pay. $2,000,000

P8-4B 4. Interest pay. $7,750
Bonds pay., net $305,500

P8-5B 2. Bond carry. amt. 12/31/04
$473,000

P8-6B 2. Bond carry. amt. 9/30/Yr. 4
$124,423

P8-7B 1. Bond carry. amt. 12/31/X3
$314,688
3. Convertible bonds pay., net
$104,896

P8-8B NCF

P8-9B 1. Total current liab. $66,200
Total long-term liab. $767,000
3. Times-interest-earned 1.5 times

Cases

DC1 EPS: Plan A $3.22; B $3.09; C $3.03

DC2 1. Debt ratio after .93; Times-interest-earned after 1.3 times

FSC 4. Debt ratio .31

AC 1. Debt ratio .32
3. Est. interest rate 3.9%

Chapter 9

Check Points

CP9-1 NCF

CP9-2 NCF

CP9-3 NCF

CP9-4 Total increase in PIC $615 mil.

CP9-5 NCF

CP9-6 Total SE $758 mil.

CP9-7 a. $255 mil.
b. $2,149 mil.
c. $2,907 mil.

CP9-8 PIC from T/S Transactions $4 mil.

CP9-9 NCF

CP9-10 During 20X6, RE increased by $60,500

CP9-11 4. Pfd. $450,000 Com. $100,000

CP9-12 1. Cr. PIC in Excess $3,447 mil.

CP9-13 $63.05

CP9-14 NCF

CP9-15 ROA 23.3%
ROE 192.4%

CP9-16 Net cash provided $160 mil.

Exercises

E9-1 NCF

E9-2 2. Total SE $20,000

E9-3 Total SE $161,500

E9-4 Total PIC $640,000

E9-5 Total SE $415 mil.

E9-6 Overall effect on SE $46,100

E9-7 1. $5.86
3. RE, 12/31/01 $3,961 mil.

E9-8 NCF

E9-9 Total SE $13,036 mil.

E9-10 3. 378.3 mil. shares
4. $48.85 per share
5. Dividends $406 mil.

E9-11 Total divs.: pfd.–A $23,200; B $752,000; com. $24,800

E9-12 2. Total SE $6,446 mil.

E9-13 a. Decrease SE by $8,500

E9-14 Total SE $1,584 mil.

E9-15 1. $10.13 2. $10.06

E9-16 ROA .136 ROE .328

E9-17 ROA .062 ROE .100

E9-18 NCF

E9-19 NCF

E9-20 NCF

E9-21 Bal. 12/31/X6: C/S $11 mil.; APIC $17 mil.; RE $58 mil.

Problems

P9-1A NCF

P9-2A 2. Total SE $308,000

P9-3A Total SE $429,000

P9-4A NCF

P9-5A Total SE $2,341,000

P9-6A 4. $221,080

P9-7A 2. Total SE $99,010

P9-8A NCF

P9-9A 1. Total assets $486,000
Total SE $348,000
2. ROA .083; ROE .113

P9-10A 2. Net decrease in liab. $249 mil.; Net increase in SE $1,084 mil.

P9-1B NCF

P9-2B 2. Total SE $298,800

P9-3B Total SE $755,000

P9-4B NCF

P9-5B Total SE $6,180,000

P9-6B 4. $22,500,000

P9-7B 2. Total SE $80,300

P9-8B NCF

P9-9B 1. Total assets $535,000
Total SE $477,000
2. ROA .096; ROE .084

P9-10B 2. Net increase in liab. $593.9 mil.; Net decreae in SE $565.5 mil.

Cases

DC1 3. Debt ratio, as reported 0.82; as adjusted 0.87

DC2 3. Total SE—Plan 1 $371,000; Plan 2 $386,000

DC3 NCF

FSC 3. $15,544 thou.
4. ROE 18.0%; ROA 12.8%

AC 1. Avg. price paid $10.98
Avg. price rec'd. $11.30

Chapter 10

Check Points

CP 10-1 1. 12/31/X4 Unrealized loss $751

CP 10-2 Gain on sale $300

CP 10-3 3. $151 mil.

CP 10-4 Loss on sale $13.5 mil.

CP 10-5 NCF

CP 10-6 NCF

CP 10-7 2. Cash interest $70,000
4. Interest rev. $68,000

CP 10-8 c. Amortiz. amt. $2,000

CP 10-9 May 10 FC Transaction gain $2,000

CP 10-10 Sept. 29 FC Transaction loss $240

CP 10-11 NCF

CP 10-12 NCF

Exercises

E 10-1 d. Gain on sale $1,308

E 10-2 2. Unrealized loss $47,750

E 10-3 End bal. $1,655,000

E 10-4 Loss on sale $255,000

E 10-5 2. LT investment, at equity $171,400

E 10-6 2. Total SE $621,000

E 10-7 3. LT investment in bonds $19,490

E 10-8 Dec. 16 FC Transaction Loss $100

E 10-9 FC translation adj. $(13,500)

E 10-10 Net cash used in investing $3,498 mil.

E 10-11 NCF

E 10-12 3. b. $755 mil.
c. $700 mil.

E 10-13 3. Accum. other comp. inc. at 5/31/X0 $(36) mil.

Problems

P 10-1A 2. LT invest., at equity $643,300; Unrealized loss on invest. $3,400

P 10-2A 2. LT invest. in UPS $384,000

P 10-3A 1. .727
3. .900

P 10-4A 1. Consol. totals $1,033,000

P 10-5A 2. LT invest. in bonds $614,250
Interest rev. $26,250

P 10-6A Feb. 22 FC Transaction Gain $2,460; May 24 FC Transaction Loss $3,000

P 10-7A 1. FC translation adj. $364,000

P 10-8A NCF

P 10-1B 2. LT invest., at equity $716,300; Unrealized loss on invest. $1,800

P 10-2B 2. LT invest. in Affiliates $783,000

P 10-3B 1. .824
3. .891

P 10-4B 1. Consol. totals $1,146,000

P 10-5B 2. LT invest. in bonds $464,314
Interest rev. $31,814

P 10-6B July 21 FC Transaction Gain 3,000; Aug. 17 FC Transaction Loss $7,000

P 10-7B 1. FC translation adj. $(83,000)

P 10-8B NCF

Cases

DC1 2. Gain on sale of bonds $6,200
Gain on sale of Microsoft $80,000

DC2 NCF

FSC NCF

AC NCF

Chapter 11

Check Points

CP 11-1 NCF

CP 11-2 NCF

CP 11-3 Net inc. $33,000

CP 11-4 Est value of one share $25.33

CP 11-5 EPS for net inc. $3.00

CP 11-6 NCF

CP 11-7 Comp. inc. $34,000

CP 11-8 2. Net inc. $60,000

CP 11-9 RE, 12/31/X5 $470,000

CP 11-10 1. $993,000
2. $85,000
3. Sold T/S for $11,000

Exercises

E 11-1 Net inc. $1,501 mil.

E 11-2 1. Net inc. $3,288 mil.
2. Est. value of one share $74.20

E 11-3 NCF

E 11-4 2.9%

E 11-5 EPS $5.77

E 11-6 1. EPS for net inc. $0.84
2. Investment cap. rate .083

E 11-7 Income tax exp. $168,000
Income tax pay. $120,000
Deferred tax liab. $48,000

E 11-8 2. $92 mil.
3. $773 mil.

E 11-9 RE, 12/31X3 $429.4 mil.

E 11-10 Total SE 12/31/X5 $6,432,000

E 11-11 1. Total SE 2/1/X2 $6,674.4 mil.
2. 51.4%
4. $23.23 per share

E 11-12 NCF

Problems

P 11-1A 1. Net inc. $73,800
EPS for net inc. $3.39

P 11-2A RE, 12/31/X3 $95,800

P 11-3A Est. value of stock $800,000
Current market value $840,000

P 11-4A 1. EPS for net inc. $3.07
2. Est. value at 5% $58.20

P 11-5A Comp. inc. $55,200
EPS for net inc. $2.88

P 11-6A 1. Taxable inc. $120,000
3. Net inc. $84,500

P 11-7A 1. £800 mil.
2. £1.40 per share
3. £10.60 per share
4. Increase £33 mil.
5. 10%

P 11-1B 1. Net inc. $35,000
EPS for net inc. $1.04

P 11-2B RE, 9/30/X3 $102,000

P 11-3B Est. value of stock $762,500
Current market value $810,000

P 11-4B 1. EPS for net inc. $1.54
2. Est. value at 8% $13.75

P 11-5B Comp. inc. £91,200
EPS for net inc. £1.70

P 11-6B 1. Taxable inc. $185,000
3. Net inc. $130,000

P 11-7B 1. $560 mil.
2. $1.30 per share
3. $4.90 per share
4. Increase $28 mil.
5. 5%

Cases

DC1 EPS for prediction $2.75

DC2 NCF

FSC 3. Est. value at 6% $24.17

AC 2. Est. value at 6% $17.67

Chapter 12

Check Points

CP 12-1 NCF

CP 12-2 NCF

CP 12-3 NCF

CP 12-4 Net cash, oper. $71,000

CP 12-5 NCF

CP 12-6 Net cash, oper. $40,000

CP 12-7 Net cash, oper. $40,000
Net increase in cash $39,000

CP 12-8 a. $100,000
b. $15,000

CP 12-9 a. Payment $2,000
c. Dividends $84,000

CP 12-10 Net cash, oper. $180,000
Cash bal., end. $94,000

CP 12-11 Net cash, oper. $40,000

CP 12-12 Net cash, oper. $40,000
Net increase in cash $39,000

CP 12-13 a. $704,000
b. $331,000

CP 12-14 a. $48,000
b. $154,000

Exercises

E 12-1 NCF

E 12-2 NCF

E 12-3 NCF

E 12-4 Net cash, oper. $(8,000)

E 12-5 Net cash, oper. $76,000

E 12-6 Net cash, oper. $80,000
Net cash, finan. $4,000

E 12-7 NCF

E 12-8 a. $26,000
b. $6,000

E 12-9 NCF

E 12-10 NCF

E 12-11 Net cash, oper. $(8,000)

E 12-12 NCF

E 12-13 1. Net cash, oper. $80,000
Net cash, finan. $4,000

E 12-14 a. $85,000
b. $89,000

E 12-15 All in millions:
a. $24,440 e. $1,186
b. $18,516 f. $14
c. $4,793 g. $230
d. $507 h. $143

E 12-16 1. Loss of $39 mil.
2. $19 mil.
3. $961 mil.

Problems

P 12-1A NCF

P 12-2A 1. Net inc. $30,000
2. Total assets $375,000
3. Net cash, oper. $(49,000)

P 12-3A Net cash, oper. $75,200
Net cash, invest. $(90,200)
Net cash, finan. $43,000
Noncash inv. and fin. $172,000

P 12-4A Net cash, oper. $96,900
Net cash invest. $(112,000)
Net cash, finan. $31,000

P 12-5A 1. Net cash, oper. $72,900
Net cash, invest. $(37,100)
Net cash, finan. $(30,600)

P 12-6A 1. Net cash, oper. $115,700
Net cash, invest. $(27,600)
Net cash, finan. $(70,800)
Noncash inv. and fin. $79,400

P 12-7A 1. Net inc. $30,000
2. Total assets $375,000
3. Net cash oper. $(49,000)

P 12-8A 1. Net cash, oper. $72,900
Net cash, invest. $(37,100)
Net cash, finan. $(30,600)

P 12-9A 1. Net cash, oper. $67,800
Net cash, invest. $(10,200)
Net cash, finan. $(47,600)
Noncash inv. and fin. $99,100

P 12-10A 1. Net cash, oper. $69,100
Net cash, invest. $42,000
Net cash, finan. $(95,200)
Noncash inv. and fin. $19,000

P 12-1B NCF

P 12-2B 1. Net inc. $120,000
2. Total assets $303,000
3. Net cash, oper. $81,000

P 12-3B Net cash, oper. $94,000
Net cash, invest. $(91,300)
Net cash, finan. $11,100
Noncash inv. and fin. $207,400

P 12-4B 1. Net cash, oper. $48,300
Net cash, invest. $(173,000)
Net cash, finan. $120,600

P 12-5B 1. Net cash, oper. $70,600
Net cash, invest. $(47,600)
Net cash, finan. $(29,900)

P 12-6B 1. Net cash, oper. $(30,000)
Net cash, invest. $(47,200)
Net cash, finan. $91,700
Noncash inv. and fin. $142,800

P 12-7B 1. Net inc. $120,000
2. Total assets $303,000
3. Net cash, oper. $81,000

P 12-8B 1. Net cash, oper. $70,600
Net cash, invest. $(47,600)
Net cash, finan. $(29,900)

P 12-9B 1. Net cash, oper. $77,200
Net cash, invest. $(51,500)
Net cash, finan. $(30,300)
Noncash inv. and fin. $83,200

P 12-10B 1. Net cash, oper. $30,400
Net cash, invest. $800
Net cash, finan. $(37,100)
Noncash inv. and fin. $48,300

Cases

DC1 1. Net cash, oper. $140,000
Net cash, invest. $(141,000)
Net cash, finan. $(37,000)

DC2 NCF

FSC 2. a. $534,382 thou.
b. $293,294 thou.

AC NCF

Chapter 13

Check Points

CP 13-1 Rev. increase 2001 5.5%

CP 13-2 Rev. trend 2001 147%

CP 13-3 20X6 Cash 3.3%; PPE 52.7%

CP 13-4 Net inc. %: Nike 6.2%;
Home Depot 4.8%

CP 13-5 Current ratio 20X2 3.20

CP 13-6 1. Acid-test ratio
2001 1.09

CP 13-7 a. 3.4 times
b. 72 days

CP 13-8 1. 0.60 2. 13.7 times

CP 13-9 b. 0.247 c. 0.527

CP 13-10 1. EPS $0.48
P/E ratio 56

CP 13-11 a. $4,264 mil.
d. $698 mil.

CP 13-12 a. $631 mil.
e. $857 mil.

CP 13-13 1. $4,241 mil.

Exercises

E13-1 W/C increase in 2006 14.3%

E13-2 Net inc. increased by 58.8%

E13-3 Trend % for net inc., Year 5 155%

E13-4 Current assets 13.0%; PPE 76.2%

E13-5 2005 net inc. is 18.8% of rev.

E13-6 NCF

E13-7 b. 55 days d. 0.70 e. 4.01 times

E13-8 20X4 ratios: a. 1.56
b. 0.69 c. 0.59 d. 3.44

E13-9 20X6 ratios: a. 0.103
b. 0.137 c. 0.162 d. $0.75

E13-10 20X4 ratios: a. 20
b. 0.013 c. $4.75

E13-11 2. EVA of Oracle
$1,597.7 mil.

E13-12 Total assets $19,565 mil.
Current liab. $6,752 mil.

E13-13 Sales $6,639 mil.
Pretax inc. $1,183 mil.

Problems

P 13-1A 1. Trend % for net sales of 20X8
127%
2. Return on sales of 20X8 0.081

P 13-2A 1. Gross profit is 31.9% of net sales.
Net inc. is 9.2%.
Current assets are 77.1% of total assets.

P 13-3A NCF

P 13-4A 2. a. Current ratio 2.23; Debt ratio
0.49; ESP no effect

P 13-5A 1. For 20X6 b. 1.18 d. 0.152
e. 0.253

P 13-6A 1. Blues ratios: 1. 0.60
2. 2.16 3. 100 6. 0.196

P 13-7A NCF

P 13-1B 1. Trend % for net rev. of 2008
118%
2. ROE for 2008 0.142

P 13-2B 1. Gross profit is 36.4% of net sales.
Net inc. is 14.7%.
Current assets are 77.8% of total assets.

P 13-3B NCF

P 13-4B 2. a. Current ratio 1.35; Debt ratio
0.61; EPS No effect

P 13-5B 1. For 20X9 b. 1.48
d. ROE 0.357

P 13-6B 1. Caremark ratios: 1. 0.78
2. 2.32 3. 40 6. 0.349

P 13-7B NCF

Cases

DC1 NCF

DC2 NCF

DC3 NCF

DC4 NCF

FSC Ratios for 2001:
1. Trend % for sales 223%
2. GP% 49.8% Turnover 3.0 times
Days' sales in rec. 46 ROE 18.0%

AC NCF

Glossary

Accelerated depreciation method. A depreciation method that writes off a relatively larger amount of the asset's cost nearer the start of its useful life than the straight-line method does *(p. 326)*.

Account. The detailed record of the changes that have occurred in a particular asset, liability, or stockholders' equity during a period. The basic summary device of accounting *(p. 56)*.

Account format. A balance-sheet format that lists assets on the left and liabilities and stockholders' equity on the right *(p. 142)*.

Account payable. A liability backed by the general reputation and credit standing of the debtor *(p. 16)*.

Accounts receivable turnover. Measures a company's ability to collect cash from credit customers. To compute accounts receivable turnover, divide net credit sales by average net accounts receivable *(p. 623)*.

Accounting cycle. The process by which accountants produce an entity's financial statements for a specific period *(p. 112)*.

Accounting equation. The most basic tool of accounting: Assets = Liabilities + Owners' Equity *(p. 16)*.

Accounting. The information system that measures business activities, processes that information into reports and financial statements, and communicates the results to decision-makers *(p. 9)*.

Accrual. An expense or a revenue that occurs before the business pays or receives cash. An accrual is the opposite of a deferral *(p. 119)*.

Accrual accounting. Accounting that recognizes (records) the impact of a business event as it occurs, regardless of whether the transaction affected cash *(p. 113)*.

Accrued expense. An expense incurred but not yet paid in cash *(pp. 124, 369)*.

Accrued liability. A liability incurred but not yet paid by the company. Another name for *accrued expense (p. 57)*.

Accrued revenue. A revenue that has been earned but not yet received in cash *(p. 125)*.

Accumulated Depreciation. The cumulative sum of all depreciation expense from the date of acquiring a plant asset *(p. 122)*.

Acid-test ratio. Ratio (of the sum of cash plus short-term investments plus net current receivables) to (total current liabilities). Tells whether the entity can pay all its current liabilities if they come due immediately. Also called the *quick ratio (pp. 241, 621)*.

Adjusted trial balance. A list of all the ledger accounts with their adjusted balance *(p. 128)*.

Adjusting entry. Entry made at the end of the period to assign revenues to the period in which they are earned and expenses to the period in which they are incurred. Adjusting entries help measure the period's income and bring the related asset and liability accounts to correct balances for the financial statements *(p. 111)*.

Adverse opinion. An audit opinion stating that the financial statements are unreliable *(p. 516)*.

Aging-of-accounts receivable. A way to estimate bad debts by analyzing individual accounts receivable according to the length of time they have been receivable from the customer *(p. 233)*.

Allowance for Doubtful Accounts. Also called *Allowance for Uncollectible Accounts (p. 231)*.

Allowance for Uncollectible Accounts. A contra account, related to accounts receivable, that holds the estimated amount of collection losses. Another name for *Allowance for Doubtful Accounts (p. 231)*.

Allowance method. A method of recording collection losses based on estimates of how much money the business will not collect from its customers *(p. 231)*.

Amortization. The systematic reduction of a lump-sum amount. Expense that applies to intangible assets in the same way depreciation applies to plant assets and depletion applies to natural resources *(p. 337)*.

Asset. An economic resource that is expected to be of benefit in the future *(p. 16)*.

Audit. A periodic examination of a company's financial statements and the accounting systems, controls, and records that produce them *(p. 182)*.

Available-for-sale investments. All investments not classified as held-to-maturity or trading securities *(pp. 224, 467)*.

Bad-debt expense. Another name for *uncollectible-account expense (p. 231)*.

Balance sheet. List of an entity's assets, liabilities, and owners' equity as of a specific date. Also called the *statement of financial position (p. 23)*.

Balance sheet approach. Another name for *aging-of-accounts receivable (p. 228)*.

Bank collection. Collection of money by the bank on behalf of a depositor *(p. 188)*.

Bank reconciliation. A document explaining the reasons for the difference between a depositor's records and the bank's records about the depositor's bank account *(p. 188)*.

Bank statement. Document showing the beginning and ending balances of a particular bank account listing the month's transactions that affected the account *(p. 187)*.

Board of directors. Group elected by the stockholders to set policy for a corporation and to appoint its officers *(pp. 13, 419)*.

Bonds payable. Groups of notes payable (bonds) issued to multiple lenders called *bondholders (p. 374)*.

Book value (of a plant asset). The asset's cost minus accumulated depreciation *(p. 116)*.

Book value (of a stock). Amount of owners' equity on the company's books for each share of its stock *(p. 434)*.

Book value per share of common stock. Common stockholders' equity divided by the number of shares of common stock outstanding. The recorded amount for each share of common stock outstanding *(p. 630)*.

Brand name. See *trademark, trade name (p. 338)*.

Budget. A quantitative expression of a plan that helps managers coordinate the entity's activities *(p. 197)*.

Bylaws. Constitution for governing a corporation *(p. 419)*.

Callable bonds. Bonds that the issuer may call (pay off) at a specified price whenever the issuer wants *(p. 386)*.

Capital charge. The amount that stockholders and lenders charge a company for the use of their money. Calculated as (Notes payable + Loans payable + Long-term debt + Stockholders' equity) × Cost of capital *(p. 631)*.

Capital expenditure. Expenditure that increases an asset's capacity or efficiency or extends its useful life. Capital expenditures are debited to an asset account *(p. 321)*.

Capital lease. Lease agreement that meets any one of four criteria: (1) The lease transfers title of the leased asset to the lessee. (2) The lease contains a bargain purchase option. (3) The lease term is 75% or more of the estimated useful life of the leased asset. (4) The present value of the lease payments is 90% or more of the market value of the leased asset *(p. 391)*.

Capital. Another name for the *owners' equity* of a business *(p. 16)*.

Cash equivalents. Highly liquid short-term investments that can be converted into cash with little delay *(p. 547)*.

Cash flows. Cash receipts and cash payments (disbursements) *(p. 546)*.

Cash. Money and any medium of exchange that a bank accepts at face value *(p. 16)*.

Cash-basis accounting. Accounting that records only transactions in which cash is received or paid *(p. 113)*.

Chairperson. Elected by a corporation's board of directors, usually the most powerful person in the corporation *(p. 420)*.

Chart of accounts. List of all a company's accounts and their account numbers *(p. 81)*.

Check. Document instructing a bank to pay the designated person or business the specified amount of money *(p. 186)*.

Classified balance sheet. A balance sheet that shows current assets separate from long-term assets, and current liabilities separate from long-term liabilities *(p. 139)*.

Clean opinion. See *unqualified (p. 516)*.

Closing entries. Entries that transfer the revenue, expense, and dividends balances from these respective accounts to the Retained Earnings account *(p. 137)*.

Closing the accounts. The process of preparing the accounts to begin recording the next period's transactions. Closing the accounts consists of journalizing and posting the closing entries to set the balances of the revenue, expense, and dividends accounts to zero *(p. 137)*.

Closing the books. The process of preparing the accounts to begin recording the next period's transactions. Closing the accounts consists of journalizing and posting the closing entries to set the balances of the revenue, expense, and dividends accounts to zero. See *closing the accounts (p. 137)*.

Common-size statement. A financial statement that reports only percentages (no dollar amounts) *(p. 612)*.

Common stock. The most basic form of capital stock. Common stockholders own a corporation *(pp. 17, 422)*.

Comprehensive income. A company's change in total stockholders' equity from all sources other than from the owners of the business *(p. 21)*.

Conservatism. The accounting concept by which the least favorable figures are presented in the financial statements *(p. 279)*.

Consistency principle. A business must use the same accounting methods and procedures from period to period *(p. 278)*.

Consolidated statements. Financial statements of the parent company plus those of majority-owned subsidiaries as if the combination were a single legal entity *(p. 474)*.

Contra account. An account that always has a companion account and whose normal balance is opposite that of the companion account *(p. 122)*.

Contract interest rate. Interest rate that determines the amount of cash interest the borrower pays and the investor receives each year. Also called *stated interest rate (p. 376)*.

Contributed capital. See *paid-in capital (pp. 17, 421)*.

Controller. The chief accounting officer of a business *(p. 181)*.

Controlling (majority) interest. Ownership of more than 50% of an investee company's voting stock *(p. 473)*.

Convertible bonds (or notes). Bonds (or notes) that may be converted into the issuing company's common stock at the investor's option *(p. 387)*.

Copyright. Exclusive right to reproduce and sell a book, musical composition, film, other work of art, or computer program. Issued by the federal government, copyrights extend 50 years beyond the author's life *(p. 338)*.

Corporation. A business owned by stockholders. A corporation is a legal entity, an "artificial person" in the eyes of the law *(p. 12)*.

Cost of capital. A weighted average of the returns demanded by the company's stockholders and lenders *(p. 631)*.

Cost of goods sold. The cost of the inventory that the business has sold to customers. Also called *cost of sales (p. 264)*.

Cost of sales. Another name for *cost of goods sold (p. 264)*.

Cost principle. Principle that states that acquired assets and services should be recorded at their actual cost *(p. 14)*.

Cost-of-goods-sold model. Brings together all the inventory data for the entire accounting period: Beginning inventory + Purchases = Cost of goods available for sale. Then, Cost of goods available − Ending inventory = Cost of goods sold *(p. 266)*.

Credit. The right side of an account *(p. 69)*.

Creditor. The party to whom money is owed *(p. 224)*.

Cumulative preferred stock. Preferred stock whose owners must receive all dividends in arrears before the corporation can pay dividends to the common stockholders *(p. 432)*.

Current asset. An asset that is expected to be converted to cash, sold, or consumed during the next 12 months, or within the business' normal operating cycle if longer than a year *(pp. 23, 139)*.

Current installment of long-term debt. The amount of the principal that is payable within one year *(p. 368)*.

Current liability. A debt due to be paid within one year or within the entity's operating cycle if the cycle is longer than a year *(pp. 24, 139)*.

Current ratio. Current assets divided by current liabilities. Measures a company's ability to pay current liabilities with current assets *(pp. 143, 619)*.

Days' sales in receivables. Ratio of average net accounts receivable to one day's sale. Indicates how many days' sales remain in Accounts Receivable awaiting collection. Also called the *collection period (pp. 240, 623)*.

Debentures. Unsecured bonds—bonds backed only by the good faith of the borrower *(p. 375).*

Debit. The left side of an account *(p. 69).*

Debt instrument. A payable, usually some form of note or bond payable *(p. 224).*

Debt ratio. Ratio of total liabilities to total assets. States the proportion of a company's assets that is financed with debt *(pp. 144, 625).*

Debtor. The party who owes money *(p. 224).*

Deferral. A category of miscellaneous assets that typically espire or get used up in the near future. Examples include prepaid rent, prepaid insurance, and supplies. See *prepaid expense (pp. 56, 118).*

Deficit. Debit balance in the Retained Earnings account *(p. 430).*

Depletion expense. That portion of a natural resource's cost that is used up in a particular period. Depletion expense is computed in the same way as units-of-production depreciation *(p. 337).*

Deposit in transit. A deposit recorded by the company but not yet by its bank *(p. 188).*

Depreciable cost. The cost of a plant asset minus its estimated residual value *(p. 323).*

Depreciation. Expense associated with spreading (allocating) the cost of a plant asset over its useful life *(p. 119).*

Direct method. Format of the operating activities section of the statement of cash flows; lists the major categories of operating cash receipts (collections from customers and receipts of interest and dividends) and cash disbursements (payments to suppliers, to employees, for interest and income taxes) *(p. 548).*

Direct write-off method. A method of accounting for bad debts in which the company waits until the credit department decides that a customer's account receivable is uncollectible and then debits Uncollectible-Account Expense and credits the customer's Account Receivable *(p. 235).*

Disclaimer. An audit opinion stating that the auditor was unable to reach a professional opinion regarding the quality of the financial statements *(p. 516).*

Disclosure principle. A business must use the same accounting methods and procedures from period to period *(p. 278).*

Discount (on a bond). Excess of a bond's maturity (par value) over its issue price *(p. 375).*

Dividend. Distribution (usually cash) by a corporation to its stockholders *(p. 431).*

Dividends. Distributions (usually cash) by a corporation to its stockholders *(p. 18).*

Dividend yield. Ratio of dividends per share of stock to the stock's market price per share. Tells the percentage of a stock's market value that the company returns to stockholders as dividends *(p. 629).*

Double taxation. Corporations pay income taxes on corporate income. Then, the stockholders pay personal income tax on the cash dividends that they receive from corporations *(p. 419).*

Double-declining-balance (DDB) method. An accelerated depreciation method that computes annual depreciation by multiplying the asset's decreasing book value by a constant percentage, which is 2 times the straight-line rate *(p. 326).*

Double-entry system. An accounting system that uses debits and credits to record the dual effects of each business transaction *(p. 68).*

Doubtful-account expense. Another name for *uncollectible-account expense (p. 231).*

Earnings per share (EPS). Amount of a company's net income per share of its outstanding common stock *(pp. 387, 628).*

Economic value added (EVA). Used to evaluate a company's operating performance. EVA combines the concepts of accounting income and corporate finance to measure whether the company's operations have increased stockholder wealth. EVA = net income + interest expense − capital charge *(p. 618).*

Effective interest rate. Another name for *market interest rate (p. 376).*

Efficient capital market. A capital market in which market prices fully reflect all information available to the public *(p. 632).*

Electronic funds transfer (EFT). System that transfers cash by electronic communication rather than by paper documents *(p. 187).*

Entity. An organization or a section of an organization that, for accounting purposes, stands apart from other organizations and individuals as a separate economic unit *(p. 14).*

Equity method for investments. The method used to account for investments in which the investor has 20–50% of the investee's voting stock and can significantly influence the decisions of the investee *(p. 471).*

Equity securities. Stock certificates that represent the investor's ownership in a corporation *(p. 224).*

Estimated residual value. Expected cash value of an asset at the end of its useful life. Also called *residual value, scrap value,* or *salvage value (p. 323).*

Estimated useful life. Length of a service that a business expects to get from an asset. May be expressed in years, units of output, miles, or other measures *(p. 323).*

Expense. Decrease in retained earnings that results from operations; the cost of doing business; opposite of revenues *(p. 17).*

Extraordinary gain or loss. Also called *extraordinary items,* these gains and losses are both unusual for the company and infrequent *(p. 504).*

Extraordinary item. A gain or loss that is both unusual for the company and infrequent *(p. 504).*

FIFO (first-in, first-out) method. Inventory costing method by which the first costs into inventory are the first costs out to cost of goods sold. Ending inventory is based on the costs of the most recent purchases *(p. 271).*

Financial accounting. The branch of accounting that provides information to people outside the firm *(p. 10).*

Financial statements. Business documents that report financial information about a business entity to decision-makers. *(p. 9).*

Financing activities. Activities that obtain from investors and creditors the cash needed to launch and sustain the business; a section of the statement of cash flows *(pp. 25, 548).*

Foreign-currency exchange rate. The measure of one country's currency against another country's currency *(p. 481).*

Foreign-currency translation adjustment. The balancing figure that brings the dollar amount of the total liabilities and stockholders' equity of the foreign subsidiary into agreement with the dollar amount of its total assets *(p. 485).*

Franchises and licenses. Privileges granted by a private business or a government to sell product or service in accordance with specified conditions *(p. 339)*.

Free cash flow. The amount of cash available from operations after paying for planned investments in plant, equipment, and other long-term assets *(p. 573)*.

Generally accepted accounting principles (GAAP). Accounting guidelines, formulated by the Financial Accounting Standards Board, that govern how accountants measure, process, and communicate financial information *(p. 13)*.

Going-concern concept. Holds that the entity will remain in operation for the foreseeable future *(p. 15)*.

Goodwill. Excess of the cost of an acquired company over the sum of the market values of its net assets (assets minus liabilities) *(p. 339)*.

Gross margin method. A way to estimate inventory based on a rearrangement of the cost-of-goods-sold model: Beginning inventory + net purchases = Cost of goods available for sale. Cost of goods sold = Ending inventory. Also called *gross profit method (p. 284)*.

Gross margin percentage. Gross margin divided by net sales revenue. Also called the *gross profit percentage (p. 282)*.

Gross margin. Sales revenue minus cost of goods sold. Also called *gross profit (p. 265)*.

Gross profit method. See *gross profit method (p. 284)*.

Gross profit percentage. See *gross margin percentage (p. 282)*.

Gross profit. Another name for *gross margin (p. 265)*.

Hedging. To protect oneself from losing money in one transaction by engaging in a counterbalancing transaction *(p. 484)*.

Held-to-maturity investments. Bonds and notes that an investor intends to hold until maturity *(pp. 224, 476)*.

Horizontal analysis. The study of percentage changes in comparative statements *(p. 606)*.

Imprest system. A way to account for petty cash by maintaining a constant balance in the petty cash account, supported by the fund (cash plus disbursement tickets) totaling the same amount *(p. 196)*.

Income statement approach. Another name for *percent-of-sales method (p. 227)*.

Income statement. A financial statement listing an entity's revenues, expenses, and net income or net loss for a specific period. Also called the *statement of operations (p. 19)*.

Indirect method. Format of the operating activities section of the statement of cash flows; starts with net income and reconciles to cash flows from operating activities. Also called the *reconciliation method (p. 548)*.

Intangible asset. An asset with no physical form, a special right to current and expected future benefits *(p. 318)*.

Interest. The borrower's cost of renting money from a lender. Interest is revenue for the lender, expense for the borrower *(p. 236)*.

Internal control. Organizational plan and all the related measures adopted by an entity to safeguard assets, encourage adherence to company policies, promote operational efficiency, and ensure accurate and reliable accounting records *(p. 180)*.

Inventory profit. Difference between gross margin figured on the FIFO basis and gross margin figured on the LIFO basis *(p. 275)*.

Inventory turnover. Ratio of cost of goods sold to average inventory. Indicates how rapidly inventory is sold *(pp. 283, 622)*.

Inventory. The merchandise that a company sells to customers *(p. 264)*.

Investing activities. Activities that increase or decrease the long-term assets available to the business; a section of the statement of cash flows *(pp. 25, 548)*.

Investment capitalization rate. An earnings rate used to estimate the value of an investment in the capital stock of another company *(p. 502)*.

Journal. The chronological accounting record of an entity's transactions *(p. 72)*.

Just-in-time system. A system in which a company schedules production just in time to satisfy needs. Materials are purchased and finished goods are completed only as needed to satisfy customer demand. *(p. 283)*.

Lease. Rental agreement in which the tenant (lessee) agrees to make rent payments to the property owner (lessor) in exchange for the use of the asset *(p. 390)*.

Ledger. The book of a company's accounts and their balances *(p. 73)*.

Legal capital. Minimum amount of stockholders' equity that a corporation must maintain for the protection of creditors. For corporation's with par-value stock, legal capital is the par value of the stock issued *(p. 422)*.

Lessee. Tenant in a lease agreement *(p. 390)*.

Lessor. Property owner in a lease agreement *(p. 390)*.

Leverage. Another name for *trading on the equity (pp. 388, 628)*.

Liability. An economic obligation (a debt) payable to an individual or an organization outside the business *(p. 16)*.

LIFO (last-in, first-out) method. Inventory costing method by which the last costs into inventory are the first costs out to cost of goods sold. This method leaves the oldest costs—those of beginning inventory and the earliest purchases of the period—in ending inventory *(p. 271)*.

Limited liability. No personal obligation of a stockholder for corporation debts. A stockholder can lose no more on an investment in a corporation's stock than the cost of the investment *(p. 418)*.

Liquidity. Measure of how quickly an item can be converted to cash *(p. 138)*.

Long-term asset. An asset that is not a current asset *(p. 139)*.

Long-term debt. A liability that falls due beyond one year from the date of the financial statements *(p. 17)*.

Long-term investment. Any investment that does not meet the criteria of a short-term investment; any investment that the investor expects to hold longer than a year or that is not readily marketable *(p. 467)*.

Long-term liability. A liability that is not a current liability *(p. 139)*.

Lower-of-cost-or-market (LCM) rule. Requires that an asset be reported in the financial statements at whichever is lower—its historical cost or its market value (current replacement cost for inventory) *(p. 279)*.

Majority interest. See *controlling interest (p. 473).*

Management accounting. The branch of accounting that generates information for the internal decision-makers of a business, such as top executives *(p. 10).*

Market interest rate. Interest rate that investors demand for loaning their money. Also called *effective interest rate (p. 376).*

Market value (of a stock). Price for which a person could buy or sell a share of stock *(p. 434).*

Market value method of accounting (for investments). Used to account for all available-for-sale securities. These investments are reported at their current market value *(p. 467).*

Marketable security. Another name for *short-term investments (pp. 220, 466).*

Matching principle. The basis for recording expenses. Directs accountants to identify all expenses incurred during the period, to measure the expenses, and to match them against the revenues earned during that same period *(p. 115).*

Materiality concept. A company must perform strictly proper accounting only for items and transactions that are significant to the business's financial statements *(p. 279).*

Maturity. The date on which a debt instrument must be paid *(p. 224).*

Merchandise inventory. See *inventory (p. 16).*

Minority interest. A subsidiary company's equity that is held by stockholders other than the parent company *(p. 476).*

Modified Accelerated Cost Recovery System (MACRS). A special depreciation method used only for income tax purposes. Assets are grouped into classes, and for a given class depreciation is computed by the double-declining-balance method, the 150%-declining balance method, or, for most real estate, the straight-line method *(p. 331).*

Multi-step income statement. An income statement that contains subtotals to highlight important relationships between revenues and expenses *(p. 143).*

Net earnings. Another name for *net income* or *net profit (p. 18).*

Net income. Excess of total revenues over total expenses. Also called *net earnings* or *net profit (p. 18).*

Net loss. Excess of total expenses over total revenues *(p. 18).*

Net profit. Another name for *net income* or *net earnings (p. 18).*

Nominal account. Another name for a *temporary account (p. 137).*

Nonsufficient funds (NSF) check. A "hot" check, one for which the payer's bank account has insufficient money to pay the check. NSF checks are cash receipts that turn out to be worthless *(p. 188).*

Note payable. A liability evidenced by a written promise to make a future payment *(p. 17).*

Objectivity principle. See *reliability principle (p. 14).*

Operating activities. Activity that creates revenue or expense in the entity's major line of business; a section of the statement of cash flows. Operating activities affect the income statement *(p. 25).*

Operating cycle. Time span during which cash is paid for goods and services that are sold to customers who pay the business in cash *(p. 139).*

Operating lease. Usually a short-term or cancelable rental agreement *(p. 391).*

Outstanding check. A check issued by the company and recorded on its books but not yet paid by its bank *(p. 188).*

Outstanding stock. Stock in the hands of stockholders *(p. 421).*

Owners' equity. The claim of the owners of a business to the assets of the business. Also called *capital* for proprietorships and partnerships and *stockholders' equity* for corporations. Sometimes called net assets *(p. 16).*

Paid-in capital. The amount of stockholders' equity that stockholders have contributed to the corporation. Also called *contributed capital (p. 17, 421).*

Par value. Arbitrary amount assigned by a company to a share of its stock *(p. 422).*

Parent company. An investor company that owns more than 50% of the voting stock of a subsidiary company *(p. 473).*

Partnership. An association of two or more persons who co-own a business for profit *(p. 12).*

Patent. A federal government grant giving the holder the exclusive right for 20 years to produce and sell an invention *(p. 338).*

Payroll. Employee compensation, a major expense of many businesses *(p. 369).*

Pension. Employee compensation that will be received during retirement *(p. 392).*

Percentage-of-sales method. Computes uncollectible-account expenses as a percentage of net sales. Also called the *income statement approach* because it focuses on the amount of expense to be reported on the income statement *(p. 232).*

Periodic inventory system. An inventory system in which the business does not keep a continuous record of the inventory on hand. Instead, at the end of the period, the business makes a physical count of the inventory on hand and applies the appropriate unit costs to determine the cost of the ending inventory *(p. 267).*

Permanent account. Asset, liability, and stockholders' equity that are not closed at the end of the period *(p. 137).*

Perpetual inventory system. An inventory system in which the business keeps a continuous record for each inventory item to show the inventory on hand at all times *(p. 277).*

Petty cash. Fund containing a small amount of cash that is used to pay minor expenditures *(p. 268).*

Plant asset. Long-lived assets, such as land, buildings, and equipment, used in the operation of the business. Also called *fixed assets (p. 318).*

Posting. Copying amounts from the journal to the ledger *(p. 74).*

Preferred stock. Stock that gives its owners certain advantages, such as the priority to receive dividends before the common stockholders and the priority to receive assets before the common stockholders if the corporation liquidates *(p. 422).*

Premium (on a bond). Excess of a bond's issue price over its maturity (par) value *(p. 375).*

Prepaid expense. A category of miscellaneous assets that typically expire or get used up in the near future. Examples include prepaid rent, prepaid insurance, and supplies. Also called a *deferral (pp. 56, 118).*

Present value. Amount a person would invest now to receive a greater amount at a future date *(p. 376).*

President. Chief operating officer in charge of managing the day-to-day operations of a corporation *(p. 420).*

Pretax accounting income. Income before tax on the income statement *(p. 508).*

Price/earnings ratio. Ratio of the market price of a share of common stock to the company's earnings per share. Measures the value that the stock market places on $1 of a company's earnings *(p. 629).*

Principal. The amount borrowed by a debtor and lent by a creditor *(p. 236).*

Prior-period adjustment. A correction to beginning balance of retained earnings for an error of an earlier period *(p. 510).*

Proprietorship. A business with a single owner *(p. 12).*

Purchase allowance. A decrease in the cost of purchases because the seller has granted the buyer a subtraction (an allowance) from the amount owed *(p. 269).*

Purchase discount. A decrease in the cost of purchases earned by making an early payment to the vendor *(p. 270).*

Purchase return. A decrease in the cost of purchases because the buyer returned the goods to the seller. *(p. 269).*

Qualified opinion. An audit opinion stating that the financial statements are reliable, except for one or more items for which the opinion is said to be qualified *(p. 516).*

Quick ratio. Another name for the *acid-test ratio (pp. 241, 621).*

Rate of return on common stockholders' equity. Net income minus preferred dividends, divided by average common stockholders' equity. A measure of profitability. Also called *return on equity (pp. 436, 627).*

Rate of return on net sales. Ratio of net income to net sales. A measure of profitability. Also called *return on sales (p. 626).*

Rate of return on total assets. Net income plus interest expense, divided by average total assets. This ratio measures a company's success in using its assets to earn income for the persons who finance the business. Also called *return on assets (pp. 436, 627).*

Real account. Another name for a *permanent account (p. 131).*

Receivables. Monetary claims against a business or an individual, acquired mainly by selling goods and services and by lending money *(p. 227).*

Reliability principle. The accounting principle that ensures that accounting records and statements are based on the most reliable data available *(p. 14).*

Report format. A balance-sheet format that lists assets at the top, followed by liabilities and stockholders' equity below *(p. 142).*

Retained earnings. The amount of stockholders' equity that the corporation has earned through profitable operation of the business and has not given back to stockholders *(pp. 17, 421).*

Return on assets. Another name for *rate of return on total assets (pp. 436, 627).*

Return on equity. Another name for *rate of return on common stockholders' equity (pp. 436, 627).*

Return on stockholders' equity. Another name for *rate of return on common stockholders' equity (p. 627).*

Revenue principle. The basis for recording revenues; tells accountants when to record revenue and the amount of revenue to record *(p. 115).*

Revenue. Increase in retained earnings from delivering goods or services to customers or clients *(p. 17).*

Securities. Notes payable or stock certificates that entitle the owner to the benefits of an investment *(p. 224).*

Segment of the business. One of various separate divisions of a company *(p. 504).*

Serial bonds. Bonds that mature in installments over a period of time. *(p. 375).*

Shareholder. Another name for a *stockholder (pp. 12, 418).*

Short-term investments. Investments that a company plans to hold for one year or less. Also called *marketable securities (pp. 224, 466).*

Short-term note payable. Note payable due within one year *(p. 367).*

Single-step income statement. An income statement that lists all the revenues together under a heading such as Revenues or Revenues and Gains. Expenses appear in a separate category called Expenses, Costs, and Expenses, or perhaps Expenses and Losses *(p. 143).*

Specific-unit-cost method. Inventory cost method based on the specific cost of particular units of inventory *(p. 271).*

Stable-monetary-unit concept. The basis for ignoring the effect of inflation in the accounting records, based on the assumption that the dollar's purchasing power is relatively stable *(p. 15).*

Stated value. An arbitrary amount assigned to no-par stock; similar to par value *(p. 422).*

Stated interest rate. Another name for the *contract interest rate (p. 376).*

Statement of cash flows. Reports cash receipts and cash disbursements classified according to the entity's major activities: operating, investing, and financing *(pp. 25, 546).*

Statement of earnings. Another name for *income statement (p. 19).*

Statement of financial position. Another name for *balance sheet (p. 23).*

Statement of operations. Another name for *income statement (p. 19).*

Statement of retained earnings. Summary of the changes in the retained earnings of a corporation during a specific period *(p. 21).*

Statement of stockholders' equity. Reports the changes in all categories of stockholders' equity during the period *(p. 512).*

Stock dividend. A proportional distribution by a corporation of its own stock to its stockholders *(p. 432).*

Stock split. An increase in the number of authorized, issued, and outstanding shares of stock coupled with a proportionate reduction in the stock's par value *(p. 433).*

Stock. Shares into which the owners' equity of a corporation is divided *(pp. 12, 421).*

Stockholder. A person who owns stock in a corporation. Also called a *shareholder (pp. 12, 418).*

Stockholders' equity. The stockholders' ownership interest in the assets of a corporation *(p. 420).*

Straight-line (SL) method. Depreciation method in which an equal amount of depreciation expense is assigned to each year (or period) of asset use *(p. 324).*

Strong currency. A currency whose exchange rate is rising relative to other nations' currencies *(p. 482).*

Subsidiary company. An investee company in which a parent company owns more than 50% of the voting stock *(p. 473).*

Taxable income. The basis for computing the amount of tax to pay the government *(p. 509)*.

Temporary account. Another name for a *nominal account.* The revenue and expense accounts that relate to a particular accounting period and are closed at the end of the period are temporary accounts. For a corporation, the Dividends account is also temporary *(p. 137)*.

Term bonds. Bonds that all mature in installments over a period of time *(p. 375)*.

Term. The length of time from inception to maturity *(p. 224)*.

Time-period concept. Ensures that accounting information is reported at regular intervals *(p. 114)*.

Times-interest-earned ratio. Ratio of income from operations to interest expense. Measures the number of times that operating income can cover interest expense. Also called the *interest-coverage ratio (pp. 390, 625)*.

Trademark, trade name. A distinctive identification of a product or service. Also called a *brand name (p. 338)*.

Trading investments. Stock investments that are to be sold in the near future with the intent of generating profits on the sale *(pp. 224, 467)*.

Trading on the equity. Earning more income on borrowed money than the related interest expense, thereby increasing the earnings for the owners of the business. Also called *leverage (pp. 388, 628)*.

Transaction. An event that both affects the financial position of a business entity and can be reliably recorded *(p. 58)*.

Trend percentages. A form of horizontal analysis that indicate the direction a business is taking *(p. 609)*.

Treasury stock. A corporation's own stock that it has issued and later reacquired *(p. 428)*.

Trial balance. A list of all the ledger accounts with their balances *(p. 80)*.

Uncollectible-account expense. Cost to the seller of extending credit. Arises from the failure to collect from credit customers. Also called *doubtful-account expense* or *bad-debt expense (p. 231)*.

Underwriter. Organization that purchases the bonds from an issuing company and resells them to its clients or sells the bonds for a commission, agreeing to buy all unsold bonds *(p. 375)*.

Unearned revenue. A liability created when a business collects cash from customers in advance of doing work for them. The obligation is to provide a product or a service in the future *(p. 126)*.

Units-of-production (UOP) method. Depreciation method by which a fixed amount of depreciation is assigned to each unit of output produced by the plant asset *(p. 320)*.

Unqualified (clean) opinion. An audit opinion stating that the financial statements are reliable *(p. 516)*.

Vertical analysis. The study of a financial statement that reveals the relationship of each statement item to a specified base *(p. 610)*.

Weak currency. A currency whose exchange rate is falling relative to that of other nations *(p. 482)*.

Weighted-average cost method. Inventory costing method based on the weighted average cost of inventory during the period. Weighted-average cost is determined by dividing the cost of goods available for sales by the number of units available. Also called the *average-cost method (p. 271)*.

Company Index

Real company names are in bold type.

T

U

V

W

X

Y

Subject Index

C

D

H

I

J

K

L